STONE
ROAD
PRESS

This is Your Guide to
the National Parks

Come and Explore
Your National Parks

Your Guide to the National Parks, Third Edition
ISBN 978-1-62128-076-7
Library of Congress Control Number (LCCN): 2021922368

Printed in the United States of America
Published by Stone Road Press
Author/Photographer/Designer: Michael Joseph Oswald
Editor: Derek Pankratz

Corrections/Contact

This guidebook has been researched and written with the greatest attention to detail in order to provide you with the most accurate and pertinent information. Unfortunately, travel information—especially pricing—is subject to change and inadvertent errors and omissions do occur. Should you encounter a change, error, or omission while using this guidebook, we'd like to hear about it. (If you found a wonderful place, trail, or activity not mentioned, we'd love to hear about that too.) Please contact us by sending an e-mail to corrections@stoneroadpress.com. Your contributions will help make future editions better than the last.

Find us online at StoneRoadPress.com or follow us on Facebook (facebook.com/thestoneroadpress), Twitter (@stoneroadpress), Instagram (@stoneroadpress), and Flickr (stoneroadpress).

Disclaimer

Your safety is important to us. If any activity is beyond your ability or threatened by forces outside your control, do not attempt it. The maps in this book, although accurate and to scale, are not intended for hiking. Serious hikers should purchase a detailed, waterproof, topographical map (or download them from USGS). It is also suggested you write or call in advance to confirm information when it matters most.

The primary purpose of this guidebook is to enhance our readers' national park experiences, but the author, editor, and publisher cannot be held responsible for any experiences while traveling.

Cover and Introduction Photo Descriptions

Front cover: Bruce the Moose at Wonder Lake (Denali)
Introduction Pages: Many Glacier (Glacier), Devil's Hall (Guadalupe Mountains), Grand Canyon of the Yellowstone (Yellowstone)
Opposite About the Author: A lone horse near River Road (Big Bend)
Opposite Contents: Mesquite Flat Sand Dunes (Death Valley)
Page 34: Bear Gulch (Pinnacles)
Page 39: Gateway Arch (Gateway Arch)
Page 40: Spruce Flat Falls (Great Smoky Mountains)
Page 475: Motor-bikers riding Titus Canyon Road (Death Valley)
Page 622: Bear at Brooks River (Katmai)
Page 686: Waimoku Falls (Haleakala)
Page 725: Mohave Point (Grand Canyon)
Page 726: Chicago Skyline from West Beach (Indiana Dunes)
Page 727: Jordan Cliffs (Acadia)
Page 728: Notch Trail (Badlands)
Back Cover: Pedersen Lagoon (Kenai Fjords), Denali Park Road (Denali), Brooks Falls (Katmai)

Acknowledgments

Bear-play at Katmai National Park

I need to thank you, the reader, traveler, and United States National Park enthusiast. None of this is possible without your support, taking a chance on a book by some curious farm boy from Wisconsin who loves the outdoors. Quite often I feel like the bear on the right, wondering what in the world I've gotten myself into. This career path is both thrilling and frightening. Lonely yet fulfilling. Demanding but addictive. It's non-stop ups and downs, and nothing lifts me up more than your support. An e-mail about a successful trip. An image of a well-worn book. Or simply a "thank you." And for that, I thank you. I'm working to repay your support by making the best book I can. Hopefully you like it. Sorry about the price hike. Went to print with paper prices at historic highs (for what it's worth, we're sharing it—hoping prices come back down for the next print run).

Special thanks to Powder and Steel! I'm pretty sure neither of you can read but you still deserve mention. Unconditional companionship makes a person better and you guys are two of the best companions around!

Cherish your partners, people ... and if you don't have a trusty travel companion yet, I'm always here!

About the Author

Admiring the clouds banked against Haleakala

You might be wondering "why in the world should I listen to this guy staring into a volcano that's been dormant for centuries?" Allow me to tell you … while touring the parks I quickly realized most visitors only explore areas accessible by car. Families zip through, stop at the occasional pull-out or parking lot for a quick photo-op, and then continue on their merry way. While most parks cater to motorists, one cannot experience their essence from the comfort of your driver's seat. You must walk among the trees and the mountains. Listen to nature all around you. Sit back, close your eyes, and immerse yourself in its beauty. America's 63 national parks are irreplaceable treasures, yet they are our parks, preserved for our enjoyment. And if you want to experience them to their fullest, you're going to need a good guide.

That's where I come in. I admit my first trip to a national park was your typical affair. A group of friends drove to the South Rim of the Grand Canyon. We peered in, snapped a few photos, shrugged, and returned to our rental car. Did we know adventurous hikers were resting their tired legs at Phantom Ranch 5,000 feet below? No. Did we know how to reach the North Rim? Probably not. The point is, we didn't know much about the Grand Canyon. In all we spent no more than a few hours in the park. We were your typical visitors, and each year millions follow in our footsteps.

I've come a long way since those first steps atop the South Rim. I've spent years exploring and photographing the parks. Traveling from park-to-park I learned this was much more than an assignment; it became an awakening. It was a communion with life and land as I learned to immerse myself in nature. (I also learned how to get to the North Rim, and even hiked down to Phantom Ranch to prove to myself people were making regular trips to the canyon floor.) Did I hike all the trails and participate in all of the activities listed in this book? No, but I'm working on it! I have logged thousands of miles hiking, paddling, and pedaling across America and through its parks, revisiting them for each edition. More importantly, I've exhaustively researched every site in this book, integrating those findings with my unique perspective and with the opinions of hundreds of park patrons and National Park Service employees. These are the footsteps you should follow, and holding this book is the first step to an unforgettable adventure.

Table of Contents

Bryce Canyon's Inspiration Point

Plan Your Trip

Denali

Park Passes

Most United States National Parks require guests to pay an entrance fee. Entrance fees vary from park-to-park, and rates may be per individual, per vehicle, and a few rates are even charged per day. If you plan on visiting several national parks in a calendar year or visiting the same (fee-required) national park several times, the America the Beautiful Passes can minimize the damage to your wallet. A pass is not only your ticket to the national parks, it provides access to more than 2,000 federal recreation sites including national monuments (e.g., Devil's Tower), national memorials, national recreation areas, and all other lands managed by the Bureau of Land Management and Bureau of Reclamation.

Annual Pass • $80: This pass is valid for one year, beginning from the month of purchase. It is available to the general public and provides access to, and use of, federal recreation sites that charge an entrance fee or standard amenity fee. It does not provide discounted camping or program/tour rates. The pass can be purchased in person or online at store.usgs.gov.

Don't automatically purchase an annual pass if you're planning a multi-park vacation. No entrance fee is charged at the following national parks: Cuyahoga Valley, New River Gorge, Mammoth Cave, Great Smoky Mountains, Congaree, Biscayne, Indiana Dunes, Gateway Arch, Voyageurs, Wind Cave, Hot Springs, Great Basin, Channel Islands, Redwood, North Cascades, Glacier Bay, Wrangell–St. Elias, Kenai Fjords, Lake Clark, Katmai, Gates of the Arctic, Kobuk Valley, U.S. Virgin Islands, and American Samoa.

4th Grade Pass • Free: Have a 4th grader in the family? Let your son or daughter take care of entrance fees. Print your child's pass at everykidoutdoors.gov. It can be exchanged for the Annual 4th Grade Pass at any federal recreation sites that charge an entrance or standard amenity fee.

Senior Pass • $80 (Lifetime)/$20 (Annual): U.S. citizens or permanent residents 62 and older can choose from a lifetime ($80) or annual ($20) pass. Annual Senior Passes can be exchanged at any time for a lifetime pass, deducting $20 per annual pass you've purchased. Each pass provides access to, and use of, federal recreation sites that charge an entrance fee. It also may provide a 50% discount on camping fees and certain park programs/tours. Passes can be purchased in person or online at store.usgs.gov.

Access Pass • Free: This is a lifetime pass for U.S. citizens or permanent residents with permanent disabilities (documentation required). The pass provides lifetime access to, and use of, federal recreation sites that charge an entrance or standard amenity fee. It also may provide a 50% discount on camping fees and some park programs/tours. It can be purchased in person or online at store.usgs.gov ($10 fee, proof of permanent disability is required).

Military Pass • Free: This pass is available to all current U.S. military members and their dependents. The pass provides access to, and use of, federal recreation sites that charge an entrance fee. It can be obtained in person or online (store.usgs.gov) with a Common Access Card (CAC) or Military ID.

Volunteer Pass • Free: This pass is given to volunteers who accumulate 250 service hours on a cumulative basis. The pass provides access to, and use of, federal recreation sites that charge an entrance fee for a year, beginning from the date of award. The volunteer pass does not provide discounted camping or tour/program rates.

If you plan on visiting one national park several times in a calendar year you may be better off purchasing an individual park annual pass. They range from $55–70 and are typically good for one year from the month of purchase. Even if you think you might return just one more time within a year it is almost always worthwhile to purchase the park's annual pass.

Another way to save a few dollars is to visit during National Park Service Free Entrance Days (you can find a list of fee-free dates at nps.gov).

What to Pack
If you're like me, you probably wait until the night before your vacation to begin packing. You grab everything you might need and throw it in a suitcase or backpack. Anything left behind won't be noticed until you need it on your trip. Avoid these situations by compiling packing lists (for each family member) and packing a few days in advance. Everyone knows to pack the essentials like cell phone charger, money, hygiene products, and clothes, so here are a few suggestions that you may not think of.

For Any Trip
Garbage/Small Resealable Bags: Not only are bags incredibly useful storage devices, they add a bit of water resistance. I still use a small resealable bag as my wallet. Its combination of transparency, durability, and low-cost-to-quantity ratio cannot be beat. One bag can last years!

Duct Tape: I always have a roll of duct tape in my car. It's also a good practice to wrap the base of a water bottle or hiking pole with duct tape for when you venture into the wilderness.

Headlamp: Reading in your tent or searching under a car seat for the National Park Pass you just dropped, a headlamp is always useful. And kids love them.

For the National Parks
Binoculars, clothes that layer and rain gear (temperature and winds change dramatically based on elevation, location, and time), insect repellent, sunscreen, snacks and water, first-aid kit, pocketknife, journal or sketchpad, a good book, and camera (plus extra batteries and memory cards).

For Hiking
Backpack, hydration system/water bottle, compass and map and/or GPS (know how to use them), hiking stick/poles, pocketknife, whistle, and water filter.

For Camping
Camp stove with fuel, toilet paper, rope, clothes pins, flashlight(s), folding chairs, hammock, water jug, tarp, ear plugs, and a deck of cards.

For Biking
Water, spare tube, patch-kit, lights, high-vis clothing, pump, tire irons, multi-tool, and bike shorts.

For Paddling
Bilge pump, rescue bag, knife, booties, gloves, helmet, and whistle.

Electric Charging Stations
The East and West Coasts are ahead of the charging station curve, but with careful planning you should be able to reach remote parks like Big Bend or Voyageurs. You'll also find charging stations inside huge parks like Yellowstone, Death Valley, and Everglades. And if charging stations aren't available, you can always reserve an RV campsite with suitable electric hookups.

Leave No Trace
Remember the national parks are for everyone. Whether you're an avid outdoorsman or just passing through, all visitors should practice Leave No Trace principles.

1. Plan Ahead and Prepare
2. Travel/Camp on Durable Surfaces
3. Dispose of Waste Properly
4. Leave What You Find
5. Minimize Campfire Impacts
6. Respect Wildlife
7. Be Considerate of Other Visitors

Proper waste disposal is commonly referred to as "Pack It In, Pack It Out" or "Leave Only Footprints, Take Only Photographs." That includes human waste. If "nature calls" and you don't have access to a designated restroom, get off trail (and away from any freshwater source), dig a hole, and take care of your business (or bring a packable disposable toilet bag along, if you think this might be a problem). Practice these simple and sensible principles and our most remarkable and irreplaceable treasures will remain for the enjoyment of future generations.

Vandalism
Vandalism in our public spaces dramatically increased in 2020. Don't do it. Don't carve your name into a tree. Don't spray paint your next masterpiece on a rock. Don't. If you see any vandalism (even if it's human waste along a trail), please report it to a ranger.

Thar she blows! Anacapa Island (Channel Islands)

Economical Travel

Vacations can be expensive. A trip to a national park is often seen as an affordable adventure, but the costs of lodging, dining, tours, entrance fees, and gas can add up quickly. Some costs are unavoidable; others can be minimized using these practical tips.

Lodging: Park lodges are beautiful but expensive. Discounts are rarely available during peak-season and many lodges book months in advance. Travel during off-season for the best rates on in-park lodging.

If you aren't a camper and are willing to splurge in one area, make it lodging. Staying in the park is almost always worth the premium, especially at large, remote parks like Yellowstone, Yosemite, Death Valley, Grand Canyon, etc.

Less expensive lodging is often found beyond park boundaries. Most gateway cities offer everything from chain hotels to B&Bs. Before making reservations, price check your options using online tools (don't forget about airbnb and couchsurfing). It's usually best to make reservations a few weeks in advance. Book too early and you'll pay the standard rate. Book too late and you might pay standard or more depending on availability and demand. If you're making an unplanned stop at a hotel and unable to check pricing online, the best way to receive a discount is to ask. Occasionally a hotel will have a room that is not up to their typical standards (e.g., no air conditioning) that they'll offer at a deep discount. If you don't mind the room's defect, the hotel will not mind checking you in.

Another option is to take the money you would have spent on a hotel room and use it on a tent, sleeping bag, and mat. Camping isn't for everyone, but it's worth a try. You can avoid campground fees (and truly explore the park) by camping in the parks' backcountry. Popular parks typically charge a fee and have an application process for backpacking permits. Others offer free permits. By no means must you be a seasoned backpacker to enjoy backpacking. However, you may want to consult with a park ranger to help plan an itinerary suitable for your experience, as well as get a brief overview of backcountry regulations. Most parks require setting up camp at designated sites or a minimum distance from roads, trails, and water sources. You must also practice Leave No Trace principles.

If "free" is the price you're looking for, you can often find free dispersed camping no federal land (typically National Forest or BLM) nearby (particularly for western parks). In between parks, travelers and truckers are often permitted to sleep in many Walmart parking lots. Walmart's intent is to provide a safe location for weary travelers and truck drivers, so they don't endanger other motorists. Do not take advantage of this benefit by getting comfortable and camping out in the parking lot for an extended period.

Dining: The best way to minimize dining expenses is to pack a cooler. Bringing a loaf of bread, jam or honey, and peanut butter can prevent a few trips to the nearest town for a snack or meal. My preferred low-maintenance/high-energy backpacking/traveling meal is a stick of salami, package of tortillas, and a few candy (or protein) bars. Of course, many vacationers like to treat themselves to more sophisticated meals. There are plenty of ways to do that too (even at a campground).

Activities: Discounts are more difficult to come by for activities. Asking is the place to start, especially if your group is large. Outfitters would rather get your business than see you walk out their door. Many outfitters offer "early-bird" discounts or "online only" specials. It's also a good idea to browse their website and/or social media accounts looking for coupons.

Entrance Fees: These are non-negotiable, but the National Parks Service offers a few free entrance days (search nps.gov for a list of fee free dates). If you plan on visiting several federal fee areas in the same year, consider buying an annual pass (page 2).

Gas: Most national parks are vast regions located in extremely remote sections of the U.S. It will take a lot of gas simply to get to the park much less around it. Remember to top off your tank before entering. A few parks have gas stations but expect to pay a premium.

Acadia, Indiana Dunes, Glacier, White Sands, Rocky Mountain, Bryce Canyon, Zion, Grand Canyon, Pinnacles, Sequoia, Yosemite, Mount Rainier, and Denali offer free shuttle services during peak tourism season. Take advantage of these shuttles. Not only are they free, they give you the chance to enjoy the magnificent vistas along the way without the added stress of driving your car.

Camping Regulations
Camping is a national park staple. Children and adults alike love the freedom of spending a night under the stars. To do so, campers must adhere to a few basic regulations that help protect park resources and ensure an enjoyable stay for all the campground's patrons and your fellow park visitors.

1. Camp only in designated sites.
2. Leave something of little value to indicate occupancy (important for vans and RVs).
3. Store all food and cooking equipment in an enclosed vehicle or hard-sided food locker (particularly in parks with healthy bear, raccoon, or mouse populations).
4. Do not leave fires unattended.
5. Observe campground-specific quiet hours and generator hours.
6. Check out on time.
7. Lock valuables in your vehicle and out of sight.

Regulations regarding maximum length of stay, speed limits, gathering wood, and pets change from campground to campground. Specific regulations should be posted at self-check-in stations or handed out when you register for your campsite upon arrival, or they can be found prior to arrival at each park's website.

Road Construction
All the most popular parks are developed with the modern motorist in mind. Paved roadways venture across regions once declared impassable by foot. Ingenuity, perseverance, hard work and thousands of miles of concrete and asphalt allow automobiles to twist and turn along rugged mountain slopes and craggy coastlines through some of the most beautiful scenery you'll find anywhere in the world. Roads were built to increase tourism and accessibility, but they were also carefully designed to retain aesthetic beauty. You won't find a bridge across the Grand Canyon or a parking lot next to Half Dome, but roads lead to stunning viewpoints of these iconic settings.

Park roads require regular maintenance. Repairing roads in these remote and rugged regions can be a difficult task—a task made more challenging since construction and tourism seasons coincide with one another. To get the most of your vacation, try to plan around road construction. Current and upcoming construction plans are typically listed on park websites. If you can't find construction information there, a friendly park ranger is just a phone call away.

Safety
It is important that park visitors follow safety precautions and park regulations to enjoy a safe visit and prevent injuries. In the unlikely event someone is injured, know where to go to receive proper medical treatment. A few parks have medical facilities on-site, but most do not. Carry a cell phone, but do not rely on it; cell coverage is spotty in most parks.

Accidents happen. And occasionally an accident results in death. Fatality statistics vary from park to park, but there are three common causes: drowning, falling, and car accidents. Out of more than 300 million annual guests, about three hundred die each year (on average). Come prepared, behave responsibly, and you shouldn't have a problem. Still, it's good to know about the inherent risks.

Drowning: Visitors should use extreme caution near water. River crossings can be challenging due to uneven footing, moss covered rocks, and slippery logs. One misstep could lead to being swept down river or over a waterfall. Be especially careful in spring when creeks and streams swell with snowmelt/rain. Do not mix intoxicants and water activities.

Falling: Falls are common, especially at parks like Yosemite and Grand Canyon, where the terrain is extreme, and climate can be unforgiving. No where you're going. Watch your step. And do not take unnecessary risks to get that enviable Instagram image. Have someone else take your photo when you're on ridgelines or near a cliff edge.

Car Accidents: Drive with awareness (there are many distracted drives in the parks). Wear your seat belt. Obey the rules of the road. And take advantage of the park's free shuttles when you can.

Hypothermia: Rivers and lakes. High elevations. Alaska. These places have one thing in common: they're cold. Extended exposure to any cold environment (especially water) can lead to hypothermia, the progressive degradation, both physically and mentally, caused by chilling your body's core. To help prevent hypothermia, wear water-resistant clothing or clothing that wicks away moisture. It's also a good idea to pack a sweater, warm hat, rain gear, headlamp, fire starter, and emergency blanket for any hike, just in case you get lost and have an unexpected night in the wilderness.

Dehydration: It's important to stay hydrated. Remember to carry a day pack with ample water and snacks.

Giardia: Giardia is caused by a parasite found in lakes and streams. If consumed it causes persistent, severe diarrhea, abdominal cramps, and nausea. To prevent giardia, use an approved filter, boil water, or drink from sources clearly labeled "potable" (e.g., water fountains). Filters should be capable of removing particles as small as one micron.

Falling Trees/Rocks: Parks do their best to proactively close trails that pose a significant threat due to falling rocks or trees, but hikers must always be aware of their surroundings. Also, don't kick or throw rocks off cliffs or ledges. There may be hikers below. Rare they may be, but these things do happen. Fall 2019 while hiking in the Smokies, I heard a crash on the trail behind me. Going back to investigate, a tree fell on the trail I crossed not even a minute earlier.

Wildlife: Do not approach wildlife. This is particularly true of bears. Know the differences between grizzly and black bears. Grizzlies are blond to nearly black and sometimes have silver-tipped guard hairs. They have a dished-in face and a large hump of heavy muscle above the shoulders. There claws are around 4 inches. Black bears also range from blond to black. They are typically smaller with a straighter face from tip of the nose to ears. They do not have a prominent hump

above their shoulders and their claws are about 1.5 inches long. Most bear–human encounters occur when hikers startle or provoke the animal. Visitors often wear bells to scare away bears. But your best bet is to hike with a group and talk as you go. Carrying bear spray, a non-lethal pepper spray dilution, is a good idea too.

Firearms: People who can legally possess firearms under applicable federal, state, and local laws, can carry firearms in the national parks.

COVID-19
The global pandemic did not leave our national parks unscathed. Timed entry systems were put in place for extremely popular destinations (Going-to-the-Sun Road at Glacier, Trail Ridge Road at Rocky Mountain, Cadillac Mountain at Acadia, Zion Canyon Shuttles, and Yosemite). Visitor Centers closed. Boat and cave tours were canceled. Everyone was short staff. And on top of that, there was a substantial influx of visitors in 2021. Zion has returned to first-come, first-served shuttle service. Timed entry was a pilot program, so there's no guarantee it's here to stay (my guess is it's not). But there's no knowing what 2022 (and beyond) will bring. So, when planning your trip, be sure to check park websites for up-to-date COVID information.

Wildlife Viewing
Wildlife is transient. The best way to pinpoint your desired animal is to ask a park ranger about current activity and feeding areas. Dawn and dusk are typically prime viewing times for large mammal species.

When you do spot wildlife, remember that these are not tame animals, and should not be approached. Visitors are often injured when they get too close. Stay at least 100 yards away from bears and wolves and 25 yards away from all other animals (like bison, elk, bighorn sheep, moose, deer, and coyotes). Absolutely do not feed wildlife. It's illegal for good reason.

Photography Tips
With over 100,000 photos, I might have the world's largest collection of mediocre national park gallery. It also suggests I'm not a great source for photography tips, but I've learned a lot during the last twelve years.

Every year smartphones cameras become better. Current phones are more than good enough to capture high-quality photos for social media. They nail exposure and focus almost every single shot, and software balances out most scene's dynamic range. There's no shame in relying on your phone for photos.

Gateway Arch from Mississippi Overlook

If you choose to use a DSLR or mirrorless camera, spend time using it, changing settings, figuring out what works for you. While it's fine to operate on "auto," you aren't going to get the most out of it.

Photography is all about light. When using a camera's manual settings, you have three ways to control how much light reaches the sensor. They are aperture, shutter speed, and ISO. Aperture is the opening in the lens. A low f-stop (2.8) means a large aperture (and a lot of light is let in). When you shoot at a low f-stop, you'll have minimal depth of field (good for portraits to focus on the subject, or to create bokeh effects). A high f-stop (22) means a small aperture (and a little light is let in). When you shoot at a high f-stop, you'll have maximum depth of field (good when you have content in the foreground and background you'd like to be in focus). Shutter speed is exactly what it sounds like. It's how long the shutter is open. Shutter speed is often adjusted when you're dealing with motion. If you would like to freeze a subject (or you're in a moving vehicle), you want a fast shutter speed). If you'd like to introduce blurred motion or turn a waterfall into a glossy ribbon, you want a slow shutter speed. ISO is slightly more abstract. It's the sensitivity of the camera's sensor. Keep the sensitivity low (100 ISO) and your images will have little noise. Noise/graininess increases with ISO. That's photography in a nutshell. Cameras allow you to shoot full manual (you set the aperture, shutter speed, and ISO for a proper exposure), aperture priority (you choose the aperture, your camera chooses ISO and shutter speed for a proper exposure), or shutter priority (you choose the shutter speed, your

camera chooses aperture and ISO). For sharp hand-held images you want low ISO (100) and fast shutter speed, which requires a bright scene and/or low aperture. And shutter speed depends on the length of your lens. The rule of thumb is to set your shutter speed at least twice the lens length. Wide angle (16mm), shoot at 1/30 second or faster. 200mm, shoot at 1/400 second or faster. If you have a camera with Auto ISO minimum shutter speed (adjusts ISO to maintain minimum shutter speed), use it.

The next logical question is, what is a proper exposure? Your camera figures that out too. It reads the available light based on a selected metering mode. It's important to understand your camera's metering modes. Most offer multi-metering (full screen but weighing areas differently), center-metering (full screen but emphasizes the central area), and spot-metering (measures light in a spot you control). So, taking a photo using aperture priority and spot-metering, you select the aperture and move the "spot" to where you'd like light to be metered. Your camera selects the ISO and shutter speed for a correct exposure. If that doesn't make sense, read your manual and fool around with your camera.

Photos typically aren't very interesting if they aren't in focus. Your camera will have at least three focus modes. Manual allows you to manually adjust the focus using the focus ring on your lens. Single-shot autofocus locks focus on a subject. Use single-shot AF when your subject is motionless. Continuous autofocus continues to focus while the shutter button is pressed halfway down. Use continuous when your subject is in motion.

White Sands

Keep interesting subject matter away from the edges of your image, especially when using a wide-angle lens. Most wide angle lenses introduce distortion around the frame's perimeter. It's fun to place a subject in a corner, but place that subject a third of the way into the frame and crop it later. You'll get better results. When shooting landscapes with subjects in them, it's often best to keep the people out of the center of the frame as well. Many photographers follow the Rule of Thirds, dividing the frame into a 3x3 grid and placing subjects at any one of the four intersections (as illustrated in the inset photo above of a rock being thrown near Green River Lakes, Bridger-Teton National Forest).

Zoom lenses are your friends. People love to use prime lenses because they take the sharpest images and widest apertures (plus we have legs to move around). This is true, but zoom allows you to adjust the framing on the fly, and that extra focal length can bring in the background, making shots more interesting (plus, changing lenses outside sucks). Take photos at different focal lengths and see what you like.

Many professionals like to say they don't even think about picking up their cameras any time outside of the golden hours (an hour before sunset and an hour after

sunrise). Let them stay home! The easiest time to get sharp photos is in the middle of the day with blue skies and a radiant sun. You'll be shooting at ISO 100 with plenty of speed to get tack-sharp shots from even the least steady set of hands. Mix in some cool clouds and you'll be in heaven. Overcast days are when you might want to forget about your camera. Although, that is a good time to take portraits (excluding the sky) thanks to soft even lighting.

Golden hour photography takes some practice. So does Blue Hour (the hour before sunrise/after sunset). While cameras continue to improve in low-light situations, using a tripod (or monopod) is a good idea. During these periods you'll have long shadows, often creating a scene with large lit and unlit areas. Anytime I'm taking photos with large areas in the shade, I like to take one image exposed for the shadows and another image exposed for direct sunlight. This is where your camera's light metering mode is important. If it's evaluating the entire screen, it will average things out and you'll have underexposed lit areas and overexposed dark areas. Taking two shots, allows you to have the shadows and light exposed properly, but it requires some work to make a good image out of it. A tripod will also make it easy to align your images if you decide to make a composite of the two images later when you're at a computer.

Speaking of processing. Do it. Use Lightroom. Use Photoshop. Find a program you like and get to know it. I used very few of my own photos for the first edition because, quite frankly, they weren't any good. The vast majority of the second edition's photos were mine, but I did very little processing and the quality of work suffered for it. This time almost all the images are mine and I spent a considerable amount of time making them look better (and closer to reality) thanks to Lightroom. It's impressive software!

Powell Point (Grand Canyon)

Don't carry a tripod with you wherever you go because you have it. Almost every time I've brought a tripod on a backpacking trip or long hike, I've regretted it. Now I leave the tripod in my car and get creative with rocks or logs to find a stable surface to set my camera. Sure, your perspective will be limited, but you cut weight and free up valuable space. If there's space and I'm left to choose between packing a long lens or tripod, I'm taking the lens 99 times out of 100.

Pay attention to the light. Today, when I visit a park, I think about where I'm headed, what I'd like to shoot, from what angle, and then what timeframe should I try to be there to have the desired lighting. It's also important to check the weather. Many professionals also like to say to get out and shoot on overcast days as you'll have soft, even light. Overcast days are blah and depressing. Give me interesting clouds or blue skies. Now I wouldn't stay in your tent on an overcast day because your photos aren't going to pop. But, if you have a couple days with variable cloud cover, I'd go to your least exciting destinations on the overcast day(s). Generally speaking, you want the sun at your back for properly exposed images (especially when you're taking a picture of yourself or others), but it can be fun to play around shooting into the sun, too.

That's the basics. This is what works for me. I'm usually shooting landscapes, so most of my time is in aperture priority at f/9 or f/11 (where the lenses I have are sharpest), with spot metering (focus point linked), and single-shot autofocus. I'd guess 90% of my current photos are taken with these settings. The other 10% are wildlife. For wildlife I switch to continuous autofocus (and the focus area and mode changes depending on the situation), but I'm still in aperture priority. If you're a slow learner like me, it may take some time, but hopefully this information helps you avoid a few of my early mistakes. I had no clue what I was doing with my first DSLR. Photos for my first tour of the parks were shot almost entirely in full auto. My second tour, I shot almost everything in aperture priority at f22 because a traveler said I was wasting my camera's capability. That isn't a good strategy either. While you may want more depth of field (higher f-stop), using f22 requires slower shutter speeds to shoot at ISO 100 (less noise). And for sharp handheld shots, you probably want to be shooting at 1/60 of a second or faster. When looking at images in Lightroom, I scroll right past almost every photo taken at f22. They aren't sharp. Photography is not extremely complicated. If you know how ISO, aperture, and shutter speed are related, and spend some time practicing, you'll figure out what you like a few hundred photos into it (not 100,000 like me!).

Social Media

NPS sites have social media accounts. It's a good idea to follow them or at least check posts prior to arriving for potential travel complications (wildfires or road construction) and interesting special events. Facebook tends to be the most useful platform, but it varies for each park.

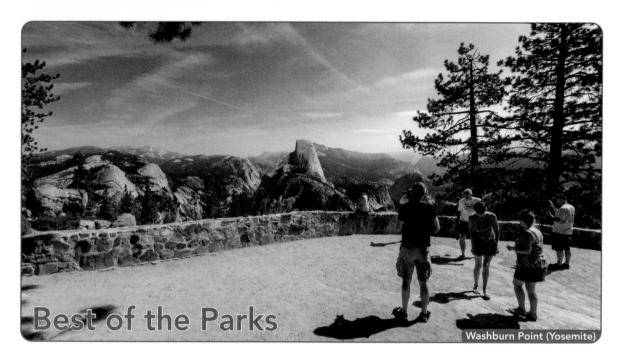

Best of the Parks

Washburn Point (Yosemite)

Best Parks
Tier 1 – Superlative

Yellowstone (page 238)
Glacier (page 264)
Yosemite (page 536)

Tier 2 – The next best
Parks you can't wait to get back to.

Acadia (page 42)
Great Smoky Mtns (page 104)
Grand Teton (page 224)
Big Bend (page 294)
Rocky Mountain (page 350)
Zion (page 430)
Grand Canyon (page 442)
Joshua Tree (page 476)
Death Valley (page 508)
Mount Rainier (page 584)

Tier 3 – Amazing but…
They're missing something. Maybe that "wow" factor. Or they're too big. Too small. Too seasonal …

Shenandoah (page 70)
New River Gorge (page 82)
Everglades (page 134)

Dry Tortugas (page 144)
Isle Royale (page 172)
Voyageurs (page 184)
Badlands (page 194)
Theodore Roosevelt (page 212)
Carlsbad Caverns (page 312)
White Sands (page 322)
Great Sand Dunes (page 366)
Black Canyon of the Gunnison (page 374)
Arches (page 390)
Canyonlands (page 398)
Capitol Reef (page 410)
Bryce Canyon (page 420)
Great Basin (page 466)
Channel Islands (page 488)
Pinnacles (page 498)
Sequoia & Kings Canyon (page 522)
Lassen Volcanic (page 558)
Redwood (page 566)
Crater Lake (page 576)
Olympic (page 596)
North Cascades (page 610)
Glacier Bay (page 624)
Wrangell-St. Elias (page 634)
Denali (page 640)
Kenai Fjords (page 652)
Lake Clark (page 660)
Katmai (page 666)

Gates of the Arctic (page 674)
Kobuk Valley (page 680)
Virgin Islands (page 688)
Haleakala (page 696)
Hawaii Volcanoes (page 704)

Tier 4 – Still great but…
not as strikingly beautiful. Still, it shows our country's embarrassment of geographical riches.

Cuyahoga Valley (page 60)
Mammoth Cave (page 94)
Congaree (page 118)
Biscayne (page 126)
Indiana Dunes (page 154)
Wind Cave (page 204)
Guadalupe Mountains (page 304)
Petrified Forest (page 330)
Saguaro (page 338)
Mesa Verde (page 382)
American Samoa (page 718)

Tier 5 – Good but…
I'm not sure they meet the stereotypical idea of a "national park."

Gateway Arch (page 164)
Hot Springs (page 286)

Above Grinnell Glacier (Highline Trail, Glacier)

Top Attractions

Some of the best easily-accessible attractions (sites you can basically drive your car or boat right up to).

Cadillac Mountain (Acadia)
Skyline Drive (Shenandoah)
Grandview (New River Gorge)
New River Gorge Bridge
Mammoth Cave (Mammoth Cave)
Synchronous Fireflies ("")
Fort Jefferson (boat, Dry Tortugas)
Gateway Arch (Gateway Arch)
Grassy Bay Cliff (boat, Voyageurs)
The Wall (Badlands)
Wind Cave (Wind Cave)
Jenny Lake Overlook (Grand Teton)
Schwabacher Landing (Grand Teton)
Moulton Barns (Grand Teton)
Grand Prismatic Spring (Yellowstone)
Grand Canyon of the Yellowstone
Old Faithful/Upper Geyser Basin
Goat Haunt (boat, Glacier)
Many Glacier (Glacier)
Apgar (Glacier)
Chisos Mountains (Big Bend)
Santa Elena Canyon (Big Bend)

White Sands (White Sands)
Forest Canyon (Rocky Mountain)
Great Sand Dunes
Painted Wall (Black Canyon of the Gunnison, South Rim)
Cliff Palace (Mesa Verde)
Double Arch (Arches)
Park Avenue Viewpoint (Arches)
Grand View Point (Canyonlands)
Shafer Canyon Overlook ("")
Green River Overlook ("")
Gooseneck Overlook (4x4, "")
Goosenecks (Capitol Reef)
Temple of the Sun/Moon (4x4, "")
Inspiration Point (Bryce Canyon)
Bryce Point (Bryce Canyon)
Sunset Point (Bryce Canyon)
Zion Canyon (Zion)
Toroweap (4x4, Grand Canyon)
Lipan Point (Grand Canyon)
Desert View (Grand Canyon)
Cape Royal (Grand Canyon)
Keys Ranch (ranger-led, Joshua Tree)
Badwater Basin (Death Valley)
Mesquite Flat Sand Dunes ("")
Titus Canyon (4x4, Death Valley)
Racetrack (4x4, Death Valley)

Mineral King (Sequoia)
Roads End (Kings Canyon)
Glacier Point (Yosemite)
Tunnel View (Yosemite)
Valley View (Yosemite)
Yosemite Falls (Yosemite)
Tenaya Lake (Yosemite)
Watchman Overlook (Crater Lake)
Sinnott Memorial Overlook ("")
Paradise (Mount Rainier)
Sunrise (Mount Rainier)
Second Beach (Olympic)
Hurricane Ridge (Olympic)
Stehekin (boat, North Cascades)
Johns Hopkins Inlet (boat, Glacier Bay)
Root Glacier (Wrangell–St. Elias)
Copper Center (Wrangell–St. Elias)
Stony Hill Overlook (Denali)
Reflection Pond (Denali)
Exit Glacier (Kenai Fjords)
Trunk Bay (U.S. Virgin Islands)
Haleakala Summit (Haleakala)
Kilauea Volcano (Hawaii Volcanoes) – check eruption status, it's started and stopped several times in the last couple of years)
Ofu (boat/plane, American Samoa)

Buck Canyon Overlook (Canyonlands)

More Top Attractions

The parks offer attractions galore, so here are more favorites. (Listed in order of appearance.)

Sand Beach (Acadia)
Jordan Pond (Acadia)
Thunder Hole (Acadia)
Brandywine Falls (Cuyahoga Valley)
Cuyahoga Valley Scenic Railroad
Big Meadows (Shenandoah)
Sandstone Falls (New River Gorge)
Thurmond (New River Gorge)
Green River Ferry (Mammoth Cave)
Cades Cove (Great Smoky Mtns)
Cataloochee (Great Smoky Mtns)
Stiltsville (Biscayne)
West Beach (Indiana Dunes)
Chellberg Farm (Indiana Dunes)
Old Courthouse (Gateway Arch)
Kettle Falls Hotel (boat, Voyageurs)
Sheep Mtn Table (4x4, Badlands)
River Bend Overlook (Theodore Roosevelt)
Painted Canyon ("")
Oxbow Overlook ("")
Beef Corral Bottom ("")
Snake River Overlook (Grand Teton)
Jackson Lake (Grand Teton)
Mammoth Terrace (Yellowstone)
Hayden Valley (Yellowstone)
Lamar Valley (Yellowstone)
Great Fountain Geyser ("")
Gibbon Falls (Yellowstone)

Two Medicine (Glacier)
Bowman Lake (Glacier)
Wild Goose Island Overlook (Glacier)
Bathhouse Row (Hot Springs)
Boquillas Canyon (Big Bend)
River Road (4x4, Big Bend)
Fossil Discovery Exhibit (Big Bend)
Sam Nail Ranch (Big Bend)
Williams Ranch (4x4, Guadalupe Mtns)
Chinde Point (Petrified Forest)
Giant Logs (Petrified Forest)
Red Hills Visitor Center (Saguaro)
EZ-Kim-In-Zin Picnic Area ("")
Rainbow Curve (Rocky Mountain)
Sprague Lake (Rocky Mountain)
Medano Pass (4x4, Great Sand Dunes)
Chasm View (Black Canyon of the Gunnison, North Rim)
Balcony House (Mesa Verde)
Long House (Mesa Verde)
Spruce Tree House (Mesa Verde)
Park Point Overlook (Mesa Verde)
Balanced Rock (Arches)
Skyline Arch (Arches)
Buck Canyon Overlook (Canyonlands)
Horseshoe Canyon (4x4, "")
Capitol Gorge (Capitol Reef)
Burr Trail Switchbacks (4x4, "")
Fairyland Point (Bryce Canyon)
Sunset Point (Bryce Canyon)
Lava Point Overlook (Zion)
Mather Point (Grand Canyon)
Point Imperial (Grand Canyon)
Lehman Caves (Great Basin)

Mather Overlook (Great Basin)
Keys View (Joshua Tree)
Indian Cove (Joshua Tree)
Hidden Valley (Joshua Tree)
Painted Cave (boat, Channel Islands)
Arch Rock (boat, Channel Islands)
Rainbow Canyon (Death Valley)
Aguereberry Point (Death Valley)
Eureka Dunes (4x4, Death Valley)
Artist's Palette (Death Valley)
Crystal Cave (Sequoia)
Hetch Hetchy (Yosemite)
Lake Helen (Lassen Volcanic)
Manzanita Lake (Lassen Volcanic)
Hat Lake (Lassen Volcanic)
Butte Lake (Lassen Volcanic)
Gold Bluffs Beach (Redwood)
Klamath River Overlook (Redwood)
Crescent Beach Overlook ("")
Discovery Point (Crater Lake)
Pinnacles Overlook (Crater Look)
Mowich Lake (Mount Rainier)
Lake Crescent (Olympic)
Hoh Rain Forest (Olympic)
Rialto Beach (Olympic)
Ruby Beach (Olympic)
Diablo Lake Overlook (N Cascades)
McCarthy (Wrangell–St. Elias)
Wonder Lake (Denali)
Dog Sled Demo (Denali)
Aialik Bay (Kenai Fjords)
Maho Bay (U.S. Virgin Islands)
'Ohe'o Gulch (Haleakala)
Vatia Bay (American Samoa)

Skyline Drive (Shenandoah)

Best Scenic Drives

National parks have become motorists' favorite travel destinations. This book would not be complete without a list of the absolute best paved stretches they have to offer.

Park Loop Road • Acadia (page 49): 27 miles of pure bliss as it loops around the eastern half of Mount Desert Island with a spur road to Cadillac Mountain, the tallest peak in the park.

Skyline Drive • Shenandoah (page 75): The 105-mile highway is Shenandoah's main attraction.

Badlands Loop Road • Badlands (page 198): A severely underrated detour from I-90.

Teton Park Road • Grand Teton (page 229): It offers so many dramatic Teton views.

Going-to-the-Sun Road • Glacier (page 271): Mountain layers and jaw-dropping scenery, but the road is only open completely in summer.

Trail Ridge Road • Rocky Mountain (page 357): It travels above 11,000 feet elevation for 8 miles, with unreal mountain views.

Glacier Point/Wawona Road • Yosemite (page 549): Any road to Yosemite Valley is a good one, but the view from Glacier Point is truly spectacular.

US-101 • Redwood (page 573): For my gallons of gas, there are more scenic stretches of the Pacific Coastline along CA-1 and US-101, but the park's towering redwoods add contrast to California's rocky and rugged coast.

Rim Drive • Crater Lake (page 578): I absolutely love everything about this lake. In summer you can drive around the caldera filled with the bluest water you'll ever see.

McCarthy Road • Wrangell–St. Elias (page 637): A long, gravel road leads to America's Alps. Treat yourself and stay at one of the lodges at the end of the road.

Denali Park Road • Denali (page 645): Only accessible via shuttle/tour bus from late May through mid-September (most years) with a "Road Lottery" in late September.

Best Lodges

Most lodges in the parks were built not just to serve a purpose, but to compliment the environment. These lodging facilities are works of architecture worthy of the landscapes they accent.

Skyland Resort • Shenandoah
Le Conte Lodge • Great Smoky Mtns
Rock Harbor Lodge • Isle Royale
Jenny Lake Lodge • Grand Teton
Old Faithful Snow Lodge • Yellowstone
Many Glacier Lodge • Glacier
Glacier Park Lodge • Glacier
Chisos Mtns Lodge • Big Bend
Zion Lodge • Zion
El Tovar • Grand Canyon
The Oasis at Death Valley
Ahwahnee • Yosemite
Crater Lake Lodge • Crater Lake
Paradise Inn • Mount Rainier
Glacier Bay Lodge • Glacier Bay
Denali Backcountry Lodge • Denali

Saddle Pass via Castle Trail (Badlands)

Best Trails

It's nice to see the parks from the comfort of your vehicle or lodge, but to really explore wilderness you need to hit the trails. (Ratings: E = Easy, M = Moderate, S = Strenuous, X = Extreme)

Tier 1

Unfortunately, many of the national parks' most thrilling trails skew toward the strenuous side.

Precipice (Acadia, X)
Old Rag (Shenandoah, X)
Long Point (New River Gorge, M)
Alum Cave (Great Smoky Mtns, S)
Lake Solitude (Grand Teton, S)
Amphitheater Lake ("", S)
Hidden Lake (Glacier, M)
Grinnell Glacier (Glacier, M)
Highline (Glacier, S)
Sky Pond (Rocky Mountain, S)
Chasm Lake (Rocky Mountain, S)
Delicate Arch (Arches, M)
Grand View Point (Canyonlands, E)
Queen's/Navajo Loop (Bryce Canyon, M)
Observation Point (Zion, S)
High Peaks Loop (Pinnacles, S)
Rae Lakes (Kings Canyon, S)
Half Dome (Yosemite, X)

Tall Trees (Redwood, M)
Skyline Loop (Mount Rainier, S)
Cascade Pass (North Cascades, S)
Sliding Sands (Haleakala, S)

Tier 2

Time on the trails is time well spent, but not all trails are created equal. You'll like these too.

Beehive (Acadia, X)
Dorr (Acadia, X)
Giant Slide (Acadia, S)
Ledges (Cuyahoga Valley, M)
Blue Hen/Buttermilk Falls (Cuyahoga Valley, M)
Passamaquoddy (Shenandoah, M)
Castle Rock (New River Gorge, M)
Tunnel (New River Gorge, E)
Kaymoor (New River Gorge, M)
Charlie's Bunion (Great Smoky Mountains, M)
Dune Succession (Indiana Dunes, M)
Cowle's Bog (Indiana Dunes, S)
Anderson Bay (Voyageurs, S)
Notch (Badlands, M)
Castle (Badlands, M)
Phelps Lake Loop (Grand Teton, M)
Avalanche Peak (Yellowstone, S)
Electric Peak (Yellowstone, X)
Ptarmigan Tunnel (Glacier, S)
Lake Francis (Glacier, M)

Cracker Lake (Glacier, M)
Avalanche Lake (Glacier, M)
Gunsight Pass (Glacier, S)
Dawson Pass (Glacier, S)
Swiftcurrent Pass (Glacier, S)
Santa Elena Canyon (Big Bend, E)
Emory Peak (Big Bend, S)
South Rim (Big Bend, S)
Ward Spring (Big Bend, E)
Mariscal Canyon (Big Bend, S)
Devil's Hall (Guadalupe Mountains, M)
Guadalupe Peak ("", S)
Alkali Flat (White Sands, M)
Hugh Norris (Saguaro, S)
Longs Peak (Rocky Mountain, X)
Dream Lake (Rocky Mountain, E)
Hallet Peak (Rocky Mountain, S)
Lower Cathedral Valley ("", M)
Left Fork/Subway (Zion, M)
The Narrows (Zion, S)
Angel's Landing (Zion, S)
Cape Royal (Grand Canyon, E)
Rim (Grand Canyon, E)
Bristlecone (Great Basin, M)
Wheeler Peak (Great Basin, S)
Boy Scout (Joshua Tree, M)
Bear Gulch Cave (Pinnacles, M)
Juniper Canyon (Pinnacles, S)
Golden Canyon (Death Valley, E)
Mount Whitney (Sequoia, X)
Mosquito Lakes (Sequoia, S)
General Sherman (Sequoia, M)

Dunanda Falls (Yellowstone)

Sentinel Dome (Yosemite, M)
Cathedral Lakes (Yosemite, M)
Cinder Cone (Lassen Volcanic, M)
Lassen Peak (Lassen Volcanic, S)
Burroughs Mtn (Mount Rainier, S)
Pinnacle Peak (Mount Rainier, S)
Gobbler's Knob (Mount Rainier, S)
Second Beach (Olympic, E)
Thornton Lakes (North Cascades, M)
Exit Glacier (Kenai Fjords, M)
Harding Icefield (Kenai Fjords, S)
Pipiwai (Haleakala, M)
Mauna Loa (Hawaii Volcanoes, S)

Tier 3
There's more. Much more.

Gorham Mountain (Acadia, M)
Bar Island (Acadia, E)
Little Devil's Stairs (Shenandoah, S)
Endless Wall (New River Gorge, M)
Chimney Tops ("", S)
Indian Creek ("", E)
Big Plateau (T. Roosevelt, S)
Petrified Forest ("", S)
Jenny Lake Loop (Grand Teton, E)
Bunsen Peak (Yellowstone, S)
Dunanda Falls (Yellowstone,)
Union Falls (Yellowstone,)
Blue Mesa (Petrified Forest, M)
Black Lake (Rocky Mountain, S)
Star Dune (Great Sand Dunes, S)
Warner Point (Black Canyon, M)
Long Draw ("", S)

North Vista ("", M)
Petroglyph Point (Mesa Verde, M)
Devil's Garden (Arches, S)
Murphy Point (Canyonlands, E)
Chesler Park (Canyonlands, S)
Goosenecks (Capitol Reef, E)
Fairyland Loop (Bryce Canyon, S)
Mosaic Canyon (Death Valley, M)
Badwater Flat (Death Valley, E)
Telescope Peak (Death Valley, S)
Monarch Lakes (Sequoia, M)
Eagle Lake (Sequoia, M)
Boy Scout Tree (Redwood, M)
Fern Canyon (Redwood, E)
Watchman Peak (Crater Lake, M)
Discovery Point (Crater Lake, E)
Mount Storm King (Olympic, X)
Lind Point (U.S. Virgin Islands, E)
Kilauea Iki (Hawaii Volcanoes, M)

See the individual park sections for more great hiking trails.

Best for Hiking
Try one of these parks if you're looking to hit the trails.

Best for Backpacking
Big, beautiful backcountries.

Having a paddle (Kenai Fjords)

Intro to Backpacking

Smaller parks. Difficult to get lost. Few dangerous animals. Backpacking training wheels!

New River Gorge (page 89)
Mammoth Cave (page 100)
Isle Royale (page 179)
Wind Cave (page 209)
Theodore Roosevelt (page 219)
Guadalupe Mountains (page 309)
Bryce Canyon (page 425)
Channel Islands (page 495)
Redwood (page 572)

Best for Paddling/Boating

Watery wonderlands.

Acadia (page 52)
Congaree (page 122)
Biscayne (page 130)
Everglades (page 138)
Dry Tortugas (page 148)
Isle Royale (page 180)
Voyageurs (page 190)
Grand Teton (page 232)
Yellowstone (page 255)
Glacier (page 278)
Big Bend (page 300)
Channel Islands (page 493)
Lassen Volcanic (page 563)
Olympic (page 604)
Glacier Bay (page 629)
Kenai Fjords (page 656)

Best for Whitewater

Parks with commercial trips.

New River Gorge (page 87)
Great Smoky Mtns (page 112)
Yellowstone (page 263)
Glacier (page 278)
Canyonlands (page 406)
Grand Canyon (page 451)
North Cascades (page 618)
Glacier Bay (page 630)
Wrangell–St. Elias (page 638)
Denali (page 646)

Best for Biking

Pedaling is a great way to explore these parks.

Acadia (page 53)
Cuyahoga Valley (page 65)
Shenandoah (page 77)
New River Gorge (page 90)
Great Smoky Mtns (page 112)
Everglades (page 139)
Theodore Roosevelt (page 220)
Grand Teton (page 232)
Yellowstone (page 257)
Glacier (page 279)
Saguaro (page 344)
Zion (page 439)
Grand Canyon (page 458)
Death Valley (page 519)
Mount Rainier (page 592)
Denali (page 646)

Best for Horseback Riding

Check out the parks like the earliest explorers, on horseback.

Acadia (carriage) (page 53)
Shenandoah (page 78)
Mammoth Cave (page 101)
Great Smoky Mtns (page 113)
Theodore Roosevelt (page 220)
Grand Teton (page 233)
Yellowstone (page 256)
Glacier (page 279)
Saguaro (page 344)
Rocky Mountain (page 361)
Great Sand Dunes (page 371)
Capitol Reef (page 417)
Bryce Canyon (page 426)
Zion (page 439)
Grand Canyon (mule) (page 457)
Joshua Tree (page 484)
Death Valley (page 519)
Sequoia & Kings Canyon (page 531)
Yosemite (page 553)

Best for Fishing

Anglers will find plenty of fish here.

Shenandoah (page 78)
Great Smoky Mtns (page 113)
Biscayne (page 131)
Everglades (page 139)
Isle Royale (page 181)
Voyageurs (page 191)
Grand Teton (page 233)

Plenty of granite at Yosemite

Yellowstone (page 257)
Rocky Mountain (page 361)
Yosemite (page 553)
North Cascades (page 618)
Alaska Parks (page 622)
Virgin Islands (page 693)

Best for Rock Climbing
Take the direct (and much more difficult) way up rock faces.

Acadia (page 51)
New River Gorge (page 89)
Grand Teton (page 233)
Rocky Mountain (page 361)
Black Canyon of the Gunnison (page 380)
Arches (page 395)
Canyonlands (page 407)
Capitol Reef (page 417)
Zion (page 439)
Joshua Tree (page 483)
Pinnacles (page 504)
Sequoia & Kings Canyon (page 531)
Yosemite (page 552)

Best for Mountain Climbing
Summits at these parks range from multi-day treks requiring specialized equipment to day-hikes.

Grand Teton (page 233)
Yellowstone (page 250)
Glacier (page 273)

Rocky Mountain (page 357)
Sequoia & Kings Canyon (page 529)
Yosemite (page 551)
Mount Rainier (page 592)
Olympic (page 596)
North Cascades (page 618)
Wrangell–St. Elias (page 637)
Denali (page 646)
Lake Clark (page 661)

Best for Stargazing
Stargazing is so underrated. Most parks offer plenty of stars on a clear night; these feature especially dark skies.

Isle Royale (page 172)
Voyageurs(page 184)
Big Bend (page 300)
Utah Parks (page 390–441)
Grand Canyon (page 442)
Great Basin (page 471)
Joshua Tree (page 484)
Death Valley (page 508)
Haleakala (page 701)

Best Off-Roading
A high-clearance 4x4 unlocks some pretty interesting roads at these parks.

Big Bend (page 299)
Great Sand Dunes (page 368)
Arches (page 390)

Canyonlands (page 405)
Capitol Reef (page 415)
Grand Canyon (page 442)
Great Basin (page 470)
Joshua Tree (page 481)
Death Valley (page 517)

Best for SCUBA
Spend some time underwater at any of these parks.

Biscayne (page 130)
Dry Tortugas (page 148)
Isle Royale (page 180)
Channel Islands (page 493)
Virgin Islands (page 693)
American Samoa (page 722)

Best for Beaches
Seldom do you need to pack your swimsuit for a trip to a national park; these are the exceptions.

Acadia (page 54)
Biscayne (page 126)
Dry Tortugas (page 144)
Indiana Dunes (page 158)
Great Sand Dunes (page 371)
Channel Islands (page 493)
Redwood (page 566)
Olympic (page 607)
Virgin Islands (page 688)
Hawaii Volcanoes (page 704)
American Samoa (page 722)

Maho Bay (U.S. Virgin Islands)

Best for Waterfalls
Visit these parks for the soothing sight of plummeting water.

Cuyahoga Valley (page 60)
Shenandoah (page 70)
New River Gorge (page 82)
Great Smoky Mtns (page 104)
Yellowstone (page 238)
Glacier (page 264)
Rocky Mountain (page 350)
Sequoia–Kings Canyon (page 522)
Yosemite (page 536)
Mount Rainier (page 584)
Olympic (page 596)
North Cascades (page 610)
Haleakala (page 696)

Best for Caves
Children love the dark mysterious passages and ornate rock formations found at these parks.

Mammoth Cave (page 99)
Wind Cave (page 208)
Carlsbad Caverns (page 317)
Great Basin (page 471)
Channel Islands (page 493)
Pinnacles (page 503)
Sequoia & Kings Canyon (page 529)
Hawai'i Volcanoes (page 712)

Best for Culture
These parks have a variety of cultural and/or archaeological sites.

Shenandoah (page 70)
New River Gorge (page 82)
Great Smoky Mtns (page 104)
Indiana Dunes (page 154)
Badlands (page 194)
Theodore Roosevelt (page 212)
Big Bend (page 294)
Guadalupe Mountains (page 304)
White Sands (page 322)
Mesa Verde (page 382)
Channel Islands (page 488)
Kobuk Valley (page 680)
Hawai'i Volcanoes (page 704)

Best for Winter
Summer isn't the only good time for a national park trip. Many are just as wonderful in winter.

Warm Winters
Biscayne (page 126)
Everglades (page 134)
Dry Tortugas (page 144)
Hot Springs (page 286)
Big Bend (page 294)
Saguaro (page 338)
Joshua Tree (page 476)

Channel Islands (page 488)
Death Valley (page 508)
Virgin Islands (page 688)
Haleakala (page 696)
Hawai'i Volcanoes (page 704)
American Samoa (page 718)

Cold Winters
Cuyahoga Valley (page 60)
Voyageurs (page 184)
Yellowstone (page 238)
Rocky Mountain (page 350)
Sequoia & Kings Canyon (page 522)
Yosemite (page 536)
Crater Lake (page 576)
Mount Rainier (page 584)
Olympic (page 596)

Best for Birdwatching
A few parks are well-known for the diversity and abundance of our flying friends.

Acadia (page 54)
Congaree (page 123)
Everglades (page 141)
Dry Tortugas (page 149)
Big Bend (page 300)
Channel Islands (page 496)
Pinnacles (page 504)
Haleakala (page 701)

Zabriskie Point (Death Valley)

Best for Wildlife
Fishing bears. Migrating caribou. Grazing bison. Feeding whales. Plenty of wildlife in the wilderness.

Great Smoky Mtns (page 104)
Everglades (page 134)
Isle Royale (page 172)
Yellowstone (page 238)
Rocky Mountain (page 350)
Glacier Bay (page 624)
Denali (page 640)
Lake Clark (page 660)
Katmai (page 666)
Kobuk Valley (page 680)

Best for Photography
Some parks are simply more photogenic than others.

Grand Teton (page 224)
Yellowstone (page 258)
Big Bend (page 294)
White Sands (page 327)
Arches (page 396)
Canyonlands (page 398)
Bryce Canyon (page 420)
Zion (page 430)
Grand Canyon (page 442)
Joshua Tree (page 476)

Death Valley (page 508)
Yosemite (page 553)
Glacier Bay (page 624)
Denali (page 640)

Best Sunrise Spots
Wake-up with the sun at these sites.

Cadillac Mountain • Acadia
Ocean Path • Acadia
Clingman's Dome • Great Smoky Mtns
Delicate Arch • Arches
Landscape Arch • Arches
Mesa Arch • Canyonlands
Sunset Point (Thor's Hammer) • Bryce Canyon
Jumbo Rocks • Joshua Tree
Zabriskie Point • Death Valley
Watchman Overlook • Crater Lake
Haleakala Summit • Haleakala

Best Sunset Spots
Bring a chair and watch the sun set.

Hawksbill Mountain • Shenandoah
Clingman's Dome • Great Smoky Mtns
Lake View • Indiana Dunes
Snake River Overlook • Grand Teton
Crystal Point • Glacier
The Window • Big Bend

Hot Springs • Big Bend
West Filming Area • White Sands
Gates Pass Road • near Saguaro
Delicate Arch • Arches
Cape Royal • Grand Canyon
Hopi Point • Grand Canyon
Shoshone Point • Grand Canyon
Yavapai Point • Grand Canyon
Queen Valley Road • Joshua Tree
Dante's View • Death Valley
Glacier Point • Yosemite
Shi Shi and Rialto Beaches • Olympic

Best for Couples
Couples will find these parks exciting, adventurous, and romantic.

Acadia (page 42)
New River Gorge (page 82)
Great Smoky Mtns (page 104)
Indiana Dunes (page 154)
Grand Teton (page 224)
Yellowstone (page 238)
Glacier (page 264)
White Sands (page 322)
Rocky Mountain (page 350)
Mount Rainier (page 584)
Virgin Islands (page 688)
Haleakala (page 696)
Hawai'i Volcanoes (page 704)

Towpath Trail (Cuyahoga Valley)

Best for Families

Some parks are more family-friendly than others thanks to easy accessibility, short trails, and sights and sounds guaranteed to spark your child's imagination.

Cuyahoga Valley (page 60)
New River Gorge (page 82)
Mammoth Cave (page 94)
Everglades (page 134)
Indiana Dunes (page 154)
Gateway Arch (page 164)
Badlands (page 194)
Wind Cave (page 204)
Theodore Roosevelt (page 212)
Grand Teton (page 224)
Yellowstone (page 238)
Glacier (page 264)
Carlsbad Caverns (page 312)
White Sands (page 322)
Great Sand Dunes (page 366)
Pinnacles (page 498)
Sequoia & Kings Canyon (page 522)
Mount Rainier (page 584)
Olympic (page 596)
Hawai'i Volcanoes (page 704)

Best for Daytrips

Located near major metropolitan areas, it isn't too difficult to pop-in to these parks for a nice hike.

Cuyahoga Valley • Cleveland/Akron
New River Gorge • PA/VA/OH
Shenandoah • Washington D.C.
Congaree • Columbia
Everglades • Miami
Indiana Dunes • Chicago/Gary
Gateway Arch • St. Louis
Saguaro • Tucson
Rocky Mountain • Denver
Joshua Tree • Los Angeles
Channel Islands • Los Angeles
Pinnacles • San Francisco
Mount Rainier • Seattle
Olympic • Seattle

Best for Train Travel

Railroads played an important role establishing parks. They still play an important role at a few.

Cuyahoga Valley (page 64)
New River Gorge (page 82)

Indiana Dunes (page 154)
Glacier (page 264)
Grand Canyon (page 442)
Denali (page 640)

Best Ranger Programs

All ranger programs are recommended, but these are a few favorites. The price is almost always right, too, as most are free.

Wild Cave Tours (fee) • Mammoth Cave, Wind Cave, and Carlsbad Caverns
Slough Slog • Everglades
Guided Canoe Tour • Congaree
Ranger III (fee) • Isle Royale
North Canoe Voyage • Voyageurs
Adventure Hikes • Yellowstone
Grinnell Glacier Hike • Glacier (fee for ferry rides)
Bat Flight Program • Carlsbad Caverns
Lake Lucero • White Sands
Cliff Palace (fee) • Mesa Verde
Balcony House (fee) • Mesa Verde
Sled Dog Demonstration • Denali
Discovery Hikes (fee) • Denali

◀ Hall of the White Giant (Carlsbad Caverns)

Best Concessioner Tours
Even though they cost some money, concessioner tours are incredibly good ways to explore our parks.

Dive-In Theater • Acadia
Carriage Rides • Acadia
Top of the Arch • Gateway Arch
Captain's Cruise • Isle Royale
Red Jammer Tours • Glacier
Canyon Raft Trip • Grand Canyon
Mule Ride • Grand Canyon
Snowcoach Tours • Yellowstone
Crater Lake Boat Tour

Most Underrated
A handful of parks hog most the park love. These deserve a bit more.

Isle Royale (page 172)
Voyageurs (page 184)
Big Bend (page 294)
Great Sand Dunes (page 366)
Black Canyon of the Gunnison (page 374)
Capitol Reef (page 410)
Great Basin (page 466)
Joshua Tree (page 476)
Channel Islands (page 488)

Death Valley (page 508)
Lassen Volcanic (page 558)
North Cascades (page 610)

Worst for Traffic
Other parks get unbelievably busy. We're talking full parking lots, bumper-to-bumper traffic, make arrangements one year in advance.

Acadia: Summer
Great Smoky Mtns: Summer & Oct
Grand Teton: Summer
Yellowstone: Summer
Glacier: Summer
Rocky Mountain: Summer
Arches: Spring–Fall
Zion: Spring–Fall
Grand Canyon: Spring–Fall
Yosemite: Spring–Fall
Mount Rainier: Summer

Worst for Bugs
Warm, wet, fertile environments breed bugs. Pack your bug spray when visiting these parks.

Acadia: mid-May–mid-June
Everglades: Summer

Sequoia & Kings Canyon: Summer
Yosemite: early Summer
Isle Royale: late June–late July
Voyageurs: late June–late July
Alaska Parks: June–mid-July

Backcountry Cabins
Looking to get away from it all without sleeping in a tent? Several parks have backcountry cabins only accessible by foot (or boat). Most lack electricity and other luxuries.

Le Conte Lodge • Great Smoky Mtns
Sperry/Granite Park Chalet • Glacier
Phantom Ranch • Grand Canyon
High Sierra Camps • Yosemite and Sequoia & Kings Canyon
Drakesbad Ranch • Lassen Volcanic
Glacier Bay
Wrangell–St. Elias
Denali
Kenai Fjords
Lake Clark
Katmai
Holua, Kapalaua, and Paliku Cabins • Haleakala
Mauna Loa, Pu'u'ula'ula, & Red Hill • Hawai'i Volcanoes

Grand Prismatic Spring (Yellowstone)

Best Campgrounds

Many of the parks' campgrounds are nondescript accommodations lacking scenic views and privacy. Others are exceptional with stunning vistas, access to great hiking trails, and well-equipped facilities. These are some of the best.

Isle au Haut • Acadia
Isle Royale
Voyageurs
Cottonwood • Theodore Roosevelt
Jenny Lake • Grand Teton
Many Glacier • Glacier
Devil's Garden • Arches
Squaw Flats • Canyonlands
Jumbo Rocks • Joshua Tree
Hidden Valley • Joshua Tree
Indian Cove • Joshua Tree
Paddle-in Sites • North Cascades
Wonder Lake • Denali

Best Oddities

Many weird and unexplainable oddities exist within the parks.

Synchronous Fireflies • Great Smoky Mtns and Congaree
Triple Divide • Glacier
Waterpocket Fold • Capitol Reef
Arches/Canyonlands
The Racetrack • Death Valley
Badwater Basin • Death Valley

Best Superlatives

The national parks are brimming with superlatives. These are some of the most impressive.

Mammoth Cave (page 94): With more than 415 miles of passageways, it's the world's longest known cave system.

Yellowstone (page 238): World's largest concentration of geysers.

Kolob Arch • Zion (page 430): The largest free-standing arch in the park system.

Bristlecone Pines • Great Basin (page 466): Some of the world's oldest living organisms grow here.

Badwater Basin • Death Valley (page 508): Lowest point in North America at 282 feet below sea level.

General Sherman • Sequoia (page 522): The largest known tree by volume at 52,600 ft3 (roughly the size of 16 blue whales).

Mount Whitney • Sequoia (page 522): Highest mountain peak in the contiguous U.S. with an elevation of 14,505 ft.

Yosemite Falls • Yosemite (page 536): The tallest waterfall in North America. Sentinel Falls, the second tallest waterfall, is also located at Yosemite.

Hyperion • Redwood (page 566): The tallest known tree at 379.3 ft.

Crater Lake (page 576): Deepest lake in the U.S., with a 1,943-ft maximum depth and average depth of 1,148 ft. It's also one of the purest lake in North America.

Mount Rainier (page 584): Rising to 14,410 ft, Mount Rainier is the tallest volcano in the contiguous United States.

Wrangell–St. Elias (page 634): Largest unit in the national park system and continent's largest quantity of glaciers.

Denali (page 640): Highest mountain peak in North America, with a summit elevation of 20,320 ft.

Harding Icefield • Kenai Fjords (page 652): The largest icefield contained entirely in the U.S.

Rafting the Gauley River

Best Beyond the Parks

United States wonders don't begin and end with the national parks. (NM = National Monument, NME = National Memorial, NR = National River, NRA = National Recreation Area, NL = National Lakeshore, NS = National Seashore, NVM = National Volcanic Monument, NCA = National Conservation Area, NF = National Forest, SP = State Parks)

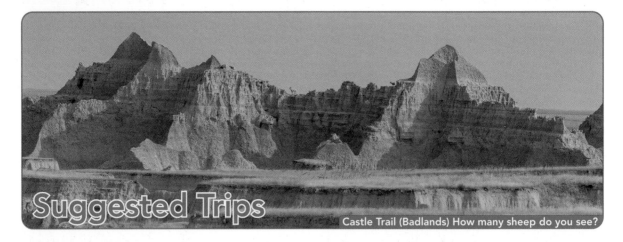

Suggested Trips

Castle Trail (Badlands) How many sheep do you see?

Quite a few people are setting off on "collect them all" National Park adventures these days. As someone who's made three tours around the country working on this book, I don't recommend it. If you already have a travel companion and savings (or passive income), consider exploring the country by region, breaking free from the "national park or bust" mentality. There's a lot more to this country than national parks. With that said, that's not what this book is about, so, if you're going to go for them all in one go, here's what I think. 365 days is more than enough time to check them all off, but one calendar year doesn't include enough summer in the Rockies and Alaska (in my opinion). You'd be better served to make it 15 months, spanning two summers to properly explore the Rockies, High Sierra, Cascades, and Alaska, which are all somewhat limited the rest of the year. Another spring or fall in the southwest would also be nice.

I like to start out east and work west, allowing everything to get bigger and more spectacular along the way, with the stunning crescendo at Glacier National Park (as it's planned below). Note that you could just as easily go up the Cascades and down the Rockies, hopping over to Great Basin, and then making Yosemite your trip's equally amazing conclusion.

For the more traditional travelers, I've highlighted a few areas where you can make a 1- or 2-week national park holiday. These vacations may require a flight or long drive to reach the initial destination, but once you're there, the next stop is usually a manageable drive away. You'll find a few notes giving you a head start in planning your next adventure, but you'll want to dig into the meat of this book to flesh out a full plan for your upcoming national park holiday. However you choose to travel, I hope you have fun!

Sept

Short but intense storms are fairly common spring through summer

Book specialty cave tours up to one month in advance

Sturgis Motorcycle Rally is typically in August

#1 – Theodore Roosevelt (4 days, page 212)
300-mile, 5-hour drive to Wind Cave
to Wind Cave

#2 – Wind Cave (3 days, page 204)
130-mile, 2.25-hour drive
to Badlands

#3 – Badlands (3 days, page 194)
700-mile, 11-hour drive
to Voyageurs

VACATION IDEA – Badlands are Good Lands
Combine these three parks in late summer/early fall (or late spring) for a very nice week-long vacation, spending two nights at each destination. Drive yourself or fly into Rapid City, SD and rent a car.

Elkhorn Ranch is interesting, but if you're looking for something to cut from your itinerary at Theodore Roosevelt, skip it and focus your time on the North and South Units.

Catch a rodeo in Medora (ND), stop at Mount Rushmore or Custer State Park, hike Black Elk Peak (in Black Hills NF), or spend more time underground at Jewel Cave NM! Devil's Tower NM isn't that far away too!

Best of the Midwest

Drive yourself or fly into Minneapolis, Milwaukee, Chicago, or St. Louis to make this 4-park loop that requires about one week to complete.

Notes: This isn't a get-in-your-car-and-go vacation. It'll take some planning and advance reservations. Voyageurs is best explored by boat or canoe, camping on islands inaccessible to motorists (or in a houseboat). You can also stay in the park at Kettle Falls Hotel. Likewise, Isle Royale can only be reached by ferry or seaplane from Grand Portage, MN (best for this itinerary); or Houghton or Copper Harbor, MI. You can get by with just one day at Indiana Dunes and Gateway Arch, but exploring Chicago and St. Louis can be fun.

With a few extra days, adding Cuyahoga Valley to the above vacation is a great idea!

Acadia is close to a lot of amazing outdoor attractions, but no other national parks.

Appalachian Explorer

The newest national park, New River Gorge, conveniently breaks up the long drive from Shenandoah to Mammoth Cave. You'll want to schedule this trip around bookings (whitewater rafting at New River Gorge or the nearby Gauley River and cave tours at Mammoth Cave). Try to plan at least two full days at Shenandoah and three at Great Smoky Mountains. The amount of time you spend at New River Gorge and Mammoth Cave depends on how much rafting/cave touring you want to do. The other kicker is that Great Smoky Mountains should often be its own vacation, because there's nearly infinite attractions/activities in the park and nearby communities. On the other side of the itinerary, you could spend a couple extra days at Washington, D.C. as well.

Congaree is cool because it's a change of pace to the Appalachian and Florida national parks, but it isn't as spectacular.

#4 – Voyageurs (3 days, page 184)
250-mile, 4.5-hour drive to Grand Portage plus a 2-hour ferry ride to Isle Royale

#5 – Isle Royale (4 days, page 172)
2-hour ferry ride to Grand Portage plus a 950-mile, 15.75-hour drive to Gateway Arch

#6 – Gateway Arch (2 days, page 164)
310-mile, 4.75-hour drive to Indiana Dunes

#7 – Indiana Dunes (3 days, page 154)
310-mile, 4.75-hour drive to Cuyahoga Valley

#8 – Cuyahoga Valley (3 days, page 60)
915-mile, 14.25-hour drive to Acadia

#9 – Acadia (7 days, page 42)
800-mile, 13.5-hour drive to Shenandoah

#10 – Shenandoah (7 days, page 70)
200-mile, 3.5-hour drive to New River Gorge

#11 – New River Gorge (3 days, page 82)
375-mile, 6-hour drive to Mammoth Cave

#12 – Mammoth Cave (3 days, page 94)
240-mile, 4.5-hour drive to Great Smoky Mountains

#13 – Great Smoky Mtns (5 days, page 104)
255-mile, 4.5-hour drive to Congaree

#14 – Congaree (3 days, page 118)
655-mile, 10-hour drive to Biscayne

Sept
Book boat tours in advance

Hours are reduced in September and the island closes in October

Catch a Cardinals game

Take the train into Chicago

Many live events to look into at Blossom Music Center and Porthouse Theater

October

Foliage peaks mid-to-late October

Fall foliage peaks late October (avoid weekends)

Book rafting trips in advance and consider rafting the Gauley as well

Book cave tours in advance (better tour options on weekend)

Fall foliage peaks late October (avoid weekends)

Synchronous fireflies in late May/early June

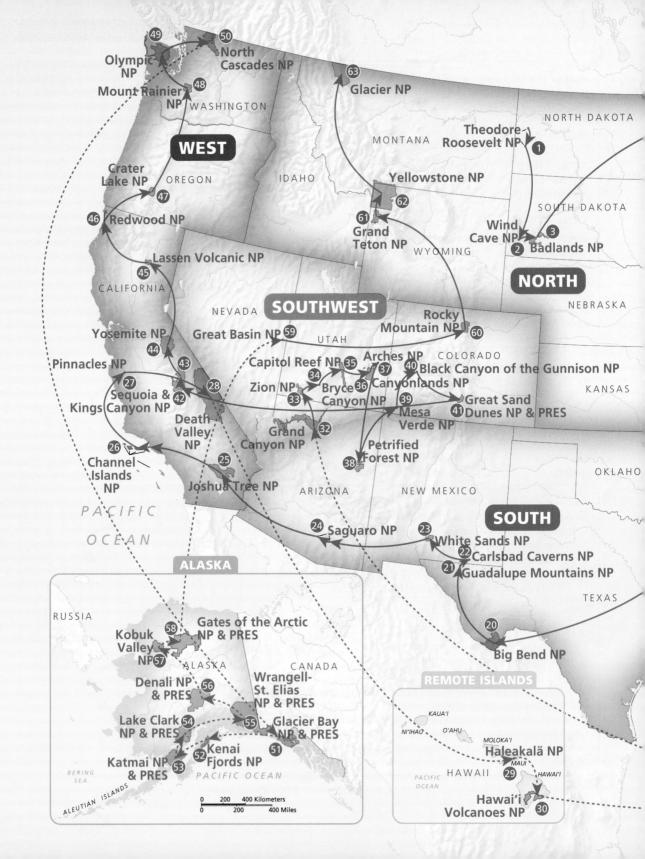

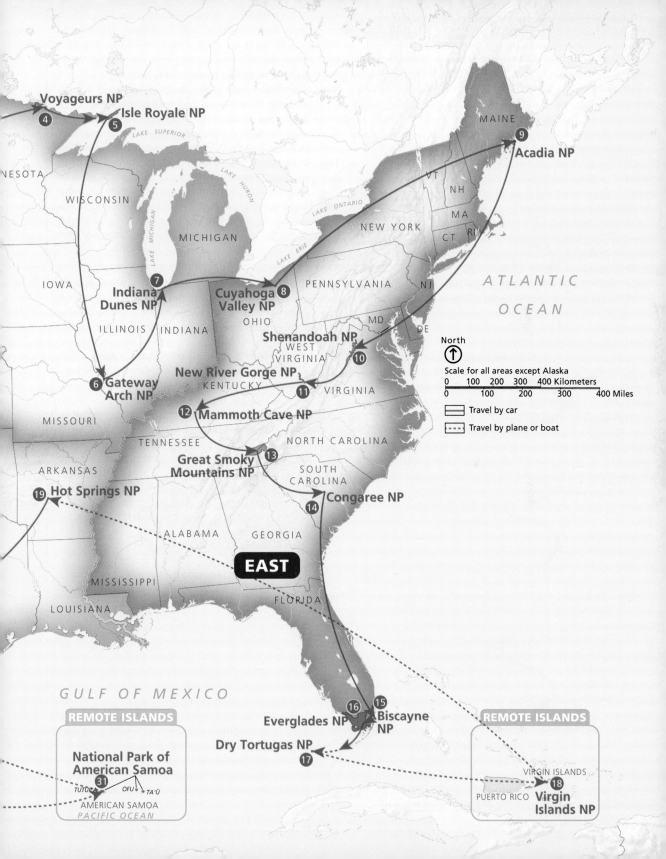

Voyageurs NP
④

Isle Royale NP
⑤

LAKE SUPERIOR

MAINE

⑨ Acadia NP

MINNESOTA

WISCONSIN

VT

NH

LAKE HURON

LAKE ONTARIO

NEW YORK

MA

RI

CT

IOWA

MICHIGAN

LAKE MICHIGAN

LAKE ERIE

⑦ Indiana
Dunes NP

⑧ Cuyahoga
Valley NP

PENNSYLVANIA

NJ

ATLANTIC

OCEAN

ILLINOIS

INDIANA

OHIO

Shenandoah NP

MD

DE

WEST
VIRGINIA

⑩

North

↑

Scale for all areas except Alaska

0   100   200   300   400 Kilometers

0   100   200   300   400 Miles

⑥ Gateway
Arch NP

New River Gorge NP

KENTUCKY

⑪   VIRGINIA

MISSOURI

⑫ Mammoth Cave NP

TENNESSEE

NORTH CAROLINA

Travel by car

Travel by plane or boat

ARKANSAS

Great Smoky
Mountains NP

⑬

SOUTH
CAROLINA

⑲ Hot Springs NP

Congaree NP

⑭

ALABAMA

GEORGIA

EAST

MISSISSIPPI

LOUISIANA

FLORIDA

GULF OF MEXICO

REMOTE ISLANDS

⑯   ⑮ Biscayne
NP

Everglades NP

REMOTE ISLANDS

National Park of
American Samoa

Dry Tortugas NP

⑰

㉛

TUTUILA   OFU   TA'Ū

VIRGIN ISLANDS

⑱

AMERICAN SAMOA

PACIFIC OCEAN

PUERTO RICO

Virgin
Islands NP

Nov

Book water activities in advance

Reserve boat tours/rentals in advance

Make camping reservations as early as possible

Hurricane season is June through October

Fall foliage peaks late October/early November

Holidays, spring break, and winter weekends get busy at both these Texas parks - Parking areas and campgrounds fill early -

Lodging/ camping books early at Big Bend

Bat Flight Program is typically mid-April until mid-October

December
Lake Lucero Ranger Tours offered once a month, November through April

Saguaro bloom at night May/ June

#15 – Biscayne (3 days, page 126)
55-mile, 1.3-hour drive to Everglades

#16 – Everglades (4 days, page 134)
173-mile, 3.5-hour drive to Key West plus a 2-hour ferry ride or 40-minute flight to Dry Tortugas

#17 – Dry Tortugas (3 days, page 144)
3-hour flight from Miami plus a short ferry ride to St. John and U.S. Virgin Islands

#18 – U.S. Virgin Islands (7 days, page 688)
1,250-mile, 18-hour drive from Miami to Hot Springs

#19 – Hot Springs (3 days, page 286)
850-mile, 13-hour drive to Big Bend

#20 – Big Bend (5 days, page 294)
260-mile, 4-hour drive to Guadalupe Mountains

#21 – Guadalupe Mtns (3 days, page 304)
40-mile, 40-minute drive to Carlsbad Caverns

#22 – Carlsbad Caverns (3 days, page 312)
210-mile, 3.5-hour drive to White Sands

#23 – White Sands (3 days, page 322)
300-mile, 4.5-hour drive to Saguaro

#24 – Saguaro (4 days, page 338)
430-mile, 6.5-hour drive to Joshua Tree

The Scenic Side of South Florida

For these three parks, I like to arrange a base camp in Homestead or Florida City and set out exploring Biscayne and Everglades. While you could make Dry Tortugas a day-trip with a 3-hour drive to Key West from Homestead and catching a seaplane or even waking up early enough to catch the 8am ferry, you should spend at least one night in Key West. In fact, an entire vacation could be planned visiting State Parks and/or vacation rentals along the way. You can also spend the night at Dry Tortugas. Primitive campsites are available, but they aren't for everyone.

It'd be easy enough to tack the U.S. Virgin Islands on to the South Florida trip, but you're better off using any extra time you might have to have a look around other Virgin Islands (U.S. or British).

Hot Springs is the odd park out, hanging out in Arkansas. The park is neat and Northwest Arkansas has plenty of cool outdoor attractions.

West Texas Wilderness

If you're looking for a relatively easy trip, fly in and out of El Paso, and spend two nights a piece at Guadalupe Mountains, Carlsbad Caverns, and White Sands. It's a real fun loop around the Guadalupe Mountain Range, combining mountains, caves, and some of the most beautiful sand dunes you'll ever see. Altogether it's a little more than 400 miles and seven hours in a car.

Now, if you want to spend a whole lot more time behind the wheel, begin and end in different cities, and require an extra week of vacation time, add Big Bend and Saguaro National Parks. Big Bend is an incredible place. It offers great hiking, river rafting, and lots of interesting landscapes. If you can only add one of these destinations, I'd choose Big Bend. And note that Big Bend is even better with a high-clearance 4x4, so that's another thing to think about. Saguaro is fun too. It just isn't as bold. Tucson is a relaxed city with a couple of mountains, where you'll find the park's two units and an awful lot of cacti. A bonus for heading in Saguaro's direction is you'll pass Chiricahua National Monument, another worthwhile destination in this beautiful corner of the country.

Hiking above Prisoner's Harbor (Channel Islands)

Southern California Spectacular

A lot of people spend a week at Death Valley, and return home wanting more. But for the "more is more" crowd, fly into San Francisco, spend two nights at Pinnacles, two at Channel Islands, three at Joshua Tree, three at Death Valley, and Fly out of Las Vegas. It's an ambitious trip (and you might be tempted to spend some time in/around San Francisco, Yosemite, Los Angeles, or Las Vegas). It takes about 11 hours of driving just to reach the destinations, much less explore them (and Death Valley is HUGE!).

If you'd rather slow down and go with the "less is more" crowd, break it in half, and make Pinnacles and Channel Islands a short-ish trip (5 days), which is pleasant almost any time of year, and combine Death Valley and Joshua Tree for a long-ish trip (10 days), which is really only nice fall through spring.

If you're flying all this way and spending this much time traveling, it's a good idea to budget for an extended stay and spend a good chunk of winter exploring the islands while you're here. If you aren't a beach/ocean person, hole up somewhere else for winter. You could stretch out your time in the mainland's desert (although even that can get expensive) or parks like Yellowstone or Yosemite make great winter destinations too, as long as you don't mind snow.

Among a book filled with remote and isolated destinations, American Samoa is the most remote of all. You'll want to spend a fair amount of time, not just because it's so far away (for most people), it takes some time and logistics to sort out how to reach Ofu.

#25 – Joshua Tree (5 days, page 476)
195-mile, 3-hour drive plus a ferry ride to the Channel Island(s) of your choice

#26 – Channel Islands (3 days, page 488)
240-mile, 4-hour drive to Pinnacles

#27 – Pinnacles (3 days, page 498)
400-mile, 7-hour drive to Death Valley

#28 – Death Valley (7 days, page 508)
8+ hour flight from Las Vegas to Maui

#29 – Haleakala (7 days, page 696)
40-minute flight from Maui to the Big Island (Hawaii)

#30 – Hawaii Volcanoes
(7 days, page 704)
9+ hour flight from Hawaii

#31 – American Samoa
(7 days, page 718)
20+ hour flights back to Las Vegas plus a 280-mile, 4.5-hour drive to Grand Canyon

Very busy during holidays and weekends

Book ferry tickets in advance

Not the best time to visit Pinnacles Bear Gulch is usually fully open in March and October

Wildflowers (rain dependent) beginning in February

January & February

If you like the ocean/beach and breathtaking scenery, spend as much time as you can in Hawaii

Silverswords at Haleakala typically bloom July through October

This is American Samoa's rainy season

March

North Rim is closed November to May

Zion Canyon Scenic Drive only open to the park shuttle (and Zion Lodge guests) from mid-March through October

Bryce Canyon runs a free shuttle from mid-April through October

Pick your own fruit June through October

#32 – Grand Canyon (7 days, page 442)
325-mile, 5.75-hour drive to Zion

#33 – Zion (5 days, page 430)
85-mile, 1.75-hour drive to Bryce Canyon

#34 – Bryce Canyon (3 days, page 420)
115-mile, 2.25-hour drive to Capitol Reef

#35 – Capitol Reef (3 days, page 410)
150-mile, 2.5-hour drive to Canyonlands

Cruising Canyon Country

This is another ambitious national park tour, but if you like to hustle, fly into Flagstaff (or Las Vegas), spend a few nights at the South Rim of the Grand Canyon (consider stopping at the North Rim for a more peaceful experience), spend a few nights at Zion, spend a night or two at Bryce Canyon, and finish with a night or two at Capitol Reef (depending on what you feel like doing), before flying home from Salt Lake City. Proceed in this order if traveling in spring and reverse it for fall. Goblin Valley State Park, Grand Staircase-Escalante National Monument, and Kodachrome Basin State Park are pretty neat nearby destinations you may want to check out.

April/May or September/October are great times to visit all these Southwestern United States national parks too, but you have a lot of parks to visit

April

Petrified Forest closes overnight

Cliff Palace Tour available late May through September

Road beyond Gunnison Point and North Rim Road typically don't open until April

Medano Pass Road closes for winter, typically opening in late spring

#36 – Canyonlands (5 days, page 398)
30-mile, 35-minute drive to Arches

#37 – Arches (3 days, page 390)
300-mile, 5-hour drive to Petrified Forest

#38 – Petrified Forest (3 days, page 330)
260-mile, 4-hour drive to Mesa Verde

#39 – Mesa Verde (2 days, page 382)
155-mile, 3-hour drive to Black Canyon of the Gunnison

#40 – Black Canyon of the Gunnison (2 days, page 374)
200-mile, 3.75-hour drive to Great Sand Dunes

Canyons and Culture

Petrified Forest is a little bit of an outlier in the quest to collect all the national parks. I've driven to it from Flagstaff. I've driven to it from Saguaro. But coming at it from this direction, you get the chance to drive through Monument Valley (AKA "where Forest Gump ran"). While there are a lot of interesting National Park Service units in the area, it's no easy decision to add on another 400 miles and seven hours of driving time to see where Forest Gump ran and stop at Petrified Forest. Personally, I'd go for the less-aggressive loop, starting and ending in Moab, spending time at Canyonlands (2–4 nights), Arches (2 nights), Mesa Verde (1 night), and Black Canyon of the Gunnison (1–2 nights). That circuit will have you on the road for about 9 hours and 500 miles in between destinations. And remember Capitol Reef and Bryce Canyon aren't too far from Moab either.

#41 – Great Sand Dunes (3 days, page 366)
1,055-mile, 17.5-hour drive to Sequoia & Kings Canyon

Another odd park out. You could include it in the above itinerary, but it adds some serious distance and then you're left wondering where to find an airport. Drive up to Denver? Down to Santa Fe or Albuquerque? Great Sand Dunes is great, but visiting it messes up a nice loop trip.

Crater Lake

Cascades and Coastland

This is a serious national park vacation, requiring more than 30 hours and 1,600 miles in your car to reach these destinations. But that's what the west coast is, it's park after park after park, as you go up or down the coast. A better way to do things is to break things into three separate trips:

Combine Sequoia & Kings Canyon (3 nights) and Yosemite (3–5 nights), flying in and out of San Francisco. (Spending a night at Pinnacles National Park to hike into the High Peaks makes for a nice side-trip.) You'll also be close by Golden Gate National Recreation Area, Alcatraz, Muir Woods National Monument, Point Reyes National Seashore, and Devil's Postpile National Monument.

Spend a solid week looping around Lassen Volcanic (2 nights), Redwood (2 nights), and Crater Lake (2 nights). Along the way you'd pass nearby Whiskeytown National Recreation Area, Lava Beds National Monument, Oregon Caves National Monument, and there's waterfalls, whitewater and mountains galore.

Finally, explore Olympic (3–5 nights), Mount Rainier (3–4 nights), and North Cascades. I won't suggest how many days at North Cascades because it's a different kind of park, with remote reaches accessible by boat, vast backcountry open to adventurous backpackers and mountaineers, and even tranquil paddling opportunities.

#42 & 43 – Sequoia & Kings Canyon (5 days, page 522)
170-mile, 3.5-hour drive to Yosemite

#44 – Yosemite (7 days, page 536)
350-mile, 6.25-hour drive to Lassen Volcanic

#45 – Lassen Volcanic (3 days, page 558)
235-mile, 4.75-hour drive to Redwood

#46 – Redwood (3 days, page 566)
215-mile, 4.5-hour drive to Crater Lake

#47 – Crater Lake (3 days, page 576)
400-mile, 7.25-hour drive to Mount Rainier

#48 – Mount Rainier (7 days, page 584)
180-mile, 4.5-hour drive to Olympic

#49 – Olympic (7 days, page 596)
160-mile, 4.25-hour drive to North Cascades

#50 – North Cascades (5 days, page 610)
Land, sea, and air options from Seattle to Alaska

High Sierra will be packed in with snow yet

May
Tioga, Glacier Point, and Mariposa Grove Roads close from November until May

Lassen Volcanic National Park Highway closes for winter, typically opening in late spring

Should see many migratory birds

Rim Drive typically remains closed into July

Wildflowers peak in July

June
Dry season starts in June

Ferry to Stehekin operates from mid-March into fall

Momma bear and cubs (Katmai)

June sees 24-hour daylight

Humpback whale sightings peak in July

Consider cruising up the Inside Passage - many cruises would take you to Glacier Bay and Kenai Fjords

Most bears at Brooks Falls in late July

July

Mosquitoes might be pretty bad

Services are extremely limited September through May

Buses run from late May until early September

Caribou migration begins in September

Gnats and mosquitoes will most likely be bad

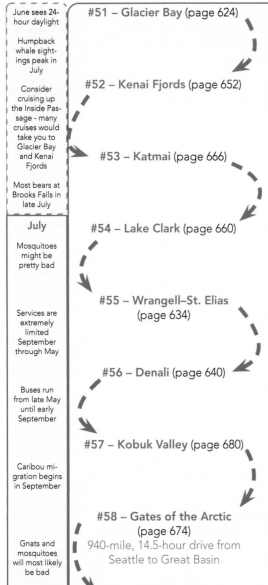

#51 – Glacier Bay (page 624)

#52 – Kenai Fjords (page 652)

#53 – Katmai (page 666)

#54 – Lake Clark (page 660)

#55 – Wrangell–St. Elias (page 634)

#56 – Denali (page 640)

#57 – Kobuk Valley (page 680)

#58 – Gates of the Arctic (page 674)
940-mile, 14.5-hour drive from Seattle to Great Basin

Exploring the Last Frontier
Alaska is known for its wilderness and wildlife. It's untamed and unforgiving, but you don't need a particularly unique set of survival skills, a bottomless budget, or unlimited vacation time to experience it.

Motorists can reach three of the eight national parks: Denali, Wrangell–St. Elias, and Kenai Fjords. If you think Texas is big, Alaska will blow your mind. It's twice the size of Texas. If you want to drive to these three parks, you're going to have some serious windshield time. Starting and ending in Anchorage, it's at least 1,200 miles to drive around a very small corner of Alaska. And then each park's road(s) access(es) only a tiny portion of the respective park. Wrangell–St. Elias has two access roads. Nabesna enters the park's northern boundary, providing excellent vistas and access to trails like Skookum Volcano. McCarthy Road enters the park from the west and terminates at McCarthy, near Kennecott Visitor Center (and Kennecott Copper Mine). From the main park Visitor Center, between Glennallen and Copper Center, you'll be treated to views of Mount Drum. Denali is a little different. Motorists are allowed to drive the first 15 miles of Denali Park Road to Savage River, beyond that it's only open to shuttle buses (save for a couple days in September when there's a road lottery), which makes for much more orderly park operation. At Kenai Fjords, you can drive to Exit Glacier (and continue hiking from there). Consider taking the train from Anchorage. It's an incredibly scenic stretch of rail, and from Seward you can book boat or land tours, without having to get a car (although car rental is available at the train station).

The other five Alaskan national parks cannot be accessed by car. Most visitors arrive by plane or simply fly over. Kobuk Valley and Gates of the Arctic are continually in the running for "Least Visited National Park." Two of these parks are quite well known. Katmai, thanks to bears who "fish" at Brooks Falls, and Glacier Bay, frequented by many cruise ships (and hundreds of thousands of passengers) each summer, are quite popular in summer. Alaska is huge and not particularly motorist friendly. Enjoy it!

You'll find more than hikers on Glacier's Highline Trail (Thanks Sam & Katie!)

Great Basin is great, but it doesn't fit in with any of the travel itineraries due to its location and climate.

Rocky Mountain High

Like other "flagship" national parks, each of these could be its own singular week-long (or more) vacation destination and it's highly unlikely you'd return home disappointed. Focusing on the popular highlights, you can get more bang for your vacation days by hustling up (or down) the Rockies. Still, unless you have a full two weeks, I'd recommend saving Rocky Mountain or Glacier for another trip, so you aren't too rushed (or forced to miss out on a whole lot of spectacular attractions due to time constraints).

Grand Teton and Yellowstone are the classic combo. They're nearly contiguous, and Grand Teton's prominent range is the perfect complement to Yellowstone's alpine lakes and geothermal wonders. Deciding how much time to spend at any of these parks is difficult. And, quite frankly, that's one of the beautiful things about them. Even if you think you've done everything, they're always changing, and always worth visiting again and again.

#59 – Great Basin
(2 days, page 466)
630-mile, 11-hour drive
to Rocky Mountain

#60 – Rocky Mountain
(5 days, page 350)
530-mile, 8-hour drive
to Grand Teton

#61 – Grand Teton
(5 days, page 224)
80-mile, 2-hour drive
to Yellowstone

#62 – Yellowstone
(7 days, page 238)
400-mile, 7-hour drive
to Glacier

#63 – Glacier (7 days, page 264)

August
Wheeler Peak Road opens completely in May

Trail Ridge Road typically closes from October through May

This is prime time at Grand Teton, Yellowstone, and Glacier - You'll want to reserve campgrounds/lodgings/activities as early as possible

Going-to-the-Sun Road typically closes from October until June/July

How to Use This Book

Beef Corral Bottom (Theodore Roosevelt)

About the Guide
The United States has 63 national parks. Each one uniquely beautiful, brimming with life, adventure, and fun. Activities and attractions differ from park-to-park and season-to-season, and the possibilities are nearly limitless. But most visitors only have a few days to explore these vast expanses of unspoiled wilderness. To make those few days count, plan your trip wisely with the help of a guide familiar with the park's trails and history.

Let this book be *Your Guide to the National Parks*. The 63 national parks are broken into seven regions: East, North, South, Southwest, West, Alaska, and Remote Islands (map on following page). Within these sections the parks are included in geographical order (not alphabetical), allowing parks that are commonly visited on the same trip to be found adjacent to one another. Each park section includes an introduction, basic logistical information, maps, popular activities, the basics (accessibility, pets, and weather), and a few tips and recommendations. You'll also find a short list of attractions beyond the park. All information has been researched and assembled with the greatest attention to detail, so each park's most interesting facts and exciting activities are right here at your fingertips.

Introductions
"There is nothing more practical than the preservation of beauty, than the preservation of anything that appeals to the higher emotions of mankind."

– Theodore Roosevelt

President Theodore Roosevelt was a practical man who liked big things, so it comes as no surprise that he was one of the most influential individuals in the history of the national parks. Each introduction tells stories about men and women like President Roosevelt and events—both natural and historic—that helped shape the parks as we know them today.

Logistics
Logistical data like contact information, accommodations, operating hours, and entrance fees are listed right up front alongside the introduction. Close by you'll find a "When to Go" section. It includes practical information about peak visitation, seasonal changes, and closures. A "Transportation & Airports" section covers all pertinent information about how to travel to and around each park. Everything you need to know about park shuttles, airports, and Amtrak is found here. Driving directions are typically provided to the park's most popular entrance(s) and are often accompanied with a regional map displaying major highways and interstates. If a park has multiple units or popular developed regions you can expect to find a "Regions" section describing each one. Names, locations, dates, and rates of campgrounds and lodges found within the park are often listed in an easy-to-read table.

Maps
Large legible maps are included to aid in planning your trip. Markers help pinpoint trailheads and popular attractions.

The maps in this book are not intended for hiking. You can purchase a high-quality topographical park map at most visitor centers. Always use a road map or GPS when traveling.

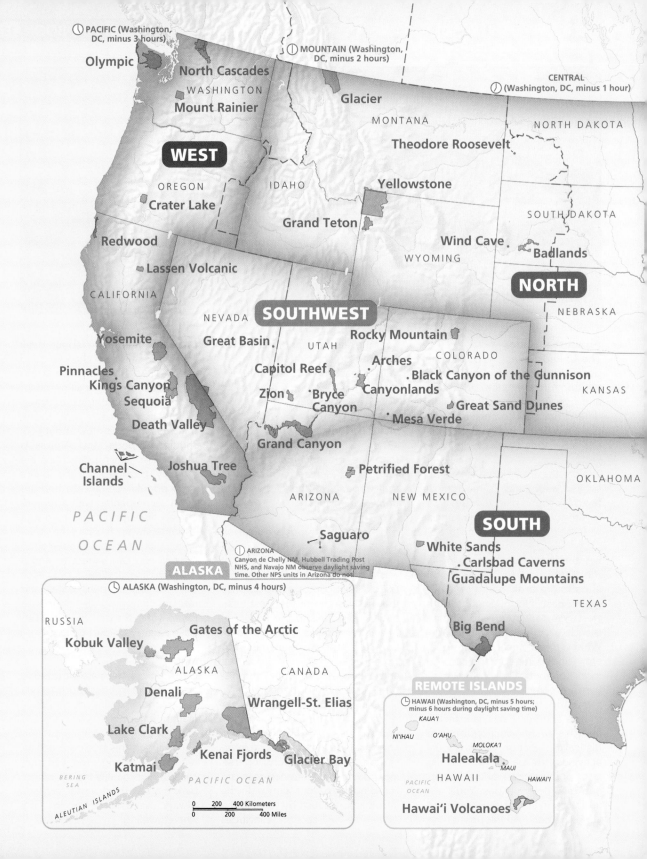

PACIFIC (Washington, DC, minus 3 hours)

MOUNTAIN (Washington, DC, minus 2 hours)

CENTRAL (Washington, DC, minus 1 hour)

Olympic

North Cascades

WASHINGTON

Mount Rainier

Glacier

MONTANA

Theodore Roosevelt

NORTH DAKOTA

WEST

OREGON

IDAHO

Yellowstone

SOUTH DAKOTA

Crater Lake

Grand Teton

Redwood

WYOMING

Wind Cave

Badlands

Lassen Volcanic

CALIFORNIA

NORTH

NEVADA

SOUTHWEST

NEBRASKA

Yosemite

Great Basin

UTAH

Rocky Mountain

COLORADO

Pinnacles

Capitol Reef

Arches

Black Canyon of the Gunnison

KANSAS

Kings Canyon

Zion

Bryce Canyon

Canyonlands

Great Sand Dunes

Sequoia

Death Valley

Mesa Verde

Grand Canyon

Joshua Tree

Channel Islands

PACIFIC

Petrified Forest

OKLAHOMA

OCEAN

ARIZONA

NEW MEXICO

SOUTH

Saguaro

ARIZONA
Canyon de Chelly NM, Hubbell Trading Post NHS, and Navajo NM observe daylight saving time. Other NPS units in Arizona do not.

White Sands

Carlsbad Caverns

Guadalupe Mountains

TEXAS

ALASKA

ALASKA (Washington, DC, minus 4 hours)

RUSSIA

Gates of the Arctic

Big Bend

Kobuk Valley

ALASKA

CANADA

Denali

Wrangell-St. Elias

REMOTE ISLANDS

HAWAII (Washington, DC, minus 5 hours; minus 6 hours during daylight saving time)

Lake Clark

KAUA'I

NI'IHAU

O'AHU

MOLOKA'I

Katmai

Kenai Fjords

Glacier Bay

Haleakala

MAUI

BERING SEA

PACIFIC OCEAN

HAWAII

HAWAI'I

ALEUTIAN ISLANDS

0   200   400 Kilometers
0   200   400 Miles

PACIFIC OCEAN

Hawai'i Volcanoes

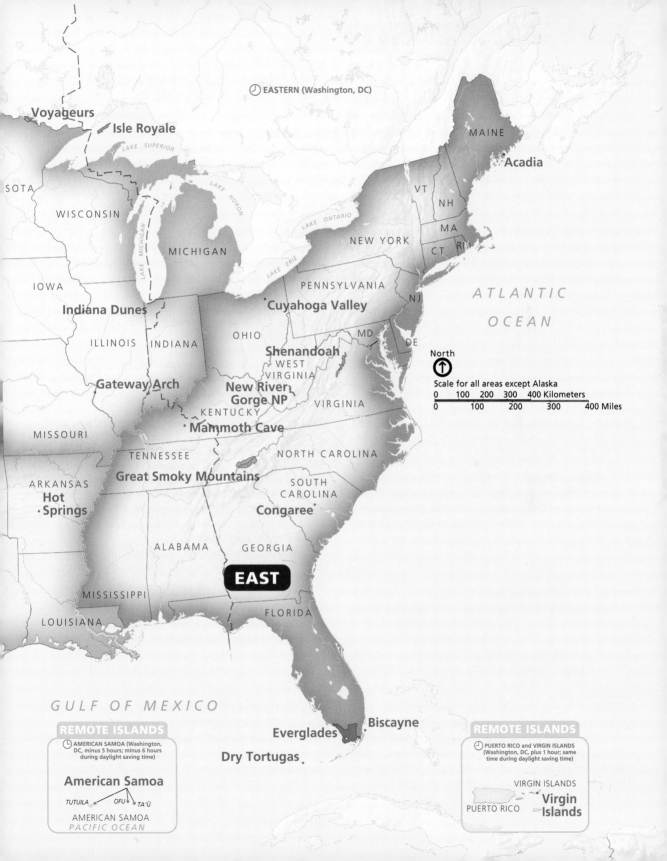

EASTERN (Washington, DC)

Voyageurs

Isle Royale

LAKE SUPERIOR

MAINE

Acadia

SOTA

WISCONSIN

LAKE HURON

VT

NH

MICHIGAN

LAKE MICHIGAN

MA

NEW YORK

CT RI

IOWA

LAKE ONTARIO

Indiana Dunes

LAKE ERIE

PENNSYLVANIA

NJ

ATLANTIC

OCEAN

ILLINOIS

INDIANA

OHIO

Cuyahoga Valley

MD

DE

North

Gateway Arch

Shenandoah

WEST
VIRGINIA

New River
Gorge NP

VIRGINIA

Scale for all areas except Alaska

0   100 200 300 400 Kilometers

0   100   200   300   400 Miles

MISSOURI

KENTUCKY

Mammoth Cave

TENNESSEE

NORTH CAROLINA

ARKANSAS

Great Smoky Mountains

SOUTH
CAROLINA

Hot
Springs

Congaree

ALABAMA

GEORGIA

EAST

MISSISSIPPI

FLORIDA

LOUISIANA

GULF OF MEXICO

Everglades

Biscayne

Dry Tortugas

Activities

The activity most often associated with a trip to one of our national parks is hiking. (Don't forget to pack your hiking shoes.) This guidebook chronicles hiking in great detail. Most park sections include a hiking table with essential information like trailhead location, distance, and difficulty. More often than not trailheads are assigned a number corresponding to a marker on the park map at the trailhead location. Hiking is often the main attraction, but there's much more to do. You can do everything from SCUBA diving to flightseeing, mule rides to train excursions, biking to snowmobiling. All the most popular activities are discussed, and outfitter information (including pricing) is included whenever applicable.

The Basics

Visitor Centers: Whether it's your first visit or your 40th, every national park trip should begin at a visitor center. This section provides basic information like location, operating hours, and a short description of what you can expect to find at each facility. You'll also find details on museums and cultural exhibits here.

Ranger Programs & For Kids: Ranger Programs vary from park-to-park, but expect a variety of walks, talks, and evening programs to be offered, especially if you're traveling during peak tourism season. Park rangers often live in the parks and they love to show off their homes. Ranger programs are highly recommended. They provide a chance to learn more about these special places and share the enthusiasm, knowledge, and humor of friendly park rangers. Most of the programs are free. Ranger program schedules change from week-to-week and year-to-year. For a current schedule of events, check the park's website, free newspaper, or bulletin boards conveniently located at campgrounds, visitor centers, and sometimes along roadways.

Kids of all ages are invited to participate in each park's Junior Ranger Program. Activity booklets are typically free. These hard copies allow families to complete the Junior Ranger activities on their own terms. Activities may direct children to places especially interesting to younger visitors, or to other ranger-guided programs. After completing a specific number of activities for the child's age, participants return the booklet to a visitor center and he or she is awarded a patch/badge and certificate. While these activities are designed specifically for kids, your entire family may discover the importance of the park and gain a more intimate connection with these natural wonderlands.

Flora & Fauna: A brief discussion of plants and animals you're likely to encounter to invasive, endangered, and reintroduced species found within park boundaries.

Pets & Accessibility: Next up are the animals we bring with us, our pets. I love pets and can understand why you'd want to bring them, but I'd explore every avenue available to leave them at home for your national park vacation. Simply put, they will limit what you can do. In general, pets are only allowed where your car can go, but over the years I've noticed more trails opening to leashed pets. Most buildings and the backcountry are off limits to pets. They must be kept on a leash (less than six feet). A few parks offer boarding facilities for a nominal fee. Or you can usually find a boarding facility in the nearest town.

The parks are constantly working to increase accessibility of trails, attractions, and facilities. If you or someone you are traveling with has any special needs, it is always best to discuss them with a park employee at least a week before arriving. I provide a brief overview of accessible facilities and trails.

Weather: A small graph of average temperatures and precipitation provides a quick glimpse of what you can expect weather-wise throughout the year. Weather is difficult to predict, so these averages only provide a baseline for planning. Whether you're departing on a 2-hour hike or a multi-day trek, make a habit of checking the local forecast before departing.

Tips & Recommendations

Each park section closes with a bit of subjectivity about how to visit each park, including short lists of favorite trails, among other things.

Beyond the Parks

The United States is huge, and there's much more to it than national parks. I've included a short list of nearby (mostly) outdoor attractions you might want to add to your travel itinerary. By no means is it exhaustive. (I'm sure there's plenty of wonderful places I don't know about.) This little section highlights one of my biggest mistakes. I don't visit nearly enough destinations in between parks (or nearby). Now, I put a lot of pressure on myself to make the best possible book, and I've always felt like that meant hiking more trails, taking more photos, spending more nights in the parks. But I also can't count how many times I've driven past a place thinking, "man, that looks amazing," only to drive right past it to the next park. These recommendations are going to improve with each new edition.

Welcome to Your
National Parks

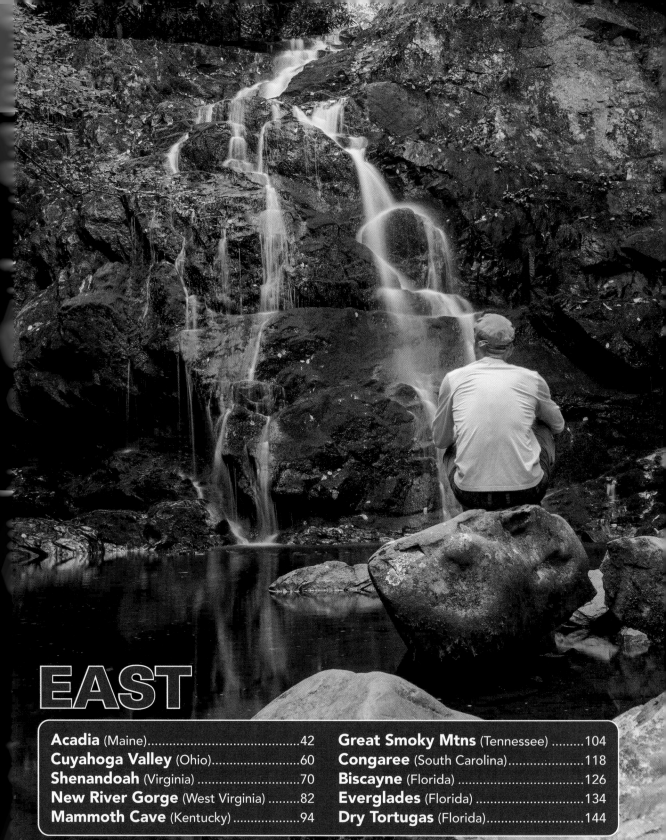

EAST

EASTERN (Washington, DC)

Isle Royale NP

LAKE SUPERIOR

Apostle Islands NL
Keweenaw NHP
Pictured Rocks NL
Portage NM

WISCONSIN

MICHIGAN
Sleeping Bear Dunes NL
LAKE MICHIGAN
LAKE HURON

MILWAUKEE
MADISON
LANSING
DETROIT
CHICAGO
River Raisin NBP
TOLEDO
CLEVELAND
Perry's Victory and International Peace Memorial
James A. Garfield NHS
Cuyahoga Valley NP
AKRON

Pullman NM
Indiana Dunes NP
INDIANA
INDIANAPOLIS

ILLINOIS

Lincoln Home NHS
SPRINGFIELD

Arch NP
ST. LOUIS
Ulysses S. Grant NHS
George Rogers Clark NHP

OHIO
COLUMBUS
Dayton Aviation Heritage NHP
Charles Young Buffalo Soldiers NM
CINCINNATI
Hopewell Culture NHP
William Howard Taft NHS

FRANKFORT
LOUISVILLE
Abraham Lincoln Birthplace NHP
KENTUCKY

Lincoln Boyhood N MEM

MAINE

Katahdin Woods and Waters NM
Appalachian NST
Saint Croix Island IHS
AUGUSTA
Acadia NP

BURLINGTON
MONTPELIER
VT
NH
CONCORD

Marsh-Billings-Rockefeller NHP
Saint-Gaudens NHS
Lowell NHP
BOSTON
MA
Cape Cod NS
Springfield Armory NHS
Blackstone River Valley NHP
PROVIDENCE
New Bedford Whaling NHP
HARTFORD
CT
RI
Roger Williams N MEM

LAKE ONTARIO
Fort Stanwix NM
Harriet Tubman NHP
ROCHESTER
SYRACUSE
ALBANY
Women's Rights NHP
BUFFALO
Martin Van Buren NHS
NEW YORK
Theodore Roosevelt Inaugural NHS
Vanderbilt Mansion NHS
Eleanor Roosevelt NHS
Home of Franklin D. Roosevelt NHS
Weir Farm NHS
Sagamore Hill NHS
Fire Island NS
Upper Delaware SRR
Middle Delaware NSR
Steamtown NHS
Delaware Water Gap NRA
Paterson Great Falls NHP
Morristown NHP
NEW YORK CITY
Thomas Edison NHP
N.J.

LAKE ERIE

PENNSYLVANIA
Allegheny Portage Railroad NHS
Johnstown Flood N MEM
PITTSBURGH
Flight 93 N MEM
HARRISBURG
PHILADELPHIA
First Ladies NHS
Friendship Hill NHS
Fort Necessity NB
Gettysburg NMP
Eisenhower NHS
First State NHP
DOVER
Great Egg Harbor SRR
BALTIMORE
MD
WASHINGTON, D.C.
Harpers Ferry NHP
Cedar Creek and Belle Grove NHP
Thomas Stone NHS
Assateague Island NS
Harriet Tubman Underground Railroad NHP
George Washington Birthplace NM
Fredericksburg and Spotsylvania Co. Battlefields Mem. NMP

WEST VIRGINIA
Shenandoah NP
CHARLESTON
New River Gorge NP
Gauley River NRA
Bluestone NSR

VIRGINIA
RICHMOND
Richmond NBP
Maggie L Walker NHS
Colonial NHP
Fort Monroe NM
Petersburg NB
Appomattox Court House
Booker T. Washington NM
Wright Brothers N MEM
Fort Raleigh NHS
Cape Hatteras NS

Mammoth Cave NP
Big South Fork NRRA
Cumberland Gap NHP
Andrew Johnson NHS
Blue Ridge PKWY
Guilford Courthouse NMP
RALEIGH
NORTH CAROLINA

Manhattan Project NHP
Fort Donelson NB
Obed WSR
Stones River NB
NASHVILLE

Carl Sandburg Home NHS
CHARLOTTE
Kings Mountain NMP
Cowpens NB
Moores Creek NB
Cape Lookout NS

Great Smoky Mountains NP
TENNESSEE
Shiloh NMP
MEMPHIS
Chickamauga and Chattanooga NMP
Russell Cave NM
Little River Canyon N PRES
Appalachian NST
Chattahoochee River NRA
Ninety Six NHS
SOUTH CAROLINA
COLUMBIA
Congaree NP

Brices Cross Roads NBS
Tupelo NB
Natchez Trace PKWY & NST
Freedom Riders NM
Kennesaw Mountain NBP
Horseshoe Bend NMP
BIRMINGHAM
Birmingham Civil Rights NM
ATLANTA
Martin Luther King, Jr., NHS
Ocmulgee NM
Charleston
Charles Pinckney NHS
Fort Sumter NM
Reconstruction Era NM

MISSISSIPPI
ALABAMA
MONTGOMERY
Tuskegee Airmen NHS
Tuskegee Institute NHS
GEORGIA
Andersonville NHS
Jimmy Carter NHS
Fort Pulaski NM

VICKSBURG
Vicksburg NMP
JACKSON
EAST
Fort Frederica NM
Cumberland Island NS

ATLANTIC OCEAN

Natchez Trace PKWY & NST
Natchez NHP

Timucuan Ecological and Historic Preserve
Fort Caroline N MEM
TALLAHASSEE
JACKSONVILLE
Castillo de San Marcos NM
Fort Matanzas NM

BATON ROUGE
LOUISIANA
Gulf Islands NS
NEW ORLEANS
New Orleans Jazz NHP
Jean Lafitte NHP & PRES

FLORIDA
Canaveral NS

GULF OF MEXICO

North

ST. PETERSBURG
TAMPA
De Soto N MEM

Big Cypress N PRES
MIAMI

Everglades NP
Biscayne NP

Dry Tortugas NP

NORTHEAST

BOSTON AREA
Adams NHP
Boston African American NHS
Boston Harbor Islands NRA
Boston NHP
Frederick Law Olmsted NHS
John Fitzgerald Kennedy NHS
Longfellow House-Washington's Headquarters NHS
Minute Man NHP
Salem Maritime NHS
Saugus Iron Works NHS

NEW YORK CITY AREA
African Burial Ground NM
Castle Clinton NM
Federal Hall N MEM
Gateway NRA (also NJ)
General Grant N MEM
Governors Island NM
Hamilton Grange N MEM
Saint Paul's Church NHS
Statue of Liberty NHS
Stonewall NM
Theodore Roosevelt Birthplace NHS

PHILADELPHIA AREA
Edgar Allan Poe NHS
Hopewell Furnace NHS
Independence NHP
Thaddeus Kosciuszko N MEM
Valley Forge NHP

BALTIMORE AREA
Fort McHenry NM and Historic Shrine
Hampton NHS

NATIONAL CAPITAL

DISTRICT OF COLUMBIA
Belmont-Paul Women's Equality NM
Carter G. Woodson Home NHS
Constitution Gardens
Ford's Theatre NHS
Franklin Delano Roosevelt Memorial
Frederick Douglass NHS
Korean War Veterans Memorial
Lincoln Memorial
Lyndon Baines Johnson Memorial Grove
Martin Luther King, Jr. Memorial
Mary McLeod Bethune Council House NHS
National Capital Parks
National Mall
Pennsylvania Avenue NHS
Rock Creek Park
Theodore Roosevelt Island
Thomas Jefferson Memorial
Vietnam Veterans Memorial
Washington Monument
White House
World War I Memorial
World War II Memorial

MARYLAND
Antietam NB
Catoctin Mountain Park
Chesapeake and Ohio Canal NHP (also DC and WV)
Clara Barton NHS
Fort Washington Park
Greenbelt Park
Monocacy NB
Piscataway Park
Potomac Heritage NST (also PA, VA, and DC)

VIRGINIA
Arlington House, The Robert E. Lee Memorial
George Washington Memorial PKWY (also MD)
Manassas NBP
Prince William Forest Park
Wolf Trap National Park for the Performing Arts

0   100   200   300   400 Kilometers
0   100   200   300   400 Miles

Acadia

On The Precipice

Phone: (207) 288-3338
Website: nps.gov/acad

Established: February 26, 1919
July 8, 1916 (National Monument)
Size: 47,390 Acres
Annual Visitors: 3 Million
Peak Season: July–September
Hiking Trails: 120+ Miles
Carriage Trails: 45 Miles

Activities: Hiking, Rock Climbing, Paddling, Boat & Carriage Tours, Biking, Flightseeing, Swimming, Fishing, Birdwatching

Campgrounds: Blackwoods and Seawall (Mount Desert Island, $22–30/night), Schoodic Woods (Schoodic Peninsula, $22–40), Duck Harbor (Isle au Haut, $20)
Backcountry Camping: None

Park Hours: All day, every day
Entrance Fee (May–October): $30/25/15 (car/motorcycle/individual)

The coast of Maine and Mount Desert Island (MDI) has an allure, a gravity that draws people away from their big city lives and frenetic lifestyles. Here time slows down; visitors are given the chance to enjoy the little things that often go unnoticed. Nature is heard. Waves cracking against granite cliffs. A bullfrog's guttural croak. The rat-a-tat-tat of a woodpecker. A choir of singing sparrows. While it can feel like your first time truly experiencing nature, today's tourists are far from the first to enjoy the beauty of Maine's Atlantic Coast. The deep blue lakes, bald granite mountaintops, and surf-splashed cliffs of Acadia National Park have been treasured for more than a century.

About 25,000 years ago, MDI wasn't even an island. It was continental mainland, occupied by a massive sheet of ice. The ice receded, but not without leaving a number of visible scars. Slow moving glacial ice carved Somes Sound, the only fjord along the U.S. Atlantic Coast. And then, when the glacier melted, Somes Sound filled with water. Glaciers also carried Bubble Rock, a 14-ton glacial erratic, 19 miles from its original resting place, depositing it precariously near the top of South Bubble. As the ice melted, water poured down the slopes of the recently shaved mountaintops; lakebeds filled, seas rose, and as the coast drowned in melt water an island formed.

Long after glaciers covered the coast, the Abenaki people used the island as their seasonal home. A home they called "Pemetic" or "the sloping land." Food was abundant. Fishing and hunting were relatively simple. Shellfish, plants, and berries were easily gathered. For the Abenaki people, life was good along the coast of Maine. It also was an appropriate home for them. Abenaki translates to "People of the Dawn" and MDI's Cadillac Mountain, the tallest peak along the U.S. Atlantic Coast, is the first place in the continental U.S. to experience dawn.

In 1604, Samuel de Champlain spotted the barren peak of Cadillac Mountain from his ship. Not noticing the forested hills around it, he declared the island "l'Isle des Monts Déserts" or "island of bare mountains." Barren or not, nations quarreled over the region for the next 150 years, with these islands changing hands between Natives, French, English, and Americans, but they were never permanently occupied and seldom visited.

Thomas Cole and Frederic Church, painters from the Hudson River School, helped rediscover MDI in the mid-19th century. And their work brought public attention. At first, artists, professors, and other intellectuals known as "rusticators" made the multi-day journey. Travelers required little in terms of accommodations, hiking from place-to-place, enjoying the area's simple lifestyle and sublime beauty.

Not long after the rusticators exposed MDI's beauty, developers were clamoring to increase island access. Direct steamboat service from Boston arrived in the 1860s. Construction of a new rail line completed in the 1880s. By this time MDI was the place to be for the East Coast's elite. Some of the wealthiest visitors, known locally as "cottagers," purchased large tracts of land and built lavish summer homes they ironically called "cottages." "Millionaires' Row," a stretch of "cottages" near Bar Harbor, burned to the ground during the great fire of 1947. Before blowing into the Atlantic, the blaze razed more than 17,000 acres, including 10,000 acres of park land.

Still, development was MDI's main threat, not nature. Residents believed its scenic beauty needed to be protected. Fortunately, John D. Rockefeller, Jr. and George B. Dorr, both cottagers-turned-conservationists, became two of the park's greatest advocates. Rockefeller built 57 miles of carriage roads, donated thousands of acres of land, and spent $3.5 million on the potential park. Dorr blazed trails, donated land, and became the park's first superintendent. Acadia National Park was eventually created, cobbled together entirely from private donations, successfully protecting some of the area's most rugged shorelines and beautiful landscapes for the enjoyment of the people.

Bubble Rock

When to Go
Acadia is open all year. The park experiences heavy traffic during July and August. Fall foliage attracts large crowds from September through mid-October. **Hulls Cove Visitor Center** is closed from November through mid-April. Most of Park Loop Road is closed from December through mid-April.

Transportation & Airports
Help reduce traffic congestion and air pollution by riding the free **Island Explorer Shuttle**. The shuttle runs from late June through mid-October. Ten regularly scheduled routes link hotels, inns, campgrounds, and Bar Harbor Airport with popular park destinations (but not Cadillac Mountain). Maps and timetables are available at the visitor center and Island Explorer's website (exploreacadia.com).

Bar Harbor Airport (BHB) is 10 miles from Hulls Cove Visitor Center. Bangor International (BGR) is 49 miles away. Portland International (PWM) is about 3 hours away. Logan International (BOS) in Boston is 5–6 hours away.

Directions
To arrive at **Mount Desert Island** from the south, take I-95 north to Augusta, then Route 3 east through Ellsworth and on to Mount Desert Island.

To arrive at **Schoodic Peninsula** from Ellsworth, take Route 3 south and turn left onto US Hwy 1. Continue east to West Gouldsboro. Go south on Route 186 to Winter Harbor, and then follow signs to the park.

Isle au Haut is accessible via the Mail Boat from Stonington. Take Route 172 south from Ellsworth to Route 15 and on to Stonington (and the Mail Boat).

Mansell Mountain

Regions of Acadia

There are three distinct regions: Mount Desert Island (MDI), Schoodic Peninsula (SP), and Isle au Haut (IAH). Each region offers camping, but MDI is the park's centerpiece, where you'll find the vast majority of attractions, restaurants, lodgings, and visitors. Somes Sound breaks this large island into east (busy) and west (quiet) sides. The free Island Explorer Shuttle connects many of MDI's most popular sites and SP. SP possesses views similar to those found at MDI but slightly less spectacular and with considerably smaller crowds (it's also much smaller). Located east of MDI, across Frenchman Bay, it's the only park territory on the mainland. MDI and SP are accessible by car. Seven smaller islands, including IAH, are preserved by the park, but can only be reached by boat. Make camping reservations early for IAH.

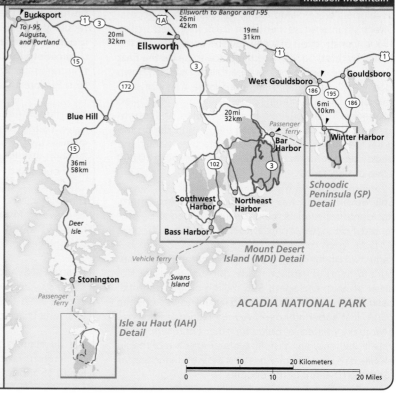

ACADIA NATIONAL PARK

Mark Island

Schoodic Peninsula

Roughly one of every ten Acadia visitors makes the trip to Schoodic Peninsula. Here you'll find a more secluded and intimate experience. Less visitation also means fewer facilities. There are four restrooms one picnic area, and **Schoodic Woods Campground**. The campground, located 3 miles southeast of Winter Harbor, offers tent and RV sites from $22 (primitive, hike-in) to $40 (full hookups) per night. It is open from late May until Columbus Day. In summer, **Downeast Windjammer Cruises** (207.288.4585, downeastwindjammer.com) operates a passenger ferry between Bar Harbor and Winter Harbor (one hour each way). **Island Explorer Shuttle** stops at the ferry terminals. By car, the 45-mile route around Frenchman Bay from Bar Harbor also takes about an hour. After reaching the peninsula, a six-mile, one-way loop road offers stunning views of the dramatic Maine coastline. You'll immediately be treated to views of **Winter Harbor Lighthouse** and **Cadillac Mountain** across the bay. A narrow gravel road weaves up toward the highest point on the peninsula, **Schoodic Head** (you can also hike to it).

Isle au Haut

Named by Samuel de Champlain in 1604, Isle au Haut or "High Island" is a rugged and relatively remote island five miles south of Stonington. Today, a few thousand day-trippers and some 500 campers travel aboard the **Mail Boat** (207.367.5193, isleauhaut.com) from Stonington each year. About half the island is park land; the rest is owned and occupied by summer residents and a year-round fishing community. At times the relationship between visitors and residents has been contentious, forcing the adoption of a visitor capacity limit. Isle au Haut visitors should exit the Mail Boat at **Duck Harbor Landing**, stay within park boundaries, and camp at one of five designated sites (each with its own lean-to). Camping costs $20/night with a 3-night maximum stay. You can disembark at Town Landing and walk 1,500 feet (uphill) to the park Ranger Station, but Duck Harbor Landing is the better option.

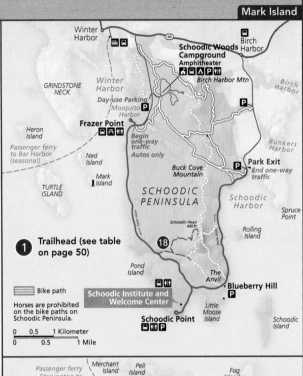

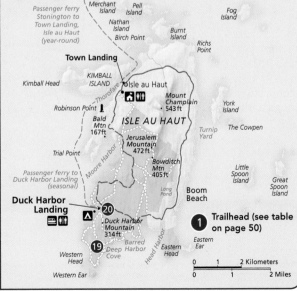

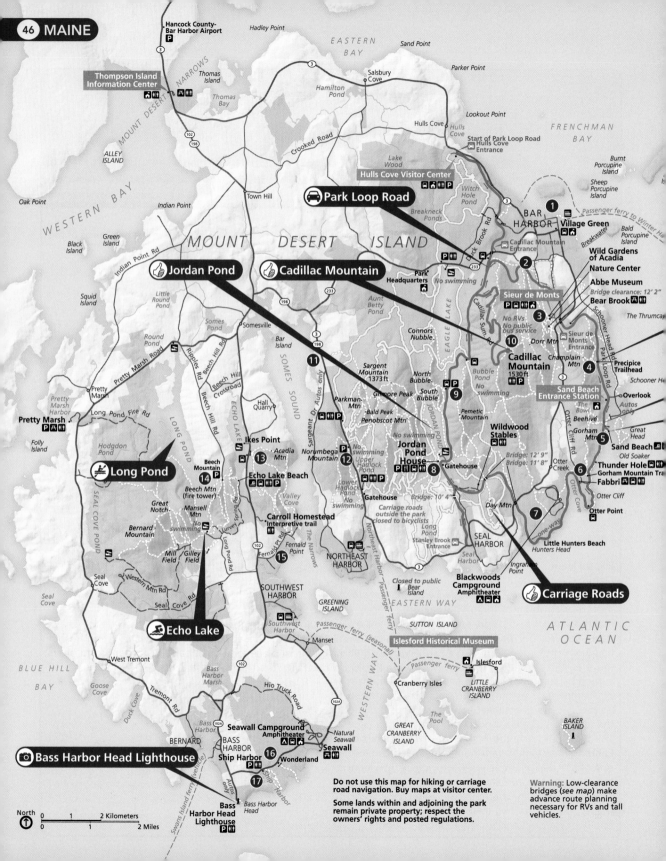

Hancock County-
Bar Harbor Airport

Hadley Point

*EASTERN
BAY*

Sand Point

Parker Point

**Thompson Island
Information Center**

Thomas
Island

Salsbury
Cove

Hamilton
Pond

Lookout Point

*FRENCHMAN
BAY*

Thomas
Bay

Hulls Cove

Burnt
Porcupine
Island

Sheep
Porcupine
Island

Crooked Road

Lake
Wood

Start of Park Loop Road
Hulls Cove
Entrance

Bald Porcupine
Island

Hulls Cove Visitor Center

Witch
Hole
Pond

①

*ALLEY
ISLAND*

Town Hill

Park Loop Road

Breakneck
Ponds

Cadillac Mountain
Entrance

**BAR
HARBOR**

Village Green

Passenger ferry to Winter Harbor

**Wild Gardens
of Acadia**
Nature Center

WESTERN BAY

Oak Point

Indian Point

MOUNT DESERT ISLAND

②

Abbe Museum
Bridge clearance: 12' 2"

Black
Island

Green
Island

Indian Point Rd

Jordan Pond

Cadillac Mountain

Park
Headquarters

No swimming

Sieur de Monts

③

Bear Brook

Squid
Island

Little
Round
Pond

Aunt
Betty
Pond

⑩

No RVs
No public
bus service

The Thrumcap

Somesville

Connors
Nubble

Sieur de
Monts
Entrance

④

Precipice
Trailhead

Round
Pond

Bar Island

Sargent
Mountain
1373 ft

North
Bubble

Dorr Mtn

**Cadillac
Mountain**
1530 ft

Champlain
Mtn

Schooner Head

Pretty Marsh Road

⑪

Gilmore Peak

South
Bubble

Bubble
Pond

⑨

**Sand Beach
Entrance Station**

Pretty
Marsh

Parkman
Mtn

Bald Peak
Penobscot Mtn

No
swimming

*The
Beehive*

Overlook

Pretty Marsh
Harbor

Beech Hill Crossroad

Pemetic
Mountain

Pretty Marsh

Long Pond Fire Rd

Ikes Point

⑬

Acadia
Mtn

Norumbega
Mountain

Upper
Hadlock
Pond

No
swimming

**Wildwood
Stables**

Gorham
Mtn

⑤

Long Pond

Hodgdon
Pond

Beech
Mountain

⑭

⑫

**Jordan
Pond
House**

Sand Beach

Old Soaker

Thunder Hole

Folly
Island

Beech Mtn
(fire tower)

Echo Lake Beach

Lower
Hadlock
Pond
No
swimming

Gatehouse

⑧

Otter
Creek

Bridge: 12' 9"
Bridge: 11' 8"

⑥

Gorham Mountain Trail

Fabbri

Great
Notch

Mansell
Mtn

No
swimming

Carroll Homestead
Interpretive trail

Gatehouse

Bridge: 10' 4"

Otter Cliff

Bernard
Mountain

Fernald
Point

⑮

Carriage roads
outside the park
closed to bicyclists

Day Mtn

⑦

Otter Point

Mill
Field

Gilley
Field

Long
Pond

Stanley Brook
Entrance

Little Hunters Beach
Hunters Head

Seal
Cove

**NORTHEAST
HARBOR**

Carriage Roads

The Narrows

Western Mtn Rd

Seal Cove Rd

**SOUTHWEST
HARBOR**

*GREENING
ISLAND*

Closed to public
Bear Island

**Blackwoods
Campground
Amphitheater**

*ATLANTIC
OCEAN*

West Tremont

Echo Lake

Southwest
Harbor

EASTERN WAY

**SEAL
HARBOR**

Ingraham
Point

*BLUE HILL
BAY*

Goose
Cove

Manset

Passenger ferry (seasonal)

SUTTON ISLAND

Islesford Historical Museum

Tremont Rd

Duck Cove

Bass
Harbor
Marsh

Hio Truck Road

WESTERN WAY

Cranberry Isles

*LITTLE
CRANBERRY
ISLAND*

Passenger ferry

Islesford

*The
Pool*

*BAKER
ISLAND*

*GREAT
CRANBERRY
ISLAND*

**Seawall Campground
Amphitheater**

BERNARD

**BASS
HARBOR**

Natural
Seawall

Seawall

⑯

Wonderland

Ship Harbor

Bass Harbor Head Lighthouse

Bass
Harbor

⑰

Swans Island ferry (vehicle)

Bass
Harbor
Head

**Bass
Harbor Head
Lighthouse**

North

0   1   2 Kilometers
0   1   2 Miles

Do not use this map for hiking or carriage
road navigation. Buy maps at visitor center.

Some lands within and adjoining the park
remain private property; respect the
owners' rights and posted regulations.

Warning: Low-clearance
bridges (*see map*) make
advance route planning
necessary for RVs and tall
vehicles.

Bald Peak

STAVE
ISLAND

Jordan
Island

GRINDSTONE
NECK

ONBOUND
ISLAND

Precipice

Beehive

Sand Beach

	Acadia National Park
	Park Loop Road
	Unpaved road
	Carriage road
	Hiking trail
	Locked gate
	Ranger station
	Picnic area
	Campground
	Swimming (seasonal)
	Boat launch
	Restrooms
	Lighthouse
	Food service
	Parking
	Bus stop
	Ferry to park areas
	Park Loop Road Entrance
1	**Trailhead (see table on page 50)**

Mount Desert Island (MDI)

To many visitors, MDI and Acadia National Park are synonymous. Almost two thirds of the park is on MDI and it is the only destination for most of the 3+ million people who flock here each year. About half of the island is protected under park ownership. The boundary raggedly weaves its way around private property and the Atlantic seashore. The park and island are nearly split in half by a natural, glacially-carved barrier, Somes Sound, the only fjord on the U.S. Atlantic Coast.

Within park boundaries lies an enchanting place where granite cliffs and angry seas, mountaintops and clear blue skies, people and wildlife come together. Eight mountains exceed 1,000 feet. Diminutive in stature compared to their western counterparts, they still find a way to take your breath away. Hiking from sea level to summit can leave avid hikers gasping for air, especially on **ladder trails** which are more vertical than horizontal. And if that fails to do the trick, the panoramic views afforded from these barren mountaintops definitely will. Should you only go to one mountaintop, make it the **Cadillac**. Its summit can be reached by car, bike, or foot. Many visitors drive to the summit before the sun rises in order to bask in the first rays of sun as they peek over the Atlantic Ocean. Don't worry if you aren't a morning person; the views overlooking Bar Harbor, Frenchman Bay, and the Porcupine Islands are spectacular rain or shine, sun or fog, morning until evening. On a clear day you can see Mount Katahdin, Maine's tallest mountain, standing some 100 miles away. **Starting May 2021, the park installed a reservation system for driving to Cadillac Mountain during peak summer season.** Reservations cost $6/car and can be made at recreation.gov. Thrill-seekers unafraid of heights and searching for adventure should scale Champlain Mountain via **Precipice Trail**. Steel rungs, ladders, and railings aid hikers along the harrowing journey. The Trail is often closed during winter, and it closes once more from late spring through summer when peregrine falcons nest on the precipitous mountain's face.

Twenty-six freshwater lakes and ponds are found on MDI, providing a wide variety of activities. You can swim in the Atlantic at **Sand Beach** or the much warmer and fresher water of **Echo Lake**. **Long Pond** is a great place for a quiet paddle. **Jordan Pond** offers stunning views of the **Bubble Mountains** (South and North Bubble). View the bubbles from **Jordan Pond House** while enjoying one of their famous pastries, a popover, or just down the road at the boat landing.

A trip to Acadia is not complete without touring the 27-mile **Park Loop Road**, but if you'd like to escape the hum of automobiles go out and explore the **carriage roads**. These crushed stone paths are enjoyed by bikers, hikers, and horse-drawn carriages. A carriage road map is available at Hulls Cove Visitor Center, located just north of Bar Harbor on Route 3. You'll find most park facilities on MDI, but you won't find any lodging within park boundaries. Bar Harbor, the island's largest city, is the most popular destination for dining, lodging, shopping, and nightlife. Additional accommodations are available in Northeast Harbor and Southwest Harbor.

Park Loop Road (near Champlain Mountain)

Acadia Camping (Fees are per night)

Name	Location	Open	Fee	Sites	Notes
Blackwoods*	Mount Desert Island (MDI) Route 3, 5 miles south of Bar Harbor	May–October (peak) April & November Winter (closed)	$30	281 (60 RV) 6 people, 2 tents, 1 car limit per site	No hookups Showers 0.5 mile away 35-ft max RV Make reservations from May–October
Seawall*	MDI, Route 102A, 4 miles south of Southwest Harbor	late May–mid-October	$30 (drive-in) $22 (walk-in)	202 (59 RV) 6 people, 2 tents, 1 car limit per site	No hookups Showers 1 mile away 35-ft max RV Make reservations from May–October
Schoodic Woods*	SP, 3 miles southeast of Winter Harbor	late May–Columbus Day	$30 (drive-in) $22 (walk-in)	89 (65 RV)	31 sites with RV electric and water ($40/night) and 34 sites with electric ($36/night)
Duck Harbor**	Isle au Haut, take boat from Stonington	mid-May–mid-October	$20	5 6 people/site	Primitive Camping, 3 night max per permit, Reservation required

Backcountry Camping is prohibited at Acadia National Park

*Reservations can be made up to three months in advance at 877-444-6777 or recreation.gov

**Reservations are required (book early!) and can be made beginning April 1 at 877-444-6777 or recreation.gov

Camping & Lodging

The park has four campgrounds. **Blackwoods**, located on MDI near Otter Creek at the foot of Cadillac Mountain is closest to Bar Harbor. Showers are located near the Blackwoods entrance, a short walk from the far end of B-Loop (sites B124, B126). Reservations are a good idea (and often necessary) if you plan on visiting between June and mid-October. Blackwoods is busy because its location is exceptional. **Seawall Campground** is on MDI's quiet side, but it still fills up in summer. Across Frenchman's Bay is **Schoodic Woods**, a relatively new campground. It's more peaceful yet and the best destination for RVers. The **Island Explorer Shuttle** (exploreacadia.com) stops at all three of these campgrounds from June through mid-May, which is a great service to park guests. To reach Schoodic Woods from MDI, or vice versa, using the Island Explorer Shuttle, you'll have to use the Bar Harbor-Winter Harbor ferry. Finally, the most peaceful option is to spend a few nights on Isle au Haut at **Duck Harbor**. There are only five sites, each has a lean-to shelter. Most people reach the isle using the Mail Boat (isleauhaut.com) out of Stonington. Camping at Isle au Haut is popular. Try to secure reservations as soon as they become available (April 1). But remember it isn't car camping. You'll have to pack everything you need with you. All campgrounds close for winter.

You won't find any lodging within the park, but there's plenty nearby in Bar Harbor (on Mount Desert Island) or Ellsworth (back on the mainland, roughly 30 minutes from the visitor center).

Driving

MDI's 27-mile **Park Loop Road** is a must-see for first-time visitors. There are a number of turnouts and parking and picnic areas where you can stop and enjoy the scenery. Parking is also allowed along the road's right-hand side wherever it's one-way (unless signs state otherwise). Watch for evidence of the great fire of 1947 as you drive. Thick evergreen forests give way to sun-loving deciduous trees that replaced thousands of acres of pine lost in the flames. One of the most popular Park Loop Road experiences is to drive up **Cadillac Summit Road** for sunrise. Map it out and set your alarm to arrive at least 30 minutes early. Grab a blanket, coffee, and a loved one, and wait atop the barren peak for the first rays of light. Testament to its popularity, beginning in 2021, you must reserve a ticket online ($6, recreation.gov) to drive to Cadillac's summit during the peak summer season. If you missed out on a permit, there are many great locations to watch the sunrise along Ocean Path. Either way, waking with the

Boulder Beach

sun is a good idea. An early start allows you to visit popular destinations like Jordan Pond, Otter Cliffs, and Sand Beach before the afternoon crowds. Traffic typically peaks between 10am and 3pm.

Be sure to plan ahead if you will be arriving in an RV or tall vehicle, as there are four low-clearance bridges (the lowest is 10' 4"). If you'd like to escape Park Loop Road gridlock, drive over to **Schoodic Peninsula**. Here you'll find a 6-mile, one-way coastal loop featuring scenery that's nearly as dramatic as MDI. You'll also find campsites with ample space and hookups for RVs.

Anyone visiting during the busy season (late June through mid-October) should consider parking your car and hopping aboard the **Island Explorer Shuttles** (exploreacadia.com). They're free, frequent, and connect just about everything a visitor could possibly want to visit (except Cadillac Mountain's summit).

Acadia is more than manageable on your own, but if you'd like to be in the company of a knowledgeable guide, narrated tours are available. **Acadia National Park Tours** (207.288.0300, acadiatours.com) offers tours of Park Loop Road (stopping at Sieur de Monts Spring, Thunder Hole, Cadillac Mountain) from $40 (2.5 hours, bus) to $70 (3.5 hours, smaller coach) per person. **Oli's Trolley** (207.288.9899, olistrolley.com) runs a similar route, adding a stop at Jordan Pond for $48 (2.5 hours) to $73 (4 hours).

Hiking

Acadia is truly a day-hiker's paradise, featuring some of the best-maintained trails of all the national parks. Thanks to a dense network of more than 120 miles of short trails and the **Island Explorer Shuttle** (exploreacadia.com), creative hikers can come up with all sorts of fun one-way hiking itineraries. Backcountry

Acadia Hiking Trails (Distances are roundtrip unless noted otherwise)

	Name	Location (# on map)	Length	Difficulty Rating & Notes
Mount Desert Island	Bar Island - 🐾	Bar Harbor, located at the end of Bridge Street (1)	~1.4 miles	E – A sandbar to Bar Island appears at low tide, be sure to check tide tables
	Great Meadow	Bar Harbor, located off Cromwell Harbor Road (2)	2.0 miles	E – A loop trail across private land connecting Bar Harbor to Acadia
	Cadillac North Ridge	Park Loop Road, 3.2 miles from the start of Park Loop Road (2)	4.4 miles	M – Views of Bar Harbor • Shorter and steeper than South Ridge Trail
	Tarn	Sieur de Monts Spring, Tarn Parking Lot off Route 3 (3)	2.4 miles	M – Hike through woods along Otter Creek and by beaver ponds
	Precipice - 🐾	Park Loop Road, 1.75 miles past Sieur de Monts Spring entrance (4)	2.1 miles	X – Iron rungs and ladders • Not for children or anyone afraid of heights
	Beehive - 🐾	Sand Beach Area, across Park Loop Road from Sand Beach parking lot (5)	1.6 miles	X – Iron rungs and ladders • Not for children or anyone afraid of heights
	Great Head	East end of Sand Beach (5)	1.5 miles	M – Loop trail with cliff and beach views
	Ocean Path - 🐾	Sand Beach Upper Lot (5, 6, 7)	4.4 miles	E – Passes Thunder Hole and Otter Cliffs
	Gorham Mtn - 🐾	Gorham Mtn Lot, 1 mile past Sand Beach on Park Loop Road (6)	1.8 miles	M – Wide open views of the ocean • Connects to The Bowl, Beehive, and Cadillac Cliffs
	Cadillac South Ridge	Route 3, about 100 feet south of Blackwoods Campground (7)	7.0 miles	S – Hike to Cadillac from Blackwoods Campground on one of the park's longer trails
	Jordan Pond - 🐾	Jordan Pond Boat Ramp (8)	3.2 miles	M – Loop along the edge of Jordan Pond
	Jordan Cliff/ Penobscot Mtn	Behind Jordan Pond Gift Shop (8)	3.7+ miles	X – Ascend Jordan Cliff (ladder) or Jordan Pond/Deer Brook, descend Penobscot Mtn
	Sargent Mtn	Many Options (8, 9, 11, 12)	Varies	S – 2nd tallest park summit, long, difficult hike (regardless of route) by Acadia standards
	Bubble Rock - 🐾	Park Loop Road, Bubble Rock Parking Lot (9)	1.0 mile	M – Steep, short hike up South Bubble to a peculiar glacial erratic (big rock)
	Summit Path	Cadillac Mtn Summit Parking Lot (10)	0.3 mile	E – A paved path around the summit
	Giant Slide - 🐾	1.1 mile from the junction of Route 198 and 233 (11)	2.8 miles	S – Challenging trail along Sargent Brook to Sargent Mtn (via Grandgent) or Gilmore Peak
	Acadia Mtn - 🐾	Acadia Mountain Parking Lot, west side of Route 102 (13)	2.5 miles	S – Best views of Somes Sound in the park, return via fire road
	Beech Mtn - 🐾	Beech Mtn Parking Lot, off Beech Hill Road (14)	1.1 miles	M – Alternate from Long Pond Road: ascend West Ridge, return via Valley (~3 miles)
	Flying Mtn	Fernald Cove Parking Area, Fernald Point Rd (15)	1.2 miles	M – Explore tide pools at Valley Cove
	Wonderland	Seawall Campground, off Route 102A, 0.9 miles from Seawall (16)	1.4 miles	E – Rocky shoreline, cobble beach, and spruce forests
	Ship Harbor	Rte 102A, 2 miles from Seawall (17)	1.2 miles	E – A good spot for blueberries and birds
SP	Schoodic Head - 🐾	Schoodic Peninsula, Blueberry Hill Parking Lot (18)	2.5 miles	M – Combine Alder, Schoodic Head and Anvil Trails for a loop to Schoodic Head
IAH	Goat Trail	Isle au Haut, via Western Head Road and Duck Harbor Mountain Trail (19)	2.1 miles (one-way)	M – Rugged and rocky hike with spectacular coastal vistas
	Duck Harbor Mountain	Isle au Haut, accessible from Western Head Road (20)	2.4 miles	S – Panoramic views of Isle au Haut • Most strenuous hike on the isle

Difficulty Ratings: E = Easy, M = Moderate, S = Strenuous, X = Extreme

camping is not permitted within park boundaries. Trails—many of which were trod by Native Americans or the park's first superintendent, George Dorr—are well marked with cairns (small, pyramid-like rock piles) and blue blazes courtesy of Acadia Trails Forever (please don't build or alter cairns).

One of the ways Dorr is remembered is by a mountaintop: **Dorr Mountain**, the third tallest peak in the park. Four trails lead to its summit, including the short and steep **Ladder Trail**. The ascent is aided by three sets of steel ladders and numerous granite steps that were carved and placed in 1893 and restored by the Civilian Conservation Corps (CCC) in the 1930s. The trailhead is found at **Sieur de Monts Spring** directly behind the Spring House. To complete the 3.3-mile journey to Dorr Mountain summit, take Ladder Trail to Schiff Path (East Face Dorr Trail) and return via South Ridge Dorr Trail and Canon Brook Trail.

There are more ladder trails. **Precipice Trail** is the most fun ladder trail (or terrifying for anyone with a fear of heights/exposure). It begins 7.3 miles from Hulls Cove Visitor Center on Park Loop Road. It quickly climbs the steep east face of Champlain Mountain. Ascend 0.9 mile along Precipice Trail and return via Champlain Mountain North Ridge Trail and Orange & Black Path, making a 2.5-mile loop. The trail closes from mid-March to mid-August to protect nesting peregrine falcons. During this time, you'll often find a park ranger conducting Peregrine Watch in the Precipice Trail parking area. Continuing along Park Loop Road, you will arrive at another popular ladder trail climbing up **The Beehive**. It begins across the road from Sand Beach Parking Area. Follow Beehive Trail 0.8 mile to its summit, and then take Bowl Trail back to Park Loop Road, completing a 1.6-mile loop. **Jordan Cliff Trailhead** is found behind Jordan Pond Gift Shop at Carriage Road junction #15. This hike begins with excellent views of Jordan Pond as you start the 2.2-mile (one-way) ascent to the top of Penobscot Mountain. Take in the 360° panoramic views at the summit before heading back down Penobscot Mountain Trail, which loops back to Jordan Pond Gift Shop. The 2.2-mile **Perpendicular (Mansell Mountain) Trail** begins at the south end of Long Pond near Southwest Harbor. It's more of a granite staircase, but there is a ladder, and the views are nice. The sixth and final ladder trail, 0.5-mile **Beech Cliff Trail**, begins behind the ranger house at Echo Lake Parking Area. These are some of the park's most challenging trails and should not be attempted by small children, anyone afraid of heights, or pets. Hike something else if conditions are unsafe.

Beehive Trail

Most trails don't require climbing ladders, but that doesn't mean they aren't unique. **Bar Island** can be reached at low tide by crossing a sand bar right from downtown Bar Harbor. Have your kids pose next to a precariously-positioned 14-ton boulder at the steep but short, 1.0-mile **Bubble Rock Trail**. About two or three hours before high tide you may want to head down **Ocean Path** to listen to waves explode at **Thunder Hole**. And **Giant Slide** is a riot as you follow Sargent Brook up to Gilmore Peak and/or Sargent Mountain (via Grandgent Trail). (You can easily reach Parkman and Bald Mountains from here, too, and Penobscot and Cedar Swamp Mountains aren't out of the question if you like to get after it!) Giant Slide begins on private property. Respect it just the same as you should respect all public land. See the hiking table for the location and difficulty of these and many other trails.) **Carriage roads** provide much more relaxed hiking possibilities. Concentrated around the Jordan Pond Area, 45 miles of crushed stone roads stretch from Hulls Cove to Seal Harbor.

Rock Climbing

Acadia's mountains may not be big, but they are steep. Sheer granite walls offer some of the most unique rock climbing opportunities in the United States. **Otter Cliffs** is a popular climbing spot. The South Wall of Champlain Mountain, Central Slabs, South Bubble, and Great Head are also serviceable climbing destinations. Climbers at Otter Cliffs, Canada Cliffs, and South Wall should sign in at daily use logs, available at the climbing areas, park headquarters, visitor center, and campgrounds. With a wide variety of climbing routes Acadia is a wonderful destination for beginners to learn how to rock climb. Give it a try by contacting an outfitter: Atlantic Climbing School (207.288.2521, climbacadia.com) or Acadia Mountain Guides (207.288.8186, acadiamountainguides.com).

Docking at Isle au Haut

Both have similar offerings and rates. Expect a family of four to pay about $300 for a half-day course (2–3 hours of climbing).

Paddling

Acadia National Park has paddling in spades for people of all experience levels. Inexperienced paddlers are sure to enjoy the glacially-carved lakes and ponds or perhaps a guided tour with a local outfitter. Eagle Lake, Long Pond, Jordan Pond, and Echo Lake are a few of the most popular freshwater paddle-spots, with at least one boat launch at each.

Experienced paddlers can take to the open waters of the Atlantic Ocean where you are free to explore Acadia's islands, inlets, and coves. Somes Sound and the entire eastern coast (from Mount Desert Narrows to Moose Island) are good ideas. Isle au Haut campers may want to consider paddling the five miles of water separating it from Stonington.

Paddling allows visitors to see the park from a different perspective and gain a new appreciation for this scenic land. It's also an excellent way to view the park's wildlife. Enjoy the tranquility of these majestic waters but remember to use caution, especially when paddling alone. Cold water, swift currents, erratic weather, and dense fog can make paddling at Acadia challenging. Check the weather and tide tables before heading out. If you plan to explore any of Acadia's remote smaller islands, be sure to discuss your itinerary with a park ranger, because birds may be nesting on the shorelines.

A number of places offer kayak rental. National Park Canoe & Kayak Rental (207.244.5854, nationalparkcanoerental.com) has the perfect quiet-side location on Pretty Marsh Road at the northern tip of Long Pond, with reasonable (3-hour) rates:

canoe ($38), solo kayak ($36), tandem kayak ($42), paddleboard ($39). You can save a few bucks by getting out there early (8am–11am), which is a good idea. Another option is to have Acadia 1 Watersports drop off a kayak or canoe for you. A canoe costs $170/week. A tandem kayak or SUP costs $215/week.

Similarly, if you'd like to take a kayak tour, Coastal Kayaking Tours (800.526.8615, acadiafun.com, 4 hours, $60/person) is a good choice to paddle about Frenchman Bay from Bar Harbor. Maine State Kayak (207.244.9500, mainestatekayak.com, 4 hours, $73), National Park Sea Kayak Tours (800.347.0940, acadiakayak.com, 4 hours, $55–60/person, 12 paddlers max), and Aquaterra Adventures (207.288.0007, aquaterra-adventures.com) also offer guided paddling tours. And Acadia Outfitters (207.288.8118, acadiaoutfitters.com) offers a little bit of everything, including rentals (scooters, bikes, kayaks) and tours (hiking: $51/5.5 hours up Cadillac Mountain and paddling: $58/4 hours).

Boat Tours

Baker Island Cruise (5 hours, $49/adult) explores the island's unique natural and cultural history with the help of a park ranger. You'll have the chance to see marine life before spending an hour on the island on a one-mile walking tour. Reservations and additional information are available at barharborwhales.com or (207) 288-2386.

Dive-In Theater Boat Cruise (2 hours, $42/adult) searches for underwater life. Passengers scour the surface of Frenchman Bay for seals, porpoises, and seabirds, while a diver hunts for marine life on the ocean floor. Occasionally the diver returns with live specimens for a real hands-on experience. It's an excellent choice for anyone with kids (or anyone who remains a kid at heart). Reservations and additional information are available at divered.com or (207) 288-3483.

Downeast Windjammer offers Frenchman Bay cruises aboard a four-mast schooner. You'll search for wildlife and enjoy the views of the surrounding islands. Tours last about two hours and cost $42–48/adult. Reservations and additional information are available at downeastwindjammer.com or (207) 288-4585. Downeast Windjammer also runs passenger ferries, and offers private charters and fishing excursions.

Discover Acadia's past on the **Islesford Historic and Scenic Cruise** (2.75 hours, $32/adult), which takes you to Little Cranberry Island's Islesford Historical Museum. This tour is provided by Sea Princess Scenic Nature

Cruises. They offer a few other cruises in Somes Sound, starting at $27/person. Reservations and additional information are available at cruiseacadia.com or (207) 276-5352.

Bass Harbor Cruises (207.244.5785, bassharborcruises.com) offers a variety of wildlife and historical cruises (2–3.5 hours, $40/adult), as well as sailboat and fishing charters. **Sail Acadia** (207.266.5210, sailacadia.com) will take you lobstering aboard the oldest working friendship sloop with Downeast Friendship Sloop Charters or a more modern vessel, you choose. **Bar Harbor Whale Watching** (207.288.2386, barharborwhales.com) also offers a variety of cruises, including wildlife (whales, puffins, etc.), lighthouses, and lobstering. **Acadian Boat Tours** (207.801.2300, acadianboattours.com) offers sunset, sightseeing, fishing, lighthouse, and wildlife tours starting at $33/adult. You can also learn about lobstering with **Lulu Lobster Boat** (207.288.3136, lululobsterboat.com). Tours last two hours and cost $35/adult.

Reservations are recommended for all cruises. Schedules and fees vary. All tours are seasonal.

Biking

Eastern **MDI's carriage roads** are your best bet for a relaxing bike ride. The 45-mile network of broken-stone roads extends from Hulls Cove Visitor Center to Seal Harbor, including 17 carefully-crafted stone-faced bridges. Some of the most scenic stretches skirt Jordan Pond and Eagle Lake. The 8-mile circuit (roundtrip) to Day Mountain, the only summit reached by carriage road, begins at Jordan Pond Gatehouse. No matter where you go, be sure to carry a map of the carriage roads (available at Hulls Cove Visitor Center or the park's website), because you'll encounter several junctions even on short rides. Also note that the 12 miles of carriage roads south of Jordan Pond are on private property and off-limits to cyclists. (However, horseback riders and walkers are allowed on these gravel roadways.)

The quieter western side of MDI has two gravel roads. **Seal Cove Road** (4 miles) connects Southwest Harbor and Seal Cove. **Hio Road** (2.5 miles) connects Seawall Campground with Highway 102 at Bass Harbor Marsh.

The 27-mile **Park Loop Road** offers scenic and hilly terrain for road cyclists. If you feel like challenging yourself, take the 3.5-mile Mountain Loop Road to the summit of Cadillac Mountain. It's seriously tough pedaling going up, but the return trip downhill is a breeze

Sand Beach

(make sure your brakes work well). Due to Park Loop Road's steep grades, tight turns, and abundance of tourist traffic during the summer, offseason pedaling is best. For less congested biking try the loop around Schoodic Peninsula's scenic coastline or Route 102/102A on MDI's western side. Biking at Isle au Haut is not encouraged. Biking is not allowed on hiking trails and you won't find singletrack within park boundaries. Bike rental is available in Bar Harbor at Bar Harbor Bicycle Shop (207.288.3886, barharborbike.com, $30/day) and Acadia Bike (800.526.8615, acadiabike.com, $30/day), in Southwest Harbor at Southwest Cycle (207.244.5856, southwestcycle.com, $25/day), and in Northeast Harbor at Island Bike Rental (207.276.5611), which is closest to the carriage roads. Acadia Bike also offers ranger-guided bike tours (2.5 hours, $57/person).

Carriage Tours

Wildwood Stables (877.276.3622) offers carriage tours along the park's crushed stone carriage roads. They offer a Day Mountain Summit Tour (2 hours, $40/adult) and a tour of Mr. Rockefeller's Bridges (2 hours, $40/adult). Wild Iris Horse Farm (207.288.5234, wildirishorsefarm.com) offers carriage tours in downtown bar harbor, as well as farm tours and driving lessons.

Flightseeing

Acadia is filled with dramatic contours and sharp transitions that are incredibly difficult to appreciate from up close. Well, there's a solution for that. Take to the air! Scenic Flights of Acadia (207.667.6527, scenicflightsofacadia.com) offers flights ranging from a 15-minute glimpse of Bar Harbor for $49/person to a 75-minute lighthouse enthusiast's route for $229/person, and a few other options in between. Acadia Air Tours (207.288.0703, acadiaairtours.com) has similar offerings, ranging from $149–399/person. Planes fly out of Bar Harbor Airport.

Jordan Pond

Swimming

On hot summer days many of Acadia's guests migrate to the beaches. Sand Beach and Echo Lake Beach are staffed with a lifeguard in summer. The 55°F water found at Sand Beach might be refreshing to some, but it's downright frigid to others. The freshwater of Echo Lake is considerably warmer, especially near the end of summer. For more secluded swimming head to the park's western side where you can paddle yourself to swimming holes in Seal Cove, and Round and Hodgdon Ponds. Lake Wood, on the north end of the island, also has a small beach with vehicle access.

Swimming is prohibited at all lakes used for drinking water. These include Upper and Lower Hadlock Ponds, Bubble and Jordan Ponds, Eagle Lake, and the southern half of Long Pond.

Fishing

To fish any of the freshwater lakes in Acadia, you'll need a freshwater fishing license. Maine residents 16 and older and non-residents 12 and older require a license. Licenses are available at Walmart in Ellsworth and Paradis True Value in Bar Harbor or online (maine. gov/ifw). Freshwater fishing season is generally from April until September. Trout, salmon, perch, and bass are commonly caught in freshwater lakes and ponds.

A license is not required for saltwater fishing. Sargent Drive (Somes Sound) and Frazer Point (Schoodic Peninsula) are two saltwater fishing areas within the park. Mackerel typically run from mid-July to September at these locations.

Be sure to respect private property and follow all boating and fishing regulations.

Birdwatching

Acadia is a premier birdwatching destination. More than 300 bird species have been identified on MDI and the surrounding waters.

Reintroduced in the 1980s, peregrine falcons have been nesting on the cliffs of Champlain Mountain since 1991. If you'd like to observe these magnificent birds, join a park ranger or volunteer for Peregrine Watch. The program takes place at Precipice Trail Parking Area and is offered intermittently from mid-May through mid-August, weather permitting, when nesting falcons have been identified. Other popular nesting locations include Beech Cliffs (above Echo Lake) and Jordan Cliffs (above Jordan Pond).

Birds are everywhere, but a few locations are better than others. Sieur de Monts Springs is an excellent choice if you're looking to spot cedar waxwings, pileated woodpeckers, and the minuscule ruby-throated hummingbird. Beaver Brook and Beaver Dam Pond are popular habitats for herons, ducks, and bald eagles.

Birdwatchers will definitely want to walk around the Otter Cliffs area. Here you might find any number of seabirds, including double breasted cormorant, black guillemot, and northern gannet. Schoodic Peninsula, Wonderland, Ship Harbor, and Seawall provide bird enthusiasts with promising chances of seeing seabirds. Songbirds serenade cyclists, carriage riders, and hikers along the many miles of carriage roads.

Cadillac Mountain's wide-open summit offers an excellent vantage point to see bald eagles and peregrine falcons as they patrol the sky high above the park's granite peaks. In fact, birdwatching is so good here the park has a Hawk Watch station at Cadillac's summit from late August until mid-October. Park rangers aid visitors in spotting raptors as they make their winter migration from Maine and Canada to warmer locales down south.

Birdwatchers on a trip to Acadia will not want to forget their binoculars and bird book. Also, be sure to stop at Hulls Cove Visitor Center to get the latest information on migratory birds, peregrine falcons, and ranger-led bird watch programs.

Winter Activities

Winter activities at Acadia are hit or miss. The park averages about five feet of snow each year, but rain is just as likely during the winter months. January and February are the most reliable months for winter weather. When there is snow, Acadia becomes a winter wonderland with plenty to do. Two short sections of Park Loop Road remain open through winter for motorists. Snowmobiles are allowed on Park Loop Road and most fire roads. However, the maximum speed is 35 mph on Park Loop Road, and 25 mph on all unpaved roads. Snowmobilers must follow all state snowmobile laws. Dog sleds may be pulled by no more than four dogs. Ice fishing is popular. Carriage roads are good for snowshoeing and cross-country skiing. Winter hiking is an option. Microspikes and hiking poles are good ideas. Stay away from rocky, vertical trails when they're slippery. Rental equipment is available in Bar Harbor at Cadillac Mountain Sports (207.288.0682, cadillacsports.com, skis: $20/day, snowshoes: $15/day, ice skates: $8/day).

Lighthouses

There are five lighthouses near MDI. Of these, Bass Harbor Head Lighthouse is the easiest to access. It marks the entrance into Blue Hill Bay and is located at the end of Route 102A on the western half of MDI near Bass Harbor. Egg Rock Lighthouse is located at the mouth of Frenchman Bay. It can be seen from Park Loop Road. Baker Island is the oldest lighthouse in the area. It's located seven miles from MDI, and can be accessed by kayak or boat. Bear Island Lighthouse is closed to the public, but it can be viewed on boat cruises departing from Northeast Harbor. Mark Island's Winter Harbor Lighthouse comes into view from the west side of Schoodic Peninsula. Cadillac Mountain looms behind it.

Visitor Centers & Museums

Thompson Island Information Center resides on the tiny island just north of MDI along with a picturesque picnic area. It's open from mid-May to mid-October and serves as a good place to orient yourself to the region (and learn about any upcoming events) as the building is shared with chambers of commerce.

Hulls Cove Visitor Center (207.288.3338), located on Route 3 just south of Hulls Cove, should be your first stop upon arriving at the park on Mount Desert Island. Its standard hours are from 8am–4:30pm, extending to 6pm in summer (July–August). The visitor center closes for winter (November–April). A long staircase leads up to its entrance. There is an alternate parking area for individuals with disabilities. Look for the access road near the south end of the main lot.

In **Sieur de Monts Spring** you'll find the privately-run **Abbe Museum** (abbemuseum.org), the community-

A fawn near Seal Harbor

cared-for **Wild Gardens of Acadia**, and the park's **Nature Center**. Abbe Museum is a small building, housing a collection of Native American artifacts. Entry is $3/adult. They have a larger museum in downtown Bar Harbor (26 Mt Desert Street) that costs $10/adult. Wild Gardens of Acadia displays hundreds of native plant species, and it's complemented quite nicely by the park's Nature Center. Even if none of these attractions interest you, Sieur de Monts Spring is worth visiting, as it provides access to several excellent hiking trails. You can also walk here from Bar Harbor via Great Meadows/Jesup Trails.

Jordan Pond House (207.276.3316 for reservations, jordanpondhouse.com) is an Acadia institution. And for good reason, it's located at the nexus of carriage roads and several popular hiking trails. The setting, at the south end of Jordan Pond, is delightful. And, most importantly, tea and popovers ($12) on the Pond House lawn is an Acadia tradition! Reservations are a good idea.

Schoodic Institute (schoodicinstitute.org) has a beautiful campus near the tip of Schoodic Peninsula. This non-profit's primary purpose is research, but you'll find a welcome center and bookstore at Rockefeller Hall, and they routinely offer public programs and events.

Islesford Historical Museum (207.288.3338, islesford-historicalmuseum.org), located on Little Cranberry Island, explores the history of island life. The island is accessible via ferry out of Northeast or Southwest Harbor.

Park Headquarters, located on Route 233 near Eagle Lake, isn't something you need to know about, except that it serves as the park's visitor center in winter.

Bass Harbor Head Lighthouse

Ranger Programs & For Kids

Be sure to check with a park ranger or at the visitor center to view a current schedule of ranger-led programs. You'll find a wide variety of regularly scheduled educational walks, bike rides, and even a photography tour. Most of the programs are free of charge. The knowledge and enthusiasm exhibited by park rangers makes activities—from hiking to stargazing—more exciting and interesting. If you have an extra hour or two and aren't sure what to do, you cannot go wrong with a ranger program.

Kids of all ages can become Junior Rangers from mid-May through mid-October. Acadia also offers numerous children's programs exploring the park's ecology, geography, and history. Families also enjoy playing at Sand Beach, picking blueberries, hiking, or taking a boat tour. I've seen kids on the ladder trails. I'd suggest starting with Mansell Mountain and see how that goes. There's a point of no return on these things, and you don't want to have a panic attack (kids or adults). You also might want to check out the park's website to learn more about Acadia Quest, a new family-oriented program.

Flora & Fauna

Many of Acadia's picturesque attractions are named for their occupants: Seal Harbor, Beaver Pond, Eagle Lake, and Otter Cliffs. All these creatures reside in the park (although "otter" areas were named for river dwellers, not playful sea otters). Fortunate visitors might spot moose, black bear, red fox, porcupine, deer, whale, sea urchin, starfish, or lobster while exploring the park. Black flies and mosquitoes are two pests you'd rather not encounter on vacation, but, if you plan on traveling

between May and June, chances are you'll be greeted by these winged nuisances, so pack bug repellent.

Over 1,100 plant species live in Acadia, and 25 of these are state-listed rare plants. Walking about the park you're sure to notice a wide variety of trees, wildflowers, ferns, shrubs, mosses, lichens, and freshwater plants. The favorite plant of many visitors is the wild blueberry bush. Maine is the country's number one producer of wild blueberries, and these delectable snacks can be found all over MDI. They are typically ready-to-pick in late summer.

Pets & Accessibility

Pets are permitted but must be kept on a leash (less than six feet). They are not allowed at Sand Beach (mid-June to mid-September), Echo Lake (mid-May to mid-September), in public buildings, at ranger-led programs, on ladder trails, at Wild Gardens of Acadia, or at Duck Harbor Campground. Pets (and humans) are not allowed to swim in any lakes used as a public water supply. Be sure to pick up after your pet.

Hulls Cove Visitor Center, some restrooms, carriage paths, and Island Explorer Shuttle are wheelchair accessible. Blackwoods and Seawall Campgrounds have a few accessible sites. The Wild Gardens of Acadia, Jesup Path, and carriage roads are accessible to wheelchair users, but may require some assistance. Wildwood Stables operates two wheelchair-accessible carriages. Please call the park information center at (207) 288-3338, ext. 0 if you have accessibility questions.

Weather

Acadia's weather is extremely unpredictable and can change without warning any day of the year, so come prepared for all conditions. Rainfall is common in every month. MDI is often shrouded in fog during summer, when highs have a huge variance.

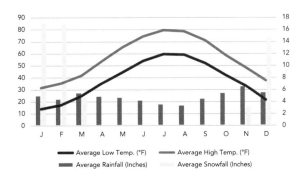

Eagle Lake

Tips & Recommendations

About one-third of the park's visitors arrive in July or August. That's the peak rush, but it's busy from June until mid-October. Late October is cool, but crowds are sparse, trails are quiet, and trees are usually holding onto some color.

Use the Island Explorer Shuttle.

It's completely understandable if you'd like to drive Park Loop Road in your own car, but if you're going to be driving around during mid-day, peak season, be sure to have a backup activity plan. Parking can be difficult to find, especially at popular spots like Sand Beach (found on a one-way stretch of Park Loop Road). Don't get discouraged. For this specific instance, there are several locations further down the road, where you can park and walk back to Sand Beach/Beehive Trail via Ocean Path or Gorham Mountain/Bowl Trail. And you can always park and hop on the Island Explorer Shuttle.

It isn't a guarantee, but if you want to see "thunder" at Thunder Hole, arrive in between high and low tides.

Cadillac Mountain (reservation required in summer from recreation.gov) is The Place to see the sunrise (and sunset), but Ocean Path provides many excellent sunrise viewing locations (including Thunder Hole). Or bring a headlamp and hike up Gorham Mountain.

Speaking of Gorham Mountain, if you have your heart set on hiking The Beehive or Precipice but aren't sure you can overcome the inherent fear factor, start by hiking Cadillac Cliffs (a short spur running parallel to Gorham Mountain Trail) or a less ladder-y ladder trail like Mansell Mountain or Beech Cliff.

Weather can be temperamental, but it's often short-lived, so don't let rain get you down. Come prepared, but also, if it's raining, go in the park, drive Park Loop Road, go up to Cadillac Mountain (just remember, as of 2021, you'll need a reservation during peak summer season). Views of the Acadia Coast can be more interesting in less-than-ideal weather. Plus, you never know when those clouds are going to break, allowing you to get back out there for some enjoyable hiking/exploring. But remain vigilant and watch the weather. You don't want to be up on a bald mountaintop in a thunderstorm or hiking any of the ladder trails (they're more dangerous when wet or icy).

Check with the park about trail closures (there are routine closures for maintenance and nesting birds).

I love Acadia! It's a great big playground, filled with low-mileage, high-reward hikes that are easy to bundle thanks to a well-designed trail network and the Island Explorer Shuttle. Before going into a list of favorites, I want to let you know how I'd spend three days (strictly visiting for fun). I'd climb mountains. They're relatively

Giant Slide

small, so you can climb a few hills in a couple of days (without wearing yourself out). Maybe start with Dorr Mountain and The Beehive. Drive up Cadillac or watch the sunset over Eagle Lake from Park Loop Road. Wake up in time to catch sunrise along the coast or up Gorham Mountain, then climb Jordan Cliffs before the crowds roll in. Next, head to the quiet side. Hike (there are plenty of good trails over here too!), relax at Echo Lake, or poke around the coast, looking for a good place to watch the sunset. Save the best for last, hiking Precipice (if it's open) before returning home. Squeeze in Giant Slide if you have the time and energy. Or maybe Pemetic Mountain (the mountain just east of Jordan Pond). It's the next trail on my hiking list. With that said, whether you're paddling, biking, or hiking, Acadia is sure to impress.

Three days is enough time to start thinking about the one-hour drive (or ferry ride) to Schoodic Peninsula or hopping aboard the Mail Boat to get a taste of Isle au Haut, but I'd suggest sticking to Mount Desert Island for your first visit. Here's a broader menu of activities and attractions to jump start your planning.

Easy Hikes: Bar Island (1.4 miles), Ocean Path (4.4), Summit Path (0.3)
Moderate Hikes: Gorham Mountain (1.8 miles), Bubble Rock (1)

Strenuous Hikes: Giant Slide (2.8 miles), Penobscot (3.7), Sargent Mountain (many routes)
Extreme Hikes: Precipice (2.1 miles), Beehive (1.6), Ladder/Dorr (3.3), Jordan Cliffs (3.7)
Family Activities: Become Junior Rangers, ride the ferries, hike to Bar Island, play at Sand Beach, watch the waves at Thunder Hole, climb to Bubble Rock, bike the carriage roads, play at Echo Lake Beach, paddle one of the inland lakes or ponds
Guided Tours: Say Kayak (acadiafun.com), Bike Tour (acadiabike.com), Trolley Tour (olistrolley.com), Rock Climbing Class (acadiaclimbing.com)
Rainy Day Activities: Drive Park Loop Road, stop at the visitor center, explore Abbe Museum, Drive to Schoodic Peninsula (and Schoodic Institute), explore Bar Harbor, dine at Jordan Pond
History Enthusiasts: Sieur de Monts Spring, Baker Island Cruise (207.288.2386), Isleford Historical Cruise (barharborcruises.com or take the ferry)
Sunset Spots: Cadillac Mountain, Park Loop Road pullout above Eagle Lake, Bass Harbor Head Lighthouse, Indian Point
Sunrise Spots: Cadillac Mountain, Ocean Path (Sand Beach, Thunder Hole, Boulder Beach, Otter Cliff), Gorham Mountain, Bass Harbor Head Lighthouse
Wildlife: Dive-In Theater Boat Cruise (divered.com), Bar Harbor Whale Watching (barharborwhales.com), Frenchman Bay Cruise (downeastwindjammer.com)

Beyond the Park...

Dining

Lompoc Café & Brew Pub
36 Rodick St, Bar Harbor
(207) 288-9392
lompoccafe.com

2 Cats • (207) 288-2808
130 Cottage St, Bar Harbor
twocatsbarharbor.com

Lunch Bar Harbor
8 Mt Desert St, Bar Harbor
(207) 901-0018
lunchbarharbor.com

The Barnacle • (207) 801-9249
112 Main St, Bar Harbor
thebarnaclebarharbor.com

Café This Way • (207) 288-4483
14 ½ Mount Desert St, BH
cafethisway.com

CIAO food|drink • (207)
901-9110
135 Cottage St, Bar Harbor
ciaobarharbor.com

Bar Harbor Lobster Bakes
10 ME-3, Bar Harbor
(207) 288-4055
Barharborlobsterbakes.com

The Stadium • (207) 801-9477
62 Main St, Bar Harbor
thestadiumbh.com

Quietside Café & Ice Cream
360 Main St, Southwest Harbor
(207) 244-9444

MDI Lobster and BBQ
126 Clark Point Rd, SW Harbor
(207) 266-9419
mdilobsterco.com

Peter Trout's Tavern and Inn
48 Shore Rd, Southwest Harbor
(207) 244-8619
petertrouts.com

Thurston's Lobster Pound
9 Thurston Rd, Bernard
(207) 244-7600
thurstonslobster.com

Saltmeadow Farm
221 Tremont Rd, Bass Harbor
(207) 244-4158 • Pizza

Fisherman's Galley
7 Newman St, Winter Harbor
fishermansinnmaine.com

The Pickled Wrinkle
9 E Schoodic Dr, Birch Harbor
thepickledwrinkle.com

Grocery Stores

Hannaford Supermarkets
86 Cottage St, Bar Harbor
(207) 288-5680

Town Hill Market
1339 ME-102, Bar Harbor
(207) 288-5136

Pine Tree Market
121 Main St, Northeast Harbor
(207) 276-3335

Walmart Supercenter
17 Myrick St, Lamoine
(207) 667-6780

Lodging

Bar Harbor Inn • (844) 814-1668
7 Newport Dr, Bar Harbor
barharborinn.com

Emery's Cottages
181 Sand Point Rd, Bar Harbor
(207) 288-3432
emeryscottages.com

Bar Harbor Motel
100 Eden St, Bar Harbor
(800) 388-3453
barharbormotel.com

Moseley Cottage
12 Atlantic Ave, Bar Harbor
(800) 458-8644
moseleycottage.net

Bass Cottage Inn
14 The Field, Bar Harbor
(207) 288-9552
basscottage.com

Asticou Inn • (207) 276-3344
15 Peabody Dr, NE Harbor
asticou.com

Colonels Suites • (207) 288-4775
143 Main St, Northeast Harbor
colonelssuites.com

Harbourside Inn • (207) 276-3272
48 Harbourside Rd, NE Harbor
harboursideinn.com

Harbour Cottage Inn
9 Dirigo Rd, Southwest Harbor
(207) 244-5738
harbourcottageinn.com

Winter Harbor Inn
298 Main St, Winter Harbor
(207) 562-7837
winterharborinn.com

*Many chain restaurants and
hotels can be found in Ellsworth,
a few miles west of MDI*

Camping

Bar Harbor / Oceanside KOA
136 Count Rd, Bar Harbor
koa.com • (207) 288-3520

Bar Harbor Campground
409 ME-3, Bar Harbor
(207) 288-5185
thebarharborcampground.com

Mainstay Cottages & RV Park
66 Sargent St, Winter Harbor
(207) 963-2601
mainstaycottages-rvpark.com

Hadley's Point Campground
33 Hadley Point Rd, Bar Harbor
(207) 288-4808
hadleyspoint.com

Mount Desert Campground
516 Sound Dr, Mt Desert
(207) 244-3710
mountdesertcampground.com

Somes Sound View Camp
5 Spinnaker Way, Mt Desert
ssvc.info • (207) 244-3890

Smuggler's Den • (877) 244-9033
20 Main St, Southwest Harbor
smugglersdencampground.com

Narrows Too Camping Resort
1150 Bar Harbor Rd, Trenton •
(877) 570-2267

Timberland Acres RV Park
57 Bar Harbor Rd, Trenton
(207) 667-3600
timberlandacresrvpark.com

Festivals

Birding Festival • June
acadiabirdingfestival.com

Windjammer Days • June
boothbayharbor.com

Fourth of July • pancake
breakfast, parade, lobster bake,
lobster races, and fireworks

Bar Harbor Music Festival • July
barharbormusicfestival.org

Maine Lobster Festival • August
mainelobsterfestival.com

Acadia Night Sky Festival • Sept
acadianightskyfestival.com

MDI Marathon • October
NE Harbor • mdimarathon.org

Oktoberfest • October
acadiaoktoberfest.com

Attractions

Atlantic Brewing Co
15 Knox Rd, Bar Harbor
(207) 288-2337
atlanticbrewing.com
Seasonal • Admission: Free

Timber Tina's Lumberjack Show
127 Bar Harbor Rd, Trenton
mainelumberjack.com

Baxter State Park
*Mt Katahdin, the northern
terminus of the Appalachian
Trail, is this park's centerpiece*
(207) 723-5140
baxterstatepark.org

Camden Hills State Park
280 Belfast Rd, Camden
(207) 256-3109

Maine Coastal Islands NWR
*5 separate refuges, protecting
more than 73 offshore islands
that provide outstanding habitat
for birds and marine life*
9 Water St, Rockland
(207) 594-0600

North Country Rivers
*Whitewater rafting on the
Kennebec, Penobscot, and
Dead Rivers*
36 Main St, Bingham
(800) 348-8871
northcountryrivers.com
Open: Seasonal • Rafting: $79+

Rockland Breakwater Light
rocklandharborlights.org

Pemaquid Point Lighthouse
Bristol • (207) 677-2492

Cabbage Island Clambakes
Boat ride to the island for food
Pier 6, 22 Commercial St,
Boothbay Harbor
cabbageislandclambake.com

Burnt Island Light
Boothbay Harbor

Bowdoin College
Historic liberal arts college
255 Maine St, Brunswick
bowdoin.edu

Popham Beach State Park
711 Popham Rd, Phippsburg
(207) 389-1335

Portland Museum of Art
7 Congress Sq, Portland
(207) 775-6148
portlandmuseum.org

Cuyahoga Valley

A spider perched atop a turtle's nose (Towpath Trail)

Phone: (440) 717-3890
Website: nps.gov/cuva

Established: October 11, 2000
Size: 33,000 Acres
Annual Visitors: 2.2 Million
Peak Season: Summer
Hiking Trails: 186 Miles

Activities: Train Rides, Hiking, Biking, Paddling, Fishing, Horseback Riding, Golfing, Birdwatching, Cross-Country Skiing, Snowshoeing, Downhill Skiing, Sledding, Concerts, Theater, Art Exhibits, Museums, Festivals

Campgrounds: None (but there are several public campgrounds within 30 miles of the park)

Park Hours: All day, every day (some areas close at dusk) Cuyahoga Valley Scenic Railroad offers train excursions year-round
Entrance Fee: None

Northeastern Ohio might not be a place you expect to find a national park. Towering mountains and gaping gorges are nowhere to be found. But our parks are filled with surprises, and considering its location deep in the middle of the rust belt, Cuyahoga Valley might be the greatest surprise of all. Miles of undeveloped land nestled between the sprawling cities of Akron and Cleveland lack the sheer size and wild feeling found at the natural wonders of the West, but this area is rich in history, culture, and beauty. Now a recreational escape, Cuyahoga Valley endured decades of development, trade, industry, and pollution before conservationists began pushing for a new era of preservation and protection. The valley's history is its own unique story, but its present is the same: the area has been restored and protected for the enjoyment of future generations.

As the Cuyahoga River twists and turns for 22 miles through the center of the park, it lives up to its name, the Iroquois word for "crooked." The same Native Americans who named the river used it for trade and transportation. By 1795 the river formed the northern boundary between Indian Territory and the United States.

Imaginary boundaries were drawn and erased. Treaties written then ignored. The region developed and Ohio became the hub of American industrialization. In 1827, the Ohio & Erie Canal was completed, connecting the Great Lakes region with the Gulf of Mexico via the Mississippi, Ohio, and Cuyahoga Rivers, dramatically improving shipping of goods and people to the Great Plains States. Companies like BF

Goodrich and Standard Oil prospered. The Cuyahoga River perished.

The region's rapid development, booming industry, alarming population growth, and inadequate infrastructure spawned a river filled with sewage and industrial waste. So saturated with oils, gases, and chemicals, it was infamously referred to as "the river that burned," catching fire at least thirteen times between 1868 and 1969. A fire in 1969 was short in duration, lasting only 24 minutes, but huge in environmental impact, prompting *Time Magazine* to write that the water "oozes rather than flows" and that a person "does not drown but decays." The pointed article helped galvanize an environmental movement, which spurred the passing of water quality legislation. State and federal environmental agencies and Earth Day were established thanks to the "river that burned" and the activism it inspired. President Gerald Ford signed a bill creating Cuyahoga Valley National Recreation Area in 1974, and in 2000 Congress changed its designation to a national park. Decades of treatment and restoration efforts have improved water quality. Wildlife has returned. But it's far from the pristine waterway it once was. Boating and swimming are still not recommended and fish caught in these waters are not to be eaten.

Since the late 19th century, Cuyahoga Valley has been used for recreational purposes, beginning with modest boat trips and carriage rides. Railroads led to obsolescence of the Ohio & Erie Canal, but the path used by horses and mules to tow seafaring vessels is used today by hikers and bikers. Twenty miles of the 101-mile Towpath Trail passes through Cuyahoga Valley and it is one of the park's most popular attractions. The railway also serves as a tourist attraction. Cuyahoga Valley Scenic Railroad travels from Canton to Akron and on to Cleveland, making seven stops within the park. Themed excursions, including everything from beer tasting to book reading, are offered throughout the year. The park's urban location lends itself to some atypical attractions like golfing, a music center and theater, and a ski resort. You can also explore several original and re-created heritage sites where guides don time-period wardrobe and pretend like they grew up during a drastically different era.

Cuyahoga Valley's unique combination of nature, history, development, destruction, and restoration provides a park that is as much a walk through history as it is a walk in nature. Join some of the park's ranger-led experiences and you almost certainly will have an entertaining, educational, and memorable visit.

Blue Hen Falls

When to Go
Cuyahoga Valley is open all year. While visitation peaks in July/August, it's steady from March through November. Weekends are busiest. Spring wildflowers and fall foliage attract above-average crowds.

Transportation & Airports
Cuyahoga Valley National Park is located in an urban area. Many roads provide access to the park. Greyhound (800.231.2222, greyhound.com) has a bus station in downtown Cleveland and Akron. Amtrak (800.872.7245, amtrak.com) serves Cleveland. **Cuyahoga Valley Scenic Railroad** (800.468.4070, cvsr.com) travels from Canton–Akron–Cleveland, making seven stops within park boundaries.

The closest airports are Cleveland Hopkins International Airport (CLE) and Akron–Canton Regional Airport (CAK).

Directions
Canal Visitor Center (7104 Canal Road, Valley View) is roughly 11 miles from downtown Cleveland. Traveling by car from the north, take I-77 south to exit 157 for OH-21/Granger Road/Brecksville Road toward OH-17. Merge onto OH-21/Brecksville Rd. Turn left at Rockside Road. Turn right at Canal Road. The visitor center will be on your right

Boston Store Visitor Center (1550 Boston Mills Road, Peninsula) is about 18 miles from downtown Akron. Driving from the south, take OH-8 north. Turn left at E Hines Road and continue on to Boston Mills Road. The visitor center will be on your left.

Buttermilk Falls

Bridal Veil Falls
Brandywine Falls

Leonard Krieger
CanalWay Center

Canal VC

Canal Exploration Center
Information

Rockside Station

OHIO & ERIE CANAL

Lock 39

BACCI PARK
Village of Cuyahoga Heights

OHIO & ERIE CANAL
RESERVATION
Cleveland
Metroparks

Cuyahoga River

To Cleveland

Brecksville
Nature Center

Brushwood
Lake

Boston Mill VC

Squire Rich
Historical Museum

Sleepy Hollow
Golf Course

Deer Lick
Cave

Brecksville
Stables

BRECKSVILLE
RESERVATION
Cleveland
Metroparks

Overlook

Brecksville
Station

Terra Vista
Natural Study Area

Canal Corners
Farm &
Market

Fitzwater

Alexander's Mill
(Wilson's Mill)

Tinkers Creek
Gorge

BEDFORD
RESERVATION
Cleveland
Metroparks

Tinker Creek

Boston Mill Visitor Center

National Park Service
Administrative Headquarters
Jaite

Coonrad

Spice
Acres

Ohio & Erie Canal Towpath Trail

Cuyahoga Valley Scenic Railroad

Station Road
Bridge

Frazee House
(building closed)

Overlook
Lake

Bridal Veil
Falls

Overlook

Lost Meadows

Great
Falls

Shawnee Hills
Golf Course

Viaduct
Park

Boston Mills
Ski Resort

BOSTON

Hines Hill Center

Red Lock

Inn at Brandywine Falls
(lodging)

Brandywine
Ski Resort

Stanford House
(lodging)

Cuyahoga Valley Scenic Railroad

Brandywine
Falls

Boston Store and
MD Garage

Blue Hen Falls

Brandywine Falls

SOUTH CHAGRIN
RESERVATION
Cleveland
Metroparks

To Cleveland

Indigo Lake Train Station

Camping & Lodging

Camping is not available within the park, however there are a few public campgrounds nearby. Nimisila Reservoir Metro Park (30 minutes south, 29 sites, $25–35/night), and Punderson (40 minutes northeast, 90 sites, $25+/night) and West Branch (40 minutes east, 198 sites, $27+/night) State Parks (ohiodnr.gov) are options. If you want to go backpacking, Buckeye Trail (buckeyetrail.org) passes through the park, and backcountry sites are located along it, just none within Cuyahoga Valley.

There are two lodging options. **Inn at Brandywine Falls** (innatbrandywinefalls.com, 330.467.1812) features exceptional location next to beautiful Brandywine Falls. It's a family-run bed and breakfast with rooms starting around $150. The Conservancy for Cuyahoga Valley National Park (conservancyforcvnp. org, 330.657.2909) rents out the 9-room, 30-bed **Stanford House** ($400–600/night) for events or your family vacation. Just a short walk from Brandywine Falls, it also has prime location.

Scenic Railroad

One of the most unique and entertaining experiences in the valley is taking a ride aboard the **Cuyahoga Valley Scenic Railroad** (CVSR). Owned by the National Parks Service (NPS), it's one of the oldest, longest, and most scenic tourist excursions the NPS offers. The hard part isn't deciding whether you ride the CVSR, it's choosing which excursion to take. Most common is National Park Scenic Excursion ($15–35), which provides visitors a relaxing, enjoyable trip to see the wildlife and scenery of Cuyahoga Valley. You'll find beer and wine tasting excursions or breakfast, brunch, or lunch trips. There are social evening rides, including Ales on Rails ($50–90), Grape Escape ($60–90), and Murder Mystery ($50–60/person). And then there are special programs for families like "Royalty on the Rails" ($15–35/person), featuring appearances from your children's favorite characters (Cinderella, Snow White, the Little Mermaid) or "Superheroes on the Train" ($15–35/ person), where passengers are encouraged to dress up in costume. In winter they offer The Polar Express and children are welcome to wear pajamas aboard the train while the popular children's book is read out loud. It's common for National Park rangers to narrate train rides, and they never fail to make any park activity enlightening and entertaining through their knowledge and spirit. Depth and variety of excursions make CVSR an appealing attraction to just about everyone.

Stations are located between Independence and Akron, including seven within the park. General passengers can board at Rockside Station (the park's north end), Peninsula Depot (central), and Akron Northside Station (south end, outside the park). Free parking is available near each station. The rest are Bike Aboard stops. **Bike Aboard** allows cyclists to use the train for $5/person (one-way). It's a unique opportunity to complete a one-way bicycle trip along the Towpath Trail. More information and reservations are available at (330) 439-5708 or cvsr.com.

Hiking

Many city dwellers search out sites of natural beauty to escape the stress and hectic pace of an urban lifestyle. Cuyahoga Valley provides such a location for the people of Akron and Cleveland. With 186 miles of hiking trails, it's a great place to clear your mind and enjoy some fresh air.

Nature seekers visited Cuyahoga Valley as early as the late 1800s, but the region wasn't developed as a park until the early 1900s. In 1929, Hayward Kendall, a Cleveland coal baron, willed 430 acres around Ritchie Ledges to the state of Ohio, stipulating the "property should be perpetually used for park purposes." His generous donation created Virginia Kendall Park, named in honor of Hayward's mother. Here you'll find one of the park's premier hikes, **Ledges Trail**. Its trailhead is located at Ledges Parking Area, just off Kendall Park Road, which becomes Truxell Road. This moderate 2.2-mile hike leads to dramatic eroded sandstone formations known as The Ledges (AKA Ritchie Ledges).

Haskell Run Trail is located near The Ledges. Parking is available at Happy Days Lodge Parking Area on the north side of Route 303. The trailhead for this moderate 0.5-mile hike is in the southeast corner of the parking lot directly adjacent to the lodge.

Haskell Run and Ledges Trail intersect the short spur to **Ice Box Cave**. It's not exactly a cave, but kids enjoy the trek to a cool, moist, 50-foot deep slit in solid rock. To pick up the trail from Haskell Run, simply take a short connector trail up a hill and to the left after crossing the first wooden bridge. Wooden steps make the climb easier, and the connector trail intersects Ledges Trail. Turn left along the base of Ritchie Ledges and continue about 0.4-mile to the cave. An excursion to Ice Box Cave adds about one mile to the total hiking distance of either Ledges or Haskell Run. It may not be a cave, but it still can be cold and dark in the Ice Box, so remember to pack a jacket and flashlight. With that said, Ice Box Cave remains closed to help protect the bat population. Ice Box or no Ice Box, Ledges is one of the best hikes in the park.

There are more than 70 waterfalls in Cuyahoga Valley. The most popular is 60-foot **Brandywine Falls**, which you can view from overlooks opposite Inn at Brandywine Falls. Most visitors simply view Brandywine from the overlooks, but there is a moderate 1.5-mile loop around Brandywine Gorge, providing waterfall-views from a few different perspectives. Either way, begin at Brandywine Falls Parking Area on Stanford Mills Road, west of Brandywine Road. Plan to visit in the middle of the week or early/late on the weekend.

Blue Hen is next on the pecking order of popular waterfalls. Compared to Brandywine, Blue Hen is merely a trickle, but the small amount of cascading water is exactly what's so appealing. Three narrow ribbons of water fall over a wide, rocky face before dropping into a shallow pool. The 1.2-mile trail is easy to moderate, and its trailhead is located in Boston, on Boston Mills Road, one mile west of Riverview Road. The trailhead parking area is quite small, but overflow parking has been added on the south side of the road. A viewing area offers excellent views of the falls. A bit of scrambling will get you to the waterfall's base. The equally impressive 20-foot **Buttermilk Falls** is less than one mile downstream from Blue Hen. The path to Buttermilk is more rugged and not as easy to follow, but most hikers should make it there just fine. Take your time and pay careful attention to the path.

Tinkers Creek Gorge is a National Natural Landmark in the northeast corner of the park. Here you'll find the **Great Falls** of Tinkers Creek in Viaduct Park and **Bridal Veil Falls**. Bridal Veil Falls Trailhead is located on Gorge Parkway, 1.4 miles northwest of Egbert Road and about one mile east of Overlook Lane in Bedford Reservation. It's an easy 0.25-mile hike to the falls.

Chippewa Creek Trail begins at Brecksville Nature Center parking lot on Chippewa Creek Drive, about 0.5-mile south of State Route 82. This scenic 2.5-mile

Kendall Lake

loop follows both sides of Chippewa Creek. Note that the creek may be impassable during periods of high water. For a moderate to difficult hike, try the **Old Carriage Trail** between Jaite and Boston. This 5.25-mile trip starts at Red Lock Trailhead located on Highland Road, 0.5-mile east of Riverview and Vaughn Roads.

The 1,300-mile **Buckeye Trail** circles the state of Ohio and 30 miles pass through Cuyahoga Valley, briefly joining Towpath Trail in the park's southern half. It is well maintained by the Buckeye Trail Association and can be accessed from eight locations within the park. Stretches vary from easy to difficult and anywhere from 1.5 to 7 miles between access points. **Towpath Trail** is another great hiking choice. The segments north of Ira Road Trailhead or south of Boston Mill Visitor Center are particularly nice.

Biking

There are four major bicycle trails in Cuyahoga Valley. Most popular is the **Ohio & Erie Towpath Trail**. This 101-mile crushed stone path follows the historic Ohio & Erie Canal Route, and 20 of its most scenic miles span the length of the park. Along the way you'll find picnic areas, restrooms, and train depots. Thanks to the Cuyahoga Valley Scenic Valley Railroad you can have an incredibly unique biking experience. Bike from depot to depot and then take the train back to where you started. With the railroad's **Bike Aboard!** Program, cyclists and their bikes ride the train for the reasonable price of $5/person. All you have to do is flag down a train at one of the boarding stations.

East Rim Trail (2.3 miles) and **Lamb Loop** (4.7 miles) are two trail additions with intermediate (and up) mountain bikers in mind. The trails straddle I-80. East Rim Trailhead is located at 281 Boston Mills Road. To protect the trail, it closes when wet or muddy.

There are more than 70 miles of paved paths. **Summit County Bike & Hike Trail** follows the park's border for nearly 16 miles. Between Brecksville and Bedford Metroparks, you'll find over 60 miles of paved trails alone.

If you would like to rent a bike or join a group ride, there are a few nearby shops: Century Cycles (330.657.2209, centurycycles.com, Bike Rental: $10+/hour), Blimp City Bike & Hike (330.836.6600, blimpcitybikeandhike.com, $10+/hour, group rides available), and Ernie's Bicycle Shop (330.832.5111, erniesbikeshop.com, $6+/hour, group rides available).

Paddling
Restoration efforts continue to improve water quality of the Cuyahoga River, but high pollutant levels are frequently recorded, especially after heavy rainfalls. The river is navigable, but there are several permanent hazards, including Lock 29 dam remnants, metal pylons that regularly collect wood debris upstream of Rockside Road/Lock 39, and downed trees between Red Lock and Station Road (which can be navigable at high water levels). The park has five river access locations: Lock 29, Boston Store Trailhead, Red Lock, Station Road Bridge, and Lock 39. From Lock 39 it's a 12-mile paddle into Cleveland. Remember that you are responsible for your own safety. Strainers are common. If you're thinking about paddling the river, scout your route if you can't find someone who's done it recently. When in doubt, take it out! Always portage around hazards. After rain, the river may be contaminated with sewer overflow. Alternatively, paddlers are also welcome in the park's ponds.

Fishing
Fishing is permitted. More than 65 species of fish are found in the park. Catch-and-release fishing is encouraged. Eating your catch from the river is not. Motorboats are prohibited within the park, and lakes are occasionally closed for resource management. A fishing license is required in accordance with Ohio regulations. Kendall Lake, Indigo Lake, Brushwood Lake, Conrad Farm Pond, Goosefeather Pond, and Armington Pond are recommended fishing locations.

Horseback Riding
Exploring the park on horseback provides an interesting perspective of the park's landscapes and wildlife, and there are about 50 miles of designated horse trails at Cuyahoga Valley. However, horse rental and guide services are not available within the park, so visitors keen on riding must trailer in their own stock. Station Road parking lot, close to Brecksville

Reservation, has large pull-through parking spots allowing easy access. Here you'll find several miles of trails around Brecksville Stables Area. It's always a good idea to inquire about trail closures, difficulty, and access before heading out for a ride.

Golf
Near the park, you'll find two public golf courses: Shawnee Hills (440.232.7184, clemetparks.com, $16–20/9 holes), and Sleepy Hollow (440.526.4285, clemetparks.com, $19–27/9-holes). The Conservancy of Cuyahoga Valley National Park is working on converting Brandywine Country Club into public park lands. Astorhurst Country Club shares a similar future, but as part of Bedford Reservation.

Birdwatching
Birdwatchers like Cuyahoga Valley. The park's varied landscapes provide habitat for more than 248 species. After an extended absence due to excessive pollution, blue herons and bald eagles have returned to nest. Herons are often seen in February scavenging for materials to build or repair their nests. Many nests have been found perched high above the Cuyahoga River at sites north of Route 82 and just south of Bath Road. From February until July, you may see herons at either Bath Road heronry (from a pullout along Bath Road) or Pinery Narrows heronry (from Towpath Trail, 0.5-mile north of Station Road Bridge). Nesting bald eagles can also be found in this area. They returned in 2006 after an absence of more than 70 years.

Beaver Marsh is a great place to spot wood ducks and other waterfowl during their migrations in March and November. Solitary vireos, winter wrens, hermit thrushes, and black-throated warblers frequent the hemlocks near Ledges in late spring. Red-breasted nuthatches and golden-crowned kinglets call Horseshoe Pond their home from late October through early March. Grassland around the former Coliseum site (near the intersection of I-80 and I-271 on W. Streetsboro Rd/OH-303) is now habitat for eastern meadowlark, bobolink, savannah sparrow, grasshopper sparrow, and Henslow's sparrow. These species can be seen during their summer breeding season, and it is asked that you stay on the edge of the grassland from April to August because many of these birds nest on the ground.

Winter Activities
There are nearly as many ways to enjoy Cuyahoga Valley National Park in winter as there are in summer. **Winter Sports Center** at Kendall Lake Shelter offers cross-country skiing and snowshoeing. It's located

in Peninsula at 1000 Truxell Road, two miles west of Akron Cleveland Road. The Sports Center offers ski rental for $15/day or $7.50/half-day. It is open daily (when snow depth is four or more inches), Dec 26–31; Sat & Sun, Jan 2–Feb 28; Martin Luther King Day, and President's Day, 10am–4pm. Call (330) 657-2752 to confirm. Towpath Trail is straight, flat, and popular among skiers and snowshoers. Another popular winter hike is Ledges, where you may see spectacular icicle formations. **Snowshoe rental** is available at Boston Store Visitor Center (open daily from 10am–4:30pm except Christmas and New Year's) when snow depth is four or more inches. Snowshoes cost $5 per pair per day.

Ice fishing is permitted at lakes and ponds. **Sledding** is available at Kendall Hills on Quick Road, with parking at Pine Hallow (5465 Quick Road, Peninsula) or Little Meadow (5249 Quick Road, Peninsula) Parking Areas.

Boston Mills/Brandywine (330.657.2334, bmbw.com) offers **downhill skiing** and **snowboarding** (daily), and **polar blast tubing** (Friday–Sunday). They are two separate ski hills, located in the Brandywine Falls area, close to one another on opposite sides of the Cuyahoga River. In 2019 these ski hills (and other midwestern resorts) were purchased by the largest ski resort company in the country, Vail Resorts. If you love to ski/board, this may be a benefit to you, as they sell an Epic Pass ($999), which grants access to all 37 of their resorts.

Visitor Centers, Museums & The Arts

Canal Exploration Center takes visitors back to the booming canal era centered around the mid-19th century. You can also peruse the rehabilitated **Lock 38** here. The visitor center is open 10am–4:00pm, every day in summer, Saturdays and Sundays from fall through spring.

Frazee House, located along Towpath Trail at 7733 Canal Road in Valley View, is another historic structure preserved by the national park. It's neat to look at, but this is a better place to park and hike **Sagamore Creek Loop Trail** (in Bedford Reservation), which is worth the effort, especially if the creek is flowing.

Brecksville Nature Center (440.526.1012, cleveland-metroparks.com), located at 9000 Chippewa Creek Dr, isn't part of the national park, but it's some more parkland to explore. The Nature Center is nice, and they offer regular walks and nature programs.

The new **Boston Mill Visitor Center** opened on October 25, 2019 (and I strolled through on the 29th!). It's a great central location. From here, a walk to Brandywine Falls, heading north along Towpath Trail and east on Stanford Trail, is less than three miles (one-way). Or hike Buckeye Trail west to Blue Hen Falls, which is less than two miles (one-way). The section of Towpath Trail to the south is fun as well. Bring bikes, and you could lose track of time, spending the whole day here no problem. The visitor center is open every day except Thanksgiving and Christmas, from 10am–4:00pm, with extended hours in spring and summer.

Peninsula Depot Visitor Center (216.524.1497) is a good place to board the Cuyahoga Valley Scenic Railroad. The short walk to **Lock 29** is a decent idea. You'll also find a gift store, cafe, and there's a bike shop (Century Cycles) across the street, where you can rent bikes.

Cuyahoga Valley Historical Museum (330.657.2892, peninsulalibrary.org), located in Peninsula at 1775 Main St, isn't part of the park, but it dives into the history of the area. It's open noon until 5, Friday through Sunday.

Hunt Farm Visitor Information Center is located along Towpath Trail at the southern end of the park not far from **Everett Road Covered Bridge**. It's a small building with a few exhibits, restrooms, and a place to rest (if you're biking/hiking the Towpath). It's open from 10am–4pm, daily in summer, Saturdays and Sundays in spring and fall, and it's closed in winter.

Hale Farm & Village (330.666.3711, wrhs.org), located in Bath at 2686 Oak Hill Rd, is a beautiful property centered around an early 19th-century farmhouse. On tours you'll get the chance to meet farm animals, learn how to make candles, brooms, and bricks, and observe pottery glassblowing, blacksmithing, and spinning demonstrations. It'll feel like you've travelled back in time as you interact with historians in time-period clothing. Admission costs $12 per adult, a fair price for an interesting experience.

Blossom Music Center (330.920.8040, clevelandamphitheater.com), located in Cuyahoga Falls at 1145 W Steels Corners Rd, is an outdoor amphitheater that hosts major productions for tens of thousands of guests. At the very least, take a quick look at who will be performing during your trip.

Porthouse Theatre Co (330.672.3884, kent.edu/porthouse), located near Blossom Music Center at 3143 O'Neil Rd, is another wonderful outdoor venue that puts on a variety of plays and musicals. Similarly, check them out while planning your trip.

Heron (sweet hair!) near Beaver Marsh (Towpath Trail)

Ranger Programs & For Kids

If land is the park's body, rangers are its soul. Joining a ranger-led excursion is one of the best ways to enhance your visit. You have myriad choices, ranging from birdwatching to monarch butterfly monitoring, alien invasions (invasive plant and animal species) to surveying a cemetery. Check the park's schedule online or at a visitor center, and then let the rangers make your visit a little more memorable.

Kids (ages 7–12) are invited to take part in the park's Junior Ranger Program and children (ages 4–6) can participate in the Junior Ranger, Jr. Program. These programs are typically offered during summer. Ohio & Erie Canalway (ohioanderiecanalway.com) created 40 quests along the canalway, one is part of the Junior Ranger Guidebook. Try it and do more if you had fun. The park also offers multi-day camps and ranger-led hikes throughout summer. Check online or at a visitor center for an up-to-date listing of all the great programs geared for children. Hiking to Blue Hen Falls (and Buttermilk Falls) or Ledges or riding the rails are excellent family activities. If you'd like to do things as a group, Get Up, Get Out & Go! arranges free recreational programs for 11–14 year olds and their families every Tuesday and Thursday.

Flora & Fauna

More than 900 plant species thrive in Cuyahoga Valley. Spring, when wildflowers are in bloom, and fall, when deciduous trees are shedding their leaves, are the most popular seasons to view the valley's plant life. Wildflowers are most abundant in moist areas near creeks and streams, far from trees whose leaves block the sun's light. You may encounter these flowers: spring beauty, yellow trout lily, toothwort, hepatica, bloodroot, dwarf ginseng, Virginia bluebells, spring cress, purple cress, rue anemone, foam flower, twin leaf, bishop's cap, squirrel corn, violets, jack-in-the-

pulpit, and many species of trillium. The grasses, trees, and wildflowers play an important role in making this a special place, so appreciate them, or at the very least, don't step on or pick any flowers.

Just as the park serves as a retreat for weary city-dwellers, it is a refuge for a variety of wildlife. For the most part mammals consist of small critters like squirrels, chipmunks, and mice. But you'll also find white-tailed deer, raccoons, and woodchucks scurrying about. You may not see beavers, but you will see their handiwork in the form of felled trees and dammed streams. If you're lucky you may catch a glimpse of a coyote or river otter. These species naturally returned to the park in recent years. Also residing here are hundreds of species of reptiles, amphibians, insects, and birds.

Pets & Accessibility

Pets are allowed on hiking trails but must be kept on a leash (less than six feet). Only service animals are allowed in park buildings and on the train.

Canal and Boston Store Visitor Centers, as well as Hunt Farm Visitor Information Center, Frazee House, and Towpath Trail are accessible to wheelchair users. And Horseshoe Pond has an accessible fishing pier near the parking lot.

Weather

Weather at Cuyahoga Valley is typical of the Midwest. Winters are cold and snowy. The Cleveland area averages 61 inches of snowfall, but annual accumulation varies greatly from year-to-year. Average annual precipitation is 35 inches, with 20 inches accumulating between the months of April and September. Summers are typically hot and humid with unpredictable thunderstorms. Most guests travel to the park in summer, but fall might be the ideal time to visit, when cool, crisp, clear days and colorful foliage make the valley particularly inviting.

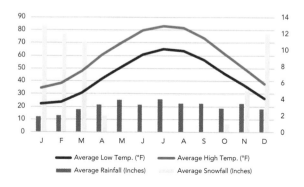

Average Low Temp. (°F) Average High Temp. (°F)
Average Rainfall (Inches) Average Snowfall (Inches)

Tips & Recommendations

Cuyahoga Valley is incredibly diverse in its activities and attractions. It has the staples: hiking, biking, and paddling. But it also has many uncommon attractions like train rides, farms, concerts, plays, even snowboarding. So, to get the most from any visit to Cuyahoga Valley, you have to do a little planning. Before arriving, consider doing a couple of things:

1). Check cvsr.org to see what special events the Cuyahoga Valley Scenic Railroad is putting on while you'll be here.
2). Check nps.gov/cuva for a schedule of events.
3). Check clevelandamphitheater.com to see if there are any concerts at Blossom Music Theater They bring in major performers as well as the Cleveland Orchestra (clevelandorchestra.com).
4). Check kent.edu/porthouse to see what shows they'll be putting on during your visit.
5). Reserve tickets for Hale Farm and Village.
6). Winter travelers should consider checking out the ski resorts (bmbw.com).

Use the Bike Aboard program so you can pedal further along Towpath Trail and eliminate having to do an out-and-back. Plus, trains are cool!

Try to plan your trip around ranger programs and special events, but you could stay a couple days doing typical national park things like the ones listed below.

Easy Hikes: Brandywine Falls (0.3 mile), Bridal Veil Falls (0.25), Towpath Trail (Boston and Ira areas are favorites)
Moderate Hikes: Ledges (2.2 miles), Blue Hen (3) and Buttermilk Falls (1.3 beyond Blue Hen), Haskell Run (0.5), Brandywine Gorge (1.5)
Family Activities: Ride the Cuyahoga Valley Scenic Railroad, Bike Towpath Trail, Hale Farm and Village, become Junior Rangers
Guided Tours: Cuyahoga Valley Scenic Railroad
Rainy Day Activities: Ride the rails, waterfall hikes (be careful), learn about the area's history (see below), explore Akron and/or Cleveland
History Enthusiasts: Hale Farm & Village, Boston Mill Visitor Center, Cuyahoga Valley Historical Museum, Canal Exploration Center, Towpath Trail
Sunset Spots: Ledges Overlook
Sunrise Spots: Maybe Indigo Lake. This is a good park to sleep in at. You're in a forested valley, and most of the attractions don't open until late morning. While the sky can always impress, really good sunrises/sunsets are hard to come by.
Wildlife: Towpath Trail (Beaver Marsh, Stumpy Basin)

Beyond the Park...

Dining
Trail Mix • (330) 657-2277
1565 W Boston Mills Rd, Peninsula
conservancyforcvnp.org

The Wine Mill • (234) 571-2594
4964 Akron Cleveland Rd, Peninsula
thewinemill.com

Flip Side • (330) 655-3547
49 Village Way, Hudson
flipsideburger.com

3 Palms Pizzeria • (330) 342-4545
60 Village Way, Hudson
3palmspizzeria.com

Creekside Rest • (440) 546-0555
8803 Brecksville Rd, Brecksville
creeksiderestaurant.com

Farinacci Pizza • (330) 467-7919
9385 Olde 8 Rd, Northfield
farinaccipizza.com

Loose Moose Grub and Pub
500 W Aurora Rd, Northfield
(330) 748-0431

Tinkers Tavern • (216) 642-3900
14000 Tinkers Cr Rd, Walton Hills
tinkerstavern.com

Grocery Stores
Heinen's Fine Foods
8383 Chippewa Rd, Brecksville
(440) 740-0535

Giant Eagle Supermarket
4428 Broadview Rd, Richfield
(330) 659-6134

Costco Wholesale
6720 Bass Pro Dr, Hudson
(330) 341-7000

Lodging
Shady Oaks Farm B&B
241 W Highland Rd, Northfield
(330) 468-2909
shadyoaksfarmbnb.com

Many chain restaurants and hotels can be found nearby in Macedonia and Richfield.

Campgrounds
Streetsboro / Cleveland SE KOA
187 OH-303, Streetsboro
koa.com • (330) 650-2552

Silver Springs Campground
5238 Young Rd, Stow
(330) 689-5100

Festivals
Riverfront Irish Festival • June
riverfrontirishfest.org

Duct Tape Festival • June
Avon • ducttapefestival.com

Italian American Festival • July
festaitalianacf.com

Twins Day Festival • August
Twinsburg • twinsdays.org

Oktoberfest • September
oktoberfestcfo.com

Covered Bridge Fest • October
coveredbridgefestival.org

Attractions
Gorge Metro Park (*Mary Campbell Cave*), Sand Run Metro Park, Cascade Valley Metro Park, and F.A. Seiberling Nature Realm • (330) 867-5511
Beautiful parks around Akron, featuring waterfalls and valleys
summitmetroparks.org

Bedford Reservation
Great Falls of Tinkers Creek
clevelandmetroparks.com

Stan Hywet Hall & Gardens
714 N Portage Path, Akron
stanhywet.org • (330) 836-5533

James A. Garfield NHS
8095 Mentor Ave, Mentor
nps.gov/jaga • (440) 255-8722

Hocking Hills State Park
19852 OH-664, Logan
thehockinghills.org

Cedar Point • (419) 627-2350
Amusement park with 17 roller coasters and a waterpark!
1 Cedar Point Dr, Sandusky
cedarpoint.com

A Christmas Story House
3159 W 11th St, Cleveland
achristmasstoryhouse.com

Nelson-Kennedy Ledges SP
Small park with cliffs and waterfalls similar to Cuyahoga
12440 OH-282, Garrettsville
parks.ohiodnr.gov

Kelleys Island • (419) 798-9763
See Glacial Grooves
510 W Main St, Lakeside
kelleysislandferry.com

Shenandoah

Sunset from Skyline Drive

Phone: (540) 999-3500
Website: nps.gov/shen

Established: December 26, 1935
Size: 199,000 Acres
Annual Visitors: 1.4 Million
Peak Season: October
Hiking Trails: 516 Miles
Horse Trails: 201 Miles
Driving: 105-Mile Skyline Drive

Activities: Hiking, Backpacking, Biking, Rock Climbing, Horseback Riding, Fishing, Birdwatching

Campgrounds ($15–20/night): Big Meadows, Mathews Arm, Loft Mountain, and Lewis Mountain
Backcountry Camping: Permitted
Lodging ($118–233/night): Big Meadows Lodge, Skyland Resort, and Lewis Mountain

Park Hours: All day, every day
Entrance Fee: $30/25/15 (car/motorcycle/individual)

Shenandoah National Park is centered on a long narrow stretch of the Blue Ridge Mountains. Forested mountaintops give way to the Shenandoah River Valley to the west and the Virginia Piedmont's gentle hills to the east. 105-mile Skyline Drive bisects the park as it follows the mountains' crest. Located just 75 miles from the nation's capital, it may come as no surprise that the park's creation had as much to do with politics and personalities as with natural forces.

Long before it received federal government protection, the Shenandoah region served many purposes to many people. Native Americans hunted and gathered for survival. Loggers and miners tapped the land for its resources. Union and Confederate soldiers shed blood deep in the Shenandoah Valley.

Eventually resorts began to crop up high atop the mountains, and for the past century Skyland Resort has served as recreational hub of Shenandoah. Ironically, Skyland never intended to be a company specializing in tourism. Between 1854 and 1866, a large tract of land within present park boundaries exchanged hands between numerous mining companies on speculation of substantial copper and iron deposits. Miners Lode Copper Company found the land to be commercially unsuccessful. However, George Freeman Pollock, son of one of the primary shareholders, convinced his father the land had value as a resort. On October 1, 1889, Pollock's father and Stephen M. Allen formed the Blue Ridge Stonyman Park Preserve. Guests paid $9.50 per week to sleep in tents outfitted with cots, chairs, washstands, and pitchers. An idea far more prosperous than mining ever was, but not enough to cover debt owed on the land's initial purchase. Stonyman Preserve had to be put up for sale at public auction to satisfy the mortgage. George Freeman Pollock, jobless and unsure of his future, was allowed to buy the Blue Ridge land on credit. He renamed it Skyland Resort, but his attempts at business fared much like his father's. He found himself in continuous debt, never actually gaining title to the land. Pollock may not have been much of a businessman, but he was a successful marketer. He threw elaborate balls, costume parties, jousts, musicals, pageants, and bonfires. His other skill was pandering to Washington's politicians. He became one of the most influential local advocates for the construction of Skyline Drive and the formation of a national park, but at the time of the park's establishment in 1935, Pollock had $67,107 in outstanding liens against a property appraised at less than $30,000.

Growth and success of western national parks sparked Congress's commissioning of the Southern Appalachian Committee to perform a thorough and wide-ranging survey of prospective locations in the east. The committee's survey proposed that land of present-day Mammoth Cave, Shenandoah, and the Great Smoky Mountains met the ideals of a U.S. National Park, and on May 22, 1926, Congress authorized establishment of Shenandoah once Virginia donated at least 327,000 acres of land to the federal government. Authorization was easy; procuring land was not. More than 4,000 privately owned tracts had to be turned over to federal ownership, a drastic change compared to western parks where most land was already federally owned. The state of Virginia responded by acquiring 1,088 tracts of land through condemnation and eminent domain, then donating all of it to the federal government. Some 465 mountain residents moved or were forced to move, but a few were allowed to live out their lives within the park. The last life-long resident, Annie Bradley Shenk, passed away in 1979 at the age of 92.

By the time the park was officially established in 1935, development was underway thanks to the effort of George Freeman Pollock and President Roosevelt's New Deal. Forty miles of Skyline Drive were already completed. Ten CCC camps, housing as many as 1,000 workers, were set-up. The CCC built trails and facilities around Skyland and Skyline Drive, the primary attractions of the successful park it is today. It took more than a decade of political posturing to establish, but today the park is a welcome escape for more than one million annual visitors.

Skyline Views

When to Go
Shenandoah is open all year, but most visitors arrive from May through November, peaking in October for fall foliage. If you plan on visiting during this time, a mid-week trip is a good idea or else you'll want to arrive early. Skyline Drive, the only public road through the park, closes occasionally for inclement weather. Several park facilities operate seasonally.

Transportation & Airports
You can find shuttle services to reach Shenandoah, but it was designed with motorists in mind. You'll want to drive or rent a car at the airport.

The closest airports are Washington Dulles International (IAD) (56 miles east of Front Royal) and Reagan International (DCA) (70 miles east of Front Royal). Closer to the park you'll find two smaller airports: Shenandoah Valley Regional Airport (SHD) (27 miles west of Swift Run Gap), and Charlottesville–Albemarle (CHO) (31 miles east of Rockfish Gap).

Directions
Shenandoah has four entrances along Skyline Drive.

Pittsburgh, PA to North Entrance (~190 miles): Travel east on I-76 to exit 161. Take I-70 East to US-522 South. Continue on US-522 to Route 37 South to I-81. Take I-81 South to I-66 East. Take I-66 to Front Royal, and follow signs to the entrance.

Washington, D.C. to North Entrance (~70 miles): Travel west on I-66 to Front Royal. Exit onto Route 34, where signs will direct you to the entrance.

D.C. to Thornton Gap Entrance (~81 miles): Travel west on I-66 to exit 43A. Take US-29 South to Warrenton. Take US-211 West into the park.

Richmond, VA to South Entrance (~90 miles): Travel west on I-64 to exit 99, where signs guide you to the entrance.

Richmond, VA to Swift Run Gap Entrance (~95 miles): Travel west on I-64 to Charlottesville. Take the exit to US-29 North. Turn left onto US-33 West into the park.

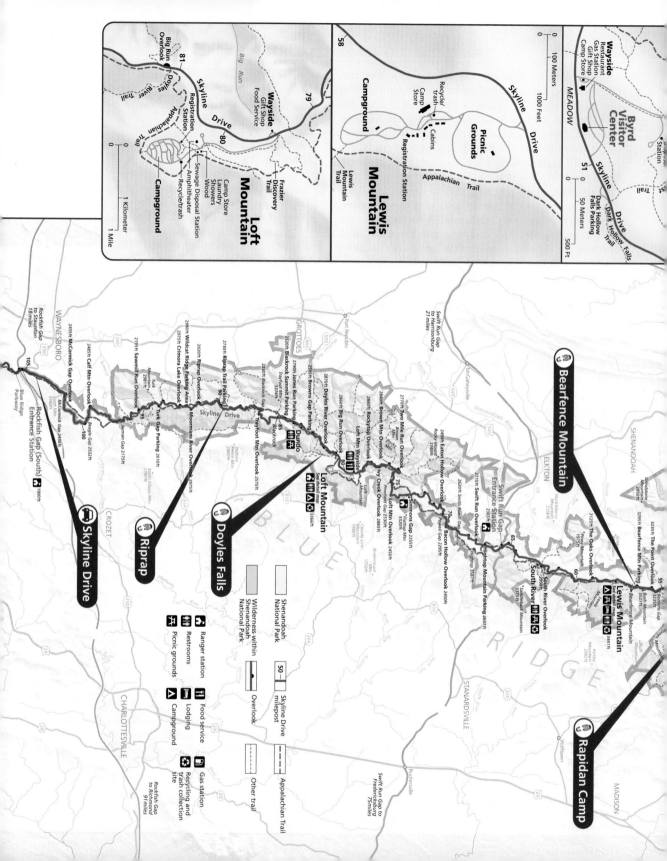

Byrd Visitor Center

Wayside
Restaurant
Gas Station
Gift Shop
Camp Store

MEADOW

51

Skyline Drive

Dark Hollow Falls Parking

Dark Hollow Falls Trail

0   50 Meters
0   500 Ft

Lewis Mountain

58

Lewis
Campground

Picnic
Grounds

Recycle/
trash

Camp
Store

Cabins

Registration Station

Appalachian Trail

Skyline Drive

Lewis
Mountain
Trail

0   100 Meters   1000 Feet
0

Loft Mountain

Big Run
Overlook

81

Doyles River Trail

79

Skyline Drive

80

Wayside
Gift Shop
Food Service

Frazier
Discovery
Trail

Appalachian Trail

Registration
Station

Gift
Shop

Camp Store
Laundry
Showers
Wood

Sewage Disposal Station
Amphitheater
Recycle/trash

Campground

0   1 Kilometer
0   1 Mile

WAYNESBORO

Rockfish Gap
to Staunton
18 miles

105

Blue Ridge Parkway

Rockfish Gap (South)
Entrance Station

1900ft

2455ft McCormick Gap Overlook
McCormick Gap 2434ft
100
Beagle Gap 2532ft

2485ft Calf Mtn Overlook
Jarman Gap 2175ft

CROZET

2195ft Sawmill Run Overlook
95
Turk Gap Parking 2610ft
Turk Gap 2175ft

2950ft Crimora Lake Overlook
Turk
Mountain
2981ft

2975ft Moormans River Overlook
90
Wildcat Ridge Parking Area

2920ft Riprap Overlook
Riprap Trail Parking 2790ft
Blackrock 3092ft

2730ft Riprap Trail Parking
Blackrock Gap 2321ft
2933ft Blackrock Gap

3250ft Blackrock Summit Parking
Trayfoot Mtn 3374ft

2790ft Jones Run Parking
85
Trayfoot Mtn Overlook 2575ft
Blackrock

GROTTOES
340

2955ft Browns Gap Overlook
Dundo
Skyline Drive

2870ft Doyles River Overlook
2860ft Big Run Overlook
80

Loft Mtn Wayside

CHARLOTTESVILLE

Horsehead
Mtn 2358ft

Rocky
Mtn 2864ft

Rocky Mtn
Overlook 2738ft

Austin
Mtn 2656ft

Big Flat
Mtn 2926ft

Loft Mountain
3336ft
See detail map

BLUE

2600ft Rockytop Overlook

Rockytop
1086ft

Brown Mtn
2850ft

2860ft Brown Mtn Overlook

2700ft Two Mile Run Overlook

Loft
Mountain
2851ft

Loft Mtn Overlook 2530ft

2620ft Loft Mtn Overlook
320ft
75
Ivy Creek Overlook 2851ft

2490ft Eaton Hollow Overlook
2740ft

Simmons Gap 2255ft
Simmons
Gap

Powell Gap 2294ft
Pinefield Gap 2585ft

Pinefield
Hut 2430ft

Weaver
Mtn 1750ft

Brokenback
Mtn 2800ft

Port Republic
605

McGaheysville
653

Swift Run Gap
to Harrisonburg
21 miles
33

Swift Run Gap 2365ft
Swift Run Gap
Entrance Station

2520ft Smith Roach Gap
Bacon Hollow Overlook 2450ft
70

2710ft Swift Run Overlook

Saddleback
Mountain 3275ft

Hightop Mountain Parking 2637ft
Hightop
Mountain 3587ft

65
South
River

STANARDSVILLE
230

Flattop 3325ft

South River Overlook 2935ft
60
See detail map

Bush
Mountain 3525ft

RIDGE

Rockfish Gap
to Richmond
91 miles

Skyline Drive

Riprap

Doyles Falls

Loft Mountain

Bearfence Mountain

3135ft The Oaks Overlook 1975ft
Bearfence Mtn Parking 3395ft
55
3325ft Bearfence Mtn 3527ft

ELKTON

Grandstone
Mountain 2850ft

Huckleberry
Mtn 2558ft

Piney Mountain 1975ft

SHENANDOAH
340

Shenandoah
River

Hawksbill
Mountain 2993ft

Lewis Mountain
See detail map

Bearfence Mountain

Karlins
Mtn 2093ft

Roundtop
Mtn 2880ft

Rapidan Camp

Swift Run Gap
to Fredericksburg
75 miles
33

MADISON

Wolftown
230

Ruckersville
29

---

50 — Skyline Drive milepost

Overlook

Appalachian Trail

Other trail

Shenandoah
National Park

Wilderness within
Shenandoah
National Park

Ranger station

Restrooms

Picnic grounds

Food service

Lodging

Campground

Gas station

Recycling and
trash collection
site

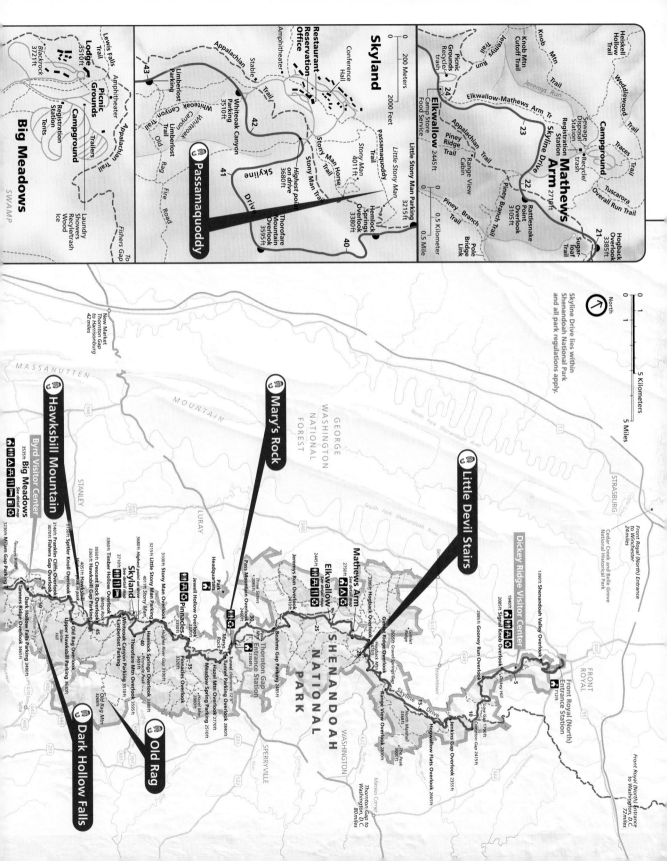

Presidents in the Park

Before becoming a national park, this region provided recreation, refuge, and a backdrop to promote political agendas for several U.S. Presidents.

In the summer of 1929, Herbert Hoover, the 31st President, bought Rapidan Camp. At the time, it was a 164-acre parcel on the eastern slope of the Blue Ridge Mountains. Hoover envisioned using the camp as a place of rest and recreation for himself and his wife during difficult times. Unfortunately, difficult times were the norm during his term. The stock market crashed in October of 1929, less than eight months after inauguration. The remainder of his first and only term was spent combatting the Great Depression that ensued.

But life at Rapidan Camp wasn't all trials and tribulations. Friends, family, and politicians were frequently entertained there during Hoover's presidency. Charles Lindbergh, Mrs. Thomas A. Edison, the Edsel Fords, and British Prime Minister Ramsay MacDonald all show up in the cabin's guest registry. Being just a 3-hour drive from Washington, Rapidan Camp was used as a meeting place for Hoover and his cabinet members and department heads. It was a fully functional Summer White House; an airplane dropped off mail and telephones were conveniently located in the President's Cabin.

In 1932, the Hoovers donated Rapidan Camp to the Commonwealth of Virginia for use as a Presidential summer retreat. It officially became part of Shenandoah National Park in 1935. Jimmy Carter was the last sitting President to visit the camp, but the "Brown House" or President's Cabin and the Prime Minister's Cabin still stand today. These structures have been restored to their original appearance and are only open to the public during ranger-led tours.

Franklin D. Roosevelt, the 32nd President, used the region as part of a highly visible public relations effort to buoy the negative psychological impact of the Great Depression. He visited a CCC camp in 1933, and three years later he returned to officially dedicate the park.

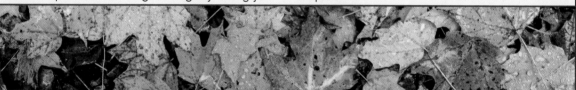

Shenandoah Camping (Fees are per night)

Name	Location	Open	Fee	Sites	Notes
Mathews Arm*	Mile 22.1	mid-May–October	$15	165	No Showers, No Laundry
Big Meadows*	Mile 51.2	late March–November	$20	51 Tent/170	Showers, Laundry, and Store
Lewis Mountain	Mile 57.5	mid-April–October	$15	30	Showers, Laundry, and Store
Loft Mountain*	Mile 79.5	mid-May–October	$15	50 Tent/167 RV	Showers, Laundry, and Store
Backcountry	A free permit is required. Backcountry planning information and application form are available at any visitor center, the park website, or call (540) 999-3500.				
Group	Mathews Arm, Big Meadows and Dundo (mile 83.7). Reserve at recreation.gov or (877) 444-6777.				

*Reservations can be made up to six months in advance at (877) 444-6777 or recreation.gov
Each campground is near a section of the Appalachian Trail, and has at least one accessible site. No campgrounds have hookups for water, electricity, or sewage. Mathews Arm, Big Meadows, and Loft Mountain have dump stations and sites that can accommodate large RVs. Many sites at Mathews Arm and Loft Mountain are first-come, first-served.

Shenandoah Lodging (Fees are per night during peak season)

Name	Open	Fee	Location & Notes
Skyland Resort	March–November	$127–233	Mile 41.7 • 179 guest rooms, rustic cabins, modern suites
Big Meadows Lodge	late April–November	$118–221	Mile 51.2 • 25 main lodge rooms, 72 rustic cabins rooms
Lewis Mtn Cabins	March–November	$145	Mile 57.6 • Simple cabins with private baths and grills

Additional information and reservations available at goshenandoah.com or (877) 847-1919

Camping & Lodging

Campgrounds are located at Mathews Arm (Mile 22.1), Big Meadows (Mile 51.2), Lewis Mountain (Mile 57.5), and Loft Mountain (Mile 79.5). Reservations can be made at (877) 444-6777 or recreation.gov. Mathews Arm, Big Meadows, and Loft Mountain campgrounds have pull-through sites that accommodate RVs. No sites have hookups.

Rustic lodging can be found at Big Meadows Lodge, Skyland Resort, and Lewis Mountain Cabins. For details refer to the table on the opposite page.

We highly recommend spending your nights in the park at one of the lodges or campgrounds and maybe spending one night east of the park at a bed and breakfast to be closer to the trailhead for Old Rag. Of course, there's plenty of lodging/camping outside the park, and it isn't a huge inconvenience.

Skyline Drive

Skyline Drive is a National Scenic Byway that runs 105 miles spanning the entire length of the park. Milepost markers, located on the west side of the road, make locating the park's facilities and services on Skyline Drive a snap. They're also an important tool for using this guidebook as the location of park trailheads, campgrounds, and lodgings are all defined by their milepost. When travelling this scenic drive, be sure to follow the 35-mph speed limit. Typical to mountain driving, you'll find steep hills, sharp turns, and frequent stops (75 overlooks!). Be aware of Mary's Rock Tunnel (Mile 32)—RVs, horse trailers, and other vehicles taller than 12' 8" will have to detour around it.

In 1931, crews broke ground on Skyline Drive. Political posturing and the Great Depression slowed the project's pace. The stretch from Rockfish Gap to Front Royal wasn't completed until 1939 at a cost of nearly $5 million or $50,000 per mile. Contractors built the highway, but it would not have been completed without the CCC's help. They graded the slope on either side of the roadway and built many of the guardrails and guard walls. Other sections of road were built simply to see if it was possible. Legend says the 670-foot Mary's Rock Tunnel was designed to settle a challenge between the Bureau of Public Roads and National Park Landscape Architects. After completion, facilities were needed to accommodate guests. In western parks infrastructure was developed independently by powerful railways. Shenandoah didn't have the luxury of a railroad's deep pockets. In 1937, with no plan and few ideas, Congress turned to a concessioner, Virginia Sky-Line Company

Skyline Views

(now Aramark). Sky-Line dictated much of the park's direction and development from 1937 to 1942.

There are two **visitor centers**: Dickey Ridge (Mile 4.6) and Harry F. Byrd (Mile 51). They're typically open from March through November. Loft Mountain Information Center (Mile 19.5) is open on weekends and holidays, mid-May until October.

You'll also find a number of **picnic grounds** along Skyline Drive. Elkwallow (Mile 24.1), Pinnacles (Mile 36.7), South River (Mile 62.8) and Dundo (Mile 83.7) Picnic Grounds are open all year. Dickey Ridge (Mile 4.6), Big Meadows (Mile 51.2) and Lewis Mountain (Mile 57.6) are open from May until November.

Food, gifts, and camping supplies can be found at three **waysides** along Skyline Drive. Elkwallow (Mile 24.1) and Loft Mountain (Mile 79.5) are open from mid-April until early November. Big Meadows, the only place to get gas in the park, is open from mid-March until late November (24/7 pay at the pump is available).

Dining is available at Skyland (Mile 41.7) and Big Meadows Lodge (Mile 51.2). Each restaurant offers traditional sit-down dining as well as quick meals to take with you. They're typically open March through November. All establishments are operated by the park's concessioner, Delaware North. You can find more information at goshenandoah.com.

Hiking & Backpacking

Leave Skyline Drive in favor of Shenandoah's wilder side. Yes, some of the views from the road are postcard-perfect, especially in October, but you won't see a single waterfall and wildlife sightings are limited to deer, squirrels, and birds. To witness the depth of history and nature Shenandoah has to offer, one must

From Old Rag

Shenandoah Hiking Trails (Distances are roundtrip)

Skyline Drive

Name	Location	Length	Difficulty Rating & Notes
Fox Hollow Nature	Mile 4.6	2.0 miles	E – Leads to Fox Home Site • Cemetery and old farm fence remnants are visible (can be shortened to 1.2 miles)
Dickey Ridge	Mile 4.6	2.7 miles	E – Hike along a small stream through overgrown fields
Snead Farm	Mile 4.6	1.4 miles	E – Gravel fire road leads hikers to an old farm and orchard
Hickerson Hollow	Mile 9.2	2.2 miles	E – A horse trail leads into an old mountain resident's hollow
Compton Peak - 👣	Mile 10.4	2.4 miles	M – Fairly steep and rocky hike to scenic views
Little Devil Stairs - 👣	Mile 19.4	7.7 miles	S – Follow Keyser Run Fire Road to Little Devil Stairs
Overall Run Falls	Mile 21.1	6.5 miles	S – Hike to the tallest waterfall in the park (93-ft tall)
Traces Nature	Mile 22.2	1.7 miles	E – Trail through a mature oak forest and old homesteads
Mary's Rock - 👣	Mile 32.7	2.8 miles	M – Outstanding panoramic views
Little Stony Man Cliffs	Mile 39.1	0.9 mile	E – Excellent views along this extremely short hike
Passamaquoddy - 👣	Mile 41.7	3.4 miles	M – Take Furnace Spring Horse Trail to Passamaquoddy, return via AT
Stony Man - 👣	Mile 41.7	1.6 miles	E – Easy climb to the park's second highest point (4,011 ft)
Cedar Run/ Whiteoak Circuit	Mile 42.6	8.2 miles	S – One of the most strenuous hikes in the park • From Hawksbill Gap, take Cedar Run–Link–Whiteoak–Whiteoak Fire Road–Horse Trail • Multiple waterfalls and cascades
Limberlost	Mile 43	1.3 miles	E – A gravel loop, accessible to strollers and wheelcharis
Crescent Rock	Mile 45.6	3.3 miles	E – Lightly traveled, treks north to Limberlost Trail
Hawksbill Mtn Summit - 👣	Mile 46.7	2.1 miles	M – Park's tallest peak (4,051 ft) • You can also find a 1.7-mile (roundtrip) and 2.9-mile circuit to Hawksbill at Mile 45.6
Rose River Falls - 👣	Mile 49.4	4.0 miles	M – See as many as four cascades after a heavy rain
Dark Hollow Falls - 👣	Mile 50.7	1.4 miles	M – Shortest waterfall hike in the park
Lewis Falls	Mile 51.4	2.0 miles/ 3.3 miles	M – Out-and-back from Skyline Drive to the 81-ft falls • 3.3-mile circuit begins from Big Meadows Amphitheater
Mill Prong - 👣	Mile 52.8	4.0 miles	M – Roundtrip hike to Hoover's Rapidan Camp
Bearfence Mountain - 👣	Mile 56.4	0.8 mile	M – Short scramble over rocks to broad panoramic views
South River Falls - 👣	Mile 62.8	2.6 miles	M – Third tallest waterfall in the park (83-ft tall)
Frazier Discovery	Mile 79.4	1.4 miles	E – Leads to a spectacular overlook atop Loft Mountain
Doyles River Falls - 👣	Mile 81.1	3.2 miles	S – Rigorous hike to the 28-ft upper falls and 63-ft lower falls
Jones Run Falls - 👣	Mile 84.1	3.4 miles	M – A nice casual hike to 42-foot cascade
Blackrock Summit - 👣	Mile 84.8	0.8 mile	E – Short hike to rock outcroppings and beautiful views
Riprap/Wildcat Ridge - 👣	Mile 90 or 92.1	9.8 miles	S – Fun loop, watch for the correct trail junctions with the AT
Old Rag - 👣	Near Nethers on Route 600	5.6 miles	X – Challenging and popular hike/scramble • Parking area is at the park's eastern boundary, not Skyline Drive • Start on Ridge Tr and return via Saddle Tr (7.2 miles)

Difficulty Ratings: E = Easy, M = Moderate, S = Strenuous, X = Extreme

lace up a pair of hiking shoes and ramble a few miles beyond the road and mountain's ridgeline. Appalachia offers a wealth of hiking opportunities.

There are 516 miles of trails here, ranging from short strolls through open meadows to steep, rocky scrambles atop exposed mountains. All trails are marked with colored blazes. White is for the **Appalachian Trail**; roughly 101 miles of the 2,184-mile trail run through the park, mostly paralleling Skyline Drive. Blue indicates park hiking trails and yellow marks trails designated for horse use, which are also open to hikers. Most of the trailheads are located at parking areas along Skyline Drive, and are downhill going out and uphill coming back. A few, like that of immensely popular Old Rag Trail, are located near the park boundary. **Old Rag** is a long (5.6 miles roundtrip) and challenging scramble to the summit of Old Rag Mountain (3,268 feet). The shortest route begins near Nethers on Route 600 which terminates at the park's eastern boundary. Old Rag can also be reached from the park's interior via Old Rag Fire Road, but it's longer (15+ miles) and less fun.

The most Old Rag-like hike from Skyline Drive is the 9.8-mile **Wildcat Ridge/Riprap Loop**. You can begin at Wildcat Ridge (Mile 92.1) or Riprap (Mile 90) parking area. Wildcat Ridge and Riprap Trails are connected by the Appalachian Trail. Which direction you go isn't too important, but choosing clockwise makes it more difficult to miss the Riprap/Appalachian trail junction to return to whichever parking area you started at. Along the way you'll cross streams, pass a small waterfall, and visit Chimney Rock.

Old Rag-like hikes aren't for everyone, but there are trails to satisfy hikers of all interests and abilities along Skyline Drive. The shortest and most popular waterfall hike is **Dark Hollow Falls Trail**. Thomas Jefferson once admired this 70-ft falls. **Limberlost Trail** is accessible to wheelchair users and provides an excellent stroll in June when mountain laurel is in bloom. Hiking on **Fox and Hickerson Hollow Trails** allows hikers with an active imagination to travel to the times of early mountain residents who lived in the hollows for more than 100 years before being moved off their land for the creation of the park. Remnants of their presence still stand to this day. Simple mountain folk weren't the only occupants of these hills. **Rapidan Camp** served as the Summer White House for President Herbert Hoover. **Mill Prong Trail** leads to the historic structure. You can hike there any time but the house is only open and accessible during ranger programs (reservations required via recreation.gov).

Riprap Trail

Backpackers have more than 500 miles of trails and 190,000 acres of wilderness at their disposal. A free permit is required for all overnight stays in the backcountry. Permits are available online or in person at a visitor center. It's always a good idea to make a plan, and then consult with a park ranger. Being a park with a high degree of weekend visitation, backpackers will typically have a better selection of sites by visiting during the week. Also try to avoid choosing camping locations along the Appalachian Trail during May, June, and September, when thru-hikers are passing through. The Potomac Appalachian Trail Club also has six backcountry cabins within park boundaries (and many more beyond) that can be reserved through patc.net for $30–45/night.

Biking

The twists, turns, and hills of Skyline Drive are a welcome challenge to road cyclists. Bikes are permitted on all paved surfaces within the park, but Skyline Drive experiences heavy motorist traffic from May through October, especially on weekends. Skyline Drive isn't a great place to ride. It's fairly narrow and busy, but if you visit on a weekday and start early (before 9am), traffic should be manageable. However, morning is also prime time for poor visibility. Fog is common, and you'll encounter darkness any time of year at 600-foot-long Mary's Rock Tunnel (Mile 32). Bikes are prohibited on unpaved roads, grass, and trails. No mountain bike trails exist within the park. If you'd like to join a group on a multi-day bicycle adventure, Carolina Tailwinds (carolinatailwinds.com) occasionally offers tours of Shenandoah (along with many other bike trips).

Rock Climbing

It's no Yosemite, but Little Stony Man Cliffs is a great place for beginners to learn the basics of climbing and rappelling. From April through October,

Upper Doyle's Falls

visitors can take part in an introductory rock climbing course offered by Shenandoah Mountain Guides (877.847.1919, goshenandoah.com). Classes cost $150/person and generally start at 9:00/9:30am, departing from Skyland Resort. Advance reservation is required.

Horseback Riding
Horses are allowed on more than 180 miles of trails. Horse trails are marked with yellow blazes and a complete list can be found at the park website. While this all may sound like a warm welcome to horse owners, you must be aware that the park's lodges and campgrounds do not accommodate horses and they are not allowed to sleep in their trailer. You are allowed to camp in the backcountry with your equine partners, but it's discouraged by the park. Your best bet is to find a nearby boarding stable. Bringing your own horse gives riders the freedom to explore deeper into Shenandoah's wilderness, but know that trails are steep and strenuous. Both you and your horse should be fit for the conditions. Travel with a map and ride trails suitable to your ability.

Or leave your horses at home and visit Skyland Stables (877.847.1919, goshenandoah.com) for a guided horse ride. An hour-long ride costs $50 per person, while a 2.5-hour ride costs $110. Pony rides are available for children 5 and under (as long as their feet reach the stirrups and they wear a helmet). The stable is open from early April until November, and the long ride is only given on weekends. Skyland Stables is located at mile 42.5, near Skyland Resort. All riders must be at least 4'10" and weigh less than 250 pounds.

Fishing
Some 70 streams begin in the Blue Ridge Mountains and flow into the surrounding valleys. These streams are inhabited by a variety of species, including the popular eastern brook trout. When fishing in the park, anglers must adhere to Virginia fishing regulations. All Virginia residents 16 years and older and non-residents 12 years and older are required to have a Virginia state fishing license. A 5-day non-resident license can be purchased at Big Meadows Wayside or from local sporting goods stores. If you're looking for sound fishing advice or to hire a guide, check out Murray's Fly Shop (540.984.4212, murraysflyshop.com, $425/full day) or Page Valley Fly Fishing (540.743.7952, pagevalleyflyfishing.com, $300/full day).

Birdwatching
About 95% of Shenandoah National Park is forested and 40% of the total area is designated wilderness, providing an excellent habitat for birds. About 200 species of resident and transient birds use the park. Nearly half of the species breed here, but only thirty make the park their year-round home. Local species include tufted titmice, red-tailed hawk, Carolina chickadee, wild turkey, barred owl, and downy woodpecker.

Exotic species also call the park home. In the summer of 2000, the park resumed its Peregrine Falcon Restoration Program. It has been a success and today visitors may spot these beautiful raptors soaring high above the Blue Ridge Mountains. Cerulean warbler and scarlet tanager also reside in the park but are seldom seen. The Cerulean warbler, once common in the lower Mississippi valley, has declined in numbers due to loss of habitat. The park hosts a healthy population of scarlet tanagers, but most bird watchers wouldn't know it. These feathered friends spend most of their time in the upper canopy.

Winter Activities
Shenandoah is more or less neglected during the brief winter season. All campgrounds, lodging, and waysides are closed. Skyline Drive occasionally closes during inclement weather. Big Meadows averages more than thirty inches of snow each year. Still, many hardy hikers enter the park to view a completely different environment. Few humans. Ground covered in snow. Trees without leaves. Waterfalls turned to ice. Bears holed up for winter. Facilities may be closed, but there's 196,000 acres of land open for backcountry camping, you just need to be better prepared to make for a comfortable night's stay.

Visitor Centers
It's a good idea to begin your trip at one of the park's visitor centers: **Dickey Ridge** (mile 4.6) or **Harry F. Byrd, Sr.** (mile 51). Both locations are situated along

Skyline Drive and offer exhibits, an information desk, a bookstore, and an orientation film. You'll also find access to restrooms, first aid, and backcountry permits. But the best resource is the staff. There's also a mobile visitor center, allowing park rangers to bring their expertise directly to you!

Ranger Programs & For Kids
The best way to see the park is under the thoughtful guidance of a park ranger. They are happy to share their knowledge of bears, raptors, and other wildlife and plant life on a series of walks, talks, and evening programs. You can learn about the history of Skyland Resort on a tour of Historic Massanutten Lodge, hike the Appalachian Trail, or stroll through CCC-era structures as Shenandoah rangers shower you with entertaining and educational anecdotes that have been passed down through generations of park stewards. The only way to tour Rapidan Camp (accessed via Mill Prong Trail) is in the presence of a ranger. Reservations are required and can be made through recreation.gov. Be sure to stop in at a visitor center for a current schedule of all the programs.

Children (ages 7–12) have the opportunity to become Shenandoah National Park Junior Rangers. Kids (ages 13 and older) will enjoy the entire set of Ranger Explorer Guides. Activity booklets can be picked up in the park or are available for print at the park website. Ranger-led tours and talks are another family favorite. In fact, attending a ranger program may be the spark your child needs to ignite interest in the Junior Ranger Program. The personalities of the rangers are so infectious they may inspire your child to one day don the iconic "Smoky the Bear" hat that has become the symbol of the park ranger and National Park Service. If they like the hats, but don't want the job that comes with it, you can pick one up at a nearby visitor center. If you'd like a little more interactive hiking experience on your own, a few of the park's trails have Track Trails. You can find them at kidsinparks.com.

Flora & Fauna
Shenandoah's forests are classified as "oak-hickory," but many other trees take root within the park. Pine, maple, birch, basswood, blackgum, tulip poplar, chestnut, and a few stands of hemlock can all be found here. Mountain laurel, which blooms in June, can be found along Skyline Drive. It is a native species, but these shrubs were planted by the CCC in the 1930s. Variation in latitude and elevation help create astounding diversity. More than 1,000 species of ferns, grasses, lichens, mosses, fungi, and wildflowers exist in the park.

Deer along Skyline Drive

The creation of Shenandoah National Park helped reestablish the area as a refuge for wildlife. In the 1700s, early European settlers noted the region's abundance and diversity of animals. By the late 1800s, American bison, elk, beaver, and river otter were extirpated. Many over-hunted species have now returned or been reintroduced. Shenandoah is home to one of the densest populations of black bears in the United States. A few hundred bear reside here. In all there are more than 50 species of mammals in the park. White-tail deer and gray squirrels are often seen along the roadway, while bobcats, black bears, moles, and shrews are more elusive. Ten species of toads and frogs and fourteen species of salamanders and newts live here. Twenty-five species of reptiles have found refuge in Shenandoah including eighteen snakes, five turtles, three skinks, and one lizard. Viewing and photographing wildlife is a popular activity, but please help keep wildlife wild. Be sure to stay a safe distance from animals and never feed or provoke them.

Pets & Accessibility
Pets are allowed in the park but must be kept on a leash (less than six feet). Pets are allowed on all trails except Fox Hollow, Stony Man, Limberlost, Old Rag, Dark Hollow Falls, Story of the Forest, Bearfence Mountain, and Frazier Discovery Trails. Only service animals are permitted in park buildings. Campgrounds and lodging are pet-friendly, but you cannot bring them to any ranger-led programs.

Sites accessible to wheelchair users are available at all picnic areas and campgrounds. Most facilities and restrooms are accessible with assistance. Lewis Mountain, Skyland Resort, and Big Meadows Lodge offer wheelchair-accessible lodging. Many ranger programs are accessible, including a van tour to Rapidan Camp. Limberlost Trail is accessible.

Below Dark Hallow Falls

Weather

Come prepared for all kinds of weather. Storms are common throughout the year, but peak in September. Snow can fall any day from November to April but is most common in January and February. Roads are often slippery with ice in winter and foggy in spring. The mountains in Shenandoah are usually 10°F cooler than the valley.

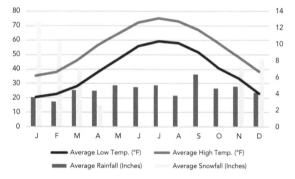

Tips & Recommendations

Shenandoah is a very popular weekend getaway, pretty much from April through November, peaking in October for fall foliage. Planning a weekday trip is a good idea.

I forget this one all the time even though it's obvious. Most trails begin along Skyline Drive at the crest of the Blue Ridge Mountains, meaning you'll almost always be hiking downhill on the out, and uphill on the back. Don't get carried away, lost in nature's beauty, and forget about having to make that uphill climb out of Shenandoah's valleys. So, remember to turn around well before you're tired (or hungry).

Old Rag is fantastic. Go for it, if you enjoy challenging hikes, just remember the trailhead isn't located along

Skyline Drive. In fact, it's almost an hour from the nearest park campground. Plan accordingly or consider staying at a B&B closer to the trail. The parking area fills early on weekends.

With 75 overlooks along Skyline Drive, it isn't particularly difficult to find a good place to watch the sunrise/sunset, but three of our favorite sunset locations are in the same vicinity. The park's highest point, Hawksbill Mountain, is a good choice. It takes a short hike to reach the viewpoint, so wear layers and bring a headlamp for the return trip. The other two are Skyline Drive Overlooks. Point Overlook (mile 55.5) is great. You'll probably notice the point referenced in its name a short walk from the parking area. Hazeltop Ridge (mile 54.5) is also nice.

With that said, if you're on Skyline Drive while the sun is setting, don't race to any of those locations. Pull over and get comfortable at the first overlook you find with clear views to the west.

I'd be remiss if I didn't suggest stopping at Washington, D.C. Even though I feel like I become more cynical every year, our national parks may be the best example of doing something for the benefit of others, and walking around our nation's capital can be an even more persuasive argument to work, not only for yourself and your family, but for your community, your country, and to help move us in a positive direction.

With hundreds of miles of hiking trails and dozens of scenic overlooks, it isn't easy choosing how to spend your time. The recommendations listed below help point you in the right direction.

Easy Hikes: Stony Man (0.9 mile), Black Rock Summit (0.8), Frazier Discovery (1.4)
Moderate Hikes: Passamaquoddy (3.4 miles), Mary's Rock (2.8), Compton Peak (2.4), Hawksbill Mountain (2.1), Dark Hollow Falls (1.4)
Strenuous Hikes: Riprap/Wildcat Loop (9.8 miles), Little Devil Stairs (7.7), Doyle's River Falls (3.2)
Extreme Hikes: Old Rag (5.6 miles)
Family Activities: Become Junior Rangers, go horseback riding, hike to the park's tallest peak (Hawksbill Mountain), hike Old Rag if your kids are go-getters who like to play on rocks
Guided Tours: Rock Climbing (goshenandoah.com), Horseback Riding (goshenandoah.com)
Rainy Day Activities: Drive Skyline Drive, stop at a visitor center, head to Washington, D.C. or Luray Caverns (540.743.6551, luraycaverns.com, $30/adult)

History Enthusiasts: Visit Rapidan Camp on a ranger-led tour (reservation required via recreation.gov), hike Fox Hollow Nature Trail
Sunset Spots: Hazletop Ridge Overlook (mile 54.5), The Point Overlook (mile 55.5), Hawksbill Mountain (hike, bring a light for return trip)
Sunrise Spots: Pinnacles Overlook (mile 35), Thorofare Mountain Overlook (40.5), Bearfence Mountain (hike, rocky, bring a light)
Wildlife: Big Meadows, Skyline Drive

The Appalachian Trail

Beyond the Park...

Dining
Spelunker's • (540) 631-0300
116 South St, Front Royal
spelunkerscustard.com

Hawksbill Diner • (540) 778-2006
1388 E Main St, Stanley

Triple Crown BBQ • (540) 743-5311
1079 US-211, Luray

Ciro's Italian Eatery
101 Downey Knolls Dr, Elkton
(540) 298-1205
cirositalianeatery.com

Three Blacksmiths
20 Main St, Sperryville
(540) 987-5105
threeblacksmiths.com

Gathering Grounds
24 E Main St, Luray
ggrounds.com • (540) 743-1121

Off the Grid • (540) 987-5114
11692 Lee Hwy, Sperryville
offthegridva.com

Grocery Stores
Lots of grocery options in every direction from the park.

Lodging
Graves Mountain Farm
205 Graves Mountain Lane, Syria
(540) 923-4231
gravesmountain.com

Foster Harris House B&B
189 Main St, Washington
fosterharris.com • (540) 675-3757

Gay Street Inn • (540) 316-9220
160 Gay St, Washington
gaystreetinn.com

South Court Inn B&B
160 S Court St, Luray
(540) 843-0980
southcourtinn.com

Piney Hill B&B • (540) 860-8470
1048 Piney Hill Rd, Luray
pineyhillbandb.com

Mimslyn Inn • (540) 743-5105
401 W Main St, Luray
mimslyninn.com

Inn at Sugar Hollow Farm
6051 Sugar Hollow Rd, Crozet
(434) 260-7234
sugarhollow.com

Iris Inn B&B • (540) 943-1991
191 Chinquapin Dr, Waynesboro
irisinn.com

Many chain restaurants and hotels can be found nearby in Harrisonburg, Luray, Waynesboro, Front Royal, and Dulles International Airport is about one hour from Front Royal

Campgrounds
Riverside Camping
4298 US-340, Shenandoah
(540) 652-1075
riversidecampingcanoeing.com

Outlanders River Camp
4253 US-211, Luray
(540) 743-5540
outlandersrivercamp.com

Jellystone Park • (540) 300-1697
2250 US-211 E, Luray
campluray.com

Shenandoah Valley KOA
12480 Mtn Valley Rd, Broadway
koa.com • (540) 896-8929

Luray KOA
3402 Kimball Rd, Luray
koa.com • (540) 743-7222

Graves Mountain Farm
3822 Old Blue Ridge Tpke, Syria
(303) 877-9659
gravesmountain.com

Festivals
Highland Maple Fest • March
50+ year tradition explores maple syrup-making
highlandcounty.org/maple

National Cherry Blossom Fest
One of the best times to visit Washington DC
nationalcherryblossomfestival.org

Virginia Wine & Craft Fest • May
wineandcraftfestival.com

Virginia Gold Cup • May
Horse steeplechase races
vagoldcup.com

Night Sky Festival • August
goshenandoah.com

Apple Butter Festival • Sept
goshenandoah.com

Attractions
Shenandoah River Outfitters
Rafting, canoeing, kayaking
6502 S Page Valley Rd, Luray
shenandoahriver.com

Luray Caverns • (540) 743-6551
101 Cave Hill Rd, Luray
luraycaverns.com

Bear Mountain Ziplines
2354 US-211, Luray
bearmountainadventure.com

Skyline Caverns • (540) 635-4545
10344 US-340, Front Royal
skylinecaverns.com

Sky Meadows State Park
Pretty park, Appalachian Trail
11012 Edmonds Ln, Delaplane
dcr.virginia.gov

Assateague Island N Seashore
Barrier island with wild-ish horses
7206 National Seashore Ln
nps.gov/asis

Grayson Highlands State Park
Entrance fee, Appalachian Trail, mountains, and horses
829 Grayson Highlands Ln
dcr.virginia.gov

George Washington & Jefferson
National Forest • (540) 291-2188
Humpback Rocks, Crabtree Falls
27 Ranger Ln, Natural Bridge

Natural Tunnel State Park
Cave used as a railway tunnel
1420 Natural Tunnel Pkwy
dcr.virginia.gov

Natural Bridge State Park
90-ft natural stone arch
6477 S Lee Hwy, Natural Bridge
dcr.virginia.gov

Foamhenge • (540) 464-2253
A to-scale foam Stonehenge
Hwy 11 South, Natural Bridge

The Pentagon • (703) 571-3343
1400 Defense Pentagon •
pentagontours.osd.mil

Arlington National Cemetery
arlingtoncemetery.org

Lincoln Memorial • (202) 426-6841
All of National Mall is great!
2 Lincoln Memorial Cir NW

Newseum • (202) 292-6100
555 Pennsylvania Ave
newseum.org

Washington Mon • (202) 426-6841
nps.gov/wamo • Free

Smithsonian National Museum
of Natural History
1000 Constitution Ave NW
mnh.si.edu • Free

Smithsonian National Zoo
3001 Connecticut Ave
nationalzoo.si.edu • Free

New River Gorge

Long Point

Phone: (304) 465-0508
Website: nps.gov/neri

Established: December 21, 2020
November 10, 1978 (National River)
Size: 72,808 Acres
Annual Visitors: 1.2 Million
Peak Season: June–October

Activities: Whitewater Rafting,
Rock Climbing, Hiking,
Backpacking, Biking, Fishing

9 Primitive Campgrounds: Free,
first-come, first-served
Backcountry Camping: Permitted
Lodging: None

Park Hours: All day, every day
Entrance Fee: None

In December 2020, Congress folded legislation redesignating New River Gorge National River as a National Park and Preserve into a larger stimulus package. Just like that, with a stroke of the President's Sharpie, the newest U.S. National Park was established. In reality, the park formed on November 10, 1978 by President Jimmy Carter, protecting the area "for the purpose of conserving and interpreting natural, scenic, and historic values and objects in and around the New River Gorge and preserving as a free-flowing stream an important segment of the New River in West Virginia for the benefit and enjoyment of present and future generations."

The park may have a shiny new title, but "new" isn't a word you'd use to describe the 53 miles of fast-flowing water bisecting the Appalachian Mountains. Wild. Relentless. Picturesque. Those words work. But when it comes to age, the New is ancient. In fact, people who study this stuff believe it is one of the oldest rivers on the planet. For anyone celebrating its next birthday, you'll need a cake with room for about two hundred million candles. Scientists believe the New is so old because it didn't form with the Appalachian Mountains—although the Appalachian Mountains may be the oldest mountains on Earth—it rose with them. But the river responsible for this rugged countryside isn't the oldest thing you'll find in the gorge. Raft the river or walk its shoreline and you'll likely pass 330-million-year-old rocks.

If the river is so old why is it called "New?" Don't blame Native Americans. They nicknamed the waterway "river of death" and "river of evil spirits." And English fur traders weren't looking to rebrand the river with a more welcoming term. Two fur traders, after returning from an exploratory mission, handed their map to a map maker. On it, they labelled a "new" river. The map maker called it the New River, and the rest, as they say, is history. At least that's how the story goes. Adding to the naming confusion, just after the Gauley River flows into the New, its name changes to Kanawha, continuing across West Virginia, through Charleston, and into the Ohio River.

For anyone stubborn enough to try and eke out a life in this isolated region before railroads and roadways increased access, the river meant life. Trees were cut for pastures and farmland, lumber used to warm their homes and cook their meals. Meals hunted in the forests or caught in the waterways. Days were just long enough to complete the work necessary to subsist on a small tract of Appalachia. Things changed when C&O Railroad arrived in 1873. Railway, logging, and mining booms caused towns to pop up, seemingly overnight. You couldn't go half a mile downriver without running into another company mining town. Coal from these mines fueled the nation's Industrial Revolution. Thousands of immigrants and newly freed slaves, equipped with pick and shovel, excavated the mines. Already struggling through the Great Depression, the coal industry suffered as locomotives transitioned from steam to diesel and humans fell in love with the automobile. The booms went bust, and dozens of company towns became ghost towns…seemingly overnight.

Today, the river that carved the gorge continues to shape its civilization. As the New River flows through the park, it drops some 750 feet, providing ample excitement for thrill-seeking whitewater rafters. Hard sandstone cliffs rise from its banks 30 to 120 feet, offering a surface for gravity-defying rock climbers to map out and ascend more than 1,400 routes. Hiking trails explore the park's shore, cliffs, valleys, and mining ruins. Some trails afford sublime views of the New River Gorge Bridge, the third highest bridge in the country. Today's natural resource is adventure, and it draws hundreds of thousands of travelers from around the globe to the New River Gorge.

Canyon Rim

When to Go
About half all park visitors arrive between June and October, but there are plenty of reasons to visit any day of the year. Spring brings a swollen New River and beautiful wildflowers (Catawba rhododendron in May, great rhododendron in late June/early July). Summer is the busy rafting and rock climbing season. Fall offers changing leaves, Bridge Day, and the nearby Gauley River's rafting season. Winter offers a different landscape when trees drop their leaves and the gorge is blanketed in snow.

Transportation & Airports
Amtrak's (amtrak.com) Cardinal Line, traveling between Chicago and New York, stops at Hinton and Prince, and if you have a reservation it will stop at Thurmond. Greyhound (greyhound.com) has a bus terminal in Beckley. And you'll find taxi services in Oak Hill and Beckley.

The closest major airport is Yeager Airport (CRW), 60 miles to the northwest, in Charleston, WV. Car rental is available at the airport.

Directions
New River Gorge National Park is a long sliver of land following the twists and turns of the New River. With more than 20 road-accessible sites of interest, navigating the park can be a challenge. A great place to start your trip to New River Gorge is **Canyon Rim Visitor Center** at the park's north end.

To Canyon Rim Visitor Center: From I-64 take Exit 60 for WV-612 toward Mossy/Oak Hill. Travel east on WV-612 for about 8 miles, and then turn left onto US-19 N. After about 10 miles you'll cross the New River Gorge Bridge. After the bridge, turn right onto County Route 85/9 and take an immediate right into the Visitor Center Parking Area.

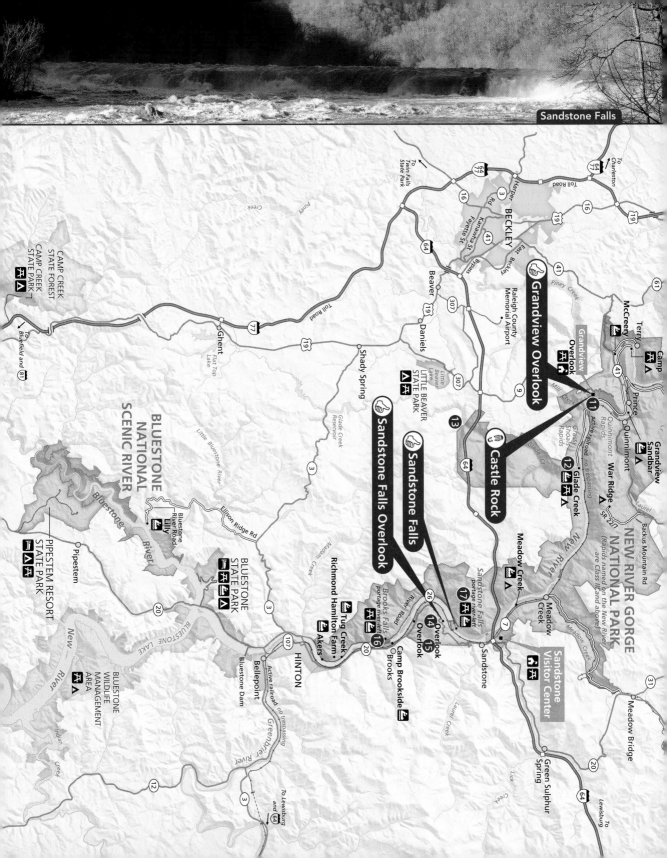

Sandstone Falls

To Charleston

BECKLEY

Harper Rd

Kanawha St
East Beckley Bypass
Fayette St

Toll Road

Raleigh County Memorial Airport

Beaver

Daniels

Shady Spring

Ghent

To Twin Falls State Park

To Bluefield and

CAMP CREEK STATE PARK
CAMP CREEK STATE FOREST

Piney Creek

Little Beaver Lake

LITTLE BEAVER STATE PARK

Grandview Overlook

Grandview Overlook

Castle Rock

Glade Creek

Prince
Quinnimont

War Ridge
SR 25/1

McCreery

Terry

Camp

Grandview Sandbar

NEW RIVER GORGE NATIONAL PARK

Backus Mountain Rd

(rapids named on the New River are Class III and above)

Active railroad no trespassing

Quinnimont Rapids

Grass Shoals Rapids

Meadow Creek

Sandstone Falls
portage riverleft

Sandstone Falls Overlook

Sandstone Falls

Sandstone Falls Overlook

Brooks Falls
portage riverleft

Tug Creek

Akers

Richmond Hamilton Farm

Camp Brookside

Brooks

Overlook

Sandstone

Sandstone Visitor Center

Meadow Creek

Green Sulphur Spring

Meadow Bridge

To Lewisburg

BLUESTONE NATIONAL SCENIC RIVER

Bluestone River

Little Bluestone River

Glade Creek Reservoir

Flat Top Lake

Piney Creek

Ellison Ridge Rd

Bluestone River Road
Lily

Pipestem

PIPESTEM RESORT STATE PARK

BLUESTONE STATE PARK

BLUESTONE LAKE

Bluestone Dam

Bellepoint

HINTON

Greenbrier River

Active railroad no trespassing

BLUESTONE WILDLIFE MANAGEMENT AREA

New River

Indian Creek

To Lewisburg and

Lick Creek

Laurel Creek

Laurel Creek

Thurmond

New River Gorge Bridge

To travel down into the gorge and back up use WV 82; begin in Lansing. For most of the distance between Lansing and Fayetteville the road is one-way, narrow, and winding.

Thurmond

GAULEY RIVER NATIONAL RECREATION AREA
(Rapids named on the Gauley River are Class V and above)

Long Point

Lower New

The Gauley

Canyon Rim Visitor Center

PLUM ORCHARD WILDLIFE MANAGEMENT AREA

To Mossy and Charleston

To Montgomery and Charleston

To Charleston

Kanawha River

Gauley Bridge

Belva

Dixie

Plum Orchard Lake

Whipple

OAK HILL

FAYETTEVILLE

Cotton Hill

HAWKS NEST STATE PARK

Hawks Nest Dam

Overlook

ANSTED

Victor

GAULEY RIVER

Gauley River

Jodie

Swiss

Upper Swiss

Pure Screaming Hell Rapids

Upper and Lower Mash Rapids

Heaven Help You Rapids

Peters Junction

Gauley River

Peters Creek

Minden

Dunglen

Thurmond

Kaymoor Mine Site

Burnwood

Ames Heights

Lansing

Fayette Station

Greyhound Rapids

Nuttallburg Mine Site

Overlook

Edmond

Woods Ferry

Koontz Flume Rapids

Panther Mountain Road

Masons Branch

CARNIFEX FERRY BATTLEFIELD STATE PARK

Overlook

Glen Jean

National Park Headquarters

SUMMIT BECHTEL FAMILY NATIONAL SCOUT RESERVE

Stone Cliff

Brooklyn

Cunard

Sewell

Thurmond Historic District

BEURY MOUNTAIN WILDLIFE MANAGEMENT AREA

Winona

Lookout

Hico

Edmond

Iron Ring Rapids

Sweets Falls Rapids

Paddle Rapids

Pillow Rock Rapids

Insignificant Rapids

Summersville Dam

SUMMERSVILLE LAKE WILDLIFE MANAGEMENT AREA

Summersville Lake

Summersville Airport

Gauley Tailwaters

BABCOCK STATE PARK

CAMP WASHINGTON CARVER

Clifftop

Grist Mill

Danese

Meadow Bridge

RAINELLE

To Lewisburg and 64

Mount Nebo

To Summersville and 79

Homily Creek

Gauley River

North

0 | 5 Kilometers
0 | 5 Miles

1 Trailhead (see table on page 88)

Much of the land within the National Park Service areas remains private property; please respect the owners' rights.

The degree of difficulty varies from rapid to rapid and with water level. River users should consult with an experienced river runner or ranger before attempting river running.

Rapids

National Park Service area

Unpaved road

Ranger station

Picnic area

Public river access

Lodging

Campground

Primitive campsite

Grandview sunrise

Regions

New River Gorge isn't a particularly easy park to explore. Access is often via a narrow, winding (often unpaved) road, where, if you encounter oncoming traffic, you may have to go in reverse to get out of the way. Below you'll find the park's most popular areas (listed from north to south), along with how to reach them and what you'll find.

Canyon Rim

Easily accessible via US-19, you'll find a visitor center (year-round), excellent hiking opportunities, river access, and the famous **New River Gorge Bridge**.

Nuttalburg Mine Site

Accessed via the narrow, winding Lansing-Edmond or Keeneys Creek Roads, where you'll have to drive cautiously and cooperate with oncoming traffic. Once you arrive, you'll be able to walk freely around one of West Virginia's best-preserved coal mining sites.

Kaymoor Mine Site

An interesting site but only accessible on foot. Kaymoor Trail from Wolf Creek (Fayette Station Road) is great, but it was closed when we went to print (although people were still using it). It can also be reached via Kaymoor Miner's Trail (short and steep) from Cunard Road (not far from Long Point Trailhead).

Cunard/Brooklyn

Continuing past the Kaymoor trailhead, you'll reach Cunard, and Cunard River Access Road. As you'd imagine, the unpaved road winds its way down to the river and continues on to a small primitive campground.

Thurmond

Accessible via WV Route 25 (continuing past park headquarters), the road follows an active railroad past a waterfall and to Thurmond Historic District. A single-lane bridge leads to the small town. The old Train Depot has been turned into a visitor center (open seasonally). The area is pretty neat, especially if you're interested in mining history.

Army Camp

Army Camp, just west of Prince, is accessed via unpaved Prince Army Camp Road. This site used to serve as an Army training ground for the quick assembly of floating bridges. Today you'll find a picnic area and primitive campground.

Prince

Located along WV Route 41, Prince was important for its location, serving as a transportation and commerce hub. Today, there's a small residential community and a train (Amtrak) depot.

Quinnimont

Located east of Prince, Quinnimont was New River Gorge's first mining town. Today, all that remains are railroad switching and holding yards, a monument honoring Colonel Joseph Beury (the first mining operator), and two formerly segregated churches.

Grandview

Accessed via WV Route 9 (Grandview Road), Grandview offers a visitor center (open year-round), scenic overlooks, and hiking trails. **Grandview Overlook** is great for sunrise or a couple hours before sunset.

Glade Creek

Located directly below Grandview, Glade Creek is accessed from WV Route 41 via unpaved Glade Creek Road. Once a prime site for logging, today it's a popular place for fishing, hiking, biking, and camping.

Sandstone Falls

Located just off I-64, Sandstone Visitor Center was built on the grounds of the former Sandstone School. To the north, you'll find a primitive campground at Meadow Creek. To the south, via WV Route 20, you'll find an overlook of Sandstone Falls. You'll pass another overlook and Camp Brookside. What used to be a camp for children of all the mining company's employees is now an Environmental Education Center. You cross the river at Hinton and can drive back up its western shoreline using River Road, concluding at Sandstone Falls Boardwalk and Island Loop.

Camping & Lodging

Just like navigating the park, camping isn't straightforward. There are eight small primitive campgrounds, sprinkled along the park's unpaved roadways. All but War Ridge are located next to the river, providing easy access for boaters and fishermen. From north to south, these are the camping areas: Brooklyn (4 walk-in sites, 1 drive-in), Stone Cliff (6 walk-in, 1 drive-in), Thayer (4 walk-in), Army Camp (11 drive-in, tent or RV), Grandview Sandbar (6 walk-in, 10 drive-in, 2 accessible, small–Medium RV), Glade Creek (6 walk-in, 5 drive-in, 1 accessible, small–Medium RV), War Ridge/Backus Mountain (8 drive-in, tent or small RV), and Meadow Creek (26 drive-in). Meadow Creek is the largest and easiest campground to access, but the park does not recommend large RVs (due to a dangerous railroad crossing). Gauley River National Recreation Area, located north of the park, also has a small primitive campground with 18 drive-in sites. All sites are free (except Meadow Creek) and available on a first-come, first-served basis. Water and hookups are not available. Most whitewater rafting outfitters offer a variety of overnight accommodations.

There are no in-park lodges, but there are many nearby in Fayetteville, Oak Hill, Mount Hope, and Beckley.

Driving

Driving around the park is its own adventure. It'll probably feel like the only flat roadways are bridges and short stretches along the river's shoreline. And that isn't too far from the truth. Come prepared for an abundance of ups and downs, twists and turns, and a whole lot of "oohs" and "ahhhs," especially if you visit in fall (late October) when leaves have turned. An 83-mile (3-hour) New River Gorge Scenic Drive circles the gorge, stopping at many popular destinations. Take US-19 and 60; WV Route 41, 31, and 20; and I-64. Add side-trips to Thurmond Historic District, Fayette Station Road, Canyon Rim Visitor Center, Babcock State Park, Sandstone Visitor Center, Sandstone Falls, Grandview, and a couple hiking trails, and you're talking about more than a daytrip. Mix in whitewater rafting and/or rock climbing (if you're into those things) and your New River Gorge vacation itinerary is set.

Three roads should not be skipped. First, drive across the iconic **New River Gorge Bridge** (US-19) at the park's northern tip. Next is **Fayette Station Road**. This narrow (mostly one-way) road twists and turns its way to the river, crossing it just south of New River Gorge Bridge. Along the way you'll pass rocky cliffs, waterfalls, and Wolf Creek Trailhead. Since it's mostly

Rafting the Lower New River

one-way, you'll want to access it on the east side of the river. The easiest way is to turn right when leaving Canyon Rim Visitor Center (a left returns to US-19). Finally, Grandview Road. It's accessed via a well-marked off-ramp from I-64 near the park's southern end. **Grandview Road** leads to the Main Overlook and ends at Turkey Spur (a popular overlook with limited parking). Be prepared for narrow, winding roads. US-19 and WV Route 16 are your friends.

Whitewater Rafting

A trip to New River Gorge takes you into the heart of American whitewater excitement. The New River drops 750 feet in 50 miles through the gorge, with about two dozen major rapids. Downstream but outside the park you'll find the (dam-controlled) Gauley River, a tributary to the New that is often regarded as the best whitewater rafting in the country. It drops more than 600 feet in 25 miles, with more than 100 serious rapids. Between the two you can find everything from a mellow day on the river to a hair-raising, paddle-gripping death-ride filled with class IV-V rapids. Young kids and anyone afraid of big rapids should start with the upper New River. It's pretty smooth-going, with some ripples mixed in and the occasional class I, II, or III rapid. Outfitters have an age limit around 6 years old for the upper New. The New gets a little wilder below Thurmond. The lower New isn't too wild for first-timers, but two class IV+ rapids (Keeneys and Double Z) keep seasoned paddlers plenty entertained. Lower New River trips end at the New River Gorge Bridge and have a minimum age around 10 years old. One of the best things about the New River is that it almost always has enough water to run. Most outfitters offer trips from April through October on the New. Spring is when you'll get cold water and big rapids (typically reserved for return rafters wanting to experience the New River at its wildest).

New River Gorge Hiking Trails (Distances are roundtrip)

Region	Name	Location	Length	Difficulty Rating & Notes
Fayetteville	Long Point - 👍	Newton Road (1)	3.2 miles	M – Leads to rock outcrop with panoramic views
	Craig Branch	Kaymoor No. 1 (1)	2.4 miles	M – Gorge and river views, connects to Kaymoor Trail
	Kaymoor Miner's - 👍	Kaymoor No. 1 (1)	2.0 miles	S – Stairs and switchbacks to Kaymoor coal mine site
	Butcher Branch	Kaymoor No. 1 (1)	0.8 mile	M – Connects Kaymoor to Long Point Trail
	Timber Ridge	Newton Road (1)	1.0 mile	E – Rhododendron tunnels in spring
	Kaymoor - 👍	Cunard/Wolf Creek (1, 2)	8.6 miles	M – Parallels gorge, Craig Br and Kaymoor Mine spurs
	Fayetteville	Kaymoor/Wolf Cr (1, 2)	4.0 miles	S – Connects Fayette Station Road with Kaymoor
	Park Loop	Park Drive (2)	1.1 miles	E – Connects to Fayetteville Trail
	Burnwood	Burnwood (3)	1.2 miles	E – Loop, across from Rim Visitor Center, rhododendron
	Canyon Rim - 👍	Canyon Rim VC (3)	0.1 mile	E – Accessible ramp to first overlook, stairs to second
	Bridge	Fayette Station Rd (3)	0.9 mile	S – Steep and rocky, views of New River Gorge Bridge
	Endless Wall - 👍	Fern Creek, Nuttall (4, 4)	2.9 miles	M/X – Make loop with road, rock climbers' playground
Nuttallburg	Headhouse	Short Creek (5)	0.7 mile	M – Leads to historic coal mine
	Conveyor	Headhouse Spur (6)	0.8 mile	S – Steep, connects Headhouse and Keeneys Creek Rail
	Keeneys Creek Rail	Keeneys Creek Rd (6)	3.3 miles	E – Follows former rail line that connected to C&O main
	Town Loop	Nuttallburg (6)	0.5 mile	M – Loops around old Nuttallburg town ruins
	Tipple	Nuttallburg (6)	0.6 mile	E – See remains of old mine site and community
	Seldom Seen	Tipple Trail (6)	0.3 mile	E – Ruins of a small community of Nuttallburg families
Thurmond	Brooklyn Mine	Brooklyn (7)	2.7 miles	M – Follows old road through forest to mine site
	Southside	Brooklyn (7)	7.0 miles	E – Shoreline trail past several old mining sites
	Rend	Thurmond/Minden (8, 9)	6.4 miles	E – Old rail line, bridge out one mile from Minden
	Church Loop	Rend Trail (9)	0.1 mile	E – Visits the First Baptist Church of Thurmond
	Stone Cliff	Stone Cliff Picnic (10)	2.7 miles	M – Follows river, stone cliffs on opposite side
Grandview	Grandview Rim - 👍	Main Overlook (11)	3.2 miles	M – Ends at Turkey Spur Overlook (can drive there)
	Castle Rock - 👍	Main Overlook (11)	1.2 miles	M – Cool rocks, 1-mile loop with Grandview Rim
	Tunnel - 👍	Main Overlook (11)	0.5 mile	E – Loop, tunnels (closed), rocks and rock overhang
	Woodland	Shelter #2 (11)	0.6 mile	E – Forested Loop
	Big Buck	Shelter #2 (11)	0.9 mile	E – Forested loop exploring the area's tree diversity
	Little Laurel	Shelter #3 & 4 (11)	3.0 miles	S – Descends 1,400 ft to river banks/Glade Creek Road
Glade Cr	Glade Creek - 👍	Glade Creek (12, 13)	11.2 miles	M – Swiming hole, waterfalls, backpacking area
	Kate's Falls	Glade Creek (13)	0.2 mile	M – Short spur from Glade Creek to a pleasant waterfall
	Kate's Plateau	Glade Creek South (13)	5.1 miles	M – Lollipop semi-loop forested hike
	Polls Plateau	Kate's Plateau (13)	4.9 miles	M – Semi-loop continuation from Kate's Plateau
Sandstone	Sandstone Overlook	WV Route 20 (14)	0.1 mile	E – Stairs, see Sandstone Falls 600 feet above the river
	Gwinn Ridge	Brooks Mtn Rd (15)	3.0 miles	S – Up and down loop, trail can be difficult to follow
	Big Branch - 👍	Brooks Falls (16)	2.0 miles	S – Steep, loop with waterfall and wildflowers (spring)
	Boardwalk - 👍	Sandstone Falls (17)	0.25 mile	E – Largest (1,500 feet across) waterfall on New River
	Island Loop - 👍	Boardwalk (17)	0.5 mile	E – Circles the largest island below Sandstone Falls

Difficulty Ratings: E = Easy, M = Moderate, S = Strenuous, X = Extreme

The Gauley River's water-volume is controlled by Summersville Dam. The season is short (six weeks in September/October), but it's also guaranteed great rafting. The upper Gauley is the most extreme section of water, featuring more than 50 rapids over 12 miles. Paddlers must be at least 15 years old and should have previous whitewater experience. The Lower Gauley is comparable to the lower New, except with more rapids squeezed into less river.

There are several licensed outfitters ready to show you an incredible time on the New and/or Gauley Rivers. ACE Adventure Resort (800.787.3982, aceraft.com) can take care of lodging and all your adventure needs (rock climbing, mountain biking, hiking, kayaking, fishing, and more), of course your bill will add up in a hurry, especially if you have a large group. Adventures on the Gorge (855.379.8738, adventuresonthe-gorge.com) also has camping and cabin options, and offers unique adventures on Summersville Lake. Alpine Ministries (800.806.2180, alpineministries. com) is your faith-based adventure outfitter. Cantrell Ultimate Rafting (304.877.8235, cantrellultimateraft-ing.com) can take care of your rafting and lodging/camping needs. New and Gauley River Adventures (800.463.9873, gauley.com) offers all the rafting you can handle, and they'll also take you horseback riding, fishing, and/or mountain biking. West Virginia Adventures (800.292.0880, trywva.com) has your rafting and lodging covered, and if you want to get in the New River early, they'll take your group down in March (conditions permitting). With considerable competition, pricing is fairly consistent across the board. Expect to pay about $100 per paddler for the most popular lower New River trip (wetsuits, splash jackets, photos, and tips not included).

Rock Climbing

Even with more than 1,400 established routes, most of them favor the highly-experienced climber. If that's you, pick up a rock climbing guidebook or stop at Water Stone Outdoors (waterstoneoutdoors.com) in Fayetteville. Or consider joining New River Mountain Guides (newriverclimbing.com) or Blue Ridge Mountain Guides (blueridgemtnguides.com) for a climbing course (or book a combo with a whitewater outfitter listed above). If you'd just like to see climbers in their natural habitat, Endless Wall Trail is the place to go. Buttress Trail near Canyon Rim is another option.

Hiking & Backpacking

There are plenty of interesting hiking opportunities. Starting at the park's northern end, **Canyon**

Castle Rock Trail

Rim Boardwalk is a short and easy stroll to sweeping views of the New River Gorge Bridge. It features two overlooks. The first is a long, fully-accessible ramp, the second requires descending (and then ascending) a few flights of stairs. For even better New River Gorge views, hike **Long Point Trail**. It begins on Newton Road (Cunard), just south of Fayetteville. This 3.2-mile roundtrip trek leads to an open rock promontory facing New River Gorge bridge. Bikes are allowed until the final narrow descent to the point. Mid-week, early in the day is the best time to hike. Not only will you have the morning sun illuminating the bridge, but you should also get a parking space in the relatively large parking area at the trailhead (it's popular, obey the parking signs). On the other side of the river, you can hike **Endless Wall Trail** for panoramic views. There are two trailheads (Fern Creek and Nuttall), both located on Lansing-Edmond Road. It's 2.4 miles from trailhead to trailhead, with another half-mile walking along the road to return to your car. Expect to hike more than this distance to explore viewpoints along the way.

If you'd like to hike to a mining site, go for **Kaymoor**. There are a few ways to reach it. You can hike about two miles (one-way) from Wolf Creek Trailhead (Fayette Station Road), which is a wonderful trail, passing a waterfall, and following the river with the New River Gorge Bridge behind you. However, there's only space for two vehicles (one, if it's large or parked poorly) at the trailhead. There is a public parking area down the road at the river access point. Just know Fayette

Big Branch Trail

Station Road is one-way here, so, if you go to Wolf Creek Trailhead and don't find a parking space, you'll have to make another lap around Fayette Station Road to return to the river access parking area. You can also reach Kaymoor via **Kaymoor Miner's Trail**. It's short (one mile) and steep, and also passes a waterfall near its trailhead. The trailhead is located on Kaymoor No. 1 Road, not far from Long Point Trailhead. Both of these trails get you to Kaymoor Top, where coal was mined. From there you can descend 821 stairs to Kaymoor Bottom, where the coal was processed and shipped. It's interesting, but the trail is no joke. You're hiking into and out of the gorge.

Nuttallburg is another old mining site option. It's basically on the other side of the river from Kaymoor. Similarly, you can hike down to it via **Headhouse Trail**. It begins at Short Creek Trailhead, not far from the trailheads for Endless Wall. You should see a sign for Short Creek driving down Lansing-Edmond Road. Like with Kaymoor, there is a top and a bottom. Headhouse Trail descends to the headhouse, mine, and conveyor. From there you can continue down the extremely steep switchbacks of Conveyor Trail to Keeneys Creek Rail Trail. Continuing downhill, you will finally reach a large home, the tipple and ruins of schools, churches, homes, and coke ovens. Again, if you're thinking of hiking here, it's almost 2.5 miles (one-way) from the trailhead to the river and around the mining sites, and then you have to hike 2.2 miles back up to the parking area. (Note that you can drive to Nuttallburg Mine Site via Keeneys Creek Road.)

An easier old mining town to explore on foot is the **Thurmond Historic District**. While it's located on the same side of the gorge as Nuttallburg, you'll have to drive around the gorge to access it via WV Route 25 near the park's headquarters in Glen Jean. Near its

conclusion, the road narrows to one lane before crossing the river and reaching the visitor center. From there, you are free to explore the area. Many signs describe what life was like when business was booming.

Continuing upriver (south), **Grandview** is another popular point of interest. From the Main Overlook you can hike out on **Castle Rock Trail** and return via Grandview Rim Trail for an excellent loop. You'd also have the option to continue north on **Grandview Rim** to Turkey Spur (definitely worth a stop). You can reach Turkey Spur by car as well. However, it only has three parking spaces and hikers are rewarded with a couple New River overlooks along the way. Hike it. Beneath Grandview is Glade Creek. **Glade Creek Trail** is a relatively long moderate hike that follows an old narrow-gauge rail line. You can access the trail from the north at Glade View Camp or from the south about two miles from the Grandview Road I-64 off-ramp. From the south it's a short hike to a spur trail to **Kate's Falls**, but a high-clearance 4WD vehicle is recommended to reach the trailhead. To reach Kate's Falls from the north (Glade View Camp), you're looking at a ten-mile hike.

At the park's southern end, you can drive up River Road to hike the short and easy **Sandstone Falls Boardwalk** and **Island Loop**. **Big Branch Trail** is a more strenuous loop in the area, featuring a beautiful waterfall. Just know that you must cross the stream and it may be impassable at high-water levels. Begin the loop in a clockwise direction to hit the stream early and you can assess the creek-crossing conditions.

Backpacking is somewhat forgotten with all the area's more extreme activities. Your best options are boat-in locations along the upper New. Be sure to camp above the high-water line and know that camping is prohibited on Brookside Island (just downstream from Brooks Falls). Or hikers can find tent-space at Glade Creek, Southside, and Stone Cliff Trails, as long as you're at least 100 feet away from trails, roads, and any other developed area. Make a plan and then discuss it with a park ranger before heading out.

Biking
New River Gorge is one of the most mountain bike-friendly national parks. First you have **Arrowhead Trails**. It's a series of four mountain biking loops, ranging from easy to intermediate, totaling 12.8 miles. These trails were built over the course of 78,544 volunteer hours from the Boy Scouts' Order of the Arrow. Clovis (green) is a 1-mile loop. Adena (blue) is a 3.1-mile loop. Dalton (blue) is a 6.4-mile loop with tighter

turns, narrow trail, and steeper hills (including a wide set of switchbacks). LeCroy (blue) is a 1.8-mile loop featuring a rock bridge and a rhododendron tunnel on the connector with Dalton Trail. These are trails built with mountain biking in mind. Additionally, the park allows mountain bikes on many hiking trails: Kaymoor, Fayetteville, Long Point, Headhouse, Rend, Stone Cliff, Glade Creek, and Southside, just to name a few. It's always a good idea to stop in at a visitor center to discuss trail conditions or hike the trail first to see if it's suitable and safe for your ability.

Arrowhead Bike Farm (arrowheadbikefarm.com) has your biking needs covered. They offer rentals ($35-75/day), clinics ($20-85), tours ($69-90) from their bike shop in Fayetteville (conveniently situated near trailheads for Long Point and Arrowhead Trails). If you're serious about mountain biking, talk to them about other trails in the area!

Fishing
New River Gorge is a popular fishing destination. And although you are permitted to fish year-round, spring and fall (mornings and evenings) are the best times to fish. You'll find bass in the river and trout in its tributaries. There are a number of public river access points labelled on the map, including (from north to south) Fayette Station, Cunard, Dunglen, Stone Cliff, McCreery, Grandview Sandbar, Mill Creek, Glade Creek, Meadow Creek, Sandstone Falls, Brooks Falls, and Tug Creek Beach. Anyone fishing in the park must have a West Virginia fishing license and follow the state's fishing regulations. Nearby Babcock State Park is another popular fishing spot.

Visitor Centers
New River Gorge has four visitor centers. On the park's north end, near the New River Gorge Bridge, you'll find **Canyon Rim Visitor Center**. It's open from 9am until 5pm, year-round. It's a beautiful facility, filled with exhibits, an auditorium, bookstore, and restrooms. Stop here first to get oriented, ask park rangers your questions, watch two short videos on the park, peruse a current schedule of ranger programs, and take a look at the gorge and bridge. On the other end of the park is **Sandstone Visitor Center**, located just off I-64. It's also open year-round from 9am until 5pm but closes intermittently between December and March. Inside you'll find information about the park's natural and cultural history, as well as a bookstore. Outside is a monarch waystation, a native grassland planted with milkweed to entice monarch butterflies to stopover. In between you'll find **Grandview Visitor Center**, a small

Endless Wall Trail

facility perched high above the river. It's open seasonally between Memorial Day through Labor Day, from noon until 5pm. Nearby you'll find a large amphitheater where outdoor performances take place. Finally, **Thurmond Depot** harkens back to the days when coal was king and train whistles regularly rang out in the air. Today, the depot is open June through August, from 10am until 5pm.

Ranger Programs & For Kids
New River Gorge offers a variety of free walks, talks, and activities within the park. They occur year-round but most are offered during the busy summer season. Additionally, the park hosts two annual events: Wildflower Weekend (late April) and Hidden History Weekend (late September). The former celebrates Appalachian plant life's annual renewal. The latter digs deeper into the area's rich history, from subsistence farming to substantial mining and logging operations. Check them out and stop in at a visitor center for a current schedule of ranger programs.

New River Gorge and its raucous river is a real treat for teenagers, but you'll find plenty of attractions for kids of all ages. Summer is the best time for family paddling, when the water is warm and the rapids have flattened out a bit (spring is a little wilder). One of the National Park Service's institutions is the Junior Ranger Program. Stop in at a visitor center to pick up a booklet. Complete the necessary requirements and return to become an official Junior Park Ranger and receive a badge and certificate. Like fishing? New River Gorge offers the unique Junior Ranger Angler Program. Booklets are available online or at Canyon Rim or Sandstone Visitor Centers. There's also a Girl Scout Ranger Program and Scout Ranger Program. Families will also enjoy the diverse collection of short hiking trails New River Gorge has to offer.

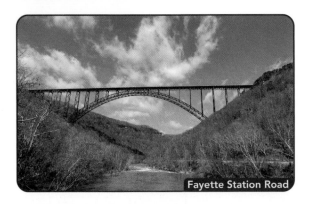

Fayette Station Road

Flora & Fauna

New River Gorge boasts more than 1,400 plant species. Spring wildflower blooms draw a crowd. Stars of the show are the dense rhododendron thickets like you'll find at Burnwood and Timber Ridge Trails. Catawba rhododendron typically bloom in mid- to late May. Great rhododendrons usually bloom in late June/early July. Mountain laurel bloom from late May through early July. Fall is equally spectacular, when the forested gorge, now recovered from being clear-cut during the logging boom, explodes in color.

Common wildlife includes white-tail deer and squirrels. You might spot a fox, black bear, or river otter if you're lucky. Abandoned mines provide good habitats for bats, including two endangered species (Virginia big-eared and Indiana bats). Bald eagles and peregrine falcons are occasionally spotted. Many migratory birds like the cerulean warbler stopover for a visit. More than 40 species of reptiles live here, including two venomous snakes (copperhead and timber rattlesnake). Nearly 50 species of amphibians have been documented, including the frightening hellbender (AKA Allegheny alligator, snot otter, or devil dog). Hellbender numbers are declining (along with their habitat). The park is home to 89 species of fish, split almost evenly between native and introduced species.

Pets & Accessibility

New River Gorge is a pet-friendly place. Your furry companions are allowed on park trails, but they must be kept on a leash (less than six feet). Just remember to pick up your pet's waste. Pets are prohibited from visitor centers and ranger programs.

New River Gorge is all ups and downs, so it isn't a particularly accessible destination for anyone with mobility restrictions but there are a few exceptions. All visitor centers are accessible. Glade Creek and Grandview

Sandbar offer an accessible campsite. Canyon Rim (first overlook) and Sandstone Falls Trails are accessible, as well as the first quarter-mile of Long Point and Glade Creek Trails. You'll also find a wheelchair accessible fishing area at Glade Creek Campground.

Weather

You're going to want to come prepared for all types of weather. Storms are common year-round, but temperature and precipitation peak in July. Just don't get caught out on any of the sandstone cliffs when a thunderstorm passes through. Water temperature lags behind air temperature, but it usually warms up nicely into the 70s°F by the end of July, and then stays there until the end of August.

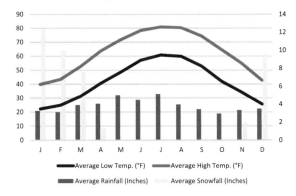

Tips & Recommendations

Everyone says it, but it's actually true that there's no bad time to visit New River Gorge (although you could be temporarily inconvenienced if you happen to visit during a snowstorm). Spring and fall are the prettiest seasons, with personal preference tipping to fall's colorful foliage (and the short Gauley River rafting season). Spring is about wildflowers and wild water, when the snowmelt's surge draws experienced rafters to the lower New River. Summer is for families to enjoy the river when the air and water are most pleasant. Winter offers unobscured gorge views, snowcapped mountains, and relief from the summer crowds (but no fun extreme sports activities).

Even though the park is relatively small, driving to its most popular sites takes a solid day because of the number of access points, the nature of roads (unpaved, narrow, steep, winding), and the number of photo-worthy viewpoints. The Express Tour to The Bridge (near Canyon Rim Visitor Center) and Sandstone Falls would only take a couple hours. With that said, you should spend a few days. Hike the trails. Travel back in time at Thurmond Historic District. Raft the river. Watch rock climbers scale the gorge's vertical walls. Join a few ranger programs. And do whatever else you have your eyes on. Maybe hop back in a raft for another trip down the river?

If you're planning on whitewater rafting, reservations are a good idea, especially if you have some experience and want to raft the Upper Gauley during Bridge Day (mid-October). What's Bridge Day? It's West Virginia's largest single-day festival when a bunch of maniacs jump off the bridge (with parachutes!). That's cool. It's also cool that spectators are free to walk across the bridge to watch the crazy spectacle.

New River Gorge isn't just a playground for adrenaline junkies. There's a rich history of the railroad, mining, and logging to be found at the park's ghost towns and historic sites. It's a good idea to begin your history lesson at a visitor center. After that, move along to Thurmond Historic District and Nuttallburg. These sites are accessible by car. If you're up for it, Kaymoor is another mining site worth exploring, but the hike to reach it is quite strenuous. You can also visit old subsistence farmsteads like Richmond-Hamilton Farm (located north of Hinton along River Road).

Be prepared for narrow, winding roads. If you stick to US-19, WV Route 16, Grandview Road, and Fayette Station Road, you'll be fine. Although you may have problems on Fayette Station Road if your vehicle is long (the road is narrow with switchbacks, but mostly one-way). Basically, all other roads heading to or into the gorge are narrow and sinuous (and often unpaved).

The Lower New

Easy Hikes: Tunnel (0.5 mile), Canyon Rim (0.1), Boardwalk/Island Loop (0.75)
Moderate Hikes: Long Point (3.2 miles), Castle Rock (1.2), Kaymoor (8.6), Endless Wall (2.9), Glade Creek (11.2), Grandview Rim (3.2)
Strenuous Hikes: Kaymoor Miner's (2 miles), Big Branch (2)
Family Activities: Go rafting!, watch for trains in Thurmond, become Junior Rangers, go mountain biking
Guided Tours: Whitewater Rafting, Rock Climbing
Rainy Day Activities: Go rafting!
History Enthusiasts: Thurmond Historic District, Kaymoor Mine, Nuttallburg,
Sunset Spots: Canyon Rim Overlook
Sunrise Spots: Grandview (Main Overlook)
Wildlife: Sandstone Falls/Overlook (raptors, heron, otter, turtle), Grandview (birds, bats in summer, deer), Glade Creek

Beyond the Park...

Dining
The Station Market & Bistro
312 N Court St, Fayetteville
thestationwv.com • (304) 900-5516

Wood Iron Eatery • (304) 900-5557
129 S Court St, Fayetteville
woodironeatery.com

The Char • the-char.com
100 Char Dr, Beckley

The Dish Café • dishcafewv.com
1466 Ritter Dr, Daniels

Lodging
Hawks Nest Lodge
18408 Midland Trail, Ansted
wvstateparks.com • (304) 658-5212

Country River Inn • (304) 574-0055
9060 Gatewood Rd
countryriverinn.com

The Resort at Glade Springs
255 Resort Dr, Daniels
gladesprings.com • (304) 763-2000

Fayetteville, Oak Hill, and Beckley: groceries, food, hotels

Campgrounds
Rifrafters Campground
448 Laurel Creek Rd, Fayetteville
rifrafters.com • (304) 574-1065

New River Camp • (877) 762-1523
101 Milroy Grose Rd, Lansing
newrivercampground.com

AAC • (304) 693-2667
97 Pudds Rd, Lansing
americanalpineclub.org

Little Beaver State Park
1402 Grandview Rd, Beaver
wvstateparks.com • (304) 763-2494

Berry's Campground
1211 New River Rd, Hinton
berryscamp.com • (304) 466-4199

Camp Creek State Park
2390 CH-19/5, Camp Creek
wvstateparks.com • (304) 425-9481

Bushcreek Falls RV Resort
5127 Eads Mill Rd, Princeton
bushcreekfalls.com • (304) 431-1950

Festivals
New River Birding Fest April
birding-wv.com

New River Gorge Fest • aceraft.com

Mountain Music Festival • June
mountainmusicfestwv.com

Bridge Day October • Fayetteville
officialbridgeday.com

Attractions
Bluestone National Scenic River
nps.gov/blue • (304) 465-0508

Babcock State Park
Glade Creek Grist Mill
486 Babcock Rd, Clifftop
wvstateparks.com • (304) 438-3004

Gauley River NRA
36 Fayette Station Rd, Victor
nps.gov/gari • (304) 465-0508

Cathedral Falls
short hike near Gauley Bridge

Three Rivers Avian Center
Brooks Mountain Rd, Brooks
tracwv.org • (304) 466-4683

Burning Rock Off-Road Park
171 Burning Rock Dr, Sophia
burningrockwv.com • (304) 683-9242

Mammoth Cave

A Park Ranger leads the River Styx Tour

Phone: (270) 758-2180
Website: nps.gov/maca

Established: July 1, 1941
Size: 52,830 Acres
Annual Visitors: 570,000
Peak Season: Summer/Weekends
Total Cave Length: 415+ Miles
Public Cave Trails: ~14 Miles
Hiking Trails: 80 Miles

Activities: Cave Tours ($8–66), Hiking, Backpacking, Horseback Riding, Biking, Paddling, Fishing

3 Campgrounds: $15–25/night
Lodging: The Lodge ($71–136)

Park Hours: All day, every day with Cave Tours available daily from 8am–5pm (extended hours summer and holidays, closed Christmas)
Entrance Fee: None

At more than 400 miles in length, Mammoth Cave is the longest cave system in the world, and the competition isn't close. Mammoth earns its name by being nearly twice as long as its next closest rival, Sistema Sac Actum in Mexico. And several new miles of passages are discovered each year, leaving geologists to believe there could be as many as 600 additional miles of cave yet to be discovered.

The first known cave exploration took place some 4,000 years ago. Native Americans mined the cave's upper levels for more than two millennia. They sought gypsum, selenite, and mirabilite, among other minerals. Proof of their presence was left in the form of ancient artifacts: cane torches, gourd bowls, cloth, a handful of petroglyphs, and even their remains. Constant temperature, humidity, and salty soil make caves a particularly good environment for preserving human remains. Several "mummies" were buried in an organized fashion. Others, like the remains of a primitive man pinned beneath a rock, tell stories about the lives and times of these ancient people. Decades of exploration have uncovered thousands of artifacts but few answers about the purpose of minerals they sought. Perhaps a greater mystery is why—after 2,000 years—they left Mammoth Cave and never returned.

Mammoth Cave was rediscovered by John Houchins near the turn of the 19th century. Legend states he shot and wounded a black bear near the cave's entrance. The injured animal led its hunter to the cave, and the rest, as they say, is history.

In 1812, after 2,000 years of anonymity, the cave's underground passageways were once again being mined. The War of 1812 was brewing, and the British successfully cut-off America's gunpowder supplies in the east. Fortunately for the American Army, Mammoth Cave had large deposits of calcium nitrate, which, through a simple process, could be converted into gunpowder. This cave and its minerals ended up playing a pivotal role in a war hundreds of miles away.

As a result, Mammoth Cave received considerable publicity, and by 1816 visitors began showing up to tour the mysterious labyrinth. But local citizens had other uses in mind. An enthusiastic clergyman used the cave as a church, and a doctor from Louisville purchased it for use as a tuberculosis treatment center. These ventures failed, but cave tours were an undeniable success—so successful they have been conducted without interruption through the Civil War to the present day. Slaves led many of the tours. Stephen Bishop, a slave with quick wit, good humor, and a curious spirit, was one of the most passionate guides. He became the first to map the cave system and cross Bottomless Pit. Along the way, he discovered and named many of the cave's features, including Gorin's Dome and 192-ft-tall Mammoth Dome. In 1908, Max Kämper, a German geologist and mapmaker, picked up where Bishop left off, setting out to create a comprehensive map of the cave. Guided by Ed Bishop, great-nephew of Stephen, Kämper discovered Kämper Hall, Elizabeth's Dome, and Violet City. Together, they mapped and surveyed all the passages known at the time.

By 1920, tens of thousands of tourists visited Mammoth Cave each year, causing locals to seek a piece of the tourism pie. George Morrison, a wealthy oilman, found the cave's "New Entrance." He "found" it using drills and explosives. Floyd Collins, pioneer and explorer, was determined to find a lucrative new cave. While exploring Sand Cave, a rock wedged his ankle, leaving him trapped near the cave's entrance. After 17 days of failed rescue attempts Collins died of exposure. The event created a "carnival atmosphere" rife with dozens of journalists and sensational stories, which sparked the movement to make Mammoth Cave a national park. When this idea came to fruition in 1941, only 40 miles of passageways had been surveyed. Since then, several cave networks have been connected, creating the largest such area in the world, of which about fourteen miles of passages are available for tours.

Old Guide's Cemetery

When to Go
Mammoth Cave National Park is open all year. The temperature underground is a nearly-constant 54°F. The park is busiest in summer and holiday weekends. During this time reservations are recommended for cave tours (especially Wild Cave, River Styx, and Intro to Caving Tours). Tours are given daily throughout the year, except Christmas Day. Tour choices will be limited during the slow winter season.

Transportation & Airports
Mammoth Cave Railroad Bike and Hike Trail connects Mammoth Cave Hotel to Park City. There are no bridges across Green River within the park, but it can be crossed with the aid of a free ferry. Green River Ferry operates year-round (6am–9:55pm). Houchin's Ferry is seasonal. It's a good idea to call the Ferry Hotline at (270) 758-2166 for current information.

The nearest large commercial airports are Louisville International (SDF) and Nashville International (BNA). Both are approximately 90 miles from the park. Bowling Green-Warren County Regional (BWG) is a smaller airport located 35 miles southwest of the park.

Directions
Arriving from the north: Take I-65 South to Exit 53 (Cave City). Turn Right onto KY-70. Follow KY-70/255 as it becomes Mammoth Cave Parkway. Mammoth Cave Parkway leads directly to the Visitor Center.

Arriving from the south: Take I-65 North to Exit 48 (Park City). Turn left onto KY-255. Follow KY-255 until it becomes Park City Road, which leads into the park. Turn left where Park City Road joins Mammoth Cave Parkway and follow it to the Visitor Center.

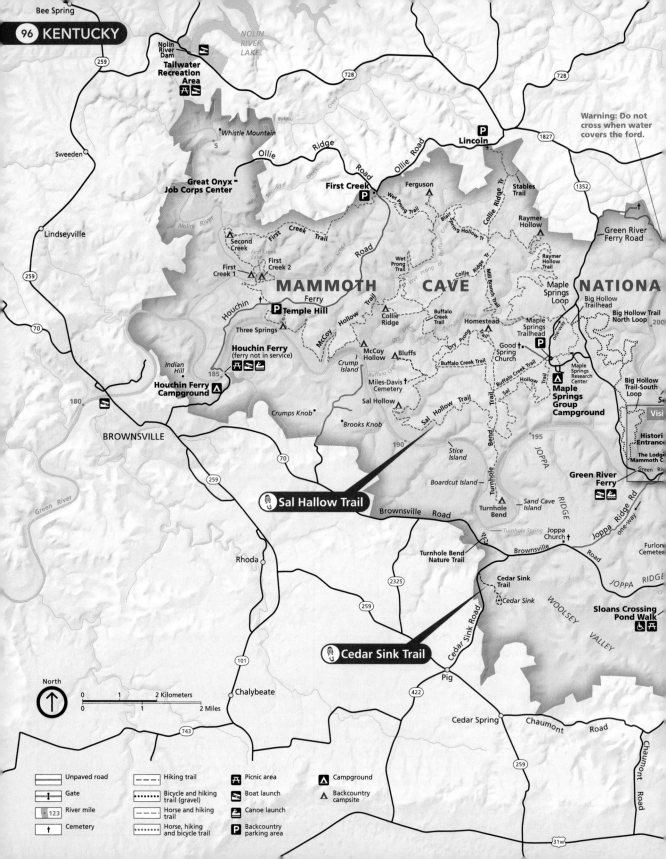

Bee Spring

259

NOLIN RIVER LAKE

Nolin River Dam

Tailwater Recreation Area

728

728

1827

Warning: Do not cross when water covers the ford.

Whistle Mountain
5

Sweeden

Ollie Ridge Road

Ollie Road

P Lincoln

1352

Great Onyx - Job Corps Center

First Creek P

Ollie Road

Ferguson

Blair Spring Hollow Tr

Wet Prong Trail

Buffalo Creek Trail

Collie Ridge Tr

Stables Trail

Raymer Hollow

Raymer Hollow Trail

Green River Ferry Road

Lindseyville

Nolin River

First Creek Trail

Second Creek

First Creek Lake

First Creek 2

Wet Prong Trail

Collie Ridge Tr

Mill Branch Trail

Maple Springs Loop

Big Hollow Trailhead

Big Hollow Trail North Loop

200

259

First Creek 1

MAMMOTH   **CAVE**   **NATIONA**

70

Houchin Ferry Road

P Temple Hill

Three Springs

McCoy Hollow Trail

Collie Ridge

Buffalo Creek Trail

Homestead

Dry Prong Trail

Maple Springs Trailhead

P

Maple Springs Research Center

Big Hollow Trail-South Loop

Houchin Ferry (ferry not in service)

Indian Hill

185

McCoy Hollow

Bluffs

Buffalo Creek Trail

Good Spring Church

Maple Springs Group Campground

Visi

Houchin Ferry Campground

180

Crump Island

Miles-Davis Cemetery

Buffalo Creek Trail

Sal Hollow

Histori Entrance

BROWNSVILLE

Crumps Knob

Sal Hollow

Sal Hollow Trail

195

JOPPA

The Lodge Mammoth C

Green Riv

Brooks Knob

190

Turnhole Bend Trail

Green River Ferry

Sal Hallow Trail

Stice Island

Boardcut Island

Sand Cave Island

RIDGE

Joppa Ridge Rd one-way

Furlon Cemeter

70

Brownsville Road

Turnhole Bend

Turnhole Spring

Joppa Church †

Brownsville Road

JOPPA RIDGE

259

Turnhole Bend Nature Trail

2325

Cedar Sink Trail

Cedar Sink

WOOLSEY VALLEY

Sloans Crossing Pond Walk

Rhoda

259

Cedar Sink Trail

Cedar Sink Road

Pig

101

422

North

259

Chalybeate

Cedar Spring

Chaumont Road

743

31w

Chaumont Road

0   1   2 Kilometers
0   1   2 Miles

Legend

Unpaved road	---- Hiking trail
Gate	····· Bicycle and hiking trail (gravel)
River mile	--- Horse and hiking trail
Cemetery	····· Horse, hiking and bicycle trail

Picnic area
Boat launch
Canoe launch
Backcountry parking area

Campground
Backcountry campsite

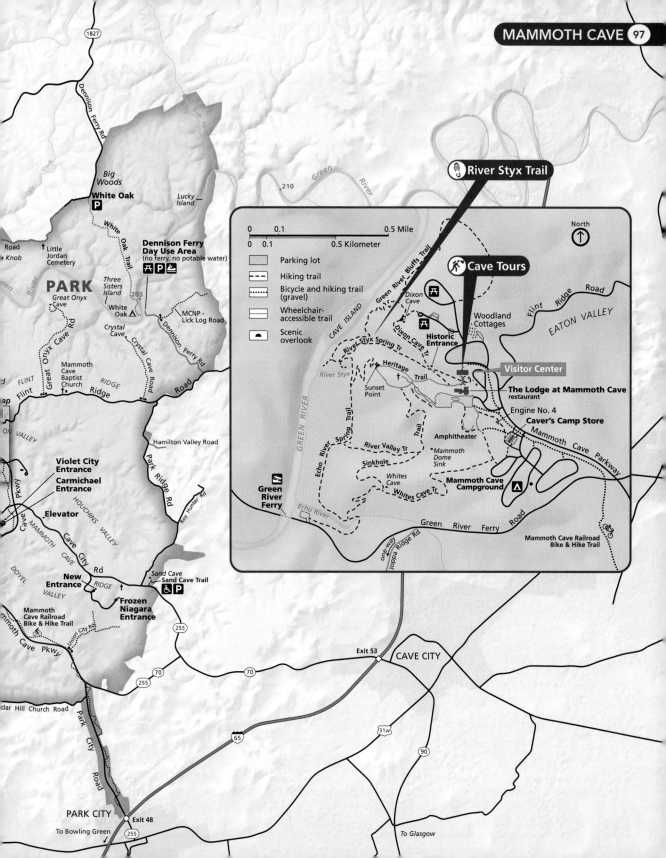

River Styx Trail

Cave Tours

North

Map Legend

	Parking lot
- - -	Hiking trail
···	Bicycle and hiking trail (gravel)
===	Wheelchair-accessible trail
⌒	Scenic overlook

Scale:
0   0.1   0.5 Mile
0   0.1   0.5 Kilometer

PARK

1827

Dennison Ferry Rd

Big Woods

White Oak P

Lucky Island

Road
Little Jordan Cemetery
Knob

White Oak Trail

Three Sisters Island

Dennison Ferry Day Use Area
(no ferry, no potable water)

205

White Oak △

Great Onyx Cave

Crystal Cave

Crystal Cave Road

Great Onyx Cave Rd

Mammoth Cave Baptist Church

FLINT
Flint   RIDGE
Ridge

MCNP - Lick Log Road

Dennison Ferry Rd

Green River
210

Green River Bluffs Trail

CAVE ISLAND

Dixon Cave

Woodland Cottages

Flint   Ridge   Road

EATON VALLEY

Dixon Cave Tr

Historic Entrance

River Styx Spring Tr

Heritage Trail

Visitor Center

River Styx

Sunset Point

The Lodge at Mammoth Cave
restaurant

Engine No. 4

Caver's Camp Store

Echo River Spring Trail

GREEN RIVER

River Valley Tr

Sinkhole

Amphitheater

Mammoth Dome Sink

Mammoth Cave Parkway

Whites Cave

Mammoth Cave Campground △

Green River Ferry

Echo River

Whites Cave Tr

Joppa Ridge Rd

Green   River   Ferry   Road

one-way

Mammoth Cave Railroad Bike & Hike Trail

Hamilton Valley Road

Park Ridge Rd

Violet City Entrance
Carmichael Entrance

Elevator

VALLEY

MAMMOTH

Cave City Rd

HOUCHINS VALLEY

Roy Hunter Rd

Sand Cave
Sand Cave Trail

New Entrance
RIDGE

DOYEL
VALLEY

Frozen Niagara Entrance

Mammoth Cave Railroad Bike & Hike Trail

Mammoth Cave Pkwy

Union City Rd

Park City Road

255

70

255

70

65

Exit 53

CAVE CITY

31w

90

Cedar Hill Church Road

PARK CITY   Exit 48

255

To Bowling Green

To Glasgow

Violet City Lantern Tour

Mammoth Cave Camping (Fees are per night)

Name	Location	Open	Fee	Sites	Notes
Mammoth Cave	0.25 mile from the Visitor Center	March–Nov	$25 $40	105 4 Group	Showers at Service Center (March–Nov)
Houchin's Ferry	15 miles from the Visitor Center	All Year	$15–20	12	Water and Pit Toilets No RVs, No Showers
Maple Springs (Horse/Group)	6 miles from Visitor Center	March–Nov	$50	8	Water, Pit Toilets, No Showers, Water/Electric Hookups
Backcountry	To camp at any of the park's 13 primitive backcountry sites requires a $10 permit (available in-person or at recreation.gov). Boat-accessible-only island/riverside camping requires a free permit (in-person).				

Mammoth Cave Lodging (Fees are per night)

Name	Open	Fee	Location & Notes
The Lodge	All Year	$71–136	Next to the Visitor Center • Rooms and cottages • mammothcavelodge.com

Mammoth Cave Tours

Name	Fee	Duration	Notes
Mammoth Cave Access	$22 (Adult)/ $16 (Youth)	2 hours	This tour is designed for people with a disability or limited mobility, using the elevator entrance to reach the Snowball Room
Mammoth Passage	$8/6	1.25 hours	Easy tour delving into the cave's cultural and natural history
Discovery - ♿	$8/6	0.5 hour	Self-guiding version of Mammoth Passage to the Rotunda
Broadway	$11/8	2 hours	Visits Rotunda, Methodist Church, Booth's Amphitheater, and more
Frozen Niagara	$18/14	1.25 hours	Short trek, with only 12 stairs to visit the cave's main formations
Historic	$20/15	2 hours	Learn about 19th- and early 20th-century visitors, 540 stairs
Extended Historic	$18/13	2.25 hours	Historic tour plus a side trip to an 1840s treatment ward (there is a self-guided option, same price, 1.5 hours)
Domes and Dripstones	$21/16	2 hours	Domes, pits, and dripstone formations, 500 stairs
Grand Avenue	$35/27	4 hours	Strenuous tour providing idea of the cave system's size, 670 stairs
Cleaveland Avenue	$22/16	2 hours	See various gypsum formations, follows Grand Avenue route
Gothic Avenue	$19/15	2 hours	Portions of Star Chamber, Historic, and Violet City Lantern tours
Violet City Lantern - ♿	$25/20	3 hours	Strenuous trip lit only by lanterns
Great Onyx Lantern	$23/18	2.25 hours	Explore dripstone gypsum and helicitite formations by lantern
River Styx - ♿	$22/16	2.5 hours	View a few underground waterways
Star Chamber	$25/20	2.5 hours	Visit site of the Tuberculosis Hospital by lantern light
Focus on Frozen Niagara	$16/12	1.5 hours	Photo-friendly tour of cave's most famous formations
Trog	–/$25	2.75 hours	Kids-only trip of rarely used passages
Intro to Caving	$35/28	3.5 hours	Hiking boots required, chest/hip measurement less than 42"
Wild Cave - ♿	$66	6 hours	Hiking boots , less than 42" chest/hip, and 16+ years old required

Youth is 6–12 years of age. Golden Age, Golden Access, and America the Beautiful Senior and Access Passes receive a 50% discount from the listed adult tour prices. Tour availability changes. Check online for a current schedule.

Campground and tour reservations can be made at (877) 444-6777 or recreation.gov

Camping & Lodging

Mammoth Cave Campground is the place to pitch your tent. Standard sites cost $25/night and can be reserved up to six months in advance at (877) 444-6777 or recreation.gov. Many standard sites accommodate RVs or trailers, but they do not have hook-ups. There are two RV-only sites (38-foot max) with full hookups available on a first-come, first-served basis for $50/night. It is the only campground with flush toilets. Showers are available at the nearby service center from March through November (a necessity if you plan on doing the Wild Cave Tour). It's also just a quarter mile from the visitor center, where all cave tours depart.

If you want to stay even closer to the visitor center, **The Lodge** (844.760.2283, mammothcavelodge.com) is located right next door. They offer simple cottages without heat, A/C, wi-fi, or TV starting at $71/night or more modern accommodations with all those things for $136+/night. They also offer a boarding kennel if you plan to bring your pet.

Cave Tours

Tours began in 1816 and have continued to the present day without interruption. All original tours entered the cave's Historic Entrance. Native Americans from some 4,000 years ago, wealthy easterners under the guidance of a slave named Stephen Bishop, and patients hoping an extended stay underground at Dr. Croghan's Tuberculosis Hospital would cure what ailed them, all have at least one thing in common: They walked through the Historic Entrance to the dark and mysterious Mammoth Cave. Today, it's reserved for tourists. Broadway, Gothic Avenue, Historic, Discovery, Star Chamber, Violet City Lantern, River Styx, and Trog tours all begin here. Park rangers guide visitors through the passages, slowly satisfying guests' curiosities while regaling them with stories of the cave's incredible history and geology.

Images of caves usually begin with dripping stalactites hanging from the ceiling; stubby, rounded stalagmites protruding from the floor; and a collection of other-worldly rock formations, but most of Mammoth Cave is drab and undecorated. Its plainness is caused by a hard, thick layer of sandstone just above the passageways. This cap prevents water, the key component of cave feature formation, from seeping in. However, there are a few locations, like Frozen Niagara, where the sandstone cap rock has dissolved, allowing water to seep through the cave's limestone strata. In these sections, formations were slowly created by water combined with carbon dioxide, which can dissolve

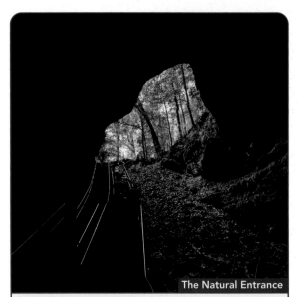
The Natural Entrance

World's Longest Caves

1). Mammoth Cave (USA, 415 Miles)
2). Sistema Sac Actum (Mexico, 372 Miles)
3). Jewel Cave (USA, 208 Miles)
4). Sistema Ox Bel Ha (Mexico, 168 Miles)
5). Shuanghedong Cave (China, 160 miles)
6). Optymistychna (Ukraine, 160 Miles)
7). Wind Cave (USA, 154 Miles)
8). Lechuguilla Cave (USA, 150 Miles)
9). Clearwater Cave (Malaysia, 147 Miles)
10). Fisher Ridge (USA, 130 Miles)

How was the cave formed?

Mammoth Cave's limestone was laid down 325 million years ago by an ancient sea covering much of the central U.S. The sea disappeared and a river proceeded to deposit a sandstone and shale cap on top of the limestone. Erosional forces slowly wore away the sandstone. About 10 million years ago cracks and holes formed, exposing limestone and allowing rainwater to work its way underground. Sinking streams began to hollow out the cave, and underground rivers formed.

Erosional forces played a part in the cave's formation, but they were not responsible for carving the passageways. The cave was created and continues to grow because limestone is soluble in groundwater under the right conditions. Water combined with carbon dioxide forms a weak carbonic acid able to dissolve limestone. Rainwater dissolved and carried away limestone previously inhabiting Mammoth's subterranean passages.

Fat Man's Misery

limestone. These solutes precipitate and over time—tens of thousands of years—accumulation of precipitates leads to cave formations. The most noteworthy of which can be seen on these tours: Frozen Niagara, Focus on Frozen Niagara (for photographers), Domes and Dripstones, Grand Avenue, and Great Onyx (a lantern tour of Great Onyx Cave).

Kentucky Cave Shrimp are the park's most notable occupants. These eyeless, albino shrimp were discovered by Stephen Bishop, and it was later determined that they live exclusively in the water of the cave's lower levels. While no tours explore these regions, you can walk the banks of River Styx, the Dead Sea, and Lake Lethe on the River Styx Tour.

While exploring the cave take note of the names of each room. Many names come from their shape or appearance, but others are derived from the cave's unique history. Names of owners, explorers, and visitors are all found among the passages and rooms. Booth's Amphitheater is named for Edwin Booth, who recited Hamlet's famous soliloquy there. Edwin is overshadowed by his infamous brother, John Wilkes Booth, who assassinated President Lincoln. Ole Bule Concert Hall is named for the famous violinist. John Muir, conservationist, writer, and national park advocate, visited in September of 1867, but he was just an "unknown nobody" walking to Florida at the time.

Tours come in all lengths and difficulties. Frozen Niagara is the easiest, and it is suitable for visitors who require the aid of a cane or walker. There's also an accessible tour, which utilizes an elevator to the Snowball Room. Wild Cave is the most strenuous. It's a real caving adventure. Participants spend much of the six-hour tour crawling on hands and knees as they squeeze through tight spaces. All Wild Cave participants must be at least 16 years old, meet certain size requirements (to fit through openings), and wear high-top, lace-up hiking boots. Bring a second pair of tennis shoes for the boot-cleaning session at the end of the tour. An

adult must accompany visitors under age 18. Cameras are not allowed, because there isn't an opportunity to use them. It is recommended that you wear gym shorts and a t-shirt under coveralls (provided). You will get dirty, but coin-operated showers are available at the service center on Mammoth Cave Parkway. All tours can be reserved at (877) 444-6777 or recreation.gov.

White-nose syndrome, a bat-killing fungal disease spreading through the United States, is present in Mammoth Cave. Do not wear clothing or carry objects that have been in another cave or mine to help prevent spread of this disease that has already resulted in the death of millions of bats. Likewise, whatever clothing and objects go into Mammoth Cave with you should not enter any other cave or mine. Be prepared to clean your shoes at the white-nose station after completing your tour. (It only takes a minute or two.) White-nose syndrome is not known to be harmful to humans.

Hiking & Backpacking

Above the dark caverns lies a world of trees, water, and light that is best enjoyed on foot. On a busy day several thousand visitors explore the park's underground world, but few of them experience what's right out in the open, just waiting to be hiked. Above ground are signs of the caves beneath your feet. Trails skirt alongside rivers that disappear into the earth via sinkholes.

There are 23 miles of hiking trails south of the Green River. Most of these begin at or near the visitor center or Mammoth Cave Campground. If you don't plan on taking a cave tour that enters through the Historic Entrance be sure to hike **River Styx Spring Trail**. This 0.6-mile trail leads past the Historic Entrance, which is worth a quick look. The trail continues to the site where River Styx exits Mammoth Cave. Eventually it leads to the banks of the Green River before looping back to the visitor center. If you care to extend River Styx Spring Trail, continue north along the 1.1-mile **Green River Bluffs Trail**. From this stretch you'll see Cave Island protruding from the Green River. Continue past the island to a scenic overlook. The trail concludes at the visitor center picnic area. Just south of the visitor center is **Heritage Trail**, a 0.3-mile loop around "Old Guides Cemetery," where tour guides like Stephen Bishop are buried. It terminates at sunset point, and then loops back to the visitor center. The 2.2-mile Echo River Trail and 2.0-mile Mammoth Dome Sink Trail connect to Heritage Trail Loop. **Cedar Sink Trail** is another good hiking opportunity. Its trailhead is located on Cedar Sink Road just south of Brownsville Road.

About 60 miles of trails are found north of the Green River. To reach them you must cross the river—using Green River Ferry—to Maple Springs Group Campground, which serves as a hub for many hiking trails. This is the best area of the park to escape crowds that may form near the visitor center. Even during peak season you may feel like you're the only person around (which might be true). The 8.1-mile **Sal Hollow Trail** and 2.8-mile **Buffalo Trail** are two of the most beautiful and secluded hikes. This region also provides excellent backpacking opportunities thanks to 13 campsites sprinkled throughout the backcountry. A backcountry permit is required. They cost $10 and can be reserved at recreation.gov during peak season and at the visitor center in winter.

Domes and Dripstones

Horseback Riding

The network of trails north of Green River is open to horse use. Campsites approved for stock are available at Maple Springs Group Campground. Day-use riders can park trailers at Lincoln Trailhead, First Creek Trailhead, Maple Springs Trailhead, Maple Springs Campground (across from the bulletin board), and Temple Hill Trailhead. Note that your trailer may be too long for the Green River Ferry. Be sure to follow all rules specific to visitors with horses. Double J Stables (270.286.8167, doublejstables.com) and Jesse James Riding Stables (270.773.2560) offer guided trail rides. Double J even rents horses.

Biking

Mammoth Cave Railroad Bike and Hike Trail is popular among pedalers. It follows the route used by early visitors arriving at Mammoth Cave from Park City by rail and stagecoach. You can also bike on 101 miles of roadway found in the park. During the off-season, the 10-mile circuit leaving the visitor center via Flint Ridge Road to Park Ridge Road to Cave City Road is a pleasant pedal with easy to moderate climbs. Bicycles are prohibited on hiking trails south of Green River and around the visitor center. Mountain biking is allowed on some trails north of the Green River including Big Hollow Trail. You'll find the trailhead near Maple Springs Campground.

Paddling

Paddling is another way to enjoy the park's above ground attractions. At normal water levels Green and Nolin Rivers provide a casual float for paddlers of any experience level. Green River meanders through the park for 25 miles, with boat landings at Dennison Ferry, Green River Ferry, and Houchin's Ferry. Be aware that there is an unmarked lock and dam past Houchin's Ferry

just a short distance beyond the park boundary. For a nice paddle launch your canoe or kayak on Nolin River just below Nolin River Dam at Tailwaters Recreation Area. Paddle downstream to the confluence of Nolin and Green Rivers. When you reach Green River paddle upstream a short distance to the take-out at Houchin's Ferry. Riverside and Island camping is permitted, but you'll need a free permit that you can pick up in-person at the visitor center. To rent a canoe or hire a guide, contact Big Buffalo Crossing Canoe (270.774.7883, bigbuffalocrossingcanoe.com), Cave Country Canoe (270.773.5552, cavecountrycanoeky.com), Green River Canoeing (270.773.5712, mammothcavecanoe.com), or Adventures of Mammoth Cave (270.773.6087, adventuresofmammothcave.com).

Fishing

A state fishing license is not required for fishing in Green and Nolin Rivers as long as you are within park boundaries. Bass, crappie, bluegill, muskellunge, and catfish are commonly caught in these waters.

Live bait other than worms is prohibited at Sloan's Crossing Pond, Green Pond, Doyle Pond, and First Creek Lake. Minnows and worms are allowed for river fishing. Fish size and quantity restrictions follow Kentucky Department of Fish & Wildlife regulations.

Visitor Center

Skip out on visiting the visitor center and you're missing the whole underground experience at Mammoth Cave. It is the point of departure for all cave tours and ranger programs. It also offers the standard fare (gifts, restrooms, backcountry permits, information), as well as a bunch of cool cave exhibits. If you have some free time and aren't joining a tour that uses the Natural Entrance, it's a short walk down the hill west of the visitor center. Standard hours are 9am until 5pm,

The River Styx

with extended hours on a few holidays. And the park is closed on Christmas Day.

Ranger Programs & For Kids

In addition to all the ranger-led cave tours, Mammoth Cave offers ranger-led walks, campfires, evening programs, and auditorium programs. All the activities (outside of cave tours) are free of charge and highly entertaining. Check a current schedule of events (available at the visitor center or park website) and join a program if you can.

Mammoth Cave offers a few kid-centric tours and programs. Trog is a kid-only (ages 8–12) cave tour. Introduction to Caving is open to children 10 and up, as well as their parents. Kids can also participate in the park's Junior Ranger Program. Grab a free Junior Ranger booklet at the Visitor Center Information Desk, and then complete enough activities to receive a Junior Ranger badge and certificate. There's also a Junior Cave Scientist Program for kids (ages 5–12). Download the booklet at the park website before arriving.

Flora & Fauna

More than 1,300 species of flowering plants grow here. This extreme biodiversity is due to the park's location in a transitional zone between cooler climates to the north and sub-tropical climates to the south. In spring, meadows erupt in a colorful display of wildflowers. Between February and March, more than 60 species of herbaceous wildflowers bloom to the delight of hikers. During this time, the park hosts an annual wildflower day, with programs focusing on flowers, ecology, and conservation held throughout the day by park rangers and volunteers. Refer to the park's website for event details. The park also protects a few swaths of grassland similar to what once covered 3 to 5 million acres of neighboring land before it was settled and developed.

You'll find several species of grasses including the western dwarf dandelion, which is common in western prairie states, but can only be found in Kentucky at Mammoth Cave National Park.

About 45 species of mammals inhabit this park. You'll probably see white-tailed deer and squirrels, while bobcats, coyotes, foxes, raccoons, skunks, beaver, and mink are seldom spotted. Wild turkeys, bald eagles, and blue herons are just a few bird species that make for decent birdwatching. Several species of bat reside in the cave. It also supports a variety of creepy-crawly insects, crustaceans, and fish. About 130 animal species are regular inhabitants of the cave system.

Pets & Accessibility

Pets are permitted on hiking trails but must be kept on a leash (less than six feet). All pets, except service animals, are prohibited in the cave and park buildings. The Lodge at Mammoth Cave allows them in Woodland Cottages, but they are not allowed in any other facilities. The hotel also operates a kennel for visitors with pets ($3.50 for the first hour).

The park offers wheelchair-accessible camping, picnicking, lodging, trails (Heritage, Sand Cave, and Sloan's Crossing Pond), dining, and visitor center facilities. Mammoth Cave Access Tour opens the cave up to individuals with limited mobility (with aid from a traveling companion). Wheelchairs, walkers, and canes will have to be decontaminated upon exciting the cave to limit the spread of White Nose Syndrome.

Weather

The weather above ground is moderate. Wet springs, hot summers, dry falls, and cold winters are the norm. While the weather above ground is difficult to predict, weather in the cave is easily anticipated. Subterranean temperatures only fluctuate a degree or two from 54°F. Cave temperature doesn't stabilize until you're a fair distance from its entrance.

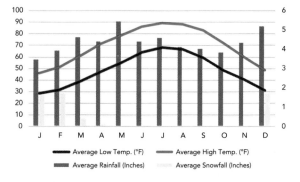

Average Low Temp. (°F) — Average High Temp. (°F) — Average Rainfall (Inches) — Average Snowfall (Inches)

Tips & Recommendations

Make cave tour reservations as soon as you've set the dates for your trip. While you can just show up and join a tour, the small, less-frequent tours fill early.

With that said, if your heart was set on a limited tour like Wild Cave but couldn't get tickets, it's a good idea to inquire about cancellations at the reservations desk (especially if you're a small group).

Summer visitors should consider hiking/paddling in the morning/evening (when it's coolest) and touring the cave in the middle of the afternoon/late afternoon (when it's hottest).

Sunset Point

Mammoth Cave is the main attraction, but there's plenty to do above ground, too. Here are a few recommendations to help with your trip planning.

Moderate Hikes: River Styx Spring (0.6 mile), Cedar Sink (1), Green River Bluffs (1.1)
Family Activities: Intro to Caving Tour, Bike Mammoth Cave Railroad Bike & Hike Trail, canoe the Green River
Guided Tours: Cave Tours!

Rainy Day Activities: Cave Tours, drive Flint Ridge Road and Park Ridge Road
History Enthusiasts: Violet City Lantern Tour, Old Guides Cemetery, Mammoth Cave Baptist Church
Sunset Spots: Sunset Point (Heritage Trail)
Sunrise Spots: Nothing's real reliable for sunsets/sunrises as the area is heavily wooded with a lot of hollows
Wildlife: Deer sightings are common around the visitor center and surrounding trail network

Beyond the Park...

Dining
Mammoth Cave Railway Café
5 Old Dixie Hwy, Park City
(270) 544-7873

The Dog Pound • (270) 773-8600
810 Sanders St, Cave City

Landers Pots Bottom • (270) 308-8655
105 Broadway St, Cave City

Cave City Creamery • (270) 547-8312
201 Hubbard Ln, Cave City

5 Broke Girls • (270) 786-8768
904 E Main St, Horse Cave
5brokegirls.com

Farmwald's Dutch Bakery & Deli
3678-3876 L and N Turnpike Rd,
Horse Cave • (270) 786-5600

Blue Holler Café • (270) 286-0013
7713 Nolin Dam Rd, Mam Cave

Lincoln County Corner
80 Stockholm Rd, Mam Cave
(270) 286-9005

Groceries
Save-A-Lot • (270) 773-2402
1445 KY-259 N, Brownsville

Walmart • (270) 678-1003
2345 Happy Valley Rd, Glasgow

Lodging
Grand Victorian Inn
5 Old Dixie Hwy, Park City
(270) 590-1935
grandvictorianinnky.com

Horse Cave Motel
319 S Dixie St, Horse Cave
(270) 786-2151

Serenity Hill B&B • (270) 597-9647
3600 Mam. Cave Rd, Brownsville
serenityhillbedandbreakfast.com

Campgrounds
Diamond Caverns RV Resort
1878 Mam Cave Pkwy, Park City
(270) 749-2891

Rock Cabin • (270) 773-4740
5091 Mam Cave Rd, Cave City
rockcabincamping.com

Singing Hills RV Park
4110 Mam Cave Rd, Cave City
(270) 773-3789
singinghillsrvpark.com

Jellystone Park • (270) 773-3840
950 Mam Cave Rd, Cave City
jellystonemammothcave.com

Horse Cave KOA
489 Flint Ridge Rd, Horse Cave
koa.com • (270) 786-2819

Festivals
Hillbilly Days • April
hillbillydays.com • Pikeville, KY

International Bar-B-Q Fest • May
bbqfest.com • Owensboro, KY

Nat'l Jug Band Jubilee • Sept
jugbandjubilee.com • Louisville

Kentucky Bourbon Fest • Sept
kybourbonfestival.com

World Chicken Fest • Sept
Dedicated to the first KFC
chickenfestival.com • London, KY

Attractions
Daniel Boone National Forest
Lots of beautiful sites (Red River Gorge Geological Area, Natural Bridge, Creation Falls, Chimney Top) • fs.usda.gov

Diamond Caverns • (270) 749-2233
1900 Mam Cave Pkwy, Park City
diamondcaverns.com

Onyx Cave • (270) 773-2323
93 Huckleberry Knob Rd, Cave City • onyxcave.com

Raven's Cross Escape Games
907 Mam Cave Rd, Cave City
ravenscrosshauntedvillage.com

Dinosaur World • (270) 773-4345
711 Mam Cave Rd, Cave City
dinosaurworld.com

KY Down Under • (270) 786-1010
3700 L&N Tpke Rd, Horse Cave
kentuckydownunder.com

Blue Holler Offroad Park
1494 Ollie Rd, Mammoth Cave
blueholleroffroadpark.com

Skyline Drive-in Theatre
5600 Hodgenville Rd, Summersville
skylinedrivein.com • (270) 670-5851

Lost River Cave • (270) 393-0077
2818 Nashville Rd, Bowling Green
lostrivercave.com

Corvette Museum • (270) 781-7973
350 Corvette Dr, Bowling Green
corvettemuseum.org

Bourbon Trail
kybourbontrail.com

Abraham Lincoln Birthplace NHS
2995 Lincoln Farm Rd, Hodgenville
nps.gov/abli • (270) 358-3137

Keeneland • (859) 254-3412
Thoroughbred racing
4201 Versailles Rd, Lexington
keeneland.com

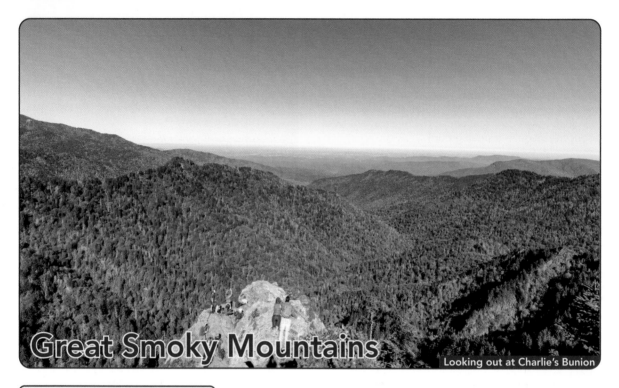

Looking out at Charlie's Bunion

Great Smoky Mountains

Phone: (865) 436-1200
Website: nps.gov/grsm

Established: June 15, 1934
Size: 521,621 Acres
Annual Visitors: 12 Million
Peak Season: June–October
Hiking Trails: 800+ Miles
Horse Trails: 500+ Miles

Activities: Hiking, Backpacking, Biking, Paddling, Fishing, Horseback Riding

Synchronous Fireflies: Elkmont (usually mid-June, permit required)

10 Campgrounds: $17.50–27/night Only Cades Cove and Smokemont are open year-round
Backcountry Camping: Permitted (reservation required)
Lodging: Le Conte Lodge ($159 per person per night, hike-in only)

Park Hours: All day, every day
Entrance Fee: None

The location and geography of Great Smoky Mountains National Park (GRSM) have led to two incredible phenomena: mass tourism and unparalleled biodiversity. Straddling the Smoky Mountains on the Tennessee–North Carolina border, the park is less than a day's drive from one-third of the U.S. population. On a busy day it might feel like they're visiting at the same time. They aren't, but the park's 12+ million annual visitors remains intimidating. That's more than double the next closest national park's annual total. Ten million more pass through each year for non-recreational purposes. These staggering numbers lead to frequent bouts of bumper-to-bumper traffic and occasional gridlock, making the park feel constrictive and small even though it is one of the largest protected areas in the country.

This region sought national park status to spare trees covering the mountains' slopes from logging and paper companies bent on stripping the land bare. Both sides got what they wanted. Many trees were clear-cut. Others were saved by a park. Eventually the region was designated an International Biosphere Reserve and a UNESCO World Heritage Site due to its biodiversity. GRSM is home to the greatest diversity of plant, animal, and insect life of any region in a temperate climate zone. A fact largely due to abundant annual precipitation (as much as 85 inches in some locations) and varied elevation (ranging from 876 feet at the mouth of Abrams Creek to 6,643 feet at the summit of Clingman's Dome). A hiker travelling from these two extremes experiences the same flora and fauna diversity as hiking from Georgia to Maine along the Appalachian Trail— 2,184 miles! That same hiker passes one of the largest blocks of deciduous old-growth forest in North

America, home to 100 species of trees, more than any other U.S. National Park.

For centuries Cherokee Indians have lived among these trees, hunting and gathering what they needed to survive. Mining claims and the Indian Removal Act forced them to Oklahoma on what came to be known as the "Trail of Tears." A few small American settlements sprang up, but substantial amounts of gold were never found. As the East continued to develop, industry's eye focused on the area's most abundant natural resource, its trees. By the mid-1920s, 300,000 acres had been clear-cut by logging and paper companies. Dramatic changes caused by reckless logging inspired Horace Kephart, author and park supporter, to ask the question "Shall the Smoky Mountains be made a national park or a desert?"

A question demanding an immediate answer. In 1926, President Calvin Coolidge signed a bill authorizing the formation of Great Smoky Mountains National Park, with the provision that no federal funds would be used to procure land. It was a serious hurdle to overcome. Parks in the West were formed mostly from land already owned by the federal government. Here on the East Coast, some 6,600 tracts of land needed to be purchased from more than 1,000 private landowners and a handful of logging and paper companies for a total price of $10 million. People from all walks of life banded together, donating every penny they could spare. Overwhelming public support prompted Tennessee and North Carolina to promise $3 million for the potential park, bringing the total to $5 million—still only half the required sum.

Thankfully, a philanthropist with deep pockets came to the park's aid. John D. Rockefeller, Jr., son of the wealthiest man in America, ultimately donated the remaining $5 million balance. He made just one request: that a plaque honoring his mother be placed within the park (Rockefeller Memorial at Newfound Gap).

Despite this promising turn, the stock market crash in 1929 resulted in North Carolina and Tennessee being unable to honor their pledges to the new park. During these troubling times, Franklin D. Roosevelt intervened, allocating $1.5 million of federal funds to complete the land purchase. This marked the first time the U.S. government spent its taxpayer dollars to buy land for a national park. Effort, time, and money from small communities to wealthy philanthropists and governments helped create what is now the most popular national park in the United States.

When to Go

The park is open all year and it's nearly perfect in summer and fall. This near perfection is nobody's secret. A typical weekend summer day draws more than 60,000 visitors. Visitation is strong all year long, but it peaks from June through October. During this time, there are plenty of reasons to visit: synchronous fireflies (June at Elkmont, permit required), wildflowers (spring–summer, specifically flame azaleas in June at Gregory Bald and Andrew's Bald), and fall foliage (October). Regardless when you visit, an early start is a good idea. The vast majority of visitors get out and about between 9am and 6pm, and during this time you may want to avoid popular destinations like Cades Cove, Newfound Gap, and Roaring Fork. As always, the best way to escape the crowds is to park your car and hike. Relatively speaking, few visitors explore the park's interior on foot.

Transportation & Airports

Public transportation is not available, but Gatlinburg offers a trolley service (gatlinburgtrolley.org, Tan Route to park, $2 fare, June–October).

Asheville Regional Airport (AVL) is 55 miles east of the park's Cherokee Entrance. McGhee Tyson Airport (TYS), just south of Knoxville in Alcoa, TN is 50 miles west of the Gatlinburg Entrance.

Directions

There are many park entrances, including a handful of dead-end roads that provide more peaceful experiences, but the vast majority of visitors enter via US Highway 441, which bisects the park. US-441 enters the park less than 3 miles from Gatlinburg, TN. And exits the park less than four miles from Cherokee, NC. There are many routes to reach the park, but one of the most scenic is to take Blue Ridge Parkway (nps.gov/blri) from the Asheville, NC area.

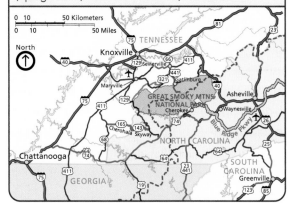

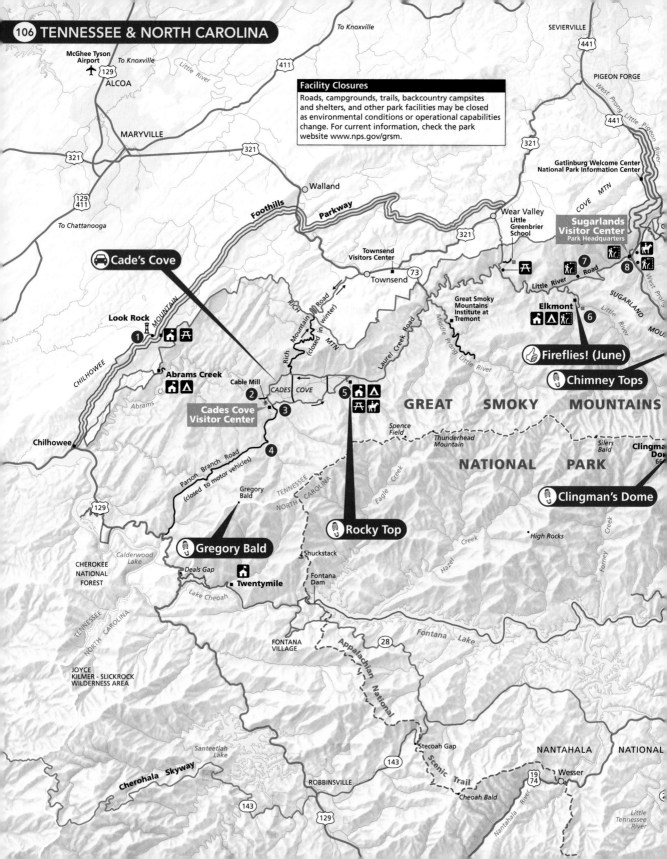

Facility Closures
Roads, campgrounds, trails, backcountry campsites and shelters, and other park facilities may be closed as environmental conditions or operational capabilities change. For current information, check the park website www.nps.gov/grsm.

McGhee Tyson Airport
To Knoxville
ALCOA
MARYVILLE
To Chattanooga

SEVIERVILLE
PIGEON FORGE
Gatlinburg Welcome Center
National Park Information Center

Walland

Little Greenbrier School

Townsend Visitors Center
Townsend

Wear Valley

Sugarlands Visitor Center
Park Headquarters

Foothills   Parkway

Great Smoky Mountains Institute at Tremont

Cade's Cove

Look Rock

Elkmont

Fireflies! (June)

Chimney Tops

Abrams Creek
Cable Mill

CADES COVE

Cades Cove Visitor Center

CHILHOWEE
Abrams

Chilhowee

GREAT   SMOKY   MOUNTAINS

Spence Field

Thunderhead Mountain

Silers Bald

Clingmans Dome

Clingman's Dome

NATIONAL   PARK

Gregory Bald

Gregory Bald

Rocky Top

CHEROKEE NATIONAL FOREST

Calderwood Lake

Deals Gap

Twentymile

Lake Cheoah

Shuckstack

Fontana Dam

Fontana Village

High Rocks

JOYCE KILMER - SLICKROCK WILDERNESS AREA

FONTANA VILLAGE

Appalachian   National

Fontana   Lake

Santeetlah Lake

Cherohala   Skyway

ROBBINSVILLE

Scenic   Trail

Stecoah Gap

Cheoah Bald

NANTAHALA   NATIONAL

Wesser

Nantahala River

Little Tennessee River

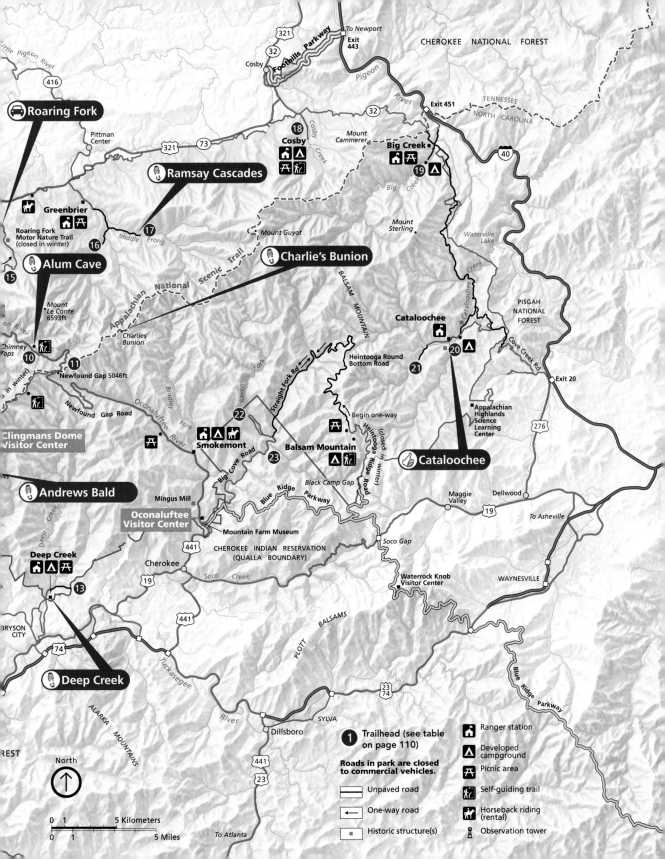

CHEROKEE NATIONAL FOREST

321
32
Cosby
Foothills Parkway
To Newport
Exit 443

Exit 451

TENNESSEE
NORTH CAROLINA

32

Pigeon

River

Mount Cammerer

40

18 Cosby

Cosby Creek

Big Creek

19

Big Creek

416

🚗 **Roaring Fork**

Pittman Center

Little Pigeon River

321 **73**

🦶 **Ramsay Cascades**

Big Creek

Greenbrier

Roaring Fork Motor Nature Trail (closed in winter) **16**

17

Middle Prong

Mount Guyot

Mount Sterling

Waterville Lake

PISGAH NATIONAL FOREST

🦶 **Alum Cave**

15

Mount Le Conte 6593ft

Appalachian National Scenic Trail

Charlies Bunion

🦶 **Charlie's Bunion**

BALSAM MOUNTAIN

Cataloochee

Cataloochee

Cove Creek Rd

20

🏕 Chimney Tops
10

11

Raven Fork

Straight Fork Rd

21

Heintooga Round Bottom Road

Newfound Gap 5046ft

in winter
🏕

Newfound Gap Road

Oconaluftee River

Bradley Fork

Begin one-way

(closed in winter) Heintooga Ridge Road

Appalachian Highlands Science Learning Center

Exit 20

276

Clingmans Dome Visitor Center

22

🏕🐎 **Smokemont**

🏕

🦶 **Andrews Bald**

Mingus Mill

23

🏕 **Balsam Mountain**

Black Camp Gap

Blue Ridge Parkway

🏕

Cataloochee

Maggie Valley

Dellwood

To Asheville

Oconaluftee Visitor Center

Mountain Farm Museum

Soco Gap

19

🦶 **Deep Creek**

441

CHEROKEE INDIAN RESERVATION (QUALLA BOUNDARY)

Cherokee

19

Soco Creek

Waterrock Knob Visitor Center

WAYNESVILLE

Deep Creek

🏕🏕🏕

13

BRYSON CITY

74

PLOTT

BALSAMS

Blue Ridge Parkway

441

Tuckasegee

ALARKA MOUNTAINS

River

23 74

Dillsboro

SYLVA

🦶 **Deep Creek**

North

↑

441

23

To Atlanta

1 **Trailhead** (see table on page 110)

Roads in park are closed to commercial vehicles.

Unpaved road

One-way road

Historic structure(s)

🏕 Ranger station

🏕 Developed campground

🏕 Picnic area

🏕 Self-guiding trail

🐎 Horseback riding (rental)

🗼 Observation tower

0 1   5 Kilometers

0 1   5 Miles

There's smoke in those hills

Great Smoky Mountains Camping (Fees are per night)

Name	Location	Open	Fee	Sites	Notes
Abrams Creek	West side, NE of Chilhowee	mid-March–October	$17.50	16	RVs up to 12'
Balsam Mtn	Heintooga Ridge Rd, SE corner	mid-May–mid-October	$17.50	46	RVs up to 30'
Big Creek	NE corner, take Exit 451 (I-40)	mid-March–October	$17.50	12	Tent-only
Cades Cove	Entrance of Cades Cove Loop	All Year	$25	159	RVs up to 40'
Cataloochee	East side off Cove Creek Road	mid-March–October	$25	27	RVs up to 31'
Cosby	NE corner, just south of TN-73	mid-March–October	$17.50	157	RVs up to 25'
Deep Creek	North of Bryson City	April–October	$25	92	RVs up to 26'
Elkmont	Near Sugarlands Visitor Center	mid-March–November	$25–27	220	RVs up to 32'
Smokemont	Near Oconaluftee VC	All Year	$25	142	RVs up to 40'
Backcountry	A permit is required for all overnight stays in the park's backcountry. It costs $4 per person, per night, with a maximum fee of $20/person. Apply online or in-person at the Backcountry Office at Sugarlands Visitor Center up to 30 days in advance. You must stay at a designated campsite or shelter. For more information and trip planning help call the Backcountry Information Office at (865) 436-1297.				

Frontcountry camping reservations can be made up to six months in advance at 877-444-6777 or recreation.gov. There are no showers or electric/water hookups in the park. Shower facilities are available in nearby communities. Inquire about the nearest facilities upon check-in. Group sites are available at Big Creek, Cades Cove, Cataloochee, Cosby, Deep Creek, Elkmont, and Smokemont (15–30 people/site, $30–75/night, reservations required)

Great Smoky Mountains Lodging

Name	Open	Fee	Location & Notes
Le Conte Lodge (Hike-in only)	March–November	$159/person per night	Shortest hike is 5.5 miles one-way (Alum Cave) • Meals included • 2 and 3 bedroom cabins available • Reserve one year in advance

More information and reservations are available at (865) 429-5704 or lecontelodge.com

Camping & Lodging

The park has nine frontcountry campgrounds. If you're looking for a central location, the best choice is Elkmont or Smokemont. But, considering the park's size, it's better to decide what you want to do, and then choose your camping locations accordingly. Personal favorites are Big Creek, Cataloochee, and Deep Creek, but they're in relatively remote regions. All campgrounds have running water and flush toilets. Reservations can be made up to six months in advance at recreation.gov. Reservations are a good idea, especially if you're planning on visiting between June and October. Cades Cove and Smokemont are the only year-round options.

As for lodging, you have one option: **Le Conte Lodge**. It's absolutely glorious, but, and this is a big but, you can only reach it by foot. The shortest route is hiking 5.5-miles up Alum Cave Trail, which is a steep, steady climb to the top of Mount Le Conte. That isn't stopping park enthusiasts. You'll want to make reservations a year in advance to stay here. And this unique privilege has a price tag. It costs about $159 per person per night (meals included). Not bad, when you think about running a lodge disconnected from civilization.

Driving

Great Smoky Mountains is a motorists' park. Indeed, the idea of a park in the Smoky Mountains drew much of its support from the people's demands for a highway between Knoxville and Asheville. Today, more than 384 miles of drivable roads, most of them paved, provide unprecedented access to the Smokies' interior. Cades Cove Loop is the park's most popular destination, and Roaring Fork Motor Nature Trail isn't far behind. Both routes allow visitors to see wildlife and nature from the comfort of their vehicle.

The perimeter of **Cades Cove** is traced by an 11-mile, one-way loop road, beginning and ending at the eastern terminus of Laurel Creek Road. If you'd like to conclude your driving tour of Cades Cove prematurely (maybe because of excessive traffic), you can exit the loop via two seasonal, steep, winding, unpaved roads: Rich Mountain Road and Parson Branch Road. A pair of bisecting roads also give you options to cut the loop short. If traffic is manageable, you'll want to stick around, because Cades Cove provides some of the best opportunities to spot white-tailed deer and black bear. You'll also find the largest open-air museum in the Smoky Mountains, where pioneer homesteads, barns, churches, and mills have been restored to their 19th-century appearances. While many of these

Clingman's Dome

structures are removed from the road, all of them are well-marked and easily accessible.

The loop starts where Smoky Mountain settlement began. First stop is also the first cabin built in the Smokies, John Oliver Place. Next, you'll find Primitive Baptist Church, which was established in 1827, but the congregation worshiped in a small log structure until 1887 when the larger white frame church (seen at this stop) was erected. A small cemetery where many of the early settlers are buried is located nearby. Religion was the cause of many disagreements in the Cove. In 1839, expelled members of Primitive Baptist Church formed Missionary Baptist Church (site 7). (Once the Civil War began, the church was forced to close its doors because the congregation was mostly Union sympathizers, but Confederate support also ran deep among the cove's 700 citizens.) Continuing along the loop is a short spur road to Abrams Falls Trailhead and Elijah Oliver Place. A 0.5-mile hike leads to the homestead of another Oliver family. It's five miles (roundtrip) to 20-foot Abrams Falls. John Cable Mill and Cades Cove Visitor Center are located near the loop's midway point. Rangers, gifts, and restrooms make this one of the more popular stops, but you shouldn't leave without browsing the time-period exhibits on display. The only original building left behind is the mill where early settlers ground corn. All others were brought here by the National Park Service to aid in their demonstrations of early farm life (schedules are available at the visitor center). Energy and attitudes permitting, there are a few more sites to see on the second half of the loop. You'll pass Henry Whitehead Place, Cades Cove Nature Trail, Dan Lawson Place, and Carter Shields Cabin before completing the full circle. The loop is open from sunrise until sunset, and you'll often find cars lined up at the gate before it opens. Cars are not permitted on Wednesdays, mid-June through September. These are designated vehicle-free days for pedestrians (hikers and bikers). It can still be busy, even with bikers. While the loop is only 11 miles, with modest hills, it's a workout, especially in the summer heat.

Great Smoky Mountains Hiking Trails (Distances are roundtrip)

Name	Location (# on map)	Length	Difficulty Rating & Notes
Look Rock	Foothills Parkway (1)	0.5 mile	E – Less scenic than Clingman's Dome, fewer visitors
Abram's Falls	Cades Cove Loop, past Stop #10 (2)	5.0 miles	M – Flat, popular, well-maintained trail leading to a 20-foot waterfall
Cades Cove Nature Trail	About 1 mile past Cades Cove Visitor Center (3)	2.0 miles	E – Great family hike • Brochures explain the area's cultural and historical significance
Gregory Bald - 🥾	Cades Cove, Parson Branch Road (4)	11.3 miles	S – Bald named for a man murdered by Confederate troops, wildflowers (usually in June)
Rich Mountain	Cades Cove (5)	8.5 miles	S – Excellent views of Cades Cove and wildlife
Rocky Top - 🥾	Cades Cove Picnic Area, Anthony Creek Trailhead (5)	13.9 miles	S – Uphill, Follow Anthony Creek Trail (past horse camp), right on Bote Mtn Trail, left on Appalachian Trail (Spence Field) to Rocky Top, wildflowers (June)
Cucumber Gap	Elkmont/Little River (6)	5.6 miles	E – Wildflowers in spring and a 20-foot waterfall
Laurel Falls - 🥾	Laurel Falls (7)	2.6 miles	E – One of the park's most popular destinations
Sugarlands Valley Nature Trail	Sugarlands Visitor Center (8)	0.5 mile	E – Self-guiding nature trail that is accessible to individuals in wheelchairs
Chimney Tops - 🥾	Newfound Gap Road (9)	4.0 miles	S – One of the most popular hikes in the park, stairs!
Alum Cave - 🥾	Alum Cave Bluffs (10)	4.6 miles	S – Views to the west from Cliff Top and to the east from Myrtle Point • 11 miles to Mount Le Conte
Charlie's Bunion - 🥾	Newfound Gap (11)	8.1 miles	M – Follows the Appalachian Trail to a rock outcropping named for Charlie Conner's bunion
Clingman's Dome - 🥾	Clingman's Dome (12)	0.5 mile	M – Short but steep hike to an observation tower atop the highest peak in the Smoky Mountains
Andrews Bald - 🥾	Clingman's Dome (12)	3.5 miles	M – Great, wildflowers (usually in June)
Indian Creek - 🥾	End of Deep Creek Rd (13)	1.6 miles	E – Toms Branch Falls and Indian Creek Falls
Rainbow Falls - 🥾	Rainbow Falls (14)	5.4 miles	M – 80-foot falls produces rainbows when sunny
Bullhead	Cherokee Orchard Loop (14)	14.4 miles	S – Least traveled route to Mount Le Conte
Grotto Falls - 🥾	Roaring Fork Motor Nature Trail Stop #5 (15)	2.8 miles	M – Pass old-growth hemlock forest to a 25-foot high falls that you hike above and below
Porter's Creek	Greenbrier Entrance (16)	4.0 miles	M – Spring wildflowers, old-growth forest and waterfalls • Spur trail (1 mile) to cantilevered barn
Ramsay Cascades - 🥾	Greenbrier Entrance (17)	8.0 miles	S – Tallest waterfall in the park at 100 feet
Hen Wallow Falls - 🥾	Cosby Picnic Area (18)	4.4 miles	M – Hike to a narrow 90-foot high waterfall
Mt Cammerer - 🥾	Cosby, Lower Gap Trailhead (18)	12.0 miles	S – Panoramic views and a fire tower built by the CCC in the 1930s
Mouse Creek Falls - 🥾	Big Creek Trail, Waterville Road, Exit 451 from I-40 (19)	4.0 miles	M – Follows an old railroad grade, there's a nice swimming hole (Midnight Hole) at 1.4 miles
Boogerman Loop	Cataloochee Camp (20)	7.4 miles	M – Good hike in a less popular portion of the park
Little Cataloochee	Just west of Cataloochee Campground (20)	6.0 miles	M – Hike through remnants of Little Cataloochee Cove where 1,200 people used to live
Woody Place - 🥾	End of Cataloochee Rd (21)	2.0 miles	E – Follow the Rough Fork Trail to an 1880s home
Smokemont Loop	Smokemont Camp (22)	6.5 miles	M – The journey begins on Bradley Fork Trail
Mingo Falls - 🥾	Qualla Boundary (23)	0.4 mile	E – Spectacular 120-foot waterfall (outside the park)

Difficulty Ratings: E = Easy, M = Moderate, S = Strenuous

Roaring Fork Nature Trail is a 6-mile one-way road beginning and ending in Gatlinburg. Its 10 mph speed limit is testament to the amount of twists, turns, and traffic you'll encounter. Along the way you'll pass several restored homes and buildings and Rainbow Falls Trailhead. Rainbow Falls is best seen on a sunny day after a heavy rain, when the trail lives up to its name and the Place of a Thousand Drips will be dripping. Rain or shine, the hike is pleasant any time of year.

Newfound Gap and Clingman's Dome Roads are must-sees. Balsam Mountain and Heintooga Ridge Roads around Balsam Mountain, and Cove Creek Road to the Cataloochee Valley are great places to avoid summer and fall crowds while enjoying similar majestic views of the Smoky Mountains.

🚶🚶 Hiking & Backpacking

The Smokies offer more than 800 miles of hiking trails, including 70 miles of the Appalachian Trail. Many of which either start at or lead to 9 frontcountry campgrounds, dozens of backcountry campsites, or 15 backcountry shelters. Whether it's a multi-day trek along the Appalachian Trail, a short jaunt through historic settlements; a knee-jarring, mountain-climbing work-out to a 6,000-foot summit; or a casual creek-side stroll to a cascading waterfall, the Smokies have it all.

Spring brings about some of the most colorful wildflower displays on the East Coast. Creekside trails are ideal locations to see wildflowers due to cool moist air and wet ground. **Oconaluftee River Trail** (begins at Oconaluftee Visitor Center), **Deep Creek Trail** (begins at the end of Deep Creek Road), **Kanati Fork Trail** (begins just north of Kephart Prong footbridge on Newfound Gap Road), **Little River Trail** (begins just before Elkmont Campground Entrance), **Middle Prong Trail** (begins at the end of Tremont Road), and **Porters Creek Trail** (begins at Greenbrier Entrance) are all excellent spring wildflower hikes. In the Smokies, bald is beautiful! Andrew and Gregory are two of the best balds in town, providing spectacular late spring/early summer flame azalea and rhododendron blooms. To reach **Andrews Bald**, follow Forney Ridge Trail for 1.8 miles (one-way) from its trailhead located along the paved trail to Clingman's Dome. Beginning near the park's highest point, the trail starts with a fairly steep descent, levels off, and then climbs up to the bald. Views from the bald are often diminished by fog. The trail to **Gregory Bald** is no less stunning, especially when wildflowers are in bloom (typically in June), but it is considerably longer and more difficult. It's possible to reach the bald from either Gregory Ridge or Gregory

Indian Creek Falls

Bald Trails. Ridge is longer (11.3 miles roundtrip), but hiking a bit further prevents you from committing to exiting the park via Parsons Branch Road (one-way). Both routes are strenuous.

The park's waterfalls are popular hiking destinations all year. Spring snowmelt causes streams and waterfalls to swell, but trails are often muddy and busy. Crowds subside from late fall to early spring, and trees have shed their leaves opening up panoramic views. **Cataract Falls** is a short hike departing from Sugarlands Visitor Center. The paved path to **Laurel Falls** is one of the easiest and most popular waterfall hikes in the park. The routes to **Grotto** and **Abrams Falls** are a little more challenging, but nothing to intimidate the average hiker. Then there's **Ramsay Cascades**, the tallest waterfall in the park, and a fairly strenuous day-hike. There's plenty of beautiful scenery along the way, and most of the hike is a gradual climb, before a little optional scrambling near the cascades.

Late Spring/early summer is a great time to hike to one of the park's sun-soaked, wind-swept balds or 6,000-foot summits. To reach a summit you must inevitably head uphill, but not all these trails are difficult. **Clingman's Dome Trail** (0.5 mile) leads to the park's highest point, but it's also one of the easiest summit hikes. One of the most difficult trails is the 14.4-mile **Bullhead Trail** to Mount Le Conte. It's sure to make you sweat as you gain 3,993 feet in elevation along the way. **Rocky Top** is another strenuous summit (follow the trails listed in the hiking table), but it rewards hardy hikers with exceptional views. With a pinch of planning you can take one of four trails to the top of **Mount Le Conte** (the park's third highest peak) and spend a night at Le Conte Lodge (lecontelodge.com). The pinch is that you'll need to make reservations up to a year in advance (or get lucky and secure a cancelled spot). **Alum Cave**

Rainbow Falls

Trail is relatively short, steep, and strenuous, but it provides some of the most majestic scenery anywhere in the park. **Trillium Gap** and **Boulevard Trails** are longer and more gradual. Bullhead Trail is both long and difficult. No matter which route you choose it's a workout, but your effort will be rewarded with a night at Le Conte Lodge, a Smoky Mountain paradise. **Chimney Tops Trail** begins near Alum Cave Trailhead, on the opposite side of Newfound Gap Road. Chimney Tops is an outdoor Stairmaster, leading to panoramic views. In the past, hikers would scramble up a rocky outcropping, but stay on the correct side of the posted signs.

For **easy hikes** look no further than the old homesteaders' villages. Woody Place, Cades Cove (Nature), Porter's Creek, and Little Cataloochee Trails are relatively flat hikes that allow visitors to reimagine life in the Smokies during the 1800s.

Backpackers must obtain a permit (available online or in person at Sugarlands Visitor Center's Backcountry Information Office) and stay at designated campsites or shelters. Permits cost $4 per person, per night, with a maximum fee of $20 per individual. They can be reserved up to 30 days in advance. To plan your

backpacking trip, visit the park's website or call the Backcountry Information Office (865.436.1297). It's always a good idea to discuss your plans with a park ranger before setting out to get more accurate trail conditions.

Biking
Bicycles are allowed on most of the roads within the park, but that doesn't mean you should bike them. **Cades Cove Loop Road**—the one recommended location—is narrow, hilly, and packed with motorists, but it gets better during scheduled motor-free periods (Wednesday and Saturday mornings from mid-June through September). During these times, cyclists are free to enjoy the sights and sounds of the Cove, without having to navigate motorist traffic. (You may want to check if this is still going on for your visit as it was just a pilot program in 2020.) Regardless when you visit, try to pedal the loop early in the day, but expect it to be busy pretty much any time during peak season or any pleasant weekend. Bicycles can be rented ($7.50/hour) from Cades Cove Campground Store (865.448.9034, cadescovetrading.com) near the campground, which is open every day from 9am until 4pm.

If you're lucky and catch Clingman's Dome Road when it's free of snow but not open to motorists, it's a great challenge for cyclists. Generally I'd say biking early or late when it's open to motorists, but Clingman's Dome is a popular sunrise/sunset destination. You'd be better off dealing with the cold and trying it during the shoulder seasons.

Bikes are prohibited on all park trails except Gatlinburg, Oconaluftee River, and Lower Deep Creek Trails.

Paddling
Mountain lakes and streams provide water activities ranging from leisurely flatwater paddling to adrenaline-pumping whitewater runs. Paddling offers an unobtrusive, peaceful, and less stressful way to view wildlife and fall colors. Fontana and Calderwood Lakes are the most popular locations for flatwater. Both lakes skirt the park's southeastern boundary. Fontana Lake has a handful of marinas between Bryson City and Fontana Dam where you can launch your boat. At Calderwood Lake, a 5-mile dammed section of the Little Tennessee River, you'll find a boat ramp near Cheoah Dam. It's an ideal location for an out-and-back paddle.

Steep mountain slopes and an abundance of rain and snow make for some of the East Coast's best whitewater paddling. River Rat Tubing (865.448.8888, smokymtnriverrat.com), Smoky Mountain Outdoors (800.771.7238, smokymountainrafting.com), and Rafting in the Smokies (800.771.7238, raftinginthesmokies.com) offer whitewater rafting, kayaking, and tubing trips on the north side of the park. Nantahala Outdoor Center (828.785.4839, noc.com), Endless River Adventures (828.488.6199, endlessriveradventures.com), Adventurous Fast Rivers Rafting (800.438.7238, nantahalarafting.com), and Wildwater Rafting (866.319.8870, wildwater-rafting.com) offer rafting trips on the south side of the park. Deep Creek Tube Center (828.488.6055, deep-creekcamping.com) rents tubes for $7 to take down Deep Creek, which looks pretty fun.

Fishing

Fishing is allowed year-round in all the park's 2,900 miles of streams and open waters. Depending on which state you are in, a valid Tennessee or North Carolina fishing license is required. Trout (brook, brown, and rainbow) and smallmouth bass have a seven-inch minimum and possession limit of five. You must use artificial flies or lures with a single hook. Outfitters like Smoky Mountain Angler (865.325.6036, smokymoun-tainangler.com), Fly Fishing the Smokies (828.488.7665, flyfishingthesmokies.net), Fightmaster Fly Fishing (865.607.2886, fightmasterflyfishing.com), and R&R Fly Fishing (865.448.0467, randrflyfishing.com) can help you catch your limit.

Horseback Riding

More than 500 miles of trails are open to horses. Five drive-in horse campgrounds are open from April through October: Anthony Creek (near Cades Cove Campground), Big Creek, Cataloochee, Round Bottom (near Oconaluftee), and Tow String (near Oconaluftee).

Horseless guests would be making an excellent choice by joining Cades Cove Riding Stables (865.448.9009, cadescovestables.com) or Smokemont Riding Stables (828.497.2373, smokemontridingstable.com) for a ride. Cades Cove offers a 1-hour ride ($35), carriage rides ($15), and even hayrides ($15). Smokemont offers hour-long rides for $35, 2.5-hour waterfall rides for $87.50, or a 4-hour ride for $140. They also offer wagon rides along the Oconaluftee River for $15 per rider. There are also two horseback riding outfitters near the Gatlinburg entrance. Smoky Mountain Riding Stable (865.436.5634, smokymountainridingstables.com) offers a 45-minute ride for $26.50 per rider. Sugarlands Riding Stables (865.436.3535, sugarlandsridingstables.com) offers 1-hour ($35), 1.5-hour ($52.50), 2-hour, and 4-hour ($140) rides. All horseback tours are walking only and typically offered from March through November.

Ramsay Cascades (Thanks, Sam & Kaylin!)

Visitor Centers & Museums

Sugarlands Visitor Center is located right along US-441, two miles south of Gatlinburg. It's open every day except Christmas, and holds standard hours from 9am until 5pm (until 4:30pm in winter, until 6pm in spring). You'll find exhibits, a park film, bookstore, gift shop, and restrooms. It's also the location of the park's Backcountry Information Office (865.436.1297). They're your one-stop shop for backpacking information, but backpackers can also reserve permits up to 30 days in advance through the park's website as well.

Elk near Oconaluftee

Cades Cove Visitor Center is located at the mid-way point of Cades Cove Loop. It's open every day except Christmas, and holds standard hours of 9am until 5pm (shortened to 4:30 in winter, and extended until 5:30 in November, and 6:30 in March, September, and October). You'll find a variety of outdoor and indoor structures, bookstore, gift shop, and restrooms.

Cable Mill is located in Cades Cove and is open daily from mid-March through October, and on weekends in November from 9am until 5pm.

Clingman's Dome Visitor Center, located at Clingman's Dome, the highest peak in the Smokies, is open from April through November from 10am until 6pm (until 4 in summer, and until 5 in November). It's a small facility with a bookstore, gift shop, and restrooms.

Mingus Mill is located along US-441, just a few miles north of Oconaluftee Visitor Center. It's open from April through October, and on weekends in November from 9am until 5pm. It's an old water-powered grist mill, and a pretty interesting stop that shouldn't take you more than an hour to check out.

Oconaluftee Visitor Center is located on US-441, two miles north of Cherokee, NC. It's open every day except Christmas, and holds standard hours from 8am until 5pm (shortened to 4:30 in winter, and extended to 6 in April and May). The Mountain Farm Museum, where you'll find various early farm-life structures and even a few farm animals, is located right behind the visitor center. Bookstore, gift shop, and restrooms are also on site.

Great Smoky Mountains Association runs Visitor/ Welcome Centers in **Sevierville** (3099 Winfield Dunn Pkwy), **Gatlinburg** (1011 Banner Rd), and **Townsend**

(7906 E Lamar Alexander Pkwy). All three hold pretty standard hours (about 9am-5pm) and are open every day except Christmas (Townsend also closes for Thanksgiving). They're convenient locations to help get oriented before entering the park (or exploring the respective gateway community).

Great Smoky Mountains Institute at Tremont (9275 Tremont Rd, Townsend, TN, gsmit.org) is a national park partner offering educational programs, including photography workshops and hiking/backpacking outings. You'll also find the trailhead for Spruce Flat Falls nearby, but there are only a handful of parking spaces.

Appalachian Highlands Science Learning Center (107 Purchase Road, Waynesville, NC) is a research center that studies things like air quality and biodiversity. There are also a few hiking trails in the area.

Ranger Programs & For Kids
Attending a ranger program should be a mandatory requirement at all national parks. Be sure to browse a current schedule of ranger-led activities online or at a visitor center, and then pick out which program(s) you'll attend. You'll find ranger-led Cable Mill Demonstrations and hayrides ($17) in Cades Cove, but there are many other hikes, lunches, talks, and campfires held throughout the park where rangers impart their wisdom and humor to those willing to listen. One ranger program even invites visitors to learn to play the hog fiddle. Seasonal programs like Autumn Arrives and The Smokies Synchronous Fireflies (mid-June) are so unique and enjoyable you may want to plan your trip around them.

The park offers ranger-led programs for children from spring to fall (check online or in person at a visitor center for a current schedule of events). Children between the ages of 5 and 12 can become Junior Rangers. Junior Ranger Activity Booklets can be purchased for $2.50 at any visitor centers or at Elkmont and Cades Cove Campgrounds. Complete the booklet, and then return to a visitor center to receive a junior ranger badge. The junior ranger program runs all year long.

Flora & Fauna
Incomparable biodiversity resulted in the park's designation as a UNESCO World Heritage Site and International Biosphere Reserve. It is home to more than 1,600 species of flowering plants, which helped inspire billing as "the Wildflower National Park." Spring/early summer is the ultimate time to view an abundance of colorful blossoms. The week-long

Wildflower Pilgrimage Festival celebrates these living decorations and features programs and guided walks that explore the park's amazing biodiversity. You can help save the wildflowers by staying on hiking trails. It is illegal to pick wildflowers. Beyond flowers, you'll find more than 100 native tree species and over 100 native shrub species. There are more tree species here than any other U.S. National Park, and more species than in all Northern Europe.

More than 200 species of birds, 50 native species of fish, 80 types of reptiles and amphibians, and 66 species of mammals are protected in the park. Spotting wildlife is often easiest in winter after trees have shed their leaves. During the remainder of the year, open areas like Cataloochee and Cades Cove are great spots for wildlife viewing. White-tailed deer, wild turkey, squirrels, and bats are your most probable sightings, but don't count out seeing the symbol of the park, the black bear. The Smokies provide the largest protected bear habitat in the East, and it's home to approximately 1,500 of them. The park's 30 species of salamander are enough to earn the title of "Salamander Capital of the World." However, the most unique wildlife display comes from one of its smallest occupants, the **Smoky Mountain Synchronous Fireflies**. The name sounds like a circus act—a description not far from reality—but these tiny insects aren't performing for you; their flashing light patterns are part of a mating display. It's special because the individual fireflies are able to synchronize their lights. Such a spectacle is only known to occur in a few other places in the world (like Congaree National Park). These phosphorescent flies perform nightly for a two-week period around the middle of June (dates change from year-to-year). To view it, you'll have to win the parking lottery to park at Sugarlands. A lottery application is available at recreation.gov and costs $1. Successful applicants will be charged $24 for a parking pass. From there, it's $2 per person to take a trolley to Elkmont to see the show. (Personal vehicles are not permitted.) Visitors should follow a few simple rules, so you do not disrupt the fireflies or other guests. Use a red light or cover your flashlight with red cellophane. Only use your flashlight (pointed toward the ground) when walking to your viewing spot. Stay on the trail. Do not catch fireflies. Pack out your garbage.

Pets & Accessibility
Pets are allowed in the park but must be kept on a leash (less than six feet). Basically, they can go where your car can (picnic areas, campgrounds, etc.). They are not allowed on hiking trails except for Gatlinburg Trail and Oconaluftee River Trail.

Bears in Cade's Cove

Temporary Parking Permits are available at Sugarlands and Oconaluftee Visitor Centers for visitors with disabilities. Elkmont, Smokemont, and Cades Cove have campsites accessible to wheelchair users. Much of the park is accessible by car, but almost all trails are rugged and inaccessible. Cades Cove Complex and Amphitheater, Oconaluftee Mountain Farm Museum, and Sugarlands Valley Nature Trail are fully accessible.

Weather
Visitors can receive current park weather forecasts by calling (865) 436-1200 ext. 630. The area's temperate climate makes the park a pleasant place to visit just about any time of year. However, high elevation areas receive considerable precipitation (85" annually). Lower elevations average 55" of precipitation each year. October is the driest month.

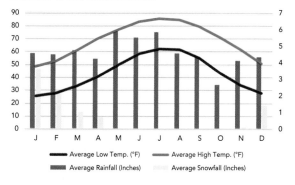

— Average Low Temp. (°F)   — Average High Temp. (°F)
■ Average Rainfall (Inches)   Average Snowfall (Inches)

Clingman's Dome sunset

Tips & Recommendations

Great Smoky Mountains is the most visited national park, so crowds and traffic are things you are likely to encounter. You may want to consider visiting midweek in the off-season. March and November see about half as many visitors as the park receives during its peak June, July, October rushes.

Cades Cove is incredibly popular. People love it. Many motorists finish a lap only to drive back in and do it again. In peak season you better pack your patience. The road is one lane, and people inevitably stop to check things out (everyone's looking for bears but they'll settle for turkey and white-tail deer). Your only options are to wait or take one of two quick-exit roads bisecting the loop for an early retreat. Abrams Falls, the visitor center, Gregory Bald, and a bunch of historic sites are neat, but, quite frankly, during peak season, you may find yourself fighting the urge to exit ASAP. With that said, you never know what you're going to see. Some visitors might be ogling deer, leading you to duck into a spot like Primitive Baptist Church, where you could find yourself alone with a family of bears. Still, get an early start if you want to get to a trailhead.

If you wake up early for Cade's Cove, you'll probably find a line of vehicles waiting at the gate at sunrise, but you will be able to find parking spaces, and drive the loop with fewer fits and starts.

If you're planning on visiting during peak season, you really need to make a plan, a backup plan, and a backup to the backup plan, or, at the very least be flexible. It can be a real challenge to find parking at popular spots like Newfound Gap, Alum Cave, Chimney Tops, Laurel Falls, Clingman's Dome, and a slew of sites along Roaring Fork Motor Nature Trail.

The best argument to camp inside the park is to be there when the day starts so you don't need to spend any time packing up and driving into the park. Traffic in Pigeon Forge, Sevierville, and Gatlinburg often reaches gridlock status.

Easy Hikes: Indian Creek (1.6 miles), Laurel Falls (2.6), Mingo Falls (0.4)
Moderate Hikes: Charlie's Bunion (8.1 miles), Andrew's Bald (3.5), Grotto Falls (2.8), Clingman's Dome (0.5), Mouse Creek Falls (4), Little Cataloochee (6), Rainbow Falls (5.4), Hen Wallow Falls (4.4)
Strenuous Hikes: Alum Cave (4.6 miles), Chimney Tops (4), Gregory Bald (11.3+), Ramsay Cascades (8), Rocky Top (13.9), Mount Cammerer (12)
Family Activities: Go on a hayride or carriage ride at Cades Cove, drive Cades Cove Loop, go river tubing, become Junior Rangers, explore the Mountain Farm Museum at Oconaluftee Visitor Center, pedal Cades Cove when cars are prohibited
Guided Tours: Horseback riding at Smokemont, river rafting, photography workshop with the Great Smoky Mountains Institute
Rainy Day Activities: You could drive around the park or explore the time-period exhibits, but, if you get a rainy day or two, this is the time to check out all the tourist traps in Sevierville, Gatlinburg, and Pigeon Forge, it's also a good time to hike to waterfalls
History Enthusiasts: Cades Cove Loop, Mountain Farm Museum at Oconaluftee Visitor Center
Sunset Spots: Clingman's Dome, Le Conte Lodge (spend the night!), Morton Overlook (0.7 mile north of Newfound Gap)
Sunrise Spots: Clingman's Dome, Le Conte Lodge, Luftee Overlook (0.8 mile south of Newfound Gap)
Wildlife: Cades Cove, Cataloochee

Beyond the Park...

Grocery Stores
Food City • (865) 430-3116
1219 E Parkway, Gatlinburg

Kroger • (865) 429-0874
220 Wears Valley Rd, Pigeon Forge

Walmart • (865) 429-0029
1414 Parkway, Sevierville

Townsend IGA • (865) 448-3010
7945 E L Alexander Pkwy, Townsend

Walmart • (828) 456-4828
135 Town Center Loop, Waynesville

There are nearly unlimited lodging and dining options in and around Great Smoky Mountains National Park. I feel like this space serves you better by listing more attractions and camping options. As they can be harder to sort through. There are many good alternative resources to choose where to eat and spend the night. (Although I always recommend staying within the park—with that said, it's only camping or hiking up Mount LeConte here.)

Campgrounds
Imagination Mtn Camp-Resort
4946 Hooper Hwy, Cosby
imaginationmountaincamping.com

Smoky Mtn Premier RV Resort
4874 Hooper Hwy, Cosby
smokymountainpremierrvresort.com

Adventure Bound Camping
4609 E Pkwy, Gatlinburg
abccamping.com • (865) 436-4434

Smoky Bear Camp and RV Park
4857 East Pkwy, Gatlinburg
smokybearcampground.com

Foothills RV Park • (865) 428-3818
4235 Huskey St, Pigeon Forge
foothillsrvparkandcabins.com

Pine Mountain RV Park
411 Pine Mtn Rd, Pigeon Forge
pinemountainrvpark.com

Up the Creek • (865) 453-8474
1919 Little Valley Rd, Pigeon Forge
upthecreekrvcamp.com

Great Smokies KOA
8533 TN-73, Townsend
koa.com • (865) 448-2241

Great Smokies KOA
92 KOA Campground Rd, Cherokee
koa.com • (828) 497-9711

Festivals
Wildflower Pilgrimage • April/May
wildflowerpilgrimage.org

Biltmore Blooms • April/May
biltmore.com • Asheville, NC

Scottish Festival & Games • May
smokymountaingames.org

Bloomin' BBQ • May
bloominbbq.com • Sevierville

Tomato Festival • July
graingercountytomatofestival.com

Scottish Highland Games • July
gmhg.org • Linville, NC

Folkmoot USA • July
folkmootusa.org • Maggie Valley

Secret City Festival • September
secretcityfestival.com • Oak Ridge

Bonnaroo • September
One of the premier music festivals in the U.S.
bonnaroo.com • Manchester

Attractions
Blue Ridge Parkway
More great mountain scenery and a drive you won't want to skip when you're in the area
nps.gov/blri

Cape Hatteras National Seashore
70 miles of coast with beaches and the eponymouse lighthouse
nps.gov/caha

Cape Lookout National Seashore
Requires a boat ride to reach, but you'll find horses, beach, fishing, and more
nps.gov/calo

Pisgah National Forest
Appalachian Forest in western North Carolina. Home to Looking Glass Rock • fs.usda.gov

Chattahoochee National Forest
Appalachian Trail's southern terminus, Long Creek Falls
fs.usda.gov

There are a many interesting state parks in Tennessee (TN), North Carolina (NC), Georgia (GA), and Kentucky (KY). These are just a few.

Pilot Mountain State Park (NC)
Very unique mountain popular for rock climbing and rappelling
ncparks.gov

Chimney Rock State Park (NC)
Hickory Nut Falls, Chimney Rock, Devil's Head, and more
ncparks.gov

Gorges State Park (NC)
A bunch of waterfalls not too far from the South Carolina border
ncparks.gov

Burgess Falls State Park (TN)
Centered around 250-ft falls
tnstateparks.com

Fall Creek Falls State Park (TN)
Tall waterfall • tnstateparks.com

Rock Island State Park (TN)
Features Caney Fork Gorge below Great Falls Dam
tnstateparks.com

Tallulah Gorge State Park (GA)
1,000-ft-deep gorge near Tallulah Falls • gastateparks.org

Black Rock Mtn State Park (GA)
Georgia's Blue Ridge Mountains
gastateparks.org

Moccasin Creek State Park (GA)
Very small park with a waterfall
gastateparks.org

Cumberland Falls State Park (KY)
Home to the Little Niagara
parks.ky.gov

CLIMB Works Zipline
155 Branam Hollow Rd, Gatlinburg
climbworks.com • (865) 325-8116

Hillbilly Golf • (865) 436-7470
340 Pkwy, Gatlinburg

Ripley's Odditorium
800 Parkway, Gatlinburg
ripleys.com • (865) 436-5096

Sugarlands Distilling Company
805 Pkwy, Gatlinburg
sugarlands.com • (865) 325-1355

Rowdy Bear Mountain Coaster
386 Pkwy, Gatlinburg
rowdybearmountain.com

Outdoor Gravity Park
203 Sugar Hollow Rd, Pigeon Forge
outdoorgravitypark.com

Smoky Mtn Zipline • (865) 429-9004
509 Mill Creek Rd, Pigeon Forge
smokymountainziplines.com

WonderWorks • (865) 868-1800
100 Music Rd, Pigeon Forge
wonderworksonline.com

Comedy Barn Theater
2775 Parkway, Pigeon Forge
comedybarn.com • (865) 428-5222

Parrot Mountain and Gardens
1471 McCarter Hollow Rd, PF
parrotmountainandgardens.com

Foxfire Mtn Adventures
3757 Thomas Lane, Sevierville
foxfiremountain.com

Wahoo Zip Lines • (865) 366-1111
605 Stocton Dr, Sevierville
wahooziplines.com

Adventure Park at Five Oaks
1628 Parkway, Sevierville
adventureparkatfiveoaks.com

Parkway Drive-In • (865) 379-9865
2909 E L Alexander Pkwy, Maryville
parkwaydrivein.com

Nantahala NF • (828) 524-6441
90 Sloan Rd, Franklin • Nice hiking (*Dry, Bridal Veil, and Whitewater Falls*)

Nantahala Outdoor Center
13077 US-19 W, Bryson City
noc.com • (828) 785-4964

Nantahala Rafting • (828) 321-4037
1965 US-19 W, Topton
nantaharalarafting.com

Tweetsie Railroad
300 Tweetsie RR Ln, Blowing Rock
tweetsie.com • (800) 526-5740

WTT Motorcycle Museum
62 Vintage Ln, Maggie Valley
wheelsthroughtime.com

Ijams Nature Center
2915 Island Home Ave, Knoxville
ijams.org • (865) 577-4717

Minister's Treehouse
The World's Biggest Treehouse
Beehive Lane, Crossville, TN

Raccoon Mtn Caverns
319 West Hills Dr, Chattanooga
raccoonmountain.com

NASCAR Hall of Fame
400 E MLK Blvd, Charlotte, NC
nascarhall.com • (704) 654-4400

Biltmore Estate
1 Lodge St, Asheville, NC
biltmore.com • (800) 411-3812

U.S. National Whitewater Center
5000 Whitewater Center Pkwy,
Charlotte, NC • usnwc.org

Congaree

Phone: (803) 776-4396
Website: nps.gov/cong

Established: November 10, 2003
Size: 24,000 Acres
Annual Visitors: 150,000
Peak Season: Spring

Activities: Hiking, Paddling, Fishing, Biking, Birdwatching
Ranger Programs: Big Tree Hike*, Owl Prowl*, Guided Canoe Tour*

Campgrounds: Longleaf** (walk-in, $10/night) and Bluff** (walk-in, $5/night)
Group Camping: 4 Sites ($20/night)
Backcountry Camping: Permitted with a free permit (available via e-mail or in-person)

Park Hours: All day, every day
Visitor Center Hours: 9am–4pm, every day

Entrance Fee: None

*Reservations required (check the park website for schedule and reservation information)

**Reservations required at 877.444.6777 or recreation.gov

Congaree is akin to a less popular, scaled-down combination of Redwood and Everglades National Parks. It protects the largest contiguous expanse of old growth bottomland hardwood forest left in the United States. You'll never confuse the towering bald cypress and loblolly pine for their West Coast compatriots, the redwood and giant sequoia, but they are massive by East Coast standards. Several national and state champion trees reside within the park's boundary. Congaree's canopy averages an impressive 130 feet, making it as tall as any temperate deciduous forest in the world. When navigable, Cedar Creek provides a narrow, maze-like waterway reminiscent of the Everglades' "River of Grass" (minus the grass, mix in some moss). Trees and waterways provide habitat for a multitude of plants and animals. In fact, the park was recognized as an International Biosphere Reserve in 1983 and was designated a Globally Important Bird Area in 2001. A floodplain forest draped in Spanish moss, invokes illusions of traveling back in time to a primeval setting. These waterways and trees have helped shape the history of not only a park, but the region. Water protected and nourished trees. Trees attracted conservationists. And now this unique environment is protected and preserved for future generations to enjoy.

Hernando de Soto was first to detail an encounter with Congaree Natives in 1540. His exploration continued north through Appalachia, but Natives stayed, living along what is now named the Congaree River. Around the turn of the 18th century, The Congaree were decimated by smallpox. By 1715, the tribe consisted of 22 men and 70 women and children. Today they are gone. What's left is a river and park bearing their name. The name of the area's original inhabitants.

Frequent flooding renewed the soil's nutrients. Trees thrived, reaching record heights. Floods weren't beneficial to area farmers. They spent decades trying to coax crops from the nutrient-rich land, but standing water stifled most agricultural activities. Farmers moved out of the floodplain. Santee River Cypress Logging Company moved in. They

Cypress knees of Congaree

When to Go
Congaree is open all year. It rarely receives large crowds, but if you intend to join a park ranger on an Owl Prowl, canoe trip, or hike, you'll need to reserve your place online or give the park a call at (803.776.4396) to check on availability. Don't and you'll likely be disappointed when you show up to a fully-booked program. Visitation is low but steady throughout the year. Summers are often hot, humid, and buggy, but the Congaree floodplain is considerably cooler than the surrounding area (so it can be surprisingly refreshing in summer). Things get more comfortable in fall, but you'll rarely find a crowd. Flooding is most common in late winter/early spring. Cedar Creek can be impossible to navigate during periods of high and low water. If you plan on paddling, call the park for current conditions before departing. Recently, visitation spikes in May thanks to a bunch of synchronous fireflies and the park's spectacle-long Fireflies Festival.

Transportation & Airports
Public transportation does not provide service to or around the park. The closest airports are Columbia Metropolitan (CAE), Charlotte Douglas International (CLT), and Charleston International (CHS), 24, 96, and 100 miles away, respectively.

Directions
Congaree National Park is located 20 miles southeast of Columbia, SC.

From Columbia/Spartanburg (~20 miles): Take I-26 E (toward Charleston) to Exit 116. Turn onto I-77 N toward Charlotte (left exit). After about five miles, take Exit 5. Turn off onto SC-48 E (Bluff Road), following the brown and white Congaree National Park signs. Continue southeast toward Gadsden for approximately 14 miles before turning right onto Mt View Road. Turn right onto Old Bluff Road. Turn left at the large park entrance sign and proceed to Harry Hampton Visitor Center.

From Charleston (~115 miles): Take I-26 W (toward Spartanburg) to Exit 116. Turn onto I-77 N toward Charlotte, taking exit 5. Follow the directions above for Columbia/Spartanburg (from Exit 5) to the visitor center.

From Charlotte (~110 miles): Take I-77 S to Exit 5. Follow the directions above for Columbia/Spartanburg (from Exit 5) to the visitor center.

purchased an exceptional tract of hardwood along the Congaree River in 1905, but regular flooding proved to be as troublesome to loggers as it was to farmers. Heavy logging equipment couldn't move across the wet and muddy earth. They could only access trees along the waterways where a new problem arose. They sank. Many of these trees were too green to float. Some remain where they fell along the riverbank to this day. After ten years of logging, the floodplain was left relatively unscathed. In 1969, high timber prices and advancements in logging equipment brought attention back to the uncut lumber of the Congaree River. This time floodwaters wouldn't be enough to save the trees. Thankfully, the Sierra Club stepped in. Their grassroots campaign to save the trees culminated in establishment of Congaree Swamp National Monument in 1976. Incorrectly labeled a swamp, the area does not contain standing water throughout most of the year, so it's actually a floodplain. Regardless, new legislation protected this land, its trees, and its waterways from future logging interests.

Nothing could protect the monument from Hurricane Hugo. In 1989 winds toppled many champion trees, permanently changing the park's landscape. But with tragedy came new life and diversity. Sunlight could once again penetrate the canopy. Nature ran its course, and new growth sprang up across the floodplain. Downed trees became habitat for plants and animals. Land unsuitable for farming and logging proved to be suitable for life. A flourishing ecosystem for bobcat, white-tailed deer, river otter, snakes and insects, fungi and ferns, is on display at Congaree National Park.

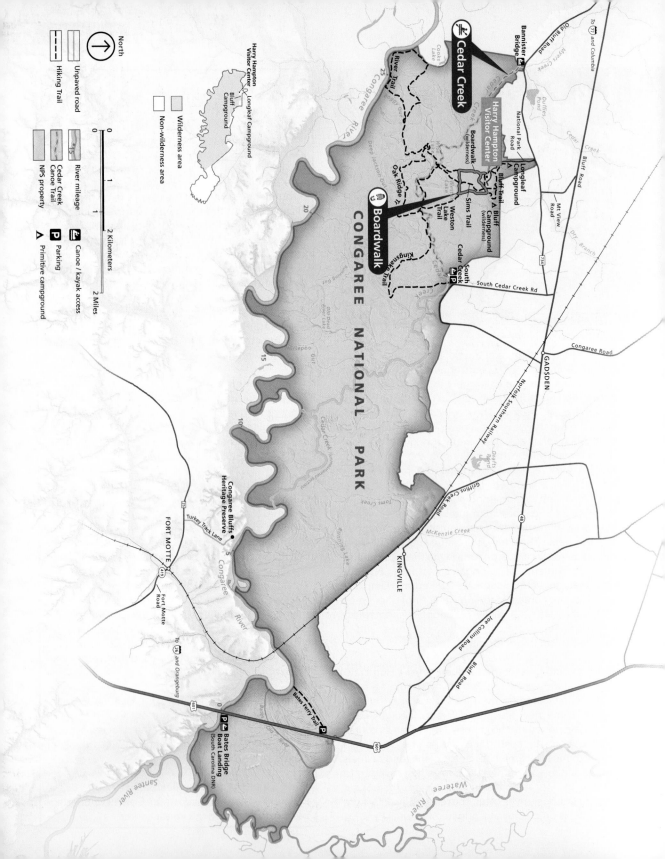

Camping

The park has three camping options: Longleaf Campground, Bluff Campground, and backcountry camping. **Longleaf Campground** is located on the east side of National Park Road, near the park gate. All ten individual sites and four group sites are walk-in, not more than 50 yards from the parking area. Chemical toilets are nearby. Drinking water is available from a spigot outside the visitor center when it's open. Tent sites cost $10 per night. Group sites cost $20 per night. **Bluff Campground** has six designated walk-in sites for $5 per night, located about one mile from the visitor center parking area. Restrooms and water are not available. Reservations are required to camp in the frontcountry at Longleaf and Bluff campgrounds. You cannot pay for camping inside the park. Make reservations at (877) 444-6777 or recreation.gov. Camping is tent-only. RV and/or car camping is not permitted. **Backcountry camping** is allowed with a free backcountry permit (available through e-mail or in person). There are no designated campsites. You must camp on the south side of Cedar Creek, at least 100 feet from creeks, lakes, and trails.

Hiking

The park is small and wet, allowing just over 20 miles of hiking trails to lead you through primeval forests and wetland. An ambitious hiker with an early start can hike Congaree's entire trail network in a weekend.

The Boardwalk is the only trail most visitors hike. It's an elevated, wheelchair-accessible walkway. Self-guided brochures for this 2.6-mile circuit through old-growth forest to Weston Lake are available at the visitor center. The forest drips with Spanish moss and cypress knees protrude from the earth, creating a setting worthy of a mystical fairy tale. (Knees are part of the bald cypress root system and they have been measured up to six feet tall.) The Boardwalk is elevated, but sections can be inaccessible during periods of flooding.

The 1.8-mile **Bluff Trail** connects with The Boardwalk for a short distance before reaching the campground. You'll pass through a young stand of loblolly pines.

The 3.2-mile **Sims Trail** is an old gravel road, running between Bluff Trail and Cedar Creek.

The 4.4-mile **Weston Lake Loop** departs via The Boardwalk and continues from Weston Lake to the north shore of Cedar Creek, skirting along for a short distance through old-growth forest before returning to the visitor center via The Boardwalk.

Heading down River Trail

Oak Ridge Trail is a 7-mile hike, looping around the south shore of Cedar Creek before joining River Trail and returning to the visitor center via The Boardwalk.

River Trail is 10.1 miles long. As the name suggests, this trail reaches the shores of the Congaree River. Along the way you'll be able to see successional stages of forest life, since much of the forest along the river was logged prior to the park's establishment.

The 12-mile **Kingsnake Trail** connects South Cedar Creek Road Canoe Landing to the visitor center. It's an excellent choice for bird watching or spotting wildlife as you pass through a large cypress–tupelo slough.

Bates Ferry Trail covers 2.2 miles from US-601 at the park's eastern boundary to the shore of the Congaree River at the site of a now-non-existent river ferry. The riverbank is steep and potentially slippery.

And there are two new trails. **Fork Swamp Trail** is 0.6 miles long, following a narrow section of Bates Old River. And high schoolers built a trail connecting the visitor center parking lot with Bluff Trail.

Paddling Cedar Creek

Paddling

Paddling is an excellent way to explore the park and to view its record holding trees. You are welcome to bring your own canoe or kayak to explore Cedar Creek or the Congaree River, but a better alternative is to join a park ranger on one of the free regularly-scheduled canoe trips (check online for a current schedule of events). The park provides everything you need: canoes, life jackets, and paddles. Children must be at least six years old to attend. Reservations are required. They can be made through the park's website. Always check the weather before leaving, because trips are cancelled if it's 45°F or below, the water level on Cedar Creek is 10 feet or above, or wind speed is 30 mph or greater.

Two landings on Cedar Creek within the park, and another landing on the Congaree River outside the park, allow paddlers to create a variety of trips. Cedar Creek slowly meanders through Congaree's old-growth forest, making it perfect for an out-and-back paddle. Start at **South Cedar Creek Landing**, just east of the park entrance at the end of South Cedar Creek Road. Pick your pleasure, upstream or downstream, and then paddle until your heart's content (half content, actually) before turning around. Even though the current is slow, remember paddling upstream will be more difficult and take more time than paddling downstream.

By putting in at **Bannister's Bridge**, west of the park entrance on Old Bluff Road, paddlers can float along Cedar Creek as it winds through swaths of bald cypress. The trail is fairly well marked, but there's always a chance you paddle into a dead end or two, especially when the water level is high. Near the half-way point you can take a narrow passage to Wise Lake, which was a channel of the Congaree River some 10,000 years ago before the river altered course to its current location. It is located on the right-hand side of Cedar Creek, shortly after you pass beneath a small hiking bridge. Note that it may be inaccessible at low water levels. The entire trip is roughly 7 miles (4–6 hours) to the take-out at **South Cedar Creek Landing**. You will need to arrange transportation between landings.

A 20-mile trip from **South Cedar Creek Landing** to the **601 Landing** is perfect for tireless or overnight paddlers. If you plan on spending the night, be sure to stop at the visitor center for a camping permit. Cedar Creek eventually joins the Congaree River, but the paddle trail takes a safer detour following Mazyck's Cut to the Congaree. Beyond the junction with Mazyck's Cut, Cedar Creek is unmarked and uncleared, so we highly recommend paddlers follow the trail. Three trail markers and a wooden sign point paddlers in the appropriate direction. Once you've reached the Congaree, you've got another 13 miles to the 601 bridge take-out. Again, you'll have to arrange transport.

If that isn't enough, paddlers can take the **Congaree River Blue Trail**. It's a 50-mile adventure beginning in Columbia, the capital of South Carolina, continuing downstream to Congaree National Park. If you're floating the Columbia River and plan to camp out, camping permits are available by calling (803) 776-4396.

Finally, several outfitters provide guided paddling tours. Palmetto Outdoors (803.404.8254, palmettooutdoor.com), JK Adventure Guides (803.397.000, jkadventureguides.com), River Runner Outdoor Center (803.771.0353, shopriverrunner.com), and Carolina Outdoor Adventures (803.381.2293, carolinaoutdoor-adventures.com) have Cedar Creek paddling excursions for about $80/person (as well as other offerings).

Fishing

Fishing is permitted within the park. A valid South Carolina State Fishing License is required, and all state laws and limits apply. To help prevent introduction of non-native species, live bait, such as minnows, amphibians, and fish eggs, are prohibited. Do not fish from or within 25 feet of manmade structures, including bridges, boardwalk, and overlooks.

Congaree's fish are almost as varied as the species of trees lining the shores. Largemouth bass, striped bass, perch, and crappie are a few of the commonly caught game fish. Prehistoric fish like garfish, mudfish, and shortnose sturgeon can also be found lurking beneath the surface of the murky water. Congaree River has a healthy population of white perch, white bass, catfish, carp, and suckers. Catch and release is encouraged.

Biking

Bicycles are allowed in the park but all trails, including The Boardwalk, are closed to cyclists. That leaves 1.5-miles of National Park Road as the lone stretch of pavement for bikers. A few roads surrounding the park offer decent, flat pedaling, but it's not really worth the effort of bringing a bike.

Birdwatching

Remember to pack your binoculars. Congaree is a park for birds and bird watchers, with more than 170 species spotted here. This includes eight species of woodpeckers: red-bellied, red-cockaded, red-headed, pileated, downy, hairy, yellow-bellied sapsucker, and yellow shafted flicker. Even the legendary ivory-billed woodpecker is believed to reside among the old-growth forest.

Owls are one of the most popular residents. More than 20 years ago a park ranger decided to lead a night-time "**Owl Prowl**." It was a hit then, and still is today. Online reservations are required and can be made through the park website.

Visitor Center

Stop in at **Harry Hampton Visitor Center**. You'll find exhibits, a short film, bookstore, park rangers, and the ever-important Mosquito Meter is hanging outside by the restrooms. Hours are 9–4, every day except Labor Day, Columbus Day, Veterans Day, Thanksgiving, and Christmas. If the visitor center and ranger programs are important to you (and they should be), double check the operating hours before departing as hours have changed over the years/seasons since I've been a regular visitor.

Ranger Programs & For Kids

A little bit of planning is required for a few of the park's ranger programs: Big Tree Hike, Guided Canoe Tour, and Owl Prowl require reservations through the park website. If you miss out on one of these programs, don't worry, there are additional regularly scheduled, ranger-led hikes, chats, lectures, and campfires that are all free and do not require reservation. A current schedule of events can be found at the park's website.

Congaree's Junior Ranger Program gives kids of all ages the opportunity to receive a badge for completing a free activity booklet (available at the visitor center). The booklet takes approximately three hours to complete. These activities help engage children in their surroundings while you're all off exploring. It's also filled with interesting park facts. If workbooks

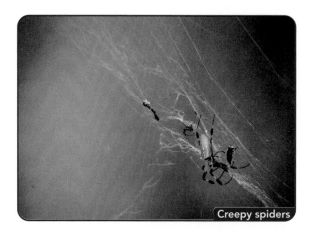
Creepy spiders

aren't your kid's style, a short introductory film plays regularly at the visitor center.

Flora & Fauna

The park's skyline is dominated by many of the eastern United States' tallest trees. About 20 trees hold state or national records for size. The largest is a 169-foot-tall, 17-foot-diameter loblolly pine. More than 98% of park land is designated wilderness covered with 75 species of trees, including: cherrybark oak, paw, water oak, bald cypress, tupelo, American holly, laurel oak, and ironwood. The Congaree River flows through the park for 23 miles, with a miniscule elevation change of 20 feet. The elevation difference, no matter how slight, affects vegetation growth. You'll find that loblolly pines grow on higher ground, while bald cypress and tupelo thrive in low areas of standing water. The park isn't all about trees. There are 22 distinct plant communities filled with fungi, ferns, flowers, and shrubs flourishing beneath the dense canopy.

Most animals found in the park are commonly described with words like creepy, crawly, or nocturnal. For the most part insects aren't bothersome until the middle of summer, when mosquitoes rule the wetlands. Four venomous snake species inhabit the park. These include coral snake, copperhead, canebrake rattler, and cottonmouth. Use caution when near rocks, holes, downed trees, or other spots where a snake might be hiding. Bobcats, raccoons, opossums, and owls are most active at night. In the morning and evening you may see white-tailed deer, squirrels, or river otter. You might be tempted to stare at the ground searching for poisonous snakes, but look up from time to time. The park is loaded with interesting moths, butterflies, and birds. A good spotting can be the fondest memory of a trip to Congaree.

Cedar Creek

Pets & Accessibility

Pets are allowed but must be kept on a leash (less than six feet). Pets, except service animals, are not permitted in park buildings. They are allowed in campgrounds and on all trails, including The Boardwalk.

The park's two most popular attractions, Harry Hampton Visitor Center and The Boardwalk, are completely accessible to individuals in wheelchairs. Congaree Campfire Chronicles is also accessible.

Weather

Summers are hot and humid. Memorial Day and Thanksgiving are the two busiest days due to comfortable weather during spring and fall. Winters are mild. On average the park floods ten times each year. Most flooding occurs in winter.

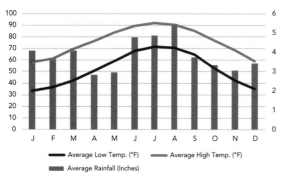

- Average Low Temp. (°F) — Average High Temp. (°F)
- Average Rainfall (Inches)

Tips & Recommendations

Congaree is a small national park most commonly visited by daytrippers. There are two primitive frontcountry campgrounds, but it's a day-trippin' park for a reason: you don't need to allocate a whole lot of time for your visit. So, it isn't difficult to drive-in, hike around a bit, and drive-out in the same day. With that said, if you want to paddle Cedar Creek (or the Congaree River) or join one of the unique ranger programs, plan on spending one night.

If you're trying to decide between camping at Congaree versus a hotel in Columbia, camp. Just know all sites are walk-in and reservations are required. You can show up, take a look at the campsites, and then reserve one the same day over the phone or online (cell coverage is spotty but wi-fi is available in and around the visitor center).

Check online (or give the visitor center a call) to see if you can join a ranger-guided Owl Prowl or Canoe Tour. Either one is worth the effort to get here. If your schedules don't align, don't skip the trip. The park is beautiful, and it's still fun to admire the huge trees.

Late May/early June offers a unique treat: synchronous fireflies. They don't perform during the same time each year, so it's a good idea to check-in with the park before making the trip. The park recently built a trail to help protect the firefly habitat, and when the show goes on, visitor center hours are extended, and a Firefly Festival takes place until they stop performing.

Paddling Cedar Creek is definitely recommended. I'm not sure why, but the bald cypress feel even more impressive from the water.

If you're in the area, do stop by. In about two hours you can hike The Boardwalk Loop to Weston Lake and watch the short film at the visitor center. Both activities are a decent use of your time.

Easy Hikes: All trails are flat and easy (to moderate, depending on length) as long as they are not flooded. If you only have time for one trail, hike The Boardwalk.
Family Activities: Become Junior Rangers, Ranger-guided Owl Prowl or Canoe Trip
Rainy Day Activities: Watch the short film at the Visitor Center
Sunrise/Sunset Spots: The park's road dead ends at the visitor center, and trails are heavily forested. There aren't any reliably good sunset/sunrise locations.
Wildlife: Boardwalk/River or Kingsnake Trail

Reflecting at Wise Lake

Beyond the Park...

Dining
Big T's Bar-B-Q • (803) 353-0488
2520 Congaree Rd, Gadsden
bigtbbq.com

Eric's San Jose Mexican Rest
4478 Rosewood Dr, Columbia
(803) 783-6650

Blue Marlin • (803) 799-3838
1200 Lincoln St, Columbia
bluemarlincolumbia.com

Motor Supply Co Bistro
920 Gervais St, Columbia
motorsupplycobistro.com

Julia's German Stammtisch
120 Sparkleberry Crossing Rd
(803) 738-0630

Za's Brick Oven Pizza
2930 Devine St, # E, Columbia
zasbrickovenpizza.com

Saluda's • (803) 799-9500
751 Saluda Ave, Columbia
saludas.com

Grocery Stores
Piggly Wiggly • (803) 456-4154
615 Harry C Raysor Dr, St Matthews

Food Lion • (803) 695-9757
9013 Garners Ferry Rd, Hopkins

Walmart • (803) 783-1277
7520 Garners Ferry Rd, Columbia

Publix • (803) 806-8839
2800 Rosewood Drive, Columbia

Lodging
The Inn at USC • (803) 779-7779
1619 Pendleton St, Columbia
innatusc.com

Chestnut Cottage • (803) 256-1718
1718 Hampton St, Columbia
chesnutcottage.com

*Chain restaurants and hotels in
Columbia and Orangeburg*

Campgrounds
River Bottom Farms
357 SC-32-45, Swansea
riverbottomfarms.com

Elliott's Landing • (803) 452-5336
2010 Elliott's Landing Rd, Rimini
elliottscampground.com

Sweetwater Lake • (803) 874-3547
58 Campground Tr, St Matthews

Barnyard RV Park • (803) 957-1238
201 Oak Dr, Lexington
barnyardrvpark.com

River Oaks • (803) 535-6565
524 Neeses Hwy, Orangeburg

Home Stay RV Park
332 Webber Farm Rd, Orangeburg
homestaycamping.com

Festivals
Spoleto USA • May/June
spoletousa.org • Charleston, SC

Greek Festival • September
columbiasgreekfestival.com

South Carolina State Fair • Oct
scstatefair.org • Columbia, SC

Attractions
Poinsett State Park
*Lake, waterfall, and interesting
ecology*
Poinsett Park Rd, Wedgefield
southcarolinaparks.com

Sesquicentennial State Park
Water fun near Columbia
9564 Two Notch Rd, Columbia
southcarolinaparks.com

Santee State Park
251 State Park Rd, Santee

House Museum • (803) 252-7742
1616 Blanding St, Columbia
historiccolumbia.org

Riverbanks Zoo • riverbanks.org
500 Wildlife Parkway, Columbia

SC State Museum • (803) 898-4921
301 Gervais Street, Columbia
scmuseum.org

The Comedy House
2768 Decker Blvd, Columbia
comedyhouse.us • (803) 798-9898

Marionette Theatre
401 Laurel St, Columbia
cmtpuppet.org • (803) 252-7366

Saluda Shoals Park
5605 Bush River Rd, Columbia
icrc.net • (803) 772-1228

World's Largest Fire Hydrant
1404 Taylor St, Columbia

Johns Island County Park
2662 Mullet Hall Rd, Johns Island
ccprc.com

One of the Stiltsville shacks seen from Bill Baggs Cape Florida State Park

Biscayne

Phone: (305) 230-1114
Website: nps.gov/bisc

Established: June 28, 1980
Size: 172,971 Acres
Annual Visitors: 500,000
Peak Season: Winter and Spring

Activities: Hiking, SCUBA, Snorkeling, Paddling, Fishing, Birdwatching

Campgrounds: Boca Chita Key (restrooms, no showers), Elliott Key (restrooms and cold-water showers)
Camping Fee: $25/night
Backcountry Camping: Prohibited
Lodging: None within Park

Park Hours: Varies by area
Entrance Fee: None

In the 1960s, Biscayne Bay's mangrove forests were declared "a form of wasteland" by well-to-do businessmen, who saw roads, bridges, buildings, and an oil refinery as the only way to revitalize an otherwise useless wilderness. Thankfully, a swell of opposition rose up from the public. Politicians, actors, writers, and environmentalists banded together to help preserve the longest undeveloped shoreline on Florida's east coast. Today, 40 small emerald isles and their mangrove shorelines remain untethered to civilization thanks to the creation of Biscayne National Park. But there's more here than unaltered islands and forests. More than 95% of the park is water, and beneath its surface lies an underwater wilderness completely unique among United States National Parks. A vast array of wildlife seeks refuge here. And not a single one of the thousands of escape-seeking visitors would consider this priceless landscape a "form of wasteland."

Israel Jones was among the first to enjoy the seclusion and wilderness of Biscayne. He moved to Florida in 1892, searching for work. After nine years as caretaker for a well-to-do businessman, handyman at the Peacock Inn, and foreman of a pineapple farm, he chose to work for himself. With his savings, he purchased two islands on the southern edge of Caesar Creek. Two years later he moved his family to Old Rhodes Key, where he started a business, raised a family, and left a legacy. Israel cleared gumbo-limbo, palmetto, and mahogany trees to reveal a coral limestone base suitable for farming key limes and pineapples. Weathering several years of indebtedness, he eventually became one of the largest producers of pineapples and limes on the east coast of Florida. Reinvesting his profits into real estate, he purchased Totten Key for $1 an acre. The property, all 212 acres, later sold for $250,000. Good, lucky, or both, Israel had proven himself to be a keen businessman who understood the value of an education. He hired a live-in teacher for his sons and helped create the Negro Industrial School in Jacksonville. His children used their education to follow in their father's footsteps. Arthur and Lancelot Jones continued to farm limes after the death of their parents. They also began guiding visitors on fishing excursions. Lancelot's fishing expertise was well known in the area and he was often hired to guide wealthy visitors of the Cocolobo Club on Adams Key. During the 1940s and 50s Lancelot served as fishing guide to the likes of Herbert Hoover, Lyndon B. Johnson, Richard Nixon, and other well-known politicians.

Other prominent people wanted to use the region for more than its fish. Daniel Ludwig, a billionaire developer, announced plans for an industrial seaport called Seadade in 1962. Development included an oil refinery and dredging a 40-foot-wide channel through Biscayne Bay. Fill from the dredging project would be used to form new islands, which would eventually connect North Key Largo to Key Biscayne by a series of roads and bridges. The project drew considerable support thanks to the prospect of new jobs and increased property value. But it also had opponents. Herbert W. Hoover, vacuum cleaner magnate and childhood visitor to the area, led legislators on dramatic blimp rides over the proposed development. As the park movement gained momentum, Seadade supporters razed a 6-lane "spite highway" the entire 7-mile length of Elliott Key. (Today, Elliott Key Boulevard follows Spite Highway, and it is the only significant hiking trail in the park.) In 1968 Congress, led by Representative Dante Fascell (the visitor center's namesake), passed a bill to protect "a rare combination of terrestrial, marine, and amphibious life in a tropical setting of great natural beauty." On October 18, 1968, President Lyndon Johnson, who decades earlier had gone fishing with Lancelot Jones, signed a bill creating Biscayne National Monument. Lancelot Jones sold his property to the National Parks Service in 1970 and was granted the right to live out his life in his family home.

Off on a boat tour

When to Go
95% of the park is water, and the water is open 24 hours a day. However, Convoy Point—where you'll find the visitor center, guided tours, and kayak launch—is open from 8:30am until 5:30pm, every day of the week. Adams Key (accessible by boat) is a day-use area, open 9am until sunset. Visitation is pretty steady throughout the year. In summer, visitors must brave mosquitoes, high temperatures and humidity, frequent thunderstorms, and the occasional hurricane. Hurricane season stretches from June through November.

Transportation & Airports
Most visitors reach the park's islands by private boat, but you can join a guided tour.

Miami International (MIA) is the closest large commercial airport (about 35 miles away).

Directions
Most visitors enter the park by private boat, but Convoy Point serves as hub for all excursions.

From Miami to Convoy Point (37 miles): Take FL-821 South (Partial Toll Road) to Exit 6 for SW 137th Ave toward Speedway Blvd (Toll Road). Keep left at the fork, following signs to Air Reserve Station/Job Cargs Canter. Turn left at SW 137th Ave. Turn left at SW 328th St/N Canal Drive, which leads to the park entrance and visitor center.

From Everglades National Park/Flamingo Area (56 miles): Follow the Main Park Rd east to Ingraham Hwy. Continue on Ingraham Hwy until Tower Rd. Turn left on Tower Rd. After about 2 miles, turn right onto SW 344th St. Continue onto W Palm Dr, which will turn into SW 138th Ct and then Speedway Blvd, and finally SW 137th Ave. Turn right at SW 328th St/N Canal Dr, which leads to the park entrance and visitor center.

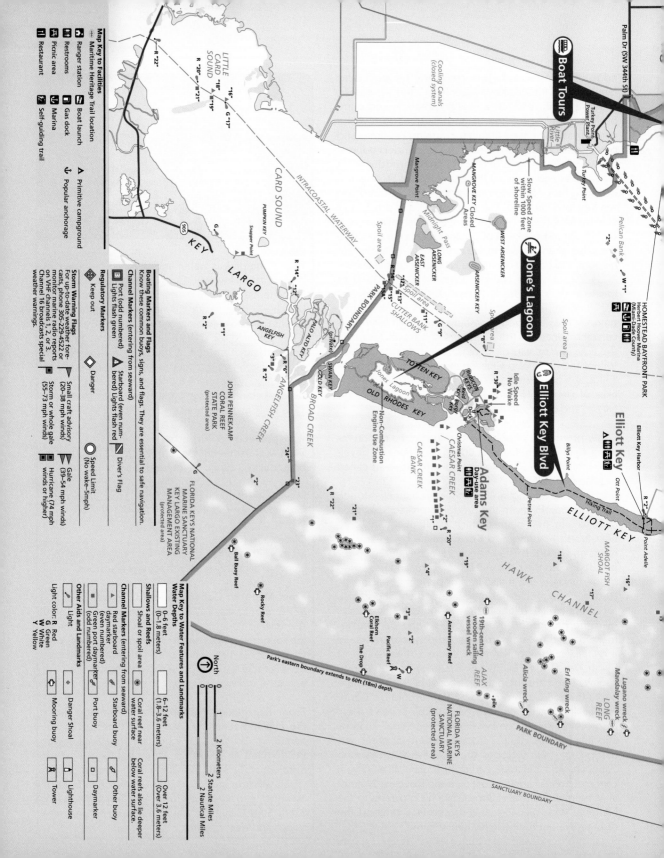

Dante Fascell Visitor Center

Park Headquarters

Convoy Point

BLACK POINT PARK (Miami-Dade County)

Fender Point

Breakwater

Black Point

R "2"

Goulds Canal

Black Creek

Coconut Palm Dr (SW 248th St)

SW 107th Ave

SW 304th St

SW 107th Ave

Florida's Turnpike (toll)

821

CUTLER RIDGE

SW 87th Ave

SW 184th St

SW 168th St (SW 152nd St)

Coral Reef Dr

Don Shula Expy

874

KENDALL

Palmetto Expy

826

SW 144th St

Old Cutler Road

Ludlum Rd (SW 67th Ave)

SOUTH MIAMI

SW 57th Ave

Old Cutler Road

*DEERING ESTATE AT CUTLER (Miami-Dade County)

CHICKEN KEY

Cutler Power Plant

R "2"

Shoal Point

G "1"

Fairchild Tropical Botanic Garden

MATHESON HAMMOCK PARK (Miami-Dade County)

R "2"

Slow Speed Zone within 1000 feet of shoreline

B I S C A Y N E   N A T I O N A L   P A R K

PARK BOUNDARY

Black Ledge

Black Ledge

INTRACOASTAL WATERWAY

R "2"

Y "C"

Y "B"

Stiltsville

G "1A"

G "1"

Y "A"

Y "2"

R "4"

R "2"

B I S C A Y N E   B A Y

Spoil area

W

W

Non-Combustion Engine Use Zone

R "6"

"4"

G "3"

"5"

FEATHERBED BANK

"X"

W "5"

R "2"

"1"

Idle Speed No Wake

University Dock

G "18"

W

G "21"

"19"

R "20"

"3"

"18"

"16"

"14"

"12"

"10"

G "15"

"13"

"8"

BISCAYNE CHANNEL

W

SANDS KEY

SANDS CUT

"2"

G "3"

"3"

harbor

ornamental lighthouse

Boca Chita Key

LEWIS CUT

RAGGED KEYS (private)

BOWLES BANK

BACHE SHOAL

G "11 BC"

R "8"

"9"

"7"

W "21B"

Triumph Reef

ANCHORAGE

Restricted Area

Boca Chita Key

LEGARE

STAR REEF

BREWSTER REEF

BOWLES BANK

SOLDIER KEY

@Closed Area

S A F E T Y   V A L V E

STILTSVILLE

G "1"

R "2"

W

W

BILL BAGGS CAPE FLORIDA STATE PARK

KEY BISCAYNE

W

G "3"

R "6"

"4"

"2"

Boundary marker

N "N"

FOWEY ROCKS

Arratoon Apcar wreck

W

"2"

"3"

"4"

G "6"

Do Not Use This Map For Navigation

Zones and regulations are subject to change. For safe boating, National Ocean Survey charts are indispensable. Use chart 11451 (purchase at visitor center) or charts 11462, 11463, and 11465.

A distant Miami skyline

Camping

Boca Chita and Elliott Campgrounds are open all year. Boca Chita is the park's most popular island. Its campground features waterfront sites and toilets, but drinking water, showers, and sinks are not. Elliott Key is the park's largest island. Its campground features forested sites, restrooms, sinks, cold-water showers, and drinking water (although the system isn't always reliable). Travel with animal-proof food containers, and do not sleep with food in your tent. Sites fill early on a first-come, first-served basis, especially between December and April. Camping costs $25/night, which includes docking a boat. There's one group site on Elliott Key available for $25/night. Payment should be made upon arrival at the kiosks near the harbor. All camping and docking fees are waived from May through September. You must bring your own food and water to the islands. RV camping is not available; the islands can only be reached by boat.

Hiking

Biscayne isn't a hiking park. You'll find a 0.25-mile trail at Convoy Point, which begins north of the visitor center and continues along the coast. Depending on the time of year, you might be able to catch the sunrise if you show up when the gate opens (8:30am). Then there's a half-mile trail at Boca Chita Key. However, when we went to print a bridge was out (closer to the start going counterclockwise). If this is still the case on your visit, you'll have to turn around or get wet. The trail is not spectacular and is often muddy. On Elliott Key, you'll find a 7-mile trail running the length of the island, with a couple short spurs. On Adams Key, you'll find a 0.25-mile trail.

Guided Tours

Biscayne National Park Institute (786.465.4058, biscaynenationalparkinstitute.org) offers a selection of paddle, snorkel, and boat tours. For $79 you can go on a 3.25-hour kayaking trip of Jones Lagoon. For $99 you can go on a 3.5-hour snorkel tour (location changes with conditions). Then there's a combo 6-hour sail, paddle, snorkel, and Island tour or a 6-hour snorkel and paddle trip, $159 each. You can save some cash and paddle along the mangrove coast for 1.5 hours for $39. Half an hour of that time is guided by a naturalist. Finally, they offer a cruise around Biscayne Bay (3.5 hours, $79), a cruise to Boca Chita (3 hours, $56), a lighthouses cruise (4 hours, $70), and a guided tour of Stiltsville (2 hours, $56). Many of the tours are offered daily, so, regardless when you visit, you should be able to find something to suit your interests. Biscayne Institute is great and they operate out of Convoy Point. A few other outfitters are authorized to give boat tours. Ocean Force Adventures (305.372.3388, oceanforceadventures.com) offers private tours of Biscayne Bay from Miami Beach Marina. Explore Miami (305.714.2121, exploremiamiboatrental.com) offers customized private charters. Miami Sailing Charters (305.714.0401, miamisailing.us) offers private sailing charters to Boca Chita, Stiltsville, or Elliott Key. They sail out of Dinner Key Marina in Coconut Grove.

If you're looking for something different, South Florida Kiteboarding (305.834.0595, southfloridakiteboarding.com) offers kiteboarding lessons from Key Biscayne.

SCUBA & Snorkel

More than 50 shipwrecks and a significant portion of the third largest barrier reef in the world make Biscayne National Park one of the best SCUBA and snorkel destinations in the United States. Wreck-diving was first made popular by treasure hunters who inhabited Elliott Key. Today, a Maritime Heritage Trail connects six of the park's wrecks. Mooring buoys, maps, and site cards aid divers and snorkelers on their exploration of each site. All sites except the *Mandalay* are best suited for SCUBA divers. The best option for snorkeling is to join one of the Biscayne National Park Institute tours listed above. Tropic SCUBA (305.669.1645, tropicscuba.com) and Horizon Divers (800.984.3483, horizondivers.com) are SCUBA options.

Paddling

Paddling is a great way to explore the mangrove shorelines and shallow flats surrounding Jones Lagoon, where you might see sharks, rays, upside-down jellies, and wading birds. North of Jones Lagoon, between Porgy and Old Rhodes Keys is Hurricane Creek, another good site to explore. Visitors with their own boats can launch for free from the visitor center. Overnight parking is available for anyone planning on camping at either of the park's primitive campgrounds, but you must obtain a free permit (available at the visitor center) prior to departure. Elliott Key is approximately seven miles from shore. Do not attempt to cross the bay during periods of inclement weather or adverse water conditions. Or play it safe and avoid having to rent or haul kayaks by joining the Biscayne National Park Institute on a guided tour.

Fishing
Biscayne Bay's fishing is nearly as good today as it was when Lancelot Jones guided future presidents to local hotspots. For the most part, fishing and harvesting is regulated by state law. All anglers 16 and older require a Florida State Saltwater Fishing License to fish in Biscayne National Park, and they must follow regulations pertaining to size, season, limit, and method. While there aren't any charter services offered out of nearby Herbert Hoover Marina, you can find outfitters like Shallow Tails (786.390.9069, shallowtails.com) that'll take you fishing out on the flats of Biscayne Bay. And Angler Obsession (360.485.3334, anglerobsession.com) offers guided fly-fishing expeditions out of Key Largo each year starting in April.

Or exchange your fishing pole for a bow and arrow and join Arrow Assault Bowfishing (786.708.4973, arrowassaultbowfishing.com) and go hunt some fish at night in Biscayne National Park!

Birdwatching
More than 170 species of birds have been recorded. Convoy Point and Black Point are two of the better mainland birding locations, but, to really experience the multitude of sea birds, visitors must hit the water. Jones Lagoon, just south of Caesar Creek, is the park's premier birding location. Here you'll likely spot cormorants, brown pelicans, and anhinga.

Visitor Center
Dante Fascell Visitor Center, located at Convoy Point, is open Wednesdays, Fridays, Saturdays, and Sundays from 9am–5pm. Boat and kayak tours depart from this location, and Biscayne National Park Institute has a small office at the back of the building. A stop at the visitor center alone isn't worth a trip to Biscayne, but, if you come, you certainly should stop.

Ranger Programs & For Kids
Ranger-led activities are periodically offered at several locations within the park, so it's always a good idea to check the online schedule of events.

Boca Chita

Kids will enjoy boat tours, snorkel trips, and paddling, but there are also several attractions geared especially for children. On the second Sunday of each month, from December to April, the park holds a Family Fun Fest. It's a free program at Dante Fascell Visitor Center highlighting the region's diverse resources with five hands-on activity booths. Participants receive a "passport" that is punched each time they complete a station. Complete all five stations and receive a prize.

Children can also participate in the park's Junior Ranger Program. An activity booklet can be downloaded from the park website or hard copies are available free of charge at Dante Fascell Visitor Center. The program is jointly administered between Big Cypress National Preserve, Biscayne National Park, and Everglades National Park. Complete the activities for Biscayne and earn a badge. Complete the entire book and you earn a South Florida National Parks Junior Ranger Patch.

Flora & Fauna
Hundreds of species of plants can be found here. Most obvious are the mangrove forests lining the shores, a cornerstone of the entire ecosystem. Birds, manatees, and crocodiles visit these masses of twisted roots and branches with great frequency. Smaller fish seek protection from larger predators among the half-sunken mangrove roots where trapped leaves provide nourishment for a variety of sea-life. If you go on a SCUBA, snorkel, or boat tour, chances are you'll see beds of sea grass. These underwater pastures are all-you-can-eat, self-service buffets for sea turtles and manatees, and a nursery for small fishes and invertebrates. The park's islands and mainland contain numerous cacti, ferns, trees, shrubs, and wildflowers. Many appear on lists of threatened and endangered species while others are non-native, exotic plants introduced by humans. Non-native species pose a serious threat to native plants as they compete for the same limited supply of water and nutrients.

A heron in Biscayne Bay

The majority of wildlife at Biscayne National Park is hidden beneath the sea. Underwater inhabitants include 512 species of fish, a handful of crustaceans like crabs and lobsters, dolphins, manatees, a few species of whale, and several mollusks like squid, snails, and oysters. Lucky snorkelers or SCUBA divers may spot a graceful sea turtle. Green, loggerhead, leatherback, and hawksbill turtles, all endangered species, can be found here. The American crocodile is another endangered species that finds refuge among the park's mangrove islands. Harvest, harassment, harm, or any other interference with these species is strictly prohibited.

Rare creatures also live above the water. For example, there are just a few dozen Schaus swallowtail butterfly adults remaining in the world, and they are only found on North Key Largo and some of the park's small Keys. That said, most animals living above sea level fall under the category of pests. Mosquitoes are common year-round, but are particularly pesky during summer. Raccoons inhabit the islands and are frequently found rummaging through visitors' coolers and picnic baskets. Do not feed the wildlife and travel with animal-proof food containers.

Pets & Accessibility

Pets are only allowed in the developed areas of Elliott Key and Convoy Point. They must be kept on a leash (less than six feet). Pets, except service animals, are prohibited from all other areas of the park.

More than 95% of the park is covered by water, so accessibility is directly dependent on your transportation (usually a boat). Dante Fascell Visitor Center and Jetty Trail are fully accessible to wheelchair users. Boca Chita Key is the only island within the park with sidewalks.

Weather

When visiting Biscayne National Park be especially observant of the weather. A subtropical climate provides abundant sunshine all year long, but thunderstorms with massive amounts of lightning are common, and hurricanes batter the land occasionally. Winters are generally dry and mild, with average highs in the 70s°F. Summers are often hot and humid with average highs in the 80s°F. Scattered thunderstorms are most common in summer. Hurricane season lasts from June to November. Biscayne Bay is relatively well protected, but if skies grow dark or the wind begins to pick up, boaters should head for shore rather than get caught in a thunderstorm.

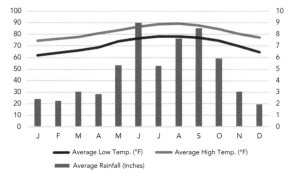

Tips & Recommendations

Biscayne National Park visitation is pretty steady throughout the year. Pests tend to be worst in summer, but if you're out on the water, you don't have to worry about them as much. Summer is actually a good time to visit as the water will be cool and refreshing compared to the hot/humid mainland. One major concern is hurricanes. They occasionally sweep through this area between June and November.

This isn't the kind of park you show up, stop at the visitor center, and then figure out what to do. Do that and you're almost sure to leave disappointed. Know what you can do and book your trips early. If you're going to come here, you have to get out on the water. And if you have a group of around six people, think about hiring a charter. It'll cost about the same as a trip with Biscayne National Park Institute, but you'll get a private/customized experience.

With that said, Biscayne National Park Institute is great. I'd encourage you to check out their tours. The Boca Chita tour is a good place to start if you'd like to learn a little bit about the area's unique history and spend some time on a beautiful island. Jones Lagoon paddle trip is great if you're looking to do some exploring.

How much time you spend here depends on what you plan to do. If you bring your own kayaks and want to camp out on the islands, you'll want a few days. If you aren't going to join a tour but still want to stop at Convoy Point, an hour will probably suffice. Look through these pages. Take a closer look at some of the tour opportunities and figure out what you really want to do (staying within your travel budget).

Stiltsville is pretty neat, and, while you can arrange tours, you can get a good view from Bill Baggs Cape Florida State Park on Key Biscayne (about an hour from the visitor center). It also features a great beach and lighthouse.

Don't forget your sunscreen!

Beach at Boca Chita

Hikes: This isn't a hiking park, but you'll find short trails on Boca Chita and Adams Keys, as well as a trail running the length of Elliott Key (note the bridge on Boca Chita's half-mile trail was out when we went to print)

Family Activities: Become Junior Rangers, Biscayne National Park Institute offers tours for families with kids of all ages and (most) interests (Boca Chita Key is a particularly good choice as you can tour an ornamental lighthouse, explore the key, or enjoy a small beach)

Guided Tours: Small Group Snorkel/Island Visit (3.5 hours, $99, biscaynenationalparkinstitute.org), Boca Chita Key Cruise (3 hours, $56)

Rainy Day Activities: Explore the visitor center

History Enthusiasts: Boca Chita Key Cruise (3 hours, $56), Stiltsville Guided Historic Tour (2 hours, $56)

Sunset/Sunrise Spots: Elliott Key or Boca Chita Key

Wildlife: Snorkel or Paddle

Beyond the Park...

Dining
Shiver's BBQ • (305) 248-2272
28001 S Dixie Hwy, Homestead
shiversbbq.com

Mamma Mia • (305) 248-3133
538 Washington Ave, Homestead
mammamiapizza2.com

Royal Palm Grill • (305) 246-5701
806 N Krome Ave, Homestead
royalpalmhomestead.com

Casita Tejas • (305) 248-8224
27 N Krome Ave, Homestead
casitatejas.com

Mario's Latin Café • (305) 247-2470
1090 N Homestead Blvd
marioscubancuisine.com

Black Point Ocean Grill
24775 SW 87th Ave, Homestead
blackpointoceangrill.com

Rosita's • (305) 246-3114
199 W Palm Dr, Florida City
rositasmexicanrestaurantfl.com

Grocery Stores
Costco • (305) 964-4227
13450 SW 120th St, Miami

Publix • (305) 242-0954
3060 NE 41st Terrace, Homestead

Winn-Dixie • (305) 246-3998
30346 Old Dixie Hwy, Homestead

Walmart • (305) 242-4447
33501 S Dixie Hwy, Florida City

Lodging
Hoosville Hostel • (305) 363-4644
20 SW 2nd Ave, Florida City
hoosvillehostel.com

Chain restaurants and hotels in Florida City and Homestead

Campgrounds
Miami Everglades RV Resort
20675 SW 162nd Ave, Miami
(305) 233-5300

Goldcoaster • (305) 248-5462
34850 SW 187th Ave, Homestead

Palm Garden RV Park
28300 SW 147th Ave, Homestead
palmgardenrv.com • (305) 247-8915

Southern Comfort RV Resort
345 Palm Dr, Florida City
socorv.com • (305) 248-6909

Festivals
Renaissance Festival • Feb/March
ren-fest.com • Miami

Sunfest • April/May
sunfest.com • West Palm Beach

Biketoberfest • October
biketoberfest.org • Daytona Beach

Attractions
Bill Baggs Cape Florida State Park
Beautiful park with sandy beaches and Stiltsville views
1200 Crandon Blvd, Key Biscayne
floridastateparks.org

Morikami Museum and Gardens
4000 Morkami Park Rd, Delray Beach
morikami.org • (561) 495-0233

Oleta River State Park • (305) 919-1846
Large urban park
3400 NE 163rd St, Miami
floridastateparks.org

Miami Culinary Tours • (786) 942-8856
1000 5th St, Ste 200, Miami Beach
miamiculinarytours.com

Vizcaya Museum & Gardens
3251 S Miami Ave, Miami
vizcaya.org • (305) 250-9133

Everglades Alligator Farm
40351 SW 192nd Ave, Homestead
everglades.com • (305) 247-2628

Miami Gliders • miamigliders.com
28790 SW 217th Ave, Homestead

R F Orchids • rforchids.com
28100 SW 182nd Ave, Homestead

Blue Springs State Park
All kinds of water activities near Orlando (manatees!)
2100 W French Ave, Orange City
floridastateparks.org

Everglades

A baby gator found along Shark Loop Road

Phone: (305) 242-7700
Website: nps.gov/ever

Established: December 6, 1947
Size: 1,509,000 Acres
Annual Visitors: 1 Million
Peak Season: December–April
Hiking Trails: 50+ Miles
Wilderness Waterway: 99 Miles

Activities: Paddling, Boat Tours, Fishing, Biking, Hiking, Birdwatching

Campgrounds* ($25/night): Long Pine Key and Flamingo
Flamingo Eco-Tents*: $90/night
*Reserve at flamingoeverglades.com
Backcountry Camping: Permitted at designated sites with a permit ($21 plus $2 per person per night)
Lodging: None

Park Hours: All day, every day
Entrance Fee: $30/25/15 (car/motorcycle/individual)

Wherever you look the circle of life is on display in the Everglades. From alligator holes to mangrove coasts, lofty pine to dwarf cypress forests, grassy waterways to man-made canals, life flourishes and flounders, thrives and perishes, dies and is reborn. When Americans began to develop South Florida in the late 19th century, humans threw this circle of life into a century-long tailspin. Amazingly resilient, it's not too late to recover, but our actions will ultimately destroy or preserve this irreplaceable wilderness.

Whether you're looking at the Everglades from above, atop the 45-foot-high observation deck at Shark Valley, or from the seat of a kayak in a maze of waterways, one thing you're sure to notice is its flatness. At 1,509,000 acres, it's the largest wilderness area east of the Mississippi River, and its highest elevation is just eight feet. Hidden among this vast river of grass are amazing pockets of life.

Alligators reside at the top of the food chain for good reason. Their vise-like jaws and razor-sharp teeth make a fearsome predator. Alligators burrow in mud creating small pools of water. When the dry season sets in, water levels decrease so much that alligator holes are often the only available source of freshwater, providing an important habitat for fish and amphibians trying to survive from one year to the next. Mammals congregate at these gator holes, drinking water and feeding on smaller prey. Meanwhile, alligators lay motionless, waiting to attack as they feed. Eventually, the region floods again, and fish and amphibians, survivors of life in a gator hole, are free to repopulate the freshwater prairies.

Quantity, quality, and type of water shape the plant and animal life of the Everglades' ecosystems. Cypress trees adapted to survive in areas frequently covered with standing fresh water. These hearty conifers are surrounded by woody, conical protrusions called "knees" that provide oxygen to the roots below. Dwarf cypresses reside in areas with less water and poorer soil. Spanish moss, orchids, and ferns grow from the trees' branches and trunks. Along the saltwater coast you'll find jungle-like mangrove forests. The park protects the largest continuous system of mangroves in the world. These plants have also acclimated to extreme conditions. They acquired a high tolerance for saltwater, winds, tides, temperatures, and muddy soils. Mangroves also serve as the first line of defense against hurricanes. Sturdy roots and dense branches are capable of absorbing and deflecting flood water, helping prevent coastal erosion. They also act as a nursery and food depot for marine and bird species.

Sadly, human actions are altering many of the area's natural life cycles. Nearly all of the park land's pine forests were logged. Dade County was once covered with more than 186,000 acres of pine rockland forest. Today, only 20,000 acres remain. Florida panthers have been ravaged by loss of habitat, poor water quality, and hunting. Now, perhaps ten exist in the park. In the early 1900s, alligators, birds, frogs, and fish were hunted on a massive scale. Since the 1930s, the number of nesting wading birds in the southern Everglades has declined by 93% from 265,000 to 18,500. Most were killed for their plumes, commonly used to decorate women's hats. More recently, non-native Burmese pythons are decimating the region's small mammal populations. Still, the greatest threat the Everglades faces is depletion and diversion of water. Man-made dikes, levees, and canals have been constructed to bring water to South Florida's urban areas, cutting off the region's water supply. A park brochure offers a sad and honest description of the state of the Everglades' water: "Freshwater flowing into the park is engineered. With the help of pumps, floodgates, and retention ponds along the park's boundary, Everglades is presently on life support, alive but diminished." Come to the Everglades. Witness the abundance of life still struggling to survive. See for yourself if condos, strip malls, and roadways are worth destroying one of the world's most magnificent natural wonders. It's not too late to save the Everglades. Changing its course is up to us. All we need to do is act, before it really is too late.

A storm brewing over Florida Bay

When to Go

Everglades is open all year, but some tours, attractions, and hours of operation are seasonal. Southern Florida experiences two seasons. Most guests visit during the dry season (December–April). It's typically comfortable with fewer bugs, thunderstorms, and hurricanes. The wet season (March–November) is hot and humid, and mosquitoes may be a nuisance. Thunderstorms are common and hurricanes do occasionally pass through the area. Hurricane season spans from June to November. Needless to say, you do not want to be camping when hurricane-force winds rip through the Everglades. Fewer people come to the park during the wet season, but it's still tens of thousands each month.

Ernest F. Coe Visitor Center Entrance and Gulf Coast Entrance are open 24 hours per day. Shark Valley is open daily from 8:30am–6pm. Chekika is closed indefinitely due to insufficient resources.

Transportation & Airports

Public transportation is not available to or around Everglades National Park.

Miami International Airport (MIA) is about 40 miles northeast of Ernest F. Coe Visitor Center. On the Gulf Coast, Southwest Florida International Airport (RSW), located in Fort Myers, is about 80 miles northwest of Everglades City. The smaller Naples Municipal Airport (APF) is just 35 miles northwest of Everglades City.

Map Labels

To Naples 25 mi
Big Cypress Bend
Carnestown
Gulf Coast Visitor Center
Everglades City
Tiger Key
Picnic Key
Jewell Key
Lopez River
Chokoloskee
Crooked Creek Chickee
Rabbit Key
THOUSAND ISLANDS
Big Cypress Swamp Welcome Center
Ochopee
Halfway Creek
Tamiami Trail
H.P. Williams Roadside Park
Burns Lake
Kirby Storter Roadside Park
Monument Lake
Florida National Scenic Trail
Oasis Visitor Center
Gator Hook Trail
Midway
Monroe Station
BIG CYPRESS NATIONAL PRESERVE
CYPRESS
Loop Rd (scenic drive)
Tree Snail Hammock
Pinecrest
Mitchell Landing
Miccosukee Cultural Center
Miccosukee Reserve Area
PINELAND

Air Boat Tours
Water Conservation Area 3A
Water Conservation Area 3B
Everglades Safari Park
Gator Park
Coopertow

Boat Tours
GULF OF MEXICO
The Watson Place
Darwins Place
Mormon Key
New Turkey Key
Turkey Key
Sweetwater Bay Chickee
Plate Creek Bay Chickee
Lostmans Five Bay

Shark Valley Visitor Center
Bobcat Boardwalk
Otter Cave Hammock Trail
Bicycles allowed on tram trail
13
Observation Tower

Tram Tours
Tram Trail

Recent construction of elevated bridges along this portion of Tamiami Trail is designed to deliver more sheet flow of water into the park.

HARDWOOD HAMMOCK
SHARK RIVER SLOUGH
Chekika (closed)

Anhinga Trail
AGRICULTURAL DEVE
Homestead Airport
Park Headquarters
Ernest F. Coe Visitor Center

Pa-hay-okee
FRESHWATER SLOUGH
EVERGLADES NATIONAL PARK
FRESHWATER MARL PRAIRIE

Pa-hay-okee Overlook
4
Rock Reef Pass
3
Pinelands
Long Pine Key
2
Long Pine Key Trail
Pine Glades Lake
Robertson Building
Snail Pond
Nike Missile Base Historic Area
Daniel Beard Center
Hole in the Donut wetlands restoration area
1
Park Entrance Station
9336
Royal Palm
Anhinga Trail
Gumbo Limbo Trail

South Florida National Parks
Lake Okeechobee
Big Cypress National Preserve
EVERGLADES NATIONAL PARK
Dry Tortugas National Park
Biscayne National Park

Wilderness Waterway
A well-marked inland water route runs from Flamingo to Everglades City. Sequentially numbered markers guide you along its 99 miles (160 kilometers). Boats over 18 feet (6 meters) long or with high cabins and windshields should not attempt the route because of narrow channels and overhanging foliage in some areas. The route takes a minimum of six hours with an outboard motor or seven days by canoe. One-day round trips are not advised. Campsites are available on the route; backcountry permits are required.

Coe Visitor Center to Areas in the Park
Royal Palm	4mi	6km
Long Pine Key	6mi	10km
Pinelands	7mi	11km
Pa-hay-okee Overlook	13mi	21km
Mahogany Hammock	20mi	32km
Paurotis Pond	24mi	39km
Nine Mile Pond	27mi	43km
West Lake	31mi	50km
Flamingo Visitor Center	38mi	61km
Florida Bay Ranger Station	38mi	61km
Chekika	26mi	42km
Shark Valley Visitor Center	50mi	80km
Gulf Coast Visitor Center	92mi	148km

Coe Visitor Center to Other Areas
Homestead	11mi	18km
Miami International Airport	45mi	72km
Key West	135mi	217km

Message to Boaters
Do not use this map for navigation. For safe boating, National Ocean Survey charts are indispensable. Charts 11430, 11432, 11433, 11451 are for sale at the Coe Visitor Center, Flamingo, and in the Everglades City area. Keys and beaches in Florida Bay are closed to landings unless otherwise designated. Commercial fishing is prohibited in the park. Recreational fishing requires a license in both freshwater and saltwater. Where backcountry camping is allowed, a camping permit is required.

More Map Labels
Highland Beach
Broad River
Camp Lonesome
Rodgers River Bay Chickee
Willy Willy
Hog Key
Harney River Chickee
Canepatch
COASTAL MARSH
Graveyard Creek
PONCE DE LEON BAY
Shark River Chickee
Little Shark River
Oyster Bay
Watson River Chickee
North River Chickee
Mahogany Hammock
5
Sweet Bay Pond
Hells Bay Canoe Tr
Nine Mile Pond
Nine Mile Pond Canoe Trail
Noble Hammock Canoe Tr
TAYLOR SLOUGH
CYPRESS
'Ficus' Pond
Old Ingraham Hwy

Oyster Bay Chickee
MANGROVE
Mud Bay
Joe River Chickee
WHITEWATER BAY
Roberts River Chickee
Lane Bay Chickee
Paurotis Pond
Pearl Bay Chickee
Hells Bay Chickee
Lard Can
West Lake Restrooms
6
Coot Bay Pond
West Lake Canoe Trail
Long Lake
Alligator Creek
North Nest Key
7
Shark Pt Chickee
Snake Bight Trail
Mrazek Pond
Rowdy Bend Trail
8
Christian Point Trail
10

Northwest Cape
CAPE SABLE
South Joe River Chickee
Tarpon Creek
Middle Cape Canal
Middle Cape
East Cape Canal
East Cape
Clubhouse Beach
Bear Lake Canoe Trail impassable
Mud Lake Canoe Trail
Homestead Canal
Bear Lake
Buttonwood Canal
9
Coot Bay
POLE/TROLL ZONE
Eco Pond
12
11
Flamingo
Coastal Prairie Trail

Eco Pond

Flamingo Visitor Center

Boat Tours
FLORIDA BAY
Johnson Key Chickee
Little Rabbit Key

North scale
North 0 1 5 10 Kilometers
0 1 5 10 Miles

Everglades Ecosystems
- Marine and Estuarine
- Freshwater Slough
- Hardwood Hammock
- Freshwater Marl Prairie
- Coastal Prairie
- Coastal Marsh
- Mangrove
- Pineland
- Cypress

Water Depths
- 0-3 feet (0-1 meter)
- 3-6 feet (1-2 meters)
- Over 6 feet (Over 2 meters)

1 Trailhead (see table on page 140)

- Hiking trail
- Unpaved road
- Wilderness Waterway and canoe trail
- Pumping station
- Lighted marker
- Canal and gate
- Wildlife protection area (limited access)
- Water detention area

- NPS Campground
- Private campground
- Interpretive trail
- Bike trail
- Tram tour
- Airboat tour
- Boat tour
- NPS primitive campsite
- Picnic area
- Marina
- Boat launch
- Gas station
- Lodging
- Food service

Florida Keys National Marine Sanctuary
Humiguitate Key State Aquatic Preserve
Islamorada
Plantation Key
Intracoastal Waterway
To Key West 70 mi
Anne's Beach
Long Key

Regions

Everglades is an expansive wilderness, much of which is completely inaccessible to automobiles. However, there are four entrances dispersed along the park's perimeter. Main Entrance and Shark Valley are the most popular entry points due to a variety of attractions and proximity to Miami.

Main Entrance/Ernest F. Coe/Flamingo: The main entrance is your number one choice for hiking, biking, and paddling trails. Flamingo is situated at the end of Main Park Road, 38 miles southwest of the entrance. Flamingo marks the southeast terminus of the 99-mile Wilderness Waterway, which leads into big open water of Whitewater Bay. It's also a spot where boat tours and rentals (canoe, kayak, boat, and houseboat) are offered. Both park campgrounds (as well as more comfortable eco-tents and by the time you read this a hotel may be completed), numerous hiking/biking/paddling trails, and three picnic areas are found between the Main Park Entrance and Flamingo.

Shark Valley: Shark Valley is popular for its 15-mile paved loop road. Visitors are no longer allowed to drive the loop, but you are encouraged to bike or walk as much as time and attitudes allow. The only vehicles permitted on the loop are open-sided trams (fee) that transport visitors to and from an observation tower at the loop's half-way point. This is arguably the best location to see vast sawgrass prairies that have become synonymous with the Everglades. Shark Valley also provides excellent opportunities for alligator viewing and bird watching. Nearby you'll find several non-park affiliated attractions, including air-boat tours and alligator farms.

Gulf Coast: This region is the gateway to Ten Thousand Islands and the northwestern end of the Wilderness Waterway. Boat tours and kayak rentals are available for those wishing to explore the maze of mangrove islands. Turner River Canoe Trail is a good place to paddle. There are no hiking trails. If you aren't interested in paddling or boat tours, you can skip this area. A visitor center provides backcountry permits, brochures, exhibits, and an introductory film.

Directions

Main Entrance/Ernest F. Coe Visitor Center/Flamingo Visitor Center (from Miami): Take Florida Turnpike/Route 821 (Toll Road) south until it ends and merges with US-1 at Florida City. Turn right at the first traffic light. Follow the signs to the park.

If arriving from the Florida Keys, turn left on Palm Drive in Florida City and follow signs to the park.

Ernest F. Coe Visitor Center is on your right just before the park entrance station. Flamingo is another 38 miles southwest of the entrance station. Allow an hour to drive from the Main Entrance Station to Flamingo.

Shark Valley Visitor Center (from US-41/Tamiami Trail): US-41 crosses the Florida peninsula from east to west, providing access to Shark Valley and its visitor center. Follow US-41 (~40 miles from downtown Miami and 75 miles from Naples). Shark Valley Loop Road is south of US-41. The visitor center and Tram Tour departure point are a short distance from the highway.

Gulf Coast Visitor Center (from I-75): Gulf Coast Visitor Center is located on the very western edge of the park, 5 miles south of US-41 (Tamiami Trail). From I-75 (Toll Road), take exit 80 to merge onto FL-29 S. Follow FL-29 for 20 miles to Everglades City and follow signs to the park.

Flamingo Eco-Tents

Camping

Long Pine Key Campground is located seven miles from the main entrance. It's open seasonally from November until May. The camp has 108 sites for tents and RVs (up to 45 feet) and one group site. Restrooms, showers, water, grills, picnic tables, and a dump station are available. There's a small pond for fishing, an amphitheater, and several hiking trails in the area. Hookups are not available. Reservations can be made at flamingoeverglades.com. Regular sites cost $25/night, the group site is $35/night.

Flamingo Campground is located at the end of Main Park Road. It has 234 drive-in sites (55 with a view of the water, 41 with electric hookups) and 11 eco-tents (glamping with queen bed, electricity, fan, and deck area). Restrooms, cold water showers, grills, picnic tables, dump stations, and an amphitheater are available. Full hookups are not. Hiking, paddling, and saltwater fishing are popular activities. Reservations can be made at flamingoeverglades.com. RV sites with electricity cost $45/night, regular sites cost $25/night. Eco-tents run $90–150/night.

Backcountry camping is available at several designated sites throughout the park (most only accessible by water). A permit is required. Permits can be reserved at recreation.gov, and several sites are reserved for first-come, first-served visitors. All permits must be obtained in-person at the Flamingo or Gulf Coast Visitor Centers during regularly scheduled hours (but less than 24 hours before your trip). Permits cost $21 plus $2 per person per night.

Paddling

The essence of the Everglades is found in its grassy waterways. To get there you must paddle. Daytrips or multi-day adventures? You'll find some of the best in the world. Whitewater? Look somewhere else. There's little to no current; it's all paddling here. These creeks and rivers flow into Florida Bay at the blistering speed of 0.25-mile per day. At that rate, it would take more than a year to float the 99-mile Wilderness Waterway. Low water levels can impede your paddling goals. If you plan on departing between late February and March, discuss your itinerary with a park ranger to assure your desired route is completely navigable. Also be prepared for strong winds and tides.

Flamingo has the most paddling variety. **Nine Mile Pond** is a great place to spot birds and alligators. Access to the 5.2-mile trail is just off Main Park Road at Nine Mile Pond Picnic/Parking Area. A little further south is **Noble Hammock Canoe Trail**. This 2-mile loop requires good maneuvering skills (or a small kayak) to navigate a maze of mangrove-lined creeks and ponds. Opposite this launch site is **Hells Bay Canoe Trail** (5.5 miles, one-way), another extremely narrow trail through dense mangroves. Hells Bay is an excellent location to test yourself for the Wilderness Waterway. One campsite and two chickees (permit required) are found along the way. Anyone looking on the trail from above might wonder how this maze of mangroves is navigated. Park employees help by placing more than 160 poles marking the way. Continuing along Main Park Road is **West Lake Trail** (7.7 miles, one-way), which leads to Alligator Creek backcountry campsite. Next up is **Mud Lake Loop**, a 7-mile trail with excellent birding opportunities (requires a short portage between Bear Lake and Buttonwood Canal). You can also venture out into Florida Bay for more wide-open paddling. Gulf Coast also offers a wealth of paddling opportunities. Like the 5-mile loop to **Sandfly Island** from the visitor center. **Turner River** is another popular destination, where you can launch from Big Cypress (off US-41), Chokoloskee Island, or the Gulf Coast Visitor Center. **Halfway Creek** is another option, and you can make a few loops in this area. Trail maps of canoe/kayak trails are available at the park website. Kayak and canoe rentals are available at Flamingo (flamingoeverglades.com, canoe: $20/2 hours) and Gulf Coast (evergladesfloridaadventures.com, canoe: $25/2 hours). Shurr Adventure Kayaking (239.300.3004, shurradventures.com) in Everglades City offers guided paddle trips.

Wilderness Waterway

The Wilderness Waterway is a 99-mile trail connecting Flamingo and Everglades City. The best time to paddle is between December and April. It takes around eight days to complete. Do not consider this to be the sort of adventure you can complete on a whim. You must plan ahead. There are many routes and dozens of campsites along the way. The park's website provides a trip planning guide to make sure you are properly prepared. Park rangers at Flamingo and Gulf Coast Visitor Centers are also happy to help with planning. Backcountry permits are required. Permits can be obtained online at recreation.gov and cost $21 plus $2 per night per person. You must pick up the permit in-person no more than 24 hours before departing. You'll be in the backcountry, but solitude can still be difficult to find. Remember that motorboats are allowed in most wilderness areas, and some campsites have capacity for as many as 60 campers.

Boat Tours & Boating

Tours depart from Flamingo (855.708.2207, flamingoeverglades.com) and Gulf Coast (855.793.5542, evergladesfloridaadventures.com). Flamingo's 1.5-hour tour leads through Buttonwood Canal to Whitewater Bay's backcountry. Tickets cost $40/adult and reservations can be made online. On the opposite end of the park visitors can enjoy a tour of Ten Thousand Islands (1.5 hours, $40/adult). While sailing the seas, you may see all sorts of wildlife, including bottle-nosed dolphins, manatees, ospreys, and pelicans. As you pass the sea of islands (far fewer than 10,000) imagine a time when Calusa Indians paddled from island to island and fished these waterways. It has been hundreds of years since they inhabited the area, but archaeological evidence remains to this day, including mountains of shells left on small tree islands. Boat rentals, including houseboats (sleeping up to 4 adults and 2 children), are available in the marina at Flamingo. Pontoon boats start at $125 for a half-day. Houseboats start at $400/night. From the marina, you're free to head north up the Buttonwood Canal and into Whitewater Bay.

Fishing

More than one-third of the park is covered by navigable water, creating ample fishing opportunities. Whether it's fresh- or saltwater you're fishing in, a Florida State Fishing License is required for anyone 16 and older. A few of the fish frequently caught within the park include snapper, sea trout, bass, and bluegill. It is possible to fish from shore but good locations are extremely limited. There are unlimited fishing spots for those with a boat (rentals available at Flamingo marina starting at $125/half-day, reserve online at flamingoeverglades.com). Before heading out on the water, be sure to know the state fishing regulations and catch limits. No boat? No problem. Fishing the Everglades (239.280.9085, fishingtheeverglades.com, $450/half-day), Everglades Fishing Charters (239.695.2029,

A look down Shark Loop Road from Shark Tower

evergladesfishingcharters.com, $450/half-day), Everglades City Fishing Charters (239.253.9926, evergladescityfishingcharters.com, $500/half-day), and Everglades Backwater Fishing (239.695.0687, gofishguides.com, $450/half-day) provide guide service from Everglades City for guests looking to get out on the water.

Tram Tours

The 2-hour narrated Shark Valley tram tour is the highlight of many Everglades vacations. The open-sided tram allows unobstructed views of your surroundings. It's likely you'll see alligators and several species of birds. You'll make two stops along the way. One at the half-way point where you'll find restrooms and a look-out tower. The other for a brief educational lesson. Tours cost $27/adult (13-61), $21/senior (62+), and $14/child (3–12). Reservations can be made at (305) 221-8455 or sharkvalleytramtours.com.

Biking

If you're looking for grueling mountain climbs, this isn't the place for you. The park's maximum elevation is 8 feet above sea level, and no, that is not a typo. What you will find are flat paved roads and a handful of dirt hiking trails that allow bicycles. The 15-mile Shark Valley Loop is the most popular biking destination. Taking a bike to the 45-foot observation tower is a great alternative to the tram tour, allowing you to go at your own pace. Bike rental is available at Shark Valley Tram Tours (350.221.8455, sharkvalleytramtours.com) for $20. A few miles east of Shark Valley Entrance is the L-67 Canal. The gravel road is an excellent destination for bicycling and wildlife viewing.

Snake Bight, Rowdy Bend, and Long Pine Key Trails permit bicycles. Use caution when biking on trails to avoid hikers who share these paths. Main Park Road is a longer option for early risers. During peak-season,

Behind Long Pine Key

Everglades Hiking Trails (Distances are roundtrip unless noted otherwise)

	Name	Location (# on map)	Length	Difficulty Rating & Notes
Pine Key	Anhinga - 🐾	Royal Palm Visitor Center (1)	0.8 mile	E – Wildlife opportunities • Ranger-led tours
	Gumbo-Limbo - 🐾	Royal Palm Visitor Center (1)	0.4 mile	E – Self-guided trail • Hardwood hammock
	Old Ingraham Highway	Royal Palm Visitor Center (1)	11.0 miles (one-way)	M – Provides access to backcountry campsites and Nike Missile Base • Bikes allowed
	Long Pine Key	Begins west of Long Pine Key Camp/Ends at Pine Glades Lake along Main Park Road (2)	6.7 miles (one-way)	M – Running parallel to Main Park Road you travel from the campground to Pine Glades Lake • Bikes allowed
	Pineland	About 7 miles from the Main Park Entrance (3)	0.4 mile	E – A short loop through a forest of pines, palmettos, and wildflowers
	Pa-hay-okee Overlook - 🐾	About 13 miles from the Main Park Entrance (4)	0.2 mile	E – A great hike to a bird's eye view of the vast "river of grass"
	Mahogany Hammock - 🐾	About 20 miles from the Main Park Entrance (5)	0.5 mile	E – Self-guided trail • Largest living mahogany tree in the U.S.
Flamingo	West Lake - 🐾	About 7 miles north of Flamingo on Main Park Road (6)	0.5 mile	E – Self-guided boardwalk trail passing through mangroves to the edge of West Lake
	Snake Bight	About 4 miles north of Flamingo on Main Park Road (7)	1.6 miles (one-way)	E – Tropical hardwood hammock, another excellent birding location • Bikes allowed
	Rowdy Bend	About 3 miles north of Flamingo on Main Park Road (8)	2.6 miles (one-way)	E – Connects Snake Bight Trail • Bikes allowed
	Bear Lake	About 2 miles north of Flamingo on Main Park Road (9)	1.6 miles (one-way)	E – Ends at Bear Lake, meanders through a hardwood hammock mixed with mangroves
	Christian Point	About 1 mile north of Flamingo on Main Park Road (10)	1.8 miles (one-way)	E – Excellent location for bird watching
	Eco Pond	Flamingo (11)	0.5 mile	E – Freshwater pond often frequented by wading birds, song birds, and alligators
	Guy Bradley	Flamingo (11)	1.0 mile (one-way)	E – Connects the visitor center and the amphitheater along the shore of Florida Bay
	Bayshore Loop	Flamingo (11)	2.0 miles	E – Butterfly and bird opportunities
	Coastal Prairie	At the back of Flamingo Campground's Loop C (12)	7.5 miles (one-way)	E – An old settlement road leading to Clubhouse Beach and a backcountry campsite
Shark Valley	Bobcat Boardwalk	Behind Shark Valley Visitor Center (13)	0.5 mile (one-way)	E – Short, self-guiding trail passes through a sawgrass slough and hardwood forest
	Otter Cave Hammock	Behind Shark Valley Visitor Center (13)	0.25 mile (one-way)	E – Limestone trail passes through a tropical hardwood forest • Often flooded in summer
	Tram Road - 🐾	Shark Loop Road (13)	15.0 miles	M – Paved road to 45-ft tower • May spot alligators, egrets, and snail kites • Bikes allowed

Difficulty Ratings: E = Easy, M = Moderate

traffic begins to pick up around 10am and die down around 5pm. Old Ingraham Highway, near Long Pine Key Camp, is a more peaceful stretch of pavement.

Hiking

The best way to explore the park may be on the water, but that doesn't mean great hiking trails don't exist. Most trailheads are found along Main Park Road between Ernest Coe Visitor Center and Flamingo. **Anhinga Trail** is an absolute must hike. It's a short and easy stroll beginning at Royal Palm Visitor Center. It immediately immerses hikers into the park's amazingly unique biodiversity. You'll likely see alligators along this 0.8-mile semi-loop. The parking area is a popular spot where vultures hang out to pick the rubber seals from car windows. Many visitors bungie a tarp around their vehicle to protect it.

If toothy, prehistoric-looking creatures aren't your cup of tea, try **Mahogany Hammock Trail**. It's a 0.5-mile boardwalk located 20 miles from the Main Park Entrance. Trees are the main attraction, including the largest living mahogany tree in the United States. **West Lake Trail** (31 miles from the Main Park Entrance) is a short boardwalk through mangroves. Visitors will also find good hiking opportunities at Long Pine Key and Flamingo Campgrounds. Hiking is more enjoyable if you see a little wildlife (at a safe distance), so always discuss your intentions with a park ranger to learn the best hiking locations to see animals during your visit. A more complete list of the park's hiking trails is provided on the previous page.

Birdwatching

Everglades is the most important breeding ground for tropical wading birds in North America. Sixteen species inhabit the park. Most common is the white ibis, but you may also encounter wood storks, great blue herons, green-backed herons, and roseate spoonbills. Birds of prey, such as ospreys, short-tailed hawks, bald eagles, red-tailed hawks and snail kites also soar high above the "river of grass." In all more than 350 species of birds have been identified within the park, making it a favorite destination among birdwatchers. Anhinga, Christian Point, and Eco Pond Trails are excellent birding destinations. Along with Shark Valley's Tram Road and the entire Flamingo area.

Visitor Centers

Ernest F. Coe Visitor Center (305.242.7700) and **Flamingo Visitor Center** (239.695.2945) are on the main entrance near Homestead. They are open from 8am–5pm and 8am–4:30pm, respectively, during peak

Watch where you step on Anhinga Trail

tourism season (mid-November through mid-April). **Shark Valley Visitor Center** (305.221.8776) is open daily from 9am–5pm. The Shark Valley entrance gate is open from 8:30am until 6pm each day. **Gulf Coast Visitor Center** (239.695.3311) is open from 8am–5pm. All four hold slightly shorter hours in the off-season.

Ranger Programs & For Kids

Guests are able to enjoy a variety of programs from canoe trips to starlight walks at Ernest F. Coe and Flamingo Visitor Centers. Gulf Coast Visitor Center offers canoe trips, walks, and talks. Guests are invited to join an "Anhinga Amble" or "Glades Glimpses," which depart from the Royal Palm benches (three miles from the main entrance). Shark Bites Program offers hands on learning at Shark Valley. Everglades is also home to a park oddity, A **Nike Missile Site** (a side effect of the Cuban Missile Crisis). Guided tours are offered most afternoons between December and March. Note that you'll need to bring your own watercraft or rent one for ranger-led canoe trips. A current schedule of ranger programs can be found at the park website. You can also call or stop in at a visitor center.

Kids get a kick out of seeing alligators. The best chance to see these reptilian friends is at Shark Valley Loop Road, Anhinga Trail, or outside the park along Tamiami Trail (US-41). Children ages 12 and older will love the ranger-led Slough Slog. Slough sloggers must bring water, sturdy close-toed, lace up shoes, and long pants. The program is limited to 15 participants. To sign up or receive additional information, visit Ernest F. Coe Visitor Center or call (305) 242-7700.

Children are encouraged to participate in the Junior Ranger Program. Junior Ranger booklets are available online or at a visitor center. Complete the activities for Everglades National Park to earn a park badge. The

An anhinga drying its wings

There are more than 50 other species of reptiles inhabiting the park, including the endangered or threatened American crocodile, green sea turtle, and eastern indigo. With so many flying and swimming attractions, the park's 40 species of mammals often go unnoticed. Florida panthers are rarely seen because of their stealth and diminished numbers (maybe 10 left in the park) due to habitat loss. Other popular mammals include white-tailed deer, river otter, cottontail, and manatee.

A world of life exists beneath the water's surface. Nearly 300 species of fresh and saltwater fish swim in the park's waters. You won't find any sweeping mountain panoramas here, but you'll definitely find some of the world's most diverse and interesting wildlife.

Pets & Accessibility
Pets must be kept on a leash (less than six feet) and are only permitted on public roadways, roadside campgrounds and picnic areas, maintained grounds surrounding public facilities and residential areas, and aboard private boats.

All the park's visitor centers are accessible to individuals in wheelchairs. Several hiking trails have a paved or boardwalk surface allowing wheelchair accessibility. They include Anhinga Trail, Gumbo Limbo Trail, Pineland Trail, Pa-hay-okee Overlook, Mahogany Hammock Trail, West Lake Trail, and Bobcat Hammock. Long Pine Key and Flamingo Campgrounds have accessible campsites, restrooms, and parking. Only one backcountry campsite is accessible to individuals with mobility impairments, Pearl Bay Chickees, located about four hours (by canoe) from Main Park Road. The site features handrails, a canoe dock, and an accessible chemical toilet. Many of the ranger-led programs are fully accessible. Check the park website for details. Boat and Shark Valley Tram Tours (350.221.8455, sharkvalleytramtours.com) are accessible.

Weather
Everglades enjoys the same tropical climate as the rest of southern Florida. Summers are hot and humid with frequent thunderstorms. Hurricane season stretches from June to November. Thunderstorms and hurricanes are bad news. Mosquitoes are another summer nuisance. If you plan on traveling to the Everglades between May and November pack bug spray. Most visitors choose to visit between December and April, when temperatures are comfortable and regular winds keep the bugs at bay. This time frame also features the widest variety of attractions and longest hours of operation.

program is jointly administered by Big Cypress National Preserve, Biscayne National Park, and Everglades National Park. Completing the entire book earns a South Florida National Parks Junior Ranger Patch.

Flora & Fauna
Visitors constantly pass from one ecosystem to the next while exploring the Everglades. Each has its own unique plant and animal life. A multitude of trees, lichens, ferns, fungi, and wildflowers combine to total more than 1,000 species of documented plants. Sawgrass marshes cover the heart of the park. These marshes are the largest of their kind in the world and the reason it is known as "the river of grass." The region is uncommonly flat, yet "high" ground plays an important role in its biodiversity. Slash pines and palmetto trees occupy the elevated regions, while other trees have adapted to grow in marshy areas. Hardwood hammocks of mahogany, gumbo-limbo, and cocoa palm trees are able to grow within the marsh in places where limestone is situated slightly above sea level. Trees capable of surviving in standing water are also found here. Cypress trees manage to live in freshwater, while mangroves have become resilient to the extreme and salty conditions along the coast.

For many, alligators steal the show. Alligators only reside in the park's freshwater. Anhinga Trail and Shark Valley are two of the best locations to spot a gator. The lower the water level, the farther north you have to go to find these freshwater reptiles. Invasive Burmese python are unwelcome visitors who have decimated the small animal population in recent years.

Chart showing Average Low Temp. (°F), Average High Temp. (°F), and Average Rainfall (Inches) across months J F M A M J J A S O N D.

— Average Low Temp. (°F)   — Average High Temp. (°F)
■ Average Rainfall (Inches)

A few airboat companies are allowed in the park

Tips & Recommendations

If you only have time to visit one area, I'd choose Shark Valley. It's closest to Miami, and, once there, you'll have the option to bike, hike, or tram along the 15-mile Shark Loop Road that concludes with a lookout tower high above the river of grass, and wildlife is abundant all along the way.

The next stop would be Flamingo. Long Pine is a nice campground, plus there's a bounty of hiking, paddling, pedaling, and boating opportunities.

The Gulf Coast region's paddling and boating opportunities are excellent, but if you aren't interested in those things, you can skip this part of the park, especially considering how far it is from the other side.

With elevation maxing out at eight feet, none of the hiking trails are especially difficult, but some, particularly those closer to Flamingo, can be muddy.

With so little topography, sunsets and sunrises are good from just about anywhere, as long as you aren't in a stand of trees.

It's a great idea to tour early in the morning, when wildlife is most active and temps are comfortable.

You can often see manatee in the Flamingo Marina, so look in the water too.

West Lake's Boardwalk will be closed for repairs until somewhere around spring 2022. And they're working on a hotel which may be open when you read this.

Hikes: Anhinga Trail (Easy, 0.8 mile), Shark Loop Road (Moderate, 15, bikes allowed)
Family Activities: Junior Ranger Program, Boat Tours (Flamingo or Gulf Coast),
Guided Tours: Boat (Flamingo or Gulf Coast), kayak (shurradventures.com), or airboat tours!
Rainy Day Activities: Storms are typically brief but intense … wait them out.
History Enthusiasts: Nike Missile Base (only accessible on Ranger Programs between December and March)
Sunrise Spots: West Lake, Long Pine Key, Christian Point, Clubhouse Beach, Eco Pond
Sunset Spots: West Lake
Wildlife: Shark Loop Road, Anhinga Trail, Buttonwood Canal, Eco Pond

Beyond the Park...

See Biscayne NP for businesses on the east side of the park.

Dining
Joanie's Blue Crab Café
39395 Tamiami Tr E, Ochopee
(239) 695-2682

Camellia Street Grill • (239) 695-2003
208 Camellia St, Everglades City
camelliastreetgrill.com

Little Bar • (239) 394-5663
205 Harbor Pl, Goodland
littlebarrestaurant.com

Hoot's Breakfast & Lunch
563 E Elkcam Circle, Marco Island
hootsbreakfastandlunch.com

Grocery Stores
Walmart • (239) 793-5517
3451 Tamiami Trail E, Naples

Costco • (239) 596-6404
6275 Naples Blvd, Naples

Lodging
Ivey House B&B • (239) 695-3299
605 Buckner Ave N, Everglades City
iveyhouse.com

Rod and Gun Club • (239) 695-2101
200 W Broadway, Everglades City
rodandguneverglades.com

Marco Beach Ocean Resort
480 S Collier Blvd, Marco Island
marcoresort.com • (239) 393-1400

Campgrounds
Trail Lakes Camp • (239) 695-2275
40904 Tamiami Trail E, Ochopee
evergladescamping.net

Chokoloskee Island Park and Marina
1150 Hamilton Ln, Chokoloskee
chokoloskee.com • (239) 695-2414

Festivals
Big "O" Birding Fest • March
bigobirdingfestival.com • LaBelle

Sandsculpting Festival • Nov
fmbsandsculpting.com • Fort Myers

Attractions
The next three listings offer airboat tours in the park.

Gator Park • (305) 559-2255
gatorpark.com

Everglades Safari • (305) 226-6923
evergladessafaripark.com

Coopertown Airboats
coopertownairboats.com

Big Cypress National Preserve
Multiple campgrounds here too
33100 Tamiami Trl E, Ochopee
nps.gov/bicy • (239) 695-2000

Delnor-Wiggins Pass State Park
Naples • floridastateparks.org

Island Hopper • (239) 961-2473
islandhopperboatrentalandtours.com

Dry Tortugas

Phone: (305) 242-7700
Website: nps.gov/drto

Established: October 26, 1992
January 4, 1935 (Nat'l Monument)
Size: 64,700 Acres
Annual Visitors: 70,000
Peak Season: April–May

Activities: Paddling, SCUBA, Snorkeling, Fishing, Birdwatching

Campgrounds: 10 primitive campsites on Garden Key
Camping Fee: $15/night
Overflow camping and one group site are also available
Lodging: None

Access: Ferry ($190–210/adult) or Seaplane (half-day: $361/adult, full-day: $634/adult) • Entrance fee included in transportation cost

Park Hours: All day, every day
Entrance Fee: $15/person (16+)

The collection of United States national parks is best defined by its awe-inspiring vistas, deep canyons, rugged mountains, and spouting geysers, natural wonders whose imagery proved America's beauty matched its prosperity. Among this collection hides an aberration of sorts. Just 70 miles from Key West is a park formed around a military fort. Fort Jefferson is a man-made military relic, whose massive brick structure serves as centerpiece of the Dry Tortugas. Many visitors are attracted to the area's military past, but there's also a unique world of natural wonders to be enjoyed above and below the sea. Seven low-lying keys and their surrounding waters provide sanctuary for an array of bird and marine life. Beneath the water is a snorkeler's playground filled with colorful corals, corroding shipwrecks, and chill sea turtles.

Now endangered, the region's once dense population of sea turtles provided inspiration for the archipelago's name. In 1513, Juan Ponce de León claimed to have caught some 160 turtles in the waters surrounding the islands, declaring them "las Tortugas (The Turtles)." Years later the word "Dry" was added to warn mariners of the island's lack of freshwater. As American productivity increased, the 75-mile-wide strait between the Gulf of Mexico and Atlantic Ocean became a busy shipping route, moving massive amounts of cotton, meat, livestock, coffee, tobacco, and other merchandise from the Gulf Coast. Something was needed to suppress piracy and protect trade.

Fort Jefferson was the solution. Construction began in 1847, and after 16 million bricks and 30 years of intermittent work, the fortress

God Bless the USA from Fort Jefferson

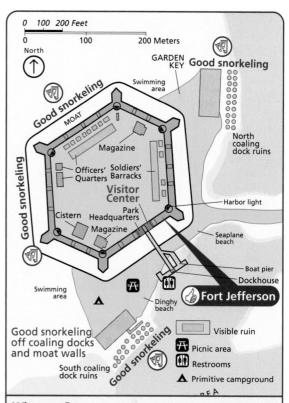

remained unfinished. Even in its incomplete state, it was the most sophisticated coastal fortress from Maine to California and the largest masonry structure in the western hemisphere. Its design called for 420 heavy-guns and 2,000 soldiers. But those guns were never fired and the fort's main use was as a prison for deserters of the Union Army during the Civil War. In 1888, the Army turned the fortress over to the Marine Hospital Service to be used as a quarantine station. In 1908, President Theodore Roosevelt observed the area's importance as a refuge for birds and created Tortugas Keys Reservation.

Nearly a quarter of a century later, the area's recreational usefulness was recognized when President Franklin D. Roosevelt established Fort Jefferson National Monument in 1935, and in 1992 it was designated as a national park. Fort Jefferson, although in need of maintenance, is still standing guard over the gulf. Life is teeming beneath the sea. Thousands of migratory birds flock to the islands, including about 100,000 sooty terns nesting here between March and September. In fact, more sooty terns visit the park each year than tourists, making Dry Tortugas an excellent choice for a relaxing vacation in a tropical paradise with a military past.

When to Go
The park is open all year. April and May are considered the best months to visit due to calm seas, few thunderstorms, and comfortable temperatures. Fort Jefferson and Loggerhead Key are open daily from dawn until dusk. Bush Key is closed seasonally from mid-January through mid-October during the sooty tern nesting season. East Key, Middle Key, Hospital Key, and Long Key are closed for nesting wildlife. Hurricane season is June through November. Florida Keys Eco Discovery Center is open Tuesday through Saturday from 9am–4pm. Garden Key Visitor Center is open daily from 8:30am–4:30pm.

Directions & Transportation
The park is 70 miles southwest of Key West. It can only be reached by seaplane or boat. **Dry Tortugas National Park Ferry** (day-trip: $190/adult, camping: $210/adult, 800.634.0939, drytortugas.com), located at Key West Ferry Terminal (100 Grinnell St), provides water transportation and **Key West Seaplane Adventures** (half-day: $361/adult, full-day: $631/adult, 305.293.9300, keywestseaplanecharters.com) provides air transportation. Rates include the park entrance fee. Show your National Park Pass upon arrival to receive an entrance fee refund.

TORTUGAS ECOLOGICAL RESERVE
TORTUGAS NORTH

NORTHWEST CHANNEL

Y "H"
Fl Y 2.5s
24°43'00"N
82°54'00"W

Y "I"
Fl Y 4s
24°43'32"N
82°52'00"W

W "A"
24°43'32"N
82°51'00"W

Y "J"

Y "G"

PARK BOUNDARY

Y "F"

Texas Rock

Brilliant Shoal

RESEARCH NATURAL AREA BOUNDARY

Northkey Harbor

DRY TORTUGAS NATIONAL PARK

Y "E"
Fl Y 6s
24°39'00"N
82°58'00"W

Loggerhead Key

□ "7"

Middle Ground

Hospital Key
(closed to public)

△ "4"

East Ke
(closed to publi

Middle Key
(closed to public)

Loggerhead Key
Fl W 20s 167ft 24M

Windjammer wreck

White Shoal

Fort Jefferson
on Garden Key
(see inset below right)

Loggerhead Reef

□ "3"

△ "4"

DRY
TORTUGAS

G "1"

Bird Key

RESEARCH NATURAL AREA BOUNDARY

SOUTHEAST CHANNEL

R "2"
Fl R 4s

RESEARCH NATURAL AREA BOUNDARY

W "C"
24°36'00"N
82°58'00"W

W "B"
24°36'00"N
82°51'00"W

W "P"

Y "D"

Fl G 2.5s 19ft 5M "1"

SOUTHWEST CHANNEL

"6" △

Fo
on

Y "Q"

"2"

PARK BOUNDARY

FLORIDA KEYS
NATIONAL MARINE
SANCTUARY

"2BK

"3B

Brick wreck

24°34'00"W
82°58'00"W
Y "C"
Fl Y 4s

Y "B"

Y "A"
Fl Y 2.5s
24°34'00"N
82°54'00"W

This map is an orientation aid for
visitors to Dry Tortugas National Park.
It should not be used in place of
National Ocean Survey chart 11438,
which is indispensable for safe
boating on these waters.

GOOD
SNORKELING

Bird Ke
Bank

Light characteristics
Fl Flashing
W White
R Red
Y Yellow

Buoy characteristics
R Red
G Green
Yellow

▲ Red daymark   □ White daymark   Buoy   Light   Sunken wreck

□ Green daymark   △ Daybeacon   Lighted buoy   Lighthouse   • Rock

Fort Jefferson

Fort Jefferson

In the early 19th century, the U.S. was in search of an ideal location for a fort to protect the profitable Gulf Coast–Atlantic Ocean trade route. Dry Tortugas was just the place, but when U.S. Navy Commodore David Porter visited these remote keys in 1825, he declared them completely unsuitable. He called the islands specks of land without a trace of freshwater among a sea of blue, and probably not even stable enough to build the fort they desired.

Four years later, Commodore John Rodgers revisited the Dry Tortugas. He believed it to be the perfect location. In 1847, after 17 years of engineering studies and bureaucratic delays construction of Fort Jefferson began. The fort, named for the third president, was to be the scourge of the seas, equipped with 420 heavy-guns and a fleet of warships capable of running down ships wise enough to remain beyond firing range. It took a huge workforce to build such an immense structure, including blacksmiths, machinists, carpenters, and masons. Even the resident prisoners and slaves helped build the behemoth. By 1860, more than $250,000 (~$10 million today) had been spent on a fort that wasn't half completed. During the Civil War, an influx of prisoners, mostly Union deserters, caused the fort's population to peak at more than 1,500, and new prisoners were immediately put to work.

In 1865, the fort welcomed its most famous prisoner, Dr. Samuel Mudd, who was convicted of conspiracy in the assassination of President Abraham Lincoln. It is believed he set, splinted, and bandaged John Wilkes Booth's broken leg shortly after Booth shot the President at Ford's Theater. Not long after his arrival, the prison's doctor died during an outbreak of yellow fever. Mudd temporarily took over the position. Soldiers, feeling indebted to Mudd, petitioned the president on his behalf, and four years after he arrived, Mudd was pardoned by President Andrew Johnson.

By 1888, the usefulness of Fort Jefferson was waning, and damage caused by the corrosive tropical environment and frequent hurricanes created high maintenance costs. The Army decided to turn the fort over to the Marine Hospital Service. They used it as a quarantine station up until the 1930s when it was officially handed over to the National Park Service. The fort was never completed and never fired upon, but this long-since-obsolete maritime base is an interesting piece of American military history set in a tropical paradise.

North

0 _____ 1 Kilometer
0 _____ 1 Statute Mile
0 _____ 1 Nautical Mile

'32''N
'00''W

Pulaski Shoal
Fl W 6s 49ft 9M

GOOD SCUBA DIVING

24°42'00''N
82°46'00''W
Y "L"
Fl Y 2.5s

Y "M"
Fl Y 4s
24°40'00''N
82°46'00''W

FLORIDA KEYS
NATIONAL MARINE
SANCTUARY

Y "N"

O"
6s
'37'00''N
'48'00''W

5 Kilometer
0.5 Statute Mile
0.5 Nautical Mile

Fl G 4s 16ft 5M "3"
Iowa Rock

son
Key

Shoal
Bush Key

Light

"9" "11"
"10" "12"

Tortugas
anchorage

Long Key
(closed to public)

Nurse Shark Special
Protection Zone
(closed to public June
through October)

Coral Special
Protection Zone
(closed to public)

Snorkeling back to the beach

Camping

There are 10 primitive campsites on Garden Key. Sites are available on a first-come, first-served basis for $15 per night, paid with your ferry ticket (the ferry only brings a limited number of campers, so make reservations eight to ten months in advance). If the primitive sites are full, an overflow camping area is available. One group site is available for groups of 10–20 campers by reservation (available online or at 305.242.7700). Campers must bring all food and water required for the duration of their stay. Composting toilets are available in the campground. Wood fires are prohibited. Be sure to pack your food and scented items in a hard-sided container to protect it from rats and crabs. There are posts to hang trash and food, but some rats have figured those out.

Hiking

Besides underwater, the primary place to explore Dry Tortugas is Fort Jefferson. Here you'll find a self-guided tour that takes visitors through the history of the 50-foot-tall, three-story, heavily-armored fort. Visitors can walk along the 0.6-mile-long seawall and moat, where you may spot some sea creatures.

Paddling

Paddling allows observant visitors to keep an eye on what's happening above and below the water. Crystal clear waters provide a window to life beneath the sea. When you aren't watching the creatures stirring below your boat, look along the horizon for migratory birds. Bush and Long Keys are the closest islands to Fort Jefferson and where you are most likely to find nesting birds. **Loggerhead**, the largest key of the Dry Tortugas, is three miles away. It's perfect for swimming and snorkeling, and you can take a look at the *Windjammer* wreck near the southwest tip of the key, and its beaches will be empty (not that Garden Key's will

be packed, but how often do you get a beach to yourself?). To get to Loggerhead Key you must pass deep open water with a swift current. (Inexperienced paddlers should not head out into open water.) No matter where you paddle, a boating permit is required. If you plan on paddling to Loggerhead Key, it must be listed on your permit. Permits are free and may be obtained on arrival from a park staff member. Shark and Coral Special Protection Zones are closed to paddling. You should ask where these areas are in order to avoid them. The ferry will transport your kayak(s) to Dry Tortugas, but there is limited space. Confirm space requirements prior to arrival.

SCUBA Diving

Located at the far western end of the Florida Keys, these islands are not tethered to the mainland by roads and bridges, so SCUBA divers must arrive by private boat or charter.

Beneath the water, divers find the Caribbean's largest and healthiest reef system. One of the highlights is Sherwood Forest, featuring a canopy of mushroom-shaped formations. More than 400 species of fish reside here; of them, hammerhead sharks, barracuda, and Goliath grouper are frequently seen. Dolphins and turtles are also common to the area. Sea Clusive (305.744.9928, seaclusive.com) and Adventure Watersport Charters (305.453.6070, adventurewatersportcharters.com) are permitted to conduct dives within the park.

Snorkeling

More than 99% of the park is water, so you have to get in or under the water to experience it. Dry Tortugas just might be the best snorkeling the Florida Keys have to offer. The water is clean, clear, and warm. A boat or seaplane trip is required to reach them, but once you're there, the water is yours to explore whenever you want. A designated snorkel area is available on Garden Key, southwest of Fort Jefferson along its outer wall. You can walk right into the water from the main swimming area north of Fort Jefferson. The area features chest-deep water, turtle grass, and coral. Coral reefs make up a small fraction of the underwater environment, but they provide habitat for more than 25% of the area's fish population. Snorkeling is best along the moat wall (north and west walls of Fort Jefferson) and along the north and south coaling docks. *Yankee Freedom* has snorkel sets for their passengers, but one opinionated snorkeler said several masks didn't seal well, so you may want to bring your own snorkel gear (or at least the mask). Camp and you'll have hours to snorkel at your leisure.

Fishing

Due to excessive commercial fishing new regulations prohibit fishing in about half of the park's waters. The ban was required to help repopulate a once thriving fish community. Good fishing is still possible in and around Dry Tortugas, and the scenery and climate is a serious bonus. Calm water makes spring and summer the preferred seasons for fishing. Grouper and snapper are commonly caught. On Garden Key you are permitted to fish from the seaplane dock (east of the main dock) when the seaplane is absent, the dinghy beach west of the main dock (as long as you're at least 50 feet from the old coaling dock ruins). You can also fish from a boat within the one-mile Historic Use Area of Garden Key. Spearfishing and lobstering are prohibited. Delph Fishing (305.304.7574, delphfishing.com), Y Knot Charters (305.923.6134, yknotkeywest.com), Fish Andy (fishandy.com), and Two Fish Charters (305.797.6396) offer overnight fishing charters to Dry Tortugas.

Boat Tours

If you want to get to the island, you're probably going to come with *Yankee Freedom* (800.634.0939, drytortugas.com). They provide boat service to the park from Key West Ferry Terminal on Grinnell Street. Tickets cost $190 per adult and $135 per child (ages 4–16). The park fee is included in these prices, so if you have a National Parks Pass, present it at the ticket booth for a $15 refund. The trip takes approximately 2.5 hours each way and check-in begins at 7am for 8am departure (campers should arrive at 6:30am). Breakfast and lunch are served aboard the boat. They have limited space available to transport personal kayaks. Snorkel gear is provided. Knowledgeable guides provide tours of Fort Jefferson. Snorkelers and swimmers will be able to rinse off with freshwater onboard the boat. Complimentary soft drinks, water, and tea are available throughout the day. Alcohol is available for purchase.

Birdwatching

Nearly 300 bird species have been identified within park boundaries. Only seven species nest here regularly; most commonly seen are brown and black noddies, magnificent frigatebirds, and masked and brown boobies. Spring is prime time for bird watching. Between March and September 100,000 sooty terns nest on Bush Key. Bush Key is visible from Garden Key and Fort Jefferson, but bringing a set of binoculars remains a good idea.

Visitor Centers

Garden Key Visitor Center houses a small shop, a few historical and ecological exhibits, and a lionfish

An invasive lionfish

in a tank. It's open daily from 8:30am–4:30pm. Florida **Keys Eco Discovery Center** examines South Florida life. It's open Tuesday through Saturday, 9am–4pm.

Ranger Programs & For Kids

Check online or with a park ranger upon arrival to see what ranger-led activities are taking place the day you visit. Several rangers live on the island, and they provide intermittent tours. Guests who arrive with *Yankee Freedom* are offered a complimentary 45-minute guided tour of the fort.

Dry Tortugas is a great park for kids. Many children love the water, the beach, the wildlife, and they might even love Fort Jefferson. If the fort's history isn't holding their attention, they will at least have fun climbing the spiral staircases, gazing into the moat, and pretending to fire 19th century cannons.

Children can become Junior Rangers. A free workbook is available online, at the visitor center, or aboard the *Yankee Freedom*. Complete it to earn a park badge. The program is recommended for children ages 8–13.

Flora & Fauna

The park's vegetation is fairly limited. You'll find a variety of palms and succulents, but several islands are nothing more than sand, almost completely devoid of life. Sea grasses and other marine plant life can be found underwater.

Nearly 300 species of birds have been identified in the park, but only 7 species nest here regularly. The park protects the most active turtle nesting site in the

Florida Keys. Hawksbill, loggerhead, and green sea turtles are commonly seen swimming in the park's waters. Each year female sea turtles climb onto sandy beaches of Middle and East Keys to lay their eggs before retreating to the sea. You'll also find an amazing variety of coral, fish, and other marine life underwater. Sea fans, anemones, lobster, and sponges are often found on the sea floor. Coral reef inhabitants may include numerous colorful reef fish and their predators: amberjacks, groupers, wahoos, tarpon, sharks, and barracudas. You may also spot the invasive (and venomous) lionfish. For a guaranteed lionfish sighting, stop in at the visitor center, where one is on display.

Pets & Accessibility

Pets are permitted on Garden Key but not inside Fort Jefferson. And they are not permitted on any other key in the park. They must be kept on a leash (less than six feet). Keep in mind that pets are not permitted aboard the *Yankee Freedom* or seaplane, so, to bring a pet, you'll have to arrive by charter or private boat.

The dock, campground, visitor center, bottom level of Fort Jefferson, and tour boats are accessible to individuals in wheelchairs. The *Yankee Freedom* has lifts at the dock to help board the boat in Key West, but they'll need advance notice to get it setup for any passengers in need of assistance.

Weather

The park experiences three seasons. December to March is the winter season when you can expect windy weather and angry seas. The tropical storm season spans from June to November. It is marked by hot and humid days with occasional thunderstorms. Hurricane activity is not unheard of during this time. Finally, there's birding season, which includes April and May. This period provides nearly perfect weather for a tropical vacation. Due to the highly erratic nature of the area's weather, visitors should always check an extended weather forecast the day before leaving.

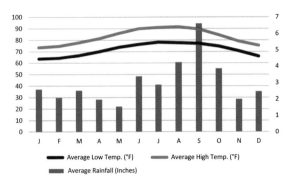

- Average Low Temp. (°F)
- Average High Temp. (°F)
- Average Rainfall (Inches)

Tips & Recommendations

Everyone (including me) says April and May are the best months to visit, but visitation is pretty steady throughout the year. A few thousand people arrive each month, so if you're headed to Florida, don't discard Dry Tortugas because the calendar won't be flipped to April or May, come down to Key West and check the place out.

While the water is never crowded, you can essentially have the fort, beach, and water to yourself by taking advantage of the primitive campsites. If you like solitude but dislike camping, take the first or last seaplane flight and you'll miss the ferry crowd for much of your stay.

Arrive via the ferry and you'll have approximately five hours on the island. That should be plenty of time to join the narrated tour (about an hour), snorkel, eat lunch (served on the boat), and enjoy the beach.

If you spend the night, travel light and be sure to pack your food (and all scented items) in an animal-proof container (rats are a problem).

Or minimize the rat problem by camping in the overflow area (the large, grassy space, southeast of the primitive sites). The downside is no shade.

If you have your own snorkel mask that fits well, bring it. While most masks fit most faces, the amount of luggage space required to pack your own is worth eliminating the chance of less-than-enjoyable snorkeling. Should you go out and buy a mask if you don't have one? No. Only do so if you know you're going to do more snorkeling in your future. Then it's worth the investment.

Don't forget your sunscreen! Chances are good, it will be hot and sunny.

Sunrise/Sunset Spots: Campers get the opportunity to watch the sun rise from the Atlantic Ocean and sink into the Gulf of Mexico. Garden Key is small, allowing you to walk anywhere in minutes, selecting the spot of your choice. There's no wrong answer here (unless you choose to stand behind a tree or right next to Fort Jefferson on the opposite side of the show) during a brilliant sunrise/sunset.

Wildlife: The coaling docks and moat wall are the best locations to find marine life. Visit late February through April and you'll see impressive bird life (in comfortable weather).

Entering Fort Jefferson

Beyond the Park...

Dining
Square Grouper • (305) 745-8880
22658 Overseas Hwy, Cudjoe Key
squaregrouperbarandgrill.com

HogFish Bar & Grille
6810 Front St, Stock Island
hogfishbar.com • (305) 293-4041

El Siboney • (305) 296-4184
900 Catherine St, Key West
elsiboneyrestaurant.com

Better Than Sex • (305) 296-8102
906 Simonton, Key West
betterthansexdesserts.com

Sarabeth's Kitchen
530 Simonton St, Key West
sarabeth.com • (305) 293-8181

Santiago's Bodega • (305) 296-7691
207 Petronia St, Key West
santiagosbodega.com

BO's Fish Wagon • (305) 294-9272
801 Caroline St, Key West •
bosfishwagon.com

Caroline's • (305) 294-7511
310 Duval St, Key West
carolinescafe.com

Grocery Stores
Publix • (305) 451-0808
101437 Overseas Hwy, Key Largo

Winn-Dixie • (305) 852-5904
92100 Overseas Hwy, Tavernier

Publix • (305) 289-2920
5407 Overseas Hwy, Marathon

Winn-Dixie • (305) 872-4124
251 Key Deer Blvd, Big Pine Key

Publix • (305) 296-2225
3316 N Roosevelt Blvd, Key West

Winn-Dixie • (305) 294-0491
2778 N Roosevelt Blvd, Key West

Lodging
Parmer's Resort • (305) 872-2157
565 Barry Ave, Little Torch Key
parmersresort.com

Harbor Inn • (305) 296-2978
219 Elizabeth St, Key West
keywestharborinn.com

Mermaid & The Alligator B&B
729 Truman Ave, Key West
kwmermaid.com • (800) 773-1894

Orchid Key Inn • (305) 296-9915
1004 Duval St, Key West
orchidkeyinn.com

Campgrounds
Keys Palms • (305) 440-2832
104200 Overseas Hwy, Key Largo
keyspalmrvresort.com

Keys Ventures @96
96401 Overseas Hwy, Key Largo
keys.ventures • (305) 451-2911

Riptide RV Resort • (305) 852-8481
97680 Overseas Hwy, Key Largo
sunrvresorts.com

Royal Palm RV Park • (305) 872-9856
163 Cunningham Ln, Big Pine Key
royalpalmrvpark.com

Festivals
Underwater Music Festival • July
31020 Overseas Hwy, Big Pine Key

Attractions
Capt. Sterling Everglades Tours
101900 Overseas Hwy, Key Largo
(305) 394-7422

John Pennekamp Coral Reef SP
*Snorkel/SCUBA destination with
Christ of the Abyss (an 8.5-ft
Jesus statue in 25-ft of water)*
102601 Overseas Hwy, Key Largo
pennekamppark.com

Skydive Key West • (305) 876-6302
skydivekeywest.com

Wild Bird Center • (305) 852-4486
92080 Overseas Hwy, Tavernier
keepthemflying.org

Dolphin Plus • (305) 451-4060
101900 Overseas Hwy, Key Largo
dolphinsplus.com

History of Diving Museum
82990 Overseas Hwy, Islamorada
divingmuseum.org • (305) 664-9737

Bahia Honda SP • (305) 872-2353
36850 Overseas Hwy, Big Pine Key
bahiahondapark.com

Curry Hammock • (305) 289-2690
56200 Overseas Hwy, Marathon
floridastateparks.org

Turtle Hospital • (305) 743-2552
2396 Overseas Hwy, Marathon
turtlehospital.org

Catch Em' All • (305) 481-4568
catch-em-all.com

Skins and Fins • (305) 393-0363
skinsandfinscharters.com

Long Key SP • (305) 664-4815
67400 Overseas Hwy, Long Key
floridastateparks.org

Great White Heron NWR
fws.gov

Butterfly Conservatory
1316 Duval St • (305) 296-2988
keywestbutterfly.com

Truman Little White House
111 Front St • (305) 294-9911
trumanlittlewhitehouse.com

Fort Zachary Taylor Historic SP
601 Howard England Way
floridastateparks.org

Wild about Dolphins • (305) 294-5026
6000 Peninsular Ave, Stock Island
wildaboutdolphins.com

Edward B Knight Pier
White St, Key West

Schooner Appledore
205 Elizabeth St, Key West
appledore2.com • (305) 509-9047

Ingham Maritime Museum
Southard St, Key West
uscgcingham.org • (305) 292-5072

Yoga on the Beach • Key West
yogaonbeach.com • (508) 737-3211

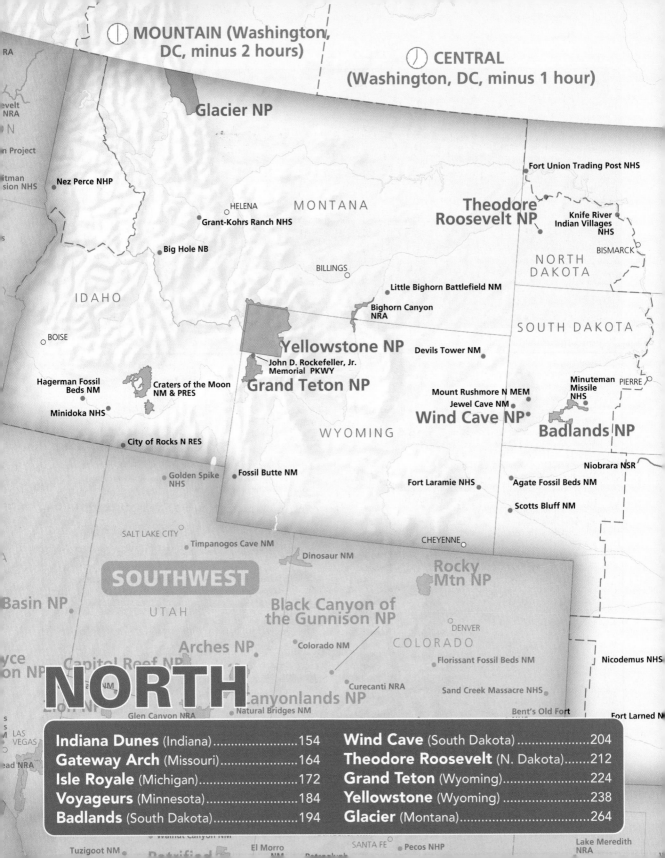

MOUNTAIN (Washington, DC, minus 2 hours)

CENTRAL (Washington, DC, minus 1 hour)

Glacier NP

Fort Union Trading Post NHS

Nez Perce NHP

MONTANA

HELENA

Grant-Kohrs Ranch NHS

Theodore Roosevelt NP

Knife River Indian Villages NHS

BISMARCK

Big Hole NB

NORTH DAKOTA

BILLINGS

IDAHO

Little Bighorn Battlefield NM

Bighorn Canyon NRA

SOUTH DAKOTA

BOISE

Yellowstone NP

Devils Tower NM

Hagerman Fossil Beds NM

John D. Rockefeller, Jr. Memorial PKWY

Grand Teton NP

PIERRE

Minuteman Missile NHS

Mount Rushmore N MEM

Jewel Cave NM

Craters of the Moon NM & PRES

Minidoka NHS

Wind Cave NP

WYOMING

Badlands NP

City of Rocks N RES

Niobrara NSR

Golden Spike NHS

Fossil Butte NM

Fort Laramie NHS

Agate Fossil Beds NM

Scotts Bluff NM

SALT LAKE CITY

Timpanogos Cave NM

CHEYENNE

SOUTHWEST

Dinosaur NM

Rocky Mtn NP

Basin NP

UTAH

Black Canyon of the Gunnison NP

DENVER

Arches NP

Colorado NM

COLORADO

Capitol Reef NP

Florissant Fossil Beds NM

Nicodemus NHS

NORTH

Canyonlands NP

Curecanti NRA

Sand Creek Massacre NHS

Glen Canyon NRA

Natural Bridges NM

Bent's Old Fort

Fort Larned N

LAS VEGAS

Tuzigoot NM

El Morro NM

SANTA FE

Pecos NHP

Lake Meredith NRA

Voyageurs NP

Isle Royale NP

Grand Portage NM

LAKE SUPERIOR

Apostle
Islands
NL

Keweenaw NHP

Pictured Rocks
NL

FARGO

MINNESOTA

Saint Croix NSR

LAKE HURON

Sleeping Bear Dunes
NL

Mississippi NRRA   ST PAUL

MINNEAPOLIS

WISCONSIN

LAKE MICHIGAN

Pipestone NM

MICHIGAN

Effigy Mounds NM

MADISON

MILWAUKEE

LANSING

DETROIT

Missouri NRR

IOWA

Herbert Hoover NHS

CHICAGO

River Raisin NBP

TOLEDO

Cuyahoga
Valley N

NEBRASKA

DES MOINES

Pullman NM

Indiana
Dunes NP

First Ladies N

OMAHA

OHIO

LINCOLN

NORTH

ILLINOIS

INDIANA

Dayton
Aviation
Heritage
NHP

COLUM

Charles Young
Buffalo Soldiers

Homestead NM
of America

SPRINGFIELD
Lincoln Home NHS

INDIANAPOLIS

Hope
Cultu

CINCINNATI

William Howard Taft
NHS

Gateway Arch NP

KANSAS CITY

George Rogers
Clark NHP

FRANKFORT

Brown v. Board
of Education NHS

TOPEKA

Harry S Truman NHS

ST LOUIS

LOUISVILLE

JEFFERSON CITY

Ulysses S.
Grant NHS

Abraham Lincoln Birthplace
NHP

KANSAS

Tallgrass Prairie
N PRES

MISSOURI

Lincoln Boyhood N MEM

KENTUCKY

WICHITA

Fort Scott NHS

Wilson's Creek
NB

Ozark NSR

Mammoth
Cave NP

Cumberla
NHP

Big South Fork NRRA

George Washington Carver NM

Fort Donelson NB

Manhattan
Project
NHP

NASHVILLE

Obed WSR

Pea Ridge NMP

Stones River NB

TULSA

TENNESSEE

Buffalo NR

Great Smoky Mountains NP

field NHS

Indiana Dunes

Dune Succession Trail

Phone: (219) 395-1882
Website: nps.gov/indu

Established: February 15, 2019
Nov. 6, 1966 (National Lakeshore)
Size: 15,067 Acres
Annual Visitors: 1.8 Million
Peak Season: June–August
Hiking Trails: 50+ Miles
Beach: 15 Miles

Activities: Swimming, Hiking, Biking, Horseback Riding

Dunewood Campground: $25/night
Backcountry Camping: None

Park Hours: 6am to 11pm (varies)
Entrance Fee: None
West Beach: $6 per vehicle per day
(Memorial Day–Labor Day)

Like every "new" national park of the past three decades, the National Park Service (NPS) already protected Indiana Dunes prior to receiving the NPS's flagship status. For most visitors, the name change is a matter of semantics. The park operates exactly as it did before February 15, 2019 when it was a national lakeshore. However, the name change has two significant effects: the park's digital and physical media materials need to be updated and local tourism departments enjoy a free marketing boon. One chamber of commerce believes the name change could boost visitation by as many as 800,000 additional visitors each year. For better or worse, national parks collectively get far more attention from travelers, journalists, and guidebooks like this, compared to every other group of NPS units.

Interestingly, Indiana Dunes attracted the attention of Stephen Mather, first director of the NPS and sentimental father of the national parks, in 1916, the same year the NPS was established. At the time, all national parks were in remote regions out West. Mather was determined to add eastern parks of similar scenic character and inherently more accessible due to their proximity to most of the U.S. population. More visitors meant more support for the "National Park Idea." In his Sand Dunes National Park Proposal, Mather stated he has "never seen sand dunes that equal them in any degree," that they are "beautiful at all times of year," and that they "attract the scientist, the teacher, and the student, as well as the individual who merely seeks rest and recreation and communion with nature." Teachers, researchers, outdoors enthusiasts, artists, and dunes-area property owners recited affection for this unusual environment. Scenic beauty and recreational opportunities found at the dunes were indisputable; property was the problem. Out West, most, if not all, park land was already owned by the government. Here, money would need to be allocated to purchase land from private parties, some uninterested in selling to the government for nothing short of extortionate rates. It didn't matter. WWI happened, preoccupying Congress with more pressing matters. And the dunes region was a center of much more than recreation. It was a site of industry.

Times haven't changed much. Today, industrial structures are far more prominent than the dunes they're built on. Working your way east along Lake Michigan's coast from Gary to Michigan City, first you'll see a power plant, then a steel mill, a couple miles of national park land sneak into frame before giving way to a harbor and another steel mill. A few more miles of uninterrupted sand terminate at another power plant in Michigan City. Railroad tracks run parallel to the coast, connecting industrial hubs. This is the modern story of Indiana Dunes. Industry and recreation cohabiting with one another. No national park so clearly depicts the American pursuit of wealth and development, and the side effects of those pursuits: the need for recreation and relaxation—the need to escape. Even the park's establishment as a national lakeshore in 1966 featured a tit-for-tat exchange with industry. Industry received a port. The people received a park.

In 1916, Stephen Mather's Sand Dunes National Park Proposal asked whether these dunes "were worthy of inclusion in a national park?" His national park definition required "scenic features of supreme magnificence or scientific or historical features of transcendent importance," as well as being distinctive and accessible. These are his words: "My judgment is clear, however, that their characteristics entitle the major portion of their area to consideration as a national park project." He went on to discuss the area's distinct beauty, unlike any existing national park, as well as its incomparable accessibility. More than 100 years have passed, but—thanks to four lines of text tucked away in a U.S. Homeland Security Budget—today Indiana Dunes is a national park. Is it worthy of the title? Visit and decide for yourself.

Where industry meets recreation

When to Go
Indiana Dunes is open year-round, but nearly half its visitors arrive in summer. Spring brings wildflowers. Fall sees colorful foliage. Winter dusts the dunes with snow. The park has its appeal every day of the year and only gets crowded during summer and weekends (especially the holidays).

Transportation and Airports
The park runs two 16-passenger beach shuttles Saturdays and Sundays from Memorial Day through Labor Day. Both operate between 10am and 6pm, taking a 30-minute break at 2pm. The East Shuttle stops at Dunewood Campground, USGS Great Lakes Research Center, and Kemil Beach Parking Lot. The West Shuttle stops at Miller Train Station, Marquette Park, Paul H. Douglas Center, 5th Avenue and Lake Street, and Lake Street Beach.

The South Shore Line (mysouthshoreline.com) conducts regularly scheduled trains between Chicago and South Bend, with two stations (Dune Park and Beverly Shores) near the park. One-way fare is about $10 per person from Chicago (Millennium Station). The train is a fantastic way to sneak in a Chicago trip. Passengers can bring a bicycle free-of-charge during certain non-peak fares. Even with the summer weekend shuttle and Beverly Shores South Shore Railroad Station a short walk from Dunewood Campground, most visitors will want a car to explore the park in depth due to its disjointed nature.

Gary/Chicago International Airport (GYY) is closest to the park, but O'Hare (ORD), Midway (MDW), and South Bend (SBN) International Airports are less than two hours away by car (traffic permitting). Car rental is available at each airport.

Directions
I-94 runs parallel to Lake Michigan's shoreline and Indiana Dunes National Park. Whether traveling east or west on I-94, take Exit 26B onto IN-49 N, which leads directly to the visitor center (and Indiana Dunes State Park). The national park has many disjointed regions.

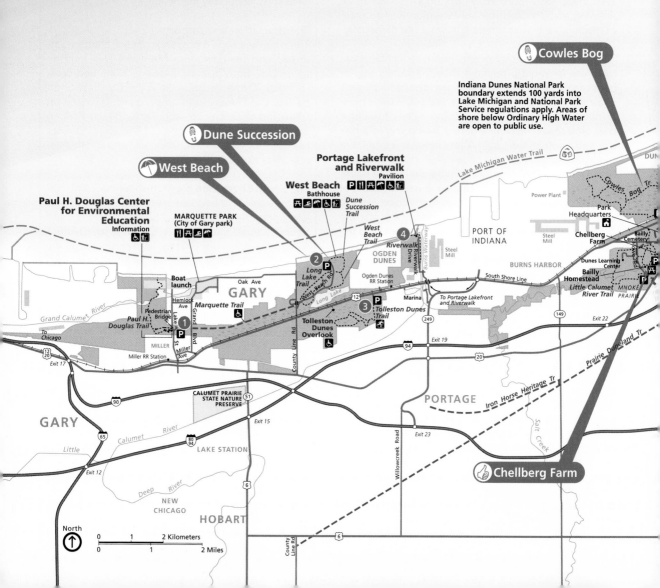

LAKE MICHIGAN

Cowles Bog

Indiana Dunes National Park boundary extends 100 yards into Lake Michigan and National Park Service regulations apply. Areas of shore below Ordinary High Water are open to public use.

Dune Succession

Portage Lakefront and Riverwalk
Pavilion

West Beach

West Beach
Bathhouse

Dune Succession Trail

Paul H. Douglas Center for Environmental Education
Information

MARQUETTE PARK
(City of Gary park)

West Beach Trail

Riverwalk

OGDEN DUNES

PORT OF INDIANA

Power Plant

BURNS HARBOR

Park Headquarters

Chellberg Farm

Bailly Cemetery

Dunes Learning Center

Bailly Homestead

Little Calumet River Trail

MNOKE PRAIRIE

Lake Michigan Water Trail

Steel Mill

Steel Mill

Ogden Dunes RR Station

South Shore Line

Long Lake Trail

Long Lake

Boat launch

Hemlock Ave

Pedestrian Bridge

Paul H. Douglas Trail

Grand Calumet River

To Chicago

GARY

Oak Ave

Marquette Trail

MILLER

Miller RR Station

Miller Ave

Tolleston Dunes Overlook

Tolleston Dunes Trail

Marina

To Portage Lakefront and Riverwalk

Exit 19

Exit 22

Prairie Duneland Tr

Chellberg Farm

Iron Horse Heritage Tr

PORTAGE

Salt Creek

Exit 23

Willowcreek Road

CALUMET PRAIRIE STATE NATURE PRESERVE

Exit 15

GARY

Calumet River

LAKE STATION

Little

Deep River

NEW CHICAGO

HOBART

Exit 12

Exit 17

County Line Rd

North

| 0 | 1 | 2 Kilometers |
| 0 | 1 | 2 Miles |

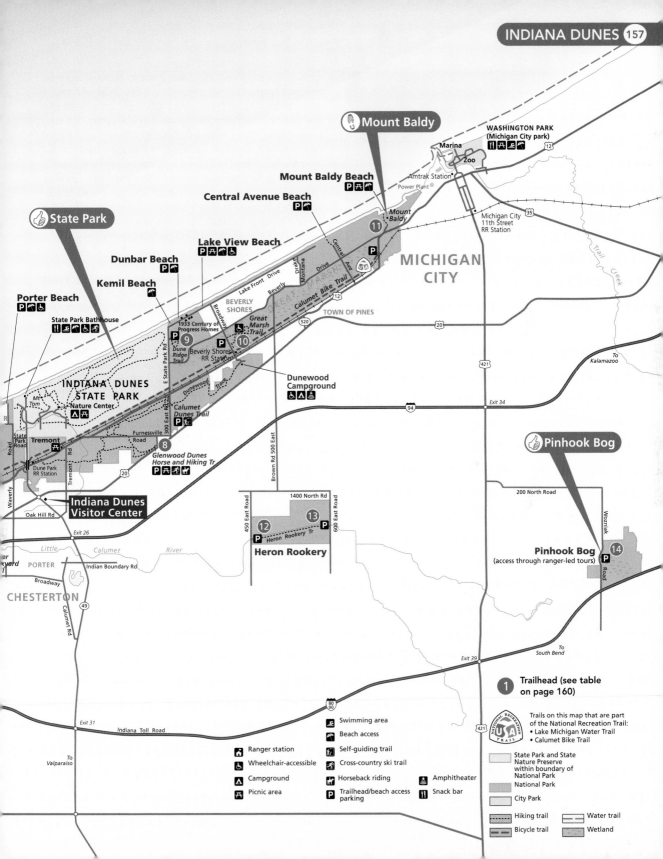

Mount Baldy

WASHINGTON PARK
(Michigan City park)

Marina

Zoo

Amtrak Station

Power Plant

Mount Baldy Beach

Central Avenue Beach

State Park

Lake View Beach

Dunbar Beach

Kemil Beach

Porter Beach

State Park Bathhouse

1933 Century of Progress Homes

Lake Front Drive

BEVERLY SHORES

Beverly Shores RR Station

Great Marsh Trail

Dune Ridge Trail

Michigan City 11th Street RR Station

MICHIGAN CITY

Mount Baldy

Drake

Montana

Beverly

Central Ave

Calumet Bike Trail

GREAT MARSH

TOWN OF PINES

Dunewood Campground

INDIANA DUNES STATE PARK

Mt. Tom

Nature Center

Dune Park RR Station

Tremont

State Park Road

Calumet Dunes Trail

Glenwood Dunes Horse and Hiking Tr

Furnessville Road

Dunewood Trace

E State Park Rd

300 East Rd

Indiana Dunes Visitor Center

Oak Hill Rd

Exit 26

Little Calumet River

Indian Boundary Rd

PORTER

Broadway

CHESTERTON

Calumet Rd

To Valparaiso

Exit 31

Indiana Toll Road

Waverly

Brown Rd 500 East

450 East Road

600 East Road

1400 North Rd

Heron Rookery Tr

Heron Rookery

To Kalamazoo

To South Bend

Exit 34

Exit 39

Pinhook Bog

200 North Road

Wozniak Road

Pinhook Bog
(access through ranger-led tours)

Trailhead (see table on page 160)

Trails on this map that are part of the National Recreation Trail:
• Lake Michigan Water Trail
• Calumet Bike Trail

Swimming area

Beach access

Self-guiding trail

Cross-country ski trail

Horseback riding

Trailhead/beach access parking

Ranger station

Wheelchair-accessible

Campground

Picnic area

Amphitheater

Snack bar

State Park and State Nature Preserve within boundary of National Park

National Park

City Park

Hiking trail

Bicycle trail

Water trail

Wetland

Mount Baldy

Camping

Dunewood is the only campground in the park. Located in Beverly Shores at the intersection of Golf Wood Road and Dunewood Parkway, it features 66 sites (54 drive-in, 12 walk-in, 4 fully accessible), restrooms, and showers. Electric and water hookups are not available. The campground is open from April 1 through November 1. Each site costs $25 per night for up to 8 people. More than half the sites can be reserved at recreation.gov, the rest are first-come, first-served via an automatic kiosk (credit or debit card required). Senior and Access Pass holders receive a 50% discount.

Indiana Dunes State Park offers year-round camping with more than 100 sites. All sites feature water and electric hookups for $30 per night (plus $7 resident or $12 non-resident entrance fee per vehicle). Reservations can be made at reserveamerica.com.

Swimming

With 15 miles of shoreline, Indiana Dunes has plenty of sand to sink your toes into. All beaches are open from 6am until 11pm. West, Portage, Porter, Kemil, Dunbar, Lake View, Central Avenue, and Mount Baldy Beaches (listed from west to east) have parking areas and restrooms. West, Porter, Dunbar, and Lake View are easiest to access. The rest require slightly longer walks from their respective parking areas. Hardest among them is the short trail to Mount Baldy Beach. It's less than a half-mile roundtrip, but you'll have to descend (and then ascend) a fairly steep dune to reach the waterfront. Portage (along with the adjacent Riverwalk) and Lake View Beaches are superb sunset destinations. When we went to print, Portage Beach was closed due to storm damage, but the views remain pleasant. Driving to Portage Beach, you may think you're on the wrong path. At first it will feel like you're

going to a steel mill. You are. Prior to redevelopment, this site hosted settling ponds for the steel mill and a sewage treatment facility. At Lake View, be sure to use the national park's parking area (the western lot with restrooms). Park in Beverly Shores lot and you might get ticketed. Dunbar Beach parking area used to be a homesite. From here, walking east along the beach, you'll pass five historic homes from the 1933 Century of Progress World's Fair. In 2019, one of these historic homes known as The House of Tomorrow offered a "free" 50-year sublease to anyone willing to restore it (at an estimated cost of $2-3 million).

You are welcome to swim anywhere within the park, but lifeguards only monitor the primary swim area, **West Beach** (from Memorial Day through Labor Day). It features the largest parking area, as well as a bathhouse with showers and lockers. As the park's most popular destination, it is also blessed with an amenity fee, $6 per vehicle per day (only collected between Memorial Day and Labor Day). Every inch of beach provides views of the distant Chicago skyline, but my favorite views are from West Beach's Dune Succession Trail. For more secluded options, consider hiking Paul H. Douglas (Miller Woods) or Cowles Bog Trails. Each trail features a remote beach. (The sandy conclusion of Paul H. Douglas Trail is also accessible to motorists via Marquette Park.) Indiana Dunes State Park possesses some of the best Lake Michigan shoreline, but you'll encounter a $7 (Indiana State Resident) or $12 (non-Resident) entrance fee. Complete the 3 Dune Challenge, relax on the beach, and cool off in the water, and you'll get your money's worth.

Be sure to respect rip current warnings. If caught in a rip, remain calm and swim perpendicular to the current until you're free of its push. Strong winds are common, so have a plan to protect your inflatables or leave them at home. Do not feed the birds.

Hiking

The park provides more than 50 miles of well-maintained trails. None are extreme, but almost all of them—even the flat trails—are made slightly more challenging because of their sandy surface. West Beach offers the widest variety of trails. **Dune Succession Trail** is excellent. Short yet difficult, it leads into the dunes, providing examples of the four stages of dune development and stunning views of Chicago's skyline. Be aware, it includes 250+ stairs up and down the dunes. Consider going in spring or fall to avoid summer's swarm of beach enthusiasts. When the beach is hopping, it's possible to escape the crowds on **Long**

Lake Loop, which connects to Dune Succession Trail via West Beach Loop. Long Lake Loop isn't spectacular, but it is surprisingly peaceful, providing opportunities to spot birds or deer just a few miles from throngs of crazed beachgoers. Park at West Beach and walk through the picnic area at the back of the lot, where you'll intersect West Beach Loop. You should notice a wide, sandy path heading up and into the woods. There wasn't a trail marker when we hiked it, but that's Long Lake Loop. We prefer going clockwise to scamper down the dune at the end. Heading clockwise, follow signs for Long Lake Loop. The trail is obvious until you cross West Beach Road the second time. A pedestrian walkway leads to Marquette Trail Parking Area. Turn right, passing in front of a maintenance building and picnic table, where you should notice a Long Lake Loop sign leading you back into the woods, which leads back to the picnic area.

Cowles Bog is the most intense trail in the park. At 4.7 miles, it isn't the longest, but it is fairly challenging. However, there are many easier options thanks to two trailheads and a pair of connector trails. The highlight isn't Cowles Bog. It's a remote beach (bordered by a power plant). The most direct beach route is to do an out-and-back from the main lot (look for a gravel access road on the east side of North Mineral Springs Road near Dunes Acres Entrance Guardhouse). It's 3.4 miles. The best route is to park at the main lot, and immediately get the half-mile stretch along Mineral Springs Road out of the way. Walk south on Mineral Springs Road to the South Parking Lot on the west side of the road. (The lot is difficult to miss. Just to make sure, look for it on the way to the main lot.) From here, hike west on a wide gravel path. (Do not walk east along Calumet Rail Trail!) You should be walking toward a steel mill, following powerlines, with a pond to the south and Cowles Bog to the north. You will encounter two spur trails on your right. They're connectors for smaller loops. Walk past them, obeying signs pointing toward the "Beach." From the beach, walk east, away from the power plant. There are a few large, weathered trees near the shore, providing a perfect place to rest or eat lunch. To complete the loop, look for a wide sandy path leading up and into the woods. That's the trail. You should notice a brown park sign reminding you not to litter. Below it is a smaller trail sign, putting you on the correct path.

Dune Succession and Cowles Bog Trails are favorites, but there's something for everyone. **Paul H. Douglas Trail** (formerly Miller Woods) leads through black oak savanna and open dunes, terminating at Lake

Chellberg Farm

Michigan's shore. Or walk on the park's oldest dunes, **Tolleston Dunes** (you'd hardly know you were in a dunefield). **The Riverwalk** is a leisurely paved path along Burns Waterway, suspended below the riverbank opposite a steel mill. It's also a popular fishing destination. For a bit of history, head to **Chellberg Farm**, where you can walk to Bailly Homestead and Cemetery. Joseph Bailly was the first white settler. He established a fur trading post right here along the banks of the Little Calumet River in 1822. Swedish immigrants established Chellberg Farm in the 1870s. **Pinhook Bog** and **Mount Baldy** are great hikes, but only accessible on ranger-led tours. The park imposes these restrictions due to the delicate nature of each ecosystem. Pinhook Bog is important due to its rare plant species. Meanwhile Mount Baldy is an aspiring snowbird, moving south at a pace of four feet each year. This movement creates an unstable surface, susceptible to erosion. Limiting foot traffic helps preserve the dunes. The park is working to preserve, and, in the case of Mount Baldy, restore these unique environments.

But bounding down massive sand dunes is one of life's simple joys. The national park prohibits this type of duneplay. Things are slightly less restrictive at Indiana Dunes State Park. They welcome any and all visitors to take on the **3 Dune Challenge**, a 1.5-mile loop summitting Indiana's three tallest dunes: Mount Jackson (176 feet), Mount Holden (184 feet), and Mount Tom (192 feet). For comparison, Mount Baldy, the national park's tallest dune, is 126 feet.

Biking

Leave your fat tire bike at home because you can't pedal across the beaches or dunes, but there are 37 miles of bicycle paths in the area. Calumet Trail is the most notable within park boundaries. It's 9.5 miles (one-way) paralleling railroad tracks and Highway 12 between North Mineral Springs Road (at Cowles Bog South Lot, Trailhead #6) and Highway 12 (near Mount Baldy). The gravel path is not suitable for road bikes. Cyclists can continue south to Bailly Homestead via Porter Brickyard Trail (paved, 3.5 miles one-way) and beyond park borders thanks to connections (a mixture of sidewalks, streets, and dedicated paths) to Prairie Duneland (paved, 11.2 miles one-way), Oak Savannah (paved, 8.9 miles one-way), and Iron Horse Heritage (paved, 2.4 miles one-way) Trails. Dunes Kankakee Trail is presently 1.8 miles of pavement between Indiana Dunes State Park and Dorothy Buell Memorial Visitor Center on State Road 49. The goal is to continue south to Kankakee River, tying into the American Discovery Trail, which crosses the country.

Horseback Riding

Bring your horse and you can explore nearly 15 miles of trails at Glenwood Dunes. The main trailhead and parking area (with ample space for horse trailers) are located on North Brummitt Road, near Highway 20 (Trailhead #8). Equestrians are permitted from March 16 through December 14. Glenwood Dunes is designated for cross-country skiers the rest of the year, and any day with suitable snow cover. Equestrians should ride in a counterclockwise fashion, allowing for one-way traffic. Carry a map and study it prior to departure, as there are 13 trail junctions within the system. Glenwood Trail System connects to Dunewood Campground, but equine sites are not available. However, sites for humans with horses are offered at Indiana Dunes State Park.

Cross-Country Skiing

Cross-country skiers take over Glenwood Dunes Trail System once it's covered in snow. Like horseback riders, skiers are expected to follow the trails in a counterclockwise manner, and you'll need to bring your own equipment. Glenwood Dunes is mostly flat and suitable for beginners. More advanced skiers should head to Tolleston Dunes, featuring a few more challenging hills. You can also enjoy sledding at West Beach or in the state park. And, if you don't mind the cold, the lake is often quite interesting in winter.

Indiana Dunes Hiking Trails (Distances are roundtrip)

Name	Location (# on map)	Length	Difficulty Rating & Notes
Paul H. Douglas - 🚲	Paul H. Douglas Center (1)	3.2 miles	M – Formerly Miller Woods, crosses dunes to beach
Dune Succession - 🚲	West Beach (2)	1.0 mile	M – Wonderful Chicago skyline views on clear days
Long Lake	West Beach (2)	1.7 miles	M – Peaceful alternative to beach-time
West Beach	West Beach (2)	1.2 miles	E – Loop connects beach, trails, and parking area
Tolleston Dunes	Highway 12 (3)	2.6 miles	M – Oldest dunes in park, forested trail
Riverwalk	Portage Lakefront (4)	0.9 mile	E – Partially paved loop near pavillion
Bailly Homestead	Chellberg Farm (5)	3.7 miles	E – Short hike to homestead, continues to cemetery
Cowles Bog - 🚲	Mineral Springs Rd (6, 7)	4.7 miles	S – Loop or out-and-back to secluded beach
Glenwood Dunes	N Brummitt Rd (8)	6.4 miles	M – Flat horse/ski trail, many junctions
Dune Ridge	E State Park Rd (9)	0.7 mile	M – Short loop up dune to wetland views
Great Marsh	S Broadway (10)	1.3 miles	E – Flat birding trail in marsh, two access points
Mount Baldy - 🚲	Rice St (11)	1.1 mile	M – Steep, sandy conclusion to beach (can only access the dune on ranger-led tour)
Heron Rookery	450 East Rd (12) 600 East Rd (13)	3.3 miles	E – Herons no longer nest here, but still good for birders, also frequented by fishermen
Pinhook Bog - 🚲	Wozniak Rd (14)	2.1 miles	M – Only accessible via ranger-led tour
Hobart Woodland	Liverpool Rd (not on map)	2.2 miles	E – Begin at Robinson Lake Park, visits Lake George
Oak Savannah	Liverpool Rd (not on map)	3.9 miles	E – Begin at Robinson Lake Park, paved rail trail

Difficulty Ratings: E = Easy, M = Moderate, S = Strenuous

Birdwatching

Birding opportunities abound. Bank swallows nest in the dunes near Central Avenue Beach and can be seen regularly in spring and summer. Great blue heron, sandhill crane, and egret are often spotted from Great Marsh Trail. I saw kingfishers along Paul H. Douglas trail in spring. While heron no longer nest at Heron Rookery, it's a good site for woodpeckers and many species of small birds. And, who knows, maybe heron will find the area to their liking in the future and return?

Visitor Center

Dorothy Buell Memorial Visitor Center is open daily from 9am to 4pm, with extended hours from 8am to 6pm between Memorial Day and Labor Day. It is closed Thanksgiving, Christmas, and New Year's days. You'll find a few exhibits, two orientation videos, and a bookstore. **Paul H. Douglas Center for Environmental Education** (100 North Lake Street) holds the same hours as the visitor center. It's home to nature exhibits and serves as a departure point for ranger walks (using the eponymous trail).

Ranger Programs & For Kids

Parks near large urban areas tend to have a more diverse menu of ranger programs and events. Indiana Dunes takes it to another level, offering more than 400 interpretive programs and ranger-guided hikes. There are standard offerings like hiking to the top of Mount Baldy or through Pinhook Bog, which are only accessible with a park ranger. And then there are one-off events, like Art in the Park, Animal Feeding at Chellberg Farm, Movie Screenings, and a Maple Syrup Festival. During one of my visits, rangers rounded up children (and a few non-muggle parents) for a quidditch match! Checking the event calendar at the park's website or Facebook page prior to arriving is highly recommended. Otherwise, stop in at the visitor center to see what's happening. More importantly, join in the fun! Even if an event doesn't excite you, we bet you'll have a blast fooling around with the park rangers.

Thanks to enough sand to build a few million sandcastles, Indiana Dunes is a great place for the entire family. In addition to beaches, hiking trails are generally short, flat, and accessible to most visitors. As noted above, investigate the ranger programs. Many are geared toward children. And, like all parks, children (ages 5 to 15) can become Junior Rangers. Discovery Guides are available at the park's visitor center, located on State Road 49. Return once it's completed to be sworn in and receive a badge.

Bailly Homestead

Flora & Fauna

As you might expect of the birthplace of ecology in the United States, Indiana Dunes is a fascinating living laboratory. More than 100 years ago, research began with Henry Cowles and his University of Chicago students, who frequented the area (especially Cowles Bog before it was given his name) to study plant succession. For its relatively small size, this corner of Indiana contains an incredibly wide range of ecosystems. From just about anywhere in the park, you're a short stroll from plants of the desert, pine woods, swamps, oak woods, and prairies. Cactus are found living among plants of the Arctic. The dunes themselves create a wide range of habitats, from bare dunes to primeval forests. Most hikers at Tolleston Dunes wouldn't realize they're walking atop a dune if it wasn't in the name. At 4,700 years, they're the park's oldest dunes, completely covered with vegetation. Human influence is the primary threat endangering these ecosystems. Oak savannas used to cover 50 million acres from Michigan to Nebraska. Today, they occupy about 30,000 acres. Some of the last surviving black oak savannas are found in the park, like the one Paul H. Douglas (Miller Woods) Trail passes through. Let's be honest, superficiality is important to many nature lovers. In that regard, more than 500 blooming plant species reside here. Blooms depend on many variables, including, species, temperature, and moisture, but most colorful displays are found between April and July. Do not pick or trample flowers. Predicting peak Fall foliage isn't an exact science either, but it's usually in October.

Birds are the most compelling wildlife. Nearly 300 species can be spotted throughout the year as the Great Lakes serve as a pit-stop for many migratory species. Woodpeckers, hawks, and warblers tend to be the most sought-after. As for mammals, they're mainly small critters and bats, but, if you're fortunate, you may spot a red fox or white-tailed deer.

Five points for Gryffindor!

Pets & Accessibility

Pets must be on a leash (less than six feet). They are permitted on all trails and beaches, with the exception of West Beach lifeguard swim area, Pinhook Bog Trail, and Glenwood Dunes Trail System (to prevent interaction with horseback riders). During special events, other areas may be temporarily closed to pets.

Dorothy Buell Memorial Visitor Center and Paul H. Douglas Center are accessible to wheelchair users. Dunewood Campground offers four accessible sites. Riverwalk Trail and the nearby pavilion are also accessible. A beach wheelchair can be checked out at West Beach from the lifeguards.

Weather

Lake Michigan helps stabilize the weather, but summers remain hot and humid, with an abundance of sun. Winters get cold, but not unbearably so. Wind greatly affects general comfort level. Consistent northwest winds are welcome in summer as they'll cool you off and push warm surface water close to shore, but they'll also turn a cool day cold. Water temperature peaks just above 70°F in August, and then gradually cools. As always, check the forecast before going out and dress in layers any time of year.

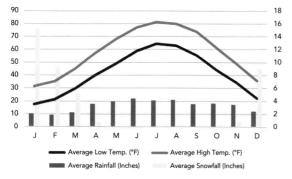

- Average Low Temp. (°F)
- Average High Temp. (°F)
- Average Rainfall (Inches)
- Average Snowfall (Inches)

Tips & Recommendations

If you'd like to get the most out of a trip to Indiana Dunes, you really should visit in summer, so the lake is at its most inviting state. With that said, the park is wonderful all year long, with advantages to each season. Spring, it's wildflowers. Fall, it's foliage. Winter, it's snow and small crowds.

The disadvantage of summer is that it's busy. Indiana Dunes is within a 3-hour drive of more than 30 million people, and half the park's visitors arrive from June through August.

Traveling on a weekday is always a good idea but it's an excellent one when your destination is close to a large urban area like Chicago.

There's 15 miles of sandy shoreline so don't feel like West Beach is the only place to relax and/or swim. Porter, Kemil, Lake View, Central Avenue, Mount Baldy, and the beach fronting the state park are all excellent alternatives.

Be sure to check the park's Facebook page or website for a current calendar of events prior to arrival.

With several restaurants and hotels, Michigan City is a good place to spend the night outside the park.

At $7 for Indiana residents and $12 for non-residents, Indiana Dunes State Park is worth the price of admission. You can play more freely on the dunes here, including attempting the 3 Dune Challenge. Plus, they offer year-round camping. The state park and national park are operated independently from one another, but they do collaborate on public programming, prescribed burns, and invasive species control.

Easy Hikes: West Beach (1.2 miles), Riverwalk (0.9)
Moderate Hikes: Dune Succession (1 mile), Mount Baldy (1.1), Pinhook Bog (2.1), Paul H. Douglas (3.2)
Strenuous Hikes: Cowle's Bog (4.7 miles)
Family Activities: Become Junior Rangers, swim at West Beach, ride the rails, join a ranger program, go biking, complete the 3 Dune Challenge at Indiana Dunes State Park
Rainy Day Activities: Take the South Shore Line to South Bend or Chicago
History Enthusiasts: Chellberg Farm, Bailly Homestead and Cemetery
Sunset Spots: West Beach, Lake View, Portage Lakefront, Porter Beach
Sunrise Spots: Mount Baldy

Cowles Bog Trail

Beyond the Park...

Dining
Craft House • (219) 929-5570
711 Plaza Dr, Chesterton
crafthouse.beer

Third Coast Spice • (219) 926-5858
761 Indian Boundary Rd, Chesterton
thirdcoastspice.com

Duneland Pizza • (219) 926-1163
520 Broadway, Chesterton
dunelandpizza.com

Ivy's Bohemia House • (219) 929-4319
321 Broadway, Chesterton
ivysbohemiahouse.com

George's Gyros • (219) 926-5435
325 N Calumet Rd, Chesterton
georgesgyrosspot.com

Lucrezia Café • (219) 926-5829
428 S Calumet Rd, Chesterton
lucreziacafe.com

Musashi Sushi Bar • (219) 728-1529
757 Indian Boundary Rd, Chesterton
musashichestertoon.com

Chesterton Brewing Co
1050 Broadway, Chesterton
chestertonbrewery.com

Dune Billies • (219) 809-6592
201 Center St, Michigan City
dunebilliesbeachcafe.com

Grocery Stores
Jewel-Osco • (219) 926-7172
747 Indian Boundary Rd, Chesterton

Strack & Van Til • (219) 929-1717
1600 Pioneer Trail, Chesterton
strackandvantil.com

Nature's Cupboard • (219) 926-4647
761 Boundary Rd, Chesterton

Lodging
Riley's Railhouse • (219) 395-9999
123 N 4th St, Chesterton
rileysrailhouse.com

Bridge Inn • (219) 561-0066
510 E 2nd St, Michigan City
bridgeinnmc.com

The Brewery Lodge
5727N N 600 W, Michigan City
brewerylodge.com • (866) 625-6343

Serenity Springs • (219) 861-0000
5888 US-35 La Porte
serenity-springs.com

Arbor Hill Inn • (219) 362-9200
263 W Johnson Rd, La Porte
arborhillinn.com

Campgrounds
Michigan City RV • (219) 872-7600
1601 US-421, Michigan City
michigancitycampground.com

Last Resort • (219) 797-2267
4707 W 1300 S, Hanna
camplastresort.com

Lakeside RV Resort
7089 N Chicago Rd, New Carlisle
(574) 654-3260

Festivals
Indiana Dunes Birding Festival
indianaaudubon.org • May

Crown Beer Fest • June
crownbeerfest.com • Crown Point

Pierogi Fest • July
pierogifest.net • Whiting

Attractions
Indiana Dunes State Park
Well worth a visit
1600 N 25 E, Chesterton
in.gov • (219) 926-1952

Turkey Run State Park
Excellent hiking through gorges
8121 Park Rd, Marshall
turkeyrunstatepark.com

Potato Creek State Park
25601 IN-4, North Liberty
in.gov

Old Lighthouse Museum
1 Washington St, Michigan City
oldlighthousemuseum.org

Mascot Hall of Fame
1851 Front St, Whiting
mascothalloffame.com

Barker Mansion • (219) 873-1520
Essentially started Michigan City
631 Washington St, Michigan City
barkermansion.com

Friendship Botanic Gardens
2055 E US-12, Michigan City
friendshipgardens.org

Millennium Park • *The Bean*
201 E Randolph St, Chicago
Chicago.gov • (312) 742-1168

Willis Tower
233 S Wacker Dr, Chicago
theskydeck.com

Navy Pier • (312) 595-7437
600 E Grand Ave, Chicago
navypier.org

Shedd Aquarium
1200 S Lake Shore Dr, Chicago
sheddaquarium.org

Museum of Science and Industry
5700 S Lake Shore Dr, Chicago
msichicago.org

Frank Lloyd Wright Studio
951 Chicago Ave, Oak Park
flwright.org

Gateway Arch

A St. Louis sunset from the Mississippi Overlook in Illinois

Phone: (314) 655-1600
Website: nps.gov/jeff

Established: February 22, 2018
Size: 91 Acres
Annual Visitors: 2 Million
Peak Season: March–November

Park Grounds: 5am–11pm
Gateway Arch Museum and Tram Tours*: 8am–10pm (Memorial Day–Labor Day), 9am–6pm (rest of year)
Old Courthouse*: 8am–4:30pm
No Camping or Lodging

Entrance Fee ($3/person), **Tram Tour** ($12–16), **Movie** ($7), **Riverfront Cruise** ($21–51), **Helicopter Tour** ($43–169)

*Closed Thanksgiving, Christmas, and New Year's Day

In 2018, an act of Congress redesignated Jefferson National Expansion Memorial as Gateway Arch National Park. Reading only its former name, even some park enthusiasts would be left scratching their heads, wondering "What park is that?" Or "Where is it?" See an image of the Arch and you immediately know … St. Louis. In fact, it's most commonly called the St. Louis or Gateway Arch. Naming confusion isn't completely abated, but the next subject for debate is its designation. Why does a park the size of a small family farm—just 91 acres—warrant the capital 'N', capital 'P', National Park designation, hobnobbing with the likes of Yosemite and Yellowstone?

Indeed, a valid question. The Arch is extremely impressive. Standing as tall as it is wide—an impressive 630 feet—it is the tallest structure in Missouri. A structure possessing an uncommon elegance thanks to its curves and highly-reflective stainless-steel exterior. Unique trams running up and down each leg make the monument even more engaging. Visitors can take a four-minute ride to an observation deck within the Arch's keystone, serving up stunning views of the city and Mississippi River. Gateway Arch deserves considerable merit as a world-renowned monument, but it's manmade. Height, beauty, and novelty form a fascinating combination for any structure, but the Arch has transcended architecture and become the defining characteristic of St. Louis's skyline, recognized around the globe. The Arch is something many proud Missourians hang their hats on. It's become the symbol of St. Louis.

Symbolism could also be a matter of dollars and cents, indicating national wealth, power, and exceptionalism. When asked about the recently acquired national park designation, one ranger suggested the "largest renovation project in NPS history" was reason enough. The $380 million project—more than four times the cost to build the arch in today's dollars—added paths and trees, razed a parking ramp, modernized the underground museum, and, most importantly, connected the arch to downtown St. Louis. Prior to the project, the Arch was its own island, cut off from St. Louis by Interstate 44, except for a pair of narrow pedestrian bridges. Today, a massive land bridge allows visitors to stroll unimpeded from the Old Courthouse in downtown St. Louis to the bank of the Mississippi River, walking under the Arch along the way (and, often unknowingly, over I-44). Hoping to boost overall tourism, the renovation project connected the iconic Arch to downtown St. Louis. Another impressive feat of engineering, but hardly the idea our national parks were founded on.

Long before landscape architects were challenged to solve the problem of the Arch's isolation, this land was French (and Spanish) Territory. The only thing separating it from a young, growing nation was an international border, the Mississippi River. Returning to the park's original name, Jefferson National Expansion Memorial, you get an idea why the Arch was built. It was made as a monument to the third President of the United States, Thomas Jefferson. Park advocates believed the monument should be constructed on a site with direct ties to one of his greatest accomplishments, the Louisiana Purchase. A purchase that expanded the United States nearly 1,000 miles west to the Rocky Mountains. Prior to 1803, the Mississippi River was the United States' version of Interstate 44. After 1803, St. Louis experienced rapid growth as a booming trade hub and outfitting stop for fur traders and homesteaders preparing to head west. It is the perfect site to memorialize President Jefferson and the Louisiana Purchase. Completed in 1965, the Arch symbolizes a Gateway to the West, built in honor of a man with a vision of westward expansion, creating a nation from sea to shining sea. The Arch rises from the same soil where homesteaders and explorers—many more than Meriwether Lewis and William Clark—departed civilization seeking adventure, the great unknown, and incomparable scenic beauty. That symbol rings true with the National Park Idea.

Fluffy clouds accent a brilliant Arch

When to Go
Nearly one-half all Gateway Arch National Park visits occur between June and August, with huge crowds for the fourth of July. Summers are commonly hot and humid. Air conditioning found in the museum and riverboats provide a welcome escape from the summer's heat. Our favorite seasons are spring and fall, when weather is mild, and crowds seldom reach overwhelming levels (although that can change on weekends or with a few weekday school field trips). Winter is also quite nice. St. Louis receives little snow and few days with high temps below freezing.

Transportation & Airports
Most visitors arrive by car, but it is possible to use lightrail (metrostlouis.org) from the airport (or any station) or MetroBus. A 2-hour public transit pass costs $3–4. A One-Day Adventure Pass costs $7.50 (stladventurepass.com). The Arch is a short walk from Laclede's Landing Station. The Downtown Trolley runs every 20 minutes, Monday through Sunday, from the Civic Center Transit Center to the City Museum, stopping on 4th Street near the Arch. It costs $2 per adult and $1 per child or senior.

St. Louis Lambert International Airport (STL) is 16 miles from Gateway Arch. Rent a car, catch a taxi, or use MetroLink from there.

Popular field trip destination

Directions

Most visitors park off-site and enter on foot from 4th Street. However, there isn't a single entry point or parking area. As the tallest structure in the state, it's difficult to miss the Arch. And accessing downtown from I-64 or I-44 is fairly straightforward. The more painful prospect is determining where to park.

Prior to the 2018 renovation project, most visitors used an on-site parking ramp, visited the Arch and left St. Louis. Today, after the demolition of the ramp and construction of a land bridge between the Arch and downtown St. Louis, motorists must seek out a parking space. Metered spaces are available, but they're difficult to get, nearly impossible on Cardinals gamedays. More reliable options include two parking structures on 4th Street. Mansion House Garage (200 N 4th Street), two blocks from the Arch (roughly 0.3-mile to the Museum), is a good choice if your vehicle is less than 6' 2" tall. It costs $16 per day. Across the street, Quick Park Garage offers parking space for $18 per day. Surface lots can be found north of the Arch at Citi Park (605 N 2nd Street, $7/day) and Laclede's Landing (801 N 1st Street, $6/day) about 0.75-mile from the museum. It's trickier if you have an RV. You can park along Leonor K. Sullivan Boulevard, south of Poplar Street Bridge to the flood wall. The roadway was raised two feet to better withstand flooding, but it was underwater when I visited in fall 2019 (after an uncommonly wet year). You can also park across the river in Illinois at the Casino Queen (casinoqueen.com) and walk or take the train (metrostlouis.org) across the Mississippi River. The lot has security, and many commuters use it, but parking is at your own risk, and, as always, do not leave behind anything you value. More complicated yet, you could find a nearby store parking lot and hire a ride to the Arch. If you'd like to drop off passengers, there's a designated drop-off area alongside the Old Cathedral parking lot (accessed from Memorial Drive).

Arch & Museum/Visitor Center

Regardless how you feel about Gateway Arch's national park status, there's no denying it is one of the world's most fascinating manmade structures. It's uniquely beautiful from every angle of perspective and light. A few favorite Arch-viewing locations are near either leg, in front of the museum entrance, from Kiener Plaza Park (west of the Old Courthouse), and from the Mississippi Overlook (in Illinois). Be sure to spend an hour or two strolling around the grounds. Quickly you'll notice every element—from the ponds to the paths to the Museum's entrance—possesses a curve. Designers took great care to accentuate and pay homage to the monumental steel Arch.

Of course, the highlight of any trip to Gateway Arch is a **tram ride** to its 630-foot peak (two times the height of the Statue of Liberty) and the subsequent views of St. Louis! Tram tickets cost $12-16/adult and $8-12/child. Subtract $3 with a National Parks Pass. Pricing varies depending on demand. Nonrefundable tickets can be purchased in advance at gatewayarch.com. Make reservations if you have a rigid schedule or plan to visit on a summer/holiday weekend. Even during peak season, mornings and evenings tend to be quiet. Our preference is morning, when the sun is at your back as you peer down upon St. Louis from the observation deck. Tickets can be purchased on-site at the Visitor Center/Museum Entrance or, after entering the museum, near the North Exit. Reservations aren't necessary most of the time because they hustle as many as 3,500 people to the observation deck every 8 hours. Trams, located at the far end of the museum, run up each leg. Only one tram operates outside of peak hours. The experience begins with striking a pose for your standard amusement-park-style photo-op and a brief educational animation. While boarding the cozy 5-seat pods, pay attention to the chairs. They're shaped like a tulip, another creation of Eero Saarinen, the Arch's architect. Dick Bowser designed the pods, incorporating elements of an elevator, escalator, and Ferris wheel. You'll feel all three on the 4-minute ascent and 3-minute descent. When you're ready to leave, line up for the next available tram (south or north). Guests are free to spend as much time as operating hours allow at the observation deck, but the entire experience lasts 45 minutes on average.

The new **museum** is pretty neat. The entrance is located between the Arch and Old Courthouse. It's impossible to miss if you're arriving from the west. However, it's almost impossible to notice standing under the Arch. Not to interfere with the park's

👍 Kiener Plaza Park

👍 Old Courthouse

OLD COURTHOUSE

Dred and Harriet Scott statue

LUTHER ELY SMITH SQUARE

👍 Visitor Center/Museum

OLD CATHEDRAL

Visitor Center Entrance

**VISITOR CENTER
Museum at the Gateway Arch**
(Underground)

South Exit

North Exit

To the North Gateway

Accessible Route to the Arch ♿

THE GRAND STAIRCASE

To Lewis and Clark statue

Accessible Route to the Arch ♿

Mississippi River

The Museum is underground

greenspace, the museum is beneath it. The museum is free, but a **35-minute documentary** on the Arch's construction costs $7/adult or $3/child. It rolls every hour in the museum's theater. There's a $3 discount with a Tram/Cruise package or National Park Pass. The film is interesting, its tone refreshingly candid. Continuing the candor, it should probably be free. The museum features six exhibit galleries: Colonial St. Louis, Jefferson's Vision, New Frontiers, The Riverfront Era, Manifest Destiny, and Building the Dream. Each one is filled with compelling displays (some interactive) and video interviews. Plan on spending at least an hour exploring the museum. Additionally, there's a gift store and café. Museum exits deposit guests at the north and south legs of the awe-inspiring Arch.

Don't feel pressure to buy a combo package at the museum entrance. There's another ticket counter inside the museum and the combo isn't a bargain. It only appears that way because the $3 park entrance fee is included once. (You'll pay the same price buying each activity individually.) Particularly for individuals with tram reservations, be aware that all visitors must pass through an airport-style security checkpoint to access the museum and trams. It can take more than 30 minutes to enter on a busy day. Use the restroom prior to your tram ride. You won't find one at the observation deck. The tram is not fully accessible. All guests are required to negotiate 96 steps over the course of six flights of stairs. Any tram-goers bringing a stroller should put a label (or unique identifier) on it, because many guests leave strollers at the tram loading zones.

Old Courthouse

The Old Courthouse (11 N 4th Street) is situated opposite Gateway Arch on the west end of the newly built land bridge over I-44. Architecturally, the courthouse is a mishmash of styles as multiple renovations tried to keep up with St. Louis's rapid population growth. An original brick courthouse was incorporated into a four-wing Greek-Revival-style building in 1839. In 1851, the old brick structure was demolished and replaced with the present east wing. In 1861, the dome was replaced with one similar to that found in St. Peter's Basilica in Rome (also used as inspiration for the Capitol Building dome in Washington, D.C.). The city moved out in 1930, and tenants like St. Louis Art League moved in before the building formally became part of the future Jefferson National Expansion Memorial in 1940. The Old Courthouse contained as many as twelve courtrooms. Today, two are restored to their 1910 appearance. In addition, you'll find a bookstore and four mediocre exhibits on the ground level. Exhibits include: Early St. Louis (French colonization), Exploring the West (fur trade and Lewis and Clark Expedition), Clash of Cultures (Native American life and interaction with pioneers), and Legacy of Courage: Dred Scott & the Quest for Freedom (including a 17-minute History Channel video). If you're short on time, start at the Legacy of Courage exhibit. The Dred Scott Case is one of the most important cases in United States History. In short, Scott sued (with help from social justice advocates) for his family's freedom on grounds "once free, always free" (he lived in several free territories with his owner). The Circuit Court of St. Louis County, in the Old Courthouse's West Wing, awarded Dred Scott and his family their freedom on January 12, 1850. His owner, Irene Emerson, appealed to the Missouri Supreme Court. The decision was overturned. A new suit led all the way to the United States Supreme Court. By seven-to-two decision, the court ruled Scott should remain a slave. They went a step further and declared the Missouri Compromise of 1820 unconstitutional (effectively sanctioning slavery everywhere in the United States). These decrees and ensuing civic unrest sparked election of Abraham Lincoln as President and the Civil War. A sympathetic friend (and abolitionist) gave the Scotts their freedom in 1857, but Dred died in 1858, years before the abolition of slavery. Architecture and exhibits aren't for everyone, but the view from Kiener Plaza Park, just west of the Old Courthouse, seems to be universally appreciated.

Old Cathedral

The Basilica of Saint Louis, commonly referred to as the Old Cathedral, is the fourth Catholic Church built on this site. The first, constructed in 1764, was a one-room log cabin. The present version, completed in 1834, became the first cathedral west of the Mississippi River. Today, it is the oldest building in St. Louis, earning its descriptor. Amazingly, it remains in the hands of its original owner, the Archdiocese of St. Louis. While it is not part of the national park grounds, it sits on adjacent land, southwest of the Arch. It remains an active parish with mass offered twice daily. Visitors are welcome. There is a small museum with irregular hours. If you'd like to visit, please contact the office (314.231.3250) prior to arrival.

Riverboat Cruises

From March through early December (water level permitting), you can cruise the Mississippi aboard replica steamboats named *Tom Sawyer* and *Becky Thatcher*. The boats were brought to St. Louis in 1964 to accommodate Arch-oglers seeking a better view of construction. More than 50 years later, the boats continue to satisfy Arch-ogling needs. Gateway Arch remains the highlight of the hour-long standard tour ($21/adult, $11/child), unless it's a summer scorcher, then the air-conditioning might be your favorite attraction. With agreeable weather, the best place to be is the top deck for fresh air and 360-degree views. However, you won't be the only one with this idea. It's a race to the top. Mandatory pre-cruise photo-ops are the most polarizing event of the entire operation. They'll hawk these photos to you when you return. Some love it. Some don't.

In summer, they offer a 2-hour lunch cruise ($39/adult, $15/child) on Wednesdays and Saturdays. From April through October, they offer a 2-hour dinner cruise with music ($51/adult, $20/child) on Fridays and Saturdays. They add a dinner cruise on Sundays from June through August. Sunday Brunch ($48/adult, $20/child) is available on select Sundays between April and October. Food is served buffet-style and snacks and drinks are sold at a cash bar. Finally, there's a mixed bag of themed cruises throughout the year, including blues, theater, DJs, even a drag show and Halloween costume party. Check gatewayarch.com for a complete list, schedule, pricing, and to make reservations. Reservations are required for every offering except the basic hour-long riverfront tour. Tickets are nonrefundable. It is possible to walk down to the riverfront from the Arch via Grand Staircase. Cash-only parking, accessed via South Leonor K. Sullivan Blvd,

Manmade but still beautiful

is available near the riverboat docks. Paddlewheel Café, located at the dock, is open from April through October. They offer burgers, chicken strips, salads, ice cream, and more. Pricing is fair, all things considered.

Helicopter Tours

They aren't associated with the park, but Gateway Helicopter (gatewayhelicoptertours.com) has a helipad along the riverfront. They offer a 2-3-minute Riverfront Tour for $43 per person. They also provide longer experiences: Anheuser-Busch (5-6 minutes, $72/person), Botanical Gardens (10-12 minutes, $118/person), and St. Louis (18-20 minutes, $169/person). No, the helicopter does not fly through the Arch. You must purchase at least two seats, and there is a 300-pound weight limit per passenger. They're open 11am to 5pm (or later), daily, from April through November (water level permitting). Walk to the helipad via Grand Staircase or use a cash parking lot near the riverboat dock on South Leonor K. Sullivan Blvd.

Ranger Programs & For Kids

Rangers provide daily tours of the Old Courthouse. Times vary, so you'll have to check with the information desk for a schedule. The park also hosts several recurring and one-off events, covering subjects ranging from women's suffrage to astronomy. The best place to view up-to-date event information is Gateway Arch's official Facebook page.

Impressive any way you look at it

Kids love riding the tram up to the Arch's observation deck to view St. Louis from the top of the tallest structure in Missouri. Children (ages 5-18) can become Junior Rangers. Pick up Junior Ranger activity sheets at the information desk found at the Arch or Old Courthouse. Complete the selected activities and return to an information desk to receive a badge.

Flora & Fauna

Gateway Arch is a 91-acre urban park with limited flora and fauna. Ash trees, threatened by the ash borer beetle, lining the park's paths were recently replaced with London plane trees. As part of the renovation, the park also planted hundreds of flowering species, including redbuds, magnolias, and buckeyes. Animals are limited to birds and critters common to many Midwestern urban greenspaces, like robins, bluebirds, cardinals, and squirrels.

Pets & Accessibility

Pets must be kept on a leash (less than six feet). All pets, except service animals are prohibited from the riverboats and all park buildings, including the Arch, Museum, and Old Courthouse.

The top of the Arch is not accessible to wheelchair users. However, as part of the 2018 renovation, the museum features a model of the keystone piece, complete with live video feed east and west from the Arch's observation deck. There is a wheelchair lift at the Old Courthouse's Broadway entrance (west side), but only the ground level is accessible. The riverfront, where riverboats and helicopters depart, is not ADA accessible from the park grounds due to a steep grade. Accessible parking is available on the levee near the riverboat dock for a cash fee. The lot is located off South Leonor K. Sullivan Blvd between Poplar Street and the Grand Staircase.

Weather

St. Louis's climate is quite delightful. Precipitation is moderate throughout the year with a slight uptick in spring. Weather is mostly comfortable year-round aside from the hot, humid, and sunny summers. Winters are relatively mild, with only a few weeks when high temperatures dip below freezing. On average, about a foot of snow falls each year. Flowers begin to bloom in April. Fall foliage typically peaks in late October.

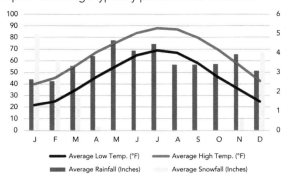

Tips & Recommendations

Don't leave without riding the tram to the top. My preference is to go up the Arch in the morning (when the sun is east of the city and the Arch's shadow falls on the lawn above the museum), but it's pretty cool any time of day, including sunset or even when it's dark.

It wouldn't be difficult to spend a day loafing around the park's new greenspace; another day in the museum, taking the tram up the Arch, and checking out the Old Courthouse; and another day exploring St. Louis, but, if you're in a hurry, you can hit the highlights (museum, greenspace, tram) in a couple hours.

If you know when you'll be arriving and the general timeframe you'd like to take the tram, book it in advance, especially during peak season. They send a lot of people to the top each day. Most days you can show up and you'll be loaded in a tram in a matter of hours. Other days, their timeline may not work with your timeline, so plan ahead. Just make sure you arrive at least

30 minutes before your designated tram ride time (earlier in peak season). It takes a while to file visitors through the airport-style security checkpoint.

The movie is a little expensive, but it's jam-packed with interesting information. If you're going to watch it, watch it before riding the tram to the top. It'll help put the work required to build this monument into perspective as you ratchet up one of the Arch's steel legs.

Kiener Plaza Park (Thanks Erik, Jacci, Ethan & Logan)

Family Activities: Ride the tram, become Junior Rangers, play in the park

Guided Tours: Helicopter Tour, Riverboat Cruise

Rainy Day Activities: While the views may not be as grand, rain doesn't completely ruin a visit to the arch, in fact it's probably pretty fun to be at the top of the Arch during a thunderstorm. And, no matter what, you always have the museum.

History Enthusiasts: Old Courthouse, Arch Museum

Sunset Spots: Mississippi River Overlook at Malcolm W. Martin Memorial Park (across the river in Illinois)

Sunrise Spots: Kiener Plaza Park or out in front of the museum entrance

Beyond the Park...

Dining
Chili Mac's Diner
510 Pine St •(314) 421-9040

Anthony's Bar • (314) 231-7007
410 Market St • tonysstlouis.com

Sugarfire Smoke House
605 Washington Ave • (314) 394-1720
sugarfiresmokehouse.com

Pickle Deli • (314) 241-2255
200 N Broadway • picklesdelistl.com

Sauce on the Side
411 N 8th St • (314) 241-5667
sauceontheside.com

Broadway Oyster bar
736 S Broadway • (314) 621-8811
broadwayoysterbar.com

Medina Grill • (314) 241-1356
1327 Washington Ave
medinagrill.com

Blues City Deli • (314) 773-8225
2438 McNair Ave • bluescitydeli.com

Grocery Stores
Schnucks Downtown
315 N 9th St • (314) 436-7694

Lodging
Many name brand hotels near the park. Also Airbnb/VRBO.

Campgrounds
Casino Queen RV Park
200 Front St, East St Louis
casinoqueen.com • (800) 777-0777

Cahokia RV Parque • (618) 332-7700
4060 Mississippi Ave, Cahokia
cahokiarvparque.com

Trails End RV • (618) 931-5041
3225 W Chain of Rocks Rd, Granite City

Granite City KOA
3157 W Chain of Rocks Rd, Granite City
koa.com • (618) 931-5160

Festivals
The Loop Ice Carnival • January
visittheloop.com

Circus Flora • June
circusflora.org

Brewers Festival • July
stlbeer.org

Great Forest Park Balloon • Sept
greatforestparkballoonrace.com

Budweiser Taste of St Louis
tastestl.com • September

Attractions
Missouri Botanical Garden
4344 Shaw Blvd • (314) 577-5100
missouribotanicalgarden.com

Anheuser-Busch
1200 Lynch St • (314) 577-2626
budweisertours.com

St Louis Cardinals
700 Clark Ave • (314) 345-9600
stlouis.cardinals.mlb.com

City Museum
750 N 16th St • citymuseum.org

St Louis Art Museum
1 Fine Arts Dr • slam.org

St Louis Science Center
5050 Oakland Ave • slsc.org

Missouri History Museum
5700 Lindell Blvd
mohistory.org • (314) 746-4599

Citygarden Sculpture Park
801 Market St • (314) 241-3339
stlouis-mo.gov

Tower Grove Park
4257 Northeast Dr
towergrovepark.org

Laumeier Sculpture Park
12580 Rott Rd • (314) 615-5278
laumeiersculpturepark.org

Magic House Children's Museum
516 S Kirkwood Rd
magichouse.org • (314) 822-8900

Forest Park • 5595 Grand Dr
forestparkforever.org

Cathedral Basilica
4431 Lindell Blvd • cathedralstl.org

Ullysses S Grant National Historic Site
7400 Grant Rd
nps.gov/ulsg • (314) 842-1867

The Butterfly House
15193 Olive Blvd • (314) 577-0888
missouribotanicalgarden.org

The World Chess Hall of Fame
4652 Maryland Ave
worldchesshof.org • (314) 367-9243

Cahokia Mounds State Historic Site
Site of a large pre-Columbian city
30 Ramey St, Collinsville
cahokiamounds.org • (618) 346-5160

Meramec State Park
Caves 60 miles from St. Louis
115 Meramec Park Dr, Sullivan
mostateparks.com

Johnson's Shut-Ins State Park
148 Taum Sauk Tr, Middle Brook
mostateparks.com

Starved Rock State Park
Waterfalls & sandstone canyons
2678 E 875th Rd, Oglesby, IL
illinois.gov

Isle Royale

Phone: (906) 482-0984
Website: nps.gov/isro

Established: April 3, 1940
Size: 571,790 Acres
Annual Visitors: 25,000
Peak Season: July–August
Hiking Trails: 165 Miles

Activities: Hiking, Backpacking, Paddling, Boat Tours, SCUBA Diving, Fishing

Campgrounds: 36 Campgrounds accessible by boat and trail (free permit required, permit is $25 for groups of 7–10 people)
Lodging: Rock Harbor Lodge (Rooms and Cottages available for $227–341/night), Windigo Camper Cabins (no plumbing, no heat, no A/C, $52/night)

Open: mid-April–October
Entrance Fee: $7/person per day (please pay in advance at pay.gov)

Isle Royale, born of fire, sculpted by glaciers, nearly drowned in water, is a wilderness wonderland left mostly unaltered by man. Millions of years ago this archipelago of about 400 islands was created by what scientists believe to have been the world's largest lava flow. An amount of lava so immense the earth's surface sunk under its weight, forming the Superior basin. As the basin formed, Isle Royale began to rise and tilt. Today, effects of this ancient geologic activity can still be seen in Isle Royale's ridgelines. Northwest ridges are generally steep and rugged because the lagging edge ripped away from the crust. The leading edge (southeast slope) is more gradual, as it faces the point of compression.

About 10,000 years ago, the last glacier to reach Lake Superior receded. As it scraped the island's ridgelines, pulverizing rock, a thin layer of soil was left behind. The glacier melted and Isle Royale "appeared" as water filled Lake Superior. Wind and water brought plant life to the island. Birds and insects arrived. Moose and caribou swam 15 miles from Canada's shoreline. Unseasonably cold winters allow wolves to reach the island by crossing a frozen sheet of ice.

The trip to these remote islands, while not nearly as difficult as it was for plants and animals, is still challenging for humans. Isle Royale remains untethered to the mainland, inaccessible to motorists. The only way to reach the park is by boat or seaplane. Diehard backpackers and paddlers make the trip across Lake Superior to immerse themselves in something increasingly scarce: undeveloped wilderness.

Sun setting over Pie Island

Thousands of shallow pits indicate Natives were mining copper here more than 4,000 years ago, long before tourists stepped foot on the island. They mined for some 1,500 years. No one knows why. Benjamin Franklin was aware of the mineral's value. Historians believe Franklin insisted the Treaty of Paris draw the border between a newly formed United States and England's Canada north of Isle Royale because of its copper. By the 1920s, lumber and mining companies—having exhausted most of Michigan's mainland's dollarable resources—eyed the island's trees and minerals. Albert Stoll, a journalist for The Detroit News, wanted to preserve what commercial interests sought to exploit. Inspired by Stoll's passion and enthusiasm, the newspaper backed his interest, launching a decade-long campaign to protect the region as a national park. In 1931 the federal government acted upon their pleas. President Hoover signed into law a bill creating Isle Royale National Park, provided no federal funds were used to acquire land. Timing couldn't have been worse as the economy was reeling during the Great Depression and money was hard to appropriate. President Franklin D. Roosevelt ignored the federal mandate and steered funds from the New Deal to buy land for the park, preserving one of the most majestic and undeveloped regions of the Lower 48.

When to Go
Isle Royale is the only national park that closes for winter (November until mid-April). August is the best time of year. Weather is typically warm, pests like black flies and mosquitoes diminish, and blueberries are often ripe for the picking.

Transportation & Airports
Most visitors reach Isle Royale by ferry from one of three locations: Houghton (MI), Copper Harbor (MI), or Grand Portage (MN). **Grand Portage Transportation Line** (218.475.0024, isleroyaleboats.com) is located at 402 Upper Road in Grand Portage. **Isle Royale Ferry Services** (906.289.4437, isleroyale.com) is located at 14 Waterfront Landing in Copper Harbor. **Isle Royale National Park** (906.482.0984) and the *Ranger III* are located at 800 East Lakeshore Drive in Houghton, MI.

Thunder Bay International (YQT) in Ontario, Canada is approximately 40 miles northeast of Grand Portage. Houghton County Memorial (CMX) is located in Houghton, MI, about 40 miles southwest of Copper Harbor.

Directions
Vehicles are not allowed on Isle Royale. Parking is available at departure locations (for a nominal fee).

To Grand Portage, MN (145 miles from Duluth): From the south, follow MN-61 northeast along the coast of Lake Superior. Turn right onto Stevens Road to enter Grand Portage. Follow County Road 73/Store Road to the right. Turn left on Mile Creek Road. Turn right onto Bay Road. After a little more than one mile, turn right onto Upper Road, which leads to the ferry terminal.

From Thunder Bay, travel southwest on MN-61. Turn left onto County Rd 73/Store Rd to head into Grand Portage, which leads to Mile Creek Road. Continue with the directions listed above from this point.

To Houghton/Copper Harbor (215/261 miles from Green Bay, WI): US-41 passes Isle Royale Visitor Center in Houghton. To arrive at the visitor center, turn right onto Franklin Street just after US-41 becomes one-way. Continue onto Lakeshore Drive. The visitor center is located along the south bank of the river. US-41 continues north to Copper Harbor. In Copper Harbor take the first left onto 5th St to reach the ferry terminal.

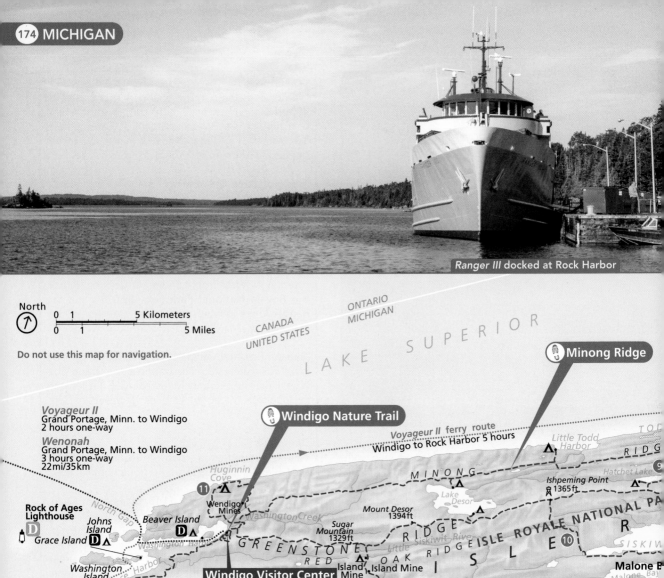

Ranger III docked at Rock Harbor

North

0   1   5 Kilometers

0   1   5 Miles

Do not use this map for navigation.

CANADA   ONTARIO
UNITED STATES   MICHIGAN

LAKE SUPERIOR

Minong Ridge

Voyageur II
Grand Portage, Minn. to Windigo
2 hours one-way

Wenonah
Grand Portage, Minn. to Windigo
3 hours one-way
22mi/35km

Windigo Nature Trail

Voyageur II ferry route
Windigo to Rock Harbor 5 hours

Little Todd Harbor

TODD

RIDGE

Huginnin Cove

MINONG

Ishpeming Point
1365ft

Hatchet Lake

9

11

Wendigo Mines

Lake Desor

Washington Creek

Rock of Ages Lighthouse

North Gap

Johns Island

Beaver Island

Mount Desor
1394ft

RIDGE

ISLE ROYALE NATIONAL PA

Grace Island

GREENSTONE

RED

Sugar Mountain
1329ft

Little Siskiwit River

OAK RIDGE

ISLE

R

10

SISKIW

Washington Island

Grace Harbor

Windigo Visitor Center

Island Mine

Island Mine

Malone B

12

Hay Bay

Wright Island

Malone Bay

Cumberland Point

Rainbow Cove

Feldtmann Lake

Big Siskiwit River

SISKIWIT BAY

FELDTMANN RIDGE

Lake Halloran

no alcohol

Point Houghton

Long Island

The Head

HOUGHTON RIDGE

Fishermans Home

Voyageur II ferry route
Rock Harbor to Windigo 4.5 hours

To reduce noise and wake impacts
the park has designated certain areas
around the island as Quiet/No-wake
Zones. For detailed information on
the zones, contact a park ranger.

The Isle Royale National Park
boundary extends 4.5 miles into Lake
Superior from Isle Royale and the
outer islands, or to the international
boundary.

1   Trailhead (see table
on page 178)

- - - - Trail

▨ Quiet/no wake
zones

▲ Campsite

🗼 Lookout tower

🚨 Lighthouse

D Overnight dock

D Day-use only dock

⚓ Marina

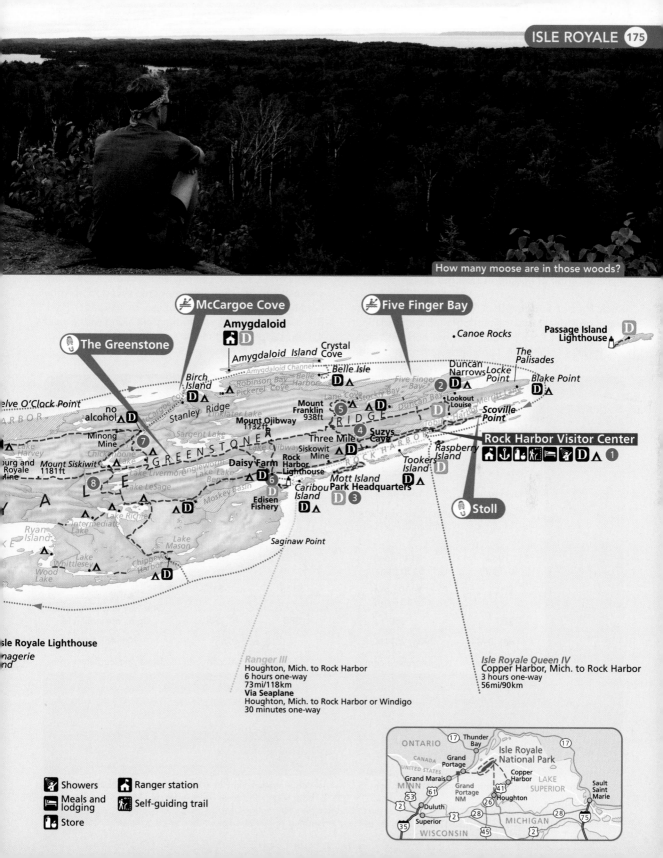

How many moose are in those woods?

The Greenstone

McCargoe Cove

Five Finger Bay

Amygdaloid

Canoe Rocks

Passage Island Lighthouse

Crystal Cove

Amygdaloid Island

Amygdaloid Channel

The Palisades

Duncan Narrows

Locke Point

Blake Point

Belle Isle

Belle Harbor

Robinson Bay

Picketel Cove

Five Finger Bay

Duncan Bay

Birch Island

Stanley Ridge

Twelve O'Clock Point

no alcohol

Linklater Lake

Mount Franklin 938ft

RIDGE

Lane Cove

Stockly Bay

Lookout Louise

Merritt Lane

Scoville Point

Mount Ojibway 1132ft

Sargent Lake

Mount Siskiwit 1181ft

GREENSTONE

Chickenbone Lake

Lake Livermore

Lake LeSage

Moskey Basin

Minong Mine

Lake Harvey

Isle Royale Mine

Three Mile

Siskiwit Mine

Rock Harbor Lighthouse

Suzys Cave

ROCK HARBOR

Raspberry Island

Rock Harbor Visitor Center

Daisy Farm

Lake Benson

Edisen Fishery

Caribou Island

Mott Island
Park Headquarters

Tookers Island

Stoll

Lake Richie

Intermediate Lake

Lake Mason

Saginaw Point

Ryan Island

Lake Whittlesey

Wood Lake

Chippewa Harbor

Isle Royale Lighthouse
Menagerie Island

Ranger III
Houghton, Mich. to Rock Harbor
6 hours one-way
73mi/118km
Via Seaplane
Houghton, Mich. to Rock Harbor or Windigo
30 minutes one-way

Isle Royale Queen IV
Copper Harbor, Mich. to Rock Harbor
3 hours one-way
56mi/90km

Showers

Meals and lodging

Store

Ranger station

Self-guiding trail

ONTARIO

Thunder Bay

CANADA

UNITED STATES

Grand Portage

Grand Marais

Isle Royale National Park

Copper Harbor

LAKE SUPERIOR

Sault Saint Marie

Grand Portage NM

Houghton

MINN

Duluth

Superior

MICHIGAN

WISCONSIN

 **Camping & Lodging**

Camping is free and sites are assigned on a first-come, first-served basis. July and August are the busiest months, but visitation is relatively modest throughout the tourism season and sites are always available. However, shelters go pretty quickly in July and August. I wouldn't recommend leaving your tent at home and banking on having a shelter for the duration of your stay. Sites closest to the docks/harbors usually fill first. If you want to get away from the small crowd at Daisy Farm, use the water taxi to explore less popular areas. A free permit is required for all camping trips. Groups of 7–10 people must make camping reservations and pay a $25 fee through pay.gov. Permits are obtained at a visitor center or aboard the *Ranger III*.

Rock Harbor Lodge (906.337.4993, rockharborlodge.com) provides more comfortable accommodations. It is located at Rock Harbor, near the northeast tip of Isle Royale. Location is superlative; accommodations are basic. Considering the remote nature of this lodge, pricing is more than fair starting at $227/night. At the same time, if you have even the slightest interest in backpacking, now's the time to do it. Take that $227 per night and invest it in a tent, sleeping bag, and mat, unlocking more spectacular settings thanks to 36 backcountry campsites littered across the 45-mile long, 9-mile-wide Isle Royale and a few smaller islands. **Windigo Camper Cabins** offer more economical lodging. Two no-frills cabins go for $52/night. They feature bunk beds and electricity, but no plumbing, heat or A/C.

Whether camping, lodging, or making a daytrip, all visitors 12 and older must pay a $7 per person per day entrance fee. It's best to pay your entrance fee in advance at pay.gov. Entrance fees are waived for anyone holding an annual, Senior, Access, or Volunteer Pass. Bring your pass with you to the park along with a valid ID. You can also pay the entrance fee at Rock Harbor or Windigo Visitor Center upon arrival.

Isle Royale Transportation Services

		Ranger III	Isle Royale Queen IV	Voyageur II	Sea Hunter	Seaplane
Operator		National Park	Private	Private	Private	Private
Departs		Hougton, MI	Copper Harbor, MI	Grand Portage, MN		Houghton, MI
Duration		6 hours	3 hours	2 hours	1.5 hours	1 hour
Open		May–Sept	May–Sept	May–Sept	June–Sept	May–Sept
Schedule		9am*	8am (Copper Harbor) 2:45pm (Rock Harbor)	7:30am	8:30am (Grand Portage) 2pm (Windigo)	Every day, May 23 through September 18
Rates (roundtrip)	Adults	$110 (low) $140 (high)	$135 (low) $150 (high)	$152	$152	$342 roundtrip from Hancock Portage Canal $300 from Grand Marais to Windigo One-way and intra-island flights are available
	Children	$70	$110 (low) $115 (high)	$136	$136	
	Kayak	$60	$60	$80	$80	
Phone		(906) 482-0984	(906) 289-4437	(218) 600-0765		(906) 483-4991
Website		nps.gov/isro	isleroyale.com	isleroyaleboats.com		isleroyaleseaplanes.com

Trips to Isle Royale are not made every day. Check the operator's website or call to confirm departure schedules. Trip duration is one-way. Fares are roundtrip. You can buy one-way fares if you'd like a shorter/longer stay, but you'll have to arrange transportation between different ferry terminals. Make reservations for *Ranger III* via pay.gov.
*Departs at 9am from Houghton on Tuesdays and Fridays and from Rock Harbor on Wednesdays and Saturdays.

Isle Royale Lodging (Fees are per night)

Name	Open	Notes
Rock Harbor Lodge	May–September	Lodge and cottages ($227+) available at Rock Harbor • Primitive camper cabins available at Windigo ($52) • Dining, boat tours, and boat rental available at Rock Harbor

More information and reservations are available at (906) 337-4993 or rockharborlodge.com

Isle Royale Camping

Campground	Max Nigths	Tent Sites	Shelters	Group Sites	Fire Pit	Boat Access
Merritt Lane	3	1	1	0	No	Yes
Duncan Narrows	3	1	2	0	Yes	Yes
Rock Harbor	1	11	9	3	No	Yes
Tookers Island	3	0	2	0	No	Yes
Duncan Bay	3	1	2	0	Yes	Yes
Lane Cove - 🔥	3	5	0	0	No	Yes
Belle Isle	5	1	6	0	Yes	Yes
Three Mile	1	4	8	3	No	Yes
Caribou Island	3	1	2	0	No	Yes
Daisy Farm - 🔥	3	6	16	3	No	Yes
Pickerel Cove	2	1	0	0	No	Yes
Birch Island	3	1	1	0	No	Yes
Moskey Basin - 🔥	3	2	6	2	No	Yes
Chippewa Harbor - 🔥	3	2	4	1	Yes	Yes
McCargoe Cove - 🔥	3	3	6	3	Yes	Yes
Chickenbone East	2	3	0	1	No	Yes
Chickenbone West	2	6	0	3	No	Yes
Lake Richie Canoe	2	3	0	0	No	Yes
Lake Whittlesey	2	3	0	0	No	Yes
Lake Richie	2	4	0	2	No	Yes
Intermediate Lake	2	3	0	0	No	Yes
Wood Lake	2	3	0	0	No	Yes
Todd Harbor - 🔥	3	5	1	3	Yes	Yes
Malone Bay - 🔥	3	0	5	2	Yes	Yes
Hatchet Lake	2	5	0	3	No	No
Little Todd - 🔥	2	4	0	0	Yes	Yes
Desor North	2	3	0	0	No	No
Desor South	2	7	0	3	No	No
Hay Bay	3	1	0	0	No	Yes
Siskiwit Bay - 🔥	3	4	2	3	Yes	Yes
Island Mine	3	4	0	2	Yes	No
Huginnin Cove	3	5	0	0	No	No
Washington Creek (Windigo)	3	5	10	4	No	Yes
Beaver Island	3	0	3	0	No	Yes
Feldtmann Lake	2	5	0	2	No	No
Grace Island	3	0	2	0	No	Yes

Listed by Location on Isle Royale from the Northeast to Southwest

A moose at McCargoe Cove

Isle Royale Hiking Trails (Distances are one-way unless loop)

Name	Location (# on map)	Length	Difficulty Rating & Notes
Tobin Harbor	Near Rock Harbor Seaplane Dock (1)	3.0 miles	E – Alternative to Rock Harbor Trail
Stoll - ♨	Northeast corner of Rock Harbor (1)	4.2 miles	E – Two loops cross back and forth from the shorelines of Lake Superior and Tobin Harbor to Scoville Point
Suzy's Cave	Southwest of Rock Harbor's Dock (1)	3.8 miles	E – Take Rock Harbor Trail to the spur trail to Suzy's Cave • Loop back to Rock Harbor via Tobin Harbor Trail
Rock Harbor and Lake Ritchie	Southwest of Rock Harbor's Dock (1)	12.9 miles	M – Combine Rock Harbor and Lake Ritchie Trails to hike past busy camps at Three Mile and Daisy Farm to more remote locations near the center of the island
Lookout Louise	Northeast terminus of Greenstone Ridge (2)	1.0 mile	S – Seldom visited corner of the park, outstanding views overlooking Duncan Bay
Greenstone Ridge - ♨	Spans from Windigo to Lookout Louise (2, 5)	42.2 miles	M – Best known trail on Isle Royale
Mott Island Circuit	Mott Island Seaplane Dock (3)	2.6 miles	E – Short, seldom-hiked loop trail accessible by boat
Mount Franklin	0.2 mile west of Three Mile Camp (4)	2.0 miles	M – Hike between Rock Harbor and Greenstone Ridge to a dramatic view of the Island's north side
Lane Cove - ♨	Continues north from Mount Franklin (5)	2.4 miles	S – Great destination for hikers leaving Rock Harbor
Daisy Farm and Mount Ojibway	Daisy Farm Camp (6)	5.1 miles	M – Loop trail starting and ending at Daisy Farm • Passes Mount Ojibway Tower on Greenstone Ridge
East Chickenbone	0.5 mile from McCargoe Cove (7)	1.6 miles	E – Connects McCargoe Cove and Greenstone Ridge Trail
Minong Ridge - ♨	Spans from Windigo to McCargoe Cove (7, 11)	26.0 miles	S – Less traveled alternative to The Greenstone • Forested and exposed ridgeline • Excellent chance of seeing moose
Indian Portage and Lake Mason	Spans the island's width from McCargoe Cove to Chippewa Harbor (8)	10.6 miles	M – Isolated trail accessible by The Greenstone and Rock Harbor Trail or by boat at McCargoe Cove and Chippewa Harbor • South section is lightly traveled
Hatchet Lake	Greenstone and Minong Connector (9)	2.6 miles	M – Short connecting trail between ridgelines
Ishpeming	Malone Bay Camp to Ishpeming Point (10)	7.0 miles	S – Steady climb to the park's second highest point
Huginnin Cove	Near Washington Creek Campground (11)	9.4 miles	M – Loop trail passes ridges, wetlands, and a mine
Windigo Nature Walk	Up the hill past Windigo Visitor Center (12)	1.2 miles	E – Self-guided nature trail through hardwood forest
Feldtmann Lake/ Ridge and Island Mine	Near the main dock at Windigo (12)	23.5 miles	M – A loop that leads to Grace Creek Overlook, Feldtmann Lake, Siskiwit Bay, Island Mine, and 3 campgrounds, before returning on Greenstone Ridge

Difficulty Ratings: E = Easy, M = Moderate, S = Strenuous

Hiking

More than 99% of the park is designated wilderness, making Isle Royale and its 165-mile network of trails one of the best hiking regions in the Midwest. Most trails are hidden in the backcountry, only trafficked by backpackers and overnight paddlers. But there are a few extremely rewarding short hikes around Windigo and Rock Harbor. **Windigo Nature Walk** is a great first hike and introduction to the island. Trail guides for the 1.2-mile walk are available at the visitor center. Another pleasant hike near Windigo is the 3.6-mile (roundtrip) trek along **Feldtmann Lake Trail** to Grace Creek Overlook. The rest of Feldtmann Lake/Island Mine Trail is seldom hiked, but the first 1.8 miles is a popular destination for day-hikers seeking views of Grace Harbor from this majestic overlook. Adventurous day-hikers may want to try taking **Minong Ridge Trail** to Minong Ridge Overlook. After hiking up and down over rocky and rugged terrain for 3 miles (one-way) you'll be rewarded with spectacular vistas of Canada's shoreline.

Rock Harbor is precariously positioned on a thin slice of land between Tobin Harbor and Lake Superior. There's more water than land, but you can find several good hiking trails in the area. **Stoll Memorial Trail** starts just northeast of the dock. It recognizes the time and energy Albert Stoll, a *Detroit News* journalist, spent in his effort to protect the region. About 2 miles of it are self-guided. In all, it's nearly 5 miles to the trail's terminus at Scoville Point and back. You'll pass craggy cliffs, harbor views, and remnants of ancient mines along the way. Heading southwest from Rock Harbor are **Tobin Harbor** and **Rock Harbor Trails**. They run parallel to one another, weaving from shoreline to thick forests as they follow alongside the bodies of water that share their names. Regardless which trail you choose, you'll have the opportunity to take a short spur to **Suzy's Cave**. It's more of an eroded arch, but still worth a quick peek. Both trails are among the park's busiest. Rock Harbor is usually the busier of the two because it serves backpackers, daytrippers, lodge guests, and park rangers. From here, hikers often beeline to Three Mile or Daisy Farm to secure a shelter. Raspberry Island, only accessible by boat, has a short interpretive trail to **Rock Harbor Lighthouse** near Edisen Fishery.

Backpacking

Isle Royale is a great place to try backpacking. For starters, it's nearly impossible to get seriously lost. The island is roughly 45 miles long and 9 miles wide; unless you're walking in circles, you can only go so far. With that said, don't just show up here to

The shelters are wonderful

give backpacking a try. Simulate the experience at home, setting up a tent in your apartment or backyard, experimenting with food, and loading up your pack to see how much weight is reasonable for you.

Greenstone Ridge, commonly referred to as "The Greenstone," follows the spine of the island and is as long as trails get here. There aren't any campsites located directly on its 42-mile length, but several short spurs lead to more secluded and less exposed camping locations. It is reasonable for strong hikers to cover the entire length of the trail from Lookout Louise to Windigo in 3 days, camping at Chickenbone Lake and Lake Desor. Less intense hikers should plan things more conservatively. Hiking up and down to the Greenstone with a full pack is more draining than you might imagine. Regardless, plan a longer trip allowing more time to explore the many bays and lakes, and to wait out bad weather (if needed).

Running parallel to The Greenstone from McCargoe Cove to Windigo is **Minong Ridge Trail**. It covers 26 miles of forest and ridgeline. The challenge, abundance of wildlife, and lack of hikers attract backpackers to Minong, but these adventurous souls are few and far between. You have a better chance of spotting moose than another hiker. Just don't get lost while looking for wildlife; pay close attention to the cairns lining barren ridgelines. Also, watch where you step because the terrain is uneven and the trail is undeveloped, lacking bridges and walkways that are integrated into most of Isle Royale's other trails. Minong Trail is best hiked from east to west (McCargoe Cove to Windigo). *Voyageur II* makes scheduled stops at McCargoe Cove. You can also hike in or take a water-taxi.

Backpackers must stay at established campsites unless off-trail arrangements are made in advance while obtaining your backcountry permit. Permits are required for all overnight stays at campgrounds, off-trail sites

The *Sandy* ready to go

(only recommended for experienced backpackers), docks, or at anchor, and can be obtained aboard the *Ranger III* or upon arrival at Rock Harbor or Windigo Visitor Centers. It's nice if you pay the $7 per person per day entrance fee prior to arriving via pay.gov.

Paddling

Experienced paddlers will find some incredibly unique open water paddling opportunities. Bringing your kayak or canoe with you unlocks a multitude of campsites, coves, and bays that cannot be reached on foot. You can explore the island's inland lakes, but you better have sturdy shoulders or a kayak cart. Portages can be up to two miles, covering steep and rugged terrain. However, the rewards are always worth the effort. After putting a mile or two of dirt path behind you, you'll be left to enjoy the tranquil side of the island from the seat of your watercraft. One of the more rigorous routes beginning at Rock Harbor takes paddlers southwest past Rock Harbor Lighthouse into Moskey Basin. From Moskey Basin dock, it's a two-mile (mostly flat) portage to Lake Ritchie (a popular paddle site). Four more portages take you from Lake LeSage to Lake Livermore to Chickenbone Lake and finally to McCargoe Cove, crossing the width of the island to its northern shoreline. Five Fingers is another great destination for paddlers departing Rock Harbor. Remember, weather and waves can change in an instant. *Voyageur II* offers paddler and boat transportation (fee) to several locations.

Rock Harbor Marina (rockharborlodge.com) has canoes and kayaks available for rent. Canoes cost $23 (half-day) and $40 (full-day), while kayaks cost $33 (half-day) and $58 (full-day). Woods & Waters (888.502.8373, woodswaterecotours.com) offers multi-day kayaking tours departing from Grand Marais (MN) or Hancock (MI), that include seaplane transportation, equipment, and all meals, starting at $4,510 (4 nights for two paddlers in a tandem kayak).

Boat Tours

A unique and easy way to explore the park's coastline and harder to reach regions is to hop aboard the *M.V. Sandy* on a sightseeing tour. Four tours are offered throughout the week. Passage Island (4.5 hours) motors over to Passage Island Lighthouse (built in 1881). You'll be required to hike about 2 miles and traverse a few steep inclines. Hidden Lake/Lookout Louise (3.5 hours) visits the northeastern terminus of The Greenstone Trail. Edisen Fishery/Rock Harbor Lighthouse (4 hours) is a guided tour of the oldest lighthouse at Isle Royale (built in 1855) and a historic fishery site. Raspberry Island/Sunset Cruise (2.5 hours) makes a stop at Raspberry Island before rounding Blake Point to Isle Royale's northern shoreline to watch the sunset. All tours depart from Rock Harbor dock. Cost is the same for each at $38.75/adult and $19.50/child (11 and under). Visit rockharborlodge.com for a complete schedule of tours.

M.V. Sandy is also available for use as a one-way water bus to Hidden Lake ($16/passenger) or Daisy Farm ($18). They'll drop you off or pick you up from any spot on the island (weather permitting). You can make reservations for water taxi service at Rock Harbor Marina. Rates are based on number of passengers and mileage. For example, it costs 1–2 people $58 to be taxied five miles or less. It'll cost $326 for a 21–25-mile water taxi ride. There is a maximum of six people with backpacks or four people and two canoes per trip. Rock Harbor Lodge also offers boat rentals out of Rock Harbor Marina. It'll cost $62 to rent a 14' aluminum boat with a 15hp engine for a half-day.

SCUBA Diving

Isle Royale's rugged landscape is enough to include it with the United States' great natural landmarks, but there's a completely different world to be explored beneath the frigid waters of Lake Superior. The park boundary extends 4.5 miles from the islands' shorelines. More than 25 ships have run aground or wrecked on the surrounding reefs, and most are relatively well-maintained due to the cool, clean, freshwater. Mooring buoys are available at nine wrecks, including the 183-foot *SS America*, the park's most popular wreck. This passenger and package steamer ran aground in the North Gap of Washington Harbor, and its bow is visible from above water (its bow sits just two feet below the surface, while its stern is some 80 feet deep). Visitors arriving at Windigo aboard the ferry from Grand Portage will stop to view the massive steamer without having to jump into Lake Superior's water, which ranges from 34–55°F.

Even though it's some of the best wreck diving around, only a few hundred visitors experience this underwater world each year. Divers must be experienced and prepared for the lake's cold water and potentially tight confines of its many shipwrecks. No facilities are available to fill air tanks within the park. All divers must register at one of the visitor centers before diving. Isle Royale Charters (855.348.3472, isleroyalecharters.com) is available on the mainland to take you on an ultimate Isle Royale underwater adventure.

Fishing

Isle Royale's lake trout populations are the most productive and genetically diverse in all of Lake Superior. Waters within park boundaries provide excellent opportunities for catching both trout and salmon. Catch and release all brook trout and coaster brook trout caught in Isle Royale Lake Superior waters. Interior lakes offer habitat for a healthy population of walleye and northern pike. Anglers (17 and older) must have a Michigan State Fishing License if you plan to fish in Lake Superior. A license is not required to fish inland lakes and streams (only use barbless hooks and artificial bait). Rock Harbor Lodge (906.337.4993, rockharborlodge.com) provides fishing charter services ($431 for up to four anglers for four hours).

Visitor Centers

Rock Harbor and Windigo Visitor Centers are open from 8am–6pm every day in July and August. Hours are reduced in May, June, and September. Please call (906) 482-0984 for a current schedule. **Houghton Visitor Center** is open from 8am–6pm, Monday–Friday and from 10am–6pm on Saturdays, June–mid-September. It's open from 8am–4pm, Monday–Friday, for the rest of the year. It closes for all federal holidays in fall through spring. Windigo and Rock Harbor are similar. You'll find showers, a camp store, gift shop, potable water, park rangers, and backcountry permits.

Ranger Programs & For Kids

In addition to the *M.V. Sandy* Boat Tours from Rock Harbor Marina and the ranger narrated boat ride to Isle Royale aboard the *Ranger III*, there are many ranger-led programs offered at the park's Windigo and Rock Harbor Visitor Centers. It's amazing how much more enjoyable a park ranger can make a simple walk along the shorelines. If you have the chance to join one of these activities, do it! Check online or at the visitor center for a current listing of programs.

Most children will like the boat ride across Lake Superior (unless the water is rough, or perhaps enjoy it even

Mount Ojibway

more when the water is rough?). You'll also find activities specifically designed for children once you arrive at Rock Harbor or Windigo. The park's Junior Ranger Program is meant for children ages 6–12, but kids of all ages are welcome to participate. Complete the free activity booklet with the help of parents and the park rangers to receive a unique certificate and badge. There's also a Wilderness Ranger Program for older children to complete during a backcountry stay.

Flora & Fauna

Compared to the rest of the contiguous U.S., Isle Royale is extremely isolated. It's so isolated only a few mammal species reside here. There are more than 40 mammals on the surrounding mainland, but only 18 inhabit the park. Species like caribou and coyote have disappeared. Others, like moose and wolves, have found a way to reach the island within the last century. It's widely believed moose, excellent swimmers among the animal kingdom, swam to the island, motivated by the scent of vegetation. Wolves arrived a few decades later when an exceptionally cold winter left the passage between Ontario, Canada and Isle Royale frozen solid. The presence of moose and their natural predator, wolves, in a closed environment creates an ideal setting to study predator-prey relationships. Scientists have studied the park's wolves and moose since 1958. Today, you can lend a hand by joining a moosewatch expedition (isleroyalewolf.org). In 2016, only two wolves remained on the island. By 2019, scientists introduced 19 genetically diverse wolves. Several of them survived, formed packs, staked out territory, and even had pups. Over time they should moderate the moose population, which, in turn, protects the park's vegetation. In addition to these larger mammals, snowshoe hare, beaver, red fox, red squirrel, at least 40 species of fish, and a handful of amphibians and reptiles reside in the park. Pests are also abundant. Bugs are usually worst in June and July.

Taking a look in Minong Mine

The island is primarily forested with a mixture of boreal and northern hardwoods. Spruce, fir, pine, birch, aspen, maple, and ash are commonly found. Blueberries and thimbleberries grow wild on open ridge tops. They typically ripen between late July and August, providing a tasty snack while hiking about the island.

Pets & Accessibility
Pets are not allowed within the park. However, special conditions do apply to service dogs. Please contact the park (906.482.0984) for additional information.

All transportation services and Rock Harbor Lodge are accessible with assistance to individuals in wheelchairs. Trails are narrow and rugged with limited access.

Weather
The park's weather is moderated by Lake Superior. Its massive body of water has an average temperature of 45°F, cooling summer highs and warming winter lows. Ambient temperature seldom reaches 80°F on the islands. Dense fog and thunderstorms are common during spring and summer. Paddlers should be prepared to head to shore if the wind changes abruptly. Lake Superior's rough waters have received notoriety, thanks in part to the *Edmund Fitzgerald* and Gordon Lightfoot, but weather rarely delays or postpones a departure to or from the island.

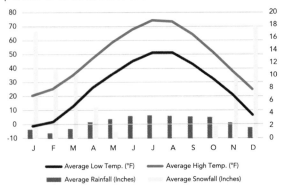

- Average Low Temp. (°F)   — Average High Temp. (°F)
- Average Rainfall (Inches)   Average Snowfall (Inches)

Tips & Recommendations
I always forget Isle Royale (and Michigan's Upper Peninsula) is in the Eastern Time Zone. Don't be like me if you're departing from Houghton or Copper Harbor. Fortunately, I'm also an early riser and haven't missed a boat yet! A real trait worth imitating.

Definitely consider arriving via seaplane. Yes, it's more expensive, but it will save you several hours, and seeing Isle Royale from above is a real treat.

All ferries have different schedules. Pay careful attention to them when planning your trip. The schedules alone may make your ferry selection(s) for you.

The trip aboard the NPS's *Ranger III* out of Houghton is the longest (6 hours), least expensive, and often the most enjoyable (a park ranger is onboard to tell stories and issue backcountry permits). The other ferries arrive earlier, allowing eager backpackers the chance to get deeper into the park on day one.

You can make a daytrip to Isle Royale using the *Queen Royale IV* or *Seahunter III*, but think about spending the night. If camping isn't your thing, Rock Harbor Lodge or the Windigo Camper Cabins are options. Or try backpacking. This is a great location to do so.

The *Voyageur II* (out of Grand Portage) makes stops at Windigo, McCargoe Cove, Belle Isle, Rock Harbor (leaves the next morning), Daisy Farm, Chippewa Harbor, Malone Bay, and Windigo. This allows you to do an easy one-night camping trip to Windigo. It also allows you to see the entire island (from Lake Superior) as it circumnavigates Isle Royale.

The best moose-spotting tip is to use your ears. I've stumbled upon many moose by going off trail after hearing something sloshing around in water or hearing them charging past my campsite early in the morning. But I've also seen moose near Rock Harbor all three trips since I first made this book, so, whether you're backpacking or staying at the lodge, you'll have a good chance of spotting these massive mammals.

And here are a few sample itineraries. Three nights (with a fourth night at the lodge for a good meal and shower before ferrying back to the mainland) is a good place to start, but if it suits you better, make them 4-night trips and spend the first night at the arrival location (Rock Harbor, Washington Creek, or where a water taxi or *Voyageur II* drops you off). It's always nice to sleep a night in the wilderness before putting on some miles. For the long trips from Rock Harbor, you'll have to arrive early via the *Isle Royale Queen IV* from Copper Harbor or seaplane, or stop short of the initial destination because it's unlikely you'd make it to Moskey Basin from Rock Harbor arriving on the *Ranger III* (even if you ran the whole way with your pack).

Begin/End at Rock Harbor
Short 3-Night Itinerary: Three Mile to Lane Cove to Rock Harbor
Long 3-Night Itinerary: Moskey Basin to McCargoe Cove to Daisy Farm
Short One-way 3-Night Itinerary: Water taxi drop off at Todd Harbor to McCargoe Cove to Moskey Basin to Daisy Farm (or Three Mile or Rock Harbor)
Long One-way 3-Night Itinerary: Water taxi drop off at Malone Bay to Hatchet Lake to Moskey Basin to Daisy Farm (make it a 4-night itinerary if you can't get to Malone Bay early enough to make it to Hatchet Lake on Day 1)

Begin/End at Windigo
Short 3-Night Itinerary: Washington Creek to Huginin Cove to Washington Creek
Long 3-Night Itinerary: Feldtman Lake to Siskiwit Bay to Island Mine
Long One-way 3-Night Itinerary: Water taxi drop off at McCargoe Cove to Little Todd to Huginin Cove

Miles of boardwalk help keep your feet dry

Beyond the Park...

Dining
Harbor Haus • (906) 289-4502
77 Brockway Ave, Copper Harbor
harborhaus.com

Joey's Seafood & Grill
304 Shelden Ave, Houghton
joeys-grill.com • (906) 483-0500

Four Seasons Tea • (906) 482-3233
606 Shelden Ave, Houghton
fourseasonstearoom.com

Hungry Hippie Tacos • (218) 387-3382
15 MN-61, Grand Marais
hungryhippiehostel.com

World's Best Donuts • (218) 387-1345
10 Wisconsin St, Grand Marais
worldsbestdonutsmn.com

Grocery Stores
Walmart • (906) 482-0639
995 Razorback Dr, Houghton

Festival Foods • (906) 482-7500
47401 M-26, Houghton

Trading Post • (218) 475-2282
77 Mile Creek Rd, Grand Portage

Lodging
Bella Vista Motel • (877) 888-8439
180 6th St, Copper Harbor
bellavistamotel.com

Hollow Rock • (218) 475-2272
7422 MN-61, Grand Portage

MacArthur House • (218) 260-6390
520 W 2nd St, Grand Marais
macarthurhouse.net

Naniboujou Lodge
20 Naniboujou Tr, Grand Marais
naniboujou.com • (218) 387-2688

Campgrounds
Fort Wilkins State Park
15223 US-41, Copper Harbor

Sunset Bay RV Resort
2701 Sunset Bay Beach Rd, Allouez
sunset-bay.com • (941) 232-4832

McLain State Park
18350 M-230, Hancock

Hancock Recreation Area
2000 Jasberg St, Hancock
(906) 482-7413

City of Houghton RV Park
1100 W Lakeshore Dr, Houghton
cityofhoughton.com • (906) 482-8745

Grand Portage Marina and RV
41 Marina Rd • (218) 475-2476

Attractions
Keweenaw Adv • (906) 289-4500
155 Gratiot St, Copper Harbor
keweenawadventure.com

Copper Harbor Lighthouse
Fort Wilkins Historic State Park
Hunter's Point Park, Manganese
Falls, Devil's Washtub
Copper Harbor

Keweenaw Brewing Co
408 Shelden Ave, Houghton
kbc.beer • (906) 482-5596

Pictured Rocks National Lakeshore
Great kayaking and hiking
N8391 Sand Point Rd, Munising
nps.gov/piro • (906) 387-3700

Palms Book State Park
Kitch-iti-kipi (freshwater spring)
Manistique, MI • michigan.org

Bond Falls Scenic Site
Haight Township, MI

Mackinac Island State Park
Fun fact: It was made a National Park in 1875, the world's second after Yellowstone (went back to the state in 1895)
7029 Huron Rd, Mackinac Island
mackinacparks.com

Tahquamenon Falls State Park
41382 W M-123, Paradise MI
michigan.org

Sleeping Bear Dunes
9922 Front St, Empire, MI
nps.gov/slbe • (231) 326-4700

Apostle Islands National Lakeshore
415 Washington Ave, Bayfield, WI
nps.gov/apis • (715) 779-3397

Grand Portage National Monument
170 Mile Creek Rd, Grand Portage
nps.gov/grpo • (218) 475-0123

For anyone arriving via Grand Portage, more Minnesota parks are listed on page 193

Voyageurs

Grassy Bay Cliff

Phone: (218) 283-6600
Website: nps.gov/voya

Established: April 8, 1975
Size: 218,054 Acres
Annual Visitors: 240,000
Peak Season: Summer

Activities: Hiking, Backpacking, Boating, Paddling, Fishing

Drive-in Campgrounds: None
270+ Campsites: $16–35/night + $10 Reservation Fee, Boat Access Only, Permit Required
Kettle Falls Hotel: $70–90/night (room), $210–390/night (villa, 3 day min), Boat or Seaplane Access Only

Park Hours: All day, every day
Entrance Fee: None

It's appropriate that Minnesota, the land of 10,000 lakes, is home to a national park made mostly of islands and lakes. At Voyageurs travel is by boat, not car. Visitors carry a paddle in their hands rather than a walking stick. After a long day's journey, adventurers sit by a campfire resting their tired arms and blistered hands (instead of their sore feet).

One other thing about this place that feels like Minnesota: the winters. They are numbingly cold. Freezing temperatures can make the region feel downright unbearable, but it's far from uninhabitable. In fact, people have lived here since glacial waters of Lake Agassiz receded some 10,000 years ago. Cree, Monsoni, and Assiniboin tribes were living here in the late 17th century. In 1688, these tribes were the first Native American contacts of French–Canadian explorer Jacques de Noyon. He and his band of voyageurs, known for their strength and endurance, were seeking beaver pelts. Fur trade was the leading industry in the New World, and animal populations in the east were approaching extinction due to overhunting. Trappers like de Noyon were continually pushing west in search of new animal populations to harvest. By the mid-18th century, Ojibwa Indians took up residence in the Rainy Lake area, supplying fur traders with food, furs, and canoes in exchange for manufactured goods.

Over the course of the next century rapid development stressed the United States' resources. By the 1880s, a logging frenzy had reached Minnesota's U.S.–Canada border and the present-day site of Voyageurs National Park. Forests were clear-cut as fast as humans could cut them, with logs rafted down the rivers to increase efficiency. Hoist Bay was named for the act of hoisting floating logs from the waters of Namakan Lake, where they were loaded onto a train.

While loggers were clear-cutting trees, miners were blasting through rock hoping for gold. Several gold mines, most notable being Little American Mine, were constructed beginning in the 1880s. Rainy Lake City, a town bustling with miners and their families, sprang up overnight. By 1898 gold mines went bust, and in 1901 Rainy Lake City was a ghost town.

The next enterprise to take the region by storm was commercial fishing, especially for caviar (lake sturgeon eggs). Without refrigeration there was no way to transport their catch. Fishing fizzled and gave way to bootlegging during the era of Prohibition. The maze of waterways along the United States–Canada border proved to be a perfect location for boaters to smuggle alcohol.

Today's industry is tourism. As early as 1891, legislation had been written to protect the area now known as Voyageurs National Park, but the request fell on deaf ears. Trees were harvested. Minerals were mined. Dams were constructed at International Falls, Kettle Falls, and Squirrel Falls. Commercial interests scarred the scenic landscapes, and Ernest Oberholtzer stood in opposition. He championed the park idea and was one of eight founding members of the Wilderness Society. He used his position to lobby Washington to create a national park of the region he explored as a child by canoe. It took decades, but in 1975—when Oberholtzer was 90 years old—the park was finally established.

Voyageurs is a place changed by human enterprises, but nature itself is a powerful agent of change. In summer, boats glide across the water as loons float on its surface. Bald eagles soar above the lakes and trees. Quietly, leaves turn yellow, brown, and orange, before falling to crunch beneath your shoes. Rain turns to snow. Water becomes ice. Year-to-year, day-to-day, the park is in a constant state of flux. But one thing remains the same: visitors find peace and solace on the water. They are at home in the wilderness, much like the voyageurs and Ernest Oberholtzer were before them.

Snowmobiling Crane Lake

When to Go
The park is open all year, but its weather and landscapes are dramatically different from summer to winter. In summer, most visitors explore the region by houseboat, boat, canoe, or kayak. In winter, snowmobilers race across the frozen lakes while cross-country skiers and snowshoers make use of snow-covered hiking trails.

Transportation & Airports
Most of the park—including all campsites and Kettle Falls Hotel—is only accessible by boat or seaplane. Public transportation does not reach this remote location. The closest airport is International Falls (INL), located about 25 miles northwest of Kabetogama. Taxis and rental cars are available at the airport.

Directions
The park is best explored by boat, but all three visitor centers can be reached by car.

To Rainy Lake Visitor Center (13 miles from International Falls): Take MN-11 east out of International Falls and it will lead you to the visitor center.

To Ash River Visitor Center (145 miles from Duluth): Take US-53 North about 131 miles. Turn right at Ash River Trail/Ness Road. Continue for 8 miles before turning left onto Mead Wood Road, which leads directly to the visitor center.

To Kabetogama Lake Visitor Center (140 miles from Duluth): Take US-53 N 134 miles. Turn right onto Gamma Road/Salmi Road. After 1.3 miles, turn right onto Gappa Road. Keep left at the fork, and then turn right into the visitor center parking lot.

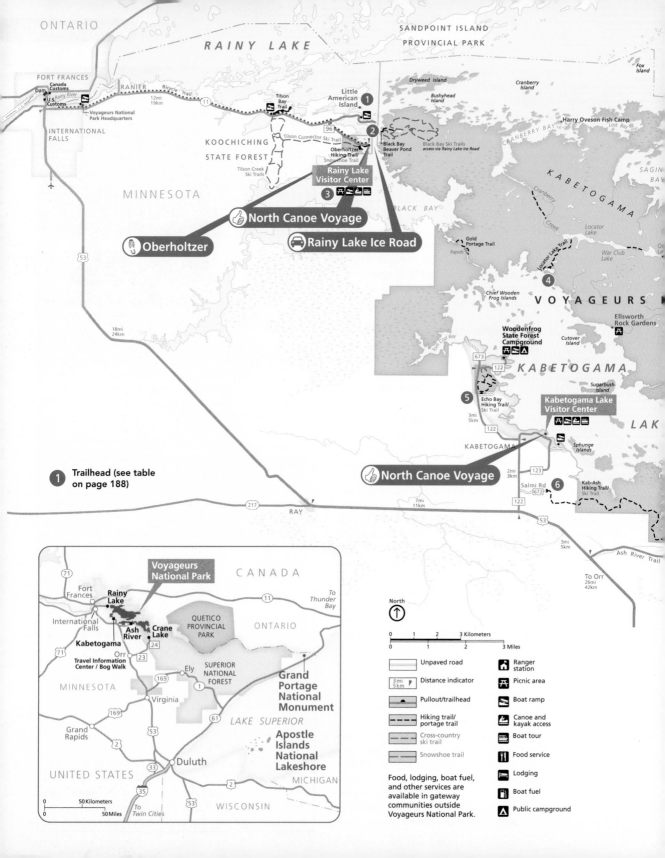

Map Labels

ONTARIO

RAINY LAKE

SANDPOINT ISLAND
PROVINCIAL PARK

Fox Island

FORT FRANCES

Canada Customs
U.S. Customs
Dam
Rainy River
RANIER
Bicycle Trail
12mi
19km
11
Voyageurs National Park Headquarters

INTERNATIONAL FALLS

Dryweed Island

Cranberry Island

Bushyhead Island

Harry Oveson Fish Camp

Lost Bay

Little American Island **1**

2

96

CRANBERRY BAY

KABETOGAMA

SAGIN BAY

KOOCHICHING STATE FOREST

Tilson Bay Trail

Tilson Connector Ski Trail

Tilson Creek Ski Trails

Oberholtzer Hiking Trail/ Snowshoe Trail

Black Bay Beaver Pond Trail

Black Bay Ski Trails
access via Rainy Lake Ice Road

MINNESOTA

Rainy Lake Visitor Center

3

👍 **North Canoe Voyage**

👣 **Oberholtzer**

🚗 **Rainy Lake Ice Road**

BLACK BAY

Gold Portage Trail

Rapids

Cranberry Creek

Locator Lake Trail

Locator Lake

War Club Lake

VOYAGEURS

4

Chief Wooden Frog Islands

Ellsworth Rock Gardens

53

18mi
24km

Lost Bay Cod Bay

Woodenfrog State Forest Campground

673

Cutover Island

KABETOGAMA

122

Sugarbush Island

Echo Bay Hiking Trail/ Ski Trail

5

Kabetogama Lake Visitor Center

LAK

122

KABETOGAMA

Sphunge Islands

123

1 Trailhead (see table on page 188)

👍 **North Canoe Voyage**

3mi
5km

2mi
3km

Salmi Rd

672

Kab-Ash Hiking Trail/ Ski Trail

6

217

RAY

7mi
11km

122

53

3mi
5km

Ash River Trail

To Orr
26mi
42km

Inset Map

71

Fort Frances

Rainy Lake

Voyageurs National Park

CANADA

11

To Thunder Bay

International Falls

71

Ash River

Crane Lake

24

QUETICO PROVINCIAL PARK

ONTARIO

Kabetogama

Travel Information Center / Bog Walk

Orr

23

Ely

1

SUPERIOR NATIONAL FOREST

Grand Portage National Monument

MINNESOTA

169

Virginia

LAKE SUPERIOR

61

Apostle Islands National Lakeshore

Grand Rapids

169

2

53

33

Duluth

MICHIGAN

UNITED STATES

35

53

WISCONSIN

To Twin Cities

0   50 Kilometers
0   50 Miles

Legend

North
⬆

0   1   2   3 Kilometers
0   1   2   3 Miles

Unpaved road

3mi 5km ▸ Distance indicator

Pullout/trailhead

- - - Hiking trail/ portage trail

Cross-country ski trail

Snowshoe trail

Food, lodging, boat fuel, and other services are available in gateway communities outside Voyageurs National Park.

🏠 Ranger station

🪑 Picnic area

🛶 Boat ramp

🛶 Canoe and kayak access

Boat tour

🍴 Food service

🛏 Lodging

⛽ Boat fuel

⛺ Public campground

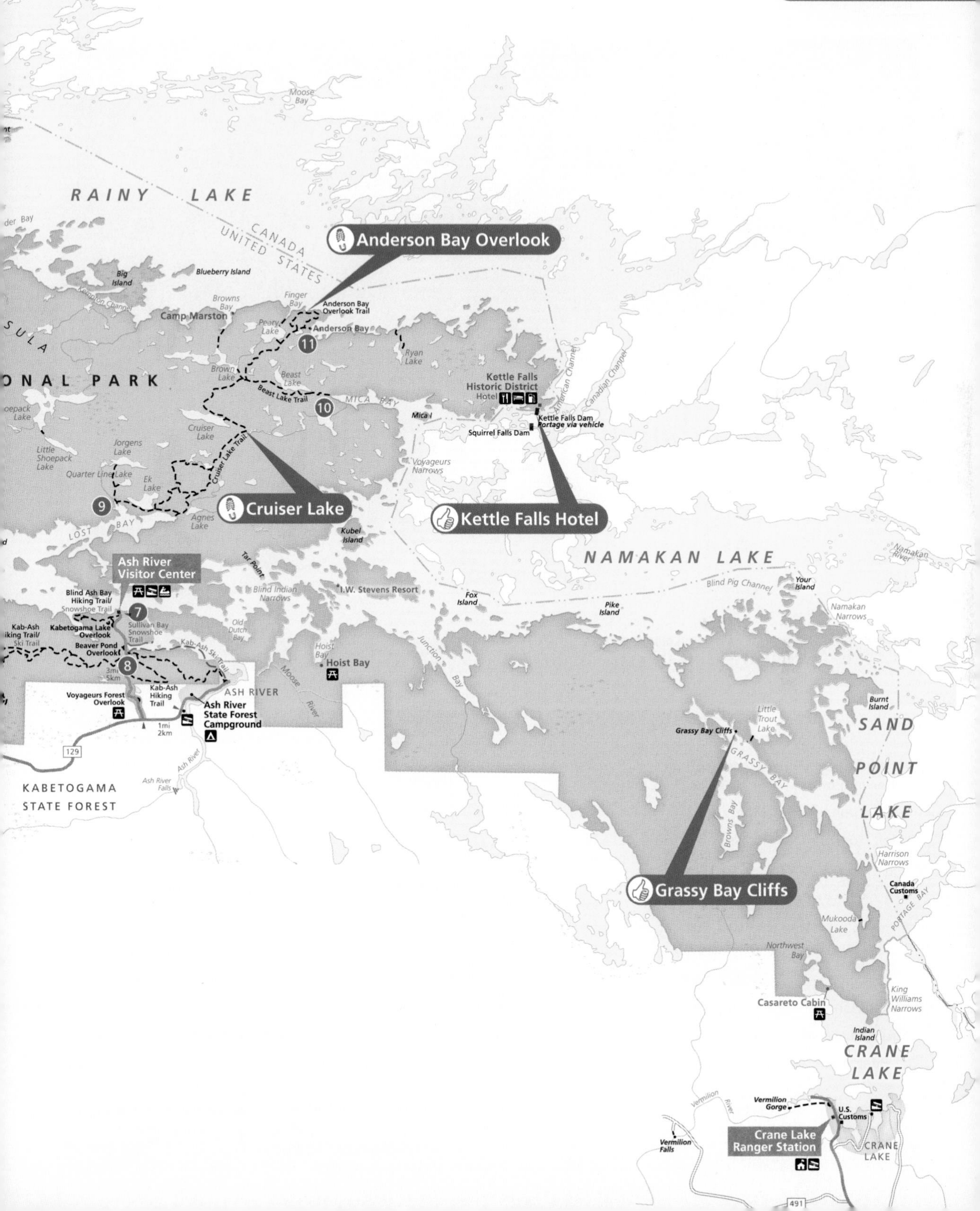

RAINY LAKE

der Bay

Moose
Bay

CANADA
UNITED STATES

Big
Island

Blueberry Island

SULA

Browns
Bay

Camp Marston

Finger
Bay

Peary
Lake

Anderson Bay Overlook

Anderson Bay
Overlook Trail

Anderson Bay

11

Ryan
Lake

ONAL PARK

Brown
Lake

Beast
Lake

MICA BAY

Beast Lake Trail

10

Mica I.

Kettle Falls
Historic District
Hotel

Voyageurs
Narrows

Kettle Falls Dam
Portage via vehicle

Squirrel Falls Dam

Kettle Falls Hotel

epack
Lake

Jorgens
Lake

Cruiser
Lake

Cruiser Lake Trail

Little
Shoepack
Lake

Quarter Line Lake

Ek
Lake

Cruiser Lake

9

LOST

BAY

Agnes
Lake

Kubel
Island

NAMAKAN LAKE

Namakan
River

Tar Point

**Ash River
Visitor Center**

Blind Ash Bay
Hiking Trail/
Snowshoe Trail

7

Blind Indian
Narrows

I.W. Stevens Resort

Fox
Island

Pike
Island

Blind Pig Channel

Your
Island

Namakan
Narrows

Kab-Ash
Hiking Trail/
Ski Trail

Kabetogama Lake
Overlook

Beaver Pond
Overlook

Sullivan Bay
Snowshoe
Trail

Kab-Ash Ski Trail

Old
Dutch
Bay

Hoist
Bay

Hoist Bay

Junction
Bay

SAND

8

3mi
5km

ASH RIVER

Moose
River

Burnt
Island

Voyageurs Forest
Overlook

Kab-Ash
Hiking Trail

Ash River
State Forest
Campground

Little
Trout
Lake

Grassy Bay Cliffs

POINT

129

1mi
2km

Ash
River

GRASSY BAY

LAKE

KABETOGAMA
STATE FOREST

Ash River
Falls

Browns
Bay

Harrison
Narrows

Grassy Bay Cliffs

Mukooda
Lake

Canada
Customs

Northwest
Bay

King
Williams
Narrows

Casareto Cabin

Indian
Island

PORTAGE

CRANE

LAKE

Vermilion
Gorge

U.S.
Customs

**Crane Lake
Ranger Station**

Vermilion
Falls

Vermilion
River

CRANE
LAKE

491

Blind Ash Bay Trail

Voyageurs Hiking Trails (Distances are roundtrip unless noted otherwise)

Name	Location (# on map)	Access	Length	Difficulty Rating & Notes
Little American Island	Rainy Lake (1)	Boat	0.25 mile	E – Self-guided loop exploring Minnesota's late 19th-century gold rush
Black Bay Beaver Pond	Across Black Bay north of Rainy Lake Visitor Center (2)	Boat	1.2 miles	E – Visits an active beaver pond
Oberholtzer	Rainy Lake Visitor Center (3)	Land/Car	1.7 miles	E – Hikes to two scenic overlooks
Locator Lake	Across Kabetogama Lake North of the Visitor Center (4)	Boat	4.0 miles	S – A hilly out-and-back that passes through forests and wetlands
Echo Bay	Off County Rd 122, 3 miles from Kabetogama Lake VC (5)	Land/Car	2.5 miles	E – Excellent birdwatching trail • Good site for cross-country skiing
Kab-Ash	Connects Kabetogama Lake and Ash River Visitor Centers (6)	Land/Car	28.0 miles	S – Four separate trailheads are located along the trail (one-way & loops)
Sullivan Bay	Ash River Visitor Center (7)	Land/Car	1.5 miles	E – Tracked snowshoe trail in winter
Blind Ash Bay	Kabetogama Lake Overlook (8)	Land/Car	3.3 miles	M – A pleasant wooded semi-loop
Cruiser Lake - ⌂	Rainy or Kabetogama Lake (9)	Boat	9.5 miles	S – Crosses Kabetogama Peninsula (1-way)
Beast Lake	Namakan Lake (10)	Boat	2.5 miles	M – Steep climbs at the beginning and end to reach ridgeline (1-way)
Anderson Bay - ⌂	East end of Rainy Lake just past Kempton Channel (11)	Boat	1.8 miles	M – This short loop rewards hikers with a clifftop view of Rainy Lake

Difficulty Ratings: E = Easy, M = Moderate, S = Strenuous

Camping & Lodging

Camping is a fantastic way to see the stars and hear the wildlife of Minnesota's Northwoods. More than 270 campsites dot the shorelines of Voyageurs National Park. Not a single one is accessible by car (except possibly during winter, via Rainy Lake Ice Road). With 655 miles of shoreline, that's roughly one campsite every other mile.

A permit is required for all overnight stays in the park (including houseboats). Permits can be reserved at (877) 444-6777 or recreation.gov. No matter what time of year you'd like to visit, you will have to pay a $10 reservation fee. During high season (May through September) you'll also have to pay an amenity fee ranging from $16 per night for a small campsite with no tent pad to $35 per night for a group campsite. Houseboats require a $10/night amenity fee (but the reservation fee is included). There are four group sites and four handicap accessible sites. The park provides backcountry canoes at the Chain of Lakes (Locator, War Club, Loiten, and Quill Lakes), Ek Lake, Shoepack and Little Shoepack Lake, and Brown Lake. The canoes are locked on racks near the respective lake. You will receive a key with your permit for Chain of Lakes, and Shoepack and Little Shoepack Lakes as a canoe is required to access the site. For other sites, you will have the option to reserve a canoe with your backcountry permit. Once you've made your reservations, you must print your permit and bring it with you, placing it inside the site's waterproof box. You can make same-day reservations at self-help kiosks at any of the visitor centers for that night only. Any additional nights must be reserved through (877) 444-6777 or recreation.gov.

The only lodging within park boundaries is **Kettle Falls Hotel** (218.240.1724, kettlefallshotel.com), which has been in operation since 1918. Just like the rest of the park it's only accessible by boat or plane. The shortest water route is from Ash River, but shuttle service (starting at $45 roundtrip) is available from Rainy, Kabetogama, and Crane Lakes as well. The hotel is situated near Kettle Falls on the Canada–U.S. border. They have a variety of lodging accommodations, ranging from basic rooms ($70–90/night) to villa suites ($210–390/night). There is a three-night minimum stay for all villas and suites. Kettle Falls closes for winter, but can still be contacted at (218) 875-2070. They also offer canoe ($15/day), kayak ($25/day), and boat ($170/day for a 70hp fishing boat with GPS/depth finder) rental.

Drive-in camping is available near the park's southern boundary at Woodenfrog State Forest Campground

Reflections on Kabetogama Lake

(59 sites, 218.235.2520, CR-22, Kabetogama State Forest) on Kabetogama Lake and Ash River Campground (8 sites, 218.235.2520, CR-126, Orr) in Ash River. Camping at either location costs $15 per night.

Hiking & Backpacking

Voyageurs is dominated by water, making its hiking trails more afterthought than main attraction. Even so, you'll find some great opportunities within the park and a boat isn't needed to reach all of them. **Oberholtzer Trail** begins near Rainy Lake Visitor Center before passing through forests and wetlands. The first quarter-mile is wheelchair accessible and you'll find two overlooks along its 1.7-mile length.

Not surprisingly, most trailheads are only accessible by boat. **Cruiser Lake Trail System**, a 9.5-mile network, is the best way to explore Kabetogama Peninsula by foot. It leads to several inland lakes as the path crosses from Kabetogama Lake to Rainy Lake. It's also a great trail for backpackers. Campsites are available at Little Shoepack, Jorgens, Quarter Line, Ek, Agnes, Cruiser, Beast, Brown, and Oslo Lakes—many of which have boats available for rent ($12/day • reserve at 877.444.6777 or recreation.gov). **Black Bay Beaver Pond**, near the northwest point of Kabetogama Peninsula, provides a fairly short hike through pine forest to an active beaver pond.

Not your ordinary camping trip

Boat Tours

More than a third of the park is water, and much of its beauty and mystique cannot be grasped without heading out to sea. Boat tours are the perfect way to explore Voyageurs if you don't have your own.

Kettle Falls Cruise (6.5 hours, $45/adult, $22.50/child) and Grand Tour (2.5 hours, $30/adult, $15/child) depart from Rainy Lake Visitor Center. Kettle Falls Cruise (5.5 hours, $40/adult, $20/child) also departs from Kabetogama Lake Visitor Center. Kettle Falls tours spend two hours at historic Kettle Falls Hotel, dining and exploring the dam area. Grand Tour stops at Little American Island. Ellsworth Rock Garden Tour (1.5 hours, $25/adult, $12.50/child) departs from Kabetogama Lake Visitor Center and motors to a quirky garden, where a park ranger will lead you on a quarter-mile tour of the unique sculptures and the property. Life on the Lake Tour (2 hours, $25/adult, $15/child) departs from Rainy Lake Visitor Center and explores an old commercial fishing camp.

Reservations can be made in person at each respective visitor center or until midnight the night before the tour at (877) 444-6777 or recreation.gov. Reservations are recommended. Tickets first become available for the upcoming tourism season on April 15th.

Paddling/Boating

Voyageurs is an anomaly among national parks in that there are only 8 miles of paved roadways within its boundaries. If you're going to get out there and explore the region, you'll have to head out on the open water, by canoe, kayak, motorboat, or houseboat.

Water exploration occurs in five main lakes: Kabetogama, Namakan, Rainy, Sand Point, and Crane. More than 500 islands, 84,000 acres of water, and infinitely many boating possibilities make it easy to get lost in a maze of forests and water. If your intent is a multi-day or even a half-day trip, be sure to travel with a good map and compass (GPS is optional, just know how to use it). If you don't have your own boat, think about taking a water taxi to Kabetogama Peninsula where you can hike to any one of 17 inland lake campsites. Rental canoes ($12/day) are provided by the park for your enjoyment at nine of these sites. Like campsites, canoes can be reserved at recreation.gov. You can also rent boats at many of the nearby resorts, Kettle Falls Hotel, or marinas like Handberg's (218.993.2214, handbergs.com) near Crane Lake. Be sure to plan your route out in advance and carry one life jacket for each person using a boat or canoe.

No boat. No problem. Check at a visitor center for a current schedule of ranger-led activities. **Free guided canoe trips** are offered regularly. One trip takes visitors back in time by traveling aboard a 26-foot North Canoe similar to those used by original voyageurs. You can also find full-service outfitters like Border Guide Service (218.324.2430, borderguideservice.com) to take you into the backcountry.

If you believe the strength and endurance of the voyageurs is in you, consider navigating around Kabetogama Peninsula. This 75-mile voyage requires two short portages, one at Gold Portage, a rapid between Kabetogama and Rainy Lake, and another at Kettle Falls Dam. Other than that, it's all wide-open water as you trace the jagged shoreline for seven-ish days.

Houseboats

You can find floating motorhomes at Voyageurs. Before renting one, know you'll need to have a backcountry permit ($10/night) for all overnight stays within the park. Make your reservations at (877) 444-6777 or recreation.gov. Houseboat sites are available on a first-come, first-served basis, two houseboats per site. You must be moored to shore from dusk to dawn, so you'll want to find a site well before the sun is setting. You cannot moor overnight at docks inside the park or simply anchor in the middle of a lake, but you are permitted to stay at undesignated sites as long as you are at least 200 yards away from any developed site or structure. You can have campfires using the metal rings at designated houseboat sites. Houseboat rentals are available at many locations, including Voyagaire (Crane Lake, 800.882.6287, voyagaire.com), Ebel's (Ash River, 888.883.2357, ebels.com), Rainy Lake Houseboats (Rainy Lake, 800.554.9188, rainylakehouseboats.com), and Northernaire Houseboats (Rainy Lake, 218.286.5221, northernairehouseboats.com). Expect one to cost anywhere from $300 to more than $1,000 per day. There are additional expenses for food, fuel, and a smaller boat (you must tow). And you definitely should have some boating experience before renting one of these things.

Fishing

Voyageurs is home to some of the best fishing in the Midwest. Walleye, northern pike, muskie, panfish, yellow perch, and bass are commonly caught. Visitors with their own boat can launch at any of ten boat ramps lining the southern shorelines of the park's lakes. If you don't have your own boat or would like access to a knowledgeable guide, consider contacting Border Country Outfitters (218.324.0668, bcoaonline.com) on Rainy Lake or Northern Limits Guiding (320.266.4514, northernlimitsguiding.com) or Kabetogama Angling Adventures (218.875.2075, kabetogamaangling.com. com) on Kabetogama Lake and Ash River.

Winter Activities

In winter, canoes and hiking boots are retired in favor of cross-country skis and snowshoes. Black Bay and Echo Bay Trails are two popular destinations for **cross-country skiing**. Tilson Connector Trail, accessible from Rainy Lake Visitor Center, is a 10-mile network of well-groomed trails. Kab-Ash Trail from Kabetogama Lake to Ash River is a long, ungroomed trail for experienced skiers. Trail maps and conditions are available at the park website. Park personnel maintain three **tracked snowshoe trails**: Blind Ash Bay, Sullivan Bay, and Oberholtzer. Rainy Lake Visitor Center has snowshoes and cross-country skis they'll lend out on a first-come, first-served basis for free. You may want to call the visitor center at (218) 286-5258 for sizing and availability.

Ice fishing is also popular. Winter anglers must come prepared for northern Minnesota's brand of cold. Temperatures are frequently below zero, snow drifts and the wind whips, leaving even the hardiest of fishermen dreading the thought of exiting their warm fishing shanties. Woody's Fairly Reliable Guide Service (218.286.5001, fairlyreliable.com) will take you out in winter and show you how ice fishing is done.

Snowmobilers are allowed on frozen lake surfaces and Chain of Lakes Scenic Trail. In all, there are 110 miles of staked and groomed trails to explore the vast expanses of snow, ice, and forests. Boyum Performance (218.324.0566, boyumperformance.com) offers rentals or tours from Thunder Bird Lodge on Rainy Lake. Voyagaire Lodge (800.882.6287, voyagaire.com) offers rentals on Crane Lake.

Snowmobilers aren't the only motorized vehicles driving on ice, as the magic of wintertime turns a paddler's paradise into a motorist's retreat. Automobiles can take ice roads, driving straight down the boat ramps

Ice Road Truckin'

at Rainy Lake, Kabetogama Lake, Ash River, and Crane Lake. They are open to cars and trucks weighing less than 7,000 pounds. Islands usually only accessible by boat can be viewed from the warmth of your car. Winter also provides the only opportunity for drive-up camping. You can park and camp along the ice road if you can endure the cold. An overnight permit (reserve at 877.444.6777 or recreation.gov) is required for winter camping. Even without spending the night, driving an ice road is a unique national park experience. A trip that becomes even more memorable if you're lucky enough to spot a lone gray wolf crossing the ice surface, or more likely, a pack of fishing shanties where ice fishermen escape the harsh Minnesotan winter. Routes vary depending on conditions, so it's a good idea to call the park to discuss what's plowed and what's open.

My first ice road choice would be Kabetogama Lake, as you'll find a **sledding hill** at Sphunge Island along with a nearby **skating rink**. It can be accessed by taking Kabetogama–Ash River Ice Road. There are two hills (one for older children and adults, the other for young children), picnic tables, and a fire ring. But it is a unique experience surrounded by all kinds of natural beauty, whichever ice road you choose. Or choose them all. Just know it's a 92-mile drive (on pavement) from Rainy Lake to Crane Lake.

Visitor Centers

Rainy Lake (218.286.5258), **Kabetogama** (218.875.2111), and **Ash River** (218.374.3221) **Visitor Centers** are open daily from 9am–5pm from late May until late September. Kabetogama and Ash River are closed the rest of the year. Rainy Lake remains open but with shorter hours. Each visitor center offers a free public boat launch, exhibits, restrooms, information desk, short film, and a children's activity table.

Modern-day Voyageurs

Ranger Programs & For Kids

In addition to boat tours, the park offers numerous free ranger-led activities. Visitors can explore the history of the voyageurs, for whom the park is named, on the free North Canoe Voyage departing from both Rainy Lake (218.286.5258) and Kabetogama Lake (218.875.2111) Visitor Centers. Paddling is required. Minimum age is 5. All tours are weather dependent. Reservations, available beginning in late May by calling the respective visitor center, are recommended.

Campfire programs are held frequently, and special speakers are often invited to discuss topics suitable to their expertise. Check out the park's online calendar to view a current schedule of events. If you don't have a boat and no ranger programs or boat tours are offered, activities here are limited to a few short hiking trails.

Voyageurs has more activities geared to children than the average park. For starters, children of all ages can dress up in traditional voyageurs' clothing at any of the park's visitor centers. To feel like a modern-day voyageur, sign up for the free ranger-led North Canoe Voyage. Children's tables are available at each visitor center, filled with kid-friendly activities like coloring and stamping. Children also have the opportunity to become Junior Rangers by completing a free activity booklet (available online or at any of the visitor centers). Upon completion, children are rewarded with a certificate and badge. Discovery Packs are also available at the visitor centers. They help families explore the park's geology, wildlife, and history through an assortment of educational materials. Packs are loaned out, free of charge. They must be checked out by an adult with a valid driver's license. The park also holds an annual Kids' Art Show.

Flora & Fauna

Wildlife has attracted visitors to Voyageurs since the first European explorers arrived in 1688. In summer,

bear, deer, Canadian lynx, and moose are roaming about. But you're more likely to see some of the 240 species of birds. Two of the most frequently spotted popular species are the common loon and bald eagle. In winter you'll probably see tracks of snowshoe hare or gray wolf. Maybe see them if you're lucky.

The park is dominated by water, but you can find forests, marshes, and peatlands. Spruce, fir, pine, aspen, and birch are common trees.

Pets & Accessibility

Pets are not allowed at any backcountry campsites (campsites within the Kabetogama Peninsula). They are allowed at frontcountry sites (sites along the main lakes' shoreline) and the short recreational trail running parallel to County Road 96. They are allowed in developed areas like visitor centers, picnic areas, and boat ramps, but must be on a leash (less than six feet).

The park's visitor centers, Kettle Falls Hotel, the first quarter-mile of Oberholtzer Trail, four campsites, and most boat tours are wheelchair accessible. Most of the park is reached by boat, making accessibility dependent on your personal method of transportation. National Park Service boat tours are accessible, but the land portion may not be. If you plan on hiring the services of an outfitter, discuss any potential accessibility requirements with them prior to arrival.

Weather

International Falls, the closest city to Voyageurs National Park, holds the title for coldest city in the Lower 48. This standard should give you a pretty good idea what the weather is going to be like. Summers are short and comfortable with average highs reaching the upper 70s°F in July and August. Winters tend to be long and cold. Temperatures below 0°F are common and average January highs are in the teens.

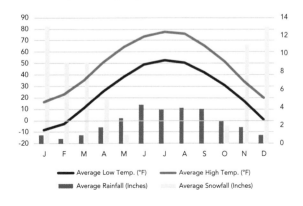

Tips & Recommendations

Summer is the busiest time of the year at Voyageurs National Park. Roughly 85% of all visitors arrive between May and September. And June, July, and August are about twice as busy as May and September. With that said, visitation is always manageable and rarely feels over-crowded with everyone dispersed across the lakes (they're massive and very deep).

Lakes typically begin to freeze in November/December. If you want to have a park to yourself, visit in December, when ice is typically too thin for vehicles and snowmobiles. Plus, it's cold. Visitation picks up in February, when ice is thick and snowmobilers are racing across the frozen lakes. April is another transition month, where the lakes thaw and travelers stay away.

You'll want to have a plan for visiting Voyageurs. Making daytrips out of boat tours and ranger programs is one way to experience the park. The other is to get out there on the water with your boat or a rental. For this you'll need a good map and campsite reservations.

For boat rental, bigger is better (maybe not houseboat big though). Also inquire if its depth finder has GPS. If not, it's a very good idea to bring one (or download maps on your phone). It's very easy to get lost on the water, and a challenge to find your destination.

If you're visiting in summer, you're going to find all kinds of boats. Big (houseboats). Small (canoes). Fast (speedboats). Slow (rowboats). And they all have to get along. Be courteous. Use common sense.

If you're thinking about paddling. A good first trip is to paddle from Ash River up Lost Bay to the Cruiser

King Williams Narrows

Lake Trail. If you're thinking about using a motorboat, people like to visit Grassy Bay Cliffs in Sand Point Lake or Kettle Falls Hotel. For either site, you'll have to navigate some narrows. Be mindful of other boaters. Slow down, give them space, especially houseboats and canoes. Anderson Bay Overlook is another popular site.

Remember your passport if you plan to visit the Canadian coast or fish in Canadian waters.

Hikes: Anderson Bay (Strenuous, 1.8), Cruiser Lake (Moderate, 9.5 miles)
Family Activities: North Canoe Voyage, rent a houseboat, boat tours, go paddling, visit in winter, become Junior Rangers
Guided Tours: Boat tours (recreation.gov), go snowmobiling, go paddling, go fishing
Rainy Day Activities: Considering much of the park is water, you may want to stay indoors (in-tent) when it rains (especially during thunderstorms)
History Enthusiasts: Kettle Falls Hotel (kettlefallshotel.com), Little American Island
Sunset/Sunrise Spots: Most of the park is good for sunrise and sunset since you're usually on the water

Beyond the Park...

Dining
The Rocky Ledge • (218) 875-3481
10064 Gappa Rd, Kabetogama
therockyledgeonkab.com

Crane Lake Grill • (218) 993-2900
7546 Gold Coast Rd, Crane Lake

Grocery Stores
Super One • (218) 283-8440
1313 3rd St, International Falls

County Market • (218) 283-4475
1907 Valley Pine Circle, Int'l Falls

Lodging
Harmony Beach • (218) 875-2811
10002 Gappa Rd, Kabetogama
harmonybeachresort.com

Voyageur Lodge • (218) 875-2131
10436 Waltz Rd, Kabetogama
voyageurparklodge.com

Arrowhead Lodge • (218) 875-2141
10473 Waltz Rd, Kabetogama
arrowheadlodgeresort.com

Voyagaire Lodge
7576 Gold Coast Rd, Crane Lake
voyagaire.com • (800) 882-6287

Festivals
Eelpout Festival • February
Walker • eelpoutfestival.com

Homegrown Music Festival • May
Duluth • duluthhomegrown.org

Dylan Fest • May
Duluth • bobdylanway.com

Campgrounds
Trails End Resort • (218) 993-2257
6310 Crane Lake Rd
trails-end-resort.com

Arnold's Campground & RV Park
2031 2nd Ave, International Falls
arnoldsfishing.com • (218) 285-9100

Attractions
Boundary Waters • fs.usda.gov

Superior NF • fs.usda.gov
Many interests, including fishing, boating, and hiking (Vermillion Gorge Trail near Crane Lake)

Temperance River State Park
Beautiful park along the north shore of Lake Superior
dnr.state.mn.us

There are many outstanding parks along the north shore of Lake Superior, including Grand Portage National Monument (nps.gov/grpo), Grand Portage State Park (dnr.state.mn.us), Split Rock Lighthouse State Park, Tettegouche State Park, Judge C.R. Magney State Park, Gooseberry Falls State Park ... and many more. Check them out, you'll be chasing waterfalls for days. There are interior parks too, but Lake Superior is nice.

Badlands

Castle Trail to Saddle Pass

Phone: (605) 433-5361
Website: nps.gov/badl

Established: November 10, 1978
Size: 244,000 Acres
Annual Visitors: 1 Million
Peak Season: Summer

Activities: Hiking, Biking,
Horseback Riding, Stargazing

2 Campgrounds: free–$38/night
Backcountry Camping: Permitted
Cedar Pass Lodge: $176/night
(mid-April–mid-October)

Park Hours: All day, every day
Entrance Fee: $30/25/15
(car/motorcycle/individual)

Badlands is a swath of semi-arid land bisected by a 60-mile rock wall with steep pinnacles and spires that used to be a daunting site to Indians, fur trappers, and homesteaders. Lack of water, scorching sun, arctic winters, and bone-chilling north winds make the mixed-grass prairies and colorful rock formations of western South Dakota uncommonly hostile. Lakota Sioux and French fur trappers felt the same way. Lakota called it "mako sica." To trappers, it was "les mauvaises terres à traverser." Two languages, one translation: "bad lands." Spanish explorers were even less complimentary. They referred to the rugged buttes, dusty siltstones, and gaping gullies as "tierra baldía" or "waste land." But as they say, one man's trash is another man's treasure.

For more than 150 years, the Badlands have been treasured by archaeologists and paleontologists. Buried in layers of shale, sandstone, volcanic ash, and siltstone are millions of years of history. Ancient fossils, some 35 million years old, retell the story of a shallow sea that once covered the region. Geologic forces caused the sea to drain. Subtropical forests began to grow and rivers and streams deposited layers of debris. Ash from volcanic eruptions in the West was carried by the wind, adding to the geologic stratification. Within it you'll find fossils of small saber-toothed cats, hornless rhinos, three-toed horses, ancient camels, squid, and turtles. As water and wind wear away the earth's surface new fossils are exposed. Each discovery is another page turned in the history of the Badlands, a story scientists are eager to read. Today, the park's White River area is widely regarded as one of the richest mammal fossil beds in the world.

Erosion and deposition have also played a part in this extreme topography. Intense rains and piercing winds have worn away layers of loose, fine-grained rock. Steep slopes funnel water and sediment to the valley floor rapidly and efficiently. Vegetation capable of slowing these erosional forces is unable to grow in the semi-arid climate, silty soil, and jagged rock formations. It's the perfect storm of climatic and geologic conditions, resulting in an inch of rock eroding each year. It will continue for centuries until the "Badlands Wall" is nothing at all. Perhaps, as these Badlands are ground down to dust, new Badlands will form. While these uniquely special formations may look the same day-to-day, week-to-week, year-to-year, they're constantly changing, and they'll continue to change until the Badlands are dust in the wind.

A perfectly flat plain may have been all homesteaders were expecting. Drawn to the Badlands by promises of free land and prospect of gold in the Black Hills, easterners began gobbling up lots of land, 160 acres at a time. An abundance of land didn't make up for the harsh conditions. Much like the lives of Lakota Indians and French fur trappers before them, it was a struggle to survive and nearly impossible to coax enough crops out of the ground to support a family. But they tried; cattle replaced bison and wheat fields displaced grasslands. They tended to the land as best they could, but the land never gave back, and only the hardiest homesteaders hung on to life in the Badlands.

Homesteaders and other 19th-century developments left their mark on South Dakota's prairies. Today only one in every 50 prairie areas remain, and Badlands protects the largest prairie in the National Park System. Inexplicably, the prairie is teeming with life. Bison and pronghorn graze. Prairie dogs scurry about their burrows. Sure-footed bighorn sheep traverse the rocky slopes. Swift fox and black-footed ferret (once thought to be extinct) have been reintroduced by biologists. Where humans failed to survive, a healthy prairie ecosystem flourishes, showing the land might not be so bad after all.

Sheep near Door Trail

When to Go
The park is open all year, but extreme weather conditions can cause uncomfortable or difficult touring. Summer high temperatures can exceed 110°F. Winter lows may dip below -40°F.

Transportation & Airports
Public transportation does not serve the park. The closest airport is Rapid City Regional (RAP), located 67 miles west of the park on Hwy 44. Car rental is available at the airport.

Directions
Badlands National Park is located in southwestern South Dakota, just south of Interstate 90.

Arriving on I-90 from the east, take Exit 131 (Interior) and follow park signs to the Northeast Entrance. From the west, take Exit 110 (Wall) and follow signs leading to the park's Pinnacles Entrance. Highway 44 (from Rapid City) provides a more scenic alternate route. Take Hwy 44 east to Interior. Continue on Hwy 377, which leads directly to the park's Interior Entrance.

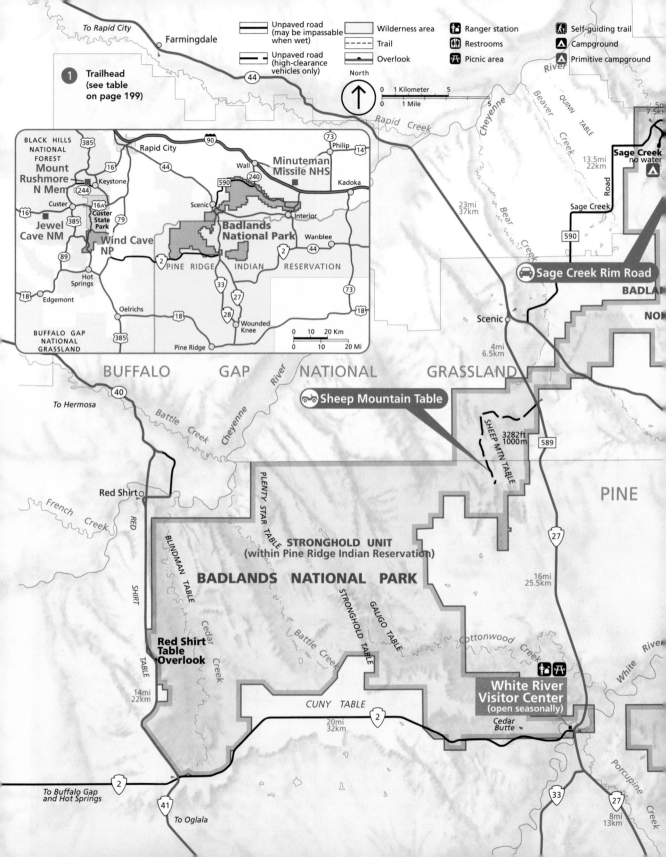

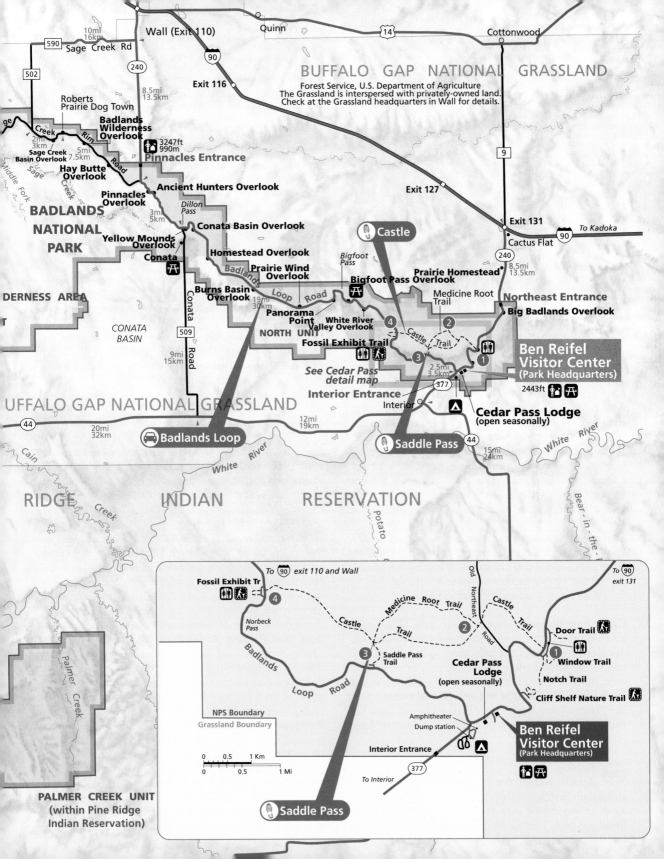

BUFFALO GAP NATIONAL GRASSLAND
Forest Service, U.S. Department of Agriculture
The Grassland is interspesed with privately-owned land.
Check at the Grassland headquarters in Wall for details.

Wall (Exit 110)
Quinn
Cottonwood
590
10mi 16km
Sage Creek Rd
502
240
Exit 116
8.5mi 13.5km
14
90
9
Exit 127
Exit 131
To Kadoka
90
240
Cactus Flat
8.5mi 13.5km

Roberts Prairie Dog Town
Badlands Wilderness Overlook
3247ft 990m
Pinnacles Entrance

Creek
Rim
2mi 3km
Sage Creek Basin Overlook
5mi 7.5km
Hay Butte Overlook
Pinnacles Overlook
Dillon Pass
3m 5km
Ancient Hunters Overlook

BADLANDS NATIONAL PARK

Yellow Mounds Overlook
Conata
Conata Basin Overlook
Homestead Overlook
Prairie Wind Overlook
Bigfoot Pass
Castle

Burns Basin Overlook
Bigfoot Pass Overlook
Prairie Homestead
Northeast Entrance
Big Badlands Overlook

DERNESS AREA

Panorama Point
White River Valley Overlook
Fossil Exhibit Trail
4
Castle Trail
2
Medicine Root Trail
3
1
Ben Reifel Visitor Center
(Park Headquarters)

509
9mi 15km
Conata Road
NORTH UNIT

CONATA BASIN

See Cedar Pass detail map
2.5mi 3.5km
Interior Entrance
Interior
377
2443ft
Cedar Pass Lodge
(open seasonally)

UFFALO GAP NATIONAL GRASSLAND

44
20mi 32km
19mi 30km
Badlands Loop
12mi 19km
White River
Saddle Pass
44
15mi 24km
White River

Cain
Creek

RIDGE   **INDIAN**   **RESERVATION**

Potato

Bear-in-the-

To 90 exit 110 and Wall
Fossil Exhibit Tr
4
Norbeck Pass
Castle Trail
Medicine Root Trail
2
Castle Trail
Old Northeast Road
To 90 exit 131
Door Trail
1
Window Trail
Notch Trail

Badlands Loop Road
3
Saddle Pass Trail
Cedar Pass Lodge
(open seasonally)
Cliff Shelf Nature Trail

NPS Boundary
Grassland Boundary
Amphitheater
Dump station
Ben Reifel Visitor Center
(Park Headquarters)

0   0.5   1 Km
0   0.5   1 Mi

Interior Entrance
377
To Interior
Saddle Pass

PALMER CREEK UNIT
(within Pine Ridge
Indian Reservation)

Palmer Creek

Sheep Mountain Table

established in 1939. For your gallon of gas, Badlands is one of the best scenic detours you'll find in the country. While driving along I-90, you can take Hwy 240 for a 42-mile scenic detour through the Badlands between Exits 110 and 131. From the interstate it's not obvious one of the most amazing natural wonders in the world is a few miles to the south. Once you reach Pinnacles or Northeast Entrance, eroded stone formations appear and Hwy 240 becomes Badlands Loop Road. It provides access to 11 overlooks, Ben Reifel Visitor Center, Cedar Pass Lodge and Campground, and trailheads for the park's most popular hikes. Door, Window, Notch, Cliff Shelf, and Fossil Exhibit Trails are pleasant short hikes found along Badlands Loop Road. Visitors should allow at least 60 minutes to drive the 42-mile loop, but it wouldn't be difficult to spend an entire day hiking trails and poking around the visitor center.

Visitors searching for a more primitive experience should drive **Sage Creek Rim Road**. This unpaved and washboard road intersects Badlands Loop Road just south of Pinnacles Entrance. It features a bunch of overlooks, Robert's Prairie Dog Town, and it's your best bet for seeing wildlife like bison, deer, bighorn sheep, and fox. Shortly before the road exits the park, there is a spur road leading to Sage Creek Campground. The Road closes at times in winter and after heavy rains in spring. **Sheep Mountain Road**, four miles south of Scenic on CR-589, is unreal, but it's only passable in dry conditions with a high-clearance 4WD vehicle.

Camping & Lodging

Badlands National Park has two maintained drive-in campgrounds, both are open year-round. Backcountry camping is also allowed (no permit required). Open campfires are not permitted due to the flammable nature of prairie grass. **Cedar Pass** is the only developed campground. It is located near Ben Reifel Visitor Center. All 96 sites have covered picnic tables and exceptional views of Badlands Wall. Cold running water, flush toilets, and pay showers are available nearby. Tent sites cost $23 per night. RV sites cost $37 per night (electric hookups only). There is a dump station ($1.00 per use). There are four group sites for up to ten occupants that cost $40 per night. Group sites remain available through winter for $15 per night. Sites can be reserved at cedarpasslodge.com or (877) 386-4383. **Sage Creek Campground** is accessed via Sage Creek Rim Road (unpaved). Camping is free on a first-come, first-served basis. Water is not available. Pit toilets and picnic tables are located nearby.

Cedar Pass Lodge (cedarpasslodge.com, $176/night), located on Badlands Loop Road near Ben Reifel Visitor Center, provides the only lodging, gift store, and restaurant in the park. It's seasonal, only open in summer. Before its first incarnation burned down in the 1930s, Cedar Pass Lodge was a dance hall where bands like "Hotsy Totsy Boys" and "Honolulu Fruit Gum Orchestra" were conducted by a bandleader named Lawrence Welk.

Driving

A park was authorized here in 1929 with the stipulation that South Dakota construct a road through its most significant rock formations. **Badlands Loop Road** was built, and Badlands National Monument was

Hiking & Backpacking

If the temperature is 110°F or you've arrived in the middle of a "gully washer," not leaving your car is understandable. If not, get out and meet the Badlands face-to-face. Hiking is a perfect way to commune with this unique landscape. On a comfortable day you may be tempted to take a long, casual hike on **Castle Trail**. A few miles south of Northeast Entrance is **Door/Window Trail Parking Area** where three excellent trails (Door, Window, and Notch) begin. Each one is less than a mile roundtrip, supplying its own perspective of Badlands Wall and the erosional forces responsible for it. Short on time, sure-footed guests in search of fantastic views should drive no further than **Saddle Pass Trailhead**. It's a 0.25-mile strenuous climb up and into the Badlands. You can also reach Saddle Pass via Castle or Medicine Root Trails. To shorten the trek, start on Castle from Northeast Road. A few more trails are listed in the table. You are allowed to explore beyond designated trails, but be aware of hidden canyons and cracks in the floor. Off-trail hikers must have exceptional map reading skills, as route finding is difficult.

Notch Trail

Badlands Hiking Trails (Distances are roundtrip)

Name	Location (# on map)	Length	Difficulty Rating & Notes
Door - 👆	Badlands Loop Road (1)	0.75 mile	E – Self-guided trail accesses other side of Badlands Wall
Window	Badlands Loop Road (1)	0.25 mile	E – Peek the Badlands from an eroded "window"
Notch - 👆	Badlands Loop Road (1)	1.5 miles	M – Views of White River Valley, must climb a wooden ladder or scramble up a gully
Cliff Shelf	Badlands Loop Road (1)	0.5 mile	M – Short loop follows a boardwalk and climbs stairs
Castle - 👆	Badlands Loop Road (1, 4)	10.0 miles	M – Passes mostly level terrain and Badlands formations, connects Fossil Exhibit and Door/Window Parking Areas
Medicine Root	Spur from Castle Trail (2)	4.0 miles	M – Detour through a mixed-grass prairie
Saddle Pass - 👆	Badlands Loop Road (3)	0.25 mile	S – Short, steep climb straight up the Badlands Wall
Fossil Exhibit	Badlands Loop Road (4)	0.25 mile	E – View replicas of fossils that were unearthed here

Difficulty Ratings: E = Easy, M = Moderate

Big Badlands Overlook in the morning light

Camping in the park's backcountry is allowed and does not require an overnight permit. However, backpackers should contact a staff member at Ben Reifel Visitor Center or Pinnacles Entrance Station before setting out on an overnight trip. Backcountry users are also advised to register at Medicine/Castle Trail Loop, Saddle Pass Trailhead, Conata Picnic Area, Sage Creek Basin Overlook, or Sage Creek Campground before departing. Set up your campsite at least 0.5-mile from roads and trails and make sure it cannot be seen from the roadway. There is little to no water in the backcountry, so carry in enough for the duration of your trip.

Biking

Biking is not a common activity. For starters, bicycles are not permitted on any of the park's hiking trails. They are only allowed on paved and unpaved roadways. Badlands Loop Road can be a challenging and scenic bike ride when motorists aren't racing back and forth at 45 mph. The road is narrow and filled with twists, turns, and climbs. It's best to pedal early in the morning or closer to evening when fewer vehicles are out and about. Sage Creek Rim Road is an option for mountain bikers, but this rutted roadway is not the most posterior-friendly biking surface. Another reason to skip Sage Creek Rim Road is Sheep Mountain Road. Located about 4 miles south of the tiny town of Scenic, it's a better mountain biking destination. The road follows Sheep Mountain Table for 7 miles (one-way). Biking the Badlands may sound uninviting, but you may want to seriously consider toting your two-wheelers for other trails located nearby. George S. Mickelson Trail in Deadwood and Centennial Trail in Sturgis are excellent pedaling alternatives.

Horseback Riding

Horseback Riding is allowed anywhere in the park except on marked trails, roads, highways, and developed areas. You must trailer in your own horses, as guided rides are not offered. A portion of Sage Creek Campground is designated for horse use, and there is a watering hole 0.5-mile southwest of camp.

Stargazing

Stargazing is one of the most underrated activities in any location far from big city lights that tend to drown out nightscapes. At Badlands you can admire otherworldly rock formations by day, and gaze into another world at night. Enjoy an evening stargazing program with a park ranger or simply sit outside your tent, staring up at the stars.

Visitor Centers

Ben Reifel Visitor Center, located on Badlands Loop Road (Hwy 240), is open every day except Thanksgiving, Christmas, and New Year's. It is typically open from 8am to 5pm, but hours are extended in summer (7am–7pm) and shortened in winter (9am–4pm). Inside you'll find exhibits, a bookstore, restrooms, and an air-conditioned theater. On South Dakota Hwy 27, about 20 miles south of the town of Scenic, you'll find **White River Visitor Center**. It's open seasonally (May to mid-October) from 8am to 5pm. It focuses on Lakota heritage. Inside you'll find exhibits and restrooms.

Ranger Programs & For Kids

From June to mid-September Badlands' rangers give walks, talks, and presentations. You can find a weekly listing of ranger-led activities on white bulletin boards along Badlands Loop Road, at visitor centers (call or stop-in), or at the park's website. If you're enchanted by the spires and buttes of Badlands Wall, you may want to join a ranger on "Geology Walk." Confused about why fossils of ancient sea creatures were found in the middle of this prairie land? "Fossil Talk" is the ranger program for you. Curious about more recent life on the prairie, including today's wildlife? Hop aboard a "Prairie Walk." In addition to these activities the park offers a Night Sky Program, and a Junior Ranger Program. Most programs take place at Cedar Pass Campground's Amphitheater.

Fossils and kids are almost always a winning combination, so Fossil Exhibit Trail and Ben Reifel Visitor Center are two good destinations for families. Everyone's favorite fossils, dinosaurs, have yet to be unearthed here, but many other prehistoric beasts have been found fossilized in Badlands' soft rock layers. (However, notable T-Rex fossils have been found nearby!) The elephant-sized titanothere and the ancient scavenger archaeotherium (nicknamed the "big pig" even though it's not genetically related to pigs) lived in the area millions of years ago. A three-toed horse, an ancient camel, a small sabre-tooth cat, and several other mammals and sea creatures have also been found. As the ground continues to erode, new fossils are exposed and discovered by paleontologists and visitors. The White River Area is one of the world's most productive fossil beds.

If your children are more interested in animals that are still scurrying about, stop at Robert's Prairie Dog Town on Sage Creek Rim Road. These little critters are sure to draw a few giggles as they pop in and out of their burrows, barking among their friends.

Kids also can become Junior Rangers. Your child can join this exclusive club one of two ways: by completing the free junior ranger activity book (available online or at Ben Reifel Visitor Center) or by attending an official Junior Ranger Program during summer. Check online or at a visitor center for an up-to-date schedule of events. When completed, return the booklet to the visitor center, where your child will be awarded an official Badlands National Park Junior Ranger badge. You can also pick up a GPS Adventure booklet at Ben Reifel Visitor Center!

Fossils

Multi-colored layers of fragile sedimentary rock made more than spectacular scenery, they made spectacular fossils. Prehistoric fossils are extremely rare around the world, but in Badlands they are common. So common, a visitor occasionally stumbles upon one. In summer of 2010, a seven-year-old girl from Atlanta discovered a museum-quality skull of a small saber-toothed cat. Should you unearth the next amazing fossil, leave it where it is and notify a ranger. It is illegal to collect fossils, flowers, rocks, and animals from federal property.

If you don't spark the next big dig, you can still learn all about paleontology, fossils, and the park's ancient history by viewing exhibits and replicas at Ben Reifel Visitor Center and Fossil Exhibit Trail. Fossil Exhibit is the last hiking trail on Badlands Loop Road if you entered via Northeast Entrance, or the first trail from Pinnacles Entrance. It is educational in nature, but expect your kids to be playing on the Badlands formations rather than learning about extinct animals found within the rock's layers. Regardless, it's a great stop for families.

Sheep near Sage Creek Rim Road

Flora & Fauna

There was a time when prairie sprawled across more than a third of North America. These areas were too wet to be deserts and too dry to support trees. Today, most are gone, but the largest remaining prairie protected by the National Park System is located at Badlands. Nearly 50% of the park is mixed-grass prairie, a combination of short and tall grass. The other half is Badlands rock formations with small areas of woodlands, wetlands, and shrublands mixed in. More than 400 species of plants survive in this dry and rocky environment. Of these, nearly 60 are grasses.

Semi-arid land also provides habitat for a surprising diversity of wildlife: 55 mammal species, 120 bird species, and 19 species of reptiles and amphibians. Park biologists have determined these prairies can sustain nearly 800 bison, far fewer than the original herds that numbered more than one million but a healthy population by today's standards. Bighorn sheep, swift fox, pronghorn, mule deer, coyotes, and prairie dogs also reside here. Among Badlands' animals, black-footed ferrets have the most remarkable story. These nocturnal critters—once thought to be extinct—were accidentally

Why's that lady in my hole?

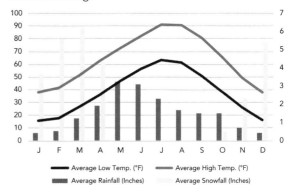

in summer, and the first signs of snow typically show up in October. Average high temperatures in July and August reach the low 90s°F but it's not uncommon to crack 100°F. Winter is cold but not unbearably so. January is the coldest month with average highs right around freezing.

rediscovered in Wyoming. About 12 ferrets were taken into captivity, and search for suitable habitats began. Badlands was selected because its prairie dog population (black-footed ferrets' primary food source) was healthy and free of diseases. Today, park biologists monitor the ferret population. They are reproducing naturally and in an apparent state of self-sustainability. The seldom-visited Badlands Wilderness Area, accessed via Sage Rim Road (unpaved), is a good location to view wildlife.

Pets & Accessibility
Pets are permitted in the park but must be kept on a leash (less than six feet). They are allowed in developed areas like campgrounds and picnic areas. Pets are not allowed on hiking trails, in public buildings, in the backcountry, or near prairie dog towns.

Ben Reifel and White River Visitor Centers are accessible to wheelchair users. Cedar Pass Campground has two fully-accessible sites. Cedar Pass Lodge is fully accessible. Fossil Exhibit and Windows Trails as well as the first section of Door and Cliff Shelf Trails have accessible boardwalks. Ranger programs held at Cedar Pass Campground Amphitheater are accessible, but ranger-led walks and hikes generally are not, due to rugged terrain.

Weather
The Badlands received its name due to relatively inhospitable living conditions. Lack of water and extreme weather made even the hardiest homesteaders pack up and move elsewhere. Things haven't changed much. The region is semi-arid, receiving an average of 18 inches of rain each year, but it's known for brief, intense rainfalls, commonly called "gully-washers." Spring showers extend into June. It gets hot and dry

Tips & Recommendations
It gets hot in summer. Almost all trails are completely exposed. And you won't find any water sources. So, come prepared for the heat. Bring sunscreen. Wear a hat with a brim. Carry plenty of water.

Nearly two-thirds of all park visitors arrive between June and August. Practically no one visits from October through April. So, if you'd like a quiet national park experience, try Badlands in the off-season.

Storms are typically brief but intense. Watch weather reports and the sky. Look for cover if things get dark.

Badlands is often a drive-thru park, treating Badlands Loop Road as an hour-long detour from I-90, but you definitely should consider spending at least one night. That'll allow time to hike a few trails, observe the prairie dogs, catch a sunset/sunrise, drive Sage Creek Rim Road, and maybe even enough time to take things off the pavement to head up Sheep Mountain Table (if you have a high-clearance 4x4).

I wouldn't blame you if you treated Badlands as a drive-thru park in the middle of summer (although it cools down quite nicely after dark) or during the harsh (often windy) winter months.

There's a excellent picnic area with badlands views near Ben Reifel Visitor Center. Pack a lunch and stick around for a while.

Stargazing is another reason to spend the night!

And Cedar Pass Lodge offers extremely comfortable accommodations if you aren't interested in camping. If you're on a tight budget, there's free camping at Sage Creek Primitive Campground! Or many people like to camp for free on BLM land near the Pinnacles entrance (look for the cell towers to the east).

To see wildlife, drive Sage Creek Rim Road in the morning/evening. Prairie dogs, bison, pronghorn, and bighorn sheep are all commonly spotted along the way.

You don't have to stick to the trails. If you see some interesting badlands formations, stop, grab your camera, and check them out. Just don't stray too far from where you started without a map or GPS. People have gotten lost and died out here, so use common sense and don't do anything beyond your comfort level.

Don't go feeling underneath rocks or any place a snake might hang out. Prairie rattlesnakes do reside here.

Easy Hikes: Door (0.75 mile), Fossil Exhibit (0.25)
Moderate Hikes: Notch (1.5 miles), Castle (10), Saddle Pass (0.25, can be extreme if you're afraid of heights)
Family Activities: Observe the prairie dogs, play on the badlands, go looking for bison, become Junior Rangers, check out long-extinct animals at Ben Reifel Visitor Center
Rainy Day Activities: Drive the park roads and enjoy the show if it's a gully washer!

Saddle Pass

History Enthusiasts: Stop at the visitor centers (Ben Reifel explores the parks natural history from ancient fossils to modern life, while White River is more of a cultural center, helping to preserve Lakota history)
Sunset Spots: Pinnacles Overlook, Castle Trail, Bigfoot Pass, Burns Basin, Conata Basin Overlook, Sheep Table Mountain, Hay Butte Overlook, Old Northeast Road
Sunrise Spots: Big Badlands Overlook, Castle Trail, Window Trail, Panorama Point, Door Trail, Big Badlands Overlook
Wildlife: Robert's Prairie Dog Town, Sage Creek Rim Road

Beyond the Park...

Dining
Red Rock • (605) 279-2388
506 Glenn St, Wall

Kathmandu Bistro • (605) 343-5070
727 Main St, Rapid City
kathmandubistro.com

Firehouse Brewing • (605) 348-1915
610 Main St, Rapid City
firehousebrewing.com

Delmonico Grill • (605) 791-1664
609 Main St, Rapid City
delmonicogrill.com

Golden Phoenix • (605) 348-4195
2421 W Main St, Rapid City
goldenphoenixrc.com

Colonial House • (605) 342-4640
2315 Mt Rushmore Rd, Rapid City
colonialhousernb.com

Tally's Silver Spoon • (605) 342-7621
530 6th St, Rapid City
tallyssilverspoon.com

Piesano's Pacchia • (605) 341-6941
3618 Canyon Lake Dr, Rapid City
piesanospacchia.com

Grocery Stores
Badland's Grocery • (605) 433-5445
101 Main St, Interior

Wall Food Center • (605) 279-2331
103 W South Blvd, Wall

Lodging
Circle View • (605) 433-5582
20055 E SD-44, Interior
circleviewranch.com

Frontier Cabins • (605) 279-2619
1101 S Glenn St, Wall
frontiercabins.net

Sunshine Inn • (605) 279-2178
608 Main St, Wall

American Buffalo • (605) 342-5368
13752 S US-16, Rapid City
americanbuffaloresort.com

Campgrounds
Sleepy Hollow Campground
118 4th Ave, Wall • (605) 279-2100

Triangle Ranch • (605) 859-2122
RV sites, volleyball, fishing
23950 Recluse Rd, Philip

Badlands/White River KOA
20720 SD-44, Interior
koa.com • (605) 433-5337

Lake Park • (800) 644-2267
Lodge, RV, camping
2850 Chapel Ln, Rapid City
lakeparkcampground.com

Rapid City KOA
3010 E SD-44, Rapid City
koa.com • (605) 348-2111

Festivals
Motorcycle Rally • August
sturgismotorcyclerally.com • Sturgis

Black Hills Pow Wow • October
blackhillspowwow.com • Rapid City

Attractions
Wall Drug Store • (605) 279-2175
510 Main St, Wall • walldrug.com

1880 Town • (605) 344-2236
24280 SD-63, Midland
1880town.com

Minuteman Missile NHP
24545 Cottonwood Rd, Philip •
nps.gov/mimi • (605) 433-5552

Giant Prairie Dog Statue
Pretty much what it says
SD-240, Philip

Bear Country USA • (605) 343-2290
13820 S US-16, Rapid City
bearcountryusa.com

Storybook Island • (605) 342-6357
1301 Sheridan Lake Rd, Rapid City
storybookisland.org

Reptile Gardens
8955 S US-16, Rapid City
reptilegardens.com

Wind Cave

Phone: (605) 745-4600
Website: nps.gov/wica

Established: January 9, 1903
Size: 28,295 Acres
Annual Visitors: 600,000
Peak Season: Summer

Activities: Cave Tours, Hiking, Biking, Horseback Riding

<u>Cave Tours*</u>
Open: All Year
Fee: $10–30
Duration: 1–4 hours

Campgrounds: Elk Mountain
Fee: $18/night ($9/night in winter)
Backcountry Camping: Permitted**
Lodging: None

Park Hours: All day, every day
Entrance Fee: None

*Tickets are available at the visitor center. Reservations are only available (and required) for Candlelight and Wild Cave Tours

**Backcountry camping is restricted to the northwest corner of the park and requires a free permit

Long before European fur traders and eastern miners arrived, Lakota Sioux considered the area now known as Wind Cave National Park sacred. They spoke of a "hole that breathes cool air" and left tipi rings near the cave's only natural entrance. Indian legend describes this opening as the site where bison first emerged to roam the prairies. While evidence bison originated from the cave is scant, scientists know, with some certainty, why the cave is so "windy." It's all about air pressure. Air flows into the abyss when pressure outside the cave is greater than pressure inside. However, when pressure is greater inside the cave, gusts of air blow out of its natural opening.

One summer day, a strong wind blowing out of this opening knocked a hat from the top of Tom Bingham's head. Tom and his brother, Jesse, rediscovered the cave in 1881. And so the story goes. While displaying their find to a few locals, Tom leaned over the small chasm only to have a gust of wind blow off his hat, ultimately falling into the cavern below. Tom and Jesse were first to rediscover the cave, but they weren't willing to be first to enter the unknown world below. That honor was left for Charlie Crary, a local miner who entered Wind Cave with a small lantern and a ball of twine to trace his path. Shortly after this discovery, South Dakota Mining Company took an interest in the cave. The company hired J. D. McDonald to lay claim to a homestead directly above the cave and begin examining its passages for gold. His 16-year-old son, Alvin, did most of the exploring. Much to the mining company's dismay he wasn't seeking gold. Alvin charted new passages for the simple pleasure of witnessing and exploring a place never seen before by human eyes.

Things turned contentious in 1899. J. D. McDonald and a partner entered a dispute over land ownership with South Dakota Mining Company. The Department of Interior ruled that no one was entitled to the land, as it was not being used properly for mining nor did it comply

Remember to share the road

Natural Entrance Tour

with the terms of the Homestead Act. Two years later, 1,000 acres surrounding the cave became federal property and tours were given for free by Elmer McDonald (another son of J. D.). On January 9, 1903, legislation passed creating Wind Cave, the eighth national park of the United States and first created to protect a cave, ensuring visitors could satisfy their own curiosities exploring the mysteries of the unknown just like Alvin McDonald did.

Very few visitors explore the rolling grasslands and ponderosa pine forests above this subterranean labyrinth. These landscapes and the wildlife living here are worthy of federal protection by themselves. Lakota called this region "Pahá Sápa" or "Black Hills," named because the pine-covered hills look black compared to a sea of grass surrounding them. By the time the park was established in 1903, bison, elk, and pronghorn were gone. Park employees attempted reintroduction programs to restore the habitat to its original state. Today, Wind Cave National Park is home to one of four free-roaming, genetically pure bison herds on publicly owned lands. Pronghorn are seen in the prairies and elk can be heard bugling in the backcountry. Whether your curiosity takes you to the backcountry or underground passages, you'll begin to realize why Lakota Sioux considered this area sacred. It's the same indescribable gravitational force that drew Alvin McDonald deeper and deeper into the cave. While forces of nature caused Tom Bingham's hat to fall into the cave, that same figurative gravity got ahold of him too. Now it's your turn to be drawn to this special place.

When to Go
The park is open all year. Most visitors arrive in summer, but the best times to visit might be April/May (when bison calves are born) and September/October (when leaves begin to change colors). Off-season brings smaller crowds and comfortable temps. The cave is comfortable year-round and tours are offered daily at the park's visitor center.

Transportation & Airports
Public transportation does not serve the park. The closest airport is Rapid City Regional (RAP), located about 60 miles to the northeast.

Directions
Wind Cave is located at the southern tip of South Dakota's Black Hills. It is six miles north of Hot Springs and 1.5 hours (driving) from Rapid City. Several routes are available if traveling from the north (two are listed below).

Via US-385/US-16 (60 miles): The longest and fastest route provides opportunity for a short detour to Mount Rushmore. Follow US-16 W for 40 miles. Turn right at Custer St/Mt Rushmore Rd. Continue for 0.5 mile before turning left at US-385 S, which leads into the park.

Via SD-79/SD-87 (55 miles): Take SD-79 S from Rapid City. Turn right at SD-36W and continue onto US-16 Alt W. Turn left to follow SD-87 S, which leads into the park.

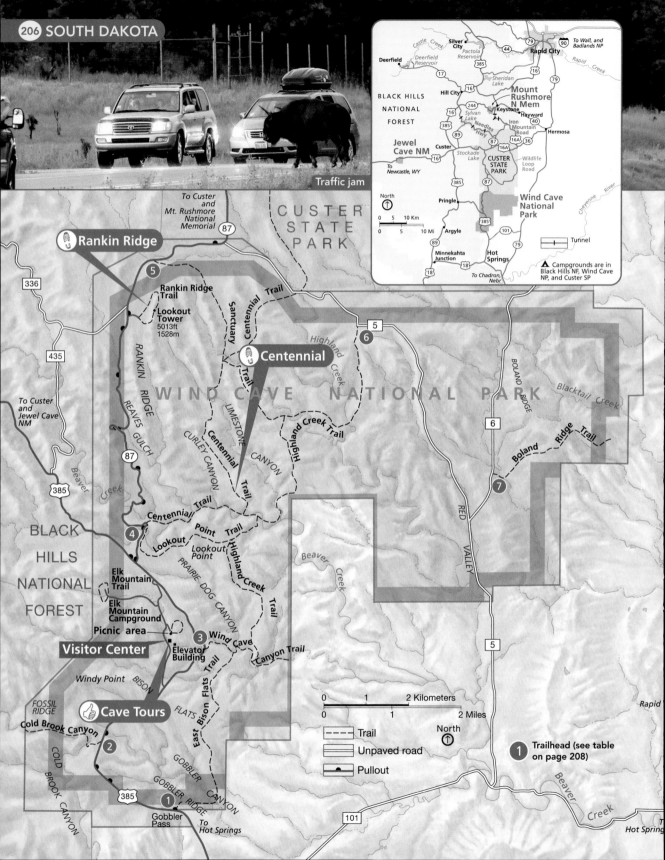

Traffic jam

CUSTER STATE PARK

To Wall, and
Badlands NP

Castle Creek • Silver City • Pactola Reservoir • Rapid City

Deerfield • Deerfield Reservoir

Rapid Creek

BLACK HILLS NATIONAL FOREST

Sheridan Lake

Hill City • Mount Rushmore N Mem

Sylvan Lake • Keystone

Needles Hwy • Iron Mountain Road • Hayward • Hermosa

Jewel Cave NM • Custer

Stockade Lake

CUSTER STATE PARK • Wildlife Loop Road

To Newcastle, WY

Pringle

Wind Cave National Park

Cheyenne River

North

0 5 10 Km
0 5 10 Mi

Argyle

Minnekahta Junction

Hot Springs

To Chadron, Nebr

Tunnel

▲ Campgrounds are in Black Hills NF, Wind Cave NP, and Custer SP

To Custer and Mt. Rushmore National Memorial — 87

CUSTER STATE PARK

👣 **Rankin Ridge**

336

⑤

Rankin Ridge Trail

Centennial Trail

Lookout Tower 5013ft 1528m

Sanctuary Trail

⑤

Highland Creek

⑥

435

RANKIN RIDGE

REAVES GULCH

👣 **Centennial**

BOLAND RIDGE

Blacktail Creek

To Custer and Jewel Cave NM

87

W I N D   C A V E   N A T I O N A L   P A R K

LIMESTONE CANYON

Centennial Trail

Highland Creek Trail

Boland Ridge Trail

385

Beaver Creek

CURLEY CANYON

⑥

④

Centennial Trail

Point Trail

⑦

Lookout

Lookout Point

Highland Creek Trail

RED VALLEY

Elk Mountain Trail

PRAIRIE DOG CANYON

Elk Mountain Campground

Beaver Creek

BLACK HILLS NATIONAL FOREST

Picnic area

③ Wind Cave

Visitor Center

Elevator Building

5

Canyon Trail

Windy Point

BISON

East Bison Flats Trail

FLATS

FOSSIL RIDGE

👍 **Cave Tours**

Cold Brook Canyon

②

COLD BROOK CANYON

GOBBLER RIDGE

GOBBLER CANYON

0   1   2 Kilometers
0   1   2 Miles

- - - Trail

═══ Unpaved road

●━● Pullout

North

385

①

Gobbler Pass

To Hot Springs

101

Beaver Creek

Hot Spring

① **Trailhead** (see table on page 208)

Rapid

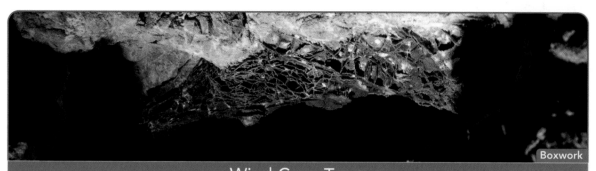

Boxwork

Wind Cave Tours

Name	Fee (Adult/Youth)	Duration	Notes
Garden of Eden - ♿	$10 / 5	1 hour	Least strenuous tour visits small samples of boxwork, popcorn, and flowstone • Enter/exit by elevator
Natural Entrance - ♿	$12 / 6	1.25 hours	A quick hike to the natural entrance before entering via a man-made entrance • Exit by elevator • 300 stairs
Fairgrounds - ♿	$12 / 6	1.5 hours	Explore boxwork, popcorn, and frostwork in two levels of the cave • Enter and exit by elevator • 450 stairs
Candlelight* - ♿	$12 / 6	2 hours	Harken back to the original cave tours by Alvin McDonald • Each visitor carries a candle bucket • Minimum age of 8
Wild Cave* - ♿	$30 / Not Permitted	4 hours	Cavers get dirty as you crawl, squeeze, and climb through sections of the cave very few visit • Minimum age of 16

Youth is 6–16 years of age. Senior or Golden Age/Access Pass holders pay youth rates.
*Tours are limited to groups of 10. Reservations are required and can be made up to one month in advance by calling (605) 745-4600. These tours are only available from early June to early September. Long pants, long-sleeved shirts, and sturdy boots are required apparel for the Wild Cave Tour. Gloves are recommended. Helmets, lights, and kneepads provided. Tickets are sold at the visitor center. All tours except Wild Cave and Candlelight Tours are sold on a first-come, first-served basis. The cave is a constant 53°F all year, so dress accordingly. Sandals are not recommended footwear.

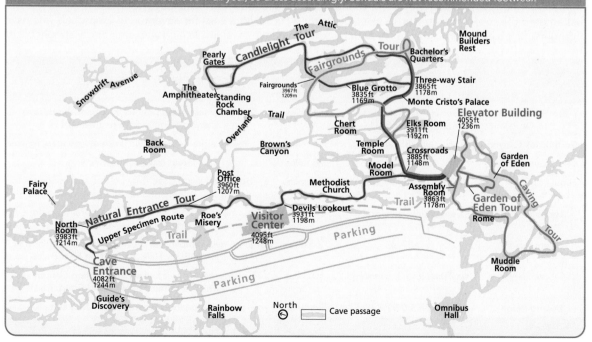

Camping

For the reasonable price of $18 per night visitors can camp at **Elk Mountain Campground**, located near the park's western boundary, one mile north of the visitor center. All sites are available on a first-come, first-served basis, but the camp rarely fills to capacity. Pull-through sites are available for RVs. Hookups, dump stations, and showers are not available. Restrooms with cold water are located nearby. Water is turned off from late fall through early spring. During this time vault toilets are available and the camping fee is reduced to $9/night. Campfire wood is available near the camp's entrance. No cost is associated with wood, but donations are accepted. Group camping is available by reservation only. Reservations can be made by calling (605) 745-4600.

Driving

You don't have to hit the trails to get a good view of prairie dog towns, bison, and undulating hills. The park is extremely accessible to motorists. Pullouts along US-385 and SD-87 provide outstanding views of underappreciated scenery. Obey the speed limits and watch for wildlife. In the past 20 years more than 80 bison have been hit by motorists, and you don't want an ornery bison on your hands, do you?

Cave Tours

In 1891, Alvin McDonald, self-proclaimed "permanent guide" of Wind Cave, began a systematic exploration of the cave's passageways. The young man first entered the cave when he was 16 years old with a candle and a ball of twine to trace his path back to the surface. For the next three years he spent several hours per day mapping passages, inspecting chasms, and exploring the unknown. In March of 1891 alone, he registered 134 hours in the cave over the course of 34 trips. By the end of that year he surveyed several miles of passages and wrote in his diary…"have given up the idea of finding the end of Wind Cave." Sadly, Alvin died at the age of 20 while in Chicago with his father showing cave specimens. His body was returned to the place he loved so much, buried near the cave's natural entrance where a bronze plaque marks his grave. His diary is on display at the visitor center. In all, Alvin McDonald explored 8 to 10 miles of the cave, naming many of its rooms and passages. Alvin gave up on finding the cave's end, but modern explorers have not. Today, it measures 154 miles in length, the 7th longest cave in the world, and experts believe that only 5 percent of the entire network has been discovered. Each year, a few new miles are mapped out, with no end in sight.

The only way for guests to explore the cave is on a guided tour, many of which follow routes Alvin McDonald and Katie Stable (guide for 11 years) pioneered more than a century ago. If you'd like to share a similar experience, take the **Candlelight Tour**. A park ranger leads groups of no more than 10 through an unlit section of the cave. The candle bucket you hold in your hand provides the only light. It's an excellent tour and one of two where reservations are allowed (and required). **Wild Cave Tour** also requires reservations. It's a blast for adventurous individuals who have a little caver inside (and who are not claustrophobic or

Wind Cave Hiking Trails (Distances are roundtrip)			
Name	Location (# on map)	Length	Difficulty Rating & Notes
East Bison Flats	Gobbler Pass near the South Entrance (1)	7.4 miles	M – Traverses rolling prairies then joins Wind Cave Canyon 0.5 mile from its trailhead
Cold Brook Canyon	US-385 (2)	2.8 miles	E – Passes a prairie dog town, ends at boundary fence
Wind Cave Canyon	US-385 (3)	3.6 miles	E – Great trail for birdwatching
Highland Creek - ⚇	US-385 (3) and NPS 5 (6)	17.2 miles	S – Begins off Wind Cave Canyon Trail and continues to NPS 5, crosses prairies and pine forests
Lookout Point	Centennial Trailhead (4)	4.4 miles	M – Views of 1999 wildfire and vast prairies before ending at Beaver Creek
Centennial	SD-87 (4)	12.0 miles	M – A 6-mile sampling of the 111-mile Centennial Trail through the Black Hills that ends at Bear Butte
Sanctuary	Near the North Entrance (5)	7.2 miles	M – Cross rolling hills before intersecting Centennial Trail, which continues to Highland Creek Trail
Boland Ridge	NPS 6 (7)	5.4 miles	S – Guaranteed excellent views • May see elk
Difficulty Ratings: E = Easy, M = Moderate, S = Strenuous			

afraid of getting dirty). The trip lasts four hours. Much of the time will be spent on your hands and knees or in other precarious positions as you traverse sections of the cave few visitors get the chance to see. Tour schedules are subject to change. Call (605) 745-4600 to make reservations or confirm tour times. Long waits are common during peak visitation in summer. Try to tour early in the day. Clothing worn in any other cave is not permitted to prevent the spread of White-Nose Syndrome.

Hiking & Backpacking

Hiking is one of the most underrated and underutilized activities. These badlands are a transitional region, highlighted by the convergence of western ponderosa pine forests and eastern mixed-grass prairies. Three self-guided nature trails (featuring interpretive signs along the way) help you learn about the park's ecology. **Rankin Ridge Nature Trail** is located on SD-87 near the North Entrance. It's a short loop leading to the highest point in the park and extraordinary views. **Elk Mountain Nature Trail** begins at the campground. It provides the perfect example of overlapping pine and prairie ecosystems. **Prairie Vista Nature Trail** begins near the visitor center, and then loops around a quiet prairie grassland. All three of these trails are about one mile long.

The remaining trails are longer out-and-back treks, but a nice scenic loop (< 5 miles) can be formed by connecting a few together. Begin on Centennial Trail and loop back to the area via Lookout Point Trail. Going counter-clockwise can lead to some trail-finding confusion near the end along Beaver Creek (GPS standard maps contour back to Lookout Point Trail). The park's northwest corner is open to **backcountry camping**. Backpackers can extend this smaller loop by making a figure 8. Hike in on Lookout Point Trail but continue east on Highland Creek Trail. Return via Centennial Trail, and this time use Sanctuary Trail as the connector. A free permit is required for backcountry stays. Pick one up from the visitor center before heading out.

Biking

Paved roadways are open to cyclists. If there's heavy traffic, you may want to stick to pedaling US-385, because it has wider shoulders. SD-87 is winding and narrow, but it can be fun (and challenging) to bike up to Rankin Ridge, the highest point in the park at 5,013 feet. The other two roads (NPS-5 and NPS-6) pass through rolling grasslands. Wind Cave is small and very manageable by bike, but they are not permitted on hiking trails or in the backcountry. Do not approach

Cold Brook Canyon

bison on your bicycle. If possible, use a vehicle for protection when they block traffic.

Horseback Riding

An alternative method of transportation is to travel by horse. The entire park, except for hiking trails, near water sources, on roadways, and in campground and picnic areas, is open to horseback riding. All visitors must obtain a free permit from the visitor center prior to riding. Currently no outfitters provide guided horse rides within the park.

Visitor Center

Wind Cave Visitor Center is open daily from 8am to 4:30pm, with extended hours in summer. It closes on Thanksgiving, Christmas, and New Year's Day. Cave tours depart daily from the visitor center all year long, but popular tours like Wild Cave and Candlelight are only offered during the peak summer season. In addition to cave tours and friendly staff, you'll find exhibits, a bookstore, a short film, and restrooms.

Ranger Programs & For Kids

The park's most notable tours are those that occur in the cave's passageways, but you'll also find quality ranger programs above the surface. Prairie hikes (2 hours long) are offered daily during summer. Occasionally, the park offers evening hikes to a nearby prairie dog town. You arrive at dusk because the goal is to spot the endangered (and nocturnal) black-footed ferret. Remember to bring a flashlight. Evening hikes depart from Elk Mountain Campground Amphitheater. Interested visitors should call or stop by the visitor center (605.745.4600) for more details. Additionally, campfire programs and Ranger Talks are offered throughout summer. Check the park's website for a current schedule of ranger-led activities.

Hello!

Wind Cave is one of the best national parks for children. Below the surface lies the 7th longest cave network in the world. Children can explore these dimly lit passageways on any one of the park's guided cave tours (as long as they meet the age requirements). If confined dark spaces aren't for you, there's just as much to do back on the surface. A relatively small area and healthy animal populations make Wind Cave a great place to view wildlife. Sometimes you see them up-close and personal without even trying. Bison are often found lumbering alongside (or on) the road. Children up to age 12 may participate in the Junior Ranger Program. Free activity booklets are available online or at the visitor center. Once completed, return to the visitor center to receive a certificate and badge. And now the park offers Adventures in Nature, an educational program about a ranger-selected topic geared for children ages 4 to 10. Reservations are required. Call (605) 745-4600 to reserve your space.

Flora & Fauna

Today, Wind Cave is one of the best national parks for animal watching and its small size makes wildlife viewing easy and quite predictable. This wasn't the case in 1903 when it was established. At the time bison, pronghorn, bear, and elk were all extirpated from the region. In 1913, 14 bison were donated to the park by the New York Zoological Society. Black-footed ferret, a predator of prairie dogs, was reintroduced in 2007. The reintroduction program has been successful and now you can attend evening programs, where visitors—armed with a flashlight—try to spot these mink-like critters. Sometimes a brigade of bison forms a roadblock holding up traffic. Even though they are the largest terrestrial animal in North America, a motivated bison can reach speeds up to 40 mph. On the other end of the size spectrum, prairie dogs scurry from burrow to burrow squawking all the while.

Ponderosa pine forests, common to the American West, occur in great abundance. Prairies, covering more than half the park, erupt in a sea of color from late spring to summer when wildflowers are in bloom.

Pets & Accessibility

When in the park, pets must be kept on a leash (less than six feet). They are prohibited from public buildings, the backcountry, and all hiking trails (except Elk Mountain and Prairie Vista Nature Trails). Pets are allowed at Elk Mountain Campground.

The cave and visitor center are accessible to wheelchair users. A special cave tour ($5) is offered for visitors with special needs if you call ahead (605.745.4600). Elk Mountain Campground has two accessible campsites.

Weather

Situated at the southern tip of South Dakota's Badlands, Wind Cave enjoys a much warmer and drier climate than the northern hills. January is the coldest month, with average high temperatures around 40°F. Average annual snowfall is 30 inches, fairly evenly distributed from December through April. May and June are the wettest months of the year, receiving roughly 3 inches of rain per month. It gets hot in July/August when highs reach the upper 80s°F. However, warm afternoons can quickly turn into brisk evenings with strong winds blowing from the north.

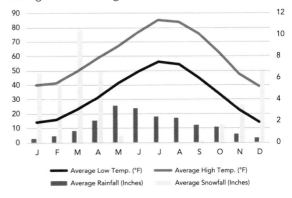

Tips & Recommendations

There's plenty to see above ground to warrant a visit to Wind Cave, but you're missing out if you don't spend a little time under the earth (unless, of course, you don't think you'll be comfortable underground).

Standard tours are first-come, first-served, so you can simply show up and join a cave tour, but the Candlelight and Wild Cave Tours are worth the effort to plan your trip early and make reservations (up to one month

Bison are everywhere

in advance). Again, choose a tour that's appropriate for you. You spend nearly the entire Wild Cave Tour on your hands and knees. Some people find that fun. (It was a blast!) Others see it as cruel and unusual punishment.

There are many prairie dog towns within the park. There's one along NPS-5 near its intersection with SD-87. There's another one near the visitor center at Bison Flats near the US-385 junction. You'll find an interpretive exhibit near the intersection of US-385 and SD-87. And you'll find more along hiking trails like Cold Brook Canyon and Lookout Point.

Hikes: Highland Creek (Strenuous, 17.2 miles), Cold Brook Canyon (Easy, 2.8), East Bison Flats (Moderate, 7.4), Lookout Point (Moderate, 4.4)
Family Activities: Explore the cave, observe some prairie dogs, watch bison (from a safe distance), become Junior Rangers
Rainy Day Activities: Tour the cave
Sunset Spots: Gobbler Pass
Sunrise Spots: Rankin Ridge, Gobbler Pass
Wildlife: Rankin Ridge

Beyond the Park...

Grocery Stores
Safeway • (605) 342-8455
730 Mtn View Rd, Rapid City

Safeway • (605) 348-5125
2120 Mt Rushmore Rd, Rapid City

Walmart • (605) 342-9444
1200 N Lacrosse St, Rapid City

Walmart • (605) 877-3291
100 Stumer Rd, Rapid City

Sonny's Super Foods
801 Jensen Hwy, Hot Springs

Lodging & Camping
Log Cabin • (605) 745-5166
500 Pacific Ave, Hot Springs
historiclogcabinsinc.com

Red Rock River • (605) 745-4400
603 N River St, Hot Springs
redrockriverresort.com

Bavarian Inn • (605) 961-0201
855 N 5th St, Custer
bavarianinnsd.com

Powder House • (800) 321-0692
24125 US-16A, Keystone
powderhouselodge.com

Alpine Inn • (605) 574-2749
133 Main St, Hill City

Mount Rushmore KOA
12620 SD-244, Hill City
palmergulch.com

Rafter J Bar Ranch
12325 Rafter J-Bar Rd, Hill City
rafterj.com • (605) 574-2527

Horse Thief Campground
24391 SD-87 S, Hill City
horsethief.com • (605) 574-2668

Heartland RV Park • (605) 255-5460
heartlandrvpark.com

Festivals
Mt Rushmore • July 4th
mountrushmoresociety.com

Attractions
Chapel In the Hills • (605) 342-8281
3788 Chapel Ln, Rapid City
chapel-in-the-hills.org

Bear Country USA • (605) 343-2290
13820 S US-16, Rapid City
bearcountryusa.com

Sylvan Rocks Climbing School
301 Main St, Hill City
sylvanrocks.com • (605) 484-7585

Rabbit Bike Rental
175 Walnut Ave, Hill City
rabbitbike.com • (605) 574-4302

Palmer Gulch • (605) 574-3412
Horseback riding loacated at the KOA/resort
12620 SD Highway 244, Hill City
ridesouthdakota.com

SD Air and Space Museum
2890 Davis Dr, Ellsworth AFB
sdairandspacemuseum.com

Mount Rushmore • (605) 574-2523
13000 SD-244, Keystone
nps.gov/moru

Rushmore Cave
More attractions than the cave
13622 Hwy 40, Keystone
rushmtn.com • (605) 255-4384

Crazy Horse Mem • (605) 673-4681
Unfinished but still neat
12151 Ave of the Chiefs, Crazy Horse
crazyhorsememorial.org

Rockin R Rides • (520) 349-6078
Guided horseback rides
24853 Village Ave, Custer
rockingrtrailrides.com

Custer State Park
Great place for sightseeing, wildlife, and hiking (Black Elk Peak, Cathedral Spires)
13438 US-16A, Custer
gfp.sd.gov • (605) 255-4515

Black Elk Wilderness
Black Elk Peak • Keystone

Bear Butte State Park
Another odd geological site
NE of Sturgis off SD-79

Jewel Cave NM
World's third-longest cave
11149 US-16, Custer
nps.gov/jeca • (605) 673-8300

Black Hills Balloons
Hot air balloon rides!
Custer • (605) 673-2520
blackhillsballoons.com

Mammoth Site • (605) 745-6017
Paleontological site and museum
1800 US-18 Bypass, Hot Springs
mammothsite.org

Black Hills Wild Horse Sanctuary
12165 Highland Rd, Hot Springs
wildmustangs.com • (605) 745-5955

Devil's Tower NM
Extremely peculiar place. It's popular with rock climbers, but if you're anywhere within a few hours, it's worth the detour. Watch Close Encounters of the Third Kind before visiting.
WY-110, Devils Tower, WY
nps.gov/deto • (307) 467-5283

Theodore Roosevelt

Phone: (701) 623-4466
Website: nps.gov/thro

Established: November 10, 1978
Size: 70,447 Acres
Annual Visitors: 700,000
Peak Season: Summer

Activities: Hiking, Backpacking, Horseback Riding, Paddling, Biking, Fishing, Cross-country Skiing, Snowshoeing

Campgrounds: Cottonwood and Roundup Horse Camp (South Unit) and Juniper (North Unit)
Fee: $14/night (peak season) $7/night (off-season)
Backcountry Camping: Permitted*
Lodging: None

Park Hours: All day, every day
Entrance Fee: $30/25/15 (car/motorcycle/individual)

*A free permit is required for backcountry camping and multi-day horseback trips

Cliffs, gullies, and badlands formations of Theodore Roosevelt National Park are as rugged and relentless as its namesake. September of 1883, Theodore Roosevelt arrived in the town of Little Missouri a bespectacled, affluent New York City kid. Time spent in the Dakota badlands influenced him so deeply he later wrote, "I would not have been President if it had not been for my experiences in North Dakota." Roosevelt came to "bag a buffalo," but he would do much more than hunt. Romanced by the West's lawless lifestyle and potential for economic success, Roosevelt bought into the booming cattle industry, purchasing Maltese Cross Ranch for $14,000. The one-and-a-half story cabin with wooden floors and separate rooms was, to locals, a "mansion." Today, it is preserved at the park's South Unit.

Roosevelt returned to New York, where tragedy struck on February 14, 1884. Just hours apart, Theodore's mother and wife passed away. Stricken by grief, all Roosevelt could write in his diary was a large "X" and one sentence: "The light has gone out in my life." Searching for solace, he returned to Maltese Cross Ranch. However, the ranch's location on a busy carriage road near the train station lacked the sort of solitude he desired for thought and reflection, prompting him to establish Elkhorn Ranch.

Roosevelt's days as a ranchman were short-lived. Nearly 60 percent of his cattle froze or starved to death during the winter of 1886–87. (His livestock's fate was better than most; nearly 80 percent of the area's cattle died that year.) Within two years, the small meat-packing town of Medora turned into a ghost town. Roosevelt closed Elkhorn Ranch, and, in 1898, sold his remaining cattle interests. Today, his ranch is

River Bend Overlook

Mind the traffic

part of the park. The structures' materials have been scavenged, leaving nothing more than sections of foundation. Interpretive panels provide insight into Roosevelt's domain that once stood proudly above the banks of the Little Missouri.

Roosevelt may have left Elkhorn Ranch a failure in cattle business, but he returned to New York a hardened ranchman with newfound appreciation of wilderness and the strenuous life of a frontiersman, which helped him ascend to the presidency. He is often referred to as America's "Conservationist President," earning this title by preserving and protecting an estimated 230 million acres of land of ecological and scenic value.

Through the National Park Service's efforts, visitors can experience these badlands just as Theodore Roosevelt did (except while driving in cars rather than riding on horseback). Bison (or buffalo), pronghorn, and elk have been reintroduced after being overhunted. Artifacts from Roosevelt's time are on display, including rifles and ranch clothing. Period pieces and several of Roosevelt's personal effects, including a traveling trunk, remain in Maltese Cross Cabin, which can be toured with a park ranger. For all he has done for future generations of Americans and the welfare of the nation's irreplaceable resources, it is fitting the land that helped mold such an extraordinary man now bears his name.

When to Go
The park is open all year. In winter, portions of the South Unit's Scenic Loop Drive and the North Unit's Scenic Road may be closed due to snow and ice. May and June are typically the best months to see wildflowers and to paddle the Little Missouri River.

Transportation & Airports
Public transportation does not serve the park. There are small regional airports at Williston and Dickinson. Bismarck Municipal Airport (BIS) is 136 miles east of the South Unit.

Directions
The park consists of three separate units, all of which are in western North Dakota, north of I-94.

South Unit's entrance is in the old meat-packing town of Medora. Medora can be reached by taking Exits 24 or 27 from I-94 (depending which direction you're traveling). South Unit Visitor Center and Maltese Cross Cabin are located on the west side of East River Road near the entrance.

South Unit's Painted Canyon Visitor Center is located just off I-94 at Exit 32, 7 miles east of Medora. The visitor center, overlook, and Painted Canyon hiking trail are all found at the dead end on the north side of the interstate.

North Unit's entrance is just off US-85, 69 miles north of the South Unit. Head east on I-94 to Exit 43. Take US-85 North to the park's entrance and North Unit Visitor Center.

Elkhorn Ranch is more difficult to reach. From I-94, take Exit 10. Turn right onto County Road 11 and continue for 8.8 miles. Turn right onto Westerheim Road and follow it for 6.5 miles. Turn left on Bell Lake Road. Continue for 11.7 miles. Turn right onto FH 2 towards the USFS Elkhorn Campground. Continue for 3 miles (past the campground) to the parking area. (High-clearance vehicle recommended.)

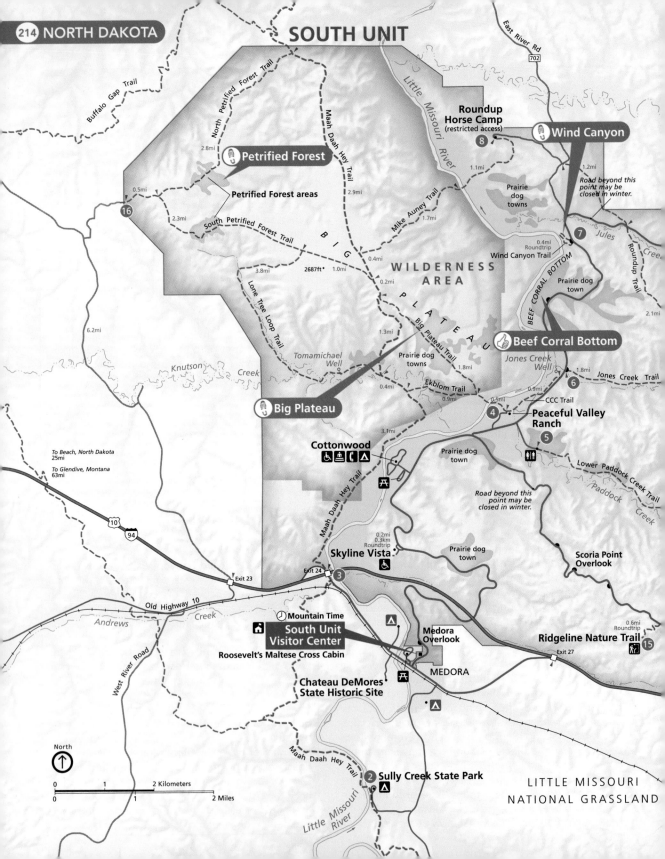

SOUTH UNIT

East River Rd
702

Buffalo Gap Trail

North Petrified Forest Trail

2.8mi

Petrified Forest

Petrified Forest areas

0.5mi

16

2.3mi

South Petrified Forest Trail

Maah Daah Hey Trail

2.9mi

Mike Auney Trail

1.7mi

B I G

2687ft • 1.0mi

3.8mi 0.4mi

0.2mi

Roundup Horse Camp
(restricted access)

8

1.1mi

Prairie dog towns

Wind Canyon

1.2mi

Road beyond this point may be closed in winter.

Jules Creek

7

0.4mi
Roundtrip
Wind Canyon Trail

BEEF CORRAL BOTTOM

Prairie dog town

Roundup Trail

2.1mi

W I L D E R N E S S
A R E A

P L A T E A U

1.3mi

Big Plateau Trail

Prairie dog towns

1.8mi

Lone Tree Loop Trail

6.2mi

Knutson Creek

Tomamichael Well

0.4mi

Ekblom Trail

0.9mi

0.5mi

4

Beef Corral Bottom

Jones Creek Well

1.8mi

Jones Creek Trail

6

0.9mi

CCC Trail

Peaceful Valley Ranch

5

Big Plateau

3.1mi

Cottonwood

Prairie dog town

Lower Paddock Creek Trail

Paddock Creek

To Beach, North Dakota
25mi

To Glendive, Montana
63mi

10

94

Maah Daah Hey Trail

0.2mi
0.3km
Roundtrip

Skyline Vista

Road beyond this point may be closed in winter.

Prairie dog town

Scoria Point Overlook

Exit 23

Exit 24

3

Old Highway 10

Andrews   Creek

West River Road

• Mountain Time

South Unit Visitor Center

Roosevelt's Maltese Cross Cabin

Chateau DeMores State Historic Site

Medora Overlook

MEDORA

0.6mi
Roundtrip

Ridgeline Nature Trail

15

Exit 27

North

↑

0   1   2 Kilometers
0   1   2 Miles

Maah Daah Hey Trail

2

Sully Creek State Park

Little Missouri River

LITTLE MISSOURI NATIONAL GRASSLAND

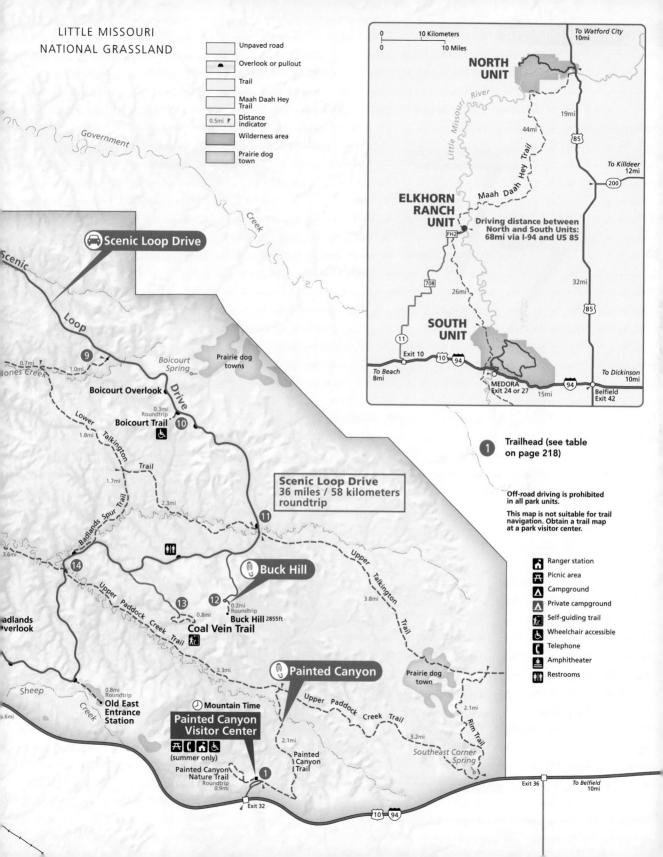

LITTLE MISSOURI NATIONAL GRASSLAND

Unpaved road

Overlook or pullout

Trail

Maah Daah Hey Trail

0.5mi ▶ Distance indicator

Wilderness area

Prairie dog town

Inset map

To Watford City 10mi

NORTH UNIT

Little Missouri River

19mi

44mi

Maah Daah Hey Trail

85

To Killdeer 12mi

200

ELKHORN RANCH UNIT

FH2

Driving distance between North and South Units: 68mi via I-94 and US 85

708

26mi

SOUTH UNIT

32mi

85

11

Exit 10

To Beach 8mi

10 94

MEDORA Exit 24 or 27

15mi

94

To Dickinson 10mi

Belfield Exit 42

Main map

🚗 Scenic Loop Drive

Scenic

Loop

Government

Creek

Drive

9

0.7mi

Jones Creek

1.0mi

Boicourt Spring

Prairie dog towns

Boicourt Overlook

0.3mi Roundtrip

Boicourt Trail ♿

10

Lower

1.8mi

Talkington

Trail

1.7mi

2.3mi

Badlands Spur Trail

3.6mi

**Scenic Loop Drive
36 miles / 58 kilometers
roundtrip**

11

Upper

Talkington

🚻

3.8mi

Trail

14

👟 **Buck Hill**

13

12

0.2mi Roundtrip

Buck Hill 2855ft

0.8mi

Coal Vein Trail 🚶

Badlands Overlook

Upper

Paddock

Creek

Trail

3.3mi

👟 **Painted Canyon**

Upper Paddock Creek Trail

Prairie dog town

2.1mi

Sheep

Creek

0.8mi Roundtrip

Old East Entrance Station

🕐 Mountain Time

Painted Canyon Visitor Center
🧺🚻♿
(summer only)

2.1mi

Painted Canyon Trail

3.2mi

Southeast Corner Spring

Rim Trail

1 Trailhead (see table on page 218)

Off-road driving is prohibited in all park units.

This map is not suitable for trail navigation. Obtain a trail map at a park visitor center.

Painted Canyon Nature Trail
Roundtrip 0.9mi

1

Exit 32

10 94

Exit 36

To Belfield 10mi

Legend (right side)

🏠 Ranger station
🍽 Picnic area
⛺ Campground
⛺ Private campground
🚶 Self-guiding trail
♿ Wheelchair accessible
☎ Telephone
🎭 Amphitheater
🚻 Restrooms

NORTH UNIT

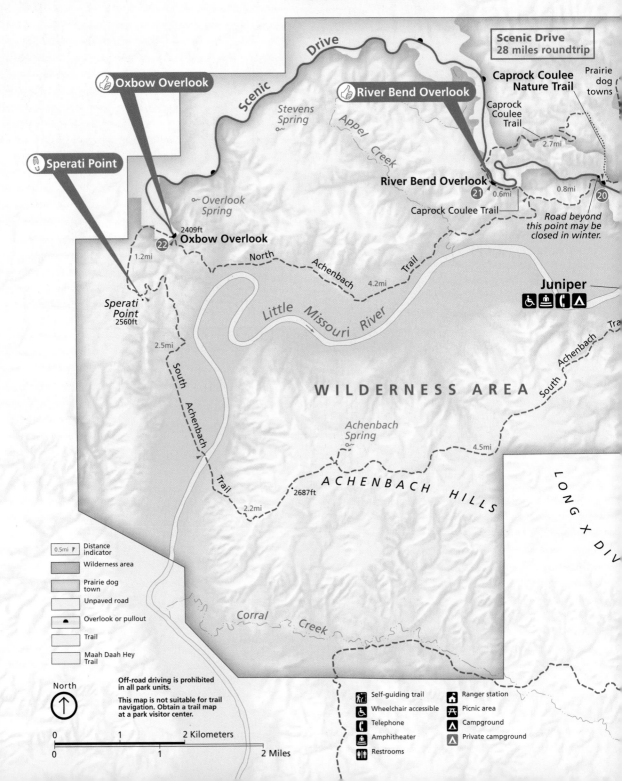

Scenic Drive
28 miles roundtrip

👍 **Oxbow Overlook**

👍 **River Bend Overlook**

Caprock Coulee Nature Trail

Prairie dog towns

Stevens Spring

Caprock Coulee Trail

2.7mi

👟 **Sperati Point**

Appel Creek

River Bend Overlook

21 0.6mi

Overlook Spring

2409ft

22 **Oxbow Overlook**

1.2mi

Caprock Coulee Trail

0.8mi

20

Road beyond this point may be closed in winter.

North Achenbach 4.2mi Trail

Sperati Point 2560ft

Juniper ♿ 🚻 ☎ ⛺

2.5mi

Little Missouri River

South Achenbach

South Achenbach

W I L D E R N E S S   A R E A

Trail

4.5mi

Achenbach Spring

2.2mi 2687ft

A C H E N B A C H   H I L L S

L O N G   X   D I V

Corral Creek

0.5mi	Distance indicator
▨	Wilderness area
▨	Prairie dog town
▢	Unpaved road
•▬	Overlook or pullout
▢	Trail
▢	Maah Daah Hey Trail

North ↑

Off-road driving is prohibited in all park units.

This map is not suitable for trail navigation. Obtain a trail map at a park visitor center.

🚶 Self-guiding trail	🏠 Ranger station
♿ Wheelchair accessible	🍽 Picnic area
☎ Telephone	⛺ Campground
🎭 Amphitheater	⛺ Private campground
🚻 Restrooms	

0   1   2 Kilometers

0   1   2 Miles

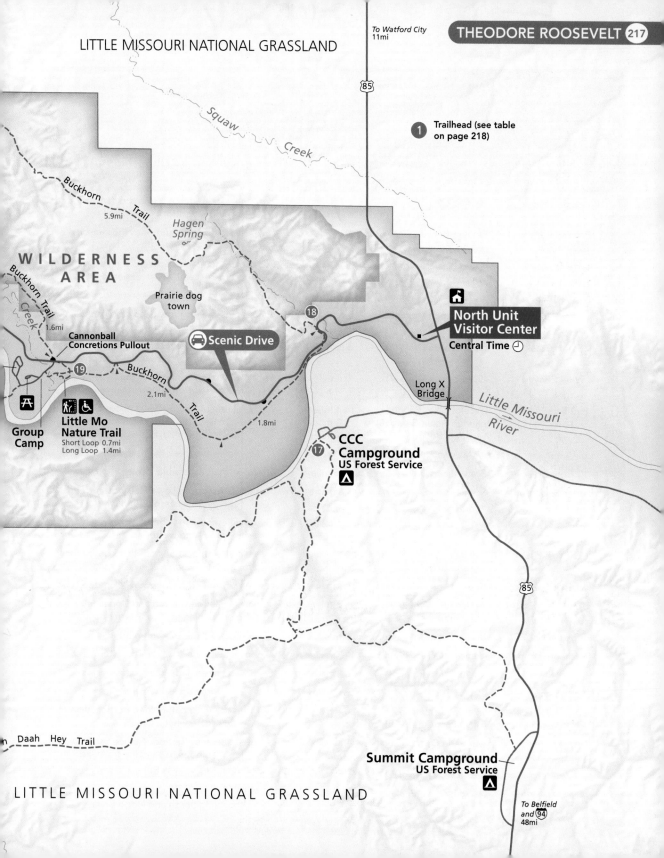

LITTLE MISSOURI NATIONAL GRASSLAND

To Watford City 11mi

THEODORE ROOSEVELT 217

85

1 Trailhead (see table on page 218)

Squaw Creek

Buckhorn Trail 5.9mi

Hagen Spring

WILDERNESS AREA

Buckhorn Trail Creek 1.6mi

Prairie dog town

18

Scenic Drive

North Unit Visitor Center
Central Time 🕐

Cannonball Concretions Pullout

19

Buckhorn Trail 2.1mi

Long X Bridge

Little Missouri River

Group Camp

Little Mo Nature Trail
Short Loop 0.7mi
Long Loop 1.4mi

1.8mi

17 **CCC Campground**
US Forest Service

85

Daah Hey Trail

Summit Campground
US Forest Service

To Belfield and 94 48mi

LITTLE MISSOURI NATIONAL GRASSLAND

Peaceful Valley Ranch

Theodore Roosevelt Hiking Trails (Distances are one-way unless loop)

	Name	Location (# on map)	Length	Difficulty Rating & Notes
South Unit	Painted Canyon - ♿	Painted Canyon Visitor Center (1)	2.1 miles	M – Extremely steep descent into the canyon • Ends at Upper Paddock Creek Trail
	Painted Canyon Nature Trail - ♿	Painted Canyon Visitor Center (1)	0.9 mile	M – Short loop descends into the canyon
	Lone Tree Loop	Maah Daah Hey Trail (3) Peaceful Valley Ranch (4)	13.1 miles 10.2 miles	S – Two choices to reach a scenic 6.3-mile loop, river crossing from Peaceful Valley (easier for horses)
	Big Plateau - ♿	Peaceful Valley Ranch	3.2 miles	M – Crosses Little Mo, you have some loop options
	Lower Paddock Creek	Scenic Loop Drive (5)	3.6 miles	M – Passes a prairie dog town and crosses the creek numerous times
	Jones Creek	Scenic Loop Drive (6)	3.5 miles	M – Follows Jones Creek, crossing it twice, creek can be muddy and wet (especially in spring)
	Wind Canyon	Scenic Loop Drive (7)	0.4 mile	E – Short climb to an overlook of the Little Missouri River and a wind sculpted canyon
	Petrified Forest Loop - ♿	Peaceful Valley Ranch (4) Roundup Horse Camp (8) West Park Boundary (15)	14.4 miles 15.0 miles 10.4 miles	S – Crosses Little Mo (bring water shoes and towel) S – Crosses Little Mo (horse route) M – Remote trailhead, but easier hiking
	Lower Talkington	Multiple (9, 10, 13)	4.1 miles	M – Follows a creek that is usually dry
	Boicourt	Scenic Loop Drive (10)	0.15 mile	E – Wheelchair accessible, pretty good views
	Upper Talkington	Scenic Loop Drive (11)	3.8 miles	M – Continues east from Lower Talkington • Ends at the park's eastern boundary
	Buck Hill - ♿	Buck Hill (12)	0.1 mile	E – Note differences in vegetation between drier south-facing slopes and wetter north-facing slopes
	Coal Vein Loop	Coal Vein (unpaved) (13)	0.8 mile	E – Visible after-effects of a fire that burned here from 1951 to 1977 when a coal seam caught fire
	Badlands Spur - ♿	Scenic Loop Drive (14)	1.7 miles	E – Allows Lower Paddock/Lower Talkington Loop
	Upper Paddock Creek	Scenic Loop Drive (14)	6.5 miles	M – Intersects Painted Canyon and Upper Talkington Trails before ending at the eastern boundary
	Ridgeline Nature	Scenic Loop Drive (15)	0.6 mile	M – Steep climb to a self-guided loop
North Unit	Buckhorn Loop	Scenic Drive (16, 17, 20)	11.4 miles	S – Loops around the park's northeastern section
	Little Mo	Juniper Campground (19)	1.1 miles	E – Paved (inner) and unpaved (outer) loops
	Achenbach - ♿	Scenic Drive (19, 20, 22)	18.0 miles	S – Loop crosses the river twice
	Caprock Coulee Nature Trail	Scenic Drive, 1.5 miles west of Juniper Camp (20)	0.8 mile	M – This is the trail's self-guided portion, where you'll learn what a "coulee" is
	Upper Caprock Coulee Loop - ♿	River Bend Overlook (21)	4.3 miles	M – A continuation of Caprock Coulee's self-guided portion that loops back to the trailhead
	Sperati - ♿	Oxbow Overlook (22)	1.5 miles	M – Short portion of Achenbach Trail
	Maah Daah Hey	South Unit (2, 3) North Unit (17)	96.0 miles	S – Hikers, bikers, and horses can take this trail connecting South and North Units

Difficulty Ratings: E = Easy, M = Moderate, S = Strenuous

Camping

Cottonwood (76 sites) and **Juniper** (50 sites) are the primary campgrounds in the South and North Units, respectively. Both campgrounds have pull-through sites for RVs, but hookups are not available. Restrooms, water, grills, and picnic tables are located nearby. The camping fee is $14/night. It is reduced to $7/night during the off-season (October–April), when there's limited services. Odd-numbered sites at Cottonwood can be reserved at (877) 44-6777 or recreation.gov from May through September. Even-numbered sites at Cottonwood (South Unit) and all sites at Juniper (North Unit) are available first-come, first-served. Cottonwood fills by noon most days from mid-May through mid-September. Each campground has a group campsite that accommodates a minimum of 6 campers for $30/night. **Roundup Group Horse Campground** (South Unit) is intended for horseback riders. It may also be used by groups of 7–20 campers for $40/night. During peak season (May through September), all group sites must be reserved at (877) 444-6777 or recreation.gov.

Backcountry camping is allowed with a free permit available at North or South Unit Visitor Center.

Driving

Driving is the most popular activity. **South Unit** visitors circle the park via 36-mile Scenic Loop Drive, stopping at pullouts to read interpretive signs and soak in the views. It begins just beyond East River Road and provides access to many hiking trails and overlooks. Drive slowly to spot bison, pronghorn, elk, and wild horses. Residents you can't miss are playful prairie dogs who scurry about their little prairie dog towns.

The **North Unit** offers a 14-mile (one-way) Scenic Drive ending at Oxbow Overlook, where you'll find outstanding panoramic views. As you make your way, watch for wildlife. Mule deer are frequently seen crossing the upper grasslands. Witness the power of erosion at Cannonball Concretions Pullout. Eye the main agent of erosion, the Little Missouri River, from River Bend and Oxbow Overlooks.

Hiking & Backpacking

A multitude of hiking opportunities exists at both the North and South Unit of Theodore Roosevelt National Park. Whether by horse or foot, all visitors should leave the roadways and explore a few miles of trails that provide a closer look at eroded badlands, bustling prairie dog towns, steep canyons, colorful rock layers, and lush bottomlands. These are the landscapes that

Buck Hill

helped transform Theodore Roosevelt into the United States' "Conservationist President."

Most of the **South Unit's hiking trails** are accessed via Scenic Loop Drive. Jones Creek, Lower Talkington, and Paddock Creek Trails bisect the loop drive as they follow (usually) dry creek beds. If you arrive after a heavy thunderstorm or recent snow melt check trail conditions prior to hiking, as the creeks occasionally run, causing trails to be muddy or impassable. At times you may have to cross running water.

Paddock and Talkington Trails continue east past Scenic Loop Drive all the way to the park's eastern boundary. The boundary is difficult to miss because you'll encounter a 7-foot fence meant to keep bison and wild horses in and grazing cattle out.

You'll find the nation's 3rd largest petrified forest in the South Unit's northwest corner. Take the 10.4-mile **Petrified Loop Trail**, accessed by taking exit 23 on I-94 and heading north along Forest Service Road 730. Turn left at a "Petrified Forest" sign to follow Road 730. Continue until you reach 730-2. Turn right at another "Petrified Forest" sign and take an immediate left. Veer left at the next Y-intersection to the parking area. The trail begins at the lift gate in the fence. Pack plenty of water if you intend to hike the entire loop. Or do a shorter out-and-back following the loop to the north, where you'll find abundant petrified wood specimens. An excellent alternative is to access the Petrified Forest from Peaceful Valley Ranch via Ekblom and Big Plateau Trails. Bring a towel and water shoes because you'll have to cross the Little Missouri.

North Unit's Buckhorn Trail is great for seeing bison, prairie dogs, and deer. It's fairly long (11.4 miles) but can be completed in a day. If you really want to push

Petrified stump near Jones Creek

day-hiking to the limits, try **Achenbach Trail**. Check with park rangers about Little Missouri River crossing conditions before you begin.

Backcountry camping is allowed with a free backcountry permit. There are no approved water sources, so you'll have to carry in all your cooking and drinking water. Camp must be set up at least a quarter-mile from any road and trailhead and 200 feet from any water source. Campsites must not be visible from any roadway or trail. Purchase a good map. Plan your trip. Get your permit (at the South Unit Visitor Center for trips in the South Unit or Elkhorn Ranch Unit and at the North Unit Visitor Center for North Unit backpacking trips). Winter backpacking is an option, but you better be prepared for bitterly cold weather, and teeth-chattering winds. When your trip is over, call (701.623.4730 ext. 1422) or stop by the visitor center to let them know you're safe.

Horseback Riding
You can explore North Dakota's badlands by horse just like Theodore Roosevelt did more than 100 years ago. All hiking trails, except developed nature trails, are open to stock. The South Unit is better suited for horse riders thanks to a larger network of trails and Roundup Group Horse Campground ($40/night). You can also camp in the backcountry (8 horse/rider maximum). Permits are required and can be obtained at the North or South Unit Visitor Center. Another option is to board your horse(s) at Lone Butte Ranch (701.863.6864, lonebutteranch.com) near the North Unit. The CCC campground near the North Unit is horse-friendly too. Peaceful Valley Ranch, located near the beginning of South Unit's Scenic Loop Drive, was one of the United States' first "dude" ranches. They used to offer guided tours and horse boarding, but they were closed for business at time of publication. So, horseless folks or anyone who left theirs at home itching for a ride

will have to go to a place like Medora Riding Stables (800.633.6721) to get in the saddle.

Paddling
Just as Maah Daah Hey Trail connects South and North Units for hikers, the Little Missouri River connects the two for paddlers. A trip from Medora (South Unit) to Long X Bridge (North Unit) on US-85 is 108 miles. The journey takes about five days and requires considerable planning, as you are traversing relatively uncivilized terrain where cell phones rarely work and there are no reliable drinking water sources. The river is not navigable all year round. You'll want a river depth of 2.5–3.5 feet for good boating. May and June are the best months to paddle, as temperatures are comfortable, and the water is usually navigable after spring thaw. It's a trip that you won't soon forget. The route is filled with spectacular scenery and wildlife viewing opportunities abound. There are no designated campsites along the way, but camping is allowed on National Forest land. Camping is prohibited on adjacent private property. You will have to portage around the wildlife fence crossing the river at park boundaries.

Biking
All park roads are open to bicycles. Biking is a really nice alternative to driving, due to small crowds, abundant wildlife, and varied terrain. Both park units' Scenic Drives are hilly, but the North Unit is a bit more strenuous. Bicycles are not allowed off road in the park. However, bikers can take Maah Daah Hey Trail through Little Missouri National Grasslands between North and South Units. Check out Dakota Cyclery (888.321.1218, dakotacyclery.com) for guided tours and bike rentals. They can even hook you up with a lockable trailer, and they'll move it from stop-to-stop so you don't have to carry heavy gear. Altogether this is some of the best pedaling you'll find in the Dakotas.

Fishing
Blue gills and catfish can be caught in the Little Missouri River. You must abide by North Dakota state law and license requirements.

Winter Activities
The Little Missouri River is good for cross-country skiing. Frozen water can create a flat, well-defined surface to explore on skis during winter (which can extend from October to April). Park Roads are also used for skiing. With 30 inches of annual snowfall, snowshoeing is possible, but snow tends to blow and drift. There are no groomed trails within the park. You'll have to blaze your own (or follow someone else's).

Visitor Centers

South Unit Visitor Center is open daily from 8am–6pm from Memorial to Labor Day. It's open daily from 8am until 5pm in spring and fall, and from 8am until 4:30pm in winter. It closes for Thanksgiving, Christmas, and New Year's Day. Here you'll find staff, the Maltese Cross Cabin, bookstore, film, exhibits, and restrooms. **Painted Canyon Visitor Center** is open from April to mid-November from 8:30am–4:30pm. Here you'll find staff, a few exhibits, a gift shop, and restrooms. **North Unit Visitor Center** is open daily from Memorial Day to Labor Day, and it typically closes from November through April. Here you'll find staff, a bookstore, park film, and restrooms.

Ranger Programs & For Kids

Park rangers provide guided walks, talks, and campfire programs from June to early September. A current schedule of activities is available online or at a visitor center. A typical talk or walk exposes visitors to a ranger's perspective regarding the life and land you are about to explore. South Unit visitors can tour Roosevelt's Maltese Cross Cabin (available daily in summer).

The park is a wonderful place for children to see wildlife and appreciate nature. Children (ages 6 and up) are invited to become Junior Rangers. Pick up a free Junior Ranger Activity Booklet from either visitor center, complete the activities, and return to a visitor center to receive a certificate and an official Junior Ranger Badge. During summer, Junior Ranger Family Fun Days are offered about once a month.

Flora & Fauna

Badlands are known for their inhospitable conditions, but a visit to Theodore Roosevelt National Park reveals a world of great plant and animal diversity. More than 400 species of plants are found in the park. Prairies burst with life when wildflowers bloom in spring. They also help sustain healthy populations of large grazing mammals.

Bison, wild horses, elk, pronghorn, mule deer, and white-tailed deer all reside in the wide-open prairies. The North Unit keeps a small herd of longhorn steers as a living history exhibit. Stop at a prairie dog town and you'll hear the occupants barking from the stoop of their burrows. This region wasn't always as rich in wildlife as it is today. Westward expansion led to severe overhunting. Several species were eliminated from North Dakota only to be reintroduced by the National Park Service. Bison were restored at the South Unit in 1956 and the North Unit in 1962. Elk were next to return

Pronghorn near Elkhorn Ranch

to the South Unit in 1985 and bighorn sheep eventually followed at the North Unit. Through the park's conservation efforts, the land and wildlife are much like they were when a wealthy easterner named Theodore Roosevelt arrived in September of 1883.

Pets & Accessibility

Pets are permitted in the park but must be kept on a leash (less than six feet). They are not allowed in park buildings, on trails, or in the backcountry.

The visitor centers and Maltese Cross Cabin are wheelchair accessible. Accessible sites and restrooms are available at Cottonwood and Juniper Campgrounds. A few shorter trails like Skyline Vista Overlook and Boicourt Overlook in the South Unit and Little Mo Nature Trail in the North Unit are wheelchair accessible.

Weather

The three park units share similar climates. Summers are hot with average highs in the 70s and 80s°F. Winters are cold with average lows in the single digits. It's fairly dry, receiving only about 15 inches of precipitation each year, but thunderstorms in summer and blizzards in winter can occur with little to no warning.

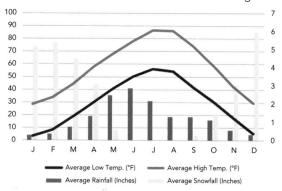

Legend:
— Average Low Temp. (°F) — Average High Temp. (°F)
■ Average Rainfall (Inches) □ Average Snowfall (Inches)

Crossing the Little Mo via Ekblom Trail

Tips & Recommendations
About 80% of all visitors arrive between May and September. Only a few thousand people show up each month from December through March. Modest visitation makes a park that is rarely crowded, so you can choose to go with the flow and enjoy warm summer days with everyone else or take the opportunity to have the place to yourself and plan an off-season trip.

Wild horses are in the southern unit and they move around quite a bit. I've seen them on both sides of Loop Drive as well as at Beef Corral Bottom, so keep your eyes open for horses off in the distance while touring the South Unit. Due to a scarcity of trees, views are expansive, but some wildlife blend in (or hide) among the surrounding badlands.

If you're going to make the drive to Elkhorn Ranch, it's a good idea to ask a ranger about road conditions. Most park fans are huge admirers of Theodore Roosevelt, but Elkhorn Ranch is just okay. Ruins are all that's left. The scenery is nice, displays are interesting, and you may see wildlife, but focus on Painted Canyon and the North and South Units before venturing here.

Maltese Cross Cabin can only be visited with a park ranger in summer. There are regularly scheduled tours. And, if things are slow, tours may be available on demand (just ask). It's open to self-guided touring the rest of the year.

Wildlife is easier to spot in the South Unit. For one, there's more wildlife here (the bison herd is about twice the size of the North Unit's herd), and the road provides access to a greater percentage of the park, which creates more encounters, and more encounters makes more animals that are conditioned to and comfortable with human interaction.

Whether you're traveling with children or not, you'll want to stop at a prairie dog town. If you're lucky, you may see them on high alert when a predator or two is lurking about. There are towns along the scenic drives or trails like Big Plateau.

Easy Hikes: Buck Hill (0.1 mile), Little Mo (1.1)
Moderate Hikes: Big Plateau (3.2 miles), Painted Canyon (2.1), Lower Paddock Creek (3.6), Upper Caprock Coulee Loop (4.3), Sperati (1.5)
Strenuous Hikes: Petrified Forest Loop (10.4 miles), Lone Tree Loop (12.8), Achenbach Loop (18), Buckhorn Loop (11.4)
South Unit Viewpoints/Stops: Maltese Cross Cabin, a prairie dog town, Beef Corral Bottom, Wind Canyon, Boicourt Overlook, Buck Hill, and Scoria Point
North Unit Viewpoints/Stops: Cannonball Concretions, River Bend Overlook (tremendous view!), and Oxbow Overlook
Family Activities: Prairie Dogs!, look for wildlife at Beef Corral Bottom, become Junior Rangers
Rainy Day Activities: Check out Theodore Roosevelt's Maltese Cross Cabin
History Enthusiasts: Medora Visitor Center, Elkhorn Ranch, Maltese Cross Cabin
Sunset Spots: Painted Canyon, River Bend Overlook, Wind Canyon
Sunrise Spots: River Bend Overlook, Painted Canyon, Peaceful Valley
Wildlife: Beef Corral Bottom, any of the prairie dog towns

Coyotes invade a prairie dog town

Beyond the Park...

Grocery Stores
Walmart • (701) 225-8504
2456 3rd Ave W, Dickinson

Walmart • (701) 572-8550
4001 2nd Ave W, Williston

Lodging
Roosevelt Inn • (701) 842-3686
600 2nd Ave SW, Watford City
rooseveltinn.com

El Rancho Hotel • (701) 572-6321
1623 2nd Ave W, Williston
elranchowilliston.com

Rough Riders Hotel • (701) 623-4444
301 3rd Ave, Medora

Campgrounds
Medora Campground
3370 Pool Dr • (701) 623-4444

Buffalo Gap Campground
fs.fed.us • (701) 227-7800

Oleo Acres RV Park • (701) 290-5763
1967 ND-85, Belfield

Tobacco Gardens • (701) 842-4199
4781 ND-1806, Watford City

Festivals
Roughrider Days • June
roughriderdaysfair.com • Dickinson

Badlands Ukranian Days • July
badlandsukraniandays.com

Attractions
Little Missouri National Grassland
*Largest grassland in the country
surrounds Theodore Roosevelt
National Park. You'll probably
find prairie dogs!*

Little Missouri State Park
Near Lake Sakakwea confluence
ND-22, Southeast of Watford City
parkrec.nd.gov

Lake Sakakwea State Park
Country's third-largest reservoir
parkrec.nd.gov

Fort Stevenson State Park
*Located on Lake Sakakwea
(boating, fishing, hiking)*
parkrec.nd.gov

Cowboy HOF • (701) 623-2000
250 Main St, Medora
northdakotacowboy.com

Medora Musical
An outdoor musical
Burning Hills Amphitheater
medora.com • (800) 663-6721

Chateau de Mores
*Summer residence of Medora's
founder*
3426 Chateau Rd, Medora
history.nd.gov • (701) 623-4355

Medora Riding Stables
Guided badlands trail rides
Pacific Ave • (800) 633-6721

Fort Union Trading Post NHS
Reconstructed trading post
15550 ND-1804
nps.gov/fous • (701) 572-9083

Knife River Villages NHS
Major Native trade hub
nps.gov/knri • (701) 745-3300

Makoshika State Park • fwp.mt.gov
More badlands formations
1301 Snyder St, Glendive, MT

Grand Teton

Looking across Jenny Lake to Cascade Canyon

Phone: (307) 739-3399
Website: nps.gov/grte

Established: February 26, 1929
Size: 309,995 Acres
Annual Visitors: 3.4 Million
Peak Season: June–September
Hiking Trails: ~230 Miles

Activities: Hiking, Backpacking, Boating, Biking, Horseback Riding, Rock Climbing, Mountaineering, Fishing, Cross-country Skiing, Snowshoeing

7 Campgrounds: $36–84/night
8 Lodges: $210–1,000+/night
Backcountry Camping: Permitted*

Park Hours: All day, every day
Entrance Fee: $35/30/20
(car/motorcycle/individual)

*Permit ($35 in-person, $45 online) and approved bear-resistant food canister required

"If you have ever stood at Jenny Lake and looked across to Cascade Canyon weaving its sinuous way toward the summit of the Tetons, you will know the joy of being in a sacred place, designed by God to be protected forever."

– Horace Albright

Thanks to the tireless efforts of Horace Albright and deep pockets of John D. Rockefeller, Jr., Grand Teton National Park now preserves one of America's iconic landscapes, allowing future generations to stand at Jenny Lake, looking across to Cascade Canyon and Grand Teton. But creating the park was no easy task. The Teton's remarkable, if not sacred, appearance was indisputable, however not all residents believed it should be protected.

Native Americans camped along Jackson Lake while hunting game more than 11,000 years ago. In the 17th century, French fur trappers named the range's three tallest peaks "Les Trois Tetons" or "The Three Nipples." Would you expect anything less from rugged frontiersmen removed from society (and women) for long periods? By the 18th and 19th centuries, trappers had thoroughly explored the Three Tetons, and the valley below had become fur trapper David Jackson's favorite place to "hole-up." Today this valley is known as Jackson Hole, named after David in 1829. In the late 19th century, homesteaders began trickling into the Hole. Only the hardiest—or most stubborn—were able to endure unforgiving winters, living off crops grown during the brief summer. That very same Jackson-Hole brand of stubbornness would greet Horace Albright head on in the 1920s, when he made it his mission to preserve the Tetons under protection of the recently created National Park Service.

Albright's pet project took shape while serving as Superintendent of Yellowstone, where he had the opportunity to escort congressmen, dignitaries, and two Presidents to the southern expanses of Yellowstone. From Yellowstone, the Tetons could be seen looming in the background. It wasn't until 1926 that Albright met a man with the resources and ambition to make his dream a reality. John D. Rockefeller, Jr. and his wife toured the Tetons with Albright and then invited him to New York to discuss his project. Rockefeller, convinced of the park idea, formed Snake River Land Company of Salt Lake City and began buying up properties surrounding the Tetons under the guise of a cattle ranch. Subterfuge was required because a vast majority of ranchers were anti-park. Bull-headed and stubborn, they refused to cede rights to the land.

In 1929, Congress redesignated national forest land consisting of the Teton Range and six glacial lakes at its base to form a small Grand Teton National Park. Rockefeller tried to donate his properties, only to have it refused. Undeterred, he continued to purchase land, acquiring an additional 35,000 acres for $1.4 million. In 1943, more than a decade later, he became increasingly frustrated that donating his land was more difficult than acquiring it. He wrote a letter to President Franklin D. Roosevelt suggesting he would sell the land if the government would not accept it. That same year President Roosevelt invoked the Antiquities Act to create Jackson Hole National Monument. It placed 221,610 acres of land east of Grand Teton National Park under Park Service control, but once again failed to include Rockefeller's holdings.

Many locals were outraged by use of executive order, and in protest they drove 500 cattle across the monument. The dispute wasn't settled until 1950. After WWII the economy in Jackson Hole improved largely due to tourism to the new National Monument. Anti-park sentiment began to wane and finally the monument, park, and Rockefeller's properties were merged to form today's Grand Teton National Park. To this day the Rockefellers' conservation efforts have continued. In 2001, Laurance Rockefeller, son of John D. Rockefeller, Jr., donated the family's JY Ranch, which is now open to the public as Laurance S. Rockefeller Preserve (just as his father would have wanted it).

Cunningham Cabin

When to Go
Grand Teton National Park is open all year. The park is incredibly crowded from June through August. Campgrounds and parking areas fill early. Roads become congested. Even hiking trails can be busy. It's possible to find peace and quiet a few miles from roadways, but traveling during September and October, when weather is pleasant but temperamental, is a good alternative to summer touring.

Transportation & Airports
Grand Teton Lodge Co. (307.543.2811, gtlc.com) provides complimentary guest shuttle transportation throughout the park and Jackson, as well as narrated bus tours (fee). Alltrans (800.443.6133, jacksonholealltrans.com) provides shuttle service (year-round) and narrated park tours (June–September).

Jackson Hole Airport (JAC) is located inside the park. Car rental is available on-site. The nearest large airport is Salt Lake City International (SLC), more than 300 miles to the south.

Directions
The most popular entry points are from the north, south, and east. But there are also trailheads on the west side accessible near Driggs, ID, too.

From the North: Arriving from Yellowstone National Park's South Entrance (~6 miles away) leads you down John D. Rockefeller, Jr. Memorial Parkway, one of the most scenic highways in the United States.

From the South: From Jackson, WY (~4 miles) take US-26/US-89/US-191 north, which leads directly to the south entrance station and Craig Thomas Discovery & Visitor Center.

From the East: US-26/287 enters from the east at Moran where it intersects US-26/89/191, at Moran Entrance Station.

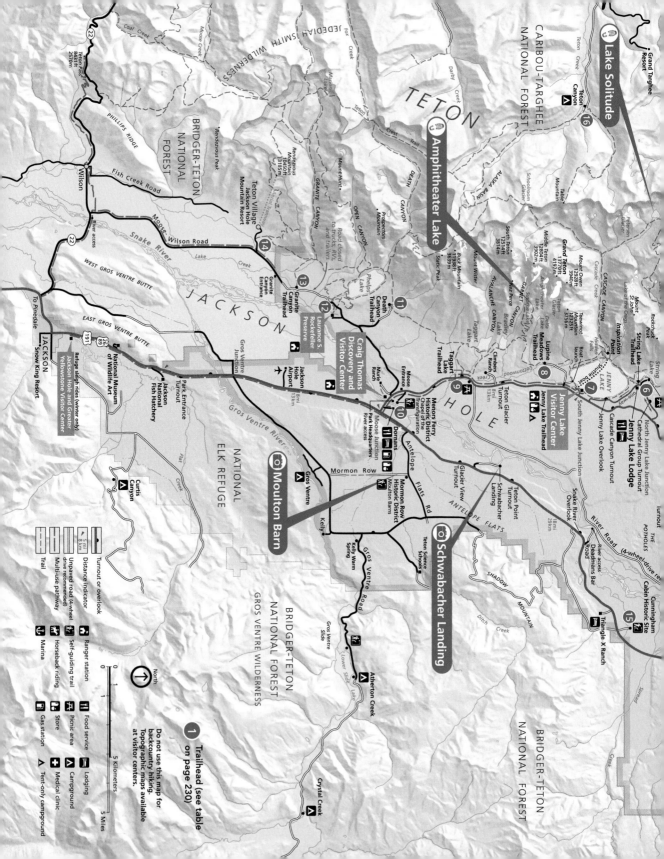

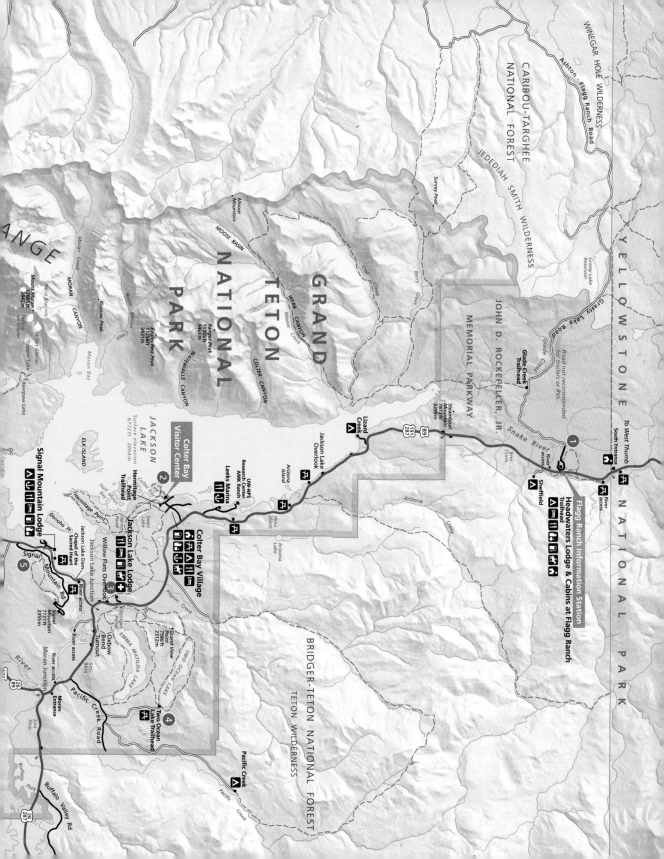

Moulton Barn sunrise

Grand Teton Camping (Fees are per night)

Name	Location	Open	Fee	Sites	Notes
Gros Ventre (gltc.com)	11.5 miles SE of Moose	May–early Oct	$38 (tent) $60 (RV)	302	Typically last campground to fill
Jenny Lake - ♿ (gltc.com)	8 miles N of Moose	early May–Late Sept	$36	51	Tents only, 10 walk-in sites available
Signal Mountain - ♿ (signalmountainlodge.com)	9 miles N of Jenny Lake	mid-May–mid-Oct	$40 (tent) $79 (RV)	86	23 RV hookup sites available
Colter Bay Campground (gltc.com)	US-89, 25 miles north of Moose	late May–late Sept	$38 (tent) $60 (RV)	335	Walk-in sites available ($13/night)
Colter Bay RV Park (gltc.com)	Colter Bay Village	early May–early Oct	$88	112	Full hookups available
Lizard Creek - ♿ (signalmountainlodge.com)	32 miles N of Moose	mid-June–mid-Sept	$41	60	$12/night for hikers or bikers w/o a car
Headwaters at Flagg Ranch (gltc.com)	Just south of Yellowstone NP	early June–late-Sept	$35 (tent) $70 (RV)	175	Full hookups available
Backcountry Camping	Permitted at designated sites and regions of the park with a permit obtained in person from Craig Thomas Discovery & Visitor Center, Jenny Lake Ranger Station, or Colter Bay Visitor Center ($35) or online at recreation.gov ($45). Approved bear canisters must be used.				
Group Camping	Group sites (10+ people, $13 per night per person) are available at Colter Bay and Gros Ventre Campgrounds. Reservations are required and can be made at recreation.gov.				

Grand Teton Lodging (Fees are per night)

Name	Open	Fee	Notes
Dornan's Spur Ranch (307.733.2415, dornans.com)	Closed November & April	$375 (peak) $125 (off season)	Dining, grocery, deli, gasoline, and equipment rental available
AAC Climber's Ranch - ♿ (307.733.7271, americanalpineclub.org)	June–early Sept	$22/32	Lower rate is for AAC members
Jenny Lake Lodge - ♿ (307.543.3100, gltc.com)	early June–early Oct	$855+	Dining, horseback riding, cruiser bicycles available to guests
Signal Mountain Lodge (307.543.2831, signalmountainlodge.com)	mid-May–mid-Oct	$330–530	Dining, float trips, guided fishing excursions available
Jackson Lake Lodge - ♿ (307.543.3100, gltc.com)	mid-May–early Oct	$356–881	Restaurants, adventure outfitters, and park tours
Triangle X Ranch (307.733.2183, trianglex.com)	mid-May–Oct late Dec–mid-March	$2,057+/person per week	Lodging, meals, horseback riding, and activities included
Colter Bay Cabins (307.543.3100, gltc.com)	late May–late Sept	$210–289	Also have 4-bunk primitive tent cabins available for $83/night
Headwaters Lodge & Resort (307.543.3100, gltc.com)	early June–late Sept	$248–335	Also have 4-bunk primitive tent cabins available for $83/night

Camping & Lodging

All campsites can be reserved up to six months in advance at (877) 444-6777 or recreation.gov. While there are more than 1,000 sites, demand is incredibly high during summer. Make reservations as early as possible for pretty much any trip between Memorial Day and Labor Day. Jenny Lake and Signal Mountain are campgrounds with the most desirable locations, but each location has its benefits. Coin-operated showers and laundry are available at Signal Mountain, Colter Bay, and Headwaters Campgrounds. Campground opening dates are weather dependent. All established campgrounds close for winter. Simple tent cabins are available at Colter Bay and Headwaters for $83/night. A few free primitive campsites are dispersed throughout the park, like those located along unpaved Grassy Lake Road near Flagg Ranch Information Station. And camping is available in the National Forest to the east.

The unique, and often contentious, history of Grand Teton's creation has allowed a variety of commercial interests to be tucked away within park boundaries. From Dornan's Spur Ranch at the park's southern reaches to Headwaters Lodge & Resort (at Flagg Ranch) near the northern boundary, you can find lodging accommodations to suit your itinerary, if not your budget. Jenny Lake Lodge has earned the title of "most expensive lodging in the National Park System." Warranted or not, it's usually booked to capacity months in advance. Many guests are drawn to the lodge's incomparable combination of fine dining and majestic scenery, and they choose to return annually. It should be noted that their most expensive packages include a 5-course dinner, gourmet breakfast, horseback riding, and use of cruiser style bicycles. On the other end of the spectrum, American Alpine Club Climber's Ranch caters to rock climbers. It's affordable. And its location is exceptional, merely three miles south of Jenny Lake and four miles north of Park Headquarters. If it's a horseback riding vacation you're looking for, Triangle X Ranch offers horses and rides for all levels of rider. Additional ranch activities include cookouts, square dancing, trout fishing, and much more.

Driving

There are miles upon miles of roadways with strategically placed pullouts and picnic areas allowing motorists to enjoy the park's magnificence through their windshield. Beginning at the north end you'll encounter John D. Rockefeller, Jr. Memorial Parkway (NPS Unit connecting Grand Teton and Yellowstone). After entering the park, you'll skirt around Jackson Lake until Teton Park Road veers west of the Snake

Cascade Canyon

River and US-89/US-191/US-287 continues along its eastern shore. Teton Park Road follows the base of the Teton Range to Moose Junction. In between are side trips up Signal Mountain Road and one-way Jenny Lake Scenic Drive. As you approach Moose Junction you'll come across Moose–Wilson Road, which leads to fantastic hiking trails and Laurence S. Rockefeller Preserve. Views from US-26/US-89/US-191 on the east side of Snake River are equally amazing. We recommend exploring Schwabacher Landing or catching the sunset from Snake River Overlook (site of a well-known Ansel Adams photograph). If you'd rather let someone else do the driving, Alltrans (800.443.6133, jacksonholealltrans.com) offers full day (7 hours) bus tours for $245/adult.

Hiking

Spectacular views of the Teton Range and amazing hiking trails are everywhere. More than 230 miles of trails cross the flats of Jackson Hole, wind through picturesque canyons into the Teton Range, and weave their way to majestic mountaintops. Jenny Lake's postcard-perfect backdrops set the stage for a few of the park's most popular hiking trails: **Jenny Lake Loop, Hidden Falls Trail, Inspiration Point, and Cascade Canyon Trail**. (Extreme beauty also makes them four of the most heavily trafficked trails.) If you'd like to enjoy the sites with a little less walking, shorten these trails by taking a **shuttle boat** (307.734.9227, jennylakeboating.com) across Jenny Lake to the mouth of Cascade Canyon. The shuttle departs near Jenny Lake Visitor Center from mid-May through September, running every 10–15 minutes, starting at 7am during peak season (June–August). This shortcut—sparing your feet four miles of hiking—costs $18 (roundtrip) per adult and $10 for children. (Subtract four miles from Hidden Falls/Inspiration Point hikes if you take the boat.) Still,

Grand Teton Hiking Trails (Distances are roundtrip)

Name	Location (# on map)	Length	Difficulty Rating & Notes
Polecat Creek Loop	Flagg Ranch (1)	2.5 miles	E – Short, flat hike above a marsh
Flagg Canyon	Flagg Ranch (1)	4.0 miles	E – Out-and-back along Snake River
Lakeshore	Colter Bay (2)	2.0 miles	E – Views of Teton Range across Jackson Lake
Heron Pond & Swan Lake	Colter Bay (2)	3.0 miles	E – Hike to two ponds through bird habitat
Hermitage Point	Colter Bay (2)	9.7 miles	M – Long but easy hike to Jackson Lake shore
Lunch Tree Hill	Jackson Lake Lodge (3)	0.5 mile	E – Self-guiding trail overlooking Willow Flats
Christian Pond Loop	Jackson Lake Lodge (3)	3.3 miles	E – Nice loop to Teton views and pond
Two Ocean Lake	Two Ocean Lake (4)	6.4 miles	M – Trail loops around Two Ocean Lake
Emma Matilda Lake	Two Ocean Lake (4)	10.7 miles	M – Trail loops around Emma Matilda Lake
Signal Mountain	Signal Mountain (5)	6.8 miles	M – Hike to motorist-friendly summit
Leigh Lake - ⛵	Leigh Lake (6)	1.8 miles	E – Hike along String and Leigh Lake's shores
Bearpaw Lake - ⛵	Leigh Lake (6)	8.0 miles	M – Views of Mount Moran and alpine lakes
Holly Lake	Leigh Lake (6)	13.0 miles	S – Through Paintbrush Canyon to lake
String Lake	String Lake (6)	3.7 miles	E – Trail loops around the lake
Paintbrush–Cascade Loop/Lake Solitude - ⛵	String Lake (6)	19.2 miles	S – Phenomenal but difficult circuit to Lake Solitude (spur trails to Inspiration Point and Hidden Falls)
Jenny Lake Loop - ⛵	Jenny Lake (7)	7.1 miles	E – Trail follows the park's second largest lake
Hidden Falls - ⛵	Jenny Lake (7)	5.2 miles	M – Hike around Jenny Lake to 200-ft cascade
Inspiration Point	Jenny Lake (7)	6.0 miles	S – Past Hidden Falls overlooks Jenny Lake
Forks of Cascade Canyon	Jenny Lake (7)	13.6 miles	S – Excellent mountain views (popular)
South Fork Cascade	Jenny Lake (7)	24.8 miles	S – Leads to Schoolroom Glacier
Amphitheater Lake - ⛵	Lupine Meadows (8)	10.1 miles	S – Difficult but incredible hike to glacial lakes
Garnet Canyon - ⛵	Lupine Meadows (8)	8.4 miles	S – Hike through a Teton Range Canyon
Taggart Lake - ⛵	Taggart Lake (9)	3.0 miles	E – Hike across sagebrush flats
Taggart Lake–Beaver Creek	Taggart Lake (9)	3.9 miles	M – To Taggart Lake, returns via Beaver Creek
Taggart Lake–Bradley Lake	Taggart Lake (9)	5.9 miles	M – Very nice loop to two glacial lakes
Menors Ferry District - ⛵	Menors Ferry (10)	0.3 mile	E – Homesteaders lived here in 1894
Phelps Lake Overlook	Death Canyon (11)	2.0 miles	M – Climbs to an overlook of Phelps Lake
Phelps Lake Loop - ⛵	Death Canyon (11)	6.3 miles	M – Passes rock people jump off
Death Canyon–Static Peak	Death Canyon (11)	7.9 miles	S – To Phelps Lake and back to Death Canyon
Static Peak Divide	Death Canyon (11)	16.3 miles	S – A series of switchbacks leads to high ridge
Lake Creek–Woodland	Rockefeller Preserve (12)	3.1 miles	E – Loop leads to north shore of Phelps Lake
Aspen–Boulder Ridge	Rockefeller Preserve (12)	5.8 miles	M – Loop Reaches the shore of Phelps Lake
Phelps Lake Loop	Rockefeller Preserve (12)	6.6 miles	M – Travels around Phelps Lake
Granite Canyon	Trailhead/Tram (13, 14)	12.3 miles	M – Downhill from mountaintop to village
Marion Lake	Trailhead/Tram (13, 14)	11.8 miles	S – Follows Granite Creek to a pristine lake
Cabin Loop	Cunningham Cabin (15)	0.8 mile	E – Preserved historic homestead
Table Mountain - ⛵	Teton Canyon (16)	12.0 miles	S – Great views of Grand Teton

Difficulty Ratings: E = Easy, M = Moderate, S = Strenuous

with an early start, an ambitious hiker can complete the loop through Cascade Canyon (past Inspiration Point and Hidden Falls) to Lake Solitude and back to String Lake Trailhead via Paintbrush Canyon in a day without taking the boat. Another hiking option is to continue along the south fork of Cascade Canyon to Schoolroom Glacier at the park's western boundary (and then return as you came or continue up the north fork of Cascade Canyon to Lake Solitude and return via Paintbrush Canyon, time and energy permitting, of course).

Many of the park's features have been named accurately, like Surprise and Amphitheater Lakes. Others, I'm sure were accurate at one time, but you'll almost always have company hiking to Lake Solitude. The trails through Paintbrush and Cascade Canyons continue to increase in popularity. We aren't talking shoulder-to-shoulder traffic, but you're going to run into similarly adventurous hikers along the way. It's a great, albeit slightly challenging hike, so why shouldn't a lot of people enjoy it?

There's more beyond the tourism hubs centered on Jenny and Jackson Lakes. **Emma Matilda Lake and Two Ocean Lake Trails** can be combined to make a large 13.2-mile loop around the lakes. To see what the area looked like in the early 20th century when hardy homesteaders were moving in, hike around **Menor's Ferry Historic District** or take the short **Cunningham Cabin Loop**. Or drive down to Death Canyon Trailhead on Moose–Wilson Road. Solitude is not a common commodity at Grand Teton during peak season. Parking areas at popular trailheads like Jenny Lake, String and Leigh Lakes, Lupine Meadows, Death Canyon, and Granite Canyon fill early. Although there is extra parking along the road at Jenny Lake, Taggart Lake, and Lupine Meadows. At sites like Rockefeller Preserve (Phelps Lake), one car parks when one car leaves. Get up and get going on your vacation. Not only will you score a parking space, but you'll be able to watch the Tetons light up with the first rays of sunlight. If you get a later start, obey the posted parking regulations.

🏃🏕 Backpacking

Many of the listed hikes can be combined into multi-day backpacking loops, which are ideal treks. Loops eliminate repeating scenery, arranging a shuttle service, or using multiple cars. From String Lake Trailhead (Trailhead # 7) backpackers can combine Cascade Canyon and Paintbrush Canyon Trails to make a 19.2-mile loop to Lake Solitude (extend it through the south fork of Cascade Canyon with an out-and-back to Schoolroom Glacier). If you're a little wary of being

Phelps Lake

in the backcountry alone this is a good option as it's quite busy in summer. The loop passes Hidden Falls, Inspiration Point, Lake Solitude, and Holly Lake. Alternatively, from Granite Canyon Parking Area (Trailhead # 14) backpackers can hike a 19.3-mile loop, the Granite Canyon and Open Canyon Circuit via Valley Trail. Hikers looking to add a few more miles should continue past the junction on Open Canyon Trail to Marion Lake. And Teton Crest Trail (which includes Cascade Canyon–Paintbrush Canyon Trails) is one of the classic backpacking routes in all the national parks.

There are more than 230 miles of hiking trails here and many more extend beyond park boundaries. The wilderness is to be explored, but it must also be respected. Permits are required for all overnight stays in the backcountry. Walk-in permits are available no more than one day before the start of your trip at Jenny Lake Ranger Station, and Craig Thomas and Colter Bay Visitor Centers for $35. Reservations are accepted for one-third of all designated backcountry sites (and group sites). Reserve your site at recreation.gov for a one-time $45 reservation fee (from early January to mid-May). Even if you reserve your permit, you still must pick it up at Craig Thomas or Colter Bay Visitor Center, or Jenny Lake Ranger Station before 10am the day of your trip. Any permit involving camping in Garnet Canyon, climbing, or mountaineering must be picked up at Jenny Lake Ranger Station. If you aren't going to use a permit, cancel it so someone else can.

Always travel with a good topographic map. Always err on the side of caution when planning your trip, and deciding how much ground you can cover in a day. Be sure to consider the ability of every member of your group and the weight of your pack. Snow cover can persist in the high country well into summer; prospective hikers must carry (and know how to use) an ice axe

Chapel of the Transfiguration (Menor's Ferry)

if they wish to pass these regions. It's also bear country. Food must be stored in approved, portable bear-proof canisters. Canisters are available to check out from ranger stations and visitor centers.

Boating & Floating

Grand Teton National Park provides an incredible array of water adventures. **Float trips** down the winding Snake River are a peaceful way to enjoy mountain vistas and view wildlife. The standard ten-mile route is offered by many of the park's lodging facilities: Grand Teton Lodge Company (307.543.2811, gtlc. com, $80/adult, $55/child), Signal Mountain Lodge (307.543.2831, signalmountainlodge.com), Triangle X Ranch (307.733.5500, trianglex.com, $82/62), and Lost Creek Ranch (included in lodging rate). Barker Ewing Float Trips (307.733.1800, barkerewing.com, $80/50) and Solitude Float Trips (307.733.2871, grand-teton-scenic-floats.com, $80/60) are also authorized park outfitters. These trips cover ten of the most picturesque miles of water you'll ever see. Grand Teton looms in the background for the entire three-hour journey. Trips are generally available from mid-May until late September. To make things confusing, Barker Ewing (by Jackson Hole Whitewater) (307.733.1000, barker-ewing.com) offers a scenic float & whitewater combo ($167/145) outside of the park from mid-June through mid-August. Yes, it's the same name, different company.

You can make the same float trip on your own. All you have to do is launch your craft at Deadman's Bar Road and take out at Moose Landing. This stretch of water is not especially technical or treacherous and current is generally gentle as you wind your way across Jackson Hole. As long as you have some paddling experience and can read the river to stay in the main channel, you should be fine. You may encounter eddies, bars,

and the occasional downed tree, but, again, it isn't anything that wild. Water volume changes, so if you don't like what you see, don't put your boat in the water. There are other paddling options. If you want **flatwater**, String and Jenny Lakes are great. You can also paddle Jackson, Phelps, Emma Matilda, Two Ocean, Taggart, Bradley, Bearpaw, and Leigh Lakes. Rendezvous River Sports (307.733.2471, jacksonholekayak. com) offers multi-day paddling trips of Jackson Lake and the Snake River for about $999/person for a 3-day trip. Motorboats are only allowed on Jenny (10hp max) and Jackson Lakes. If you bring your own watercraft (including SUPs), you must obtain a non-motorized boat permit ($12/season) and an Aquatic Invasive Species inspection ($5 WY residents, $15 non-residents). Motorized boats also require permits ($40/season) and AIS inspection ($10 WY, $30 non-residents).

If you don't have your own boat or you'd rather leave it at home, **canoe or kayak rental** is available from Jenny Lake Boating (307.734.9227, jennylakeboating. com), Grand Teton Lodge Co (307.543.2811, gtlc.com), and Signal Mountain Lodge (307.543.2831, signalmtnlodge.com). Rentals are available for use at Jenny or Jackson Lake on a first-come, first-served basis for $20–40 per hour. Signal Mountain Marina also provides fishing boats ($42/hour), pontoon boats ($115/hour), and deck cruisers ($145/hour) for rent. Grand Teton Lodging Company also offers scenic cruises of Jackson Lake that are exceptional. They'll even feed you breakfast, lunch, or dinner along the way. Cruises depart daily from late May through late September and cost anywhere from $40–74 per adult.

Biking

Biking is permitted on all park roads. Pedaling is relatively easy because most roads cross the flat expanse of Jackson Hole rather than working their way into the mountains, rewarding cyclists with beautiful mountain landscapes without all the heavy cranking. Roads are often crowded (especially in summer), but early morning or late evening and off-season rides can be splendid. The Multi-Use Pathway (designed for bikers, rollerbladers, and walkers) runs from Jackson to Jenny Lake (it opens for the season as soon as weather allows it, and staff has time to run a sweeper down it). Teton Park Road is recommended for road cyclists, and the 52-mile unpaved Grassy Lake Road (Ashton–Flagg Ranch Road) is a hot-spot for mountain bikers (but it's not single track). Adventure Sports (307.733.2415, dornans.com) at Dornan's Spur Ranch provides bike rental for $16 (hour), $38 (half-day), or $44 (24 hours). (They also rent kayaks and SUPs.)

Horseback Riding

Dude ranches are alive-and-well here. In fact, business ranches are often booked months in advance. These ranches are hardly inexpensive, but horse enthusiasts seeking "all-you-can-ride" accommodations will not find a better destination in the National Park System. Triangle X Ranch (307.733.2183, trianglex.com) offers an all-inclusive modern western adventure for $2,057+ per person per week. Lost Creek Ranch (307.733.3435, lostcreek.com) offers an all-inclusive package for $13,900 for up to 4 people per week. (Additional guests, taxes, alcohol, spa treatments, rodeo tickets, skeet shooting, transportation for non-Lost Creek activities, and other activities cost extra. And tips are not included.) Heart Six Ranch (307.543.2477, heartsix.com), located outside the park near the south entrance to Yellowstone National Park offers all-inclusive dude ranch experiences, and they also offer multi-day pack trips into Yellowstone (starting at $1,155 per person for a 3-day trip). They offer the standard fare like float trips, fly fishing, and driving tours, as well as snowmobiling (half-day to week-long tours) and dog-sledding in winter. A more affordable alternative for the horse enthusiast is to take a **trail or wagon ride** provided by Grand Teton Lodge Company (307.543.2811, gtlc.com) at Colter Bay Village, Jackson Lake Lodge or Headwaters Lodge & Resort, which costs $48–80 (1–2 hours). Pony Rides ($5) are also available at Jackson Lake Lodge. Horseback riding is also available at Jenny Lake Lodge, but only to their guests. Regardless how you do it, this is a great place to ride a horse.

Rock Climbing & Mountaineering

Grand Teton has plenty of granite to go around. It's one of the premier rock climbing parks, drawing climbers from all around the world. Everyone from beginners to experts will find routes suitable to their ability level. A climbing permit is not required unless you plan on an overnight trip. Check the park's climbing and backcountry website at tetonclimbing.blogspot.com for additional information, routes, and conditions. Information can also be obtained at Jenny Lake Ranger Station in-person or on the phone by calling (307) 739-3343 in summer and (307) 739-3309 in winter. Exum Mountain Guides (307.733.2297, exumguides.com) and Jackson Hole Mountain Guides (307.733.4979, jhmg.com) offer guided rock climbing classes for about $225 per person (group pricing must reach a minimum # of people). They'll also take you out for day climbs or summit adventures (like climbing to the top of the mighty Grand Teton!) matched to your ability level. While you don't need to hire a guide to climb the Grand Teton, ropes are required (and comfort/experience with exposure.)

Grand sunsets

Fishing

50 miles of the 1,056-mile-long Snake River and more than 100 alpine lakes provide ample opportunity for anglers searching for the catch of the day. Fishermen must follow Wyoming regulations and licensing requirements. Licenses are available at Colter Bay Marina, Signal Mountain Lodge, and Dornan's Fly Shop. Grand Fishing Adventures (307.734.9684, grandfishing.com, $475/half-day), Grand Teton Fly Fishing (307.690.0910, $575/half-day), Snake River Angler (307.733.3699, snakeriverangler.com, offers, lessons, fly-tying, and rental equipment), Grand Teton Lodge Company (307.543.2811, gtlc.com, $525/half-day), and Triangle X Ranch (307.733.2183, trianglex.com, $495/half-day) can help get you out on the water to catch some fish. Lost Creek Ranch also leads fishing trips but exclusively for their guests.

Winter Activities

A few park lodges remain open during winter. It's quite the contrast from summer when lodges are filled to capacity and parking spots are hard to come by. Cars and visitors may be few and far between, but activities are everywhere. The best way to explore the park in winter is with the aid of a set of **cross-country skis or snowshoes**. Moose–Wilson, Signal Mountain, and Teton Park roads close in winter, providing a proper surface for skiers and snowshoers. Phelps Lake Overlook, Jenny Lake Trail, Taggart Lake/Beaver Creek Loop, Swan Lake–Heron Pond Loop, and Polecat Creek Loop are popular ski/snowshoe trails. If you don't want to explore the Tetons on your own, you can join a park ranger for a guided snowshoe trek. Trips usually take place from late December to mid-March and depart from Craig Thomas Discovery & Visitor Center. Each year, reservations can be made starting in December by calling (307) 739-3399. These excursions are free, but a donation is recommended.

Schwabacher Landing

Grand Teton Visitor and Information Centers

Name	Location	Open	Notes
Craig Thomas Discovery & Visitor Center (307.739.3399)	In Moose, 0.5-mile west of Moose Junction on Teton Park Road	March–October Daily from 9am–5pm Extended hours in summer	Primary Visitor Center, boat and backcountry permits available
Jenny Lake Visitor Center (307.739.3392)	On Teton Park Road, 8 miles north of Moose Junction	mid-May–late September Daily from 8am–5pm Extended hours in summer	Boat permits available
Jenny Lake Ranger Station (307.739.3343)	On Teton Park Road, 8 miles north of Moose Junction	June–early September Daily from 9am–5pm	Rock climbing info and backcountry permits available
Colter Bay Visitor Center & Indian Arts Museum (307.739.3594)	On Highway 89/191/287, 0.5-mile west of Colter Bay Junction	mid-May–mid-October Daily from 9am–5pm Extended hours in summer	Boat and backcountry permits available, museum tours
Flagg Ranch Information Station (307.543.2372)	On Highway 89/191/287, 16 miles north of Colter Bay	early June–early Sept Daily from 9am–4pm	Info on John D. Rockefeller, Jr. Memorial Parkway
Laurence S. Rockefeller Preserve Center (307.739.3654)	On Moose-Wilson Road, 4 miles south of Moose	June–late September Daily from 9am–5pm	Interactive exhibits, sales and permits are not available

Some areas of the park allow **snowmobiling**. It's a somewhat controversial due to the noise and air pollution, but it's fun. Contact a visitor center for current information. **Backcountry skiing and snowboarding** are allowed within the park, and many of its lakes are open for ice fishing. Heart Six Ranch (307.543.2477, heartsix.com) will take you snowmobiling ($302.50/half-day) or dogsledding ($489.25 to learn to mush). Triangle X Ranch (307.733.2183, trianglex.com) also typically opens for winter (2020 was an atypical year). It's the only in-park lodge open for winter.

Visitor Centers

Craig Thomas Discovery & Visitor Center is a modern facility, where you can peruse the exhibits, get backcountry permits, talk to a ranger, watch a short film, or shop at the bookstore. It's a great place to begin your trip to Grand Teton. **Laurence S. Rockefeller Preserve Center** is filled with unusual exhibits, but its parking area is more often used for the area's hiking trails, including the popular Phelps Lake Loop. Recently-renovated **Jenny Lake Visitor Center** is a popular departure location for ranger-led activities, and a good place to pick up permits, get general information, browse a few exhibits, shop at the bookstore, or use the restrooms. **Colter Bay Visitor Center** offers friendly staff, exhibits, a short film, permits, a bookstore, and restrooms. At the northern end of the park, you'll find **Flagg Ranch Information Station**, which is a small, staffed building, where you can get basic information and purchase maps or souvenirs.

Ranger Programs & For Kids

It probably seems like it costs a fortune to experience the Tetons, but the best way to discover them is free. Join a park ranger on one of their guided programs! They are often enjoyable for children and adults. From June until early September, you'll find a variety of programs offered in and around the park's visitor centers and Laurance S. Rockefeller Preserve.

Activities range from a 30-minute talk about the park's biology to a 3-hour ramble on a trail. There are also campfire programs, a boat cruise, museum tours, and all sorts of walks and talks. The hike to Hidden Falls from Jenny Lake can be enhanced by joining a ranger on a first-come, first-served basis for the first 25 hikers. They take Jenny Lake Boat Shuttle (307.734.9227, jennylakeboating.com) to shorten the hike, so show up prepared with your shuttle token ($18 round-trip/$10 one-way for adults, $10/$8 for children ages 2–11). There are dozens of programs. To get a current schedule of activities you'll have to visit the park's

Lake Solitude

website or stop in at any visitor center. So, for your trip to the Tetons, don't fret if the commercial excursions aren't in your budget, there's always a park ranger available to take you on an adventure in this natural wonderland.

Children like the Tetons. They'll enjoy just about everything: floating Snake River, paddling Jenny Lake, watching wildlife, joining a park ranger on a guided tour, and much more. In addition to child-oriented ranger activities, the park offers a Junior Ranger Program. Children of all ages can participate in this unique program exploring the wonders of Grand Teton. Upon completion of the Junior Ranger Activity Booklet (available online or at a visitor center), return to a visitor center so your child can be christened as the park's newest Junior Ranger and receive a badge.

Flora & Fauna

More than 1,000 species of vascular plants inhabit Grand Teton National Park, including 900 flowering species. The park's forests are mostly coniferous, with whitebark pine, limber pine, subalpine fir, and Englemann spruce capable of surviving at elevations up to 10,000 feet. Lodgepole pine, Douglas fir, and blue spruce are found closer to the valley floor where the soil is deep enough to support tree growth. A smaller sampling of deciduous trees resides along rivers and lakeshores.

Seeing the park's wildlife in its natural environment is just as enthralling as a brilliant Teton sunset. Moose, bear, and elk are the most popular residents, but there are 61 mammals inhabiting the park. Bison, pronghorn, and mule deer are often seen grazing along the roadside. Motorists should pass with caution as some of these animals have become indifferent to traffic. Car accidents kill more than 100 large mammals each year at Grand Teton.

Delta Lake

Pets & Accessibility

Pets are permitted but must be kept on a leash (less than six feet). They are prohibited from all hiking trails, pathways, visitor centers, other public buildings, and the backcountry. They are not allowed to swim in the park either. Pets are allowed at campgrounds, picnic areas, and parking lots.

All visitor centers are wheelchair accessible. In-park lodges have accessible rooms. Accessible campsites are available at Gros Ventre, Jenny Lake, Colter Bay, and Headwaters. The Multi-use Pathway and South Jenny Lake Trail are accessible paved trails. Colter Bay, Jackson Lake Dam, Laurance S. Rockefeller Preserve, Menor's Ferry Historic District, and String Lake are other areas of the park suggested for wheelchairs users. Most ranger programs are accessible.

Weather

Most visitors arrive between May and September. Jackson Hole has a semi-arid climate, receiving about 20 inches of precipitation annually, fairly evenly distributed. No matter what time of year, it's best to wear multiple layers of clothing while exploring the park. Temperatures change with wind, elevation, and time of day, and afternoon thunderstorms are common.

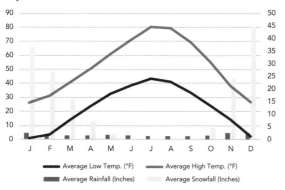

Tips & Recommendations

The Teton Range is one of the most iconic landscapes in the country, and many visitors come to see it, particularly during the busy summer season. Places like Jenny Lake can become uncomfortably busy to many guests. Have a backup plan for when that happens. The best bet is to simply move on. If there are too many people at Jenny Lake, head to Jackson Lake. Snake River Overlook is full, stop at Glacier View Turnout down the road. While it may not feel like it at times, the park is big enough for everyone. And, if you really would like to enjoy a more peaceful experience, visit after Labor Day or wake up before the sun.

About 95% of visitors arrive from May through October. The park is open all year, and you can find in-park lodging at Triangle X Ranch in winter. Winter provides some of the most memorable moments for park-goers, but you have to come prepared for shorter days and freezing cold. Do this and you can really enjoy those afternoon highs in the 30s°F.

Another great way to shake the crowds is to join an outfitter on a rafting/floating, fishing, or horseback trip.

If you're primary destination is Yellowstone and you're considering a daytrip to Grand Teton, recalibrate your thinking and spend at least one night. Drive in for a look, and you're guaranteed to be driving away wishing you had more time (of course you could come back?).

For anyone thinking about hiking Cascade Canyon/Paintbrush Canyon Loop to Lake Solitude, Paintbrush Canyon is prettier and steeper. Many hikers choose to hike the loop counterclockwise to have the sun at your back hiking up Paintbrush Canyon (and getting the view of Lake Solitude from above earlier in the day), but it's pretty darn good either way (as long as you're watching the weather and prepared for any conditions you might encounter). Just be sure to get an early start if you're doing it as a day hike.

Along the way to Surprise and Amphitheater Lakes is an unmarked spur trail to Delta Lake. It's unreal but the trail is extreme and not maintained. You cross boulder fields and scale steep sandy/muddy slopes. I'm not sure what the park's stance is, so I'll leave it to you to find the trail junction if that's something you're interested in (there are plenty of sources).

Everyone goes ga-ga for Teton views, but Mount Moran is no slouch. Be sure to spend some time around (or on) Jackson Lake too.

There are two parking areas near the end of the road to Schwabacher Landing. Most people drive to the end. The other spot is beautiful too.

Taking the 100-passenger aerial tram at Jackson Hole Mountain Resort (jacksonhole.com) to the top of Rendezvous Mountain is an easy way to climb a mountain.

Easy Hikes: Jenny Lake Loop (7.1 miles), Leigh Lake (1.8), Menor's Ferry (0.3), Taggart Lake (3)
Moderate Hikes: Phelps Lake Loop (6.3 miles), Hidden Falls (5.2), Bearpaw Lake (8)
Strenuous Hikes: Delta Lake (Extreme, ~9 miles), Lake Solitude Loop (19.2), Amphitheater Lake (10.1), Table Mountain (12), Garnet Canyon (8.4)
Family Activities: Float the Snake River, become a Junior Ranger, ride the aerial tram at Jackson Hole Mountain Resort (jacksonhole.com), rent a boat at Jackson Lake, stay at a dude ranch, bike the Multi-Use Pathway, give rock climbing a try
Guided Tours: Float the Snake River, ride a horse across Jackson Hole, climb the Tetons
Rainy Day Activities: Chase waterfalls by car, stop in at the visitor centers, spend a few hours in Jackson, check out the Indian Arts Museum in Colter Bay
History Enthusiasts: Mormon Row, Menor's Ferry, Cunningham Cabin

Take my picture (moose at Gros Ventre)

Sunset Spots: Mormon Row, Snake River Overlook, Schwabacher Landing, Chapel of the Transfiguration
Sunrise Spots: Any of the locations above, Signal Mountain Lodge, Jenny Lake, pretty much anywhere with a clear view of the Teton Range (bonus points if you find some reflective water or interesting foreground subjects—like found at the listed sunset spots)
Wildlife: Moose–Wilson Rd, Antelope or Willow Flats

Beyond the Park...

Dining
Miazga's • (307) 733-2784
399 W Broadway, Jackson
miazgas.com

Glorietta • (307) 733-3888
242 Glenwood St, Jackson
gloriettajackson.com

Coelette • (307) 201-5026
85 S King St, Jackson
coelette.com

Hand Fire Pizza • (307) 733-7199
120 N Cache St, Jackson
handfirepizza.com

China Fun • (307) 734-8988
826 W Broadway, Jackson
chinafun.kwickmenu.com

Persephone Bakery • (307) 200-6708
145 E Broadway Ave, Jackson
persephonebakery.com

Grocery Stores
Albertsons • (307) 733-5950
105 Buffalo Way, Jackson

Smith's • (307) 733-8908
1425 US-89, Jackson

Lodging
Huff House Inn • (307) 733-7141
240 E Deloney Ave, Jackson
huffhousejh.com

Rusty Parrot Lodge
175 N Jackson St, Jackson
rustyparrot.com • (307) 733-2000

Sassy Moose Inn • (307) 413-4110
3895 Miles Rd, Wilson
sassymoose.com

Teton View B&B • (307) 733-7954
2136 Coyote Loop, Wilson
tetonview.com

Campgrounds
Snake River RV Village
9705 US-89, Jackson • (307) 733-7078
snakeriverrvpark.com

Virginian RV Park • (307) 733-7189
750 W Broadway, Jackson
virginianlodge.com

Bridger-Teton National Forest
Granite Hot Springs and Camp, plus additional camping just east of Grand Teton
fs.usda.gov

Attractions
National Elk Refuge • (307) 733-9212
Animal habitat and hunting
675 E Broadway • fws.gov

Bridger-Teton National Forest
Wind River Range is one of the best backpacking destinations in the country—Patagonia vibes— there's also good day-hiking, paddling, and just sightseeing

Shoshone National Forest
2-million-acre wilderness with an abundance of waterfalls and alpine lakes

Sinks Canyon State Park
Interesting site in the Wind River Mountains where the Pop Agie River disappears into a limestone cavern
3079 Sinks Canyon Rd, Lander
sinkscanyonstatepark.org

Teton Mountain Bike Tours
tetonmtbike.com • (307) 733-0712

Wilderness Trails • (307) 733-5171
Horseback trips, big game hunts
wildernesstrailsinc.com

Mill Iron Ranch • (307) 733-6390
Horses, hunting, sleigh rides
3495 E Horse Creek Rd, Jackson
millironranch.net

Scenic Safaris • (307) 734-8898
scenic-safaris.com • *Winter Tours*

Lewis & Clark River Expeditions
lewisandclarkriverrafting.com

Jackson Hole Rodeo
Bi-weekly rodeos from Memorial Day through Labor Day
jhrodeo.com • (307) 733-9727

Jackson Hole Rafting & Whitewater
jhww.com • (800) 700-7238

Buffalo Roam Tours • (307) 413-0954
buffaloroamtours.com

Vintage Adventures • (307) 732-2628
Sleigh rides, tipis, boat tours
woodboattours.com

Craters of the Moon National Mon
Stark, otherworldly landscape of past lava flows
US-26, Arco, ID • (208) 527-1300
nps.gov/crmo

Yellowstone

Phone: (307) 344-7381
Website: nps.gov/yell

Established: March 1, 1872
Size: 2,221,766 Acres
Annual Visitors: 4 Million
Peak Season: July–August
Hiking Trails: 900+ Miles

Activities: Hiking, Backpacking, Boating, Horseback Riding, Biking, Swimming, Fishing, Photography, Snowmobiling, Snowcoach Tours, Snowshoeing, Cross-country Skiing

12 Campgrounds: $15–35
9 Lodges: $109–1,126
10 Visitor Centers/Ranger Stations
Backcountry Camping: Permitted*

Park Hours: All day, every day
Entrance Fee: $35/30/20
(car/motorcycle/individual)

*Must obtain a permit in-person no more than 48 hours prior to departure or select sites are available for reservations ($25 application fee)

Long after Americans reached the Pacific Ocean, explorers, fur trappers, and frontiersmen began filling in blank spots left on maps between the East and West Coasts. In the 1850s—before Wyoming became a state—one of these unmapped regions was reported as a rugged wilderness of boiling mud, steaming rivers, and petrified birds. Such reports were promptly disregarded as myth in the East, colorful yarns spun by colorful men, and publishers curtly responded, "We do not print fiction." Still, these landscapes captured the curiosity of several expedition parties. In 1871, the U.S. government deployed the Hayden Geological Survey to uncover the truth. Ferdinand V. Hayden, painter Thomas Moran, and photographer William Henry Jackson were sent to assess what really existed. Less than one year later, President Ulysses S. Grant signed the Act of Dedication, effectively making Yellowstone the world's first national park. This large tract of land in northwestern Wyoming Territory, barely extending into Montana and Idaho Territories, was set aside, preserved for the enjoyment of the people. Much like the area's first explorers, today's visitors come across steaming rivers, towering waterfalls dropping into deep canyons, bubbling mud-pots, hot spring terraces, and boiling water gushing from the earth. Sights so amazing they inspire the same disbelief of 19th-century publishers and politicians. But it is real. Guests can see it. Touch it. Smell it. It is Yellowstone.

The first people known to have explored this land called Yellowstone were Native Americans. Discovery of obsidian arrowheads dating back 11,000 years suggests they hunted here shortly after glaciers from the last great ice age receded. By the time of the Lewis and Clark Expedition in 1805, trappers had already named the river "Roche Jaune"

Grand Prismatic Spring

N. P. Langford became the park's first superintendent (allowing him to sign his name "National Park Langford"). It was not a glamorous position. He was denied salary, funding, and staff. Without resources to protect the park, it was vulnerable to poachers, vandals, and others seeking to raid its resources. Philetus Norris was appointed as Yellowstone's second superintendent, and first to receive a salary. Although meager, he received enough funding to begin construction on a system of roads and to hire Henry Yount as gamekeeper. Yount is widely regarded as the first park ranger, but he resigned when it was obvious the job of preventing poaching and vandalism was far too great a task for one man.

Protecting the park would only become more difficult as tourism increased. Completion of the Northern Pacific Railroad line to Livingston, MT and the park's northern entrance had dramatic results. Visitation increased from 300 in 1872 to more than 5,000 in 1883. The railroad sought to develop the area's prime locations with help from an amiable superintendent named Rufus Hatch. Under Hatch's leadership, trash was discarded in streams and fumaroles, tourists were charged exorbitant amounts, animals were killed for food, trees were chopped for construction, and coal was mined from park land. America's first and only national park was being exploited by visitors, developers, poachers, and its stewards. Many Americans believed Hatch was destroying the park. To prove this point, Civil War hero General Phillip Sheridan invited President Chester A. Arthur to join him on a Yellowstone camping trip. The first Presidential visit led to legislation appropriating $40,000 for the park, regulating Hatch's development, and allowing the Secretary of the Interior to summon troops to prevent vandalism and hunting. A more imposing presence than one ranger.

To protect the country's last free-roaming bison herd, General Sheridan and Troop M of the 1st United States Cavalry, summoned by order of the Secretary of the Interior, rode to the rescue. Their temporary residence lasted 32 years, during which they built structures, enforced regulations, oversaw construction of Roosevelt Arch, and created many of the management principles adopted by the National Park Service when it assumed control in 1918. More than half a century after its establishment, the park idea was beginning to take shape. It was a long and arduous journey to form a park that is truly "for the Benefit and Enjoyment of the People," as Roosevelt Arch states, but this too has become as real as the yarn-spinners' tales of bubbling mud, towering geysers, and golden canyons.

or "Yellow Stone" in English, referring to yellow sandstones found along the river's banks. They didn't come up with the name. Its carried over from the Minnetaree tribe who called it "Mi tse a-da-zi" or "Rock Yellow River." In 1806, John Colter left Lewis and Clark's Expedition to work for the Missouri Fur Company, exploring the regions comprising present-day Yellowstone and Grand Teton National Parks. He is believed to be the first white man to see Yellowstone Lake, at least one geyser, and the Teton Range. While Lewis and Clark would have believed Colter's accounts, many jokingly referred to the land of boiling mudpots and steaming rivers as "Colter's Hell."

Few explorers ventured into Colter's Hell until 1871, when Hayden's Geological Survey explored the region. During the expedition, a party member suggested the area should be set aside as a national park. Hayden agreed and became the most enthusiastic and devoted advocate of this newly conceived park idea. His report declared the land unsuitable for farming because of its high elevation. Mining was impossible because of its volcanic origins. These findings combined with images and paintings collected during the expedition were enough to convince Congress to withdraw this region from public auction. On March 1, 1872, President Grant signed a law creating Yellowstone National Park, the first of its kind anywhere in the world.

When to Go

Yellowstone is open all year, but the park receives nearly one million visitors per month in summer. Visiting in September or October is a nice alternative. It's less crowded, wildlife is active, and the weather is decent (although temperamental). About 120,000 people visit the park each winter to see an enchanting wonderland created by the combination of snow and geothermal features. Mammoth Campground is open all year. Year-round lodging is available at Old Faithful and Mammoth Hot Springs. North and Northeast Entrance provide the only year-round access to wheeled vehicles. All other entrances close, allowing roads to be groomed for the winter season. The road between North and Northeast Entrances and the road from Mammoth Hot Springs to the parking area at Upper Terraces are the only roads plowed for wheeled vehicles during winter. All interior roads can only be accessed by over-snow vehicles in winter. The open/close dates for over-snow vehicle roads are subject to change based on the amount of snowfall. Park entrances are closed once again in late March or early April to clear roads for the upcoming summer season.

Transportation & Airports

Public transportation is available to several gateway cities. Visitors can reach West Yellowstone aboard a bus/shuttle from Salt Lake City (208.656.8824, saltlakeexpress.com). Yellowstone Roadrunner (406.640.0631, yellowstoneroadrunner.com) provides airport shuttle, taxi, and van service. Currently, the park does not provide a public shuttle to explore its 142-mile Grand Loop Road.

Yellowstone Regional (COD) in Cody, WY is close to the East (27 miles) and Northeast Entrances (76 miles). Jackson Hole Airport (JAC), located in Grand Teton National Park, is about 50 miles from the Southern Entrance. Gallatin Field (BZN) just outside Bozeman, MT, is about 90 miles from the North Entrance. Billings' Logan International (BIL) is 67 miles from the Northeast Entrance. Idaho Falls Regional (IDA) is about 110 miles from the West Entrance. Between June and early September, Yellowstone Airport, (WYS) located in West Yellowstone, MT, is serviced from Salt Lake City International Airport (SCL) in Utah.

Directions

Yellowstone is huge. It's larger than the states of Delaware and Rhode Island combined. Five roads lead into the park: one from each side, and another from the northeast corner. Current road conditions are available by calling (307) 344-2117. Below you'll find short descriptions of traveling directions to each entrance from the nearest major city.

North Entrance (40 miles from Livingston, MT): From I-90, take Exit 333 near Livingston, MT for US-89 S toward City Center/Yellowstone. Turn onto US-89 S. Drive about 52 miles through Gardiner, MT, under Roosevelt Arch, and into the park's North Entrance.

West Entrance (108 miles from Idaho Falls, ID): From Idaho Falls (I-15), take US-20 E more than 100 miles to West Yellowstone, MT. Turn left at US-191 S/US-20 E/US-287 S/Yellowstone Ave, which leads across the Montana–Wyoming border and into the park.

South Entrance (57 miles from Jackson, WY): You'll take a very scenic highway (US-191 N/US-287 N/US-89 N/John D. Rockefeller, Jr. Parkway) about 38 miles north through Grand Teton National Park to South Entrance. (Remember to spend time in the Tetons.)

East Entrance (52 miles from Cody, WY): Take US-14 W/US-16 W/US-20 W/Sheridan Avenue (following signs to Yellowstone) about 25 miles west to the park entrance. (This route is gorgeous, too.)

Northeast Entrance (81 miles from Cody): Take WY-120/Depot Rd north about 16 miles. Turn left at Chief Joseph Hwy/WY-296, which turns into Crandall Road then Dead Indian Hill Road, and finally Sunlight Basin Road before intersecting with US-212 W/Beartooth Highway (closed seasonally). Turn left onto Beartooth Highway to Cooke City and Northeast Entrance (also very beautiful).

Go where the buffalo roam

Developed Areas

Yellowstone has eight developed areas centered on the most breathtaking natural attractions. Each area is located on or near Grand Loop Road (GLR). GLR forms a giant figure-8 connecting all five entrances.

Mammoth Hot Springs: Located just 5 miles from the North Entrance, you'll find spectacular terraces formed of travertine (calcium carbonate—the main ingredient in heartburn relief tablets). Lodging, dining, gas, campground, post office, shopping, visitor center, and medical station are available.

Tower–Roosevelt: Located at the NE corner of GLR, you'll find Petrified Tree, Specimen Ridge, Tower Fall, and some of the best hiking trails. Lodging, camping, store, and gas are available.

Canyon Village: Located near GLR's center, this is one of the most popular regions, including Grand Canyon of the Yellowstone. Gas, lodging, dining, store, visitor center, and showers are available.

Norris: Situated opposite Canyon Village at the center of GLR is Norris, the oldest and hottest thermal area, and home to Steamboat, the world's tallest geyser. Camping and Park Ranger Museum are available.

Madison: Located southwest of Norris, where Madison and Firehole Rivers converge. Thermal features, a 75–80°F swimming hole just below Firehole Falls, campground, and information station are available.

Old Faithful: Iconic Old Faithful is located in Upper Geyser Basin (southwest corner of GLR). Nearby is Midway Geyser Basin (Grand Prismatic Spring). Just about everything is available at Old Faithful Village (except a campground).

West Thumb & Grant Village: At the southern end of GLR is West Thumb Geyser Basin on Yellowstone Lake. Campground, store, lodging, showers, gas, and visitor center are available.

Fishing Bridge, Lake Village, & Bridge Bay: At the north end of Yellowstone Lake, Fishing Bridge is a popular place to watch cutthroat trout, but fishing is banned. An RV park, gas, store, and dining are available at Fishing Bridge. You will find lodging, dining, medical station, store, and a Ranger Station at Lake Village. Bridge bay has a campground and marina.

Lost in the Park

In 1870, Truman C. Everts joined an expedition exploring present-day Yellowstone. At Yellowstone Lake, Everts wandered away from the group. After being lost for two days, his horse ran away. Left with little more than the clothes on his back, Everts began walking aimlessly. A month passed without success from the expedition's search attempts; they decided to complete their work and return East to confirm the existence of "Colter's Hell" and spread word of the unfortunate predicament of their companion.

Everts's situation worsened when he broke through brittle ground while crossing a geyser basin, scalding his hip. Next, he managed to start a fire with an opera glass, only to severely burn his hands. Consuming only elk thistle, he withered away to skin and bones. A full 37 days after his separation, a man, no more than 50 pounds, was spotted crawling along a hillside. Incoherent but alive, Everts was able to make a full recovery and later pen the book *Thirty-Seven Days in Peril*. His adventure created considerable publicity for Yellowstone and helped create the world's first national park. He was even given the opportunity to be its first superintendent. (Not surprisingly, he declined.) Today, the legend lives on. Elk thistle is called Everts Thistle and a 7,831-ft peak in northwestern Wyoming is named Mount Everts.

Don't expect to be rewarded for getting lost. It's a huge inconvenience, not only to you, but to park staff. Be prepared. Carry a compass and quality map. GPS users should know how to use it and carry extra batteries. Plan your route, stay on marked trails, and always keep track of your group.

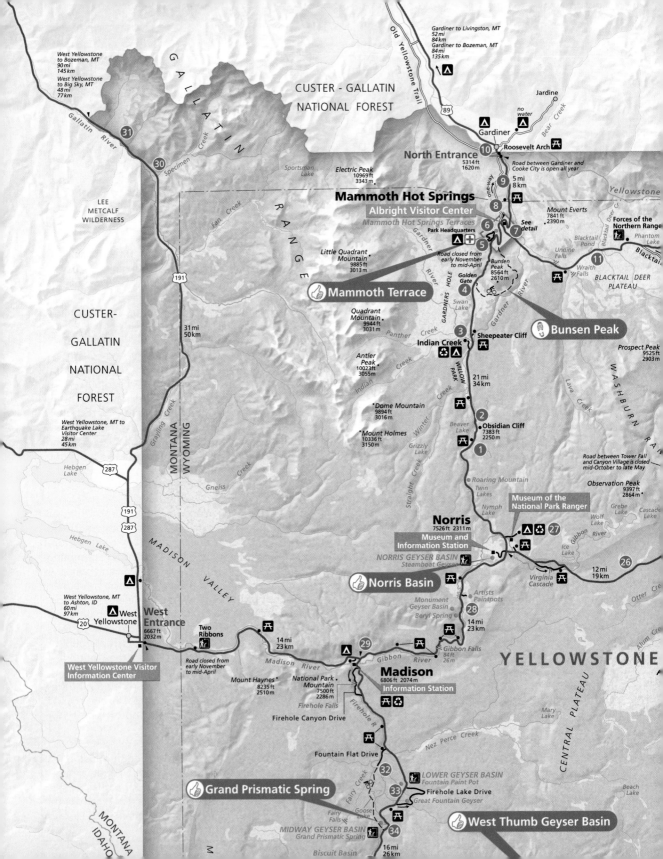

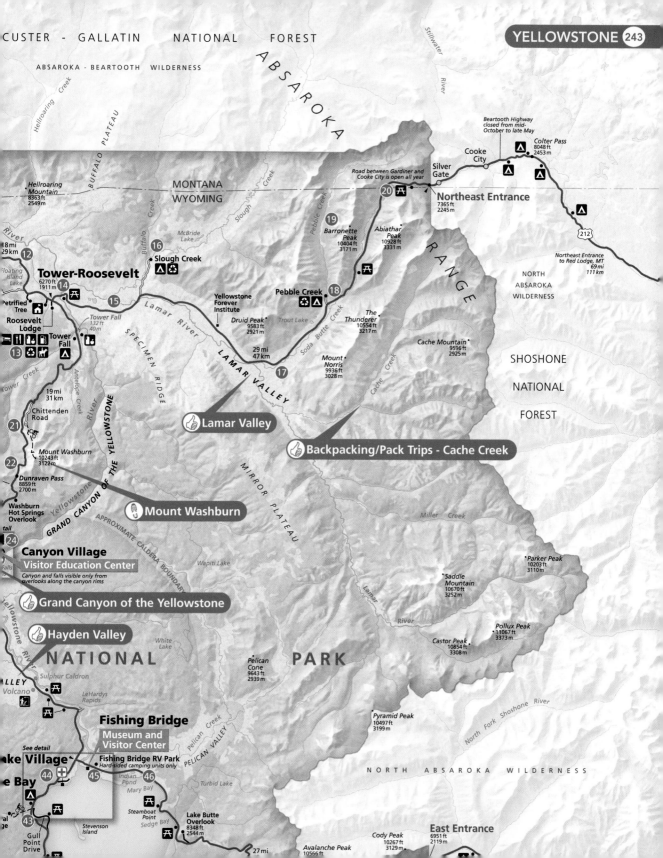

CUSTER - GALLATIN NATIONAL FOREST

ABSAROKA - BEARTOOTH WILDERNESS

Hellroaring Creek

Stillwater River

ABSAROKA

Buffalo Plateau

Beartooth Highway closed from mid-October to late May

Cooke City

Colter Pass
8048 ft
2453 m

MONTANA
WYOMING

Hellroaring
Mountain
8363 ft
2549 m

Road between Gardiner and Cooke City is open all year

Silver Gate

Northeast Entrance
7365 ft
2245 m

20

Slough Creek

McBride Lake

16

19

Barronette Peak
10404 ft
3171 m

Abiathar Peak
10928 ft
3331 m

RANGE

NORTH ABSAROKA WILDERNESS

Northeast Entrance to Red Lodge, MT
69 mi
111 km

212

8 mi
29 km

12

Floating Island Lake

Slough Creek

Tower-Roosevelt
6270 ft
1911 m

14

Yellowstone Forever Institute

Pebble Creek

18

The Thunderer
10554 ft
3217 m

Cache Mountain
9596 ft
2925 m

SHOSHONE

NATIONAL

FOREST

Petrified Tree

Roosevelt Lodge

13

Tower Fall
132 ft
40 m

Tower Fall

15

Druid Peak
9583 ft
2921 m

Trout Lake

29 mi
47 km

17

Mount Norris
9936 ft
3028 m

Soda Butte Creek

Cache Creek

Lamar Valley

Backpacking/Pack Trips - Cache Creek

Tower Creek

19 mi
31 km

Chittenden Road

21

Mount Washburn
10243 ft
3122 m

22

Dunraven Pass
8859 ft
2700 m

Washburn
Hot Springs
Overlook

Mount Washburn

MIRROR PLATEAU

Miller Creek

Parker Peak
10203 ft
3110 m

24

Canyon Village

Visitor Education Center
Canyon and falls visible only from overlooks along the canyon rims

Grand Canyon of the Yellowstone

Wapiti Lake

Saddle Mountain
10670 ft
3252 m

Pollux Peak
11067 ft
3373 m

Hayden Valley

White Lake

NATIONAL

PARK

Pelican Cone
9643 ft
2939 m

Castor Peak
10854 ft
3308 m

Sulphur Caldron

LeHardys Rapids

Pyramid Peak
10497 ft
3199 m

North Fork Shoshone River

VALLEY
Volcano

Fishing Bridge

Museum and Visitor Center

Pelican Creek

PELICAN VALLEY

ke Village

e Bay

44

45

Fishing Bridge RV Park
Hard-sided camping units only

Indian Pond

Mary Bay

46

Steamboat Point

Sedge Bay

Lake Butte Overlook
8348 ft
2544 m

NORTH   ABSAROKA   WILDERNESS

Turbid Lake

43

Gull Point Drive

Stevenson Island

27 mi

Cody Peak
10267 ft
3129 m

Avalanche Peak
10566 ft

East Entrance
6951 ft
2119 m

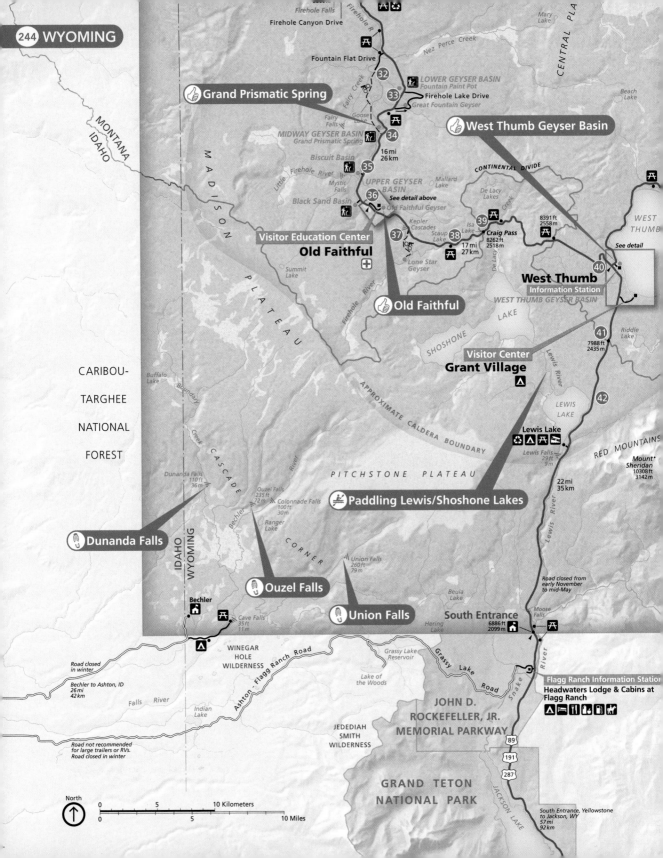

Firehole Falls
Firehole Canyon Drive
Firehole R
CENTRAL PLA
Nez Perce Creek
Mary Lake

Fountain Flat Drive
32
LOWER GEYSER BASIN
Fountain Paint Pot
Firehole Lake Drive
Great Fountain Geyser
Beach Lake

👍 **Grand Prismatic Spring**
33

👍 **West Thumb Geyser Basin**

Fairy Creek
Goose Lake
Fairy Falls
34
16 mi
26 km
CONTINENTAL DIVIDE
WEST THUMB

MIDWAY GEYSER BASIN
Grand Prismatic Spring
Biscuit Basin
35
Mallard Lake
De Lacy Lakes
8391 ft
2558 m

Little Firehole River
Mystic Falls
36
UPPER GEYSER BASIN
See detail above
Old Faithful Geyser

Black Sand Basin
Craig Pass
8262 ft
2518 m
39
See detail

Visitor Education Center
Old Faithful
37
Kepler Cascades
Isa Lake
38
17 mi
27 km
West Thumb
Information Station

Scaup Lake
Lone Star Geyser
WEST THUMB GEYSER BASIN
40

Summit Lake
Firehole River
SHOSHONE LAKE
7988 ft
2435 m
41
Riddle Lake

👍 **Old Faithful**

Visitor Center
Grant Village

Lewis River
LEWIS LAKE
42

CARIBOU-

TARGHEE

NATIONAL

FOREST

Buffalo Lake
Boundary Creek
CASCADE
APPROXIMATE CALDERA BOUNDARY
PITCHSTONE PLATEAU
Lewis Lake
Lewis Falls
29 ft
9 m
RED MOUNTAINS
Mount Sheridan
10308 ft
3142 m

Dunanda Falls
110 ft
36 m

Ouzel Falls
235 ft
72 m
Colonnade Falls
100 ft
30 m

Bechler River
Ranger Lake
🥾 **Paddling Lewis/Shoshone Lakes**

🥾 **Dunanda Falls**

CORNER
Union Falls
260 ft
79 m
22 mi
35 km

IDAHO
WYOMING
🥾 **Ouzel Falls**
Beula Lake

🥾 **Union Falls**
South Entrance
6886 ft
2099 m

Bechler
Cave Falls
35 ft
11 m
Hering Lake
Moose Falls

Road closed from
early November
to mid-May

WINEGAR
HOLE
WILDERNESS
Grassy Lake Reservoir
Snake River
Flagg Ranch Information Station
Headwaters Lodge & Cabins at Flagg Ranch

Road closed
in winter
Bechler to Ashton, ID
26 mi
42 km

Ashton–Flagg Ranch Road
Lake of the Woods
Grassy Lake Road

Road not recommended
for large trailers or RVs.
Road closed in winter

Falls River
Indian Lake
JEDEDIAH
SMITH
WILDERNESS
JOHN D.
ROCKEFELLER, JR.
MEMORIAL PARKWAY
89
191
287

North
0   5   10 Kilometers
0   5   10 Miles

GRAND TETON
NATIONAL PARK

Jackson Lake

South Entrance, Yellowstone
to Jackson, WY
57 mi
92 km

MONTANA
IDAHO
MADISON PLATEAU

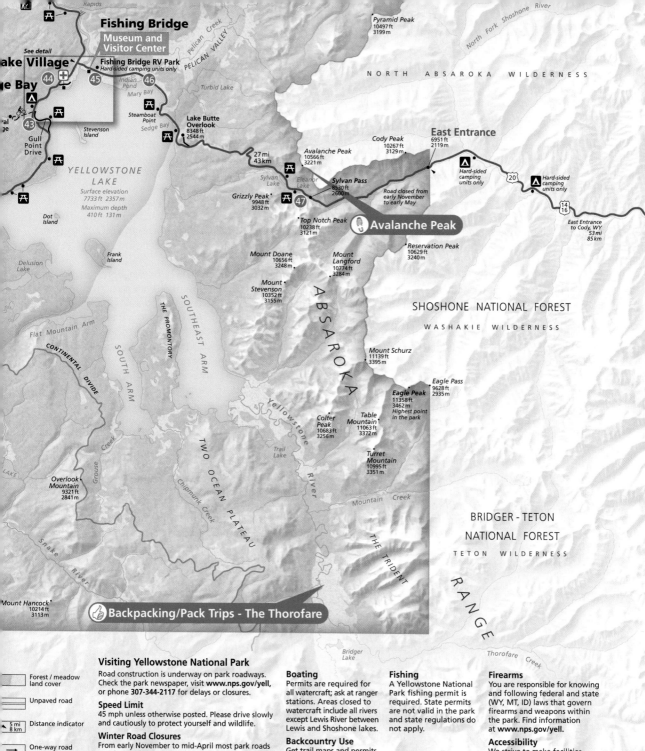

Fishing Bridge
Museum and Visitor Center

Fishing Bridge RV Park
Hard-sided camping units only

See detail

44
45
46

ake Village
ge Bay

43

Indian
Pond
Mary Bay

Steamboat
Point
Sedge Bay

Lake Butte
Overlook
8348 ft
2544 m

Gull
Point
Drive

YELLOWSTONE
LAKE

Surface elevation
7733 ft 2357 m

Maximum depth
410 ft 131 m

Stevenson
Island

Dot
Island

Frank
Island

Delusion
Lake

PELICAN VALLEY

Pelican Creek

Turbid Lake

27 mi
43 km

Sylvan
Lake

Eleanor
Lake

47

Grizzly Peak
9948 ft
3032 m

Top Notch Peak
10238 ft
3121 m

Avalanche Peak
10566 ft
3221 m

Sylvan Pass
8530 ft
2600 m

Pyramid Peak
10497 ft
3199 m

North Fork Shoshone River

NORTH ABSAROKA WILDERNESS

Cody Peak
10267 ft
3129 m

East Entrance
6951 ft
2119 m

Road closed from
early November
to early May

Hard-sided
camping
units only

20

Hard-sided
camping
units only

14
16

East Entrance
to Cody, WY
53 mi
85 km

👣 **Avalanche Peak**

Reservation Peak
10629 ft
3240 m

Mount Doane
10656 ft
3248 m

Mount Langford
10774 ft
3284 m

Mount
Stevenson
10352 ft
3155 m

A B S A R O K A

SHOSHONE NATIONAL FOREST

WASHAKIE WILDERNESS

Flat Mountain Arm

SOUTHEAST ARM

THE PROMONTORY

SOUTH ARM

CONTINENTAL DIVIDE

Grouse Creek

Chipmunk Creek

Snake River

Mount Schurz
11139 ft
3395 m

Yellowstone River

Eagle Pass
9628 ft
2935 m

Eagle Peak
11358 ft
3462 m
Highest point
in the park

Colter
Peak
10683 ft
3256 m

Table
Mountain
11063 ft
3372 m

Turret
Mountain
10995 ft
3351 m

TWO OCEAN PLATEAU

Trail
Lake

Mountain Creek

BRIDGER - TETON
NATIONAL FOREST

TETON WILDERNESS

Overlook
Mountain
9321 ft
2841 m

THE TRIDENT

R A N G E

Mount Hancock
10214 ft
3113 m

👍 **Backpacking/Pack Trips - The Thorofare**

Bridger
Lake

Thorofare Creek

Visiting Yellowstone National Park

Road construction is underway on park roadways. Check the park newspaper, visit www.nps.gov/yell, or phone 307-344-2117 for delays or closures.

Speed Limit
45 mph unless otherwise posted. Please drive slowly and cautiously to protect yourself and wildlife.

Winter Road Closures
From early November to mid-April most park roads are closed. The exception is the road between Gardiner and Cooke City. It is open all year.

From mid-December to mid-March, oversnow vehicles may be used only on the unplowed, groomed park roads. Call park headquarters for regulations or check the park website, www.nps.gov/yell.

Boating
Permits are required for all watercraft; ask at ranger stations. Areas closed to watercraft include all rivers except Lewis River between Lewis and Shoshone lakes.

Backcountry Use
Get trail maps and permits, required for backcountry camping, at most ranger stations. Do not use this map for backcountry hiking. There are almost 1,000 miles of trails.

Fishing
A Yellowstone National Park fishing permit is required. State permits are not valid in the park and state regulations do not apply.

Firearms
You are responsible for knowing and following federal and state (WY, MT, ID) laws that govern firearms and weapons within the park. Find information at www.nps.gov/yell.

Accessibility
We strive to make facilities, services, and programs accessible to all. Service animals are allowed but require a permit in the backcountry. Find information at visitor centers and on our website.

Forest / meadow land cover

Unpaved road

5 mi
8 km — Distance indicator

One-way road

Geothermal feature

Trail or boardwalk

Day-use hiking/
bicycling trail
ask for more information)

1 — Trailhead (see tables on pages 251–254)

Geysers & Hot Springs

The park is centered on Yellowstone Caldera, the largest supervolcano on the continent, measuring 45-by-30 miles. It's an active volcano. "Active" is generous. It's erupted three times in the last 2 million years. The last one, 640,000 years ago, was 1,000 times larger than Mt St. Helens' eruption in 1980. The Yellowstone hotspot, consisting of the heat source (earth's core), plume, and magma chamber, have endowed the park with more than 10,000 geothermal features, including 300 geysers. These features and one-to-three thousand annual earthquakes (all undetectable to visitors) are proof of present-day volcanic activity.

Now that you're scared silly, remember, scientists are constantly monitoring these activities, and it is very unlikely an eruption will occur in the next thousand or even 10,000 years. So, scratch "witness an apocalyptic volcanic eruption" off your Yellowstone To-Do List. It's highly unlikely. However, you'll definitely want to visit the ever-changing geyser basins.

Mammoth Hot Springs is located in the northwest corner just beyond the caldera boundary. A road leads through the upper terrace, but there's also a self-guided boardwalk that winds its way through the terraced pools and travertine formations.

Traveling south on Grand Loop Road from Mammoth you'll encounter **Norris Geyser Basin**. Its unique acidic (opposed to alkaline) waters nurture different classes of bacterial thermophiles. Thermophiles create the different color patterns you see in and around the basin's water. Norris is home to several geysers. Among them is Steamboat, the world's tallest active geyser. Its eruptions hurl super-heated water more than 300 feet into the air, but they occur irregularly, often separated by more than a year. Echinus Geyser is also on the unpredictable side, but it may erupt multiple times per day. There's no guarantee that you'll see a geyser erupt like at Old Faithful/Upper Geyser Basin, but Norris's self-guided boardwalk is a "must-do" activity. There's just something about it that feels different than other basins (it actually is different!). Its baby blue pools surrounded by white rocks are inviting and comforting, even as steam ominously billows from vents.

Monument Geyser Basin is between Norris and Madison. Contrary to the name, there are no active geysers. Its monuments are rocky spires containing silica (glass) that have also been discovered on the floor of Yellowstone Lake. Scientists believe these spires formed thousands of years ago when the area was submerged by a glacially dammed lake. Reach this basin by taking a steep 1-mile trail beginning just south of Artists' Paint Pots. The Paint Pots are two bubbling mudpots.

You'll find, in order, Lower, Midway, and Upper Geyser Basins between Madison and Old Faithful. **Lower Geyser Basin** has a lower concentration of geothermal features. Its highlights are Fountain Paint Pots and Great Fountain Geyser (an extremely popular sunset destination). You'll find a self-guided trail explaining the four types of geothermal features: geysers, hot springs, fumaroles, and mud pots. Mud pots are hot springs containing boiling mud rather than water. **Midway**

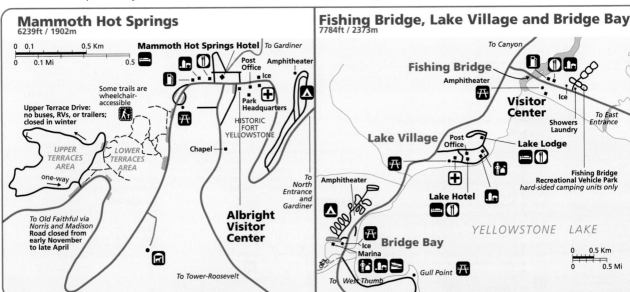

Geyser Basin is small in size, but its geothermal features are large and colorful. Midway is home to **Grand Prismatic Spring**, the largest hot spring in Yellowstone (370-ft wide, 121-ft deep). From up-close its beauty is obscured by its size. Of all the geothermal features to see, the sight of Grand Prismatic Spring is most likely to leave you breathless. Excelsior Geyser, which pours hot water into the Firehole River, is another noteworthy site. The best Grand Prismatic vantage point is from a new overlook accessed via Fairy Falls Trail (south of the spring). While they expanded the parking area, it still fills and you may have to wait for space. Normally I'd suggest an early arrival. This is an exception. Grand Prismatic's colors don't pop in the early-morning sun.

Upper Geyser Basin boasts **Old Faithful** and the highest concentration of geothermal features in the park. If you want to see a geyser erupt, this is the spot. Old Faithful pumps 200+°F water 100–185 feet in the air once every 60–110 minutes. Prediction times are posted at most buildings in the area. Observation Point (accessed by a short but steep 1-mile trail) is a more peaceful position to watch the eruption. Castle, Daisy, Grand, and Riverside geysers erupt regularly. Check the park website for daily eruption predictions (or you'll find eruption windows posted near each geyser). There are many other features to see here (Beehive Geyser, Chromatic Pool, Giant Geyser, Grotto Geyser, Morning Glory Pool, and Punch Bowl Spring, just to name a few.)

East of Old Faithful is **West Thumb Geyser Basin**. Thermal features extend from the shoreline to beneath the surface of Yellowstone Lake, which is pretty neat.

There are many more geothermal areas. Mud Volcano and Sulfur Cauldron are located near Hayden Valley. Gibbon, Heart Lake, Lone Star, and Shoshone Geyser Basins are all found in the backcountry.

Camping

There are 12 campgrounds and more than 2,000 campsites. That sounds like a lot, but as many as 50,000 visitors can enter the park on a single day in summer. Congested roads, competitive parking, and full campgrounds are common. Five campgrounds accept reservations (307.344.7311, yellowstonenationalparklodges.com). The rest are first-come, first-served (filling before noon in summer). Showers are available at Canyon, Fishing Bridge, and Grant Village. Full hookups are only available at Fishing Bridge RV Park (but it's closed for renovations until the summer of 2022). Yellowstone does not offer overflow camping areas, but there are several campgrounds and RV parks outside the park.

Services and Facilities

Winter road closures
From early November to early May most park roads are closed. The exception is the road between the North Entrance and Cooke City. It is open all year.

From mid-December to early March, oversnow vehicles may be used only on the unplowed, groomed park roads. Call park headquarters for regulations or check the park website, www.nps.gov/yell.

Emergencies
For medical or other emergencies contact a ranger or call 307-344-7381 or 911.
Check the park newspaper or website for seasonal dates of services and facilities.

Medical clinic
Ranger station
Campground
Horse rental
Boat launch
Lodging
Food service
Gas station (some have auto repair)
Self-guiding trail
Picnic area
Store

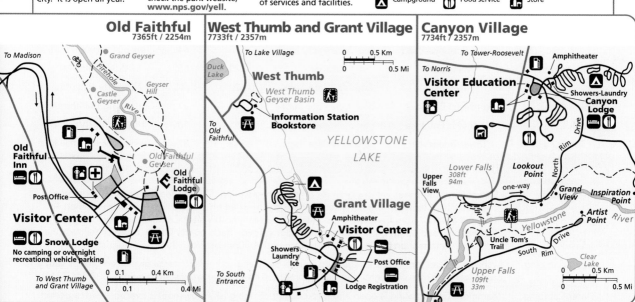

Reservations are recommended (if not required) as only about 20% of the park's sites are available on a first-come, first-served basis (and expect them to fill early). If you're willing to rise early (and wait) to get a site or deal with weather that's a little more hit-or-miss than usual by traveling in the off-season, by all means go for it. Visiting Yellowstone with a certain amount of flexibility can be a great joy, as you can move around more freely. Stick around if you're having fun in one area. Leave if you aren't. With that said, I've been burned before with this strategy, and it's no fun driving out of the park to find a place to camp. The added cost of reservable sites is worth a little peace of mind. If you don't want to move your camp around, stay at Canyon Village. You'll still end up doing a ton of driving to see the park, but it's centrally located, Grand Canyon of the Yellowstone is amazing for sunrises, and it's huge so you don't have to make your reservations the second they're available, but you should make them as soon as possible, especially for summer travel plans.

Indian Creek, Lewis Lake, Pebble Creek, Slough Creek, and Tower Fall are primitive campgrounds with vault toilets. Their small size, small fees, and stunning environments cause them to fill early in summer. The three "Creek" camps are particularly nice. A camper who secures a site at one of these locations is also more likely to spend a few nights, making them harder to come by.

Most campgrounds have many pull-through sites, but few can accommodate RVs longer than 30 feet. It is recommended that visitors with large RVs make reservations at Fishing Bridge RV Park. This campground is for hard-sided vehicles only. Tents and tent-trailers are prohibited. Unfortunately, Fishing Bridge RV Park is closed for renovations until the 2022 season.

Backcountry camping is also popular. A backcountry user permit is required. Permits can be reserved ($25 application fee), but they must be obtained in person at one of the locations listed in the camping table. Pick

Yellowstone Camping (Fees are per night)

Name	Location	Open	Fee	Sites	Notes
Bridge Bay*	Bridge Bay	late May–early Sept	$28	432	Dump station
Canyon*	Canyon Village	late May–mid-Sept	$33	273	Shower and laundry
Fishing Bridge RV*	Fishing Bridge	early May–mid-Sept (reopens summer 2022)	TBD	346	Hookups, sewer, shower and laundry
Grant Village*	Grant Village	mid-June–mid-Sept	$33	430	Dump station, shower and laundry
Madison*	Madison	late April–mid-Oct	$28	278	Dump station, no hookups
Indian Creek	Near Sheepeater Cliff	mid-June–mid-Sept	$15	70	10 sites for RVs (<35') 35 sites for RVs (<30')
Lewis Lake - ⚓	South Entrance Road	mid-June–early Nov	$15	84	few pull-through (<25')
Mammoth	Mammoth	All Year	$20	85	RVs less than 30'
Norris	Norris	late May–late Sept	$20	111	7 sites for RVs (<30')
Pebble Creek - ⚓	Northeast Entrance	mid-June–late Sept	$15	27	Some long pull-throughs
Slough Creek - ⚓	Northeast Entrance	mid-June–early Oct	$15	16	14 sites for RVs (<30')
Tower Fall	Tower/Roosevelt	late May–late Sept	$15	31	Best for tents/small RVs

*Run by Xanterra Parks & Resorts and available for reservation (307.344.7311, yellowstonenationalparklodges.com) All other campgrounds are operated by the National Park Service and available on a first-come, first-served basis

Backcountry	Backcountry campsites are available for advance reservation ($25/trip fee). Permits ($3/person per night for trips between Memorial and Labor Day) must be obtained in person not more than 48 hours in advance from Canyon, Grant Village, and Mammoth Visitor Centers; Bechler, Bridge Bay, Old Faithful, and South Entrance Ranger Stations; Tower Backcountry Office, or West Yellowstone Information Center, daily from 8am until 4:30pm between June and August.
Group Camping	Available at Madison, Grant Village, and Bridge Bay Campgrounds for large organized groups with a group leader ($136–399/night, depending on group size). Reservations are required (307.344.7311).
Winter Camping	Mammoth Campground is open and backcountry camping (ski/snowshoe) is available with a permit

up your permit at the location closest to where your trip begins to receive up-to-date information regarding trail conditions and wildlife activity. Most backcountry campsites have a maximum stay of three days. Permits issued for trips between Memorial Day and September 10 cost $3 per person per night (with a max of $15/night) for backpackers and boaters and $5 per person per night (no max) for stock parties (horses/mules/llamas). Fees are collected when the permit is issued.

Yellowstone is bear country. Do not keep food in your tent, keep a clean camp, and store food in air-tight containers (bear canisters for backpackers).

Elk near Grand Canyon of the Yellowstone

Lodging

Yellowstone's lodging facilities are attractions themselves, worthy of standing side-by-side with the most wonderful natural architecture the United States has to offer. Many visitors find **Old Faithful Inn** more impressive than the eponymous geyser visible from many of the rooms. It's priced reasonably, with rooms starting at $153/night. Stopping in to admire the architecture is free. Other lodgings are equally rustic and more secluded. If it's a true Wild West experience you seek, **Roosevelt Lodge** is where you'll find it. The Lodge's Roughrider Cabins—the park's most economical lodging—are suitable for 2–4 adults and cost just $109/night. Inspired by President Theodore Roosevelt, who frequented the park, they provide no-frills lodging with few furnishings, no bathroom, and heat supplied by a wood burning stove. Mammoth Hot Springs Hotel and Old Faithful Snow Lodge are the only **winter accommodations**. Recent renovations at Mammoth Hot Springs Hotel resulted in a mixture of cabins (some with hot tubs) to suites with all the trappings. All accommodations are non-smoking, and televisions, radios, and air conditioning are not available in most rooms. Cell service is available in developed areas. Verizon provides the best coverage, except in Canyon Village (AT&T). Service is less reliable in summer when visitation is high. Wi-Fi is available for guests at Mammoth Hot Springs Hotel, Canyon Lodge, Grant Village, Lake Lodge, Lake Yellowstone Hotel, Old Faithful Snow Lodge, Old Faithful Lodge, and Old Faithful Inn. Registered campers, staying at any of the campgrounds operated by Yellowstone National Park Lodges, can access the internet at these locations with an access code. Similarly, Wi-Fi bandwidth is limited, so expect slow download speeds in summer. Get your downloading in before arriving at the park if you feel like an evening show/movie before going to sleep or want to be prepared in case of inclement weather.

Yellowstone Lodging (Fees are per night)			
Name	Open	Fee	Notes
Canyon Lodge - ♨	late May–early Oct	$182–659	Canyon Village's Dunraven Lodge is often regarded as the best lodging in the park
Grant Village	late May–early Oct	$291	Overlooks Yellowstone Lake
Lake Lodge	early June–late Sept	$170–260	Cozy cabins with cafeteria style dining
Lake Hotel	mid-May–late Sept	$235–865	Basic rooms to a Presidential Suite
Mammoth Hot Springs Hotel	late April–mid-Oct mid-Dec–late Feb	$112–632	Motel-style rooms with shared restrooms to suites with cable TV
Old Faithful Lodge	mid-May–early Oct	$110–183	Simple accommodations
Old Faithful Inn	early May–early Oct	$153–1,126	Most requested lodging in the park
Old Faithful Snow Lodge - ♨	late April–late Oct mid-Dec–late Feb	$132–348	Stays true to park style design • Only accessible in winter via snow transportation
Roosevelt Lodge	early June–early Sept	$109+	Primitive Lodging based on 2–4 people

For reservations call Xanterra Parks and Resorts at (866) 439-7375 or click yellowstonenationalparklodges.com
Rates are per night, for up to 2 adults and do not include tax and utility fee

Artist Point

Driving

Driving Yellowstone is all about 142-mile **Grand Loop Road**. It makes a giant "figure-eight," connecting all the park's developed areas. Much of this loop was planned during the park's early days when it was still under U.S. military administration. All five park entrances lead to the loop. The top half takes visitors to locations such as Mammoth Hot Springs, Petrified Tree, Tower Fall, Norris Geyser Basin, and Sheepeater Cliff. Lamar Valley is located along Northeast Entrance Road, which is an immensely popular hiking and wildlife viewing area. The lower half passes Grand Canyon of the Yellowstone, Hayden Valley, Fishing Bridge, West Thumb Geyser Basin, Upper Geyser Basin (Old Faithful), Midway Geyser Basin (Grand Prismatic Spring), and Lower Geyser Basin. Motorists cross the Continental Divide twice between West Thumb and Old Faithful. South Entrance Road leads to Lewis Lake (popular for paddling), coming from John D. Rockefeller, Jr. Memorial Parkway and Grand Teton National Park. One of the biggest mistakes Yellowstone visitors can make is to believe they can drive Grand Loop Road in one day (sure, it's physically possible, but you'll spend most of the day in your car). Plan to spend a minimum of three days. In summer, the roadway can be extremely busy. Start touring early, and don't forget to pull completely off the road when you stop to view wildlife. Finally, drive safely and have fun.

Hiking

More than 900 miles of trails makes selecting one challenging. To begin whittling down your options, consider which regions you plan on visiting. Trails have been sorted geographically into six distinct regions. Many trails close seasonally due to poor conditions or increases in bear activity. It's a good idea to stop in at a visitor center prior to hiking to inquire about trail conditions and wildlife activity. Boardwalks connect the most interesting geothermal features. Dirt-packed, tree-covered, gloriously natural hiking trails lead far away from traffic-filled roads and bustling facilities.

For geothermal features, circle around the lower half of the figure eight. While elevation is high throughout the park, the most prominent mountains are found along the park's eastern boundary, as well as a few trails. Hike around the East and Northeast Entrances for mountain hiking (and there are a few serious trails around Mammoth as well). Waterfalls are everywhere, from the park's southwest corner to northern entrance, many of them, including Undine Falls, Wraith Falls, Gibbon Falls, Firehole Falls, Tower Fall, Upper and Lower Falls of the Yellowstone River, Kepler Cascades, and Lewis Falls are all just a short walk from parking areas along Grand Loop Road. And they're great places to take short strolls to get acclimated to elevation before heading deeper into the park. Others are more remote like Dunanda and Union Falls in Cascade Corner.

Canyon, one of the busiest areas, is often filled with motorists. All short trails around Upper and Lower Falls have been omitted from the table; you can't miss them while driving along the north and south rims. They'll be busy too. **Uncle Tom's Trail** is a must-hike (even though it's quite strenuous). It descends 500 feet via a series of paved inclines and more than 300 steps to an up-close look at Lower Falls. **Brink of Lower Falls** and **Brink of Upper Falls** are also worth a visit, but my favorite spot is **Artist Point**. If you're determined to get down to the Yellowstone River from the canyon area, **Seven Mile Hole** is the only way to get there. The trailhead is accessed from the North Rim loop. This is one of those trails that suffers from its easily-accessible surroundings. If you spent any time admiring Lower Falls, there's a good chance you may come away from this strenuous hike feeling a little underwhelmed, but it isn't bad and you'll get a good workout. But I'd stay on the rim if you're short on time. Go to **Artist Point** on the South Rim, and **Lookout Point** (and/or **Red Rock Point**) on the South Rim. Trails connect viewpoints on the South and North rims.

To appreciate the size of Yellowstone Lake, drive to Lake Butte (East Entrance Road) or hike to **Lake Overlook**, where on a clear day you can see clear across Yellowstone Lake to the Teton Range. You'll also have a bird's eye view of West Thumb, a smaller caldera created by volcanic eruption some 100,000 years ago that has since filled with water. If you're looking to challenge yourself, try the 2-mile, 2,100-ft-nearly-vertical climb to the top of **Avalanche Peak**. It's a real thigh burner! If you want to truly explore the park, you should get a dedicated hiking guidebook. I realize I'm only scratching the surface of what you can do here. My eyes are on the park's northeast corner for the next trip!

Mammoth Terraces

Mammoth Area Hiking Trails (Distances are roundtrip unless noted otherwise)

Name	Location (# on map)	Length	Difficulty Rating & Notes
Grizzly Lake	1 mile south of Beaver Lake Picnic Area on Mammoth–Norris Road (1)	4.0 miles	E – Hike into a valley and to Grizzly Lake • Trail continues, joining Mt Holmes Trail
Mount Holmes	3 miles south of Indian Creek Camp (2)	20.0 miles	S – Hike to 10,336-ft summit of Mt Holmes
Bighorn Pass	Indian Creek Campground (3)	16.0 miles	S – Through grizzly country to 9,022-ft pass
Bunsen Peak - 🐾	Mammoth–Norris Road (4, 6 alt.)	4.6 miles	M – Fairly easy summit to panoramic views
Osprey Falls - 🐾	Mammoth–Norris Road (4, 6 alt.)	8.0 miles	M – Alt. Sheepeater Canyon to 150-ft falls
Electric Peak	4 miles south of Mammoth on Mammoth–Norris Road (5)	18.0 miles	X – Take Snow Pass/Sportsman Lake Trail to a 3.1-mile spur trail that leads to the summit
Beaver Ponds Loop	Just north of Liberty Cap (6)	5.0 miles	M – Nice loop through meadows and aspen
Sepulcher Mtn Loop	Between Liberty Cap and the stone house next to Mammoth Terraces (6)	11.0 miles	S – Follows Beaver Ponds Trail to Sepulcher Mt Trail junction and to the 9,652-ft summit
Lava Creek Canyon	Across from Lava Creek Picnic Area on Mammoth–Tower Rd (7, 11)	4.2 miles (one-way)	M – Pass 60-ft Undine Falls (located close to the southern trailhead), follows Gardner River
Boiling River - 🐾 (closed)	Parking Area near 45th parallel sign north of Mammoth Hot Springs (8)	1.0 mile	E – Short hike to a swimming area where hot spring water and Gardner River meet
Rescue Creek	7 miles east of Mammoth on Mammoth-Tower Road (9, 11)	8.0 miles (one-way)	M – Ends 1 mile south of NE Entrance
Black Canyon of the Yellowstone - 🐾	Hellroaring Trailhead 3.5 miles west of Tower Junction (10, 11, 12)	18.5 miles (one-way)	M – Long day or 2-day hike from Hellroaring Trailhead to Gardiner, MT
Wraith Falls - 🐾	0.5-mile east of Lava Cr Picnic Area (11)	1.0 mile	E – Short hike to beautiful waterfall
Blacktail Creek/ Yellowstone River	7 miles east of Mammoth on Mammoth–Tower Road (11, 12)	12.0 miles (one-way)	M – Crosses a river, joins Yellowstone River Trail, and ends in Gardiner, MT

Difficulty Ratings: E = Easy, M = Moderate, S = Strenuous, X = Extreme

Bison near Lamar Valley

Tower Hiking Trails (Distances are roundtrip unless noted otherwise)

Name	Location (# on map)	Length	Difficulty Rating & Notes
Hellroaring - ♨	3.5 miles west of Tower Junction (12)	6.2 miles	S – Great trail, suspension bridge
Lost Lake	Behind Roosevelt Lodge (13)	2.8 miles	M – Loop trail skirts Lost Lake, reaches Petrified Tree before returning to the lodge
Garnet Hill Loop	50 yards north of Tower Junction on Northeast Entrance Road (14)	7.6 miles	M – Follows an old dirt coach road, then Elk Creek to intersection with Hellroaring Trail
Yellowstone River Overlook - ♨	Yellowstone River Picnic Area (14)	3.7 miles	M – Follows rim of Yellowstone Canyon
Specimen Ridge	East of Yellowstone River Picnic Area or Lamar Valley (14, 17)	17.5 miles (one-way)	S – Long point-to-point hike climbs out of Lamar Valley and follows Specimen Ridge back to road
Petrified Forest	5.3 miles east of Roosevelt Junction (15)	3.0 miles	S – Climbs 1,200 feet rapidly to petrified trees
Slough Creek	On dirt road toward Slough Creek Camp where the road bears left (16)	1.7/4.3 mi. (one-way)	M – Follows old wagon trail • Distances are to the first two meadows • Trail continues beyond
Trout Lake - ♨	1.5 mi south of Pebble Cr Camp (15)	1.2 miles	E – Nice and short semi-loop trail
Pebble Creek	Near Pebble Creek Bridge (18) and Warm Creek (20) on NE Entrance Road	12.0 miles (one-way)	M – Do a portion of this trail between Pebble Creek Camp and Warm Creek Trailhead
Bliss Pass	Pebble Creek Trail intersects Bliss Pass at mile 6.6 (19)	20.6 miles (one-way)	S – Connects Slough Creek and Pebble Creek Trails over Bliss Pass
Mt Washburn - ♨	Chittenden Road (21, for bikers) or Dunraven Pass (22, for hikers)	2.5/3.0 mi. (one-way)	S – Bike from Chittenden Road Parking Area or hike from Dunraven Pass Parking Area, popular

Canyon Hiking Trails (Distances are roundtrip unless noted otherwise)

Name	Location (# on map)	Length	Difficulty Rating & Notes
Cascade Lake	Just south of Cascade Lake Picnic (23)	4.4 miles	E – Walk through meadows to secluded lake
Observation Peak	Cascade Lake Trailhead (23)	9.6 miles	S – 1,400-ft climb, follow Cascade Lake Trail
Seven Mile Hole	Glacial Boulder Pullout near Inspiration Point (24)	10.0 miles	S – Follow Glacial Boulder Trail, only trail leading into Grand Canyon of the Yellowstone
Point Sublime	Artist Point Overlook (25)	2.5 miles	E – Follow South Rim Trail to this point
Grebe Lake	3.5 miles west of Canyon Junction (26)	6.2 miles	M – Follows an old fire road

Difficulty Ratings: E = Easy, M = Moderate, S = Strenuous

Fairy Falls

Old Faithful–Norris Hiking Trails (Distances are roundtrip unless noted otherwise)

	Name	Location (# on map)	Length	Difficulty Rating & Notes
Norris	Artists' Paint Pot	4.5 miles south of Norris Junction (28)	1.0 mile	E – Peculiar geothermal features
	Solfatara Creek	Norris Campground (27)	6.5 miles	M – One-way trail along creek
	Mon Geyser Basin	5 miles south of Norris Junction (28)	2.0 miles	M – Tough, views of Gibbon River
	Purple Mountain	0.25-mile north of Madison Junction (29)	6.0 miles	S – Convenient trail for Madison Camp
Old Faithful	Fairy Falls - ⚲	End of Fountain Flat Drive (32) Fairy Falls Trailhead (34)	6.7 miles 5.4 miles	E – Off the beaten path route E – Grand Prismatic Overlook nearby
	Sentinel Meadows	End of Fountain Flat Drive (32)	3.8 miles	M – Skirts along Firehole River
	Mallard Creek	3.8 miles north of Old Faithful Junction toward Madison (34)	9.2 miles	S – Alternate route to Mallard Lake across hilly terrain and burned forest
	Mystic Falls - ⚲	Back of Biscuit Basin Boardwalk (35)	2.4 miles	M – 70-ft falls of the Firehole River
	Observation Pt - ⚲	Behind Old Faithful (36)	1.6 mile	M – Better spot to view Old Faithful
	Mallard Lake	South of Old Faithful Lodge Cabins (36)	7.0 miles	M – Leads to a remote lake
	Howard Eaton	Across Grand Loop Road from Old Faithful Ranger Station (36)	6.3 miles	M – Out-and-back traverses spruce forests down to Lone Star Geyser
	Lone Star Geyser - ⚲	Near Kepler Cascades Parking Area (37)	4.8 miles	E – Partially paved along Firehole River
	Divide	6.8 miles south of Old Faithful Junction (38)	3.4 miles	M – Views of Shoshone Lake en route to the Continental Divide
Other	High Lake Loop	Access via Specimen Creek Trail at Milepost 26 of US-191 (30)	23.0 miles	S – Multi-day hike to two alpine loops through mountain country
	Sky Rim Loop - ⚲	Access via Dailey Creek Trail at Milepost 31 of US-191 (31)	18.0 miles	S – Steep, rocky, exposed trail with superb mountain scenery and wildlife

A storm on its way to Storm Point

Yellowstone Lake Hiking Trails (Distances are roundtrip unless noted otherwise)

	Name	Location (# on map)	Length	Difficulty Rating & Notes
Fishing Bridge/Lake Village	Shoshone Lake	8.8 mi W of West Thumb Junction (39)	5.8 miles	E – The park's largest backcountry lake
	Lake Overlook	West Thumb Geyser Parking Lot (40)	1.7 miles	M – View of Yellowstone's West Thumb
	Duck Lake	West Thumb Geyser Parking Lot (40)	0.8 mile	E – Views of Duck and Yellowstone Lake
	Riddle Lake	3 miles south of Grant Village intersection (41)	4.8 miles	E –Trail crosses the Continental Divide to a pretty little lake
	Lewis River Channel/ Dogshead Loop	5 miles south of Grant Village intersection (42)	10.8 miles	S – 7-mile out-and-back through rugged terrain with a 4-mile loop at the end
	Heart Lake - ♨	5.4 miles south of Grant Village (42)	15.0 miles	S – Day-hike to the lake and return
	Mt Sheridan	Continues south of Heart Lake (42)	6.0 miles	S – Leads to a fire lookout station
West Thumb/Grant Village	Natural Bridge	Bridge Bay Marina Parking Lot (43)	2.5 miles	E – Convenient for campers at Bridge Bay
	Elephant Back Mtn	South of Fishing Bridge Junction (44)	3.5 miles	M – Views of massive Yellowstone Lake
	Howard Eaton	East side of Fishing Bridge (45)	7.0 miles	M – Ends at LeHardy's Rapids
	Pelican Creek	West end of Pelican Cr Bridge (46)	0.6 mile	E – Traverses several different habitats
	Storm Point - ♨	Indian Pond Pullout (46)	2.3 miles	E – Views Indian Pond & Yellowstone Lake
	Pelican Valley	End of a gravel road across from Indian Pond (46)	6.2 miles	M – Prime grizzly habitat above Pelican Valley and into the park's backcountry
	Avalanche Peak - ♨	Pullout at west end of Eleanor Lake toward East Entrance (47)	4.2 miles	S – 2,100-ft climb in just 2 miles to view some of the park's tallest peaks

Difficulty Ratings: E = Easy, M = Moderate, S = Strenuous

Backpacking

There are more than 900 miles of trails and 300 designated backcountry campsites. Backpackers planning on spending the night in the backcountry must obtain a Backcountry Use Permit ($3 per person per night). Only with special permission are you allowed to camp beyond designated sites. Reservations are accepted at some sites from January through October for a one-time $25 non-refundable permit fee. All reservations received prior to March 31 are processed in a random lottery. Reservations received after March 31 are processed in the order they are received. From May through October, the rest of the sites are available in-person at the park's backcountry offices no earlier than two days prior to the start of your trip. Even with reservations, you'll have to pick up your backpacking permit from a backcountry office at Canyon, Grant Village, and Mammoth Visitor Centers; Bechler, Bridge Bay, Old Faithful, and South Entrance Ranger Stations; Tower Backcountry Office, or West Yellowstone Information Center. They're open daily from 8am until 4:30pm between June and August. Use the closest location to your backpacking itinerary for the most accurate information on trail and weather conditions. Fires are only allowed in established fire rings, and dead and down wood may be used as firewood. Orange metal tags on trees and posts mark established trails. Very few of Yellowstone's rivers and streams have bridges. Seal important items in plastic bags and use a long sturdy stick when attempting to ford a river. If a waterway looks impassable, you probably shouldn't attempt to cross it. Water is cold and swift (especially after it rains). Much of the park's backcountry is unprotected and experiences severe winds. Carry a tent suitable for windy conditions. Finally, Yellowstone is grizzly bear country. Obey the closures/restrictions. Keep your camp clean and sleep at least 100 yards up wind from where you cook. For additional information and permit reservation form, download the Backcountry Trip Planner from the park website.

Yellowstone isn't a great place for first-time backpackers. It's huge. There are a lot of grizzlies. Then there's the scalding hot geothermal features. This isn't meant to discourage you. It's meant to take this seriously. Know your group. Plan carefully. Use caution. Do those things and you'll have a great time. If you're worried, stay close to developed areas (maps with locations of all backcountry campsites and trailheads are available online in the park's Backcountry Trip Planner). Call and talk to a park ranger about your intentions prior to submitting reservations. If you still aren't feeling comfortable, a bunch of outfitters are ready to take you on

Dunanda Falls Hot Pots

an adventure in Yellowstone's backcountry. There are the name brands like NOLS (nols.edu) and REI (rei.com/adventures). And others like Big Wild Adventures (406.823.0337, bigwildadventures.com), Wildland Trekking (800.715.4453, wildlandtrekking.com), Yellowstone Guidelines (406.599.2960, yellowstoneguidelines.com), Yellowstone Tour Guides (406.995.2399, yellowstonetourguides.com), and In Our Nature Guiding Services (406.579.3838, in-our-nature.com).

The **Thorofare Area** is fantastic for backpacking. Start at Nine Mile Trailhead, located nine miles east of Fishing Bridge on East Entrance Road. From here, the trail leads 34 miles to Bridger Lake, just past Thorofare Ranger Station (presently holding the distinction of "most remote location in the Lower 48" by being 20 miles from the nearest road of any kind). **Cache Creek** (southeast of Pebble Creek Campground) and the **Bechler Area** (southwest corner of the park, like highly prized site 9A3 near Dunanda Falls) are other popular backpacking destinations. **Shoshone Lake Area** is another good spot. Sites along the lake's shoreline are occupied almost every night in summer. Several land trails lead to the lake, but it's also accessible to paddlers via Lewis Lake and Lewis River Channel. Yellowstone National Park Lodges (307.242.3893, yellowstonenationalparklodges.com) also offers backcountry boat shuttle service to some of the more remote locations along Yellowstone Lake.

Boating

Whether you use a motorized boat, kayak, canoe, or even a float tube, you must obtain a permit before hitting the water. They are available in person at Lewis Lake Ranger Station, Grant Village Backcountry Office, and Bridge Bay Ranger Station. Float tube-only permits are available at North Entrance, Northeast

Avalanche Peak

Entrance, and Bechler Ranger Station. Permits are $20/$10 (annual/7-day) for motorized boats and $10/$5 for non-motorized crafts. Motorized boats are only allowed on Lewis and Yellowstone Lakes. Jet-skis and watersports (e.g., waterskiing) are prohibited. Canoes, kayaks, and SUPs are permitted on all lakes except Sylvan, Eleanor and Twin Lakes, and Beach Springs Lagoon. All types of watercraft are prohibited from streams and rivers except for the channel between Lewis and Shoshone Lakes where non-motorized boats are allowed. Kayak Yellowstone (307.413.6177, geyserkayak.com) offers guided day and overnight trips. Shurr Adventures (239.300.3004, shurradventuresyellowstone.com) offers paddling (and hiking) daytrips.

Motorized boats are permitted on most of Yellowstone Lake and Lewis Lake. Boat launches are located at Lewis Lake and Bridge Bay Marina. Yellowstone National Park Lodges (307.344.7311, yellowstonenationalparklodges.com) offers hour-long cruises on Yellowstone Lake for about $20/adult. They also have motorized boats (40hp, $60/hour) and rowboats ($10/hour) for rent at Bridge Bay Marina. Cruises and rentals are available from mid-June to early September. Rentals are available on a first-come, first-served basis and the office opens at 8am.

Horseback Riding

Yellowstone National Park Lodges (307.344.7311, yellowstonenationalparklodges.com) offers 1-hour ($55) and 2-hour ($75) trail rides departing from Roosevelt Lodge and Cabins, and Canyon Lodge and Cabins. A favorite activity from Roosevelt Lodge is the 1–2-hour ($92–102) trail ride to a western style cookout. Both are interpretive rides featuring knowledgeable guides who educate riders on the park's history and geography. Minimum age is 8 years old. Riders ages 8–11 must be accompanied by an adult. Minimum height is 4-ft. Maximum weight is 240 pounds. Helmets are available upon request. They also offer Stagecoach rides ($15.50/adult) from Roosevelt Corral.

If you'd like to get away from the standard equine offerings, consider a multi-day pack trip into the Yellowstone backcountry. You're in the heart of American dude ranch country and there are plenty to choose from. Elkhorn Ranch (North Entrance, 406.995.4291, elkhornranch-montana.com) is a family-focused ranch. Nine Quarter Circle Ranch (North Entrance, 406.995.4276, ninequartercircle.com) has been living and ranching in southern Montana for 75 years now, so they should know how to show you a good time. Dry Ridge Outfitters (Jackson Hole, 208.351.1796, dryridge.com) will take you to Grand Teton and/or Yellowstone. Sunrise Pack Station (Bozeman, 406.579.9642, sunrisepackstation.com) offers everything, trail rides, pack trips, hayrides, even sleigh rides! Rockin HK (406.333.4933, rockinhk.com) will take you just about anywhere in Yellowstone horses can get to on 3–12-day pack trips. Rand Creek Ranch (East Entrance, 307.587.3200, randcreekranch.com) can satisfy your horseback riding needs near Cody, WY. The same family has been running Covered Wagon Ranch (North Entrance, 406.995.4237, coveredwagonranch.com) since 1925. Mountain Sky Ranch (North Entrance, 800.548.3392, mountainsky.com) and Lone Mountain Ranch (North Entrance, 406.995.4644, lonemountainranch.com) are more luxurious "ranching" options. Even though they don't operate in Yellowstone, it'd be wrong not to mention Bitterroot Ranch (Dubois, WY, 800.545.0019, bitterrootranch.com) as another destination for the serious horse enthusiast. They provide cattle drives and all sorts of horse-riding fun.

Guided Bus/Van Tours

Yellowstone National Park Lodges (307.344.7311, yellowstonenationalparklodges.com) offers **yellow bus tours** like "Evening Wildlife Excursion" (Mammoth, 4 hours, $75/adult), "Wake Up to Wildlife" (Mammoth, 5 hours, $102), "Twilight on the Firehole" (Old Faithful Inn, 2 hours, $42/adult), "Firehole Basin Adventure" (Old Faithful Inn, $61, 3 hours), "Geyser Gazers" (Old Faithful Inn, 1.5 hours, $31.50), and "Lake Butte Sunset Tour" (Lake Hotel, 2 hours, $43.50). The signature tour is "Circle of Fire" (8 hours, $92.50). It departs from Old Faithful Inn, Grant Village, and Lake Hotel, and circles the lower loop of Grand Loop Road. There's also a "Yellowstone In a Day" tour (10 hours, $127). Tours are half price for children ages 3–11, and children 2 and under are free. Don't see anything you like? They can also help you plan a custom guided tour ($686–1,650 for 8 hours depending on the size of your group). Yellowstone Association (406.848.2400, yellowstone.org) offers private customizable tours exploring the parks wilderness with an Institute naturalist guide, if you're looking for someone to show you around.

Biking

Bicycles (and e-bikes) are allowed on all park roads and a few trails but prohibited from backcountry trails and boardwalks. Two gravel roads are ideal for mountain bikes: Old Gardiner Road, which connects Mammoth Hot Springs and Gardiner, and Blacktail Plateau Drive, which (is known for bear sightings and) runs parallel to a short section of Grand Loop Road (GLR) between Tower and Mammoth. These roads are one-way for motorists, but cyclists may travel in either direction. They're also a good alternative to the busy GLR.

To explore some of the park's 300 miles of paved roadways by bike, it's best to deal with temperamental weather and visit in fall. Or between mid-April and mid-May (when the snowmobiling season has ended, and roads remain closed to motorized vehicles to prepare for the upcoming tourist season), cyclists can pedal between West Entrance and Mammoth Hot Springs (weather permitting). If you're thinking about it, make sure you come prepared. Weather is unpredictable, and all the park's services and facilities will be closed. Dress in layers and stock up on supplies in Gardiner or West Yellowstone before you arrive. Also be sure to wear safety gear and high-visibility clothing as high snowbanks make travel more dangerous. To pedal when the weather is more pleasant, try going early in the morning or later in the evening during the busy tourist season. Occasionally, bicycle clubs hold evening full moon rides. The moon may be bright, but not bright enough. You'll need front and rear lights. Still, pedaling GLR at night is not the best idea.

The easiest options are found at bike-approved trails. Bunsen Peak Road (10 miles) near Mammoth, Riverside Trail (1.4 miles) near the West Entrance, Fountain Freight Road (3 miles) and Lone Star Geyser Road (4.8 miles) near Old Faithful, Morning Glory Pool from Old Faithful Inn (2 miles), Natural Bridge (2.5 miles) near Bridge Bay, and Mount Washburn (5 miles) from Chittenden Road to its summit near Tower, are open to bikes. Yellowstone National Park Lodges has bike rentals ($10/hour, $30/4-hour, $40/24-hour) at Old Faithful Snow Lodge. Touring cyclists receive discounted rates at many campgrounds with biker/hiker campsites.

Swimming

There are two popular swimming holes. One spot is located on Gardner River, two miles north of Mammoth on North Entrance Road at a spot known as Boiling River (closed when we went to print). The other is a pool below Firehole Falls near Madison Junction. Swimming in Yellowstone Lake is not advised because

Firehole River

water temperature rarely exceeds 60°F. As you can imagine there are many many more hot springs and "hot pots" (like Dunanda Falls) inside and outside the park, but I don't know about them. You'll have to get a dedicated guidebook for that. Speaking of, "buy my Yellowstone Hot Springs …" just kidding.

Fishing

Fishing has been a popular activity since the park was established. Before dipping your line in the water hoping to catch the renowned Yellowstone cutthroat, all anglers 16 and older must obtain a permit (3-day: $18, 7-day: $25, season: $40). Children under 15 can fish without one if they are observed by an adult with a permit or they can obtain a free permit (signed by a responsible adult). Permits are available at visitor centers, ranger stations, and several area fly shops. Anglers should visit the park website or discuss their plans with a park ranger prior to fishing to receive accurate regulations. Popular locations for watching trout like LeHardy's Rapids (June only) and Fishing Bridge prohibit fishing. The northeast corner is widely regarded as The Place to fish, but the park is humongous, and you'll find fish ready

Old Faithful

to put up a fight throughout. And there are nearly unlimited guides: Three Rivers Ranch (Warm River, ID, 208.652.3750, threeriversranch.com), Firehole Ranch (West Yellowstone, 406.646.7294, fireholeranch.com), Arrick's Fly Shop (West Yellowstone, 406.646.7290, arricks.com), Hubbard's Lodge (North Entrance, 406.848.7755, hubbardslodge.com), Montana Angler (North Entrance, 406.522.9854, montanaangler.com), Gallatin River Guides (North Entrance, 406.995.2290, montanaflyfishing.com), Montana Angling Co. (North Entrance, 406.579.9553, montanaanglingco.com), Long Outfitting (North Entrance, 406.220.6775, longoutfitting. com), Nelson's (North Entrance, 406.222.6560, nelsonsguidesandflies.com), Trout on the Fly (North Entrance, 406.580.7370, montanatroutonthefly.com), Angler's West Fly Fishing (North Entrance, 406.333.4401, montanaflyfishers.com), and Montana Trout Wranglers (North Entrance, 406.580.6050, troutwranglers.com). Yellowstone National Park Lodges provides charter fishing on Yellowstone Lake for $103 per hour departing from Bridge Bay Marina.

Photography

What better way to remember Yellowstone than a collection of your own professional-quality photographs? Regardless of your camera (or phone), a Yellowstone photo tour is sure to send you home with jaw-dropping images you can't wait to decorate your home with. While the scenery does most of the work, an experienced photo tour guide can teach subtle tips and techniques to make your vacation shots pop. Yellowstone National Park Lodges offers a 5-hour Picture Perfect Photo Safari. Tours depart from Old Faithful Inn and Lake Hotel, and require a minimum of two paying customers. They are generally available from late May until late September. They meet at the hotel between 5:45am and 6:30am to take advantage of the soft morning light. Rates are $102.50 per adult. Outfitters like Alpenglow Tours (307.739.1914, alpenglowtours.com) lead specialized photography tours if you'd like a pro at your side. They have the advantage of spending most days in the park, knowing the land

and where wildlife has been active. You could also join a wildlife-specific outfitter like Yellowstone Wild Tours (406.224.0001, yellowstonewildtours.com) or Yellowstone Wolf Tracker (wolftracker.com). Rather do it on your own? Grand Prismatic Spring and Grand Canyon of the Yellowstone rarely disappoint.

Winter Activities

There are limitations, but the park can be even more incredible in winter. North Entrance, Northeast Entrance, and Mammoth–Tower are the only roads open to wheeled vehicles during winter. Cars are left behind in favor of **snowmobiles** and **snowcoaches**. There are many licensed guides who lead snowmobile (and snowcoach) tours of Yellowstone or, through the Non-commercially Guided Snowmobile Access Program, up to four groups (of five or less) can enter the park each day (one group per oversnow entrance—the West Entrance is the most popular). Backcountry Adventures (406.646.9317, backcountry-adventures.com) offers snowmobile tours and rentals, and snowcoach tours from West Yellowstone. Yellowstone Vacations (406.848.5171, yellowstonevacations.com) offers all that from West Yellowstone and Gardiner (north). Gary Fales Outfitting (307.587.3970, garyfalesoutfitting.com) is the only option for snowmobile tours and rentals on the east (more mountainous) side of the park. And Scenic Safaris (307.734.8898, scenic-safaris.com) has snowmobile and snowcoach tours from the south side of the park (including Grand Teton). Refer to the park's website for a complete list of snowmobile guides and rental outfitters (you must use BAT snowmobiles, so your sleds may not suffice). A permit is required for private groups. They are awarded via lottery through recreation.gov. Permits cost $40/day plus a $6 application fee, a small price to pay to avoid the throngs of summer visitors.

Yellowstone National Park Lodges offers an array of snowcoach tours from Mammoth and Old Faithful between late December and early March. Rates listed below are for adults. Children (ages 3–11) cost about half the adult rate. Mammoth to Old Faithful ($266) and Tour of the Grand Canyon of the Yellowstone ($230.50) are two of the basic trips. From Mammoth you can take tours of Norris Geyser Basin ($101.50) and Wake Up to Wildlife ($85.50). A few of the parks most popular hiking trails are groomed for skiers during winter. Yellowstone National Park Lodges offers a cross-country skier shuttle from Mammoth for $24 (each way). Snowshoe and ski rental, guided tours, trail info, as well as ski repair and instruction are available at Bear Den Ski Shop at Mammoth Hot Springs.

Fountain Paint Pots

Yellowstone Visitor and Information Centers

Name & Phone	Open	Notes
Albright Visitor Center (Mammoth) (307) 344-2263	Daily, All Year, 9am–5pm extended hours in summer	Museum of people in the park (Natives to NPS Rangers), Thomas Moran Gallery, Theater, free Wi-Fi
West Yellowstone Info Center (307) 344-2876	mid-April–early November	Information for West Entrance users, located at West Yellowstone Chamber of Commerce
Old Faithful Visitor Center (307) 344-2751	mid-April–early November mid-December–mid-March	Newest facility features exhibits on hydrothermal features and other geologic phenomena
Canyon Visitor Education Center (307) 344-2550	mid–April–early November	Explores the geology of Yellowstone, including its volcanoes, geysers, hot springs, and geologic history
Fishing Bridge Visitor Center (307) 344-2450	late May–mid-October	Explores the park's wildlife • Backcountry office and bookstore are available
Grant Visitor Center (307) 344-2650	late May–mid-October	Named for President Ulysses S. Grant, it explores the role of fire at Yellowstone
Madison Information Station (307) 344-2876	late May–mid-October	Information and Yellowstone Association bookstore
Museum of Park Rangers (Norris) (307) 344-7353	May–late September	Short movie and exhibits about Park Rangers
Norris Geyser Basin Museum (307) 344-2812	May–mid-October	Explores the park's unique geothermal geology
West Thumb Info Station (307) 344-2650	May–mid-October	Information and Yellowstone Association bookstore

Visitor Centers & Services

All developed areas have a visitor center or ranger station. They're listed in the table on the previous page along with contact info, seasons, and a few basic notes. Additionally, you'll find year-round medical services at Mammoth Clinic, and medical services at Lake Clinic and Old Faithful Clinic in summer. Post Offices are available at Mammoth Hot Springs, Canyon Village, Lake Village, Grant Village, and Old Faithful. 24-hour gas is available at Mammoth Hot Springs, Tower Junction, Canyon Village, Fishing Bridge, Grant Village, and Old Faithful. Refueling in the park will cost noticeably more than surrounding gateway towns (except Cooke City). Electric vehicle charging stations are available at Yellowstone Forever (Gardiner), Mammoth Hot Springs, Canyon Village, Lake Village, and Old Faithful. General Stores are located in Mammoth Hot Springs, Tower, Canyon Village, Fishing Bridge, Lake Village, Grant Village, and Old Faithful.

Ranger Programs & For Kids

Yellowstone is brash and exuberant. Water drops hundreds of feet before passing through a beautiful yellow canyon. Water and mud boil vigorously. Bison and grizzlies lumber along roadways. Geysers send columns of water shooting into the air. And then there's the smell. Many of the geothermal features are accompanied with the smell of sulphur, similar to rotten eggs. Yellowstone gets in your face and your nose. It's screaming for attention. And the best way to immerse all your senses is on a ranger-led activity.

Rangers entertain guests with talks, walks, adventure hikes, and evening programs from the busy summer season through winter. Programs take place in all areas. To find out exactly what, when, and where they are, visit the park's website or stop in at a visitor center as soon as you arrive. Almost all programs are free of charge. One exception is Yellowstone Lake Scenic Cruise, which requires a fee and advance reservation. Yellowstone National Park Lodges operates the tour, while a park ranger narrates. It costs $19.25 for adults and $11.25 for children (ages 3–11). For reservations call (307) 344-7311 or stop by the Bridge Bay Marina.

Talks, walks, and evening programs are all great, but the Adventure Hikes are where it's at. If your schedule permits, join a ranger on at least one of the following: Hayden Valley Venture, Gem of the Rockies, or Fairy Falls Frolic. Tours are limited to 15 people. You must sign up in-person, in advance, at a specific visitor center. Refer to the park website for details. Most Adventure Hikes are available from mid-June through

August. The selection is reduced for fall, but programs are still available at all major areas. In winter only evening programs, afternoon talks, and snowshoe walks are available. Since there are dozens of programs, all of which are incredibly rewarding, it's a good practice to take your favorite (or what you think will be your favorite) Yellowstone attraction and join a ranger-led activity for that feature/region. Ultimately you can't go wrong. You can close your eyes and point to the list of activities if you'd like. Park rangers can even help plan your vacation before you arrive through a series of free videos and podcasts available at the park website and iTunes, respectively. They even have an app!

Yellowstone provides several online and in-park activities designed specifically for kids. You'll find things like a virtual stamp online. "Ask a Ranger" provides answers to frequently asked questions. And there's an interactive map to help with the travel plans. It's educational fun for all ages that can help build excitement for your Yellowstone vacation.

Once you've arrived, children (ages 4 and up) can become a Yellowstone National Park Junior Ranger. The program introduces kids to the wonders of Yellowstone and their role in preserving these treasures for future generations. Children must complete a 12-page activity booklet to become a Junior Ranger. The booklet is available at any visitor center for the reasonable price of $3. Once your child completes the activities, attends a ranger-led program, and hikes a park trail, he/she will receive a Junior Ranger Badge, marking admission into the Yellowstone Junior Ranger Club. You may need to check out one of the Junior Ranger Snowpacks to become a Junior Ranger during winter. Snowshoes may also be required. Packs and snowshoes are available at Mammoth and Old Faithful Visitor Centers. There's also a Young Scientist program designed for children five and up. Like with Junior Rangers, you buy a booklet (at Canyon or Old Faithful Visitor Education Center), and then use it to go on a science-based adventure throughout the park and visitor center. A job well-done is awarded with a patch or key chain.

Flora & Fauna

The landscape is covered with forests (80% of the park), grasslands (15%), and water (5%). Forests are dominated by lodgepole pines, but much of the plant life is still recovering from a forest fire that burned more than one-third of the park in 1988.

Yellowstone is more zoo than park. There are over 1,350 plant species and 67 species of mammals. It is home to the highest density of mammals in the contiguous United States, making Yellowstone one of the absolute best locations to view wildlife.

Bison, grizzly bears, and wolves are the stars. You may see Yellowstone cutthroat trout, elk, moose, coyote, and bighorn sheep. Lynx, mountain lion, and bobcat also reside here, but it's highly unlikely you'll cross their paths. There are two easily accessible areas for wildlife viewing: Hayden Valley, located between Canyon and Lake Villages, and Lamar Valley, located along Northeast Entrance Road just east of Tower. Lamar Valley is one of your best bets to spot a wolf. Be careful when viewing wildlife. You should stay at least 25 yards away from all mammals, and 100 yards away from predatory species like bears and wolves. If you'd like some help from the experts, you can join Yellowstone Wolf Tracker (wolftracker.com) on a private wildlife tour or join a group trip during the park's offseason.

Pets & Accessibility
Pets are allowed in the park but must be kept on a leash (less than six feet). They are prohibited from trails, boardwalks, the backcountry, and all hydrothermal areas. They are only allowed in developed areas and must remain at least 100 feet from roads, parking areas, and campgrounds. If you choose to bring your pet, it cannot be left unattended or tied to an object. Visitors with pets must be careful. There's a possibility pets could become prey or fall into a boiling spring (which happened in 2021). Unfortunately, there are no boarding kennels in Yellowstone, but some are available nearby, like Yellowstone Pet Boarding (406.578.3279, yellowstonepetboarding.com) in Livingston, MT. Service animals for people with permanent disabilities are allowed throughout the park and in all park facilities, but they must remain on a leash.

Wheelchair-accessible lodging is available in all areas of the park. Most campgrounds have at least one wheelchair-accessible campsite. Accessible restrooms are available in all developed areas. Accessible showers are available at Grant Village Campground, Old Faithful Inn, and Fishing Bridge RV Park. Old Faithful, Canyon, Grant, and Albright (Mammoth), West Thumb, and West Yellowstone Visitor Centers are accessible. A wheelchair-accessible fishing ramp and platform are available on Madison River at Mount Haynes Overlook (3.5 miles west of Madison Junction). Many of the walkways and self-guided trails have at least one wheelchair-accessible walkway. Accessible ranger programs are offered. Wheelchairs are available for loan at Old Faithful, Canyon, Albright (Mammoth), Grant, Fishing

Near the Northeast Entrance

Bridge, and Norris Visitor Centers, as well as all lodging facilities (while staying in these areas). Mammoth, Canyon, and Old Faithful are the most accessible areas of the park. Wheelchairs can be rented on a first-come, first-served basis at all medical clinics.

Weather
Yellowstone has a typical mountain climate: long, cold winters and short, hot summers. Average highs in summer max out around 80°F, and average winter lows hover around 10°F. Snow is common from fall to spring, with an annual average accumulation of 72 inches. It's not a secret that the best months to visit (weather-wise) are July and August. The weather is great, but crowds can be thick. May and September are nice alternatives. Or, if you have a bit more travel flexibility, you can find traveling during the offseason to be much more enjoyable than June through August when 75% of all visitors come to the park.

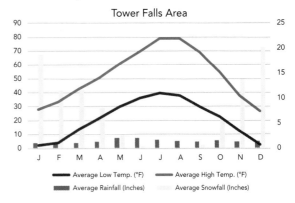

Tower Falls Area

Average Low Temp. (°F) — Average High Temp. (°F)
Average Rainfall (Inches) — Average Snowfall (Inches)

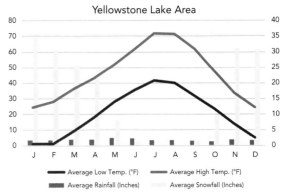

Yellowstone Lake Area

Average Low Temp. (°F) — Average High Temp. (°F)
Average Rainfall (Inches) — Average Snowfall (Inches)

Tips & Recommendations

Yellowstone is not a one-day-visit kind of park. You should be thinking about three days at a minimum. That much time and you can quickly hit a lot of the highlights. Spend five or more and you'll really have time to get a taste of Yellowstone.

But remember, almost one million visitors show up at Yellowstone each month from June through August. That's nearly 75% of annual visitation. And maybe one out of every hundred visitors goes deeper into the park than the day-hikes and roadways. All the popular destinations will be busy. You'll have to make some compromises. Pack your patience and deal with the crowds? Wake up before the sun? Plan a trip in the offseason?

You shouldn't do this, but if you're racing through the park, the couple of easy sights to see that should not be missed are Grand Canyon of the Yellowstone, Grand Prismatic Spring, and Old Faithful (you may have to stick around up to 90 minutes for it to go off—check the online predictions for other geyser eruptions). A quick look or two at Yellowstone Lake, Mammoth Hot Springs Terrace, and Tower Fall would be nice too.

If you're thinking of arriving at West Yellowstone via US-20, try ID-47 instead. It's very scenic with some big waterfalls (Upper and Lower Mesa Falls) along the way.

A big part of any trip to Yellowstone is spotting wildlife. Best times are morning and evening, and the two most reliable locations are Hayden and Lamar Valleys (thanks to bison). Elk are regularly spotted in Mammoth Hot Springs and by the west entrance. Bring binoculars. Continually scan the perimeter. (If you see a car pulled over, possibly looking at wildlife, don't stop in the middle of the road. If it's safe to pull over, do so, otherwise, move along to the next designated parking area, if that's possible.)

Go to Old Faithful and Grand Canyon of the Yellowstone early in the morning to avoid the crowds. Evening is often less crowded too, but I prefer morning light at both these locations.

Grand Canyon of the Yellowstone is a natural wonder, and guests are always looking for the best vantage point. Via South Rim Drive: Be at Artist Point for sunrise and hike Uncle Tom's Trail. Via North Rim Drive: Stop at Lookout Point and Red Rock Point, and hike to the Brink of Lower Falls. They're all great. Enjoy them. Come back later to see the waterfall under different light. There's a good reason artists love this spot.

All the geyser basins are interesting and unique in their own way. Midway is many visitors' favorite solely due to Grand Prismatic Spring (it's truly magnificent). Norris Geyser Basin is cool because it looks, feels, and smells different than the others. Upper (Old Faithful) and Lower have reliable geysers that are awesome. West Thumb is fun as it's right on Yellowstone Lake. You won't see anything like Mammoth Hot Springs Terrace anywhere else in the United States. And Monument Geyser Basin, Biscuit Basin, and Black Sand Basin each have their charm. Visit them all if you have time. But be sure to mix in some mountains, waterfalls, and wildlife.

You are allowed to soak in bodies of water fed by run-off from hydrothermal features. The two most popular are Boiling River (north of Mammoth Hot Springs, closed when we went to print) and a swimming area just south of Firehole Falls on Firehole Canyon Drive.

Cascade Corner is wonderful but there is a substantial cost of entry: it's remote, accessed via a long gravel road, and trails are rather long by day hike standards. It's a popular area for horseback riders, and, if you hike here, you'll notice trails often lead to deep stream crossings (for horses). Off to the side you'll usually find a better crossing for hikers. Regardless bring a towel and water shoes for the creek crossings to Dunanda and Union Falls.

If you hike to Dunanda Falls, the trail leads to the top of the falls (which is also pretty cool). To get to the bottom you'll have to walk through site 9A3, descend to the river, and then continue upstream to the falls (be careful of hot spring water).

Drive to Cooke City. Beartooth Highway (MT-212) is impressive. (The east entrance is great as well.)

Remember to spend a few days at Grand Teton National Park directly to the south.

Easy Hikes: Fairy Falls (6.7 miles), Wraith Falls (1), Boiling River (1), Storm Point (2.3), Trout Lake (1.2), Lone Star Geyser (4.8)
Moderate Hikes: Dunanda Falls (16 miles from Bechler Ranger Station), Union Falls (multiple fairly long options), Bunsen Peak (4.6), Osprey Falls (8), Black Canyon of the Yellowstone (18), Yellowstone River Overlook (3.7), Mystic Falls (2.4), Observation Point (1.6)
Strenuous Hikes: Avalanche Peak (4.2 miles), Mount Washburn (5), Hellroaring (6.2), Seven Mile Hole (10), Sky Rim Loop (18), Heart Lake (15)
Extreme Hikes: Electric Peak (18 miles)

Family Activities: Visit in winter, admire the captivating colors of Grand Prismatic Spring, become Junior Rangers, watch Old Faithful, view animals at Lamar and/or Hayden Valleys

Guided Tours: Snowcoach Tours, Yellowstone Lake Cruises, ride a horse

Rainy Day Activities: Duck into a Visitor Center, drive the roads, admire the fantastic architecture of the Old Faithful Inn, or take advantage of a bunch of visitors being in their lodges/tents and hit the trails as long as it's safe

Sunset Spots: Lower Geyser Basin (Great Fountain Geyser, Fountain Paint Pot), Upper Geyser Basin, Hayden Valley, Norris Geyser Basin, Yellowstone Lake (Steamboat Point)

Sunrise Spots: Grand Canyon of the Yellowstone (Artist Point), Mammoth Hot Springs Terrace, Yellowstone Lake (West Thumb Geyser Basin), West Entrance (along the Madison River), Upper Geyser Basin

Riverside Geyser (Upper Geyser Basin)

Wildlife: You're pretty much guaranteed bison viewing at Hayden Valley and usually elk at Mammoth Hot Springs; Lamar Valley is great for bison, pronghorn, and wolves, West Entrance can be good for wolves and elk, beyond that it's luck of the draw, wake up early and stay out late for the best wildlife chances

Beyond the Park...

Dining
Firehole BBQ • West Yellowstone
fireholebbqco.com • (406) 641-0020

Tumbleweed Bookstore & Café
501 Scott St, Gardiner • (406) 848-2225

MontAsia • (406) 838-2382
montasia.ninja • Cooke City

Wy Thai • Cody • (307) 250-6725
1928 Big Horn Ave • wythai.com

The Breadboard • (307) 527-5788
breadboardcody.com • Cody

Fat Racks BBQ • (940) 453-8840
fatracksbbq.com • Cody

Noon Break 2 Go • Cody
noonbreak.com • (307) 578-7247

Grocery Stores
Food Roundup • (406) 646-7501
107 Dunraven St, West Yellowstone

Gardiner Market • 701 Scott St

Albertsons • (307) 527-7007
1825 17th St, Cody

Walmart • (307) 527-4673
321 Yellowstone Ave, Cody

Lodging
1872 Inn • 1872inn.com
603 Yellowstone Ave, W Yellowstone

Gateway Inn • (406) 848-7100
103 Bigelow Ln, Gardiner
yellowstonegatewayinn.com

High Country • (406) 838-2272
113 Main St W, Cooke City
highcountrymotelandcabins.com

The Cody Hotel • (307) 587-5915
232 Yellowstone Ave, Cody
thecody.com

Campgrounds
West Gate KOA
3305 US-20, West Yellowstone
koa.com • (406) 646-7606

Yellowstone Grizzly RV Park
210 S Electric St, West Yellowstone
grizzlyrv.com • (406) 646-4466

Yellowstone RV Park • Gardiner
121 US-89 • (406) 848-7496
rvparkyellowstone.com
Eagle Creek Campground
Custer Gallatin National Forest

Red Lodge KOA
7464 US-212, Red Lodge
koa.com • (406) 446-2364

Ponderosa Camp • (307) 587-9203
codyponderosa.com • Cody

Cody KOA
5561 Greybull Hwy, Cody
koa.com • (307) 587-2369

Parkway RV Campground
132 Yellowstone Ave, Cody
(307) 527-5927

Buffalo Bill State Park
4192 N Fork Hwy, Cody

Festivals
Cody Stampede • June–August
codystampederodeo.com

Red Ants Pants Festival • July
redantspantsmusicfestival.com

Attractions
Caribou-Targhee National Forest
Over three million acres of non-continuous wilderness in Idaho, Wyoming, and Utah. Forest land extends along the western boundary of Yellowstone and Grand Teton National Parks. You'll find many campgrounds, as well as popular sites like Upper and Lower Mesa Falls (near West Yellowstone).
fs.usda.gov

Sawtooth National Forest
Collection of wilderness areas with great backpacking and hiking, especially near Stanley, ID (Tin Cup Trailhead and Hell Roaring Lake).

Bighorn National Forest
Another wilderness area with superb hiking and backpacking. This one is east of Yellowstone.

Gallatin National Forest
Alpine lakes and waterfalls

Lewis and Clark Caverns State Park
Largest known limestone cave in the northwest
25 Lewis & Clark Caverns Road, Whitehall, MT • fwp.mt.gov

Shoshone Falls State Park
Interesting Snake River waterfall
4155 Shoshone Falls Grade, Twin Falls • tfid.org

Grizzly & Wolf Discovery Center
201 S Canyon St, West Yellowstone
grizzlydiscoveryctr.org

Wild West Rafting • (406) 848-2252
Whitewater, float, trail rides
wildwestrafting.com

Flying Pig Rafting • (888) 792-9193
Whitewater, trail rides, and tours
511 Scott St, Gardiner
flyingpigrafting.com

Montana Whitewater Rafting
Whitewater, kayak, trail rides, fly fishing, and ziplining
603 Scott St, Gardiner • (406) 763-4465
montanawhitewater.com

Jake's Horses • (406) 995-4630
200 Beaver Creek Rd, Gallatin
jakeshorses.com

Big Sky Resort • (800) 548-4486
Skiing, Yellowstone tours
50 Big Sky Resort Rd, Big Sky
bigskyresort.com

The Cody Cattle Co • (307) 272-5770
Country music and dinner
1910 Demaris Dr, Cody
thecodycattlecompany.com

Buffalo Bill Center • (307) 587-4771
720 Sheridan Ave, Cody
centerofthewest.org

Glacier

The hike to Grinnell Glacier

Phone: (406) 888-7800
Website: nps.gov/glac

Established: May 11, 1910
Size: 1,013,594 Acres
Annual Visitors: 3 Million
Peak Season: July–September
Hiking Trails: 745 Miles

Activities: Hiking, Backpacking, Red Jammer Tours, Boat Tours, Fishing, Horseback Riding, Biking, Cross-country Skiing, Snowshoeing

13 Campgrounds: $10–23/night
Backcountry Camping: Permitted*
6 Lodges: $70–229/night

Park Hours: All day, every day
Entrance Fee: $35/30/20 (car/motorcycle/individual)

*A $7 per person per night Backcountry Permit is required

George Bird Grinnell came to northwestern Montana on a hunting expedition; he found a land so beautiful and majestic he named it "the Crown of the Continent." More than 100 glaciers capped the mountains' rugged peaks. Turquoise lakes dotted the high country. Green forests spread out as far as his eyes could see. It was a land completely unspoiled by human hands. Grinnell returned again and again. He was drawn by the prominence of the mountains, purity of the lakes, and peacefulness of his surroundings. These Rocky Mountain landscapes inspired him to spend the better part of two decades working to protect this special area as a national park.

Grinnell found an unlikely ally in the Great Northern Railway. Following the blueprint created by Southern Pacific Railroad at Yosemite National Park, the Great Northern hoped to stimulate passenger service by promoting scenic wonders like Glacier. In 1891, rail crossed the Continental Divide at Marias Pass, just south of the present-day park boundary. That same year, George Bird Grinnell wrote in his journal that the land surrounding St. Mary Lake should be a national park. The Great Northern couldn't agree more. They knew it would be much easier to deal with the federal government rather than negotiating with hundreds of private landowners.

In 1897, land was set aside as the Lewis and Clark Forest Preserve, largely due to lobbying by Grinnell and the railway. Grinnell continued to pursue the idea of a national park, and his efforts proved successful on May 11, 1910, when President William Howard Taft signed legislation establishing Glacier, the nation's tenth national park.

The Great Northern Railway had gotten their wish too, receiving sole rights to develop the area. Glacier Park Lodge and Many Glacier Hotel were erected. Chalets were built in the backcountry at Sperry, Granite Park, Cut Bank, and Gunsight Lake. Blackfeet Indians, who once hunted the Rockies' western slopes and performed ceremonies on the shores of St. Mary Lake, sold more than 800,000 acres of their land to the U.S. government for $1.5 million. Not long after, tribal members were camped in tipis atop McAlpin Hotel in New York City as a publicity stunt for the railroad. They rode the subway and visited the Brooklyn Bridge. They danced at the annual *Travel and Vacation Show*. Everywhere they went, people referred to them as "the Indians of Glacier National Park." Blackfeet were at the park too, standing in traditional clothing, waiting to greet visitors. This advertising campaign was yet another attempt by the Great Northern Railway to get Americans to "See America First."

The campaign worked. Upper-middle class Americans were flocking to these wonders of the western frontier. Tourists arrived by train and were catered to by the railway's subsidiary companies. George Bird Grinnell believed tourism ruined Yellowstone and Glacier. Stephen Mather, the first director of the National Park Service, understood that tourism was the only thing that could save them. The parks needed to be made dollarable or the government would give in to constant pressures of commercial interests like mining, logging, and oil. Mather envisioned park roads as spectacular feats of engineering, an attraction in and of themselves. At Glacier, the goal was to build a road through the center of the park, across the Continental Divide, and Mather approved construction of a much more expensive route carved into the face of Garden Wall.

Dedicated on July 15, 1933, Going-to-the-Sun Road still serves as the park's main attraction. It crosses the crown of the continent, providing access for millions of guests to the awe-inspiring alpine lakes, knife-edge ridgelines, and craggy mountaintops George Bird Grinnell so admired. It connects lodges originally established by the Great Northern Railway, the very same places where today's visitors spend a night or two after exploring Glacier National Park and taking the time to "See America First." Now it's your turn. Come and see the Crown of the Continent for yourself.

Logan Pass sunrise

When to Go
Glacier is open all year, but long winters cause road and facility closures from fall through spring. Most roads and facilities are open from late May to early September, but Going-to-the-Sun Road (GTSR) first opens for public use around late June/early July and it usually stays open until October. Exact dates vary from year-to-year. Most park visitors arrive in July and August (about one million each month), when weather is best and GTSR is open. Not even one hundred thousand guests arrive between November and March to enjoy the park covered in snow.

Free Shuttles, Amtrak, and Airports
To reduce pollution and congestion, the park provides free shuttle service along Going-to-the-Sun Road from late June/early July through early September. Shuttles make several stops in between Apgar Transit Center (west) and St. Mary Visitor Center (east). They depart every 15–30 minutes. They're extremely convenient, especially considering parking at stops like Logan Pass fill by 8am on busy days. But shuttles fill too. You must reserve a shuttle ticket in advance through recreation.gov for a reservation fee of $1 per ticket. Most tickets for the entire season are released on June 1. The rest are released two days ahead of time on a rolling window.

Amtrak (800.872.7245 or amtrak.com) serves East Glacier, West Glacier, and Whitefish. One-way fare from Chicago costs about $200. Glacier Park Inc. (406.892.2525, glacierparkinc.com), operates shuttles on the east side ($15–75, one-way). Glacier National Park Lodges (855.733.4522, glaciernationalparklodges.com) provides shuttle service from West Glacier Train Station to Apgar ($5–10, one-way).

The nearest airport is Glacier Park International (GPI), located near Kalispell, 30 miles from the West Entrance. Great Falls International (GTF) is the closest airport to the eastern boundary (about 140 miles from East Glacier Village). Spokane International (GEG), 280 miles to the west, is the closest large airport. Car rental is available at each location.

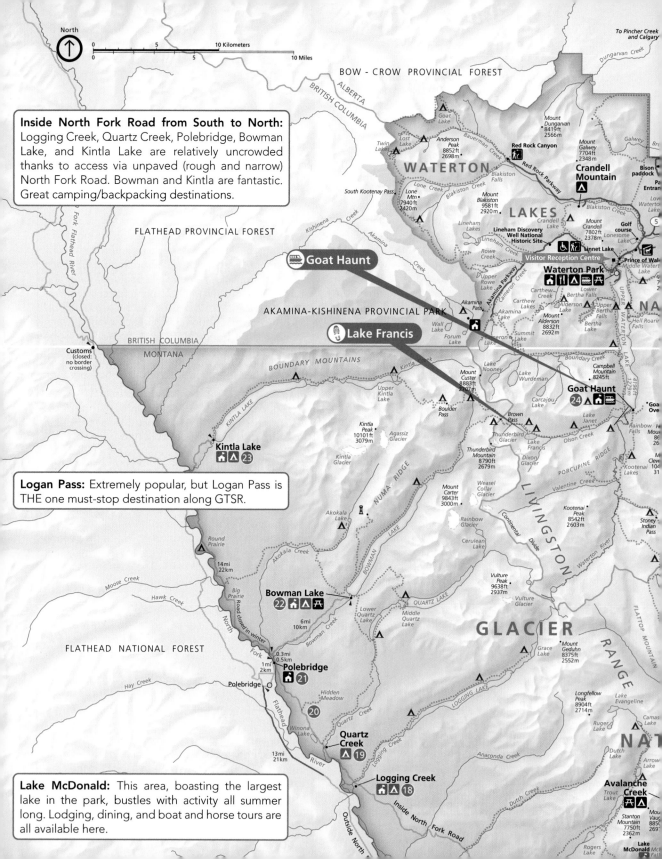

Inside North Fork Road from South to North: Logging Creek, Quartz Creek, Polebridge, Bowman Lake, and Kintla Lake are relatively uncrowded thanks to access via unpaved (rough and narrow) North Fork Road. Bowman and Kintla are fantastic. Great camping/backpacking destinations.

Logan Pass: Extremely popular, but Logan Pass is THE one must-stop destination along GTSR.

Lake McDonald: This area, boasting the largest lake in the park, bustles with activity all summer long. Lodging, dining, and boat and horse tours are all available here.

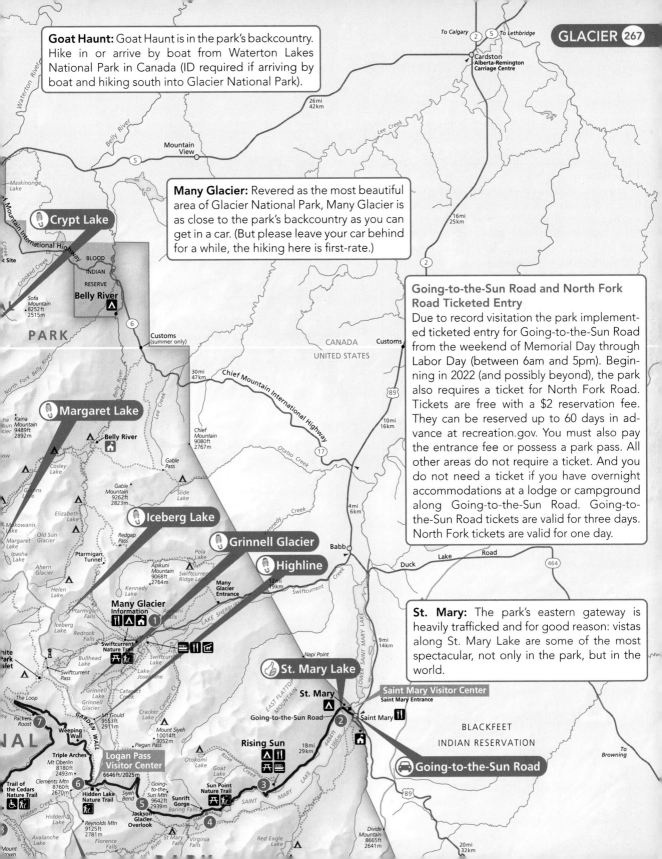

Goat Haunt: Goat Haunt is in the park's backcountry. Hike in or arrive by boat from Waterton Lakes National Park in Canada (ID required if arriving by boat and hiking south into Glacier National Park).

Crypt Lake

Many Glacier: Revered as the most beautiful area of Glacier National Park, Many Glacier is as close to the park's backcountry as you can get in a car. (But please leave your car behind for a while, the hiking here is first-rate.)

Going-to-the-Sun Road and North Fork Road Ticketed Entry
Due to record visitation the park implemented ticketed entry for Going-to-the-Sun Road from the weekend of Memorial Day through Labor Day (between 6am and 5pm). Beginning in 2022 (and possibly beyond), the park also requires a ticket for North Fork Road. Tickets are free with a $2 reservation fee. They can be reserved up to 60 days in advance at recreation.gov. You must also pay the entrance fee or possess a park pass. All other areas do not require a ticket. And you do not need a ticket if you have overnight accommodations at a lodge or campground along Going-to-the-Sun Road. Going-to-the-Sun Road tickets are valid for three days. North Fork tickets are valid for one day.

Margaret Lake

Iceberg Lake

Grinnell Glacier

Highline

St. Mary: The park's eastern gateway is heavily trafficked and for good reason: vistas along St. Mary Lake are some of the most spectacular, not only in the park, but in the world.

St. Mary Lake

Going-to-the-Sun Road

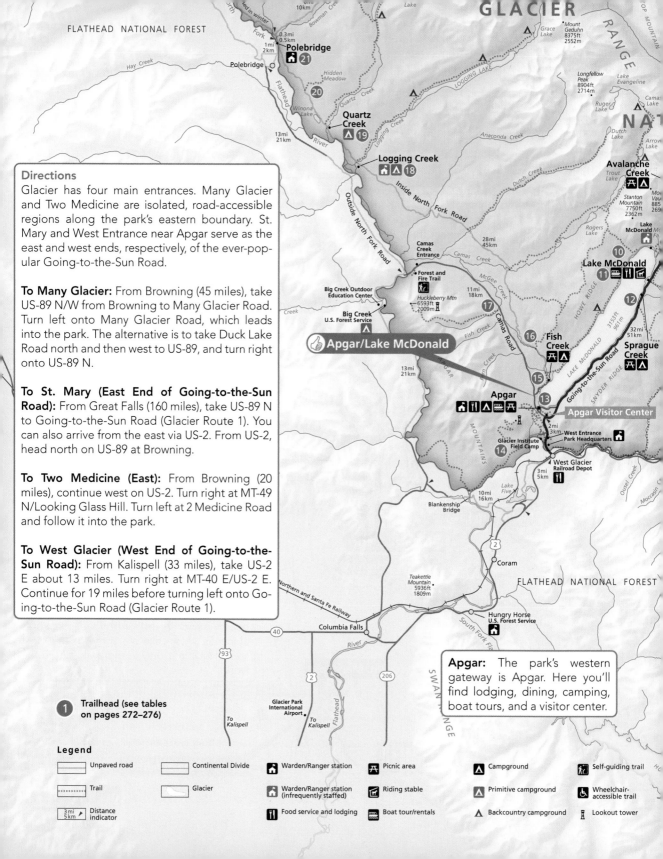

Directions

Glacier has four main entrances. Many Glacier and Two Medicine are isolated, road-accessible regions along the park's eastern boundary. St. Mary and West Entrance near Apgar serve as the east and west ends, respectively, of the ever-popular Going-to-the-Sun Road.

To Many Glacier: From Browning (45 miles), take US-89 N/W from Browning to Many Glacier Road. Turn left onto Many Glacier Road, which leads into the park. The alternative is to take Duck Lake Road north and then west to US-89, and turn right onto US-89 N.

To St. Mary (East End of Going-to-the-Sun Road): From Great Falls (160 miles), take US-89 N to Going-to-the-Sun Road (Glacier Route 1). You can also arrive from the east via US-2. From US-2, head north on US-89 at Browning.

To Two Medicine (East): From Browning (20 miles), continue west on US-2. Turn right at MT-49 N/Looking Glass Hill. Turn left at 2 Medicine Road and follow it into the park.

To West Glacier (West End of Going-to-the-Sun Road): From Kalispell (33 miles), take US-2 E about 13 miles. Turn right at MT-40 E/US-2 E. Continue for 19 miles before turning left onto Going-to-the-Sun Road (Glacier Route 1).

Apgar: The park's western gateway is Apgar. Here you'll find lodging, dining, camping, boat tours, and a visitor center.

1 Trailhead (see tables on pages 272–276)

Legend

Unpaved road	Warden/Ranger station	Picnic area
Trail	Warden/Ranger station (infrequently staffed)	Riding stable
Distance indicator	Food service and lodging	Boat tour/rentals
Continental Divide	Campground	Self-guiding trail
Glacier	Primitive campground	Wheelchair-accessible trail
	Backcountry campground	Lookout tower

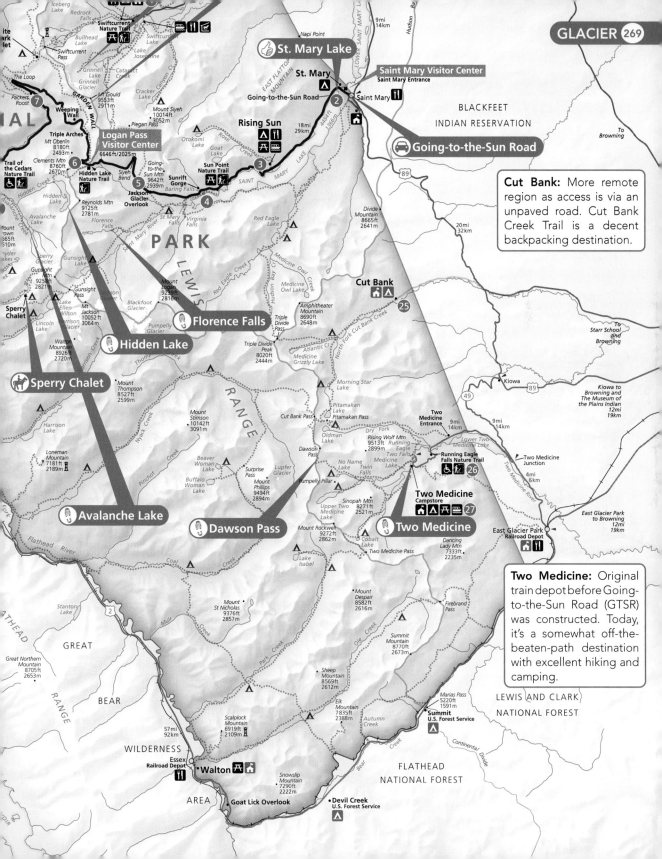

Glacier Camping (Fees are per night)

Name	Location	Open	Fee	Sites	Notes
St. Mary* - 🦽	GTSR	All Year	$23	148	Up to 40-ft parking space • F, DS, PC, HB
Rising Sun	GTSR	mid-June–mid-Sept	$20	84	Up to 25-ft parking space • F, DS, PC, HB
Avalanche	GTSR	mid-June–mid-Sept	$20	87	Up to 26-ft parking space • F, HB
Sprague Creek	GTSR	early May–mid-Sept	$20	25	No towed units, Up to 21-ft space • F, HB
Apgar - 🦽	Apgar	All Year	$20	194	Up to 40-ft parking space • F, DS, PC, HB
Two Medicine - 🦽	East Side	mid-April–late Sept	$20	100	Up to 35-ft parking space • F, DS, PC, HB
Cut Bank	East Side	early May–late Sept	$10	14	Dirt road, primitive camping, no potable H_2O
Many Glacier* - 🦽	East Side	late May–late Sept	$23	109	Up to 35-ft parking space • F, DS, PC, HB
Fish Creek* - 🦽	West Side	late June–early Sept	$23	178	Up to 35-ft parking space • F, DS, PC, HB
Logging Creek	West Side	early July–late Sept	$10	7	Dirt road, primitive camping, no potable H_2O
Quartz Creek	West Side	early July–late Oct	$10	7	Dirt road, primitive camping, no potable H_2O
Bowman Lake - 🦽	West Side	late May–mid-Sept	$15	46	Dirt road, large units not recommended • PC
Kintla Lake - 🦽	West Side	early May–mid-Sept	$15	13	Dirt road, large units not recommended • PC

*Campsites can be reserved up to six months in advance, June through Labor Day, at (877) 444-6777 or recreation.gov
F = Flush Toilets, DS = Dump Station, PC = Primitive Camping (after the open dates), HB = Hike/Bike Sites ($5–8/night)

Backcountry	A Backcountry User Permit is required for all overnight camping in the backcountry. Between June 15 and September 30 about half the sites can be reserved for a $40 application fee. Reservations can only be made online via pay.gov. All permits must be obtained in-person from one of these locations: Apgar Backcountry Permit Center (opens late June), St. Mary Visitor Center, Many Glacier Ranger Station, Two Medicine Ranger Station, Polebridge Ranger Station, or Waterton Lakes National Park Visitor Reception Center.
Group Camping	Available at Apgar*, Many Glacier, St. Mary, and Two Medicine ($65 plus $5 per person after first 9 campers)
Winter Camping	Available at St. Mary and Apgar from December 1–March 31

Glacier Lodging (Fees are per night)

Name	Open	Fee	Location & Notes
Glacier Park Lodge	early June–late Sept	$189–469	East Glacier • Golf, spa, and dining are available
St. Mary Lodge	early June–late Sept	$149–390	St. Mary • Just outside the park's east entrance
Apgar Village Lodge	mid-May–early Oct	$149–349	Apgar • Located inside the park at Apgar Village
West Glacier Motel	early May–early Oct	$119+	West Glacier • Just outside the park's west entrance
Motel Lake McDonald	early June–mid-Sept	$199	Lake McDonald • Inside park, 10 miles from west entrance
Grouse Mountain Lodge	All Year	$219	Whitefish • 30 miles from Apgar Visitor Center
Prince of Wales Hotel	early June–mid-Sept	CA$279+	Waterton Lakes National Park (Canada) • Unreal setting

For reservations contact Glacier Park Collection at (844) 868-7474 or glacierparkcollection.com

Name	Open	Fee	Location & Notes
Many Glacier Hotel - 🦽	mid-June–mid-Sept	$191–400	Many Glacier • Dining and boat tours on-site
Swiftcurrent Motor Inn	mid-June–mid-Sept	$182	Many Glacier Area • some rooms have a shared bathroom
Rising Sun Motor Inn	mid-June–mid-Sept	$179–195	Going-to-the-Sun Road, 5.5 miles from St. Mary
Lake McDonald Lodge	late May–late Sept	$118–324	SW region of park on Going-to-the-Sun Road • Cabins available, dining on-site • Swiss chalet-style design
Village Inn at Apgar	late May–mid-Sept	$182–264	Apgar • All rooms are rustic yet comfortable
Cedar Creek Lodge	All Year	$100–405	Outside the park in Columbia Falls

For reservations contact Glacier National Parks Lodges (Xanterra) at (855) 733-4522 or glaciernationalparklodges.com

Camping & Lodging

Drive-in campgrounds are located along Going-to-the-Sun Road and the park's east and west boundaries. **Many Glacier** is highly recommended but sites are snapped up the second they become available. St. Mary, Fish Creek, and Many Glacier are the only campgrounds that allow reservations (up to six months in advance). Make reservations at (877) 444-6777 or recreation.gov. All sites at Many Glacier were available via reservation for 2020/2021, they may return to half the sites being available on a first-come, first-served basis in 2022. All other campgrounds are first-come, first-served. Anyone can use the showers at Rising Sun and Swiftcurrent Campstores for a fee. Showers at St. Mary, Fish Creek, and Apgar campgrounds are only available to campground guests.

Two hike-in chalets located in the backcountry allow visitors to access the heart of the park, miles from roads and automobiles, without sacrificing a bed and warm meal. **Granite Park Chalet** (graniteparkchalet. com, $117/night) is located just west of the Continental Divide, a few miles north of Going-to-the-Sun Road. It can be accessed via Highline, Loop, Swiftcurrent, and Fifty Mountain/Waterton Lake Trails. A kitchen with stove is available for guests to cook their own meals (carried in or chosen from the chalet's menu of freeze-dried foods). **Sperry Chalet** (sperrychalet.com, $241/ night per person) sits on a ledge overlooking Lake McDonald. Dinner and breakfast are served at specified times, and all guests receive a trail lunch. Sperry Trail starts at Lake McDonald Lodge's parking lot and heads southeast to the chalet. Horse trips from the park's concessioner are also available from Lake McDonald Horse Barn to Sperry Chalet. An alternative hiking route is Gunsight Pass Trail (more scenic, but longer). All visitors must pack out what is packed in. If you only intend on staying at a chalet, a Backcountry User Permit is not required. These chalets provide a unique opportunity to explore hiking trails that relatively few guests take the time to enjoy, but the chalets are reserved to capacity within minutes of becoming available each year. Consider spending two nights. You can spend the extra day exploring Highline Trail from Granite Park or Gunsight Pass from Sperry.

Glacier has several in-park lodges available for summer visitors. All properties are operated by Glacier Park Collection (844.868.7474, glacierparkcollection. com) and Glacier National Park Lodges (855.733.4522, glaciernationalparklodges.com). Glacier Park Lodge and Many Glacier Hotel are original structures built by the Great Northern Railway in the early 1900s, a few

Waterton–Glacier International Peace Park

On June 18, 1932, Waterton Lakes National Park in Canada united with Glacier National Park to form the world's first International Peace Park. The parks retain separate borders and independent staffs, but they cooperate in wildlife management, scientific research, and some visitor services (like a ranger-led International Peace Park Hike). Waterton Lakes' activities are not covered in this guide, but the hike to **Crypt Lake** is worth a quick mention. It is one of the best hikes in the world, but not one to be attempted by individuals scared of heights or confined spaces. A short boat ride (CA$55/adult, CA$27/child) leads to the trailhead, where you'll hike past running streams and sparkling waterfalls before a steel ladder climbs to a tunnel. Next, you traverse a narrow, completely exposed cliff-edge with the aid of a cable. Continuing, you end at a perfect cirque nestled on the Canada–U.S. border. Remember to leave Crypt Lake with enough time to catch the return ferry (hikers have been left behind). Also remember to bring your passport. You'll need it to pass through the customs station where you drive in and out of Canada.

Glacier's Glaciers

In 1850 there were 150 glaciers in the park. Today, there are 26, all of which are shrinking in size. The climate is changing, and glaciers are receding. If current climate patterns persist, their demise at Glacier National park isn't a matter of if but when.

years after the park was established. John Lewis established Lewis Glacier Hotel in 1913-1914. He envisioned Glacier as "America's Switzerland," and used traditional Swiss chalet-style architecture. In 1930 it was bought by Great Northern Railway and renamed Lake McDonald Lodge. Today, the park's lodges are as popular as ever. Reservations are recommended (and imperative for summer traveling). Most are booked to capacity during the brief tourist season months in advance. While the lodges may seem expensive at first glance, you're paying for location, and there's no better way to visit this park than sleeping within its boundaries.

Driving

Going-to-the-Sun Road (GTSR) exists because of the foresight of Stephen Mather, the National Park Service's first Director, who chose to construct a more expensive, less obtrusive route across the divide. This route unlocks many of the most spectacular landscapes to motorists. Whether it's in your own car, a Red Jammer, or the park's free shuttle, do not skip touring

Grinnell Glacier

Many Glacier, St. Mary, and Logan Pass Hiking Trails (Distances are roundtrip)

Name	Location (# on map)	Length	Difficulty Rating & Notes
Apikuni Falls - ⬧	1.1 miles east of Many Glacier Hotel (1)	2.0 miles	E – Short hike, stunning waterfall
Redgap Pass - ⬧	1.1 miles east of Many Glacier Hotel (1)	12.8 miles	M – Distance to Poia Lake
Grinnell Lake - ⬧	Grinnell Glacier TH or Many Glacier Hotel (1) With boat rides from Many Glacier Hotel	6.8 miles 1.8 miles	E – Hike in and out, or take shortcut via boat trip
Redrock Falls	Swiftcurrent Trailhead (1)	3.6 miles	E – Short leisurely hike
Ptarmigan Falls	Iceberg Ptarmigan Trailhead (1)	5.4 miles	E – Falls on Iceberg Lake route
Swiftcurrent Nature	Grinnell Glacier TH or Many Glacier Hotel (1)	4.6 miles	E – Short and flat path
Cracker Lake - ⬧	South end of Many Glacier Hotel Parking Area (1)	12.8 miles	M – Beautiful setting
Grinnell Glacier/ Viewpoint - ⬧	Grinnell Glacier TH or Many Glacier Hotel (1) With boat rides from Many Glacier Hotel	10.6 miles 7.2 miles	M – Definitely one of the best hikes in the park
Iceberg Lake - ⬧	Iceberg Ptarmigan Trailhead (1)	9.6 miles	M – Another day hiker's favorite
Ptarmigan Lake - ⬧	Iceberg Ptarmigan Trailhead (1)	8.6 miles	M – Veers from Iceberg Lake Trail
Piegan Pass - ⬧	South end of Many Glacier Hotel Parking Area (1) Piegan Pass TH (Siyeh Bend Shuttle Stop) (5)	16.6 miles 9.0 miles	M – East side of the Garden Wall, absolutely extraordinary
Granite Park Chalet - ⬧	Swiftcurrent Trailhead at Many Glacier (1) Cross GTSR at Logan Pass (Shuttle Stop) (6) Loop Trailhead on Going-to-the-Sun Road (7)	15.2 miles 15.2 miles 8.4 miles	S – Tedious Swiftcurrent Pass S – The amazing Highline Trail M – Shortest route via the Loop
Ptarmigan Tunnel - ⬧	Iceberg Ptarmigan Trailhead (1)	10.6 miles	S – Doors usually open mid-July
Swiftcurrent Pass - ⬧	Swiftcurrent Trailhead (1)	13.6 miles	S – Leads to Granite Park Chalet
St Mary Falls - ⬧	St. Mary Falls Trailhead (Shuttle Stop) (2) With boat ride from Rising Sun	1.6 miles 3.2 miles	E – Very popular trail with multiple access options
Virginia Falls - ⬧	St. Mary Falls Trailhead (Shuttle Stop) (2) With boat ride from Rising Sun	3.6 miles 4.8 miles	E – Switchbacks from St Mary Falls lead to Virginia Falls
Beaver Pond Loop	1913 Ranger Station Parking Area (2)	6.6 miles	E – Popular, flat loop trail
Red Eagle Lake	1913 Ranger Station Parking Area (2)	16.2 miles	E – Easy hike, but long
Otokomi Lake	Next to Rising Sun Campstore (3)	11.0 miles	M – Meadows lead to scenic lake
Baring Falls - ⬧	Sunrift Gorge Pullout (Shuttle Stop) (4)	0.6 miles	E – Short descent to falls
Sun Point Nature - ⬧	Sun Point Parking Area (Shuttle Stop) (4)	1.6 miles	E – Skirts along St Mary Lake
Sunrift Gorge	Sunrift Gorge Pullout (Shuttle Stop) (4)	400 feet	E – Very short, easily accessible
Siyeh Pass - ⬧	Sunrift Gorge Pullout (Shuttle Stop) (4) Piegan Pass TH (Siyeh Bend Shuttle Stop) (5)	11.0 miles 9.2 miles	S – Good steep hike following along Garden Wall's east side
Gunsight Pass - ⬧	Gunsight Pass Trailhead (Shuttle Stop) (5)	18.4 miles	S – More difficult (and more beautiful) route to Sperry Chalet
Hidden Lake / Overlook - ⬧	Logan Pass Visitor Center (Shuttle Stop) (6)	7.0/2.8 mi	M – One of the best, with views of iconic Bearhat Mountain
Highline Trail - ⬧	Cross GTSR at Logan Pass (Shuttle Stop) (6)	15.2–40+ miles	S – Meets Continental Divide to U.S.–Canada Border

Difficulty Ratings: E = Easy, M = Moderate, S = Strenuous

GTSR. A word of warning about taking your own car: parking areas fill up (very early in July and August). During peak season Logan Pass parking area fills by 9am. Consider taking the free shuttle. **Inside North Fork Road**, which nearly parallels the park's western boundary from Fish Creek to Kintla Lake (portions of it are sometimes closed), and provides solitude, but at a price: the gravel road is narrow and bumpy.

Hiking

Glacier is the ultimate hiking destination. More than 700 miles of trails crisscross one million acres of mountainous terrain, providing access to an unparalleled collection of blue-green alpine lakes, knife-edge arêtes, rugged and prominent mountains, and textbook examples of glacial geology. A hiker could spend a month here and still be left in awe of the many layers of mountainous majesty.

Every area has its gems, but **Many Glacier** is without a doubt the best of the best. The second you pass through the entrance you feel like you've driven into a postcard, and it only gets better. The prominence and jagged nature of these mountains is overwhelming. Here you'll find many of the best treks: Grinnell Glacier, Iceberg Lake, and Ptarmigan Tunnel Trails, just to name a few favorites. Ambitious hikers can power through each of these trails in less than six hours, but pack a lunch and make a day of it. **Grinnell Glacier Trail** allows hikers to view one of the park's endangered species: glaciers. It begins near Many Glacier Hotel and once you reach the shores of Lake Josephine, you are showered with spectacular mountain views as snowmelt pours from their steep slopes. Just beyond the lake is a viewpoint/picnic area, where you can continue to Upper Grinnell Lake (usually open by mid-July). Glacier Park Boat Co. (glacierparkboats.com) offers guided tours of Grinnell Lake and Grinnell Glacier for $33.25/adult and $16.75/child (ages 4–12). Tours include boat rides across Swiftcurrent Lake and Lake Josephine. Walk-up tickets can be purchased based on availability, but reservations are recommended.

Iceberg Lake Trail begins at Iceberg/Ptarmigan Trailhead and continues to Ptarmigan Falls before passing through a field of beargrass, along a babbling creek, and up into the high-country. Left in the shadows of Mount Wilbur and the Continental Divide, Iceberg Lake features blue water and massive icebergs (sometimes into August) beneath a perfect glacial cirque.

Lake McDonald Hiking Trails (Distances are roundtrip)

Name	Location (# on map)	Length	Difficulty Rating & Notes
Avalanche Lake - ♿	Avalanche Gorge Bridge on Trail of the Cedars (8)	4.6 miles	M – Extremely popular hike
Trail of Cedars	Avalanche Picnic Area (Shuttle Stop) (8)	1.4 miles	E – Wheelchair-accessible loop
Johns Lake Loop	Johns Lake Trailhead (9)	6.0 miles	E – Short loop off GTSR
Trout Lake	Trout Lake Trailhead (10)	8.0 miles	M – Popular horse trail
Snyder Lakes	Sperry Trailhead (Shuttle Stop) (11)	8.6 miles	S – Breaks north of Sperry Trail
Sperry Chalet - ♿	Sperry Trailhead (Shuttle Stop) (11)	12.6 miles	S – Shortest route to the chalet
Mt Brown Lookout	Sperry Trailhead (Shuttle Stop) (11)	10.4 miles	S – Steep, but spectacular
Fish Lake	Sperry Trailhead (Shuttle Stop) (11)	5.4 miles	M – Just south of Sperry Trail
Lincoln Lake - ♿	Lincoln Lake (12)	16.0 miles	M – Secluded/Beaver Chief Falls
Apgar Lookout - ♿	At the end of Glacier Institute Road, about 2.0 miles from Going-to-the-Sun Road (13)	7.2 miles	M – Hike up switchbacks to a view of several 10,000-ft peaks
Apgar Bike Path	Apgar Visitor Center (Shuttle Stop) (14)	3.0 miles	E – Apgar–West Glacier
Lake McDonald West Shore	Lakeshore at Fish Creek Campground (15) 2.8 miles west on North Lake McDonald Rd (9)	14.0 miles	E – A mostly level and easily accessible trail around the lake
Fish Creek Bike Path	Near McDonald Cr Bridge (Shuttle Stop) (14, 15)	2.4 miles	E – Fish Creek–Apgar
Rocky Point	0.2 miles north of Fish Creek Campground (16)	2.2 miles	E – Overlook of Lake McDonald
Howe Lake	Howe Lake TH on Inside North Fork Road (16)	3.2 miles	E – Continues past lake to ridge
Huckleberry Lookout	Huckleberry Mt Trailhead on Camas Road (17)	12.0 miles	S – Look for a huckleberry snack

Difficulty Ratings: E = Easy, M = Moderate, S = Strenuous

Bowman Lake

Goat Haunt and North Fork Hiking Trails (Distances are roundtrip)

Name	Location (# on map)	Length	Difficulty Rating & Notes
Logging Lake	Logging Creek Ranger Station (18)	9.0 miles	E – This trail is popular among fishermen
Hidden Meadow	3 miles south of Polebridge Ranger Station (19)	2.4 miles	E – Short and flat hike through nice meadow
Covey Meadow	Polebridge Ranger Station (21)	3.0 miles	E – Short and easy loop through meadow
Lower Quartz Lake	Bowman Lake Picnic Area (22) North of Quartz Creek Camp (19)	6.0 miles 13.8 miles	M – Combine with Quartz Lake Trail for a strenuous (but exceptional) 12+ mile loop
Quartz Lake - ♨	Bowman Lake Picnic Area (22)	12.0 miles	M – Most scenic of the three Quartz Lakes
Numa Lookout	Bowman Lake Ranger Station (22)	11.2 miles	M – Views across Bowman Lake
Akokala Lake	Bowman Lake Ranger Station (22)	11.6 miles	M – Crosses Akokala Creek to small lake
Bowman Lake - ♨	Bowman Lake Ranger Station (22)	14.2 miles	M – Flat, easy, long hike to lake and camp
Kintla Lake	Near Kintla Lake Campground (23)	13.2 miles	M – Easy, but long hike along lakeshore
Lake Francis - ♨	Goat Haunt Ranger Station (24)	12.4 miles	M – Continuing beyond Lake Janet
Lake Janet	Goat Haunt Ranger Station (24)	6.6 miles	E – Backcountry hike to alpine lake
Kootenai Lakes	Goat Haunt Ranger Station (24)	5.0 miles	E – Backcountry hike to a small lake
Goat Haunt Overlook	Goat Haunt Ranger Station (24)	2.0 miles	E – Climb to overlook of Upper Waterton Lk
Waterton Townsite	Goat Haunt Ranger Station (24)	17.0 miles	E – Crosses U.S.–Canada Border to Waterton
Rainbow Falls	Goat Haunt Ranger Station (24)	2.0 miles	E – Short hike to falls on Waterton River

Difficulty Ratings: E = Easy, M = Moderate, S = Strenuous

Ptarmigan Tunnel Trail shares the same trailhead and is an equally stunning trek. The tunnel connects to the park's Belly River area and the doors typically first open in mid-July, closing again in late September.

Highline Trail begins at Logan Pass (Going-to-the-Sun Road) and follows Garden Wall along the Continental Divide. This hike is outstanding, especially the short but thigh-burning ascent to **Grinnell Glacier Overlook**. (You'll know the junction when you see it. The trail goes up, up, and up to a notch in Garden Wall.) The only drawback for some visitors is that Highline follows the road for a considerable distance, which means you can get similar views from your car seat. Still, we'll take the trail any day! After the spur to Grinnell Glacier Overlook, you continue on to Granite Park Chalet (which can also be reached via Swiftcurrent Pass from Many Glacier—another great hike!), and you can return to Going-to-the-Sun Road via The Loop (free shuttle back to Logan Pass required). **Hidden Lake**, also beginning at Logan Pass, might be my favorite hike.

Even though Grinnell Glacier, Iceberg Lake, Ptarmigan Tunnel, and Highline Trails are fairly long day hikes, don't anticipate much solitude. These are four of the park's most beautiful and popular adventures.

Many of the park's easiest (and most popular) trails are found in the **St. Mary Area**. Most St. Mary Lake boat tours (glacierparkboats.com, $33.25/adult) usually hike to St. Mary Falls and Baring Falls. Or hike in from St. Mary Falls Trailhead on Going-to-the-Sun Road. It adds some distance and elevation, but you can continue on to Virginia Falls and/or Florence Falls (with an early start).

The **Lake McDonald Area** has a fairly dense collection of trails of all difficulty levels. Apgar Lookout Trail provides expansive panoramas. And Sperry Trailhead, located on Going-to-the-Sun Road, serves as an access point to the region's most beautiful hikes, including the 6.3-mile (one-way) trail to Sperry Chalet, where you can spend a night in the wilderness and enjoy a warm dinner and breakfast before returning to civilization.

North Fork is located along the park's western boundary, north of Going-to-the-Sun Road. It's a nice, somewhat secluded area with a variety of easy and relatively flat hikes exploring the western foothills. **Goat Haunt** is located in the backcountry at the south end of Upper Waterton Lake near the U.S.–Canada Border. It's a popular stop for backpackers but can also be reached as a day hike from Canada's Waterton

Hidden Lake

Lakes National Park. Here, an out-and-back trek to Goat Haunt is possible thanks to Waterton Shoreline Cruise's (403.859.2362, watertoncruise.com) boat rides back to Waterton. One-way fare is CA$55/adults and CA$27/youth (ages 12 and under). Boats typically run from June until September.

Cut Bank is the place to go if you are looking for solitude. Located in the southeast corner, it is seldom visited (relatively speaking). Even though it doesn't attract swarms of tourists like Going-to-the-Sun Road, there's plenty of majestic mountain scenery (if you're willing to hike). Triple Divide Pass is one of the more unique hiking destinations. Depending on where a drop of water lands within a one-square-foot area of Triple Divide Peak, that droplet could end up in Hudson Bay, the Gulf of Mexico, or the Pacific Ocean. The views along the way to the peak are equally amazing. But it's really a backpacking destination. **Two Medicine**, just a bit further south, is a much better area to find day-hiking trails (and boat service to shorten the journey).

There are so many more incredible trails at Glacier. Even more than those listed in the hiking tables. Trails at Glacier are more difficult than those found at most parks. Expect a trail listed as strenuous here to be extremely demanding, traversing several steep climbs with the potential for switchbacks. Moderate trails are likely to include more than 1,000 feet in elevation change. And remember you're in grizzly country. Hike in groups, and know what to do should you encounter an aggressive bear. If you're feeling uncomfortable about bears or difficult terrain, start with one of the popular trails (Highline, Iceberg, Grinnell Glacier) where you'll have plenty of company, and let things progress from there. But don't let your guard down. Hiking in this remote region is not without dangers.

Two Medicine

Cut Bank and Two Medicine Hiking Trails (Distances are roundtrip)

Name	Location (# on map)	Length	Difficulty Rating & Notes
Atlantic Falls	Cut Bank Trailhead (9)	8.0 miles	E – Waterfall seen en route to Pitamakan Pass
Medicine Grizzly Lake	Cut Bank Trailhead (9)	12.0 miles	M – Spur trail from Triple Divide Trail
Triple Divide Pass	Cut Bank Trailhead (9)	14.4 miles	S – From here water flows west, south, and north
Running Eagle Fall - ♿	Running Eagle Falls TH (10)	0.6 mile	E – A short wheelchair-accessible trail
Appistoki Falls	0.25-mile east of Two Medicine Ranger Station (11)	1.2 miles	E – Short and easy waterfall hike
Scenic Point	0.25-mile east of Two Medicine Ranger Station (11)	7.8 miles	S – Short climb to a wonderful viewpoint
Aster Park/Falls - ♿	South Shore Trailhead (11)	4.0 miles	E – Views of Two Medicine Lake
Rockwell Falls	South Shore Trailhead (11)	7.0 miles	M – Follow South Shore Trail to Cobalt Lake
Cobalt Lake - ♿	South Shore Trailhead (11)	11.6 miles	M – Last two miles to the lake are steep
Twin Falls - ♿	North Shore Trailhead (11) Using concession boat	7.0 miles 1.8 mile	E – A short spur trail from Upper Two Medicine Lake Trail leads to Twin Falls
Upper Two Medicine Lake	North Shore Trailhead (11) Using concession boat	10.0 miles 4.4 miles	E – After Twin Falls the trail continues to Upper Two Medicine Lake
No Name Lake	North Shore Trailhead (11)	9.8 miles	M – Pretty lake north of Upper Two Medicine
Dawson Pass - ♿	North Shore Trailhead (11)	13.0 miles	S – Combine with Pitamakan Pass for 18.8-mi loop
Pitamakan Pass - ♿	North Shore Trailhead (11)	15.2 miles	S – Follows Cut Bank Creek to two lakes
Oldman Lake	North Shore Trailhead (11)	12.8 miles	S – Follows Dry Fork to lake near Pitamakan Pass

Difficulty Ratings: E = Easy, M = Moderate, S = Strenuous

Any trailhead followed by a (Shuttle Stop) means it is on or near the park's shuttle route that follows Going-to-the-Sun Road. Get an early start or use the shuttle in July/August. Xanterra operates a hiker shuttle between Many Glacier and the free Going-to-the-Sun Road shuttle system (at St. Mary Visitor Center). It costs $14/adult each way. And whenever you hike, come prepared for all kinds of weather.

Backpacking

The one sure-fire way to escape the sea of summer tourists along Going-to-the-Sun Road is to strap a pack to your back, and head into the wilderness (more than 95% of the park's area). That's not to say backpacking isn't popular here. It is. All backpackers must camp in designated sites with an overnight backcountry use permit. Permits cost $7 per person per night (from May through October). Half the sites can be reserved for a $40 application fee (including $10 nonrefundable administrative fee) only through pay.gov. Reservations are highly recommended. Permits must be obtained in person no sooner than one day before your trip's departure. You cannot request a backcountry permit without planning your route. Along the park's trails there are more than 60 backcountry campgrounds and 200+ campsites. Choose a route with every member of the group in mind. If it's your first time camping in the backcountry think about staying near Going-to-the-Sun Road or one of the park's developed areas. If your plans change and you can no longer use your permit, please call (406) 888-7900 to cancel your trip. You won't receive a refund, but karma will be in your favor as your site will become available to another visitor. **Popular routes** include a semi-loop from Bowman Lake to Kintla Lake (adding on a stop at Lake Francis), but you'll need to cache a car, arrange a shuttle, or hitch back to where you started. You could make a loop from Many Glacier using Redgap and Ptarmigan Trails or make an even bigger loop down to Glenns Lake and return on the Continental Divide Trail. Gunsight Pass to Lake McDonald is another great option. So is Cracker Lake. And then there's the Belly River area. Or combine Dawson Pass and Pitamakan Pass Trails in Two Medicine. Just like with day-hiking, there's nearly a bottomless buffet of choice scenery at Glacier, so, make a plan and be ready to request your permit as soon as the reservation period opens up (or take your chances in-person).

All campgrounds have tent sites, pit toilets, food hanging or storage devices, and food preparation areas. Set up camp and prepare and store food where you're supposed to. Fires are only allowed in designated fire pits, which are not available at all camps. For the most

Apikuni Falls

part, all that is expected of you is simple courtesy toward your surroundings and fellow backpackers.

Very few incidents occur, but backpackers must be well aware of the inherent dangers. To some, the danger is part of the allure; to others, it's a reason to stay away. Weather, wildlife, and accidents are all unpredictable forces of nature that can cause serious problems in the backcountry. Check the extended weather forecast before your trip. Travel with a group and carry a first-aid kit, a good topographic map, and a compass (most importantly, know how to use them). Treat your water (boil or filter). Know how to react should you encounter a bear or mountain lion. In reality these dangers are nothing to be afraid of. While there are no guarantees, with a little bit of knowledge and ample preparation you can nearly assure yourself a safe once-in-a-lifetime experience in a one-of-a-kind environment. Every first-

Fire turning the evening sky pink

time, multi-day expedition should be planned carefully, well in advance (no exceptions!). If you'd like to get deeper in the park but could use a little help/company, hire a guide like Glacier Guides (406.387.5555, glacierguides.com).

Red Jammer & Bus Tours

Red Jammers are 17-passenger convertible touring sedans, forming the oldest fleet of passenger carrying vehicles. Operating since the late 1930s, these antique autos have earned the name "red jammers," because of the gear jamming that occurred while scaling the steep grades of Going-to-the-Sun Road. Do not let their antique status deter you from the tour. The entire fleet was rebuilt to run on propane, and they've been going strong ever since.

If you only have a day, a red jammer tour is the most relaxing, informative, and comprehensive way to experience the park. (Please plan more than a day here.) A variety of tours are offered departing from various lodging facilities on both sides of the park. The most inclusive is Big Sky Circle Tour ($102/adult, $51/Child). In 8.5 hours you'll loop around the southern boundary following US-2, crossing the Continental Divide at Marias Pass, and then you'll return through the heart of the park via all 50 miles of Going-to-the-Sun Road, crossing the divide once more at Logan Pass. Eastern Alpine Tour is the least expensive offering. This 2.5-hour-long tour departs Rising Sun Motor Inn, takes you up GTSR to Logan Pass and brings you right back for $40/adult and $20/child. It's also available from St. Mary Lodge, Many Glacier Hotel, and Swiftcurrent Motor Inn, but is longer and more expensive from these locations. All tours typically run from mid-June until mid-September. A complete list of departure locations, rates, and dates are available at glaciernationalparklodges.com.

Sun Tours (406.732.9220, glaciersuntours.com) offers park tours aboard 25-passenger, large windowed, air-conditioned coaches. Trips departing East Glacier are 8.5 hours and cost $120/adult. A 3.5-hour tour of the park's east side costs $60/adult, while a 4-hour tour of the west side costs $70. They also offer custom tours.

Boat Tours

Not to be outdone by the "Red Jammers," many of the wooden tour boats have been in operation since before the Great Depression. From these historic boats you can sit back and enjoy some of the most majestic alpine scenery found anywhere in the world (without having to trudge up a steep mountain trail). Boat tours are available at Lake McDonald Lodge (Lake McDonald), Many Glacier Hotel (Swiftcurrent Lake and Lake Josephine), Rising Sun Motor Inn (St. Mary Lake), and Two Medicine (Two Medicine Lake). Cruises range from 45 minutes to 1.5 hours, and cost between $16.75 and $33.25 per adult (about half that for children ages 4–12). Tours typically operate from June through Labor Day. A complete listing of tour descriptions, rates, and dates are available at glacierparkboats.com. Reservations are available online and they are highly recommended. Walk-up tickets are issued at location ticket offices based on availability. Waterton Shoreline Cruise Co. (403.859.2362, watertoncruise.com) can get you to Goat Haunt from Waterton Lakes National Park (in Canada). They also offer a few other boat tours.

Boating & Rafting

Hundreds of streams originate and flow from these mountains. Triple Divide Peak, just west of Cut Bank, is essentially the apex of the continent. Within one square-foot, water from the peak can become part of the Columbia, Mississippi, and Saskatchewan River systems. Respectively, these rivers flow into the Pacific Ocean, Gulf of Mexico, and Hudson Bay. Altogether there are more than 700 lakes here, but only 131 are named. Lake McDonald is the largest at 9.4 miles long and 1.5 miles wide. It's also the deepest at 464 feet. A few lakes are popular spots for **boating** and **paddling**. You can bring your own boat and use it on a few lakes, but it'll need to pass an invasive species inspection and then be quarantined for 30 days. Waterton Lake allows motorized boats too, but they must undergo a 90-day quarantine after inspection. Non-motorized boats are permitted after same-day inspection by park staff, no quarantine period required. Considering the devastation zebra and quagga mussels can cause, these restrictions seem fair. And there is an alternative to bringing your own boat. Motorboats (8–10hp, $28–30/hour), rowboats ($22/hour), canoes ($22/hour), kayaks ($18–22/hour), and paddleboards ($15/hour) are available for rent at Many Glacier, Lake McDonald Lodge, Apgar, and Two Medicine Lake. Rentals are provided by Glacier Boat Co. (406.257.2426, glacierparkboats.com).

Glacier Guides (406.387.5555, glacierguides.com), Glacier Raft Company (406.888.5454, glacierraftco.com), Great Northern Resort (800.735.7897, greatnorthernresort.com), and Wild River Adventures (406.387.9453, riverwild.com) offer **rafting trips** on the Middle and North Forks of Flathead River. North Fork forms the park's western boundary. Middle Fork is just outside the park. Each outfitter has similar offerings. A half-day trip costs $60–70 and a full-day is $100+/paddler.

🐎 Horseback Riding

Guided trail rides are available at Many Glacier, Lake McDonald, and Apgar. Swan Mountain Outfitters (877.888.5557, swanmountainglacier.com) is the park's concessioner. Stables are typically open from late April until late October. Rides come in a variety of lengths for reasonable prices: 1-hour ($55), 2-hour ($80), half-day ($125), and full-day ($200). They'll even take you on an overnight trip ($350) if you're up for it!

🚴 Biking

Biking Going-to-the-Sun Road (GTSR) is gaining popularity. Cross-country pedalers often choose Logan Pass to cross the Continental Divide because its breathtaking scenery. However, it typically first opens in late June, depending on the amount of spring snow, so you should have an alternate route in mind if you're heading out on a transcontinental bike ride. Several campgrounds along GTSR have reduced fee campsites for cyclists traveling without a vehicle. After opening, it is immediately flooded with motorists. Traffic is heaviest between 9am and 3pm, and GTSR is closed to bike use from 11am to 4pm (mid-June until Labor Day). This closure affects the road from Apgar Campground to Sprague Creek Campground and eastbound from Logan Creek to Logan Pass, meaning you'll have to squeeze in your heart-pumping, leg-burning ride in the morning or evening. In spring, some portions of GTSR are closed to vehicles, but open to bicycles. You'll have to check the park website to receive accurate information on road status. Winds can be extremely strong, especially on the park's eastern side. Portions of GTSR can be under construction, and often unpaved, so use extreme caution when approaching blind corners and steep downhill stretches. The road is narrow, and cyclists must pull to the shoulder if four or more vehicles stack behind you.

Avalanche Lake

Bikes are prohibited from all trails, except for the paved path between Park Headquarters and Apgar Village, Fish Creek Bike Path (between Apgar Village and Fish Creek Campground), and Old Flathead Ranger Station Trail (west of Apgar). Inside North Fork Road is a good choice to bike (except no road bikes, it's gravel). Personally, I believe hiking is the best use of your time at Glacier. Bike rental is not available in the park.

🎣 Fishing

Fishing is allowed, but regulations are enforced to preserve the native fish populations. A few areas close to aid in repopulating certain species. River and stream fishing season is from the third Saturday in May through November 30. Lake fishing is open all year. All native fish caught must be released. A fishing license is not required, but park regulations must be followed. Stop at a visitor center to obtain a copy of current regulations and to be briefed on fishing closures. Glacier Park Collection offers full-day and half-day fishing excursions starting at $400 for two anglers. More information is available at (844) 868-7474 or glacierparkcollection.com. Or Glacier Guides (406.387.5555, glacierguides.com) will take you fly fishing ($425/half-day).

🏃 Winter Activities

In winter, Going-to-the-Sun Road is buried beneath several feet of snow, but trails remain open to intrepid snowshoers and cross-country skiers. If you plan on visiting in winter, it's a good idea to check online about trail closures and avalanche conditions before heading out. Information is available at Apgar Information Center on weekends, and Park headquarters (near West Glacier) and Hudson Bay District Office (near St. Mary) on weekdays. Ranger stations are open intermittently depending on staffing. You'll find cross-country skiing and snowshoeing opportunities at Apgar, Lake

Going-to-the-Sun Road

McDonald (including Avalanche Lake), Polebridge, Two Medicine, and St. Mary. Generally, you can follow the paths of others. Be sure to sign the trail registry before heading out. Backcountry camping is allowed (with a free permit) during winter, but it should only be attempted by experienced, well-equipped parties. Ice fishing is allowed within park boundaries.

Visitor Centers

Glacier has three visitor centers. All three are situated along Going-to-the-Sun Road: one on each end, and another in the middle. **St. Mary Visitor Center** is located at the scenic byway's eastern end. It's open daily, late May through early October, from 8am–5pm. Hours are extended to 8am–6pm from late June to late August. It houses a variety of interactive exhibits on Native Americans, a short film, bookstore, Wi-Fi, and restrooms. It also has a large parking lot with plenty of room to leave your car and use the park's free Going-to-the-Sun Road Shuttle Service. **Logan Pass Visitor Center** is located on the Continental Divide. It's opening date depends on the amount of spring snow, but it usually opens by late June. Hours are typically 9:30am–5pm. You'll find exhibits, bookstore, and restrooms. **Apgar Visitor Center** is located on the western end of GTSR. It's open daily from mid-May until mid-October, and weekends fall through winter. Typical hours are 8am until 5pm. It has exhibits, a bookstore, Wi-Fi, restrooms, and a large parking lot (shuttle stop). Ranger stations at Many Glacier and Two Medicine are open from late May until mid-September, 7am–5pm. Glacier Institute (406.755.1211, glacierinstitute.org), located in Columbia Falls, provides educational adventures for children and adults.

Ranger Programs & For Kids

Intimidated by the vast network of trails? Unsure what activities are worth the money? Scared of bears? Join a Ranger Program. They're structured, free (unless a boat trip is required), and safe. Check online for a current listing of ranger-led activities.

The highlight of many visitors' vacation is an **International Peace Park Hike.** On this adventure, you'll join rangers from Waterton Lakes (Canada) and Glacier National Parks and hike across the U.S.–Canada border to Goat Haunt. The tour begins at Waterton Lakes and includes a boat ride (fee). Remember your passport (or Real ID). You won't need it to cross the backcountry border, but it is required at all roadway customs stations found along the U.S.–Canada border. Each hike is limited to 35 people. Registration is required. Check online for availability and details. Of course you can do it on your own as well.

Many Glacier is a great area for ranger programs. The best hikes are made better with a ranger to Grinnell Glacier or Iceberg Lake. The trip to Grinnell Glacier includes boat trips for a moderate fee.

Two Medicine area offers programs less frequently than sites like Many Glacier or Logan Pass, but they are no less spectacular. Full-day hikes to Cobalt Lake, Dawson Pass, and Fireband Pass are a few of the highlighted programs. At St. Mary, the "History in the Making" program is great for families. In just three hours you'll explore the park's past, present, and future. You'll even get to write a letter that will be placed in a time capsule. At Logan Pass you can join a ranger on a Highline Trail Hike to Granite Park Chalet or skirt Garden Wall to Haystack Butte. An assortment of walks, talks, and evening programs are available at Lake McDonald Valley. In short, you can't go wrong wherever you go. You'll find engaging ranger programs in any developed area in summer.

For children, whether it's the rugged magnificence of the Rocky Mountains, coming face-to-face with a mountain goat, or catching a glimpse of a grizzly bear as it runs away, Glacier National Park is often a spellbinding place. To help introduce them to these experiences and other natural wonders, a Junior Ranger Program is offered for children 5 and older. To become a Junior Ranger, children are asked to complete five activities from the free Junior Ranger booklet (available online or at any visitor center), and to attend a Ranger-led Program. Children receive an official Junior Ranger badge and certificate upon completion.

Flora & Fauna

About 1,000 species of plants exist at Glacier. Wildflowers are seen spring through fall. Beargrass is commonly found between June and July. Trees are dominated by conifers, but deciduous cottonwoods and aspens can be found in the lower elevations.

Grizzly bears are constantly on the minds of visitors. You might be afraid of them? Are you intrigued by them? Maybe you want to cuddle with a grizzly (not recommended)? A healthy population of some 700 grizzlies roams the northern continental divide area. For the most part, bears are shy and skittish, just like the rest of the animal kingdom. But some can be extremely dangerous, especially if you startle one or find yourself between a mother and her cub. Still, bears have only been responsible for a handful of deaths. Grizzlies are abundant, but it's more likely you'll see mountain goats, bighorn sheep, deer, maybe a moose. Glacier protects a remarkably intact ecosystem. Nearly all its known plant and animal species still exist. Woodland caribou and bison are the only missing mammals. Gray wolf naturally returned to the area in the 1980s. Canadian lynx, wolverine, moose, elk, coyote, and mountain lion also call glacier home. More than 270 species of birds visit or reside here as well.

Pets & Accessibility

Pets are allowed in the park but must be kept on a leash (less than six feet). They are only allowed in drive-in campgrounds, along park roads open to motor vehicles, and in picnic areas. Pets are prohibited from all hiking trails, the backcountry, and all shores (outside of developed areas). It's probably better to leave your pets at home with a loved one, but Columbia Mountain Kennels (406.897.7197, columbiamountainkennels.com) will board them for you while you're here, should you need their services.

Apgar and St. Mary Visitor Centers are wheelchair accessible. A few of the park's interpretive programs are accessible. Apgar Bike Bath, Trail of the Cedars, Lake McDonald, Running Eagle Falls, and Swiftcurrent Nature Trail are accessible. Ten of the thirteen campgrounds offer accessible sites.

Weather

Visitors should come prepared for all weather conditions. The temperature difference from low altitude to high altitude is usually about 15°F. Most rain falls in the park's western valleys. The eastern slopes are normally sunny and windy. Summer highs can reach 90°F, but overnight lows can drop into the 20s°F. Snow

Granite Park Chalet

is possible any month of the year. In August of 2005, eight inches fell in one night, forcing hundreds of backpackers out of the backcountry. Winter snowpack averages 16 feet. It closes Going-to-the-Sun Road for most of the year. The scenic byway is usually completely open by late June.

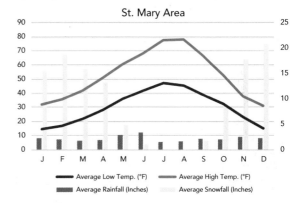

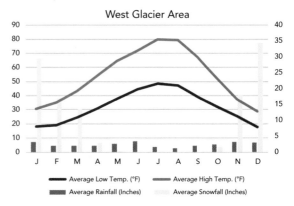

Cracker Lake

Tips & Recommendations

Coming from Yellowstone, consider taking MT-83. It's great, with plenty to see and do along the way.

If you're traveling early in the peak tourism season (June/July), you must accept the fact Going-to-the-Sun Road may not be open completely. It opens on Mother Nature's (and the people operating the plows) schedule, not yours. Sometimes that's June. Sometimes that's July.

Same goes for trails. Some high elevation trails remain snow-covered (and closed) well into summer (bring microspikes). For example, Grinnell Glacier Trail usually fully opens in mid-July.

Glacier has a relatively short peak tourism season and during that time it sees many tourists (almost one million each month for July and August!), so you need to plan your trip in advance. Hopefully you're reading this more than six months before your intended travel plans as camping and lodging accommodations (and backpacking permits) fill fast.

There are more overnight accommodations beyond park boundaries, but it's a huge advantage to sleep at the park's campgrounds or lodges. The park is big and it's generally slow-going on Going-to-the-Sun Road. Plus, having the option to walk to a trailhead (or shuttle stop) from your campsite or lodge is a valuable perk you'll appreciate once you arrive.

Popular parking areas (like Avalanche Lake and Logan Pass) fill early during peak season. Use the free shuttle to access trailheads along Going-to-the-Sun Road, and, if you don't, have a few backup plans ready to go in case you can't access the area you were aiming for.

Hiking here is an unbelievable experience and it isn't just a trail or two that will make you feel an indescribable sense of wonder, it's dozens of trails (covering hundreds of miles). Have a plan. Have a backup plan. Be patient. And have fun.

There's more than enough great hiking for you at Glacier but you should consider crossing the border into Canada to take the boat cruise to Goat Haunt or Crypt Lake. However, this opens a can of worms, because then you'll probably start thinking about heading further into the Canadian Rockies and you'll be begging your employer for more time off.

If there are a few hikes that you really want to do (like Hidden Lake, Avalanche Lake, or Grinnell Glacier), simply make it a priority. Wake up early, get to the trailhead, and then enjoy the heck out of it. 2021 was a unique year, so it might not be the best measuring stick, but people were camping out in the very early morning at Logan Pass and the parking lot was usually full by 8am (and this was in September when the park closed Hidden Lake Trail due to bear activity).

Don't feel like there's a "best" single destination to stay or visit. Many Glacier, St. Mary, Two Medicine, Logan Pass, and Apgar are all incredibly special places. Just because Going-to-the-Sun Road isn't fully open doesn't mean you shouldn't visit. If you're thinking about late spring/early fall, it's likely most of the road will be clear of snow. But you'll have to drive around the park via US-2 to get from side to side (if you want). There's more than enough to see and do on either side, but US-2 is a scenic route in its own right, too.

Speaking of US-2, if crowds are getting you down, take a look at the park map and pick a trail or two beginning near US-2. You'll have much less company.

Easy Hikes: Grinnell Lake (6.8), Apikuni Falls (2), St Mary's Falls (1.6), Running Eagle Fall (0.6), Virginia Falls (3.6), Baring Falls (0.6), Sun Point (1.6), Aster Park (4), Twin Falls (7)
Moderate Hikes: Grinnell Glacier (10.6 miles), Hidden Lake Overlook (2.8), Cracker Lake (12.8), Lake Francis (12.4), Avalanche Lake (4.6), Redgap Pass (12.8), Bowman Lake (14.2), Iceberg Lake (9.6), Quartz Lake (12), Piegan Pass (16.6), Cobalt Lake (11.6), Lincoln Lake (16), Apgar Lookout (7.2)
Strenuous Hikes: Highline Trail (15.2 miles), Ptarmigan Tunnel (10.6), Gunsight Pass (18.4), Dawson Pass (13), Swiftcurrent Pass (13.6), Sperry Chalet (12.6), Pitamakan Pass (15.2), Siyeh Pass (11)

Family Activities: Ride in a Red Jammer, cruise a lake (St. Mary, Swiftcurrent, McDonald, or Two Medicine Lakes), head up to Canada and cruise across Upper Waterton Lake to Goat Haunt, become Junior Rangers

Guided Tours: Joyride up and down the Rockies in a historic Red Jammer, saddle up and let a horse carry you into the wilderness, go rafting

Rainy Day Activities: As long as you're careful about swollen streams and lightning, don't let a little rain get in the way of your Glacier vacation. Put on your rain gear and enjoy the thinned-out crowds by hiking to a waterfall-y destination (like Avalanche Lake or Cracker Lake). Maybe the clouds will break and you'll be treated to rainbows and ephemeral waterfalls! Rafting is a good option too. You're already going to get wet.

Sunset Spots: Crystal Point (Going-to-the-Sun Road), Apgar (Lake McDonald), Bowman Lake

Sunrise Spots: Hidden Lake Overlook, Swiftcurrent Lake, Two Medicine Lake, St. Mary Lake (Wild Goose Island Overlook), Logan Pass

Photography Note: You could also sit out at any of the lakes waiting for the sun to rise behind the mountains (east side lakes for sunset, west side lakes for sunrise). You may get a dazzling display, but even if it's simply

Many Glacier Hotel

a clear morning/evening, watching the light pierce throught the mountains is a treat.

Wildlife: Logan Pass Area (bighorn sheep, mountain goats, possibly grizzly), pretty much any trail east of the Garden Wall from Many Glacier to Two Medicine (bear, moose), but we've seen bear in the Apgar/Inside North Fork Road area too, so keep your eyes open, and be mindful of your surroundings

Beyond the Park...

Dining
Two Medicine Grill • (406) 226-9227
314 US-2, East Glacier Park

Leaning Tree Café & Campground
MT-464, Babb • (406) 338-5322

Eddie's Café • (406) 888-5361
eddiescafegifts.com • Apgar

Northern Lights Saloon & Café
255 Polebridge Loop, Polebridge
thenorthernlightssaloon.com

Grocery Stores
Glacier Park Trading • (406) 226-9227
316 US-2, East Glacier Park

Super 1 Foods • (406) 892-9996
2100 9th St W, Columbia Falls

Safeway • (406) 862-3006
6580 US-93, Whitefish

Walmart • (406) 257-7535
170 Hutton Ranch Rd, Kalispell

Lodging
Mountain Pine Motel
909 US-49, East Glacier Park
mtnpine.com • (406) 226-4403

Travelers Rest Lodge • (406) 226-9143
20987 US-2 E, East Glacier Park
travelersrestlodge.net

Glacier Guides Lodge
120 Highline Blvd, West Glacier
glacierguides.com • (406) 387-5555

Great Northern • (406) 387-5340
12127 US-2, West Glacier
greatnorthernresort.com

Great Bear Inn • (406) 250-4220
5672 Blankenship Rd, West Glacier
thegreatbearinn.com

Glacier Wilderness
13400 US-2 E, West Glacier
glacierwildernessresort.com

Campgrounds
St Mary-Glacier Park KOA
koa.com • (406) 732-4122 • St. Mary

Moose Creek RV • (406) 387-5280
11505 US-2 E, West Glacier
moosecreekrv.com

Glacier Camp • (406) 387-5689
12070 US-2, West Glacier
glaciercampground.com

W Glacier RV Park • (406) 888-5580
350 River Bend Dr, West Glacier

North American RV Park
10640 US-2 E • (800) 704-4266
northamericanrvpark.com

West Glacier KOA • West Glacier
koa.com • (406) 387-5341

Columbia Falls RV Park
103 US-2 • (406) 892-1122
columbiafallsrvpark.com

Mountain Meadows RV Park
9125 US-2, Hungry Horse
mountainmedowrv.com

Festivals
Whitefish Winter Carnival • Feb
whitefishwintercarnival.com

Wildlife Film Festival • April
Missoula • wildlifefilms.org

Attractions
Wayfarers (8600 MT-35, Big Fork) and West Shore State Parks offer boating, fishing, hiking, and camping along Flathead Lake
fwp.mt.gov

Museum of the Plains Indian
19 Museum Loop, Browning
(406) 338-2230

Giant Springs State Park
Huge freshwater spring
Great Falls • (406) 727-1212

Flathead National Forest
fs.usda.gov • (406) 758-5200

Bitterroot Backpacking
Great guide who will take you on day hikes of Glacier or back-packing in the Bitterroots. He'll even bring an inflatable kayak along to splash around in the backcountry.
bitterrootbackpacking.com

Discovery Ski • (406) 563-2184
skidiscovery.com

C M Russell Museum
400 13th St N, Great Falls
cmrussell.org • (406) 727-8787

Kruger Helicopter Tours
Columbia Falls • (406) 857-3893
krugerhelicopters.com

Amazing Fun Center • (406) 387-5902
10265 US-2 E, Coram
amazingfuncenter.com

Conrad Mansion • (406) 755-2166
330 Woodland Ave, Kalispell
conradmansion.com

Dog Sled Adv • (406) 881-2275
8400 US-93 N, Whitefish
dogsledadventuresmontana.com

Glacier Cyclery • (406) 862-6446
326 E 2nd St, Whitefish
glaciercyclery.com

NM
LAS
VEGAS
Pipe Spring NM
Rainbow Bridge
NM
Navajo NM
Yucca House NM
Great Sand Dur
NP & PRES

Lake Mead NRA
Grand Canyon NP
Mesa Verde NP

Aztec Ruins NM

Canyon de Chelly NM
Capulin Volcano
NM

Wupatki NM
Hubbell Trading
Post NHS
Chaco Culture NHP
Manhattan Project
NHP

Sunset Crater Volcano NM
Valles Caldera N Pres
Fort Union NM

Walnut Canyon NM
Bandelier NM
SANTA FE
Pecos NHP

tains NM
Mojave
N PRES
Tuzigoot NM
Petrified
Forest NP
El Morro
NM
Petroglyph
NM
ALBUQUERQUE

Montezuma Castle NM
El Malpais
NM

ARIZONA
NEW MEXICO

PHOENIX
Tonto NM
Salinas Pueblo Missions NM

Hohokam Pima NM
Casa Grande Ruins NM
Gila Cliff Dwellings NM

Organ Pipe Cactus
NM
Saguaro NP
White Sands NP

Fort Bowie NHS

Chiricahua NM
Carlsbad Caverns NP

Tumacacori NHP
EL PASO
Guadalupe
Mountains NP

Coronado N MEM
Chamizal N MEM

ⓘ ARIZONA
Canyon de Chelly NM, Hubbell Trading Post
NHS, and Navajo NM observe daylight saving
time. Other NPS units in Arizona do not.

Fort Davis NHS

ⓘ MOUNTAIN (Washington,
DC, minus 2 hours)

Rio Grande WSR

Big Bend
NP

SOUTH

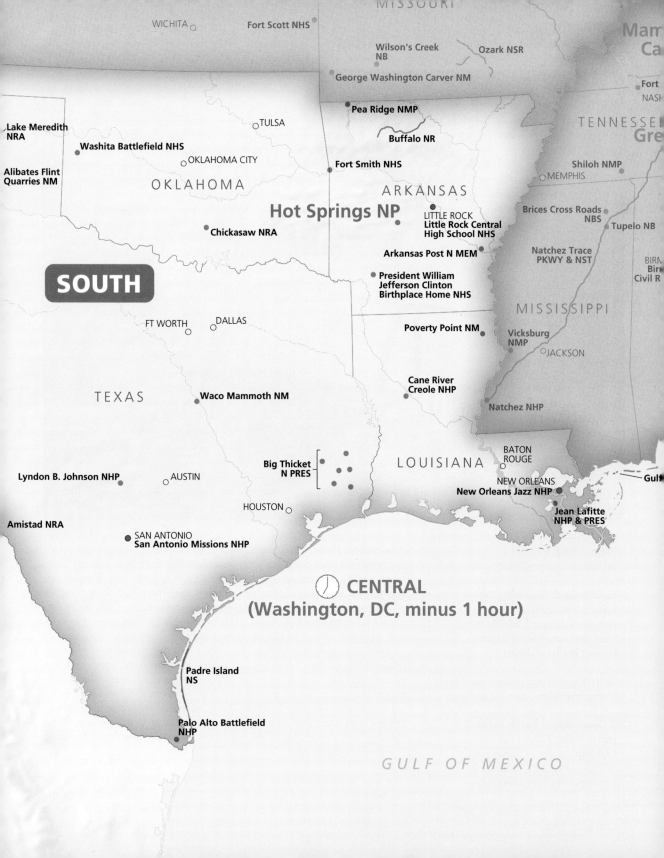

WICHITA ○

Fort Scott NHS ○

MISSOURI

Ma Ca

Wilson's Creek NB ○

Ozark NSR

Fort NASH

George Washington Carver NM ●

TENNESSEE Gre

Lake Meredith NRA ●

Washita Battlefield NHS ●

TULSA ○

Pea Ridge NMP ●

Buffalo NR

Shiloh NMP ●

MEMPHIS ○

Alibates Flint Quarries NM ●

OKLAHOMA CITY ○

Fort Smith NHS ●

ARKANSAS

OKLAHOMA

Hot Springs NP

LITTLE ROCK ●
Little Rock Central High School NHS

Brices Cross Roads NBS

Tupelo NB ●

Chickasaw NRA ●

Arkansas Post N MEM ●

Natchez Trace PKWY & NST

BIR
BIR
Civil R

SOUTH

President William Jefferson Clinton Birthplace Home NHS ●

MISSISSIPPI

FT WORTH ○

DALLAS ●

Poverty Point NM ●

Vicksburg NMP ●

JACKSON ○

TEXAS

Waco Mammoth NM ●

Cane River Creole NHP ●

Natchez NHP ●

Lyndon B. Johnson NHP ●

AUSTIN ○

Big Thicket N PRES

LOUISIANA

BATON ROUGE ○

NEW ORLEANS ●
New Orleans Jazz NHP ●

Gul

Amistad NRA

HOUSTON ○

Jean Lafitte NHP & PRES ●

SAN ANTONIO ●
San Antonio Missions NHP

🕐 **CENTRAL**
(Washington, DC, minus 1 hour)

Padre Island NS

GULF OF MEXICO

Palo Alto Battlefield NHP

Hot Springs

The view from Goat Rock

Phone: (501) 620-6715
Website: nps.gov/hosp

Established: March 4, 1921
Size: 5,550 Acres
Annual Visitors: 1.5 Million
Peak Season: May–October
Hiking Trails: 26 Miles

Activities: Hiking, Bathhouse Tours, Baths, Massages, Spa Treatments

2 Operational Bathhouses: $38+
Hotel Hale: $270–385/night
Campgrounds: Gulpha Gorge ($30/night with full hookups)
Backcountry Camping: None

Park Hours: All day, every day
Entrance Fee: None

Tree-covered mountains, natural hot springs, and ridgeline hiking trails are common ingredients for a national park. Hot Springs possesses these traits, but it's far from typical. Mountains crest at 1,400 feet. Mineral-rich hot springs water is collected, monitored, and managed via a complex plumbing system. Trails connect the area's mountains, but the entire network measures about 30 miles, a day of hiking for an industrious individual. So, what attracted Native Americans to this spot for thousands of years? The answer is hidden underground. In a gap between Hot Springs Mountain and West Mountain, rainwater seeps into the earth at a rate of one foot per year. After some 4,400 years, water has traveled a mile below the surface where it achieves a high temperature, naturally heated by rock under immense pressure. Pressure builds and what took several millennia to flow down now takes one year to return to the surface. Water flowing from the springs today fell as rain when ancient Egyptians were building the pyramids.

The first European to see the springs arrived after an epic journey of his own. It is believed Native Americans led Hernando de Soto to the place they called "Valley of the Vapors" in 1541, after the famed Spanish explorer had sailed half-way around the world. More than a century later,

Father Jacques Marquette and Louis Jolliet explored the area and claimed its land for France. Ownership exchanged hands between French and Spanish several times before becoming American territory in 1803 as part of the Louisiana Purchase. Less than one year later, President Thomas Jefferson sent a scientific team led by Dr. George Hunter and William Dunbar to explore the region known to them as "the hot springs of Washita." They discovered a log cabin and several small huts of canvas and wood, built by visitors who believed in the water's healing properties.

The first baths were nothing more than excavated rock, spanned by wooden planks where bathers sat and soaked their feet in 150°F water. A true log bathhouse wasn't built until 1830. In 1832, prompted by 12 years of requests by Arkansas Territory, President Andrew Jackson signed a law giving the hot springs federal protection as a reservation. This act makes Hot Springs the oldest National Park Service unit, 40 years older than Yellowstone, the world's first national park.

During the early days of government operation, hot springs' water was declared federal property and subsequently sold to bathhouses. Even with having to pay for their water, the baths of Hot Springs proved profitable, and by the late 19th century, facilities on Bathhouse Row rivaled the finest establishments found anywhere in Europe. Opulent structures and rejuvenating waters attracted sports heroes, politicians, and mobsters. From the late 1800s to mid-1900s, Hot Springs became known for organized crime such as gambling, prostitution, and bootlegging. Some of the nation's most infamous gangsters moved in. Al Capone, Frank Costello, and Bugs Moran are just a few who sought refuge at Hot Springs—the original Sin City.

Stephen T. Mather, first director of the National Park Service, remained unfazed by the area's corruption. He was actually quite enthusiastic about the hot springs, largely due to his affinity for rubdowns. Shortly thereafter Mather ordered construction of a new, free bathhouse and persuaded Congress to redesignate the reservation as Hot Springs National Park in 1921. Business on Bathhouse Row waxed and waned over the years. Only one bathhouse has endured, operating continuously since its inception, and just two are open today.

Hot Springs is an anomaly among its fellow parks whose calling cards are indescribable natural beauty. It's small and established around a commercialized natural resource. And that's exactly what's refreshing about Hot Springs—it's different. Oh, and the baths are nice too.

The Observation Tower

When to Go
The park is open all year. If you're passing nearby, it can provide a nice break from the road for a couple hours. Visitation is steady throughout the year with a summertime surge, but, be warned, summers can be uncomfortably hot and humid. Fall, when leaves are changing color, is my favorite time to visit.

Transportation & Airports
Greyhound has a bus station in Hot Springs (1001 Central Ave, Suite D), just one mile south of the park on Central Ave. Contact Greyhound at (800) 231-2222 or greyhound.com.

Hot Springs Memorial Field is located just 4 miles from the park. Little Rock National Airport is located 55 miles to the east.

Directions
Hot Springs National Park Visitor Center is located at Fordyce Bathhouse (369 Central Ave). Hot Springs is easily accessed via US-70 from the east and west. Arriving from the west, take US-70 E/Airport Road into Hot Springs and follow the signs to the park. From the east, take US-70 to US-70 Business W/E Grand Ave. Turn right onto Spring St. Continue onto Reserve St, then turn right onto Central Ave, which leads to the visitor center.

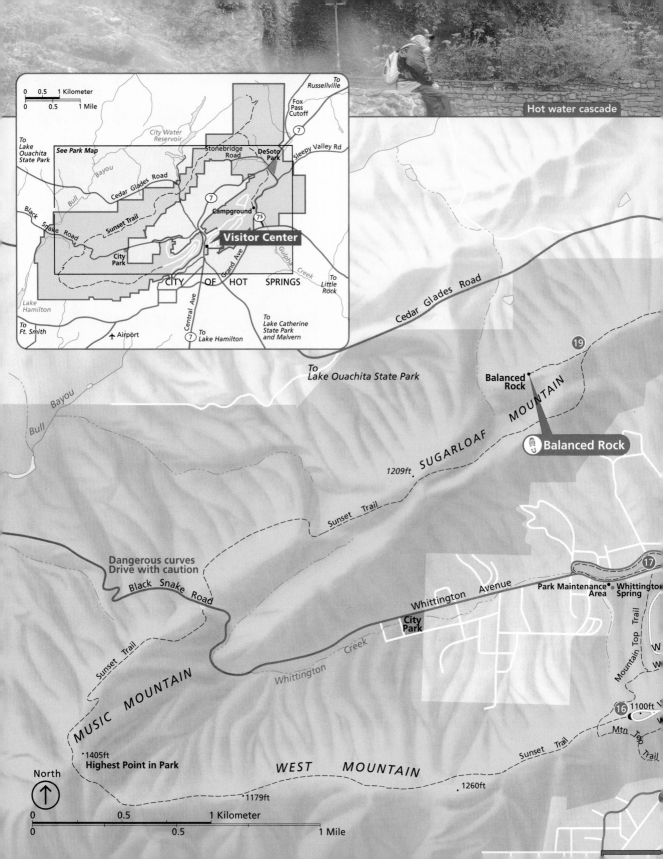

Hot water cascade

See Park Map

0 0.5 1 Kilometer
0 0.5 1 Mile

To Russellville

Fox Pass Cutoff

7

To Lake Ouachita State Park

City Water Reservoir

Stonebridge Road

DeSoto Park

Sleepy Valley Rd

Bull Bayou

Cedar Glades Road

7

Campground

7S

Visitor Center

City Park

Sunset Trail

Black Snake Road

CITY   OF   HOT   SPRINGS

Central Ave

Grand Ave

Gulpha Creek

To Little Rock

Lake Hamilton

To Ft. Smith

Airport

7

To Lake Hamilton

To Lake Catherine State Park and Malvern

To Lake Ouachita State Park

Cedar Glades Road

19

Balanced Rock

SUGARLOAF   MOUNTAIN

1209ft

Sunset   Trail

👣 **Balanced Rock**

Bull Bayou

**Dangerous curves
Drive with caution**

Black   Snake   Road

Sunset   Trail

Whittington   Avenue

Park Maintenance Area

Whittington Spring

17

City Park

Whittington   Creek

Mountain Top Trail

16   1100ft

MUSIC   MOUNTAIN

Sunset   Trail

•1405ft
Highest Point in Park

WEST   MOUNTAIN

•1179ft

•1260ft

Sunset   Trail

Mtn. Top Trail

North

↑

0   0.5   1 Kilometer

0   0.5   1 Mile

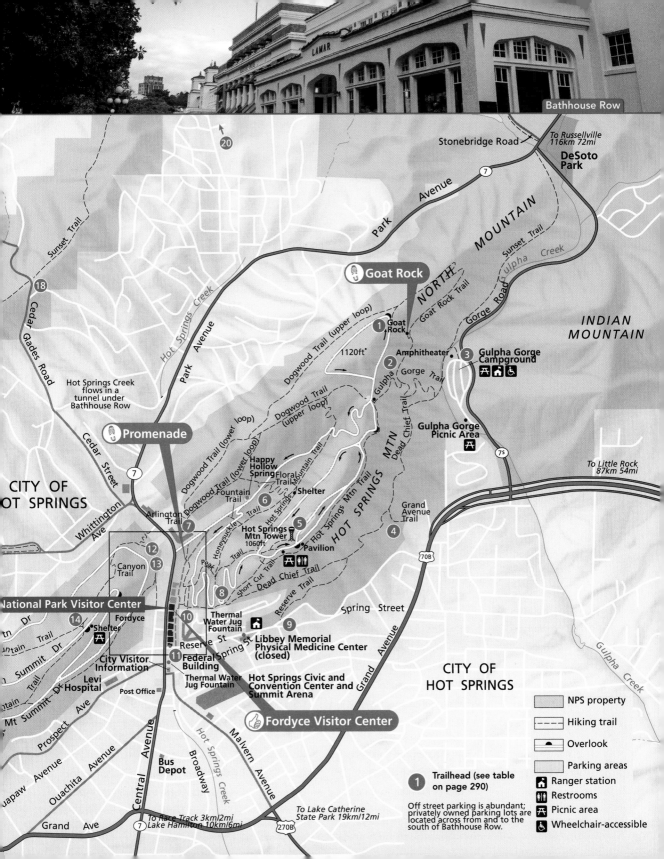

Bathhouse Row

To Russellville
116km 72mi

Stonebridge Road

DeSoto
Park

Park Avenue

NORTH MOUNTAIN

INDIAN
MOUNTAIN

Sunset Trail

Gulpha Creek

Goat Rock

Sunset Trail

Gorge Road

1 Goat
Rock

Goat Rock Trail

1120ft

2

Amphitheater

3 Gulpha Gorge
Campground

Dogwood Trail (upper loop)

Gulpha Gorge Trail

Dead Chief Trail

Gulpha Gorge
Picnic Area

Cedar Glades Road

18

Sunset Trail

Hot Springs Creek

Dogwood Trail (upper loop)

Park Avenue

Promenade

Hot Springs Creek flows in a tunnel under Bathhouse Row

Dogwood Trail (lower loop)

Dogwood Trail (lower loop)

Happy Hollow Spring

Floral Trail

Mountain Trail

HOT SPRINGS MTN

Dead Chief Trail

Grand Avenue Trail

75

To Little Rock
87km 54mi

CITY OF
HOT SPRINGS

Cedar Street

7

Arlington Trail

Whittington Ave

Dogwood Trail (lower loop)

Fountain Trail

6

Shelter

Hot Springs Mtn Trail

5

4

7

12

13

Canyon Trail

Honeysuckle Trail

Hot Springs
Mtn Tower
1060ft

Pavilion

70B

Peak Trail

Short Cut Trail

Dead Chief Trail

Reserve Trail

National Park Visitor Center

14

Shelter

Fordyce

Mt Summit Dr

Summit Trail

8

Spring Street

Grand Avenue

CITY OF
HOT SPRINGS

City Visitor
Information

10

Thermal Water Jug Fountain

Libbey Memorial
Physical Medicine Center
(closed)

9

Gulpha Creek

Levi Hospital

Prospect Ave

Mt Summit Dr

Ouapaw Avenue

11

Federal
Building

Reserve St

Spring St

Post Office

Thermal Water
Jug Fountain

Hot Springs Civic and
Convention Center and
Summit Arena

Ouachita Avenue

Grand Ave

7

Bus
Depot

Central Avenue

Broadway

Hot Springs Creek

Malvern Avenue

To Race Track 3km/2mi
Lake Hamilton 10km/6mi

To Lake Catherine
State Park 19km/12mi

270B

Fordyce Visitor Center

1 Trailhead (see table
on page 290)

Off street parking is abundant;
privately owned parking lots are
located across from and to the
south of Bathhouse Row.

NPS property

Hiking trail

Overlook

Parking areas

Ranger station

Restrooms

Picnic area

Wheelchair-accessible

Grand Promenade

Hot Springs Hiking Trails (Distances are one-way unless loop)

	Name	Location (# on map)	Length	Difficulty Rating & Notes
Hot Springs & North Mountains	Upper Dogwood	North Mountain Overlook (1)	1.0 mile	M – Ends at Hot Springs Mountain Trail
	Goat Rock - ♿	Gulpha Gorge Camp (1, 2)	1.1 miles	M – Up North Mountain to Goat Rock
	Gulpha Gorge	Camp Amphitheater (3)	0.6 mile	S – Intersects Goat Rock/Hot Springs Mtn
	Oertel (Dead Chief)	Camp/Bathhouse Row (3, 10)	1.4 miles	M – Combine with Gulpha Gorge to hike from the campground to Bathhouse Row
	Grand Avenue	Spur Trail (4)	0.2 mile	E – Spur from Oertel Trail to Grand Ave
	Hot Springs Mtn - ♿	Hot Springs Mtn Tower (5)	1.7 miles	M – One of the better hiking trails
	Carriage Road	Hot Springs Mtn Tower (5)	0.1 mile	E – Old Carriage Road from Army–Navy Hospital to the summit of Hot Springs Mtn
	Peak	Hot Springs Mtn Tower (5, 10)	0.6 mile	M – Steep climb, Tufa Terrace to Mtn Tower
	Floral	Connector Trail (6)	0.7 mile	M – Connects Dogwood and Honeysuckle
	Fountain	Honeysuckle Trail (6)	0.2 mile	M – Short and steep trail, concrete steps
	Honeysuckle	Connector Trail (6, 8)	0.5 mile	M – Connects Peak, Fountain, and Floral Tr
	Arlington	Arlington Hotel (7)	0.1 mile	E – Continues to Lower Dogwood Trail
	Lower Dogwood	Arlington Hotel (7)	0.7 mile	M – Steep gravel trail that climbs North Mtn
	Shortcut	Hot Springs Mtn Picnic Area (8)	0.2 mile	M – Connects Oertel Trail and Picnic Area
	Reserve	Dead Chief Trail (9)	0.3 mile	M – Shortcut to Gulpha Gorge Camp
	Tufa Terrace	Near Grand Promenade (10)	0.3 mile	E - Pass calcium carbonate (tufa) deposits
	Grand Promenade - ♿	Reserve Street (11)	0.5 mile	E – Brick path through historic Hot Springs
West & Sugarloaf Mtn	Canyon	West Mountain (12)	0.7 mile	M – Old carriage road to Bathhouse Row
	Oak	Mountain Street (13)	1.0 mile	M – Intersects Canyon Trail
	West Mountain	West Mtn Summit Drive (14)	1.2 miles	M – Trail loops around the road
	Mountain Top	Whittington/Prospect Ave (15, 17)	1.5 miles	M – Crosses West Mtn and Sunset Trails
	Sunset	West Mtn Summit Drive/Cedar Glades Rd (16, 18)	10+ miles	M – Passes Ricks Pond and varied terrain along the park's longest trail
	Whittington	Whittington Park (17)	1.2 miles	E – Loop with unmaintained jogging path
	Balanced Rock Spur - ♿	Spur Trail (19)	0.2 mile	E – Spur from Sunset to a balanced rock
	Pullman	End of Pullman Avenue (20)	0.7 mile	E – Mountain bike trail, opened in 2020
	Fordyce Peak Spur	Spur Trail (off map)	1.5 miles	M – Spur from Sunset Trail to Fordyce Peak

Difficulty Ratings: E = Easy, M = Moderate, S = Strenuous

Camping & Lodging

Gulpha Gorge (305 Gorge Road), located off US-70B on the east side of Hot Springs, is the park's only campground. All sites are available on a first-come, first-served basis. Restrooms are located nearby. Showers are not available. Camping fees are $30/night for a site with electric, water, and sewer hookups. Sites are not pull-through. The Historic Hale Bathhouse has been renovated into a nine-suite luxury hotel, **Hotel Hale** (501.760.9010, hotelhale.com). It's conveniently located on Bathhouse Row, two buildings away from Fordyce Visitor Center. Each suite features a large soaking tub. Rates range from $270–385/night.

Driving

On your visit, you definitely should drive down Central Avenue, turn right on Fountain Street, and take another right onto the one-way Hot Springs Mountain Drive (you can hike up Hot Springs Mountain as well). Formerly a carriage road, this scenic route leads to Hot Springs Mountain Tower and a number of overlooks. West Mountain Summit Drive, accessed from Prospect Avenue or Whittington Avenue, is another scenic route to explore, providing access to hiking trails and scenic overlooks. These are also good roads to bike.

Hiking

Hot Springs has a total of 26 miles of hiking trails. **Sunset Trail** (10+ miles) circles the mountains surrounding Hot Springs, passing the highest point in the park, Music Mountain (1,405 ft). It traverses the park's most remote areas, providing good opportunities to see white-tailed deer and wild turkeys, but it's often broken into smaller sections. One of the better stretches is the 2.8 miles following Sugarloaf Mountain's ridge. It's located in the northwest corner and can be accessed via Cedar Glades Road or Black Snake Road. Here you'll also find a short spur to Balanced Rock, a large novaculite boulder precariously positioned atop another sloped boulder. The remainder of park trails are less than 2 miles in length, forming very manageable networks on Hot Springs, North, and West Mountains. The brick path known as **Grand Promenade** is the one trail you should not skip.

Bathhouse Row

The first bathhouses were nothing more than small canvas and lumber structures situated on openings cut into rock. But by the late 19th century, Hot Springs' bathhouses could go toe-to-toe with the best Europe had to offer. Health seekers, wealthy and indigent alike, sought Hot Springs Mountain's rejuvenating waters. Doctors prescribed a strict bathing regimen for

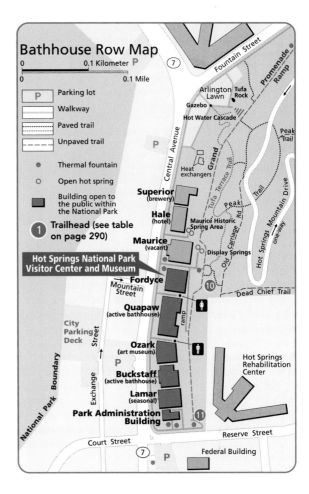

all sorts of ailments including rheumatism, paralysis, syphilis, gout, and bunions. Hot Springs reemerged as a popular destination in the 1920s when it was brought into the fold of national parks, and when construction began on a free government bathhouse in 1922. Each successive bathhouse was more extravagant than the last. During Hot Springs' heydays in the mid-1940s as many as 24 bathhouses were open for business at one time. They gave more than one million baths in a single year. In time, medical advancements led to a severe decrease in visitation. Penicillin and other modern medicines were being prescribed rather than frequent baths in mineral rich water.

In its prime, **The Fordyce** was the most elegant of all the bathhouses, and today it serves as the park's visitor center and museum. **Buckstaff Baths** still provides traditional treatment and is the only bathhouse in continuous operation since being established in 1912. **Quapaw Baths & Spas** reopened as a modern spa. It

Bathhouse Tour at the Visitor Center

Flora & Fauna

Forested mountain slopes are dominated by oak and hickory. Pines cover the southern slope. In all, there are more than 300 acres of old growth forests consisting of shortleaf pine, blackjack oak, and white oak; many of the trees are over 130 years old, and a few exceed 200 years of age. Hot Springs is one of the smallest national parks, and unlike most, it is set in an urban environment. A portion of the Ouachita Mountain Range, including Hot Springs Mountain, lies within park boundaries. Here you'll find bats, rodents, and other small mammals typical of the region. When exploring the area near the bathhouses, you'll probably only encounter squirrels and a few of the park's 100+ species of native birds. In more remote regions northwest of Bathhouse Row, you may encounter wild turkeys, deer, opossum, gray fox, coyote, or nine-banded armadillo.

Pets & Accessibility

Hot Springs is very pet-friendly. Pets are allowed on all trails and in the campground, but must be kept on a leash (less than six feet). Pets, except for service animals, are not allowed in the visitor center or other park buildings.

The visitor center is wheelchair accessible and has a wheelchair available for loan. There is one wheelchair-accessible campsite. The Grand Promenade is paved with ramps off Fountain Street and behind the Fordyce Bathhouse.

Weather

Arkansas summers are what visitors need to be prepared for. They are hot and humid. Standing in the Arkansas heat can feel an awful lot like a steaming hot bath. Average high temperatures in July and August reach the 90s°F. Fall and spring are mild. Winter is comfortable with average highs in the 50s°F and lows around freezing.

is the first bathhouse to open under the park's lease program. Like the Quapaw, old bathhouses are being restored by private lease. **Lamar Bathhouse** is a seasonal office and bookstore. **Ozark Bathhouse** hosts community events. And **Superior Bathhouse** (superiorbathhouse.com) is now home to a craft brewery.

Buckstaff Baths (501.623.2308, buckstaffbaths.com) is open year-round. You can take a mineral bath for $38 or get a Swedish massage for $40. **Quawpaw Baths** (501.609.9822, quawpawbaths.com) is open year-round. An individual mineral bath costs $30 or you can visit their public thermal pool for $20/person. A Swedish massage costs $80 for 50 minutes. Many other treatments are available at each bathhouse.

Visitor Center

Fordyce Bathhouse is the park's visitor center, but it was also the most highly regarded bathhouse on Bathhouse Row during the early 1900s. You'll find a variety of modern and historic bathhouse exhibits inside. The visitor center is open daily from 9am to 5pm, except New Year's Day, Thanksgiving, and Christmas. Even if you don't join a tour of Fordyce Bathhouse (although you should), the visitor center is a good place to stop, get yourself oriented, and speak with a friendly park ranger.

Ranger Programs & For Kids

Outdoor tours of Bathhouse Row are offered periodically during summer. Tours of Fordyce Bathhouse are offered daily (staff permitting).

Free Junior Ranger activity booklets are available online and at Fordyce Bathhouse Visitor Center. Children can earn a Junior Ranger patch by completing a number of activities while exploring the park.

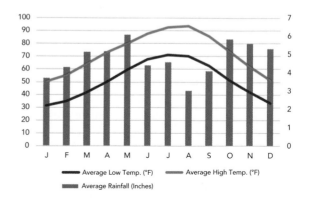

Tips & Recommendations

Hot Springs isn't a park that demands a great deal of time. Stop, get a spa treatment if you feel like treating yourself, tour the visitor center (Fordyce Bathhouse) to see what things were like in the early 1900s, do some hiking, go up the tower, bum around town (Bathhouse Row is quite nice), and continue on your way.

There is a free parking garage at 128 Exchange Street.

As long as there's staff, tours of Fordyce Bathhouse are offered every day. Join one if you can.

There are no outdoor hot springs to dip yourself into, but Quawpaw and Buckstaff Baths offer rejuvenating mineral baths and typical spa treatments. Buckstaff also offers a "traditional therapy," allowing you to travel back in time to learn exactly why everyone was fussing about Hot Springs in the 1920s.

Pullman (mountain bike) Trail opened in 2020. It connects Hot Springs to the Northwoods Trails, passing through the park. Note that it meanders near a homesite, featuring "historic" trash. Leave things as they are. Oddly, the cans, bottles, toys, and car are considered archeological artifacts. (Don't add to the trash.)

Drink some water! There's a water fountain at either end of the Grand Promenade. Fill your water bottles! Filling stations are located in front of Libbey Memorial Physical Medicine Center on Reserve Street, at the National Park Service Administration Building on Reserve Street, between Hale and Maurice Bathhouses on Bathhouse Row, and outside park boundaries at Hill Wheatley Plaza on Central Avenue.

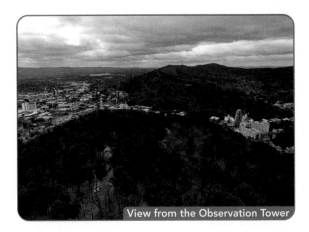
View from the Observation Tower

In the end, Hot Springs isn't for everyone, but it's a unique part of our national park history as the first national reservation, and it's worth a quick stopover on your way to more adventurous locales (although, in my opinion, some of these spa treatments are plenty "adventurous" in their own right).

If you're looking for outdoor activities, consider looking into the destinations listed in the "Beyond the Park" section at the bottom of the page.

Easy Hikes: Grand Promenade (1 mile), Balanced Rock (1.6+, depends on where you begin Sunset Trail)
Moderate Hikes: Goat Rock (2.2 miles), Hot Springs Mountain (3.4), Sunset Trail (10+ miles)
Family Activities: Become Junior Rangers
Guided Tours: Tour Fordyce Bathhouse
Rainy Day Activities: Explore the Bathhouses
History Enthusiasts: Bathhouse Row

Beyond the Park...

Dining
Mama Vee's • (501) 612-2211
420 Malvern Ave, Hot Springs

Emma Lee's • 765 Park Ave

SQZBX Brewery & Pizza
236 Ouachita Ave, Hot Springs
sqzbx.com • (501) 609-0609

Alexa's Creperie •
238 Cornerstone Blvd, Hot Springs
alexascreperie.com

Grocery Stores
Harp's • (501) 760-1233
146 Thornton Ferry Rd, Hot Springs

Kroger • (501) 624-0259
3341 Central Ave, Hot Springs

Lodging & Camping
Hot Springs Treehouses
142 Jubilee Trail • (501) 538-3394
hotspringstreehouses.com

Fox Pass Cabins • (501) 545-0344
1287 Fox Pass Cutoff, Hot Springs
foxpasscabins.com

Best Court • (501) 293-0086
638 Ouachita Ave, Hot Springs
bestcourthotsprings.com

Catherine's Landing
1700 Shady Grove Rd, Hot Springs
rvcoutdoors.com • (501) 262-2550

Hot Springs KOA
838 McClendon Rd, Hot Springs
koa.com • (501) 624-5912

Young's Lakeshore RV Resort
1601 Lakeshore Dr, Hot Springs
rvhotsprings.com • (800) 470-7875

J&J RV Park
2000 E Grand Ave, Hot Springs
jjrvpark.com • (501) 321-9852

Festivals
Rodeo of the Ozarks • June
roadeooftheozarks.com

Attractions
Garvan Woodland Gardens
550 Arkridge Rd, Hot Springs
garvangardens.org

Lake Catherine State Park
1200 Catherine Park Rd, Hot Springs
arkansasstateparks.com

Lake Ouachita State Park
Large man-made lake just 10 miles from Hot Springs
5451 Mtn Pine Rd, Mtn Pine
arkansasstateparks.com

Little Rock Central HS NHS
2120 W Daisy L Gatson Bates Dr
nps.gov/chsc • (501) 374-1957

Buffalo National River
Beautiful, undammed river
402 N Walnut St, Harrison
nps.gov/buff • (870) 439-2502

Mount Magazine State Park
Arkansas's highest point, in the Ozark National Forest
16878 AR-309, Paris
arkansasstateparks.com

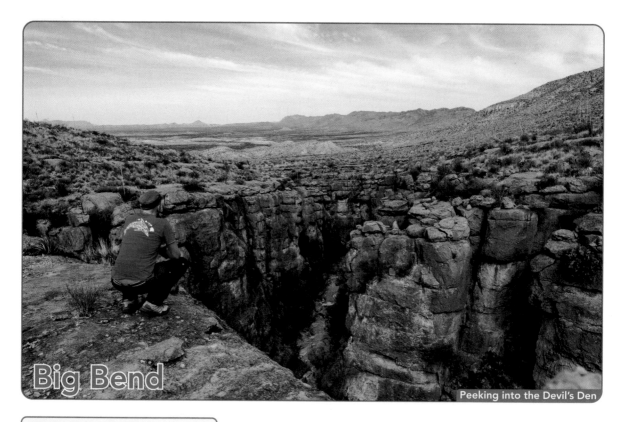

Big Bend

Peeking into the Devil's Den

Phone: (432) 477-2251
Website: nps.gov/bibe

Established: June 12, 1944
Size: 801,163 Acres
Annual Visitors: 450,000
Peak Season: November–April
Hiking Trails: 150+ Miles

Activities: Hiking, Backpacking, Biking, Paddling/Rafting, Stargazing, Birdwatching

3 Campgrounds: $16/night (tent sites), $37/night (RV sites)
Backcountry Camping: Permitted at primitive road (high-clearance 4WD required for some) and trailside campsites with a Backcountry Permit ($10/night, recreation.gov)
Chisos Mtns Lodge: $156–176/night

Park Hours: All day, every day
Entrance Fee: $30/25/15 (car/motorcycle/individual)

"I wish you would take a map of the State showing the counties, put your pencil point on the Rio Grande, just where the Brewster and Presidio County line hit that stream; then draw a line due East and at a distance of sixty miles it will again strike the River. My dream is to make the area south of this line into a park and I shall live to see it done."

– Everett Townsend, 1933

Congress authorized the park in 1935, but it wasn't until 1944 that Everett Townsend's dream came true. Since its establishment, Big Bend has had its fair share of admirers, including geologists, paleontologists, botanists, and birdwatchers. But it is seldom visited by the average national park-goer. Looking at a county map of Texas like Townsend did, you begin to understand why only the most dedicated visitors reach this scenic wilderness in the southwest corner of Texas. It isn't close to anything unless you count the United States–Mexico border. Then there's the stigma associated with desert; it's known for being a barren wasteland, not the diverse wonderlands national parks have been made out to be. But the park's faithful continue to return time and time again. They drive dirt roads, hike dusty trails, and run the Rio Grande in canoes and rafts. To them the steep limestone canyons, mountain vistas, and desert wilderness of Big Bend are every bit as wondrous as the western parks. It simply hasn't been marketed like Yosemite and the Grand Canyon, and that's perfectly fine. To understand Big Bend, you have to visit. You can't truly comprehend its size and desolation through a 4" x 6" image. But those willing to make the long journey, almost immediately feel what inspired Townsend's big dream.

Over the years, people have freely crossed the Rio Grande, observing this area's beauty, hunting its wildlife, and, seasonally, farming its land. Artifacts date back some 9,000 years. In the 16th and 17th centuries, Spanish explorers passed through current parkland, crossing the Rio Grande in search of gold, silver, and fertile soil. In the 19th century, Comanche blazed a path across the desert into Mexico where they carried out raids. Today, when visitors enter at Persimmon Gap, they follow a section of the same Comanche Trail. In the early 1900s Mexican settlers lived on both sides of the river. Some tried to eke out a life farming an arid land. Others chose ranching.

After a mining settlement was established at Boquillas in 1898, more attention was given to the United States–Mexico border. Mounted inspectors began to patrol the boundary. Everett Ewing Townsend was one of them. He grew up on a ranch, eventually joining Company E Frontier Battalion of the Texas Rangers. While stationed at Big Bend as a U.S. Marshall, Townsend "saw God" and realized the "awesomeness of the region" while tracking stolen mules through the Chisos Mountains. His mountaintop epiphany inspired a new hobby: lobbying politicians to protect the region. Unsuccessful as a lobbyist, he joined the ranks of politicians. Elected to the state legislature after 18 years as a ranchman, his new role allowed time to co-author legislation creating Texas Canyons State Park.

Townsend was also instrumental in establishing a CCC camp at Chisos Basin. Many of the area's trails and facilities were constructed by the CCC in the 1930s. Living during the Great Depression was a struggle, but it was incredibly difficult at Big Bend. There was no electricity, they had few reliable water sources, roads were not paved, and the nearest telephone was 100 miles away. But the CCC got by, completing much of the present-day infrastructure, setting the stage for establishment of Big Bend National Park in 1944. Townsend was eventually appointed as its first commissioner. Today, he's remembered as the "Father of Big Bend" and forever recognized thanks to Townsend Point (7,580 ft), the second highest peak in the Chisos Mountains and the site of his epiphany. Many of today's guests share the same fervor as Everett Townsend. They travel great distances to reach a barren, but uniquely beautiful region. Beauty only witnessed by those willing to make the trip to Rio Grande's Big Bend.

The Chisos Mountains

When to Go
The park is open all year, but most visitors come to Big Bend between November and April. Visitation peaks in March for spring break, but it can also be busy around holidays, fall through spring. Summer can be unbearable, with high temperatures frequently surpassing the century mark. Thunderstorms, overcast skies, and high elevations make for a more enjoyable climate than you might expect, but it's still very hot in summer.

Transportation & Airports
Public transportation does not serve Big Bend. However, Amtrak (800.872.7245, amtrak.com) and Greyhound (800.231.2222, greyhound.com) provide service to Alpine, TX (100 miles from park headquarters). Car rental is available in Alpine.

The closest airports are Midland International (MAF) in Midland, TX (223 miles away) and El Paso International (ELP) in El Paso, TX (315 miles away). Car rental is available at each destination.

Directions
Big Bend is located in southwestern Texas on the U.S.–Mexico border. Arriving from the east via I-10, the park is 125 miles south from Fort Stockton on US-385. Arriving from the west via I-10, the park is 197 miles south from Van Horn via US-90 and US-385. Due to the area's remote nature, be sure to have plenty of food, and water (there is a gas station near Panther Junction).

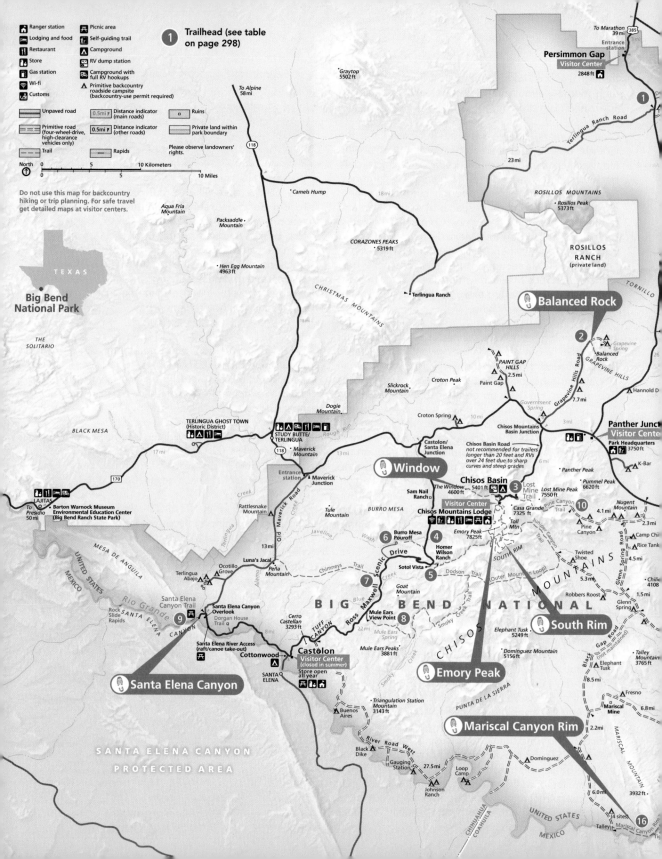

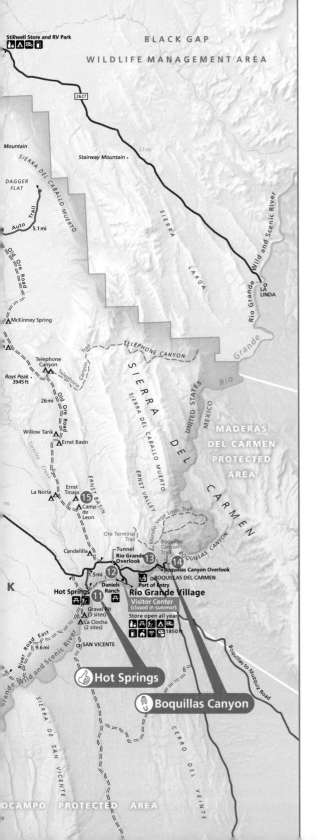

Camping & Lodging

Big Bend has three established campgrounds. **Cottonwood Campground** is located on Ross Maxwell Scenic Drive near Castolon Historic District and the Mexico–U.S. border. It has 24 sites, pit toilets, and potable water. 16 of the sites can be reserved (877.444.6777, recreation.gov) from November through April. **Chisos Basin Campground** has 60 sites (40 can be reserved year-round), running water, and flush toilets. **Rio Grande Village Campground** has 100 sites (60 can be reserved from November through April), flush toilets, and running water. All campsites listed above are available year-round for $16/night. **Rio Grande Village** has a 25-site RV Park. It's open year-round, and sites cost $37/night (plus $3/person). These are the only sites with full hookups. Reservations can be made at chisosmountainslodge.com or (877) 386-4383. Rio Grande Village is also the only location with showers and laundry. Each campground has at least one group site designed to accommodate more than nine campers. Group sites must be reserved at (877) 444-6777 or recreation.gov. All reservations are available up to six months in advance.

Chisos Mountains Lodge (877.386.4383, chisosmountainslodge.com), high in the Chisos Mountains near the center of the park, is the only in-park lodging, and your only option within a 50-mile radius. Rooms cost $156–166/night. Cottages are available for $176/night. A restaurant is located on-site.

Primitive Roadside Camping

More than 70 primitive roadside campsites are available to you with a Backcountry Permit ($10/night). These sites provide secluded camping with drive-up convenience. You'll need a high-clearance 4WD vehicle to reach sites along Old Ore, River, Pine Canyon, Juniper Canyon, Glenn Springs, and Black Gap Roads. (Pine Canyon, Twisted Shoe, Ernst Tinaja, and Talley are good choices.) These high-clearance-4WD-required sites can only be reserved in-person at Panther Junction (8:30am–5pm) or Chisos Basin (8:30am–4pm) Visitor Centers. Many others, including sites along Grapevine Hills and Old Maverick Roads, can be accessed by regular vehicles unless a recent storm has compromised the dirt road. Grapevine Hills and Terlingua Abajo are nice, but you really can't go wrong. These sites can be reserved online at recreation.gov up to six months in advance. If you're the least bit tentative about driving a primitive, high-clearance recommended road, stick to the main roads (Old Maverick and Grapevine Hills), and then check out Old Ore and/or River Road while you're there (and reserve one if you feel good about it). Remember you won't find toilets and very little shade (if any) is available. Generator use is prohibited. And you'll want to pack in more water than you'll need. Pack out everything you brough with you.

Sunrise near Dog Canyon

Big Bend Hiking Trails (Distances are roundtrip)

	Name	Location (# on map)	Length	Difficulty Rating & Notes
East	Rio Grande Village Nature Trail	Rio Grande Village Camp, Site #18 (12)	0.8 mile	E – Self-guided trail with great birdwatching opportunities and nice scenery
East	Hot Springs Canyon	Daniel's Ranch (12)	6.0 miles	M – Follows the river to Hot Springs
East	Hot Springs - 🐾	Hot Springs Road (11)	1.4 miles	E – Easy loop or just 0.25 mile to Hot Springs
East	Ore Terminal - 🐾	Boquillas Canyon Rd (13)	8.0 miles	M – Follows an old tramway that carried ore from Mexican mines
East	Marufo Vega	Boquillas Canyon Rd (13)	12.0 miles	S – Loop through mountains to Rio Grande's banks
East	Boquillas Canyon - 🐾	End of Boquillas Canyon Road (14)	1.4 miles	M – Up and down and into the canyon until the canyon's walls close in on the river
North	Dog Canyon & Devil's Den - 🐾	3.5 miles south of Persimmon Gap on the main park road (1)	4.0 miles 5.6 miles	M – After 1.5 miles you head into a wash and meet a junction • Left leads to Dog Canyon, right leads to Devil's Den (follow cairns out of the wash)
Chisos Mtns	Window View	Near Basin Store (3)	0.3 mile	E – Hike to watch the sunset through "the window"
Chisos Mtns	Lost Mine - 🐾	Mile 5 of Basin Rd (3)	4.8 miles	M – Steep, popular self-guided hike
Chisos Mtns	Window - 🐾	Basin Camp (3)	5.6 miles	M – Popular descent to a rocky window
Chisos Mtns	Emory Peak - 🐾	Near Basin Store (3)	10.5 miles	S – Park's highest point and best panoramic views
Chisos Mtns	South Rim - 🐾	Near Basin Store (3)	12–14.5 miles	S – Extremely long day hike or backpack it, taking advantage of campsites along the way
West	Ward Spring - 🐾	Ross Maxwell Drive (RMD) mile 5.5 (4)	3.6 miles	E – Seldom used trail to volcanic dike and spring, interesting geology and great Chisos views
West	Red Rocks Canyon (Also Blue Creek)	Homer Wilson Ranch Overlook (5)	3.0 miles	M – Colorful rocks and an old cabin (Trail continues beyond into the Chisos Mountains)
West	Upper Burro Mesa Pour-off	RMD mile 6 (6)	3.8 miles	M – Through a wash and two canyons • Requires a bit of scrambling, gorge's floor is mostly sandy
West	Chimneys	RMD mile 13 (7)	4.8 miles	M – Long, flat, rock formations and petroglyphs
West	Mule Ears Spring	RMD mile 15 (8)	3.8 miles	M – Nice views through foothills of the Chisos Mtns
West	Santa Elena Canyon - 🐾	End of RMD (9)	1.7 miles	M – Cross Terlingua Creek into the canyon
Backcountry	Grapevine Hills - 🐾	7 miles down Grapevine Hills Rd (2)	2.2 miles	M – Kids' favorite to balanced rock, mostly flat until you must climb into the nearby boulders
Backcountry	Pine Canyon	Pine Canyon Rd (10)	4.0 miles	M – The trail leads to a waterfall (after rain), high-clearance vehicle required
Backcountry	Ernst Tinaja - 🐾	Old Ore Rd (15)	1.4 miles	E – Interesting geology, high-clearance required
Backcountry	Mariscal Canyon - 🐾	River Rd/Talley Rd (16)	6.5 miles	S – Amazing, requires a high-clearance vehicle

Difficulty Ratings: E = Easy, M = Moderate, S = Strenuous

Driving

A considerable amount of Big Bend can be explored without leaving your vehicle, thanks to roughly 100 miles of paved roadways suitable for the average motorist. The most scenic stretch is 30-mile **Ross Maxwell Scenic Drive**, which leads to Santa Elena Canyon and Castolon. Along the way, you'll pass several stop-worthy overlooks, trailheads, and historic sites (Sam Nail Ranch, Homer Wilson Ranch). You can also reach Santa Elena Canyon via unpaved **Old Maverick Road**. Most visitors beeline to the Chisos Mountains. They're tremendous, but if you're headed here during a holiday/spring break week, expect to encounter traffic and possibly delayed entry to the region. **Chisos Basin Road** leads to a campground, lodge, restaurant, visitor center, and many of the most popular hiking trails. There are sites worth seeing along every stretch of roadway, but the other paved road to make sure you cover is the stretch from Panther Junction to Boquillas Canyon. Gas is available near Panther Junction.

Off-Roading

You'll also find a network of dirt roads; some (Grapevine Hills, Old Maverick Road) are improved to the point standard 2WD vehicles traveling at low speeds can pass. Others (River Road, Old Ore Road) can only be accessed by high-clearance vehicles. River Road loosely follows the Rio Grande and is one of the best off-road drives. Conditions change, but I find these roads to be worst in the middle, where they see the least traffic, so you may want to drive as far as you're comfortable and then turn back. Always check current road conditions at a visitor center before traveling on them, even for the improved roads as a recent storm may have made them impassable.

Hiking & Backpacking

The Chisos Mountains provide the densest network of trails, allowing visitors to choose between day-hikes and backpacking trips. The 10.5-mile roundtrip hike to the park's highest point, **Emory Peak** (7,832 feet), is challenging. Complete the journey, ending with a short exposed (and kind of frightening) scramble to the top, and you'll be rewarded with sweeping desert panoramas. **South Rim Trail** is longer and just as rewarding. It can be done as a loop by taking Pinnacles and Laguna Meadows Trails. Both begin at Chisos Basin Trailhead, located near the Lodge, Basin Store, and visitor center. A really nice shorter hike in the Chisos Mountains is **Lost Mine Trail**. This 4.8-mile walk leads to a promontory overlooking Pine and Juniper Canyons. It's one of the park's most popular hikes. And for good reason, views at the conclusion are exceptional.

Chisos Mountains near Sam Nail Ranch

Window is another popular Chisos Mountains hiking trail. It descends a canyon, aided by a few steps, ending at a window carved out of rock by the slow trickle of water (where it can get a little slick). Along the way you'll cross Oak Creek a few times (when it's running). Energetic hikers can continue beneath the Window via Oak Springs Trail. It's about 2.5 miles (one-way) to **Cattail Falls** from the junction on Window Trail (remember that you'll have to hike back up on the return trip). You can also reach Cattail Falls hiking in from Ross Maxwell Drive, beginning near Sam Nail Ranch.

Most visitors explore the Chisos Mountains by foot, but that doesn't mean it's the only place in the park worth hiking. **Santa Elena Canyon and Boquillas Canyon Trails** are located along the Rio Grande on opposite ends of the park. They provide beautiful canyon views and are as short as the canyons are impressive. If you only have enough time to drive to one, head west and hike Santa Elena Canyon Trail. It's more spectacular. **Grapevine Hills**, leading to a balanced rock, is another good hike (the rock is best scene/photographed in the morning). Something of a novelty (and often crowded), you can hike to **Hot Springs** (a small manmade 105°F pool along the Rio Grande) accessed via a short trail at the end of Hot Springs Road (also accessible via Hot Springs Canyon Trail from Daniel's Ranch).

While you can camp in the surrounding desert, most **backpackers** stick to the Chisos Mountains. There are 42 designated sites in the area, and you can make a few loops using South Rim and East Rim Trails. If you're visiting during peak season, especially during holiday/spring break weeks, you'll want to reserve your permit early. Permits are available up to six months in advance at recreation.gov for $10/night. Backpacking is good, but you're somewhat limited since you must carry ample water with you. You're also subject to huge differences in temperature between day and night.

Ward Spring Trail

Biking

Cyclists are allowed on all roads (paved and dirt). Compared to most parks, traffic is light (except during winter holidays and weekends), but cyclists should use extreme caution as roads, especially Chisos Basin, are steep and winding with narrow shoulders. Chisos Basin Road is also the most scenic and strenuous stretch of pavement. Pedal the 10 miles between Panther Junction and Chisos Basin for a nice ride. En route you'll encounter 15% grades, gaining 1,650 feet of elevation before reaching its end. Turn around and enjoy the cruise back to Panther Junction. If you can arrange a shuttle, biking between Panther Junction and Rio Grande Village is an easy 20-mile ride, most of which is downhill.

Dirt roads are suitable for mountain bikers. Old Maverick Road is easiest from north to south and its southern end reaches picturesque Santa Elena Canyon. An out-and-back of Old Maverick Road is 26 miles from Maverick Junction. You can make a 48-mile loop by combining Old Maverick Road and Ross Maxwell Drive. Mountain bikers will not find single track. Bikes are not allowed off road or on trails. However, 50 miles of the area's best single track are located nearby in Lajitas.

Floating & Rafting

For 118 miles, the Rio Grande serves double duty as Big Bend's southern boundary and natural border between the U.S. and Mexico. Many visitors find a float through Santa Elena Canyon to be the most dramatic way to view Big Bend. Picture yourself winding through 1,500-ft cliffs for 13 miles and it's easy to understand why. Then there's Rock Slide, the canyon's largest rapid, which becomes Class IV whitewater under the right conditions. This section of the Rio Grande is easily accessed with a put-in outside the park at Lajitas and take-out inside the park at Santa Elena Canyon Trail. Canyons may not be safe for all boat types during high water level.

If you have your own boat but can't arrange a shuttle between put-in and take-out, launch at Santa Elena Canyon Trail and paddle upriver for two miles to Fern Canyon before turning around (only possible at low water levels and you may have to walk your kayak through some shallow rapids to the canyon's mouth). Within the park, you'll find two established campgrounds and 11 designated campsites along the Rio Grande. To use these sites, you must first obtain a Backcountry Use Permit ($10/night) from Chisos Basin or Panther Junction Visitor Center up to seven days in advance. Even if you only plan on spending a few hours on the water, a day-use river permit is required (available at any visitor center). If Big Bend isn't big enough for you, Rio Grande Wild and Scenic River extends downstream beyond the park boundary an additional 127 miles.

Big Bend River Tours (800.545.4240, bigbendrivertours. com), Desert Sports (432.371.2727, desertsportstx.com), and Far Flung Outdoor Center (432.371.2633, bigbend-farflung.com) provide shuttles, equipment, and tours.

Stargazing

As one of the most isolated national parks, Big Bend is also one of the best locations for stargazing. Far away from busy streets and city lights, stars shimmer across the perfectly dark night sky. A night spent here can provide an especially inspiring experience for city-folk accustomed to lights and smog obscuring the stars above. Occasionally, the park offers ranger-led night sky programs that explore the heavens. Check online or at a visitor center for a current schedule, and join one if you can. If you'd rather view the stars on your own, consider spending a night in the backcountry. Many sites are available for backpackers and motorists (a few require high-clearance and 4WD).

Birdwatching

Big Bend possesses a unique location where bird species converge from three distinct geographical regions: eastern U.S., western U.S., and Mexico. It's also located along a major avian migratory route. This combination yields more than 450 documented species of birds, more than any other national park.

Birds are somewhat like humans, residing where they can find food, water, and safe habitat. That makes camping areas like Cottonwood, Chisos Basin, and Rio Grande Village a few of the best birding destinations. However, not all birds follow the vacation patterns of humans. One of the most prized species, the Colima warbler, visits Big Bend during the summer after wintering in Mexico. Fortunately, they're usually spotted in the higher elevations of the Chisos Mountains, where you'll also find a bit of relief from summer's heat. Peregrine falcons, Montezuma quail, flammulated owls, and Lucifer hummingbirds are a few other highly sought-after species found in the Chisos Mountains and along the Rio Grande. Dugout Wells, Sam Nail Ranch, and Red Rocks Canyon are other popular (and easily accessible) birding destinations.

Visitor Centers

Big Bend has five visitor centers. **Panther Junction** (432.477.2251), located at the intersection of US-385 and TX-118, is open year-round, daily from 8:30am–5pm, with reduced hours on Christmas Day. This is where you can get Backcountry Permits, watch a film, browse exhibits, pay your entrance fee, or shop at the bookstore. Water and restrooms are also available. West of Panther Junction is the park's only gas station along with a small general store. **Chisos Basin** is located near Chisos Mountain Lodge. It's also open year-round and operates from 8:30am–4pm. Hours are reduced on Christmas, and it closes from noon until 1pm for lunch every day. Backcountry Permits, exhibits, restrooms, and water are available. **Persimmon Gap**, located where US-385 enters the park, is open seasonally (November through April) from 10am to 4pm. It houses exhibits, a bookstore, small theater, and restrooms. **Rio Grande Village** and **Castolon** are the easternmost and westernmost visitor centers, respectively. Both locations are only open during the busy season (November–April). Rio Grande Village is open from 9am–4:30pm. Castolon is open from 10am–4pm. Both close for lunch and Christmas Day. They feature a few exhibits, a bookstore, and river use permits.

Ranger Programs & For Kids

Park rangers can help satisfy all your Big Bend curiosities through a series of regularly scheduled interpretive programs. Activities range from walks to talks, campfire programs to stargazing. Whatever you choose, you're sure to come away with a better understanding of Big Bend's natural and cultural history. Check the park website for an up-to-date schedule of activities or stop in at Panther Junction Visitor Center when you arrive.

Big Bend's Junior Ranger Program is for kids of all ages. Children learn about the park's history and geology as they explore its geography. To participate, pick up a Junior Ranger Activity Booklet at one of the visitor centers or download it from the park website. Complete it and return to a visitor center for a certificate and Junior Ranger patch. Kids also tend to love the new Fossil Discovery Exhibit a few miles north of Panther Junction.

Santa Elena Canyon

Flora & Fauna

Big Bend appears to be a lifeless wasteland. In reality, it's one of the most ecologically diverse areas in the country. There are two major flowering periods: spring and late summer. Flower blooms are dependent on seasonal rain; without enough, the spring bloom is postponed for another year. The summer monsoon is far more dependable. More than 1,200 species of plants, including 60 cactus species, inhabit steep mountain sides, dry desert lands, and relatively lush river floodplains. The park is also home to 11 species of amphibians, 56 species of reptiles, 40 species of fish, 75 species of mammals, 450 species of birds, and 3,600 species of insects. That's more birds, bats, and cacti than all other national parks. Mountain lions, black bear, pig-like javelinas, and coyotes are a few of the big mammals spotted each year.

Pets & Accessibility

As a general rule of thumb, pets can only go where your car can go. That includes parking areas, roadways, and drive-in campgrounds. They must be kept on a leash (less than six feet). Pets are prohibited from all hiking trails and public buildings. Kennels are available in Alpine, TX at the Veterinary Clinic (432.837.3888) and Small Animal Clinic (432.837.5416).

All visitor centers are wheelchair accessible. Both Chisos Basin and Rio Grande Village Campgrounds have an accessible campsite. Chisos Mountains Lodge has wheelchair-accessible rooms. Dugout Wells and Persimmon Gap Picnic Areas are fully accessible. Panther Path, Window View Trail, and Rio Grande Village Nature Trail Boardwalk are short, flat, relatively smooth wheelchair-friendly trails. The park's amphitheaters and auditorium, where ranger programs are held, are wheelchair accessible. A complete list of accessible ranger programs is available online or at a visitor center.

Hot Springs

Weather

Hot! That's really the only way to describe weather at Big Bend. In winter, average high temperatures reach into the 80s°F, but evening lows can drop below freezing. Most guests visit between fall and spring when temperatures are comfortable and humidity is low. During summer, temperatures max out above 110°F. What little rain the park receives usually falls between June and October. A high degree of temperature variance is also found here. Temperature in the high Chisos Mountains is typically about 20°F cooler than at Rio Grande Village, and 10°F cooler than at Panther Junction. It's also wetter in the Chisos Mountains. Cool and wet (for desert standards) make the Chisos Mountains The Place to spend the night at Big Bend (especially in summer).

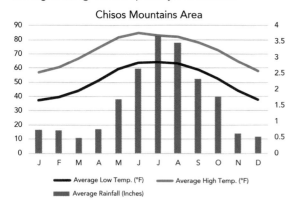

Chisos Mountains Area

— Average Low Temp. (°F)   — Average High Temp. (°F)
■ Average Rainfall (Inches)

Tips & Recommendations

Big Bend is one of the most remote national parks, so be sure to plan ahead and pack all of the necessities (plus slightly more food than you think you'll need). Still, don't stress too much about packing everything. There are a couple of camp stores, where you can pick up this and that, and any essential items.

For a park this size, visitation is light. June through September are extremely quiet (although this can be a great time to explore the Chisos Mountains). Visitation peaks in March when spring breakers are going wild. This may sound great, but you must remember accommodations are fairly limited. If you're planning a trip in March or during any holiday week from fall through spring, you're going to want to make reservations for camping or lodging.

Do your best to spend your nights in the park. Not only is it more convenient, it's a real treat sleeping under the stars in such a remote location. If you are stuck scrambling for alternatives, there are many funky accommodations in Terlingua at the park's western gate, otherwise you'll have to head all the way back to Alpine or Marathon (more than an hour away), where you'll find more typical lodgings.

I tend to fill up with gas every time I pass through Panther Junction. That level of compulsiveness isn't necessary, but you definitely want to keep your tank half full rather than half empty.

Off-roading is tempting but remember this is a remote region. You're in for a terrible vacation if you end up getting stranded on one of the dirt roads (and a big bill). While conditions vary, thru-roads like Old Ore Road and River Road are typically best at the ends where they're used most, and worst in the middle. If you're unsure about driving any of them, start out with something popular and easy (like Old Maverick or Grapevine Hills), and see what you think about that. Primitive roads like River and Old Ore require high-clearance and are considerably more rugged. However, they are worth exploring (and they unlock great camping locations). Before driving any of these roads, it's always a good idea to duck into a visitor center to inquire about road conditions.

Everyone likes the idea of Hot Springs, a medium-sized, naturally-heated hot tub along the shore of the Rio Grande. And it's neat. There's no denying that. It's also a relatively short time commitment (unless you sit and soak for hours), but if you're in a pinch and need to strike something from your itinerary, Hot Springs is a good place to start. I'd rather see Boquillas Canyon and Santa Elena Canyon, or hike through (or around) the Chisos Mountains. Or maybe do a little bit of paddling. Of course, the choice is yours. And, as I mentioned, if you drive to Hot Springs, it's only a half-mile walk to take a look at the pool, requiring no more than an hour of your time.

Backpackers must talk to park rangers about reliable water sources or pack more than enough water for the duration of your trip. This is desert-country and there are few reliable water sources.

You also have to talk to a park ranger before booking a primitive roadside campground on any of the unimproved roads (River, Old Ore, Glenn Springs, etc.). This is to make sure you don't get into a bad situation. Getting towed is never good, but it's particularly bad here.

Easy Hikes: Santa Elena Canyon (1.7 miles), Ward Spring (3.6), Ernst Tinaja (1.4), Hot Springs (1.4)
Moderate Hikes: Window (5.6 miles), Dog Canyon (4) & Devil's Den (5.6), Lost Mine (4.8), Boquillas Canyon (1.4), Grapevine Hills (2.2), Ore Terminal (8)
Strenuous Hikes: South Rim (varies), Mariscal Canyon (6.5), Emory Peak (10.5miles)
Family Activities: Go Off-Roading, Fossil Discovery Exhibit, become Junior Rangers, explore canyons Santa Elena, Boquillas, and/or Red Rock), float the Rio Grande, enjoy the stars at night
Guided Tours: River rafting, Jeep tours
Rainy Day Activities: Don't think about rain, it's a desert! If it does rain, don't let it get in the way of your fun.
History Enthusiasts: Fossil Discovery Exhibit, Mariscal

Fossil Exhibit

Mine, Sam Nail Ranch, Homer Wilson Ranch, Dugout Wells, Luna's Jackal

Sunset/Sunrise Spots: Popular opinion says Windows View at sunset and Hot Springs for sunrise. Yes, those are good spots, but the park is bracketed by imposing mountains to the east and west. If you get a good sunset/sunrise, it's going to be good from just about anywhere you can see the horizon. Personally, I like sunset from camps along Old Ore Road. Sunrise, I'd probably camp off Old Maverick Road.

Beyond the Park...

Dining
DB's Rustic Iron BBQ
23270 FM170, Terlingua
rusticironbbq.com • (432) 210-3457

Starlight Theatre • (432) 371-3400
631 Ivey Rd, Terlingua
thestarlighttheatre.com

Rio Bravo • (432) 371-2101
23302 FM170, Terlingua

Bad Rabbit Café • (432) 371-2244
16000 Terlingua Ranch Rd
terlinguaranch.com

Grocery Stores
There are small convenience stores at Chisos Mountains, Castolon, Cottonwood, Rio Grande Village, and the Panther Junction Gas Station, but it's best to come prepared.

Lajitas General Store
55 Main St, Lajitas • (432) 424-5040

Little Burro Country Store
51491 TX-118, Alpine

The French Company Grocer
206 Avenue D, Marathon

Lodging & Camping
Willow House • (432) 213-2270
23113 FM170, Terlingua
willowhouse.co

Villa Terlingua • (469) 607-9828
100 Guadalupe Loop, Terlingua
villaterlingua.com

The Buzzard's Roost Tipis
333 Goat Track Trail, Terlingua
buzzardsroostterlingua.com

Ten Bits Ranch • (432) 371-3110
6000 N County Rd, Terlingua
tenbitsranch.com

Nuevo Terlingua
23041 FM170, Terlingua
basecampterlingua.com

Terlingua Ranch • (432) 371-3146
16000 Terlingua Ranch Rd
terlinguaranch.com

RoadRunner RV • (432) 466-1036
23315 FM170, Terlingua
roadrunnertravelers.com

Paisano Village RV • (432) 371-2057
53690 TX-118, Terlingua
paisanovillagervparkandinn.com

BJ's RV Park • (432) 371-2259
FM170, Terlingua • bjrvpark.com

Maverick Ranch RV Park
10 Main St, Lajitas • (432) 424-5181
lajitasgolfresort.com

Festivals
Chili Cook-Off • November
abowlofred.com • Terlingua

Attractions
Big Bend Ranch State Park
Adjacent to the national park. Definitely worth some time.
1900 S Saucedo, Presidio
tpwd.texas.gov

Davis Mountains State Park
Excellent high desert hiking
TX-118, Fort Davis
tpwd.texas.gov

Caverns of Sonora
Very beautiful cave
1711 Private Rd 4468, Sonora
cavernsofsonora.com

Devil's River State Natural Area
Paddle spring-fed water
21715 Dolan Creek Rd, Del Rio
tpwd.texas.gov

Seminole Canyon State Park
Hiking, camping, pictographs
US-90, Comstock
tpwd.texas.gov

Big Bend & Lajitas Stables
High quality trail ride operation
TX-118, Terlingua • (800) 887-4331
lajitasstables.com

Lajita Ziplines • (432) 424-5153
lajitasgolfresort.com

These parks (tpwd.texas.gov) aren't close to Big Bend, but they deserve a quick mention.

Kickapoo Caverns State Park
Small but interesting caves
20939 Ranch to Market Rd 674
N, Bracketville

Palo Duro Canyon State Park
Scenic park near Amarillo
11450 State Hwy Park Rd 5

Brazos Bend State Park
Wildlife near Houston
21901 Farm to Market Rd 762

Caddo Lake State Park
245 Park Rd 2, Karnack

Guadalupe Mountains

The road to William's Ranch

Phone: (915) 828-3251
Website: nps.gov/gumo

Established: September 30, 1972
Size: 86,416 Acres
Annual Visitors: 200,000
Peak Season: Oct–Nov, March–April
Hiking Trails: 85 Miles

Activities: Hiking, Backpacking
Stargazing, Horseback Riding

2 Campgrounds: $15/night
Backcountry Camping: Permitted
with free Backcountry Use Permit
Lodging: None

Park Hours: All day, every day
Day-use Areas: McKittrick Canyon,
Williams Ranch (high-clearance
required), and Salt Basin Dunes
Entrance Fee: $10/person

Set on the Texas–New Mexico state line, the Guadalupe Mountains appear to be too remote, rugged, and dry to be hospitable. Certainly, they're too prominent and mysterious to be ignored. Native Americans and Spaniards brought attention to the area with elaborate stories of gold hidden deep in the mountains. The mountains had stories of their own. Mysteries about the region's underwater past were revealed rock by rock, fossil by fossil. Today, guests visit the park and create their own stories while hiking and camping in these hills of hidden gold and buried fossils.

Also hidden in the mountains is proof of more than 10,000 years of human habitation. The earliest of which were hunter–gatherers who followed game and collected edible vegetation. The only remnants of their existence are projectile points, baskets, pottery, and rock art. Spaniards passed through in the 16th century. They didn't establish settlements, but they left their mark by introducing horses to the Mescalero Apache. Horses proved to be an invaluable asset to the Apache as they tried to protect their land.

In 1858, Pinery Station was constructed near Pine Springs for the Butterfield Overland Mail. Apache considered this development and America's westward expansion an invasion. They retaliated by carrying out raids of nearby settlements and mail stagecoaches. After the Civil War, a new transportation route allowed homesteaders and miners to encroach further on Apache land. This new surge of settlers forced Mescalero Apache to take refuge in the Guadalupe Mountains, which served as their last stronghold. Here they hunted elk, mule deer, and bighorn sheep; they harvested agave (mescal), sotol, and beargrass. Eventually, Lt. H.B. Cushing and a troop of Buffalo Soldiers were ordered to stop the raids on settlements and mail coaches. The small brigade marched into the mountains, destroying two Apache camps. By the 1880s, surviving Mescalero Apache were driven onto reservations.

Many new settlers from the East took up ranching. But most found the land to be rugged and inhospitable. Frijole Ranch, built by the Rader Brothers in 1876, was the first permanent home built in the area. For much of the 20th century, Frijole Ranch remained the area's only major building, serving as community center and regional post office. Today, it has been restored as a museum of local ranching history.

The area's history changed when Wallace Pratt came to the Guadalupe Mountains. Pratt, a petroleum geologist for Humble Oil and Refining Company, visited McKittrick Canyon and fell in love with the lush oasis. He purchased nearly 6,000 acres surrounding the only year-round water source and built two homes: Ship-On-The-Desert near the canyon's mouth, and Pratt Cabin at the confluence of north and south McKittrick Canyons. Pratt and his family enjoyed the summer retreat for two decades before deciding to donate it to the federal government. His donation became the heart of Guadalupe Mountains National Park.

Since Pratt's time in McKittrick Canyon other geologists have been busy studying exposed reefs found in the mountains. The reefs help paint a picture of the area's past, when Texas and New Mexico were covered by a shallow, tropical sea. Algae, sponges, and other aquatic organisms formed a giant reef that looped around the present-day Guadalupe, Apache, and Glass Mountains. A visitor walking into McKittrick Canyon today is entering El Capitán Reef from its seaward side.

A disappearing sea. A sanctuary for Apache. A geologist's summer retreat. These are the stories of the Guadalupe Mountains' past. Today's story is about a park. A park for the enjoyment of the people. A park that protects the past and ensures its future. A park for each and every one of us.

On the way to Devil's Hall

When to Go
Guadalupe Mountains is open all year. Two periods are fairly busy. In March and April, college kids on spring break hit the trails and go backpacking. During this time, parking areas and campgrounds fill early. You may find yourself having to park at Pine Springs Visitor Center to access Pine Springs Trailhead. In October, leaf-peepers flock to McKittrick Canyon to see its colorful foliage. Spring and fall are the most pleasant seasons to visit.

Transportation & Airports
Public transportation is not available to or around the park. The closest major airports are Midland International (MAF) in Midland, TX (219 miles away) and El Paso International (ELP) in El Paso, TX (102 miles away). Cavern City Air Terminal (CNM) in Carlsbad, NM (66 miles away) offers passenger service between Albuquerque International Sunport (ABQ) and Carlsbad, NM. Car rental is available at each destination.

Directions
The park is located in West Texas on US-62/180 between Carlsbad, NM (near Carlsbad Caverns National Park) and El Paso, TX. Dog Canyon is located on the park's north side near the Texas–New Mexico border, roughly a 120-mile drive from Pine Springs Visitor Center. NM-137 leads directly to Dog Canyon Entrance, campground, and Ranger Station.

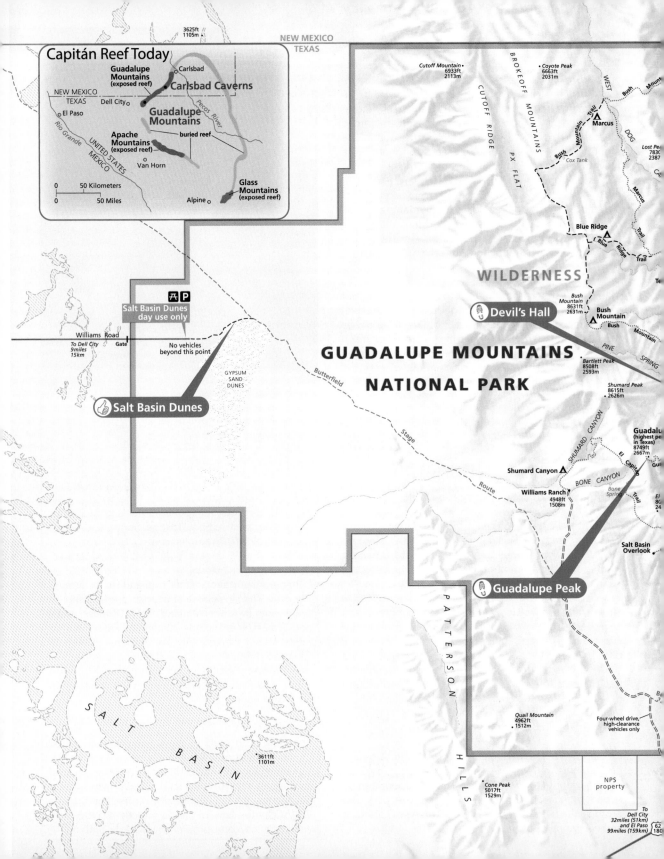

Capitán Reef Today

3625ft / 1105m

NEW MEXICO
TEXAS

Guadalupe
Mountains
(exposed reef)

Carlsbad

Carlsbad Caverns

NEW MEXICO
TEXAS

Dell City

**Guadalupe
Mountains**

El Paso

Apache
Mountains
(exposed reef)

buried reef

Van Horn

Pecos River

Glass
Mountains
(exposed reef)

UNITED STATES
MEXICO

Rio Grande

Alpine

0   50 Kilometers

0   50 Miles

Cutoff Mountain •
6933ft
2113m

BROKEOFF

• Coyote Peak
6663ft
2031m

WEST

Bush

CUTOFF

MOUNTAINS

Mountain

Mountain

Marcus

Trail

Lost Peak
7830
2387

RIDGE

PX   FLAT

Bush

Cox Tank

Marcus

Trail

Blue Ridge

Blue

Ridge

Trail

WILDERNESS

Bush
Mountain
8631ft
2631m

Bush
Mountain

🥾 **Devil's Hall**

GUADALUPE MOUNTAINS

Bartlett Peak
8508ft
2593m

PINE

SPRING

NATIONAL PARK

Shumard Peak
8615ft
• 2626m

🗺 Salt Basin Dunes
day use only

Williams Road

To Dell City
9miles
15km

Gate

No vehicles
beyond this point

GYPSUM
SAND
DUNES

Butterfield

Guadalu
(highest pea
in Texas)
8749ft
2667m

El Capitan

Stage

Shumard Canyon △

SHUMARD CANYON

Gu

👍 **Salt Basin Dunes**

Williams Ranch
4948ft
1508m

BONE   CANYON

Bone
Spring

El
80
24

Route

Salt Basin
Overlook

S A L T

🥾 **Guadalupe Peak**

Quail Mountain
4962ft
• 1512m

Four-wheel drive,
high-clearance
vehicles only

B A S I N

3611ft
1101m

P
A
T
T
E
R
S
O
N

H
I
L
L
S

• Cone Peak
5017ft
1529m

NPS
property

To
Dell City
32miles (51km)
and El Paso
99miles (159km)

62
180

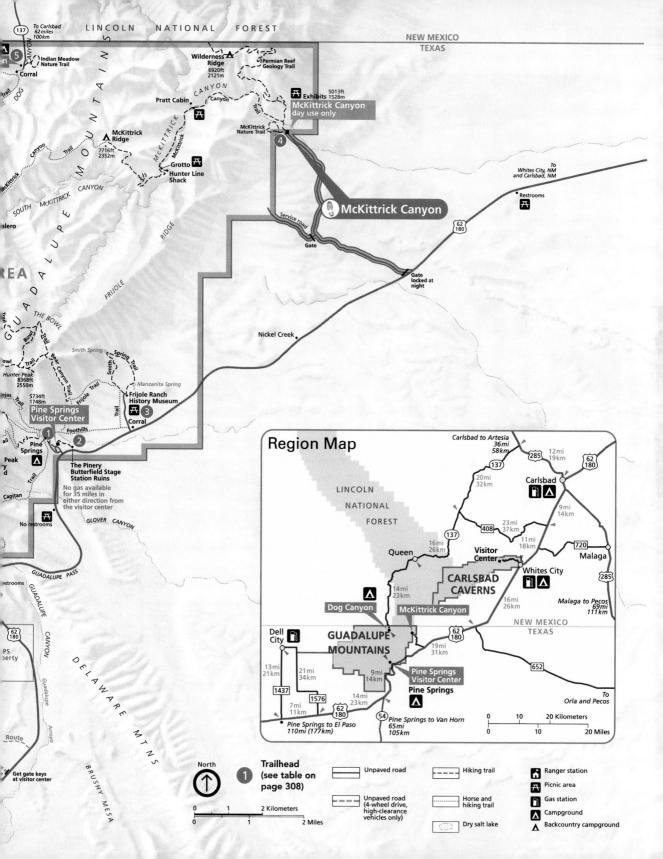

LINCOLN NATIONAL FOREST

NEW MEXICO
TEXAS

To Carlsbad
62 miles
100km
137

Indian Meadow
Nature Trail

5
Corral

Wilderness
Ridge
6920ft
2121m

Permian Reef
Geology Trail

Pratt Cabin

McKittrick
Ridge
7716ft
2352m

Grotto
Hunter Line
Shack

Exhibits 5013ft
1528m

McKittrick Canyon
day use only

McKittrick
Nature Trail

4

McKittrick Canyon

To
Whites City, NM
and Carlsbad, NM

Restrooms

Service road

Gate

62
180

Gate
locked at
night

Nickel Creek

Smith Spring

Manzanita Spring

Frijole Ranch
History Museum

Corral

Pine Springs
Visitor Center

3

1
Foothills

2

Pine
Springs

The Pinery
Butterfield Stage
Station Ruins

No gas available
for 35 miles in
either direction from
the visitor center

No restrooms

GLOVER CANYON

GUADALUPE PASS

Get gate keys
at visitor center

Region Map

Carlsbad to Artesia
36mi
58km

12mi
19km

285

62
180

LINCOLN

NATIONAL

FOREST

20mi
32km

137

Carlsbad

9mi
14km

408

23mi
37km

11mi
18km

720

16mi
26km

137

Visitor
Center

Malaga

Queen

CARLSBAD
CAVERNS

Whites City

285

14mi
23km

16mi
26km

Malaga to Pecos
69mi
111km

Dog Canyon

McKittrick Canyon

NEW MEXICO
TEXAS

Dell
City

GUADALUPE
MOUNTAINS

9mi
14km

62
180

19mi
31km

Pine Springs
Visitor Center

Pine Springs

652

13mi
21km

21mi
34km

1437

1576

7mi
11km

14mi
23km

62
180

54

To
Orla and Pecos

Pine Springs to El Paso
110mi (177km)

Pine Springs to Van Horn
65mi
105km

0   10   20 Kilometers

0   10   20 Miles

North

↑

Trailhead
(see table on
page 308)

1

Unpaved road

Unpaved road
(4-wheel drive,
high-clearance
vehicles only)

Dry salt lake

Hiking trail

Horse and
hiking trail

Ranger station

Picnic area

Gas station

Campground

Backcountry campground

0   1   2 Kilometers

0   1   2 Miles

Dog Canyon

Guadalupe Mtns Hiking Trails (Distances are roundtrip unless noted otherwise)

Name	Location (# on map)	Length	Difficulty Rating & Notes
Frijole/Foothills	1, 3	3.7 miles	E – Loop trail between Pine Springs Campground and Frijole Ranch
Devil's Hall - ♿	1	4.2 miles	M – Follow Pine Springs Canyon to a staircase and Devil's Hall
El Capitán/Salt Basin Overlooks - ♿	1	11.3 miles	M – A flat hike to the base of El Capitán and an overlook Can extend it 9.4 miles to Shumard Canyon and Williams Ranch
Guadalupe Peak - ♿	1	8.4 miles	S – Pass El Capitán and exposed cliffs to Texas's highest peak
The Bowl - ♿	1	9.1 miles	S – Follow Frijole and Bear Canyon Trails, then left on Bowl Trail to a beautiful coniferous forest along high ridges and canyons
Tejas	1, 5	11.7 miles	S – One-way distance from Pine Springs to Dog Canyon
The Pinery	2	0.8 mile	E – Paved path to the ruins of Pinery Station
Manzanita Spring	3	0.4 mile	E – Paved path to a desert watering hole
Smith Spring	3	2.3 miles	M – Potential for wildlife viewing at this shady little oasis
McKittrick Canyon - ♿	4	4.8 miles	M – Follow the park's only year-round stream to Pratt Lodge (4.8 miles), continue on to the Grotto, Hunter Cabin, and McKittrick Ridge
McKittrick Canyon Nature Trail	4	0.9 mile	M – Self-guiding trail with exhibits that help describe the area's geology and ecology
Permian Reef - ♿	4	8.4 miles	S – Geology guides for this trail are available at the visitor center
Indian Meadow Nature Loop	5	0.6 mile	E – Nearly level trail • A free trail guide educates hikers on the natural and cultural history of the meadow
Marcus Overlook	5	4.5 miles	M – Dramatic views down into West Dog Canyon via Bush Mtn Tr
Lost Peak - ♿	5	6.4 miles	S – Follows Tejas Trail from Dog Canyon to Lost Peak
Bush Mountain	5	12.0 miles	S – One-way distance from Dog Canyon to The Bowl/Tejas Trails
Juniper	N/A	2.0 miles	M – A short connector trail between The Bowl and Tejas Trails
Bear Canyon	N/A	1.0 mile	M – A short connector trail between The Bowl and Frijole Trails
Blue Ridge	N/A	1.5 miles	M – A short connector trail between Marcus and Bush Mtn Trails

Difficulty Ratings: E = Easy, M = Moderate, S = Strenuous

Camping

The park has two established campgrounds. **Pine Springs**, located just off US-62/180 near Pine Springs Visitor Center, has 20 tent sites, 19 RV sites (50-ft maximum length), and two group sites. **Dog Canyon** is located on the less visited north side of the park. It has 9 tent sites, 4 RV sites, a stock corral site, and one group site. Both campgrounds have year-round potable water, flush toilets, and sinks. They do not have showers, hookups, or dump stations. Fires are not permitted. Campsites are available on a first-come, first-served basis for $15/night. Group campsites must be reserved up to 60 days in advance by calling (915) 828-3251 between 8am and 4:30pm. They accommodate 10–20 people and cost $3 per person per night.

Hiking & Backpacking

Guadalupe Mountains is a great place to introduce yourself to hiking or backpacking. The park is extremely manageable. Hikers can trek from Pine Springs (south end) to Dog Canyon (north end) in a day. Campgrounds only fill early during peak visitation (spring break/fall foliage). Best of all, it's exceedingly difficult to get lost. Just as the park's southern sentinel, El Capitán, marked the way for homesteaders, Native Americans, and mail coaches, the mountains rising out of the Chihuahuan Desert form an extremely well-defined natural boundary to the east, south, and west. If you've been itching to give backpacking a shot or test your day-hiking limits but are intimidated by the size and wildlife of places like Rocky Mountain or Glacier National Parks, try the Guadalupe Mountains. The main precaution is to carry enough water with you, as there are few reliable sources in the backcountry. You also must be prepared for the elements. Weather is often extreme (hot, cold, windy), and many of the trails are completely exposed. Evenings in the mountains, even in summer, are often chilly.

Guadalupe Peak, the highest point in Texas at just 8,749 feet, proves not everything is bigger in Texas. However, it takes a strenuous 8.4-mile hike, gaining more than 3,000 feet in elevation, to reach its summit. Begin at Pine Springs Campground's RV loop. Make it past the first 1.5 miles and you'll have no trouble completing the hike. This stretch is steep, with switchbacks leading up the mountain. Along the way, sneak a peak of El Capitán from above. Later in the journey, you'll pass Guadalupe Peak Camp and horse-hitching posts before reaching the monument marking its summit.

McKittrick Canyon and Devil's Hall Trails are nice any time of year, but they're particularly popular between

The old Butterfield Coach Trail

late October and early November when big-tooth maple trees lining the canyons turn shades of yellow, orange, and red. **McKittrick Canyon Trail**, located in the park's northeast corner, is often called the best hike in Texas, but be aware it is a day-use area. A gated entrance opens at 8am and closes at 4:30pm in winter and 6pm in summer. The trail is 4.8 miles (roundtrip) to Pratt Cabin or 6.8 miles to the Grotto (well worth the additional 2 miles). **Devil's Hall** is accessed from Pine Springs Campground's RV loop, which is open 24/7. It is highlighted by a natural rock stairway leading to a narrow canyon called Devil's Hall.

Ten backcountry campsites (free permit required) are spread out along 85 miles of hiking trails. The closest campground to Pine Springs is found at Guadalupe Peak, just 3.1 miles from Pine Springs Trailhead and parking area. It offers 5 secluded campsites. Pine Top, located on Bush Mountain Trail near the Bowl, is another easy one-night backpacking trip. It consists of 8 campsites, and is just 6.2 miles from Pine Springs, providing some of the park's best sunset views. Tejas, Mescalero, McKittrick Ridge, Blue Ridge, Marcus, and Wilderness Ridge are other remote campsites in Guadalupe's high country. The only low elevation campground is found on the park's west side at Shumard Canyon, 9.2 miles from Pine Springs Trailhead. There are few reliable water sources in the backcountry, so carry all the water you'll need.

Stargazing

One of the best ways to enjoy the peaceful calm of a night in the Guadalupe Mountains is to look up. On a cloudless night, whether you're lying in your tent or enjoying campfire conversation, look to the sky to see the galaxy's immensity. It's slightly bigger than Texas. Stargazing is best from one of the many backcountry campsites, but the stars twinkle and shine above Pine Springs and Dog Canyon Campgrounds as well.

Salt Basin Dunes

Horseback Riding

More than 50 miles of hiking trails are open to horseback riding. If you want to explore the region on horseback, you'll have to trailer your own stock. Horse corrals are available at Dog Canyon and Frijole Ranch. They can accommodate up to ten animals. Horse corrals can be reserved up to 60 days in advance. They cost $15/night plus $10/person. All trips must start and end at one of these corrals, and stock must return to the corrals each night. All stock trips require a free backcountry use permit (available at Pine Springs Visitor Center or Dog Canyon Ranger Station).

Trails open to stock are denoted on the park map with a dotted line. Easy trails include Foothills Trail, Williams Ranch Road, and Frijole Trail. Experienced riders and animals will want to try Bush Mountain or Tejas Trails, beginning at Dog Canyon.

Birdwatching

Birding is another popular activity at Guadalupe Mountains. The best and most easily accessible locations for birders are Smith Spring Trail (near Frijole Ranch) and McKittrick Canyon Trail. These destinations reward guests with sightings of greater roadrunners, northern mockingbirds, and western scrub jays. McKittrick Canyon protects more than 40 species of nesting birds, including ash-throated flycatchers and Cassin's kingbirds in spring and summer. If you'd like to mix a lot of hiking with your birding, try the 9.1-mile roundtrip hike to the Bowl. The trail leads through a relict forest of ponderosa pine and Douglas fir, where you'll have a chance of seeing mountain chickadees, pygmy, white-breasted nuthatches, dark-eyed juncos, hairy woodpeckers, band-tailed pigeons, and red crossbills. If you make the trek in the fall, watch for Townsend's warblers. To see the birds of the high country without having to hike long trails with steep grades, drive around the park to Dog Canyon (elevation 6,290 ft).

Visitor Centers

Pine Springs Visitor Center is open daily (except Christmas Day) from 8am–4:30pm. **Frijole Ranch** is open as staffing allows, from 8am–4:30pm. McKittrick Canyon, Williams Ranch, and Salt Basin Dunes are **day-use areas**. McKittrick Canyon's gate is open daily from 8am–4:30pm (Nov–March), and 8am–6pm the rest of the year. To access Williams Ranch (high-clearance 4WD required), you must obtain a gate key from Pine Springs Visitor Center. Salt Basin Dunes is open from sunrise until 30 minutes after sunset. Dog Canyon (505.981.2418) is open all year, with a small ranger station (open intermittently).

Ranger Programs & For Kids

Ranger programs are not offered throughout the year. Typically, programs are held in March, throughout summer, and from late October to early November. These are the best times of year to visit, and ranger programs provide the best activity. Programs vary and depend on staffing, so it is a good idea to check online or at Pine Springs Visitor Center for a current schedule of activities when you visit.

The park is a great place for kids' imaginations to run wild. The wealth of fossils has inspired a new Junior Paleontologist Program. If your kids are aspiring fossil hunters, stop in at the visitor center for more information or go online to find an activity booklet. There's also a Junior Ranger Program. You can find the activity booklet online or at Pine Springs Visitor Center. Complete three activities and your child will earn a certificate and badge. Complete 6 to receive a certificate, badge, and patch. You can substitute hiking a trail, attending a ranger program, or visiting the stage ruins in place of a workbook activity.

Flora & Fauna

The most interesting flora and fauna in the Guadalupe Mountains have been dead for hundreds of millions of years. Ancient calcareous sponges, algae, and other sea organisms were growing on a 400-mile-long horseshoe-shaped reef within an ancient sea once covering much of Texas and New Mexico. After the sea evaporated, the reef was buried in eroded sediment deposited by streams and rivers. Entombed for millions of years, the reef returned to the surface when uplift raised it more than 2 miles. Today, scientists consider the exposed reef at Guadalupe Mountains and nearby Apache and Glass Mountains as one of the finest examples of ancient marine fossil reef on earth. Still, not all creatures are fossils. Black bear, elk, mountain lions, and over 1,000 species of plants live here.

Pets & Accessibility

Pets are allowed in the park but must be kept on a leash (less than six feet). They are allowed in developed areas (campgrounds, roadways, and parking lots) but are not allowed inside buildings or on hiking trails (except for Pinery Trail).

Pine Springs Visitor Center, Frijole Ranch Museum, and McKittrick Canyon Contact Station are all accessible to individuals in wheelchairs. Pinery Trail and Manzanita Spring Trail are paved, mostly flat, and accessible with assistance.

Weather

Weather can change as abruptly as the Guadalupe range rises out of the Chihuahuan Desert. Summers are hot, but more comfortable than you'd imagine thanks to occasional rain (although very limited, it does cool things down), high elevation, and strong winds. Evenings in the mountains are cool any time of year. Temperatures are typically pleasant from fall through spring, but snowstorms and freezing rain may occur in winter. The most common annoyance from winter-to-spring is gusting wind, particularly along the south and west sides of the mountain range.

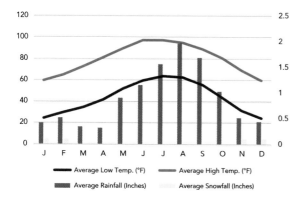

Tips & Recommendations

Be aware that a road does not cross the park. If you want to get from Pine Springs to Dog Canyon you'll have to backpack or drive the long way (through Carlsbad, 100+ miles, 2+ hours). With that said, Dog Canyon is frequented by horseback riders and backpackers, and the drive is nice, but driving here just to take a look isn't the best use of your time. You're better off heading to White Sands or Carlsbad Caverns.

And most points of interest are unique destinations, only reached by their own road. Salt Basin Dunes (gated access) is on the west side of the park (note that it's often incredibly windy south and west of the mountains, so pay attention to the forecast ... sand dunes are considerably less fun during gale-force winds). William's Ranch (gated access, requires high-clearance and key from visitor center), Pine Springs, Frijole Ranch, and McKittrick Canyon (gated) can be reached by roads from Highway 62. Dog Canyon is accessed from the north. The park is relatively small, but it takes time to visit each area, so plan a couple days if you'd like to check them all out.

Moderate Hikes: Devil's Hall (4.2 miles), McKittrick Canyon (4.8), El Capitan (11.3)
Strenuous Hikes: Guadalupe Peak (8.4 miles), Lost Peak (6.4), The Bowl (9.1), Permian Reef (8.4)
Family Activities: Become Junior Rangers or Junior Paleontologists
Rainy Day Activities: Go to Carlsbad Caverns
History Enthusiasts: Pratt Cabin, Frijole Ranch, William's Ranch, The Pinery Butterfield Stage Station Ruins
Sunrise/Sunset Spots: It's best to look for places to catch the first/last rays of light hitting the Guadalupe Mountains. Salt Basin Dunes is a good place at sunset, and there are several places to pullout along Highway 62 with ample parking and good Guadalupe views for sunrise or sunset.

Beyond the Park...

Dining
Guadalupe Mountain Brewing Co
3324 US-62, Carlsbad
gmbrewingco.com • (575) 887-8747

Spanish Angels Café
106 Main St, Dell City
(915) 964-2208

Cornudas Café
180 US-62 • (915) 964-2508

Grocery Stores
Walmart • (915) 342-9866
3590 N Zaragoza Rd, El Paso

Lodging & Camping
Taylor Motel • (432) 283-1968
900 W Broadway St, Van Horn

El Paso, Van Horn, or Carlsbad have many commercial options. I prefer Carlsbad best. See page 321 for a few choices.

Festivals
Lobster Festival • April
lobstermusicfest.com• El Paso

Ice Cream Fest • El Paso
icecreamfestep.com

Attractions
Hueco Tanks State Park
Strange rocks in the Texan desert just outside of El Paso
6900 Hueco Tanks Rd No. 1
tpwd.texas.gov

Franklin Mountains State Park
Aztec Cave, Franklin Mountain
Tom Mays Park Access Rd, El Paso
tpwd.texas.gov • (915) 566-6441

War Eagles Air Museum
8012 Airport Rd, Santa Teresa
war-eagles-air-museum.com

Ysleta Mission • (915) 859-9848
131 S Zaragoza Rd, El Paso

Tom Lea Upper Park
900 Rim Rd, El Paso • (915) 212-0092

Murchison Rogers Park
1600 Scenic Dr, El Paso

Wyler Aerial Tramway
1700 McKinley, El Paso
tpwd.texas.gov • (915) 566-6622

El Paso Museum of Art
epma.org • (915) 212-0300

Carlsbad Caverns

Phone: (575) 785-2232
Website: nps.gov/cave

Established: May 14, 1930
Size: 46,766 Acres
Annual Visitors: 500,000
Peak Season: March–November
Hiking Trails: 50+ Miles
Self-Guided Cave Trails: 2.5 Miles

Activities: Cave Tours, Caving, Hiking, Backpacking, Stargazing

Campgrounds & Lodging: None
Backcountry Camping: Permitted with a free Backcountry Use Permit

Park Hours: All day, every day (Except Thanksgiving, Christmas, and New Year's)
Entrance Fee: $15/person
Free for Children 15 and under
Audio Guide Fee: $5
Cave Tours: $7–$20 (1.5–5.5 hours)

Beneath the Guadalupe Mountains lies a magnificent world, a maze of passages and chambers decorated with indescribable rock formations. Soda straws and stalactites pierce the ceiling. Stalagmites rise from the ground. Draperies adorn the sloped walls where water dripped. Clusters of popcorn-like protrusions cover the chambers. Fragile helictites defy gravity as they twist and turn in every direction. At Carlsbad Caverns, Mother Nature, like an eccentric collector, has filled rooms upon rooms with thousands of formations. Every last bit of cave real estate is plastered, ceiling-to-floor, with what is considered the world's most wondrous collection of cave formations.

An ancient reef, visible in areas of Guadalupe Mountains National Park, made cave formation possible. Some 250 million years ago, the area was covered by a shallow, tropical sea. Changes in climate caused it to evaporate and calcite to precipitate from the water. Uplift raised the mountains and reef nearly two miles, creating many cracks and faults. Newly formed grade and openings allowed rainwater to flow through the limestone substrate. As rainwater seeped through the rock, pressurized hydrogen sulfide-rich water migrated upward from huge reservoirs of oil and gas. Mixing, they formed a sulfuric acid capable of dissolving limestone at a rapid rate. As limestone dissolved from the bottom up, cracks and faults widened, forming the large chambers and passages we walk through today. Creation began nearly one million years ago and continues today, one drop of water at a time. As rainwater

Hall of the White Giant Tour

Storytelling at Colonel Boles Formation

seeps through the layers of earth above the cave, it absorbs carbon dioxide from the air and soil forming a weak acid. This weak acid is able to dissolve a small amount of limestone and absorb it as calcite. Once the water droplet emerges in the cave, carbon dioxide is released into the air and dissolved calcite precipitates from water. Each droplet deposits its miniscule mineral load. Over hundreds of thousands of years, enough deposits are made to create the otherworldly features you see while touring Carlsbad Caverns.

Carlsbad is one of the sights you must see to believe. Indeed, the folks in Washington, D.C. didn't believe reports of the elaborate caves until 1923 when the Department of the Interior sent Robert Holley and a photographer to pay the cave a visit. Holley described it as work of the Divine Creator, invoking "deep conflicting emotions of fear and awe." One year later, President Calvin Coolidge used the power of the Antiquities Act to establish Carlsbad Cave National Monument. In 1928, additional land was added to the monument, and two years later Congress established Carlsbad Caverns National Park, protecting one of America's most unique natural treasures for future generations.

When to Go
Carlsbad Caverns is open every day of the year except Thanksgiving, Christmas, and New Year's Day. Between Memorial Day weekend and Labor Day weekend the visitor center is open from 8am–7pm, and the last cavern entry is at 3:30pm via the natural entrance, and 5pm via elevator. For the rest of the year, the visitor center is open from 8am–5pm, the last entry at the natural entrance is 2pm, and the last elevator entry is at 3:30pm.

Summer holidays tend to be the busiest periods. If you are interested in a specific tour, be sure to make reservations. Kings Palace and Left Hand Tunnel are the only tours offered daily.

Transportation & Airports
Public transportation does not serve the park. Greyhound (800.231.2222, greyhound.com) has a station in Carlsbad (24 miles away). Cavern City Air Terminal (CNM) in Carlsbad (23 miles away) offers passenger service to and from Albuquerque International Sunport (ABQ). El Paso International (ELP), in El Paso, TX, is a nice alternative (144 miles away). Car rental is available at each destination.

Directions
Carlsbad Caverns has one entrance road, NM-7, which runs west from US-62/180 at Whites City. It is 16 miles southwest of Carlsbad, NM and 151 miles northeast of El Paso, TX.

If you're looking to explore Slaughter Canyon Cave (tour required) or to hike Yucca or Slaughter Canyon Trails, take US-62/180 south from Carlsbad/Whites City. Head west on County Road 418. From here, follow signs to the parking area and trailhead.

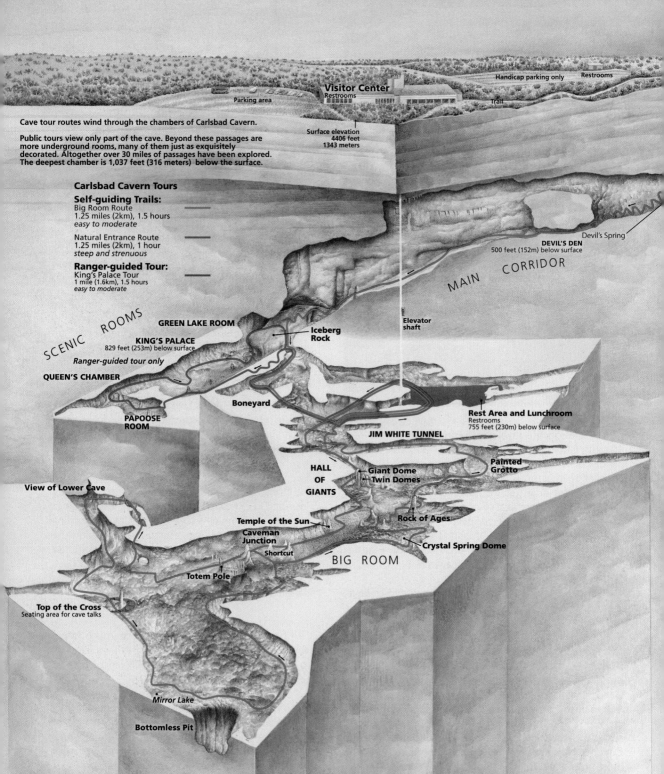

Cave tour routes wind through the chambers of Carlsbad Cavern.

Public tours view only part of the cave. Beyond these passages are more underground rooms, many of them just as exquisitely decorated. Altogether over 30 miles of passages have been explored. The deepest chamber is 1,037 feet (316 meters) below the surface.

Carlsbad Cavern Tours

Self-guiding Trails:
Big Room Route
1.25 miles (2km), 1.5 hours
easy to moderate

Natural Entrance Route
1.25 miles (2km), 1 hour
steep and strenuous

Ranger-guided Tour:
King's Palace Tour
1 mile (1.6km), 1.5 hours
easy to moderate

Visitor Center
Restrooms

Parking area

Handicap parking only   Restrooms

Trail

Surface elevation
4406 feet
1343 meters

Devil's Spring

DEVIL'S DEN
500 feet (152m) below surface

MAIN   CORRIDOR

Elevator
shaft

GREEN LAKE ROOM

Iceberg
Rock

SCENIC   ROOMS

KING'S PALACE
829 feet (253m) below surface

Ranger-guided tour only

QUEEN'S CHAMBER

Boneyard

Rest Area and Lunchroom
Restrooms
755 feet (230m) below surface

**PAPOOSE
ROOM**

JIM WHITE TUNNEL

**Painted
Grotto**

**HALL
OF
GIANTS**

**Giant Dome
Twin Domes**

View of Lower Cave

Rock of Ages

Temple of the Sun

**Caveman
Junction**

Crystal Spring Dome

Shortcut

BIG ROOM

Totem Pole

Top of the Cross
Seating area for cave talks

Mirror Lake

Bottomless Pit

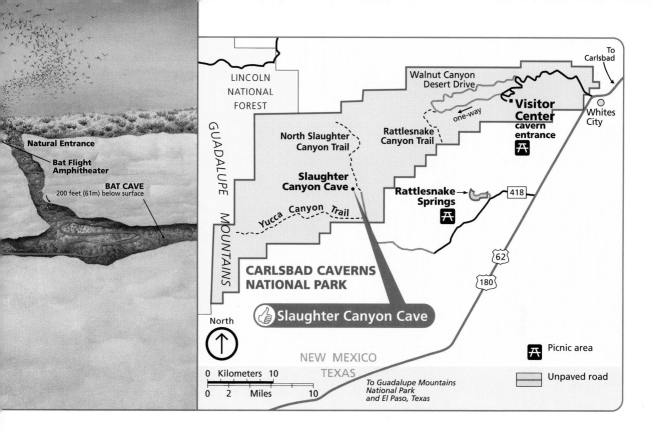

Natural Entrance

Bat Flight
Amphitheater

BAT CAVE
200 feet (61m) below surface

LINCOLN
NATIONAL
FOREST

GUADALUPE MOUNTAINS

Walnut Canyon
Desert Drive

To
Carlsbad

one-way

**Visitor
Center**
cavern
entrance

Whites
City

North Slaughter
Canyon Trail

Rattlesnake
Canyon Trail

**Slaughter
Canyon Cave**

**Rattlesnake
Springs**

418

Yucca Canyon Trail

**CARLSBAD CAVERNS
NATIONAL PARK**

👍 **Slaughter Canyon Cave**

North

62

180

NEW MEXICO
TEXAS

0 Kilometers 10

0   2   Miles   10

To Guadalupe Mountains
National Park
and El Paso, Texas

🏕 Picnic area

▬ Unpaved road

Carlsbad Caverns

Ancient artifacts indicate the area around Carlsbad Caverns has been inhabited for nearly 10,000 years, but very little is known about these early people. Native Americans entered Carlsbad more than 1,000 years ago, but it's unlikely they used the cave for anything more than shelter. They left behind drawings, including an ancient petroglyph near the natural entrance. Exploration of the cave didn't occur until the 1800s, when settlers were drawn to a mysterious cloud (of bats) rising out of the desert each summer night.

It's disputable whether Jim White was first to rediscover the cave, but, after entering in 1898 at the age of 16, he would become its primary explorer. During his expeditions he named many of the rooms: Big Room (the largest cave chamber in the United States), New Mexico Room, King's Palace, Queen's Chamber, Papoose Room, and Green Lake Room. He also named features like Totem Pole, Witch's Finger, Giant Dome, Bottomless Pit, Fairyland, Iceberg Rock, Temple of the Sun, and Rock of the Ages. White offered to take locals on tours, but few accepted. One day he crossed paths with a man who was more interested in a different kind of deposit: bat guano. Bat's natural waste is a high-quality fertilizer, and, as you can imagine, the cave's millions of bats produced an awful lot. Drop by drop, guano piles up kind of like stalagmites, just messier and faster. Jim

White started mining guano, bringing each payload out the natural entrance in a bucket via a 170-foot ascent. They even lifted burros in and out to aid production. Guano was packed in gunnysacks and shipped to California citrus groves. Unfortunately for them, this industry wasn't very profitable. Companies formed and folded, but Jim White never left.

In 1915, the first photographs of the cave were taken by Ray V. Davis. After seeing pictures of its brilliant formations, individuals who had turned down Jim White's tour offerings were now clamoring to enter. The first tourists made the 170-foot descent via the old "guano bucket." In 1924, members of National Geographic Society joined White on an extensive exploration of the caverns, bringing with them even more publicity. The following year a staircase was built, setting the stage for the current era of tourism. Today, you can enter the cave by descending stairs into the natural entrance or an elevator will drop you off in the Big Room, where you are free to explore the strategically-lit passages.

Other Caves

Caves are the last terrestrial frontier. They're full of mystery, and it's nearly impossible to know if all a given cave's passages have been mapped. Bones of Ice Age mammals, such as jaguars, camels, and giant sloths have been found near or in these caves. There

Slaughter Canyon Cave's Christmas Tree

Carlsbad Caverns Cave Tours

Tour (Group Size, Age Limit, Offered)	Fee (Adult/Youth)	Length	Notes
King's Palace (Capacity: 55, Age Limit: 4, daily, all year) - 👍	$8/4	1.5 hours	Classic 1-mile tour through several rooms named by Jim White
Left Hand Tunnel (15, 6, daily, all year) - 👍	$7/3.50	2 hours	Easiest adventure tour • Uneven/slippery surface, lit by NPS-provided lanterns
Lower Cave (12, 12, seasonal) - 👍	$20/10	3 hours	Must descend down a 10-ft flowstone using knotted rope • Wear hiking boots
Slaughter Canyon Cave (25, 8, seasonal) - 👍	$15/7.50	5.5 hours	Strenuous tour through undeveloped cave • Wear hiking boots and long pants
Hall of the White Giant (8, 12, seasonal) - 👍	$20/10	4 hours	Crawling through narrow openings • You will get dirty • Wear hiking boots

Youth is 4–15 years of age. Senior Access Pass holders pay youth rates. All tours can be reserved in advance at (877) 446-6777 or recreation.gov. Reservations are highly recommended for all tours. Pick up tickets at the visitor center.

are more than 300 caves in the Guadalupe Mountains, about 110 within Carlsbad's boundaries.

Lechuguilla Cave (whose location has not been disclosed by the National Park Service) has been the caving community's focus since its discovery in 1986. It has already surpassed Carlsbad in depth, size, and variety of cave formations, many of which have never been seen anywhere else in the world. Lechuguilla is more than 150 miles long, the 8th longest cave known to man and the deepest in the country. Carlsbad Caverns' big open rooms feel gigantic, but when all its known passageways are measured, they total just over 30 miles in length, more than 100 fewer than Lechuguilla. It has also replaced Carlsbad Caverns as the world's most beautiful cave. You'll hear all sorts of things about Lechuguilla. It's difficult to sift out the truth. But it's undeniably special. And for that reason, it is restricted to exploratory and scientific groups. However, you can explore Lechuguilla from your living room by watching the fourth episode ("Caves") of the hit BBC documentary series *Planet Earth*.

Park rangers lead guests through **Slaughter Canyon Cave**. Additionally, there are more vertical and horizontal caves open to experienced cavers with proper skills and equipment. These caves can only be accessed with a permit. To schedule a trip, interested parties must download and complete an application (available at the park website). Reservations are made on a first-come, first-served basis. All caves open to private parties are of natural significance and should not be treated carelessly. Defacing or causing irreparable damage to any cave will result in its closure. A list of open backcountry caves can be found online.

Cave Tours

Carlsbad displays some of the world's most elaborate cave formations. A little more than 3 miles of paved and lit trails weave through rooms, past fragile features. After paying the entrance fee, you are free to explore two self-guided trails: The Natural Entrance Tour and The Big Room Tour. Slightly outdated audio guides are available for $5. **The Natural Entrance Tour** begins where you would expect, the Natural Entrance. It's 1.25 miles and 750 feet down to the Big Room. Along the way you'll pass Bat Cave, Witch's Finger, Whale's Mouth, and many other features. Once you've reached the Big Room, you can take the elevator back to the surface or continue on the **Big Room Tour** (also accessible via the elevator from the visitor center), where you'll find features named Lion's Tail, Hall of Giants, Bottomless Pit, and Rock of Ages. The 1.25-mile

The Big Room

tour is paved and mostly level. Sturdy shoes are recommended for the Natural Entrance Tour, and you should be in decent physical shape without any respiratory problems. Ranger-led Cave Tours are highly recommended. **Hall of the White Giant** is the "Wild Caving" option, where adventurous guests squeeze through tight spaces and do a bit of crawling. **King's Palace Tour** is a popular, easy walk past ornate formations like helictites, draperies, columns, and soda straws. Rangers also give guests a taste of pure darkness during a "blackout." For a less developed cave experience sign up for **Slaughter Canyon Cave Tour**, where you'll see eerie formations like the Klansman. Rangers are no longer allowed to use that name, but I stand with a wise man who said, "fear of a name increases fear of the thing itself." That wise man was none other than Albus Dumbledore. I bet he would've loved these caves! As the name suggests, Slaughter Canyon Cave is its own cave. All tour participants will have to drive to the cave location and complete a short but moderately strenuous hike to reach the cave entrance.

Dress in layers because the cave's temperature remains relatively constant throughout the year. It gets hotter the deeper you go, but temperatures are always cool, ranging between the 50s and 60s°F.

Bat Flight Program

Tourists aren't the only mammals flocking to Carlsbad Caverns in summer. Roughly from mid-April through October, the Bat Cave is home to hundreds of thousands of Mexican free-tailed bats. They leave the safety of the cave at dusk to gorge on insects, returning just before dawn. Free evening Bat Flight and morning Dawn of the Bats Programs are offered (weather and bats permitting) when they are in residence. Guests fill the amphitheater near the Natural Entrance while a ranger discusses these winged friends. In the evening,

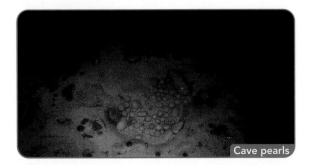

Cave pearls

just as the talk is winding down, a swarm of bats begins their mass exodus to fly about the Chihuahuan Desert in search of food. The exit flight can last anywhere from 20 minutes to 2 hours. Programs are first offered Memorial Day weekend. Evening programs typically begin at 7pm. Morning programs start around 5 am. Reservations are not required. For the exact time, check at the visitor center or call (575) 785-3012. Cameras (including cell phone cameras) and camcorders may not be used during the Bat Flight Program.

You're going to want a little bat background information before meeting Carlsbad's bats face-to-face. First, don't be afraid. These bats are not dangerous. In fact, they're amazing little creatures, being the only mammal capable of flight. They also help control the insect population. Carlsbad's Mexican free-tailed bats eat about three tons of insects each night. A single bat can eat as much as half its body weight in a single meal. One of their favorite appetizers is one of our least favorite pests: the mosquito. It has been estimated that Carlsbad's Mexican free-tailed bat population once counted in the millions, not hundreds of thousands like today. No one knows exactly what caused this dramatic decline, but use of pesticides like DDT and loss of habitat for their prey are likely causes.

Today's Carlsbad bats still live the same interesting bat-life. Days are spent hanging from the ceiling. About 250 and 300 bats huddle together in one square-foot of ceiling space. After leaving the cave, nights are spent searching for food. Their reentry at dawn is nearly as impressive as the exit. Bats at Carlsbad are considered a maternity colony because females seek the cave's safe haven to give birth. In June, females typically bear just one pup. It is born hairless and clings to the mother or ceiling after birth. The pup remains on the ceiling for 4–5 weeks before its first flight. After summer, the pups are mature enough to retreat to warmer climates in Mexico or Central America for winter with the rest of Carlsbad's bat population.

Driving
You can't drive through the cave, but most vehicles can observe the Chihuahuan Desert by driving the 9.5-mile Walnut Canyon Desert Drive (also called Desert Loop Road). This narrow one-way gravel loop is not recommended for trailers or RVs, but your typical 2WD vehicle should be able to navigate this seldom-traveled road. It also provides access to a few hiking trails.

Hiking & Backpacking
The world above Carlsbad Caverns often goes unnoticed by visitors. There are more than 50 miles of hiking trails, providing the perfect place to escape the cave-exploring crowds.

Chihuahuan Desert Nature Trail is located at the base of the hill in front of the visitor center's main entrance. It's a paved 0.5-mile loop around historic guano-mining ruins. The trail closes at dawn and dusk when Mexican free-tailed bats are occupying the cave.

Adjacent to the park entrance is **Old Guano Road**. It's suitable for hiking. This 3.7-mile (one-way) road follows the original path used by miners and burros to haul bat guano in the early 1900s. It ends at Whites City Campground, just beyond the park boundary. It closes near the cavern entrance during Bat Flight programs.

The rest of the trails fan out into the Chihuahuan Desert, where water is unavailable and shade is uncommon. Trails are marked by sporadic rock cairns. Bring plenty of water.

Juniper Ridge Trail is located on Walnut Canyon Desert Drive (also known as Desert Loop Road/DLR), about one mile past interpretive marker #15. It's a 3.5-mile (one-way) ridgeline hike ending at a canyon overlook.

Rattlesnake Canyon Trail begins on DLR, two miles from the visitor center at interpretive marker #9. This 3-mile (one-way) path descends into a deep canyon, past ruins of a 1930's homesteader's cabin. You can also make a 6-mile loop following Upper Rattlesnake Canyon to Guadalupe Ridge Road (GRR). The loop returns to DLR and Rattlesnake Canyon Trailhead by following GRR to the east. The 12-mile GRR can also be hiked in its entirety. You are allowed to leave your vehicle at the gate where GRR intersects DLR.

There's a trailhead at Slaughter Canyon Parking Area. **Slaughter Canyon Trail** continues 5.3 miles (one-way) until it intersects with Guadalupe Ridge Road. A short spur trail heads up above the canyon floor to Slaughter

Canyon Cave. (The cave is locked off and only accessible on ranger-led tours.) There are several branches within Slaughter Canyon, so know where you're going and come prepared with plenty of water if you plan on hiking extensively.

Yucca Canyon Trail branches off from the road to Slaughter Canyon at the park boundary. Here you'll find a dirt road heading west, which can only be accessed by high-clearance 4WD vehicles. The 7.7-mile (one-way) trail climbs up a canyon to a ridgeline. **Backpackers** may camp west of Rattlesnake Canyon Trailhead off DLR and south of Guadalupe Ridge Trail to the park boundary. A free Backcountry Use Permit is required (available at the visitor center).

Stargazing
Carlsbad hosts astronomy events. Like most national parks, it's far removed from city lights, providing an ideal location to gaze up at the stars. During these events, rangers guide you across the galaxy. Telescopes are available for use (weather permitting), and it's free. Arrive early, so your car's headlights don't drown out the stars. Bring a red-light flashlight or headlamp. Check the park website's calendar for details.

Visitor Center
Between Memorial Day weekend and Labor Day weekend the visitor center is open from 8am–7pm, and the last cavern entry is at 3:30pm via the natural entrance, and 5pm via elevator. For the rest of the year, the visitor center is open from 8am–5pm, the last entry at the natural entrance is 2pm, and the last elevator entry is at 3:30pm. The visitor center houses a ticket office, numerous interactive exhibits, a park film, gift shop, bookstore, and restaurant. There is a small snack bar (and restrooms) inside the cave near the elevator.

Ranger Programs & For Kids
Ranger programs consist of Cave Tours and Bat Flight Programs, and they are the primary reasons to visit Carlsbad Caverns. Do not visit the park without joining a cave tour and Bat Flight Program (if available). Reservations are not required for Bat Flight Programs. They're a good idea for cave tours.

If your children like caves, this is the place to be! If they don't, please don't force them to go on a tour. A less adventurous way to enjoy the park with your child is to take part in the Junior Ranger Program. Free activity booklets are available online or at the visitor center. Complete an age-appropriate number of activities to become an official Carlsbad Caverns Junior Ranger.

You gotta crawl on Hall of the White Giant Tour

Flora & Fauna
The park's most notable inhabitant is the Mexican (or Brazilian) free-tailed bat, but there are other living things in the desert. Reports list 67 species of mammals (17 bats), 357 species of birds, 55 species of reptiles and amphibians, 5 species of fish, at least 600 species of insects, and more than 900 species of vascular plants. Black bear, mountain lion, elk, pronghorn, Barbary sheep, and javelina are a few of the larger mammals. Barbary sheep are a non-native species, hailing from the Atlas Mountains of Northern Africa. Bighorn sheep were extirpated. Barbary sheep were introduced. As is often the case, now there's a push to remove Barbary sheep and reintroduce bighorn sheep. Humans can't seem to make up their minds about what kind of sheep they want in these mountains.

Sharing a mountain range with Guadalupe Mountains National Park, a particularly good birding destination, you'll find many similar species here. But the best birding locations are also some of the most difficult sites to reach. The southwest corner of the park, several miles into Yucca Canyon Trail, hosts a few stands of coniferous forest; this is a great place for birding, but it's only accessible to backpackers with 4WD vehicles.

Pets & Accessibility
Pets are permitted, but if you want to tour the cave, hike a trail, or attend a Bat Flight Program, it's best to leave them at home. They are not permitted in caves, on hiking trails, or at Bat Flight Programs. Pets are not to be left unattended in vehicles (citations are issued on days when ambient air temperatures are 70°F or higher). If you still choose to bring your pet, it can be boarded at the park's kennel for $10/day.

The visitor center, bookstore, theater, gift shop, restaurant, and amphitheater (site of Bat Flight Programs) are

Barbary sheep

accessible to wheelchair users. The cave's Big Room is accessible with assistance. Chihuahuan Desert Nature Trail, located near the Visitor Center, is accessible.

Weather

Temperature inside Carlsbad Caverns' Big Room is a cool 56°F all year long. It's chilly and damp in the cave, with humidity levels usually close to 100%. As the cave's passages go deeper, average temperature increases due to heat from the earth. Climate on the surface is semi-arid, typical to the Chihuahuan Desert. The park receives an average of 15 inches of precipitation each year. Summers are hot. Winters are mild, but snowstorms can occur. No matter when you visit, you'll want to dress in layers to account for differences in temperature in and out of the cave.

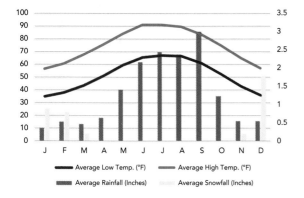

— Average Low Temp. (°F)   — Average High Temp. (°F)
■ Average Rainfall (Inches)   ■ Average Snowfall (Inches)

Tips & Recommendations

First, everyone in the area likes to say, "if you're here, you're here for the cave." It's true there isn't much nearby, but Carlsbad (the city) is alright, a whole lot of oil is being extracted nearby, and Guadalupe Mountains and White Sands National Parks are an easy drive away, so there are other reasons to be in the area. (And for

some reason I keep coming to the area to have punctured tires repaired. If you need to know where to fix a flat, send me a message, I can help.)

While there's no place to stay inside the park, you'll find a hotel and RV Park just outside the park's main entrance in White's City. It's the most convenient location to spend the night. You can also camp permit-free on Bureau of Land Management (BLM) land surrounding the park.

Even though you should book tours in advance, Carlsbad Caverns is a pretty easy trip to plan. There are five guided tours and 2.5 miles of self-guided trail (exploring Carlsbad's Big Room and Natural Entrance). Here's the tour breakdown: King's Palace is an easy walk (with one steep hill), providing a great introduction to Carlsbad. Left Hand Tunnel is fun, with the added novelty of it being lit by lanterns. Lower Cave is trending toward strenuous, where you'll have to use ropes and stairs, but I wouldn't call it extreme. Hall of the White Giant is the most strenuous tour and it'll have you crawling, high-stemming, and squeezing through narrow passages (definitely not for anyone with claustrophobia or who can't lift their own body weight). The above tours provide a little something for every type of cave enthusiast. Finally, Slaughter Canyon Cave is not located at the park's visitor center. You'll have to drive to the trailhead (in your personal car) outside the main park entrance. The hike to the cave is more strenuous than the tour itself and shouldn't be a problem for most active individuals. Each tour has its own unique appeal, but my favorites are Slaughter Canyon Cave and Hall of the White Giant.

Closed-toe shoes with good traction are recommended for exploring the Natural Entrance and Big Room trails. Some areas are naturally wet and slippery.

You will not be allowed to participate in the Lower Cave, Hall of the White Giant, or Slaughter Canyon Cave Tours if you are wearing improper footwear (flip flops, sandals, tennis shoes, etc.). You must wear hiking boots/shoes with aggressive tread.

To help slow the spread of White-nose Syndrome, you will have to wipe down your shoes and/or camera equipment if they've been in any cave in the last ten years. You also need to wear freshly washed clothes if you're going to tour Slaughter Canyon Cave.

If you're going on the Hall of the White Giant Tour, it's a good idea to keep your phone in a running belt or

The 'Natural' Entrance

fannypack. You'll be crawling on your hands and knees, and you don't want to crunch it against rocks. Or else leave it behind.

Baby strollers are not permitted in the cavern.

Canes and walking sticks are permitted on the Big Room, Natural Entrance, and King's Palace trails (if medically necessary).

Flash photography is permitted in the cave. Be mindful of your surroundings when using a flash.

It isn't necessary, but it's a good idea to bring a flashlight or headlamp with you when exploring the cave. Some cool features are obscured by darkness.

Plain water is the only food or drink permitted in the cave. And then there is a snack bar in the cave near the elevator.

This probably doesn't need to be mentioned, but, catch one of the bat flight programs if you can.

Don't leave without exploring the above ground park. Walnut Canyon Drive is a good place to spot wildlife like the non-native Barbary sheep, and it leads to a few hiking trailheads. The environment is remarkably similar to what you'll find at the Dog Canyon section of Guadalupe Mountains National Park, featuring dry washes and desert life. Still, Rattlesnake Canyon and Slaughter Canyon are two trails that you can hike out-and-back and have an enjoyable time.

Beyond the Park...

Dining
Blue House Bakery & Café
609 N Canyon St, Carlsbad
(575) 628-0555

Roque Burrito's • (575) 725-5933
1401 W Mermod St, Carlsbad

Thelma's Wants & Thangs
1618 S Canal St, Carlsbad
(575) 499-7191

Queen Café • (575) 981-2449
Off the beaten path, near Sitting Bull Falls (they also have a campground)
3670 Queens Hwy, Carlsbad

Grocery Stores
Albertsons • (575) 885-2161
808 N Canal St, Carlsbad

Walmart • (575) 885-0727
2401 S Canal St, Carlsbad

Lodging & Camping
White's City Cavern Inn
6 Carlsbad Caverns Hwy
whitescitynm.com • (575) 361-2687

Karbani Inn • (575) 200-0284
5204 US-62, Carlsbad
karbaniinn.com

Trinity Hotel • (575) 234-9891
201 S Canal St, Carlsbad
trinityhotel.com

Fiddler's Inn • (575) 725-8665
705 N Canyon St, Carlsbad
fiddlersinnbb.com

RV Park • (575) 361-3665
17 Carlsbad Caverns Hwy
whitescitynm.com

Chosa Campground
Free dispersed camping, BLM
Dillahunty Rd, Carlsbad

Hidalgo RV Park • (806) 319-2987
3402 Hidalgo Rd, Carlsbad
hidalgo-rv-park.business.site

Carlsbad RV Park • (575) 885-6333
4301 US-62 • carlsbadrvpark.com

Carlsbad KOA • (575) 457-2000
2 Manthei Rd • koa.com

Bud's Place RV • (575) 200-1865
900 Standpipe Rd, Carlsbad

Festivals
CavernFest • June
cavernfest.com

Attractions
Bottomless Lakes State Park
Southwest of Roswell (which is worth a look if you like all that alien/Area 51 stuff) where you can boat, kayak, hike, and camp
emnrd.nm.gov

Carlsbad Community Theatre
Small, non-profit theater
4713 US-62, Carlsbad
carlsbadcommunitytheatre.com

Living Desert SP • (575) 887-5516
Zoo and botanical gardens
1504 Miehls Dr, Carlsbad
emnrd.state.nm.us

Lake Carlsbad Beach Park
Fishing, boating, camping
708 Park Dr, Carlsbad
(575) 885-6262

Lincoln National Forest
More than 1 million acres, contains Sitting Bull Falls
Sitting Bull Falls Rd, Eddy, NM

Brantley Lake SP • (575) 457-2384
Boating, fishing, hiking
33 E Brantley Lake Rd, Carlsbad
emnrd.state.nm.us

White Sands

Billy Dawson filming a music video in the dunes

Phone: (575) 479-6124
Website: nps.gov/whsa

Established: December 20, 2019
January 18, 1933 (National Mon.)
Size: 145,762 Acres
Annual Visitors: 600,000
Peak Season: March–July
Hiking Trails: 9 Miles

Activities: Hiking, Sledding, Biking, Horseback Riding, Photography

Frontcountry Camping: None
Backcountry Camping: 10 Sites

Park Hours: 7am until Sunset
(closed Christmas Day)
Entrance Fee: $25/$20/$15
(vehicle/motorcycle/individual)
Annual Pass: $45

Deep in southeastern New Mexico, nestled between mountains at the northern reaches of the Chihuahuan Desert, lies a vast shimmering sea of white sand. This sea of strikingly beautiful sand is one of the most identifiable settings in the world. In fact, it's so large and easy to identify, astronauts use it as a geographic landmark from space. On December 20, 2019, Congress identified White Sands as the newest national park. Even if you don't know about White Sands, chances are you've seen it. It's an incredibly popular filming and photography location, featured in music videos by artists ranging from Pink Floyd to Puff Daddy, and major motion pictures like *Transformers* and *The Book of Eli*.

Entertainers weren't the first people drawn to the White Sands. Stone tools suggest nomads hunted along the shores of now-evaporated Lake Otero more than 10,000 years ago. They may have been hunting creatures like dire wolf, saber-tooth cat, Columbian mammoth, giant camel, Harlan's ground sloth, and American lion. Their presence is only known to us because it's documented in the largest collection of Pleistocene Era tracks found anywhere in North America. A couple hundred years after the birth of Christ, the Jornada Mogollon People arrived. They built structures and small villages, farmed the land, created pottery and rock art, and wove baskets. Drought in the 1300s caused them to move. In 1647, Spanish explorers established a salt trail from Durango (Mexico), through El Paso, to the north shore of Lake Lucero. They rarely used it because White Sands was an Apache stronghold. In the 1800s, railroads and homesteaders reached the region, and illegitimate salt claim standoffs and skirmishes between Apache and Buffalo Soldiers ensued. By the 1920s, as national park fever was sweeping the country, local businessmen began petitioning Congress to protect the White Sands.

Tourism wasn't the only industry interested in this remote region. In response to the bombing at Pearl Harbor, the United States military established present-day Holloman Air Force Base and White Sands Missile Range. Over the course of the next several decades, many military and exploration breakthroughs occurred in this arid desert. The first nuclear bomb was tested less than 100 miles away at Trinity Site. Warner Von Braun invented the V-2 rocket, which carried the first astronauts into space and landed on the moon. Before its tragic explosion, the Columbia Space Shuttle landed at White Sands Missile Range, rerouted due to poor weather conditions at primary landing locations. Today, it remains a highly active site for military training, missile defense testing, and fighter jets and drones are regularly spotted in the sky.

Human activity at White Sands is interesting, but it's hardly what makes this area so special. It's all about the dazzling dunes. And they are pure magic. Geologically speaking, the dunes are young. Less than 10,000 years young, but plenty of time for wind and water to work their magic on 4.5 billion tons of gypsum sand left behind when the Permian Sea retreated. White Sands is a desert environment, but the key to the dunes' formation is all about water, specifically the presence of a shallow water table, located inches below ground level. Gypsum is moderately soluble in water, and moisture prevents sand from blowing away. Today, the leading edge of the dunefield no longer moves but interior dunes can travel as much as 30 feet in a year. Water dependency puts these dunes—the largest gypsum dunes in the world—in a precarious position. Even the slightest decrease in soil moisture and water table level could result in the dunes blowing in the wind, quite literally. Climate change, vegetation, and desalination and geothermal plants are very real threats to this delicate landscape. Threat of an inevitable changing landscape should not be a call to visit White Sands. However, beauty is. The next time you see White Sands shouldn't be in a music video or Hollywood blockbuster. It should be in person.

Conditions constantly change

When to Go
White Sands is open every day of the year except Christmas. Standard hours of operation are from 7am until dark. However, about twice a week the park gates (and Highway 70) are closed (typically in the morning) for testing at the adjacent missile range. Backcountry campers are not allowed to spend the night prior to scheduled missile testing. Missile testing closures last no more than three hours, but you may want to call ahead about potential closures. Unsafe road and weather conditions can also cause unexpected park closures.

Weather is a particularly important consideration. Spring and Fall are our favorite seasons to visit, but they aren't perfect. Evenings are cool (40°F) and wind from the south/southwest can be downright oppressive in winter and spring.

Transportation and Airports
El Paso International (ELP) is the closest large airport at about ninety minutes away. Car rental is available at the airport. Public Transportation does not serve the park.

Directions
Dunes Drive, the Visitor Center, and park entrance are all located off US-70 between mile markers 199 and 200, 15 miles west of Alamogordo and 52 miles east of Las Cruces.

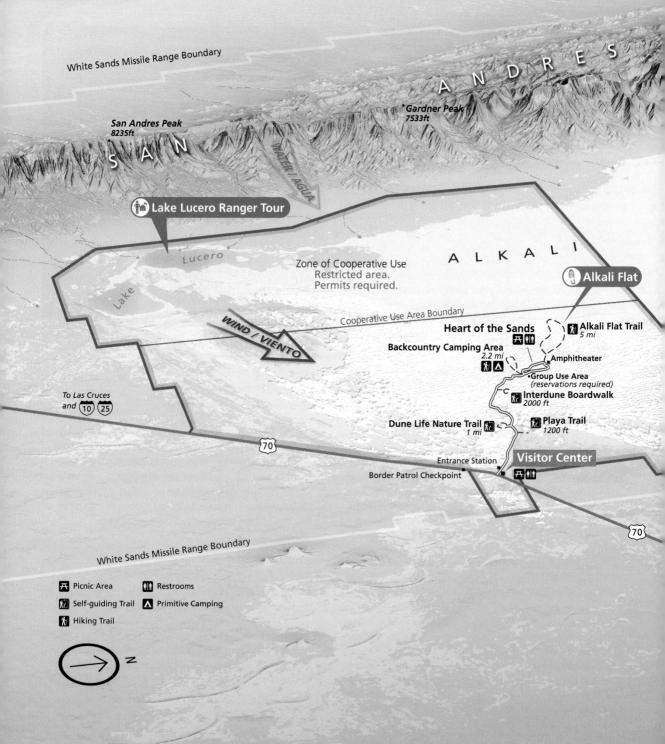

White Sands Missile Range Boundary

S A N   A N D R E S

San Andres Peak
8235ft

•*Gardner Peak*
7533ft

WATER / AGUA

Lake Lucero Ranger Tour

Lucero

Lake

Zone of Cooperative Use
Restricted area.
Permits required.

A L K A L I

Alkali Flat

Cooperative Use Area Boundary

WIND / VIENTO

Heart of the Sands

Backcountry Camping Area
2.2 mi

Alkali Flat Trail
5 mi

•Amphitheater

•Group Use Area
(reservations required)
Interdune Boardwalk
2000 ft

To Las Cruces
and ⑩ ㉕

Dune Life Nature Trail
1 mi

Playa Trail
1200 ft

Entrance Station
Visitor Center

Border Patrol Checkpoint

70

70

White Sands Missile Range Boundary

⊞ Picnic Area   ⋔ Restrooms

⬚ Self-guiding Trail   ⛺ Primitive Camping

⬚ Hiking Trail

N →

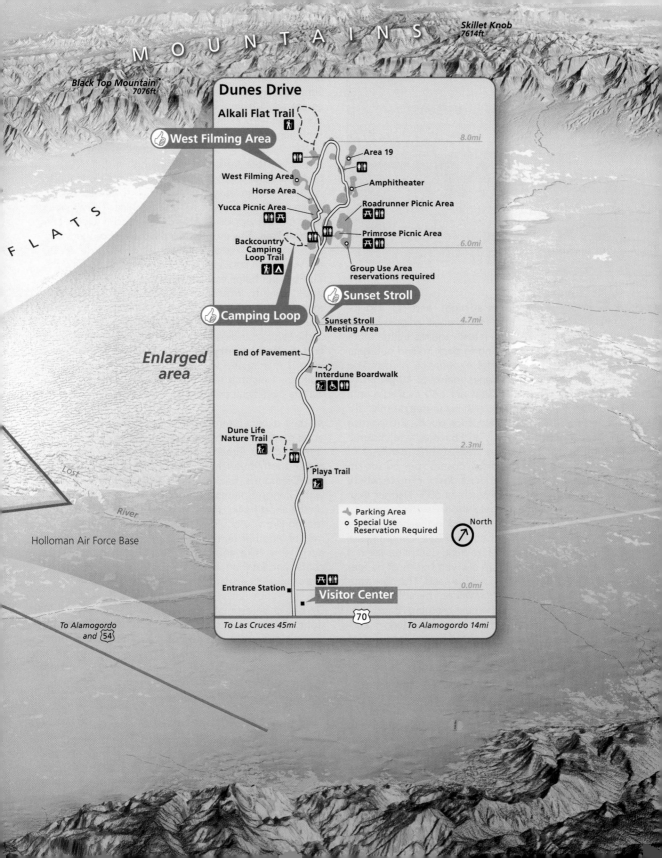

Dunes Drive

MOUNTAINS

Skillet Knob
7614ft

Black Top Mountain
7076ft

FLATS

Enlarged
area

Alkali Flat Trail

West Filming Area

Area 19

West Filming Area

Amphitheater

Horse Area

Yucca Picnic Area

Roadrunner Picnic Area

Primrose Picnic Area

Backcountry
Camping
Loop Trail

Camping Loop

Group Use Area
reservations required

Sunset Stroll

Sunset Stroll
Meeting Area

End of Pavement

Interdune Boardwalk

Dune Life
Nature Trail

Playa Trail

Parking Area
Special Use
Reservation Required

North

Lost

River

Holloman Air Force Base

Entrance Station

Visitor Center

70

To Las Cruces 45mi

To Alamogordo 14mi

To Alamogordo
and 54

8.0mi

6.0mi

4.7mi

2.3mi

0.0mi

Great place for the family (Thanks, Sam & Katie!)

Camping

White Sands closes at night, and car and RV camping are prohibited. However, it is possible to spend a night in the park. It just requires a little more work (or fun!). Visitors willing to pack in (and out) gear can enjoy the truly magical experience of camping among these glistening dunes thanks to 10 **primitive backcountry campsites**. Sites are only available on a first-come, first-serve basis, with same-day permits distributed in-person at the entrance booth. Prospective campers should arrive early and have vehicle information (make, model, license plate) for all members of your group (up to six people). It costs $3 per person (16 and older). Come prepared for a desert climate, where day-time highs can be as much as 60°F warmer than overnight lows and anticipate strong winds (especially in Spring). Campsites are situated in the heart of the dunes along Backcountry Camping Trail. Camp in your designated site. Set up before dark. Campfires are not permitted. Camp stoves are allowed but must be elevated at least six inches above the sand. The park gate will be locked overnight. You will not be able to leave the park until it reopens the next morning. Backcountry camping is not permitted the night before missile testing, so be sure to call ahead of your visit to inquire about missile testing if you plan on spending a night in the backcountry.

Hiking

White Sands is more of a 'choose your own hiking adventure' than 'follow this path' national park. With that said, you'll find five hiking trails, all located along Dunes Drive, totaling nine miles. If you'd like to climb a whole bunch of dunes and only have time for one trail, choose **Alkali Flat**. Go clockwise. Most visitors are satisfied summiting a few of the closest dunes before turning around. That's fine. This trail is about the journey, not the destination. However, reaching Alkali Flat

and the "Danger. Unexploded Munitions. Keep out." sign is pretty fun. The entire loop is 5 miles, and chances are you'll have a blast—not the unexploded munitions kind—frolicking in the dunes all the way back to the trailhead.

The other four trails are less strenuous. Entering the park via Dunes Drive, the first one you'll encounter is **Playa**. It's an easy half-mile walk to an illustration of what the area might have looked like 10,000 years ago. On the opposite side of the road is **Dune Life Nature Trail**. This moderately difficult self-guided loop ascends two dunes over the course of one mile. Along the way you'll find a variety of signs featuring Katy the Kit Fox who helps explain White Sands' ecology. Next you'll come to **Interdune Boardwalk**. It's an easy 0.4-mile stroll across an elevated boardwalk, featuring a shade canopy and signs discussing a few things that make White Sands unique. After Alkali Flat Trail, you'll find the **Backcountry Camping Trail**. While this 2-mile loop is maintained with backpackers in mind, all visitors are welcome to explore the heart of the dunes via a fairly difficult trail that climbs several steep dunes.

All trails except Interdune Boardwalk are marked by orange posts with a unique symbol and color. Playa Trail is marked with Green/Hearts. Dune Life Nature Trail is marked with Blue/Clubs. Alkali Flat Trail is marked with Red/Diamonds. Backcountry Camping Trail is marked with Orange/Spades. There isn't much to worry about on the short trails. However, if you're out on Alkali Flat feeling like you could get lost and don't see the next marker, another human, or tracks, please turn around and live to hike another day. Also stop at the visitor center and let them know a trail marker might be missing or buried beneath sand.

Do not underestimate the potentially extreme conditions. Visitors have died in the desert heat. The park recommends that you do not start a hike if the temperature is greater than 85°F, and to carry at least a gallon of water and a few high-energy snacks. But it's up to you to know your limits. The visitor center is the only place you'll find water, so plan accordingly.

Sledding

Sledding in the desert isn't just a novelty … it's fun! The most important variable is equipment. The park recommends waxed plastic saucers for the best experience and they're conveniently sold at the gift shop. It's a good idea to call (575.479.1629) in advance to check availability. The next most important variable is location. The three picnic areas are great choices and there are plenty of nice sledding hills between miles four and six, but you're free to go where you want, as long as you aren't sledding into the roadway or parking areas. Also make sure your sled hill ends in soft sand, not hazardous/delicate vegetation.

Biking

Biking is an option at White Sands, but Dunes Drive is only 8 miles (one-way), half-paved/half-hard-packed gypsum, with little-to-no shoulder. Mountain bikes are recommended as the gypsum portion of the roadway is often washboard with intermittent potholes and sand drifts. Wind and blowing sand can be a problem. And then there's the crowds. White Sands is a relatively small area that receives thousands of visitors on busy weekends. This is not to say don't pack your bicycles, but maybe don't pack them specifically to bike here. If you bike early in the morning, when weather is cool, wind is often calm, and crowds are generally thin, you can have a wonderfully peaceful pedal through the White Sands. Note that off-road travel is not permitted and subject to citation.

Horseback Riding

Unlike bikes, horses are permitted off-road! Horseback riders encounter the same difficulties as everyone else (heat, sun, wind, etc.), but it can be an extremely rewarding experience. You'll need your own horse(s) and a permit. The permit can be downloaded from the park website, and it's a good idea to fill it out in advance. You must unload/load your horse(s) at the designated area, located on Dunes Drive between West Filming Area and Yucca Picnic Area. Horses are prohibited from picnic areas, group use area, backcountry campsites, all trails, co-use area, and Dunes Drive. Overnight camping with stock is not allowed. Be sure to clean up all your debris (feed and manure) in the Horse Trailer Parking Area and dispose of it outside the park.

Photography

White Sands is an incredibly popular destinations for photographers and filmmakers. On my first trip, I witnessed Billy Dawson shooting a music video for *Sinner's Saints*. And there were a pair of photoshoots taking place on adjacent dunes. Meanwhile I sat comfortably on a tall dune (near the horse trailer parking area) waiting for the sun to set. White Sands' photogenic nature is undeniable, but sand is an archenemy of the photographer. Especially this sand. Its grains are finer than typical quartz sand. Pour a little water out on the dunefield and you'll see it ball up due to gypsum sand's solubility and water's surface tension. In

Dune photoshoot

windy conditions, it might be a good idea to leave your camera behind and rely on your cellphone. If you must bring your good camera along when sand is blowing in the dunes, protect it with a cover, do not change lenses, and use a UV filter. Your best bet to avoid the wind, is to arrive when the park opens or visit between September and November, when conditions are typically calmer. While there are plenty of dunes for everyone to enjoy the stunning sunsets, the park's limited operating hours aren't ideal for many photographers. Fortunately, you can request an Early Entry or Stay Late permit. Special access comes at the reasonable price of $50 per hour. Permit request form and instructions can be found at the park website.

Visitor Center

The visitor center is typically open from 9am to 6pm, closing an hour earlier from Labor Day to mid-March, and again from early April until Memorial Day weekend. This is the only place in the park you'll find water. Fill up before hiking! Inside you'll find exhibits, a park store (with sleds), and a short film. Restrooms are just a few steps from the visitor center's entrance.

Ranger Programs & For Kids

Every day (except Christmas) White Sands offers a Sunset Stroll. All you have to do is show up at the Sunset Stroll Meeting Area (4.7 miles from the Entrance Station) about an hour before sunset to join a park ranger on a leisurely one-mile walk across the sand to enjoy the setting sun. If you'd like to explore the park after dark, but don't want to camp in the backcountry, plan your trip around the full moon. From April through October, White Sands offers hikes the night before a full moon and live entertainment at the park amphitheater when the full moon is out. Space is limited to 40 participants for this easy-to-moderate 1.5-hour trek. Tickets are required ($8/adult). They can be purchased

Dune Life Trail

at (877) 444-6777 or recreation.gov up to 30 days in advance. Full Moon Night is free. Pack your camp chairs, a blanket, and cooler, and enjoy some music under the moonlight!

If you'd like to witness "the birthplace of the dunes," you can join a ranger-guided tour to Lake Lucero. Tours are only offered once a month in November through April. Space is limited to 50 participants for this moderate 3-hour expedition. Tickets are required. They cost $8 per adult and can be purchased up to 30 days in advance at (877) 444-6777 or recreation.gov.

Additionally, White Sands hosts an annual event called Mothapalooza, celebrating the park's vast collection of endemic moth species. Check the park website for details. Remember cancellations and schedule changes may occur due to weather or missile testing activity. If you have concerns, it is always best to call ahead and confirm your program is continuing as scheduled.

White Sands is one of the best national parks for kids. It's definitely much more than one giant sand box, but that doesn't eliminate the fact there's 4.5 billion tons of brilliant gypsum sand for kids to play in. Additionally, the park offers a Junior Ranger Program, Adventure Packs, and a few of the best picnic areas found anywhere in the United States.

Flora & Fauna

Desert life is hard. Even harder when the sand dunes you intend to live among move as much as 30 feet each year. More than 350 plant species reside in the park, but cacti—the icon of desert life—cannot survive within the dunefield. However, they are common in surrounding areas. In the dunes, life simply finds a way. Grasses like alkali sacaton thrive in the salty interdunal areas. New clusters of purple sand verbena emerge each year as dunes bury old plants. Soaptree yucca grow tall to keep their leaves above the sand. When the dune moves on, the yucca collapses on itself. Skunkbush sumac roots anchor themselves in the earth, forming pedestals of sand and root capable of remaining after the dunes move on. These pedestals provide shelter for other desert life.

The nocturnal kit fox is one species that builds their dens within the stable confines of a skunkbush sumac's pedestal. Kit fox is the largest animal living within the dunefield, but it isn't the only interesting one. Dozens of species can only be found here. They include the Apache pocket mouse, White Sands wood rat, bleached earless lizard, camel crickets, and several species of moths. Many of these species are white, an adaptation that helps them hide from predators and keep cool in summer. African oryx were introduced by the New Mexico Department of Game and Fish in 1969. Measures are in place to keep them out of the park to protect native plant species, but they are common in surrounding areas.

Pets & Accessibility

Well-behaved pets are permitted but must be kept on a leash (less than six feet). Be sure to clean up after your pet, provide it with plenty of water, do not leave it unattended (especially in your vehicle), and, unless it's a service animal, do not bring your pet inside the visitor center.

The Visitor Center, picnic areas, and Interdune Boardwalk are wheelchair accessible. An accessibility ramp is available for full moon nights as well.

Weather

White Sands enjoys a pretty typical desert climate. A brief wet season (July–September), followed by a long dry season. Fall is pleasant, featuring delightful daytime highs, cool evenings, and light winds. Spring enjoys similar temps, but it's often windy. Summer can be oppressively hot (110+°F), but evenings are comfortable. Daytime highs are fine in winter, but nights are cold, and it's often windy.

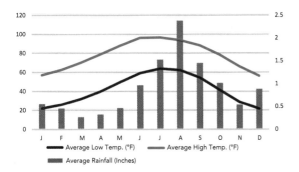

Dunes sunset

Tips & Recommendations

Visitation is pretty steady year-round, with a spring break surge in March and wintertime lull.

It's a good idea to check for missile testing closures before arriving. While they typically only delay opening by a few hours, they are common and could add a little wrinkle to your plans (especially if you're thinking about camping in the backcountry dunes).

Be prepared for the heat! Pack water. Apply sunscreen. If you're visiting in summer, limit your visits to mornings and evenings. The heat here is no joke, and the sun's rays are particularly powerful, as they reflect off the white gypsum sand.

The park is small, and you can easily hike all the trails in one day, but consider spending a night or two in nearby Alamogordo. There are many other things to do in the area, and it's fun to see the dunes in different conditions (clear skies, cloudy, stormy—although most days feature the Southwest's famed infinitely blue skies).

If you're determined to get some great photos, you really should consider taking advantage of the park's generous offer to provide special access for $50 per hour. I didn't, but it's on my mind for the next visit.

Go sledding! We're quick to discard things as childish or "not for me," bring out the kid in you and go sledding in the dunes. When are you ever going to get this chance again? Plus, it's fun! At the very least climb some dunes and frolic down them. Also fun!

Use the picnic areas. The picnic areas here are great. However, picnickers should pay close attention to weather, as you don't want all your food to be seasoned with sand if it's windy.

Hike: Alkali Flat (Moderate, 5 miles)
Family Activities: Sledding!, Become Junior Rangers
Guided Tours: Lake Lucero Ranger-Guided Tour
Sunrise/Sunset Spots: Any tall dune will do

Beyond the Park...

Dining (in Alamogordo)
Off The Wall • (575) 488-3074
1022 N White Sands Blvd

CJ's Si Senor • (575) 437-7879
2300 White Sands Blvd, Alamogordo

Brown Bag Deli • (575) 437-9751
900 Washington Ave

Grocery Stores
Albertsons • (575) 488-1200
1300 E 10th St

Walmart • (575) 434-5870
233 S New York Ave

Lodging & Camping
White Sands Motel • (575) 437-2922
1101 S White Sands Blvd
thewhitesandsmotel.com

Cabins at Cloudcroft
1006 Coyote Ave, Cloudcroft
cabinsatcloudcroft.com

White Sands KOA
412 24th St, Alamogordo
koa.com • (575) 437-3003

There are a few campsites for past and present military personnel at White Sands Missile Range, or consider camping at the national forest or state parks

Festivals
Alien Fest • July • Roswell
ufofestivalroswell.com

Balloon Fiesta • October
balloonfiesta.com • Albuquerque

Attractions
World's Largest Pistachio
7320 US-54, Alamogordo

Riverbend Hot Springs
100 Austin St, Truth or Consequences
riverbendhotsprings.com

Lincoln NF • fs.usda.gov
Lots of great mountain hikes
3463 Las Palomas Rd, Alamogordo

Trinity Site • wsmr.army.mil
1st atomic bomb test site, open for tours twice a year

White Sands Missile Range Museum
wsmr-history.org • (580) 699-4798

City of Rocks State Park
emnrd.nm.gov

Gila Cliff Dwellings NM
Highly recommended site
nps.gov/gicl • (575) 536-9461

El Malpais NM • (505) 876-2783
Peculiar volcanic landscape
1900 E Santa Fe Ave, Grants
nps.gov/elma

Bandelier NM • Los Alamos
Unique cultural site
nps.gov/band

Three Rivers Petroglyph Site
blm.gov

Organ Mountains Desert Peaks
blm.gov

Elephand Butte Lake State Park
emnrd.nm.gov

Petrified Forest

Blue Mesa

Phone: (928) 524-6228
Website: nps.gov/pefo

Established: December 9, 1962
Size: 100,000+ Acres
Annual Visitors: 800,000
Peak Season: May–September
Hiking Trails: 7 Miles

Activities: Hiking, Backpacking, Horseback Riding, Biking

Campgrounds & Lodging: None
Backcountry Camping: Permitted in the Wilderness Area with a free permit (available at visitor center)

Park Hours: 7am–dusk (February–October), 8am–dusk (November–January)
Entrance Fee: $25/20/15 (car/motorcycle/individual)

Forests of fallen trees made of stone. Ruins and petroglyphs of ancient civilizations. Fossils of prehistoric plants and animals. Pastel colored badlands. Wilderness. Peace. Solitude. Silence. All of these are found at Petrified Forest, just a short distance from the whir of traffic along Interstate 40. Nearby communities like Holbrook are sleepy ex-railway towns or ghost towns like Adamana. Oddly enough, signs of the past outnumber signs of the present. This rich history of life exists in a place that is anything but lively. Most desert animals are small rodents, amphibians, and reptiles, many of which only emerge during the summer nights, long after tourists have left the park. Plants are primarily grasses, cacti, and wildflowers that have managed to adapt to life with little water and arid soil.

Trees, some as tall as 200 feet, thrived in what was a humid and sub-tropical climate 225 million years ago. They were washed away by ancient rivers and streams, and then buried by silt, soil, and volcanic ash—conditions ripe for fossilization. Many plants and animals were cast in stone, preserved for millions of years, and today they help tell the story of prehistoric life in the Painted Desert. The story is still incomplete, but scientists believe present-day parkland was once situated near the equator. Large crocodile-like reptiles and oversized salamanders coexisted with early dinosaurs. Visitors can view fossils of these creatures and ancient plants at Painted Desert Visitor Center and Rainbow Forest Museum.

Fossils are not the only signs of life revealed through rocks. Ancient cultures, from 650 to 2,000 years ago, drew thousands of petroglyphs. There are more than 600 petroglyphs at Newspaper Rock alone. It's difficult to determine what these symbols mean; descendants of ancient Hopi, Zuni, and Navajo cultures only recognize some of them. As always, scientists are full of hypotheses regarding their meaning. Ideas ranging from trail markers to family stories to fertility charms abound. It's likely most held some spiritual significance, others more practical, like the petroglyphs near Puerco Pueblo that form a sundial signaling the summer solstice.

People have lived in the region for more than 10,000 years, but most evidence of inhabitation is from the same cultures that left behind ancient petroglyphs. Tools, pottery, and village ruins from Puebloan cultures have been found at more than 600 archeological sites. They originally lived in single-family huts built over a dug-out section of earth. Around the turn of the 13th century, climatic changes caused families to group together near reliable sources of water where they built large pueblos capable of housing as many as 200 people in about 100, 1-story rooms. The rooms were constructed without doors or windows around an open plaza. They entered using a ladder. Puerco Pueblo, located along the main park road, is home to some of the most well-preserved ruins.

Modern civilization saw value in the Painted Desert as a tourist destination. Rail was laid through the present park boundary and soon the railroad began promoting America's scenic wonders hoping to boost passenger service. Arizona's Painted Desert and Petrified Forest were near the top of the list of wonders. Tourists could take a train to Adamana, book a hotel room, and walk among the petrified trees of what was known at the time as Chalcedony Forest. Trains dropped off tourists and loaded petrified wood to be taken back East. One man even proposed to crush petrified logs turning them into an abrasive grit. John Muir, already the driving force behind creation of Yosemite National Park, conducted the first scientific excavation in Petrified Forest. What he saw was destruction of a unique resource that was clearly exhaustible. To protect the region, he enlisted service of friend and fellow conservationist, President Theodore Roosevelt. Roosevelt promptly created Petrified Forest National Monument by executive order. Fifty-six years later it was made a national park.

Newspaper Rock

When to Go
Petrified Forest is open every day of the year. However, it's not your typical 24/7 national park. It opens at 7am from mid-February until October, and at 8am from November until mid-February. The park road closes around dusk via an automated gate at the Painted Desert (north) Entrance. It's hot in summer, cool in winter, and comfortable in between. Summer thunderstorms can bring dangerous lightning and frightening thunder, but an ideal time to visit is after a storm; when sedimentary rocks of the Painted Desert are wet, their colors appear brighter and more pronounced in the soft morning or evening light. May, July, and August are typically the best months to see wildflowers.

Transportation & Airports
Public transportation is not available to or around Petrified Forest. The closest major airports are Albuquerque International Sunport (ABQ) in Albuquerque, NM (228 miles east of the park) and Sky Harbor International Airport (PHX) in Phoenix, AZ (213 miles southwest of the park). Pulliam Airport (FLG) in Flagstaff, AZ is 135 miles to the west.

Directions
Petrified Forest is located in northeastern Arizona, straddling Interstate 40 between Albuquerque, NM and Flagstaff, AZ. Visitors arriving via I-40 from the east should take Exit 311. It leads directly to the park and Painted Desert Visitor Center, where you'll find an automated gate (know the park hours). From here, begin by touring the park north of I-40 before crossing the interstate and exiting near Rainbow Forest Museum. Those traveling from the west will want to take Exit 285 into Holbrook. Drive 19 miles south on US-180 to the south entrance near Rainbow Forest Museum.

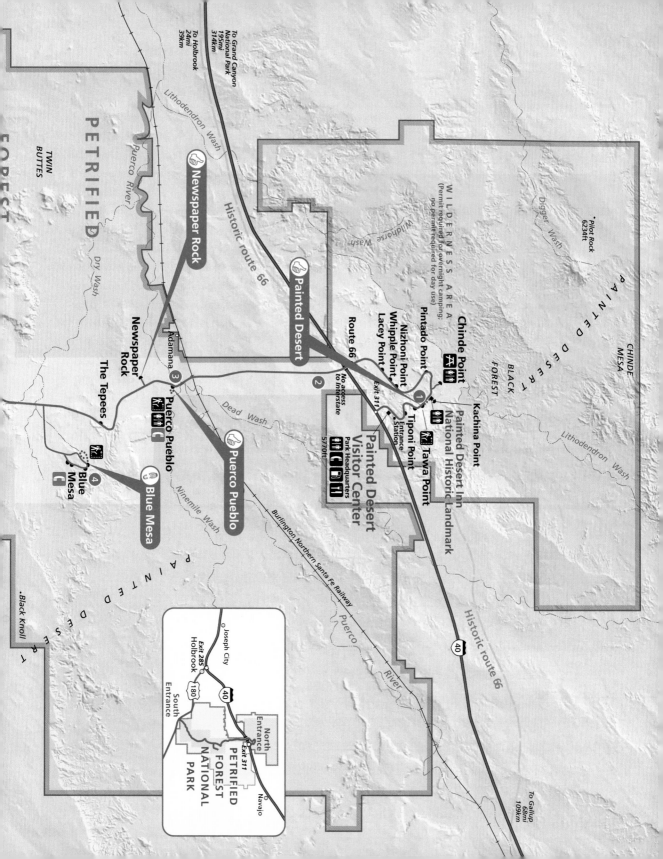

PETRIFIED FOREST

TWIN BUTTES

To Grand Canyon National Park 195mi 314km
To Holbrook 24mi 39km

Lithodendron Wash

Puerco River
Dry Wash

Historic route 66

Newspaper Rock

Adamana

Newspaper Rock

The Tepees

Painted Desert

Puerco Pueblo

Blue Mesa

Blue Mesa

Ninemile Wash

Dead Wash

PAINTED DESERT

Black Knoll

WILDERNESS AREA
(Permit required for overnight camping; no permit required for day use)

Wildhorse Wash

Pilot Rock 6234ft

Digger Wash

PAINTED DESERT

CHINDE MESA

BLACK FOREST

Chinde Point

Pintado Point
Nizhoni Point
Whipple Point
Lacey Point

Kachina Point

Painted Desert Inn
National Historic Landmark

Tiponi Point

Tawa Point

Painted Desert Visitor Center
Park Headquarters
5770ft

Entrance Station

Route 66

Exit 311

No access to interstate

Burlington Northern Santa Fe Railway

Puerco River

Historic route 66

To Gallup 68mi 109km

PETRIFIED FOREST NATIONAL PARK

Joseph City
Exit 285
Holbrook
180
40
South Entrance
North Entrance
Exit 311
Navajo

Lithodendron Wash

1
2
3
4

Petrified Forest Hiking Trails (Distances are roundtrip)

Name	Location (# on map)	Length	Difficulty Rating & Notes
Painted Desert Rim - ♨	Tawa and Kachina Points (1)	1.0 mile	E – Follows the picturesque rim
Onyx Bridge*	Painted Desert Inn (1)	4.0 miles	M – Difficult to follow, bridge collapsed in 2020
Dead Wash Overlook*	7 miles from North Entrance (2)	4.0 miles	M – Views across drainage, scrambling required
Puerco Pueblo	Puerco Pueblo Parking Area (3)	0.3 mile	E – Visits ruins of an ancient people
Blue Mesa - ♨	Blue Mesa Sunshelter (4)	1.0 mile	M – Loop trail through wood and blue badlands
Billings Gap Overlook*	Blue Mesa Loop Road (4)	3.0 miles	M – Follow the edge of Blue Mesa
Blue Forest*	Blue Mesa Loop (4)	3.0 miles	M – Connects Blue Mesa Trail to the Main Park Rd
Red Basin Clam Beds*	Blue Mesa Road (4)	8.5 miles	M – Bring GPS, park's guide provides waypoints
Jasper Forest* - ♨	Jasper Forest Parking Area (5)	2.5 miles	M – Follows an old 1930s road into the forest
First Forest Point*	Jasper Forest Parking Area (5)	2.1 miles	M – More petrified wood at Jasper Forest
Crystal Forest - ♨	Crystal Forest Parking Area (6)	0.8 mile	E – Crystals hide in a few petrified logs
Martha's Butte*	Dry Wash Bridge (mile 22) (7)	2.0 miles	M – Many petroglyphs on rocks at the butte
Long Logs - ♨	Rainbow Forest Museum (8)	1.6 miles	E – Loop trail to a large concentration of wood
Agate House	Rainbow Forest Museum (8)	2.0 miles	E – Visit a rehabilitated 700-year-old pueblo
Giant Logs	Rainbow Forest Museum (8)	0.4 mile	E – Large logs including "Old Faithful"
Devil's Playground*	Directions to access road provided with permit (call park at 928.524.6228 x 236 for status)		
Wilderness Hiking	Painted Desert Inn or Tawa Point (1)		50% of the park is designated wilderness. No trails. Permit required for overnight stays. Bring map and water.

*These are "off-the-beaten-path" routes, not maintained trails and should only be attempted with a map and/or GPS

Difficulty Ratings: E = Easy, M = Moderate

Recipe For: Petrified Wood **Ready In:** Millions of years

Ingredients: Trees (as many as you desire), sediment that includes volcanic ash

1. Take your trees and bury them in sediment (A nice layer of sediment with volcanic ash will help slow down the natural decomposition process by cutting off the amount of oxygen that reaches them)

2. Pour large amounts of water onto the sediment (Water dissolves silica from the volcanic ash - The solution of silica in water slowly replaces the wood's original tissues)

3. Let sit for a few million years (Over time silica crystalizes to quartz - Colors develop based on mineral content, like manganese, carbon, iron, cobalt, and chromium, that were in your original sediment)

4. Remove sediment and observe your tree(s) made of stone

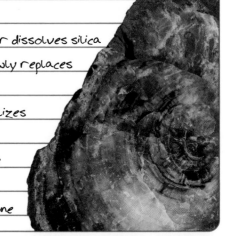

Camping & Lodging

There are no designated campgrounds or lodges within the park. However, you can find overnight accommodations nearby in Holbrook. **Backcountry camping** is allowed within Petrified Forest National Wilderness Area. Backpackers must obtain a free backcountry permit from the visitor center or Rainbow Forest Museum. Permits are not available in advance and must be obtained at least one hour before the park closes. You are required to hike at least one mile from the two designated parking locations (Painted Desert Inn or Tawa Point) before camping.

Driving

If you don't have enough time for any of the other park activities, the 28-mile Park Road and Blue Mesa Loop are worth the detour from I-40. They offer overlooks, picnic areas, and access to hiking trails. Expect it to take an hour to drive through the park.

Hiking & Backpacking

Not known for hiking, Petrified Forest can be a pleasant surprise. It features seven maintained trails, all of which are less than 3 miles long. Still, they provide access to some of the finer petrified rock specimens, badlands formations, and archaeological sites. Long Logs and Giant Logs Trails are pretty self-explanatory; you're going to see some petrified wood. **Giant Logs** leads to "Old Faithful," a petrified tree nearly ten feet in diameter. If you're interested in the area's ancient history, take **Puerco Pueblo Trail**. It leads to a hundred-room village built and occupied between 1250 and 1400 AD. **Agate House Trail** leads to a more modern habitation. About 700 years ago this structure was built using materials on hand: mud and petrified wood. It shares a trailhead with Long Logs Trail. You can combine the two to make a 2.6-mile semi-loop. My favorite hike in the park is **Blue Mesa Trail**, located off Blue Mesa Road. It's a short loop descending from the mesa to petrified wood deposits and spectacular views of badlands infused with bluish bentonite. The park added a few "Off the Beaten Path" adventures that are becoming easier to identify each year. They explore interesting areas like Jasper Forest and Blue Mesa in depth. Then there's **Devil's Playground**, which requires a permit (three available per week on a first-come, first-served basis) and driving along a rugged access road. You are also free to hike (and camp) in the park's wilderness area. **Backpackers** must obtain a free wilderness permit. Fifty-thousand acres of undeveloped desert. No trails. No water. Little shade. If you choose to blaze your own path, come prepared with a map, compass, and plenty of water.

Agate House

Horseback Riding

Bring your own horse(s) and explore Painted Desert's colorful badlands. However, riders and their stock are restricted to the wilderness area (northern half). It can be accessed via Wilderness Access Trail near Kachina Point, on the northwest side of Painted Desert Inn, two miles north of the visitor center. You and your horse are permitted to camp overnight north of Lithodendron Wash with an overnight use permit (available at the visitor center). Water is not available in the backcountry, which makes a multi-day trip with stock extremely challenging.

Biking

Motorists rule the road, but cyclists can also enjoy scenic vistas afforded by the 28-mile park road and 3.5-mile Blue Mesa Loop. These roads are relatively straight, flat, and narrow. It's best to pedal as early in the morning or as late in the evening as operating hours allow. Summer is often hot, windy, and a poor time to pedal. Cyclists are not allowed off road and may not use paved trails. Always be aware of motorists.

Visitor Centers & Museums

Painted Desert Visitor Center is located near I-40's Exit 311. Here you'll find a short orientation film, several exhibits, a bookstore, and restrooms. A restaurant, gas station, gift shop, and convenience store are also available. **Painted Desert Inn** is located at Kachina Point just north of the visitor center. It used to be a rest stop for travelers on historic Route 66, but now the Inn is a museum. Two miles north of the south entrance is **Rainbow Forest Museum**. Here you'll find fossil exhibits, a short film, bookstore, snack bar, and restrooms. Painted Desert Visitor Center and Rainbow Forest Museum are open most days from 7am–6pm. Hours extend to 7pm from early April to mid-

Agate Bridge

is dominated by grasses, but at least 400 species of plants manage to survive. However, the most fascinating plants and animals are those that lived here 225 million years ago. Their existence is recorded in rock of the Chinle Formation, one of the richest Late Triassic fossil-plant deposits in the world. More than 200 plant and animal fossils have been discovered including crocodile-like phytosaurs, large salamanders named Buettneria, and a few early dinosaurs.

Pets & Accessibility
Petrified Forest is one of few parks where pets won't limit your activities. Pets must be kept on a leash (less than six feet), but they are allowed on all developed trails (except Wilderness Access Trail). They are not allowed in buildings, but are welcome in picnic and parking areas, and along roadways.

All facilities, including visitor centers, museums, several ranger programs, restrooms, and picnic areas are accessible (assistance may be necessary) to wheelchair users. Park trails are not.

Weather
Weather is as peculiar as the Painted Desert, petrified wood, and ancient petroglyphs. A high-altitude desert with predominantly clear nights creates extreme cooling between day and night, often as much as 40°F. This effect makes for cool summer evenings and hot afternoons. Summer highs are in the 90s°F. Evening lows dip into the 50s°F. Summers can also be windy and wet. Most rain falls during the monsoon season (July and August). Summer dust devils are common. During winter, snow can fall any day, November through April, but it rarely lasts through the afternoon. Enjoy the rain and snow because moisture on the badlands can really make the Painted Desert's colors pop on a sunny day. If you're just going to drive-thru while passing by on I-40, there really is no bad time of year to visit.

September. In winter (late October–late February), hours are reduced to 8am–5pm. Painted Desert Inn National Historic Landmark is open every day from 9am–5pm.

Ranger Programs & For Kids
The area's interesting and sometimes unexplainable geology and history stirs all sorts of questions. And park rangers are ready and willing to answer them for you. "How'd the trees turn to stone?" They'll explain it to you. "Why'd the natives leave?" They'll have an answer. "Where's the restroom?" They'll point you to it. You are also invited to join their ranger programs. Rangers enlighten and entertain guests on tours of Painted Desert Inn, talks about the Triassic Period, walks at Puerco Pueblo, and hikes into the park's backcountry. Check the park website for a current schedule of programs and call them (515.724.4493) to register for one of their backcountry hikes. The park also holds a multitude of special events and cultural demonstrations throughout the year.

Children of all ages are invited to participate in the Junior Ranger and Junior Paleontologist Programs. They encourage you and your children to learn about fossils and human history while exploring the park. To join these exclusive clubs, you must first pick up a free activity booklet from Painted Desert Visitor Center, Painted Desert Inn, or Rainbow Forest Museum. Complete the activities during your visit to receive a badge or patch and be anointed the newest member.

Flora & Fauna
The park is home to more than 200 species of birds. Pronghorn, coyote, and bobcats endure the unforgiving desert climate along with dozens of other mammals, reptiles, and amphibians. This desolate terrain

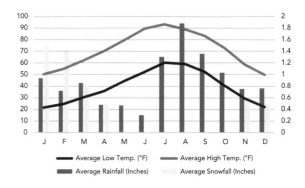

Average Low Temp. (°F)   Average High Temp. (°F)
Average Rainfall (Inches)   Average Snowfall (Inches)

Tips & Recommendations

The most important thing to know at Petrified Forest is it isn't an overnight park. Hours change with the season, but you can assume, if the sun is down, the park is closed (except for backpackers who can obtain a permit to camp in the wilderness area).

Visitation is steady from March through October, with a summertime surge that typically peaks in July. Come during the shoulder seasons for pleasant weather and smaller crowds, or stop by in winter for cool temps, no crowds, and the chance to see the Painted Desert blanketed in snow.

If you're just driving through, I prefer to start at Painted Desert Visitor Center, working south, stopping at viewpoints, hiking trails, and ending with all the petrified wood at the park's southern end. But if you're going to be in the park around sunset, you may want to reverse things and end at Painted Desert, to watch the sunset from Chinde Point. (Although, if you can hustle back from Agate House, that could be an interesting sunset location as well.)

If you enter the park from the south (Rainbow Forest), don't skip the petrified logs, thinking you'll see plenty more later. You won't. You have to hike some distance to see petrified wood in the Painted Desert area.

Ranger programs are great everywhere, but they really enhance the experience at a park like Petrified Forest. To most of us, petrified wood is just a log-like rock. To some park rangers, it is their passion. Joining one of them, you'll learn all about petrified wood and the story it can tell about the past, plus they can help get you

Painted Desert

into the park's backcountry. The Petrified Forest Field Institute (928.524.6228 ext. 239, petrifiedforestfieldinstitute.org) also offers classes and custom trips of Petrified Forest National Park. They frequent a bunch of the park's "Off the Beaten Path" destinations.

These trees have been here for more than 200 million years. Please leave them for future guests. Taking anything from a park isn't just selfish, it's illegal.

Easy Hikes: Long Logs/Agate House (1.6/2 miles), Painted Desert Rim (1), Crystal Forest (0.8)
Moderate Hikes: Blue Mesa (1 mile), Jasper Forest (2.5)
Overlooks: Chinde Point, Kachina Point
Cultural Sites: Agate House, Newspaper Rock, Rainbow Forest Museum, Painted Desert Inn National Historic Landmark, Puerco Pueblo, Route 66 Stop
Sunrise/Sunset Spots: The park typically opens after sunrise and closes around dusk, so, sunset is what you have, and you should watch it near one of the entrances. I would choose Chinde Point.

Beyond the Park...

Dining
Painted Desert Diner • at the VC
petrifiedforesttrading.com

Bienvenidos • (928) 524-1600
2600 Navajo Blvd, Holbrook

Grocery Stores
Safeway • (928) 524-3313
702 W Hopi Dr, Holbrook

Lodging & Camping
Brad's Desert Inn • (928) 224-0565
301 W Hopi Dr, Holbrook
bradsdesertinnaz.com

The View Hotel • (435) 727-5555
Views of Monument Valley
Indian Rte 42, Monument Valley
monumentvalleyview.com

Petrified Forest KOA
102 Hermosa Dr, Holbrook
koa.com • (928) 524-6689

OK RV Park • (928) 524-3226
1576 Roadrunner Rd, Holbrook
okrvholbrook.com

Festivals
Verde Valley Birding Fest • April
verderiver.org • Cottonwood

Attractions
Canyon de Chelly National Mon
Incredibly unique environment
nps.gov/cach • (928) 674-5500

Walnut Canyon National Mon
Ancient ruins, stunning vistas
nps.gov/waca • (928) 526-3367

Wupatki National Monument
Many archaeological sites
nps.gov/wupa • (928) 679-2365

Sunset Crater Volcano NM
Massive cinder cone
nps.gov/sucr • (928) 526-0502

Navajo National Monument
*Beautiful place with more
ancient cliff dwellings*
nps.gov/nava

Tuzigoot National Monument
Multi-story pueblo ruin
nps.gov/tuzi • (928) 634-5564

Montezuma Castle National Mon
More well preserved dwellings
nps.gov/moca • (928) 567-3322

Tonto National Monument
Cliff dwellings & scenery
nps.gov/tont • (928) 467-2241

Rainbow Bridge National Mon
*Huge natural bridge in SE Utah
(Glen Canyon)* • nps.gov/rabr

Northwestern New Mexico
El Morro National Monument
Sandstone bluff, cultural sites
nps.gov/elmo

Chaco Culture Nat'l Hist Park
Ancient ruins in canyon
nps.gov/chcu

Ice Cave and Bandera Volcano
12000 Ice Caves Rd, Grants
icecaves.com

Saguaro

Hugh Norris Trail

Phone: (520) 733-5153
Website: nps.gov/sagu

Established: October 14, 1994
Size: 91,440 Acres
Annual Visitors: 750,000
Peak Season: November–March
Hiking Trails: 165+ Miles

Activities: Hiking, Backpacking, Biking, Horseback Riding

Campgrounds/Lodging: None
Backcountry Camping: Permitted in the Rincon Mountains with a Backcountry Permit ($8/night)

Rincon Mountain: 5am–8pm (winter), 5am–6pm (summer)
Tucson Mountain: Sunrise–Sunset
Entrance Fee: $25/20/15 (car/motorcycle/individual)

In 1933, University of Arizona president Homer Shantz urged President Hoover to protect saguaro forests surrounding the Rincon Mountains. Several generations of saguaro had already been affected by grazing cattle, as their small hooves and immense weight compacted the ground until saguaro seeds, no bigger than a pinhead, could not penetrate the earth's surface and take root. President Hoover agreed that the "monarch of the Sonoran Desert" needed to be preserved, invoking the Antiquities Act and establishing Saguaro National Monument. Cattle no longer grazed these saguaro forests, but soon another mammal was getting too close for comfort. Tucson had once been a sleepy little town, 15 miles from present-day parkland. Today, Tucson is a bustling city, sprawling-to-and-around the park's boundaries. Humans introduced invasive plant species that need water to survive, creating competition for the desert's most valuable commodity. Vandalism and poaching increased. Cacti were stolen for landscaping projects. By 1994, still trying to protect this unique natural resource, Congress added the Tucson Mountain District, expanded both regions, and redesignated it a national park.

As conservationists try to protect the saguaro, cacti do their best to protect and provide for Sonoran Desert wildlife. To birds, the mighty saguaros are multi-tower condominiums that are constantly expanding.

Gila woodpeckers and gilded flickers drill out one-room accommodations in the saguaros' trunk and large branches. Often they make several holes, rejecting one after another before finding a home to their liking and settling down to raise a family. Other birds waste no time and begin squatting in vacant units. Elf owls, screech owls, purple martins, American kestrel, Lucy's warblers, cactus wrens, kingbirds, even honeybees seek the saguaro's protection. Not only does living within these monstrous succulents provide protection from predators, it shields them from hot summer days and cool winter nights. In summer, the inner column of a saguaro is 20°F cooler than the ambient temperature. In winter, it's 20°F warmer. Outside, red-tailed and Harris hawks build nests in the crooks of the saguaro's arms. These are the condominium's suites, custom-built with beautiful 360-degree views of the surrounding mountains.

Fruit of the saguaro is just as useful as its woody frame. For centuries the Tohono O'odham people harvested fruit to make syrup, jam, and wine; it was also dried and eaten like a fig. It is so important, they marked their new year as the beginning of the saguaro fruit harvest. Fruit are also vital to creatures that creep and fly in the cool of the night. In June and July when it ripens, for-agers like javelina, coyote, fox, harvester ants, birds, and small rodents feast on its succulent flesh.

The saguaro itself is a masterpiece of adaptation to an unforgiving environment. It's built on a wooden frame-work sturdy enough to support its weight, which can exceed 16,000 pounds. Its skin is pleated, allowing the cactus to expand as its roots sop up surrounding wa-ter. Inside is spongy flesh made of a gelatin-like sub-stance capable of absorbing large amounts of water to survive months of drought. A waxy coating covers its skin, slowing the perspiration of water. Thorny spines protrude from it, deterring hungry animals while simul-taneously providing them shade. Most importantly, the needles serve as the succulent's power plant, perform-ing the vital function of photosynthesis.

Saguaro cactus. "Monarch of the Sonoran Desert." Icon of the southwest. Not only does it enhance the desert's scenic value, it is an ecological keystone species, one that plays an integral role in maintaining the structure of its ecological community. A decline in saguaro pop-ulation would not only diminish the area's scenic value and cause devastation to a unique and iconic species, it would cripple a lively community trying to beat the odds by surviving in the desert. The same odds the saguaro has managed to overcome for centuries.

Musical cacti

When to Go
Rincon Mountain District (East) is open every day of the year from 5am until right around sunset. Tucson Mountain District (West) is open daily from sunrise to sunset. You can bike or hike in either unit at any time. Visitor Centers are open daily from 9am to 5pm except for Christmas Day. Most visitors come to the park between October and May, when weath-er is most comfortable. The desert can erupt with colorful wildflowers after a wet winter. But not all winters are wet. Saguaros bloom at night during the month of May and into June. Call the park to verify wildflower blooms before setting out.

Transportation & Airports
Public transportation is not available to or around the park. Tucson International Airport (TUS) is locat-ed along the southern outskirts of the city, less than 20 miles from either unit.

Directions
The park consists of two separate districts, one east and one west of downtown Tucson.

Rincon Mountain District/East Unit (3693 S Old Spanish Trail): From I-10, take Exit 275 (Houghton Rd). Head north on Houghton Rd for about 8 miles. Turn right at E Escalante Rd. Continue east for 2 miles before turning left onto Old Spanish Rd, which leads into the park.

Tucson Mountain District/West Unit (2700 N Kin-ney Road): Heading southeast on I-10 toward Tuc-son, take Exit 242 (Avra Valley Rd). Head west on Avra Valley Rd about 5 miles. Turn left at N Sandario Rd and continue south for 9 miles. Turn left at N Kinney Rd, which leads into the park. (Consider re-turning to Tucson via Gates Pass Road; it's extremely scenic, with saguaro, pullouts, hiking trails, etc.)

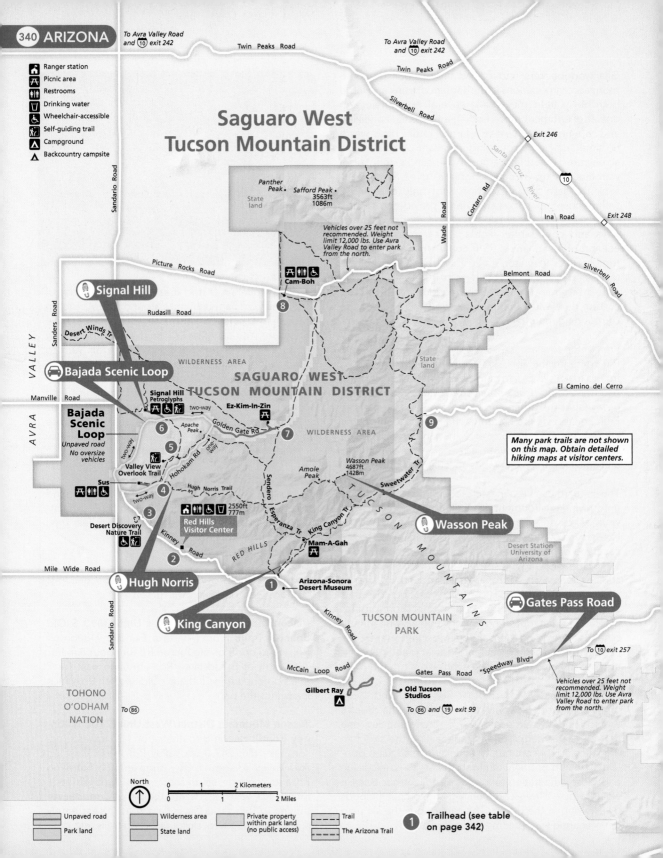

340 ARIZONA

To Avra Valley Road and ⑩ exit 242

To Avra Valley Road and ⑩ exit 242

Twin Peaks Road

Twin Peaks Road

Silverbell Road

Exit 246

⑩

Legend
- Ranger station
- Picnic area
- Restrooms
- Drinking water
- Wheelchair-accessible
- Self-guiding trail
- Campground
- Backcountry campsite

Saguaro West
Tucson Mountain District

Panther Peak

Safford Peak
3563ft
1086m

State land

Sandario Road

Vehicles over 25 feet not recommended. Weight limit 12,000 lbs. Use Avra Valley Road to enter park from the north.

Wade Road

Cortaro Rd

Santa Cruz River

Ina Road

Exit 248

Picture Rocks Road

Cam-Boh

⑧

Belmont Road

Silverbell Road

Signal Hill

Rudasill Road

Desert Winds Tr.

WILDERNESS AREA

State land

El Camino del Cerro

Bajada Scenic Loop

Manville Road

Signal Hill Petroglyphs

two-way

Ez-Kim-In-Zin

SAGUARO WEST TUCSON MOUNTAIN DISTRICT

⑨

Bajada Scenic Loop
Unpaved road
No oversize vehicles

Golden Gate Rd

⑥

Apache Peak

one-way

⑦

WILDERNESS AREA

Many park trails are not shown on this map. Obtain detailed hiking maps at visitor centers.

AVRA VALLEY

two-way

⑤

Valley View Overlook Trail

Amole Peak

Wasson Peak
4687ft
1428m

Sweetwater Tr.

Sus

⑤

Hohokam Rd

two-way

④

Hugh Norris Trail

Sendero Esperanza Tr

King Canyon Tr

TUCSON MOUNTAINS

Wasson Peak

Desert Discovery Nature Trail

③

2550ft
777m

Red Hills Visitor Center

Desert Station University of Arizona

Mile Wide Road

Kinney Road

②

Mam-A-Gah

RED HILLS

Hugh Norris

①

Arizona-Sonora Desert Museum

Gates Pass Road

King Canyon

Kinney Road

TUCSON MOUNTAIN PARK

To ⑩ exit 257

Sandario Road

McCain Loop Road

Gates Pass Road

"Speedway Blvd"

TOHONO O'ODHAM NATION

To ⑧⑥

Gilbert Ray

Old Tucson Studios

Vehicles over 25 feet not recommended. Weight limit 12,000 lbs. Use Avra Valley Road to enter park from the north.

To ⑧⑥ and ⑲ exit 99

North
↑

0   1   2 Kilometers
0   1   2 Miles

Legend
- Unpaved road
- Park land
- Wilderness area
- State land
- Private property within park land (no public access)
- Trail
- The Arizona Trail

① Trailhead (see table on page 342)

Regions

Two park regions are separated by Tucson. Tucson Mountain District is west of the city. This small mountain range is made of volcanic rock and its highest point is Wasson Peak (4,687 ft). Rincon Mountain District is on the east side of Tucson. It's about twice the size and elevation of its western counterpart. Rincon is another relatively small mountain range made of volcanic rock that has been heavily eroded over the years. Its highest peak is Mica Mountain (8,666 ft). Each region has a visitor center, picnic areas, a scenic loop drive, and many miles of hiking trails.

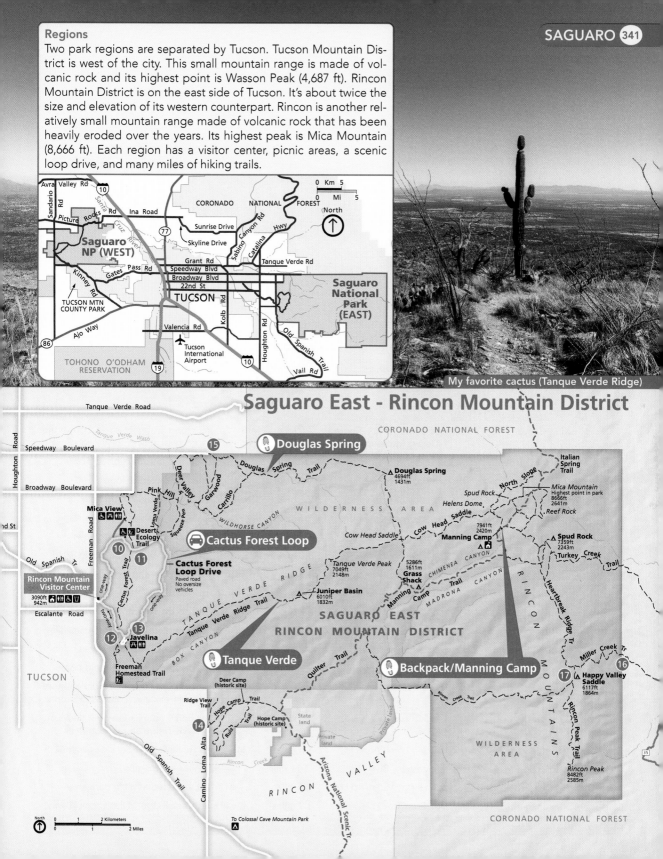

My favorite cactus (Tanque Verde Ridge)

Saguaro East - Rincon Mountain District

Signal Hill

Saguaro Hiking Trails (Distances are roundtrip unless noted otherwise)

	Name	Location (# on map)	Length	Difficulty Rating & Notes
Tucson Mountain District	King Canyon - ⛰	Across from Arizona–Sonora Desert Museum (1)	7.0 miles	M/S – 2.4-mile loop up the wash and down the trail or trek up switchbacks to Wasson Peak
	Cactus Garden	Red Hills Visitor Center (2)	0.1 mile	E – Self-guided introduction to plants
	Desert Discovery	Kinney Road (3)	0.5 mile	E – Self-guided loop
	Hugh Norris - ⛰	Bajada Loop Drive (4)	9.8 miles	S – Great hike to Wasson Peak
	Valley View Overlook - ⛰	Bajada Loop Drive (5)	0.8 mile	E/M – Cross two washes, ascend a ridge
	Signal Hill	Signal Hill Picnic Area (6)	0.5 mile	E – Passes numerous petroglyphs
	Cactus Wren - ⛰	Signal Hill Picnic Area (6)	3.0 miles	E – Flat, through washes to Sandario Road
	Sendero Esperanza - ⛰	Golden Gate Road (7)	8.2 miles	M – Cross Hugh Norris and King Canyon Trails
	Cam-Boh	Pictured Rocks Road (8)	5.4 miles	M – Leads to a small network of trails
	Sweetwater - ⛰	End of Camino del Cerro (9)	6.8 miles	M – Leads to the top of Wasson Peak
Rincon Mountain District	Desert Ecology - ⛰	Cactus Forest Drive (10)	0.3 mile	E – Paved trail, explores plant and animal life
	Cactus Forest	Cactus Forest Drive (11)	5.2 miles	E – Open to hikers, bikers, and horse riders
	Freeman Homestead - ⛰	Cactus Forest Drive (12)	1.0 mile	E – Self-guided, large saguaro, old home
	Tanque Verde - ⛰	Javelina Picnic Area (13)	18.0 miles	S – 6.9 miles to Juniper Basin Camp, continues to Tanque Verde Peak and Cow Head Saddle
	Hope Camp	Camino Loma Alta (14)	5.6 miles	M – Used by horse riders • Provides views of Tanque Verde Ridge and Rincon Peak
	Ridge View	Camino Loma Alta (14)	1.6 miles	M – Leads to views of rocky side canyons
	Douglas Spring - ⛰	Speedway Blvd (15)	16+ mi	M – 5.9 miles to Douglas Spring Camp
	Miller Creek	North Happy Valley Rd (16)	4.4 miles	M – Not accessed at main park area
	Rincon Peak - ⛰	Spur Trail (17)	3.3 miles	S – Via Heartbreak Ridge/Miller Creek (1-way)

Difficulty Ratings: E = Easy, M = Moderate, S = Strenuous

Camping & Lodging

Unless you go backpacking, you cannot spend the night in the park. There are no drive-in campgrounds or lodging facilities, but there are many options in and around Tucson.

Driving

Each unit has a well-maintained scenic drive. These stretches of road have become their primary attractions. In the west, you'll find 5-mile **Bajada Loop Drive**. It's a graded unpaved road (suitable for any vehicle) that passes through dense saguaro forest. In the east, motorists circle around 8-mile **Cactus Forest Drive**, a one-way, paved road that passes through a well-preserved desert ecosystem. Cyclists, runners, and walkers flock to Cactus Forest Drive early in the day, before the road opens and things heat up. Both roads provide access to the most popular trailheads, picnic areas, and desert vistas.

Hiking & Backpacking

Deserts offer some of the most interesting scenery for avid hikers to enjoy. You'll find trails ranging from short and flat paved loops to long-distance, rugged paths along steep, barren mountain slopes. Most of **Tucson Mountain District's trails** are short and relatively easy. **Desert Discovery Trail**, located just off Kinney Road, south of Bajada Loop Drive, is a popular loop. It has several exhibits discussing the region's native plants and animals. If you'd like to hike to the West Unit's tallest point, **Wasson Peak**, you have a couple thigh-burning choices. The easiest route is to take Sendero Esperanza Trail (located on Golden Gate Road) to its intersection with Hugh Norris Trail. Head east on Hugh Norris to the peak. This route is about 4.1 miles (one-way). Alternatively, King Canyon Trail, located near Arizona–Sonora Desert Museum, is slightly shorter but more strenuous. It's a 3.5-mile (one-way) hike to the peak, beginning with a nice gradual ascent before a series of switchbacks lead to the intersection with Hugh Norris Trail. Hugh Norris is the longest route, but also my favorite. Better yet, arrange a shuttle or cache a vehicle and go up King Canyon and down Hugh Norris. That's my preference. If, like many, you'd rather go down the steeper trail, reverse it.

Signal Hill Picnic Area, just off Golden Gate Road, has a short trail to more than 200 ancient petroglyphs (and some graffiti—don't do that!). The meaning behind these images is left to your interpretation. It connects to **Cactus Wren Trail**, which is also pleasant and easy. As you walk through the desert, imagine what stories these ancient scribes wanted to tell their descendants.

Posing with a friend atop Wasson Peak :)

Rincon Mountain District contains a much larger network of trails and six backcountry campgrounds. Several short and easy trails begin along Cactus Forest Drive. **Cactus Forest Trail** runs north–south, bisecting the loop drive. This is an excellent flat hike to see saguaro cactus up close. Another pleasant hike is **Desert Ecology Trail**, located at the southernmost point of Cactus Forest Drive. This paved path has signs describing plants and animals you might see during your visit. North of Cactus Forest Drive is a complex maze-like network of trails. Combining several short trails allows a multitude of loop routes through the foothills. You can also explore the park's wilderness area. It is most easily accessed via **Tanque Verde** or **Douglas Spring Trails**, but it's also accessible from the east via **Middle Creek Trail** through Coronado National Forest. A nice day-hike is to follow **Douglas Spring Trail** to a spur to Bridal Wreath Falls. It's less than a six-mile trip. Douglas Spring Trailhead is popular with limited parking.

Backpackers can camp in Rincon Mountain Wilderness Area at one of six designated backcountry campgrounds scattered throughout the mountains. The closest camp is a 4-mile hike along Miller Creek Trail. **Manning Camp** (13 miles via Douglas Spring Trail) is the most desirable destination, thanks to reliable water and fun trails to explore. It gets cold up there at 8,000-feet elevation in winter and is comfortable in summer (about 20 degrees Fahrenheit cooler than at the visitor center). Backpackers must obtain a backcountry permit ($8 per person per night) through recreation.gov up to six months in advance.

The Sonoran Desert provides ample terrain for exploration, but it doesn't offer shade or water. Pace yourself and drink plenty of water. Backpackers should dress in layers and discuss where to find reliable water sources with a park ranger prior to departure.

It took a long time to grow that bulb

Biking

Cyclists are limited to the park's roadways. Off-road and on-trail riding is not permitted. Road cyclists enjoy riding through saguaro forests surrounding the East Unit's 8-mile Cactus Forest Drive. It's twisty, hilly, narrow, and can become congested during peak tourism season (November–March). If you can get there early, it'll be much more enjoyable, but, since the road is one-way, it's rarely bad. The lone opportunity for mountain bike trail riding is a 2.5-mile stretch of Cactus Forest Trail that bisects Cactus Forest Drive. It's not a trail, but mountain bikers can also pedal the West Unit's Bajada Loop Drive. It's a 5-mile loop road, traversing a small portion of Tucson Mountain's lower elevations.

Horseback Riding

Horses, mules, and donkeys are allowed on more than 100 miles of trails, so don't be startled if you come face-to-face with a donkey while hiking through the desert. Stock is also permitted to camp at designated backcountry campgrounds (with a permit from Rincon Mountain Visitor Center). Don't worry if you don't have your own stock (or aren't bringing them with you). Cocoraque Ranch (520.405.5884, cocoraque. com) and Tucson Mountain Stables (520.310.2001, tucsonmountainstables.com) operate near the West Unit. All Around Trail Horses (520.298.8980, allaroundtrail-horses.com), Rocking K Ranch (520.248.2454, rock-ingkranchstablesandboarding.com), and Houston's Horseback Riding (520.298.7450, tucsonhorsebackrid-ing.com) operate near the East Unit.

Visitor Centers & Museums

Red Hills Visitor Center (520.733.5158) is located in the West Unit, on Kinney Road near the south entrance. This is a beautiful building offering up sweeping views of the nearby Tucson Mountains. Here you'll find exhibits, a bookstore, and plenty of information to help get you oriented to the area. A short introductory film is played at regularly scheduled times throughout the day. And, of course, restrooms are available. It's open every day except Christmas from 9am to 5pm. (Also located on Kinney Road near the park boundary is the popular **Arizona–Sonora Desert Museum**.) East Unit's **Rincon Mountain Visitor Center** (520.733.5153) features exhibits, a bookstore, brochures, maps, restrooms, and an updated short film that is quite good. It's also open daily, every day except Christmas, from 9am until 5pm. The most useful resource found at either visitor center is their friendly staff. Park rangers are ready to answer your questions and provide activity suggestions based on how much time you have to explore the unit, and occasionally they lead guests on walks or talks about the park.

Ranger Programs & For Kids

Many visitors have a difficult time appreciating the desert, so attending a ranger program is a good way to absorb a bit of knowledge and enthusiasm for this desolate region. Ranger-led walks, talks, and interpretive programs (offered November–March) explore the park's history, geology, and ecology, ranging from morning birdwatching tours to evening stargazing. Visitors should check online or at a visitor center for a current schedule of events.

Children (ages 5–12) are welcome to participate in the Junior Ranger Program. Complete an activity booklet (free at either visitor center or download it from the park website), aided by the contents of a Discovery Pack, to receive a ranger badge. Discovery Packs are available for check-out at either visitor center with an adult's valid driver's license or picture ID. Children (ages 6–11) can sign up for a 3-day Junior Ranger Camp held in June. It costs $30 per child and applications are available at the park website. Call (520) 733–5153 for additional information.

Saguaro Cactus

Saguaro is an icon of the American southwest and giant of the Sonoran Desert. Almost human-like, the saguaro stands tall, towering above the arid and rocky ground, arms extended in a welcoming manner. These are the redwoods of the desert, offering protection and provisions for a wealth of life in a seemingly inhospitable landscape. Their roots fan out from the trunk as far as it is tall, sopping up water with a voracious thirst. In a single rainfall, a saguaro may soak up as much as 200 gallons of water, enough to last an entire year. They can live to be more than 150 years old, 50 feet tall, and weigh up to 8 tons. That makes the saguaro not only the largest cactus in the United States, but the largest living organism in the Sonoran Desert.

In contrast, its life begins as a tiny black seed, no bigger than the head of a pin. Each year a single saguaro produces tens of thousands of seeds, which fall to the desert floor and try to take root in one of the hottest and driest regions on the continent. Hungry birds and rodents snack on these miniscule morsels. Even with an abundance of seeds, the chances of a saguaro reaching adulthood is on par with being struck by lightning. Germination odds increase if a seed falls beneath trees like palo verde and mesquite, where there's shade from the summer heat, insulation from the winter cold, and safe harbor from the constant threat of hungry animals.

Seeds that take root grow ever so slowly. After one year a saguaro may measure one-quarter inch, one foot after 15 years, and after 30 years of life in the desert, a saguaro finally begins to flower and produce fruit. There can be as many as 100 flowers on a single cactus, each blooming at sunset. They are pollinated in the night by white-winged doves, long-nosed bats, honeybees, and moths. By the following afternoon the flower has wilted in the direct rays of desert sun. Flowers turn to fruit and by June they have ripened. Each fruit contains as many as 2,000 seeds that fall to the desert floor in hope of becoming a "Sentinel of the Sonoran Desert."

Flora & Fauna
Saguaros aren't the only show in town. More than 25 species of cacti are found here. Less famous succulents include hedgehog, cholla, and prickly pear. Be careful not to be pricked by a cholla cactus. Its barbed needles are difficult to remove and extremely painful. There's also plenty of creosote bush, the most common North American desert plant. In lower elevations of the West Unit, you can find animals like desert tortoise and coyote. East Unit's higher elevations provide habitat for larger animals. Black bear, white-tailed deer, and Mexican spotted owl live among Douglas fir and ponderosa pine growing on the high mountain slopes. Birdwatchers appreciate more than 200 species of birds that live in or visit the region. One of the most sought-after birds is the elf owl. It's often seen roosting in small saguaro cavities drilled out by Gila woodpeckers or gilded flickers. High mountains also provide an opportunity to see birds not commonly found on the desert floor, like red-faced warbler and golden eagle.

Pets & Accessibility
Pets are limited to the park's roadways, picnic areas (except Mam-A-Gah), and paved trails (Desert Ecology

Hawks appreciate the saguaro

and Desert Discovery). They must be kept on a leash (less than six feet), and are prohibited from all other trails, the backcountry, and both visitor centers (except for service animals). If you choose to bring your pet and are looking to go for a walk, consider Mica View Dirt Road, Desert Ecology Trail, or Cactus Forest Loop Road in the East Unit. Bajada Loop Drive, Golden Gate Road, and Desert Discovery Trail are your best options in the West Unit.

Both visitor centers are accessible to individuals in wheelchairs. Desert Ecology Trail in Rincon Mountain District and Desert Discovery Trail in Tucson Mountain District are the only accessible trails. A few ranger-led programs are accessible.

Weather
There are a few reasons why so many Americans retire in Arizona. Mild winters is one of them. Winter average high temperatures are about 65°F before dropping into the 40s°F at night. Summers are hot and dry. Daytime highs commonly exceed 100°F in the shade. Summer visitors must remember to pack sunglasses, plenty of water, and sunscreen.

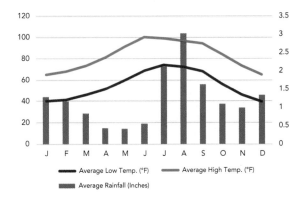

Sunset at Gates Pass Road

Tips & Recommendations

Saguaro cactus don't operate on visitors' schedules. Most guests arrive between November and April. However, saguaro cactus typically bloom in May and June. (They bloom nocturnally.) If you do visit in summer, it's a good idea to explore the park early in the morning or evening, and make sure you carry plenty of water regardless when you arrive.

The two park units are roughly 30 miles apart, one-hour drive by car. Sure, you can visit both of them easy enough on the same day, but you're far better off dedicating at least one day to each unit.

While Saguaro East (Rincon Mountain District) is considerably larger than Saguaro West (Tucson Mountain District), the eastern unit will feel smaller, because most people only visit a very small portion of the district (Cactus Forest Drive).

East of Cactus Forest Drive is a vast network of trails. Backpackers should strongly consider hiking to Manning Camp (where you'll find the most reliable water source) and some fun trails. Arrange a shuttle (or cache

a car) and you can plan a nice one-way backpacking itinerary. Just remember it's about 20 degrees cooler in the high country compared to the low. It can snow up there in winter. You have to watch the weather. Come prepared with plenty of layers and an appropriate sleeping bag. Know where water sources are (Manning Camp may be the only reliable source). If you're doing an out-and-back on the same trail, consider caching water along the way, so you have plenty on your return trip. If you're going to backpack in the Rincon Mountains to escape the summer heat, be prepared for a sweaty climb to reach them. Start your trek early, so you can get out of the completely exposed foothills as soon as possible.

Bring sunscreen. Don't overexert yourself. Hiking in extreme heat can be deadly. Even in January, daytime highs sneak into the 90s°F. And, if you're hiking in summer, know your body, listen to it, and be sure to carry plenty of water. Hiking in the morning/evening is always a good idea here.

There are no campgrounds within the park, but there are a variety of public and private camping options nearby, like Gilbert Ray Campground (Pima County Parks and Rec), Tucson/Lazydays KOA Resort (koa.com), Desert Trails RV Park (deserttrailsrvpark.com) Molino Basin Campground (recreation.gov), Sabino Canyon Campground (recreation.gov), and Whitetail Campground (recreation.gov).

Easy Hikes (West): Cactus Wren (3 miles), Signal Hill (0.5), Cactus Garden (0.1)
Easy Hikes (East): Desert Ecology (0.3 mile), Freeman Homestead (1)
Moderate/Strenuous Hikes (West): Hugh Norris (9.8 miles), King Canyon (7 miles to Wasson Peak, just doing the short hike through the wash is enjoyable as well), Valley View Overlook (0.8)
Moderate/Strenuous Hikes (East): Tanque Verde (18 miles), Rincon Peak (3.3), Douglas Spring (varies)
Family Activities: Become Junior Rangers, go find your favorite saguaro cactus!
Rainy Day Activities: Arizona–Sonora Desert Museum, explore Tucson
History Enthusiasts: Signal Hill, Freeman Homestead
Sunrise/Sunset Spots: Gates Pass is a great place for sunset but all you need is a good cactus and a clear view to the horizon and there are a bunch of setups like that. Find one and you can have your own special Saguaro National Park sunset or sunrise. Remember the gates at Cactus Forest Drive and Bajada Loop (Hohokam Road) close overnight.

Beyond the Park...

Dining (in Tucson)

Tumerico • (520) 240-6947
2526 E 6th St • tumerico.com

The Little One • (520) 612-9830
151 Stone Ave • thelittleoneaz.com

Banhdicted • (520) 389-8128
1980 W Orange Grove Rd
banhdicted.com

Street Taco and Beer
58 W Congress St • (520) 269-6266

Tito and Pep • (520) 207-0116
4122 E Speedway Blvd
titoandpep.com

Opa's Best • (520) 838-0687
4590 E Broadway Blvd
opasbest.com

Zemam's Too • (520) 882-4955
119 E Speedway Blvd
zemamsrestaurants.com

Bison Witches • (520) 740-1541
326 N 4th Ave
bisonwitchestucson.com

KUKAI • (520) 367-5982
267 S Avenida del Convento
eatkukai.com

Seis Kitchen • (520) 622-2002
130 S Avenida del Convento
seiskitchen.com

Urban Fresh • (520) 792-9355
73 E Pennington St
urbanfreshtucson.com

Raptor Canyon Café
75 E Pennington St • (520) 336-5698
raptorcanyoncafe.com

Baja Café • (520) 495-4772
7002 E Broadway Blvd
bajacafetucson.com

HUB Ice Creamery • (520) 207-8201
266 E Congress St
hubdowntown.com

Grocery Stores

Albertsons • (520) 751-7699
9595 E Broadway Blvd

Walmart • (520) 918-0087
2711 S Houghton Rd

Safeway • (520) 663-0009
9050 E Valencia Rd

Fry's • (520) 348-7125
1795 W Valencia Rd

Safeway • (520) 792-0083
2140 W Grant Rd

Walmart • (520) 573-3777
1650 W Valencia Rd

Costco • (520) 791-7340
1650 E Tucson Marketplace Blvd

Lodging & Camping

Lodge on the Desert
306 N Alvernon Way • (520) 320-2000
lodgeonthedesert.com

Hotel McCoy • (844) 782-9622
720 W Silverlake Rd
hotelmccoy.com

Canyon Ranch • (520) 749-9655
8600 E Rockcliff Rd
canyonranch.com

Hacienda del Sol • (520) 299-1501
5501 N Hacienda Del Sol Rd
haciendadelsol.com

Hotel Congress • (520) 622-8848
311 E Congress St
hotelcongress.com

Adobe Rose Inn • (520) 318-4644
940 N Olsen Ave
adoberoseinn.com

Arizona Inn • (520) 325-1541
2200 E Elm St
arizonainn.com

Rincon Country East RV Resort
8989 E Escalante Rd
rinconcountry.com • (520) 886-8431

Winter Haven RV Park
2121 S Pantano Rd • (520) 298-8024
tucsonmeadows.com

Far Horizons • (520) 296-1234
555 N Pantano Rd • cal-am.com

Rincon Country West RV Resort
4555 S Mission Rd • (520) 294-5608
rinconcountry.com

Sentinel Peak RV Park
450 N Grande Ave • (520) 495-0175
sentinelpeakrv.com

Lazydays KOA
5151 S Country Club Rd
koa.com • (520) 799-3701

Festivals

Bisbee 1000 Stair Climb • Oct
bisbee1000.org • Bisbee

All Souls Procession • Nov
allsoulsprocession.org • Tucson

Attractions

Chiricahua National Monument
*Absolutely wonderful hoodoos
and goofy rock formations*
12856 E Rhyolite Creek Rd, Willcox
nps.gov/chir • (520) 824-3560

Coronado National Forest
Sabino Canyon and more
5900 N Sabino Canyon Rd

Coronado National Memorial
*Only a few miles of trails but
there's a nice overlook*
4101 W Mont. Canyon Rd, Hereford
nps.gov/coro • (520) 366-5515

Catalina State Park
Plenty of saguaros here
1570 N Oracle Rd, Tucson
azstateparks.com

Picacho Peak State Park
Peak visible from Tucson
azstateparks.com

Kartchner Caverns State Park
Daily tours of 2-mile cave
2980 S Hwy 90, Benson
azstateparks.com • (520) 586-4100

Casa Grande National Monument
Preserved Hohokam ruins
1100 W Ruins Dr, Coolidge
nps.gov/cagr • (520) 723-3172

Organ Pipe Cactus National Mon
UNESCO Biosphere Reserve
10 Organ Pipe Dr, Ajo
nps.gov/orpi • (520) 387-6849

Tumacacori National Hist Park
1891 I-19 Frontage Rd, Tumacacori
nps.gov/tuma • (520) 377-5060

Lost Dutchman State Park
Near Superstition Mtns (great!)
6109 N Apache Tr, Apache Jct
azstateparks.com

Oracle State Park
4,000-acre wildlife refuge
3820 E Wildlife Dr, Oracle
azstateparks.com

Agua Caliente Regional Park
Milagrosa Canyon (strenuous)
12325 E Roger Rd • (520) 724-5000

Patagonia Lake State Park
Fishing, paddling, camping
400 Patagonia Lake Rd, Nogales
azstateparks.com

Tucson Petting Zoo • (520) 399-6555
2405 W Wetmore Rd
tucsonpettingzoo.com

Old Tucson • (520) 883-0100
Used to be a movie set
201 Kinney Rd • oldtucson.com

Tombstone Courthouse SHP
223 E Toughnut St, Tombstone
asstateparks.com

AZ-Sonora Desert Museum
Zoo, aquarium, garden, and more
2021 N Kinney Rd
desertmuseum.org

Foolish Pleasure Hot Air Balloon
8002 W Cortaro Farms Rd
foolishpleasureaz.com

Skydive Marana • (520) 682-4441
11700 W Avra Valley Rd, Marana
skydivemarana.com

Tohono Chul Park
7366 N Paseo del Norte
tohonochul.org • (520) 742-6455

Kitt Peak Observatory Visitor Cen
AZ-386, Sierra Vista
visitkittpeak.org • (520) 318-8726

San Xavier del Bac Mission
*Constructed in 1791, oldest
European structure in Arizona*
1950 W San Xavier Rd
sanxaviermission.org

International Wildlife Museum
4800 W Gates Pass Rd
thewildlifemuseum.org

Flandrau Science Center
1601 E University Blvd
flandrau.org • (520) 621-4516

Pima Air & Space Museum
6000 E Valencia Rd
pimaair.org • (520) 574-0462

Tucson Museum of Art
140 N Main Ave • (520) 624-2333
tucsonmuseumofart.org

Center for Creative Photography
1030 N Olive Rd
ccp.arizona.edu • (520) 621-7968

The Mini-Time Machine
Museum of Miniatures
4455 E Camp Lowell Dr
theminitimemachine.org

Colossal Cave Mountain Park
16721 E Old Spanish Trail, Vail
colossalcave.com • (520) 647-7275

Biosphere 2
32540 S Biosphere Rd, Oracle
biosphere2.org

World War II
Valor in the Pacific NM
(Tule Lake)

Hagerman Fossil
Beds NM

Craters of the
NM & PRES

Minidoka NHS

City of Rocks N RES

Golden Spike NHS

SOUTHWEST

SALT LAKE CITY
Timpanogos Cave NM

CARSON CITY

NEVADA

UTAH

Devils Postpile NM

Great Basin NP

IA

Bryce
Canyon NP

Capitol Reef NP

anyon NP
oia NP

Cedar Breaks NM

Manzanar NHS

Zion NP

Glen Canyon NRA

Tule Springs
Fossil Beds
NM

Pipe Spring NM

Rainbow Bridge NM

Death Valley NP

LAS
VEGAS

Grand Canyon NP

ávez NM

Navajo NM

Castle Mountains NM

Lake Mead NRA

Canyo

Mojave

Sa
Mo NRA

SOUTHWEST

Wupatki NM

Hubb

Sunset Crater Volcano NM

LOS ANGELES

Walnut Cany

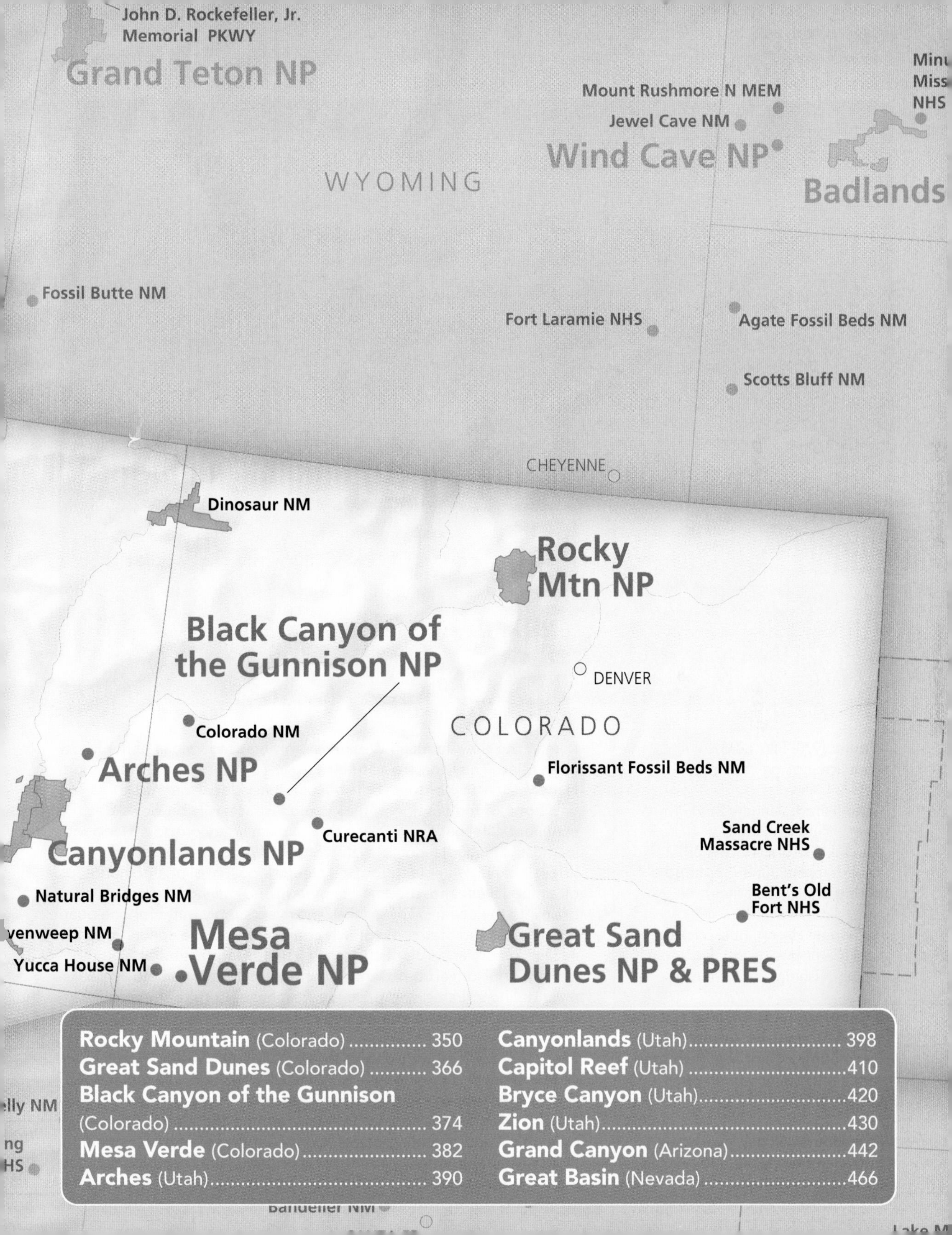

John D. Rockefeller, Jr.
Memorial PKWY

Grand Teton NP

Mount Rushmore N MEM

Jewel Cave NM

Wind Cave NP

Minu
Miss
NHS

WYOMING

Badlands

Fossil Butte NM

Fort Laramie NHS

Agate Fossil Beds NM

Scotts Bluff NM

CHEYENNE

Dinosaur NM

Rocky
Mtn NP

Black Canyon of
the Gunnison NP

DENVER

Colorado NM

COLORADO

Arches NP

Florissant Fossil Beds NM

Curecanti NRA

Sand Creek
Massacre NHS

Canyonlands NP

Natural Bridges NM

Bent's Old
Fort NHS

venweep NM

Mesa
Verde NP

Great Sand
Dunes NP & PRES

Yucca House NM

lly NM

ng

HS

Bandelier NM

Lake M

Rocky Mountain

Sky Pond Trail

Phone: (970) 586-1206
Website: nps.gov/romo

Established: January 26, 1915
Size: 265,828 Acres
Annual Visitors: 4.5 Million
Peak Season: June–September
Hiking Trails: 355 Miles

Activities: Hiking, Backpacking, Rock Climbing, Biking, Horseback Riding, Fishing, Snowshoeing

5 Campgrounds: $30/night (summer), $20/night (winter, no water)
Backcountry Camping: Permitted with a Backcountry Use Permit
Lodging: None

Park Hours: All day, every day
Entrance Fee: $25/25/15 per day (car/motorcycle/individual)

Romancing the American West inevitably leads to visions of the Rocky Mountains. They form a natural barrier, stretching 2,700 miles from New Mexico to northern British Columbia. Often referred to as the backbone of the continent, they could just as easily be viewed as the continent's lifeline. The Rockies are the main artery providing land with its most valuable resource: water. Snow collects in the rugged peaks. When it melts, water falls from the steep slopes, pooling into hundreds of alpine lakes, and streams become rivers, carving canyons as they drain into the oceans. These lakes and rivers supply water for one quarter of the United States, eventually coursing across the continent to the Pacific, Arctic, and Atlantic Oceans. Here in north-central Colorado, just a 2-hour drive from Denver, there's a collection of snowy peaks, meandering streams, and pristine lakes that epitomize the most grandiose Rocky Mountain images you can conjure.

The Rockies are as imposing as they are vast. Native Americans rarely ventured beyond the foothills. Some 6,000 years ago, Ute Indians, also known as Mountain People, were scattered throughout much of modern-day Utah and Colorado (primarily around the Grand Lake area), hunting elk and gathering plants. On the other side of the Continental Divide, Arapaho and Cheyenne lived on the plains, occasionally visiting the present-day Estes Park region to hunt. Natives dominated the area until the late 1700s. Both tribes were separated by a seemingly impenetrable barrier. A barrier they chose not to cross because food was bountiful and everything they needed was available right where they were.

Things changed following the Louisiana Purchase in 1803. Natives were moved to reservations and Americans moved in, but the Rockies failed to draw the public's attention until the gold rush of 1858. Boom towns of Denver, Boulder, and Golden were established, but mining was never very successful. Prospectors made at least one substantial discovery: the allure of the Rockies. Gold-seeking never panned out for Joel Estes either. He found a particularly beautiful location in a valley at the foot of the mountains where he hunted with his son to supply Denver's meat markets and subsidize his meager prospecting income. By 1860 he built cabins for farming and meat production, the humble beginnings of Estes Park.

In 1886, a 16-year-old boy named Enos Mills moved to Estes Park of his own accord. Enos sought what prospectors found by accident, the Rockies and life in the wilderness. In 1889 he met John Muir on a camping trip in California. Muir inspired the young man to study nature and practice conservation. Mills listened and turned his attention back to the Rockies, spending countless hours in the mountains and climbing Longs Peak more than 250 times. He established Longs Peak Inn where guests could attend trail school and be educated on the area's natural wonders. He wrote books and articles on the area's scenic value. The more time spent in the mountains, the more convinced he became that the region should be preserved for the enjoyment of the people. He needed to act because the buzz of sawmills' blades and sight of grazing cattle were closing in on his cherished landscapes.

In 1907, President Theodore Roosevelt appointed Mills to be a lecturer for the National Forest Service. An opportunity he used to spread ideas about conservation and to tell others about his beloved Rocky Mountains. Unlike parks before it, Rocky Mountain did not have a major railway lobbying its cause. Nevertheless, Mills remained dedicated to the park idea. He found allies in conservation groups like the Colorado Mountain Club. Denver Chamber of Commerce was convinced of the merits of a national park, too. Fueled by the potential for tourism and overwhelming public support, momentum was building, and in 1915 Congress approved legislation drafted by James Grafton Rogers, and President Woodrow Wilson signed it, creating Rocky Mountain National Park.

When to Go
The park is open all year. More than half of all visitors arrive between June and August. If you think Yellowstone is busy in summer, consider the fact Rocky Mountain receives just as many annual visitors but is one-eighth Yellowstone's size. September, when leaves begin to change color and elk can be heard bugling, is also popular. Escape the crowds by visiting in May or October, although Trail Ridge Road usually opens in late May and closes in mid-October. Many high elevation trails can be impassable to hikers without special equipment until well into June and again in October. Bear Lake Road is open year-round. The park is always busy in summer, but it's such a popular weekend destination that traveling early in the week often yields significantly smaller crowds. Weekends in Estes Park are usually marred with bumper-to-bumper traffic, approaching complete gridlock.

Transportation & Airports
Public transportation does not provide service to the park, but a **free shuttle** runs on Bear Lake Road between Beaver Meadows Visitor Center and Bear Lake Trailhead. There are three separate routes. Two connect Bear Lake area trailheads with Moraine Park and Glacier Basin Campgrounds. The third route ferries visitors between Estes Park Visitor Center and a central park and ride. Use the shuttles to help reduce traffic congestion (and eliminate worrying about finding a parking space). The closest airport is Denver International (DEN), about 80 miles away.

Directions
From Denver (64 miles): Take I-25 N toward Fort Collins. Exit onto CO-66. Turn left onto CO-66/Co Rd 30. It becomes US-36/CO-66. Continue through Estes Park, and follow signs to the park.

From the West (I-70): Traveling east on I-70, take exit 157 for CO-131 N toward Wolcott/Steamboat Springs. Turn left at CO-131 N/Bellyache Ridge Rd, and then another left onto CO-131 N/US-6 W. After crossing the Colorado River you'll come to a T-intersection, turn right onto County Rd 1/Trough Rd. Continue on County Rd 1 until it meets CO-9 N. Turn left and drive into Kremmling. As soon as you enter the small city, turn right onto Tyler Ave. After less than half a mile, turn right again onto US-40 E/Park Ave. US-40 follows the Colorado River to Granby. Before entering Granby, turn left onto US-34/Trail Ridge Road, which leads into the park to Grand Lake/East Entrance.

To Fort Collins

ROOSEVELT NATIONAL FOREST

To 14

Long Draw Road

Corral Creek Trailhead

Corral Creek

NPS/USFS

Long Draw

Mummy

14

Cameron Pass

RAWAH WILDERNESS
COLORADO

To Walden

STATE FOREST

NEOTA WILDERNESS

Long Draw Reservoir

Cache la Poudre River

Flatiron Mountain
12335ft
3760m

Lake Agnes

Michigan Lakes

Snow Lake

Thunder Pass

Thunder Mountain
12070ft
3679m

La Poudre Pass

Skeleton Gulch

Willow Creek

BOX CANYON

Mount Richthofen
12940ft
3944m

Tepee Mountain
12568ft
3831m

GRAND DITCH

LITTLE YELLOWSTONE

SKELETON GULCH

Trail Ridge Road

Poudre River Trail (WILD AND SCENIC RIVER)

Cache la Poudre River

Medicine Bow Curve

Fall River Pass

Alpine Ridge Trail

Chapin Creek

Chapin Creek Trailhead

Mount Cha
124.
375

ROUTT NATIONAL FOREST

Lead Mountain
12537ft
3821m

Divide

Continental

Site of Lulu City

Lake of the Clouds

Mount Cirrus
12797ft
3901m

Howard Mountain
12810ft
3904m

Specimen Mountain
12489ft
3807m

Trail Ridge Road

34

Ute Trail

Gore Range

Highest point on road
12183ft
3713m

Seasonal Snackbar

Alpine Visitor Center
11796ft
3595m

Lava Cliffs

One-way up only.

Tundra Communities Trailhead

Rock Cut

11

Forest Canyon

Mount Cumulus
12725ft
3879m

SHIPLER PARK

Colorado River

12mi
19km

Milner Pass
10758ft
3279m

Lake Irene

Poudre Lake

Iceberg Pass

Su
12
38

Red Mountain
11605ft
3537m

Red Mountain Trail

Mount Nimbus
12706ft
3873m

Mount Stratus
12480ft
3804m

Colorado River Trailhead

13

Road closed from here east to Many Parks Curve mid-October to Memorial Day

Beaver Ponds

Farview Curve

Timber Lake Trailhead

Beaver Creek

Continental Divide

Jackstraw Mountain
11704ft
3567m

Gorge Lakes

Arrowhead Lake

Azure Lake

Inkwell Lake

Doughnut Lake

Terra Tomah Mountain
12718ft
3876m

Mount Julian
12928ft
3940m

N E V E R

Parika Lake

DITCH GRAND

Baker Mountain
12397ft
3779m

Timber Creek

C

Holzwarth Historic Site

14

Timber Lake Trail

Timber Creek

Timber Lake

Mount Ida
12880ft
3926m

Highest Lake

Julian Lake

Mount Julian
12928ft
3940m

Forest Lake

THOMPSON RIVER

BIG

FOREST

S U M M E R

BAKER GULCH

Bowen Mountain
12524ft
3817m

Mineral Point
11488ft
3502m

Blue Lake

W I L D E R N E S S

Bowen Gulch

Continental Divide National Scenic Trail

Bowen Lake

ARAPAHO

NATIONAL FOREST

BLUE RIDGE

Bowen/Baker Trailhead

Coyote Valley Trailhead

15

KAWUNEECHE

Colorado River

LONG MEADOWS

8mi
13km

Onahu Creek

Onahu Trail

ROCKY MOUNTAIN

Hayden Lake

Nakai Peak
12216ft
3723m

Haynach Lake

Lonesome Lake

Sprague Glacier

Stones Peak
12922ft
3939m

Rainbow Lake

Onahu Trailhead

VALLEY

Green Mountain Trail

Big Meadows

Green Mountain Trailhead

Mount Patterson
11424ft
3482m

Snowdrift Peak
12274ft
3741m

Granite Falls

Tonahutu Creek

Continental Divide

National Trail

Scenic

BIGHORN FLA

Ptarmigan Lake

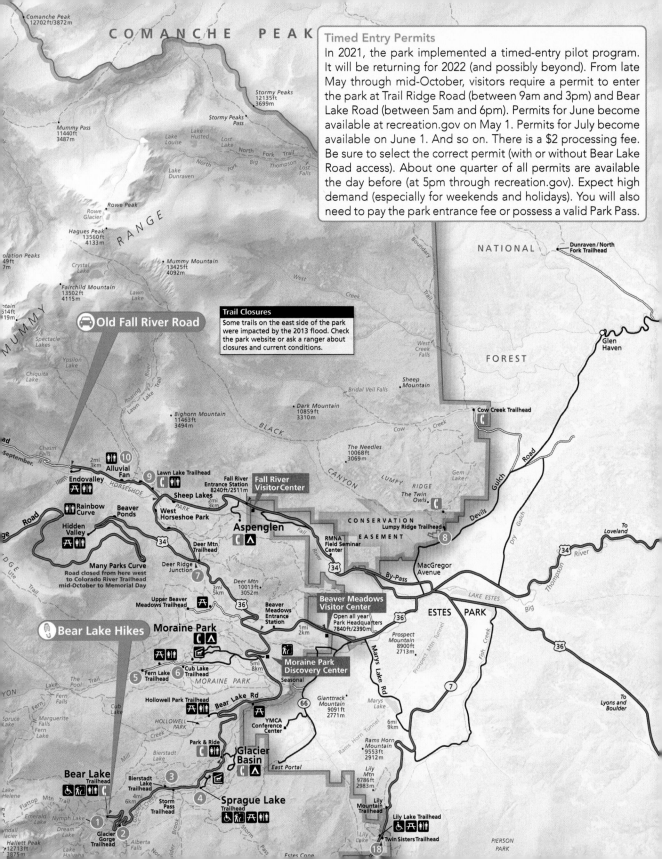

BOWEN GULCH

Bowen Lake

BLUE RIDGE

ARAPAHO

NATIONAL FOREST

Continental Divide National Scenic Trail

THE COLORADO RIVER VALLEY

8mi
13km

Onahu Creek

Onahu Trailhead

Green Mountain Trail

Green Mountain Trailhead

34

491

492

491

49

Supply Creek

Colorado River

Green Mtn
10313ft
3143 m

Harbison Meadows

Grand Lake
Entrance
Station

8720ft/2658 m
Open all year

**Kawuneeche
Visitor Center**

Tonahutu Spur
Trail

Tonahutu/
North Inlet
Trailheads

16

GRAND
LAKE

GRAND LAKE
8367ft
2550m

East Shore
Trailhead

West Portal

17

Lookout
tower

Shadow Mtn Trail

SHADOW
MOUNTAIN
LAKE

Pine Beach

Shadow
Mountain

Shadow
Mountain
Dam

Green
Ridge

Continental Divide

Colorado River

GREEN RIDGE

Cutthroat Bay
(group campground)

Stillwater

ARAPAHO NATIONAL RECREATION AREA

Table Mountain

Rainbow Bay

Sunset Point

Granby
Dam

Quinette Point

Rainbow
Bay

Willow
Creek
Reservoir

Willow Creek

Pump Canal

Willow Creek

34

Colorado River

Willow Creek

LAKE GRANBY

Knight Ridge Trail

Arapaho Bay

Roaring Fork

**Arapaho Bay-Roaring Fork Loop
Knight Ridge Trailhead**

Arapaho Bay-Moraine Loop

Arapaho Bay-Big Rock Loop

ARAPAHO

NATIONAL FOREST

Strawberry
Lake

Monarch
Lake

Continental Divide
National Scenic Trail

To Granby and 40

NATIONAL PARK

Snowdrift Peak
12274ft
3741m

Mount Patterson
11424ft
3482m

Big Meadows

Tonahutu Creek

Continental Divide

Granite Falls

Ptarmigan
Lake

Bench
Lake

North Inlet

Cascade
Falls

Summerland
Park

Pettingell
Lake

Lake
Nokoni

Ptarmigan Mountain
12324ft
3756m

Lake
Nanita

Andrews Peak
12565ft
3830m

Alva B. Adams Tunnel
(water diversion structure)

**East Inlet
Trailhead**

Adams
Falls

East Inlet

Shadow Mountain
10155ft
3095m

East Inlet

Lone
Pine
Lake

Mount Craig
12007 ft
3660m

Lake
Verna

Mount Bryant
11034ft
3363m

PARADISE PARK

Mount Adams
12121 ft
3694m

Adams
Lake

Columbine Creek

Mount Acoma
10508ft
3203m

Twin Peaks
11957ft
3644m

Watanga Mountain
12375ft
3772m

Knight Fork

Roaring Fork

I N D I A N

BIGHORN FLATS

Apiatan Mountain
10319ft
3145 m

North

| 0 | 1 | 2 | 3 Kilometers |

| 0 | 1 | 2 | 3 Miles |

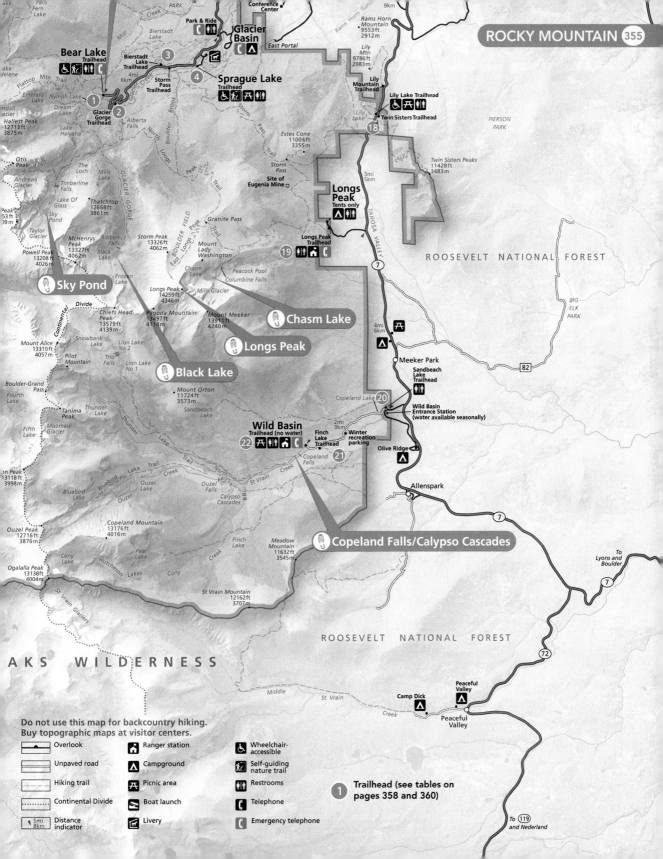

9km

Rams Horn Tunnel

Rams Horn Mountain 9553ft 2912m

Lily Mtn 9786ft 2983m

Conference Center

Park & Ride

Glacier Basin

East Portal

③

④

Bierstadt Lake

Bierstadt Lake Trailhead

Storm Pass Trailhead

Bear Lake Trailhead

Mill Creek

PARK

Bierstadt Lake

Lily Mountain Trailhead

Lily Lake Trailhead

Twin Sisters Trailhead

PIERSON PARK

Lily Lake

⑱

Falls Fern Lake

Flattop Mtn Trail

Emerald Lake

Nymph Lake

Dream Lake

①

Bear Lake Trailhead

Glacier Gorge Trailhead

②

Alberta Falls

Storm Creek

4mi 6km

North Boulder Brook

Glacier Creek

Lake Haiyaha

Peak Trail

Lake Helene

Hallett Peak 12713ft 3875m

Sprague Lake Trailhead

Storm Pass Trail

Estes Cone 11006ft 3355m

3mi 5km

Twin Sisters Peaks 11428ft 3483m

Otis Peak

Andrews Glacier

The Loch

Timberline Falls

Lake Of Glass

Thatchtop 12668ft 3861m

Storm Pass

Site of Eugenia Mine

Longs Peak Tents only

ROOSEVELT NATIONAL FOREST

Peak 53 ft 09 m

Taylor Glacier

Sky Pond

⛰ **Sky Pond**

McHenrys Peak 13327ft 4062m

Ribbon Falls

Storm Peak 13326ft 4062m

Granite Pass

Mount Lady Washington

Longs Peak Trailhead

⑲

TAHOSA VALLEY

7

BIG ELK PARK

Powell Peak 13208 ft 4026m

Black Lake

Frozen Lake

BOULDER FIELD

East Long

Longs Peak 14259ft 4346m

Peacock Pool

Columbine Falls

👣 **Chasm Lake**

4mi 6km

Continental Divide

Divide

Chiefs Head Peak 13579ft 4139m

Pagoda Mountain 13497ft 4114m

Mills Glacier

Mount Meeker 13911ft 4240m

👣 **Longs Peak**

ROOSEVELT NATIONAL FOREST

82

Mount Alice 13310ft 4057m

Pilot Mountain

Snowbank Lake

Lion Lake No 2

Lion Lake No 1

Trio Falls

👣 **Black Lake**

Mount Orton 11724ft 3573m

Meeker Park

Sandbeach Lake Trailhead

Boulder-Grand Pass

Fourth Lake

Tanima Peak

Thunder Lake

Sandbeach Lake

Copeland Lake

⑳

Wild Basin Entrance Station (water available seasonally)

Fifth Lake

Moomaw Glacier

Thunder Trail

Wild Basin Trailhead (no water)

㉒

Finch Lake Trailhead

Winter recreation parking

2mi 3km

Olive Ridge

n Peak 13118 ft 3998m

Bluebird Lake

Bluebird Creek

Ouzel Lake

Ouzel Falls

North Copeland Falls

㉑

St Vrain Creek

Allenspark

Ouzel Peak 12716ft 3876m

Ouzel Creek

Calypso Cascades

Finch Lake

7

Cony Lake

Pear Lake

Hutcheron Lakes

Cony Creek

Meadow Mountain 11632ft 3545m

👣 **Copeland Falls/Calypso Cascades**

To Lyons and Boulder

Ogalalla Peak 13138ft 4004m

St Vrain Glaciers

St Vrain Mountain 12162ft 3707m

7

AKS WILDERNESS

ROOSEVELT NATIONAL FOREST

72

Middle St Vrain

Camp Dick

Peaceful Valley

Peaceful Valley

5mi 8km

Do not use this map for backcountry hiking. Buy topographic maps at visitor centers.

To 119 and Nederland

▬ Overlook	⌂ Ranger station	♿ Wheelchair-accessible	
▭ Unpaved road	⛺ Campground	🚶 Self-guiding nature trail	
┄ Hiking trail	🏕 Picnic area	🚻 Restrooms	
┈ Continental Divide	⛵ Boat launch	☎ Telephone	
5mi 8km Distance indicator	🐎 Livery	🆘 Emergency telephone	

① Trailhead (see tables on pages 358 and 360)

Bighorn sheep near Trail Ridge Road

Rocky Mountain Camping (Fees are per night)

Name	Location	Open	Fee	Sites	Notes
Aspenglen*	Near Fall River Entrance on US-34 (Trail Ridge Rd)	late May–late Sept	$30	52	30-ft max RV length, Near visitor center
Glacier Basin*	Bear Lake Road, 6 miles south of Beaver Meadows	late May–mid-Sept	$30	150	35-ft max RV Length, Summer shuttle stop
Longs Peak	CO-7, 11 miles south of Beaver Meadows VC	late May–early Nov	$30	26	Tents Only, Access to Longs Peak Trailhead
Moraine Park*	Bear Lake Road, above Moraine Park	All Year	$30	244	40-ft max RV length, Summer shuttle stop
Timber Creek	US-34, 10 miles north of Grand Lake	late May–early Nov	$30	98	30-ft max RV length, Only west-side option

*Campsites can be reserved up to six months in advance at (877) 444-6777 or recreation.gov. Water is only available during the summer months at Moraine Park. Rates are reduced to $20/night when the water is off (starting mid-October). Cold running water and restrooms with flush toilets are available when the water is on. Otherwise vault toilets are available. All campsites have fire rings. Ice is sold at Aspenglen, Glacier Basin, and Moraine Park Campgrounds. Dump Stations are available at Glacier Basin, Moraine Park, and Timber Creek. No campgrounds have showers or hookups.

Backcountry	More than 250 sites are available with a backcountry/wilderness permit. A limited number of permits can be obtained in-person at Beaver Meadows Visitor Center's Backcountry Office or Kawuneeche Visitor Center. Online reservations are available through Pay.gov ($30 fee, May–Oct).
Group	Sites available for groups of 9–40 people at Glacier Basin in summer. Cost is $40–60 per night.

Camping

If you want to spend a night in the park, you're going to have to stay at a campground. There are five drive-in campgrounds. **Aspenglen, Moraine Park, and Glacier Basin Campgrounds** are located near Estes Park. Glacier Basin has lost much of its appeal because most trees were removed due to damage caused by the pine beetle. **Longs Peak Campground** is located south of Estes Park, just off CO-7. It features tent-only sites available on a first-come, first-served basis. It's also a good location to use as a base camp for those attempting to day hike to the summit of Longs Peak (14,259 ft), the highest point in the park. On the west side you'll find **Timber Creek Campground**. It has relatively little seclusion and shade (also because of the pine beetle), but it's the only frontcountry camping option on this side of the Continental Divide. Campgrounds often fill early during summer months. To guarantee a site, make a reservation at Aspenglen, Glacier Basin, or Moraine Park (up to six months in advance) at (877) 444-6777 or recreation.gov.

Backpackers have more than 250 backcountry sites to choose from with a backcountry permit ($30 fee). They are distributed fairly evenly between the western and eastern halves of the park. More information is provided in the backpacking section.

Driving

The park straddles the Continental Divide and driving it is all about **Trail Ridge Road** (US-34, usually closed until late May), the highest continuous paved road in the United States. This high-altitude thoroughfare unlocks the mountain range's rugged interior to motorists. Completed in 1932, the 48-mile road connects Estes Park and Grand Lake. Its grade never exceeds 7% while boasting an 8-mile continuous stretch above 11,000 feet elevation. Whether you enter from the east or west, you are sure to notice drastic changes in the ecosystem. First, you'll pass through forests of aspen and ponderosa pine. Climbing more than 4,000 feet, you cross the tree line and emerge on top of barren mountains covered with fragile alpine tundra. Overlooks and trailheads are dispersed along the scenic byway. From east to west, Many Parks Curve, Forest Canyon, and Rock Cut are pit-stops that should not be skipped. If you'd like to enjoy the Rockies at a slower pace (15 mph), take the one-way, mostly gravel **Old Fall River Road** (usually closed until late June/early July) from Endovalley to Alpine Visitor Center. Vehicles over 25 feet and trailers are prohibited from Old Fall River Road. Open/close dates change from year-to-year. Check online for current road status.

A marmot along Old Fall River Road

Hiking

No trip to the Rocky Mountains is complete without taking a little hike. This also means you're sure to run into plenty of hikers in the Rockies. Parking areas may fill up before eight in the morning. Bear Lake Hiker's Shuttle is often packed tight with like-minded individuals. But Bear Lake's incomparable beauty, vast collection of rugged lakes, meadows brimming with spring wildflowers, and majestic mountains make it easy to endure the crowds and congestion. The area is best explored by foot and all the most popular trailheads are located along Bear Lake Road. Shuttles may be cramped at times, but you should use them or get an early start. They're far better than circling the parking lots until a spot opens. Shuttles also allow easy hiking from one trailhead to another (as long as it's on the shuttle route). There's no denying the splendor of **Dream and Emerald Lakes** (most visitor's first and second destinations), but **Sky Pond** (a bit of scrambling required) and **Black Lake** are my favorites. Often times, the further you hike, the more seclusion (and beauty) you will find. A nice, fairly-long (roughly 10 miles) trek begins at Cub Lake Trailhead. Hike to **Cub Lake** and continue to The Pool, Fern Falls, and Odessa Lake, before returning to the shores of Bear Lake.

Alluvial Fan Trail, near the beginning of Old Fall River Road, is a short (and somewhat precarious) climb to dramatic views. Wild Basin is in the park's southeastern corner. The short hikes to **Copeland Falls** and **Calypso Cascades** are enjoyable. If you're feeling energetic, you can continue to three alpine lakes that lie close to the Continental Divide. The **Keyhole Route to Longs Peak** is another hike that requires plenty of energy. It's a 4,000-ft climb to the 14,259-ft summit and park's tallest peak. It begins at Longs Peak Trailhead off CO-7. From there it's 8 miles up, with the last 1.5 miles to the

View from Tundra Communities Trail

Rocky Mountain Hiking Trails (Distances are roundtrip)

	Name	Location (# on map)	Length	Difficulty Rating & Notes
South End of Bear Lake Road	Bear Lake - 🐾	Bear Lake (1)	0.5 mile	E – Self-guided nature loop
	Nymph, Dream, and Emerald Lakes - 🐾	Bear Lake (1)	1.0/2.2/3.6 miles	E – These three lakes are some of the most well-known and popular attractions in the park
	Lake Haiyaha	Bear Lake (1)	4.2 miles	M – Proof that even the lakes are rocky
	Flattop Mountain	Bear Lake (1)	8.8 miles	S – Hike to the mountain shouldering Hallet Peak
	Hallet Peak - 🐾	Bear Lake (1)	10.0 miles	S – Hike to the peak towering above Dream Lake
	Bierstadt Lake	Bierstadt Lake (3) Bear Lake (1)	2.8 miles 3.2 miles	E – Pleasant trail to alpine lake • Hike from Bear Lake to Bierstadt and use the shuttle to return
	Odessa Lake - 🐾	Bear Lake (1) Fern Lake (5)	8.2 miles 9.8 miles	M – Mountain-lined lake • 8.5-mile trek from Bear Lake Trailhead to Fern Lake Trailhead
	Alberta Falls	Glacier Gorge (2) Bear Lake (1)	1.6 miles 1.8 miles	E – Nice warm-up to venture deeper into the Rockies • Extremely enjoyable all year round
	Mills Lake	Glacier Gorge (2)	5.6 miles	M – One of the park's most beautiful lakes
	The Loch	Glacier Gorge (2)	6.0 miles	M – Beyond Alberta Falls, but before Timberline Falls
	Timberline Falls	Glacier Gorge (2)	8.0 miles	M – Can continue on to Lake of Glass and Sky Pond
	Sky Pond - 🐾	Glacier Gorge (2)	9.8 miles	S – Gorgeous! Scrambling at Timberline Falls
	Black Lake - 🐾	Glacier Gorge (2)	10.0 miles	S – Exceptional continuation beyond Mills Lake
	Sprague Lake - 🐾	Sprague Lake (4)	0.5 mile	E – Self-guided (great sunset location)
North of Glacier Basin	The Pool	Fern Lake (5)	3.4 miles	E – Pretty hike along a stream
	Fern Falls	Fern Lake (5)	5.0 miles	M – Hike through Arch Rocks to a nice falls
	Fern Lake - 🐾	Fern Lake (5)	7.6 miles	M – Continues past Fern Falls to the lake
	Cub Lake	Cub Lake (6)	4.6 miles	M – Can loop with Fern Lake Trail
	Moraine Park	Moraine Park (6)	0.8 mile	E – Self-guided nature loop
	Deer Mountain - 🐾	Deer Mountain (7)	6.0 miles	M – 10,000-ft summit, 360-degree views
	Gem Lake	Lumpy Ridge (8)	3.2 miles	M – Pass rocky terrain to a little lake
	Ypsilon Lake	Lawn Lake (9)	9.0 miles	S – Another popular mountain-lined lake
	Lawn Lake	Lawn Lake (9)	12.4 miles	S – Pristine lake in the Mummy Range
	Alluvial Fan - 🐾	Endovalley Rd (10)	0.4 mile	M – Waterfall and rocks, kids have fun here
	Tundra Communities - 🐾	Rock Cut (11)	1.0 mile	E – Paved trail across the tundra that leads to Toll Memorial (in honor of the first superintendent)
	Ypsilon Mountain	Chapin Creek (12)	7.0 miles	S – Cross Chapin and Chiquita Peaks to Ypsilon

Difficulty Ratings: E = Easy, M = Moderate, S = Strenuous

summit being the most difficult. You follow bullseyes marked on the rocks. It's no easy feat; hikers have lost their lives attempting it. Elevation change and distance from start to summit is similar to hiking out of the Grand Canyon and right back in. The trail is often impassable (without special equipment) until mid-July, so inquire about conditions at a visitor center before attempting it. You shouldn't even consider it unless you're acclimated to the elevation and get a very early start (most hikers begin before sunrise).

Most hiking is done on the busier eastern side, but some excellent hiking opportunities can be found along Trail Ridge Road and the park's west side. **Ute Trail** begins on Trail Ridge Road between Rainbow Curve and Forest Canyon. It extends 6.1 miles, descending 3,000 feet through amazing backcountry to Upper Beaver Meadows. It's recommended that you arrange a shuttle and hike one-way to Beaver Meadows. (To make things confusing, Ute Trail also runs from Alpine Visitor Center to Milner Pass. The first quarter-mile or so near Alpine Visitor Center is an exceptional sunset photography spot.) **Tundra Communities and Alpine Ridge Trails**, located on Trail Ridge Road, are worth a quick stop. They are short hikes (about one mile each) with outstanding scenery. If you came to Rocky Mountains searching for solitude, choose any of the hiking trails at **East Inlet Trailhead** located near Grand Lake. You probably won't be alone, but it won't be anything like the commotion of Bear Lake. Scenery here is nearly as inspiring, and the gentle western slopes make for easier hiking.

🚶🏕️ Backpacking

Want to enjoy a summer trip to the Rockies and evade the crowds and congestion? The most reliable solution is to pack up your gear and head into the backcountry. All day-hiking areas offer great backpacking opportunities. There are also more remote locations for experienced backpackers. The park's northeastern limits can be explored from Dunraven/North Fork Trailhead, which begins in Roosevelt National Forest off unpaved Dunraven Glade Road. From here, hike about 10 miles into the Rockies' Mummy Range to Lost Lake. This remote location can also be reached from Cow Creek Trailhead within McGraw Ranch at the end of an unpaved road north of Estes Park off Devil's Gulch Road. From Cow Creek Trailhead take North Boundary Trail to North Fork Trail to Lost Lake. Bridal Veil Falls is another popular destination from Cow Creek trailhead. The 20-ft falls is reached via a short spur from Cow Creek Trail. It is 3 miles (one-way) from the trailhead. Cow Creek Trail continues deeper into the Rockies.

Dream Lake

It follows Black Canyon all the way to Lawn and Crystal Lakes. Those looking to explore the northwestern corner should begin at Corral Creek Trailhead. It's also located in Roosevelt National Forest, along unpaved Long Draw Road. From here you can hike Poudre River and Colorado River Trails for 10.5 miles through Little Yellowstone, past Lulu City, and then to Trail Ridge Road. It is lightly traveled with two campsites along the way. Skeleton Gulch, also accessed from Colorado River Trail, is surrounded by majestic mountains. Relatively few make the steep climb to Skeleton Gulch, where you'll find peace in the form of one lone campsite.

After you've mapped out your backpacking route on a good topographical map (essential to any backpacking adventure), it's time to get a backcountry/wilderness permit. The number of permits issued is limited, so you may want to make a reservation. Reservation requests are accepted online through Pay.gov and there's a $30 (non-refundable, non-exchangeable) fee per permit reservation for travel between May and October. Walk-in permits are also available in person at the Wilderness Office at Beaver Meadows or Kawuneeche Backcountry Visitor Center for $30 per trip. For the rest of the year, you can make backcountry reservations by phone (970.586.1242) or in person at either of the permit locations. Even if you reserved your permit online, you must pick it up in-person. If you are unable to use your permit, please notify the park so your sites will be released for other campers. If you're going to arrive late, call to let them know. Your permit will automatically be cancelled and reissued if you do not pick it up before noon on the first day of your trip. Once you've secured a Wilderness Permit, get ready for fun in the backcountry, just make sure you're prepared to follow the park's backcountry regulations and equipped for the weather and environment.

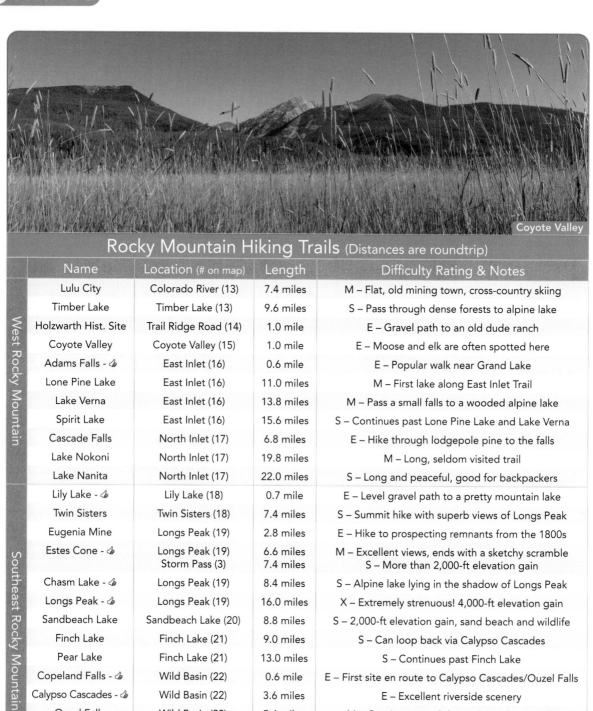

Coyote Valley

Rocky Mountain Hiking Trails (Distances are roundtrip)

	Name	Location (# on map)	Length	Difficulty Rating & Notes
West Rocky Mountain	Lulu City	Colorado River (13)	7.4 miles	M – Flat, old mining town, cross-country skiing
	Timber Lake	Timber Lake (13)	9.6 miles	S – Pass through dense forests to alpine lake
	Holzwarth Hist. Site	Trail Ridge Road (14)	1.0 mile	E – Gravel path to an old dude ranch
	Coyote Valley	Coyote Valley (15)	1.0 mile	E – Moose and elk are often spotted here
	Adams Falls - ♨	East Inlet (16)	0.6 mile	E – Popular walk near Grand Lake
	Lone Pine Lake	East Inlet (16)	11.0 miles	M – First lake along East Inlet Trail
	Lake Verna	East Inlet (16)	13.8 miles	M – Pass a small falls to a wooded alpine lake
	Spirit Lake	East Inlet (16)	15.6 miles	S – Continues past Lone Pine Lake and Lake Verna
	Cascade Falls	North Inlet (17)	6.8 miles	E – Hike through lodgepole pine to the falls
	Lake Nokoni	North Inlet (17)	19.8 miles	M – Long, seldom visited trail
	Lake Nanita	North Inlet (17)	22.0 miles	S – Long and peaceful, good for backpackers
Southeast Rocky Mountain	Lily Lake - ♨	Lily Lake (18)	0.7 mile	E – Level gravel path to a pretty mountain lake
	Twin Sisters	Twin Sisters (18)	7.4 miles	S – Summit hike with superb views of Longs Peak
	Eugenia Mine	Longs Peak (19)	2.8 miles	E – Hike to prospecting remnants from the 1800s
	Estes Cone - ♨	Longs Peak (19) / Storm Pass (3)	6.6 miles / 7.4 miles	M – Excellent views, ends with a sketchy scramble / S – More than 2,000-ft elevation gain
	Chasm Lake - ♨	Longs Peak (19)	8.4 miles	S – Alpine lake lying in the shadow of Longs Peak
	Longs Peak - ♨	Longs Peak (19)	16.0 miles	X – Extremely strenuous! 4,000-ft elevation gain
	Sandbeach Lake	Sandbeach Lake (20)	8.8 miles	S – 2,000-ft elevation gain, sand beach and wildlife
	Finch Lake	Finch Lake (21)	9.0 miles	S – Can loop back via Calypso Cascades
	Pear Lake	Finch Lake (21)	13.0 miles	S – Continues past Finch Lake
	Copeland Falls - ♨	Wild Basin (22)	0.6 mile	E – First site en route to Calypso Cascades/Ouzel Falls
	Calypso Cascades - ♨	Wild Basin (22)	3.6 miles	E – Excellent riverside scenery
	Ouzel Falls	Wild Basin (22)	5.4 miles	M – Continue past Calypso Cascades to Falls
	Bluebird Lake - ♨	Wild Basin (22)	12.0 miles	M – Long day hike or camp in the backcountry
	Thunder Lake	Wild Basin (22)	13.6 miles	S – Passes through a wildflower meadow (spring)
	Lion Lake No. 1	Wild Basin (22)	14.0 miles	S – Follows Thunder Lake Trail for much of the way

Difficulty Ratings: E = Easy, M = Moderate, S = Strenuous, X = Extreme

Rock Climbing

Boulder and Denver have earned their distinction as extreme sports hubs. Rock climbing is one of their specialties, and there are few better playgrounds for rock climbers than Rocky Mountain National Park. It is one of the area's premier climbing locations, offering everything from highly technical routes to basic scrambling. If you're interested in exploring the vertical side of the Rockies, check out the park's approved rock climbing outfitter, Colorado Mountain School (720.387.8944, coloradomountainschool.com). They offer a variety of group excursions (rates are based on group size and tour length).

Biking

Trail Ridge Road is grueling with narrow shoulders. Old Fall River Road is narrow, gravel, with no guard rails and steep drop-offs. Both are busy in summer. However, both roads are open to bicyclists from April through November, opening up two windows when they are not open to motorized vehicles. Just know that the roads are not patrolled during this time, may be closed for maintenance or emergencies, and, as always, you cycle at your own risk. The only trail bikes are permitted on is a 2-mile stretch of East Shore Trail near Grand Lake. A wide variety of bike rentals are available at Estes Park Mountain Shop (970.586.6548, estesparkmountainshop.com). They also offer camping, fishing, and rock climbing gear rentals.

Horseback Riding

Horses are allowed on approximately 260 of the 355 miles of hiking trails. Before Old Fall River Road and Trail Ridge Road were constructed, riding on horseback through the park was the way of life. Adventurous souls galloped through meadows and climbed steep summits aboard their sure-footed steeds. Horseback riding through the Rockies remains just as gratifying if not as practical as it was before automobiles arrived on the scene. Horse owners can haul in stock to explore the trails and enjoy backcountry camping (permit required), but most visitors join a group of riders on a trail ride provided by one of the park's approved outfitters. Rides range from 1–9 hours, starting at $40/rider. Multi-day trips are also available. Check out SK Horses (970.586.5890, skhorses.com, $80/2-hour ride) and Sombrero Ranch (970.533.8155, sombrero.com, $90/2-hour ride) for more information. There are several other stables nearby.

Fishing

Fishing is a popular activity even though many of the alpine lakes and streams are too high to support

Rock climbers at Sky Pond

reproducing populations of fish. But there are many fine locations to catch brown, brook, rainbow, and cutthroat trout. All anglers 16 and older require a Colorado fishing license. You can only use one rod and reel with artificial bait. Several rules and regulations regarding open and closed waters, catch and release, and possession limits are enforced. If you don't receive current information regarding rules and regulations when you purchase your fishing license (you can buy it online in advance), be sure to stop at a visitor center to discuss your plans with a friendly park ranger. A few local fishing guides include Sasquatch Fly Fishing (970.586.3341, sasquatchflyfishing.com), Estes Angler (800.586.2110, estesangler.com), and Kirk's Fly Shop (970.577.0790, kirksflyshop.com). All three are based out of Estes Park.

Winter Activities

Winter is when you'll find tranquility along the roadways and hiking trails. Most winter guests explore hiking trails with **cross-country skis or snowshoes** (but popular trails are usually packed down enough you can get by with boots with some kind of traction devices on them). Bear Lake Area remains the most popular

Moonlit elk near Gore Range Lookout

Rocky Mountain Visitor and Information Centers

Name	Open	Hours	Location & Notes
Beaver Meadows Visitor Center (closed Thanksgiving and Christmas)	November–February March–May June–October	9am–4:30pm 8am–4:30pm 8am–6pm	Located on US-36, 3 miles west of Estes Park. Designed by Frank Lloyd Wright's School of Architecture. Exhibits, short film, bookstore, backcountry permits, park rangers, and restrooms.
Fall River Visitor Center	All Year (closed Christmas and Thanksgiving)	9am–5pm	Located on US-34, 5 miles west of Estes Park. It has a bookstore, exhibits, and restrooms.
Moraine Park Visitor Center	late April–mid-June mid-June–early Sept early Sept–early Oct	9am–4:30pm 9am–5pm 9am–4:30pm	Located on Bear Lake Road, 1.5 miles from Beaver Meadows Entrance. A nature trail, exhibits, restrooms, and museum are open to visitors.
Alpine Visitor Center	late May–mid-June mid-June–early Sept early Sept–mid-Oct	10:30am–4:30pm 9:30am–4:30pm 10:30am–4:30pm	Located at Trail Ridge Rd/Old Fall River Rd Intersection. Ranger programs, exhibits, bookstore, gift store, snacks, and restrooms are available.
Kawuneeche Visitor Center	November–May June–October (closed Christmas)	9am–4:30pm 9am–5pm	Located at Grand Lake Entrance. Exhibits, short film, bookstore, backcountry permits, rangers, and restrooms. Closed Mondays and Tuesdays in winter.
Sheeps Lake Information Station	All Year	24/7	Located in Horseshoe Park, on US-34 just beyond Fall River Entrance.

destination even when it's blanketed in snow. Several trails, like Bierstadt Lake and Chasm Falls, are marked for winter use. A **winter play area** is maintained at Hidden Valley, located at the end of a short access road off Trail Ridge Road (US-34) just past Beaver Ponds Pullout. It is the only site in the park that permits sledding. Bring your own equipment or rent from one of the outdoor equipment outfitters in Estes Park, like Estes Park Mountain Shop (970.586.6548, estesparkmountainshop.com). On the west side of the park, you can rent gear from Never Summer Mountain Products in Grand Lake (919 Grand Ave, 970.627.3642, neversummermtn.com). It's a good idea to call (970) 586-1206 for snow information before visiting Hidden Valley, Estes Park, or any other low elevation area on the park's **east side**. This region receives very little precipitation because of its location just east of the Continental Divide, and winds are typically strong, resulting in patchy snow cover and drifting. It's also mostly steep and rugged terrain, not suitable for beginner cross-country skiers.

The **west side** of the park (not accessible via Trail Ridge Road in winter) is more reliable. It receives more precipitation, less wind, and features gentler slopes. Many of the west side's hiking trails remain open for hiking, snowshoeing, and cross-country skiing. Whether you visit the west or east side, it is always a good idea to stop in at a visitor center before entering the park. You'll receive current trail information and may be able to join a ranger-led ski or snowshoe tour.

Visitor Centers
Beaver Meadows and Kawuneeche Visitor Centers are open every day of the year except Thanksgiving and Christmas. Typical hours are from 8am until 5pm, with shorter hours in winter and extended hours in summer. **Fall River, Alpine, and Moraine Park Visitor Centers** close for winter. Details are provided in the table on the opposite page.

Ranger Programs & For Kids
Do not skip the park's ranger programs. A huge variety of walks, talks, and evening programs are offered regularly during summer. In winter, you can join a ranger on a snowshoe or cross-country ski tour (reservations required and you must provide your own equipment—see rental details in the Winter Activities section). Rangers are here to educate you on all sorts of subjects, including elk, lightning, geology, wildflowers, and much more. Some programs are geared toward children, birdwatchers, stargazers, and hikers. They're all free and fantastic. It's not a crazy idea to plan your entire vacation around ranger activities.

Moose near Skeleton Gulch

Maybe you've never thought much about beavers. What do they do? How do they survive? Why do they build dams? Everyone seems to know that they have an amazing set of choppers, but few people understand how they change their environment. Learn all about it at *Amazing Beavers*, a one-hour talk that takes place at Sprague Lake Picnic Area, offered every day in summer except Sundays. Dozens of other programs are offered during summer. You can find a complete list of scheduled events at the park website or stop in at a visitor center to see what's happening.

Children (12 and under) are welcome to participate in the Junior Ranger Program. Pick up a free activity booklet at any visitor center (or download it online). Complete it and show your work to a park ranger to receive an official Junior Ranger Badge. Or come in winter to go sledding at Hidden Valley, make snowmen, have a snowball fight, or come and watch some wildlife. In summer, Hidden Valley becomes the Junior Ranger Headquarters, where you can join a Junior Ranger Program or complete the activity book on your own. Programs are free to participate, and they can be fun for the whole family (an adult must be present with children at all times). Whenever you visit, Rocky Mountain is a wonderful park for children.

Flora & Fauna
The Rockies' wildlife and wildflowers are attractions worth visiting on their own. More than one-quarter of the park is alpine tundra, a seemingly barren and lifeless place for most of the year, but after the snow melts and sun thaws its frozen crust, wildflowers begin to grow. In early July, fields of flowers bloom, painting tundra in bright colors that accent the magnificence of the park's mountains standing tall in the background. 66 mammals reside here. Most popular are big and

Grand Lake

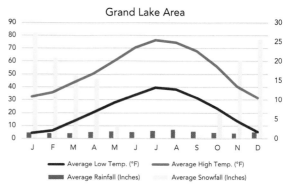

Grand Lake Area

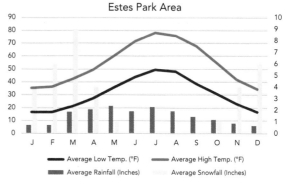

Estes Park Area

furry or small and mischievous. Elk can be seen (or heard bugling) in places like Moraine Park, where they graze around dawn and dusk. Moose are often spotted in Kawuneeche Valley, and Lilly and Sprague Lakes. Mountain lions and black bears are seldom seen. Industrious pikas live in the alpine tundra.

Pets & Accessibility

Pets are allowed in the park, but they are prohibited from all hiking trails, tundra, meadows, and backcountry. As a rule of thumb pets are permitted wherever your car can go but must be kept on a leash (less than six feet). This includes roadsides, parking areas, picnic areas, and drive-in campgrounds.

All visitor centers are fully accessible except for Beaver Meadows Visitor Center/Park Headquarters which is accessible with assistance. Glacier Basin, Moraine Park, and Timber Creek Campgrounds have accessible campsites. Most hiking trails are steep, rugged, and inaccessible to wheelchair users. The exceptions are Coyote Valley, Sprague Lake, Lily Lake, and Bear Lake Trails. They are all well-maintained, heavily trafficked, relatively flat, and accessible with assistance.

Weather

Rocky Mountain has two distinct climate patterns created and separated by the Continental Divide. The eastern region is dry and windy. The wetter western half receives about 20 inches of precipitation annually, about seven inches more than the eastern side. Both regions experience long frigid winters. Areas of high elevation can experience snowfall well into July. Expect a wide variation between day and nighttime temperatures. Summers are hot with temperatures frequenting the 70s and 80s°F. Temperatures drop into the 40s°F at night.

Tips & Recommendations

Take Peak-to-Peak Scenic Byway from Black Hawk or Boulder to Estes Park.

Estes Park is terribly busy in summer (and fall weekends). Crowds don't thin out until October, when Trail Ridge Road closes. Midweek there are noticeably thinner crowds. Don't rule out the rest of the year. Wildlife is active in fall and spring. Winter is great too, as Bear Lake Road is open year-round.

You won't find any lodges within park boundaries, but there are several campgrounds and many lodging choices in Estes Park and Grand Lake.

Colorado is hiker country. In most parks, you can hike a few miles to escape the crowds. Not here. People love to hike. That's a good thing, just letting you know to expect company on the trails.

Give yourself time to adjust to elevation. Simply driving Trail Ridge Road can take the breath out of you if you aren't conditioned for it. Spend a night at Wild Basin, then another night at Glacier Basin, and then start hiking up into the mountains, especially if you're a low-lander like me.

Exploring Trail Ridge Road (and possibly Old Fall River Road) is a full-day activity. Start early to increase your odds of seeing wildlife, pack a lunch (so you aren't tempted to go back to Estes Park in the middle of the day, although you can find food at Alpine Visitor Center), and stay out until sunset.

Old Fall River Road is a narrow, one-way, gravel road. If you're fine with some exposure, it's no big deal. If you're a bit of a nervous driver, you may want to stick to Trail Ridge Road (which offers its own excitement).

Longs Peak trailhead parking area fills extremely early. You could drive in here in the middle of the day (on a weekend), hoping to get lucky and find a parking spot, but it's better to keep driving. Not to mention, if you're serious about summiting Longs Peak (you're experienced and acclimated to elevation), you should begin before the sun rises (although spending the night here is best, but no sleeping in your car at the trailhead). That's a little bit of a bummer for anyone who wants to hike to Chasm Lake, which is a great trail.

Bear Lake is somewhat similar in the parking department. Fortunately, the park operates a few free shuttles during peak season, connecting Estes Park Visitor Center, Beaver Meadows Visitor Center, Moraine Park and Glacier Basin campgrounds, and the Bear Lake Area trailheads, through a centralized park and ride.

Easy Hikes: Dream Lake (2.2 miles), Sprague Lake (0.5), Tundra Communities (1), Calypso Cascades (3.6), Adams Falls (0.6), Bear Lake (0.5), Lily Lake (0.7)

Sunrise at Rainbow Curve

Moderate Hikes: Bluebird Lake (12 miles), Odessa Lake (8.2), Deer Mountain (6), Alluvial Fan (0.4)
Strenuous Hikes: Sky Pond (9.8 miles), Chasm Lake (8.4), Black Lake (10), Hallet Peak (10), Estes Cone (6.6)
Extreme Hikes: Longs Peak (16 miles)
Family Activities: Visit in winter and go sledding, become Junior Rangers
Guided Tours: Ride a horse, go rock climbing, catch some fish
Rainy Day Activities: Most visitors will return to Estes Park, but stick around, drive Trail Ridge Road and look for wildlife
History Enthusiasts: Holzwarth Historic Site, Lulu City
Sunset Spots: Ute Trail (Milner Pass or near Alpine Visitor Center), Sprague Lake, Forest Canyon Overlook, Gore Range Overlook, Bear Lake
Sunrise Spots: Sprague Lake, Rainbow Curve, Dream Lake, Many Parks Curve
Wildlife: Moraine Park (and Estes Park) in fall/spring, Rock Cut in summer, Old Fall River Road, the west side of the park (like Kawuneeche or Colorado River Valley) is good for moose

Beyond the Park...

Dining
Egg of Estes • (970) 586-1173
393 E Elkhorn Ave, Estes Park
eggofestes.com

Boss Burgers and Gyros
861 Moraine Ave, Estes Park
(970) 586-3137

Sagebrush BBQ • (970) 627-1404
1101 Grand Ave, Grand Lake
sagebrushbbq.com

Grand Pizza • (970) 627-8390
1131 Grand Ave, Grand Lake
grand-pizza.com

Grocery Stores
Country Market • (970) 586-2702
900 Moraine Ave, Estes Park

Safeway • (970) 586-4447
451 E Wonderview Ave, Estes Park

Mountain Market • (970) 627-3470
400 Grand Ave, Grand Lake

Lodging & Camping
Stanley Hotel • (970) 577-4000
333 E Wonderview Ave, Estes Park
stanleyhotel.com

McGregor Mountain Lodge
2815 Fall River Rd, Estes Park
mcgregormountainlodge.com

Appenzell Inn • (970) 586-2023
1100 Big Thompson Ave, Estes Park
appenzellinn.com

Winding River • (970) 627-3215
1447 CR-491, Grand Lake
windingriverresort.com

Estes Park KOA
2051 Big Thompson Ave, Estes Park
koa.com • (970) 586-3251

Elk Creek Camp • (970) 627-8502
143 CR-48, Grand Lake
elkcreekcamp.com

Camping options at Arapaho, Routt & Roosevelt Nat'l Forests

Festivals
Longs Peak Scottish-Irish Fest
scotfest.com • Sept • Estes Park

Attractions
St Catherine's Chapel on the Rock
Very photogenic spot
10758 CO-7, Allenspark

Estes Park Aerial Tramway
420 E Riverside Dr, Estes Park
estestram.com • (970) 475-4094

Rocky Mountain SUP
Lakefront Park, Grand Lake
rmsup.com • (970) 557-5150

There are quite a few large national forests (fs.usda.gov) with similar mountain scenery to Rocky Mountain National Park. Arapaho (Cascade Creek Trail, long day hike or backpack), Roosevelt, and Medicine Bow-Routt are good places to avoid the Estes Park crowds. While they are largely undeveloped, you'll still find restrooms and good day-hiking choices. There's also great backpacking, but you should be pretty comfortable in the backcountry.

You'll also find many beautiful state parks (cpw.state.co.us). Roxborough, Eldorado Canyon, Staunton, Castlewood Canyon, Golden Gate Canyon, Lory, and State Forest are a few worth looking into in the vicinity.

Great Sand Dunes

Sandy ridgelines

Phone: (719) 378-6395
Website: nps.gov/grsa

Established: September 13, 2004
(National Monument in 1932)
Size: 84,670 Acres
Annual Visitors: 500,000
Peak Season: Summer
Hiking Trails: 50+ Miles

Activities: Hiking, Backpacking,
Sand Fun, Biking, Horseback Riding

Piñon Flats Camp: $20/night
Backcountry Camping: Permitted
(with a $6 Backcountry Use Permit)

Park Hours: All day, every day
Entrance Fee: $25/20/15
(car/motorcycle/individual)

Would you guess the tallest dunes in North America are located in Colorado? They are! The Great Sand Dunes sprawl across San Luis Valley, an arid plain between the San Juan and Sangre de Cristo Mountains. This massive sand box began forming millions of years ago and the region has been inhabited for at least the last 11,000 years. Nomadic hunter–gatherers were initially drawn here by herds of mammoth and bison. Thousands of years later Ute and Jicarilla Apache lived and hunted in the San Luis Valley. Ute called the dunes "sowapopheuveha" or "the land that moves back and forth." Jicarilla Apache called them "sei-anyedi" or "it goes up and down." In 1807, an American soldier, Zebulon Pike regarded the dunes in a similar fashion, describing them as a "sea in a storm." He first encountered the dunes on the Pike Expedition, exploring land acquired in the Louisiana Purchase.

Wind drives the rise and fall of waves in a storm, and it's the impetus of these dunes' creation. Crests of sand—sinuous ridgelines—rise from the plains, crossing arid land at the foot of the Sangre de Cristo Mountains. It's a bizarre sight immediately begging the question: How were the Great Sand Dunes formed? To understand the formation of the dunes, one must first understand the formation of the mountains.

Uplift, caused by collision of two tectonic plates, forced the Sangre de Cristo Mountains to rise from the earth. The San Juan Mountains, their sister range 65 miles west of the dunefield, formed when a massive volcano erupted millions of years ago. Many scientists regard that event as the largest explosive volcanic eruption in the history of earth, with a resulting deposit 5,000 times larger than that of Mount St. Helen's. The two mountain ranges surround a vast plain, roughly the size of Connecticut, known today as San Luis Valley.

This valley used to be covered by an immense lake, which served as a collection site for massive amounts of sediment eroded away from the mountains. Climate change caused the lake to recede, a process that may have been expedited when the valley's southern end wore away, forming Rio Grande Gorge, which allowed water to drain directly into the river. A giant sheet of sand was left behind.

A huge supply of sand was completely exposed to the forces of Mother Nature. Predominant southwesterly winds went to work. This indomitable force pushed sand across the valley to the Sangre de Cristo Mountains where it funneled into Mosca, Medano, and Music Passes. Storm winds blowing from the northeast took sand pinned against the mountains' slopes and pushed it back toward the valley's floor, causing dunes to grow vertically. Additionally, and blown into the mountains is slowly collected and returned to the dunefield by Sand and Medano Creeks.

After hundreds of millennia, the opposing winds seem to have found satisfaction in their grainy masterpiece. Beneath the top layer of loose sand is a wet and cool sandy base, resilient to the forces of nature. These dunes may look like they're rising and falling like a "sea in a storm," but they're actually quite stable, having been roughly the same size and shape for more than 100 years.

A tourist's journey to Great Sand Dunes is nearly as laborious as the sand's. The park is well off the beaten path, far removed from major interstates and metropolitan areas. Like other national parks, the greatest architecture here was created by the hands of Mother Nature. Through water and wind, she's sculpted a sea of sand that is easily one of the best kept secrets among the entire parks collection. Pack up your family and come to the dunes to surf (and sled) the seas of sand and explore this natural phenomenon that has been enchanting and mystifying everyone who's passed its sandy foot for hundreds of years.

Sandy sunset

When to Go
Great Sand Dunes is open all year. Even though summer draws about half the park's annual guests, spring and fall are extremely pleasant seasons. Visitation peaks in late May/early June (particularly on weekends) when Medano Creek is flowing at its peak. During this time, plan a mid-week trip if possible. Dunes can be unbearably hot on summer afternoons (hot enough you'll want to wear shoes). Just a few thousand people visit each winter.

Transportation & Airports
Public transportation does not go to or around the park. There is a small airport in Alamosa, CO, but you are better off flying into Denver International (DEN), 250 miles to the north, or Albuquerque International Sunport (ABQ), 230 miles to the south. Car rental is available at each destination.

Directions
Great Sand Dunes has been described as the quietest park in the contiguous U.S. Even though it ought to go to Isle Royale or North Cascades, that title gives you an idea of how removed this scenic wonder is from the rest of civilization. Most visitors arrive from the north via I-25. Heading south on I-25, take Exit 52 for US-160. Turn right onto US-160. After 57 miles, turn right at CO-150 N, which leads into the park.

Regions
Great Sand Dunes is officially a National Park and Preserve. The park comprises the dunes and arid flatlands surrounding them. The preserve is the slice of Sangre de Cristo Mountains north and east of the dunefield. Congress expanded park boundaries after scientists determined the important role water played in creation of the sand dunes and continues to play maintaining them. Regulations differ between the two regions; for example you can hunt and camp at non-designated locations in the preserve, but not in the park.

Camping & Lodging

Piñon Flats is the park's only drive-in camp-ground. It's located about one mile north of the visitor center and a half-mile from the dunes (via Campground Trail). There are two 44-site loops. Sites at Loop 1 are available on a first-come, first-served basis. Sites at Loop 2 can be reserved up to six months in advance from April through October at (877) 444-6777 or recreation.gov. All sites are $20/night. Sites book extremely early for late May/June when Medano Creek should be flowing at its highest volume. Restrooms with flush toilets and sinks are available, but there are no showers. Not all sites can accommodate RVs or camping trailers over 35 feet. There are no hookups. Three group sites (15–40 people) are available from April through October by reservation only. Group sites cost $65–85/night and can be reserved up to one year in advance. Visitors with a high-clearance 4WD vehicle can access 21 campsites along **Medano Pass Primitive Road** in the national preserve region (road conditions permitting). Camping here is limited to the designated first-come, first-served campsites. Those looking to explore the backcountry by foot may camp at one of seven designated sites along **Sand Ramp Trail**. You can also camp off-trail in the dunes or national preserve. Backpackers must obtain a backcountry use permit ($6, recreation.gov). There are no lodging facilities within park boundaries, but a few options exist in nearby communities, including Great Sand Dunes Lodge (gsdlodge.com, 719.378.2900), situated near the entrance.

Driving

CO-150 enters the park along the eastern edge of San Luis Valley. Entering from the south, the Sangre de Cristo Mountains rise high above you to the east and North America's largest sand dunes come into view to the north. From the scenic byway these undulating sand hills appear to be a sand replica of the sky-scraping mountains whose foot they sit at. You'll get a closer look as the paved roadway closes in on the dunes, eventually terminating at Piñon Flats Campground. Most vehicles can make it to Point of No Return. It's high-clearance-4WD territory beyond this point, and, as the name suggests, you're committing to 22 miles of off-roading fun (or it could be a complete nightmare). It crosses the mountains at Medano Pass and exits the park on County Road 559, which leads to CO-69. Along the way you'll pass 21 designated campsites, overlooks, trailheads, and an old homestead site. It starts with some potentially deep sand (lower your air pressure, a free air station is available during the warmer months, otherwise carry

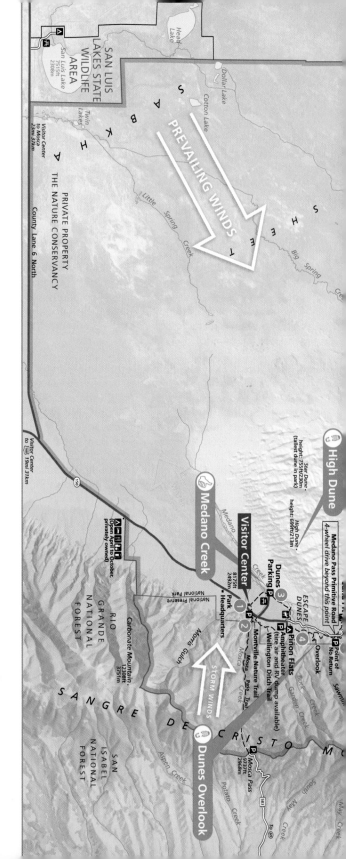

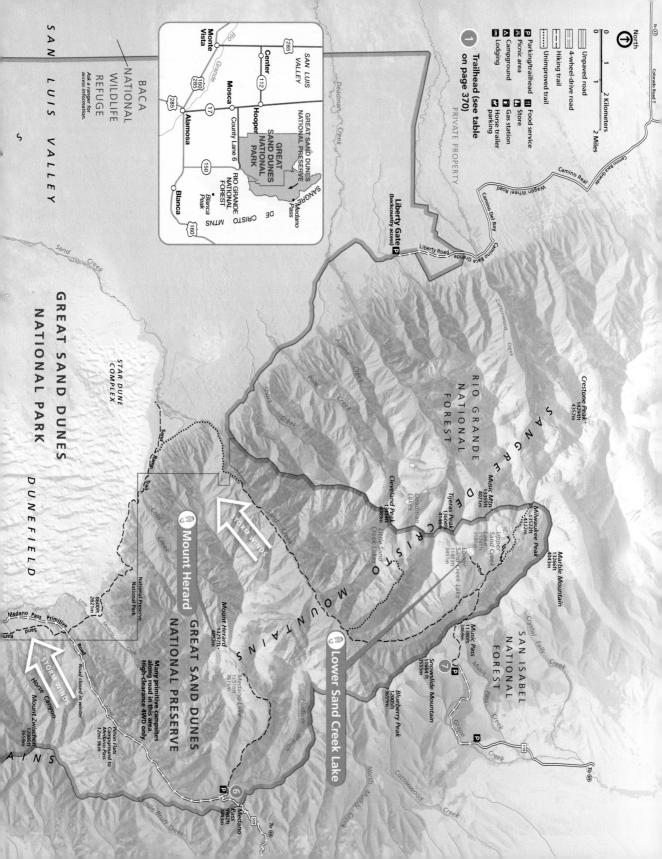

Trailhead (see table on page 370)

North

0   1   2 Kilometers
0   1   2 Miles

	Parking/trailhead
	4-wheel-drive road
	Unpaved road
	Hiking trail
	Unimproved trail
P	Parking/trailhead
▲	Picnic area
⊞	Campground
⊟	Store
⛽	Gas station
🏠	Lodging
🍴	Food service
🐴	Horse trailer parking

To 17

Colorado Road T

Camino Baca Grande

PRIVATE PROPERTY

Wagon Wheel Road

Camino Real

Camino Del Rey

Liberty Gate
(backcountry access) P

Liberty Road

Camino Baca Grande

Deadman Creek

Cottonwood Creek

SAN LUIS VALLEY

Monte Vista

SAN LUIS VALLEY

285

Center

112

Rio Grande

160
285

Mosca

Alamosa

17

285

County Lane 6

Hooper

GREAT SAND DUNES NATIONAL PRESERVE

GREAT SAND DUNES NATIONAL PARK

RIO GRANDE NATIONAL FOREST

150

Blanca

Blanca Peak

160

SANGRE DE CRISTO MTNS

Medano Pass

SAN LUIS VALLEY

BACA NATIONAL WILDLIFE REFUGE

Ask a ranger for access information.

GREAT SAND DUNES NATIONAL PARK

STAR DUNE COMPLEX

DUNEFIELD

Sand Creek

Sand Creek

Sand Ramp Trail

Cold Creek

Little Medano Creek

Medano Creek

Medano Pass Primitive

Ram Sand

Horse Canyon

Mount Zwischen
12006ft
3659m

Middle Bluff Creek

Road closed in winter

Road to Campground to Medano Pass 12mi/19km

Piñon Flats Campground to Medano Pass 12mi/19km

6 P

Medano Pass
9982ft
3043m

To 69

559

⬆ STORM WINDS

⬆ STORM WINDS

Mount Herard

Mount Herard
13297ft
4053m

8600ft
2621m

National Preserve

National Park

GREAT SAND DUNES NATIONAL PRESERVE

Many primitive campsites along road in this area. High-clearance 4WD only.

Medano Lake
11518ft
3511m

Hudson Branch

RIO GRANDE NATIONAL FOREST

Alpine Creek

Pole Creek

Short Creek

Deadman Lakes

Cleveland Peak
13414ft
4089m

Tijeras Peak
13604ft
4146m

Music Mtn
13355ft
4071m

Milwaukee Peak
13522ft
4122m

Little Sand Creek Lake

Upper Sand Creek Lake
11745ft
3580m

Lower Sand Creek Lake
11473ft
3497m

Marble Mountain
13266ft
4043m

Crestone Peak
14294ft
4357m

SANGRE DE CRISTO MOUNTAINS

Lower Sand Creek Lake

Music Pass
11380ft
3469m

7 P

Snowslide Mountain
11660ft
3353m

Blueberry Peak
12051ft
3655m

Crystal Falls Creek

Music Pass

Grape Creek

SAN ISABEL NATIONAL FOREST

119

P

North Creek

Cottonwood Creek

Muddy Creek

To 69

RAINS

your own compressor). And you'll cross Medano Creek eight times. Before attempting to drive Medano Pass, stop in at the visitor center (or call them) to assure it's not closed due to snow or high-water levels (there are several creek crossings). If that sounds like fun to you, Pathfinders4x4 (719.496.6288, pathfinders4x4.com) offers guided tours and jeep rentals. You can also reach Mosca or Medano (4WD) Pass via unpaved roads from the east. Music Pass and Liberty Gate can be reached via unpaved roads from the north. Each one ends with a stretch of 4WD road. The dunefield can be busy. These areas offer relative peace and quiet, but they're more primitive experiences.

Hiking

Great Sand Dunes is one of the National Park Service's pleasant surprises. It's easy to feel like you've been whisked away to some far away desert as you hike across the sandy ridgelines. At 750 feet, **Star Dune** is the tallest dune in the park. It's a difficult 4-mile (one-way) trudge through loose sand to the summit. Your best bet is to follow Medano Creek around the dunes for about two miles, and then head into the dunes and climb until you reach the highest peak. Summit views are phenomenal, but the return trip is where the fun begins. Forget about retracing your original footprints back to Medano Creek in favor of bounding down the

sandy slopes. As the sand gives way beneath your feet, you gain a small sense of what it must feel like to walk on the moon. However, leave the ridgelines and you'll be forced to scale several dunes (a real thigh-burning experience). The hike to **Star Dune** begins at Dunes Parking Lot, off CO-150/Medano Road. If you're looking for something easier, head to **Escape Dunes** (0.75 miles, one-way). It begins at the same trailhead and follows a portion of the 0.5-mile (one-way) Campground Trail, which connects Dunes Parking Area with Piñon Flats Campground. Another short and easy hike is **Montville Nature Trail**. This 0.5-mile loop begins on top of the hill just north of the visitor center at Montville/Mosca Pass Trailhead.

After playing in the sandbox, empty your shoes, lace them back up, and hike into the mountains. The 3.5-mile (one-way) **Mosca Pass Trail** is the most accessible mountain hike, beginning at the same trailhead as Montville Nature Trail, but it's a little underwhelming, without substantial dunes views. With a high-clearance 4WD vehicle you can really get into the mountains by traversing Medano Pass Primitive Road. Near Medano Pass, at the end of a short spur road, you'll find Medano Lake Trailhead and a small parking area. From here you can hike 3.7 miles (one-way) to **Medano Lake**, where you are free to continue an additional 1.5 miles

Great Sand Dunes Hiking Trails (Distances are roundtrip)

	Name	Location (# on map)	Length	Difficulty Rating & Notes
Medano Rd - Piñon Flats	Carbonate Peak	Visitor Center (1)	8.0 miles	S – Unmaintained trail to 12,308-ft summit
	Montville	Montville Parking Lot (2)	0.5 mile	E – Short nature trail with abundant shade
	Wellington Ditch	Montville Parking Lot (2)	2.0 miles	E – Connects visitor center and campground
	Mosca Pass	Montville Parking Lot (2)	7.0 miles	M – Forested hike, not great for dune viewing
	High Dune - 🥾	Dunes Parking Lot (3)	2.5 miles	M – No trail, tallest dune on first ridge
	Star Dune - 🥾	Dunes Parking Lot (3)	8.0 miles	S – No trail, tallest dune in the park
	Dunes Overlook - 🥾	Sand Ramp/Campground (Loop 2) (4)	2.3 miles	M – Good views of the dunes for a short hike
	Sand Ramp	Sand Ramp/Campground (Loop 2) (4)	22.0 miles	E – Backpackers access designated sites and remote dunes, can start at Point of No Return
	Sand Pit	Point of No Return (5)	1.4 miles	E – Can drive here with high-clearance 4WD
	Castle Creek	Point of No Return (5)	3.0 miles	E – Continue from Sand Pit to picnic area
Primitive Rd	Medano Lake - 🥾	Medano Lake (6)	7.4 miles	S – 4WD required • 1,900-ft elevation gain
	Mount Herard	Medano Lake (6)	10.4 miles	S – Arduous journey to 13,297-ft summit
	Music Pass - 🥾	Upper Lot (4WD req'd) (7) Lower Lot (7)	2.0 miles 7.0 miles	S – Located in the park's northeastern corner, this trail provides access to Sand Creek Lakes
	Sand Creek Lakes - 🥾	Music Pass (7)	6–16 miles	S – 3 lakes, 3 trails, Lower Sand Creek is closest

Difficulty Ratings: E = Easy, M = Moderate, S = Strenuous

to the top of looming **Mount Herard** (a spectacular viewpoint). For more mountain lakes, consider hiking to any of the **Sand Lakes**. Music Pass trailhead is located in San Isabel National Forest. If you don't have a 4WD vehicle but still want a panoramic view of the dunes, take the 2-mile (roundtrip) trail from Loop 2 of Piñon Flats Campground to **Dunes Overlook**. It's nestled in the foothills of the Sangre de Cristo Mountains, and can be accessed via a short spur trail from Sand Ramp Trail. (You can also hike back to the overlook's spur by beginning at Point of No Return.)

Backpacking

On-trail backpacking adventures are fairly limited without a 4WD vehicle. The only lengthy hike from the paved park road is **Sand Ramp Trail**, beginning at the north end of Piñon Flats Campground's second loop. From here you can hike 11 miles between the dunes and Sangre de Cristo Mountains. At the trail's end you can follow Sand Creek into the mountains. It's about 10 miles from Sand Ramp Trail to **Upper Sand Creek Lake** with optional spur trails to Milwaukee Peak, Lower Sand Creek Lake, and Little Sand Creek Lake. You must return the way you came or park a second vehicle at Music Pass Trailhead (4WD required). (Note that you'll be following an unmaintained, AKA hard to follow, section of trail from Sand Ramp to Sand Creek.) Once you're in the mountains (the preserve region), you are free to camp off-trail wherever you choose.

One of the most unique places to backpack is in the dunes. **You're welcome to camp anywhere in the dunefield outside of the day use area**. There are no marked trails, simply hike at least 1.5 miles into the dunes and pick a spot. It's easiest to follow the ridgelines, but you'll probably want to camp in a depression. It's imperative that you check the weather before departing. Blowing sand is a nuisance, and lightning is a serious threat. You can also camp at any one of seven designated sites along **Sand Ramp Trail**. They offer better protection from the elements. All overnight trips at designated backcountry sites require a permit, available up to three months in advance at recreation.gov for a $6 fee.

Sand Activities

To locals, a trip to Great Sand Dunes is like going to the beach. Pack a cooler, umbrella, beach ball, water toys, and a towel, and you're ready for some fun in the sun. When Medano Creek is at peak flow you can even play in water and surf one-foot waves when backed up water bursts through dams of sand. Don't forget your bucket and shovel; this is one of the few parks where

Medano Creek

you can build a sandcastle. It's also a popular location to write messages. Vandalism in the parks has been a widespread problem, but writing your name (or a message to outer space) in the dune's sand is encouraged. Wind will eventually wipe the slate clean. You can also sandboard, sled, or ski down these sandy slopes. It's best to use boards and sleds designed for use in the sand. Rentals are available at Kristi Mountain Sports (719.589.9759, kristimountainsports.com, $18/day) in Alamosa and at the Oasis Store (719.378.2222, greatdunes.com, $20/day), located just outside the park.

Biking

Biking is limited, but fat bikes are permitted on Medano Pass Primitive Road. Before heading out, you'll want to check road conditions as there are extended sandy sections and several creek crossings.

Horseback Riding

Horseback riders are welcome in the national preserve and most of the national park. If you have your own horse and would like to explore Great Sand Dunes, you can park your trailer at the horse trailer parking area near the beginning of Medano Pass Primitive Road. If that's full, you'll have to use the amphitheater parking area nearby. Otherwise you can access the park from the east and park at Mosca Pass or the north and park in San Isabel National Forest. Horseless visitors who would like to ride have one option: Zapata Ranch (719.257.3043, ranchlands.com), located in Mosca on CO-150, 6 miles from the visitor center. They provide all-inclusive ranch vacations for serious adventurers seeking a true western experience. Guests learn all about horsemanship at a working ranch. Adult rates range from $1,530/person for three nights to $2,765 for a week. They do some unique retreats, too. They're definitely worth checking out if you're into horses.

Visitor Center

The visitor center (719.378.6395) is where you'll want to introduce yourself to Great Sand Dunes. You'll find interactive exhibits, a short film, bookstore, and restrooms. It's also the main hub for visitor information

A mule deer near the east end of the dunefield

and the ever-popular ranger programs. Even if your children are eager to play in the sand, stop quickly to browse through the facility and its exhibits, and browse a current schedule of ranger programs before exploring the park. It's open every day, with the exception of Thanksgiving, Christmas, and New Year's Day. Spring through fall, operating hours are from 9am–4:30pm. Summer hours are 8:30am–5pm.

Ranger Programs & For Kids
Great Sand Dunes is a peculiar place. To gain a better understanding of the area, join one of its many interpretive programs. These walks and talks provide an educational exploration of the region's history, geology, and ecology. They also discuss how in the world all this sand got here. Check online or in person at the visitor center to see what programs will be offered during your visit.

To kids, Great Sand Dunes is one giant sandbox. Kids of all ages love to play in the sand, bound down the dunes, and float down Medano Creek during the spring and early summer rush. In between playing, children of all ages are welcome to participate in the park's Junior Ranger Program. To become a Junior Ranger and receive an official badge, your child must complete an activity booklet or check out a Junior Ranger Backpack (both available at the visitor center).

Flora & Fauna
Billions of grains of sand (most of which you will believe made their way into your car) may lead a person to believe that this is a desert region inhabited by cacti and reptiles adapted to life in a severe environment. This couldn't be farther from the truth; Great Sand Dunes has some of the most diverse plant and animal life of all the national parks. Hundreds of species of plants

live in the park. Most thrive in the area's wetlands or foothills, but a few species—such as Indian ricegrass and scrufpea—are capable of surviving in the dunes.

In lower elevations you may see pronghorn, bison, badgers, mule deer, elk, or the occasional beaver. Mountains are home to yellow-bellied marmots, pikas, bighorn sheep, black bears, and a small population of mountain lions. There are also more than 200 species of birds, a variety of reptiles, insects, and amphibians, and a few species of fish.

Pets & Accessibility
Pets are permitted in the preserve and main use areas of the park (Piñon Flats Campground, Dunes Overlook Trail, and along Medano Pass Primitive Road). They must be kept on a leash (less than six feet). They are prohibited from the park's backcountry (dunes and beyond Medano Pass Primitive Road).

Rolling hills of sand don't make for the most accessible park. However, there is a wheelchair-accessible viewing platform at Dunes Parking Lot. Wheelchair users hoping to get closer to the dunes can check out one of two sand wheelchairs available at the visitor center. To reserve one, call the visitor center at (719) 378-6395. The visitor center is fully accessible. Campsites suitable for wheelchair users are available at Piñon Flats and in the backcountry at Sawmill Canyon.

Weather
Temperatures in the summer average between 70 and 90°F, but the sand can get as hot as 150°F on a sunny day. Wear shoes in the dunes to protect your feet. Like most high-mountain climates, the temperature changes 30–40°F from afternoon highs to overnight lows. Spring and fall are mild. Winter is cold with significant snowfall. Visitors should be prepared for strong winds and scattered thunderstorms any time of year.

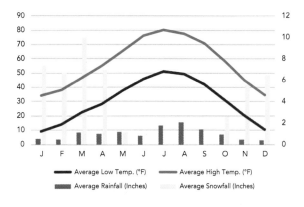

Tips & Recommendations

Visitation has increased considerably in the last few years. It peaks with Medano Creek's flow, typically in late May/early June. Expect the park to be extremely crowded during this time, with traffic lining up, full parking lots, and a crowded beach. Try to visit on a weekday if you can. The creek typically begins retreating in late June/July.

The average visit is two nights and that sounds about right. You'll want more if you're going to explore the backcountry or preserve. And, if you only want to see the dunes and get back on the road, you only need a few hours.

Pack food. Great Sand Dunes Oasis (719.378.2222, greatdunes.com) is located at the main park entrance, but it's the only restaurant within 25 miles of the park. They also offer 20 RV sites (with electric hookups), sandboard and sled rentals, tent sites, hot showers, groceries, gas, firewood, gas, motel, and cabins.

Remember that the park is at elevation. The western flats are above 7,500 ft and some Sangre de Cristo peaks rise above 13,000 feet.

Photographers will want to spend at least one whole day to witness light and shadow dancing across the dunes. If the sun is out, the dunes are interesting. They're even pretty neat at night.

These are the tallest dunes in North America and there aren't any marked trails to help navigate through them. While it's difficult to get completely lost, it is fairly easy to get disoriented. Stay on the ridges until returning to the parking area, then have some fun frolicking down them in leaps and bounds.

Unless you have board-sports experience, you (or your kids) may want to stick to sledding (or start with sledding). Sand isn't as forgiving as snow or water.

Camping in the dunes sounds great, but it can be underwhelming. Even if everything is perfectly calm, sand gets everywhere. The same stars exist above the designated campsites, but, of course, you'll have company.

Hiking Trails: Star Dune (Strenuous, 8 miles), High Dune (Moderate, 2.5), Medano Lake (Strenuous, 7.4), Music Pass (Strenuous, 2), Dunes Overlook (Moderate, 2.3)
Family Activities: It goes without saying but…make sure you spend some time playing in the sand!
Guided Tours: Horseback riding at Zapata Ranch
Sunset/Sunrise Spots: Hiking the sandy ridgelines (you'll have time in the morning as sunrise is blocked by the Sangre de Cristo Mountains), Dunes Overlook, hike along Medano Creek (it can be windy, so remember sand is not the photographer's friend)
Wildlife: West of the park at San Luis Lakes State Park and Wildlife Area

Beyond the Park…

Dining
The Colorado Farm Brewery
2070 CR-12 S, Alamosa
cofarmbeer.com • (720) 739-1168

Calvillo's Mexican • (719) 587-5500
400 Main St, Alamosa

The Rubi Slipper • (719) 589-2641
506 State Ave, Alamosa

Rendezvous BBQ • (719) 379-4380
703 4th Ave, Fort Garland

Grocery Stores
Crestone Mercantile • (719) 256-5887
182 E Galena, Crestone

Walmart • (719) 589-9071
3333 Clark St, Alamosa

Safeway • (719) 587-3075
1301 Main St, Alamosa

Lodging & Camping
Great Sand Dunes Lodge
gsdlodge.com • (719) 378-2900

Sandhill Inn • (719) 852-3585
1519 Grand Ave, Monte Vista
sandhillinn.com

Dunes Inn • (719) 589-6636
425 Main St, Alamosa
dunesinnalamosa.com

Zapata Falls Campground
Rio Grande National Forest
fs.usda.gov • (719) 852-7074

BLM Sacred White Shell Mountain
CO-150

Sand Dunes RV Park • (719) 378-2807
1991 CR-63, Hooper

Alamosa KOA
koa.com • (719) 589-9757

Cool Sunshine RV Park
coolsunshinervpark.com

Festivals
Creede Donkey Dash • June
creede.com/donkey-dash • Creede

Attractions
National Forests (fs.usda.gov):
Rio Grande (Zapata Falls is an easy hike 8 miles south of the visitor center), San Juan (Ice Lake Basin), Pike-San Isabel

Nat'l Wildlife Refuges (fws.gov): Alamosa (9383 El Ranch Ln), Monte Vista (6120 CO-15), and Baca (Crestone), and San Luis State Area (cpw.state.co.us)

Garden of the Gods • (719) 634-6666
Hiking through sandstone rocks
1805 N 30th St, Colorado Springs
gardenofthegods.com

Florissant Fossil Beds NM
Insect and plant fossils
15807 Co Rd 1 • nps.gov/flfo

Browns Canyon Nat'l Monument
New monument • fs.usda.gov

Rio Grande del Norte NM
Gorge and cinder cones • blm.gov

Scotts Bluff National Monument
Historically important landmark
190276 Old Oregon Tr, Gering, NE
nps.gov/scbl

Monument Rocks
Often called "chalk pyramids"
Gove City, KS

Pikes Peak Highway (fee) leads
to the top of a 14er or take the Cog Railway (cograilway.com)

Royal Gorge Bridge
Famous suspension bridge
4218 Co Rd 3a, Canon City

Lost Paddle Rafting • (719) 275-0884
Trips for all ages and abilities
1240 Royal Gorge Blvd, Canon City
lostpaddlerafting.com

Bishop's Castle • (719) 564-4366
Eccentric domain and longtime popular roadside diversion
12705 CO-165, Rye
bishopcastle.org

Black Canyon of the Gunnison

Phone: (970) 641-2337 x205
Website: nps.gov/blca

Established: October 21, 1999
March 2, 1933 (National Monument)
Size: 30,750 Acres
Annual Visitors: 300,000
Peak Season: Summer

Activities: Hiking, Backpacking, Kayaking, Rock Climbing, Biking, Horseback Riding, Cross-country Skiing, Snowshoeing

Camping
South Rim (1 Loop open all year)*: $16/night or $22 w/ electric hookups
East Portal (seasonal, Curecanti NRA) and North Rim (seasonal): $16/night
Backcountry Camping: Permitted with a free Backcountry Use Permit
Lodging: None

Park Hours: All day, every day
Entrance Fee: $30/25/15
(car/motorcycle/individual)

*Reserve at recreation.gov or (877) 444-6777

Western Colorado's Black Canyon of the Gunnison has been a source of frustration, irrigation, and recreation for more than a century. Its 2,200-foot walls of gray gneiss and schist rise precipitously from the raucous waters of the Gunnison River; walls so deep and narrow sunlight only penetrates their depths at midday, leaving the canyon constantly enveloped in the darkness of its own shadow. It's an ominous setting, accentuated by the angry river carving through the canyon's floor at a rate of one inch every 100 years. When the river is running, it tears through the canyon with reckless abandon, dropping 34 feet every mile. The Gunnison River loses more elevation in 48 miles than the Mississippi River does in more than 2,000. This is the Black Canyon of the Gunnison. Impassable to explorers. Incorrigible to settlers. Incredible to recreational visitors.

Fur traders and Utes undoubtedly witnessed the Black Canyon, but none were foolish enough to call such a foreboding location home. An expedition led by Captain John W. Gunnison in 1849 and the Hayden Expedition (of 1871), both declared the canyon impassable. Only a railway company, driven by the almighty dollar, had the courage to attempt passage and settlement in the midst of these mighty walls. In 1881, the Denver and Rio Grande Railroad successfully reached the small town of Gunnison from Denver. They proceeded to punch their way through the canyon, building what would be called the "Scenic Line of the World." Construction cost $165,000 per mile in 1882. The last mile of track took an entire year to construct, but they persevered through the deaths of several immigrant laborers to successfully push on to Salt Lake City. For nearly a decade it served as the main route for transcontinental travel. But the combination of a new route through Glenwood Springs and the canyon's frequent bouts of inclement weather and rock slides led to a decrease in popularity of the "Scenic Line of the World." It was finally abandoned in 1955.

Warner Point

East Portal

By the 1890s, settlers of Uncompahgre Valley began to take a serious look at the Gunnison River as a source of water for irrigation. It required new expeditions into the Black Canyon to analyze the feasibility of blasting a diversion tunnel through its walls of rock and in 1901 Abraham Lincoln Fellows, a hydrologist and Yale graduate, attempted to hike, swim, and float on a rubber mattress through the canyon. Accompanied by William Torrence, together they were the first to run the canyon, covering a distance of 33 miles in 9 days. They also declared that irrigation was possible. Construction followed thanks to funding from Theodore Roosevelt's National Reclamation Act of 1902, and a 5.8-mile, 11-foot-by-12-foot diversion tunnel was built, providing much needed water to an arid farm valley.

In 1916, Emery Kolb, a noted oarsman who, along with his brother, owned a photography studio on the rim of the Grand Canyon, attempted the first recreational trip through the Black Canyon. Years of paddling the Colorado River had left him wanting more and he set his sights on something wilder: the Gunnison. It took five attempts, several boats, canoes, and supplies, but he eventually completed the journey to Delta Bridge.

Today, a park protects the most spectacular 12 miles of the 48-mile-long canyon. A campground and visitor center sit where a railway town once thrived. Water still pours through a diversion tunnel. And thousands of visitors come to the Black Canyon of the Gunnison each year in pursuit of adventure just like Emery Kolb.

When to Go

The South Rim is open every day of the year, but South Rim Road beyond Gunnison Point closes in winter (typically mid-November until April). East Portal Road, a steep roadway down to the canyon floor, is typically closed from mid-November until mid-April. The North Rim is typically closed from late November until mid-April. Black Canyon gets busy in summer, but not wildly so like Rocky Mountain National Park.

Transportation & Airports

Public transportation isn't a viable option. Greyhound (800.231.2222, greyhound.com) has a bus station in Montrose (15 miles from the visitor center) and Grand Junction (76 miles). Amtrak (800.872.7245, amtrak.com) provides train service to Grand Junction. The closest regional airports are Montrose Regional (MTJ), 18 miles away; Gunnison-Crested Butte Regional (GUC), 62 miles to the east; and Grand Junction Regional (GJT), 82 miles northwest of the park's visitor center. Denver International (DEN) is 335 miles to the east along I-70. Car rental is available at each destination.

Directions

South Rim Visitor Center is 76 miles from Grand Junction (I-70, Exit 37). Take US-50 south through Montrose. Turn left at CO-347 N. Continue for roughly five miles before making a slight right onto South Rim Road, which leads into the park. A mere 1,100 feet separates the North and South Rims at spots (canyon walls are as narrow as 40 feet at the floor), but you will not find a bridge connecting the two. Visitors must make an 80+ mile drive to reach one rim from the other. From the south rim, return to US-50, and turn either way at the intersection of US-50 and CO-347. Heading east is about 7 miles longer, but more scenic. Regardless of which way you head on US-50, drive until you reach CO-92. Follow CO-92 to Black Canyon Road, which leads to the North Rim.

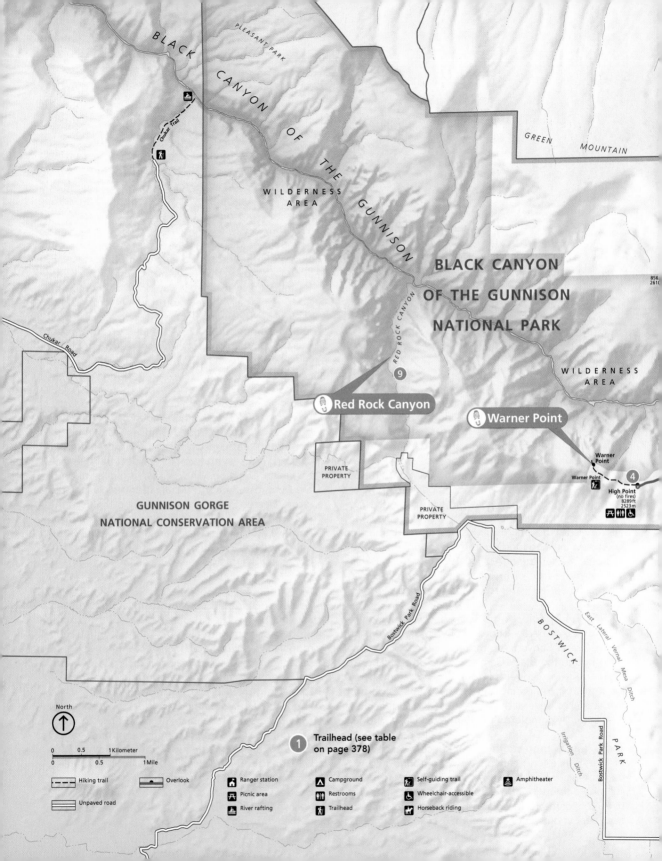

BLACK CANYON OF THE GUNNISON

PLEASANT PARK

GREEN MOUNTAIN

WILDERNESS AREA

BLACK CANYON
OF THE GUNNISON
NATIONAL PARK

RED ROCK CANYON

WILDERNESS AREA

Chukar Road

9

Red Rock Canyon

Warner Point

PRIVATE PROPERTY

Warner Point

Warner Point

4

High Point
(no fires)
8289ft
2523m

PRIVATE PROPERTY

GUNNISON GORGE
NATIONAL CONSERVATION AREA

Bostwick Park Road

BOSTWICK

East Lateral Vernal Mesa Ditch

PARK

Irrigation Ditch

Bostwick Park Road

North

0   0.5   1 Kilometer
0   0.5   1 Mile

1   Trailhead (see table
     on page 378)

Hiking trail   Overlook   Ranger station   Campground   Self-guiding trail   Amphitheater

Unpaved road   Picnic area   Restrooms   Wheelchair-accessible

                                             River rafting   Trailhead   Horseback riding

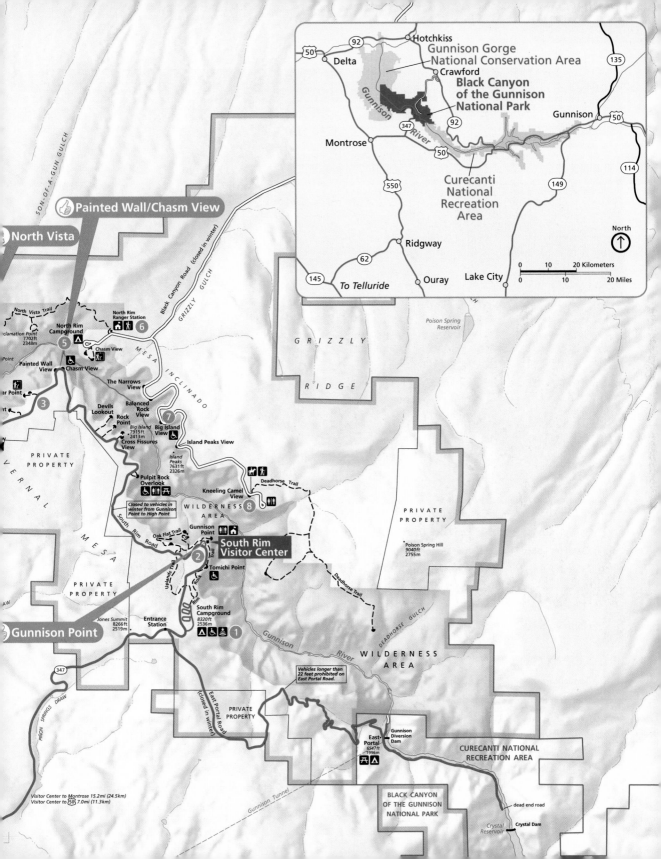

👍 **Painted Wall/Chasm View**

North Vista

SON-OF-A-GUN GULCH

Gunnison Point

Inset map (upper right)

Hotchkiss

Gunnison Gorge
National Conservation Area

Delta

Crawford

**Black Canyon
of the Gunnison
National Park**

Gunnison

50

92

135

Gunnison River

347

Montrose

550

92

50

50

114

**Curecanti
National
Recreation
Area**

149

Ridgway

62

145

To Telluride

Ouray

Lake City

North ⬆

| 0 | 10 | 20 Kilometers |
| 0 | 10 | 20 Miles |

Main map labels

Black Canyon Road (closed in winter)

North Vista Trail

Reclamation Point
7702ft
2348m

North Rim
Ranger Station

🏕 🚻 **6**

North Rim
Campground

5 🏕

Chasm View

Painted Wall
View ♿

Chasm View 🚻

The Narrows
View

GRIZZLY GULCH

MESA INCLINADO

Devils
Lookout

Balanced
Rock View

Rock
Point

*Big Island
7915ft
2413m*

Cross Fissures
View

Big Island
View ♿ **7**

Island Peaks View

*Island
Peaks
7631ft
2326m*

**PRIVATE
PROPERTY**

VERNAL

Pulpit Rock
Overlook 🚻 ⛺

*Closed to vehicles in
winter from Gunnison
Point to High Point*

**WILDERNESS
AREA**

Kneeling Camel
View 🚻 **8**

Deadhorse Trail

GRIZZLY

RIDGE

Poison Spring
Reservoir

**PRIVATE
PROPERTY**

Poison Spring Hill
9040ft
2755m

Oak Flat Trail

Gunnison
Point 🏕 🚻

South Rim Road

**South Rim
Visitor Center**

Uplands Trail

Tomichi Point ♿

Rim Rock Trail

MESA

**PRIVATE
PROPERTY**

*Jones Summit
8266ft
2519m*

Entrance
Station

South Rim
Campground
*8320ft
2536m*

🏕 🚻 **1**

Gunnison River

Deadhorse Trail

DEADHORSE GULCH

**WILDERNESS
AREA**

347

PINON SPRINGS DRAW

East Portal Road (closed in winter)

**PRIVATE
PROPERTY**

*Vehicles longer than
22 feet prohibited on
East Portal Road.*

East
Portal
*6547ft
1996m* ⛺ 🏕

Gunnison
Diversion
Dam

**CURECANTI NATIONAL
RECREATION AREA**

*Visitor Center to Montrose 15.2mi (24.5km)
Visitor Center to 50 7.0mi (11.3km)*

Gunnison Tunnel

**BLACK CANYON
OF THE GUNNISON
NATIONAL PARK**

dead end road

*Crystal
Reservoir*

Crystal Dam

Gunnison Point

Black Canyon of the Gunnison Hiking Trails (Distances are roundtrip)

	Name	Location (# on map)	Length	Difficulty Rating & Notes
South Rim	Rim Rock	Campground Loop C (1)	1.0 mile	M – Self-guided trail following the rim
	Uplands	Rim Rock Trail (1)	1.0 mile	M – Combine with Rim Rock to make a 2-mile loop
	Oak Flat Loop	Near the Visitor Center (2)	2.0 miles	S – Unmarked overlooks and narrow passages
	Cedar Point	Cedar Point (3)	0.7 mile	E – Self-guided, views of Painted Wall
	Warner Point - ✍	High Point (4)	1.5 miles	M – Wonderful trail to get great canyon views
North Rim	Chasm View	In Campground Loop (5)	0.3 mile	M – Short trail with views of Painted Wall
	North Vista - ✍	North Rim Ranger Station (6)	3.0 miles 7.0 miles	M – Route to Exclamation Point S – Continue to Green Mountain and 360° views
	Deadhorse	Kneeling Camel View (8)	5.0 miles	E/M – Follows old service road, East Portal views
Inner Canyon	Tomichi Route	Rim Rock Trail Post #13 (1)	2.0 miles	S – Steepest South Rim route with loose rock
	Gunnison Route	Near the Visitor Center (2)	3.0 miles	S – South Rim • First-timers route, still very steep
	Warner Route	Warner Point Nature Trail, just past post #13 (4)	5.5 miles	S – Out-and-back will take a full (and exhausting) day • Camp at 1 of 5 sites at the canyon floor
	S.O.B. Draw	North Rim Ranger Station (6)	3.5 miles	S – Easiest of the 3 North Rim inner canyon hikes
	Long Draw - ✍	Balanced Rock Overlook (7	2.0 miles	S – North Rim • Access to a very narrow area
	Slide Draw	Kneeling Camel View (8)	2.0 miles	S – North Rim • Extremely steep and dangerous
	Red Rock Canyon	East Parking Area (9)	6.8 miles	M – Permit Required, lottery application system

Difficulty Ratings: E = Easy, M = Moderate, S = Strenuous

Camping

South Rim Campground has a total of 88 campsites broken into three loops. Loops A and C are $16/night. Loop B sites have electric hookups and cost $22/night. Sites at Loops A and B can be reserved at (877) 444-6777 or recreation.gov from late may through mid-September (there is an additional $3 reservation fee). Sites at loop C are available on a first-come, first-served basis. Each loop has its own restroom with sinks and flush toilets. There are no dump stations and vehicles longer than 35 feet are not recommended. Loop A remains open all year while the other two loops close for winter (November–April). There's also a **small 15-site campground** on **East Portal Road** along the Gunnison River in Curecanti National Recreation Area (nps.gov/cure). Water is available from mid-May to mid-September and there are vault toilets. The fee is $16/night. **North Rim Campground** is open from spring to fall. All 13 sites are available on a first-come, first-served basis for $16/night. Maximum combined length of RV or car and trailer is 22 feet for North Rim and El Portal.

All inner canyon hiking routes (see the hiking table) end at designated camping areas with anywhere from one to six campsites. Camping in these locations requires a free Wilderness Permit.

Wilderness Permit

Whether you're planning on exploring the backcountry (including the inner canyon), paddling the Gunnison, or climbing the canyon's sheer walls, a free permit is required. Obtain yours at South Rim Visitor Center or North Rim Ranger Station on the day of your desired activity (reservations are not available). A self-registration station is available nearby each facility for anyone arriving after hours. Speak with a park ranger prior to departure if this is your first time backpacking, kayaking, or rock climbing at Black Canyon. Discussing your itinerary with a ranger helps assure you are properly prepared and experienced for your selected adventure. This is a very unforgiving place. Canyon walls are steep, the river is wild, but a safe and enjoyable adventure can be had with proper preparation.

Hiking & Backpacking

Black Canyon is too often a drive-in and drive-out attraction. Visitors should spend some time hiking the rim-top trails, if not a few days going off-trail into the wilderness or inner canyon. A number of short and moderately-difficult hikes are located along South and North Rim Roads. **Rim Rock Trail** begins at South Rim Campground and follows the rim north to Tomichi Point, Gunnison Point, and the Visitor Center. From the Visitor Center you can continue hiking on Oak Flat Loop, which provides spectacular views of the canyon as you descend slightly below the rim. After looping back to the visitor center it's possible to return to the campground via **Uplands Trail**, which veers away from the canyon on the opposite side of South Rim Road. There are a series of overlooks accessible by short hikes in between the Visitor Center and High Point. Pulpit Rock provides a nice long view of the Gunnison River as it roils beneath the canyon walls. Chasm, Painted Wall, and Cedar Point Viewpoints are exceptional. At Chasm View you're standing above the river's steepest grade, where turbulent water drops some 240 feet over a 2-mile stretch. Painted Wall View gives onlookers the opportunity to photograph Colorado's tallest cliff, standing nearly twice the height of the Empire State Building. Its name comes from pink veins of igneous pegmatite rock interrupting the layers of gneiss and schist.

South Rim Road ends at High Point and **Warner Point Nature Trail**. Mark Warner was a driving force behind the park's establishment, and this trail provides an opportunity to view the area's ecology, history, and geology through his eyes thanks to printed handouts (available at High Point, the Visitor Center, or online). Along the way, you'll notice markers corresponding to sections of the handout. The hike is well worth the effort, with amazing views looking back into the canyon. The North Rim provides longer trails with similar canyon views. Hiking to Exclamation Point via **North Vista Trail** is particularly nice.

Hikers looking for adventure (and exposure) can descend into the canyon via one of seven inner canyon routes. They are unmaintained, unmarked, steep, and littered with loose rocks. Poison ivy is practically unavoidable (wear long pants). So why hike into the canyon when you can drive there via East Portal Road? The thrill? Perhaps. The exercise? Maybe. Having such magnificent scenery to yourself is also appealing. Where each route hits the canyon floor, you'll find at least one campsite. **Gunnison Route** (South Rim) and **S.O.B. Route** (North Rim) are respectively the easiest routes on either side of the rim, but are still extremely strenuous and challenging. An 80-foot chain is anchored to the canyon wall to aid hikers attempting the Gunnison Route. Don't throw rocks from the rim, there may be hikers on their way into the canyon below.

Red Rock Canyon Route is only available to 8 visitors per day through a reservation lottery system (visit the park website for reservation request forms). This trail is

popular with fisherman and hikers because it is significantly less steep than other routes into the gorge. Restrictions are enforced to prevent overuse and because a portion of the trail crosses private land. It is only open from late May until early October and is accessed via Bostwick Park Road, located in the park's southwest corner.

If you plan on hiking the inner canyon or exploring off-trail wilderness areas, regardless of whether it's day-use or overnight, you must obtain a free wilderness permit. Permits help monitor backcountry use and aid in identifying potential emergencies.

Kayaking

Three upstream dams have tamed the Gunnison River dramatically, but the 18-mile stretch within park boundaries can still be extremely dangerous. At high water levels, several sections are unrunnable and the remainder of the corridor rates as class III–V rapids. The Gunnison should only be run by expert kayakers. Even then it should be run with individuals who are familiar with the water, its drops, and its hydraulics. All boaters must obtain a wilderness use permit.

Rock Climbing

Hard rock walls rising vertically out of the canyon floor more than 2,000 feet are sure to attract a few rock climbers. Experienced climbers love the challenge of Black Canyon's multi-pitch traditional routes. The Park Service knows about more than 145 routes, but very few are used regularly. This is largely due to difficult accessibility and general challenging nature of the routes themselves.

Black Canyon is not a place for beginners. Even the most experienced climbers will find the aid of a climbing guide helpful when making a first attempt at Black Canyon's cliffs. The most popular climbing area is north and south Chasm View. Climbing is popular from mid-April to early June, and then from mid-September through early November. All rock climbers must obtain a wilderness use permit.

Other Activities

Less popular activities include horseback riding, fishing, stargazing, biking, and winter sports. Visitors with their own horse(s) can ride North Rim's Deadhorse Trail (that's it, and the name isn't very welcoming). Cyclists are permitted on all paved roadways. In winter, snowshoers and cross-country skiers enjoy the section of South Rim Road beyond Gunnison Point, which closes to vehicles until spring.

Visitor Center

South Rim Visitor Center is open every day except Thanksgiving and Christmas. Hours are 9am until 4pm for late October through late April, but are extended to 8am until 5pm for late spring/early fall, and extended again to 8am to 6pm from Memorial Day through Labor Day. It offers exhibits, bookstore, short film, wilderness permits, and restrooms. **North Rim Ranger Station** is open intermittently during summer.

Ranger Programs & For Kids

Black Canyon provides free ranger-guided activities in summer and winter. Discussions ranging from how the canyon was formed to what birds of prey nest within its walls happen at scenic overlooks. They offer walks at East Portal or along one of the nature trails. Evening programs are performed at South Rim's Visitor Center and Amphitheater. Stargazing programs are held periodically. And in winter they lead snowshoeing treks when staffing allows. At the adjacent Curecanti National Recreation Area (nps.gov/cure), visitors can take a boat tour into Black Canyon of the Gunnison ($25/adult, $13/child). Tours are available every day but Tuesday, usually from mid-June through mid-September. Reservations (recreation.gov) are required.

Children love peering into the depths of Black Canyon (just don't let them throw rocks into the abyss, there could be unsuspecting humans below the rim). Kids are invited to become Junior Rangers. To do so, complete the free activity booklet (available at South Rim Visitor Center). Once completed, your child will be sworn into the club and receive a badge.

Flora & Fauna

It's likely you'll spot a few mule deer on your visit to the Black Canyon. Black bears have become a regular inhabitant, so be sure to use the bear-proof storage lockers for all food and scented products. Canyons aren't as prohibitive to birds as they are to humans. Peregrine falcons nest on canyon walls, occasionally forcing rock-climbing routes to close. Many different species of plants live here. Serviceberry and Gambel oak are common along the rim, while cottonwood, box elder, and Douglas fir grow in the shade of the canyon. Perhaps the most prevalent and annoying plant is poison ivy. Guests must watch diligently for the three-leafed plant when hiking the inner canyon (wear long pants).

Pets & Accessibility

Pets are permitted in several areas but must be kept on a leash (less than six feet). They are allowed on roads, in campgrounds, at overlooks, and on Rim Rock

Trail, Cedar Point Nature Trail, and North Rim Chasm View Nature Trail. From approximately June through mid-August, dogs are not allowed to be walked (or carried) around South Rim Campground or Rim Rock Trail due to potentially aggressive deer protecting their fawns. There are several boarding services available in the surrounding area if you need them.

South Rim Visitor Center, all restrooms, Tomichi Point, Chasm View, and Sunset View are fully accessible to wheelchair users. South Rim Campground has two accessible sites. The restrooms at North Rim Ranger Station and Balanced Rock Overlook are accessible.

Weather
Expect extreme variation in temperature from day-to-night, day-to-day, and canyon rim-to-floor. During summer average highs reach the 80s°F and lows dip into the 40s°F overnight. Average lows in December and January fall below zero, while highs are usually in the mid-20s°F. The canyon floor is typically 8°F warmer than its rim, even with its walls preventing sunlight from penetrating its depths except around midday.

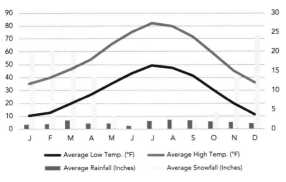

Legend:
— Average Low Temp. (°F)   — Average High Temp. (°F)
▮ Average Rainfall (Inches)   Average Snowfall (Inches)

Tips & Recommendations
Most visitors drive the south rim, stop at a few viewpoints, and continue to their next destination. Stick around for a bit. Hike to Warner Point. Drive down recently improved East Portal Road (it's very steep, 16% grade). If you're pretty intense, consider hiking into the canyon. Even if you aren't a hiker, you should still try to spend a full day here. The canyon's appearance is dramatically different as the sun moves across the sky.

The road to the North Rim is unpaved but not impassable to regular vehicles. The 2-hour drive from the South Rim is well worth it. You may even have the North Rim all to yourself for the effort.

Another way to get a different perspective of Black Canyon is to join a ranger-led boat tour at Curecanti National Recreation Area (nps.gov/cure), which encompasses Blue Mesa Reservoir, Colorado's largest lake. Curecanti National Park begins at Black Canyon's southern boundary, two miles north of Crystal Dam.

Hiking Trails: Warner Point (Moderate, 1.5 miles), Long Draw (Strenuous, 2), North Vista (Moderate, 3), Gunnison Route (Strenuous, 3)
South Rim Viewpoints: Painted Wall View, Gunnison Point, Chasm View, Pulpit Rock, Cedar Point (similar to Painted Wall View), Sunset View
North Rim Viewpoints: Chasm View, Island Peaks View, The Narrows View, Kneeling Camel View
Rainy Day Activities: Most people don't spend a lot of time here, so if it rains, it rains. The canyon is still spectacular, and maybe you'll get some rainbows.
Sunset Spots: Exclamation Point, Painted Wall View, Cedar Point Overlook, Sunset View Overlook
Sunrise Spots: Warner Point, Painted Wall View

Beyond the Park...

Dining
The Stone House • (970) 240-8899
1415 Hawk Pkwy, Montrose
stonehousemontrose.com

Trattoria Di Sofia • (970) 249-0433
110 N Townsend Ave, Montrose
trattoriadisofia.com

Himalayan Pun Hill Kitchen
710 N Townsend Ave, Montrose
himalayanpunhill.com

Grocery Stores
Safeway • (970) 249-8822
1329 S Townsend Ave, Montrose

Walmart • (970) 249-7544
16750 S Townsend Ave, Montrose

Lodging & Camping
Country Lodge • (970) 249-4567
1624 E Main St, Montrose
countrylodgecolorado.com

The Hitching Post • (970) 424-4966
313 CO-92, Crawford
thehitchingposthotel.com

River Bend RV Park • (970) 249-8235
65120 Old Chipeta Tr, Montrose
riverbend-rvpark.com

Black Canyon KOA
200 N Cedar St, Montrose
koa.com • (970) 249-9177

Black Canyon RV Park
348 US-50, Cimarron • (970) 249-1147
blackcanyonrvpark.com

Festivals
Bluegrass Festival •June
bluegrass.com • Telluride

Attractions
National Forests (fs.usda.gov) galore! Uncompahgre (mountains and waterfalls), White River (popular Maroon Bells hike), Grand Mesa, Gunnison, Pike-San Isabel, Medicine Bow-Routt (Flat Tops Wilderness/Devil's Causeway) cover millions of acres. Exploring them can be incredibly rewarding, but you'll have to do a little homework.

Curecanti National Recreation Area
Gunnison River reservoirs
nps.gov/cure • (970) 641-2337

Colorado National Monument
Some pretty wild red rock canyons are found here
nps.gov/colm • (970) 858-2800

Dinosaur National Monument
Off the beaten path from the popular Colorado attractions but you'll find good rafting, hiking, petroglyphs, and fossils
nps.gov/dino • (435) 781-7700

Crawford State Park • (970) 921-5721
Reservoir, fishing and camping
40468 CO-92, Crawford
cpw.state.co.us

Ridgeway State Park
Swimming, yurts, camping
cpw.state.co.us

Mesa Verde

Cliff Palace

Phone: (970) 529-4465
Website: nps.gov/meve

Established: June 29, 1906
Size: 52,122 Acres
Annual Visitors: 550,000
Peak Season: Summer

Ranger-Guided Tours (per person)
Cliff Palace: $8–25 (1 hour)
Balcony House (closed 2021): $8
Long House: $8 (1.5–2 hours)
Mug/Square Tower House: $25
Spring House: $45 (8 hours)

Morefield Camp: $36–50/night
Backcountry Camping: Prohibited
Far View Lodge: $102–161/night

Park Hours: All day, every day
Entrance Fee: $30/25/15
(car/motorcycle/individual)
$20/15/10 (November–April)

Let's say you arrive at Mesa Verde completely unaware of the area's history and culture. A quick drive across the mesa and you would be left scratching your head, wondering where the majestic scenery went. Mesa Verde's deep gorges and tall mesas have a bit of scenic appeal, but it pales in comparison to other southwestern national parks. What it lacks in natural beauty it redeems in cultural significance. When the park was established in 1906, it became the first tract of land set aside to protect a prehistoric culture and its ruins, pottery, tools, and other ancient artifacts.

Somewhere around 750 AD, Puebloans were living in modest pit-houses on top of the mesa, clustered together forming small villages. They found sustenance farming and hunting. Judging by the circular underground chambers called kivas, religion was important, and rituals and ceremonies were performed regularly. By the late 12th century, they began building homes in alcoves beneath the rim of the mesa. These cliff dwellings became larger and more numerous.

Scientists and volunteers are attempting to piece together the history of Ancestral Puebloan People by scouring thousands of archeological sites. To date, there are more than 4,700 archeological sites within the park; roughly 600 are cliff dwellings. About 90 percent of the cliff dwellings contain fewer than 10 rooms, but a few are enormous. Cliff

Palace, the largest and most famous dwelling, contains 150 rooms. Long House and Spruce Tree House exceed 100 rooms, and Balcony House has more than 40. These sites have attracted archeologists and vandals, pothunters and politicians, tourists and explorers.

John Moss, a local prospector, is the first person in recorded history to have seen the ruins. In 1874, he led a photographer through Mancos Canyon along the base of Mesa Verde. Resulting photos inspired geologists to visit the site in 1875. More than a decade later Richard Wetherill and his brothers began the first serious excavations. They spent the next 15 months exploring over 100 dwellings. Frederick H. Chapin—a noted mountaineer, photographer, and author—aided the excavation. Later, he wrote an article and book on the area's geologic and cultural significance. In 1889 and once again in 1890, Benjamin Wetherill wrote to the Smithsonian, warning that the area would be plundered by looters and tourists if it was not protected as a national park. He also requested that he and his brothers be placed in the employ of the government to carry out careful excavation of the ruins even though they were not legitimate archeologists.

The requests went unanswered, and the following year the Wetherills hosted Gustaf Nordenskiöld of the Academy of Sciences in Sweden. Using scientific methods and meticulous data collection, he began a thorough excavation of many ruins including Cliff Palace. Incensed locals charged Nordenskiöld with "devastating the ruins" and held him on $1,000 bond when he tried to transport some 600 artifacts, including a mummified corpse, on the Denver and Rio Grande Railroad. He was released because no laws existed to prevent treasure hunting. The artifacts were shipped to Sweden and today they reside in the National Museum in Helsinki, Finland. Upon his return home, he examined the artifacts and published a book titled *The Cliff Dwellers of the Mesa Verde.*

At this time, pothunters and vandals were becoming a serious problem. Dynamite was used to blow holes in walls to let light in or to scare away rattlesnakes. Colorado Cliff Dwelling Association (CCDA) picked up the mantle of advocating a national park. But when Virginia Donaghe McClurg, head of the CCDA, expressed her opinion that it should be a "woman's park," Lucy Peabody left the association and continued to search for support on her own. Finally in 1906, President Theodore Roosevelt signed a bill creating Mesa Verde National Park, protecting an area of unique history and culture for future generations.

Sun Temple

When to Go
Mesa Verde is open all year, but most of its more notable attractions close for the off-season (November–April). The popular Cliff Palace and Balcony House Tours are typically available from April to October (Balcony House will reopen in 2022). Wetherill Mesa Road is open from 8am–7pm (6pm in spring), typically late April through October, but all sites (including the cliff dwellings, Long House and Step House) are only accessible from mid-May until mid-October.

If you visit during the off-season, you'll be limited to exploring the visitor center, Chapin Mesa Archeological Museum, Mesa Top Loop sites, Far View sites, Petroglyph Point Trail, and the park's overlooks. Campground, showers, laundry, gas services, and Far View Lodge close for winter. Summers can be busy, but the park increases its tour offerings to accommodate increased traffic, plus Wetherill Mesa Road opens (vehicles longer than 25 feet and bicycles are not permitted). Motorists can drive as far as Step House. From there, the 5-mile Long House Loop is open to hiking and biking.

Transportation & Airports
Public transportation does not provide service to or around the park. Greyhound (800.231.2222, greyhound.com) has a bus station 35 miles from the park entrance in Durango, CO. You'll need a rental car to get the rest of the way. There are small regional airports nearby at Cortez, CO (10 miles to park entrance); Durango, CO (35 miles); and Farmington, NM (70 miles). Albuquerque International Sunport (ABQ) is located 250 miles to the southeast. Car rental is available at each destination.

Directions
Mesa Verde is located in the remote southwestern corner of Colorado. It is accessed via the Mesa Verde National Park Exit from US-160. The park entrance is 35 miles west of Durango, CO and 12 miles east of Cortez, CO. Chapin Mesa, where you'll find many of the main attractions, is located 22 miles south of the park entrance and visitor center.

Regions

Mesa Verde is essentially broken into two distinct regions: Chapin Mesa and Wetherill Mesa. **Chapin Mesa** reaches all the way down to the park's southern boundary. This is where you'll find the most recognizable cliff dwellings and Chapin Mesa Museum. A one-way loop road circles around the Museum, providing plenty of parking and access to Spruce Tree House (self-guided tours from spring to fall, free guided tours in winter). Spruce Tree House is the third largest cliff dwelling in the park. Unfortunately, it closed to the public in 2015 due to site instability. It remained closed when we went to print, and there's a good chance it will still be closed when you read this. Continuing south beyond the museum and Spruce Tree House is Mesa Top Loop. Several stops provide a tour of Ancestral Puebloan pit-houses and overlooks with views of their cliff dwellings. East of Mesa Top Loop is Cliff Palace Loop. Along this loop are parking areas for Cliff Palace and Balcony House. Both of these cliff dwellings are only accessible from spring to fall on ranger-guided tours with a ticket ($8/person • make reservations at recreation.gov).

Wetherill Mesa runs parallel to Chapin Mesa, just to its west. This quiet side of Mesa Verde is open from late April through October. Wetherill Mesa Road begins near Far View Visitor Lodge and winds its way to a collection of archeological sites in the park's southwest corner. Long House, the park's second largest cliff dwelling, is available for tour with a ticket ($8/person). Visitors are free to explore Step House, pit-houses, and nature trails on their own. Long House Loop is open to walkers and bicyclists.

Camping & Lodging

Morefield Campground has 267 campsites, 15 of them have full hookups. The campground is open from May through October. A free dump station, coin-operated showers and laundry, a general store, cafe, and gas are available nearby. Campsites are available two weeks before and after the peak season but without any services beyond restrooms. Camping fees are: $36/night (standard site) and $50/night (with hookups). Even though the campground rarely fills, reservations are always appreciated (and recommended for the RV sites). Reservations can be made at (800) 449-2288 or visitmesaverde.com.

More comfortable accommodations are available at **Far View Lodge**, located 15 miles into the park. It's open between May and late October. Rooms cost $102–161/night. The lodge features a dining room and lounge/bar. Reservations can be made at (800) 449-2288 or visitmesaverde.com. Additionally, there's a small cafe near Chapin Mesa Archeological Museum.

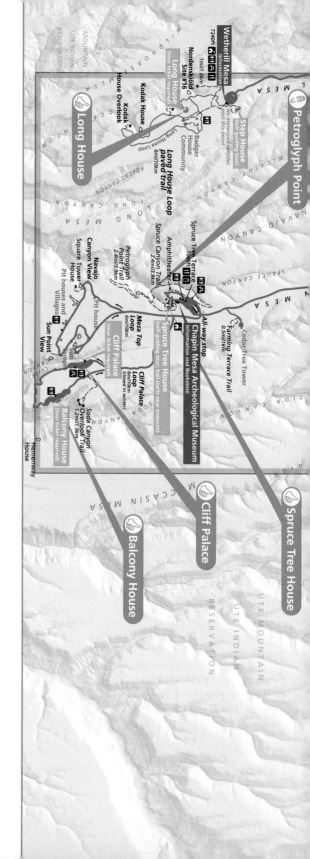

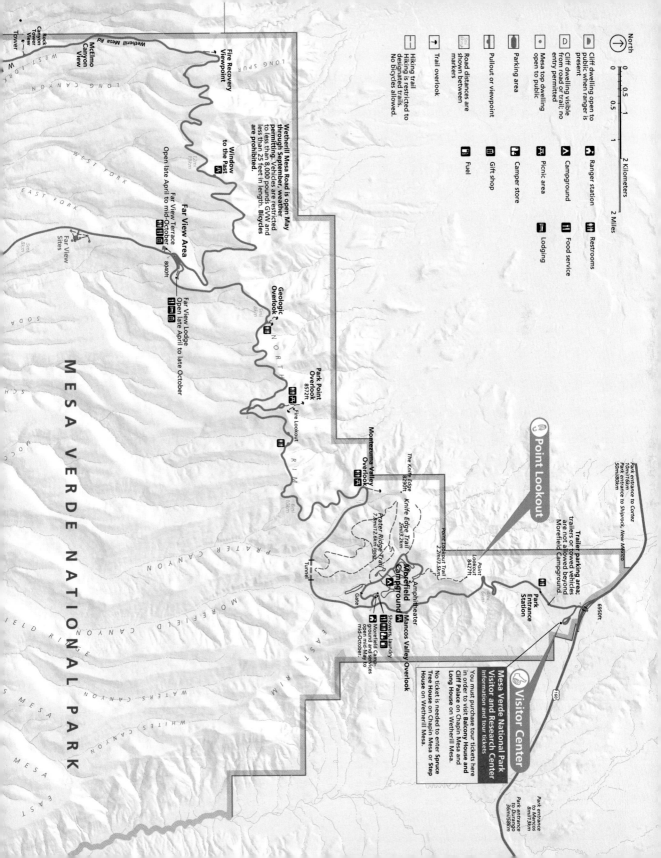

MESA VERDE NATIONAL PARK

North

0   0.5   1   2 Kilometers
0   0.5   1   2 Miles

Legend

Cliff dwelling open to public when ranger is present	Ranger station
Cliff dwelling visible from road or trail; no entry permitted	Campground
D Mesa top dwelling open to public	Picnic area
Parking area	Camper store
Pullout or viewpoint	Gift shop
Trail overlook	Fuel
Hiking trail Hiking is restricted to designated trails. No bicycles allowed.	Restrooms
Trail distances are shown between markers	Food service
Road distances are shown between markers	Lodging

Point Lookout

Visitor Center

Mesa Verde National Park Visitor and Research Center
Information and tour tickets

You must purchase tour tickets here in order to visit **Balcony House** and **Cliff Palace** on Chapin Mesa and **Long House** on Wetherill Mesa.

No ticket is needed to enter **Spruce Tree House** on Chapin Mesa or **Step House** on Wetherill Mesa.

Park entrance to Cortez 10mi/16km
Park entrance to Shiprock, New Mexico 50mi/80km

Park entrance to Mancos 8mi/13km

Park entrance to Durango 36mi/58km

Trailer parking area; trailers or towed vehicles are not allowed beyond Morefield Campground.

Point Lookout 8427ft

Park Entrance Station

6950ft

Point Lookout Trail 2.2mi/3.5km

Morefield Campground

Amphitheater

Mancos Valley Overlook

Showers, laundry

Morefield Campground and services open mid-May to mid-October

Gate

Tunnel

Prater Ridge Trail 7.9mi/12.6km loop

Knife Edge Trail 2mi/3.2km

The Knife Edge 8250ft

Montezuma Valley Overlook

Fire Lookout

Park Point Overlook 8572ft

N O R T H   R I M

Geologic Overlook

Far View Lodge Open late April to late October

Far View Terrace Open late April to mid-October

8040ft

Far View Area

Far View Sites

Window to the Past

Fire Recovery Viewpoint

Wetherill Mesa Road is open May through September, weather permitting. Vehicles are restricted to less than 8,000 pounds GVW and less than 25 feet in length. Bicycles are prohibited.

LONG SPUR

WEST FORK

EAST FORK

WEST FORK

LONG CANYON

McElmo Canyon View

Rock Canyon Tower View

Tower

Wetherill Mesa Rd

SODA CANYON

PRATER CANYON

MOREFIELD CANYON

MOREFIELD RIDGE

WATERS CANYON

WHITES CANYON

EAST RIM

SCHOOL

MOCCASIN

WHITES MESA

EAST MESA

Balcony House

Mesa Verde Cliff Dwelling Tours (Fees are per person)

Name	Dates	Duration	Fee	Notes
Cliff Palace - ♿	late May–mid-Sept	1 hour	$8	Begins at Cliff Palace Parking Area
Balcony House - ♿	late April–early Oct	1 hour	$8	Begins at Balcony House Parking Area
Spruce Tree House - ♿	All Year	N/A	Self-Guided and Guided	Access near Chapin Mesa Museum • Free guided tours are offered in winter
Long House - ♿	mid-May–mid-Oct	1.5 hours	$8	Tour begins at Wetherill Mesa Info Kiosk
Step House	mid-May–mid-Oct	N/A	Self-Guided	Access near Wetherill Mesa Info Kiosk

Tours listed above are provided by the National Park Service. Tickets can be purchased up to 14 days in advance at (877) 444-6777 or recreation.gov (Your receipt is your ticket!). Visitors must climb ladders and/or stairs at each site.

700 Years (Motor Coach Tour)	May–late Oct	4 hours	$88 (Adult) $66 (Child)	Guided tour of mesa-top sites and Cliff Palace (stairs and ladder required)

The tour listed above is offered by Aramark (800.449.2288, visitmesaverde.com). Tickets may be purchased at Far View Lodge, Far View Terrace, Morefield Campground, or online at visitmesaverde.com.

Balcony House (Sunrise)	Select Dates	1.5 hours	$25	Bring a flashlight, dress in layers, and enjoy
Cliff Palace (Twilight)	Select Dates	1.5 hours	$25	Moderate 0.25-mile trip for sunset
Sqaure Tower House	Select Dates	1.5 hours	$25	Strenuous 1-mile trip along uneven trail
Mug House	Select Dates	2 hours	$25	Strenuous 3-mile trip on unpaved terrain
Oak Tree House	Select Dates	2 hours	$25	Moderate 1-mile trip along narrow trail
Spring House	Select Dates	8 hours	$40	Strenuous 8-mile trek to unexcavated site
Yucca House	Select Dates	2 hours	$10	Easy half-mile walk to Ancestral Puebloan site

Tours listed above are special backcountry hikes offered intermittently by the National Park Service. Tickets must be purchased in advance at (877) 444-6777 or recreation.gov. Do not bring sugary snacks or drinks.

Cliff Dwellings

About 1,400 years ago Ancestral Puebloans inhabited the region that has become Mesa Verde National Park, farming and hunting on the mesa tops. Over time they moved from small communities of pit-houses on top the mesa to cliff dwellings in alcoves beneath its rim. Much can be inferred from the tools, basketry, pottery, and ruins left behind by this ancient culture, but little is certain about why they built such large structures in the canyon walls or why they abandoned them in the late 1200s. Were they seeking protection from conflict? From wildfires? From weather?

Of the 4,700 archeological sites found at Mesa Verde about 600 are cliff dwellings. These structures range from one-room houses to massive 150-room villages (like Cliff Palace). They could only be reached by hand and foot holds carved into the cliff wall. Several had kivas, ceremonial rooms used to pray for rain or prosperous hunting and farming. Ancestral Puebloans put a lot of time and effort into their homes, but they occupied these structures for less than 100 years. Success may have helped lead to their demise. Overpopulation could have stripped the farmland of its nutrients and land of its game. Climatic changes or political squabbles may have played their parts, too. Your guess is as good as anyone else's. Tour the ancient ruins and wonder to yourself why they abandoned these homes with such fantastic views. All cliff dwellings (except Spruce Tree House and Step House) are not to be entered without the accompaniment of a uniformed park ranger. Today, the park offers guided tours of Cliff Palace, Balcony House and Long House, along with a few more remote backcountry destinations (only available to small groups on select dates).

Guided Tours

A visit to Mesa Verde is not complete without touring one (or all three) of the large cliff dwellings (Cliff Palace, Balcony House, and Long House). It might be the best $8 you spend in all the parks. Tickets can be purchased at the visitor center, located near the park entrance, or online at recreation.gov. You'll also find a few unique ranger-led cliff dwelling tours only offered a few times each year. Please refer to the table for a complete listing. Rangers also lead a 4.5-hour Wetherill Mesa Bike and Hike Adventure, where you bike five miles and hike four. It can be reserved for $16/adult at recreation.gov. (Bring your bike.)

Hiking

Hiking provides an excellent retreat from the busy cliff dwellings. However, you are only allowed to

Spruce Tree House

hike on designated trails. Several originate from Morefield Campground, including **Prater Ridge Trail**, located just beyond the campground gate. It follows Prater Ridge, and then loops around the ridgetop totaling 7.8 miles. There is a short bisecting trail, allowing hikers to complete just the 3.6-mile north loop or 2.4-mile south loop. The easy 2-mile, out-and-back **Knife Edge Trail** departs from the campground's northwest corner and follows an old road that served as the main entrance beginning in 1914. Today, it provides hikers with excellent views of Montezuma Valley and a great vantage point for watching the sunset. Another excellent hike for watching the sunset is 2.2-mile **Point Lookout Trail**. It begins at the very north end of the campground.

There are four trails at Chapin Mesa. You must register at the museum or trailhead (gated, contact a ranger if closed) to hike Petroglyph Point and Spruce Canyon Trails (2.4 miles each). They are steep and somewhat difficult. **Petroglyph Point** is fun, and it leads to the only accessible petroglyphs. **Spruce Canyon** isn't as interesting but it's a different perspective as you look up at the mesa from the canyon below. **Soda Canyon** (1.2 miles) is an easy hike with distant views of Balcony House (and a telescope at the second lookout, where you can peep on tourists at Balcony House). **Farming Terrace Trail** (0.5 mile) is an easy walk through prehistoric check dams used to create farming terraces. Stop at Cedar Tree Tower while you're there. Far View Sites is another mesa top community worth exploring.

Wetherill Mesa has three short trails beginning from the information kiosk. **Step House Loop Trail** leads to pit-houses and a cliff dwelling. Nordenskiöld Site #16 (2 miles) leads to a cliff dwelling overlook. **Badger House Community Trail** (2.3 miles) passes through 600 years of pueblo development. Trail guides are available for all three.

Square Tower House

Winter Activities

Winter activities at Mesa Verde are different than those found during the rest of the year. Park rangers lead guests on tours of Spruce Tree House, but the rest of the cliff dwellings are closed until spring. You can still view many of the dwellings from a distance at overlooks. Cliff Palace Loop Road is not plowed during winter, making it an excellent location for cross-country skiing, snowshoeing, and winter hiking. Mesa Top Loop Road provides views of Cliff Palace and is open in winter. Before hiking, snowshoeing, or cross-country skiing in the park, you should discuss your plans with a ranger to receive information regarding current trail conditions. You might have to register to hike in specific areas. Overnight stays are not permitted during winter and all sites are off-limits after sunset.

Visitor Center & Museum

You'll definitely want to stop at **Mesa Verde National Park Visitor and Research Center** located near the park entrance, especially if you didn't make reservations for any of the guided tours. It's the only place to get tickets in person. The visitor center is generally open from 8am–5pm, but hours are extended from 7:30am–7pm from late May through early September, and shortened to 8:30–4:30 in winter. The visitor center also houses several impressive exhibits, a bookstore, trail guides, free Wi-Fi (in the lobby and parking area), and restrooms. **Chapin Mesa Archeological Museum** is open all year with hours from 9am–4:30pm in winter, 8am–6:30pm for spring and summer, and 8am–5pm in fall. The museum features a wealth of exhibits on Ancestral Puebloan life and numerous artifacts that were found at the park's archeological sites, and a 25-minute introductory film is shown every half-hour. The museum and visitor center close for Thanksgiving, Christmas Eve, Christmas, and New Year's Day.

Ranger Programs & For Kids

In addition to ranger-guided cliff dwelling tours, there are ranger-led walks through Far View Sites and evening programs at the Campground and Far View Lodge. Programs are offered daily from late May through early September, free of charge. Visit the park website for a current schedule of events.

Kids may or may not find the history and ruins of Ancestral Puebloans to be captivating. If not, engage your child in this unique environment by picking up a free Junior Ranger activity booklet at the visitor center or Chapin Mesa Museum. The award for a completed booklet is a Mesa Verde Junior Ranger badge. (Booklets are also available at the park website.)

Flora & Fauna

Mesa Verde was preserved for its historic culture, but its present inhabitants are nearly as interesting. About 74 species of mammals, 200 species of birds, 16 species of reptiles, and a handful of species of fish and amphibians have been documented in the park. You have a good chance of seeing animals like coyote, mule deer, spotted bat, and spotted owl.

Over 640 species of plants exist here. Cottonwood, willow, and buffaloberry survive on the banks of Mancos River and near seep springs. Over the past decade, several wildfires have cut the size of the park's piñon-juniper forests in half. A few champion-sized trees survived. One Utah juniper's trunk measures 52 inches in diameter, a record for Colorado. Another is dated at more than 1,300 years old. In the lower elevations you'll find sagebrushes. Higher up you'll find mostly shrubs, but Gambel oak and Douglas fir grow along the north rim in sheltered areas. Plants like Cliff Palace milkvetch, Schmoll's milkvetch, Mesa Verde wandering aletes, and Mesa Verde stickseed are endemic.

Pets & Accessibility

Pets are allowed in the park, but are not permitted on trails, in archeological sites, or in buildings (except for service animals). They are permitted along roadways (including the 5-mile Long House Loop), in parking lots, and at the campground but must be kept on a leash (less than six feet). Morefield Village offers a kennels ($25/day, open from May through mid-October).

Mesa Verde is tricky for individuals with limited mobility. Its cliff dwellings are built into alcoves below the rim of the mesa. Visitors must descend tall ladders or stairs carved into the steep cliff wall to access Cliff Palace and Balcony House. Many other sites are accessible with assistance. The park's scenic overlooks, Far View Visitor Center, Chapin Mesa Museum, Far View Sites, and Spruce Tree House are all potential destinations. Step House and Badger House Community are accessible with assistance. Long House is not. Morefield Campground has a few accessible campsites.

Weather

Weather is quite comfortable for most of the year. On average, every other day is clear and cloudless regardless of the month. An occasional snowstorm passes through in winter, but average high temperatures in January are above 40°F and average lows are around 20°F. In the middle of summer high temperatures can reach into the 90s°F. You may sweat during the day, but don't worry about it being too hot to sleep. Temperatures usually fall into the 50s°F at night.

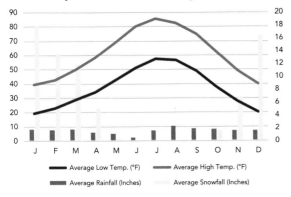

Average Low Temp. (°F)   Average High Temp. (°F)
Average Rainfall (Inches)   Average Snowfall (Inches)

Tips & Recommendations

Be sure to reserve your tickets through recreation.gov or stop at the visitor center first thing when you enter the park. It's the only place to purchase tour tickets in person. You'll spend nearly 2 hours driving back to the visitor center if you decide you'd like to tour a cliff dwelling after seeing how impressive they are from a distance. If you choose to skip the ranger-guided tours, you can still tour Spruce Tree House or Step House on your own (when they're open).

Speaking of, Spruce Tree House was closed due to potential rock falls when our last edition went to print. It remains closed when this one went to print. It's still worth checking out when you get there, even if you can only view it from the overlook

Slowing down is a good idea for every national park trip, but it's particularly good advice at Mesa Verde. Spend some time imagining what it was like living in these cliff dwellings. Spend some time exploring Chapin Mesa Museum. The more time you spend, the greater your appreciation will be for what it took to live like this hundreds of years ago.

Hiking Trail: Petroglyph Point (Moderate, 2.4 miles), Point Lookout (Moderate, 2.2), Prater Ridge (Moderate, 7.8)
Viewpoints: Cliff Palace Overlook, Square Tower House, Sun Point View (a different view of Cliff Palace), Sunset House, Soda Canyon Overlook (Balcony House)
Family Activities: Become Junior Rangers, children will probably like the Balcony House tour most as it's a little bit of an adventure
Guided Tours: They're all good!
History Enthusiasts: Mesa Verde is all about the culture! Come and enjoy it.
Sunset Spots: Point Lookout, Cliff Palace is best photographed in late afternoon (from any of the viewpoints listed above or even the Sun Temple area)
Sunrise Spots: Balcony House is best photographed in the morning and can be seen from a distance from Soda Canyon Overlook

Beyond the Park...

Dining
The Farm Bistro • (970) 565-3834
34 W Main St, Cortez
thefarmbistrocortez.com

Gustavo's Mexican Restaurant
125 E Main St, Cortez • (970) 565-4633

Mancos Brewing Co • (970) 533-9761
484 US-160, Mancos
mancosbrewingcompany.com

Grocery Stores
City Market • (970) 565-6504
508 E Main St, Cortez

Walmart • (970) 565-6138
1835 E Main St, Cortez

Lodging & Camping
Retro Inn • (970) 565-3738
2040 E Main St, Cortez
retroinnmesaverde.com

Majestic Dude Ranch • (970) 533-7900
42688 Rd N, Mancos
majesticduderanch.com

Starry Nights Ranch • (877) 314-7380
11555 Rd 39, Mancos
thestarrynightsranch.com

Sundance RV • Cortez
sundancervpark.com

The Views RV • Dolores
theviewsrvpark.com

Echo Basin RV
43747 CR M, Mancos
echobasin.com • (970) 533-7000

Attractions
Hovenweep National Monument
Several prehistoric villages
McElmo Route, Cortez
nps.gov/hove • (970) 562-4282

Aztec Ruins National Monument
Preserved Pueblo structures
725 Ruins Rd, Aztec, NM
nps.gov/azru

Canyon of the Ancients NM
Many archaeological sites
Dolores, CO • blm.gov

Mild to Wild Rafting • (970) 247-4789
Rafting, jeep tours
mild2wildrafting.com

Canyon Trails • (970) 565-1499
Horseback riding • Cortez
canyontrailsranch.com

Rimrock Outfitters • (970) 533-7588
Horseback riding • Mancos
rimrockoutfitters.com

Angel Peak • blm.gov
Badlands, peaks, and canyons in northwest New Mexico

Navajo Lakes State Park
emnrd.nm.gov

Arches

Delicate Arch

Phone: (435) 719-2299
Website: nps.gov/arch

Established: November 12, 1971
April 12, 1929 (National Monument)
Size: 76,519 Acres
Annual Visitors: 1.5 Million
Peak Season: March–October

Activities: Hiking, Backpacking, Biking, Rock Climbing

Devil's Garden Camp: $25/night
Backcountry Camping: Permitted with a Backcountry Use Permit ($7)

Park Hours: All day, every day
Entrance Fee: $30/25/15 (car/motorcycle/individual)

The only arches you see on a typical family vacation are golden, raised high above the ground, advertising the ubiquitous fast-food chain. But in southeast Utah, high atop the Colorado Plateau, is a collection of more than 2,000 natural sandstone arches, colored striking shades of pink, orange, and red. Standing tall, they frame the surrounding mountains. These natural advertisements are just as good at capturing the attention of passersby, but they have nothing to sell. In fact, all they do is give. They give inspiration to the many guests who come to admire Mother Nature's patient handiwork.

Patient is a gross understatement; these fragile features began forming more than 300 million years ago. First a massive sea covering the region evaporated, depositing a salt bed thousands of feet thick in some places. During the Uncompahgre Uplift, rivers and streams buried the salt beds with debris and sediment. Desert conditions of the early Jurassic period allowed a layer of Navajo sandstone to be covered by a layer of Entrada sandstone (the substrate of most arches). But before sandstone could be sculpted by wind, water and ice, it was buried by another 5,000 feet of sediment. The weight of material caused lower salt beds to heat up and liquefy. Layers of rock became unstable. Faulting occurred and plumes of less dense liquefied salt penetrated the upper layers of rock forming salt domes. Domes provided a curve to sections of sandstone. Years of erosion wore away the surface sediment, eventually exposing the underlying sandstone. Water seeped into cracks in its surface, gradually enlarging them until walls of sandstone called fins were left, isolated from one another. As wind and water continued to work on these fins, the salt bed layer wore away faster than sandstone. Water collected in joints and fissures. Expanding as it froze, chunks of rock would flake and crumble. Many fins collapsed into piles of rubble. Others formed magnificent arches that continue to be sculpted by wind, water, and ice. These too will concede to erosion and gravity. Since 1970, 43 arches have collapsed within the park.

The first inhabitants weren't all that interested in seeing sandstone arches. More than 10,000 years ago, nomadic people came to the region hunting and gathering. Until 700 years ago, Fremont People and Ancestral Puebloans lived here, growing crops of maize, beans, and squash. Just as they picked up and moved south, Paiute and Ute Indians moved in. Spanish missionaries encountered natives in the late 1700s while searching for a route between Santa Fe and Los Angeles. In 1855, European Americans settled in the region. Mormons established Elk Mountain Mission, but difficult farming and disputes with Native Americans led them to abandon their settlements. By the 1880s, ranchers, farmers, and prospectors were trickling into the area. John Wesley Wolfe, a Civil War veteran, was among them. He built a small ranch along Salt Wash with his son in 1898, which is still preserved in its original location near present-day Delicate Arch Trailhead.

It wasn't until 1911 that locals began to understand the recreational value of the area. Loren "Bish" Taylor, a local newspaperman, and John "Doc" Williams, Moab's first doctor, frequented the area, marveling at these sandstone formations. Bish wrote about the natural wonders just north of Moab, and eventually publicity grew to the point Denver and Rio Grande Western Railroad and the federal government took notice. Both parties were impressed, and in 1929 President Hoover signed legislation creating Arches National Monument. In 1971, Congress redesignated it as a national park. It's an eroded landscape protected from man, but not from nature, and the landscapes are constantly changing. Changes unnoticed by the average visitor. Visitors drawn to and inspired by grand natural landmarks millions of years in the making.

Private Arch

When to Go
Arches is open all day every day, and visitation is heavy from March through October, peaking between May and September. However, spring and fall are the preferred seasons. If you wish to camp inside the park anytime during peak season, you'll want to make reservations as soon as possible. They're available up to six months in advance between March and October. Campsites are first-come, first-served from November through February.

Transportation & Airports
Public transportation does not provide service to or around the park. The closest large commercial airport is Salt Lake City International (SLC), located 237 miles to the northwest. There are three regional airports nearby. Canyonlands Field (CNY) is 14 miles to the north. Grand Junction Regional (GJT) is 114 miles to the northeast. Green River Municipal (RVR) is 55 miles to the northwest.

Directions
Arches is located in southeastern Utah, just 28 miles south of I-70, between Green River, UT and Grand Junction, CO. To reach the park from I-70, take Exit 182 for US-191 toward Crescent Jct/Moab. Continue south on US-191 for approximately 27 miles, where you will see the visitor center to the east and signs for the entrance.

Visitors arriving from the southwest (Mesa Verde National Park) should take US-160 west. At Cortez, turn right onto US-491 North/North Broadway. Continue for 60 miles before turning right at US-191. Drive another 60 miles and you will pass through Moab to the park entrance and visitor center. You will also pass the entrance to Canyonlands National Park's Needles District (and Newspaper Rock) and Wilson Arch (all worthy pit-stops).

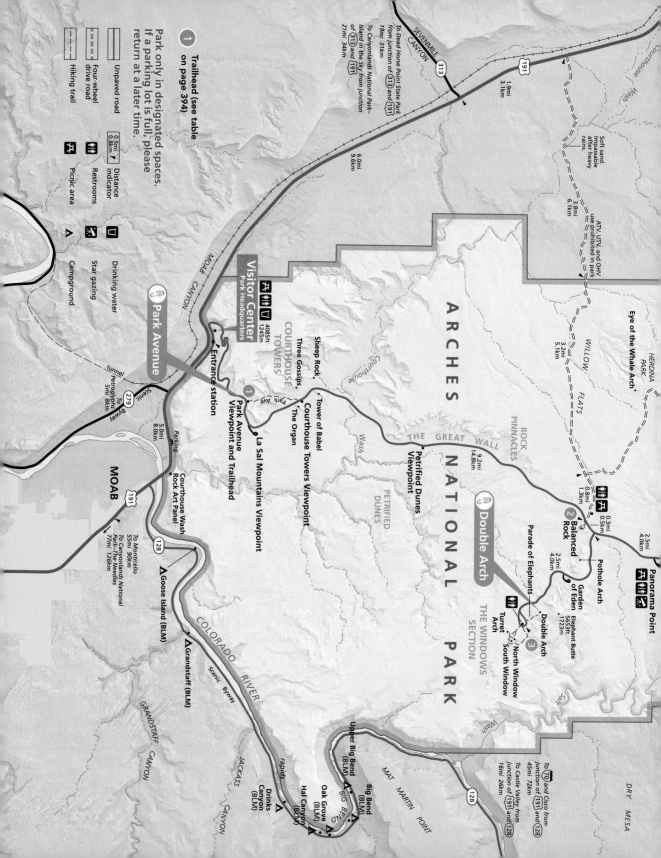

ARCHES NATIONAL PARK

① Trailhead (see table on page 394)

Park only in designated spaces. If a parking lot is full, please return at a later time.

Unpaved road
Four-wheel drive road
Hiking trail

0.5mi 0.8km ▾ Distance indicator

🚻 Restrooms

🅿 Picnic area

🚰 Drinking water

🔭 Star gazing

▲ Campground

Visitor Center
Park Headquarters
4085ft 1245m

Park Avenue Viewpoint and Trailhead

La Sal Mountains Viewpoint

Courthouse Wash Rock Art Panel

Entrance station

Park Avenue

MOAB

191

128

To Monticello 55mi 90km
To Canyonlands National Park–The Needles 77mi 126km

△ Goose Island (BLM)

△ Grandstaff (BLM)

279 Scenic Byway

Petroglyphs 5mi 8km

tunnel

5.0mi 8.0km

Parking

MOAB CANYON

COLORADO RIVER
Scenic Byway

GRANDSTAFF CANYON

JACKASS CANYON

Sheep Rock
Three Gossips
Tower of Babel
Courthouse Towers Viewpoint
The Organ

COURTHOUSE TOWERS

Courthouse Wash

THE GREAT WALL

Petrified Dunes Viewpoint

PETRIFIED DUNES

ROCK PINNACLES

WILLOW FLATS

HERDINA PARK

Eye of the Whale Arch

9.2mi 14.8km

0.8mi 1.3km
0.3mi 0.5km

Balanced Rock

② Pothole Arch

Parade of Elephants

Garden of Eden

2.5mi 4.0km

Elephant Butte 5653ft 1723m

Double Arch

THE WINDOWS SECTION

Turret Arch
North Window
South Window
③

2.5mi 4.0km

Panorama Point
🚻 🅿

To Castle Valley from junction of 191 and 128 16mi 26km

To I-70 and Cisco from junction of 191 and 128 45mi 72km

DRY MESA

MAT MARTIN POINT

BIG BEND

Upper Big Bend (BLM) ▲
Big Bend (BLM) ▲
Oak Grove (BLM) ▲
Hal Canyon (BLM) ▲
Drinks Canyon (BLM) ▲

rapids

128

SEVENMILE CANYON

313

191

To Dead Horse Point State Park from junction of 313 and 191 19mi 31km

To Canyonlands National Park–Island in the Sky from junction of 313 and 191 21mi 34km

1.9mi 3.1km

6.0mi 9.6km

Soft sand. Impassable after heavy rains.

ATV, UTV, and OHV use prohibited in park

3.8mi 6.1km

3.2mi 5.1km

Courthouse Wash

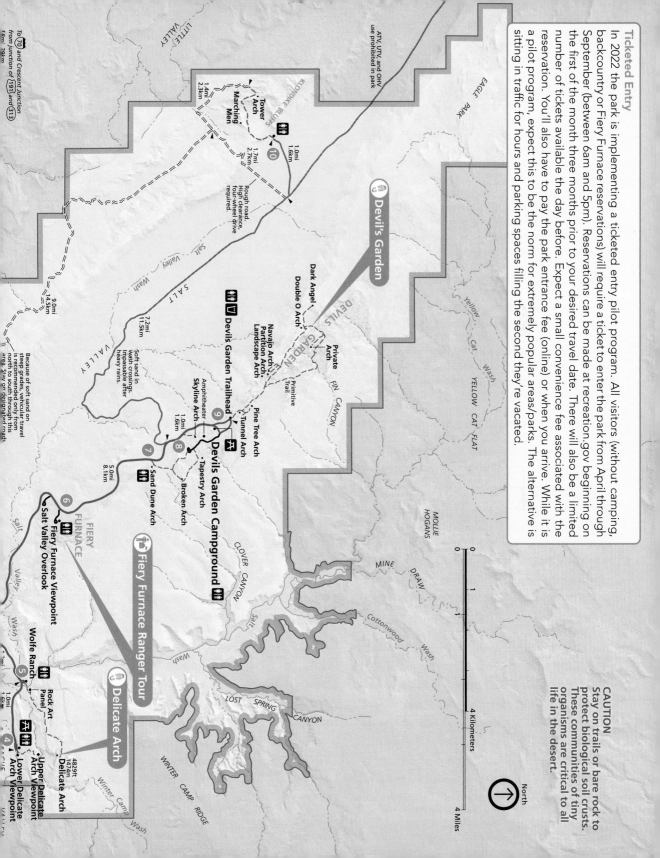

Ticketed Entry

In 2022 the park is implementing a ticketed entry pilot program. All visitors (without camping, backcountry or Fiery Furnace reservations) will require a ticket to enter the park from April through September (between 6am and 5pm). Reservations can be made at recreation.gov beginning on the first of the month three months prior to your desired travel date. There will also be a limited number of tickets available the day before. You'll also have to pay the park entrance fee (online) or when you arrive. While it is a pilot program, expect this to be the norm for extremely popular areas/parks. The alternative is sitting in traffic for hours and parking spaces filling the second they're vacated.

CAUTION
Stay on trails or bare rock to protect biological soil crusts. These communities of tiny organisms are critical to all life in the desert.

North

0
1
4 Kilometers
0
1
4 Miles

To 70 and Crescent Junction
from junction of 191 and 313
19mi 29km

ATV, UTV, and OHV use prohibited in park

Tower Arch
Marching Men
1.4mi 2.3km
1.7mi 2.7km
1.0mi 1.6km
10

KLONDIKE BLUFFS

LITTLE VALLEY

EAGLE PARK

Rough road. High clearance, four-wheel drive required.

Devil's Garden

Dark Angel
Double O Arch
Private Arch
Navajo Arch
Partition Arch
Landscape Arch
Primitive Trail
Pine Tree Arch
Tunnel Arch
Devils Garden Trailhead
9
Amphitheater
Skyline Arch
1.0mi 1.6km
7
8
Tapestry Arch
Broken Arch
Sand Dune Arch
5.0mi 8.1km
6
7.2mi 11.5km
9.0mi 14.5km

SALT VALLEY WASH

DEVILS GARDEN
FIN CANYON

YELLOW CAT WASH
YELLOW CAT FLAT

MOLLIE HOGANS

Devils Garden Campground

Because of soft sand on steep grades, vehicular travel is recommended only from north to south through this area. Stay on designated roads.

Soft sand in wash crossings. Impassable after heavy rains.

Fiery Furnace Ranger Tour

Fiery Furnace Viewpoint
FIERY FURNACE
Salt Valley Overlook
Fiery Furnace
6

CLOVER CANYON
MINE DRAW
Cottonwood Wash

Salt Wash

Wolfe Ranch
Rock Art Panel
5
4823ft 1471m Delicate Arch
1.0mi 1.6km
Upper Delicate Arch Viewpoint
Lower Delicate Arch Viewpoint
4

Delicate Arch

LOST SPRING CANYON
WINTER CAMP RIDGE
Winter Camp Wash

Camping

Devil's Garden is Arches' only designated campground. It's located at the end of the park road, 18 miles from the entrance. Flush toilets and potable water are available. There are no showers or laundry. The camp has 50 sites, each one is available for reservation up to six months in advance from March through October at (877) 444-6777 or recreation.gov. During this period, the camp fills pretty much every night. Reservations are not only recommended, but often required if you'd like to camp within the park during peak season. Sites are available on a first-come, first-served basis for the remainder of the year. Rates are $25 per night. Some sites can accommodate RVs up to 40 feet in length. There are no hookups or dump stations.

We cannot stress it enough. Make reservations early. If you intend to camp and arrive without a reservation, chances are you'll be searching for sites outside the park. Fortunately, there are several Bureau of Land Management campgrounds nearby. **Backpackers** are also welcome to camp in the backcountry ($7 permit, available at the visitor center).

Two sites are available for groups of 11 or more people. Reservations are required at a cost of $75–250 depending on group size. They can be made up to one year in advance at (877) 444-6777 or recreation.gov.

Hiking

Seeing **Delicate Arch** on Utah license plates gives an idea of its beauty, but a little paint on metal hardly does it justice. To deeply appreciate the magnificence of Utah's natural icon you need to hike to its base. Pose with it. Marvel its rocky delicateness. Even without the arch providing the crescendo, this would be one of the park's must-hike trails. It's a moderately difficult 3-mile (roundtrip) fun-filled adventure. You begin near Wolfe Ranch, where you'll cross a small wash and traverse a massive slab of unmarked slickrock. Don't worry about losing the trail, it would take considerable effort to make a wrong turn. And on most days you can simply follow the crowd. (Even if you start before the sun rises, there's usually another early-bird or two in the parking lot.) After crossing the slickrock, the trail narrows, winding its way along an exposed ledge to the rim of a large natural bowl. Your first glimpse over the rim and there it is, Delicate Arch standing proud, an anomaly that wind and water have yet to bring back to earth. Don't expect to enjoy this experience on your own. The bowl is usually busy. Hikers pose with the arch for photographs, or simply stare in admiration. A motivated person can make the hike in an hour, but allow at least two to enjoy the view. Dusk is the best time to visit Delicate Arch. As the sun sets it gives off a brilliant orange glow. Also, be aware that parking is limited. Parking is allowed alongside the road, just be

Arches Hiking Trails (Distances are roundtrip unless noted otherwise)

Name	Location (# on map)	Length	Difficulty Rating & Notes
Park Avenue - 🥾	Park Avenue Parking Area (1)	1.0 mile	M – From viewpoint to Courthouse Towers (1-way)
Balanced Rock	Balanced Rock Parking Area (2)	0.3 mile	E – Short walk around the base of balanced rock
Double Arch - 🥾	Double Arch Parking Area (3)	0.5 mile	E – Short walk to a wonderful arch
The Windows	The Windows Parking Area (3)	1.0 mile	E – Views through two windows and Turret Arch
Delicate Arch Viewpoint	Delicate Arch Viewpoint (4)	300 feet	E – Cannot reach the base of Delicate Arch, bring binoculars, the arch is off in the distance
Delicate Arch - 🥾	Wolfe Ranch Parking Area (5)	3.0 miles	M – Adventurous hike to Delicate Arch bowl/base
Fiery Furnace - 🥾	Fiery Furnace Parking Area (6)	Varies	S – Ranger-guided tour (fee, reservations)
Sand Dune Arch	Sand Dune Arch Parking Area (7)	0.3 mile	E – Also accessible from campground
Broken Arch - 🥾	Sand Dune Arch Parking Area (7)	2.0 miles	E – Also accessible from campground
Skyline Arch - 🥾	Skyline Arch Parking Area (8)	0.4 mile	E – Short but rocky hike across grassland
Landscape Arch - 🥾	Devil's Garden Trailhead (9)	1.9 miles	E – Largest arch in the park • 306-ft base-to-base
Double O Arch - 🥾	Devil's Garden Trailhead (9)	4.1 miles	S – Continue beyond Landscape Arch
Devil's Garden - 🥾	Devil's Garden Trailhead (9)	7.8 miles	S – The complete Devil's Garden Trail and its spurs
Tower Arch	Klondike Bluffs Parking Area, via Salt Valley Road (10)	2.6 miles	S – Remote area of the park accessed via Salt Valley Road or 4WD road • Moderately strenuous

Difficulty Ratings: E = Easy, M = Moderate, S = Strenuous

sure to pull all the way off to the side. Bring plenty of water (especially in summer), take your time, and enjoy yourself at this special place.

The other "must-do" activity is embarking on a ranger-guided hike through the **Fiery Furnace**. As its name implies, it gets hot here in summer. Individuals are required to carry at least one quart of water in a backpack (to free your hands to navigate sandstone obstacles). Tours of Fiery Furnace are offered twice each day from May through late September. In the morning they'll take guests on a 3-hour (2-mile), moderately-difficult loop through a sandstone maze, where a fair amount of scrambling is required. Morning tours cost $16 per adult and $8 per child (ages 5–12). It is extremely popular, and space can be reserved at (877) 444-6777 or recreation.gov. In the afternoon, they offer a shorter out-and-back hike. It costs $10/adult and $5/child, and tickets are only available in person at the visitor center up to seven days in advance. All participants must be able to squeeze through narrow spaces, pull themselves over rocks, and climb reasonably steep rock faces. Good hiking shoes are required. Visitors can explore Fiery Furnace on their own with a permit ($6/adult, $3/child). They must be obtained in person at the visitor center. Everyone in your group must watch a short orientation video.

If it's your first time in the Fiery Furnace, the park suggests joining one of the ranger-guided tours (without an experienced guide you're likely to miss most of the highlights and possibly get lost). There are several good hiking alternatives for those unable to secure a spot on a Fiery Furnace Tour. **Devil's Garden** (7.2 miles including all spur trails to rock formations) is the park's longest maintained trail. The loop passes Landscape Arch, Partition Arch, Navajo Arch, Double O Arch, Dark Angel, and Private Arch. Note that it's a primitive trail beyond Landscape Arch (the longest arch in the park). It's well maintained, but a bit of scrambling is required. If you're unsure about completing the loop, check out the first ascent past Landscape Arch. It's a decent example of the type of obstacles you'll have to traverse. Good hiking shoes are recommended. Additional trails begin at the campground and in the Windows Area.

Backpacking

Don't let the park's size fool you. You can only get a few miles away from paved roads and developed areas, but there's more than enough land to escape the crowds and find that perfect location for a night under the stars. There are no designated trails or campsites in the backcountry, and no reliable water sources.

Park Avenue

The park's small size and abundance of unique rock formations may lead you to believe that navigating the wilderness will be a snap. Do not make this assumption. In reality, the terrain is difficult to navigate, with miles and miles of sandstone decorated with shrubs and the occasional tumbling tumbleweed, so bring a good map and know how to use it. Seasoned hikers may be able to chart their way through the park's backcountry by the 2,000+ arches, but even many of them are indistinguishable to the untrained eye. A permit is required for overnight stays in the backcountry. It costs $7 and is available at the visitor center up to seven days prior to your intended trip. Note that you must pack out ALL solid waste, so come prepared with a commercial toilet bag system.

Biking

Cyclists are allowed on all park roads. The main park road would be great for road cyclists, but it's usually clogged with motorists. There isn't any singletrack, but Salt Valley and Willow Springs Roads are ideal for mountain biking (and far less congested). If it's singletrack you desire, well, you're in the right place. Moab is Mecca to mountain bikers.

Rock Climbing & Canyoneering

Climbers are encouraged to self-register for free, either online or at the kiosk outside the visitor center. There are many rules and regulations, but these are the big ones: Groups are limited to five or less. Climbers must be free or clean aid climbing. Do not physically alter the rock. White chalk is prohibited. Guided rock climbing services are prohibited. Canyoneers must complete a free self-registration permit (online or at the kiosk outside the visitor center), and regulations are similar to rock climbing (full list available online). Slacklining or "highlining" is prohibited.

Skyline Arch

Horseback Riding

Horseback riding is allowed at Arches, but you're limited to day-use along all designated 4WD roads, Salt Valley Road, Klondike Bluffs Road, and in a couple of washes (Salt Wash, Courthouse Wash, and Seven Mile Canyon). You must stay in the wash bottoms (unless quicksand is present).

Photography

Arches is one of the most photogenic parks in the United States. At dusk and dawn, sandstone illuminated by soft light glows a beautiful orange and deep blue skies provide perfect contrast. Suggestions for early morning photography include Turret Arch, Double Arch, Landscape Arch, and Double O Arch. In the evening try Delicate Arch, Fiery Furnace, Skyline Arch, Balanced Rock, and Tower Arch. Nighttime also makes for compelling photography thanks to all the prominent rock silhouettes you can place in your shot. Or simply sit back and stare at the stars.

Visitor Center

The visitor center is open every day except Christmas. Its operating hours are 7:30am to 6pm from April through October. Hours are shortened to 9am to 4pm from November through March. You'll find exhibits, a short film, bookstore, park rangers, and restrooms.

Ranger Programs & For Kids

Fiery Furnace Tours are the gem of Arches' ranger-led programs, but additional interpretive programs and activities, including night sky events, are offered spring through fall. Find a current schedule of events at the visitor center or online.

Arches is a family favorite. Most trails are short and relatively easy (even the hike to Delicate Arch is suitable for most children), and the arches are pretty cool, too. Children are invited to take part in the Junior Ranger Program. It helps encourage them to explore the park in an educational yet entertaining manner. Activity booklets are available for free online or at the visitor center. Your child will be rewarded with a badge and signed certificate for completing five or more exercises. Explorer Packs are also available at the visitor center for families who would like to learn about the park together as they go exploring.

Flora & Fauna

At first sight, Utah's high desert isn't exactly teeming with life. It's very uncommon to see large mammals grazing. Trees are few and far apart. Upon closer inspection, you may spot a skittish lizard between the cracks in a rock or a bird flying high above the desert monuments. Astute visitors will notice cacti, yuccas, and mosses built to withstand long periods of drought. Spacing between shrubs depends on the amount of seasonal rain. Most diversity is due to the Colorado River, which flows along the park's southeastern boundary. Here, and along Courthouse Wash, you'll find cottonwoods and willows.

Pets & Accessibility

Pets are permitted at overlooks, pullouts, paved roadways, parking lots, and developed campgrounds, but must be kept on a leash (less than six feet). They are prohibited from all hiking trails and the backcountry. It's a good idea to board your pet(s) at Moab Veterinary Clinic (435.259.8710, moabvetclinic.com) or Tracey's Bed and Biscuit Kennels (435.210.4466, traceysbedandbiscuit.com) if you bring them along.

Most of Arches is inaccessible to wheelchair users, but the visitor center, Park Avenue and Delicate Arch Viewpoints, and all restrooms are accessible. Devil's Garden Campground has two accessible campsites.

Weather

Arches is located in southeast Utah's high desert. The climate is extremely dry, receiving less than 10 inches of precipitation each year on average. Summers are hot, winters are cold, and the seasons in between are comfortable. Another characteristic of the high desert is extreme weather variation. A single day's temperature can vary more than 40°F. Summer highs often reach into the 100s°F, but evenings are almost always comfortable with average lows in the 60s°F. During winter, average highs are in the 40s°F with lows in the 20s°F. Spring and fall are the best seasons to visit (temperature-wise), but summer is the most popular.

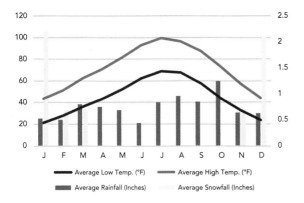

Double O Arch

Tips & Recommendations

The early bird gets the arches. If you plan on visiting between spring and fall and don't get to the park before 8am, chances are you'll have to wait at the entrance station for a bit. Arriving in the evening (after 3pm) is an alternative. Spring break, and holiday weekends (Easter, Memorial Day, Labor Day, and Utah Education Association break in mid-October) are particularly busy.

Parking is also extremely limited. Popular trailheads like Delicate Arch and Devil's Garden are full for most of the day during peak season. If you can, leave your RV or trailer in town or at the visitor center parking lot.

If you'd just like to drive through the park, plan on it taking less than two hours (depending on the line at the entrance station).

Arches is one of the most spectacularly unique parks. For stunning images, plan on waking up before the sun rises or remaining in the park until sunset at least a time or two.

If you want to camp, you'll want to make reservations as early as possible (reservations are available up to six months in advance). You should also make reservations if you'd like to join a ranger-guided tour of the Fiery Furnace (which is highly recommended).

Easy Hikes: Landscape Arch (1.9 miles), Skyline Arch (0.4), Broken Arch (2), Double Arch (0.5), Balanced Rock (0.3)
Moderate Hikes: Delicate Arch (3 miles), Park Avenue (1)
Strenuous Hikes: Devil's Garden (7.8 miles)
Family Activities: Fiery Furnace Tour with a ranger, become Junior Rangers
Sunset Spots: Delicate Arch, Skyline Arch, The Windows, Balanced Rock, Tower Arch
Sunrise Spots: The Windows, Landscape Arch, Delicate Arch, Turret Arch, Double Arch

Beyond the Park...

See page 409 for more Moab-area interests.

Dining
Thai Bella Moab • (435) 355-0555
218 N 100 W, Moab

Quesadilla Mobilla
95 N Main St • (435) 260-0289
quesadillamobilla.com

Big Don's Food Truck
39 W 100 N • (435) 650-4050

Tacos El Gordo
83 S Main St • (720) 985-6192

98 Center • (435) 355-0098
98 E Center St • 98centermoab.com

Susie's Branding Iron
2971 US-191 • (435) 259-6275

Grocery Stores
Village Market • (435) 259-3111
702 S Main St, Moab

City Market • (435) 259-5181
425 S Main St, Moab

Lodging & Camping
Moab Springs Ranch
1266 N US-191 • (435) 259-7891
moabspringsranch.com

Castle Valley Inn
424 Amber Ln • (435) 259-6012
castlevalleyinn.com

OK RV Park • (435) 259-1400
3310 Spanish Valley Dr, Moab
okrvpark.com

Goose Island, Grandstaff, Drinks Canyon, Hal Canyon, Oak Grove,

Big Bend, Upper Big Bend are *small, first-come, first-served campsites along UT-128*

Attractions
Rim Tours • (435) 259-5223
rimtours.com • *Mountain bike*

Fisher Towers
Striking sandstone towers, viewed from an easy path
Fisher Towers Road (dirt)

Sego Canyon Rock Art
Short detour from I-70 just north of Thompson Springs
21 Sego Canyon Rd

Monument Valley
AKA that place Forest Gump ran. You take US-163 near the UT-AZ border. It's just about as

far from Moab as it is from Petrified Forest National Park.

Moab Horses • (435) 259-8015
Horse or mule riding
moabhorses.com

Moab Cowboy Off-Road Adventures
Year-round off-road adventures
moabcowboy.com • (435) 220-0746

Redrock Ballooning • (801) 707-4215
A chance to get a unique perspective of Arches and Canyonlands
redrockballooning.com

Skydive Moab • (435) 259-5867
And then there's a totally different way to see this incredibly weird and wonderful place
skydivemoab.com

Canyonlands

Island in the Sky - Green River Overlook

Phone: (435) 719-2313
Website: nps.gov/cany

Established: September 12, 1964
Size: 337,598 Acres
Annual Visitors: 750,000
Peak Season: March–October
Hiking Trails: 200+ Miles

Activities: Off-Roading*, Hiking, Backpacking*, Biking, Rafting*, Rock Climbing, Horseback Riding*

<u>Campgrounds</u>
Squaw Flat (Needles): $20/night
Willow Flat (Island in the Sky): $15
Backcountry Camping: Permitted*

Park Hours: All day, every day
Entrance Fee: $30/25/15
(car/motorcycle/individual)

*Backcountry Use Permit required

Canyonlands, as its name implies, is an intricate landscape of canyons carved into the Colorado Plateau. Years of erosion have revealed colorful layers of rock and formed buttes and mesas rising high above the Colorado and Green Rivers. Their water continues to carry sediment from the canyon walls and floor west, toward the Pacific Ocean. Controversial conservationist and author, Edward Abbey, described the region best when he wrote it's "the most weird wonderful, magical place on earth—there is nothing else like it anywhere."

He's absolutely right. Proof lies in the geologic history recorded in layers of rock, and stories passed down over the course of 10,000 years of human inhabitance. Geology meets history at places like Horseshoe Canyon, where pictographs and petroglyphs are etched into the canyon's walls. These are places that weren't explored or studied until miners in search of uranium fanned out across the labyrinthine canyons.

Scientists believe at one time the Colorado Plateau region was completely flat and near sea level before layers of sedimentary rock were deposited. Millions of years ago a series of geologic events, including uplifts and volcanic activity, caused the area to rise more than 5,000 feet, on average, above sea level. This increase in elevation set the stage for the Colorado and Green Rivers to cut their way through soft sedimentary rock, revealing its geologic history in the process. Look closely at the rocks when you visit. Notice the horizontal bands of rock in the spires and canyon walls. Red and white layers seem to alternate as you move up the geologic column. Red is created from iron-rich deposits carried here by rivers from nearby mountains. White layers are mostly sand left behind from a shallow sea that covered the region millions of years ago. The park's Upheaval Dome is an anomaly in the geologic order. It's impossible to be sure what caused this crater-like formation, and scientists continue to debate its origin. Some believe it was formed by a meteorite, while others contend a giant salt-bubble, known as a salt dome, is responsible for the abnormality.

Humans have lived in the region for more than 10,000 years. Artifacts recovered in Horseshoe Canyon date back as early as 9000–7000 BC, when mammoths still roamed the American Southwest. Pictographs and petroglyphs are also present in the canyon and most notably at Great Gallery. Ancestral Puebloans and Fremont People left mud dwellings similar in style but much smaller in size than those found at Mesa Verde National Park. It is believed large populations of Ancestral Puebloans moved into this area around 1200 AD from Mesa Verde, planting maize, beans, and squash, and raising turkeys and dogs.

Paiute and Ute Indians moved in during the tail end of the Ancestral Puebloans' presence. Neither culture did much exploration of the canyons. They simply used the land to hunt game and gather plants. European Americans arrived in the early 1800s. To fur trappers and missionaries the canyons were nothing more than an impediment to collecting pelts and reaching the West Coast. By the 1880s, local ranchers used the land as winter pasture. Cowboy camps, like the one visible at Cave Spring Trail in Needles, were established to help safeguard their livestock.

After WWII, the uranium boom hit southeast Utah. Prospectors filed claims all over present-day Canyonlands and nearly 1,000 miles of roads were built thanks to incentives offered by the Atomic Energy Commission. Very little uranium was found, but this new form of exploitation caused concern for Bates Wilson, Superintendent of Arches National Monument. He passionately advocated the creation of a national park, leading jeep tours through the area hoping to gain allies. Fatefully, Secretary of the Interior Stewart Udall joined a tour after peering into the canyons while flying above the Colorado Plateau. He lobbied for the park, and in 1964 legislation was passed and signed by President Lyndon B. Johnson.

Needles - Confluence Overlook

When to Go
Canyonlands is open every day. Summers are hot and dry, winters are cold and snow poses a potential problem for hikers and drivers. Spring and fall bring temperate weather and the majority of visitors, although visitation remains high through summer.

Transportation & Airports
Public transportation does not provide service to or around the park. Salt Lake City International (SLC) is the closest large commercial airport. Grand Junction Regional (GJT), Green River Municipal (RVR), and Canyonlands Field (CNY) are nearby regional airports.

Directions
More than 94% of Canyonlands' visitors enter either Needles or Island in the Sky Districts. Their access roads are located off US-191. Island in the Sky is reached via UT-313, 20 miles south of I-70 and 6.5 miles north of the entrance to Arches National Park. Needles District is accessed via UT-212, which is 50 miles south of UT-313. From US-191 it is roughly 40 miles to the end of the park road at both Needles and Island in the Sky.

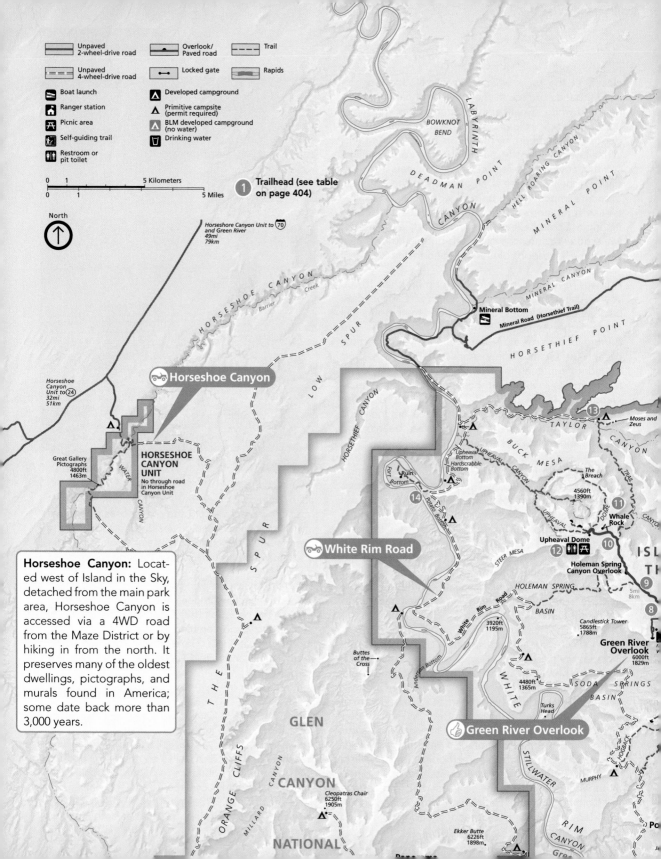

Legend

- Unpaved 2-wheel-drive road
- Unpaved 4-wheel-drive road
- Overlook/Paved road
- Locked gate
- Trail
- Rapids
- Boat launch
- Ranger station
- Picnic area
- Self-guiding trail
- Restroom or pit toilet
- Developed campground
- Primitive campsite (permit required)
- BLM developed campground (no water)
- Drinking water

0 1 5 Kilometers
0 1 5 Miles

North

1 Trailhead (see table on page 404)

Horseshore Canyon Unit to 70
49mi
79km

Horseshoe Canyon Unit to 24
32mi
51km

Horseshoe Canyon

HORSESHOE CANYON
Horseshoe
Canyon
Unit to 24
32mi
51km

Great Gallery
Pictographs
4800ft
1463m

WATER CANYON

HORSESHOE CANYON UNIT
No through road in Horseshoe Canyon Unit

BOWKNOT BEND

LABYRINTH

DEADMAN POINT

HELL ROARING CANYON

MINERAL POINT

CANYON

MINERAL CANYON

Mineral Bottom
Mineral Road (Horsethief Trail)

HORSETHIEF POINT

LOW SPUR

HORSETHIEF CANYON

TAYLOR CANYON

13 Moses and Zeus

BUCK MESA

The Breach
4560ft
1390m

Upheaval Bottom
Hardscrabble Bottom

Fort Bottom
Ruin

White Rim Road

14

Potato Bottom

STEER MESA

UPHEAVAL CANYON

Whale Rock

11

Upheaval Dome

12

10

Holeman Spring Canyon Overlook

ISLAND TH

9
5mi
8km

8

HOLEMAN SPRING BASIN

3920ft
1195m

Candlestick Tower
5865ft
1788m

Green River Overlook
6000ft
1829m

Horseshoe Canyon: Located west of Island in the Sky, detached from the main park area, Horseshoe Canyon is accessed via a 4WD road from the Maze District or by hiking in from the north. It preserves many of the oldest dwellings, pictographs, and murals found in America; some date back more than 3,000 years.

THE SPUR

Buttes of the Cross

Anderson Bottom

4480ft
1365m

WHITE RIM

SODA SPRINGS BASIN

Turks Head

Green River Overlook

STILLWATER

MURPHY

HORSEBACK

RIM CANYON

GLEN CANYON

ORANGE CLIFFS

MILLARD CANYON

Cleopatras Chair
6250ft
1905m

NATIONAL

Ekker Butte
6226ft
1898m

Green

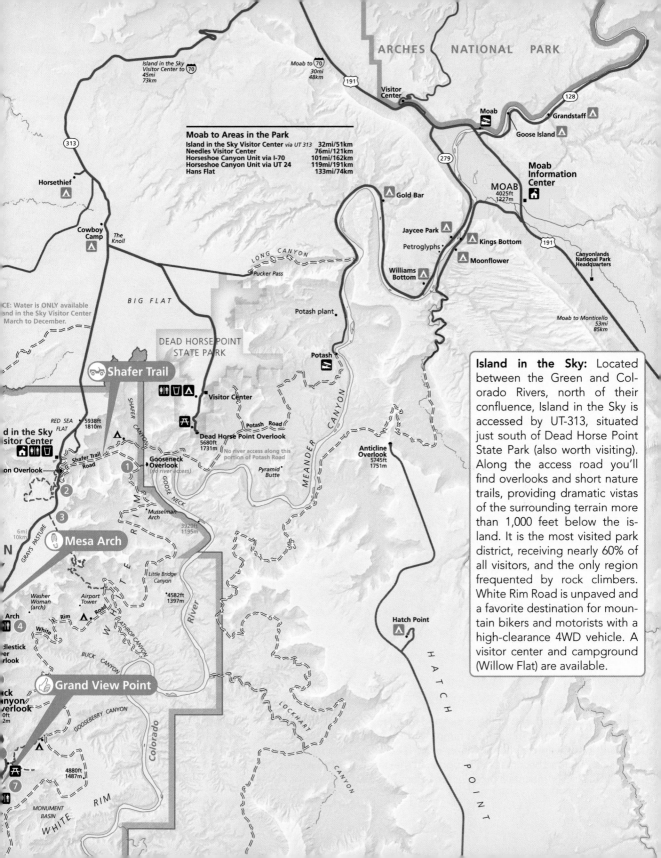

ARCHES NATIONAL PARK

Island in the Sky
Visitor Center to
45mi
73km

Moab to 70
30mi
48km

191

Visitor
Center

128

Moab

Grandstaff

Goose Island

313

Moab to Areas in the Park

Island in the Sky Visitor Center *via UT 313*	32mi/51km
Needles Visitor Center	76mi/121km
Horseshoe Canyon Unit via I-70	101mi/162km
Horseshoe Canyon Unit via UT 24	119mi/191km
Hans Flat	133mi/74km

Horsethief

279

MOAB
4025ft
1227m

Moab
Information
Center

Gold Bar

Cowboy
Camp

The
Knoll

Jaycee Park

Petroglyphs

Kings Bottom

191

LONG CANYON

Pucker Pass

Williams
Bottom

Moonflower

Canyonlands
National Park
Headquarters

CE: Water is ONLY available
and in the Sky Visitor Center
March to December.

BIG FLAT

Potash plant

Moab to Monticello
53mi
85km

DEAD HORSE POINT
STATE PARK

Potash

Shafer Trail

Visitor Center

RED SEA
FLAT

5938ft
1810m

d in the Sky
isitor Center

on Overlook

Shafer Trail
Road

Dead Horse Point Overlook
5680ft
1731m

Potash Road

No river access along this
portion of Potash Road

Gooseneck
Overlook
(no river access)

1

Anticline
Overlook
5745ft
1751m

Island in the Sky: Located between the Green and Colorado Rivers, north of their confluence, Island in the Sky is accessed by UT-313, situated just south of Dead Horse Point State Park (also worth visiting). Along the access road you'll find overlooks and short nature trails, providing dramatic vistas of the surrounding terrain more than 1,000 feet below the island. It is the most visited park district, receiving nearly 60% of all visitors, and the only region frequented by rock climbers. White Rim Road is unpaved and a favorite destination for mountain bikers and motorists with a high-clearance 4WD vehicle. A visitor center and campground (Willow Flat) are available.

2

Pyramid
Butte

MEANDER CANYON

3

Musselman
Arch

6mi
10km

GRAYS PASTURE

Mesa Arch

3920ft
1195m

Little Bridge
Canyon

Washer
Woman
(arch)

Airport
Tower

4582ft
1397m

Hatch Point

Arch

4

Rim
Road

LATHROP CANYON

River

White

Buck Canyon
Overlook

WHITE

dlestick
er
rlook

BUCK CANYON

k
Canyon
Overlook
0ft
2m

RIM

Grand View Point

GOOSEBERRY CANYON

Colorado

LOCKHART

HATCH POINT

4880ft
1487m

7

MONUMENT
BASIN

WHITE

RIM

CANYON

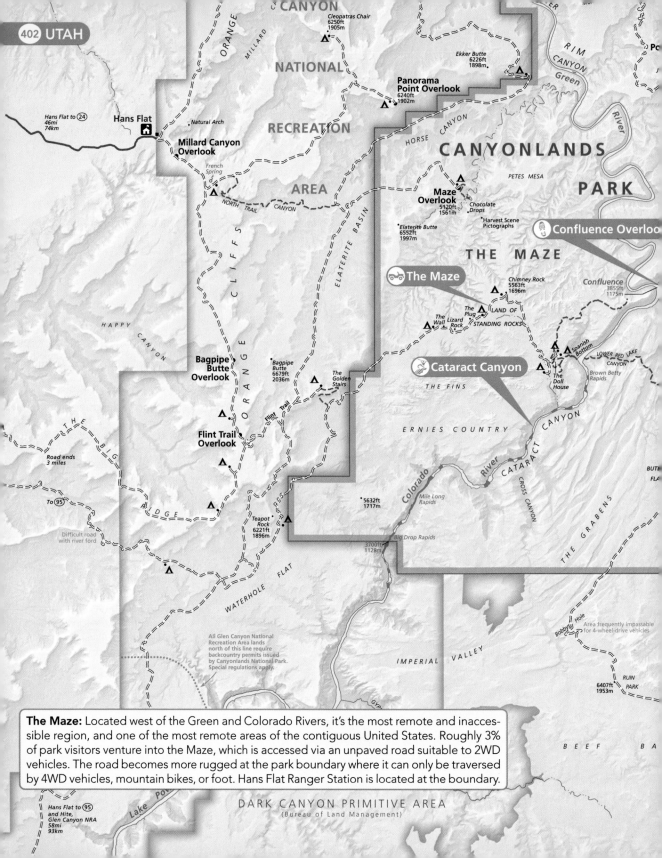

CANYON

Cleopatras Chair
6250ft
1905m

ORANGE

MILLARD

NATIONAL

Ekker Butte
6226ft
1898m

RIM

CANYON

Green

River

**Panorama
Point Overlook**
6240ft
1902m

Hans Flat to ⑳
46mi
74km

Hans Flat

· Natural Arch

RECREATION

**Millard Canyon
Overlook**

French
Spring

HORSE

CANYON

CANYONLANDS

PETES MESA

PARK

AREA

**Maze
Overlook**
5120ft
1561m

·Chocolate
Drops

·Harvest Scene
Pictographs

🏛 **Confluence Overloo**

NORTH

TRAIL

CANYON

·*Elaterite Butte*
6552ft
1997m

THE MAZE

CLIFFS

ELATERITE BASIN

🚙 **The Maze**

Chimney Rock
5563ft
1696m

Confluence
3855ft
1175m

The
Plug

LAND OF

The
Wall

Lizard
Rock

STANDING ROCKS

HAPPY

CANYON

**Bagpipe
Butte
Overlook**

·Bagpipe
Butte
6679ft
2036m

ORANGE

The
Golden
Stairs

🛶 **Cataract Canyon**

THE FINS

Spanish
Bottom

LOWER RED LAKE

CANYON

The
Doll
House

Brown Betty
Rapids

Flint

Trail

**Flint Trail
Overlook**

THE

Road ends
3 miles

BIG

To ⑳

RIDGE

Difficult road
with river ford

Teapot
Rock
6221ft
1896m

FLINT

·5632ft
1717m

ERNIES COUNTRY

Colorado

River

Mile Long
Rapids

CATARACT CANYON

CROSS CANYON

THE GRABENS

BUT
FLA

⛺

WATERHOLE

FLAT

Big Drop Rapids

3700ft
1128m

All Glen Canyon National
Recreation Area lands
north of this line require
backcountry permits issued
by Canyonlands National Park.
Special regulations apply.

Bobby
Hole

Area frequently impassable
for 4-wheel-drive vehicles

IMPERIAL

VALLEY

RUIN

PARK

6407ft
1953m

GYP

The Maze: Located west of the Green and Colorado Rivers, it's the most remote and inaccessible region, and one of the most remote areas of the contiguous United States. Roughly 3% of park visitors venture into the Maze, which is accessed via an unpaved road suitable to 2WD vehicles. The road becomes more rugged at the park boundary where it can only be traversed by 4WD vehicles, mountain bikes, or foot. Hans Flat Ranger Station is located at the boundary.

BEEF

BA

Hans Flat to ⑳
and Hite,
Glen Canyon NRA
58mi
93km

Lake Po

DARK CANYON PRIMITIVE AREA
(Bureau of Land Management)

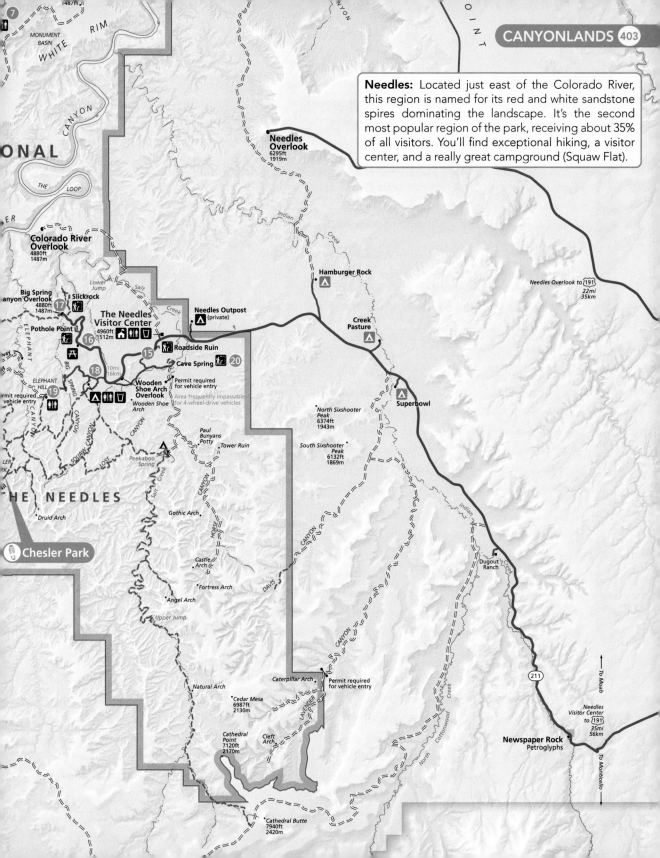

Needles: Located just east of the Colorado River, this region is named for its red and white sandstone spires dominating the landscape. It's the second most popular region of the park, receiving about 35% of all visitors. You'll find exceptional hiking, a visitor center, and a really great campground (Squaw Flat).

MONUMENT BASIN

WHITE RIM

CANYON

WHITE

THE LOOP

ONAL

Needles Overlook
6295ft
1919m

Colorado River Overlook
4880ft
1487m

Hamburger Rock

Needles Overlook to 191
22mi
35km

Big Spring Canyon Overlook
4880ft
1487m

Slickrock

The Needles Visitor Center
4960ft
1512m

Needles Outpost (private)

Creek Pasture

Pothole Point

Roadside Ruin

Cave Spring

Superbowl

ELEPHANT HILL

Wooden Shoe Arch Overlook

Permit required for vehicle entry

Area frequently impassable for 4-wheel-drive vehicles

Wooden Shoe Arch

10mi
16km

Permit required for vehicle entry

North Sixshooter Peak
6374ft
1943m

SQUAW CANYON

LOST CANYON

BIG SPRING CANYON

Paul Bunyans Potty

Tower Ruin

South Sixshooter Peak
6132ft
1869m

Peekaboo Spring

THE NEEDLES

Druid Arch

Gothic Arch

HORSE CANYON

CANYON

Chesler Park

Castle Arch

Fortress Arch

Angel Arch

DAVIS CANYON

Dugout Ranch

Upper Jump

Natural Arch

Caterpillar Arch

Permit required for vehicle entry

LAVENDER CANYON

Cedar Mesa
6987ft
2130m

Cathedral Point
7120ft
2170m

Cleft Arch

211

To Moab

Needles Visitor Center to 191
35mi
56km

Newspaper Rock
Petroglyphs

To Monticello

Cathedral Butte
7940ft
2420m

Needles

Canyonlands Hiking Trails (Distances are roundtrip)

Island in the Sky

Name	Location (# on map)	Length	Difficulty Rating & Notes
Gooseneck Overlook	NE corner on White Rim Rd (1)	0.6 mile	E – Views of the Colorado River
Neck Spring	Main Park Road (MPR) (2)	5.8 miles	M – Explores old ranch and springs (loop)
Lathrop Canyon Road	MPR • South of Neck Spring (3)	13.6 miles 21.6 miles	S – To White Rim Road S – To Colorado River (2,000 ft elevation)
Mesa Arch - ♣	MPR • North of Willow Flat (4)	0.5 mile	E – Popular self-guided trail (loop)
Murphy Point Overlook - ♣	MPR • Between Buck Canyon and Candlestick Tower Overlooks (5)	3.6 miles	E – Popular trail with continuous views
Murphy Loop	MPR • Between Buck Canyon and Candlestick Tower Overlooks (5)	10.8 miles	S – Steep trail descends from the mesa rim (1,400-ft elevation loss)
Gooseberry	MPR • White Rim Overlook (6)	5.4 miles	S – Shortest route to White Rim Road
White Rim Overlook	MPR • North of Grand View (7)	1.8 miles	E – One of the best views from the island
Grand View Point - ♣	South end of MPR (7)	2.0 miles	E – Amazing panoramic views
Aztec Butte	MPR • North of Willow Flat (8)	2.0 miles	M – Ancestral Puebloan granaries
Wilhite	MPR • West of Willow Flat (9)	12.2 miles	S – Slot canyon leads to White Rim Road
Alcove Spring	MPR • Before Upheaval Dome (10)	11.2 miles	S – Provides views of Taylor Canyon
Whale Rock	MPR • Near Upheaval Dome (11)	1.0 mile	M – Handrails aid crossing steep slickrock
Upheaval Dome	MPR • Upheaval Dome (12)	1.8 miles	M – Popular hike to two overlooks
Syncline Loop - ♣	MPR • Upheaval Dome (12)	8.3 miles	S – Optional 3- and 7-mile spur trails, great for 1-night backpack (loop)
Moses and Zeus - ♣	Alcove Spring/White Rim Rd (13)	1.0 mile	E – Strange rocks, Taylor Canyon, 4x4 req'd
Fort Bottom Ruin	NW Corner off White Rim Rd (14)	3.0 miles	M – An ancient tower ruin

Needles

Name	Location (# on map)	Length	Difficulty Rating & Notes
Roadside Ruin	Just past visitor center (15)	0.3 mile	E – Old ancestral Puebloan granary
Pothole Point	Pothole Point (16)	0.6 mile	E – Views of Needles, follow cairns
Slickrock	South of Big Spring Canyon (17)	2.4 miles	E – Self-guided trail with 360-degree views
Confluence Overlook - ♣	Big Spring Canyon Trailhead (17)	10.0 miles	S – Not the most exciting trail in the park (flat and open), but cool conclusion
Squaw Canyon	Squaw Flat Loop A (18)	7.5 miles	S – Connects with Big Spring Canyon (loop)
Elephant Canyon	Squaw Flat Loop A (18)	10.8 miles	S – Option for several spurs (semi-loop)
Lost Canyon - ♣	Squaw Flat Loop A (18)	8.7 miles	S – Scrambling and solitude (semi-loop)
Peekaboo	Squaw Flat Loop A (18)	10.0 miles	S – Arch, pictograph, and (2) ladders
Chesler Park View	Elephant Trailhead (19)	6.0 miles	M – Grassland lined with spires (popular)
Chesler Park Loop - ♣	Elephant Trailhead (19)	11.0 miles	S – Continues past viewpoint (semi-loop)
Druid Arch	Elephant Trailhead (19)	11.0 miles	S – Scrambling and a ladder, good hike
Cave Spring	Near Horse Canyon Road (20)	0.6 mile	E – Historic cowboy camp, (2) ladders

The Maze District: There are no designated trails and no reliable water sources. Come prepared.

Horseshoe Canyon District: There is a 7.5-mile roundtrip hiking trail through the canyon (ancient pictographs).

Difficulty Ratings: E = Easy, M = Moderate, S = Strenuous

Camping

Canyonlands has two established campgrounds: Willow Flat at Island in the Sky and Squaw Flat at Needles. **Willow Flat** has 12 sites available on a first-come, first-served basis. Water is not available, and the maximum RV length is 28 feet. Fees are $15 per night. **Squaw Flat** has 26 sites. 14 are first-come, first-served. 12 can be reserved up to six months in advance at (877) 444-6777 or recreation.gov from mid-March through June and September through October. Water is available. Fees are $20 per night. Group sites are available at Needles for $70–225/night, depending on group size. Group sites are open from mid-March through mid-November and can be reserved up to six months in advance at recreation.gov. Both campgrounds fill to capacity almost every day from mid-March through June and again from early September through October. Nearby camping locations include Arches National Park and Bureau of Land Management (BLM) campgrounds in and around Moab. **Backpackers** can camp in the park's backcountry with a permit ($36).

Backcountry & Day-Use Permits

River permits can be reserved up to four months in advance and no later than two days prior to your trip start date at recreation.gov. You can also get a permit in person at the Backcountry Permit Office in Moab, Monday through Friday, 8am to 4pm. Flatwater and Cataract Canyon permits cost $36 plus $20 per person. They are valid for groups up to 40 people.

Overnight **backcountry permits** are issued online at recreation.gov up to four months in advance or in person from the respective district visitor centers the day of your trip or one day before. Reservations are highly recommended for White Rim Road trips, Needles Backpacking trips, and Needles Group Camping during peak season. All backcountry permits require a $36 fee per permit. Each one is good for 7 people at Island in the Sky and Needles Districts and 5 people at the Maze. **4WD and Mountain Bike Permits** cost $36 and are good for up to 15 people and 3 vehicles at Island in the Sky, 10 people and 3 vehicles at Needles, and 9 people and 3 vehicles at the Maze. **Day-use permits** are required for all vehicles (including motorcycles and bicycles) on White Rim Road, Elephant Hill, Lavender Canyon, and Salt Creek/Horse Canyon Roads. They can be obtained up to 24 hours before your trip at recreation.gov. Day-use permits require a $6 reservation fee. Each vehicle, motorcycle, and bicycle needs a separate permit. During flood season (about May through June), White Rim Road permits are only available in-person at Island in the Sky Visitor Center.

Island in the Sky - Upheaval Dome

Off-Roading

A 4WD vehicle unlocks vast portions of Canyonlands few visitors get to see. It allows you to backpack without putting in the work. Your gear (including plenty of water!) is in your trunk, and the only things strained are the muscles of your brake foot—and maybe your nerves as you slowly make your way up and down narrow switchbacks that ascend and descend precipitous cliffs.

Island in the Sky's White Rim Road is a popular destination. Plan for this 100-mile journey to take two-to-three days in a 4WD vehicle, and three-to-four days on a mountain bike. Shafer Rim Trail near Island in the Sky's Entrance is a great (more like terrifying) 4WD alternative route to and from Moab. Routes like Elephant Hill (Needles) and the road to the Land of Standing Rocks (Maze) are more technical. A backcountry permit ($36) is required to camp at designated sites along the way, and several roads require a day-use permit ($6).

Inquire about road conditions before attempting. Fill up with gas in Moab. There are no services in the park. Rental vehicles are often restricted to paved roads, so look closely at your agreement or ask about it before driving off the lot. Be careful. A tow can exceed $1,000.

Hiking

Looking at Island in the Sky's labyrinth of eroded canyons from above may lead you to believe it is utterly impassable. Water carved its way across this arid plateau. Humans haven't been at it for millions of years, but park employees, ranchers, prospectors, and ancient inhabitants played their part blazing paths across a seemingly impenetrable landscape. Many of their trails are still used today. Most popular trails are well-maintained, marked by cairns, and have signposts

Island in the Sky - Whale Rock

at intersections. The trails are good, but few reliable water sources exist, so be sure to pack enough for the duration of your hike. One of the more popular trails at Island in the Sky is the easy 0.5-mile loop to **Mesa Arch**. Its views warrant the popularity. The arch frames distant canyons for unsurpassed photo opportunities (especially at sunrise). A great place to hike into a canyon is **Syncline Loop** (8.3 miles). This strenuous trail is short enough to complete in a day, but you can also turn it into an overnighter thanks to a few spur trails. It's also the site of most park rescues, so come prepared with plenty of water, a map, and flashlight. Hike in a clockwise direction to maximize afternoon shade.

Needles District, located on the opposite side of the Colorado River, has equally exciting hiking opportunities. **Confluence Overlook Trail** is decent. This 10-mile (roundtrip) trek leads in and out of Big Spring Canyon, across Elephant Canyon, before joining a 4WD road. Much of the scenery looks similar and it is possible to lose your way, so look closely for cairns marking the trail. The 4WD road leads to a parking area with a vault toilet. From here you make the final push to the point where sheer canyon walls and the waters of the Green and Colorado Rivers that carved them converge. The hike to **Chesler Park** is even better, and ambitious hikers can continue beyond Chesler Park Viewpoint along a sandy trail to **Druid Arch** or loop around the park via **Joint Trail** (a narrow rocky passage). The final ascent to Druid Arch is quite strenuous, and you're required to climb a ladder. The hike to Chesler Park is great and not that difficult, although terrain is uneven and you must watch the trail carefully, spotting cairns as you go.

If you prefer things that are a little more extreme, you'll enjoy the **Maze District**, where the average visitor spends three days poking around an extensive network of canyons. A 25-foot length of rope is useful (if not essential) to raise and lower your pack, and a good topographical map is indispensable in the Maze, where side canyons can be difficult to identify and getting lost is easy (as the name implies).

Backpacking

Overnight backpacking is limited to camping zones and designated sites, like those found around many of the 4WD roads. All overnight stays in the backcountry require a permit. A limited number of permits are available, and demand often exceeds supply during spring and fall, so plan your itinerary in advance and reserve one when they become available. The next hurdle is to assure you'll have plenty of water for the length of your trip, because most sources are unreliable. Inquire about potential water sources when you arrive at the park. The Maze is enjoyed, almost exclusively, by backpackers. Trails at Island in the Sky and Needles can be taken more casually or combined to make a suitable backpacking route. Chesler Park is a popular backpacking area in Needles, but Salt Creek Trail (25+ miles) to Angel Arch and Molar Rock is another option. With careful planning, considering the ability of all members of your party, you're sure to have a rewarding experience in a magnificent setting.

Biking

Located at the doorstep of Moab, the epicenter of mountain biking, it shouldn't come as a surprise that Canyonlands is a popular destination for pedalers. The 100-mile White Rim Road circling Island in the Sky is the primary biking destination. The Maze offers more secluded biking opportunities. All overnight bike trips require a permit ($36). Magpie Cycling (435.259.4464, magpiecycling.com), Holiday River Expeditions (800.624.6323, bikeraft.com), Rim Tours (435.259.5223, rimtours.com), and Western Spirit (435.259.8732, westernspirit.com) offer day and multi-day mountain biking tours of Canyonlands (White Rim, Needles, and Maze).

Rafting & Paddling

In 1869, Major John Wesley Powell became the first to officially explore Canyonlands. He traveled from Green River, WY all the way through the Grand Canyon. Much like Powell, today's visitors are inspired by the scenery and invigorated by the water's power as they float the Green River or raft the 14-mile stretch of Class III–IV rapids of **Cataract Canyon** just beyond the confluence of the Green and Colorado Rivers. All public launches are located outside the park and private parties require a permit ($36). Adrift Adventures (435.259.8594, adrift.net), World Wide River Expeditions

(435.259.7515, worldwideriver.com), Wilderness River Adventures (800.992.8022, riveradventures.com), Sheri Griffith Expeditions (800.332.2439, griffithexp.com), and many others offer a variety of rafting trips at Canyonlands (and beyond).

Rock Climbing

Climbers regularly come to Island in the Sky to test their skills against its sandstone towers and spires, and that's about it. If you're interested in climbing Canyonlands visit the park website for a list of regulations. A permit ($36) is only required if you intend on spending the night in the backcountry. Camping is not allowed at the trailhead to Moses and Zeus.

Horseback Riding

Horses and other saddle stock are permitted on all backcountry roads. A backcountry permit ($6 for day-use, $36 for overnight) is required for all stock-use, and all feed and manure must be packed out. If you would like to spend the night, you must do so at a designated vehicle campsite. Finding reliable water sources is a significant problem for hikers, and it is even more critical for horseback riders. Discuss where you might find water with a park ranger before departing, especially for overnight trips. Feed all stock pelletized feed for the duration of your trip and two days prior to prevent the spread of exotic plant species.

Stargazing

Just because it's dark at night doesn't mean there's nothing to see. Canyonlands' distinction as one of the most remote regions in the contiguous United States has its perks, one being extremely dark skies. Don't forget to look up on a cloudless night. The stargazing is phenomenal. If you're lucky, you may have the chance to join a ranger-led stargazing event during your visit.

Visitor Centers

Each district (except Horseshoe Canyon) has a visitor center or ranger station. **Island in the Sky Visitor Center** is open daily, 8am to 5pm, for most of the year, with slightly shorter hours in winter. It's closed on Christmas, MLK Day, and Presidents Day. **Needles Visitor Center** is open daily, 8:30am to 4pm, from early March through November. It's closed on Thanksgiving, and through winter. Both visitor centers feature exhibits, book and map sales, a short film, restrooms, and backcountry permits. **Hans Flat Ranger Station**, located at the Maze entry point, is open daily from 8am to 4:30pm. You'll find books and maps, but no services, food, gas, or water.

Island in the Sky - Grand View Point

Ranger Programs & For Kids

Park rangers provide various interpretive programs. They're offered daily from spring through fall at Island in the Sky, most nights at Needles in spring and fall, and most weekends at the Maze in spring and fall. Evening programs are frequently given at each of the campgrounds' amphitheaters. During the daytime, rangers give short talks on unique features or lead guests along a popular trail. At the Maze, they lead regular hikes to Horseshoe Canyon in spring and fall.

Kids are welcome to participate in Canyonlands' Junior Ranger Program. Free booklets are available online or at either visitor center. Complete the activities to receive an official junior ranger badge. You can also earn a badge by picking up a Red Rock Explorer Pack at Island in the Sky Visitor Center and using it with your whole family to explore the park. Even if you don't participate in the Junior Ranger Program, children are sure to enjoy the contrasting views of canyons and cliffs that are easily accessible along park roads. And if you have a high-clearance 4WD vehicle and the spirit of adventure, your children are sure to love a little off-roading!

Flora & Fauna

The ecology of Canyonlands is like Arches National Park. See page 407 for more information.

Pets & Accessibility

Pets are allowed in Canyonlands' developed campgrounds and along its roadways but must be kept on a leash (less than six feet). They are not permitted on hiking trails or the backcountry (including unpaved roads). It's a good idea to board your pet(s) at Moab Veterinary Clinic (435.259.8710, moabvetclinic.com) or Tracey's Bed and Biscuit Kennels (435.210.4466, traceysbedandbiscuit.com) if you bring them along.

Island in the Sky - Shafer Trail

You could spend a week paddling the Colorado River or days exploring the Maze, but most visitors only take a look at Island in the Sky and then leave. There's nothing wrong with the typical approach but you're missing out on an awful lot. Plus, Canyonlands is refreshingly uncrowded compared to Arches National Park across the street.

With that said, the campgrounds at Island in the Sky and Needles are great, but they're also small. Campgrounds fill early in spring and fall (and may not fill at all in summer/winter). If you manage to secure a spot, camping at Canyonlands is one of the best places in the country to watch the stars at night.

There are no gas stations in the park, so be sure to fill up in Moab (Island in the Sky), Monticello (Needles), or Hanksville (Maze). You also won't find food or lodging inside the park. However, there is water at Island in the Sky and Needles Visitor Centers.

If you're only spending a day in the park (at Island in the Sky), make it a full day. Try to arrive in time for sunrise at Mesa Arch and stick around for sunset at Dead Horse Point ($20 entry fee, and it's a state park, not a national park, so a National Park Pass won't help).

False Kiva has become a favorite location among photographers. It's located at Island in the Sky and accessed via an unmarked trail. It's a great moderately difficult hike, with a little bit of a scramble up to the alcove where you'll find a ring of rocks. Ask a park ranger about it for the trailhead location and current accessibility information. I'm not sure what the story is on the kiva, but it wouldn't surprise me one bit if it was made by modern man. Regardless, it's a fun hike with outstanding views.

Needles and Island in the Sky Visitor Centers and restrooms are accessible to individuals in wheelchairs. Buck Canyon, Green River and Grand View Point Overlooks, and Willow Flat Campground are accessible at Island in the Sky. Squaw Flat Campground and Wooden Shoe Overlook are accessible at Needles.

Weather
Canyonlands nearly borders Arches National Park. Both parks are situated on the Colorado Plateau in southeast Utah's high desert. See page 396 for weather information.

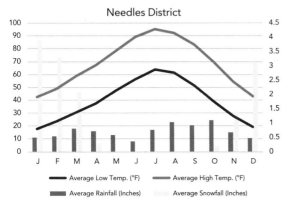

Needles District

Island in the Sky is the most popular region for good reason: it's the most accessible, featuring a nice smooth road and plenty of viewpoints and short hiking trails. If you aren't planning on hiking or off-roading, there isn't much need to visit Needles or the Maze. To visit all of Canyonlands' regions, you'll need a high-clearance 4x4 and a solid week, if not more.

Tips & Recommendations
Just a few thousand visitors reach Canyonlands each month from December through February. Visitation is heavy the rest of the year, with April, May, September, and October being the busiest. Even though most people are just stopping by on a daytrip, campgrounds fill early, and backcountry permits are reserved nearly as soon as they become available during this time. If you want to camp or explore the backcountry, you'll have to plan your trip in advance.

Put some strong consideration into going on a 4x4 adventure. There's so much more to Canyonlands than you'll see from pavement. If you want to drive White Rim Road on your own, you'll need a permit (even for a daytrip). Make reservations as early as possible if you plan on visiting in spring/fall. It's not a good idea to try and drive the entire 100-mile White Rim Road in a day. Several other 4x4 roads require a permit as well (like Elephant Hill, Salt Creek/Horse Canyon, and Lavender Canyon Roads at Needles). Jenn's Jeep Rentals (435.220.1026, jlurentals.com), Outlaw Adventures (435.260.7451, outlawjeepadventures.com), Canyonlands Jeep and Car Rentals (866.892.5337, canyonlandsjeep.com), and Twisted Jeeps (435.259.0335, twistedjeeps.com) all offer rentals. Many other outfitters provide rentals and/or off-road tours.

Make sure you have plenty of water, sunscreen, and food packed with you, regardless of region.

Needles - Newspaper Rock

Easy Hikes: Grand View Point (2 miles), Moses and Zeus (1), Murphy Point (3.6), Mesa Arch (0.5)
Moderate Hikes: Whale Rock (1 mile)
Strenuous Hikes: Chesler Park (11 miles), Syncline Loop (8.3), Lost Canyon (8.7), Confluence Overlook (10)
Family Activities: Hire a guide to take you off-roading, become Junior Rangers
Guided Tours: Go rafting!
Rainy Day Activities: Go hunting for ephemeral waterfalls (just stay safe)

History Enthusiasts: Horseshoe Canyon, Aztec Butte
Sunset Spots: Grand View Point Overlook, Dead Horse Point (outside the park, on the way to Island in the Sky), Green River Overlook, Murphy Point (bring a headlamp to hike back)
Sunrise Spots: Mesa Arch, Buck Canyon Overlook, Maze Overlook, Grand View Point Overlook, Shafer Canyon Overlook

Beyond the Park...

See page 397 for more Moab-area interests.

Dining
Hidden Cuisine • (435) 259-7711
2740 US-191 • hidden-cuisine.com

Moab Garage Go
78 N Main St • (435) 554-8467
moabgarageco.com

Sweet Cravings Bakery
397 N Main St • cravemoab.com

Desert Bistro • (435) 259-0756
36 S 100 W • desertbistro.com

Ja-Roen Thai Sushi
380 S Main St • (435) 587-4000

Grocery Stores
Blue Mountain • (435) 587-2451
64 W Center St, Monticello

Lodging & Camping
Grist Mill Inn • (435) 587-2597
64 S 300 E, Monticello
thegristmillinn.com

Roughlock Resort
7980 US-191 • (435) 587-2351
roughlockresort.com

Archview RV Resort • (435) 259-7854
13701 N US-191 • sunrvresorts.com

Moab Rim RV
1900 US-191 • (435) 259-5002
moabrimcampark.com

Moab KOA • (435) 241-7890
3225 US-191, Moab • koa.com

Up the Creek
210 E 300 S • (435) 260-1888
moabcampground.com

Canyonlands RV Resort
555 S Main St • (435) 259-6848
sunrvresorts.com

Needles Outpost • (435) 459-0777
UT-211, Monticello
needlesoutpost.com

Several first-come, first-served BLM campsites around Needles and Island in the Sky Entrances

Festivals
Skinny Tire Festival • March
skinnytireevents.com • Moab

Canyonlands Rodeo • June • Moab
moabcanyonlandsrodeo.com

Moab Music Festival • Sept
moabmusicfest.org • Moab

Moab Folk Festival • November
moabfolkfestival.com • Moab

Attractions
Bear Ears National Monument
Home to many captivating rock formations and cultural sites

Natural Bridges National Mon
Interestingly, this was Utah's first National Monument. Hiking, camping, and three massive natural bridges
nps.gov/nabr • (435) 692-1234

Dead Horse Point State Park
Great viewpoint and hiking
US-313, Moab • (435) 259-2614
stateparks.utah.gov

Edge of the Cedars State Park
Museum and archaeological site
660 W 400 N, Blanding
stateparks.utah.gov • (435) 678-2238

Corona Arch
Short trail, beginning near the Colorado River on the 4x4 route to Canyonlands

Goblin Valley State Park
Just some more whacky rocks
Goblin Valley Rd, Green River
stateparks.utah.gov • (435) 275-4584

John Wesley Powell Museum
1765 Main St, Green River
johnwesleypowell.com

Green River State Park
You can golf here
550 Green River Blvd, Green River
stateparks.utah.gov • (435) 564-3633

Anticline Overlook
Looks out over the Colorado to Dead Horse Point • blm.gov

Wilson Arch
Large Arch along US-191

Looking Glass Rock
Cool rock near Wilson Arch

Goosenecks State Park
Look into the San Juan River
UT-316, Mexican Hat
stateparks.utah.gov

Valley of the Gods
Kind of like Monument Valley, located near Mexican Hat

Navajo Twins
Huge sandstone rocks near a trading post between White Mesa and Mexican Hat

Devil's Canyon
Slot canyon in San Rafael Swell

Recapture Pocket
More goofy rocks, very few travelers

Capitol Reef

Capitol Gorge

Phone: (435) 425-3791
Website: nps.gov/care

Established: December 18, 1971
August 2, 1937 (National Monument)
Size: 241,904 Acres
Annual Visitors: 1.2 Million
Peak Season: April–October

Activities: Off-Roading, Hiking, Backpacking, Biking, Rock Climbing, Canyoneering, Horseback Riding, Stargazing

Fruita Campground: $20/night
Cedar Mesa and Cathedral Valley Primitive Campgrounds: Free
Backcountry Camping: Permitted with a free Backcountry Use Permit
Lodging: None

Park Hours: All day, every day
Entrance Fee: $20/15/10 (car/motorcycle/individual)

The name "Capitol Reef" hints that this region was once a growing, living underwater organism. However, the park's reef refers to sinuous canyons, colorful monoliths, obtrusive buttes, and giant white domes of Navajo sandstone that form the Waterpocket Fold, a 75-million-year-old warp in the earth's crust running the entire length of the park. These features make a nearly impassable rugged landscape, exactly what locals called a "reef." Today, the Waterpocket Fold defines Capitol Reef National Park, but scientists are still trying to understand its origin. No doubt the twisting of two layers of crust into S-shaped folds required exceptional force. As luck would have it, about the time the fold was created two continental plates were colliding with one another. A collision so forceful a great uplift occurred, raising the Rocky Mountains and potentially wrenching land nearly 400 miles away. From the ground you hardly notice the violence and scars at the earth's surface. From the air, it's dramatic. To view it from above without leaving the ground, stop at the visitor center where a scaled version of the park is on display.

Early inhabitants were oblivious to the area's unique geology. With only a few perennial sources of water to choose from, the Fremont People settled along the Fremont River's shores. They farmed and hunted for more than two centuries, only to abandon their granaries and dwellings in the 13th century. At the same time, Ancestral Puebloans were evacuating the region of present-day Mesa Verde and Canyonlands

National Parks, possibly pushed out by the same calamity. Scientists believe they all left because of significant change in climate, resulting in extended drought. Decades later, Paiute and Ute Indians entered the region, discovering abandoned Fremont granaries, they called moki huts (homes of tiny people known as moki).

It wasn't until the 19th century that an American crossed the Waterpocket Fold. Alan H. Thompson, a member of U.S. Army Major John Wesley Powell's expedition, completed this task in 1872. Mormons were next to settle in. Like the Fremont People before them, they lived in the Fremont River Valley, establishing settlements at Junction (later known as Fruita), Caineville, and Aldridge. Aldridge failed. Fruita prospered but was never home to more than 10 families. Caineville struggled to survive, but Mormon Bishop Ephraim Pectol operated a small convenience store that housed a private museum of Fremont artifacts.

Pectol noticed the area's finer qualities while scavenging through ruins seeking ancient relics to add to his personal museum. He and his brother-in-law, Wayne County High School Principal Joseph S. Hickman, began promoting the scenic beauty of what they called "Wayne Wonderland" in 1921. In 1933, Pectol was elected to the State Legislature, giving him a platform to pursue the park idea. Wasting no time, he contacted President Franklin D. Roosevelt, asking him to create Wayne Wonderland National Monument through executive order. For nearly a decade, tourists trickled into the proposed park, largely thanks to lectures given by J.E. Broaddus, a Salt Lake City photographer hired by Pectol and Hickman. Images piqued federal interest, and soon survey parties arrived in south-central Utah. They didn't give it "wonderland" status, but on August 2, 1937, President Roosevelt created Capitol Reef National Monument and placed it under control of Zion National Park.

At the same time, Charles Kelley retired to the area and volunteered to serve as park custodian. In 1950, he was appointed the park's first superintendent. He became leery of the National Park Service's direction as they complied with demands made by the U.S. Atomic Energy Commission to open Capitol Reef to uranium mining, but little ore was excavated.

In 1962, construction of highway UT-24 was completed, drastically increasing tourism. Momentum was finally building to permanently protect the region as a national park; in 1971, President Richard Nixon signed a bill doing exactly that.

Hickman Bridge

When to Go
Capitol Reef is most comfortable for hiking and other outdoor activities during spring and fall. You can pick fruit from Fruita Orchard between June and October. You need to be especially careful hiking slot canyons during flash flood season (typically July through September).

Transportation & Airports
Public transportation does not provide service to or around the park. The closest commercial airport is Salt Lake City International (230 miles to the north).

Directions
The park area is extremely isolated and can only be accessed by one major road, UT-24, which conveniently intersects I-70 near Aurora (Exit 48). It then loops through the park intersecting with I-70 again just west of Green River, UT (Exit 149). To reach the park from I-15 traveling south from Salt Lake City, take Exit 188. Take US-50 S for 24 miles, and then turn right at UT-260/Main St. Continue for 4 miles before turning right at UT-24. Follow UT-24 south and east about 75 miles into the park.

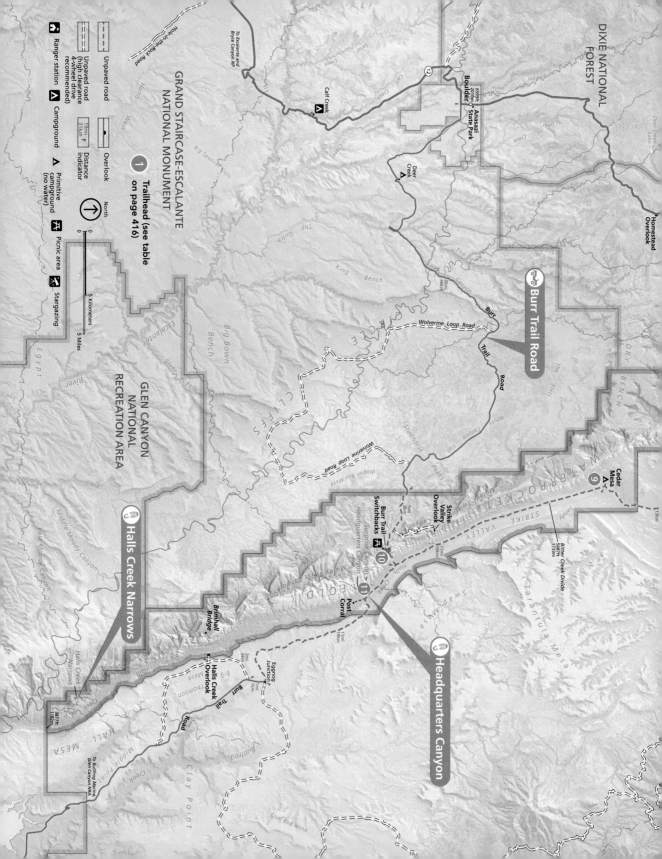

GRAND STAIRCASE-ESCALANTE
NATIONAL MONUMENT

(1) Trailhead (see table
on page 416)

North

0   5 Kilometers
0   5 Miles

	Ranger station
	Campground
	Primitive campground (no water)
	Picnic area
	Stargazing

Unpaved road

Unpaved road (high clearance 4-wheel drive recommended)

Overlook

19mi / 31km   Distance indicator

DIXIE NATIONAL FOREST

Homestead Overlook

Hole-in-the-Rock Road

To Escalante and Bryce Canyon NP

Calf Creek

12

Boulder
Anasazi State Park
6593ft 2010m

Deer Creek

The Gulch

King Bench

Horse Canyon

Long Canyon 3mi 48km

Burr Trail Road

Burr

Trail

Road

Wolverine Loop Road

Wolverine Loop Road

Wagon Box Mesa

GLEN CANYON NATIONAL RECREATION AREA

Escalante River

Silver Falls Creek

Big Bown Bench

Egypt

Moody Creek

Middle Moody Canyon

East Moody Canyon

Halls Creek Narrows

Brimhall Bridge

Halls Creek

Big Thomson Mesa

HALL MESA

Middle Point

Burr

Trail

Road

Bullfrog Creek

To Bullfrog Marina, Glen Canyon NRA

Clay Point

Goat Bed Mesa

Eggnog Junction

Halls Creek Overlook

1mi 2km

3mi 5km

387ft 118m

Post Corral

11

11mi 18km

11mi 18km

Headquarters Canyon

10

Burr Trail Switchbacks

Surprise Canyon

Muley Twist Canyon

Strike Valley Overlook

5mi 8km

Muley Twist Canyon

Halls Creek

Swap Mesa

OLD

Cedar Mesa

9

Bitter Creek Divide 5687ft 1733m

STRIKE VALLEY

WATERPOCKET

Sandy Creek

13mi

Tarantula Mesa

DRY BENCH

White Canyon

Horse Trail

Muley Twist Canyon 11mi 18km

Halls Creek Narrows

CLIFFS

Halls Creek

Whirlwind Mesa

Headquarters Canyon

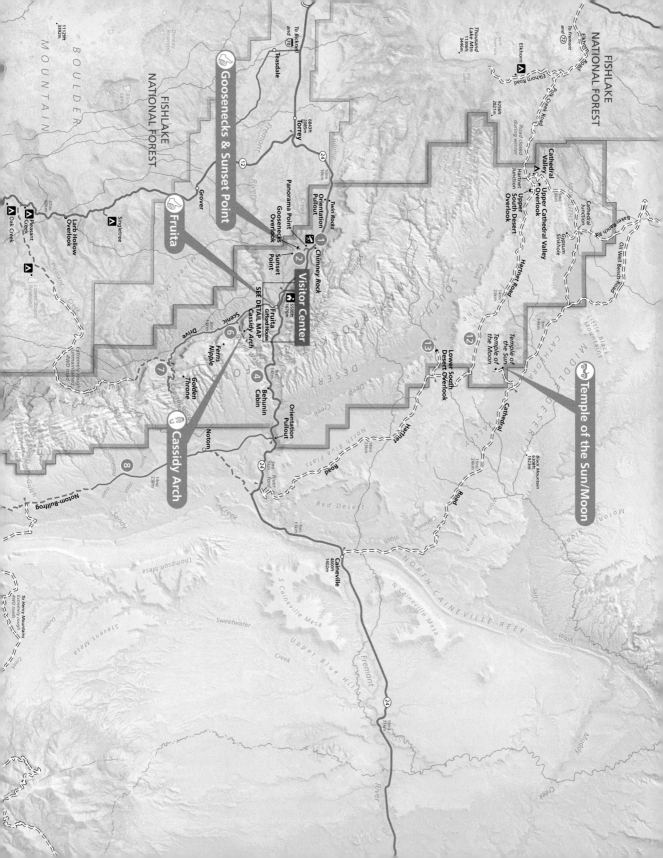

Fruita

The Castle

Hickman Bridge/Rim Overlook

Rim Overlook / Navajo Knobs Trail

Visitor Center

0.5 Kilometers

0.5 Miles

North

Hickman Bridge

Capitol Dome

Ripple Rock Nature Center

Fruita Schoolhouse

Petroglyph Panel

Sulphur Creek

Fremont River

Blacksmith Shop

Picnic Area

Gifford House

Pectols Pyramid

Cohab Canyon

Fremont Gorge Overlook Trail

Amphitheater

Frying Pan Trail

Campground

Fremont River

Group Campsite

Fremont River Trail

Cohab Canyon

Fruita

Fruita

Fruita was originally a Mormon settlement established on the banks of the Fremont River. Compared to the rest of the surrounding desert, life at Fruita was good. Even so, no more than ten families occupied the settlement at any one time. Touring Historic Fruita District will lead you to an old barn, a restored schoolhouse, **Gifford Farmhouse** (open to the public during summer, stop in for some delicious pie), a tool shed and blacksmith shop, and orchards containing almost 3,000 trees, including cherry, apple, apricot, peach, and pear. When each fruit is in season, you are welcome to pick and eat whatever you want free of charge while in the orchards. A small fee is charged for any fruit you take with you. Only pick/eat ripe fruit from orchards with a "U-Pick Fruit" sign. Fenced orchards are open from 9am until 5pm. Unfenced orchards are open from dawn to dusk. Call (435) 425-3791 for information on blossom and harvest times. Fruita Campground is also set among stands of fruit-bearing trees.

Camping

Capitol Reef's only developed campground is located at **Fruita**. All 71 sites are available on a first-come, first-served basis from November through February. The rest of the year, sites can be reserved up to six months in advance at recreation.gov. Restrooms have flush toilets and sinks, but there are no showers. Hookups are not available for RVs, but there is a dump station and a handful of sites can accommodate vehicles up to 52 feet in length. Rates are $20/night. The campground typically fills before noon from spring through fall, so reservations are a good idea. There's one group campsite in Fruita available from mid-April to mid-October. It costs $100 and can be reserved up to one year in advance at recreation.gov.

Two no-fee primitive campgrounds are available. **Cathedral Valley**, located in the northwest corner, has six sites. **Cedar Mesa**, located on Notom–Bullfrog Road 35 miles south of UT-24, has five sites. Sites are available first-come, first-served all year. They have pit toilets, but no water. Always check road conditions (435.425.3791, press 1 for information, and then 4 for road conditions) before departing, because access is via gravel roads.

If you strike out on all in-park camping options, dispersed camping is allowed on BLM land east of the park, National Forest land west of the park, at designated sites within the nearby National Forests, and at private campgrounds in Torrey. Showers are available in Torrey at Chuck Wagon General Store (and laundry),

Burr Trail

Thousand Lakes RV Park & Campground (and laundry), Sand Creek Hotel (RV Park & Campground), and Torrey Trading Post. Torrey is basically the closest place to find anything, including food, cell service, and fuel.

Driving & Off-Roading

The 10-mile **Scenic Drive**, located south of the visitor center, is the park's most popular roadway. A free brochure is available at its entrance station where visitors must pay a $20 entrance fee per vehicle. Where Scenic Drive's pavement ends, **South Draw Road** begins. This high-clearance 4WD-only road follows the Waterpocket Fold before running alongside Pleasant Creek and exiting the park. **Capitol Gorge Road** also begins at the end of Scenic Drive. There's a large parking area near the mouth of the gorge where you can park and walk or bike, but it is usually suitable for all motorists. Capitol Gorge Road ends at a popular hiking trailhead.

A 4WD vehicle is not required for Notom–Bullfrog and Burr Trail Roads. **Notom–Bullfrog Road** traces the park's eastern boundary to Post Corral where there's an equestrian staging area. It exits the park and continues south to Glen Canyon National Recreation Area (past the access point to Halls Creek Narrows). **Burr Trail Road** provides an exhilarating experience thanks to switchbacks that climb some 800 feet in just a half-mile. It's also extremely bumpy within the park, but less so west of the park boundary. Washboard or not, the drive is pretty cool as it follows the waterpocket fold. In the north, **Cathedral Loop** offers the most scenic 4WD route, combining Hartnet and Cathedral Roads (high-clearance required, must cross the Fremont River if entering from the south). It's already been mentioned, but it bears repeating, check road conditions (435.425.3791, press 1 then 4).

Cohab Canyon

Capitol Reef Hiking Trails (Distances are roundtrip unless noted otherwise)

	Name	Location (# on map)	Length	Difficulty Rating & Notes
On UT-24	Sulphur Creek - 💧	Sulphur Creek (1)	5.8 mile	S – One-way hike follows creek past waterfalls
	Chimney Rock	UT-24 (1)	3.6 miles	M – Loop trail to mesa top
	Chimney Rock Canyon	UT-24 (1)	9.4 miles	S – Backpacking route (one-way)
	Goosenecks - 💧	Panorama Point (2)	0.2 mile	E – Outstanding views for a very short hike
	Sunset Point	Panorama Point (2)	0.8 mile	E – As the name implies, sunsets!
	Hickman Bridge - 💧	UT-24 (3)	1.8 miles	M – Self-guided trail to a natural bridge
	Rim Overlook - 💧	UT-24 (3)	4.6 miles	S – Great views of Fruita
	Navajo Knobs	UT-24 (3)	9.4 miles	S – Continues beyond Rim Overlook
	Grand Wash - 💧	UT-24 (4, 6)	4.4 miles	E – Connects to Scenic Drive
	Cassidy Arch	UT-24 (4, 6)	3.4 miles	S – Can also access from Grand Wash Road
	Frying Pan	UT-24 (4, 5, 6)	5.8 miles	S – Connects Cohab Canyon with Grand Wash
Scenic Drive	Cohab Canyon - 💧	Fruita Campground (5)	3.4 miles	M – Pass through hidden canyon to overlooks
	Fremont River	Fruita Campground (5)	2.0 miles	M – Hike along river to a mesa top
	Fremont Gorge Overlook	Fruita Blacksmith Shop (5)	4.6 miles	S – 1,000-ft elevation gain to mesa top
	Old Wagon Trail	Scenic Drive (7)	3.8 miles	S – Loop west of Scenic Drive
	Capitol Gorge - 💧	Capitol Gorge Road (7)	2.0 miles	E – Short climb to waterpockets ("tanks")
	Golden Throne - 💧	Capitol Gorge Road (7)	4.0 miles	S – Short climb to viewpoint of throne
Other Areas	Burro Wash	Notom–Bullfrog Rd (8)	6.8 miles	M – Narrows
	Red Canyon	Cedar Mesa Camp (9)	5.6 miles	M – Leads into a large box canyon
	Lower Muley Twist Canyon	Burr Trail (10, 11)	23.0 miles	S – Runs parallel to Waterpocket Fold
	Surprise Canyon	Notom–Bullfrog Rd (11)	2.0 miles	E – Scrambling required but not difficult
	Lower Cathedral Valley - 💧	Off Hartnet Draw (12)	2.5 miles	M – Overlooks Temple of the Sun and Moon
	Jailhouse & Temple Rock	Lower South Desert (13)	4.5 miles	M – Mostly unmarked with unreal views

Difficulty Ratings: E = Easy, M = Moderate, S = Strenuous

Hiking

At Capitol Reef you'll find hikes similar in beauty and terrain to those at Zion National Park, but without the sometimes-overwhelming crowds. The greatest concentration of trails is found along UT-24 and Scenic Drive. Three of the best can be combined to make a 5.8-mile loop; begin at **Cohab Canyon** and connect to **Grand Wash** via **Frying Pan Trail**. This loop passes through a juniper-piñon forest and past a spur trail to **Cassidy Arch** as it traverses a narrow canyon back to UT-24. The downside of the loop is that it isn't exactly a loop. It's more like a 'C.' You exit Grand Wash 2.8 miles east of your starting point on UT-24. You'll have to plant a vehicle here, hitch a ride, hike along the road back to your car, or double back.

From Hickman Bridge Parking Area (UT-24), a small trail network leads to Hickman Bridge, Rim Overlook, and Navajo Knobs. All three share the same trail at the start before diverging. The hike begins with a gradual climb. Shortly after you've reached the flat, you'll come across the junction of Rim Overlook/Navajo Knobs and Hickman Bridge. **Hickman Bridge** is a popular destination. It's a large natural sandstone arch or bridge that is worth a quick visit. **Rim Overlook** offers spectacular panoramic views of Fruita and the surrounding desert. From Rim Overlook the trail continues an additional 4.5 miles (roundtrip), running nearly parallel to UT-24 to **Navajo Knobs** where the views are even more incredible. At the trail's end you can see for miles, beyond Gooseneck Overlook through the Fremont River Valley and on to Miners Mountain. **Cohab Canyon** is another option for an out-and-back with Fruita views. Further north, you'll find several picturesque trails in Cathedral Valley, like **Lower Cathedral Valley** (2.5 miles) and **Jailhouse & Temple Rock** (4.5 miles). A high-clearance 4WD vehicle is recommended to reach the trailheads.

Some of the most memorable sites are located less than a mile from the main roadways. Short hikes like **Goosenecks**, **Sunset Point**, and **Petroglyphs Trails** are great if you're in a rush and want to get out of the car and stretch your legs a bit. Exploring Historic Fruita District by foot is another excellent idea, especially when fruit is in season and you can treat yourself to a snack while walking through the orchard. More than an hour from Fruita via Notom-Bullfrog Road you'll find a number of narrow canyons including **Surprise Canyon** and **Headquarters Canyon**. Whether you're hiking in the busy Fruita area or the backcountry, all hikers should use caution and remember to carry plenty of water. Narrow canyons can flood quickly and should not be attempted if rain is in the forecast.

Petroglyphs

Backpacking

Visitors can camp in the backcountry with a free permit (available at the visitor center). There are nice backpacking opportunities throughout the park's 100-mile length. Upper and Lower Muley Twist Canyon Trails are two nice destinations, but you'll need a good map, and solid map-reading and cairn-spotting skills. They are located off Burr Trail Road. Halls Creek Narrows is a 22-mile multi-day adventure worth looking into. It's next on my list of Capitol Reef adventures. Pack out all human waste. Carry a commercial toilet bag system for when nature calls.

Biking

Biking is allowed, but only on designated roads. The 10-mile stretch of Scenic Drive south of the visitor center is the most popular section of roadway. It's narrow, without shoulders, and crowded with motorists between April and October. If you plan on pedaling Scenic Drive you must always be alert and proceed with caution. Mountain bikers can take on more strenuous routes like Cathedral Valley Loop, South Draw Road, or Burr Trail Road/Notom–Bullfrog Road.

Rock Climbing & Canyoneering

Rock Climbing and canyoneering are gaining popularity. Permits are required. First-timers should join someone familiar with the area or purchase a dedicated guidebook (available at the visitor center), because much of the rock is sandstone (of varying hardness).

Horseback Riding

Stock (horse, mule, and burro) are allowed in the park. However, there are no outfitters. Recommended rides include South Draw, Old Wagon Trail, Halls Creek, and the South Desert. A permit is required for overnight stays or use of Post Corral (located 35 miles south of UT-24 on Notom–Bullfrog Road.

Mule deer along Notom-Bullfrog Road

Flora & Fauna

Only a few perennial streams and rivers course through the arid region of Capitol Reef, but life finds a way. Plants have adapted to endure the harsh conditions, resulting in rare species, many of which are only found in this part of Utah. Barneby reed-mustard, Maguire's daisy, and Wright's fishhook cactus are a few rare and protected species. Mountain lions roam the mesa tops and have even been spotted in Fruita. Their main source of food is mule deer, which are quite common in Fruita's orchards. Bighorn sheep once flourished in this rocky terrain, but native sheep were hunted to extinction around the middle of the 1900s. Several reintroduction programs have infused a healthy population of desert bighorn sheep. Most animals are small rodents, bats, and birds (200+ species).

Pets & Accessibility

Pets are allowed in developed areas like Fruita Campground, parking areas, picnic areas, and along roadways, as long as they are kept on a leash (less than six feet). Pets (except service animals) are not allowed in public buildings, in the backcountry, or on trails (except for Fremont River Trail).

The visitor center, a few ranger programs, overlooks, picnic areas, and Petroglyphs Trail (located just off UT-24) are accessible (with assistance). Five accessible campsites are available at Fruita Campground.

Visitor Center & Museum

The park's **Visitor Center** is open daily (except a few federal holidays) from 8am to 4:30pm, with extended hours spring through fall. It houses exhibits, a short film, bookstore, rangers, and restrooms. **Ripple Rock Nature Center** is open from 9am until 5pm, Memorial Day through Labor Day. It offers interactive exhibits and educational programs. **Gifford House Store and Museum** is open spring through fall (with varying hours). You can get fresh-baked pies here!

Ranger Programs & For Kids

Park personnel offer interpretive walks, talks, and evening programs from spring through fall. The best of the bunch are guided hikes, star talks, and full moon walks offered from late June through October. Schedules are usually available at the visitor center or online.

Children of all ages are invited to participate in Capitol Reef's Junior Ranger Program. Free activity booklets are available online as well as at the visitor center or Ripple Rock Nature Center. Complete it and earn an official Junior Ranger Badge.

Weather

Capitol Reef spans an arid desert region. Summer days are hot, but evenings are comfortable. Winter lows fall below freezing, but average highs are around 40°F in January (the coldest month). Spring and fall bring average highs in the mid-60s to mid-70s°F. These seasons tend to be the most comfortable times of year. The region is typically dry, receiving an average of about seven inches of precipitation each year.

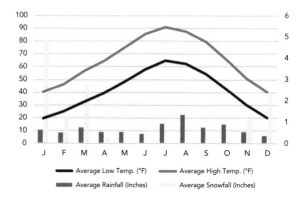

Average Low Temp. (°F) — Average High Temp. (°F)
Average Rainfall (Inches) — Average Snowfall (Inches)

Tips & Recommendations

Capitol Reef has long been overlooked among Utah's national parks. That's beginning to change. There's a lot to experience here. All it really lacks is a gateway city with all the creature comforts but Torrey isn't bad. Still, the best place to spend the night is in the park camping at Fruita or in the backcountry.

Staying on main roads, you'll only need a day or two. But most vehicles can drive Grand Wash, Capitol Gorge, and South Draw, where you'll find hiking trails.

Burr Trail and Notom–Bullfrog are more primitive but can also be accessed by most vehicles. They're highly recommended. Plan a full day to complete this drive. You'll be pulling over to take photographs, and you should also stop for a hike or two.

A high-clearance 4x4 unlocks even more. The Cathedral Valley Loop is no longer a secret, but many intrepid travelers turn around at the river you must ford immediately after turning onto Hartnet Road. Note that it is possible to access this area (and Temple of the Sun and Temple of the Moon) from the north via Elkhorn Road (also high-clearance 4x4 required). Regardless which direction you're coming from, you'll want to check on road conditions (call 435.425.3791, press 1 then 4).

Halls Creek Narrows looks very interesting. I haven't been yet (COVID sent me home, sparking a head start on the butt-work, which resulted in this edition looking as nice as it does). But I'll be out there next loop around the country. As with all canyon hikes, it's a good idea to discuss conditions and weather with a park ranger before departing. Be careful. Have fun.

Burr Trail Road

Easy Hikes: Grand Wash (4.4 miles), Capitol Gorge (2), Goosenecks (0.2)
Moderate Hikes: Lower Cathedral Valley (2.5 miles), Cohab Canyon (3.4), Headquarters Canyon (2), Hickman Bridge (1.8)
Strenuous Hikes: Sulphur Creek (5.8 miles), Golden Throne (4), Cassidy Arch (3.4), Rim Overlook (4.6)
Family Activities: Pick some fruit, hike through a slot canyon, become Junior Rangers
Rainy Day Activities: Don't change your plans unless you were planning on crossing streams or hiking slot canyons (then you need to use extreme caution, flash floods are a very real possibility)
History Enthusiasts: Fruita (Schoolhouse, Orchard, Gifford House, Blacksmith Shop), Petroglyph Panel, Behunin Cabin
Sunset Spots: Sunset Point/Goosenecks Overlook, drive Scenic Drive
Sunrise Spots: Camp at Cathedral Valley

Beyond the Park...

Dining
Outlaw's Roost • (435) 542-1763
20 N UT-95, Hanksville

Burr Trail Grill • (435) 335-7511
10 UT-12, Boulder
burrtrailgrill.menu

Grocery Stores
Chuck Wagon • (435) 425-3290
12 W Main St, Torrey

Lodging & Camping
Torrey Schoolhouse B&B
150 N Center St • (435) 491-0230
torreyschoolhouse.com

Cowboy Homestead Cabins
UT-24, Torrey • (435) 425-3414
cowboyhomesteadcabins.com

Motel Torrey • (435) 425-3800
415 W Main St • moteltorrey.com

The Lodge at Red River Ranch
2900 UT-24, Teasdale • (435) 425-3322
redriverranch.com

Wonderland RV Park
44 UT-12, Torrey • (435) 425-3665
capitolreefrvpark.com

Singletree & Pleasant Creek
Dixie National Forest

Festivals
Sundance Film Festival • January
sundance.org • Salt Lake City

Shakespeare Festival • June
bard.org • Cedar City

World of Speed • September
saltflats.com • Bonneville Salt Flats

Red Rock Film Fest • November
redrockfilmfestival.com • Cedar City

Attractions
Look at pages 397, 409, and 429 for more things to do in the area. You could spend months here and still want more time. And then Zion (page 430), Grand Canyon (page 442) and Great Basin (page 466) aren't that far either.

It's definitely worth taking UT-24 toward Hanksville. Not far from the road you'll find more strange rocks like Factory Butte.

Another place to look into is the Little Grand Canyon carved by the San Rafael River, just north-west of Green River. It's not easy to reach, but, to some, that's part of the charm, and you won't have the national park crowds.

Kodachrome Basin State Park
Just some more funky rocks
Cannonville • (435) 679-8562
stateparks.utah.gov

Red Fleet State Park
Dino tracks, paddling, camping
Vernal, UT • stateparks.utah.gov

Hondoo Rivers & Trails
Hiking, horseback, and Jeep tours
hondoo.com • (435) 425-3519

Bryce Canyon

The Navajo Loop

Phone: (435) 834-5322
Website: nps.gov/brca

Established: February 25, 1928
June 8, 1923 (National Monument)
Size: 35,835 Acres
Annual Visitors: 2.5 Million
Peak Season: April–October
Hiking Trails: 50 Miles

Activities: Hiking, Backpacking, Horseback Riding, Biking, Stargazing

Campgrounds: North and Sunset
Fee: $20/night (tent), $30 (RV)
Backcountry Camping: Permitted with a Backcountry Use Permit ($10 plus $5/person per night)
The Lodge: $176+/night

Park Hours: All day, every day
Entrance Fee: $35/30/20 (car/motorcycle/individual)

In 1918, Stephen Mather, first director and sentimental father of the National Park Service, was guided to a seldom visited attraction in southwestern Utah. His tour guides required he close his eyes before arrival. Mather had just toured Zion National Park, but Zion's colorful canyons and expanses of unspoiled wilderness could not prepare him for what he was about to see. He opened his eyes at Bryce Amphitheater, where a battalion of colorful rocky spires called hoodoos waited to greet him. Imagine having never seen a photograph of the eerie formations lining the eastern rim of Paunsaugunt Plateau. You arrive here, open your eyes, and in front of you is an indescribable masterpiece of nature. Even today, a time when everyone has seen everything on their computer or phone, this scene has the power to stop visitors dead in their tracks. These views are so divine and empowering they are inspirational to even the most casual sightseers. This is not just a place of inspiration. It's a place capable of stirring up religious sentiments. A place that invokes deep heartfelt patriotism. A place unlike all others.

To Ebenezer Bryce, it was simply "a hell of a place to lose a cow." In 1875, the Church of Jesus Christ of Latter-day Saints sent Bryce to settle the Paria Valley. He and his family chose to live right below what is known today as Bryce Amphitheater. Bryce built a home for his family, a canal for his crops and his cows, and a road to collect wood for fire to keep warm during the cool evenings and frigid winters. It became clear that Bryce and his family were sticking around, and soon locals began to call the area "Bryce Canyon." Not a true canyon, it's actually a horseshoe-shaped bowl or amphitheater formed by several creeks and streams rather than a single river and its tributaries. Life in and around Bryce Canyon was difficult. Herds of sheep and cattle quickly overgrazed the area's limited vegetation, and the region was ravaged by cycles of drought and flooding. Settlers attempted to build a water diversion channel from the Sevier River to protect their crops, cattle, and homes from seasonal floods. The effort failed. Shortly after, most settlers, including the Bryce family, left the area.

Capitulation in the face of nature has been a recurring theme in the history of southwest Utah. More than 8,000 years ago humans first visited the region, only to find it exceedingly difficult to survive for any extended period of time. Later, the Fremont Culture, hunter-gatherers who supplemented their diet with modest amounts of cultivated crops like corn and squash, lived in the area. By the mid-12th century, they also abandoned the region. Paiute Indians moved in, living much like the Fremont Culture, hunting and gathering. Paiute legends grew around the origin of the peculiar rock formations, or hoodoos. They called them "anka-ku-was-a-wits" or "red painted faces," and believed they were the Legend People turned to stone at the hands of the Coyote God.

Hoodoos may resemble beautifully colored humans sculpted from stone, but they are simply the result of thousands of years of continuous erosion. Minarets of soft sedimentary rock were left behind because they are topped by a piece of harder, less easily eroded stone. This caprock protects the column of sedimentary rock below from the erosive forces of wind, water, and ice. Several locations around the world display similar rocky spires, including nearby Cedar Breaks National Monument. But Bryce is different. It's more colorful, more abundant, and more mystical.

Bryce Canyon is a special place. A place woven into the legends of early inhabitants. A place where Ebenezer Bryce's cows got lost. A place that screamed "surprise" to Stephen Mather when he opened his eyes. A place that was almost completely inaccessible until the Union Pacific Railroad laid down track in the 1920s and the CCC built roads in the 1930s. Today, Bryce Canyon is a place accommodating to visitors, a place that will open your eyes to the natural beauty of the world around you. So come to the rim of Bryce Canyon, close your eyes, and see it for yourself.

Thor's Hammer at sunrise (located near Sunset)

When to Go
Bryce Canyon is open all year, 24 hours per day. Bryce Canyon Lodge, General Store, and Restaurant are open from April through October, with limited lodging options in winter (November and December). Wildflowers bloom between April and August, peaking in June. The park is busiest from May through September, when the weather is most pleasant and families and students are out and about. Bryce Canyon does not receive as many visitors as nearby Zion or Grand Canyon, but it is the smallest of Utah's parks and becomes congested easily. Most visitors don't stay long, and the park provides free shuttle service from mid-April until mid-October to help reduce motorist traffic.

Transportation & Airports
Public transportation does not service the park, but a **free shuttle** ferries visitors around Bryce Canyon Amphitheater (mid-April–mid-October). They also run a **Rainbow Point Tour Shuttle** (reservation required) from Ruby's Inn (outside the park) to Rainbow Point. The closest large commercial airports are Salt Lake City International (SLC), 274 miles to the north, and McCarran International (LAS) in Las Vegas, NV, 260 miles to the southwest. Car rental is available at each destination.

Directions
Bryce Canyon is located in southwestern Utah, about 75 miles northeast of Zion National Park.

From Zion National Park (86 miles): Heading east on UT-9 you will come to a T-intersection with US-89, turn left onto US-89 and continue north for 43 miles. Turn right at UT-12 East. Continue for 13 miles before turning right onto UT-63 S, which leads into the park. The visitor center is one mile beyond the park's boundary.

From Salt Lake City (270 miles): Heading south on I-15, take Exit 95 for UT-20 toward US-89. Turn left at UT-20 E. Continue 20 miles. Turn right at US-89 S. Drive 7 miles then turn left at UT-12 E. After 13 miles, turn right at UT-63 S, which leads into the park.

Camping & Lodging

Bryce Canyon has two developed campgrounds: North and Sunset. **North**, located near the visitor center, has 4 loops and 99 sites. From late May through September sites can be reserved at recreation.gov up to six months in advance. Sites are available first-come, first-served the rest of the year. **Sunset** is located 1.5 miles south of the visitor center. It has 3 loops, totaling 100 sites, available first-come, first-served from mid-April through October (closed the rest of the year). Both camps are near Bryce Amphitheater and the park's best hiking trails. Reservations are a good idea, as both campgrounds typically fill by noon during this period. Hookups are not available, but there is a dump station (free for campers, $5 otherwise) near North Campground. Campsites are $20/night for tent sites and $30/night for RV sites (about half the sites at each campground). Coin-operated shower and laundry facilities are available at the General Store, near North Campground.

The Lodge at Bryce Canyon is located in between the two campgrounds. It's typically open from March through October, and a few rooms stay open for November and December at discounted rates (come prepared with 4WD and tire chains). Rooms cost anywhere from

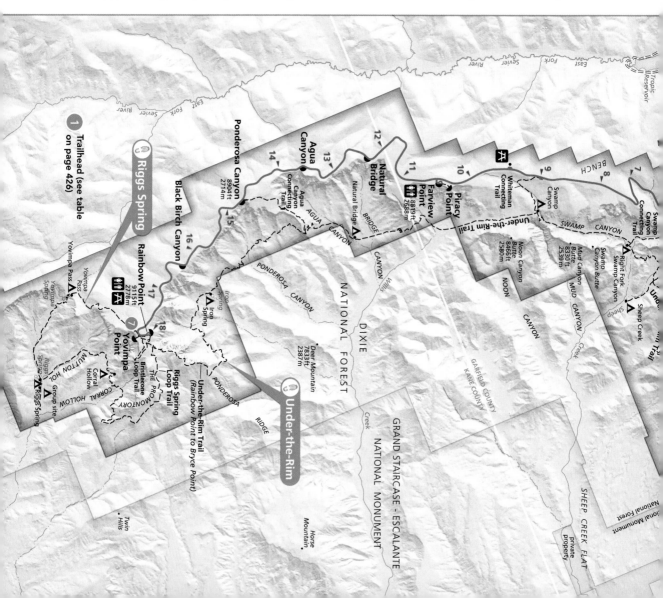

$176–271/night. There is a restaurant, cafe (serving pizzas), and general store nearby. Make reservations at (877) 386-4383 or brycecanyonforever.com.

Driving

The park's Scenic Drive is an 18-mile one-way paved road providing access to viewpoints and trailheads. All 14 viewpoints are on the east side of the road, so it's a good idea to proceed to Rainbow Point (the end) and stop at viewpoints as you head north on your return trip. Each viewpoint is unique but overlooks found around Bryce Amphitheater present the most memorable panoramas. Expect it to take at least three

hours to tour the main park road. If you don't drive the entire road, at least spend an hour or two enjoying the views between Bryce Point and Sunrise Point. During peak season you can drive to all the park's viewpoints but consider leaving your car behind and taking the shuttle.

Park Shuttle

To conserve fuel and reduce traffic and pollution, the park furnishes a free shuttle between Ruby's Inn (outside the park) and Bryce Point from mid-April to mid-October. Buses usually depart every 15 minutes between 8am and 6pm at all the most popular

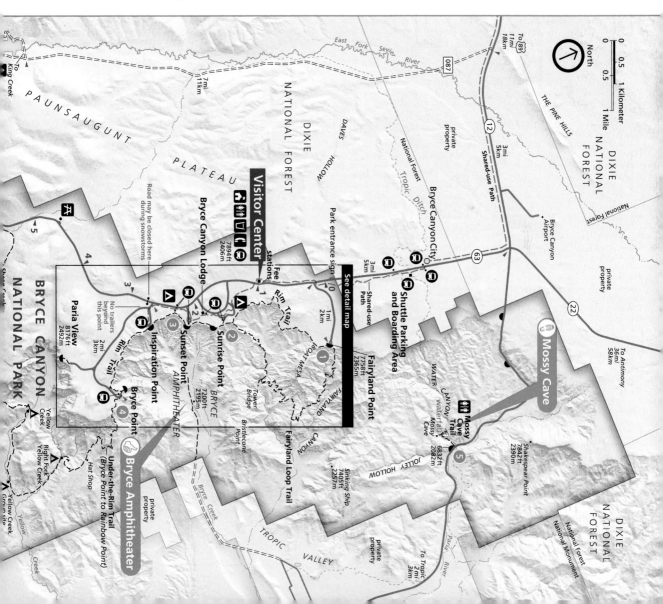

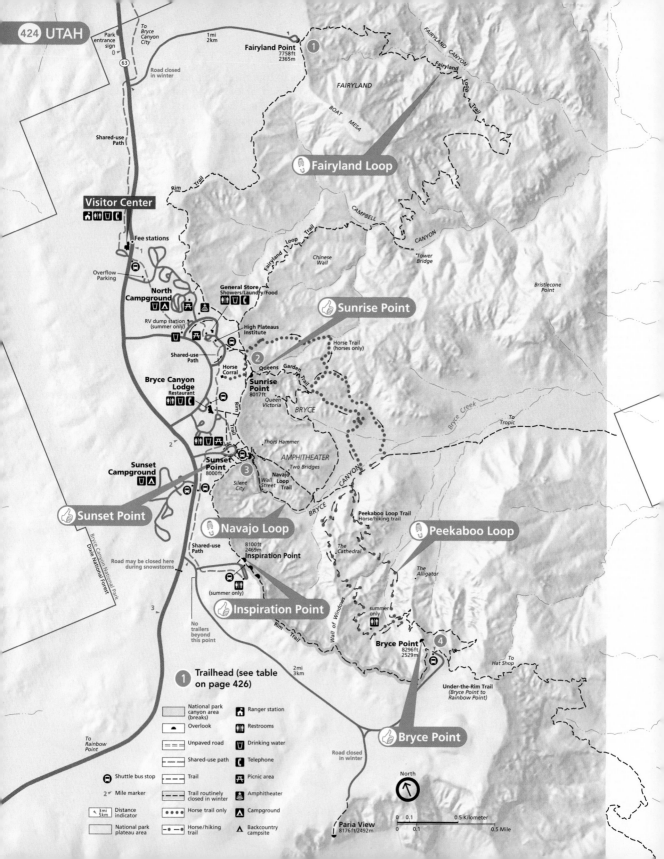

To Bryce Canyon City

Park entrance sign

Road closed in winter

63

1mi
2km

Fairland Point
7758ft
2365m
1

FAIRLAND

FAIRLAND CANYON

Fairland

BOAT MESA

Fairland Loop Trail

👣 **Fairland Loop**

Shared-use Path

CAMPBELL

Rim Trail

Fairland Loop Trail

CANYON

Chinese Wall

Tower Bridge

Bristlecone Point

Visitor Center

Fee stations

Overflow Parking

General Store
Showers/Laundry/Food

High Plateaus Institute

👍 **Sunrise Point**

Horse Trail
(horses only)

North Campground

RV dump station
(summer only)

Shared-use Path

Horse Corral

Queens Garden Trail

2

Sunrise Point
8017ft

Bryce Canyon Lodge
Restaurant

Rim Trail

Queen Victoria

BRYCE

Bryce Creek

To Tropic

Thors Hammer

AMPHITHEATER

Two Bridges

Sunset Point
8000ft

3

Silent City

Navajo Loop Trail

Wall Street

BRYCE CANYON

Sunset Campground

👍 **Sunset Point**

👣 **Navajo Loop**

Peekaboo Loop Trail
Horse/hiking trail

The Cathedral

👣 **Peekaboo Loop**

Shared-use Path

8100ft
2469m
Inspiration Point

The Alligator

Road may be closed here during snowstorms

Bryce Canyon National Park / Dixie National Forest

(summer only)

Wall of Windows

summer only

No trailers beyond this point

👍 **Inspiration Point**

Rim Trail

Bryce Point
8296ft
2529m
4

To Hat Shop

2mi
3km

1 Trailhead (see table on page 426)

Under-the-Rim Trail
(Bryce Point to Rainbow Point)

To Rainbow Point

	National park canyon area (breaks)		Ranger station
▲	Overlook	🚻	Restrooms
	Unpaved road		Drinking water
	Shared-use path		Telephone
	Trail	🌲	Picnic area
	Trail routinely closed in winter		Amphitheater
🚌	Shuttle bus stop	▲	Campground
2	Mile marker	▲	Backcountry campsite
	Horse trail only		
	Horse/hiking trail		

3mi
5km
Distance indicator

National park plateau area

👍 **Bryce Point**

Road closed in winter

North

Paria View
8176ft/2492m

0   0.1   0.5 Kilometer
0   0.1   0.5 Mile

destinations around Bryce Amphitheater. If you aren't staying at Bryce Canyon Lodge or the park's campgrounds, it's highly recommended that you leave your vehicle outside the park and use the free shuttle. Park at the shuttle station located near Ruby's Inn, pay the entrance fee, and board the next shuttle. It also stops at the two Best Westerns, Ruby's Campground, and Old Bryce Town (on the other side of the park boundary). The entire route duration is about 50 minutes, not including stops at overlooks and facilities.

Rainbow Point Tour runs from Ruby's Inn to Rainbow Point, from mid-April to mid-September, twice daily (at 9am and 1:30pm). It covers 40 miles, lasting about 3.5 hours, as it makes eight stops at scenic viewpoints along the main park road. (Note that it does not stop at the park's most popular destinations around Bryce Amphitheater.) The tour service is free, but reservations are required (available up to 24 hours in advance). Reserve your spot by calling (435) 834-5290 or stopping in at the shuttle offices at Ruby's Inn, Ruby's Campground, or the Shuttle Parking Area. Dress for the weather and pack a lunch, snacks, and anything else you require. And don't forget to stop at Bryce Amphitheater too!

Hiking

At Bryce Canyon you don't have to stare at the balanced rocks, fluted walls, and colorful hoodoos from roadside overlooks; you are free to walk among them. A variety of trails lead into and around Bryce Amphitheater. Each trail has its merits, but a few are superior. And these are some of the most outstanding trails in the entire National Park System.

Navajo Loop is tremendous, packing a whole lot of scenic bang for just 1.3 miles of hiking. The balanced rock called Thor's Hammer (near Sunset) and narrow passages of Wall Street are two of the trail's many highlights. (Note that Wall Street closes in winter, severing the loop.) Extend the experience by combining it with one of the trails at the canyon floor. Add **Queens Garden Trail** to Navajo Loop and make a 2.9-mile hike through this eroded paradise. If you don't mind hiking with horses, combine **Navajo and Peekaboo Loops**. This route leads beyond the destinations of typical Bryce Canyon day-hikers, but it merges with a path heavily trod by horses and their riders. It's dusty, steep at times, and somewhat difficult, but worth the effort and equine mingling.

If you don't want to venture into the amphitheater, enjoy it from above by hiking the 5.5-mile (one-way) **Rim Trail**. It connects all the amphitheater's viewpoints, and

Bryce Point

the free summer shuttle makes stops along the way. Views are nearly as beautiful from the trail and you may decide to continue hiking along the rim. Rim Trail closes in winter between Inspiration and Bryce Points.

The most popular hike beyond Bryce Amphitheater is **Fairyland Loop Trail**. It's excellent. Traversing two amphitheaters, Fairyland goes full-circle when combined with Rim Trail. Hikers are rewarded with a different sort of landscape as it passes through gently sloped badlands with denser tree cover. **Under-the-Rim Trail**, for its part, is not reserved for backpackers. It can be accessed via connecting trails at Sheep Creek/Swamp Canyon, Whiteman, and Agua Canyon. The latter is the most scenic, but it's rarely used due to a very steep descent. The easiest connecting trail is Whiteman. At two miles, Sheep Creek is the longest connection to Under-the-Rim Trail. Swamp Canyon and Whiteman are just under one mile, and Agua Canyon is slightly less than two miles to the trail junction.

Backpacking

There are two backcountry trails with designated campsites for backpackers. The 22.9-mile (one-way) **Under-the-Rim Trail** runs parallel to Scenic Drive from Bryce Point to Rainbow Point. (It also intersects two popular Bryce Amphitheater hiking trails: Rim and Peekaboo Trails.) Begin at Bryce Point. Check out Bryce Amphitheater viewpoint first if you haven't already, and then head away from the amphitheater on Under-the-Rim Trail. Follow it south and east to the first campsite, located just past Hat Shop. In all there are seven backcountry campsites (Sheep Creek was closed when we went to print) along Under-the-Rim Trail. Elevation ranges from 6,800 feet to 9,105 feet at Rainbow Point (highest elevation in park). The entire route can be completed easily enough in two days.

Rainbow Point Tour Shuttle is perfect for Under-the-Rim backpackers, otherwise you'll have to stash a car at Rainbow Point or double your hiking distance by doing an out-and-back. If you plan on using the shuttle, know its pickup times/locations!

Riggs Spring Loop is the other backpacking route. It's an 8.8-mile circuit beginning and ending at Rainbow Point. Hikers pass through old forests before descending into canyons east of Pink Cliffs. You return to the plateau via Yovimpa Pass. There are three designated campsites (Corral Hollow was closed when we went to print). They are the only places you can camp.

A backcountry permit is required for all overnight stays. They can be purchased at the visitor center during normal operating hours as long as you arrive at least one hour before closing. Permits are not available for reservation by mail or phone. However, they can be reserved up to 48 hours in advance, in person, at the visitor center. Permits cost $10 plus $5/person (ages 16+) per night. Open fires are not permitted in the backcountry. Reliable water sources are available at all campsites except Swamp Canyon and Natural Bridge. If you need to boil water bring a stove.

Horseback Riding

One of the most enjoyable ways to enter the amphitheater is in the saddle. Typically beginning in April and running through October (depending on weather), Canyon Trail Rides (435.679.8665, canyonrides.com) offers a 2-hour ride to the canyon floor ($75/person) and a 3-hour complete tour of the canyon on Peek-a-boo Loop Trail ($100/person). Rides are offered twice each day. Reservations can be made online or at Bryce Canyon Lodge. Visitors can bring their own stock (horse or mule), but riders must be scheduled for a specific date and time prior to entering the park. Schedule your reservation at least 72 hours in advance. Overnight stock trips are not permitted.

Biking

Cyclists are allowed on all paved roads but pedaling is not recommended as Scenic Drive is narrow

Bryce Canyon Hiking Trails (Distances are roundtrip unless noted otherwise)

	Name	Location (# on map)	Length	Difficulty Rating & Notes
Bryce Amphitheater	Rim	Fairyland to Bryce Point (1, 4)	5.5 miles	E – Connects amphitheater viewpoints (one-way)
	Tower Bridge	Sunrise Point (2)	3.0 miles	M – Follows Fairyland, spur trail to the bridge
	Queens Garden - 🐎	Sunrise Point (2)	1.8 miles	E – Easiest route into the canyon (not a loop)
	Navajo Loop - 🐎	Sunset Point (3)	1.3 miles	M – Wall Street section closed in winter
	Sunset to Sunrise	Sunset/Sunrise Points (2, 3)	1.0 mile	E – Paved portion of Rim Trail
	The 'Figure-8'	Sunset/Sunrise Points (2, 3)	6.4 miles	S – Queens Garden, Navajo, and Peekaboo
	Queens/Navajo Loop - 🐎	Sunset/Sunrise Points (2, 3)	2.9 miles	M – Extra 0.5-mile to connect Sunrise/Sunset • Check out Wall Street while you're down there!
	Navajo/Peekaboo Loop	Sunset Point (3)	4.9 miles	S – Make a smaller figure-8 than the entire Peekaboo Loop by starting/ending at Sunset Pt
	Bryce Amphitheater Traverse	Sunrise/Bryce Points (2, 4)	4.7 miles	S – Combine Peekaboo and Queens Garden and shuttle between viewpoints
	Peekaboo Loop - 🐎	Bryce Point (4)	5.5 miles	S – Horse Trail • Must go clockwise
Other Areas	Fairyland Loop - 🐎	Fairyland/Sunset Points (1, 2)	8.0 miles	S – Reduce to 5.75 miles by using the shuttle
	Hat Shop	Bryce Point (4)	4.0 miles	S – First two miles of Under-the-Rim
	Under-the-Rim	Bryce to Rainbow Point (4, 6)	22.9 miles	S – Longest backpacking route (one-way)
	Mossy Cave - 🐎	Highway 12 (5)	0.8 mile	E – Short and easy walk to a small waterfall
	Sheep Creek/ Swamp Canyon	Swamp Canyon (6)	4.0 miles	M – Not the easiest trail to follow, but it's away from the amphitheater crowds
	Bristlecone Loop	Rainbow Point (7)	1.0 mile	E – Stroll through ancient forest
	Riggs Spring Loop	Rainbow Point (7)	8.8 miles	S – 4 campsites along short backpacking route

Difficulty Ratings: E = Easy, M = Moderate, S = Strenuous

and busy (especially from mid-April through mid-October). However, an 18-mile shared use path from Red Canyon to Bryce Canyon (continuing 6.2 miles into the park) opened a few years ago. It's a great place to pedal (walk your dog, rollerblade, longboard, or cross-country ski). Bikes are available to rent just outside the park at Ruby's Inn (866.866.6616, rubysinn.com) for $10/hour, $25/half-day, and $40/day.

Stargazing

The combination of Bryce Canyon's remote location and thin desert air provide some of the darkest skies in the contiguous United States. To put things into perspective, a stargazer on a moonless night in a small town can see roughly 2,500 stars. On that same moonless night in Bryce Canyon more than 7,500 are visible without the help of a telescope. Stargazing is so exceptional here that the park offers an annual Astronomy Festival, typically held in June. Check the park's online calendar for exact dates.

Winter Activities

Cross-country skiing and snowshoeing are popular activities in winter. Skiers are not permitted on trails below the rim. Snowshoers are permitted but they aren't required unless it's snowed recently. Traction devices should be added to your hiking boots. Good locations to ski/snowshoe include Rim Trail, Bristlecone Loop, Fairyland Road, and Paria Road. The park offers ranger-led full moon snowshoe hikes. They also hold an annual Christmas Bird Count and Winter Festival. Ski and snowshoe rentals are available at Ruby's Inn.

Visitor Center

The visitor center is located on UT-63 (the park's Scenic Road), 4.5 miles south of UT-12. It's open every day except Thanksgiving and Christmas. Standard hours are 8am to 6pm. May through September, they are extended to 8pm. November through March, hours are reduced to 4:30pm. You'll find exhibits, an information desk, bookstore, a short film, restrooms, and you can obtain backcountry permits at the visitor center. Bryce Canyon Shuttles stop at the visitor center, so you can leave your car at the parking station outside the park when the free shuttle is running.

Ranger Programs & For Kids

Absolutely do not miss the chance to join at least one ranger program. Park rangers guide visitors on canyon hikes, rim walks, and the occasional Full Moon Hike (hiking boots required). Geology talks and evening programs are administered daily during summer. Evening programs take place at the lodge, visitor

Rainbow Point

center, or North Campground's Amphitheater. All these activities are very family-friendly, but discussion topics can be technical and difficult to understand for children. An alternative for families is the one-hour kid's interpretive program. Children must be accompanied by an adult. Check the park's online calendar for a current schedule of events. Tickets are required for the Full Moon Hike due to limited capacity. They are distributed via lottery the day of the hike. You must register in person at the visitor center. Each member of your group must be present (with proper footwear) at the lottery. In winter, full moon hikes become full moon snowshoe adventures (snowpack permitting).

Children can become Junior Rangers by exploring the park visitor center, attending a presentation or hike, or watching the park film and completing an age-appropriate number of activities in the park's activity booklet. Booklets are available online or for free at the visitor center. Complete these tasks and return to the visitor center to be inducted as an official Junior Ranger and receive a free badge.

Flora & Fauna

Spires, pinnacles, and hoodoos steal the show, but if you look in the air and on the ground, you'll spot a few animals and plants, too. Growing in the red rock's soil are at least 400 plant species, including a colorful array of wildflowers. In the harshest areas only limber pine and Great Basin bristlecone pine exist. Some of these ancient trees are more than 1,300 years old. Mule deer are the most common animal, but fox, bobcats, black bears, mountain lions, and Utah prairie dogs can also be found here. As a bonus, more than 170 species of birds either reside in or visit Bryce Canyon.

Sunrise Point

Pets & Accessibility

Pets are only permitted in campgrounds, parking lots, the Shared Use Path, the paved path between Sunrise Point and Sunset Point, and along paved roads. They must be on a leash (less than six feet). Pets are not allowed on unpaved trails, at viewpoints, in public buildings, or on the shuttle.

Bryce Canyon is one of the more wheelchair-friendly parks. Two campsites at Sunset Campground are reserved for wheelchair users. The summer shuttle is fully accessible. Rim Trail's first 0.5-mile is paved and level. Many of the ranger-guided activities and viewpoints are easily accessible to individuals with mobility impairments. The visitor center is fully accessible (with assistance). Accessible restrooms can be found at the visitor center, Sunset Point, Bryce Canyon Lodge, and the General Store.

Weather

Summer at Bryce Canyon is pleasant, with average high temperatures from June to August in the high 70s to low 80s°F. Only a handful of days top out above 90°F. Clear skies and high elevation make for cool evenings. The average lows during this same period range from the high 30s to mid-40s°F. Winter isn't as comfortable, but it isn't awful either. It's just that the extreme variation in temperature can make for some less-than-ideal vacations. Any given day can be sunny and 50°F, or well below freezing during winter. If you're lucky and hit Bryce on one of those 50-degree days when it's covered in snow, you'll be in for a real treat (just remember to have traction devices for your hiking boots).

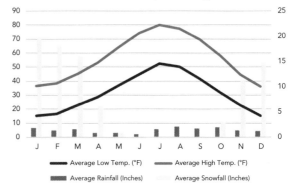

Tips & Recommendations

Bryce Canyon is a little bit of a one hit wonder, but that one hit (Bryce Amphitheater) is near the top of the charts.

Don't miss Bryce Amphitheater. This note may seem absurd, but people have visited Bryce and left wondering what all the fuss is about. Without fail, those people only drive up and down the main park road, never leaving to look at stunning Bryce Amphitheater. Don't do that.

Most visitors arrive between mid-April and mid-October. If you visit during this time, it's a good idea to park outside at the shuttle station and use the park's free shuttle. Visiting during the off-season is another good idea. Temperatures will be cooler. Crowds will be smaller. And the trails are mostly short, so you can hike them during the middle of the day when it's nicest. The park is special any time of year, but it can be truly magical covered in a blanket of fresh snow. You just have to be prepared for it (4WD, snow chains, ice scraper, traction devices for boots, etc.), in case you get dumped on while visiting. Winter also opens new opportunities for cross-country skiing and snowshoeing.

If you're only planning a quick stop on the way to Zion or Arches, spend all your time at Bryce Amphitheater. If you can spare a couple hours, it's a great idea to hike into the canyon (or let a horse carry you down there!). After a decent look around the amphitheater area, then I'd continue down the main park road to see the rest of this magical setting.

Bryce is another high elevation park, so don't get too aggressive with your hiking right off the bat, and remember to carry plenty of water.

Hiking among the hoodoos is best in the morning hours as the colorful formations will be bathed in soft light, illuminating what's already a fascinating environment. My personal favorite photography opportunity at Bryce is to be down among the hoodoos an hour or two after sunrise.

Waking up early at a high elevation in the southwestern desert, you can almost count on a crisp morning. Pack plenty of layers and bundle up if you head out for sunrise (which is a good idea).

Note that Bryce Amphitheater is east of all the park's viewpoints, so if you want to capture the sun and the stunning hoodoos, you'll need to wake up for sunrise. To catch late evening light, reach the amphitheater a several hours before sunset or else the rock formations will already be under cover of shadows. Still, the best place to be is walking among the colorful hoodoos.

A trail ride exploring Bryce

Hiking Trails: Queen's/Navajo Loop (Moderate, 2.9 miles), Fairyland Loop (Strenuous, 8), Navajo Loop (Moderate, 4.9), Queen's Garden (Easy, 1.8), Mossy Cave (Easy, 0.8), Sunset to Sunrise (Easy, 1), Peekaboo Loop (Strenuous, 5.5)
Viewpoints: Inspiration Point, Bryce Point, Sunset Point, Fairyland Point, Sunrise Point, Paria View, Yovimpa Point, Natural Bridge
Guided Tours: Ride a horse
Sunset Spots: Inspiration Point, Paria View
Sunrise Spots: Sunset (Thor's Hammer), Bryce Point, Inspiration Point, Sunrise Point

Beyond the Park...

Grocery Stores
Ruby's Inn General Store
Lodge, restaurant, store, RV park, bike rental
26 S Main St, Bryce Canyon City
rubysinn.com • (435) 834-5484

Clarke's Market • (435) 679-8633
141 N Main St, Tropic

Lodging & Camping
Stone Canyon Inn • (866) 489-4680
1380 W Stone Canyon Ln, Tropic
stonecanyoninn.com

Bryce Canyon Inn • (435) 679-8502
21 N Main St, Tropic
brycecanyoninn.com

Blueberry Inn • (435) 679-8820
412 S UT-12, Tropic
blueberryinn.com

Bryce Valley Ranch RV and Horse Park
940 UT-12, Cannonville
brycervandhorsepark.com

Bryce Valley KOA
215 Red Rock Dr, Cannonville
koa.com • (435) 679-8988

Riverside Ranch RV Park
594 US-89, Hatch • (435) 720-4464
theriversideranch.com

Bear Valley RV Resort
900 UT-20, Panguitch
bearvalleyrv.com

Panguitch KOA
555 S Main St, Panguitch
koa.com • (800) 562-1625

Hitch-N-Post • (435) 676-2436
420 N Main St, Panguitch
henrieshitchnpost.com

Kings Creek
Dixie National Forest

Festivals
Escalante Canyons Art Fest • Sept
escalantecanyonsartfestival.org

Attractions
Utah possesses an embarrassment of outdoor attraction riches. When planning your trip, I'd highly recommend looking at all these sections, and then pinning the sites you're interested in on a map, simplifying the decision of how much time to spend here. No matter what, it's a good idea to look beyond the national parks. But, I get it, time is limited. You'll probably want to return anyway.

Bryce Canyon ATV Adventures
Guided ATV tours to the rim of Bryce Canyon
450 N Airport Rd, Bryce
brycecanyonatvadventures.com

Bryce Canyon EZ Riders
Electric Bike rentals ($40/2 hours, $60/4 hours)
450 Airport Rd, Bryce
brycecanyonezriders.com

Escalante Outfitters • (435) 826-4266
Lodge, restaurant, tours
escalanteoutfitters.com

Cedar Breaks National Mon
Similar to Bryce Canyon, there's an amphitheater filled with colorful hoodoos. Also similar, it's a great place to visit.
UT-143, Brian Head
nps.gov/cebr • (435) 986-7120

Grand Staircase–Escalante National Monument (BLM)
Great trails like Lower Calf Creek Falls, Peek-a-boo Canyon, and Spooky Gulch
669 US-89A, Kanab
blm.gov • (435) 644-1300

Frontier Homestead State Park Museum • (435) 586-9290
Explores the early (pioneer) days of Utah and Cedar City
635 N Main St, Cedar City
stateparks.utah.gov

Zion

Hidden Canyon Trail

Phone: (435) 772-3256
Website: nps.gov/zion

Established: November 19, 1919
July 31, 1909 (National Monument)
Size: 146,598 Acres
Annual Visitors: 4.5 Million
Peak Season: April–September

Activities: Hiking, Backpacking, Horseback Riding, Biking, Paddling, Rock Climbing, Canyoneering

2 Campgrounds: $20–30/night*
Backcountry Camping: Permitted with a Wilderness Permit (fee)
Zion Lodge: $220–288/night

Park Hours: All day, every day
Entrance Fee: $35/30/20
(car/motorcycle/individual)

*Reservations available from late May through late October (877.444.6777, recreation.gov)

The name Zion, Hebrew for "Jerusalem" (and "the Holy Sanctuary" in Arabic), was bestowed upon a sublime red rock canyon carved by the North Fork of the Virgin River. As they say, "If the shoe fits, wear it." This region of southwestern Utah has served as sanctuary for ancient cultures, Mormon settlers, government explorers, and today's solace-seeking tourists.

People have inhabited the Virgin River Valley for at least 8,000 years. Nomadic families camped, hunted, and collected plants and seeds. About 2,000 years ago they began cultivating crops, which led to construction of permanent villages called pueblos. The only remnants of these ancient cultures are baskets, rope nets, yucca fiber sandals, tools, and simple structures dating back to 500 AD. Tools used by the Fremont Culture and Virgin Anasazi include stone knives, drills, and stemmed dart points that were hurled with atlatls (a tool similar to today's dog ball throwers). Small pit-houses and granaries have been discovered at various archaeological sites within the park's canyons. Scientists speculate a combination of extended drought, catastrophic flooding, and depleted farmland forced these people to abandon their civilization around the turn of the 14th century. As the Fremont Culture and Virgin Anasazi left the region, Paiute and Ute moved in. They migrated to the area on a seasonal basis, using its land for hunting and gathering, much like the original inhabitants. A few tribes cultivated fields of corn, sunflower, and squash, using the region as a sanctuary for hundreds of years.

It wasn't until the late 18th century that a pair of Franciscan missionaries became the first people of European descent to explore the region. Francisco Domínguez and Father Escalante led an eponymous expedition, which left Santa Fe in search of a route to Monterey, California. Before reaching the Sierra Nevada, their journey was impeded by a shortage of rations and snowstorms. Forced to turn back, they headed south, passing nearby the site of present-day Kolob Canyons Visitor Center, and then crossing the Colorado River at Marble Canyon before returning to Santa Fe.

Mormon farmers settled the Virgin River region in 1847. A few years later, Parowan and Cedar City were established, and they named the area used as a pasture and lumber yard Kolob. According to Mormon scripture, Kolob is "the heavenly place nearest the residence of God." By 1858, new settlements were established along the South Virgin River. Expansion continued when Isaac Behunin became the first to settle on the ground floor of a canyon he named Zion, referring to a place mentioned in the Bible. The Behunins and two other families summered here. They grew corn, tobacco, and fruit trees, returning to nearby Springdale for winter.

In 1872, U.S. Army Major John Wesley Powell led an expedition through the region. He named the magnificent valley Mukuntuweap, the Paiute name for "canyon." His crew took photographs, helping satisfy the East Coast's curiosity about western wonders. The East took more interest after Frederick S. Dellenbaugh displayed his paintings of the colorful canyon at the St. Louis World Fair in 1904. Five years later, President William Howard Taft decided the region should be a public sanctuary, establishing Mukuntuweap National Monument.

The region—now preserved for everyone's enjoyment—was relatively inaccessible to the average man. But in 1917 a road was completed to the Grotto. Visitation increased, and so did confusion about the canyon's name. Locals disliked Mukuntuweap, and Horace Albright felt it needed to be more manageable. Congress and President Wilson agreed; land was added, and it was redesignated Zion National Park. In 1923, a subsidiary of the Union Pacific Railroad purchased a small tent camp and replaced it with Zion Lodge. By 1930, construction crews completed Zion–Mount Carmel Highway, dramatically increasing access and visitation. Finally, Zion had become a sanctuary for everyone to enjoy.

Weeping Rock

When to Go
Zion is open all year, but visitation peaks mid-March through October. During this time, the park's facilities have maximum operating hours and Zion Canyon Scenic Drive is only accessible by the park's shuttle system (and guests of Zion Lodge). The shuttle also runs on some weekends in February, March, and November. The road is plowed and open to motorists whenever the shuttle is not running.

Transportation & Airports
Public transportation does not reach the park, but a shuttle connects the neighboring town of Springdale, providing the only access to Zion Canyon from mid-March through October. The closest large commercial airports are McCarran International (LAS) in Las Vegas, NV, 170 miles to the southwest, and Salt Lake City International (SLC), 313 miles north of the park.

Directions
Zion National Park is in the very southwestern corner of Utah. Kolob Canyons is located in the park's northwest corner and reached by taking Exit 40 from I-15. Directions are provided to Zion Canyon, the park's most popular area, which is accessed via UT-9.

From Las Vegas (167 miles): Head east on I-15 through St. George, UT, all the way to Exit 16 for UT-9 toward Hurricane/Zion National Park. Take UT-9 east 32 miles to Zion Canyon Visitor Center.

From Salt Lake City (312 miles): Head south on I-15 to exit 27 for UT-17 for Toquerville/Hurricane. Turn left at UT-17 S/UT-228. After 6 miles, turn left onto UT-9, which leads into the park.

From Kanab/Grand Canyon (42/248 miles): Head north on US-89. Turn left at UT-9 W, which leads into the park. Visitors with large vehicles should refer to page 435 for information regarding access to Zion–Mount Carmel Tunnel.

Angel's Landing and Zion Canyon

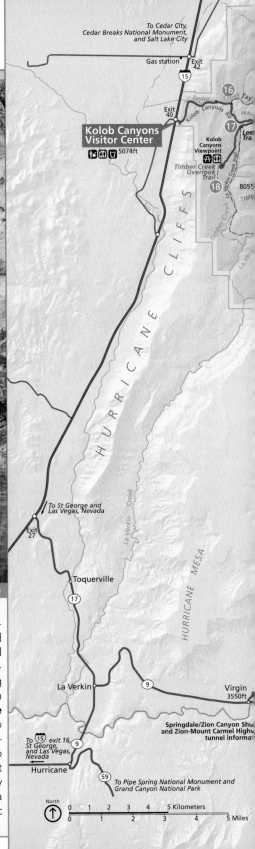

Kolob Canyons
Visitor Center
5074ft

Regions

Zion is one continuous area, but three roads lead into the park's interior. **Zion Canyon** is by far the most popular region. You will find most facilities and trailheads along Zion Canyon Scenic Drive and Zion–Mount Carmel Highway (UT-9), which provide access to the canyon. Ultra-popular hikes through Zion Narrows and to Angel's Landing are located in this region. If you follow UT-9 west, beyond the south entrance, you will reach the small town of Virgin. Here, **Kolob Terrace Road** winds its way in-and-out of the park before terminating at Kolob Reservoir. Kolob Terrace Road provides access to Lava Point Primitive Campground and numerous trailheads, including the bottom-up (non-technical) and top-down (technical) trails to The Subway (permit required, even for a day-hike). In the park's northwest corner, far away from the crowds of Zion Canyon, is **Kolob Canyons**. This region has a visitor center, a scenic drive, and a few trailheads including the scenic hike to Kolob Arch.

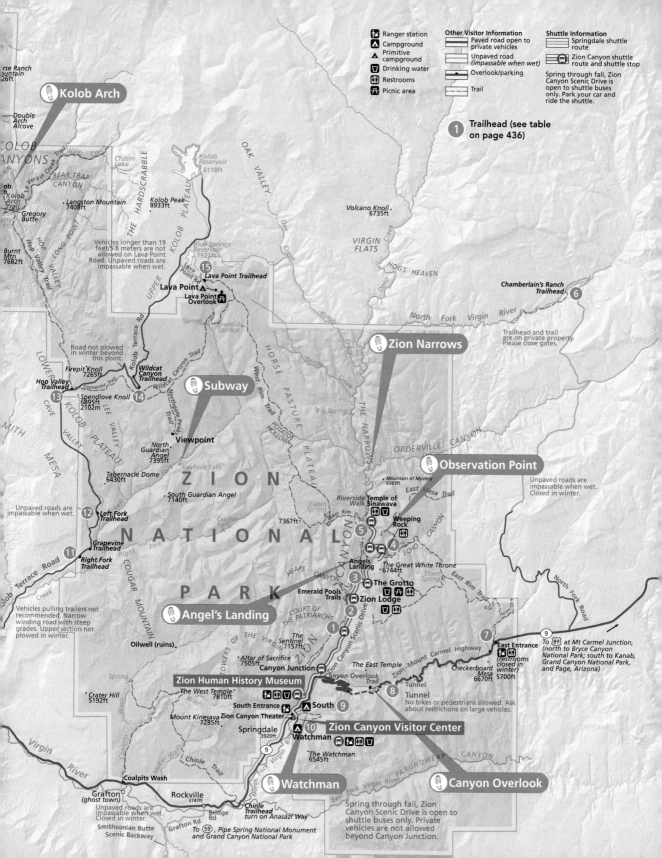

Kolob Arch

Zion Narrows

Subway

Observation Point

Angel's Landing

Watchman

Canyon Overlook

Zion Human History Museum

Zion Canyon Visitor Center

	Ranger station		Other Visitor Information		Shuttle Information
	Campground		Paved road open to private vehicles		Springdale shuttle route
	Primitive campground		Unpaved road (impassable when wet)		Zion Canyon shuttle route and shuttle stop
	Drinking water		Overlook/parking		
	Restrooms		Trail		
	Picnic area				

Spring through fall, Zion Canyon Scenic Drive is open to shuttle buses only. Park your car and ride the shuttle.

① Trailhead (see table on page 436)

Double Arch Alcove

KOLOB CANYONS

BEAR TRAP CANYON

La Verkin Creek Trail

Willis Creek

Kolob Arch Trail

Gregory Butte

Langston Mountain 7408ft

THE HARDSCRABBLE

Chasm Lake

Kolob Reservoir 8118ft

Kolob Peak 8933ft

OAK VALLEY

Volcano Knoll 6735ft

VIRGIN FLATS

Burnt Mtn 7682ft

Hop Valley Trail

LONG POINT

UPPER KOLOB PLATEAU

Blue Springs Reservoir 7921ft

Lava Point Rd

Vehicles longer than 19 feet/5.8 meters are not allowed on Lava Point Road. Unpaved roads are impassable when wet.

⑮ Lava Point Trailhead

Lava Point

Lava Point Overlook

Sawmill Springs

HOGS HEAVEN

North Fork Virgin River

Chamberlain's Ranch Trailhead ⑥

Trailhead and trail are on private property. Please close gates.

Road not plowed in winter beyond this point.

Firepit Knoll 7265ft

Kolob Terrace Rd

Wildcat Canyon Trailhead

Wildcat Canyon Trail

Northgate Peaks Trail

West Rim Trail

HORSE PASTURE PLATEAU

Goose Creek

Deep Creek

THE NARROWS

Hop Valley Trailhead ⑬

Connector Trail

Spendlove Knoll 6895ft 2102m ⑭

Big Spring

ORDERVILLE CANYON

Unpaved roads are impassable when wet. Closed in winter.

North Guardian Angel 7395ft

Viewpoint

Keyhole Falls

POTATO HOLLOW

ORDERVILLE CANYON

East Mesa Trail

Mountain of Mystery 6565ft

Tabernacle Dome 6430ft

South Guardian Angel 7140ft

Double Falls

Cabin Spring

ECHO CANYON

Weeping Rock

Riverside Walk

Temple of Sinawava

⑤

④

Unpaved roads are impassable when wet.

SMITH MESA

CAVE VALLEY

KOLOB PLATEAU

LEE VALLEY

Left Fork Trailhead ⑫

Grapevine Trailhead

Right Fork Trailhead ⑪

Right Fork

West Rim Trail

7367ft

The Great White Throne 6744ft

Angels Landing ③

The Grotto

Stave Spring

East Rim Trail

N A T I O N A L

Creek

Vehicles pulling trailers not recommended. Narrow winding road with steep grades. Upper section not plowed in winter.

COUGAR MOUNTAIN

HEAPS CANYON

Emerald Pools Trails

Zion Lodge ②

ZION CANYON

P A R K

Oilwell (ruins)

Kolob Terrace Road

The Sentinel 7157ft

COURT OF THE PATRIARCHS

①

Canyon Junction

Zion Canyon Scenic Drive

The East Temple

⑦ East Entrance (restrooms closed in winter) 5700ft

⑨ ⑧⑨ at Mt Carmel Junction, (north to Bryce Canyon National Park; south to Kanab, Grand Canyon National Park, and Page, Arizona)

Crater Hill 5192ft

The West Temple 7810ft

South Entrance

Zion Canyon Theater

Zion Human History Museum

South ⑨

Canyon Overlook Trail

Checkerboard Mesa 6670ft

Zion – Mount Carmel Highway

⑧ Tunnel

Tunnel

No bikes or pedestrians allowed. Ask about restrictions on large vehicles.

Mount Kinesava 7285ft

Springdale

3920ft

⑩ Watchman

The Watchman 6545ft

North Fork Virgin River

PARUNUWEAP CANYON

Coalpits Wash

Grafton (ghost town)

Rockville 3747ft

Bridge Rd

Chinle Trailhead turn on Anasazi Way

Chinle Trail

Grafton Rd

Unpaved roads are impassable when wet. Closed in winter.

Smithsonian Butte Scenic Backway

To ㊾ Pipe Spring National Monument and Grand Canyon National Park

Spring through fall, Zion Canyon Scenic Drive is open to shuttle buses only. Private vehicles are not allowed beyond Canyon Junction.

Virgin River

Pa'rus Trail

Zion Camping (Fees are per night)

Name	Location	Open	Fee	Sites	Notes
South*	Near South Entrance	mid-March–October	$20	117	No showers, no hookups, 4 group sites
Watchman*	Near South Entrance	All Year	$20 $30	87 (tent) 96 (RV)	RV sites have electric hookups, 18 walk-in tent-only sites, 7 group sites
Lava Point	Kolob Terrace Road	May–September	Free	6	Primitive, no water, pit toilets
*Reservations can be made at (877) 444-6777 or recreation.gov (highly recommended, all sites fill during peak season)					
Backcountry	A wilderness permit (fee) is required to camp in the backcountry. See page 438 for details.				

Zion Lodging (Fees are per night)

Name	Open	Fee	Notes
Zion Lodge (Zion Canyon Scenic Dr)	All Year	$220+	Only in-park lodging, fills early during peak season • Can drive to lodge • Make reservations at (888) 297-2757 or zionlodge.com

Camping & Lodging

Zion has three drive-in campgrounds. South and Watchman Campgrounds are located along the Virgin River's shoreline near the south entrance and main visitor center. These campgrounds have running water and flush toilets. **Watchman Campground** is open all year. It has 96 sites with electric hookups. No sites have full hookups, but a dump station is available for campers. There are seven group campsites that can accommodate 7 to 40 campers (tent-only, $50–130/night depending on group size). **South Campground** is open seasonally and none of the sites have hookups. You can reserve a standard (tent or RV) campsite up to six months in advance at Watchman or two weeks in advance at South at (877) 444-6777 or recreation.gov. Group sites can be reserved up to one year in advance. (Group sites at South were closed when we went to print.) **Lava Point** is a primitive campground located along Kolob Terrace Road, about 80 minutes from Zion Canyon Visitor Center (by car). Six free campsites are situated at 7,890 feet, where it's roughly 15°F cooler than other frontcountry campgrounds. Lava Point is typically open from May through September (weather dependent). Pit toilets are available, but water is not. Rapidly changing weather conditions can make Kolob Terrace Road impassable to 2WD vehicles, and visitors should check road conditions at the visitor center or park website prior to departure. Campgrounds fill almost every night from March through October. It's best to make reservations. If you don't, be ready with a backup plan. There are several private campgrounds nearby, and two campgrounds (Red Cliffs and Baker Dam) as well as dispersed camping on BLM land west of the park. Showers and laundry are available at Zion Outfitter (435.772.5090, zionoutfitter.com) in Springdale, just a short walk from the main visitor center.

Zion Lodge, situated in the middle of Zion Canyon, is the only in-park lodging. Prices may seem a little high compared to similar options in Springdale, but you're paying for location and it is superlative. Guests can take their own vehicles down Zion Canyon Scenic Drive to the lodge. Accommodations are basic but how much time do you plan on spending in your room anyway? It's open year-round, with slightly-reduced rates in winter. Red Rock Grill is on-site for breakfast, lunch, and dinner. There's a cafe and gift store, too. Reservations can be made at (888) 297-2757 or zionlodge.com. Make them early. Zion is incredibly popular.

Scenic Drives & Zion–Mt Carmel Highway

Zion–Mount Carmel Highway and Tunnel were built to provide a shorter route to Bryce Canyon. The

Zion Canyon

tunnel is a feat of engineering nearly as magnificent as the surrounding geography, but it poses a significant problem to large vehicles wishing to access Zion Canyon. All vehicles 7'10" or wider, or 11'4" or taller (maximum of 13'1" tall) are too large to remain in a single lane through the tunnel and require an escort. They must pay a $15 fee (good for two trips through the tunnel within seven days of purchase) at the park entrance before driving to the tunnel. Oversized vehicles are only allowed to pass through during seasonal hours when it is manned by park rangers (~8am–7pm March–April, September; 8am–8pm, late April–August). Cyclists and pedestrians are not allowed to use the tunnel.

The 10-mile Zion–Mount Carmel Highway connects the park's East and South Entrances, but the highlight of a trip for many visitors is six-mile Zion Canyon Scenic Drive. In winter, visitors can drive this stretch of road all the way to the foot of Temple of Sinawava, which is also the mouth of the famous Zion Narrows. For the rest of the year, Zion Canyon Scenic Drive is only open to park shuttle buses and guests of Zion Lodge.

Park Shuttle

The park provides two shuttle loops. They operate from mid-March through October, and select weekends in February, March, and November. Springdale Loop completes laps from the south entrance/Zion Canyon Theater to Springdale. This loop is optional, but it's extremely convenient not only for anyone staying in Springdale, but for all visitors, because parking in the park is limited (and often full early in the day). If the shuttles are running, they're the only passenger vehicles allowed in Zion Canyon (unless you're staying at Zion Lodge). However, you can also access Zion Canyon by foot or bicycle via Pa'rus Trail. The Zion Canyon

Tiny humans atop Angel's Landing

Zion Hiking Trails (Distances are roundtrip unless noted otherwise)

	Name	Location (# on map)	Length	Difficulty Rating & Notes
Zion Canyon Scenic Drive	Sand Bench Loop	Court of the Patriarchs (1)	7.6 miles	M – Sandy trail used mainly for trail rides
	Emerald Pools	Zion Lodge (2)	1.2–2.5 mi	E/M – Hike to 1, 2, or 3 small pools
	Angel's Landing - ✋	The Grotto (3)	5.4 miles	X – Adventurous hike with excellent views
	Grotto	The Grotto (3)	1.0 mile	E – Connects Zion Lodge and The Grotto
	Kayenta	The Grotto (3)	2.0 miles	M – Connects Grotto with Middle Emerald
	Weeping Rock	Weeping Rock (4)	0.4 mile	E – Paved trail to a dripping wall
	Hidden Canyon - ✋	Weeping Rock (4)	2.5 miles	X – Cliff ledge (closed when we went to print)
	Observation Pt - ✋	Weeping Rock (4)	8.0 miles	S – Great! (closed when we went to print)
	Riverside Walk	Temple of Sinawava (5)	2.2 miles	E – Paved trail along the Virgin River
	The Narrows via Riverside Walk - ✋	Temple of Sinawava (5)	9.4 miles	S – Most scenic portion of the Narrows to Orderville Canyon • You will get wet
	The Narrows - ✋	Chamberlain's Ranch to Temple of Sinawava (6, 5)	16.0 miles	X – One-way, backpack (12 campsites) or day-hike (12+ hours), wading/swimming req'd
Zion-Mt Carmel Hwy	East Rim - ✋	Near East Entrance (7)	10.8 miles	S – East Entrance to Weeping Rock, one-way
	Canyon Overlook - ✋	East of the long tunnel (8)	1.0 mile	M – Short hike with excellent scenic value
	Pa'rus - ✋	South Camp (9)	3.5 miles	E – Paved trail to Canyon Junction
	Watchman - ✋	Watchman Camp (10)	3.3 miles	M – Short trail to a perch above the camp
	Archeology	Zion Canyon VC(10)	0.4 mile	E – Small prehistoric storage buildings
Kolob Terrace Rd	Right Fork	Near Park Boundary (11)	11.8 miles	M – Follows creek to waterfalls
	Left Fork - ✋	Left Fork Trailhead (12)	9.0 miles	S – Non-technical (Bottom-up) to Subway
	Hop Valley	Hop Valley Trailhead (13)	13.0 miles	M – Walk along a sandy valley floor
	Northgate Peaks	Wildcat Canyon Trailhead (14)	4.2 miles	E – Lightly used flat trail to 7,200-ft peak
	Technical Subway	Wildcat Canyon Trailhead (14)	9.5 miles	X – 1-way, need canyoneering gear & knowledge
	Wildcat Canyon	Wildcat/West Rim (14, 15)	5.9 miles	S – Scrambling over difficult terrain
	West Rim - ✋	The Grotto/West Rim (3, 15)	14.2 miles	S – One-way Lava Point to Zion Canyon
Kolob Canyons Rd	Taylor Creek - ✋	Taylor Creek Trailhead (16)	5.0 miles	M – Leads to Arch Alcove and cabin
	North Fork Taylor Cr	Taylor Creek Trailhead (16)	5.0 miles	M – Unmaintained spur from Taylor Creek
	Kolob Arch via La Verkin Creek - ✋	Lee Pass Trailhead (17)	14.0 miles	S – Trail can be made a long day hike or an overnight backpack trip
	Timber Creek	End of Kolob Terrace Rd (18)	1.0 mile	M – Short hike, follows ridge to an overlook

Difficulty Ratings: E = Easy, M = Moderate, S = Strenuous, X = Extreme

Shuttle Loop takes roughly 90 minutes, making seven stops between the visitor center and Temple of Sinawava. The shuttle is typically free, although a $1 ticket system was initiated through recreation.gov in 2020 due to the pandemic. One ticket is required per person per boarding. Tickets are released in chunks on the 16th and last day of each month. A limited number of walk-up tickets are available from 1–3pm at Zion Canyon Visitor Center. It's a fluid situation and you'll want to check the park website to see if tickets are required during your intended trip. One thing is for sure, you do not want to miss the last shuttle out of the canyon. If you do that, you can walk out in the dark (up to eight miles) or you can stop at the lodge and they'll direct you to a list of private companies who will pick you up for a hefty fee.

Watchman Trail

Hiking

To genuinely appreciate the beauty of Zion, visitors must go for a hike. The park has a large network of well-maintained trails with trailheads conveniently located along Zion Canyon Scenic Drive (ZCSD), Zion–Mount Carmel Highway (ZMCH), Kolob Terrace Road (KTR), and Kolob Canyons Road (KCR). Whether you're looking for a casual leg-stretching stroll, or a boot-pounding multi-day backpacking adventure, you can find it here.

A few favorite short hikes are Riverside Walk (ZCSD), Hidden Canyon (ZCSD), Canyon Overlook (ZMCH), and Taylor Creek (KCR) Trails. Unfortunately, when we went to print, the main trail to Weeping Rock, Hidden Canyon, and Observation Point was closed due to a major rockfall. **Hidden Canyon Trail**, located at Weeping Rock Shuttle Stop, is relatively short but quite strenuous and not for individuals with a fear of heights. It's good training for Angel's Landing (when open). Hiking the same trail but bypassing the spur to Hidden Canyon takes you to East Rim Trail, which leads to **Observation Point** (if the rockfall still exists when you visit, you can reach Observation Point via **East Rim Trail**). It's our favorite view in the park. Less strenuous favorites include Watchman and Pa'rus Trails. Both begin near the visitor center. **Watchman** involves only modest elevation gain, as it scales to a viewpoint on the flank of The Watchman, not its peak. **Pa'rus Trail** is flat and paved, following the Virgin River from South Campground to Canyon Junction. It's wheelchair accessible, and bikes and pets are allowed. An increasingly popular trail is the bottom-up (non-technical) route to **The Subway**. The trailhead is located on KTR. All hikers require a permit (acquired via lottery). Two trails are so iconic they get their own section.

Angel's Landing

One of the most memorable hikes in the entire National Park System is the 5.4-mile (roundtrip) adventure to Angel's Landing. Calling it an adventure sells it short. The last 0.5-mile is a hair-raising experience that takes you along a knife-edge ridgeline with 500-foot drops on either side. The journey begins at Grotto Trailhead Parking Area, located just beyond Zion Lodge. After crossing the Virgin River via a short suspension bridge, head north (ignoring Kayenta Trail), making a steady climb toward the mouth of Refrigerator Canyon. Soon you will loop back and ascend the canyon wall via 21 switchbacks known as "Walter's Wiggles." The ascent leads to Scout's Lookout, providing impressive views of Zion Canyon and a closer look at the landing. West Rim Trail (also great) continues to the northwest into the backcountry and away from Angel's Landing. At Scout's Lookout you may begin to second guess your plans. The next 0.5-mile should never be attempted wearing improper footwear or in bad weather conditions. However, it is much more intimidating from a distance than up close. Only a series of chains aid passage along the Angel's Landing's spine. Once at the promontory, take a seat, a drink, and enjoy the view. If you're uncomfortable, it's probably a good idea to stay at Scout's Lookout. The trail is very popular, and the amount of fun had on knife-edge ridgelines is inversely proportional to the number of hikers. But, beginning in 2022 a permit is required to hike Angel's Landing. Permits will be distributed through recreation.gov via lottery for a $6 application fee during two application periods (quarterly and day before).

The Narrows

The Narrows follows the Virgin River as it winds its way through a 2,000-foot-deep canyon that is, as its name implies, narrow (20–30 ft). The water is cold,

The Narrows

the rocks are slippery, and the sun rarely penetrates its depths, making the trek challenging and exhilarating. You will wade through knee-high water and take the occasional swim across deep holes. Visitors can explore the Narrows three ways: day-hike from Mount Sinawava, day-hike the entire length beginning at Chamberlain Ranch, or backpack overnight. A day-hike into the canyon from Mount Sinawava Shuttle Stop via Riverside Walk is the simplest option. You are free to hike to Orderville Canyon, the most scenic and popular stretch, without a permit. The alternatives eschew crowds but require a wilderness permit. And completing the entire Narrows requires arranging a shuttle (or caching a car), since it's a one-way hike. The journey begins outside park boundaries at Chamberlain Ranch, accessed via North Fork Road, just outside the park's East Entrance. Ambitious hikers can day hike the entire 16-mile canyon in 10–14 hours. If you'd like to take your time and enjoy the scenery, spend a night at one of 12 backcountry campsites. Hiking the entire canyon provides hikers with a bit of solitude. You'll feel mostly alone until reaching Orderville Canyon, where you'll comingle with day-hikers from Mount Sinawava.

The best time of year to hike the Narrows is late spring to early summer. Cool water of the Virgin River will be refreshing as you spend more than half your hike wading. Wear sturdy shoes and carry a walking stick. Be sure to check the weather before entering the Narrows, as flash flooding and hypothermia are constant dangers. Zion Outfitter (435.772.5090, zionoutfitter.com), Zion Adventures (435.772.1001, zionadventures.com), Zion Guru (435.632.0432, zionguru.com), and Zion Rock & Mountain Guides (435.772.3303, zionrockguides.com) offer guided tours and gear rental.

Backpacking

Backpacking is allowed at designated sites along four popular trails. Zion Narrows has 12 campsites, all located above the high-water line of the Virgin River and upriver from Big Spring. West Rim Trail, from the Grotto to Lava Point Primitive Campground, is the most popular backpacking trail, with a total of nine designated campsites along the way. If you can arrange a shuttle, begin hiking at Lava Point Campground. From here, it will be a mostly downhill 14.2-mile trek that can be completed in two days without a problem. Kolob Canyons only suitable backpacking route is La Verkin/Kolob Arch Trail, including the intersecting trail through Hop Valley. There are also designated campsites in the park's southwest corner along Chinle Trail and Scoggins Wash. In addition to the designated campsites, backpackers can camp in Wildcat Canyon and East Rim areas as long as they are one mile from roads, out of sight of trails, and 0.25-mile from springs. A permit is required for all overnight stays in the backcountry.

Wilderness Permits

A wilderness permit is required for all overnight trips in the backcountry, Narrows thru-hikes, Narrows day-hikes beyond Orderville Canyon, all canyon trips requiring descending gear or ropes (including the Subway and Mystery Canyon), and all overnight trips in the backcountry. Zion Narrows and Subway permits can be obtained up to three months in advance via online lottery at zionpermits.nps.gov. If you don't secure permits through the online lottery, you can apply for Last Minute Drawing permits, seven to two days in advance. After the Last-Minute Drawing, walk-in permits become available the day before your trip. (Walk-in permits for The Subway are unlikely.) There is a $5 non-refundable application fee for the online lottery. If you won the lottery, secured a reservation, or obtained a permit the day of your trip, you will have to pay an additional wilderness permit fee. Fees are based on group size: $15 for 1–2 people, $20 for 3–7 people and $25 for 8–12 people. 12 is the maximum group size.

Camping in the Zion Wilderness requires a permit. Permits are available online (zionpermits.nps.gov) up to two months in advance (starting on the fifth of each month). There is a $5 non-refundable fee for an online reservation, plus an additional permit fee (determined by the size of your group). If you intend to camp in more than one location, you will need to make a reservation for each location. Remaining permits can be obtained in person at park visitor centers the day before or the day of your trip.

Horseback Riding

Tourists can also experience the wonders of Zion on horseback. Canyon Trail Rides (435.679.8665, canyonrides.com) offers 1-hour ($50/person) and 3-hour ($100/person) trail rides from March through October. Guided rides begin at a corral by Emerald Pools Trailhead near Zion Lodge. A one-hour ride follows the Virgin River. A three-hour ride goes deeper into the park along Sand Beach Trail. Visitors are also allowed to trailer in stock. A stock camp is available at Hop Valley Site A, located on Hop Valley Trail. A wilderness permit is required for overnight stays, but not for day use. Not all trails are approved for stock use, so check with the visitor center or online before you ride.

Biking

Biking is allowed on all the park's roadways and Pa'rus Trail, which connects South Campground with Zion Canyon Scenic Drive. Bicycles are also a great way to explore Zion Canyon Scenic Drive, just be on the lookout for shuttle buses. A few bike outfitters are located next to the park in Springdale. Zion Cycles (435.772.0400, zioncycles.com) and Bike Zion (435.772.3303, bikingzion.com) offer rentals and guided bicycle tours. Zion Outfitter (435.772.5090, zionoutfitter.com) also offers rentals. In late 2021, the first 10 miles of mountain bike trails were opened east of the park on North Fork Road (near the east entrance).

Paddling & Floating

Kayaking the Narrows is only recommended for advanced paddlers. A wilderness permit is required for all boat use in the park. They are free and available at Zion Canyon Visitor Center no more than one day before your intended trip. Zion Outfitter (435.772.5090, zionoutfitter.com) offers tubing trips outside the park (May–July). Innertubes are not permitted in the park.

Rock Climbing & Canyoneering

Rock climbing (permit not required for day climbs) and technical canyoneering (permit required) are popular activities (for experts). First-timers should hire a guide. Any of the guides listed in the Narrows section can show you all kinds of cool Zion/area rocks.

Visitor Centers & Museum

Zion has two visitor centers that are open every day of the year except Christmas. **Zion Canyon Visitor Center**, located near the park's south entrance on UT-9, is the primary destination for park information as well as the main hub for the shuttle service. Standard operating hours are from 8am to 4pm but are extended to 7:30pm during peak season. A Backcountry Desk

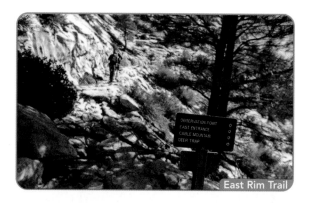
East Rim Trail

is located inside, where you can obtain backcountry information and permits (if available, you really should make reservations online). It's open from 7am to 7:30pm during summer and 8am to 4:30pm during winter. **Kolob Canyons Visitor Center** is a small facility with books and souvenirs for sale. It's staffed by a park ranger from 8am to 6pm during summer and 8am to 4:30pm during winter. **Zion Human History Museum** is located just north of Zion Canyon Visitor Center on Zion–Mount Carmel Highway. It features alternating art exhibits, a short introductory film, and book and gift stores. It's open daily, mid-March through November, from 9am to 7pm during summer and it opens intermittently through the offseason.

Ranger Programs & For Kids

From mid-March to November, park rangers administer a series of walks, talks, and interpretive programs. These activities explore the lives of resident plants and animals or discuss the difficulty of life in the desert. Walks range from a leisurely ramble along Riverside Walk to a strenuous hike up the Narrows. Evening discussions are held regularly at Watchman Campground's Amphitheater and Zion Lodge's Auditorium. A list of discussion topics is usually displayed on bulletin boards at the visitor centers, museum, and campgrounds. You can also find a current schedule of events online in the park's calendar. Many tours accept reservations up to three days in advance. To make a reservation, stop in at Zion Canyon Visitor Center. If you have the time and the opportunity to join a ranger-guided tour, don't think twice, just go.

Zion offers guided and self-guided Junior Ranger Programs for children (ages 4 and older). To participate in the self-guided program, simply pick up a Junior Ranger activity booklet from either of the park's visitor centers or Zion Human History Museum (or download it from the park's website). Complete the activities and

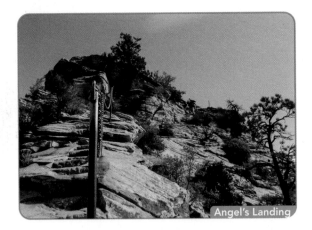
Angel's Landing

return to a visitor center to be made an official Zion National Park Junior Ranger and receive an award. Guided programs are offered daily from Memorial Day weekend through late August. These family-oriented programs are free of charge. Participants are advised to bring water and wear close-toed shoes (i.e., no flip-flops or sandals). Finally, Canyon Overlook Trail and Riverside Walk are two nice family hikes.

Flora & Fauna

Zion sits at the convergence of three geographic regions: the Colorado Plateau, Great Basin, and Mojave Desert. Geologic variance coupled with more than 4,000 feet of elevation change makes for an environment filled with incredible biodiversity. The park supports more than 900 species of plants, ranging from cacti and desert succulents to riparian trees, shrubs, and wildflowers. Zion is also home to more than 78 species of mammals, 290 species of birds, 44 species of reptiles and amphibians, and 8 species of fish. Most notable are bighorn sheep, mule deer, mountain lions, peregrine falcons, and Mexican spotted owls.

Pets & Accessibility

Pets are allowed in the park but are not permitted on the shuttle, in the backcountry, on trails (except Pa'rus), or in public buildings. These restrictions make travelling with a pet challenging. Pets are allowed in developed campgrounds, along park roads, in parking areas, and on Pa'rus Trail, but must be kept on a leash (less than six feet). Doggy Dude Ranch (435.772.3105, doggyduderanch.com) is a nearby kennel where you can keep your pet while exploring the park.

Zion Canyon Visitor Center, Zion Human History Museum, and Kolob Canyons Visitor Center are accessible to individuals in wheelchairs. All shuttle buses are accessible and equipped with a wheelchair lift. Zion Lodge has two accessible rooms, and there are seven accessible campsites at Watchman Campground. Riverside Walk and Pa'rus Trail are paved.

Weather

The weather is most comfortable between March and May, and September and November. These periods are marked by daytime highs in the low 60s to low 80s°F. Overnight temperatures drop into the 40s°F. Summer days are hot, with an average daily high of 100°F in July. It's not unheard of for the mercury to reach 110°F on the hottest days of the year. No matter how hot it gets during the day, summer nights remain comfortable with temperatures usually below 70°F. Winters are generally mild, but visitors arriving between November and March should be prepared for potentially snowy conditions. January is the coldest month with an average daily high of 52°F and a daily low of 29°F. This region does not receive much precipitation, but short thunderstorms are common throughout the year.

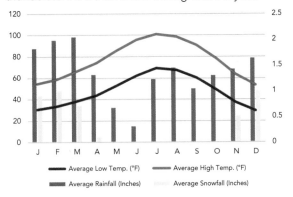

Tips & Recommendations

These days it's difficult to find a month that Zion doesn't receive at least 100,000 visitors. Things slow down a bit in January and February, but visitation is very strong from mid-March through October. Winter/early spring can be a real treat as ephemeral waterfalls adorn the canyon walls after every snowfall.

Zion is the busiest of Utah's national parks. If you plan on visiting between March and October (and some weekends in February and November), the only way to drive Zion Canyon Scenic Drive is to spend the night at the lodge or use the park's shuttle service. As of 2020, you will need a $1 ticket (a ticket per person per ride) to use the park's shuttle. It's best to reserve tickets online (recreation.gov) to know you have them. Download or print your ticket prior to boarding. A limited number are available in-person.

During peak season, parking fills up early at the main visitor center (where you board the shuttle bus to Zion Canyon). Shuttle buses also run from Springdale. Park here, board a shuttle, and you'll get dropped off at the park entrance. Then catch a shuttle into Zion Canyon.

Make reservations early! Whether it's camping, lodging, or guided trips, you should make your reservations early.

Bicyclists are also allowed to use Zion Canyon Scenic Drive, which is a good alternative but the shuttle lets you save your energy for hiking. Bikers and hikers can access Zion Canyon via Pa'rus Trail.

Once you're in the canyon, stay there by packing a lunch or dining at the lodge (although, if you eat at the lodge it's a good idea to try and avoid peak dining hours here as well).

If you have the funds, you cannot beat Zion Lodge's location, and that's why there's a premium on those accommodations. Just don't blow your entire vacation budget to stay there. The shuttle works well, and hiking/biking are good ways to reach Zion Canyon too.

Remember you're exploring the floor of Zion canyon, so you won't see sunrise or sunset (unless you go up to the rim), but it can be equally thrilling watching the sun illuminate the canyon's walls as it rises/sets.

You'll often see photographs of The Narrows and The Subway on marketing materials. They're amazing, but to hike The Narrows beyond Orderville Canyon or The Subway, you'll need a permit.

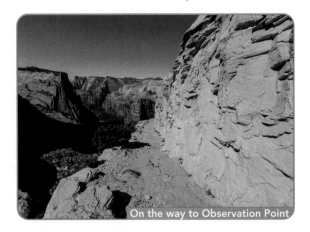
On the way to Observation Point

Easy Hikes: Pa'rus (3.5 miles)
Moderate Hikes: Watchman (3.3 miles), Canyon Overlook (1), Taylor Creek (5)
Strenuous Hikes: Observation Point (8 miles), Mouth of the Narrows (9.4), Left Fork/Subway (9), East Rim (10.8), West Rim (14.2), Kolob Arch (14)
Extreme Hikes: The Narrows (16 miles), Angel's Landing (5.4), Hidden Canyon (2.5)
Family Activities: Several of the best hikes aren't kid-friendly, but there are plenty of good ones that are, become Junior Rangers, Zion Human History Museum
Guided Tours: Hike Zion Narrows, ride a horse
Rainy Day Activities: Go into Zion Canyon and enjoy the ephemeral waterfalls (be sure to observe warnings/closures, as flash floods do happen)
Sunset Spots: Watchman, Virgin River Bridge near Canyon Junction, Kolob Canyons Viewpoint
Sunrise Spots: Canyon Overlook, Zion Human History Museum

Beyond the Park...

Dining
The Park House • (435) 772-0100
1880 Zion Park Blvd, Springdale

Oscar's Café • (435) 772-3232
948 Zion Park Blvd, Springdale

Spotted Dog Café
428 Zion Park Blvd, Springdale
flanigans.com • (435) 772-0700

Zuma Baja • (435) 772-3001
975 Zion Park Blvd, Springdale
zumazion.com

Grocery Stores
Sol Foods • (435) 772-3100
995 Zion Park Blvd, Springdale

Walmart • (435) 635-6945
180 N 3400 W, Hurricane

Lodging & Camping
Zion Park Motel • (435) 772-3251
865 Zion Park Blvd, Springdale
zionparkmotel.com

Zion Mountain Ranch
9065 W UT-9, Mt Carmel
zmr.com • (866) 648-2555

Zion Crest Camp • (435) 648-2703
Twin Knolls Rd, Orderville
zioncrestcampground.com

Zion River Resort RV Park
551 E UT-9, Virgin • (888) 822-8594
zionriverresort.com

Attractions
Kanarra Creek/Falls
Slot canyon w/ waterfall near the Kolob Canyons section

Buckskin Gulch/Paria Canyon
Backpacking and day-hiking. Permit (blm.gov) required.

Vermillion Cliffs NM (BLM)
The Wave (Coyote Buttes North)
Beautiful geologic formation requires a permit (distributed via lottery at recreation.gov). The lottery requires a $9 application fee. Winners must pay a $7 per person recreation fee. Demand far exceeds availability and winning the lottery is kind of fun. Nearby Wire Pass is great too. Details come with permit.

Coral Pink Sand Dunes SP
Unique dunes, good hiking
12500 Sand Dune Rd, Kanab
stateparks.utah.gov • (435) 648-2800

Snow Canyon SP • (435) 628-2255
Kind of like a mini-Zion
1002 Snow Canyon Dr, Ivins
stateparks.utah/gov

Sand Hollow SP • (435) 680-0715
A relatively new park for boating, fishing, and camping
3351 Sand Hollow Rd, Hurricane
stateparks.utah.gov

Gunlock State Park
Primitive park with reservoir for boating, and ephemeral falls
Gunlock Rd, Gunlock
stateparks.utah.gov

Quail Springs SP • (435) 879-2378
Another reservoir park
472 5300 W, Hurricane
stateparks.utah.gov

Grand Canyon

Phone: (928) 638-7888
Website: nps.gov/grca

Established: February 26, 1919
January 11, 1908 (Nat'l Monument)
Size: 1,217,403 Acres
Annual Visitors: 6 Million
Peak Season: March–October

Canyon Activities: River Trips ($325 for a daytrip to $6,000+ to raft the entire canyon), Backpacking (Phantom Ranch)
South Rim Activities: Flightseeing ($139+/person), Mule Rides, Hiking, Backpacking, Biking, Train Excursions/Transportation
North Rim Activities: Mule Rides, Hiking, Backpacking, Snowshoeing, Cross-country Skiing

3 South Rim Campgrounds: $12–61
1 North Rim Campground: $18–25
Backcountry Camping: Permitted with a Backcountry Permit (fee)
6 South Rim Lodges: $93–513/night
1 North Rim Lodge: $130–190/night

South Rim Hours: All day, every day
North Rim Hours: All day, every day (closes Nov/Dec–mid-May)
Entrance Fee: $35/30/20 (car/motorcycle/individual)

"There is of course no reason at all in trying to describe the Grand Canyon. Those who have not seen it will not believe any possible description. Those who have seen it know that it cannot be described..."

– J.B. Priestly (Harper's Magazine)

In Arizona's northwestern reaches, the Colorado River has carved the grandest of canyons. Measuring 277 miles long, up to 18 miles wide and more than one mile deep, the Grand Canyon is a gaping scar across the earth's surface. Theodore Roosevelt declared it "the one great sight which every American should see." One man's thought became another man's goal. Stephen Mather, first director of the National Park Service, dedicated much of his time to obtaining the land and protecting it for the general public. Since the National Park Service became custodian of the Grand Canyon in 1919, it has sought to preserve and protect this iconic landscape of the American West for the enjoyment of people, present and future.

Before the National Park Service controlled the area, cattle grazed freely above the rim and miners filed claims for any location that might produce ore. One prospector in particular had a penchant for exploiting its resources. Ralph Henry Cameron—part-time prospector, full-time spinner of colorful yarns—claimed to have spent more than $500,000 "improving" the canyon's trails, blazing the first wagon path from Flagstaff to the South Rim, and opening the first successful mining operation within the canyon. Most of his mining claims were conveniently located at scenic points along the South Rim. At Cameron Trail, today's Bright Angel Trail, he constructed Cameron's Hotel and placed a gate across the trailhead. His brother manned the gate, collecting $1 per person for its use, the first of many swindles along Cameron Trail. He also held a claim at Indian Spring, the route's only source of clean water. Hot and dehydrated, hikers had no choice but to pay exorbitant prices at Cameron's watering hole.

Lipan Point

It wasn't long until Cameron became a nuisance to the Santa Fe Railroad. Once the railway reached the South Rim, it wasted little time in constructing El Tovar Hotel. Cameron responded by filing claims all around the luxury abode. Claims were followed by lawsuits, and eventually he was bought out for $40,000. As tourism rose, Cameron watched money roll in, while neglecting the condition of his facilities. Outhouses were so appalling the Santa Fe Railroad offered to replace them free of charge. He declined the offer and filed a lawsuit on the grounds that they would have to illegally cross his claims to build the comfort stations. The court sided in favor of Cameron. When President Theodore Roosevelt created Grand Canyon National Monument, Cameron was instructed to abandon all claims not actively mined. He filed 55 more. It wasn't until 1919, more than a decade later, when Congress established the National Park, that Cameron was forced to leave.

The State of Arizona always supported Cameron. He was tied to most of northern Arizona's jobs and locals saw him as a champion against the mighty railroad and wealthy Easterners. Showing their support, he was elected a member of the Senate in 1920, where he vehemently opposed the National Park idea and made proposals for two hydroelectric dams and the development of a platinum mine in the canyon. In the end Congress tabled all dam projects and Cameron's crusade against the park finally ended when the public failed to reelect him after learning he used his position for personal gain. Today, the park is everyone's gain, protected for all mankind to see, just like President Roosevelt hoped.

Regions

Grand Canyon National Park consists of three well-defined regions: Colorado River/Canyon Floor, South Rim, and North Rim. The river and the immense canyon it carved separate the rims. As a crow flies the rims are no more than 18 miles apart, but to reach one from the other by car requires a 210-mile, 4.5-hour drive. This causes most vacationers to visit one rim or the other.

The Colorado River/Canyon Floor (page 451): Adventurous visitors run more than 150 named rapids along 225 miles of the Colorado River between Lee's Ferry and Diamond Creek. You can also hike into the canyon, spend a night on the floor (camping or at Phantom Ranch), and then return to the rim the following day.

South Rim (page 456): 90% of the park's six million guests only visit the South Rim. It's open all year and has myriad lodging, dining, and camping facilities, as well as an abundance of entertainment opportunities. The South Rim enjoys a slightly warmer and drier climate than the North Rim due to it being 1,000 feet lower in elevation. Several historic buildings, trailheads (like the popular Bright Angel and South Kaibab Trails), and numerous canyon viewpoints can be accessed via the region's free park shuttle system.

North Rim (page 461): The same great canyon views without the overwhelming crowds. It's also the best place to begin a rim-to-rim hike, since you'll spend more time going down (an extra 1,000 feet) than going up. North Kaibab Trail provides access to the inner canyon, where it connects with South Kaibab and Bright Angel Trails. The North Rim has a wide variety of above-rim trails with some excellent backpacking routes and off-roading opportunities.

Rim-to-Rim Shuttle

Transcanyon Shuttle (928.638.2820, trans-canyons-huttle.com) provides daily shuttle service between the North Rim and the South Rim, with an additional stop at Marble Canyon (Lee's Ferry). This service is ideal for rim-to-rim hikers not wanting to retrace their path back through the canyon or visitors who would rather not drive themselves. It costs $90/person (one-way). The commute between North and South Rims takes approximately 4.5 hours. One-way fare to Marble Canyon costs $80/person. Shuttle service is available between mid-May and mid-October. Reservations are required.

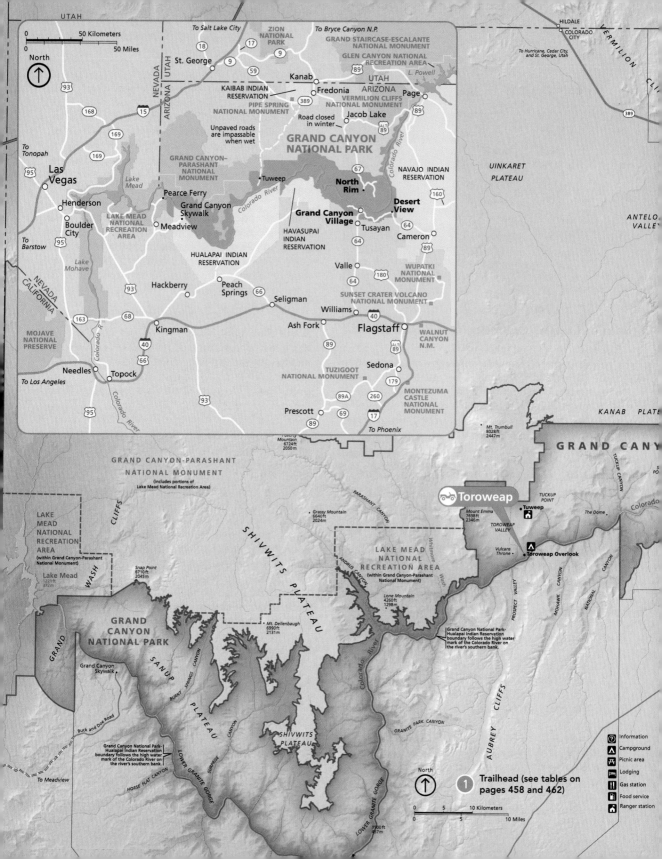

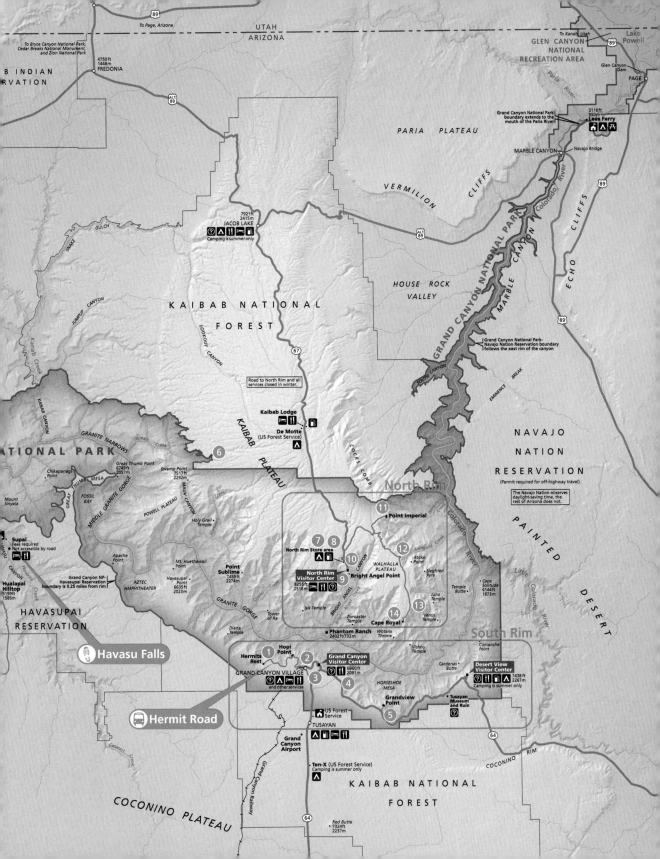

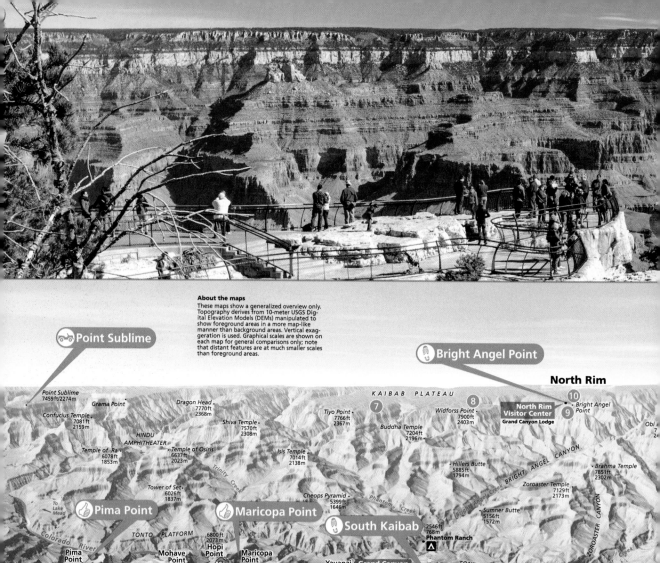

About the maps

These maps show a generalized overview only. Topography derives from 10-meter USGS Digital Elevation Models (DEMs) manipulated to show foreground areas in a more map-like manner than background areas. Vertical exaggeration is used. Graphical scales are shown on each map for general comparisons only; note that distant features are at much smaller scales than foreground areas.

Point Sublime

Bright Angel Point

North Rim

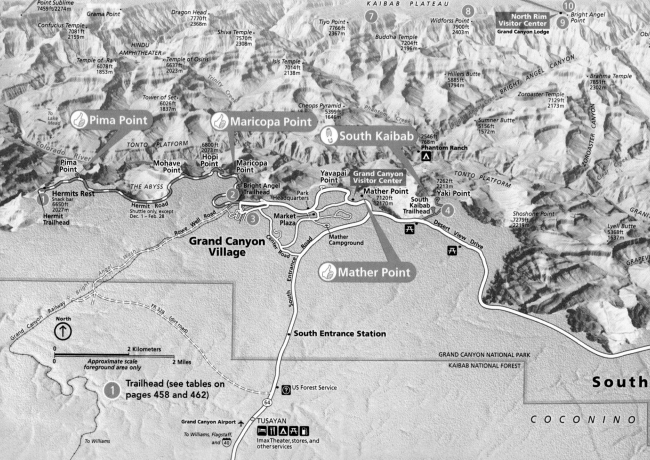

KAIBAB PLATEAU

Point Sublime
7459ft/2274m

Grama Point

Dragon Head
7770ft
2368m

Tiyo Point
7766ft
2367m

Widforss Point
7900ft
2403m

North Rim
Visitor Center
Grand Canyon Lodge

Bright Angel
Point

Confucius Temple
7081ft
2159m

Shiva Temple
7570ft
2308m

Buddha Temple
7204ft
2196m

HINDU
AMPHITHEATER

Temple of Ra
6078ft
1853m

Temple of Osiris
6637ft
2023m

Isis Temple
7014ft
2138m

Hillers Butte
5885ft
1794m

Brahma Temple
7851ft
2302m

Obi
7
2

Tower of Set
6026ft
1837m

Cheops Pyramid
5399ft
1646m

BRIGHT ANGEL CANYON

Zoroaster Temple
7129ft
2173m

To
Lake
Mead

Pima Point

Maricopa Point

South Kaibab

Phantom Creek

Sumner Butte
5156ft
1572m

ZOROASTER CANYON

Colorado River

TONTO PLATFORM

6800ft
2073m

Hopi
Point

2546ft
768m
Phantom Ranch

Clear Creek

Pima
Point

Mohave
Point

Maricopa
Point

Yavapai
Point

**Grand Canyon
Visitor Center**

7262ft
2213m

TONTO PLATFORM

GRANIT

THE ABYSS

Bright Angel
Trailhead

Park
Headquarters

Mather Point
7120ft
2170m

South
Kaibab
Trailhead

Yaki Point

Hermits Rest
Snack bar
6650ft
2027m

Hermit Road
Shuttle only, except
Dec. 1 – Feb. 28

Market
Plaza

Shoshone Point
7279ft
2219m

Lyell Butte
5368ft
1637m

Hermit
Trailhead

Rowe Well Road

Center Road

South Entrance Road

**Grand Canyon
Village**

Mather
Campground

Desert View Drive

GRAPEVIN

Mather Point

North

0   2 Kilometers
0   2 Miles

Approximate scale
foreground area only

South Entrance Station

GRAND CANYON NATIONAL PARK
KAIBAB NATIONAL FOREST

South

Grand Canyon Railway

Bright Angel Wash

FR 328 (dirt road)

**Trailhead (see tables on
pages 458 and 462)**

US Forest Service

C O C O N I N O

64

Grand Canyon Airport
To Williams, Flagstaff,
and 40

TUSAYAN
Imax Theater, stores, and
other services

To Williams

Mather Point

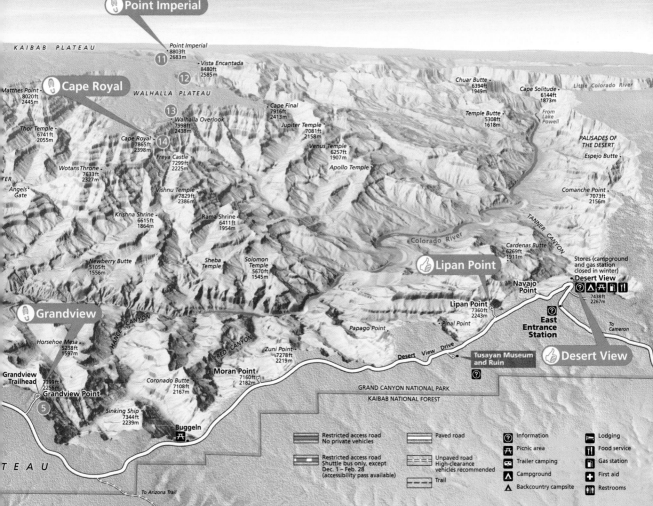

Point Imperial

KAIBAB PLATEAU

Point Imperial
8803ft
2683m

⑪

Vista Encantada
8480ft
2585m

⑫

Cape Royal

Matthes Point
8020ft
2445m

WALHALLA PLATEAU

Thor Temple
6741ft
2055m

⑬ Walhalla Overlook
7998ft
2438m

Cape Final
7916ft
2413m

Chuar Butte
6394ft
1949m

Cape Solitude
6144ft
1873m

Little Colorado River

Cape Royal
7865ft
2398m

⑭

Jupiter Temple
7081ft
2158m

Temple Butte
5308ft
1618m

From
Lake
Powell

PALISADES OF
THE DESERT

Wotans Throne
7633ft
2327m

Freya Castle
7299ft
2225m

Venus Temple
6257ft
1907m

Espejo Butte

Angels
Gate

Vishnu Temple
7829ft
2386m

Apollo Temple

Krishna Shrine
6615ft
1864m

Rama Shrine
6411ft
1954m

Comanche Point
7073ft
2156m

TANNER CANYON

Newberry Butte
5105ft
1556m

Sheba
Temple

Solomon
Temple
5670ft
1545m

Colorado River

Cardenas Butte
6269ft
1911m

Stores (campground
and gas station
closed in winter)

Lipan Point

Navajo
Point

Desert View
7438ft
2267m

🚶 🏕 🅿 🚻 🍴

Grandview

HANCE CANYON

RED CANYON

Zuni Point
7278ft
2219m

Papago Point

Lipan Point
7360ft
2243m

Pinal Point

Desert View

To Cameron

Horsehoe Mesa
5238ft
1597m

East
Entrance
Station

Grandview
Trailhead

Grandview
7399ft
2256m

⑤

Grandview Point

Coronado Butte
7108ft
2167m

Moran Point
7160ft
2182m

Desert View Drive

Tusayan Museum
and Ruin

GRAND CANYON NATIONAL PARK
KAIBAB NATIONAL FOREST

Sinking Ship
7344ft
2239m

Buggeln
🏕

TEAU

To Arizona Trail

Restricted access road No private vehicles	Paved road	Information
Restricted access road Shuttle bus only, except Dec. 1 – Feb. 28 (accessibility pass available)	Unpaved road High-clearance vehicles recommended	Picnic area
	Trail	Trailer camping

Restricted access road
No private vehicles

Restricted access road
Shuttle bus only, except
Dec. 1 – Feb. 28
(accessibility pass available)

Paved road

Unpaved road
High-clearance
vehicles recommended

Trail

Information

Picnic area

Trailer camping

Campground

Backcountry campsite

Lodging

Food service

Gas station

First aid

Restrooms

Desert View

Grand Geology

While in the area you may hear or see the term "Grand Staircase." While these geologic steps may be many visitors' perfect stairway to heaven, the term simply refers to a sequence of sedimentary rock layers that form a massive "staircase" between Bryce Canyon and Grand Canyon. Each canyon's cliff edge acts as a giant step, displaying the earth's geologic history in its layers. As you move down the geologic column, each successive rock layer is older than the previous. The oldest exposed formation in Bryce Canyon is the youngest remaining layer at Zion Canyon. Likewise, the floor of Zion Canyon is Kaibab Formation, which is the same formation you stand on at the Grand Canyon's rim. As you stand at the South Rim staring into the depths of the grandest canyon of them all, you are reviewing some 2 billion years of geologic history.

The oldest exposed layers of rock are found at the bottom of the canyon's inner gorge. They are the Vishnu Basement Rocks, a collection of hard schist and granites formed by the heat and pressure of colliding tectonic plates. Moving up the geologic column, the next set of rocks is the Grand Canyon Supergroup. Its strata accumulated in basins formed as the land mass pulled apart. These layers of shale, limestone, and lava rock can be seen from a handful of locations, such as South Rim's Lipan Point. Grand Canyon Supergroup's rocks are often pinched off and absent from the canyon's exposed walls, creating a gap in the geologic record of more than one billion years between the Vishnu Basement Rocks and adjacent Tapeats Sandstone layer. Scientists believe this irregularity marks an extended period of erosion rather than deposition. Major John Wesley Powell recognized these disjointed rock layers during his expedition of the Grand Canyon in 1869 and named it the Great Unconformity. Beginning with Tapeats Sandstone numerous layers of sedimentary rock make up the set of Layered Paleozoic Rocks occupying the upper two-thirds of the canyon walls. These layers come from a variety of sources: limestone from ancient marine life, mudstone from river deposition, and sandstone from sand dunes.

All these rock layers were formed near sea level. Some 20 million years ago, uplift that created the Rocky Mountains also raised the Colorado Plateau, encompassing present-day northern Arizona, eastern Utah, northwestern New Mexico, and western Colorado. Gravity's perpetual force caused rivers to erode the landscape. Water wore away its path and carried with it sediment stripped from the earth. By five or six million years ago, the routes of the Colorado

The easy way up South Kaibab Trail

River and its tributaries were carved in stone, draining 90 percent of the plateau. So, why is the Grand Canyon so wide? First, the canyon is not carved at a constant rate. Lava dams formed and breached, and Ice Ages came and went, both of which caused massive flows of water. Also, soft sedimentary rock erodes faster than hard rock. Today, the flow of the Colorado River is dramatically reduced by upstream dams, slowing the grinding away of layers of hard schist and granite at the canyon's floor. Meanwhile, the canyon walls are mostly soft sedimentary rock that erodes easily as rainwater and snowmelt drain into the canyon from the north and south rims. The North Rim receives more precipitation and therefore it's eroding faster than the South Rim.

Beaching near Phantom Ranch

Colorado River Outfitters

River Outfitter	Length/Rates	Craft	Notes
Arizona Raft Adventures azraft.com • (800) 786-7238	6–16 Days $2,400–5,060	Raft J-Rig	Motorized, hybrid (one paddle raft, the rest ride), & all-paddle trips offered • Offers 14–16-day kayak trip and Yoga Adventure
Arizona River Runners raftarizona.com • (800) 477-7238	6–13 Days $2,430–4,495	Raft J-Rig	Offers 6–8-day motorized J-Rig trips or 6–13-day oar-powered trips
Canyon Explorations/Expeditions canyonexplorations.com • (800) 654-0723	7–16 Days $2,775–4,975	Raft J-Rig	Hybrid and all-paddle trips • Paddle trip accompanied by a string quartet
Canyoneers canyoneers.com • (800) 525-0924	4–14 Days $1,650–4,275	Raft J-Rig	4–8-day motorized J-Rig trips or 6–14-day oar-powered trips
Colorado River & Trail Expeditions crateinc.com • (800) 253-7328	3–11 Days $1,785–4,590	Raft J-Rig	Natural history, hiking trips • Birding and Singer/Storyteller trips
Grand Canyon Expeditions gcex.com • (800) 544-2691	8–16 Days $2,930–4,579	Dory J-Rig	Specialized geology, photography, history, and ecology trips are offered
Grand Canyon Whitewater grandcanyonwhitewater.com • (800) 343-3121	4–13 Days $1,595–4,395	Raft J-Rig	Motorized J-Rig or oar-powered trips • Hike-out trips are offered
Hualapai River Runners grandcanyonwest.com • (928) 769-2636	1–5 Days $325–1,519	J-Rig	Only place to get a single-day trip in the Canyon • Can bundle with the Skywalk
Hatch River Expeditions hatchriverexpeditions.com • (800) 856-8966	4–12 Days $1,460–4,686	Raft J-Rig	Variety of motorized and paddle trips • Offer hiking focused trips (on motorized rafts)
O.A.R.S. Grand Canyon oars.com • (800) 346-6277	5–18 Days $2,799–7,399	Raft Dory	First to offer Grand Canyon rafting trips and still doing it as good as anyone
Outdoors Unlimited outdoorsunlimited.com • (800) 637-7238	5–15 Days $2,070–5,080	Raft	Oar-powered and all-paddle trips of lower, upper, and full canyon
Tour West twriver.com • (800) 453-9107	3–12 Days $1,875–4,578	Raft J-Rig	3-, 6-, and 8-night motorized J-Rig trips or 12-night oar-powered trip
Western River Expeditions westernriver.com • (800) 453-7450	3–7 Days $1,600–3,065	J-Rig	3-, 4-, and 7-day motorized J-Rig trips • Can combine with a night at a cattle ranch
Wilderness River Adventures riveradventures.com • (800) 992-8022	3.5–16 Days $1,630–5,875	Raft J-Rig	Offers 4–8-day motorized J-Rig trips or 5.5–16-day oar boat trips (full canyon)

The Colorado River

"It is not a show place, a beauty spot, but a revelation. The Colorado River made it; but you feel when you are there that God gave the Colorado River its instructions. The thing is Beethoven's Ninth Symphony in stone and magic light. I hear rumors of visitors who were disappointed. The same people will be disappointed at the Day of Judgment."

– J.B. Priestly (Harper's Magazine)

The Colorado River is sculptor of the Grand Canyon. Revealer of geologic history. Paradise to thrill-seekers. Ever so slowly these muddy waters of the Colorado dug the world's most magnificent ditch. Explorers crafted elaborate stories of impassable waterfalls, impossible portages, and inaccessible canyons. For decades it remained a blank spot on the map. Today, the map is filled in, and while Grand Canyon's beauty remains, its power is diminished by dams and irrigation.

The Colorado begins in Rocky Mountain National Park. From there it grows in size and majesty as it passes many of the United States' most treasured natural wonders. It forms the southern boundary of Arches National Park. In Canyonlands it unites with the Green River and rumbles through Cataract Canyon. It floods a red rock labyrinth at Glen Canyon National Recreation Area. And then the crescendo. The Grand Canyon, where the Colorado offers the greatest whitewater adventure in North America. The mighty river, weakened by man, still churns down below the canyon's rims.

Why investigate the canyon from above when you can meet its maker down below? Major John Wesley Powell must have shared that sentiment, as he famously set out on his namesake expedition in 1869. A most unlikely explorer, Powell lost an arm due to a Civil War injury. After the war, he worked as a geology professor, and a series of expeditions into the Rockies and around the Green and Colorado Rivers rekindled his thirst for adventure.

In 1869, he set out with nine men and four boats to explore the Colorado River. Their goal was to fill in the largest hole in the map of the United States. The journey began at Green River, Wyoming. When they arrived at the confluence of the Green and Grand Rivers (the official start of the Colorado) they had already lost one boat and a third of their supplies. Morale was low, but they had little choice but to press on. By the time they reached the Grand Canyon, Powell's men were coming apart at the seams. Starvation, summer heat, and

This is solitude

constant pounding of rapid upon rapid had taken their toll. Three men opted to climb out of the canyon into an unknown landscape most likely inhabited by Native Americans. They were never seen again. Just two days later, Powell and his crew reached the mouth of the Virgin River, where they met a few Mormon fishermen.

River Adventures

More than a dozen experienced outfitters provide guided whitewater trips through the Grand Canyon. You can choose from upper-, lower-, and full-canyon adventures. Each trip includes exciting excursions to waterfalls, beaches, and side canyons. All meals, non-alcoholic drinks, and tents are included. The upper and lower halves typically begin or end at Phantom Ranch and require hiking into or out of the canyon. (A few tours substitute a helicopter ride for the hike.) Full canyon tours cover 225 miles from Lee's Ferry near Glen Canyon Dam to Diamond Creek in Hualapai Indian Reservation. You only get to run Lava Falls, the biggest rapid, on full- and lower-canyon tours. Several outfitters offer specialized trips focusing on subjects like geology or photography. All raft adventures generally run from mid-April through October. Spring and fall are the best seasons to go. You'll avoid the summer heat and crowds, and summer trips often fully book up to a year in advance. Finally, you'll have to choose a watercraft. A wooden dory provides the wildest ride. Motorized J-Rigs smooth out the rapids and expedite the journey. Raft trips are also available, but not all trips allow passengers to paddle. If you want to have an oar in your hands look for "all-paddle" trips in the table on the opposite page.

Kolb Studio

The Kolb Brothers

Beginning in 1904, Emery and Ellsworth Kolb ran a small photography studio at the South Rim, near Bright Angel Trailhead. Their main source of income came from taking photos of mule riders as they made their descent into the canyon. Emery often boasted that the two of them had "taken more pictures of men and mules than any other living man." And it was not an easy accomplishment. A clean water supply was needed to develop the pictures, but the closest reliable source was 4.5 miles and 3,000 feet below the rim. The Kolb brothers hiked this route countless times between 1904, when their studio was constructed, and 1932 when clean water became available on the rim. During this period, one brother took pictures of the mule riders descending into the canyon, and then raced down the trail to Indian Gardens, where the pictures were developed in a makeshift dark room. Once finished, he raced back to the rim, arriving just before the mule train returned from the bottom.

Adept oarsmen and explorers at heart, the Kolb brothers set out to retrace Major John Wesley Powell's journey from Green River, Wyoming through the Grand Canyon all the way to California. First to accomplish this feat since Powell in 1869, they even captured the epic adventure on film. Together, they penned a book and took the finished film on the East Coast lecture circuit. Emery started spending more time with his family and on personal adventures (like running the Black Canyon of the Gunnison), stressing the brothers' business relationship. Soon they decided to go their separate ways, and the only fair way to determine who would leave the canyon was to flip a coin. Emery won a best of three. He kept the studio and continued to show the film of their whitewater adventure until his death in 1976. Kolb Studio remains today. The restored building houses history and art exhibits.

Phantom Ranch

One of the most unique experiences at the Grand Canyon is spending a night on the canyon's floor at Phantom Ranch. Located along Bright Angel Creek near the junction of North Kaibab, South Kaibab, and Bright Angel Trails, the only way to reach this secluded getaway is by foot, mule, or river. Designed by Mary Colter and constructed in 1922, the ranch's intent was, and still is, to provide food, lodging, and comfort to backcountry visitors.

Phantom Ranch offers men's and women's dormitories ($61/person) and 2–10 person cabins ($332) with shared showers. Hot meals and souvenirs are available for purchase. Meals cost anywhere from $26 for breakfast to $51 for a steak dinner. All meals must be reserved and are served at a designated time. If you think you might be interested in souvenirs, be sure to leave space in your backpack for them. You don't have to carry your own gear; a duffel service is available for about $76 each way.

South Rim hikers are forced to make the difficult decision of which trail to take into and out of the canyon (South Kaibab in and Bright Angel out is recommended). Remember, South Kaibab Trail, although shorter, is extremely steep and strenuous with no clean water source available along the way. Pack plenty of water or take Bright Angel Trail.

Phantom Ranch is operated by Xanterra Parks & Resorts. Demand far exceeds capacity. Reservations are made via a lottery system 15 months in advance through grandcanyonlodges.com. If you couldn't secure reservations, you can do an overnight mule ride. A one-night ride costs $1,205 for two, and $533 more for each additional rider (meals included).

Pima Point

Backpacking

The park is broken into four management zones. The Corridor Zone is recommended for hikers without previous experience at Grand Canyon. These popular trails are well-maintained and feature toilets, signs, and emergency phones. Ranger stations are also found along the way. Corridor trails include North and South Kaibab and Bright Angel Trails. All camping within the Corridor Zone must be done at designated campgrounds. Indian Garden (4.5 miles from the rim) and Bright Angel (9.5 miles) Campgrounds are located on Bright Angel Trail. Cottonwood Campground is located on North Kaibab Trail, 6.5 miles from the North Rim and 7.2 miles from Bright Angel Campground. There are no designated campsites along South Kaibab Trail.

Experienced Grand Canyon hikers may want to explore the Threshold, Primitive, and Wild Zones. Trails in these areas are either non-maintained or non-existent. Camping is available at designated sites or wherever you can find a flat space. Reliable water sources are often scarce or absent. You'll want a good map and possibly a dedicated guidebook. The other option is to hire an experienced guide like you'll find at Wildland Trekking (800.715.4453, wildlandtrekking.com).

Backcountry Permits

All overnight camping trips outside the developed campgrounds require a backcountry permit. The park receives far more permit requests than it issues, so backcountry users should apply in advance (typically as soon as they become available). Applications are accepted from the 20th of the month five months prior

to the proposed start of your trip until the end of that month. For example, if you're planning a trip for June, whether it starts on the 1st or the 30th, your application will be accepted beginning January 20th until February 1st. In-person requests are first considered three months prior to your proposed departure date. A permit request form can be found online. Permit requests may be submitted by fax (928.638.2125), through the mail, or in-person at the North or South Rim Backcountry Information Center (BIC). The South Rim's BIC is open daily from 8am–noon and 1–5pm. The North Rim BIC holds the same operating hours, but it closes for winter from mid-October until mid-May. Permit requests are not accepted by phone or e-mail.

Early consideration period permit requests are processed randomly. Allow up to three weeks for a response. Successful applicants who have met the fee requirements will receive their permit at the time of response. Permit fees include a $10 non-refundable application fee plus $8 per person per night camped below the rim or $8 per group camped above the rim. Park entrance fee is not included. Cancellations received four or more days prior to the start of your trip will receive a credit towards a future trip reserved within one year. In addition to the possibility of cancelled trips, the park holds a limited number of walk-up last-minute permits for corridor campgrounds (Indian Garden, Bright Angel, and Cottonwood). Walk-up permits are issued for a maximum of two nights. They are only issued in person and cannot be purchased earlier than one day prior to departure date. Stop by the BIC to request a waitlist number for the following day.

Upper Bright Angel Trail

To Indian Garden, Plateau Point,
and Phantom Ranch

3-Mile Resthouse
4720ft
1439m

1½-Mile Resthouse
5720ft
1743m

Trailview
Overlook

Rim Trail

Bright Angel Trail

Lower Tunnel
6250ft 1905m

Upper Tunnel
6780ft
2067m

Kolb Studio

Verkamps
Visitor Center

Rim Trail

El Tovar
Hotel

Bright Angel Lodge

**Bright Angel
Trailhead**

6840ft
2085m

0   200 Meters

0   1000 Feet

Do not swim in the Colorado
River! You could drown due to
dangerous currents and extremely
cold water temperatures.

Phantom Ranch
Canteen

Ranger Station

Bright Angel

Silver
Bridge

Pipe Creek
Rapids

River Resthouse
2500ft
762m

River Trail

1.5mi
2.4km

Plateau Point
3760ft
1146m

PLATFO

0.7mi
1.1km

Plateau Point Trail

2.9mi
4.7km

0.8mi
1.3km

TONTO

2.0mi
3.2km

2.2mi
3.5km

Tonto Trail

Skeleto

0.3mi
0.5km

3800ft
1158m

Indian Garden

Ranger Station

0.1mi
0.2km

Garden Creek

The Battleship

O'Ne

Creek

Pipe

Hopi Point
7065ft
2153m

Mojave Point
6995ft
2132m

Powell Point

Maricopa Point

Rim Trail

Hermit Road

THE
ABYSS

Bright Angel Trail

1.5mi
2.4km

3-Mile Resthouse

Grandeur
Point
7032ft
2143m

Yavapai Point
7082ft
2159m

1.5mi 2.4km

2.6mi
4.2km

Mather Point
7120ft
2170m

Grand Canyon
Visitor Center

Lower Tunnel

0.5mi 0.8km

1½-Mile Resthouse

1.0mi 1.6km

To Hermits Rest

**Bright Angel
Trailhead**

6840ft
2085m

El Tovar

Verkamps Visitor Center

Village Loop Drive

Center Road

Backcountry
Information
Center

Market Plaza Road

Clinic

Market

Campground

South Entrance Road

Rim Trail

2.3mi
3.7km

Desert View Drive

**COCONINO
PLATEAU**

South Entrance Rd

To South Entrance Station and Tusayan

SOUTH RIM

Services available year-round.

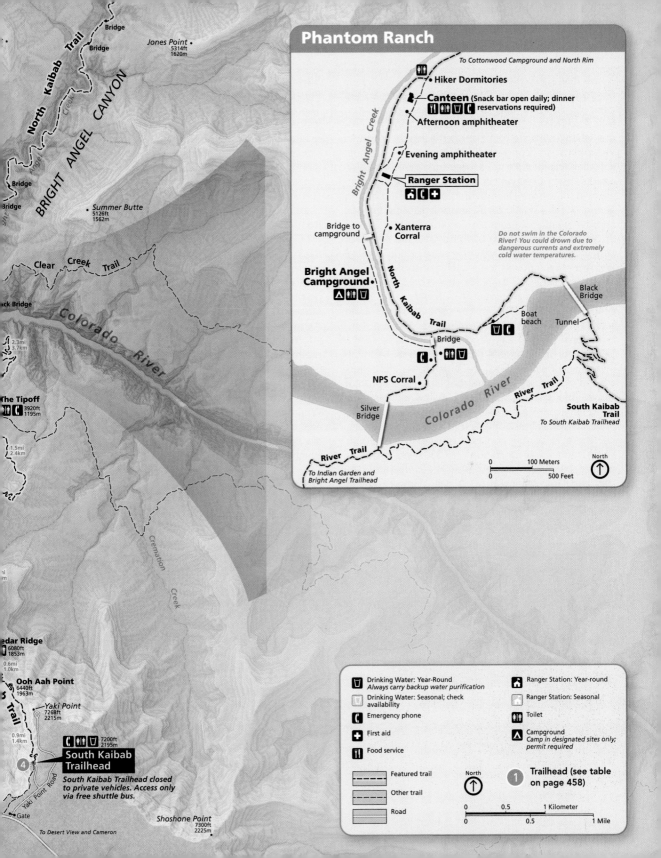

Phantom Ranch

To Cottonwood Campground and North Rim

• Hiker Dormitories

Canteen (Snack bar open daily; dinner reservations required)

Afternoon amphitheater

• Evening amphitheater

Ranger Station

BRIGHT ANGEL CANYON

Bright Angel Creek

North Kaibab Trail

Bridge to campground

• **Xanterra Corral**

Do not swim in the Colorado River! You could drown due to dangerous currents and extremely cold water temperatures.

Bright Angel Campground

Boat beach

Black Bridge

Tunnel

Bridge

NPS Corral

Silver Bridge

Colorado River

River Trail

South Kaibab Trail
To South Kaibab Trailhead

River Trail

To Indian Garden and Bright Angel Trailhead

0   100 Meters
0   500 Feet

North

Jones Point
5314ft
1620m

North Kaibab Trail

Bridge

Bridge

Summer Butte
5126ft
1562m

Clear Creek Trail

Bridge

Bridge

Black Bridge

Colorado River

Bright Angel Creek

2.3mi
3.7km

The Tipoff
3920ft
1195m

1.5mi
2.4km

Cremation Creek

Cedar Ridge
6080ft
1853m

0.6mi
1.0km

Ooh Aah Point
6440ft
1963m

Yaki Point
7268ft
2215m

0.9mi
1.4km

7200ft
2195m

South Kaibab Trailhead
South Kaibab Trailhead closed to private vehicles. Access only via free shuttle bus.

4

Yaki Point Road

Gate

Shoshone Point
7300ft
2225m

To Desert View and Cameron

Drinking Water: Year-Round
Always carry backup water purification

Drinking Water: Seasonal; check availability

Emergency phone

First aid

Food service

Ranger Station: Year-round

Ranger Station: Seasonal

Toilet

Campground
Camp in designated sites only; permit required

Featured trail

Other trail

Road

North

0   0.5   1 Kilometer
0   0.5   1 Mile

1 **Trailhead** (see table on page 458)

South Rim – When to Go

Grand Canyon's South Rim is open all year. So are camping, lodging, and dining facilities. Visitation is high from March through October, peaking in summer when hotels are often booked a year in advance. Viewpoints are congested. Shuttle buses are full. (Popular activities like mule rides and river rafting also need to be booked well in advance.) The heat (particularly in the canyon) is unbearable. Try visiting during spring or fall when crowds are only slightly thinner, and the weather is more comfortable. Winter can be an amazing time to visit. Lodging rates are reduced, and, if you're fortunate, you may see a beautiful white and red canyon thanks to a dusting of snow.

South Rim – Transportation & Airports

Amtrak (800.872.7245, amtrak.com) provides train service to Williams and Flagstaff, AZ. McCarran International (LAS) in Las Vegas, NV (270 miles away); Sky Harbor International (PHX) in Phoenix, AZ (225 miles); and Pulliam (FLG) in Flagstaff, AZ (82 miles) are the closest large commercial airports. Car rental is available at each destination. A few airlines offer direct service to Grand Canyon Airport (866.235.9422, grandcanyonairlines.com). Car rental is not available, but there is shuttle and taxi service to the South Rim. Groome Transportation (928.350.8466, groome-transportation.com) provides service between Flagstaff and Grand Canyon twice daily. Grand Canyon Shuttles (888.215.3105, grandcanyonshuttles.com) provides regular service between Flagstaff and the Grand Canyon, as well as rim-to-rim transfers. You can also reach the South Rim by train.

South Rim – Park Shuttle

Free shuttle service makes life easier at the South Rim. There are four shuttle loops. Schedules do change, so it's best to refer to the South Rim Pocket Map you'll receive at the entrance. Hermit's Rest Route runs from March through November, stopping at viewpoints along Hermit Road. (Note that Rim Trail also provides access to Hermit Road viewpoints. So, if there's a long line at the bus stop near Bright Angel Trailhead, just walk down Rim Trail and enjoy the views.) Tusayan Route runs between Tusayan and Grand Canyon Visitor Center from early May until early October. Village Route runs all year and connects all major points of interest in Grand Canyon Village. Kaibab Rim Route runs year-round, and it takes riders to canyon viewpoints, South Kaibab Trailhead, and Yavapai Geology Museum. A Hiker's Express Shuttle connects Bright Angel and South Kaibab Trails, and the Backcountry Information Center. Shuttles run every 10–15 minutes during the day and about every 30 minutes the hour before sunrise and the hour after sunset.

South Rim – Directions

Whether you're arriving at the South Rim from the east or west, you'll most likely be taking I-40. Travelers passing through Flagstaff can also take US-180, which merges with AZ-64 and heads into the park.

From I-40: Heading east or west on I-40, take Exit 165 for AZ-64 toward Williams/Grand Canyon. Head north on AZ-64 for about 55 miles. You'll pass through Tusayan and into the park. Shortly thereafter, Grand Canyon Village will come into view on your left (west).

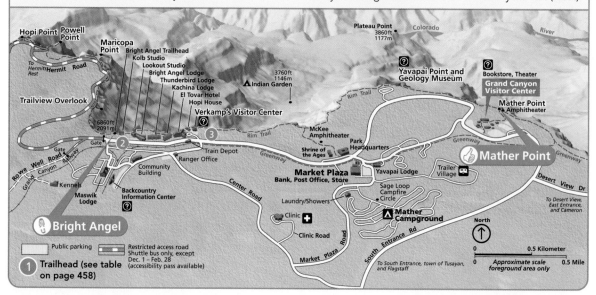

South Rim Camping & Lodging

Lodging accommodations range from Bright Angel Lodge's basic rooms with shared bathrooms to El Tovar Hotel's luxury suites. But these lodging facilities aren't about the accommodations; they're about the location. All lodges are located in Grand Canyon Village, and Maswik and Yavapai are the only ones not situated directly on the canyon's rim. Ideal location and convenience comes at a premium. Rooms on the rim with a private bath cost at least $200/night. Still, the demand is great. If you want to stay on the rim, you should make reservations early, especially if you're traveling in summer. Reservations are accepted 12–13 months in advance. Campgrounds also fill to capacity. There are three developed campgrounds at the South Rim. Reservations can be made up to six months in advance at **Mather Campground** and its neighbor, **Trailer Village**. **Desert View Campground**, located 25 miles east of the village on Desert View Road, has 50 sites available on a first-come, first-served basis.

Flightseeing & Skydiving

The Grand Canyon's size, depth, and remoteness are best understood when viewed from above. Airplane and helicopter pilots provide that unique perspective, but they must adhere to a few restrictions, including more than 75% of park airspace being off-limits to help reduce noise pollution.

Several companies provide helicopter (slower and lower) and airplane (faster and higher) tours from Grand Canyon Airport in Tusayan. Grand Canyon Airlines (702.835.8484, grandcanyonairlines.com, $159 for 40–45), Papillon (702.736.7243, papillon.com, $140+ for 40–45), and Westwind (480.991.5557, westwindairservice.com, $152 for 45) offer airplane tours. Maverick (928.638.2622, maverickhelicopter.com, $299 for 45), Papillon ($209–400 for 25–50), and Grand Canyon Helicopters (702.835.8477, grandcanyonhelicopters.com, $319 for 40–45) offer helicopter tours. All these companies offer a variety of package tours including additional land and water activities. Several offer trips departing Page, AZ and Las Vegas, NV. If you really want to get wild, Paragon Skydive (skydivegc.com, $329+) will jump out of a plane with you.

South Rim Mule Rides

Modern mule riders aren't photographed by the energetic Kolb brothers, but they still descend into the mile-deep gorge using the same trail. Xanterra Parks

South Rim Camping (Fees are per night)

Name	Location	Open	Fee	Notes
Mather*	Grand Canyon Village	All Year	$18 (peak) $15 (winter)	Laundry and showers available • No hookups, 30-ft max length
Trailer Village#	Grand Canyon Village	All Year	$61+	Full hookups, 50-ft max • No wood fires
Desert View - ♿	25 miles east of Grand Canyon Village	mid-April–mid-Oct	$12	First-come, first-served, fills by noon, flush toilets, no hookups, 30-ft max
*Reservations can be made at recreation.gov or (877) 444-6777 up to six months in advance March–November #Trailer Village reservations can be made at visitgrandcanyon.com or (877) 404-4611				
Backcountry	Permitted at designated sites or at-large areas with a permit • See page 453 for permit details			

South Rim Lodging (Fees are per night for peak season)

Name	Open	Fee	Notes
Bright Angel Lodge*	All Year	$124–179	Cabins to basic rooms with shared bathroom and shower
El Tovar Hotel* - ♿	All Year	$278–636	Premier lodging at the Grand Canyon • Exceptional views
Kachina Lodge*	All Year	$258–325	Some rooms with canyon views • Check-in at El Tovar
Thunderbird Lodge* - ♿	All Year	$232–335	Identical to Kachina • Check-in at Bright Angel Lodge
Maswik Lodge*	All Year	$179+	Renovations underway • A quarter-mile from canyon rim
Yavapai Lodge#	All Year	$115–263	Largest lodge in the park • 358 rooms

All lodging facilities are located in Grand Canyon Village. Reservations are accepted up to one year in advance.
*Make advance reservations up to one year in advance at (888) 297-2757 or grandcanyonlodges.com
#Make advance reservations up to 13 months in advance at (877) 404-4611 or visitgrandcanyon.com
Restaurants, market place, post office, clinic, bank, and pet kennel are available in the Village.

& Resorts (grandcanyonlodges.com) offers a one- or two-night mule trip down and back up Bright Angel Trail (South Rim), spending the night(s) at historic Phantom Ranch. A one-night ride costs $1,205 for two people. Each additional person is $533. The two-night ride costs $1,658 for two people. Each additional person costs $691. Fees include tax, breakfast, lunch, a steak dinner, and lodging. If you aren't interested in the steep descent or spending more than 10 hours in the saddle, there's a 2-hour trip ($153 per person) that departs from Yaki Barn (east of the Village).

South Rim mule trips are offered year-round. Riders must be at least 9 years old, 4'9" tall, and weigh no more than 200 pounds. Everyone must check-in at Bright Angel Transportation Desk at least 90 minutes prior to departure (preferably the day before). Overnight trips must be reserved and purchased in advance. Reservations can be made up to 13 months in advance by calling Xanterra's reservations center at (888) 297-2757 or (303) 297-2757 (outside the U.S.). They fill early, so plan ahead.

Biking

Bicycles are allowed on all roads open to vehicles. Roads are heavily trafficked, and narrow with little to no shoulder, making it best to bike in the early morning before motorists come out to sightsee. Better yet stick to the bike-friendly trails. You can bike on Rim Trail from Monument Creek Vista to Hermit's Rest. Then you can bike on the Greenway Trail through Grand Canyon Village (and again on Rim Trail to South Kaibab Trailhead and Yaki Point). You can also pedal between Tusayan and Grand Canyon Visitor Center via the Greenway Trail. All South Rim shuttle buses are equipped with bike racks, allowing easy bike transportation from one area to another without having to pedal. Bright Angel Bicycles (928.679.0992, bikegrandcanyon.com) in Grand Canyon Village offers bike rental ($13/hour) and guided tours to Yaki Point ($59) and Hermit's Rest ($70). Tour prices include bike and helmet rental.

Train Excursions

Santa Fe Railroad and the locomotive played a major role in the canyon's initial promotion, only to be run off the rim by the automobile. But over the past 50 years, increased tourism, congested roadways, and nostalgia have sparked resurgence in train passenger service to Grand Canyon.

Grand Canyon Railway (800.843.8724, thetrain.com) operates restored locomotives that travel from Williams, AZ directly to South Rim's Grand Canyon Village. The trip takes about 2 hours and is complete with strolling musicians, staged robberies, and shoot-outs. A roundtrip coach class ticket costs $82 for adults and $51 for children. First class seats cost $159/adult and $121/child. Observation Dome tickets cost $189/adult and $153/child. Luxury Dome costs $226/adult, and children under the age of 15 are not permitted. Grand Canyon Railway is operated by Xanterra and therefore have the resources to offer all kinds of packages and special events that are worth checking out.

South Rim Hiking

Many visitors are happy to revel in the Grand Canyon's glory from one of many well-placed viewpoints along the South Rim. Others want to immerse themselves in the canyon, hiking as far and deep as weather, attitude, and water supply allow. At the South Rim, there are three primary inner canyon hikes. **Bright Angel**, located at the west end of Grand Canyon Village near Bright Angel Lodge, is the most popular. While it's the favorite route for rim-to-rim hikers and backpackers, it also provides excellent day-hiking opportunities. Consider taking it 3 miles (roundtrip) to 1.5-Mile Resthouse or 6 miles (roundtrip) to 3-Mile Resthouse. Clean water and a restroom are available from May to October at each resthouse, and year-round a little farther down the trail at Indian Garden. If you're fit, filled with energy to trudge back up canyon, and have plenty of daylight, consider going 12 miles roundtrip to Plateau Point (it's a spur trail from Indian Garden).

South Rim Hiking Trails (Distances are roundtrip unless noted otherwise)

Name	Location (# on map)	Length	Difficulty Rating & Notes
Hermit	Hermit's Rest (1)	20.6 miles	S – Santa Maria Spring (2.5 mi), Dripping Sp (3.5 mi)
Bright Angel - ♨	Bright Angel Trailhead (2)	19.6 miles	S – Leads into the canyon to Phantom Ranch
Rim - ♨	Many Locations (3)	0–12.8 miles	E – One-way, mostly level, many access points
South Kaibab - ♨	South Kaibab Trailhead (4)	14.6 miles	S – Shortest route to the canyon floor
Grandview - ♨	Grandview Point/Trailhead (5)	6.4 miles	S – Starts steep, flattens out, 2,300-ft descent

Difficulty Ratings: E = Easy, M = Moderate, S = Strenuous

South Kaibab Trail, located near Yaki Point off Desert View Drive, is the most direct route to the canyon floor. It's steep and strenuous, but the views from the cliff-side trail and open promontories are extraordinary. Day hikers can choose to hike to Ooh-Aah Point (1.8 miles roundtrip), Cedar Ridge (3 miles), or Skeleton Point (6 miles). Water is not available along South Kaibab Trail, so fill your bottle or hydration system before hopping aboard the shuttle bus to the trailhead. Plenty of extreme hikers day-hike to the floor, but it isn't recommended for the average visitor.

For less popular inner canyon hiking, try Hermit or Grandview Trails. **Hermit Trail** is located at the west end of Hermit Road. **Grandview Trail** is located at Grandview Point on Desert View Drive. Both offer some of the finest canyon views in the park, making them ideal for a choose-your-own-distance out-and-back hike. Grandview Trail is steep (and a little suspect) at the beginning before levelling out. Note that it doesn't reach the canyon floor, but it's still a wonderful trail.

Do not overestimate your physical fitness level. Expect hiking out of the canyon to take twice the time it took to hike in (watch the time and plan accordingly). Hundreds of visitors are rescued from the canyon each year, most suffering from heat exhaustion or dehydration. Carry plenty of water, allot ample time for your hike, use a bit of common sense, and you'll love the experience. If you're daunted by the inner canyon, **Rim Trail** from Grand Canyon Village to Hermit's Rest is for you. It is South Rim's only above-rim hiking trail, and it conveniently follows a shuttle route, so you can hop aboard a bus whenever it suits you. It also follows the rim east to South Kaibab Trailhead (and Yaki Point).

Grand Canyon Field Institute (928.638.2481, grandcanyon.org) offers educational hiking/backpacking classes. Courses cost about $100 per day and discounts are available for Grand Canyon Association Members.

Visitor Centers & Museums

Kolb Studio: The former home and business of the Kolb Brothers has been restored to house free art exhibits and a bookstore. The Studio is in Grand Canyon Village's Historic District at Bright Angel Trailhead. (Open daily, 9am–5pm in winter, 8am–7pm in spring/fall, and 8am–8pm in summer)

Verkamp's Visitor Center: Occupying one of the oldest buildings on the South Rim, Verkamp's Visitor Center now features displays telling the history of Grand Canyon Village. A bookstore and information desk are available. (Open daily, 9am–5pm in winter, 8am–7pm in spring/fall, and 8am–8pm in summer)

Yavapai Geology Museum: Interested in geology, or simply curious about the canyon? If so, stop at the park's Geology Museum located one mile east of Market Plaza. (Open daily, 9am–5pm in winter, 8am–7pm in spring/fall, and 8am–8pm in summer)

Grand Canyon Visitor Center: Located near Mather Point, this is the best spot to begin your trip to the South Rim. The complex contains several outdoor exhibits, a visitor center, theater, and bookstore. Parking is limited and often fills before 10am, but the park's free shuttle system also provides transportation. (Open daily, 9am–5pm in winter, 8am–7pm in spring/fall, and 8am–8pm in summer)

Tusayan Ruins and Museum: This free museum explores more than 10,000 years of cultural history. Ancient artifacts include projectile points, split-twig figurines, pottery, and a small Ancestral Puebloan ruins site. The museum is located three miles west of Desert View. (Open daily)

Desert View Visitor Center: Located at the eastern end of Desert View Drive, this small visitor center houses a collection of art inspired by the Grand Canyon. Find your own inspiration by viewing the Colorado River from Desert View Watchtower, originally designed by Mary Colter and built in 1932. A bookstore is also available. (Open daily)

Ranger Programs & For Kids

A visit to any national park isn't complete without participating in at least one of the famous ranger programs. All programs are free, and most are in and around Grand Canyon Village. There are a few special events that take place at Desert View, Tusayan Museum, and Phantom Ranch. You'll find regularly scheduled walks and talks that explore the area's geology, history, and ecology. Check the current schedule of ranger-guided activities online or at a visitor center. All these tours are highly recommended, and you're sure to come away with a new appreciation for one of the world's most remarkable natural wonders.

Children can become official Grand Canyon National Park Junior Rangers. To become a member of this exclusive group, pick up a free activity booklet from any of the locations listed above and complete the activities required for your age group. Upon completion, bring the booklet back to a visitor center for review. If

Use Hermit Road's middle shuttle stops to avoid lines

successful, your child will earn an official Junior Ranger badge. There is a special prize for children ages 4 and up who complete the booklet's activities and make a trip to Phantom Ranch. The park also offers family oriented-summer programs.

Other Excursions

A trip to the **IMAX Theater** (explorethecanyon.com) or walking Skywalk (grandcanyonwest.com) is included in many families' vacation plans. **Skywalk** is somewhat expensive ($59), far away (4+ hours from Grand Canyon Village), and unrecordable (cameras are not allowed). It's convenient from Las Vegas, but if you're going to the park, I'd spend my time and money there instead.

On the other hand, visiting **Havasu Falls**, one of the world's finest swimming holes, is worth the time, effort, and money. But it's not easy to get to. Taking all paved roads from Grand Canyon Village, it's 195 miles to the falls' trailhead. Leave South Rim via AZ-64/US-180, heading south. Head west on I-40 about 45 miles to Exit 121 toward AZ-66/Seligman/Peach Springs. Turn right at Interstate 40 Business Loop E. After about 1 mile, take another right onto AZ-66. Continue another 30 miles to a T-intersection. Turn right onto Hualapai Hilltop Highway. After 43 miles you will come to the trailhead to Havasu Canyon. From there, it's another 8 miles by foot, mule, or helicopter.

All visitors must have reservations at the campground or lodge (havasupaireservations.com). Fees and rules change regularly. In 2020, it was about $350 to hike in and spend three nights at the campground. Those who arrive without a reservation will be charged double. You can hire a pack mule to carry your things.

South Rim – Tips & Recommendations

Grand Canyon is pretty busy all year long, but the main season is from March through October, peaking between Memorial and Labor Day. If you would like to visit when there are smaller crowds, consider the South Rim in winter or a late-season trip to the North Rim (typically open mid-May until November).

Don't skip out on South Kaibab or Bright Angel because they're long and strenuous, hike as far as you're comfortable and return to the rim. But remember hiking up may take twice as long as hiking down. My preference is South Kaibab, but each one offers spectacular views and there's water and restrooms along Bright Angel. You do not want to become a part of the park's rescue statistics. If you have any hesitations, go to Bright Angel Trailhead, hike west along Rim Trail and take in a few views of Bright Angel Trail below. That will give you a pretty good idea of what you're getting into should you choose to hike into the canyon.

As you can see below, there are many great spots to catch the sunset. Scout them out during the day, and arrive early at the spot of your choice in the evening. There are plenty of great perches within walking distance of Grand Canyon Village, if that's where you're spending the night. If a spot is too crowded for your liking, grab your things and walk east or west along Rim Trail. You'll find a place with canyon views and no crowds in between the designated "spots." The same could be said during any time of day. Mather Point is the most popular viewpoint. If you see a crowd and aren't interested in joining it, continue walking down Rim Trail, not only will you escape the crowd, but you'll find interesting vantage points to photograph them from (as well as the canyon). You'll find similar situations at Desert View, Hermit's Rest, and Yaki Point. Some spots simply require a little curiosity and exercise. For example, the road to Shoshone Point is gated off, but you can still walk there.

Hiking Trails: Rim (Easy, varies), Bright Angel (Strenuous, 19.6 miles), South Kaibab (Strenuous, 14.6), Grandview (Strenuous, 6.4)
Viewpoints: Lipan Point, Mohave Point, Desert View, Mather Point, Yaki Point, Hopi Point, Trailview Overlook
Family Activities: Take the train, become Junior Rangers, take a helicopter tour, bike along the Rim
Guided Tours: Raft the river, ride a mule, see the canyon from the sky
Rainy Day Activities: The Grand Canyon can be even more impressive during a storm, just be sure to pay attention to weather reports and trail conditions
History Enthusiasts: Tusayan Museum and Ruin, Desert View, Yavapai Geology Museum
Sunset Spots: Yavampai Point, Hopi Point, Mohave Point, Lipan Point, Desert View, Grandview Point, Mather Point, Pima Point, Shoshone Point, Yaki Point, Navajo Point
Sunrise Spots: Hopi Point, Grandview Point, Mather Point, Shoshone Point, Yaki Point

North Rim – When to Go

The North Rim is open from mid-May until the first heavy snowfall (October/November). Just like the South Rim, Summer is busiest, but there's a steady stream of visitors from opening to close. And while only 10% of guests come here, the facilities are scaled back proportionately. Fall, when leaves change colors, is one of the most pleasant times, since this rim is covered with more vegetation. The entrance road closes for winter, but the park remains open to snowshoers and cross-country skiers.

North Rim – Transportation & Airports

Public transportation does not provide service to the North Rim, but Transcanyon Shuttle (928.638.2820, trans-canyonshuttle.com) provides rim-to-rim transportation. The closest large commercial airports are McCarran International (LAS) in Las Vegas, NV, located 275 miles to the west, and Salt Lake City International (SLC), located 397 miles north of the park.

North Rim – Directions

Visitors can easily see from one rim to the other. The distance is usually about 10 miles. Hikers frequently descend into the canyon and emerge on the opposite rim after about 25 miles on foot. But, by car it's a 210-mile, 4.5-hour trip: a long, but scenic journey. You can drive yourself or hop aboard the Transcanyon Shuttle. Directions are also provided for those traveling north or south on I-15.

From South Rim (210 miles): Follow AZ-64/East Rim Drive out of the park. After 52 miles, you'll reach the small town of Cameron. Turn left onto US-89 N. Continue for another 58 miles, where you'll turn left at US-89 Alt N. After 55 miles, you'll reach a Y-intersection with AZ-67. Turn left onto AZ-67 and head south for 43 miles. Continue into the park.

From Las Vegas (256 miles): Heading east on I-15, take Exit 16 for UT-9 toward Hurricane/Zion National Park. Turn right onto UT-9 heading east. After about 10 miles, take a right onto S 100 E. Almost immediately take the first left onto UT-59. Follow UT-59 across the Utah–Arizona border where the road becomes AZ-389. After 54 miles on UT-59/AZ-389, you will reach Fredonia, turn right at US-89 Alt S. Continue south for 30 miles and then turn right at AZ-67, which leads to the North Rim.

From Salt Lake City (380 miles): Heading south on I-15, take Exit 95 for UT-20 toward US-89/Panguitch/Kanab. Turn left onto UT-20 E. Continue for 20 miles until the road terminates at US-89. Turn right onto US-89. Follow US-89 south for 76 miles to Kanab, UT. Here, US-89 follows Center St and S 100 E through the city. Do not follow US-89 to the east. Take US-89 Alt south and continue south for 36 miles to the Y-intersection with AZ-67. Turn right onto AZ-67 and continue for 43 miles into the park.

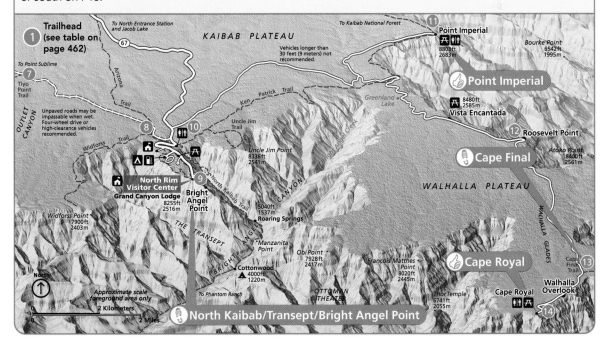

Looking straight down Bright Angel Canyon the North Rim doesn't look 1,000 feet higher from the South Rim

North Rim Camping (Fees are per night)

Name	Location	Open	Fee	Notes
North Rim* - ♨	AZ-67	mid-May–October	$18–25	Showers and laundry available, dump station, no hookups • Canyon view sites more expensive

*Campground reservations can be made at recreation.gov or (877) 444-6777 up to six months in advance

Backcountry	Permitted at designated sites or at-large areas with a permit • See page 453 for permit details

North Rim Lodging (Fees are per night)

Name	Open	Fee	Notes
Grand Canyon Lodge - ♨ (At the end of AZ-67)**	mid-May–mid-October	$186–299	Small, rustic cabins or motel-style rooms are available • North Rim's only lodging

**Lodging reservations can be made in advance at grandcanyonforever.com or (877) 386-4383

North Rim Hiking Trails (Distances are roundtrip unless noted otherwise)

Name	Location (# on map)	Length	Difficulty Rating & Notes
Thunder River	Forest Road 292/Monument Point/Bill Hall Trailhead (6)	15.2 miles	S – Backpacking Opportunities • Follows Tapeats Creek to Colorado River (steep)
Tiyo Point	Point Sublime Road (7)	12.5 miles	M – Above-rim out-and-back to Tiyo Point
Widforss	Point Sublime Road (8)	10.0 miles	M – Self-guided through forest
Bright Angel Pt - ♨	Near Visitor Center (9)	0.5 mile	E – Paved, self-guided trail to viewpoint
Transept - ♨	Lodge & Campground (9, 10)	3.0 miles	E – Flat, connects camp and lodge
Bridle	Grand Canyon Lodge/North Kaibab (9)	2.4 miles	E – Connects lodge to North Kaibab
Ken Patrick	North Kaibab/Point Imperial (10, 11)	10.0 miles	M – Imperial Pt to North Kaibab (1-way)
Uncle Jim	Ken Patrick Trail (10)	5.0 miles	M – Loop overlooking canyon (mule trail)
North Kaibab - ♨	North Kaibab Trailhead on AZ-67 (10)	14.0 miles	S – Connects to Bright Angel (1-way)
Arizona	North Kaibab Trail (10)	10.0 miles	M – Spans from Utah to Mexico (1-way)
Point Imperial	Point Imperial (11)	4.0 miles	E – Fire-damaged forest to park border
Roosevelt Point	Cape Royal Road (12)	0.2 mile	E – Loop with excellent views
Cape Final	Cape Royal Road (13)	4.0 miles	E – Spectacular canyon overlook
Cliff Springs	Cape Royal Road (14)	1.0 mile	E – Puebloan granary and steep cliffs
Cape Royal - ♨	Cape Royal Road (14)	0.6 mile	E – Angel's Window and Colorado River

Difficulty Ratings: E = Easy, M = Moderate, S = Strenuous

North Rim Camping & Lodging

It's easier to choose overnight accommodations on the North Rim. If you want to sleep in a bed, you'll have to stay at **Grand Canyon Lodge**. Perched atop Bright Angel Point, the lodge provides exceptional canyon views from a handful of cozy cabins (designed to sleep 3–4 guests) or basic motel rooms with one queen-sized bed. You'll find dining services to match your hunger and schedule. The Dining Room is a more formal setting where breakfast, lunch, and dinner are served. If you couldn't get the view for free, it'd be worth dining here just to take a peek at the canyon. Deli in the Pines offers quick meals. Rough Rider Saloon offers beverages and snacks. Reserve your space at grandcanyonforever.com.

North Rim is the only campground. Standard sites cost $18/night or upgrade to a premium site (bordering Transept Canyon) for $25/night. All 87 campsites feature picnic tables and campfire rings. Coin-operated showers and laundry and a gas/service station are available near its entrance. Campsites can be reserved up to six months in advance at recreation.gov. Whether staying at the lodge or campground, make reservations early. Rooms and campsites usually book months in advance, especially during summer.

North Rim Mule Rides

Canyon Trail Rides takes guests on 1- and 3-hour trips. One-hour rides cost $50 per person and follow the rim of the canyon along Ken Patrick Trail. Riders must be at least 7 years old and weigh no more than 220 pounds. One 3-hour ride stays above the rim following the 1-hour tour route, continuing around Uncle Jim Loop. Alternatively, another 3-hour ride leads into the canyon via North Kaibab Trail to Supai Tunnel, where you turn around and return to the rim. Both cost $100 per person. Riders must be at least 10 years of age and weigh no more than 200 pounds (220 for the Uncle Jim ride). A shuttle bus to the trailhead leaves Grand Canyon Lodge a half-hour before trip departure. Trips depart at least two times per day. North Rim mule rides are offered from mid-May through mid-October. Contact Canyon Trail Rides (435.679.8665, canyonrides.com) for reservations.

North Rim Hiking

The North Rim offers a variety of above-rim paths and one major inner-canyon trail. Ken Patrick, Uncle Jim, Widforss, and Transept Trails begin at or near North Rim Visitor Center and stay above the canyon's rim. One short trail every visitor should hike is the 0.5-mile jaunt to **Bright Angel Point**. **Bridle Trail** is the only path that allows bikes and pets. **Point Imperial**, one of the best locations to watch the sunrise, is located a few miles drive from the visitor center. Head north on AZ-67 as if you were going to exit the park. After the large S-curve, turn right onto Fuller Canyon Road and continue east until it intersects Point Imperial Road. Turn left and drive to its end, where you'll find Point Imperial. From here, you can hike two miles (one-way) through forest burned more than a decade ago to the park's northern boundary. If you're up for a significant rim-top hike, you could take **Ken Patrick Trail** all the way to Point Imperial. If you turn right at the Fuller Road/Point Imperial Road intersection, you can continue onto Cape Royal Road. The view from Cape Royal is fantastic (there's a backcountry campsite here, too). Four short and relatively easy trails are located nearby.

North Kaibab is the North Rim's corridor trail. It's a good place to begin a rim-to-rim hike because you spare 1,000 feet of elevation gain. Or day-hike to Supai Tunnel (3.4 miles, roundtrip) or Roaring Springs (6.0 miles). North Kaibab is the most difficult and least visited of the park's three corridor trails. Potable water is available at the trailhead, Supai Tunnel, Roaring Springs, the Pumphouse Residence, Cottonwood Campground, and Bright Angel Campground. Still, carry plenty of water and expect your ascent to take twice as long as your descent.

North Rim Winter Activities

The park road closes for winter, but that doesn't keep determined snowshoers and cross-country skiers out. There used to be a yurt with a wood-burning stove near North Kaibab Trailhead. A portable toilet is located nearby. If you're going to visit the North Rim in winter, you better come prepared for all conditions. Dress in layers. Watch the weather. Carry plenty of food and water.

Visitor Center

North Rim Visitor Center, located next to Grand Canyon Lodge on Bright Angel Peninsula, offers park and regional information, restrooms, and a bookstore. It is open daily, mid-May to mid-October, from 8am–6pm. The visitor center is a great place to begin a trip to the North Rim. Park rangers are available to answer your questions, and interpretive exhibits help introduce you to the region.

Ranger Programs & For Kids

Park rangers provide interpretive programs about the canyon and its environment between mid-May and mid-October. Most programs meet or take place at the

Visitor Center or Grand Canyon Lodge. What's Rock-in'? is a 30–40-minute talk about geology conducted at Grand Canyon Lodge's back porch. If you're busy hiking trails or admiring the panoramic views, you can always catch an evening program at the campground amphitheater or lodge auditorium.

Children visiting the North Rim are invited to participate in the park's Junior Ranger Program. Free activity booklets are available at the visitor center.

North Rim – Tips & Recommendations

North Rim only receives about 10% of the park's visitors, and it's loaded with things to do, especially for hikers and off-roaders. But don't beeline here because that sounds fantastic. It also has considerably fewer visitor facilities. With that said, there's good hiking, great views, and, if you can make a reservation, excellent lodging and camping accommodations.

Hike above the rim. North Kaibab is great if you've trained for a Rim-to-Rim hike and are ready to get after it, or you are taking your time and spending a few nights in the corridor. For those individuals it provides an eye-opening exposition of the canyon's massive size. But you might be better off saving up for a rafting trip or taking a flightseeing tour to get a more comprehensive idea of this uniquely grand canyon.

The North Rim's developed area is relatively small, but the views afforded at sites like Point Imperial and Cape Royal are some of the best easily-accessible points in the park. You can see/hike most of the main attractions in a full day, and then carry on to other destinations like the South Rim or Zion.

With a high-clearance 4x4 you can drive out to one of Grand Canyon's most dramatic viewpoints, Toroweap Point. It's a long trek across rugged roads that may be impassable under certain conditions. Nine primitive campsites are available at Toroweap (permit required). You'll have to get a permit from the park to spend the night, which is a good idea. Otherwise it's a day-use area, open from sunrise to 30 minutes past sunset (when the gate is locked). Depending on the route, it'll take you at least two hours to reach.

There's also a campsite at Cape Final (permit required) if you'd like extreme solitude without having to venture far from the comfort of the North Rim's civility.

If you plan on going backpacking or off-roading, be sure to stop in at the visitor center to discuss permits, trail/road conditions, and water sources with a park ranger.

Hiking Trails: Cape Royal (Easy, 0.6 mile), Bright Angel Point (Easy, 0.5), Transept (Easy, 3), North Kaibab (Strenuous, 14)
Viewpoints: Bright Angel Point, Cape Royal, Cape Final, Point Imperial, Roosevelt Point
Family Activities: Look for wildlife, become Junior Rangers
Guided Tours: Ride a mule
Rainy Day Activities: Same as the South Rim, enjoy the storm, just be wary about weather/trail/road conditions if you're thinking about any sort of extended hiking/off-roading expedition
History Enthusiasts: Wahalla Ruins
Sunset Spots: Cape Royal, Bright Angel Point
Sunrise Spots: Cape Royal, Point Imperial, Cape Final

Beyond the Park...

Flora & Fauna

Rocks are everywhere and among them is life. More than 1,737 species of vascular plants have been documented living within park boundaries. Such extreme diversity is due to the huge elevation change from rim to river and the amalgamation of ecosystems and deserts. The most prevalent plant community is desert scrub. Five of North America's seven life zones are represented at the Grand Canyon, and three of the continent's four deserts (Sonoran, Mojave, and Great Basin) converge at the canyon floor. These conditions create a diverse collection of wildlife. More than 355 species of birds, 89 mammal species, and 56 reptile and amphibian species reside in the park. Mule deer and bighorn sheep are the large mammals you're most likely to see. The largest and rarest bird in North America, the California condor, also lives here. The park offers special ranger programs that detail the reintroduction and current state of this endangered bird.

Pets & Accessibility

South Rim Visitors may walk their pets at all trails above the rim, Mather Campground, Desert View Campground, Trailer Village, and along all developed roadways and parking areas. The only location where pets are allowed at the North Rim is Bridle Trail, which connects Grand Canyon Lodge and North Kaibab Trail. Pets must be kept on a leash (less than six feet) and a kennel is available at Grand Canyon Village.

At the South Rim, free accessibility permits are available to individuals with mobility impairments so they can drive a private vehicle through areas closed to visitor traffic. However, shuttle buses are equipped with ramps. Most South Rim facilities and viewpoints are accessible. All inner canyon trails are inaccessible. Wheelchairs can be checked out for daily use from South Rim Visitor Center. Grand Canyon Lodge, North Rim Visitor Center, North Rim Campground, Bridle Trail, and Point Imperial Overlook are accessible at the North Rim.

Weather

Temperatures at the Grand Canyon vary wildly, from day-to-day, rim-to-rim, and rim-to-floor. South Rim experiences comfortable summer highs, typically in the 80s°F. On average, temperature at the higher-elevation North Rim is 7°F cooler than the South Rim and 28°F cooler than the canyon floor. An arid climate and high elevation provide cool evenings. The South Rim's average summer lows are usually in the 50s°F, while the North Rim's drop into the 40s°F. Both rims are at high enough elevation to receive snow during winter, but winter is much more severe at the North Rim. In winter,

average high temperatures drop into the 30s°F at the North Rim and 40s°F at the South Rim. It's also significantly wetter at the North Rim, receiving about 25 inches of precipitation each year compared to the South Rim's 15 inches. Seasonal patterns that typically occur in late summer and early winter contribute the majority of Grand Canyon's precipitation. All visitors should come prepared for a variety of conditions. Dress in layers and carry a raincoat. If you're headed down to the canyon floor in the middle of summer, expect the temperature to be above 100°F. Keep that in mind if you have ideas of a rim-to-rim or out-and-back hike to Phantom Ranch. Heat plus extreme exertion is a bad combination and this is no place to be exhausted.

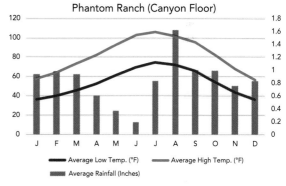

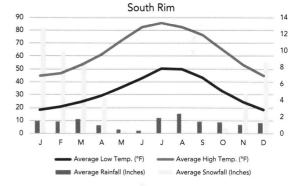

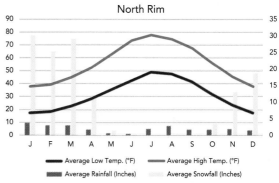

Great Basin

Phone: (775) 234-7331
Website: nps.gov/grba

Established: October 27, 1986
January 24, 1922 (Nat'l Monument)
Size: 77,180 Acres
Annual Visitors: 150,000
Peak Season: May–September
Hiking Trails: 65 Miles

Activities: Hiking, Backpacking,
Cave Tours, Stargazing, Biking,
Horseback Riding, Fishing

Cave Tours
Lodge Room: $12, 60 minutes
Grand Palace: $15, 90 minutes

5 Campgrounds ($20/night):
Upper and Lower Lehman Creek,
Wheeler Peak, Baker Creek, and
Grey Cliffs
Free Primitive Camping: Along
Snake Creek and Strawberry Creek
Roads (high-clearance 4WD)
Backcountry Camping: Permitted
(no permit required)

Park Hours: All day, every day (except Wheeler Peak and Lexington
Arch Day-use Areas)
Entrance Fee: None

In east-central Nevada near the Utah border, a 13,000-foot mountain hides a brilliantly decorated cave. Both are protected by Great Basin National Park. The park itself is just a small portion of a much larger Great Basin region extending from the Sierra Nevada in California to the Wasatch Mountains in Utah. In between, mountains and valleys form dozens of smaller basins where rivers and streams are unable to drain into an ocean. All water flows inland, eventually collecting in shallow salt lakes, marshes, and mud flats where it evaporates. The region's aridity is well known, but beautiful and unique landscapes and life forms adapt and evolve to this harsh environment. Alpine lakes fed by snowmelt from the rocky slopes accent the high mountains, where groves of bristlecone pine have been defying the odds for thousands of years. Many of these twisted elders had already celebrated their 2,000th birthday by the time Christopher Columbus discovered America.

Americans would make an indelible mark on Great Basin. In 1855, Ezra Williams claimed to be the first white man to summit the tallest mountain in the central Great Basin, naming it Williams Peak. Shortly after, Lieutenant Colonel Edward Steptoe named the same mountain Jeff Davis Peak in honor of his superior, Secretary of War Jefferson Davis. When Jefferson Davis became President of the Confederate States of America, some cartographers began to regret the name. "Union Peak" was suggested as an alternative because a ridge united the mountain's twin summits, but it was an obvious jab at Jefferson Davis' secessionist leanings. Fortunately, map publication was postponed and in 1869 a military mapping expedition resulted in George Montague Wheeler climbing the mountain and naming its summit, definitively, "Wheeler Peak."

Eight years earlier, Absalom "Ab" Lehman moved to Snake Valley. Having experienced the highs and lows of mining in California and Australia, he decided to try his hand at ranching. By the time George Wheeler hiked to the top of Wheeler Peak, Lehman's ranch had 25–30 cows and

Stella Lake

Parachute Shield

When to Go

Great Basin is open all year. Wheeler Peak Scenic Drive to Lehman Creek Campground is open all year, but the final nine miles are generally closed from November through May, depending on the weather. Cave tours are offered at Lehman Caves Visitor Center year-round except for New Year's Day, Thanksgiving, and Christmas. The park is busiest May through September, when campgrounds fill up, but crowds are rarely a problem. Leaves typically begin to change color around mid-September.

Transportation & Airports

Public transportation does not provide service to or around the park. The closest large commercial airports are Salt Lake City International (SLC), located 238 miles to the northeast, and McCarran International (LAS) in Las Vegas, NV, located 307 miles south of the park. Car rental is available at each destination.

Directions

Great Basin is located at the center of one of the most remote regions in the Lower 48.

From the West: Take US-50 or US-6. These highways converge at Ely, where you continue south/east on US-50/US-93/US-6/Great Basin Blvd for more than 55 miles to NV-487. Turn right at NV-487 and travel 5 miles to Baker. At Baker, turn right onto Lehman Caves Road, which leads into the park.

From the North: I-80 picks up US-93 at Wells (Exit 352) and West Wendover (Exit 410). Heading South on US-93 leads to Ely (follow directions from Ely).

From the East: From Delta, UT, head west on US-50/US-6 across the Utah–Nevada border to NV-487. Turn left onto NV-487 and continue for 5 miles to Baker. Turn right onto Lehman Caves Road, which leads into the park.

From the South: Heading north on US-93, turn right at US-50/US-6. Continue east for almost 30 miles to NV-487. Turn right onto NV-487, and after 5 miles turn right at Lehman Caves Road.

an orchard. Prosperity and the loneliness of Ab's second wife, Olive Smith, prompted several family members to move into the area, and a community began to develop around Lehman Ranch. A butcher shop, blacksmith shop, carpenter shop, and milk house were established, and Absalom's orchard was regarded as the best in the region. Success allowed Ab to focus his attention on his ranch's latest addition, Lehman Caves. While exploring the cave, he reached a point where stalactites and stalagmites prevented entrance to its interior chamber. Ab returned to "develop" the "passages" with a little sweat and a sledgehammer. A path was cleared, and the cave was open for tourism. After 1885, the cave received hundreds of visitors each year, nearly all of them guided by Ab.

The push to preserve the park came much later. In 1964, a graduate student searching for the world's oldest tree came to the grove of bristlecone pines at Wheeler Peak. After taking core samples, the researcher wanted to obtain a more accurate count by cutting down a tree. The Forest Service granted his request and he proceeded to fell a tree known today as Prometheus. Counting the rings proved his assumption correct. Prometheus was at least 4,862 years old; he had just cut down the oldest living single organism in the world. A cross-section of the tree resides in Great Basin Visitor Center, where you can count the rings for yourself. But all was not lost. The tragedy of Prometheus helped galvanize support for the creation of Great Basin National Park, and the young graduate student was one of the cause's leading advocates.

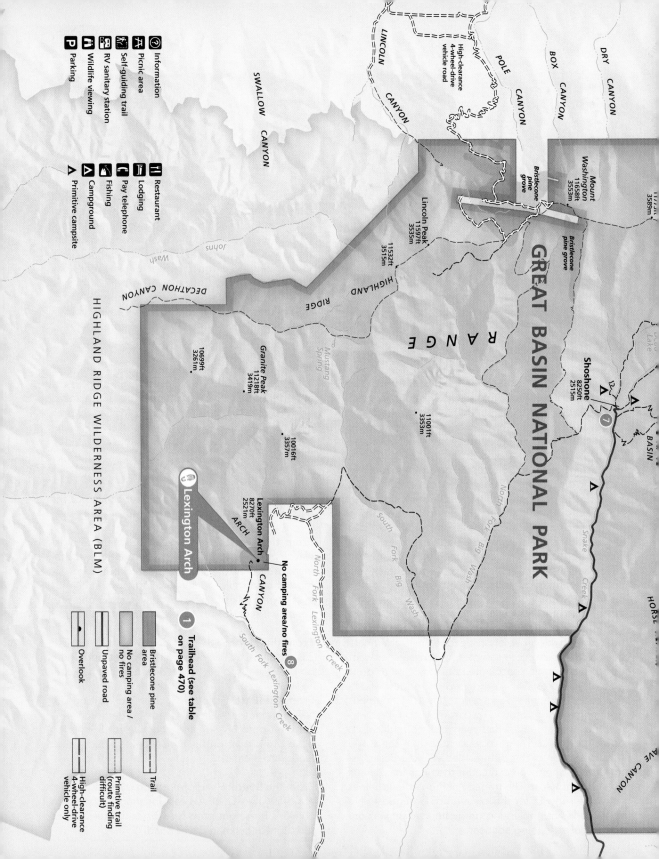

GREAT BASIN NATIONAL PARK

RANGE

SWALLOW CANYON

LINCOLN CANYON

POLE CANYON

BOX CANYON

DRY CANYON

High-clearance 4-wheel-drive vehicle road

Bristlecone pine grove

Mount Washington
11658ft
353m

358m

Bristlecone pine grove

Lincoln Peak
11597ft
3535m

11532ft
315m

HIGHLAND RIDGE

Shoshone
8250ft
251m

11001ft
3353m

Johns Wash

DECATHON CANYON

10659ft
326m

Granite Peak
11218ft
3419m

10016ft
357m

Mustang Spring

North Fork Big Wash

South Fork Big Wash

Snake Creek

HORSE CANYON

Lexington Arch
8270ft
2521m

ARCH CANYON

Lexington Arch

No camping area/no fires

North Fork Lexington Creek

South Fork Lexington Creek

HIGHLAND RIDGE WILDERNESS AREA (BLM)

Legend — symbols

🛈 Information
🖼 Picnic area
🚶 Self-guiding trail
🚐 RV sanitary station
👁 Wildlife viewing
🅿 Parking

🍴 Restaurant
🛏 Lodging
📞 Pay telephone
🎣 Fishing
🏕 Campground
🔺 Primitive campsite

① Trailhead (see table on page 470)

⑧

Map legend

Bristlecone pine area

No camping area / no fires

Unpaved road

• Overlook

Trail

Primitive trail (route finding difficult)

High-clearance 4-wheel-drive vehicle only

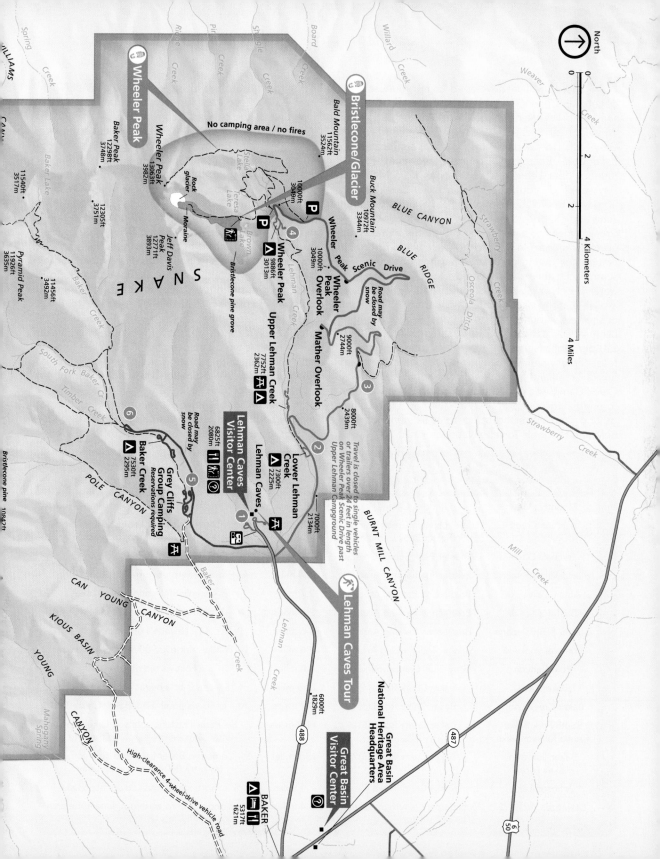

North

0
2
2
4 Kilometers
4 Miles

Wheeler Peak

Bristlecone/Glacier

No camping area / no fires

Bald Mountain
11562ft
3524m

Baker Peak
12298ft
3748m

12305ft
3751m

Wheeler Peak
13063ft
3982m

Rock glacier

Moraine

Jeff Davis Peak
12771ft
3893m

Bristlecone pine grove

11456ft
3492m

Pyramid Peak
11926ft
3635m

11540ft
3517m

Buck Mountain
10972ft
3344m

BLUE CANYON

BLUE RIDGE

Wheeler Peak Scenic Drive

10000ft
3049m

10000ft
3049m

P

P

Wheeler Peak
9886ft
3013m

④

Wheeler Peak Overlook

Mather Overlook

Upper Lehman Creek
7752ft
2362m

Road may be closed by snow

9000ft
2744m

③

8000ft
2439m

②

Travel is closed to single vehicles or trailers over 24 feet in length on Wheeler Peak Scenic Drive past Upper Lehman Campground

S N A K E

R A N G E

Baker Creek

South Fork Baker Cr.

Timber Creek

⑥

Baker Creek
7530ft
2295m

Road may be closed by snow

Grey Cliffs Group Camping
Reservations required

⑤

Lehman Caves Visitor Center

6825ft
2080m

Lower Lehman Creek
7300ft
2225m

7000ft
2134m

①

Lehman Caves

POLE CANYON

Bristlecone pine 10842ft

CAN YOUNG CANYON

KIOUS BASIN

YOUNG

CANYON

Mahogany Spring

High-clearance 4-wheel-drive vehicle road

Baker Creek

Lehman Caves Tour

BURNT MILL CANYON

Great Basin National Heritage Area Headquarters

6000ft
1825m

Great Basin Visitor Center

BAKER
531ft
1621m

488

487

6

50

Spring Creek

WILLIAMS

Creek

Baker Lake

Brown Lake

Teresa Lake

Stella Lake

Ridge Creek

Pine Creek

Shingle Creek

Board Creek

Willard Creek

Weaver Creek

Strawberry Creek

Osceola Ditch

Lehman Creek

Strawberry Creek

Mill Creek

Lehman Creek

Camping

There are five developed campgrounds. Lower Lehman Creek (11 sites), Upper Lehman Creek (24 sites), and Wheeler Peak (37 sites) are located along Wheeler Peak Scenic Drive. Baker Creek (38 sites) and Grey Cliffs (16 standard sites, 5 group) are located on Baker Creek Road. Lower Lehman Creek is open year-round. Upper Lehman Creek is open from Memorial Day weekend through September. Baker Creek is open from May to October. Wheeler Peak is open between June and October. Sites at Lower and Upper Lehman Creek, Wheeler Peak, and Grey Cliffs can be reserved up to six months in advance at (877) 444-6777 or recreation.gov during peak season. Campgrounds fill in summer. Pit toilets are located at each location, but water is only available in summer. (In winter, water is available at the visitor centers.) There are no hookups or showers. A dump station ($10 fee) is available near Lehman Caves Visitor Center in summer. All sites cost $20 per night (although they're discussing increasing fees). Free primitive campsites are available along Snake Creek and Strawberry Creek Roads. Strawberry Creek Camp was closed (fire recovery) when we went to print). If the campgrounds are full, you'll find campgrounds and dispersed camping at Sacramento Pass BLM and Humbolt-Toiyabe National Forest.

Driving

Most Great Basin visitors arrive via NV-488/Lehman Caves Road, which travels west from Baker, NV directly into the park and ultimately to Lehman Caves Visitor Center. The 12-mile Wheeler Peak Scenic Drive, which intersects **Lehman Caves Road** just beyond the park boundary, provides access to some of the most scenic viewpoints, climbing more than 3,000 feet to Wheeler Peak Campground. Vehicles longer than 24 feet are not allowed beyond Upper Lehman Creek Campground due to its steep (8% grade) and winding nature. **Wheeler Peak Scenic Drive** is open year-round to Upper Lehman Creek Campground, but usually closes beyond this point from November to May, depending on weather conditions. **Baker Creek Road** also intersects Lehman Caves Road. It's an unpaved but well-maintained road providing access to Baker Creek and Grey Cliffs Campgrounds, as well as some of the park's better backcountry hiking trails. Baker Creek Road is typically closed from December through April. Further south, running parallel to Lehman Caves Road, is the unpaved **Snake Creek Road**, which, not surprisingly, follows Snake Creek into the park. A high-clearance 4WD vehicle is recommended, but not required. A handful of primitive campsites are available along the way. **Strawberry and Lexington Arch Roads**

Great Basin Hiking Trails (Distances are roundtrip)

	Name	Location (# on map)	Length	Difficulty Rating & Notes
Wheeler Peak Scenic Dr	Mountain View	Rhodes Cabin (1)	0.3 mile	E – Nature trail through pinyon-juniper forest
	Lehman Creek	Upper Lehman Creek Camp (2) Wheeler Peak Camp (4)	6.8 miles	M – Connects Upper Lehman Creek and Wheeler Peak Campgrounds
	Osceola Ditch	Wheeler Peak Scenic Drive (3)	0.3 mile	E – Old ditch built by gold miners
	Sky Islands Forest	Bristlecone Parking Area (4)	0.4 mile	E – Paved interpretive trail of alpine forest
	Alpine Lakes - ♿	Bristlecone Parking Area (4)	2.7 miles	E – Scenic Stella and Teresa Lakes
	Bristlecone - ♿	Bristlecone Parking Area (4)	2.8 miles	M – Walk among the world's oldest trees
	Glacier & Bristlecone	Bristlecone Parking Area (4)	4.6 miles	M – Nevada's only glacier
	Wheeler Peak - ♿	Summit Trail Parking Area (4)	8.6 miles	S – Follows ridge, 2,900-feet elevation gain
Other Areas	Pole Canyon	Grey Cliffs Campground (5)	4.0 miles	E – Follows old mining road
	Baker Lake	Baker Creek Road (6)	12.0 miles	S – Leads to a beautiful alpine lake
	Baker Creek Loop	Baker Creek Road (6)	3.1 miles	M – Loop via South Fork Baker Creek Trail
	South Fork Baker Creek/Johnson Lake	Baker Creek Road (6)	11.2 miles	S – Passes historic Johnson Lake Mine structures before reaching the lake
	Baker/Johnson Lakes Loop	Baker Creek Road (6)	13.1 miles	S – Combines Baker Lake and Johnson Lake Trails • 3,000-feet elevation gain
	Johnson Lake	Snake Creek Road (7)	7.4 miles	S – Short, steep route to Johnson Lake
	Lexington Arch - ♿	Outside park, south of Baker (8)	5.4 miles	M – Longer due to wash out, limestone arch

Difficulty Ratings: E = Easy, M = Moderate, S = Strenuous

should only be accessed by high-clearance 4WD vehicles. Snake Creek, Strawberry, and Lexington Arch Roads are open year-round, but may be impassable due to snow or mud. Always check the park website for current road conditions before departing or, better yet, stop in at a visitor center to discuss your plans.

Hiking

Great Basin is a relatively small area, and all the maintained trails beginning along Wheeler Peak Scenic Drive can be completed in a day or two. The most interesting hike is **Bristlecone Trail**, a 2.8-mile (roundtrip) waltz through a forest of bristlecone pine trees, a few of which may have been growing long before the Phoenician Alphabet was created in 2,000 BC. From the end of the Bristlecone Trail, you can continue 1.8 miles (roundtrip) on **Glacier Trail** to the base of Nevada's only glacier.

For views of the Great Basin, there's no better vantage point than the summit of **Wheeler Peak**. The 8.2-mile trail begins at Summit Parking Area on Wheeler Peak Scenic Drive and steadily climbs more than 3,000 feet across rocky mountain slopes. Be sure to pack water and a jacket for this heart-pounding romp. The climb up will make you sweat, but it cools down quickly once you're soaking in the views from the completely exposed mountaintop. Another visitor favorite is **Alpine Lakes Loop**. In just 2.7 miles of fairly easy hiking, you visit two beautiful alpine lakes. Stella Lake is larger and more enchanting, but Teresa Lake is also nice and particularly pretty when snowpack remains on the surrounding slopes. They're great spots for a picnic!

Backpacking

There are more than 60 miles of hiking trails at Great Basin. Backpackers are not allowed to camp within 0.25-mile of developed areas (roads, buildings, campgrounds, etc.), within the Wheeler Peak or Lexington Arch Day Use Areas, or in bristlecone pine groves. You must set up camp a minimum of 100 feet away from all sources of water and at least 500 feet away from any obvious archeological site. Camping in the backcountry does not require a permit, but sign in at trailhead registers just in case something happens.

One of the park's best backpacking routes is to take **Baker Lake Trail**, which begins at the end of Baker Creek Road, all the way to Baker Lake. From here you can follow an unmaintained trail to Johnson Lake and return to Baker Road via Timber Creek Trail or South Fork Baker Creek Trail. The entire loop is slightly more than 13 miles. Carry a good topographic map.

Cave Tours & Caving

Ever since Absalom Lehman discovered the cave in the 1880s, tourists have marveled at its intricate and fragile formations. The National Park Service continues the cave-touring tradition. The cave is only one-quarter mile deep and two miles long, making tours heavy on information and light on walking. Lodge Room Tour ($12, 60 minutes, 20 people) covers the first 0.2 miles of cave including Gothic Palace, Music Room, and Lodge Room. Grand Palace Tour ($15, 90 minutes, 20 people) travels 0.6 miles while visiting all the rooms of Lodge Room Tour as well as Inscription Room and Grand Palace, where you will see the famous "Parachute Shield" formation. Tours are offered year-round, but only the Grand Palace Tour is offered in winter (no tours on Thanksgiving, Christmas, and New Year's Day). That's not a big deal since the Lodge Room Tour is included in it. Tickets can be purchased in advance at (877) 444-6777 or recreation.gov. You can also buy them in person at Lehman Caves Visitor Center. Reservations are a good idea, especially in summer. The cave is a constant 50°F with 90% humidity, so dress appropriately.

There are more than 40 caves in the park. Experienced cavers may be able to explore some of them by contacting the park's cave specialist. Potential cavers must show adequate caving competency to be issued a permit (no more than one wild cave permit per week will be issued for each cave).

Stargazing

Clear skies, high altitude, and 200 miles of distance from cities' light provide the perfect atmosphere for gazing into the heavens. Astronomy programs are typically held on Saturdays from May through October, as well as Tuesdays and Thursdays between Memorial Day and Labor Day. Start times change throughout the season, and occasionally an extra Sunday night astronomy program is added. Check online or at a visitor center for a current schedule. There's also an annual Astronomy Festival (usually in September). During these events, telescopes are provided and shared among guests. If you'd like to view the stars on your own, Wheeler Peak Parking Area is a great place to camp out with a blanket and a set of binoculars. Better yet, hike into the bristlecone pine grove. Watch the weather. Check the moon phase. And carry at least two light sources (use a red light when around others).

Biking

Cyclists are only allowed on park roads (and the trail between Baker and Great Basin Visitor Center). The ride up to Wheeler Peak is a relatively short

workout with a fun descent back to Lehman Caves Visitor Center or Baker, but it can get busy in summer. The park's primitive roads are a better challenge for mountain bikers, and a good way to explore areas while leaving your vehicle behind.

Horseback Riding

Horses are allowed in the backcountry, but you'll have to bring your own horse. Horses are prohibited from Wheeler Peak day use area trails, Osceola Ditch Trail, Lexington Arch Trail, and Baker to Johnson Lake Cutoff Trail. Scatter manure piles. Use certified weed-free feed, and do not camp at any of the trailheads.

Fishing

Fishing is allowed in all creeks and lakes. A Nevada state fishing license is required (not available for purchase at the park). Worms are acceptable, but all other live bait is prohibited, and use of barbless hooks is encouraged. Lehman Creek, Baker Creek, Snake Creek, and Baker Lake are suggested fishing locations.

Winter Activities

During winter, Wheeler Peak Scenic Drive and Baker Creek Road close to vehicles but open to skiers and snowshoers. You could snowshoe all the way up to Bristlecone Grove/Alpine Lakes, but it's more than a 10-mile expedition to get there and you better be aware of potential avalanche danger. However, you can camp in the closed Wheeler Peak Campground for free, just come prepared to survive the night. The Grand Palace Cave Tour is offered through winter (excluding Christmas and New Year's Day). You're almost assured a more intimate Lehman Cave experience as tours may not fill to capacity in winter.

Visitor Centers

Great Basin Visitor Center, on NV-487 just north of Baker, offers an information desk, exhibits, and a short film. It is open daily, May to September, from 9am to 5pm. **Lehman Caves Visitor Center** is on Lehman Caves Road. You can purchase cave tour tickets, browse exhibits, and view the orientation film here. It also houses a bookstore, cafe, and gift shop. It is open every day except New Year's Day, Thanksgiving, and Christmas, from 8am to 4:30pm (with shorter hours in winter, longer hours in summer).

Ranger Programs & For Kids

In addition to Cave Tours and Stargazing Programs, the park provides evening campfire programs, children's programs, and full-moon hikes, most of which are offered between Memorial Day and Labor Day. For a current schedule of events, visit the park website or stop in at a visitor center.

Children can become Junior Rangers or Junior Ranger Night Explorers. It's straightforward. Download a booklet from the park website or pick one up at a visitor center, follow the instructions to complete it, and turn it in at a visitor center to earn a patch.

Flora & Fauna

More than 800 species of plants, including 11 species of conifer trees, reside within park boundaries. Bristlecone pine are the elder statesmen of the bunch. At least one known tree, Prometheus, lived to the ripe old age of 4,862. Singleleaf pinyon trees are fruit bearers, with pine nuts that can be gathered and eaten by visitors. You'll find them in areas between 6,000- and 9,000-feet elevation. Great Basin is home to 73 species of mammals, 18 species of reptiles, 2 species of amphibians, and 8 species of fish. At least 238 species of birds reside in or visit the park, making it an excellent birdwatching destination. Mammals you're most likely to see include mule deer and squirrels, but fortunate visitors may spot a mountain lion, badger, or coyote.

Pets & Accessibility

Pets are allowed but must be kept on a leash (less than six feet). They are not allowed on trails (except Lexington Arch, high-clearance 4WD required), in the backcountry, in Lehman Caves, or at evening programs. Basically, pets are allowed where your car can go, along roads, in campgrounds, and in parking areas. You can board your dog at Park a Pooch (775.296.1432).

Both visitor centers are fully accessible to individuals with mobility impairments. Accessible campsites are available at Upper Lehman Creek, Wheeler Peak, and Baker Creek Campgrounds. Island Forest Trail is paved, but may require assistance for the second half, as the grade increases to about 8%. Cave tours are accessible with assistance (canes and walkers are allowed). The park "First Room" tour, where individuals in wheelchairs join a tour group for about 30 minutes to see the first room. Even then, a traveling companion will be needed for assistance in accessing the first room through the entrance tunnel. Wheelchair users can also enjoy evening programs at Upper Lehman Creek and Wheeler Peak Campgrounds.

Weather

With nearly 8,000 feet in elevation difference between Wheeler Peak (13,063 feet) and the valley floor, temperature varies greatly depending on where you are in the park as well as what season it is. Summer average high temperatures at Lehman Caves Visitor Center (6,825 feet) reach the low to mid-80s°F. Overnight summertime lows average in the 50s°F. Between December and February, the average highs are in the low 40s°F and average lows are right around 20°F. Even if it's 80°F at Lehman Cave Visitor Center, you should bring a jacket if you plan on hiking to Wheeler Peak or touring the cave. The temperature is usually 20 degrees cooler and it's often windy along the mountain's ridgeline. The cave is a constant 50°F all year. The region is arid, receiving about 20 inches of annual precipitation, but afternoon thunderstorms are common in summer and snow can fall in the high elevations any time of year. Most precipitation comes as snow between November and March.

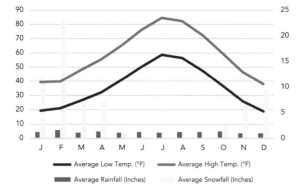

Average Low Temp. (°F) — Average High Temp. (°F)
Average Rainfall (Inches) — Average Snowfall (Inches)

Tips & Recommendations

Great Basin is a high-elevation park in a remote region of Nevada, best visited during summer. Few travelers think of adding a side trip here when heading to Utah or California, resulting in about 150,000 annual visitors. A welcome stat for many park enthusiasts, making Great Basin a refreshing trip among a vast collection of parks that continue to increase in popularity.

Deer near Strawberry Creek

Hustling, an intense visitor can hike to Wheeler Peak in the morning, tour Lehman Cave in the afternoon, and walk among some of the oldest living organisms in the evening, but, if you want to do all those things, it's better to spend a night or two, and enjoy Great Basin at a more leisurely pace (and to enjoy the stars at night!).

Great Basin is another morning park, as most activity occurs on the east side of the Snake Range, blocking out the sunset. For sunrise, you'll want to be at high enough elevation to have a view to the east and a clear view of Wheeler Peak (so you can witness it receiving the first rays of light). It's great to be in the Bristlecone Grove near Wheeler Peak, but you'll have to hike in early using a headlamp and that isn't something everyone's interested in. Although, it would also be a good opportunity to get an even earlier start to enjoy the stars from Bristlecone Grove before the sun rises.

Hiking Trails: Bristlecone (Moderate, 2.8 miles), Wheeler Peak (Strenuous, 8.6), Alpine Lakes (Easy, 2.7), Lexington Arch (Moderate, 5.4)
Family Activities: Tour the cave, stay up for the stars, become Junior Rangers
Sunrise/Sunset Spots: Mather Overlook, Bristlecone Trail (bring headlamp), Alpine Lakes Trail (bring headlamp)
Wildlife: Best chances in the grasslands around Lehman Creek and Strawberry Creek

Beyond the Park...

Dining
Kerouac's • (775) 234-7323
115 S Baker Ave, Baker
stargazernevada.com

487Grill • (775) 234-9900
120 Baker Ave, Baker
487grill.com

Sugar, Salt & Malt • (719) 237-5726
70 Baker Ave, Baker
saltandsucre.com

Lodging & Camping
Stargazer Inn • (775) 234-7323
115 S Baker Ave, Baker
stargazernevada.com

End of the Trail...er
565 Page Ave, Baker
endofthetrailer.com

Whispering Elms Motel & RV Park
120 Baker Ave, Baker
whisperingelms.com • (775) 234-9900

Sacramento Pass (BLM)
White Pine County Rd 35, Baker
free camping, no host

Attractions
Cathedral Gorge State Park
Cool, clay spires and slots
111 Cathedral Gorge Rd, Panaca
parks.nv.gov • (775) 728-4460

Spring Valley State Park
Reservoir, volcanic rock
NV-322, Pioche • parks.nv.gov

Echo Canyon State Park
Reservoir, hiking, camping
NV-322, Pioche • parks.nv.gov

Cave Lake State Park
Reservoir, camping, hiking
US-93, Ely • parks.nv.gov

Lunar Crater NNL
Access via dirt road from US-6

Ruby lake NWR
Ruby Valley, NV • (775) 779-2237

Ward Charcoal Ovens State Park
19th-century pyramid ovens
parks.nv.gov • (775) 289-1693

Kershaw-Ryan State Park
Small park, former homestead
300 Kershaw Canyon Rd, Caliente
parks.nv.gov

Humboldt-Toiyabe National Forest
6.2 million acres!
Sparks, NV • (775) 331-6444

WWII - Topaz Internment Camp
Another sad side effect of WWII
55 W Main St, Delta, UT
topazmuseum.org

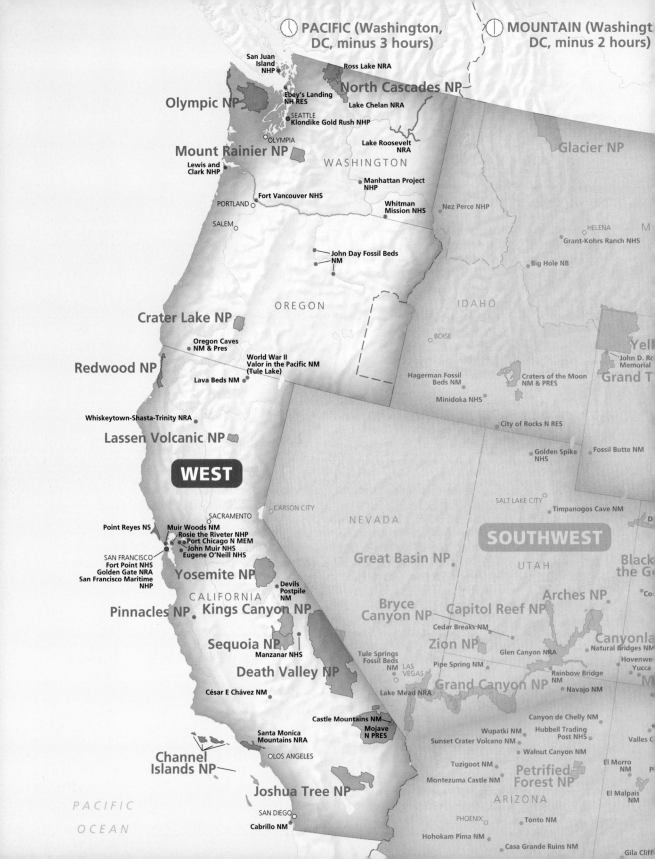

San Juan Island NHP

Ross Lake NRA

North Cascades NP

Olympic NP

Ebey's Landing NH RES

Lake Chelan NRA

SEATTLE
Klondike Gold Rush NHP

Lake Roosevelt NRA

OLYMPIA

WASHINGTON

Mount Rainier NP

Lewis and Clark NHP

Manhattan Project NHP

Glacier NP

Fort Vancouver NHS

Whitman Mission NHS

Nez Perce NHP

PORTLAND

HELENA

M

SALEM

Grant-Kohrs Ranch NHS

John Day Fossil Beds NM

Big Hole NB

OREGON

IDAHO

Crater Lake NP

BOISE

Yell

John D. R
Memorial

Oregon Caves NM & Pres

World War II Valor in the Pacific NM (Tule Lake)

Hagerman Fossil Beds NM

Craters of the Moon NM & PRES

Grand T

Redwood NP

Lava Beds NM

Minidoka NHS

City of Rocks N RES

Whiskeytown-Shasta-Trinity NRA

Lassen Volcanic NP

Golden Spike NHS

Fossil Butte NM

WEST

SALT LAKE CITY

Timpanogos Cave NM

D

Point Reyes NS

SACRAMENTO

CARSON CITY

NEVADA

Muir Woods NM
Rosie the Riveter NHP
Port Chicago N MEM
John Muir NHS
Eugene O'Neill NHS

SOUTHWEST

SAN FRANCISCO
Fort Point NHS
Golden Gate NRA
San Francisco Maritime NHP

Great Basin NP

UTAH

Black
the G

Yosemite NP

Arches NP

Co

Devils Postpile NM

CALIFORNIA

Pinnacles NP

Kings Canyon NP

Bryce Canyon NP

Capitol Reef NP

Canyonla

Cedar Breaks NM

Natural Bridges NM

Sequoia NP

Zion NP

Glen Canyon NRA

Hovenwe
Yucca

Manzanar NHS

Tule Springs Fossil Beds NM

Pipe Spring NM

Death Valley NP

LAS VEGAS

Grand Canyon NP

M

César E Chávez NM

Lake Mead NRA

Rainbow Bridge NM

Navajo NM

Castle Mountains NM

Canyon de Chelly NM

Santa Monica Mountains NRA

Mojave N PRES

Wupatki NM

Hubbell Trading Post NHS

Valles C

Channel Islands NP

Sunset Crater Volcano NM

Walnut Canyon NM

El Morro NM

OLOS ANGELES

Tuzigoot NM

Petrified Forest NP

El Malpais NM

Joshua Tree NP

Montezuma Castle NM

ARIZONA

PACIFIC

SAN DIEGO

PHOENIX

Tonto NM

OCEAN

Cabrillo NM

Hohokam Pima NM

Casa Grande Ruins NM

Gila Cliff

WEST

Joshua Tree

Boy Scout Trail

Phone: (760) 367-5522
Website: nps.gov/jotr

Established: October 31, 1994
August 10, 1936 (Nat'l Monument)
Size: 789,745 Acres
Annual Visitors: 3 Million
Peak Season: Spring–Fall

Activities: Off-Roading, Hiking,
Backpacking, Rock Climbing, Horseback Riding, Biking, Stargazing

9 Campgrounds*: $15–25/night
Backcountry Camping: Permitted

Park Hours: All day, every day,
except a few day-use areas
Entrance Fee: $30/25/15
(car/motorcycle/individual)

*Most sites can be reserved at (877)
444-6777 or recreation.gov

Joshua Tree National Park possesses some of the most unique land-scapes on the planet. Forests of twisted Joshua trees and abstract piles of rocks mark a protected region where the Mojave and Colorado deserts converge in southeastern California. For at least 5,000 years, Native Americans, missionaries, miners, ranchers, and homesteaders have had their shake at life in this arid environment. Life was difficult for all creatures: humans, animals, and plants. Only the gritty, resourceful, and adaptable survived in an inhospitable, seemingly lifeless expanse.

Inhospitable? For most…probably. Lifeless expanse? Certainly not. Hundreds of species found fascinating ways to beat the heat and con-serve moisture. Red-spotted toads reside underground for most of their lives, only escaping the sandy soil after a soaking rain. Round-tailed ground squirrels sleep through the hottest part of summer and hibernate again in winter to avoid the cold. And of course there's the iconic Joshua tree, the largest species of yucca. Endemic to the south-western United States, its primary habitat is the Mojave Desert be-tween 1,300- and 5,900-feet elevation, thriving in open grasslands. To appreciate Joshua tree "forests" you must first revisit the concept of a forest. Joshua trees are distributed sparsely across the desert allowing their roots to absorb sufficient water. For the first decade of its life a Joshua tree grows about three inches per year, an incredibly fast rate for a desert species. After its initial growth spurt, trees branch out more than up, slowing the growth rate to about an inch each year. Fortunately, they can live for hundreds of years, growing to more than 40 feet tall. The tree's name is owed to a group of Mormon settlers who crossed the Mojave Desert on their exodus west in the mid-19th century. As silhouettes, the trees appear human. Their extended limbs capped with spiky leaves evoked images of the Biblical Joshua with arms outstretched, leading his followers to the Promised Land.

Waves of miners, ranchers, and homesteaders came looking for their own promised land. Bill Keys was the most successful and colorful of the bunch. After a stint as sheriff, he settled into a life of mining and ranching in the desert of the present-day park, taking over the ranch of outlaw and cattle rustler Jim McHaney. Keys' holdings gradually expanded and eventually became known as Desert Queen Ranch. He married, had children, murdered a man in a dispute over a mill, educated himself while in prison, and was later pardoned through the efforts of Erie Stanley Gardner, author of the Perry Mason novels.

John Samuelson was another colorful desert dweller. He carved political sayings into rocks that can still be found today about 1.5 miles from the turnout west of Quail Springs Picnic Area. Forced to leave his claim when his lack of citizenship came to light, he also murdered a man over a dispute and spent time in California's State Hospital before escaping.

Minerva Hamilton Hoyt was a more refined patron of the desert. She grew up a southern belle on a Mississippi plantation before marrying a doctor and moving to Pasadena, where she spent much of her time organizing charitable and social events, gardening, and landscaping. Following the death of her husband and son, she turned her focus toward preserving the country's desert landscapes. She organized exhibitions of desert plants in New York, Boston, and London and founded the Desert Conservation League to gain support and publicity. Using her position on the California State Commission, she recommended large parks at Death Valley, Anza–Borrego Desert, and in the Joshua tree forests of the Little San Bernardino Mountains north of Palm Springs. Upon meeting President Franklin D. Roosevelt, she wasted no time expressing her opinions about the scenic and ecological value of these areas. Convinced—with the help of then Secretary of the Interior Harold Ickes—President Roosevelt created Joshua Tree National Monument in 1936, protecting the region from poachers and land developers, while preserving it for future generations.

Cholla Cactus Garden

When to Go
Joshua Tree is open every day. Unlike most national parks, summer is the least popular time to visit, with daytime high temperatures exceeding 100°F. Temperatures gradually subside, and by fall the weather is pleasant. During winter, daytime highs reach into the 60s°F, but overnight lows are often below freezing. Visitation is extremely heavy from November through April. Spring is great. Temperatures are ideal, and, depending on the amount of winter rain, you may have the opportunity to witness a spectacular array of wildflowers in bloom. Joshua Tree is often dry—after all it is a desert—receiving, on average, four inches of precipitation each year.

Transportation & Airports
Public transportation does not provide service to or around the park. The closest large commercial airport is Los Angeles International (LAX), 167 miles west of the park's South Entrance.

Directions
Joshua Tree is located in southeastern California, about 170 miles east of downtown Los Angeles. The park has three entrances, all easily accessed from I-10 and CA-62.

South Entrance: Heading east or west on I-10, take Exit 168 for Cottonwood Springs Road toward Mecca/Twentynine Palms. Turn right onto Cottonwood Springs Road into the park.

West and North Entrances: Heading east on I-10 from Los Angeles (150 miles away), take Exit 117 for CA-62/Twentynine Palms Hwy. Continue on CA-62 for almost 28 miles to Joshua Tree. Turn right at Park Blvd, which leads to the park's most popular point of entry. The North Entrance is reached by continuing on CA-62 past Park Blvd for another 17 miles to Utah Trail in Twentynine Palms. Turn right onto Utah Trail, which leads into the park.

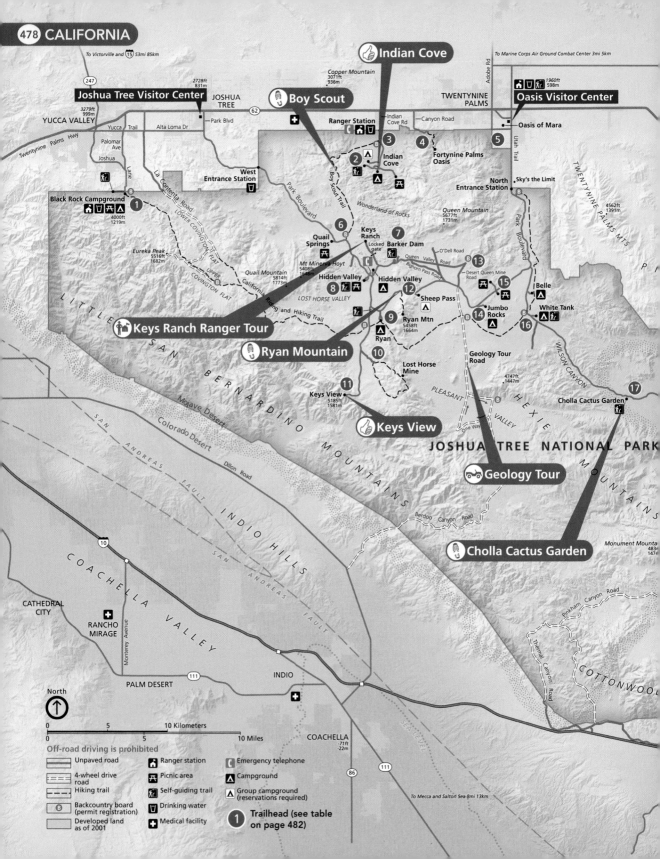

478 CALIFORNIA

To Victorville and 15 53mi 85km

247

To Marine Corps Air Ground Combat Center 3mi 5km

Adobe Rd

1960ft
598m

Oasis Visitor Center

2728ft
831m

Joshua Tree Visitor Center

JOSHUA
TREE

TWENTYNINE
PALMS

Oasis of Mara

Canyon Road

3279ft
999m

YUCCA VALLEY

Yucca Trail

Alta Loma Dr

Park Blvd

62

Boy Scout

Copper Mountain
3071ft
936m

Indian Cove

Ranger Station

Indian Cove Rd

Twentynine Palms Hwy

Palomar Ave

Joshua

West
Entrance Station

3

4

Fortynine Palms
Oasis

5

Utah Trail

Indian Cove

2

North
Entrance Station

Sky's the Limit

4562ft
1391m

Black Rock Campground

1

4000ft
1219m

La Contenta Road

LOWER COVINGTON FLAT

Park Boulevard

Boy Scout Trail

Wonderland of Rocks

6

Quail
Springs

Keys
Ranch
Locked gate

Queen Mountain
5677ft
1731m

Park Boulevard

Eureka Peak
5516ft
1682m

UPPER
COVINGTON FLAT

Quail Mountain
5814ft
1773m

California Riding and Hiking Trail

Mt Minerva Hoyt
5408ft
1648m

Keys Ranch Ranger Tour

7

Barker Dam

O'Dell Road

Queen Valley Road

13

Hidden Valley

8

LOST HORSE VALLEY

Hidden Valley

12

Sheep Pass

Desert Queen Mine Road

15

Belle

16

White Tank

Ryan Mountain

9

Ryan Mtn
5458ft
1664m

Ryan

10

14

Jumbo
Rocks

LITTLE SAN BERNARDINO MOUNTAINS

Lost Horse
Mine

Geology Tour
Road

11

Keys View
5185ft
1581m

Keys View

4747ft
1447m

PLEASANT

VALLEY

One Way Rd

JOSHUA TREE NATIONAL PARK

HEXIE

Cholla Cactus Garden

17

Mojave Desert

Colorado Desert

Dillon Road

SAN ANDREAS FAULT

INDIO HILLS

SAN ANDREAS FAULT

Geology Tour

Berdoo Canyon Road

Cholla Cactus Garden

Monument Mounta
483
147

MOUNTAINS

WILSON CANYON

Pinkham Canyon Road

COACHELLA VALLEY

CATHEDRAL CITY

RANCHO MIRAGE

Monterey Avenue

10

Thermal Canyon Road

COTTONWOOD

PALM DESERT

111

INDIO

COACHELLA
-71ft
-22m

To Mecca and Salton Sea 8mi 13km

86

111

North

0   5   10 Kilometers
0   5   10 Miles

Off-road driving is prohibited

Unpaved road	Ranger station
4-wheel drive road	Picnic area
Hiking trail	Self-guiding trail
Backcountry board (permit registration)	Drinking water
Developed land as of 2001	Medical facility

Emergency telephone
Campground
Group campground (reservations required)

1 Trailhead (see table on page 482)

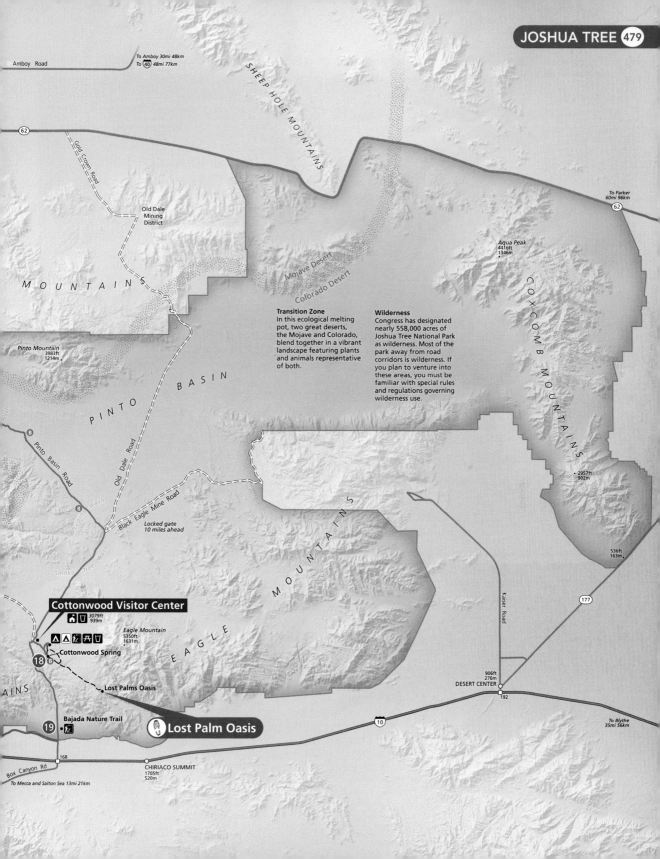

Amboy Road

To Amboy 30mi 48km
To 40 48mi 77km

SHEEP HOLE MOUNTAINS

62

To Parker
60mi 96km

62

Gold Crown Road

Old Dale
Mining
District

Aqua Peak
4416ft
1346m

M O U N T A I N S

Mojave Desert

Colorado Desert

COXCOMB MOUNTAINS

Pinto Mountain
3983ft
1214m

Transition Zone
In this ecological melting
pot, two great deserts,
the Mojave and Colorado,
blend together in a vibrant
landscape featuring plants
and animals representative
of both.

Wilderness
Congress has designated
nearly 558,000 acres of
Joshua Tree National Park
as wilderness. Most of the
park away from road
corridors is wilderness. If
you plan to venture into
these areas, you must be
familiar with special rules
and regulations governing
wilderness use.

P I N T O

B A S I N

Old Dale Road

Pinto Basin Road

B

2957ft
902m

B

Black Eagle Mine Road

Locked gate
10 miles ahead

536ft
163m

Smoke Tree Wash

177

Cottonwood Visitor Center
3079ft
939m

M O U N T A I N S

Kaiser Road

Eagle Mountain
5350ft
1631m

E A G L E

18 B
Cottonwood Spring

906ft
276m
DESERT CENTER

Lost Palms Oasis

192

19 Bajada Nature Trail

Lost Palm Oasis

10

To Blythe
35mi 56km

Box Canyon Rd

168

CHIRIACO SUMMIT
1705ft
520m

To Mecca and Salton Sea 13mi 21km

A I N S

Indian Cove

Joshua Tree Camping (Fees are per night)

Name	Location	Open	Fee	Sites	Notes
Cottonwood*	Pinto Basin Road	All Year	$25	62	Partially closed in summer • 35-ft RVs
White Tank - 🥾	Pinto Basin Road	Labor Day–Memorial Day	$15	15	First-come, first-served • 25-ft RVs
Belle - 🥾	Pinto Basin Road	Labor Day–Memorial Day	$15	18	First-come, first-served • 35-ft RVs
Jumbo Rocks* - 🥾	Park Boulevard	All Year	$20	124	Centrally located • 35-ft RVs
Sheep Pass*	Park Boulevard	All Year	$35+	6	Group tent-only sites
Ryan* - 🥾	Park Boulevard	All Year	$20	32	Horse ($15) and Bike ($5) sites
Hidden Valley - 🥾	Park Boulevard	All Year	$15	44	First-come, first-served • 25-ft RVs
Indian Cove* - 🥾	Indian Cove Road	mid-July–mid-Oct	$20	101	Partially closed in summer • 35-ft RVs
Black Rock*	Joshua Lane	All Year	$25	99	Partially closed in summer • 35-ft RVs

*Reservations can be made up to six months in advance at recreation.gov or (877) 444-6777
There are no shower or laundry facilities within the park. The only campgrounds with potable water and flush toilets are Cottonwood and Black Rock. All other campgrounds have no water and vault toilets. Water is also available at Oasis Visitor Center, West Entrance Station, and Indian Cove Ranger Station. Bring water with you into the park!

Backcountry	Permitted with a free permit in areas that are at least one mile from roads, 500 feet from trails and water sources, and not day-use only areas. There are 13 staging areas with designated parking and registration boards (where you self-register). Unregistered vehicles left overnight are subject to citation/towing.
Group*	Group campsites are available year-round at Cottonwood, Sheep Pass, and Indian Cove for $35–50/night.

Camping

Joshua Tree has nine designated campgrounds. Due to increased popularity over the last few years, most sites can be reserved up to six months in advance from September through May at recreation.gov or (877) 444-6777. During this time, campgrounds fill pretty much every single night, making reservations a great idea. **Indian Cove** is probably my favorite campground in the park, but it isn't centrally located. If you would like the perfect Joshua Tree base camp, make reservations at **Jumbo Rocks** or **Ryan**. You may want to roll the dice on first-come, first-served camping, as **White Tank**, **Belle**, and **Hidden Valley** are three of the most beautiful campgrounds you'll find in all the national parks. Water and flush toilets are only available at **Black Rock** and **Cottonwood**. Water is also available at Oasis Visitor Center, Indian Cove Ranger Station, and West Entrance. Bringing enough water with you, should be one of your primary concerns for a trip to Joshua Tree. There are no showers or hookups within the park, but you can find showers (fee) outside the park across the road from Joshua Tree Visitor Center. Group sites are available at Indian Cove, Sheep Pass, and Cottonwood (reservation are required and they are available up to one year in advance at 877.444.6777 or recreation.gov). There are fire rings, but you must bring your own wood. Campsites are in high demand from September through May, especially on weekends. If you can't find a site in the park, there is **free overflow camping** on Bureau of Land Management (BLM) land north of the park and Highway 62 at the intersection of Sunflower and Cascade Roads. It's a dry lakebed (occasionally it floods). You can also camp in the BLM's dispersed camping areas near the south entrance as long as you're at least 300 feet away from any roadway. You will not find restrooms or water at these locations, but at least you'll have a place to spend the night. You cannot sleep in your tent or vehicle in any of the park's parking areas.

Driving & Off-Roading

Park Boulevard connects West and North Entrances. It also traverses the most popular areas of the park, including Hidden Valley, Ryan, and Jumbo Rock Campgrounds, and provides access to Boy Scout Trail, Keys View Road, Ryan Mountain Trail, and Skull Rock. Split Rock and Hall of Horrors are also fun areas to look around. Park Boulevard (between the West Entrance and Pinto Basin Road intersection) and Keys View Road are where you'll find the densest collection of easily-accessible Joshua trees. If you're just driving through, this is where you want to go. In between the West and North Entrance Stations you'll find Indian

Queen Valley Road

Cove Road, which leads to an awesome secluded campground. Farther west along the park's northern boundary is Joshua Lane, which leads to another remote campground: Black Rock. To cross the park from north to south you can take Park Boulevard from either the North or West Entrance to Pinto Basin Road, which continues south to Cottonwood Springs Road. It isn't the most exciting stretch of pavement in the park, but Cottonwood Spring and Cholla Cactus Garden are worth investigating after you've thoroughly explored the park's northwestern corner.

The park also has several **dirt roads**. Geology Tour Road (18 miles) begins from Park Boulevard between Sheep Pass and Jumbo Rocks. Most vehicles can make it 5.4 miles from pavement to Squaw Tank (Marker 9 of 16) under good conditions (no mud). Beyond this point 4WD is recommended. Berdoo Canyon, Black Eagle Mine, Upper and Lower Covington Flat, Old Dale, and Pinkham Canyon–Thermal Canyon are high-clearance 4WD roads. Berdoo Canyon and Old Dale Roads are worth checking out, and a fun way to escape the traffic on Park Boulevard (if you like off-roading). If you have the right vehicle and some hesitations about heading into such a remote area, start with Geology Tour Road and see what you think. Queen Valley and Bighorn Pass Roads are excellent. They're unpaved but ordinary cars shouldn't have a problem. Stay on established roads (for your safety and to protect the environment). Off-road vehicles and all-terrain vehicles are not allowed. Carry emergency supplies and inquire about road conditions before heading out on them.

Arch Rock

Joshua Tree Hiking Trails (Distances are roundtrip)

	Name	Location (# on map)	Length	Difficulty Rating & Notes
Nature Trails (listed from NW to SW)	Hi-View	NW of Black Rock Camp (1)	1.3 miles	E – Loop, views of Mount San Gorgonio
	Indian Cove	West of Indian Cove Camp (2)	0.6 mile	E – Loop, explores history and ecology
	Oasis of Mara	Oasis Visitor Center (5)	0.5 mile	E – Accessible loop discusses oasis' history
	Barker Dam - ♿	Barker Dam Parking Area (7)	1.1 miles	E – Loop, visits early rancher's water tank
	Hidden Valley - ♿	Hidden Valley Picnic Area (8)	1.0 mile	E – Loop through a rock enclosed valley
	Cap Rock - ♿	Cap Rock Parking Area (9)	0.4 mile	E – Accessible loop, boulders and Joshua trees
	Ryan Ranch	Ryan Ranch Trailhead (9)	1.0 mile	E – Follows old ranch road to historic structures
	Keys View - ♿	Keys View Parking Area (11)	0.3 mile	E – Loop trail with expansive views
	Skull Rock - ♿	Skull Rock Parking Area (14)	1.7 miles	E – Boulder piles and the renowned Skull Rock
	Discovery	Skull Rock/Split Rock (14, 15)	0.7 mile	E – Connects Split Rock and Skull Rock
	Split Rock - ♿	Split Rock Parking Area (15)	2.0 miles	E – Fun loop, can take spur to Face Rock
	Arch Rock - ♿	Arch Rock Parking Area (16)	0.8 mile	E – Can also access from White Tank Camp
	Cholla Cactus Garden - ♿	20 miles north of Cottonwood Visitor Center (17)	0.3 mile	E – Loop through dense field of Cholla Cactus • Don't get too close to the cacti, they hurt
	Cottonwood Spring	Cottonwood Spring Camp (18)	0.1 mile	E – Short walk to palm oasis
	Bajada	Near south entrance (19)	0.3 mile	E – Loop explores plants of the Colorado Desert
Hiking Trails	Boy Scout - ♿	Indian Cove or Park Blvd (3, 6)	16.0 miles	S – Great spur trail to Willow Hole
	49 Palms Oasis	The end of Canyon Road (4)	3.0 miles	M – Desert oasis with stands of fan palms
	Lost Horse Mine - ♿	East of Keys View Rd (10)	4.0 miles	M – Visit a well-preserved defunct mining mill
	Ryan Mountain - ♿	Ryan Mtn Parking Area or Sheep Pass Camp (12)	3.0 miles	S – Leads to 5,461-ft summit with 360° views of Eagle Mountains and Salton Sea
	Pine City	Desert Queen Mine Road (13)	4.0 miles	E – Leads to an old mining site
	Lost Palms Oasis - ♿	Cottonwood Spring Camp (18)	7.5 miles	S – Oasis, canyon, scrambling, and palm stands
	Mastodon Peak - ♿	Cottonwood Spring Camp (18)	3.0 miles	S – Summit provides views of Salton Sea

Difficulty Ratings: E = Easy, M = Moderate, S = Strenuous

Hiking

You don't have to lug a heavy pack and gallons of water to enjoy the most beautiful vistas and rock formations this desert wilderness has to offer. The best way to discover the wonders of Joshua Tree is on foot, and it's easy thanks to a whole bunch of short, self-guided nature trails. Or simply pull over (completely off the road) and walk among the Joshua trees and interesting rock formations. The park's most interesting area, the entire northern region centered around Queen Mountain, is hemmed in by Park Boulevard. It's outstanding. Spend your time here and you will not leave disappointed. Check the hiking table on the left for a list of the park's Nature Trails and where to find them.

With so many great spots to explore, it's difficult to pick a favorite. It's easier to choose a trail based on what you're looking for. If you want a thigh-burning workout, head up Ryan Mountain or Mastodon Peak. If you want to look at some peculiar rocks, stop at Hall of Horrors (near the road to Key's Ranch), Cap Rock, Skull Rock, Split Rock, or Arch Rock. Or camp at Indian Cove, Hidden Valley, Jumbo Rocks, Belle, or White Tank. Each of those campgrounds is surrounded by rocky oddities.

Barker Dam explores the difficulties of desert life. This short loop passes an old cattle rancher's water tank. **Keys View** is a popular destination for sunsets and sweeping panoramic views. On a clear day you can see as far as the Salton Sea, San Andreas Fault, and Mexico's Signal Mountain. Many visitors scramble up the mountain to the north to gain a different perspective or perhaps to put some space between themselves and the carousel of cars at the lookout. You'll even find a Joshua tree or two to place in frame for a sunset photo. Key's View is nice, but I prefer exploring Park Boulevard for interesting Joshua Tree silhouettes. The 4-mile (roundtrip) **Lost Horse Mine Trail** provides a glimpse into Joshua Tree's era of mining, visiting the site of a ten-stamp mill where rock was crushed to extract its minerals. **Contact Mine Trail**, located along Park Boulevard near the North Entrance Station, ventures to another historic mining operation. It's moderately difficult and about four miles roundtrip from the parking area. And then there's **Boy Scout Trail**. From its northern trailhead at Indian Cove, things start slow but the trail quickly increases in intensity and density of spectacular rock formations. The true gem is the spur to Willow Hole and Wonderland of Rocks (closest to Boy Scout's southern trailhead). Hikers' most common problems are dehydration and getting lost. Carry plenty of water and pay attention to your route. Washes and animal paths can make route-finding difficult.

49 Palm Oasis

Backpacking

Tired of busy campgrounds? Looking for a night of the purest peace and quiet this side of the Sierra Nevada? Try backpacking in Joshua Tree's 585,000 acres of wilderness. If you plan on spending the night in the backcountry, be sure to register at one of 13 backcountry registration boards (marked with a **B** on the map). Failure to register can result in your vehicle being towed and/or cited. Backpackers must camp outside day-use areas, at least one mile from any road, and 500 feet from any trail. One of the best areas to backpack is **Big Pine**, accessed via Boy Scout Trail, which sets you up to complete as much of Boy Scout Trail (16+ miles roundtrip) as you care to do, as well as venturing into Willow Hole (another spur trail, which you should check out). You'll also find 35 miles (one-way) of **California Riding and Hiking Trail**, which runs parallel to Park Boulevard, beginning at Black Rock Canyon and terminating near the North Entrance. The environment is almost apocalyptic with sparse forests and random rubble piles, and it might feel that way when you're out there because the main difficulty is packing enough water. Park policy dictates that all water within the park boundary is reserved for wildlife. You will have to carry (or cache) enough water for the duration of your trip.

Rock Climbing

Joshua Tree is a world-class rock climbing destination, attracting thousands of climbers each year. With more than 400 climbing formations and 8,000 routes, there's something for everyone. If you are an experienced climber visiting the park for the first time you may want to pick up a comprehensive rock climbing guidebook (available at the visitor center). If you'd rather receive your information straight from the horse's mouth, there are always experienced climbers milling about the campgrounds and rock formations or there are plenty of outfitters looking to help climbers

Distant view from Geology Tour Road

of all experience levels. It's definitely a good idea for beginners to join a rock climbing course. Cliffhanger Guides (760.401.5033, cliffhangerguides.com), Mojave Guides (760.820.2806, mojaveguides.com), The Climbing Life Guides - Joshua Tree (760.780.8868, theclimbinglifeguides.com), Stone Adventures (760.364.0547, stone-adventures.com), Joshua Tree Rock Climbing School (760.366.4745, joshuatreerockclimbing.com), Joshua Tree Guides (joshuatreeguides.com), Vertical Adventures (800.514.8785, vertical-adventures.com), and Joshua Tree's Uprising Adventure Guides (888.254.6266, joshuatreeuprising.com) offer courses for climbers of all abilities. A full day costs about $200 per person. Private instruction is available with rates depending on group size. Even if you don't give rock climbing a go, it's always fun to watch them (as well as the slackliners who frequent the park). Hidden Valley is one of the best areas to see climbers in action.

Horseback Riding

Horseback riding is another excellent way to experience the park, thanks to 253 miles of designated equestrian trails. Ryan and Black Campgrounds have designated areas for horses and their riders. Grazing is not permitted within the park. Water is going to be the limiting factor for anything you plan to do with your horse(s) since stock animals are not permitted to use natural or manmade water sources within the park. Most rides explore Black Rock Canyon or the area around the park's West Entrance. You can put the planning into someone else's hands. Knob Hill Ranch (knobhillranch.com) offers vacation packages from their private ranch less than two miles from Black Rock Canyon. Cottonwood Canyon Ranch (760.447.1014, guidedtrailrides.net), Panorama Stables (886.922.5602, panoramastables.com), Coyote Ridge

Stables (760.799.5182, coyoteridgestables.com), and Crazy Horse Ranch (760.831.6450, crazyhorseranch.biz) are all located in the Morongo Valley, not far from the park's West Entrance. Each one offers guided rides and overnight accommodations. And just south of Palm Springs, Smoke Tree Stables (760.327.1372, smoketreestables.com) offers group and private rides into nearby canyons.

Biking

Biking is permitted on all park roads; unpaved and 4WD roads' limited traffic makes them ideal for mountain bikers (if you have a support vehicle following along). Like with most activities here, water is going to be your limitation. The most reasonable biking routes are to pedal Geology Tour Road (although you'll be cranking coming back out of Pleasant Valley) or to explore the Desert Queen Mine/Queen Valley Roads area (and its associated hiking trails. Both areas are open to motorists and are quite popular during peak season. Three sites are reserved for bicyclists at Ryan Campground for $5/night.

Stargazing

If you come from a busy metropolitan area like Los Angeles, there's nothing quite like a clear night sky. Bring a set of binoculars and tour the Milky Way on your own. You can also join one of the park's free Night Sky Programs, which are held regularly between October and May. A current schedule can be found at the park website, campground bulletin boards, entrance stations, and visitor centers. If you can find a way to survive the day-time heat, late summer is a great time to observe the Milky Way on a clear moonless night and the Perseid meteor shower passes through the skies every August.

Visitor Centers

Oasis (8:30am to 5pm), Joshua Tree (7:30am to 5pm), and Cottonwood (8:30am to 4pm) Visitor Centers are open all year. Black Rock Nature Center is open daily from October to May, 8am to 4pm, except on Fridays (noon to 8pm). Each site features exhibits, a bookstore, and restrooms.

Ranger Programs & For Kids

Guests can tour historic Keys Ranch, where Bill and Frances Keys thrived in the desert for nearly 60 years. The ranch is located at the end of a short spur road off Park Boulevard just east of Hidden Valley. Admission is restricted to guided walking tours. They are typically offered from October through May. Tours generally last 90 minutes and require walking a half-mile. Group size is limited to 25 people. Cost is $10 per person (ages 12 and over), $5 for children (ages 6–11), and children under 6 are free. Reservations are required and can be made at (877) 444-6777 or recreation.gov up to two months in advance. The tour is popular, so reserve your tickets early.

Throughout the year, park rangers also offer a variety of walks, talks, and evening programs. Tours range from a simple 15-minute talk at Keys View to a 2.5-hour hike to Mastodon Peak. Check online for a current schedule of events and join as many as you can.

The Desert Institute at Joshua Tree National Park (760.367.5525, joshuatree.org/desert-institute) provides educational programs. Reasonably priced courses in natural science, survival skills, arts are offered regularly. Courses do not cater to children.

Children are welcome to participate in the park's Junior Ranger Program. To get started, pick up a free activity booklet from any visitor center or entrance station. Complete the activities and return to a visitor center to earn an official Joshua Tree National Park Junior Ranger badge. Joshua Tree also participates in the Junior Paleontologist, Junior Ranger Night Explorer, and Wilderness Explorer Programs.

Flora & Fauna
More than 800 species of plants, including the park's namesake, can be found here. It's a collection so diverse and unique that park supporters originally suggested the area be called "Desert Plants National Park." There's also exceptional animal diversity. More than 50 species of mammals and 250 species of birds have been documented. Animals are commonly seen near sources of water like fan palm oases, Barker Dam, or Smith Water Canyon. You probably would love to spot a desert tortoise, but you'll need luck on your side. They spend about 90% of their life underground.

When flowers are in bloom, Joshua Tree becomes a colorful paradise. Blooms vary from year-to-year due to seasonal differences in rainfall and temperature, but they typically begin in the low elevations around February, lasting until June in the higher elevations. If you're looking for flowers, ask a ranger.

Pets & Accessibility
Pets are allowed in the park but must be kept on a leash (less than six feet). They are prohibited from all hiking trails and cannot be more than 100 feet from a road, picnic area, or campground. I love pets as much

Turn that frown upside down

as the next person, but you really don't want to bring them along on your trip to Joshua Tree. You'll be too limited in what you can do, and you absolutely do not want to leave your best friend locked in your car in the afternoon desert heat. If your pet must come along, drop him or her off at a place like Joshua Tree Pet Resort (760.219.9801, jtpetresort.com) in Joshua Tree. It's the best thing for you and your pet.

All visitor centers are accessible to individuals in wheelchairs. Lower Keys View Overlook, Bajada, Cap Rock, and Oasis of Mara Nature Trails are fully accessible. There's a designated wheelchair friendly campsite at Jumbo Rocks and Black Rock Campgrounds.

Weather
Remember you're visiting a desert. Days are usually hot, dry, and clear (unless smog from Los Angeles and the coast cause a problem). Summers are hot, over 100°F during the day and usually above 70°F through the night. Spring and fall bring perfect weather with highs around 85°F and lows averaging about 50°F.

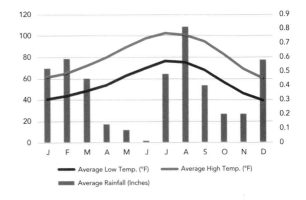
— Average Low Temp. (°F)   — Average High Temp. (°F)
— Average Rainfall (Inches)

Wonderland of Rocks

Tips & Recommendations

Joshua Tree visitation has more than doubled since 2013. It's busy from October through May, peaking in March and April. Holidays and weekends are particularly busy. If you can plan a mid-week trip, it's a good idea. But every campsite is occupied pretty much every day from October through May.

You can find some sense of solitude by reaching a trailhead early in the morning and taking a long hike, but you'll miss out on a lot of Joshua Tree's charm with that approach. All the rock/Joshua tree areas are so uniquely weird. You'll want to make many stops to experience the wide range of whacky rock formations and peculiar Joshua trees. I'd suggest sampling many areas for your first pass through Joshua Tree, and then return to explore the tastiest samples in depth.

Plan to spend a few nights. There's a pretty good chance this is one of those parks that gets in your system and you'll want to keep coming back for more.

Joshua Tree is desert country, and you must be prepared for the heat. Behave like the wildlife, being active early/late in the day. Pack plenty of water and know where to get more should you run out. The only places with water are Cottonwood, Black Rock, Indian Cove Ranger Station, West Entrance Station, and Oasis Visitor Center. Listen to your body, give it what it wants, and do not overexert yourself.

You'll find that most of the easily-accessible Joshua Trees are found between the intersection of Pinto Basin Road and Park Boulevard and the Joshua Tree (West) Entrance Station. North of this region is where you'll find a high density of wild rock formations. If your time is limited, this is where you'll want to spend it.

The Joshua Tree (West) Entrance is particularly popular. If you're visiting during peak season, think about using the Twentynine Palms (North) Entrance Station. Unless you're coming to hike from Cottonwood Spring, skip the south entrance. Eeven though it is convenient and less busy, it's less scenic.

If you like history, colorful characters, or beautiful desert scenery, try to get reservations (recreation.gov, $10/adult) for a ranger-led tour of Key's Ranch.

Even if it is hot, get out of your car and explore some of the rock features. So many people stop to take a picture of themselves in front of Skull Rock but most of the fun is had with the rocks surrounding it.

Joshua Tree has some of the best campgrounds in the entire national park system. The park also boasts reliably clear skies with limited light pollution. Camping at Joshua Tree is most highly recommended!

It's a good idea to reserve your sites early. You can wing it and hope to score one of the few-dozen first-come, first-served sites because, even if you strike out, dispersed camping is available on BLM land north and south of the park. Still, it's so much better to camp within the park's boundaries.

With that said, we know, camping isn't for everyone. There are plenty of lodging accommodations in gateway communities, and they're close enough to get into the park for sunrise (if you want). Playing around with Joshua tree silhouettes at dawn and dusk is a lot of fun. So much that you don't need a jaw-dropping display in the sky to make catching sunrise or sunset worth the effort (although, more often than not the sky is spectacular too). Give it a try. I bet you'll like it. Plus, you'll get a head start on whatever other activities you planned to do in the park.

Cholla Cactus Garden is widely panned as a delightful sunset/sunrise location. It is, but the magic happens when the sun is above the surrounding mountains. Cholla cactus glow in the low-angled direct sunlight. It's a great (morning/evening) bonus, giving you time to catch the actual sunrise/sunset up the road in the Joshua tree forests and the glowing cholla cacti back-to-back. I prefer sunset at Cholla Cactus Garden. The western view is more interesting. But they're both good. Plenty of cholla to go around.

Boy Scout Trail is great any way you do it, but there are a few junctions to know about. Starting from the southern trailhead, hike north and take the spur to Willow Hole, which leads into Wonderland of Rocks. If the name isn't obvious enough, you're in for a real treat. You'll find a lot of cool rocks starting from the north end too, but the beginning is a bit dull and it's more strenuous hiking. But starting from the north trailhead gets you to the spur to Big Pine (a popular backpacking area) quicker. Both are worth doing as day hikes. If you only have time for one, head to Wonderland of Rocks. You could hike the entire trail as an out-and-back, including Willow Hole, but you're talking a 20+-mile hike. The best bet would be to cache a car at the north trailhead (or arrange a ride). If you can't, stick to breaking it into two out-and-back hikes. You'll enjoy the trip to Indian Cove, too.

Indian Cove is fantastic, and if you drive over to the picnic area on the east end, you'll find Rattlesnake Canyon, something a little different than other Joshua Tree trails. It's unmarked. You choose where you go, and it's a full-on rock scramble. Note that it is not easy going. If you're uncomfortable, turn back. But, if you follow the water, you can find some interesting things.

If you're planning something big and need to cache water, it's best to hide your water off trail near a recognizable feature (or set a GPS waypoint). Occasionally hikers who simply don't know any better (or worse, those who do) either drink from your water stash or take them to quench their thirst. Also, rodents may chew through your containers, wasting precious water. Some people bury their cache. Others store it inside 5-gallon buckets.

Sunset off Desert Queen Mine Road

There are no services within the park. No food, gas, water, or lodging. And cell service, regardless of provider, is not available in most areas. Plan accordingly.

Easy Hikes: Hidden Valley (1 mile), Split Rock (2), Arch Rock (0.8), Skull Rock (1.7), Keys View (0.3), Cap Rock (0.4), Cholla Cactus Garden (0.3), Barker Dam (1.1)
Moderate Hikes: Lost Palms Oasis (7.5 miles), Lost Horse Mine (4)
Strenuous Hikes: Boy Scout Trail (16 miles), Ryan Mountain (3), Mastodon Peak (3)
Family Activities: Play on the rocks (Jumbo Rocks), Become Junior Rangers, go off-roading
History Enthusiasts: Key's Ranch Ranger Tour, Barker Dam, Ryan Ranch, Contact Mine
Sunrise/Sunset Spots: Find a funky Joshua Tree you can put on the open horizon and you have a good sunrise/sunset spot. There are many. I like to be just east of Skull Rock (all the way down to Pinto Basin Road) for sunrise. There are a ton of good sunset locations along Park Boulevard past Hidden Valley or along Desert Queen Mine Road.

Beyond the Park...

Dining
Pappy & Harriet's • (760) 365-5956
53688 Pioneertown Rd, Pioneertown
pappyandharriets.com

Joshua Tree Brewery • (760) 974-9274
6393 Sunset Rd, Joshua Tree
joshuatreebrewery.com

2 Guys Pies Brick Oven Pizzeria
56969 Yucca Trail A, Yucca Valley
2guyspies.com • (760) 418-5075

La Copine • (760) 289-8537
848 Old Woman Springs Rd, YV
lacopinekitchen.com

Grocery Stores
Vons • (760) 365-8998
57590 CA-62, Yucca Valley

Walmart • (760) 365-7750
58501 CA-62, Yucca Valley

Lodging & Camping
Sacred Sands • (760) 974-6008
63155 Quail Springs Rd, Joshua Tree
sacredsands.com

Joshua Tree Inn (760) 366-1188
61259 CA-62 • joshuatreeinn.com

Campbell House • (760) 367-3238
74744 Joe Davis Dr, Twentynine Palms
campbellhouse29palms.com

Joshua Tree Lake RV
2601 Sunfair Rd, JT • (760) 366-1213
joshuatreelake.com

Sportsman's Club • (760) 366-2915
6225 Sunburst St, Joshua Tree
jtsportsmansclub.com

Joshua Tree KOA
70405 Dillon Rd, Desert Hot Springs
koa.com • (760) 251-6555

Festivals
Coachella • April
coachells.com • Indio

Attractions
World Famous Crochet Museum
One of those times when "world famous" isn't an exaggeration!
61855 CA-62, Joshua Tree
sharielf.com • (760) 660-5672

Smith's Ranch Drive-In Theater
4584 Adobe Rd, Twentynine Palms
29drive-in.com • (760) 367-7713

Indian Canyons • (760) 323-6018
38520 S Palm Canyon Dr, Palm Springs
indian-canyons.com

Mecca Hills Wilderness
Great hiking (Painted Canyon, Ladder Canyon) near the park's south entrance

Salton Sea State Recreation Area
100225 State Park Rd, Mecca
parks.ca.gov • (760) 393-3059

Imperial Sand Dunes • blm.gov
Dunes near the U.S.–Mexico border (Star Wars setting)

Mojave Trail NM • blm.gov
North of park; hunting, OHV, and hiking (Amboy Crater)

Santa Rosa & San Jacinto Mtns
BLM and U.S. Forest Service land, 10,000-ft mountains

Salton Sea State Recreation Area
South of park, lake with an interesting history • parks.ca.gov

Anza-Borrego Desert State Park
Wild rocks west of Salton Sea
parks.ca.gov

Channel Islands

Yum...anchovies!

Phone: (805) 658-5730
Website: nps.gov/chis

Established: March 5, 1980
April 26, 1938 (Nat'l Monument)
Size: 249,354 Acres
Annual Visitors: 400,000
Peak Season: March–October

Activities: Paddling, Swimming,
Snorkeling, Sailing, SCUBA Diving,
Hiking, Backpacking

Camping* ($15/night): All Islands
Backcountry Camping*: Santa
Cruz and Santa Rosa with Permit

Park Hours: Open every day with
regularly scheduled ferry service
Entrance Fee: None

*Reservations required
(877.444.6777, recreation.gov)

Off the coast of California, less than 100 miles from 18 million people living in the Greater Los Angeles Area, is a group of eight magical islands. Compared to their surroundings, the Channel Islands are untouched wilderness, even after continuous inhabitation for at least the last 8,000 years. Five of these islands—Santa Barbara, Anacapa, Santa Cruz, Santa Rosa, and San Miguel—comprise Channel Islands National Park. Rich history combined with incredibly diverse and often one-of-a-kind ecology make these volcanic islands stand alone in the national park portfolio as an untouched island oasis.

The park's geology is constantly changing thanks to relentless pounding of water on rock. However, the most startling change to the islands wasn't caused by water's erosive powers, but by its absence. More than 13,000 years ago, a blink of an eye in geologic terms, the four northern islands were one super-island. North America was in the middle of the last great Ice Age when water level was much lower. Climatic changes caused the glaciers to recede. As water levels rose the lowest valleys flooded, ultimately disconnecting the islands from one another.

Geologic changes drastically altered the islands' ecology as well. Approximately 20,000 years ago, mammoths swam to the super-island, likely searching for vegetation whose scent was carried by the prevailing westward winds. As their population grew, resources became depleted. Natural selection favored smaller mammoths capable of surviving on less food. The woolly beasts lived on the islands for about 10,000 years before becoming extinct. Evidence of mammoths—once the most widely spread mammal—has been found on four continents: five-million-year-old fossils in northern Africa, an engraving on a tusk found in a rock shelter in southwestern France, the preserved carcass of a baby male frozen in Siberia's permafrost, more than 100 mammoth remains at the bottom of a sinkhole in Hot Springs, SD. When similar remains were discovered on Santa Rosa Island in 1873, scientists believed elephants must have inhabited these islands. More than 100 years later, additional fossils helped conclude they were in fact pygmy mammoths, about one-tenth the size of a typical Columbian mammoth. They measured between 4.5- and 7-feet tall, weighing about one ton. A Colombian mammoth measured up to 14-feet tall and weighed as much as ten tons. Human fossils have also been found on the Channel Islands. At Arlington Springs, on Santa Rosa Island, scientists discovered human remains dating back more than 13,000 years. This find has become known as Arlington Man, and it is among North America's oldest remains.

The islands may feel wild, but humans have had considerable effect. Early Chumash people relied on the sea for food and tools, traveling between the islands and mainland in canoes, called tomols, hollowed out from redwood trees that drifted down the coast. The Chumash were present when Juan Rodriguez Cabrillo reached San Miguel Island in 1542. Cabrillo and his fellow explorers introduced disease and overhunted sea life; by the 1820s, the remaining Chumash population moved to the mainland.

Over the course of the next century, the Channel Islands were home to Mexican prisoners, ambitious ranchers, and hermit fishermen. In 1864, the Civil War increased demand for wool, so more than 24,000 sheep grazed the hills of Santa Cruz. During prohibition, Raymond "Frenchy" LeDreau stored caches of liquor in Anacapa's caves. When Santa Cruz became part of a new National Monument, Frenchy was allowed to remain on the island as its caretaker. In 1956, at the age of 80, he left after suffering severe injuries due to a fall. In 1969, more than 100,000 barrels of crude oil spilled into the channel during the Santa Barbara oil spill, at the time the largest oil spill in United States waters. The National Park Service and Nature Conservancy have worked since to preserve this picturesque landscape and its unique ecosystem for the hundreds of thousands of visitors that arrive each year.

Prisoner's Harbor (Santa Cruz)

When to Go
The park is open every day. However, weather can be fickle. Idyllic one day. Dreary the next. High winds and rough seas can prevent scheduled transportation services from reaching the islands, but it's a rare occasion. If your plans are altered, there's much to do in the Greater Los Angeles area. Gray whales migrate through the coastal waters from late December through March. Blue and humpback whales regularly feed between July and September (but I spotted humpback in early March). With average rainfall, wildflowers peak around late winter/ early spring. Type and abundance of flowers vary from island-to-island, so call the park while making your plans if you're interested. Ocean conditions for SCUBA, snorkel, swimming, and kayaking are usually best from summer through fall. Most visitors arrive between June and August, but there's no bad time to visit the Channel Islands.

Airports
Los Angeles International (LAX) is located 70 miles southeast of park headquarters. Santa Barbara (SBA), Camarillo (CMA), and Oxnard (OXR) airports are closer, smaller alternatives.

Mainland Transportation
Amtrak (800.872.7245, amtrak.com), Metrolink (800.371.5465, metrolinktrains.com), Greyhound (800.231.2222, greyhound.com), Gold Coast Transit (805.487.4222, goldcoasttransit.org), Santa Barbara Metropolitan Transit District (805.963.3366, sbmtd. gov), and Ventura County Transportation Commission (800.438.1112, goventura.org) provide access to the park's mainland visitor centers.

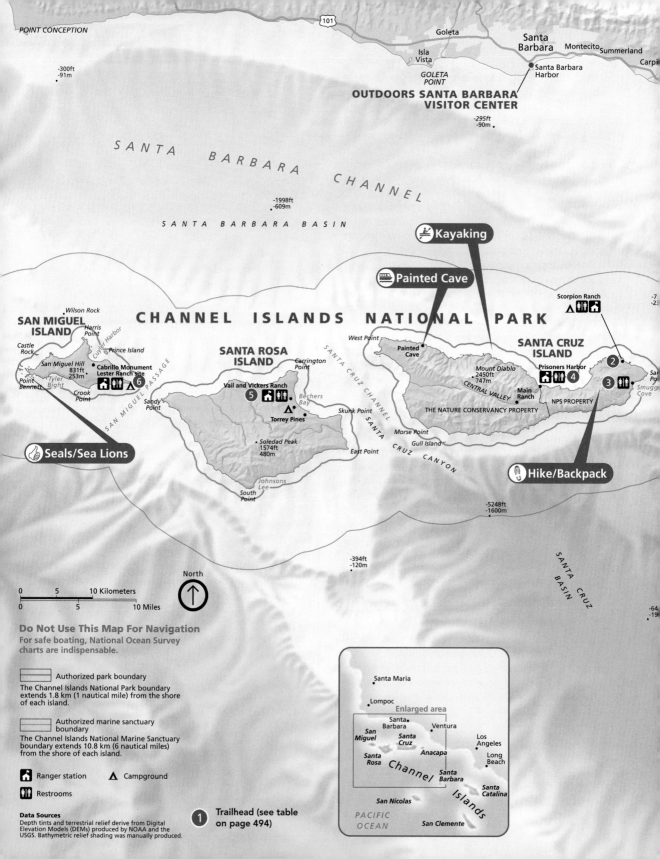

POINT CONCEPTION

101

Goleta

Isla
Vista

Santa
Barbara

Montecito Summerland

Carpi

GOLETA
POINT

Santa Barbara
Harbor

**OUTDOORS SANTA BARBARA
VISITOR CENTER**

-300ft
-91m

-295ft
-90m

S A N T A   B A R B A R A   C H A N N E L

-1998ft
-609m

S A N T A   B A R B A R A   B A S I N

Kayaking

Painted Cave

Scorpion Ranch

C H A N N E L   I S L A N D S   N A T I O N A L   P A R K

Wilson Rock

**SAN MIGUEL
ISLAND**

Harris
Point

Cuyler Harbor

West Point

Painted
Cave

**SANTA CRUZ
ISLAND**

Castle
Rock

Prince Island

Mount Diablo
2450ft
747m

2

Prisoners Harbor

San
Po

San Miguel Hill
831ft
253m

Cabrillo Monument
Lester Ranch site

**SANTA ROSA
ISLAND**

Carrington
Point

CENTRAL VALLEY

Main
Ranch

4

3

Smugg
Cove

Point
Bennett

Tyler
Bight

6

Vail and Vickers Ranch

NPS PROPERTY

Crook Point

5

THE NATURE CONSERVANCY PROPERTY

Sandy
Point

Torrey Pines

Bechers
Bay

Skunk Point

Morse Point

Seals/Sea Lions

Soledad Peak
1574ft
480m

East Point

Gull Island

Hike/Backpack

-5248ft
-1600m

Johnsons
Lee

South
Point

-394ft
-120m

S A N T A   C R U Z   B A S I N

-64
-19

North

0   5   10 Kilometers
0   5   10 Miles

Do Not Use This Map For Navigation
For safe boating, National Ocean Survey
charts are indispensable.

Enlarged area

Santa Maria

Lompoc

Santa
Barbara

Ventura

Authorized park boundary
The Channel Islands National Park boundary
extends 1.8 km (1 nautical mile) from the shore
of each island.

San
Miguel

Santa
Cruz

Anacapa

Los
Angeles

Long
Beach

Authorized marine sanctuary
boundary
The Channel Islands National Marine Sanctuary
boundary extends 10.8 km (6 nautical miles)
from the shore of each island.

Santa
Rosa

Santa
Barbara

Santa
Catalina

Ranger station   ▲ Campground

San Nicolas

Restrooms

1 Trailhead (see table
on page 494)

San Clemente

PACIFIC
OCEAN

Data Sources
Depth tints and terrestrial relief derive from Digital
Elevation Models (DEMs) produced by NOAA and the
USGS. Bathymetric relief shading was manually produced.

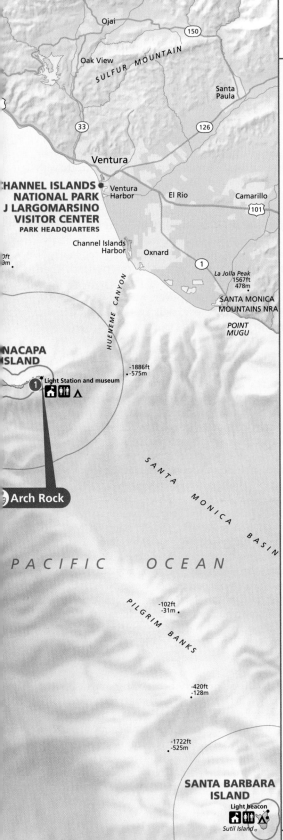

Directions

Channel Islands is located in the Pacific Ocean, off the coast of California. Most island visitors arrive via ferry with Island Packers (island-packers.com) or plane with Channel Islands Aviation (flycia.com). Most guests also visit one of the mainland visitor centers located in Santa Barbara or Ventura.

To Robert J. Lagomarsino Visitor Center (1901 Spinnaker Dr, Ventura)/Island Packers: Traveling south on US-101 toward Ventura, take Exit 68 toward Seward Ave. Turn left at Harbor Blvd. After two miles, turn right at Spinnaker Drive. Traveling north on US-101 toward Ventura, take Exit 64 for Victoria Ave. Turn left at Victoria Ave. Take the second right onto Olivas Park Drive, which turns into Spinnaker Drive. Spinnaker Drive passes Island Packers (look for the sign) and terminates at the visitor center. Free parking is available at Island Packers and the beach parking lot.

Outdoors Santa Barbara Visitor Center (113 Harbor Way, 4th Floor, 90-minute free parking at harbor parking lot): Traveling south on US-101 toward Santa Barbara, take Exit 97 for Castillo St toward Harbor. Turn right at Castillo St, and then make a right at Shoreline Dr. Turn left at Harbor Way.

Traveling north, take US-101 Exit 96B for Garden St. Turn left at Garden St, and then make a right at Cabrillo Blvd. Continue onto Shoreline Drive, and then turn left at Harbor Way.

Island Transportation

Concessioners provide boat and plane transportation to the islands. No transportation is available once you're there; all areas must be accessed by foot or kayak. **Island Packers** (805.642.1393, island-packers.com) provides year-round transportation to the Channel Islands, and specialized whale watching and harbor tours. Ferries service Santa Cruz ($63/adult for daytrip, $84/adult for camping, Scorpion Anchorage and/or Prisoners Harbor, year-round), Anacapa ($63, $84, year-round), Santa Barbara (closed when we went to print), San Miguel ($115, $168, July–October), and Santa Rosa ($85, $120, March–November) are seasonal. Santa Cruz's Scorpion Anchorage reopened in 2020. Check their website for special island trips to Nature Conservancy areas ($83–97/adult). Kayak transportation costs an additional $20 for all boats 13 feet or less and $28 for boats over 13 feet. They also offer seasonal whale/wildlife watching and birding cruises. Island Packers' Main Office is located at 1691 Spinnaker Drive, Suite 105B, just a short walk from Robert J. Lagomarsino Visitor Center.

Channel Islands Aviation (805.987.1301, flycia.com) provides year-round air transportation to Santa Rosa (25-minute flight) and San Miguel (40-minute flight) Islands. Private charter half-day (3 hours on the island) and deluxe (4.5 hours) trips, starting at $1,200 plus tax (up to 8 passengers). They also offer transportation for campers (up to 7 passengers). Campsites are located a short distance from the airstrip and must be reserved prior to arrival via recreation.gov.

Fluke!

The Islands

Some 13,000 years ago the four northern Channel Islands were united as a super-island. Glaciers from the last Ice Age receded and water levels began to rise, forming multiple distinct islands. Today, Channel Islands National Park consists of five of the eight Channel Islands: San Miguel, Santa Rosa, Santa Cruz, Anacapa, and Santa Barbara. The official boundary extends one nautical mile beyond the islands' shorelines to protect marine environments, including giant kelp forests. A trip here requires more planning than your typical national park vacation because you can't drive your car right up to them. No services or lodgings are available. You will have to pack everything you require, including food and water, and all trash must be packed out. Short descriptions of each island (listed from west to east) and its activities are provided below:

San Miguel Island (9,325 acres): If you are willing to endure the wind and the weather, San Miguel is a fantastic place for hiking and camping. At Point Bennett, tens of thousands of seals and sea lions have been seen. These gatherings represent one of the largest congregations of wildlife in the world and they usually begin in spring. Sea lions typically give birth around June, when park rangers lead guided walks to Point Bennett. Caliche 'Forest' is another interesting site. Visiting San Miguel requires a permit. Hiking is only allowed on trails and in the company of a park ranger.

Santa Rosa Island (53,000 acres): Santa Rosa is the second largest island in California. It's located 40 nautical miles from Robert J. Lagomarsino Visitor Center, and is home to substantial archeological discoveries like the pygmy mammoth and Arlington Man. Today, you can reach it via ferry (islandpackers.com) or plane (flycia.com). There's a historic ranch, and a beautiful beach is about one mile from the pier.

Santa Cruz Island (62,000 acres): Santa Cruz is the largest island in California and the only one not entirely owned by the National Park Service, with 76% controlled by the Nature Conservancy. It's also the easiest

island to get to, making it ideal for a daytrip. A network of trails (and an old military road) connects popular destinations across the park's portion of the island. Beautiful beaches, clear water, and kelp forests make this a great island for swimming and snorkeling. Kayakers also frequent the island. Painted Cave, located on Nature Conservancy property in the northwest corner of the island, is a 0.25-mile long, 100-ft wide grotto with an entrance ceiling of 160 feet. The cave is particularly beautiful after rain when water falls over its entrance.

Anacapa Island (700 acres): Early Chumash people called it "Anyapakh," which translates to "mirage." Summer fog and afternoon heat tend to cloak or change the appearance of this volcanic island. Even more deceptive is the island itself. It's composed of three smaller islets descriptively named East, Middle, and West Anacapa. These islets are separate from one another and only reachable by boat.

Even though it's the second smallest of the park's islands, it's the most visited. Anacapa is just 12 miles from the mainland, and most visits consist of a walk around East Anacapa. Two miles of trails lead to Inspiration Point (with a few scenic spots along the way), a small campground, and a lighthouse. The trail also provides excellent views of the park's most notable feature, 40-foot-high Arch Rock. It's one of many sea caves and natural bridges carved into the island's towering sea cliffs by the Pacific Ocean.

Anacapa is home to the largest breeding colony of western gulls in the world. Chicks hatch in May and June before flying away late summer. So, the island is smelly from April through mid-August. West Anacapa also boasts the largest breeding colony of endangered California brown pelicans. Sea lions and harbor seals have been known to relax on the island's rocky shorelines. The area's nutrient rich water supports a diverse underwater ecosystem including forests of kelp. Divers, snorkelers, and kayakers all have the opportunity to see the massive seaweed.

Santa Barbara Island (639 acres): The smallest of the Channel Islands is a fair distance southeast of the others and 38 nautical miles from the mainland. This small variation in location results in a significant decrease in wind and rough water. Five miles of hiking trails span the entire island. It's a fantastic site for wildlife viewing, in particular birding. The park concessioner makes infrequent trips to Santa Barbara, resulting in overnight camping trips that last a minimum of 3 days (and you'll need to pack water for the entire stay).

Camping

Channel Islands offers one designated campground on each island. Anacapa's campground (7 sites) is a half-mile from the landing, including 157 steps. Santa Cruz's campground (31 sites) is a half-mile from Scorpion Anchorage. Santa Rosa's campground (15 sites) is 1.5 miles from the pier and a quarter mile from the airstrip. San Miguel's campground (9 sites) is a steep mile-long hike from the harbor. Santa Barbara's campground (10 sites) is a steep quarter-mile hike from the harbor. The only campgrounds with access to water are Water Canyon Campground on Santa Rosa and Scorpion Canyon Campground on Santa Cruz. You must bring enough water for the duration of your stay at all other islands. Keep food and drink in rodent-proof containers (food storage boxes are provided at campsites). Regardless of where you go, you must also carry all trash off the island. Campfires are not permitted. Pit toilets are available. Wind breaks are provided at outer island campgrounds (Santa Rosa and San Miguel). Camping costs $15 per night per site. Reservations are required. They can be made up to six months in advance at (877) 444-6777 or recreation.gov.

Backcountry camping is available year-round on Santa Cruz Island and seasonally on Santa Rosa Island. Del Norte campsite (4 sites), near Prisoners Harbor on Santa Cruz Island, is a 3.5-mile hike from Prisoners Harbor and 12 miles from Scorpion Anchorage. Reservations are required ($15/night) and can be made at (877) 444-6777 or recreation.gov. Backpackers can camp on Santa Rosa's 55-mile coastline from mid-August until the end of December. Reservations for beach camping ($10 per night per site) are required and must be made in advance at (877) 444-6777 or recreation.gov. It's a good idea to contact the park when making backpacking plans, especially if you're planning to camp along Santa Rosa's shoreline, as some areas are not open during the entire backpacking period and others wash out at high tide. While water is available at campgrounds on each of these islands, you'll need to carry enough water with you for the duration of your backpacking trip.

Remember you'll need to get to the islands. Make sure ferry or plane transportation is available while making your camping/backpacking reservations.

Paddling

Sea kayaking is a common activity at Channel Islands. Island Packers can transport your boat for $20–28, depending on its size. However, it's best (and safest) to join one of the park's authorized outfitters

Painted Cave (Santa Cruz)

to explore the islands while learning about its history from a knowledgeable guide. The Scorpion Beach area on East Santa Cruz Island is the most popular kayaking destination. Here you'll find plenty of sea caves and cliffs to paddle in and out of. Sand beaches and a campground are easily accessible. San Miguel and Santa Rosa Islands are exceptional destinations, but mainly for experienced and well-conditioned sea kayakers due to consistently difficult weather and sea conditions. For your first trip to the Channel Islands, join an outfitter. If you want more, start thinking about bringing your own kayaks or maybe joining an outfitter on a private paddling excursion. Santa Barbara Adventure Company (805.884.9283, sbadventureco.com), Channel Islands Adventure Company (805.884.9283, islandkayaking.com), Channel Islands Kayak Center (805.984.5995, cikayak.com), and Wild Blue Ocean Adventures (805.585.5060, gowildblue.com) are authorized outfitters who offer a multitude of kayak trips, including daytrips to Santa Cruz (and even a few boat tours). Rates cost right around $200–250 per adult single kayak, including transportation to the island.

Water Activities

Swimming, snorkeling, and SCUBA diving are popular pastimes best done on the islands of Santa Barbara, Anacapa, and Eastern Santa Cruz. These activities are allowed at San Miguel and Santa Rosa Islands, but should only be attempted by individuals who are properly trained, conditioned, and equipped. This recommendation is issued because of consistently strong winds and rough waters typical of these two islands. There are many fantastic swimming, snorkeling, and SCUBA diving locations around the other three. The water is clear with massive curtains of kelp. However, it's possible to see what's under the water without getting wet. In summer, you can rent snorkel gear at Scorpion Anchorage on Santa Cruz, which also

Islands have ridges

Channel Islands Hiking Trails (Distances are roundtrip)

	Name	Location (# on map)	Length	Difficulty Rating & Notes
	Inspiration Point - 👍	Anacapa Island (1)	1.5 miles	E – East Anacapa Landing Cove to exceptional views
	Lighthouse	Anacapa Island (1)	0.5 mile	E – Short stroll to lighthouse from landing
Santa Cruz	Historic Ranch	Scorpion Anchorage (2)	0.5 mile	E – Casual walk around historic Scorpion Ranch
	Cavern Point	Scorpion Anchorage (2)	2.0 miles	M – Shoreline walk • Whale-watching opportunities
	Potato Harbor	Scorpion Anchorage (2)	5.0 miles	M – Secluded Harbor • No beach access
	Scorpion Canyon - 👍	Scorpion Anchorage (2)	4.5 miles	M – Loop through steep canyon walls
	Smuggler's Cove - 👍	Scorpion Anchorage (2)	7.5 miles	S – Spur trails and beach along route
	Montañon Ridge	Scorpion Anchorage (2)	10.0 miles	S – Off-trail loop • Map reading skills required
	Smuggler's Canyon	Smuggler's Cove (3)	2.0 miles	S – Leads through native vegetation
	Yellowbanks	Smuggler's Cove (3)	3.0 miles	S – Off-trail, along shoreline to overlook • No Beach
	San Pedro Point	Smuggler's Cove (3)	4.0 miles	S – Go off-trail east of Smuggler's Cove
	Prisoner's Harbor	Prisoner's Harbor (4)	0.5 mile	E – Short walk in and around Prisoner's Harbor
	Pelican Bay	Prisoner's Harbor (4)	4.0 miles	M – Permit Required • Enters Nature Conservancy
	Del Norte Camp	Prisoner's Harbor (4)	7.0 miles	S – Hike east to a backcountry camp
	Navy Road–Del Norte	Prisoner's Harbor (4)	8.5 miles	S – Loop combines Navy Road and Del Norte Trail
	Chinese Harbor	Prisoner's Harbor (4)	15.5 miles	S – Leads to only accessible beach on isthmus
	China Pines	Prisoner's Harbor (4)	18.0 miles	S – Long trek to pine grove
	Mantañon Ridge	Prisoner's Harbor (4)	21.0 miles	S – Off-trail • Map reading skills required
	Water Canyon Beach - 👍	Santa Rosa (5)	3.0 miles	E – Access 2-mile-long white sand beach (near camp)
	East Point	Santa Rosa (5)	16.0 miles	S – You'll pass torrey pines and unrestricted beaches
	Torrey Pines	Santa Rosa (5)	5.0 miles	M – Fantastic views of torrey pines
	Lobo Canyon	Santa Rosa (5)	9.6 miles	S – Amazing canyon sculpted by wind and water
	Black Mountain	Santa Rosa (5)	8.0 miles	S – View other islands and mainland from here
	Cuyler Beach	San Miguel (6)	2.0 miles	E – 1.75-mile-long white sand beach
	Lester Ranch Site	San Miguel (6)	2.0 miles	M – Exceptional views and historic sites
	Caliche Forest - 👍	San Miguel (6)	5.0 miles	S – Only allowed with a park ranger
	Point Bennett - 👍	San Miguel (6)	16.0 miles	S – Only allowed with a park ranger
	Lester Point - 👍	San Miguel (6)	5.0 miles	S – Only allowed with a park ranger
	Arch Point	Santa Barbara (7)	1.0 mile	M – Wildflowers in late winter/spring
	Sea Lion Rookery	Santa Barbara (7)	2.0 miles	M – Expansive views and (possibly) sea lions
	Elephant Seal Cove	Santa Barbara (7)	2.5 miles	S – Maybe elephant seals, definitely steep cliffs
	Webster Point	Santa Barbara (7)	3.0 miles	S – Continue beyond Elephant Seal Cove
	Signal Peak	Santa Barbara (7)	2.5 miles	S – Highest point on the island

Difficulty Ratings: E = Easy, M = Moderate, S = Strenuous

happens to be a great place to snorkel. Channel Islands Adventure Company (805.884.9283, islandkayaking.com) runs a rental booth and offers guided snorkeling tours. If you'd rather not get wet, the park has a live ocean webcam situated within the landing cove near Anacapa Island. It can be fun to watch for a little while. Truth Aquatics (805.962.1127, truthaquatics.com) offers multi-day, live-aboard excursions featuring diving, kayaking, and stand-up paddleboarding.

Dolphins and whales are often spotted swimming the waters surrounding the Channel Islands. Island Packers (805.642.1393, islandpackers.com) offers seasonal whale watching and wildlife viewing boat trips. Condor Express (805.882.0088, condorexpress.com) has similar expeditions for $65–109 per adult. Private boaters are also welcome to explore the waters, but the Marine Mammal Protection Act stipulates boats must remain at least 100 yards away from whales (unless they approach you, then turn off your engine). And moorings are not available for private parties. You can only land on San Miguel Island when National Park Service personnel are present (e-mail the park to make sure and to schedule a guided hike). Private boaters have an easier time reaching the north shores of San Miguel and Santa Rosa, where you'll find the best surfing. Sail Channel Islands (805.750.7828, sailchannelislands.com) provides a sailing school and charter services (all-day, 4 passengers, $950). There's good tidepooling at Smuggler's Cove (Santa Cruz), Cuyler Harbor (San Miguel, no ranger escort needed), and Bechers Bay (Santa Rosa).

Hiking & Backpacking
Anacapa, the park's most frequented island, has limited hiking. A 1.5-mile trail leads to East Anacapa's Inspiration Point. You can extend this walk by adding the lighthouse, Pinniped Point, and Cathedral Cove as destinations along the way. In all, it's a little more than two miles. Middle and West Anacapa are closed to hiking. **Santa Cruz** is the number one destination for campers and hikers. Trails and roads connect Scorpion Beach, Smugglers Cove, Prisoners Harbor, and many places in between. Unguided hiking is not allowed in Nature Conservancy property. But, if you take a day-trip with Island Packers to Prisoner's Harbor, you'll have the opportunity to join them on a short, moderately difficult hike on Conservancy property. The seldom visited trails on San Miguel and Santa Rosa Islands are excellent too. **San Miguel's** Caliche Forest and Bennett Point are particularly nice, but make sure you're prepared for windy weather. Hiking on San Miguel is only allowed on trails and you must be accompanied by a park ranger.

Hiking Satna Cruz's Nature Conservancy land

Camping and backpacking are essentially synonymous. All campgrounds are primitive (water is only available on Santa Cruz and Santa Rosa). Pit toilets are available (bring toilet paper). Del Norte Campground on Santa Cruz Island is the only designated backcountry campground. Backpackers visiting Santa Rosa Island can camp along the beaches between mid-August and the end of December. The closest beach is nine miles from the boat/plane drop-off location.

Visitor Centers
Robert J. Lagomarsino Visitor Center (1901 Spinnaker Dr, Ventura) is open daily from 8:30am to 5pm. It is closed on Thanksgiving and Christmas. Exhibits, an introductory film, telescopes, and a bookstore are available. **Outdoors Santa Barbara Visitor Center** (113 Harbor Way, 4th Floor) provides information, exhibits, and excellent views of Santa Barbara. It is open daily from 10am to 5pm (except Wednesdays, August 1, Thanksgiving, Christmas, and New Year's).

Ranger Programs & For Kids
Park rangers offer several free public programs at Robert J. Lagomarsino Visitor Center. Rangers and concessioner naturalists provide island hikes each day there's island transportation service. Visit the park website or a visitor center for a current schedule of events.

Children with their sea legs will enjoy a boat cruise to the islands. Whale watching and wildlife tours are favorites, but even the standard trip to the island has its thrills, and there's always a chance of seeing dolphins or whales. Children are invited to participate in the park's Junior Ranger Program. Download the activity booklet from the park website or get a free copy at the visitor center or from the boat/plane concessioner offices. Complete the activities and receive an official Junior Ranger badge.

Loose seals!

Flora & Fauna

The Channel Islands are relatively remote and home to a tempestuous climate. These factors make for an extraordinarily unique ecosystem. Even the individual islands are dramatically different thanks to variations in size and location. At least 145 endemic species of plants and animals reside within park boundaries. Most of these species have developed slight adaptations after centuries of life on a remote island. Island deer mouse is the only native terrestrial mammal common to all the Channel Islands. There are only two other endemic terrestrial mammals found here: spotted skunk and Channel Islands fox. Channel Islands fox is the smallest North American canid, only growing to about the size of your average house cat. Visitors' favorite animals tend to be those that swim in the ocean. Sea lions, seals, whales (gray, blue, and humpback), and Risso's dolphins are frequently seen patrolling the waters. The islands are also important breeding grounds for many species of bird. California brown pelicans, Scripp's murrelets, tufted puffins, western gulls, Cassin's auklets, and rhinoceros auklets all breed within park boundaries. The Island scrub jay is also endemic. In 2006, bald eagles nested on the Channel Islands for the first time in more than 50 years.

Plant life is just as interesting and unique. Nearly 800 species of plants have been documented in the park, including 75 endemic plant species, 14 of which are listed as threatened or endangered. After nearly 150 years of ranching, the park has put forth great effort to aid in the recovery of these species.

Pets & Accessibility

To protect wildlife, pets are not allowed in the park.

Both visitor centers are fully accessible to individuals in wheelchairs. However, the islands themselves have extremely limited accessibility. Santa Rosa Island is accessible via air transportation with assistance.

Weather

Weather is moderated by the Pacific Ocean, keeping average high and low temperatures relatively consistent all year. Average highs only vary about 10°F from summer to winter. Another by-product of the Pacific Ocean is high humidity and fog. Humidity often reaches 100% at night and in the early morning. Annual rainfall is about 14 inches per year with 95% of that total occurring between November and April. Fog is most common in spring and summer, especially at San Miguel and Santa Rosa Islands. Wind is the one constant on the islands, blowing primarily from the north–northwest and tending to increase throughout the daylight hours. High-velocity Santa Ana winds averaging 20–25 mph with gusts exceeding 100 mph can occur in any month but are most common from September to December. Hikers, campers, and day-visitors should come prepared to deal with a variety of elements.

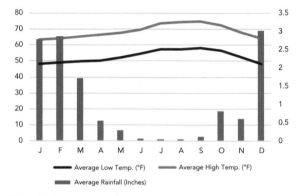

Average Low Temp. (°F) — Average High Temp. (°F) — Average Rainfall (Inches)

Tips & Recommendations

Plan ahead. It's possible to show up, get on a boat, and have a great time, but trips requiring transportation services are almost always better with a little planning. And, in the unlikely event your trip gets cancelled due to weather conditions, there's so much to do in the Los Angeles area, you won't be left on the mainland twiddling your thumbs.

Reservations are required for camping, and you'll want to make them early for summer. Also, be sure to make reservations for island transportation while reserving campsites.

Food storage boxes are provided at campsites. Use them or pack your food and scented items in a animal-proof container. Also pack a tent that can stand up to the wind.

Island Packers departs from two different harbors. Go to the one listed on your itinerary.

Even if you only have a half-day to spare, you can visit Channel Islands by ferry. Island Packers offers a few half-day express tours, one circumnavigates Anacapa Island, which may not sound that exciting, but it's pretty cool, and you'll almost certainly see marine life.

You can do much more with a full day, but chances are your choices will be determined by Island Packers schedule. You may find yourself choosing between the two primary destinations. Anacapa is known for seabirds, an arch, and a lighthouse. Santa Cruz offers more with sea caves, paddling, hiking, and snorkeling. You'll probably see marine life on either one.

Another option for a quick trip is to book a flight with Channel Islands Aviation.

With that said, Island Packers is great. Most staff in the tourism industry are the outgoing/gregarious type, and they're that, but they're also grounded and knowledgeable (from my experiences).

Daytrips are a wonderful way to see the islands but consider spending the night. Just know that water is only available at campgrounds on Santa Cruz and Santa Rosa. You'll need to carry everything you need with you (tent, water, food), and carry out all your waste.

Regardless of what time of year you go, watch for wildlife. Dolphins are common year-round. Gray whales are often seen in winter. Spring/Summer is blue and humpback whale season. Most of the year an island trip is the way to go (it's a wildlife and island adventure in one), but, if you're visiting in summer, put some thought into a dedicated whale watch tour. How often do you get a

The Visitor Center

reasonably good chance of seeing the world's largest mammal? Summer is also when seals and sea lions give birth. Summer is also the busiest time of year, so make reservations. Visitation is limited by transportation, so it isn't exactly like other popular parks.

Hiking: Santa Cruz, Santa Barbara
Solitude: All of them are pretty good in the solitude department considering what's back on the mainland, but San Miguel and Santa Rosa are particularly isolated (and backcountry campsites are available on Santa Cruz and Santa Rosa)
Family Activities: Become Junior Rangers, join Island Packers for a wildlife watching tour, Paddle the coast of Santa Cruz (exploring sea caves and sea life)
Guided Tours: Say Kayak, SCUBA, or Whale Watching
Rainy Day Activities: Suck it up and stick it out. It may not be ideal, but there are ephemeral waterfalls that show up with rain (like one right over the mouth of Painted Cave on Santa Cruz)
History Enthusiasts: Santa Rosa
Wildlife: Marine life is a big part of any trip to the Channel Islands (Island Packers will do their best to find some interesting sightings for you)

Beyond the Park...

Dining
Himalaya • (805) 643-0795
35 W Main St, Ventura
himalayacuisine.com

Lucky Thai • (805) 444-4563
1141 S Seaward Ave, Ventura
luckythaiventura.com

Sandwich Man • (805) 647-5374
1575 Los Angeles Ave, Ventura

Grocery Stores
Vons • (805) 984-0651
1291 S Victoria Ave, Oxnard

Costco • (805) 983-4200
2001 Ventura Blvd, Oxnard

Walmart • (805) 200-5224
2701 Saviers Rd, Oxnard

Lodging & Camping
Mason Beach Inn • (805) 962-3203
324 W Mason St, Santa Barbara
masonbeachinn.com

Hotel Californian • (805) 882-0100
36 State St, Santa Barbara
hotelcalifornian.com

McGrath State Beach • Oxnard
parks.ca.gov • (805) 968-1033

Hobson Beach Park
5210 PCH, Ventura
venturaparks.org • (805) 654-3951

Carpinteria State Beach
Camping, showers, beach
205 Palm Ave, Carpinteria
parks.ca.gov • (805) 684-2811

Festivals
Live Oak Fest • June
liveoakfest.org • San Luis Obispo

Aloha Beach Festival • Sept
alohabeachfestival.us • Ventura

Attractions
Los Padres National Forest
Camping and hiking (Santa Paula Punch Bowls)
fs.usda.gov

Nojoqui Falls Park
3250 Alisa Rd, Goleta
countyofsb.org • (805) 568-2460

Refugio State Beach
Nice family destination
Refugio Beach Rd, Goleta
parks.ca.gov

Griffith Park
Beautiful urban park
4730 Crystal Springs Dr, LA
laparks.org • (323) 913-4688

Carrizo Plain National Monument
Relict of what L.A. used to look like
17495 Soda Lake Rd, Santa Margarita • blm.gov

El Presidio de Santa Barbara SHP
Old Spanish military post
123 E Canon Perdido St, Santa Barbara • parks.ca.gov

Oceano Dunes SVRA
Off-roading playland
ohv.parks.ca.gov

San Buenaventura State Beach
parks.ca.gov

Pinnacles

Phone: (831) 389-4486
Website: nps.gov/pinn

Established: January 10, 2013
January 16, 1908 (Nat'l Monument)
Size: 26,606 Acres
Annual Visitors: 200,000
Peak Season: Weekends & Spring

Activities: Hiking, Rock Climbing, Birdwatching

Pinnacles Campground* (East Entrance): $35/night (standard), $45/night (w/ electric hookups), $119–129/night (tent cabins)
Backcountry Camping: Not Allowed

Park Hours
East Entrance: All day, every day
West Entrance: 7:30am–8pm
(Note: No roads cross the park)
Entrance Fee: $30/25/15
(car/motorcycle/individual)

*Reserve at recreation.gov or (877) 444-6777

Pinnacles, established on January 10, 2013, is a relatively new national park, but it's long been known to humans. Nomadic hunter-gatherers visited this area thousands of years ago. Modern-day nomads continue the tradition. Only they seek the wild, an escape from civilization.

The park's pinnacles, spires, crags, and cliffs were created through plate tectonics, earthquakes, and volcanic activity. Tens of millions of years ago, the Farallon Plate subducted beneath the North American Plate, the same process that created California's coastal range and caused volcanic activity. Scientists believe a 15-mile-long, 8,000-foot-tall volcano named Neenach existed 195 miles southeast of the present-day park. This volcanic field split at the fault between the Farallon and North American plates, and as the latter moved north at 3–6 centimeters per year it took volcanic rock with it, leaving Neenach formation behind. Millions of years of movement and erosion by heat, frost, water, and wind revealed pinnacles rock formations, originally poured from the earth at Neenach Volcano.

Humans began inhabiting this stark yet stunning landscape at least 2,000 years ago, when the Ohlone People visited for seasonal hunting and gathering. Spanish missionaries arrived in the 18th century, bringing with them new religion, education, and disease. Migrants seeking recreation in the form of picnicking, camping, and exploring, were the next wave, arriving in the late 1800s. Among them was Schuyler Hain, who followed his family from Michigan. He became the first postmaster of the Cook Post Office, located in Bear Valley. As John Muir was pushing for the preservation of Yosemite, Hain started

A California condor soars above a hiker in the High Peaks

When to Go

The East Entrance is open all day, every day. The park's West Entrance is open daily from 7:30am until 8pm. Spring is wonderful. Wildflowers accent the rocky red spires and weather is comfortable. The duration and intensity of annual blooms vary with rainfall and temperature, so check with the park before departing. Weekends and holidays are particularly busy. If you aren't fond of crowds, come on a weekday (summer through winter). Triple-digit heat isn't uncommon in summer—remember to pack plenty of water. In winter, a dusting of snow can create striking scenery, but caves can be flooded, negating a few of the more exciting attractions. Upper Bear Gulch Cave is typically only open in March and October.

Transportation & Airports

Free shuttles run between East Pinnacles Visitor Center and the Bear Gulch Area (East Side) during busy weekends and holidays. It's convenient, if not a necessity, as parking areas fill early in the morning during these times. Chances are you'll even find yourself waiting to board a shuttle bus. Expect long lines between 10am and 2pm.

Large airports are located in San Jose (SJC), San Francisco (SFO), Oakland (OAK), and Fresno (FAT), all within 150 miles of the park. Car rental is available at each destination.

to publicize Pinnacles and lead tours through its caves. Soon he was considered the unofficial caretaker of the area. One of his guests was a Stanford professor, who spoke of the region's beauty to a California congressman, who in turn reached out to Gifford Pinchot, the first chief of the U.S. Forest Service. By 1906, Pinnacles Forest Reserve was established. Quick by Congressional standards, Theodore Roosevelt made it a national monument in 1908.

The park was enlarged by Presidents Harding and Coolidge. The Civilian Conservation Corps (CCC) took up residence in the 1930s, improving roads and trails, building the dam at Bear Gulch Reservoir, even leading tours through the caves. The spirit of conservation continued, with 7,900 acres added under Bill Clinton's presidency. In 2003, Pinnacles was designated as a site for the nearly extinct California condor. On January 10, 2013, President Obama signed legislation making Pinnacles a national park and renaming Pinnacles Wilderness, Hain Wilderness, honoring the Michigan transplant affectionately known as "the father of Pinnacles."

Forged by violent volcanic eruptions. Shifted and buried by tectonic activity. Revealed and sculpted by millions of years of erosion. Hunted, explored, enjoyed, and preserved by humans. Today, you can walk among the High Peaks—land preserved by President Roosevelt—on trails created by the CCC. Enjoy their work by visiting Pinnacles and discovering caves that inspired Schuyler Hain to start a grassroots preservation movement. The park may be small, but it's packed with inspirational beauty.

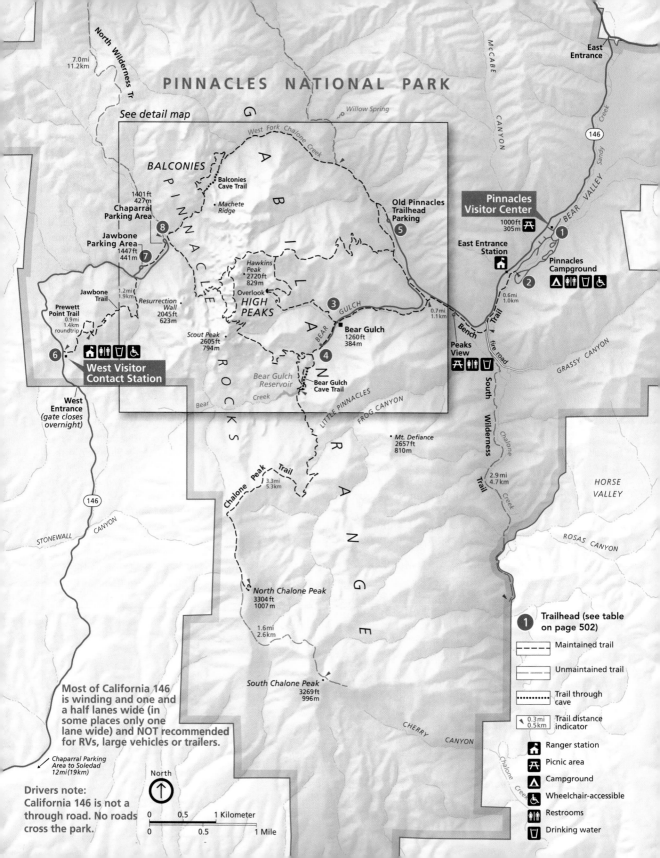

PINNACLES NATIONAL PARK

See detail map

BALCONIES

Balconies Cave Trail

1401ft
427m
Chaparral Parking Area 8

Jawbone Parking Area
1447ft
441m 7

Jawbone Trail

1.2mi
1.9km

Prewett Point Trail
0.9mi
1.4km roundtrip

6

West Visitor Contact Station

West Entrance
(gate closes overnight)

Machete Ridge

Resurrection Wall
2045ft
623m

Scout Peak
2605ft
794m

Hawkins Peak
2720ft
829m

Overlook

HIGH PEAKS

3

Bear Gulch
1260ft
384m

4

Bear Gulch Reservoir

Bear Gulch Cave Trail

North Wilderness Tr

7.0mi
11.2km

West Fork Chalone Creek

Willow Spring

Old Pinnacles Trailhead Parking
5

Pinnacles Visitor Center
1000ft
305m 1

East Entrance Station

Pinnacles Campground

0.6mi
1.0km

0.7mi
1.1km

Peaks View

LITTLE PINNACLES

FROG CANYON

• Mt. Defiance
2657ft
810m

2.9mi
4.7km

McCABE CANYON

BEAR VALLEY

146

East Entrance

Sandy Creek

GRASSY CANYON

HORSE VALLEY

ROSAS CANYON

Chalone Peak Trail
3.3mi
5.3km

North Chalone Peak
3304 ft
1007 m

1.6mi
2.6km

South Chalone Peak
3269ft
996m

STONEWALL CANYON

146

Chalone Creek

CHERRY CANYON

Chalone Creek

Most of California 146 is winding and one and a half lanes wide (in some places only one lane wide) and NOT recommended for RVs, large vehicles or trailers.

← Chaparral Parking Area to Soledad
12mi(19km)

Drivers note: California 146 is not a through road. No roads cross the park.

North
↑

0   0.5   1 Kilometer
0   0.5   1 Mile

1 **Trailhead** (see table on page 502)

- - - Maintained trail

——— Unmaintained trail

······· Trail through cave

0.3mi
0.5km Trail distance indicator

Ranger station

Picnic area

Campground

Wheelchair-accessible

Restrooms

Drinking water

Directions

Pinnacles is surprisingly remote for being just 100 miles south of San Francisco. The park's East and West regions are not connected by a through road. It's about a 2.5-hour drive to either entrance from San Francisco and another hour to get from the east entrance to the west entrance, driving around the park's southern boundary.

East Pinnacles Visitor Center

From the North: Take US-101 south to exit 353 for CA-25. Take CA-25 south, through Hollister, about 41 miles, and turn right onto CA-146 W, into the park.

From the South: Take US-101 north to exit 281 for 1st Street toward King City. Turn right onto 1st Street. After 1.3 miles it veers right, becoming Lyons Street and then Bitterwater Road. Continue for roughly 15 miles to a T-intersection and turn left onto CA-25. Drive north for 14 miles and make a sharp left onto CA-146 W, which leads into the park.

West Pinnacles Visitor Center

From the North: Take US-101 south to exit 302 (CA-146/Soledad). Continue onto CA-146 W. Turn left onto Front Street after 0.25 mile. After less than 0.5 mile turn right onto East St. Turn right onto CA-146 E/ Metz Road after 0.3 mile. Drive for 2.7 miles, and then turn left onto CA-146 E, which leads into the park.

From the South: Take US-101 north to exit 281 for 1st Street toward King City. Turn right onto 1st Street. After 1.3 miles it veers right, becoming Lyons Street. Immediately after the bend, turn left onto Metz Road. Drive north on Metz Road for 17.2 miles, and then turn right onto CA-146 W. It is 7.1 miles to the visitor center and another 2.2 miles to the end of the road.

East Pinnacles to West Pinnacles (or west to east)

No roads cross the park. The shortest route from the east to the west entrance is to take CA-25 south. Turn onto Bitterwater Road and continue to King City. Turn right onto Metz Road, and then left onto CA-146 E.

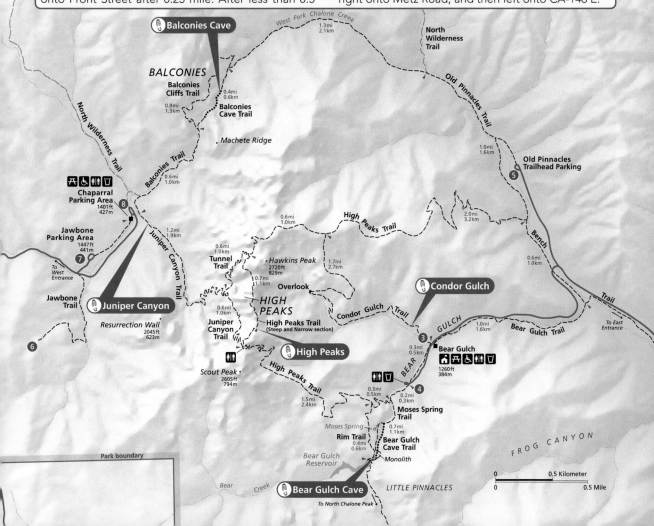

Bear Gulch

Pinnacles Hiking Trails (Distances are roundtrip)

	Name	Location (# on map)	Length	Difficulty Rating & Notes
East	Visitor Center to Bear Gulch	Visitor Center (1)	4.6 miles	M – Walk to Bear Gulch when busy
	Visitor Center to Balconies	Visitor Center (1)	9.4 miles	M – Follows Bench and Old Pinnacles Trails
	South Wilderness	Campground (2)	6.5 miles	M – Follow Chalone Creek to boundary
	Condor Gulch - 🥾	Condor Gulch (3)	3.4 miles	S – Overlook at 1 mile, high peaks beyond
	Condor Gulch–High Peaks Loop - 🥾	Condor Gulch (3)	5.3 miles	S – Great hike, steep sections, 1,300-ft gain
	Moses Spring–Rim Loop - 🥾	Bear Gulch (4)	2.2 miles	M – Loop to Bear Gulch (Reservoir) Cave
	High Peaks–Bear Gulch Loop - 🥾	Bear Gulch (4)	6.7 miles	S – Wildflowers in spring, 1,425-ft gain
	Chalone Peak - 🥾	Bear Gulch (4)	9.0 miles	S – Highest point in the park, 2,040-ft gain
	Old Pinnacles	Old Pinnacles (5)	5.3 miles	M – Hike to Balconies from the east side
West	Prewett Point	Contact Station (6)	0.9 mile	E – Short walk to lookout of High Peaks
	Jawbone	Multiple (6, 7, 8)	2.4 miles	E – Prewett Point–Jawbone–Chaparral
	Balconies Cliffs & Cave Loop - 🥾	Chaparral Trailhead (8)	2.4 miles	M – Scramble through a talus cave
	Juniper Canyon Loop - 🥾	Chaparral Trailhead (8)	4.3 miles	S – Juniper + High Peaks + Tunnel Trails
	North Wilderness Loop	Chaparral Trailhead (8)	9.3 miles	S – Unmaintained, follow the rock cairns
	High Peaks–Balconies Loop - 🥾	Chaparral Trailhead (8)	8.4 miles	S – Juniper + High Peaks + Old Pinnacles

Difficulty Ratings: E = Easy, M = Moderate, S = Strenuous

⛺ Camping

Camping is limited to **Pinnacles Campground**, located on the park's east side. Here you'll find tent, RV (most with electric hookups), group sites, and a few tent cabins (with or without electricity). Many sites offer considerable privacy and shade thanks to large old-growth oak. Potable water is available throughout the campground. Coin-operated showers and a dump station are nearby, and there's a camp store (open daily from 9:30am to 5pm) stocked with all the camping essentials (beer included). There's also something extremely uncommon among national park campgrounds, a swimming pool. The pool is typically open from mid-April through September, weather permitting. It gets hot, so the pool will be a very welcome sight after a day spent sweating your way up to the High Peaks. Depending on the fire danger level, campfires may be prohibited. Tent sites cost $35/night. RV sites cost $45. Tent cabins cost $119 without electricity, $129 with. All sites can be reserved up to 6 months in advance at (877) 444-6777 or recreation.gov.

🚶‍♂️🚶 Hiking

There are just over 30 miles of hiking trails at Pinnacles. If you're ambitious you can hike all of them in a couple of days. What the park lacks in quantity, it makes up for in quality; the NPS and the CCC (which constructed many of the trails) make those miles count.

Bench and Bear Gulch Trails, which visitors use to get from East Visitor Center to Old Pinnacles Trailhead and Bear Gulch, are easy strolls. Their primary purpose is to connect longer loops and access popular east side trailheads when parking areas fill (and the shuttle isn't running). However, there is a nice picnic spot between the parking areas at Bear Gulch and Condor Gulch. **Old Pinnacles Trail** leads into the heart of the park and is both pleasant and easy. But all the best hikes lead through High Peaks or talus caves.

On the east side, I really like the **Condor Gulch–High Peaks Loop**, which passes through a steep and narrow section of High Peaks. The nearly-vertical stairs and narrow ledges (with protective railings) that wind through peaks, pinnacles, and spires are also some of the best areas for raptor spotting. The loop simply connects High Peaks Trail (from Bear Gulch Parking Area) and Condor Gulch Trail (from Condor Gulch Parking Area). Which direction you travel doesn't make much difference, unless you want to do a slightly bigger loop and navigate a talus cave (which is really great when it's fully open, typically March and October, bring a headlamp). In that case, take Moses Spring Trail to Bear

High Peaks

Gulch Cave Trail, and continue to High Peaks via Rim Trail, and return via Condor Gulch. You'll want to hike in this order because the cave is one-way. Even better, follow that same route—Moses Spring to Bear Gulch Cave to Rim to High Peaks—hiking all of High Peaks to Old Pinnacles to Bench Trail, and taking Bear Gulch Trail back to where you began. This 8-mile loop is one of the best day hikes in the entire national park system. The lower half of Bear Gulch Cave is open most of the year, but the entire passage is only open for a few weeks each year. The largest maternity colony of Townsend's big-eared bats between Mexico and San Francisco reside here, and the park does what it can to protect them, which involves closing the trail for extended periods. Hiking past Bear Gulch Reservoir to North Chalone Peak, the park's highest point, is another wonderful hike loaded with expansive views.

On the park's less popular west side, most trails begin at Chaparral Trailhead Parking Area. **Balconies Cliffs and Cave Loop** is 2.4 miles of fun and beautiful scenery. While this route only gains 300 feet, it's considered moderate because getting through the cave requires a headlamp and some scrambling (and possibly wading through water in winter). The trek begins by traveling 0.6 mile along Balconies Trail, where you'll encounter a junction (before the cave). Right leads through the cave, left leads to the cliffs. For the loop, begin by going through the cave (it's one-way) and return via Balconies Cliffs Trail. It'll take about 2 hours. (Note: you can also reach Balconies Cave and Cliffs Trails via Old Pinnacles Trail from the east side of the park.) Old Pinnacles intersects Balconies Cave Trail at the cave's exit, 1.3 miles from Old Pinnacles Trailhead Parking Area. Another great trail on the west side is **Juniper Canyon Trail** up to High Peaks, returning to Juniper Canyon via Tunnel Trail. This loop climbs 1,215 feet over 4.3 miles

High Peaks

and takes about 2 hours. You can also ascend Juniper Canyon Trail to Scout Peak and return to Chaparral Trailhead Parking Area via High Peaks, Old Pinnacles, and Balconies Trails for an 8.4-mile loop that climbs 1,540 feet. West side hikers must exit the park before 8pm, when the gate closes. Enjoy the High Peaks. Pack a lunch. Watch for condors. It's an absolutely magnificent place to be. There's a restroom near Scout Peak, at the intersection of Juniper and High Peaks Trails. Don't forget water.

A note about the caves: these are talus caves created by earthquakes and fault action. Cave purists might find them underwhelming as they're basically boulders lodged in deep narrow gorges, forming a sun-blocking ceiling, which provides various degrees of darkness. Regardless of how cave-y they are, both cave trails are a great deal of fun (if you enjoy that sort of thing). They're relatively short and can flood depending on conditions. They're home to bats, require a bit of dexterity and scrambling to pass through, and you will need a good light source (preferably a headlamp to free your hands). They can be a bit claustrophobic, but none of the squeezes are painfully tight for most visitors. If you're excited about the caves, check with the park to make sure they're open. Upper Beach Gulch is usually only open in March and October.

Rock Climbing

Pinnacle's spires, crags, walls, and cliffs offer hundreds of routes for climbers of all ability levels. While this is a climbing hotspot, do not mistake its volcanic breccia rock with the towering granite monoliths found at nearby Yosemite. Breccia is comparatively weak, resulting in loose, flaky rocks. Longtime Pinnacles climbers are easily recognized as they tap all potential holds, listening for a response. A hollow sound means the rock may pull off the wall.

Loose rock is especially common on the park's west side at sites along Balconies Trail like the Citadel, Machete Ridge, and Elephant Rock, due to significantly less use (and longer routes). Sticking to popular areas—Tourist Trap, Discovery Wall, and High Peaks—greatly reduces the likelihood of encountering loose rocks. For an introduction to Pinnacles climbing, your best bet is Discovery Wall (on the east side of the park). Most of the climbing at Pinnacles is lead climbing, but there are a few good bouldering and top-rope climbing spots as well. Climbers come to Pinnacles year-round, with the season peaking in late January and remaining busy through May. Things pick back up again in September. No matter when you go, bring plenty of water.

Whether you are a beginner or experienced climber, please respect the park, its visitors, and its inhabitants. Dispose of your waste properly (there is a restroom near Scout Peak, along High Peaks Trail). Skip chalk altogether or use "chalk balls" to minimize chalk left on hand holds, which diminishes the rock's scenic beauty. Use the access trails. Climbing is not allowed on routes above established hiking trails. Respect route closures, which commonly occur between January and July to protect nesting raptor habitats. And don't forget to be safe. Wear a helmet. Tap your holds. Inspect the bolts. Use redundant anchor systems. And get comfortable with the rock. If you usually lead 5.10+, the park suggests you try one of the 5.6s or 5.7s for your first climb at Pinnacles. Whether you're climbing solo or with a small group, sign the climbing registers located at Moses Springs Trailhead (east side) and Balconies Trailhead (west side).

If you don't have access to a seasoned Pinnacles rock climber, check out pinnacles.org (Friends of Pinnacles) and mudncrud.com. They're two good resources for information on the park's 800+ climbing routes.

Birdwatching

Pinnacles is home to more than 180 different types of birds, but one species, the **California condor**, captivates most birders. They are the largest flying bird in North America. Its size is only surpassed by its scarcity. They are one of the rarest birds in the world. In the 1980s, California condors were pushed to the brink of extinction due to loss of habitat, poaching, and lead poisoning (contracted from carrion they feed on). In 1987, the last 22 remaining birds were captured and bred in captivity at San Diego Safari Park and Los Angeles Zoo as part of the California Condor Recovery Plan. To double reproduction rates, they fed each bird's first chick with hand puppets. The plan—although extremely expensive—has been successful. California condors were reintroduced here in 2003, and have now integrated into the Big Sur flock, numbering about 60 birds in total. California condors were also introduced in Utah and Arizona, where you'll find nesting pairs at Zion and Grand Canyon National Parks.

I was greeted by a dozen large birds my first time in the park while climbing up a High Peak's stone staircase. They soared above, occasionally swooping down close enough to hear the whoosh of their wings slicing through the hot summer air. After sitting for quite some time, enjoying the spectacle, I hiked back down to Bear Gulch, thinking "Thank goodness they saved the California condor. That was a magical moment," feeling truly connected with these rare creatures. Turns out they were turkey vultures. However, I was treated to soaring condors my next visit! And this time I knew the difference.

Mistaking turkey vultures and California condors is common among amateurs. They are in the same family and look remarkably similar from a distance. If you know what you're looking for, they're easy to distinguish. First, there's the size difference. Turkey vultures average a 6-foot wingspan and weigh 2–4 pounds. Condors have a 10-foot wingspan and can weigh up to 25 pounds. When gliding above you, they can also be identified by their underwing markings. California condors have mottled white along the leading edges of their wings, while the rest, including their wingtips, is black. The back edges of turkey vulture wings are solid silver. California condors glide with their wings flat and without rocking back and forth. Turkey vultures hold their wings in a slight "V" and rock side to side in the wind. Condors have a bright orange head, while turkey vultures have bright red heads. Still unsure? The surefire way to know you've spotted a California condor is to see a numbered wing tag. All condors are tagged and equipped with radio transmitters to help monitor their activity.

Your best bet to see these massive scavengers is to explore High Peaks, Chalone Peak Trail, and the ridge southeast of the campground in the morning and evening. My not-so-scientific approach to raptor-watching is to look for rock formations with an abundance of bird droppings. That's where raptors roost. Bring your binoculars and you might be fortunate enough to see a condor soaring in the thermal updrafts. Enjoy their presence while you can as they fly up to 55 mph and as high as 15,000 feet up. They can cruise to Big Sur, about 40 miles away, in an hour.

Balconies

Visitor Centers
Pinnacles Visitor Center (East Side) is typically open from 9:30am until 5pm, daily. **Bear Gulch Nature Center** (East Side) is typically open weekends from 10am until 4pm (January through May). **West Pinnacles Visitor Contact Station** is typically open from 9am until 4:30pm on weekends, holidays, and weekdays (January through May, staff permitting).

Ranger Programs & For Kids
Free ranger programs are fun activities for all ages. Pinnacles typically offers weekend programs on the east side from fall through spring. All ranger programs are highly recommended, so it's a good idea to check online or an Activity Board outside the East Visitor Center, Bear Gulch Nature Center, or the West Visitor Center once you arrive to see a current schedule of events.

Be sure to bring a few flashlights/headlamps along because there's a good chance your children are going to want to explore the talus caves. You'll find one cave on each side of the park: Balconies Cave on the west, Bear Gulch (or Reservoir) Cave on the east. Both are cool, but you'll have to do some scrambling and squeezing. You must be able to lift your body weight. They occasionally close due to flooding and to protect bat habitat. If hiking through them is extremely high on your list of activities, check the park's website for current closures or, better yet, call the park to hear the status firsthand from a ranger. I don't consider cave closures to be a deal-breaker (High Peaks is still a whole lot of fun), but there's no question it diminishes the overall experience.

Flora & Fauna
Much of the life found at Pinnacles has adapted to survive in this seemingly inhospitable environment. Chaparral dominates the landscape, canvassing 82% of the park's area. Some of these shrubby species have even

Horned lizard

adapted to wildfires, which are common here, evolving seeds that lie dormant for years until fire stimulates them to sprout. Pinnacles comes alive from March through May, when over 80% of the park's plants—including more than 100 species of flowers—are in bloom. The one plant you definitely want to avoid is poison oak, which is common along most trails. It's the chameleon of the plant world, growing as a shrub, vine, or small tree. Its leaves can be red, green, and any color in between. The best way to identify poison oak is that its leaves are arranged in groups of three.

You might not expect it, but Pinnacles supports a lot of animal life: nearly 200 species of birds; dozens of mammals, reptiles, butterflies, and dragonflies; a handful of amphibians; thousands of invertebrates; and about 400 species of bees. Those bees represent the world's greatest known diversity per unit area. Over 260 different species of bees have been spotted along Old Pinnacles Trail alone. The most common mammals include black-tailed deer, bobcat, gray fox, raccoon (don't leave your trash or cooler out), rabbits, squirrels, chipmunks, and bats, including Townsend's big-eared bats, which are protected in Bear Gulch (Reservoir) Cave. All visitors, but especially rock climbers, must be cautious of rattlesnakes, which commonly hole-up under rocks and in crevasses.

Pets & Accessibility
Pets must be on a leash (less than six feet). They are only allowed in picnic areas, parking lots, campgrounds, and on paved roads. They are prohibited from all trails and you must not leave them unattended, even in the campground (tied to a tree or picnic table).

Both visitor centers and their restrooms are fully accessible. Trails are another story. They're steep, often with narrow stairs carved into rock. A small portion of Bench

Trail (beginning at Peaks View Picnic Area) is accessible to wheelchair users with assistance. On the west side, Prewett Point Trail is accessible.

Weather
Being just 40 miles from the ocean (as the condor flies), you'd expect Pinnacles to have a climate moderated by the Pacific, but the intervening Santa Lucia Mountains subdue the ocean's influence, creating many summer days when it can be 60°F along the Pacific and 100°F in the park. Similarly, in winter, it can be below freezing at Pinnacles and temperate along the coast. Weather-wise, spring and fall are the most pleasant seasons.

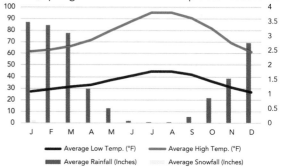

Legend:
— Average Low Temp. (°F) — Average High Temp. (°F)
▇ Average Rainfall (Inches) Average Snowfall (Inches)

Tips & Recommendations
Visitation typically peaks in March, April, and May, but it's fairly steady all year long. October weekdays are a great time, as there's a good chance Bear Gulch Cave will be fully open, and the crowds won't be huge.

Visitation is relatively modest, but the park can feel crowded at times because it's small, with only a few trailheads. Get an early start or use the shuttle when it's running. You could also start hiking from the less popular west side of the park. But those parking areas fill too. When they do, it is possible to hike to Chaparral Trailhead from Jawbone Parking Area and the Visitor Contact Station (via Prewett Point and Jawbone Trails). It'll add some miles, but you won't have to wait to park.

Visit on a weekday in spring to be treated to beautiful wildflowers without the weekend crowds. Actually, whenever you choose to travel, it's a good idea to visit Pinnacles during the middle of the week.

It's nice to take your time and relax, but, if you hustle, you can thoroughly explore the High Peaks and talus caves spending just one night in the park.

With no through road, it's just as easy to set up camp on the east side of the park (where the campground is located) and hike to Balconies/Juniper Canyon/Tunnel

Juniper Canyon

Trails as it is to drive (1.5+ hours) to Chaparral Trailhead on the west side. And CA-146 (West Entrance) is not recommended for large vehicles.

The two talus caves are highlights of the park. The lower half of Bear Gulch Cave is typically open from mid-July through mid-May. The upper half is typically only open for four weeks in March and another four weeks in October (and the upper half is pretty cool). These are just guidelines and caves may close intermittently to protect wildlife or due to flooding. If you're pumped up to explore the caves, it's a good idea to check the park website for current cave status (and don't forget your headlamps if they're open).

The High Peaks area is fun but be warned, you'll have to cross some exposed areas and use stairs and steel railings to clear precarious stretches. If this isn't for you, you might want to stick to the lowlands. If you aren't sure and want to give it a try, head up Juniper Canyon

(west) or Condor Gulch (east) to reach High Peaks and see what you think. If it's scary, turn around and head back down. If not, carry on and have fun!

Bring a set of binoculars to spot California condors. Even though it's the largest flying bird in North America, they're often seen circling high above High Peaks.

Easy Hikes: Prewett Point (0.9 mile)
Moderate Hikes: Bear Gulch Cave (2.2 miles), Balconies Cave (2.4)
Strenuous Hikes: High Peaks Loop (6.7 miles), Juniper Canyon (4.3), Condor Gulch (5.3), Chalone Peak (9)
Family Activities: Explore the talus caves, Become Junior Rangers
Sunrise/Sunset Spots: Being up in the High Peaks would be nice for sunset, just be sure to have a reliable light source to hike back down to the trailhead. Otherwise, your best bet for early/late light is to use it on the High Peaks (east side at sunrise, west side at sunset)

Beyond the Park...

Dining
Taqueria Pacheco • (831) 678-1808
325 Front St, Soledad
taqueria-pacheco.edan.io

Cocuyos • cocuyos.edan.io
185 Kidder St, Soledad

El Tamalaso • (831) 613-6895
321 B El Camino Real, Greenfield

Grocery Stores
Foods Co • (831) 678-1937
2443 H Dela Rosa Sr St, Soledad

Lodging & Camping
Bar SZ Ranch • (831) 201-2593
10001 Willow Creek Rd, Paicines
barszranch.com

Inn at the Pinnacles • (831) 678-2400
32025 Stonewall Canyon Rd, Soledad
innatthepinnacles.com

Yanks RV Resort • (855) 926-5778
40399 Livingston Rd, Greenfield
yanksrvresort.com

Attractions
So many fantastic state lands along the coast, not far from Pinnacles. In no particular order: Julia Pfeiffer Burns State Park (McWay Falls), Garrapata State Park, Point Lobos State Natural Reserve, Point Sur State Historic Park, Pomponio State Beach, Bean Hollow State Beach, Pigeon Point Light Station State Historic Park, W. R. Hearst Memorial Beach, and Limekiln State Park • parks.ca.gov

Hollister Hills SVRA
Off-road park • ohv.parks.ca.gov
7800 Cienega Rd, Hollister

Fort Ord National Monument
Former military post • blm.gov
Toro Creek Rd, Marina

Mission Soledad • (831) 678-2586
36641 Fort Romie Rd, Soledad

Puma Road Winery
32071 River Rd, Soledad
pumaroad.com • (831) 675-3548

Death Valley

Mesquite Flat Dunes

Phone: (760) 786-3200
Website: nps.gov/deva

Established: October 31, 1994
February 11, 1933 (Nat'l Monument)
Size: 3.4 Million Acres
Annual Visitors: 1.7 Million
Peak Season: November–April

Activities: Off-Roading, Hiking, Backpacking, Biking, Horseback Riding, Birdwatching

9 Campgrounds: 5 Fee ($14–36/night) and 4 Free
4 Lodges: $79–500/night
Backcountry Camping: Permitted

Park Hours: All day, every day (except day-use areas: Cottonwood Canyon, Titus Canyon, Aguereberry Point, Skidoo, Wildrose, Racetrack, West Side, and Mosaic Canyon)
Entrance Fee: $30/25/15 (car/motorcycle/individual)

In 1917, Death Valley experienced 52 days—43 consecutive—with temperatures over 120°F. In 1929, not a single drop of measurable rain was recorded. During a 40-month period from 1931 through 1934, only 0.64 inches of rain fell. It's the hottest and driest national park in the United States. Not exactly a ringing endorsement for tourism. But Death Valley's superlatives extend far beyond historical weather data. At more than three million acres, it's also the largest national park in the U.S. (excluding Alaska). Badwater is the lowest place in North America. And it's out of this world. The first rays of light dance off the mudstone of Zabriskie Point. Only the afternoon sun penetrates the depths of Titus Canyon. Signs of a volcanic past are visible at Ubehebe Crater. And Rocks move of their own accord across the flats of Racetrack Playa. And that's just the beginning of Death Valley's oddities.

People have visited Death Valley for nearly 10,000 years. Little is known of the earliest inhabitants, but it's likely they made seasonal migrations to the valley, collecting piñon nuts and mesquite beans. In 1849 the first non-Native American stepped foot in the region…completely by accident. More than 100 wagons wandered into the valley after getting lost on what they believed was a shortcut off the Old Spanish Trail. Roaming the desert for nearly two months, their oxen became weak, their wagons battered. By the time they approached present-day Stovepipe Wells, it was clear they would not be able to pass the mountains with a full complement of oxen and wagons; they made jerky of the former, burned the latter, and then set out on foot to cross Emigrant Pass, leaving "Death Valley" behind. Only one man died during the ordeal, but the name stuck thanks to *Death Valley in '49*, a book written by a member of the group, William Lewis Manly. His book became an important chapter in California's pioneer history and brought newfound publicity to this indescribable region.

Before it became a park, mining was the valley's primary activity. Boom towns (now ghost towns) sprang up around local bonanzas of gold (and misleading publicity of unimaginable wealth), but the most profitable ore was borax, used to make soap and industrial components. Today, it's an essential component in various glassware. Harmony Borax Works was the engine that opened the valley, building hundreds of miles of roads as they raked borax from the valley floor. Forty men could produce three tons each day. Next, it was hauled out 10 tons at a time by twenty-mule teams, the original semi-trailers. A single caravan stretched 180 feet. During six years of production, they hauled more than 20 million pounds of borax out of Death Valley. Stephen Mather, first director of the National Park Service, made his fortune with 20 Mule Team Borax. Success allowed him to pursue the preservation of natural wonders like Death Valley.

Walter Scott, also known as Death Valley Scotty, was a less industrious Death Valley resident. After working for Harmony Borax and the Buffalo Bill Wild West Show, he convinced wealthy easterners to invest in his "highly productive" gold mine. Unfortunately for his investors, Scotty didn't have a gold mine. He took the money and went on legendary spending sprees. With no returning profits, investors pulled funding until only Albert Mussey Johnson, an insurance magnate from Chicago, remained. He sent thousands of dollars to Scotty, only to hear of an assortment of calamities always preventing shipments of gold. Johnson decided to visit Death Valley to check on the operation. Even as he realized he had been swindled, he fell in love with Death Valley and began a long-lasting friendship with Death Valley Scotty. Johnson funded construction of a vacation home (Scotty's Castle) and Scotty's real home (Lower Vine Ranch). To Scotty and Albert Johnson, Death Valley was a magical place filled with wondrous landscapes they described with their own superlatives, not the inhospitably harsh hellscape others made it out to be. *The Death Valley Chuck-Walla*, an old mining newspaper, may have said it best when they wrote: "Would you enjoy a trip to hell? You might enjoy a trip to Death Valley, now! It has all the advantages of hell without the inconveniences." Not a ringing endorsement, but it is Death Valley after all.

A storm brewing above Badwater

When to Go

The park is open all year, but you may want to avoid summer when temps consistently rise above 100°F. Ranger programs are offered between November and April. Furnace Creek Visitor Center is open daily from 8am to 5pm. At time of publication Scotty's Castle Visitor Center was closed (at least until 2022) due to flood damage. Check status before visiting. With the right combination of well-spaced winter rainfall, sunlight, and lack of drying winds, the valley fills with a sea of gold, purple, pink, and white wildflowers typically blooming from late February (low elevations) until mid-July (high). Every year is different. 2016 was exceptional. Sometimes only a few plants bloom in the desert, but the presence of life in such a desolate place is a beautiful thing to behold, regardless the quantity.

Transportation & Airports

Public transportation does not provide service to or around the park. The closest large commercial airport is McCarran International (LAS) in Las Vegas, NV (136 miles to the east), where you can rent a car. There is a small public airfield at Furnace Creek, where private planes can land and refuel.

Directions

Death Valley is a massive remote region of eastern California, located along the California–Nevada border. The park can be entered from the west via CA-190 and CA-178 or from the east via CA-190, CA-178, NV-374, or NV-267.

From Los Angeles (235 miles): Heading east on I-15, take Exit 245 onto Baker Blvd. Turn left at CA-127/Death Valley Road. Travel north about 58 miles. Turn left at CA-178, which leads into the park.

From Las Vegas (87 miles): Head west on US-95 for about 85 miles to Amargosa Valley, and then turn left onto NV-373. Continue south for 21 miles. Turn right onto CA-190, which leads into the park.

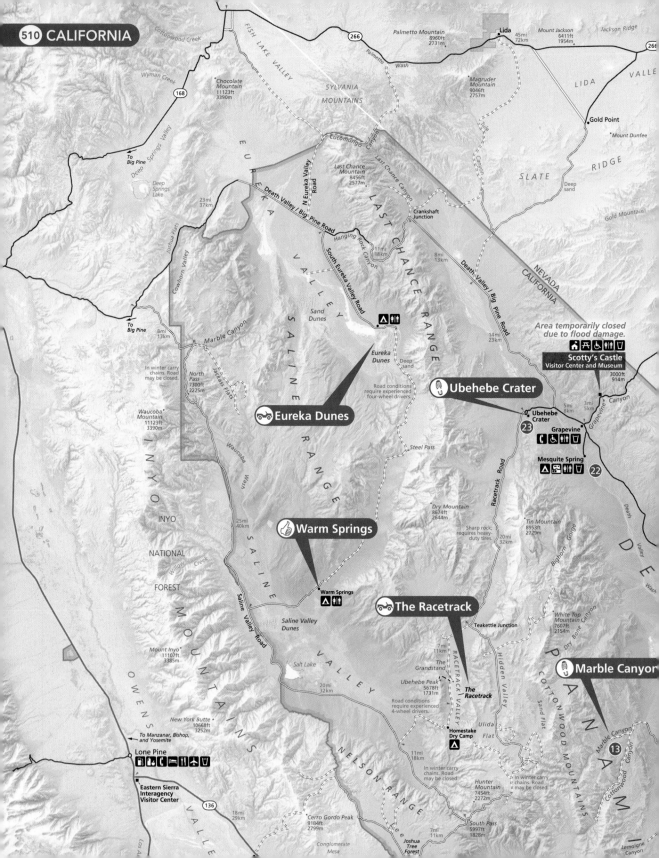

Cottonwood Creek
FISH LAKE VALLEY
Palmetto Mountain 8960ft 2731m
266
Palmetto Wash
Mount Jackson 6411ft 1954m
Jackson Ridge
Lida
45mi 72km
Mount Jackson
266

Wyman Creek
Chocolate Mountain 11123ft 3390m
SYLVANIA MOUNTAINS
Magruder Mountain 9046ft 2757m
LIDA VALLEY
Gold Point
Mount Dunfee

168

Deep Springs Valley
To Big Pine
Deep Springs Lake
Cucomungo Canyon
Last Chance Mountain 8456ft 2577m
Last Chance Canyon
SLATE RIDGE
Deep sand
Gold Mountain

23mi 37km
N Eureka Valley Road
Crankshaft Junction
NEVADA
CALIFORNIA

Death Valley / Big Pine Road
Hanging Rock Canyon
11mi 18km
8mi 13km
Death Valley / Big Pine Road
14mi 23km

Joshua Flats
South Eureka Valley Road
LAST CHANCE RANGE

Sand Dunes
⛺ 🚻

To Big Pine
8mi 13km
Marble Canyon
Jackass Flats
North Pass 7300ft 2225m
Eureka Dunes
Deep sand
Road conditions require experienced four-wheel drivers.

Area temporarily closed due to flood damage.
🏕🏖♿🚻🚽
Scotty's Castle
Visitor Center and Museum
3000ft 914m

Waucoba Mountain 11123ft 3390m
EUREKA VALLEY

🚙 **Eureka Dunes**

👢 **Ubehebe Crater**

Ubehebe Crater
23
5mi 8km
3mi 5km
Grapevine Canyon

Grapevine
🚻🍽🚽

Steel Pass
Mesquite Spring
⛺🍽🚻🚽
22

INYO
INYO
NATIONAL
FOREST
Waucoba Wash
SALINE RANGE
25mi 40km
Saline Valley Road
Willow Creek
👍 **Warm Springs**
Warm Springs
⛺🚻
Dry Mountain 8674ft 2644m
Sharp rock; requires heavy-duty tires.
20mi 32km
Tin Mountain 8953ft 2729m
Racetrack Road
Bighorn Gorge
DEE

OWENS
MOUNTAINS
Mount Inyo 11107ft 3385m
Saline Valley Dunes
SALINE VALLEY
Salt Lake
🚙 **The Racetrack**
Teakettle Junction
White Top Mountain 7607ft 2154m
Dry Bone Canyon
PANAM

New York Butte 10668ft 3252m
To Manzanar, Bishop, and Yosemite
20mi 32km
7mi 11km
The Grandstand
Ubehebe Peak 5678ft 1731m
The Racetrack
Road conditions require experienced 4-wheel drivers.
Racetrack Valley
Hidden Valley
Sand Flat
Cottonwood Canyon
COTTONWOOD MOUNTAINS
👢 **Marble Canyon**
Marble Canyon

Lone Pine
🚻♿🍽✈🚽
Homestake Dry Camp
⛺
Ulida Flat
13
Cottonwood Canyon

Eastern Sierra Interagency Visitor Center
NELSON RANGE
11mi 18km
In winter carry chains. Road may be closed.
Hunter Mountain 7454ft 2272m
In winter carry chains. Road may be closed.

136
18mi 29km
Cerro Gordo Peak 9184ft 2799m
Conglomerate Mesa
Joshua Tree Forest
7mi 11km
South Pass 5997ft 1828m
Lemoigne Canyon

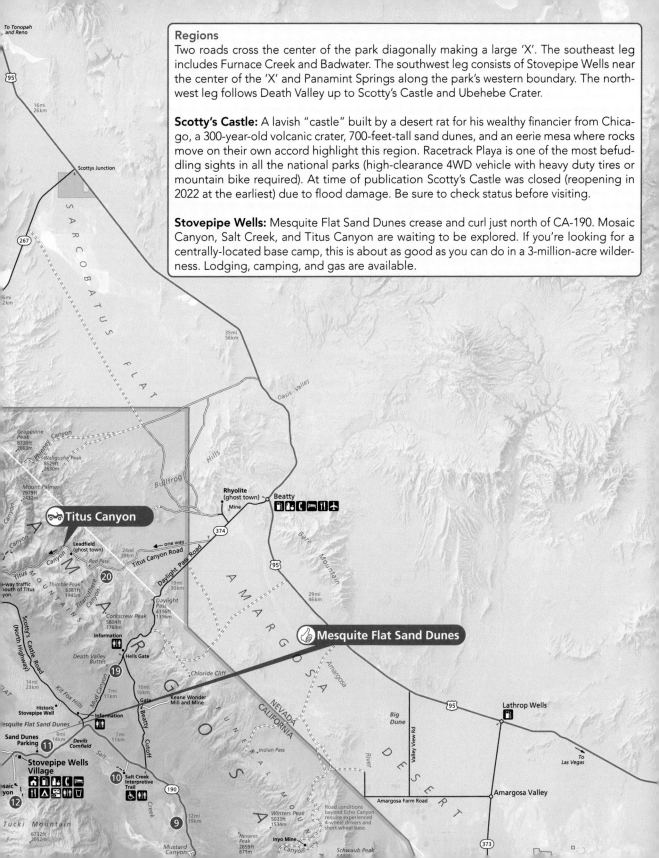

Regions

Two roads cross the center of the park diagonally making a large 'X'. The southeast leg includes Furnace Creek and Badwater. The southwest leg consists of Stovepipe Wells near the center of the 'X' and Panamint Springs along the park's western boundary. The northwest leg follows Death Valley up to Scotty's Castle and Ubehebe Crater.

Scotty's Castle: A lavish "castle" built by a desert rat for his wealthy financier from Chicago, a 300-year-old volcanic crater, 700-feet-tall sand dunes, and an eerie mesa where rocks move on their own accord highlight this region. Racetrack Playa is one of the most befuddling sights in all the national parks (high-clearance 4WD vehicle with heavy duty tires or mountain bike required). At time of publication Scotty's Castle was closed (reopening in 2022 at the earliest) due to flood damage. Be sure to check status before visiting.

Stovepipe Wells: Mesquite Flat Sand Dunes crease and curl just north of CA-190. Mosaic Canyon, Salt Creek, and Titus Canyon are waiting to be explored. If you're looking for a centrally-located base camp, this is about as good as you can do in a 3-million-acre wilderness. Lodging, camping, and gas are available.

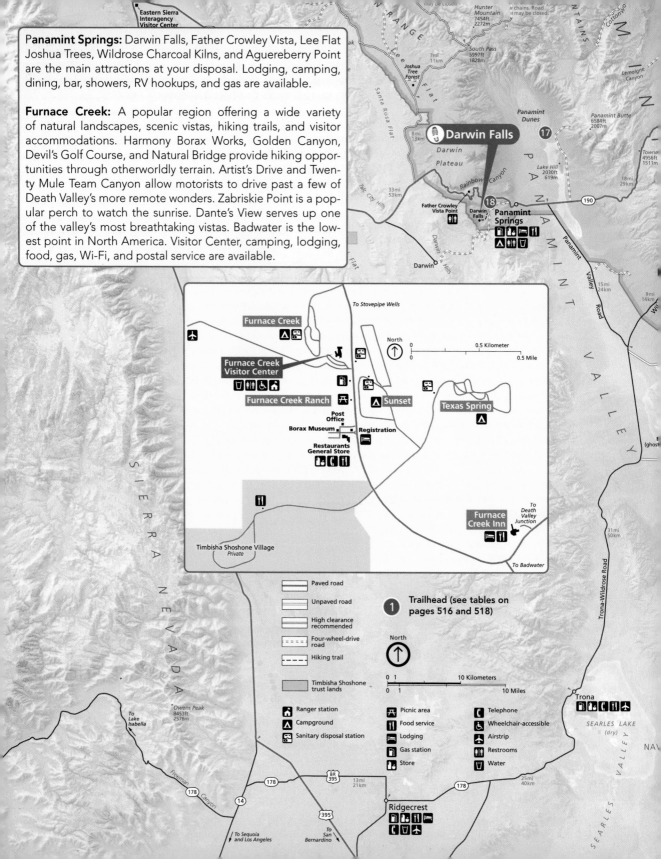

Panamint Springs: Darwin Falls, Father Crowley Vista, Lee Flat Joshua Trees, Wildrose Charcoal Kilns, and Aguereberry Point are the main attractions at your disposal. Lodging, camping, dining, bar, showers, RV hookups, and gas are available.

Furnace Creek: A popular region offering a wide variety of natural landscapes, scenic vistas, hiking trails, and visitor accommodations. Harmony Borax Works, Golden Canyon, Devil's Golf Course, and Natural Bridge provide hiking opportunities through otherworldly terrain. Artist's Drive and Twenty Mule Team Canyon allow motorists to drive past a few of Death Valley's more remote wonders. Zabriskie Point is a popular perch to watch the sunrise. Dante's View serves up one of the valley's most breathtaking vistas. Badwater is the lowest point in North America. Visitor Center, camping, lodging, food, gas, Wi-Fi, and postal service are available.

Darwin Falls

Furnace Creek

Furnace Creek Visitor Center

Furnace Creek Ranch

Post Office

Borax Museum

Registration

Restaurants General Store

Sunset

Texas Spring

Furnace Creek Inn

Timbisha Shoshone Village *Private*

To Stovepipe Wells

North

0.5 Kilometer
0.5 Mile

To Death Valley Junction

To Badwater

Trailhead (see tables on pages 516 and 518)

North

Paved road
Unpaved road
High clearance recommended
Four-wheel-drive road
Hiking trail
Timbisha Shoshone trust lands

Ranger station
Campground
Sanitary disposal station

Picnic area
Food service
Lodging
Gas station
Store

Telephone
Wheelchair-accessible
Airstrip
Restrooms
Water

0   1   10 Kilometers
0   1   10 Miles

Eastern Sierra Interagency Visitor Center

Joshua Tree Forest

Santa Rosa Flat

South Pass 5997ft 1828m

Panamint Dunes

Panamint Butte 6584ft 2007m

7ml 11km

8ml 13km

33ml 53km

Darwin Plateau

Rainbow Canyon

Lake Hill 2030ft 619m

18ml 29km

Father Crowley Vista Point

Panamint Springs

Darwin Falls

Panamint Valley Road

15ml 24km

9ml 14km

Darwin

Tal-Cry Hills

Darwin Hills

190

17

18

SIERRA NEVADA

Owens Peak 8453ft 2576m

To Lake Isabella

Froeman Canyon

178

14

395

BR 395

178

13ml 21km

Ridgecrest

To Sequoia and Los Angeles

To San Bernardino

Trona-Wildrose Road

31ml 50km

25ml 40km

178

Trona

SEARLES LAKE (dry)

SEARLES VALLEY

Hunter Mountain 7454ft 2272m

Towne 4956ft 1511m

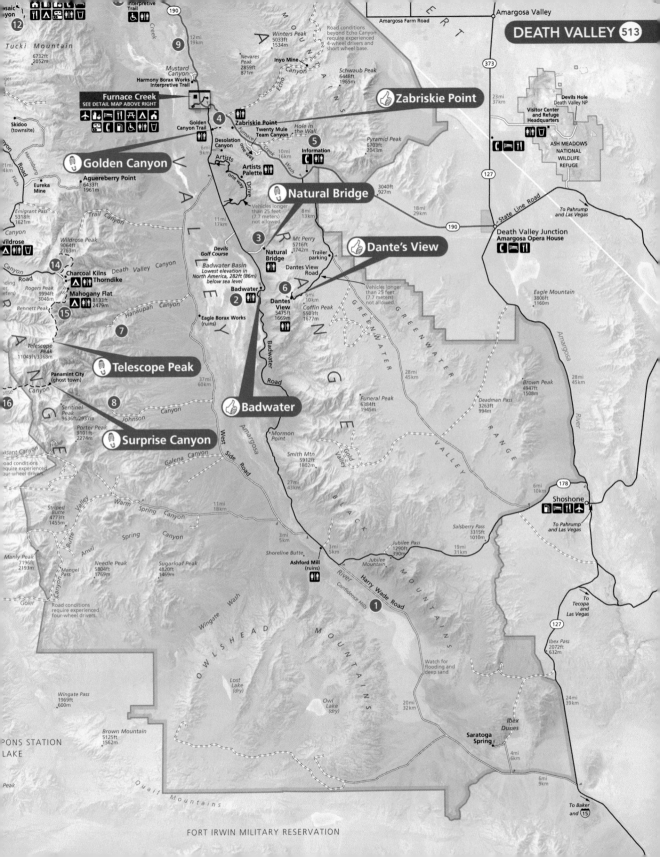

DEATH VALLEY 513

Titus Canyon Road

Death Valley Camping (Fees are per night)

Name	Location	Open	Fee	Sites	Notes
Furnace Creek*	North of Visitor Center	All Year	$22	136	W, F, DS
Sunset	Furnace Creek (CA-190)	mid-October–mid-April	$14	270	W, F, DS
Texas Spring	West of Sunset	mid-October–mid-April	$16	92	W, F, DS
Stovepipe Wells - ♿	Stovepipe Wells Village	mid-October–mid-April	$14	190	W, F, DS
Mesquite Spring - ♿	Scotty's Castle Road	All Year	$14	30	W, F, DS
Emigrant (tent only)	Near Stovepipe Wells	All Year	Free	10	W, F
Wildrose	Emigrant Canyon Road	All Year	Free	23	W, P
Thorndike	Emigrant Canyon Road	March–November	Free	6	P
Mahogany Flat	Emigrant Canyon Road	March–November	Free	10	P

*Reservations can be made up to six months in advance at (877) 444-6777 or recreation.gov
W = Water, F = Flush Toilets, P = Pit Toilets, DS = Dump Station • Furnace Creek has 18 sites with full hookups for $36/night
Private camps with RV hookups are available at Stovepipe Wells Village ($40/night, full hookups) and Panamint Springs
Resort ($80, full; $40, electric), Fiddlers' Camp (Furnace Creek) has large back-in sites ($29–34/night) without hookups.

Backcountry Camping	Permitted as long as you camp at least one mile from any developed area, paved road, or day-use area. Free voluntary permits recommended (available online or in person).
Group Camping	Two group sites are available at Furnace Creek (40 people, 10 vehicle capacity)

Death Valley Lodging (Fees are per night)

Name	Open	Fee	Notes
Stovepipe Wells Village (760) 786-7090 - ♿	All Year	$144–226	Centrally located with pool, Wi-Fi, showers, restaurant, saloon, and RV park (14 full hookup sites, $40/night) • deathvalleyhotels.com
The Inn at Death Valley (800) 236-7916 - ♿	All Year	$359–546	Fine dining, swimming pool, tennis courts, massage therapy, just completed major renovation • oasisatdeathvalley.com
The Ranch at Death Valley (800) 236-7916	All Year	$159–289	2 restaurants, saloon, swimming pool, golf course • Family-friendly, featuring standard rooms and cottages • oasisatdeathvalley.com
Panamint Springs Resort (775) 482-7680	All Year	$114–290	10–15°F cooler than valley lodging • Full hookup RV sites for $80/night, $40/night for just electric hookups • panamintsprings.com

⛺ Camping & Lodging

Death Valley has nine designated frontcountry campgrounds. All campsites, except those at Furnace Creek, are available on a first-come, first-served basis. If you'd like to secure one of the national park's full-hookup RV sites at **Furnace Creek**, you'll want to make reservations as soon as possible (up to six months in advance at recreation.gov). Furnace Creek, Sunset, and Texas Spring Campgrounds are located on CA-190 near Furnace Creek Visitor Center. Showers are not available, but you can shower at The Ranch at Death Valley's pool building for a nominal fee. Stovepipe Wells has a National Park Service-run campground and a concessioner-run RV Park/campground. A pool and showers are available to all campers for a nominal fee. A little farther west on CA-190 is **Emigrant Campground**, the only free campground with flush toilets and water. But there are just ten, tent-only sites. Continuing south on Emigrant Canyon Road leads up the Panamint Range. Located along the last five miles of road are three campgrounds: Wildrose, Thorndike, and Mahogany Flat. These are excellent locations if you're visiting in summer and want to escape the heat of the valley (and arriving in a vehicle less than 25 feet in length). Temperatures are typically 10°F cooler at Wildrose and 20°F cooler at Mahogany Flat. They're also great locations for anyone interested in climbing Telescope Peak (best from June through October). Extreme weather conditions typically close these campgrounds from December through April. A high-clearance 4x4 is a good idea for the last 1.5 miles to Mahogany Flat. If you don't have one, consider parking at Charcoal Kilns and walking the rest of the way. Considering the size of the park, it's a good idea to move your camp around a bit, but, if you're determined to stay in one place, Emigrant or Stovepipe Wells would be my choice. They're as centrally located as you can get, and it's hard to beat Mesquite Flat Sand Dunes in the morning/evening light.

Lodging is available at Furnace Creek, Stovepipe Wells, and Panamint Springs. They have all types of visitors covered. **The Inn at Death Valley** provides luxury accommodations, with a price tag to match. **The Ranch at Death Valley** is more about activities, providing a swimming pool, tennis court, shuffleboard, volleyball, bocce ball, basketball court, and the world's lowest elevation golf course is right next door. Similar to the camping situation, we like **Stovepipe Wells Village** for its location. It doesn't get much better than spending the night on the doorstep of Mesquite Flat Sand Dunes. Finally, **Panamint Springs Resort** is located near the park's western boundary, offering a variety

Golden Canyon

of cottages, cabins, and motel-style rooms. Panamint Valley is strikingly beautiful and it's significantly cooler than Furnace Creek.

🚗 Driving

Death Valley is huge! It's the largest national park in the Lower 48. More than one million acres larger than Yellowstone. Sadly, most visitors simply pass through the park on their way to other destinations. Don't be like them (unless it's summer, then you may not want to step out of your air-conditioned vehicle). If you must drive-thru, take **CA-190**. Every corner of the park offers up something interesting to see, but this stretch will take you by Rainbow Canyon (AKA Star Wars Canyon, seen from Father Crowley Vista Point), by the trailhead to Darwin Falls, through Panamint Valley, past Mesquite Flat Sand Dunes, and you'll exit the park near Zabriskie Point and Dante's View.

Having a detailed driving plan can save a lot of time in your car. First, if you're uninterested in leaving pavement (and Scotty's Castle is still closed), skip Scotty's Castle Road. Ubehebe Crater is neat, and the surroundings are otherworldly (like the rest of the park), but the area's highlights are dirt roads (Titus Canyon and Racetrack). Emigrant Canyon Road is the next least essential paved road to drive (unless it's summer and you'd like to take a shot at climbing Telescope Peak). However, it's a good place to escape the afternoon heat and Aguereberry Point and Skidoo are quite cool, but they're both situated at the end of unpaved roads and things are still more fun in the valley. So, start by planning your trip around CA-190, with a drive up to Dante's View, and down Badwater Road (as far as Badwater). If you're willing to leave payment behind, or, better yet, have a high-clearance 4WD, then you really need to spend time thinking about where you want to go and what you want to do, because there are hundreds of miles of unpaved backcountry roads.

Darwin Falls

Death Valley Hiking Trails (Distances are roundtrip)

	Name	Location (# on map)	Length	Difficulty Rating & Notes
Furnace Creek	Badwater Salt Flat - ♨	Badwater (2)	1–10 miles	E – Hot, occasionally muddy, but awesome!
	Natural Bridge - ♨	Natural Bridge (3)	1–2 miles	E – 0.5-mile to bridge, 1 mile to canyon's end
	Golden Canyon - ♨	Golden Canyon (4)	2.0 miles	E/M – Good hike, especially to Red Cathedral
	Gower Gulch Loop	Golden Canyon (4)	4.3 miles	M – Follow Golden Canyon to marker 4, and then follow gulch to complete loop
	Dante's Ridge - ♨	Dante's View (6)	8.0 miles	M – 1 mile to first summit, 8 miles to Mt Perry
	Salt Creek - ♨	Salt Creek (10)	0.5 mile	E – Interpretive Trail, may see rare pupfish
Stovepipe Wells	Mesquite Flat Sand Dunes - ♨	Sand Dunes (11)	2.0 miles	M – No trail, about 2 miles to highest dune
	Mosaic Canyon - ♨	Mosaic Canyon (12)	1–4 miles	M – Scrambling required, Day-use area
	Wildrose Peak	Charcoal Kilns (14)	8.4 miles	S – Great views, 2,200-ft elevation gain
	Telescope Peak - ♨	Mahogany Flat (15)	14.0 miles	S – Even better views, 3,000-ft elevation gain
	Darwin Falls - ♨	Darwin Falls (18)	2.0 miles	M – Hike to a year-round waterfall
Scotty's Castle	Death Valley Buttes	Hell's Gate (19)	2.4 miles	S – No trail, Narrow and exposed ridges
	Titus Canyon - ♨	Titus Canyon Mouth (21)	3.0 miles	E – Narrowest section of canyon, day-use area
	Fall Canyon - ♨	Titus Canyon Mouth (21)	6.0 miles	S – Pretty cool canyon to waterfall chutes
	Little Hebe Crater	Ubehebe Crater (23)	1.0 mile	M – Follows west rim of bizarre crater, can make extremely difficult hike into crater

Difficulty Ratings: E = Easy, M = Moderate, S = Strenuous

Off-Roading

Backcountry roads unlock some of the most fascinating remote locations in the U.S. to visitors with high-clearance 4WD vehicles. Before racing into the backcountry, make sure you are prepared. Pack basic tools, like a shovel, extra food, and water. Equip your vehicle with off-road tires. Carry at least one spare (two is better), a can of fix-a-flat or tire plug kit, a 12-volt air compressor, and a car jack and lug-wrench. Last but not least, top-off your gas tank before entering the backcountry. Gas stations are located at Panamint Springs, Stovepipe Wells, and Furnace Creek. These simple precautions could save your life or at least prevent a considerable amount of grief. Should you break down, it is usually better to stay with your vehicle and wait for another traveler. Leave the car's hood up and mark the road with a large X visible to aircraft. Traveling in a group of two or more 4WD vehicles can minimize the risks of exploring Death Valley's backcountry roads. If you come across a stranded vehicle, please stop to lend a hand. Next time, it could be you in need of help.

After making the proper preparations, choose your backcountry destination. Titus Canyon and Racetrack Valley are the most popular attractions. **Titus Canyon Road** is 26.8 miles (high-clearance recommended) and it begins at Daylight Pass Road (NV-374), 2.7 miles east of the park boundary, eventually winding its way through the Grapevine Mountains, past a ghost town and petroglyphs, and through a spectacular canyon. Titus Canyon Road is one-way until you reach the mouth of the canyon near Scotty's Castle Road (where day-hikers park). It's a beautiful journey, but I wouldn't go down this road without a high-clearance vehicle. However, I witnessed little Toyota exiting the canyon on my last visit. Still, it's a huge risk. Needing a tow would be terrible. And you won't have cell coverage.

The Racetrack, a dry lakebed located at the foot of Ubehebe Peak, is home to an unexplained phenomenon: moving rocks known as sailing stones. It's difficult to explain where they're going and how they're getting there. No one has actually seen the rocks move, but proof of movement lies in the trails left behind these heavy boulders. Some rocks have traveled more than 1,500 feet. It could be an elaborate prank, but scientists believe a combination of rain and wind allows the rocks to "move" on this extremely flat and dry lakebed. Rain reduces the friction between hard rock and the earth's surface. Winds of 50 mph or more are capable of pushing the boulders across this slippery substrate. Ironically, in a place called "Death Valley," the rocks of the Racetrack come to life and move about the valley.

Joshua Trees near Panamint

It's a sight you have to see to believe. Access it via **Racetrack Road** (high-clearance vehicle and heavy-duty tires required), beginning at Ubehebe Crater at the north end of Scotty's Castle Road. The road is rough washboard with some sharp rocks, so be prepared for a flat, and expect the 26-mile (one-way) trip on Racetrack Road to take about 2 hours each way. Stay on the road. Don't mess with the rocks (or their paths). And do not walk on the Racetrack when it's wet.

These are just two incredible destinations among hundreds of miles of backcountry roads. Eureka Dunes (easier to access from the north across Joshua Flats) and Panamint Dunes are two good off-roading destinations if you'd like a more private dunes experience.

Hiking & Backpacking

Death Valley is a desert hiker's paradise. Colorful canyons, arid flats bookended by steep sloping mountains, a volcanic crater, and rolling dunes are dispersed across the largest national park in the contiguous United Sates. All these sights are best explored on foot. So lace up your hiking shoes and hit the trails.

Dante's Ridge Trail provides hikers with a better idea of the size and scale of Death Valley, as you hike a ridgeline on the east end of the park, high above the vast valley. It's located at the end of a 13-mile (one-way) paved road that intersects CA-190 near the park's East Entrance. About halfway down the road to Dante's View is a trailer parking area. Vehicles longer than 25 feet are not allowed beyond this point. The road gets extremely steep (15% grade) near its end. From the viewpoint parking area, you can head north or south along Dante's Ridge, which follows the crest of the Black Mountains. Heading north, it is a half-mile to the first summit and another difficult 3.5 miles scrambling up and down to Mount Perry. To the south, just beyond

Dante's View, is a short rocky trail descending to a promontory with panoramic views of Badwater Basin and the Panamint Range. Elevation gain from Badwater to Telescope Peak (highest point in the park) is more than 13,000 feet. On clear days, the highest and lowest points in the Lower 48 states—Mount Whitney (14,505 feet above sea level) and Badwater (282 feet below sea level)—are visible.

Badwater Salt Flat is another good place for a short hike. It's quite peculiar to look up into the Amargosa Mountains and see a "Sea Level" sign a few hundred feet above the ground you stand on. From Badwater Parking Area on Badwater Road, you're free to walk beyond the boardwalk. Hike past the well-trod path and you can have some fun with perspective out in the salt flats. There isn't a maintained trail, but trampled ground makes it clear where people trek. If you don't want to drive Titus Canyon Road, consider hiking up from the **Titus Canyon's** mouth. This is the narrowest section of trail, and it's definitely worth a visit (in your car or on your feet). To reach the trailhead, drive north toward Scotty's Castle and take a right on Titus Canyon Road (the only section of Titus Canyon Road open to two-way traffic). You'll also find the trail leading up Fall Canyon here. It's quite good too, leading to a few waterfall chutes.

There are so many good trails. Definitely spend some time in and around Mesquite Flat Sand Dunes, especially if you enjoy photography. Golden Canyon is great. Begin the hike at Zabriskie Point or Golden Canyon trailhead on Badwater Road. I'd start at Golden Canyon and follow the signs to Red Cathedral for a brilliant vista. Mosaic Canyon is extremely popular. Darwin Falls, located near Panamint Springs is a desert oddity, a waterfall. The trail is short and easy, following a wash to the falls. This is just a small taste of Death Valley. There are canyons galore! I'm planning to explore Sidewinder and Grotto next trip.

Backpacking in Death Valley is not an easy task. Few established trails exist. Reliable water sources are hard to find. Weather conditions can be, well, deadly. But those who explore the backcountry are rewarded with complete solitude and private displays of scenic splendor found nowhere else in the world.

Marble Canyon is a great backpacking destination. **Telescope Peak** is a challenging summer/fall trek, with temperatures some 25°F cooler at the summit than the valley floor, but snow often covers its upper reaches into June. Winter hiking requires crampons and an ice axe and should only be attempted by experienced hikers. The rest of the backpacking trails

Death Valley Backpacking Trails (Distances are roundtrip)

	Name	Location (# on map)	Length	Notes
Furnace Creek	Owlshead Mountains	6.6 miles south on Harry Wade Rd (1)	16.0 miles	Return via Granite Canyon for loop, side canyons, high-clearance required
	Hole-in-the-Wall	On 4WD Road, opposite Twenty Mule Team Canyon (5)	2–10 miles	No trail, side canyons, scrambling, high-clearance 4WD required
	Hanaupah Canyon	5 miles west on Hanaupah Canyon Rd, off West Side Rd (7)	6.0 miles	Accessed via a high-clearance 4WD road, old mining area and spring
	Hungry Bill's Ranch	End of Johnson Canyon Rd (8)	14.0 miles	Informal path, historic ranch, orchard
	Indian Pass	6.5 miles north of Visitor Center (9)	16.0 miles	Gravel wash, mountain pass, canyon
Stovepipe Wells	Cottonwood–Marble Canyon Loop - 🥾	8–10 miles northwest on Cottonwood Canyon Road (13)	26–30 miles	Loop, no trail, high-clearance 4WD required, take map and compass
	Telescope Peak - 🥾	Mahogany Flat Camp (15)	14.0 miles	Maintained trail, wonderful views
	Surprise Canyon - 🥾	Outside the park, north of Ballarat (16)	10.0 miles	Ghost town, high-clearance 4WD
	Panamint Dunes - 🥾	End of dirt road, beyond CA-190 and Panamint Valley Rd Intersection (17)	6.0 miles	No trail, fighter jet training area, high-clearance required
Scotty's Castle	Titanothere Canyon	Titus Canyon Road, near Red Pass (20)	9.0 miles	No trail, high-clearance
	Fall Canyon	Mouth of Titus Canyon (21)	6–12 miles	Camp beyond first dry fall (3 miles)
	Bighorn Gorge	On Scotty's Castle Rd, 3.9 miles south of Grapevine Ranger Station (22)	20.0 miles	Out-and-back, no trail, requires some scrambling

All Backpacking Trails Are Strenuous

listed in the table follow washes, canyons, or old mining roads. One-night backpackers should try hiking **Surprise Canyon** to **Panamint City** (ghost town). The canyon is located on the park's western boundary, off CA-178 near Ballarat (ghost town). Ballarat is worth a visit by itself. It's a good idea to get a free voluntary backcountry permit at Furnace Creek Visitor Center or Stovepipe Wells Ranger Station. If you're thinking about going off the beaten path, many areas do not allow backcountry camping, including the valley floor from Ashford Mill to two miles north of Stovepipe Wells, on Eureka Dunes, Greenwater Canyon, and all day-use and historic mining areas. You must set up camp at least one mile from any paved road or day-use-only dirt road. Camp only in previously disturbed areas and park your vehicle immediately adjacent to the roadway to minimize impact. Carry water, compass, and map, and pack out your trash.

Biking
Bicycles are allowed on all the park's paved and unpaved roads. Road cyclists can cruise along Badwater Road (including Artist's Drive) or climb to Dante's View (the last ascent is a 15% grade). There's also an easy mile-long bike path from Furnace Creek Visitor Center to Harmony Borax Works. Mountain bikers like to explore Titus Canyon Road. It's all downhill if you can arrange a shuttle, but it's loose gravel and you'll be in there with quite a few vehicles and motorbikes. All the unpaved roads are open to mountain bikers (if they're closed to vehicles, they're closed to cyclists).

Horseback Riding
Furnace Creek Stables, located at the Ranch at Death Valley (760.614.1018, furnacecreekstables.com), offers guided trail rides. Two-hour guided trail rides ($120/rider) provide a taste of the desert as you travel into the foothills of the Funeral Mountains. Experienced riders who can post for a long trot and are comfortable in the canter can request a private ride for $100 per person per hour for the first two hours ($85 per person per hour after that). Just know that the pace of the ride is at the guide's discretion. They also offer Moonlight ($115), Sunrise ($85), and Sunset ($85) rides.

Scotty's Castle
Walter Scott, known as Death Valley Scotty, was a desert rat who duped wealthy easterners into investing in his "gold mine." Scotty took the money and went on infamous spending sprees, never producing an ounce of ore. All but one investor pulled their funding. Albert M. Johnson, an insurance magnate, became friends with Scotty and funded construction of what is

Rainbow Canyon (near Father Crowley Vista Point)

now known as Scotty's Castle. Scotty's Castle has been closed since 2015 due to flood damage. The earliest it will reopen for regularly-scheduled public tours is 2022. However, Death Valley Natural History Association (dvnha.org) offers occasional 2-hour-long Flood Recovery Tours ($25). Reservations are available online.

Visitor Centers
The park's primary visitor center is in **Furnace Creek**. It features exhibits, a short film, park rangers, bookstore, and restrooms. It's open year-round, typically from 8am to 5pm. Just south of the visitor center is the **Borax Museum**. It features indoor/outdoor exhibits exploring the role mining played in settlers' lives. There's a small ranger station in **Stovepipe Wells** near the gas station. It's a good place to pop-in for information or a voluntary backcountry permit. **Grapevine Ranger Station** is located on Scotty's Castle Road, just north of Mesquite Road. It's usually unmanned, but the restrooms work. There are a couple more unmanned information stations in the park, but you're better off stopping at one of these.

Ranger Programs & For Kids
Free ranger programs explore a variety of interests: photography, geology, natural history, and ecology. Mesquite Flat Dunes, Zabriskie Point, Golden Canyon, Harmony Borax Works, Badwater, and Dante's View are all sites of talks or walks. These locations are made even more memorable by the colorful stories, history, and anecdotes provided by knowledgeable park rangers. Daily programs are offered during peak season (December through March). Check online or at a visitor center for a current schedule of events.

Most kids prefer desserts to deserts, but this desert is a pretty darn cool treat. Children should enjoy exploring Badwater (the lowest spot in North America) or looking

Layers with Telescope Peak in the background

Creek, Dante's View, Sand Dunes, Ubehebe Crater, Devil's Golf Course, Charcoal Kilns, Artist's Drive, Twenty Mule Team Canyon, and Ashford Mill are accessible with assistance.

Weather
Death Valley is well known for its remarkably hot and dry climate. Average annual rainfall is about two inches. An entire year can pass without any measurable precipitation. The high mountain ranges lining the valley cause hot air to recirculate rather than dissipate. The area's low elevation is also responsible for it being the hottest spot in North America. Day-time highs in July average 115°F. Hot and dry with clear skies make the park extremely pleasant from late fall to early spring.

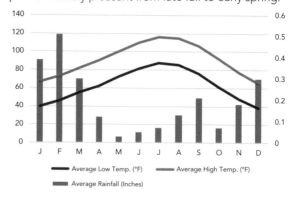

down at Death Valley from Dante's View. They can participate in the Junior Ranger Program. Booklets are available at Furnace Creek Visitor Center. Complete an age-appropriate number of activities and return to the visitor center to receive a Junior Ranger badge.

Flora & Fauna
More than 1,400 species of plants and animals have been found living in Death Valley. The most obvious animals are the park's birds. Hundreds of species of migratory birds stop at desert oases or mountains. Saratoga Spring, Furnace Creek Ranch, Scotty's Castle, Wildrose, and the High Panamints are popular birding areas. Devil's Hole and Salt Creek pupfish are endemic and noteworthy creatures residing within park boundaries. The park's famed wildflower eruption is not a regular occurrence, so check the park website for wildflower updates. They do an exceptional job of providing timely news flashes as to where the best (accessible) flower hotspots are located.

Pets & Accessibility
Pets are permitted but owners must adhere to several regulations. Pets must be kept on a leash (less than six feet). They are not allowed on trails, in the backcountry, or in public buildings (except for service animals). They must not be left unattended at any time. Owners must clean up after their pets and make sure they do not make unreasonable amounts of noise. Basically, you can take your pet anywhere your car can go: campgrounds, parking areas, and roadways.

Visitor centers, contact stations, and museums are accessible to individuals in wheelchairs. Accessible campsites are available at Furnace Creek, Texas Spring, Sunset, Stovepipe Wells, and Mesquite Spring Campgrounds. The first floor of Scotty's Castle Tour is accessible, and there is a lift to the second floor. Badwater, Zabriskie Point, Harmony Borax Works, Salt

Tips & Recommendations
Don't treat Death Valley as a drive-thru park. Unless it's summer, then you might not want to leave your car, much less stick around. With that said, mornings and evenings can be bearable, high-elevation campsites provide comfortable summer sleeping conditions, and it's prime time to hustle up Telescope Peak, so maybe spend the night. But it'll be hot from May through October. Staying true to 2020, the thermometer hit 130°F in the valley on August 16, 2020!)

If it's getting hot during the day in the valley, you don't have to stick it out. Head up to Aguereberry Point, Charcoal Kilns or Skidoo. If you plan on spending the night at elevation, it actually gets cold up there (occasionally in summer too). A good 'beat-the-heat itinerary' around Panamint/Stovepipe Wells would be to hike Mosaic Canyon in the morning, explore Emigrant Canyon Road (Aguereberry Point, etc.) in the afternoon, and return to Mesquite Flat in time for the last few hours of sunlight.

Any time of year, you must make sure you're staying hydrated, protecting yourself from the sun, and keeping the car full of fuel. Gas, food, and water are only available at Panamint Springs, Stovepipe Wells, and Furnace Creek. Make sure your tank is full before departing on any serious adventure. Unless you're coming from Alaska, gas will be more expensive than you're used to.

Superblooms are nation-wide news events. Unfortunately, they aren't that predictable. Spring flowers need winter showers. If it happens, the bloom is usually from Artist's Drive and to the south in the March/April/May timeframe.

No matter what you're going to put in some windshield time to see Death Valley's highlights. It isn't terrible to set up a base camp at Mesquite Flats, but you're better off making a plan, and moving your camp around as you explore.

They're talking about turning the airstrip at Stovepipe Wells into a space for astronomy groups. That'd be cool. No matter what, spend some time looking at the Milky Way. Checking about astronomy meetups is always a good idea when you're in a remote destination (and Death Valley certainly qualifies!).

Badwater Basin is awesome, but most people only walk a short distance before turning around. Continue a good 15–20 minutes west to where things get flat and smooth, and you can have some fun with perspective at the lowest place in the Americas.

There are a ton of seldom-explored side canyons. I'm eagerly awaiting the next Death Valley trip to poke around and see what I've been missing. Don't be afraid to look places other people aren't going. But make sure you have a reliable vehicle and you're prepared for an emergency.

Natural Bridge

Easy Hikes: Badwater Salt Flat (varies), Golden Canyon (2 miles), Titus Canyon (varies), Natural Bridge (1–2), Salt Creek (0.5)

Moderate Hikes: Mesquite Flat Sand Dunes (varies), Mosaic Canyon (1–4 miles), Darwin Falls (2), Dante's Ridge (8)

Strenuous Hikes: Telescope Peak (14 miles), Fall Canyon (6)

Family Activities: Have some fun with perspective at Badwater Salt Flat, become Junior Rangers, drive around the park (Death Valley and all its peculiar features are so much fun to look at), look for endemic pupfish at Salt Creek

Rainy Day Activities: It probably won't rain

History Enthusiasts: Scotty's Castle, Rhyolite (ghost town), Twenty Mule Team Canyon, Eureka Mine, Titus Canyon Road (Leadfield), Borax Museum, Harmony Borax Works, Historic Stovepipe Well

Sunrise/Sunset Spots: For my golden hours, it doesn't get better than Mesquite Flat Sand Dunes, Zabriskie Point and Dante's View are popular sunrise locations, and Badwater and Dante's View can be good for sunset (but the valley is bracketed by mountains, so adjust your expectations accordingly)

Beyond the Park...

Beatty, Amargosa Valley, Shoshone, Tecopa, and Lone Pine offer lodging and dining, but it's best to stay in the park due to its size. With that said, there are many interesting attractions in this region. Here's a start:

Attractions
Red Rock Canyon NCA/Spring Mountain Ranch State Park
Hiking, biking, rock climbing
1000 Scenic Loop Dr, Las Vegas
redrockcanyonlv.org

Big Bovine of the Desert
4400 NV-373, Amargosa Valley

Goldwell Open Air Museum
Near Rhyolite Ghost Town
1 Golden St, Beatty • (702) 870-9946
goldwellmuseum.org

Seven Magic Mountains
Weird rock art installation
S Las Vegas Blvd, Las Vegas
sevenmagicmountains.com

Valley of Fire SP • parks.nv.gov
Stunning photogenic park
29450 Valley of Fire Hwy, Overton

Ash Meadows Nat Wildlife Refuge
Pupfish, Devil's Hole • fws.gov
610 Spring Meadows Rd

Alabama Hills Recreation Area (BLM)
Popular Mobius Arch and Mount Whitney views/hiking, accessed via Whitney Portal Road

Mojave National Preserve
Lava Tube Trail, Mitchell Caverns
2701 Barstow Rd, Barstow
nps.gov/moja • (760) 252-6100

Manzanar National Historic Site
5001 US-395, Independence
nps.gov/manz • (760) 878-2194

Trona Pinnacles
Interesting site on BLM land near CA-178 west of the park

Lake Crowley Columns
Strange rocks found along east shore of Lake Crowley

Castle Mountains NM
Joshua trees and mountains
2701 Barstow Rd, Barstow, CA
nps.gov/camo

Barker Ranch
Inside the park near Ballarat (ghost town), the infamous last hideout of Charles Manson and his "family." Accessed via Goler Wash/Coyote Canyon Road (high-clearance 4WD recommended).

Sequoia & Kings Canyon

A Mineral King sunrise

Phone: (559) 565-3341
Website: nps.gov/seki

Established
September 25, 1890 (Sequoia)
October 1, 1890 (General Grant)
March 4, 1940 (Kings Canyon)
Size: 865,257 Acres
Annual Visitors: 2 Million
Peak Season: Summer

Activities: Cave Tours, Hiking,
Backpacking, Rock Climbing
Horseback Riding, Cross-country
Skiing, Snowshoeing, Sledding

13 Campgrounds: $12–22/night
Backcountry Camping: Permitted
with a Wilderness Permit (fee)
4 Lodges: $113+/night
Park Hours: All day, every day

Entrance Fee: $35/30/20
(car/motorcycle/individual)

Sequoia and Kings Canyon National Parks reside in a contiguous region of the southern Sierra Nevada. Each park has its own boundary and entrance, but they share the same backbone, the granite-peaked mountains. Since 1943 they have been administered jointly by the National Park Service. John Muir, one of the first American naturalists, was an early advocate of protecting regions of exceptional natural beauty. While wandering the High Sierra he formed a kinship with the trees, the rocks, and the mountains, and few areas were more important to Muir than the groves of giant sequoia and mountains of the High Sierra (including Mount Whitney, the highest peak in the lower 48 states). He spent much of his life writing, speaking, and petitioning on their behalf.

"Most of the Sierra trees die of disease, fungi, etc., but nothing hurts the Big Tree. Barring accidents, it seems to be immortal." – John Muir

Muir was just about right. The wood and bark of the park's namesake is infused with chemicals providing resistance to insects and fungi. Its bark—soft, fibrous, and more than two feet thick—is a poor conductor of heat, making the giant sequoia highly resistant to fire damage. They rarely die of old age, either. Many sequoias are more than 2,000 years old. Ironically, extreme size is its greatest threat. Most die by toppling over under their immensity. Relative to their massive size and height, the roots are shallow and without a taproot. Wet soil, strong winds, and shallow roots are a recipe for a toppled sequoia.

"God has cared for these trees, saved them from drought, disease, avalanches, and a thousand tempests and floods. But he cannot save them from fools." – John Muir

Fools found their way to the sequoia groves of the Sierra Nevada and did what they could to topple these mighty trees. In 1888, Walter Fry sought work as a logger (even though sequoias were a relatively poor wood that splintered easily). Somewhere between felling a sequoia (which took a five-man team five days to complete) and counting its 3,266 rings, he had a change of heart. At the same time conservationists were collecting signatures to protect the forest; the third signature was none other than Walter Fry, who decided to put down his axe and channel his efforts toward protecting the trees from the men he had worked alongside. Protection was achieved in 1890 thanks to establishment of a national park. Fry was hired as a road foreman in 1901 and four years later he became a park ranger. Over the next three decades, he became the first civilian superintendent (originally the park fell under army supervision) and the first nature guide, who continued to lead guests on guided walks until his retirement in 1930 at the age of 71.

"When I entered this sublime wilderness the day was nearly done, the trees with rosy, glowing countenances seemed to be hushed and thoughtful, as if waiting in conscious religious dependence on the sun, and one naturally walked softly awestricken among them."
– John Muir

John Muir didn't have to cut down a sequoia tree to understand its significance. The privilege of being able to walk among them was enough. Muir's communion wasn't just with the trees, it was with nature itself. He led energetic hikes into the High Sierra and forged a trail along the steep east face of Mount Whitney. Today, the 211-mile trail from Yosemite National Park to Mount Whitney bears his name. He dreamed of an expanded park, reaching far into Kings Canyon, but it wasn't until 1940 that Kings Canyon National Park was established. Harold Ickes, Secretary of the Interior, wanted to make a park that was impenetrable to automobiles. Kings Canyon was ideal. Today, a single road leads into the canyon and terminates abruptly at Roads End. No road within either park crosses the Sierra Nevada. Mount Whitney, the tallest point in the lower 48, cannot be seen from pavement. The park is left mostly undeveloped, allowing visitors to walk softly awestricken among its natural beauty, much like John Muir did when he first came to the Sierra Nevada.

General Grant

When to Go
Sequoia and Kings Canyon National Parks are open all year. The parks are busiest on summer weekends. Some campgrounds and lodging facilities close for winter. If you can't find a campsite in the park, campgrounds are also available at adjacent Sequoia National Forest and Monument. During winter, roads to Cedar Grove and Mineral King close. Generals Highway is open year-round, but closes during heavy snowstorms. From December to April, visitors can cross-country ski around Giant Forest. The vast majority of visitors arrive between spring and fall.

Transportation & Airports
Sequoia Shuttle (877.287.4453, sequoiashuttle.com) provides transportation between Visalia and Giant Forest Museum. Roundtrip fare is $20 and includes the park entrance fee. Reservations are required. During summer, the park operates **free shuttles** with four routes through the park's most popular sections between Dorst Campground and Crescent Meadow. The closest large commercial airport is Fresno Yosemite International (FAT) in Fresno, CA, located 83 miles from Sequoia's Ash Mountain Entrance. Car rental is available at the airport.

Directions
The parks are located in eastern California's Sierra Nevada. Ash Mountain Entrance is 34 miles from downtown Visalia. Arrive at the entrance via CA-198, which turns into Generals Highway inside the park. Generals Highway connects the two parks. It is 80 miles from Ash Mountain Entrance to the end of Kings Canyon Scenic Byway. Kings Canyon Visitor Center is 53 miles east of Fresno via CA-180.

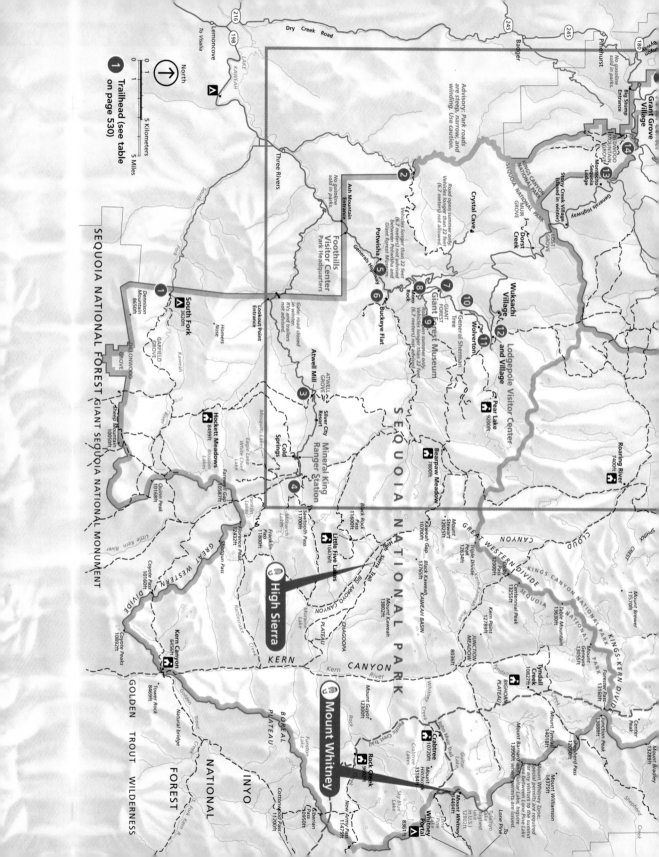

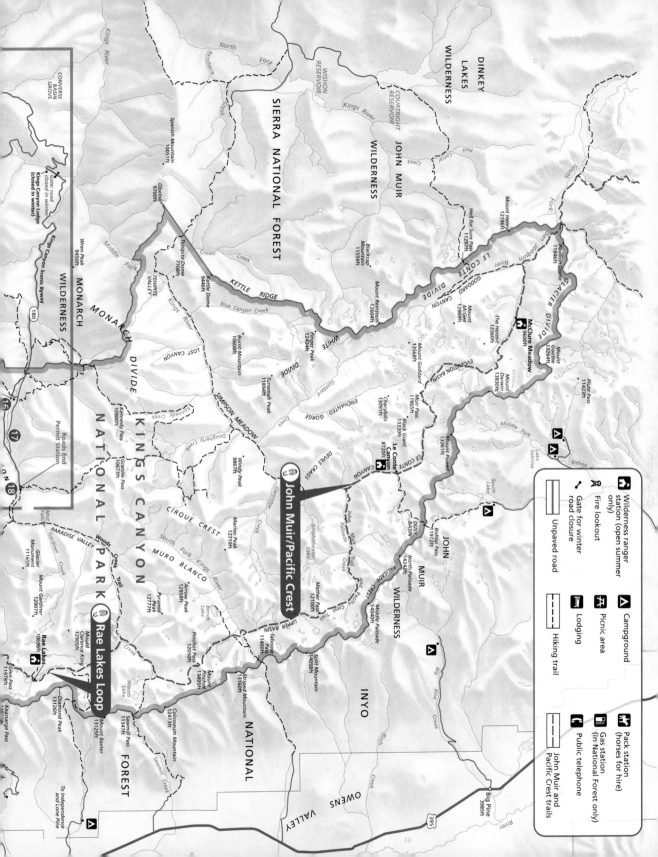

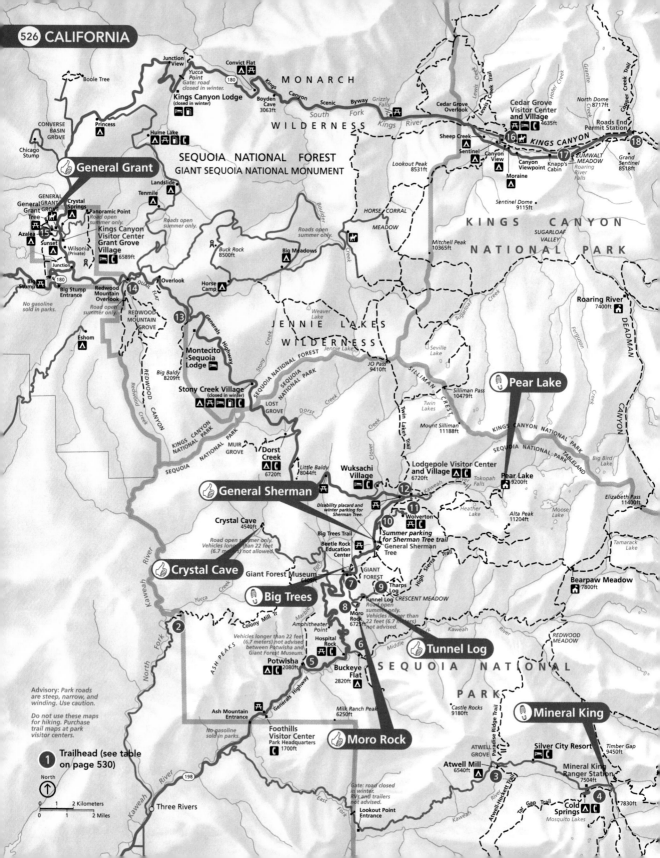

Tunnel Log

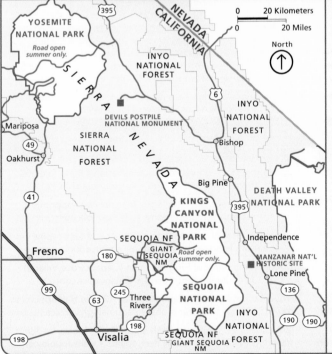

Region

Sequoia and Kings Canyon are two National Parks managed as one. Aside from a few short trails at Grant Grove and Cedar Grove Village, Kings Canyon is primarily a backpacking destination. Sequoia has great backpacking, but you'll also find cave tours, horseback riding, and quirky attractions like Tunnel Log (hard to miss, since it spans the road). Together they're a dream destination for any nature lover. The hardest part is deciding how to allocate your time. Yosemite is a quick drive to the north. Devil's Postpile National Monument is up near Mammoth Lakes (another popular vacation destination). Giant Sequoia National Monument and Sequoia National Forest share a boundary with the parks. Death Valley resides east of Mount Whitney, along with Manzanar National Historic Site, a Japanese Internment Camp during WWII. And there seems to be endless attractions along US-395. So, don't even bother trying to visit them all in one trip. Death Valley isn't much fun in summer, and the Sierra Nevada gets in the way of easy access routes.

Crescent Meadow is a good place to spot bear

Sequoia & Kings Canyon Camping (Fees are per night)

Name	Location	Open	Fee	Sites	Notes
Potwisha*	4 miles from entrance	All Year	$22	42	F, DS, RV
Buckeye Flat*	Middle Fork Kaweah	late March–Sept	$22	28	F
South Fork	South Fork Drive	All Year	$12	10	P
Atwell Mill	Mineral King Road	late May–Oct	$12	21	P
Cold Springs	Mineral King Road	late May–Oct	$12	40	P
Lodgepole*	Giant Forest	late March–Nov	$22	214	F, RV
Dorst Creek*	10 miles from Giant Forest	mid-June–early Sept	$22	210	F, DS (summer), RV
Azalea	Grant Grove (Kings Canyon)	All Year	$18	110	F, DS (summer), RV
Crystal Springs	Grant Grove	late May–September	$18	49	F, RV
Sunset	Grant Grove	late May–mid-Sept	$22	156	F, RV
Sentinel*	Cedar Grove (Kings Canyon)	late April–mid-Nov	$22	82	F, RV
Sheep Creek	Cedar Grove	late May–early Sept	$18	111	F, RV
Canyon View	Cedar Grove	late May–late Sept	$35–60	16	Groups only, F
Moraine	Cedar Grove	late May–early Sept	$18	121	F, RV

F = Flush Toilets, P = Pit Toilets, DS = Dump Station, RV = RVs & Trailers are allowed
*Summer reservations can be made up to six months in advance at (877) 444-6777 or recreation.gov

Backcountry	Allowed with a wilderness permit. Permits are free (and self-issued) from late September to late May, and $15 (+$5/person) for the remainder of the year. Reservations are allowed. Quotas are enforced.
Group	Available at Dorst Creek, Sunset, Canyon View, and Crystal Springs. Fees range from $40–70/night. All group sites must be reserved up to one year in advance at recreation.gov or (877) 444-6777.

Sequoia & Kings Canyon Lodging (Fees are per night, peak season)

Name	Open	Fee	Notes
Wuksachi Lodge (888) 252-5757	All Year	$238–359	Located in Giant Forest of Sequoia National Park, features restaurant and lounge • visitsequoia.com
John Muir Lodge (877) 436-9615	All Year	$260–272	Located in Grant Grove Village, 36 rustic, well-appointed, recently updated rooms • visitsequoia.com
Grant Grove Cabins (877) 436-9615	All Year Cabins (May–Nov)	$113–159	Located in Grant Grove Village • Timber and tent cabins (no heat or electricity in tent cabins) • visitsequoia.com
Cedar Grove Lodge (877) 436-9615	early May–late Oct	$158	Deep in the heart of Kings Canyon (Cedar Grove Village) overlooking Kings River • visitsequoia.com
Sequoia Camp (901) 486-4523	mid-June–mid-Sept	$275 per person	Unique backcountry tent cabins • 1- or 12-mile trail options to camp • ($150 per child per night) • sequoiahighsierracamp.com
Bearpaw Camp (866) 807-3598	mid-June–mid-Sept	$TBD per person	Tent cabins, 11.5 miles on High Sierra Trail • Meals, bedding included • Hot showers and flush toilets • visitsequoia.com

Camping & Lodging

There are 14 campgrounds, 4 lodges, and 2 backcountry tent-cabin camps within the two parks. **Dorst** and **Lodgepole** are the only campgrounds that accept reservations (summer only) up to six months in advance for standard sites and a year in advance for group sites. Campgrounds typically fill through summer, very early for weekends and holidays. You must use the food-storage containers. There are no RV hookups in the parks. Showers are available at Lodgepole Village and Cedar Grove Village. Two High Sierra Camps offer a glamping experience. They offer the tranquility of the backcountry with all the creature comforts of a modern lodge. The catch is you must hike-in, but Sequoia High Sierra Camp has a 1-mile hike option. See the table for a more comprehensive look at the parks' camping and lodging facilities.

Driving

Most of the parkland is inaccessible by car. That's by design. At Kings Canyon, you can drive **Kings Canyon Scenic Byway** (closed in winter) to the aptly named Roads End. That's it. Of course, there are hiking trails, lodges, campgrounds, and the ever-popular Grant Grove along the way. Most visitors explore the relatively small area between Lodgepole Visitor Center and Crescent Meadow. In summer, you'll want to use the **free shuttle** system. One route connects Lodgepole Campground with Giant Forest Museum. Another runs between the museum and Crescent Meadow, including a stop at Moro Rock. There's a route between Dorst Creek and Lodgepole Campgrounds. And a short route shuttles guests around Sherman Tree. This is the heart of the road-accessible park. CA-198 will get you there, which turns into **Generals Highway**, crossing Sequoia, and Sequoia National Forest, before entering the odd isthmus of Kings Canyon that contains Grant Grove. If you're looking for solitude, you may want to try **South Fork** (just be warned the final stretch of road is unpaved and rough, high-clearance vehicles are recommended). **Mineral King Road** is narrow, winding, and, at times, steep. It also leads deeper into the park's backcountry. It's a good place to go if you like primitive camping, backpacking, and hiking. It isn't such a great place if you don't like rugged roadways.

Caves

There are more than 265 known caves within the park and occasionally a new cave is discovered. At 17 miles in length, Liburn is the longest cave in California. **Crystal Cave** is the only one available for tours. Crystal Cave Road is about 13 miles north of Foothills Visitor Center and 3 miles south of General Sherman.

General Sherman

It's another 6.5 miles to the cave. Vehicles over 22 feet and those towing trailers are not allowed on Crystal Cave Road. Tours are given from spring through fall by Sequoia Parks Conservancy. The Standard Tour costs $17/adult and $9/child (ages 5–12). Discovery Tours are offered during summer for $25/person. Wild Cave Tours are also offered for $140/adult. Tickets are sold online at recreation.gov. It's a good idea to buy them in advance. However, any unsold tickets are available at Foothills or Lodgepole Visitor Centers. Don't drive to the cave without tickets. They are not sold at the entrance. Wear a jacket; the cave is 50°F year-round.

Hiking & Backpacking

With more than 800 miles of hiking trails, it's difficult to choose what to see and where to hike. In Sequoia, the short hike up nearly 400 stairs to the top of **Moro Rock** provides spectacular views. You'll find a short trail to **Hanging Rock** nearby. The one activity every visitor must do is stand next to a giant sequoia. **General Sherman** is the tree to visit at Sequoia. At Kings Canyon, say hello to **General Grant**, a tree President Coolidge called the "Nation's Christmas Tree." Respectively, they are the first and second largest trees in the world. More peaceful big tree options include hiking to Garfield Grove from South Fork Camp or Muir Grove from Dorst Creek Camp. **Crescent Meadow** is an easy loop with good bear-spotting opportunities. For classic High Sierra trails, go to Mineral King in Sequoia or Roads End at Kings Canyon. Note that the road to Mineral King is narrow and winding. Check out the hiking table for additional trails. You can try to day-hike to the summit of **Mount Whitney** from the park's eastern side. But you'll need a permit (recreation.gov, $6 + $15/person) and you're looking at 6,000+ feet of

Sequoia & Kings Canyon Hiking Trails (Distances are roundtrip)

	Name	Location (# on map)	Length	Difficulty Rating & Notes
Sequoia	Lady Bug	South Fork Campground (1)	6.0 miles	M – 1.75 miles to camp, 3 miles to sequoia grove
	Garfield Grove	South Fork Campground (1)	10.0 miles	S – Ends at a remote sequoia grove
	North Fork	North Fork Rec. Area (2)	8.4 miles	M – Get trailhead location from visitor center
	Paradise Peak	Atwell Mill Campground (3)	9.6 miles	S – Large sequoias, fantastic views, not popular
	Monarch Lakes - ♿	End of Mineral King Rd (4)	8.4 miles	M – Wonderful views of the southern Sierra
	Crystal Lake - ♿	End of Mineral King Rd (4)	9.8 miles	S – Branch from Monarch Lakes Trail (steep)
	Timber Gap	End of Mineral King Rd (4)	4.0 miles	M – Follows old mining route along Monarch Creek
	Franklin Lakes - ♿	End of Mineral King Rd (4)	10.8 miles	M – Popular first leg for multi-day trips
	White Chief	End of Mineral King Rd (4)	5.8 miles	M – Steep but scenic mining trail
	Eagle Lake - ♿	End of Mineral King Rd (4)	6.8 miles	M – Fairly steep but popular trail to majestic lake
	Mosquito Lakes - ♿	End of Mineral King Rd (4)	7.2 miles	S – Several small lakes in the High Sierra
	Marble Falls	Potwisha Campground (5)	7.8 miles	M – Marble Fork–Kaweah River/Deep Canyon
	Middle Fork	Off dirt road, before Buckeye Flat Campground (5)	5.5 miles	M – Views of Moro Rock and Castle Rocks, popular in spring, creek crossings required
	Paradise Creek	Buckeye Flat Camp (6)	1.5 miles	E – Popular swimming holes
	Big Trees - ♿	Giant Forest Museum (7)	1.3 miles	E – Paved loop with benches and interpretive signs
	Sunset Rock - ♿	Giant Forest Museum (7)	2.0 miles	E – Short hike to granite rock with western views
	Moro Rock - ♿	Crescent Meadow Rd (8)	0.5 mile	M – Almost 400 steps to granite dome/great views
	Crescent Meadow	Crescent Meadow Rd (9)	3.2 miles	E – Leads to Tharp's Log and Chimney Tree
	Gen. Sherman - ♿	General Sherman Tree (10)	1.0 miles	M – Handicap parking available on Generals Hwy
	Congress	General Sherman Tree (10)	2.0 miles	E – Paved loop accessed from Gen. Sherman Trail
	Alta Peak - ♿	Wolverton Picnic Area (11)	13.8 miles	S – Vews of Mount Whitney from Alta Peak
	Tokopah Falls	Lodgepole Camp (12)	3.4 miles	E – Walk along Marble Fork of the Kaweah River
	Mt Whitney - ♿	Whitney Portal (18)	22.0 miles	X – East side of park • Shortest route to the summit
Kings Canyon	Big Baldy Ridge - ♿	8 mi. S on Generals Hwy (13)	4.0 miles	M – Provides views down into Redwood Canyon
	Buena Vista Peak	Dirt road off Generals Hwy, 6 miles SE of Grant Grove (14)	2.0 miles	E – Easiest summit hike, where visitors obtain decent views of the canyon and mountains
	Redwood Canyon	Dirt road off Generals Hwy, 6 miles SE of Grant Grove (14)	16.0 miles	E/S – Network of trails through one of the largest of all Sequoia groves • Road closed in winter
	General Grant - ♿	Grant Tree Parking Area (15)	0.7 mile	E – Short loop to the Nation's Christmas Tree
	North Grove Loop	Grant Tree Parking Area (15)	1.5 miles	E – High granite walls and lush meadows
	Zumwalt Meadow	Cedar Grove Village (16)	1.5 miles	E – Popular loop/Burnt in 2015 fire
	Hotel/Lewis Creek	Cedar Grove Village (16)	8.0 miles	M – Loop includes Cedar Grove Overlook
	Roaring River Falls	3 miles east of village (17)	0.3 mile	E – Short roadside hike to powerfull waterfall
	Mist Falls - ♿	Roads End (18)	8.0 miles	M – Relatively flat trail, large waterfall
	Rae Lakes Loop - ♿	Roads End (18)	41.0 miles	S – Popular backcountry hike
	Woods Creek	Roads End (18)	28.0 miles	S – Follows Mist Falls to Paradise Valley and PCT
Both	John Muir	Backcountry	211 miles	One-way • Connects Yosemite and Mt Whitney
	Pacific Crest (PCT)	Mexico–British Columbia	2,663 mi	One-way • Follows Sierra Nevada and Cascades

Difficulty Ratings: E = Easy, M = Moderate, S = Strenuous, X = Extreme

elevation gain (and there are other fun things to investigate over there). Backpacking is a better alternative (you'll still need a permit).

Backpacking in the Sierra Nevada is an indescribable experience. This setting inspired John Muir to dedicate much of his life to the conservation of the United States' irreplaceable natural wonders. Largely thanks to Muir, Sequoia and Kings Canyon National Parks' backcountry is left as it was when he hiked these trails. Nowadays, more people have become appreciative of nature's beauty, and the backcountry is so popular a wilderness permit quota system is in place during summer (May–September). Permits cost $15 plus $5 per person and can be reserved up to six months in advance at recreation.gov. Not interested in reserving permits? A fraction of all permits is available on a first-come, first-served basis. Fees still apply. Walk-up and reserved permits must be picked up at the issuing station closest to your trailhead, no earlier than 1pm the day before you depart. From late September to late May visitors can obtain a free wilderness permit from self-issue stations located at Lodgepole Visitor Center, Foothills Visitor Center, Roads End Permit Station, and Mineral King Ranger Station. Food must be stored in a bear-resistant canister or metal food storage locker.

John Muir and Pacific Crest are legendary long-distance trails that pass through the parks. If you'd like to sample the best of the Sierra Nevada, try Sequoia's 49-mile High Sierra Trail or Kings Canyon's 41-mile Rae Lakes Loop. **Rae Lakes Loop** is often regarded as the best backpacking trail in the entire High Sierra. For a shorter, more comfortable trek, take **High Sierra Trail** 12 miles to **Sequoia High Sierra Camp** (901.486.4523, sequoiahighsierracamp.com), where you can reserve tent cabins for $275 per person per night, and $150 per child per night. If you aren't interested in a strenuous hike, there is a 1-mile trail option. Breakfast, lunch, and dinner are included. **Bearpaw High Sierra Camp** (866.807.3598, visitsequoia.com) offers a similar pampered backpacking experience with a similar per person per night price tag. Reaching Bearpaw requires an 11.5-mile (one-way) hike along High Sierra Trail, beginning at Crescent Meadow Parking Area. A wilderness permit (free to Bearpaw guests and available at Lodgepole Visitor Center) is required to park at Crescent Meadow.

If you don't feel comfortable backpacking and want to hire a guide, Wildland Trekking (800.715.4453, wildlandtrekking.com) is one of many licensed commercial outfitters that can get you out there.

A bear hiding out in Crescent Meadows

Rock Climbing

Rock found at Sequoia and Kings Canyon National Parks is similar to Yosemite in terms of quality and quantity. The main difference is that you have to pack up your gear and hike (usually a full-day) to the best climbing locations. In Kings Canyon, Bubbs Creek Trail (part of Rae Lakes Loop) is a good place to find multi-pitch climbing routes. Moro Rock and Hanging Rock (Sequoia) are easily accessible features for climbing. There are also excellent options along High Sierra Trail. Climbing in remote regions is not recommended for inexperienced climbers. Sierra Mountain Guides (760.648.1122, sierramtnguides.com) offers a variety of introductory courses and custom trips throughout the eastern and High Sierra.

Horseback Riding

Horse enthusiasts aren't excluded from the fun. Those looking to explore the Sierra Nevada on horseback have two outfitters to choose from. Grant Grove Stables (559.335.9292, grantgrovestables.com) offers 1- and 2-hour guided trips to General Grant Tree, through North Grove, Lion Meadow, and Dead Giant Meadow. Cedar Grove Pack Station (559.565.3464, cedargrovepackstation.com) has a wider range of services. You can enjoy anything from an hour-long trail ride to multi-day pack trips in Kings Canyon's backcountry. Backcountry trips include Monarch Divide and Rae Lakes Loop. Horse Corral Packers (559.565.3404, summer • 559.564.6429, winter, hcpacker.com) is located east of Big Meadows Campground in Sequoia National Forest. They offer half-day, full-day, and extended pack trips. Horseback rides are generally offered from late spring through fall. Reservations are highly recommended (and required for pack trips). Rates are about $60/rider for an hour-long ride and $100/rider for 2 hours. Multi-day backcountry trips cost about $275 per rider per day.

Tharp's Log

Winter Activities
Winter is a wonderful time of year to visit the parks. The lower foothills remain snow free year-round, but you can usually find snow for **cross-country skiing** and **snowshoeing** in the higher elevations. If you plan on visiting in winter, be prepared with tire chains.

Pear Lake Ski Hut (Sequoia) is open from mid-December through April. Located just north of Pear Lake at 9,200-feet elevation, it can be reached via a steep six-mile trail from Wolverton Meadow. The hut sleeps 10, costs $50 per person per night, and reservations are required. Sequoia Parks Conservancy (559.565.4251, sequoiaparksconservancy.org) has additional information on the reservation process. Treat it like a backpacking trip, packing along sleeping bag, stove, fuel, firestarter, light, and something to purify water. Additional ski trails are available at Giant Forest and Grant Grove (as long as there's enough snow).

The park offers ranger-guided snowshoe walks as soon as conditions permit them. Snowshoes are provided (free). These two-hour treks usually begin at Giant Forest Museum and Grant Grove. Group size is limited, and they may cancel due to conditions. It's best to check with the park, online, in person, or over the phone, to verify a snowshoe walk is happening if your heart is set on it. If conditions aren't conducive to snowshoeing, they may go out for a hike. Just be prepared with traction devices for your waterproof hiking boots. Sequoia Parks Conservancy (559.565.4251, sequoiaparksconservancy.org) also offers naturalist-guided snowshoe treks and stargazing opportunities in winter. Snowshoe trips may be difficult for small children. Snowshoe rental is available at Lodgepole Market and Grant Grove Gift Shop. Wuksachi Lodge offers ski and snowshoe rental when it's open. At Wolverton, two miles north of

General Sherman Tree, there's an open area with two sledding hills where children of all ages are welcome to race down the hills and play in the snow. There are two more snowplay areas near Grant Grove. Be sure to check road conditions before heading out to the park and carry tire chains with you in case they're required.

Visitor Centers & Museums
Sequoia has two visitor centers, a museum, and a ranger station. Entering from Three Rivers, you'll immediately meet **Foothills Visitor Center**. It's open daily, year-round. Hours are 8am to 4:30pm from mid-March through September, and from 9am until 4pm for the rest of the year. It offers exhibits, a bookstore, bear-cannister rentals, wilderness permits, Crystal Cave tour tickets (if tours didn't sell out online), and restrooms. Further down the road you'll find **Giant Forest Museum**. It offers tree-centric exhibits and is open daily, all year long. **Lodgepole Visitor Center** is located between General Sherman and Wuksachi Village. It closes for winter, with typical hours from 8am until 4:30pm from late September through mid-October. Here you'll find human-history exhibits, a short film, and wilderness permits. **Mineral King Ranger Station** is located at the end of Mineral King Road. Stop in and ask about trail conditions before heading out or maybe you'll need help if marmots get after your car (see tips).

Kings Canyon has two visitor centers. **Kings Canyon Visitor Center** is located near Grant Grove. It's open year-round, from 8am to 5pm in summer, with hours progressively shorter until they're 10am to 3pm in winter. It offers exhibits, a bookstore, and wilderness permits. **Cedar Grove Visitor Center** is typically only open in summer from 9am until 5pm.

Ranger Programs & For Kids
In addition to cave tours and snowshoe walks, the park offers a variety of free ranger-led activities. They range from moon-lit walks to climbing up Moro Rock. You may even be able to join an astronomy program. A current listing of programs can be found on bulletin boards located at each visitor center or the park's online calendar. If you're staying at a campground, be sure to check if a campfire program will be happening at its amphitheater. Most programs are offered between Memorial Day and Labor Day. But programs continue the rest of the year depending on staffing availability (and weather/snow conditions).

Almost all ranger programs are great activities for the whole family. The scenery, stories, and sweet hats topping each ranger's head can inspire children to want to join them. The Junior Ranger Program allows children of all ages to participate in some ranger fun while at the park. Pick up a free Junior Ranger Activity Booklet at a visitor center (or download it from the park website). Complete an age-appropriate number of activities and return to a visitor center to become a Junior Ranger and receive an award.

Flora & Fauna

Giant sequoias tend to steal the show for anyone's first visit to the park. Stand next to one of these towering giants and you can finally grasp their impressive size. Try to hug one (it will take more than one of you). Walk, drive, and peer through sequoias that have been hollowed out. Whatever you do, you'll be sure to come away inspired. Giant Forest (Sequoia) and Grant Grove (Kings Canyon) are the two most popular sequoia groves, but there are 75 total groves, containing more than 15,000 trees, within park boundaries along the western slope of the Sierra Nevada. Sequoias reside in the middle elevations (5–7,000 feet) with a mix of evergreens. Giant Forest is home to five of the ten largest trees in the world, including General Sherman, the world's largest tree. Grant Grove is home to General Grant, the world's second largest tree. Lower elevations are home to chaparral vegetation, and high elevations are mostly rocky and barren except for the occasional foxtail and whitebark pine.

When it comes to biodiversity, there's much more than big trees. The tallest mountain and one of the deepest canyons in the Lower 48, 265 known caves, and everything in between provide a variety of ecosystems, supporting some 1,200 species of plants and 260 vertebrate species. There's a chance you may see a bear lumbering about a sequoia grove or a bighorn sheep scaling the rocky ledges of the backcountry, but you're more likely to spot mule deer, squirrels, or marmot. The parks also provide habitat for more than 200 species of birds. Golden eagle, peregrine falcon, and blue grouse have all been spotted here. One of the best places to begin a birding expedition is Giant Forest.

Pets & Accessibility

Pets are allowed in the park but must be kept on a leash (less than six feet). They are not permitted on park trails or in the backcountry. Pets may not enter public buildings (except service animals), but are allowed along roadways, in parking areas, and in frontcountry campgrounds and picnic areas.

Accessible restrooms are available at each campground and visitor center, as well as Giant Forest Museum.

Hiking from Mineral King

General Sherman Tree (with nearby accessible parking area) and Big Trees trails are accessible to individuals in wheelchairs. Beetle Rock, Crescent Meadows, Tharp's Log, Grant Tree, Zumwalt Meadows, Muir Rock, and Roaring River Falls trails are accessible with assistance. Refer to the park's accessibility guide (available online) for a more comprehensive list.

Weather

Temperature and weather conditions change drastically depending on your elevation, which ranges from 1,500 to 14,494 feet within the park. A visitor might enter at Three Rivers (1,700 feet) wearing shorts and a t-shirt, while a hiker climbing to the summit of Mount Whitney (14,494 feet) is covered from head to toe in winter apparel. That's an extreme scenario; most areas are pleasant. The middle elevations (~4,0000–7,000 feet) feature comfortable summer temperatures with average highs in the 70s°F. Weather is rarely excessively hot, with the hottest days only sneaking into the lower 90s°F. Overnight temperatures can fall below freezing, but the average summer low is in the 50s°F. Expect the temperature to be 10–15°F warmer in the foothills than it is in the middle elevations.

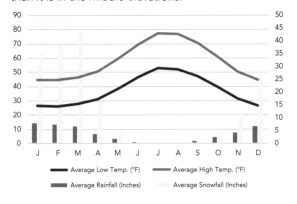

Average Low Temp. (°F) ── Average High Temp. (°F) ── Average Rainfall (Inches) ── Average Snowfall (Inches)

Tunnel Rock

Tips & Recommendations

Summer is generally the best (and most popular) time to visit, as roads and most trails will be completely free of snow. It's also the most common time for forest fires. Visibility could be an issue. Spring is a great alternative, as many of the highlights remain open, wildflowers begin to bloom, and waterfalls are super-charged by snowmelt. But if you planned on hiking, trails will be wet, muddy, and potentially impassable due to snow or dangerous water levels. Fall has its benefits. Smaller crowds and good hiking are two. You just need to be able to endure the brisk mornings. Winter can be magical, but you'll need to carry (and possibly use) tire chains, and be properly equipped should you decide to venture beyond the roadways.

As mentioned, summer is busy. Roughly 70% of the park's annual visitors arrive between May and September. While exploring the Giant Forest area, please use the park's free shuttle service during this time.

Vehicles longer than 22 feet are not advised to travel between Potwisha Campground and Giant Forest Museum (or to Crystal Cave). Additionally, vehicles longer than 24 feet are not advised to travel between Foothills Visitor Center and Potwisha Campground.

Don't leave Sequoia without getting up close and personal with its namesake trees. Most visitors are satisfied seeing General Sherman or General Grant, but spend a little more time with these giants by hiking Big Trees or Congress Trails. Or venture slightly off the beaten path to Muir Grove (Dorst Creek) or Garfield Grove (South Fork). To me, the big trees are the best easily-accessible highlight in these parks.

The next best suggestion would be to get into the park's backcountry. Yes, that isn't for everyone, but

Sequoia attracts a broader audience due to multiple backcountry options: backpacking on your own, joining an outfitter, or staying at a High Sierra camp. With proper planning, backpacking can vastly increase the quality of a national park trip. However, it is difficult to allocate a few days to hiking when there's so much to see in the area (Yosemite, Devil's Postpile, Death Valley, and Lake Tahoe aren't that far away). Remember that backpacking requires a permit (fee) from May through September. Reserve one online at recreation.gov or a portion are available in person no more than one day before your desired trip.

If you're going to stick closer to the roads. A night in each park should do just fine to see the highlights and hike a few short trails. If you don't mind narrow, winding roads, I'd suggest you add a third night, wake up early, and then drive up to Mineral King for a longer day hike to end your stay here with a breathtaking exclamation point to, say, Mosquito Lakes.

Kings Canyon is designed to be a backpacker's park, but the drive to Road's End is quite nice, and you'll find several day hikes along the way.

Similarly, Mineral King is a prime departure point for backcountry adventures at Sequoia.

If you'd like to have a more comfortable backpacking experience, there are two High Sierra Camps where you'll be treated to three full meals by an executive chef, and you sleep in a tent cabin.

In Everglades it's the vultures. At Sequoia it's the marmots. I haven't seen it personally, but a fellow traveler mentioned how cars were wrapped in tarp at Mineral King. Turns out marmots have a taste for the rubber found in today's vehicles, including seals, radiator hoses, and electrical wiring. The park suggests if you visit Mineral King, especially before August (their thirst for car parts wanes as spring turns to summer), you should first inspect underneath your vehicle for any signs of marmot sabotage (check hoses, belts, wiring, etc.). Then turn your key to "on" without starting your vehicle. Wait for the indicator lights. If things appear to be normal, start your car and listen for unusual sounds.

Having an emergency up here is a real pickle. You probably will have to rely on fellow hikers or the park ranger at the nearby ranger station (as cell service most likely will not be available). This is why it's always a good idea to be prepared for the unexpected (car-ravaging marmots including), with a few days' worth of extra food,

Mineral King

water, medications, anything you absolutely need (or find comforting).

Chances are you'll only have cell service near the Ash Mountain Entrance. Free Wi-Fi is available at Foothills and Kings Canyon Visitor Centers.

There are no gas or charging stations within park boundaries. You'll find a market, cafe, gift shop, showers, and laundry at Lodgepole Village (open spring through fall). Wuksachi Lodge has a restaurant, gift shop, and lounge. Grant Grove Village (open all year) offers a restaurant, market, post office, and gift shop. Cedar Grove Village (open late May through September) has a gift shop, market, and snack bar.

Easy Hikes: General Grant (0.7 mile), Big Trees (1.3), Sunset Rock (2)
Moderate Hikes: Monarch Lakes (8.4 miles), General Sherman (1), Eagle Lake (6.8), Big Baldy Ridge (4), Franklin Lakes (10.8), Mist Falls (8), Moro Rock (0.5)
Strenuous Hikes: Mosquito Lakes (7.2 miles), Pear Lake, Rae Lakes Loop (41 miles), Alta Peak (13.8), Crystal Lake (9.8)
Extreme Hikes: Mount Whitney (multi-day)
Family Activities: Tour Crystal Cave, pose with really big trees, look for bear at Crescent Meadow, become Junior Rangers
Guided Tours: Ride a horse, go rock climbing, tour Crystal Cave
Rainy Day Activities: Watch the weather and lay low in Three Rivers if a thunderstorm is predicted, otherwise put on your rain gear and hike
History Enthusiasts: Tharp's Log, Gamlin Cabin
Sunset Spots: Sunset Rock, Beetle Rock, Moro Rock, Panoramic Point, Hanging Rock
Wildlife: Crescent Meadow, Mineral King Road, Round Meadow (Big Trees Trail), Zumwalt Meadow

Beyond the Park...

Dining
Sierra Subs & Salad • (559) 561-4810
41651 Sierra Dr, Three Rivers
sierrasubsandsalads.com

Quesadilla Gorilla • (559) 602-6329
41119 Sierra Dr, Three Rivers
quesadillagorilla.com

Sequoia Coffee Co • (425) 802-2713
41669 Sierra Dr, Three Rivers

Smoky Mtn BBQ • (559) 338-0160
39316 Dunlap Rd, Dunlap

Bear Mountain Pizza • (559) 332-9696
31074 E Kings Canyon Rd, Squaw Valley

Grocery Stores
Village Market • (559) 561-4441
40869 Sierra Dr, Three Rivers

Costco • (559) 735-2400
1405 W Cameron Ave, Visalia

Walmart • (559) 636-2302
1819 E Noble Ave, Visalia

Lodging
Silver City Mountain Resort
Mineral King Rd, Three Rivers
silvercityresort.com • (559) 561-3223

Buckeye Tree • (559) 561-5900
46000 Sierra Dr, Three Rivers
buckeyetreelodge.com

River Dance B&B • (559) 561-4411
40534 Cherokee Oaks Dr, Three Rivers
sequoiariverdance.com

Monecito Sequoia Lodge
mslodge.com • (559) 565-3388

Campgrounds
Sequoia RV Ranch • (559) 561-4333
43490 N Fork Dr, Three Rivers
sequoiarvranch.com

Sequoia KOA
7480 Ave 308, Visalia
koa.com • (559) 651-0544

Sequoia RV Park • (559) 338-2350
35671 E Kings Canyon Rd, Dunlap

Sequoia Resort & RV Park
50616 CA-245, Badger
sequoiaresort.com • (559) 967-1755

Festivals
Gilroy Garlic Festival • July
gilroygarlicfestival.com • Gilroy

Attractions
Project Survival Cat Haven
38257 E Kings Canyon Rd, Dunlap
cathaven.com • (559) 338-3216

Boyden Cavern • (888) 854-8243
Sequoia National Forest
boydencavern.com

Sequoia National Forest & Giant
Sequoia National Monument
*National Park-adjacent land with
sequoias and hiking trails*

Sierra & Inyo National Forests
*Definitely worth looking into if
you want to hike or backpack.
Inyo features many trails as
good as, if not better, than ones
you'll find in Yosemite, King's
Canyon, and Sequoia.*

Yosemite

Prepping to hike up Half Dome

Phone: (209) 372-0200
Website: nps.gov/yose

Established: October 1, 1890
June 30, 1864 (State Park)
Size: 761,268 Acres
Annual Visitors: 4.4 Million
Peak Season: June–September
Hiking Trails: 750+ Miles

Activities: Hiking, Backpacking,
Rock Climbing, Rafting, Biking,
Horseback Riding

13 Frontcountry Campgrounds
Fee: $12–26/night
Backcountry Camping: Permitted
with a Backcountry Use Permit
**7 Lodges (and High Sierra
Camps):** $108–1,221/night

Park Hours: All day, every day,
except Hetch Hetchy (Day-Use)
Entrance Fee: $35/$30/$20
(car/motorcycle/individual)

"I have seen persons of emotional temperament stand with tearful eyes, spellbound and dumb with awe, as they got their first view of the Valley from Inspiration Point, overwhelmed in the sudden presence of the unspeakable, stupendous grandeur."

– Galen Clark

Times have changed, but the scenery remains the same. The first sight of the valley still possesses the power to leave guests weak in the knees and with a tear in their eye. These very sites were the catalyst fueling the conservation movement. The smooth granite peaks inspired a man, by his own admission an "unknown nobody," to become one of America's great naturalist writers, thinkers, speakers, and the unofficial "father of the national parks." Giant sequoias encouraged one of the country's great presidents to protect similar exhaustible resources and landscapes. Beautiful vistas motivated a photographer to capture their essence, their "unspeakable, stupendous grandeur," allowing the world to experience the spellbinding awe felt when a visitor first views the valley from Glacier Point, Tunnel View, or Valley View.

The first non-Native visitors to this majestic valley didn't come for respite or rejuvenation. In 1851, the Mariposa Battalion was called to the Sierra Nevada to settle a skirmish between Native Americans and local '49ers hoping to dispossess their land. These soldiers found the Natives, whom they believed to be the Yosemite Tribe, in a valley about one mile wide and eight miles long. Upon arrival, the battalion didn't stop to stare in bewilderment or give thanks to a greater power capable of creating such a spectacle; instead they prepared to burn it down, thus starving the Natives. Eventually the feud was settled, and it was learned that the natives were known as Ahwahneechee; Yosemite was their name for the Mariposa Battalion.

"If no man ever feels his utter insignificance at any time, it is when looking upon such a scene of appalling grandeur."

— James Mason Hutchings

James Mason Hutchings and Galen Clark shared similar sentiments when it came to Yosemite Valley. In 1855, Natives led Hutchings into the valley. He quickly became enamored with the scenery and wasted no time moving in. In his opinion, the region had "value" as a tourist attraction, so he immediately began promoting it as such. From 1855–1864, the valley was visited by just 653 tourists. Insufficient infrastructure resulted in trips from San Francisco to Yosemite Valley that took 4–5 days (on foot, horseback, and carriage).

Galen Clark's wife died young, so he too moved to California seeking his fortune. In 1853, Clark contracted a severe lung infection. Doctors gave him six months to live. "I went to the mountains to take my chances of dying or growing better, which I thought were about even (Galen Clark, 1856)." Shortly after his arrival he discovered Mariposa Grove, and from that point on much of his time was spent writing friends and Congress requesting passage of legislation to protect the area. He gained support of John Conness, a Senator from California. In 1864, in the midst of the Civil War, President Abraham Lincoln signed a bill preserving Yosemite Valley and Mariposa Grove under state control. Clark happily became guardian of the Yosemite Grant, including the grove of trees that inspired him to pursue conservation. As guardian he was expected to protect the park from overeager tourists, maintain roads and bridges, and deal with residents and businesses residing here. All this needed to be done on a meager $500 annual budget.

One business in the valley was Hutchings House Hotel. James Mason Hutchings became Galen Clark's biggest pest. He refused to abide by the $1/year government lease. Essentially squatting on public land, he expanded his operations and built a sawmill.

Hutchings hired a wandering shepherd by the name of John Muir to run his sawmill. Born in Scotland, raised in Wisconsin, Muir skedaddled to Canada to avoid

Dog Lake

When to Go
Yosemite is open all day, every day, with the exception of Hetch Hetchy Entrance Station (open during daylight hours). Yosemite Valley and Wawona are accessible by car year-round. Tioga, Glacier Point, and Mariposa Grove Roads close for winter (usually beginning in November) and do not reopen until late May. Glacier Point/Badger Pass Road to Badger Pass Ski Area is plowed from mid-December through early April. In winter, tire chains are often required to drive park roads. You must carry chains with you and know how to use them.

Spring and winter are the best times for waterfalls. Most wildflowers bloom in June. In fall, crowds thin and leaves of the few stands of maple, oak, and dogwood trees begin to change. Crowds are common, especially at Yosemite Valley in summer. Park roads, shuttles, and popular trails become extremely congested during this time. You will want to reserve accommodations well in advance or arrive early to obtain a first-come, first-served campsite.

Transportation & Airports
Amtrak (800.872.7245, amtrak.com) provides a combination of train and bus service to Yosemite Valley. Greyhound (800.231.2222, greyhound.com) provides bus service to Merced, where you can board a Yosemite Area Regional Transportation System (YARTS) (877.989.2787, yarts.com) bus to Yosemite Valley. YARTS also provides service between the park and Merced (CA-140), Sonora (CA-108/120), and Fresno (CA-41). And service is available east of Yosemite from Lee Vining, June Lake, and Mammoth Lakes (along CA-120) in summer.

Fresno–Yosemite International (FAT), Merced (MCE), and Modesto City–County (MOD) Airports are all within a 2.5-hour drive of Yosemite Valley. San Francisco International (SFO), Oakland International, San José International (SJC), Sacramento International (SMF), and Reno/Tahoe International (RNO) Airports are within a five-hour drive.

the Civil War and returned to work as an industrial engineer in Indiana. The sharp mind that had allowed memorization of the Bible's New Testament and most of the Old Testament by age 11 was on display in an industrial environment. His inventiveness and intellect helped improve many machines and processes, making life easier for the laborers at a plant manufacturing carriage parts. When a work accident nearly left him blind, Muir chose to be true to himself. He had always wanted to study plants and explore the wilderness. He set out on a 1,000-mile walk from Indiana to Florida, where he planned to board a ship to South America. Unfortunately, he contracted malaria before he could set sail across the Caribbean. While recuperating in Florida, he read about Yosemite and the Sierra Nevada. Nursed back to health, Muir booked passage to California instead. He arrived in 1868. After a brief stint as a shepherd, Muir moved into Yosemite Valley to run Hutchings' sawmill, where he built a cabin near the base of Yosemite Falls for $3, what he considered to be "the handsomest building in the valley."

As Muir was settling into his new life, Hutchings was being evicted. In 1875, Galen Clark allowed him to store his furniture in a vacant building. Hutchings moved in more than his furniture. He set up his entire operation: Wells Fargo Office, telegraph, post office, everything. Once again, he was running a hotel. This was the final straw. Hutchings, banished from Yosemite, moved to San Francisco where he started a tourist agency and wrote two best-selling books including *In the Heart of the Sierras.*

Meanwhile, Muir had become a bit of a Yosemite celebrity. All of the park's guests wanted exposure to his brand of enthusiasm and passion for the ecology and geology of the High Sierra. In 1871, Ralph Waldo Emerson, the author whose work Muir had read many a night from the light of a campfire, arrived at Yosemite. After just one day in Muir's company, Emerson offered Muir a teaching position at Harvard. Even though he had spent much of the past three years unemployed, Muir declined the offer to remain in what he called "the grandest of all the special temples of Nature I was ever permitted to enter…the sanctum sanctorum of the Sierra."

By 1889, Yosemite Valley was officially a tourist trap. A cliff-side hotel was constructed at Glacier Point. Raging fires were hurled over the cliff's edge to create a waterfall of fire. Tunnels were carved into trees. Muir had seen too much, so he set out to make Yosemite a national park. Witnessing how the establishment of

Yellowstone National Park increased passenger traffic for Northern Pacific Railroad, the Southern Pacific placed their support behind the endeavor. It worked. In 1890, Sequoia, General Grant, and Yosemite all became national parks.

James Mason Hutchings, now 82, wanted to make one last trip into Yosemite Valley. His wish was granted, but a tragic horse carriage accident resulted in Hutching's death. In what can be seen as a peculiar twist of fate in a seemingly tragic accident, the funeral service was held in the Big Tree Room, formally known as Hutchings House: the old hotel he was evicted from and the one place he loved more than any other.

In 1903, John Muir and President Theodore Roosevelt camped beneath the stars at Glacier Point. President Roosevelt stated, "it was like lying in a great solemn cathedral, far vaster and more beautiful than any built by the hands of man." It wouldn't be long until the hands of man wanted to dramatically change Yosemite. San Francisco required water to support its ballooning population. Dam proposals were focused on a tract of land within park boundaries known as Hetch Hetchy Valley. Muir found Hetch Hetchy even more appealing than the more popular Yosemite Valley. He passionately opposed the dam proposal and for years legislation was held up in a political quagmire. In 1913, Woodrow Wilson finally signed a bill approving the dam. One year later, an exhausted Muir died at the age of 76. John Muir arrived in Yosemite, "the grandest of all Nature's special temples," as an "unknown nobody." He left as president and founder of the Sierra Club, renowned writer and naturalist, and catalyst in the creation of Yosemite, Sequoia, Mount Rainier, and Grand Canyon National Parks.

In 1916, a shy 14-year-old boy, sick and in bed, decided to read James Mason Hutchings' *In the Heart of the Sierras.* Intrigued, he convinced his parents to vacation at Yosemite. What he saw left an indelible mark. Years later, the young man worked as caretaker at the Sierra Club's LeConte Memorial Lodge in Yosemite Valley, where he spent time as a photographer for Sierra Club outings and classical pianist for lodge guests, wowing them with striking imagery and wistful music. This man is Ansel Adams, one of history's great landscape photographers and a man who had a special affinity for Yosemite. A visit to Yosemite can become a life-changing experience. Its unspeakable grandeur is so overwhelming you may find yourself inspired like James Mason Hutchings, Galen Clark, John Muir, President Roosevelt, and Ansel Adams were before you.

Taft Point

Directions

Yosemite National Park is located in east-central California's Sierra Nevada. There are five park entrances. Hetch Hetchy Entrance, leading to O'Shaughnessy Dam and Hetch Hetchy Backpackers Camp, is only open during daylight hours. It does not connect to Yosemite Valley and is far less crowded. Big Oak Flat and Arch Rock Entrance enter the park from the west. South Entrance enters from the south via Oakhurst. On the eastern side you'll find Tioga Pass Entrance Station. Due to high elevation (9,945 feet) the entrance and Tioga Road usually close from November until April (depending on conditions).

To Hetch Hetchy: From CA-120, on the park's western side, turn left onto Evergreen Road just before you reach Big Oak Flat Entrance Station. Continue on Evergreen Road for about 7 miles, and then turn right at Hetch Hetchy Road, which leads to the reservoir and camp.

To Big Oak Flat Entrance: From San Francisco/Oakland, take I-580 E and continue onto I-205 E. Merge onto I-5 N. After less than a mile on I-5, take Exit 461 to CA-120. Follow CA-120 to Big Oak Flat Entrance.

To Arch Rock Entrance: From CA-99, take CA-140 E/Yosemite Pkwy at Merced, which leads into the park.

To South Entrance: From Fresno, take CA-41 N through Oakhurst into the park.

To Tioga Pass Entrance: Take US-395 north from Bishop. After about 64 miles, turn left onto CA-120/Tioga Road. It is 12 miles to the entrance.

Regions

Hetch Hetchy (all year, daylight hours only): Today's source of power and water for San Francisco was a miniature replica of Yosemite Valley before being dammed. It is often dry and hot in summer.

Tuolumne Meadows/White Wolf/Crane Flat (summer/fall): These areas, located along Tioga Road, offer amazing vistas of Yosemite's high country. Opportunities for solitude abound on backcountry hiking trails. Merced and Tuolumne Grove are two of the park's three sequoia groves.

Yosemite Valley: Waterfalls, precipitous granite cliffs, and plenty of tourists are found here. More than 90% of the park's guests visit Yosemite Valley, which comprises less than 1% of the total park land. Upon your first sight of the valley, it becomes crystal clear why this cathedral of nature is the primary destination. Plus, it possesses the majority of camping, lodging, and all other amenities.

Glacier Point: This overlook provides views of Yosemite Valley, Half Dome, and Yosemite's high country. It's a one-hour drive from Yosemite Valley or Wawona, but you can also reach it by foot from the valley via Panorama or Four Mile Trail. Excellent hiking trails (like Taft Point) and viewpoints are found along the way. Do not skip Glacier Point!

Wawona & Mariposa Grove: Mariposa Grove and Wawona are located near the park's South Entrance. Mariposa is the most popular sequoia grove in the park, and was recently reopened after the largest restoration project in park history.

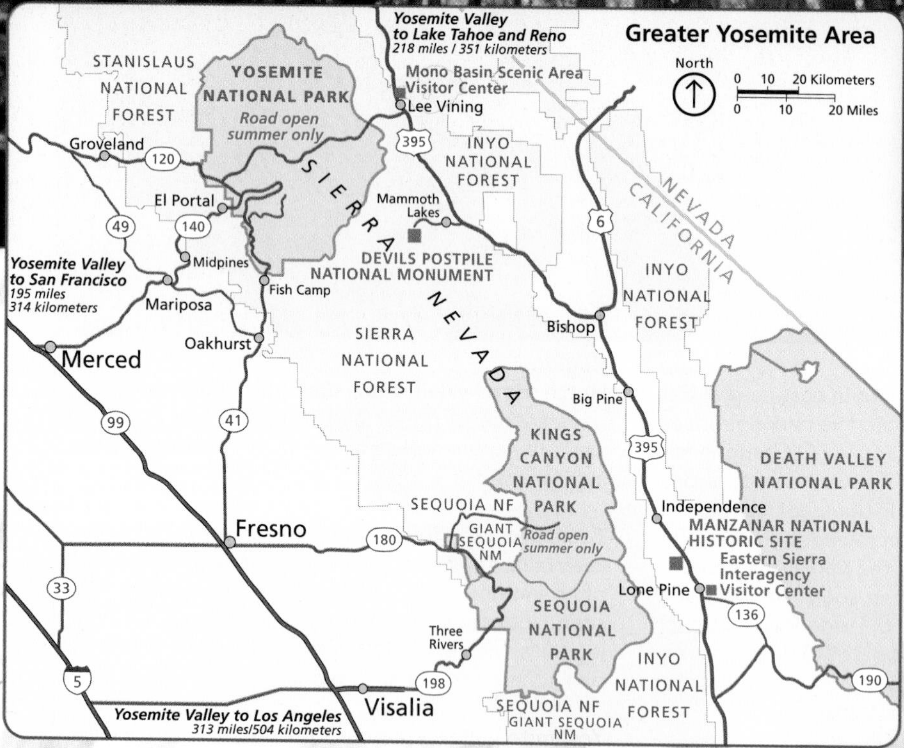

INSPIRATION POINT 0.6

Greater Yosemite Area

North ↑

0   10   20 Kilometers
0   10   20 Miles

STANISLAUS NATIONAL FOREST

YOSEMITE NATIONAL PARK
Road open summer only

Groveland

120

Yosemite Valley to Lake Tahoe and Reno
218 miles / 351 kilometers

Mono Basin Scenic Area Visitor Center
Lee Vining

395

INYO NATIONAL FOREST

El Portal

49

140

Mammoth Lakes

DEVILS POSTPILE NATIONAL MONUMENT

Midpines

Fish Camp

Yosemite Valley to San Francisco
195 miles
314 kilometers

Mariposa

Oakhurst

SIERRA NATIONAL FOREST

SIERRA NEVADA

Bishop

INYO NATIONAL FOREST

6

NEVADA
CALIFORNIA

Merced

99

41

Big Pine

395

KINGS CANYON NATIONAL PARK

DEATH VALLEY NATIONAL PARK

33

Fresno

180

GIANT SEQUOIA NM

Road open summer only

Independence

MANZANAR NATIONAL HISTORIC SITE
Eastern Sierra Interagency Visitor Center

Lone Pine

136

5

Three Rivers

SEQUOIA NATIONAL PARK

198

Visalia

SEQUOIA NF GIANT SEQUOIA NM

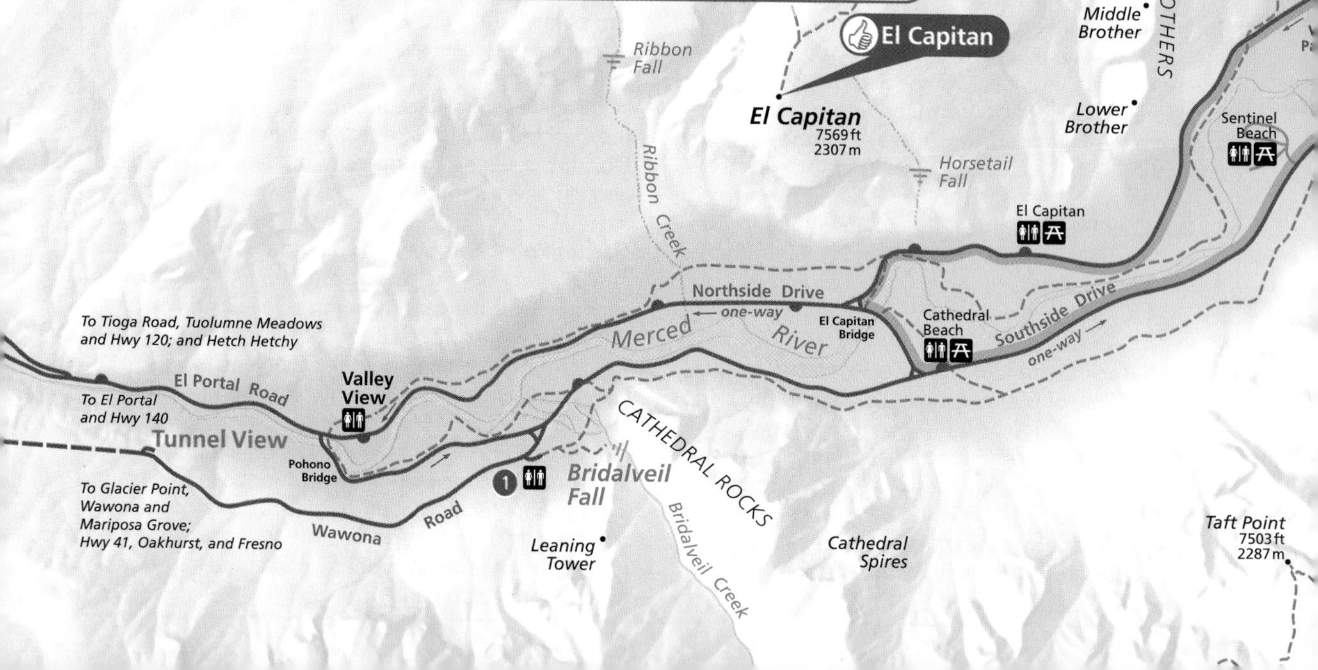

INYO NATIONAL FOREST

190

Yosemite Valley to Los Angeles
313 miles/504 kilometers

Eagle Peak
7779 ft
2371 m

THREE BROTHERS

Columb
Ro

Camp 4

Ribbon Fall

👍 El Capitan

Middle Brother

El Capitan
7569 ft
2307 m

Lower Brother

Sentinel Beach

Ribbon Creek

Horsetail Fall

El Capitan

Northside Drive
one-way

El Capitan Bridge

Cathedral Beach

Southside Drive
one-way

To Tioga Road, Tuolumne Meadows and Hwy 120; and Hetch Hetchy

El Portal Road

Valley View

Merced   River

To El Portal and Hwy 140

Tunnel View

Pohono Bridge

Wawona   Road

To Glacier Point, Wawona and Mariposa Grove; Hwy 41, Oakhurst, and Fresno

1

Bridalveil Fall

CATHEDRAL ROCKS

Leaning Tower

Bridalveil Creek

Cathedral Spires

Taft Point
7503 ft
2287 m

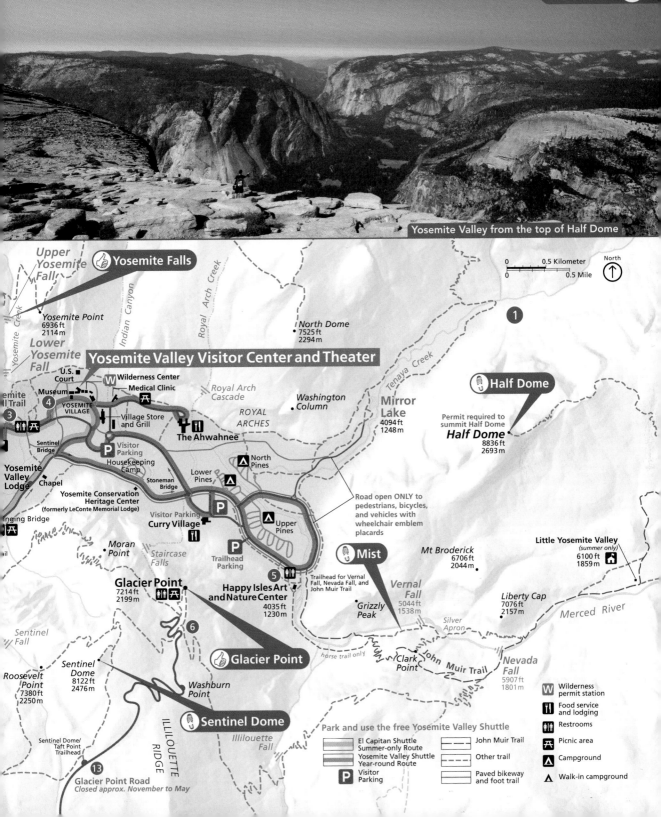

Yosemite Valley from the top of Half Dome

Upper Yosemite Fall

👍 **Yosemite Falls**

North

0   0.5 Kilometer
0   0.5 Mile

Yosemite Point
6936 ft
2114 m

Indian Canyon

Royal Arch Creek

North Dome
7525 ft
2294 m

①

Lower Yosemite Fall

Yosemite Creek

Yosemite Valley Visitor Center and Theater

U.S. Court

Ⓦ Wilderness Center

Medical Clinic

emite Trail

Museum

YOSEMITE VILLAGE

④

③

👫

Royal Arch Cascade

ROYAL ARCHES

Washington Column

Tenaya Creek

Mirror Lake
4094 ft
1248 m

🖐 **Half Dome**

Permit required to summit Half Dome

Half Dome
8836 ft
2693 m

Village Store and Grill

The Ahwahnee

Sentinel Bridge

Yosemite Valley Lodge

P Visitor Parking

Housekeeping Camp

Chapel

Stoneman Bridge

Yosemite Conservation Heritage Center
(formerly LeConte Memorial Lodge)

nging Bridge

👫

il

Moran Point

Staircase Falls

▲ North Pines

Lower Pines

▲

▲ Upper Pines

Road open ONLY to pedestrians, bicycles, and vehicles with wheelchair emblem placards

Mt Broderick
6706 ft
2044 m

Little Yosemite Valley
(summer only)
6100 ft
1859 m

Visitor Parking

Curry Village

P

🍴

P Trailhead Parking

⑤ 👫

Trailhead for Vernal Fall, Nevada Fall, and John Muir Trail

🥾 **Mist**

Vernal Fall
5044 ft
1538 m

Grizzly Peak

Liberty Cap
7076 ft
2157 m

Merced River

Glacier Point
7214 ft
2199 m

👫

Happy Isles Art and Nature Center
4035 ft
1230 m

Silver Apron

Sentinel Fall

⑥

Roosevelt Point
7380 ft
2250 m

Sentinel Dome
8122 ft
2476 m

👍 **Glacier Point**

Washburn Point

horse trail only

Clark Point

John Muir Trail

Nevada Fall
5907 ft
1801 m

ILLILOUETTE RIDGE

🥾 **Sentinel Dome**

Illilouette Fall

Sentinel Dome/ Taft Point Trailhead

⑬

Glacier Point Road
Closed approx. November to May

Park and use the free Yosemite Valley Shuttle

El Capitan Shuttle Summer-only Route

Yosemite Valley Shuttle Year-round Route

P Visitor Parking

John Muir Trail

Other trail

Paved bikeway and foot trail

Ⓦ Wilderness permit station

🍴 Food service and lodging

👫 Restrooms

🛆 Picnic area

▲ Campground

🛆 Walk-in campground

STANISLAUS NATIONAL FOREST

EMIGRANT WILDERNESS

Bond Pass

Dorothy Lake

Tower Peak

Emigrant Lake

Maxwell Lake

Cherry

Creek

Twin Lakes

Mary Lake

Tilden Lake

Pacific Crest Trail

STUBBLEFIELD CANYON

Haystack Peak

Schofield Peak

Falls Creek

Huckleberry Lake

East Fork

Styx Pass

Many Island Lake

Richardson Peak
9877 ft
3010 m

Otter Lake

(staffed intermittently)

Wilma Lake

KERRICK

Kibbie Lake

Kendrick Creek

JACK MAIN CANYON

Piute Mountain
10541 ft
3213 m

TILTILL MOUNTAIN

(staffed intermittently)

Creek

Eleanor

Laurel Lake

Lake Vernon

Mount Gibson

PLEASANT VALLEY

Table Lake

LAKE ELEANOR

Frog

Creek

Falls

Tueeulala Falls

Wapama Falls

TILTILL VALLEY

Rancheria Falls

Rancheria

RANCHERIA MOUNTAIN

GRAND CAN

Lake Eleanor
(summer only)

MIGUEL MEADOW

HETCH HETCHY RESERVOIR

3813 ft
1162 m
O'Shaughnessy Dam

28

No swimming or boating

**Hetch Hetchy
Backpackers Camp**
△ (wilderness permit required)

Smith Peak
7751 ft
2363 m

PATE VALLEY

River

POOPENAUT VALLEY

Hetchy Road

Hetch

Hetch Hetchy

YOSEMITE

NATIONAL

Harden Lake

Morrison Creek

Hetch Hetchy Entrance
(open limited hours)

Ⓦ

Tuolumne

△ Mather

27

Birch Lake

Tuolumne River

White Wolf ▣ 16
△ ⊪

Lukens Lake

YOSEMITE W

Evergreen Road

Middle

Bald Mountain
7261 ft
2213 m

ASPEN VALLEY

Tioga Road

Siesta Lake

17

18

⬟

Mou

Closed to vehicles

To Manteca

4850 ft
1478 m

Restrooms are available at picnic areas, campgrounds, trailheads, and roadside pullouts along Tioga Road

Porcupine Flat

HUMBOLDT-TOIYABE

NATIONAL FOREST

Buckeye Pass
9572 ft
2917 m

Barney
Lake

Peeler
Lake

Crown
Lake

Rock
Island
Pass

HOOVER

Slide
Mountain

SAWTOOTH RIDGE

Matterhorn
Peak

Burro
Pass

WILDERNESS

Whorl
Mountain

Virginia
Peak

Virginia Pass

Green
Lake

Summit
Lake

167

Virginia Lakes

Lundy
Lake

395

Smedberg
Lake

Benson
Pass

Volunteer
Peak

Rodgers
Lake

Pettit Peak
10788 ft
3288 m

MATTERHORN

VIRGINIA

McCabe

Creek

McCabe Lakes

Upper
McCabe
Lake

INYO NATIONAL FOREST

Return

Virginia
Lake

Pacific Crest Trail

CANYON

North Peak

Roosevelt
Lake

Mount
Conness
12590 ft
3837m

HARVEY MONROE

HALL RESEARCH

NATURAL AREA

White
Mountain

Saddlebag
Lake

Gardisky
Lake

Tioga Peak
11526 ft
3513 m

Highway 120
closed in winter

120

Ellery Lake

OF THE TUOLUMNE RIVER

RNESS

PARK

Waterwheel
Falls

COLD

CANYON

Conness

Creek

Ragged
Peak

Young Lakes

Creek

High Sierra Camps

Glen Aulin

Tuolumne

River

21

Delaney

Dog Lake

22

Pothole
Dome

TUOLUMNE

23

Lembert Dome

MEADOWS

Granite
Lakes

Gaylor
Peak

Gaylor Lakes

26

25

Tioga Lake

Tioga Pass Entrance
9945 ft
3031 m

Tioga Road closed approx. November
to May west of this point

DANA MEADOWS

Dana

Fork

Mount
Dana
13057 ft
3979 m

Elizabeth Lake

Mount Gibbs
12764 ft
3890 m

Facilities along Tioga Road
available summer only

lumne Peak
10845 ft
3306 m

May
Lake

20

Tioga Road

Fairview
Dome

Medlicott
Dome

John Muir Trail

Cathedral
Peak
10940 ft
3335 m

Cathedral
Lakes

Tresidder
Peak

Echo
Peaks

Budd
Lake

Unicorn Peak

Elizabeth Lake

Johnson
Peak

W 24

Tuolumne Meadows
Visitor Center

yell

Fork

Mammoth
Peak
12117 ft
3693 m

Creek

Rafferty

CATHEDRAL

KUNA

LYELL CA

CREST

Mono Pass
10604 ft
3232 m

Parker
Pass

May Lake

Tenaya Lake

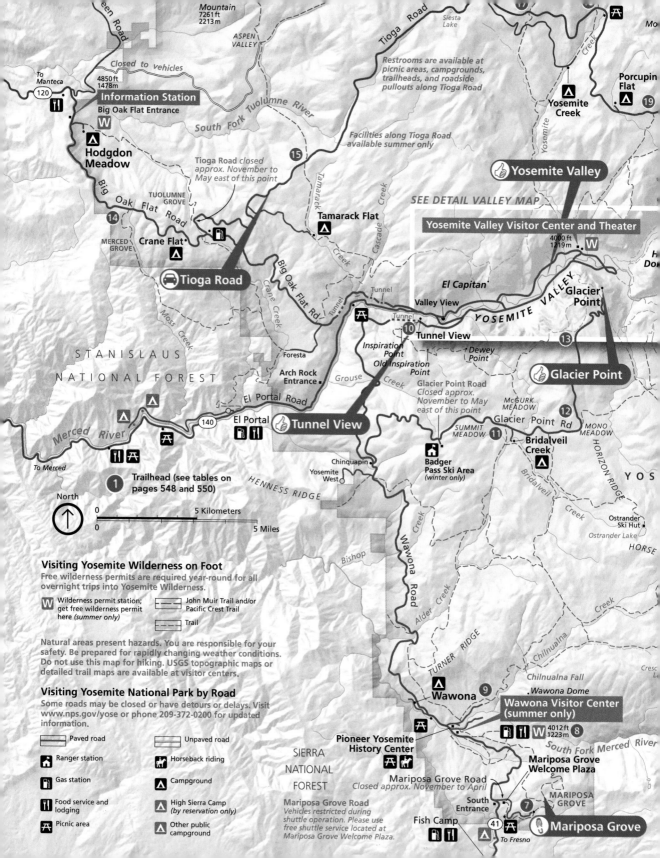

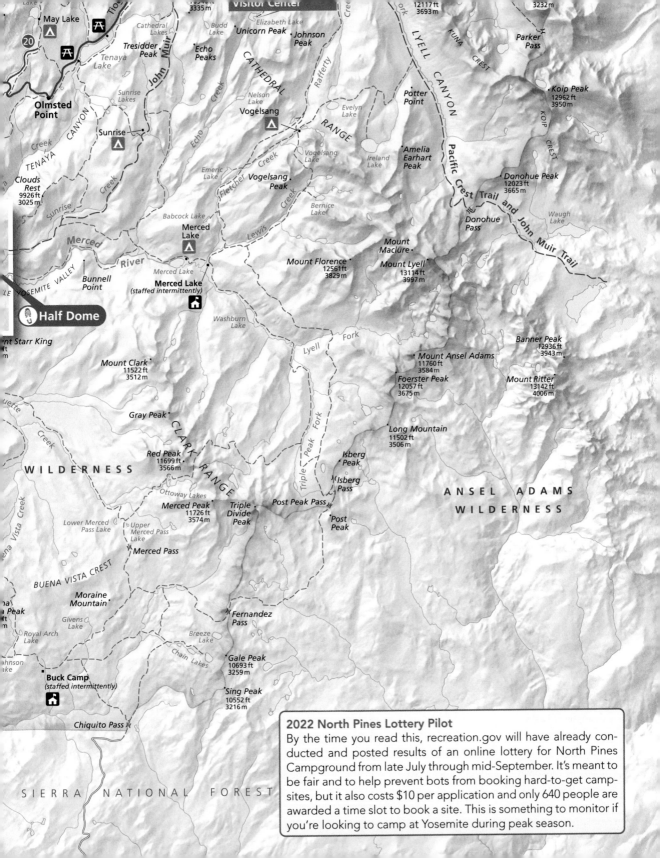

May Lake
20
Tresidder Peak
Tenaya Lake
Olmsted Point
Sunrise Lakes
Sunrise
TENAYA CANYON
Clouds Rest
9926 ft
3025 m
Creek
Sunrise Creek
Merced River
Bunnell Point
LE YOSEMITE VALLEY
Half Dome
nt Starr King
m

Cathedral Lakes
Budd Lake
Echo Peaks
Nelson Lake
Vogelsang
Vogelsang Lake
Vogelsang Peak
Emeric Lake
Fletcher Creek
Babcock Lake
Merced Lake
Merced Lake
Merced Lake
(staffed intermittently)
Washburn Lake

Unicorn Peak
Johnson Peak
Elizabeth Lake
CATHEDRAL RANGE
Echo Creek
Rafferty Creek
Evelyn Lake
Ireland Lake
Bernice Lake
Lewis Creek
Lyell Fork

3335 m
VISITOR CENTER

Potter Point
Amelia Earhart Peak
Mount Maclure
Mount Florence
12561 ft
3829 m
Mount Lyell
13114 ft
3997 m

12117 ft
3693 m
ork
LYELL CANYON
KUNA CREST
Parker Pass
Koip Peak
12962 ft
3950 m
KOIP CREST
Donohue Peak
12023 ft
3665 m
Waugh Lake
Pacific Crest Trail and John Muir Trail
Donohue Pass

3232 m

Mount Clark
11522 ft
3512 m
Gray Peak
CLARK RANGE
Red Peak
11699 ft
3566 m
Ottoway Lakes
Merced Peak
11726 ft
3574 m
Triple Divide Peak
Lower Merced Pass Lake
Upper Merced Pass Lake
Merced Pass

WILDERNESS

Lyell Fork
Triple Peak Fork
Mount Ansel Adams
11760 ft
3584 m
Foerster Peak
12057 ft
3675 m
Long Mountain
11502 ft
3506 m
Isberg Peak
Isberg Pass
Post Peak Pass
Post Peak

Banner Peak
12936 ft
3943 m
Mount Ritter
13142 ft
4006 m

ANSEL ADAMS WILDERNESS

BUENA VISTA CREST
Moraine Mountain
Givens Lake
Breeze Lake
Chain Lakes
Fernandez Pass
Gale Peak
10693 ft
3259 m
Sing Peak
10552 ft
3216 m
Royal Arch Lake
ohnson
Buck Camp
(staffed intermittently)
Chiquito Pass
na Peak

SIERRA NATIONAL FOREST

2022 North Pines Lottery Pilot
By the time you read this, recreation.gov will have already conducted and posted results of an online lottery for North Pines Campground from late July through mid-September. It's meant to be fair and to help prevent bots from booking hard-to-get campsites, but it also costs $10 per application and only 640 people are awarded a time slot to book a site. This is something to monitor if you're looking to camp at Yosemite during peak season.

The High Sierra

Yosemite Camping (Fees are per night)

Name	Location	Open (approximate)	Fee	Sites	Notes
Upper Pines*	Yosemite Valley	All Year	$26	238	F, W, 35-ft/24-ft RV/trailer
Lower Pines* - ♿	Yosemite Valley	April–October	$26	60	F, W, 40-ft/35-ft
North Pines*	Yosemite Valley	March–October	$26	81	F, W, 40-ft/35-ft
Camp 4	Yosemite Valley	All Year	$6/person	36	Walk-in, Lottery • F, W, NRV
Wawona*	Wawona Road	All Year	$26	93	F, W, 35-ft/35-ft
Bridalveil Creek	Glacier Point Road	July–mid-September	$18	110	F, W, 35-ft/24-ft
Hodgdon Meadow *	Big Oak Flat Road	All Year	$26	105	F, W, 35-ft/30-ft
Crane Flat*	Big Oak Flat Road	July–mid-Oct	$26	166	F, W, 35-ft/35-ft
Tamarack Flat - ♿	Tioga Road	June–September	$12	52	P, CW, NRV
White Wolf - ♿	Tioga Road	July–early September	$18	74	F, W, 27-ft/24-ft
Yosemite Creek	Tioga Road	July–early September	$12	75	P, CW, NRV
Porcupine Flat	Tioga Road	July–mid-Oct	$12	52	P, CW, NRV
Tuolumne Meadows	Tioga Road	July–Sept	$26	304	F, W, 35-ft/35-ft

F = Flush Toilets, P = Pit Toilets, W = Tap Water, CW = Creek Water (boil before using), NRV = No RV Sites
*Reservations are required and can be made up to five months in advance at recreation.gov
Shower and laundry facilities are available year-round in Yosemite Valley • Dump stations are available at Upper Pines (all year), near Wawona (summer), and near Tuolumne Meadows (summer) • No campsites have hookups

Backcountry	Permitted with a wilderness permit. Daily quotas are enforced due to trail popularity. 60% of each trailhead's permits are available via reservation. The remaining 40% are available on a first-come, first-served basis beginning one day before your intended departure. See page 552 for details.
Group	Group sites are available year-round at Wawona, and in summer at the following campgrounds: Hodgdon Meadow, Bridalveil Creek, and Tuolumne Meadows. Reservations are required.

Yosemite Lodging (Fees are per night)

Name	Open	Fee	Location & Notes
The Ahwahnee - ♿	All Year	$518–1221	Yosemite Valley • Four-Diamond hotel in a perfect location
Yosemite Valley Lodge	All Year	$278–298	Yosemite Valley • Close to Yosemite Falls • Family favorite
Curry Village	All Year	$143+	Yosemite Valley • Cabins, motel rooms, and tent cabins
Housekeeping Camp	All Year	$108+	Yosemite Valley • 266 basic units accommodate six guests
Wawona Hotel	All Year	$153+	Wawona • Some shared baths • Golf and swimming pool
Tuolumne Meadows	early June–early Sept	$141+	Tioga Road • A collection of private candlelit tent cabins
White Wolf Lodge	early June–early Sept	$137+	Tioga Road • Smaller complex of 24 canvas tent cabins
High Sierra Camps - ♿	early July–early Sept	$152–159	Reserved by lottery • Backpacking with beds and meals

All in-park lodging facilities are operated by Yosemite Hospitality (travelyosemite.com, 888.413.8869)

Camping

Four campgrounds are located in **Yosemite Valley**. Upper, Lower, and North Pines, located at the valley's eastern edge, require reservations (book early!). From late May through early September, sites at ever-popular **Camp 4** in Yosemite Valley are distributed via a daily lottery one day in advance through recreation.gov ($10/application lottery fee applies). Camp 4 is first-come, first-served for the remainder of the year. A ranger is there to moderate registration in spring and fall. In winter, Camp 4 shifts to self-registration (when the campground doesn't fill). Remember that Camp 4 offers walk-in, tent-only camping. You must park in a designated area a short distance from the camp, and pets are not permitted. If your heart is set on camping in Yosemite Valley, it's a good idea to make a reservation at one of the "Pines" campgrounds (as early as possible). Reservations are required and can be up to five months in advance at recreation.gov. Campsites from May through September are usually booked within minutes (sometimes seconds) of first becoming available. Have a plan for securing summertime reservations. Make sure your clock is accurate and complete as many steps of the process as possible before the sites are released for reservation. Showers (fee) are available at Curry Village and Housekeeping Camp in Yosemite Valley. Groceries are available in Yosemite Village and Curry Village.

Wawona and Bridalveil Creek Campgrounds are south of Yosemite Valley. Wawona is a nice place to spend your first night if you're entering from the south. You can explore Mariposa Grove, set up camp, and get an early start on the drive into Yosemite Valley the following day. Wawona also requires reservations (recreation.gov) during peak season (April through September). Bridalveil Creek is first-come, first-served.

Seven seasonal camps are available north of Yosemite Valley. **Tamarack Flat** is a great place to camp if you want to fool around on the Devil's Dance Floor or hike to the top of El Cap. **Tuolumne Meadows** is the largest camp in the park and it's about 1.5 hours from Yosemite Valley. Reservations (recreation.gov) are available for half its sites. The rest are first-come, first-served.

You are not allowed to park and sleep alongside the road or in a parking area. No sites have RV hookups. Pay attention to the RV/trailer length information when making reservations. Only eight sites in the park can accommodate a 40-ft RV or 35-ft trailer. Six at Lower Pines. Two at North Pines. Food must be stored in a hard-sided RV or trailer.

Tuolumne Meadows

Lodging

If you hope to reserve a room at any of Yosemite's seven lodges during peak season, book early (up to one year in advance), otherwise plan on visiting during the off-season when rooms are slightly easier to come by and may have reduced rates.

In **Yosemite Valley**, visitors have four choices for lodging: The Ahwahnee, Yosemite Valley Lodge, Curry Village, and Housekeeping Camp. **The Ahwahnee** is often regarded as the finest lodge in America. Comfort, beauty, and premium location have their price: $500+/night for a standard room. **Yosemite Valley Lodge** provides more reasonable accommodations starting at $278/night. It offers large family rooms with one king bed, two single beds, and a sofa sleeper (queen). **Curry Village** and **Housekeeping Camp** are "budget" options, with both units checking in at roughly $100 to $150 per night. Curry Village has small rustic cabins, motel-style rooms, and canvas tent cabins. Tent cabins are affordable, but the canvas is thin, providing little protection from noisy neighbors. Housekeeping Camp is simple living. Each of the 266 units has a bunk bed, a double bed, table, chairs, mirror, lights, and outlets. A curtained wall separates the living space from a covered patio. Bear-proof food storage containers are provided. Basically, you have to ask yourself what you're willing to pay to sleep in a bed. I'm not a reliable voice in the conversation because I enjoy camping.

Located near the park's southern boundary is **Wawona Hotel**. Wah-wo-nah means "Big Tree," and that's what you'll find near this Victorian-style hotel. Rooms come with or without a private bath. Golf, swimming (seasonal), horse stable, and hiking trails are available nearby. Rooms here are considerably easier to reserve than those found in the valley. Alternatively, **White Wolf** and **Tuolumne Meadows** are great High Sierra lodging options located off Tioga Road. Canvas tent

Sentinel Dome

Yosemite Hiking Trails (Distances are roundtrip)

	Name	Location (# on map)	Length	Difficulty Rating & Notes
Yosemite Valley	Bridalveil Fall - 🏞	Bridalveil Fall Parking Area (1)	0.5 mile	E – Paved trail to the base of Bridalveil Falls
	Mirror Lake	Camp 4/Shuttle Stop #7 or E2 (2)	5.0 miles	E/M – 2 miles to lake and back or 5-mile loop
	Valley Floor - 🏞	Camp 4/Shuttle Stop #7 or E2 (2)	13.0 miles	E – Loop, original trails and wagon roads
	Yosemite Falls - 🏞	Camp 4/Shuttle Stop #7 or E2 (2)	7.2 miles	S – Top of North America's tallest waterfall
	Four Mile - 🏞	Camp 4/Shuttle Stop #7 or E2 (2)	9.6 miles	S – Hike from Sentinel Rock to Glacier Point
	Lower Yosemite - 🏞	Shuttle Stop #6 (3)	1.0 mile	E – Paved trail, Yosemite Falls views
	Cook's Meadow	Shuttle Stops #5, 6, 9, or 11 (4)	1.0 mile	E – Loop, Half Dome views (sunset location)
	Vernal & Nevada Falls - 🏞	Happy Isles/Shuttle Stop #16 (5)	1.6–8.0 miles	M/S – Popular • Take Mist (600 granite steps) or John Muir Trail or loop (recommended)
	Half Dome - 🏞 (Permit Required, see page 551)	Happy Isles/Shuttle Stop #16 (5)	14.0 miles 16.4 miles 15.2 miles	X – Via Mist Trail (shortest but steepest) X – Via John Muir Trail (longest, most gradual) X – Mist up, John Muir down (compromise)
	Panorama - 🏞	Happy Isles/Shuttle Stop #16 (5)	8.3 miles	S – One-way, long way up to Glacier Point
Wawona	Grizzly Giant - 🏞	Mariposa Grove (7)	2.0 miles	M – Big trees!
	Wawona Point	Mariposa Grove (7)	7.0 miles	M – Take Mariposa Grove Trail to vista
	Guardians Loop	Mariposa Grove (7)	6.5 miles	S – Loops around Mariposa Grove
	Wawona Meadow	Big Trees Lodge/Pioneer Store (8)	3.5 miles	E – Loop follows a fire road around meadow
	Swinging Bridge	Big Trees Lodge/Pioneer Store (8)	4.8 miles	E – Self-guiding loop, swimming holes
	Alder Creek	Chilnualna Falls Road (9)	12.0 miles	S – Begin at Alder Creek Trailhead
	Chilnualna Falls	Chilnualna Falls Road (9)	8.2 miles	S – Begin at Chilnualna Falls Trailhead
	Inspiration Point	Wawona Tunnel Overlook (10)	2.6 miles	S – A little tricky to find clear valley views
Glacier Point Rd	McGurk Meadow	Glacier Point Road (11)	1.6 miles	E – Meadow and cabin of John McGurk
	Ostrander Lake - 🏞	Glacier Point Road (11)	11.4 miles	S – Beautiful backcountry lake
	Mono Meadow	Glacier Point Road (12)	3.0 miles	M – Wet through summer, log crossings
	Taft Point - 🏞	Glacier Point Road (13)	1.8 miles	M – Views of Yosemite Valley and El Capitan
	Sentinel Dome - 🏞	Glacier Point Road (13)	2.2 miles	M – Scramble, can loop with Taft for 4.9 miles

Panorama and Four Mile connect Yosemite Valley and Glacier Point. Combine them for a strenuous 13.1-mile loop.

Difficulty Ratings: E = Easy, M = Moderate, S = Strenuous, X = Extreme

cabins, sprinkled about the Sierra Nevada, are open from early June until early September. Illuminated by candlelight, they do not have electricity. Shared showers and restrooms are available. White Wolf also offers a few wooden cabins with propane heating, private baths, and limited electricity.

All lodges and hotels are operated by Yosemite Hospitality (888.413.8869, travelyosemite.com).

Finally, there are five **High Sierra Camps** in the backcountry. These comfortable camping accommodations give hikers the opportunity to enjoy the peace and quiet of the backcountry with the comforts of a bed, hot shower, and hearty home-style meals. Not having to carry a tent, sleeping bag, and food is a bonus. A night's stay at any High Sierra Camp includes a filling dinner and breakfast. Camps are located at: Merced Lake, Vogelsang, Glen Aulin, May Lake, and Sunrise Camp (see the map on pages 542–545). May Lake is the easiest to reach, just 1.2 miles from May Lake Parking Area (1.75 miles north of Tioga Road). Located 14 miles from Tuolumne Meadows, Merced Lake is the most remote camp. All camps are most easily accessed from trails along Tioga Road. Unguided trips start at $152 per person per night. Guided trips start at $706 per person for a 5-day hike or $1,320 per person for a 4-day saddle trip. You should be a fit and experienced rider for the saddle trips. High Sierra Camp reservations are made through a lottery system. Lottery details can be found at travelyosemite.com.

Driving

Hetch Hetchy Road enters from the west and dead ends at O'Shaughnessy Dam, roughly tracing the Tuolumne River. Hetch Hetchy is a particularly good location to avoid crowds, and lower elevation makes it ideal for late winter/early spring visits when the high country is cold and covered in snow. You can decide whether it's more beautiful than Yosemite Valley. The catch is that you won't find any of the creature comforts available at Yosemite Valley, and it's more of a point of departure for backpackers than prime day-hiking territory. It's definitely not a "must visit" destination.

Big Oak Flat Road (CA-120) enters from the west. After the entrance station you immediately pass Hodgdon Meadow Campground and then Crane Flat. Gas is available at its intersection with Tioga Road. A little farther south, **El Portal Road** (CA-140) follows the Merced River, merging with Big Oak Flat Road before entering the valley. El Portal is the least hair-raising option. Each entry point provides its oohs and ahhs.

Inspiration Point

Wawona Road enters from the south, passing Mariposa Grove and Glacier Point Road. Campgrounds, dining, gas, and trail rides are available near Wawona. **Glacier Point Road** provides access to some of the best views of Half Dome at Glacier Point (and Washburn Point), but it closes in winter (beyond Badger Pass Ski Area). Wawona Road continues north to **Tunnel View**, one of the most photographed vistas in the world, and finally into Yosemite Valley.

Tioga Road is the only route that crosses the Sierra Nevada within the park. Gas is available at Tuolumne Meadows. Dining is available at Tuolumne Meadows and White Wolf. Five designated campgrounds are available along the way (and High Sierra Camps are in the backcountry). Tioga Road closes seasonally.

Shuttle Service

Free and accessible shuttle buses decrease traffic congestion and pollution, and help decrease visitor frustration by connecting popular points of interest in Yosemite Valley and beyond. When we went to print it looked like shuttles would be back for 2022, but it wasn't official.

Valley Shuttle operates all year (7am to 10pm), looping around Upper Pines Campground, Curry Village, Ahwahnee, Yosemite Village, and Yosemite Lodge. El Capitán Shuttle operates in summer (9am to 5pm), completing a one-way loop between El Capitán Bridge and Valley Visitor Center. Mariposa Grove Shuttle typically operates from mid-March through November (9am to 5pm), connecting Mariposa Grove with Mariposa Grove Welcome Plaza (the grove's primary access point). Each of these shuttles runs daily every 10–20 minutes depending on the time and are free of charge. Tuolumne Meadows Shuttle typically operates

Lembert Dome

Yosemite Hiking Trails (Distances are roundtrip)

	Name	Location (# on map)	Length	Difficulty Rating & Notes
Crane Flat/White Wolf	Merced Grove	Merced Grove Parking Area (14)	3.0 miles	E – Small and secluded sequoia grove
	Tuolumne Grove	Tuolumne Grove/Crane Flat (15)	2.5 miles	E – Nature Trail through grove of sequoias
	Harden Lake	White Wolf Lodge (16)	5.8 miles	M – Can loop Grand Canyon of the Tuolumne
	Lukens Lake	Lukens Lake Trailhead (17)	1.6 miles	E – Or hike 4.6 miles from White Wolf Lodge
	North Dome - ⚲	Porcupine Creek Trailhead (18)	10.4 miles	S – Steep rocky steps, valley views, spur to arch
	Ten Lakes - ⚲	Ten Lakes Trailhead (19)	12.6 miles	S – Cross Yosemite Creek to beautiful lakes
	May Lake	May Lake Parking Area (20)	2.4 miles	E – Views of Half Dome along the way
Tuolumne Meadows	Glen Aulin - ⚲	Tuolumne Meadows (21)	11.0 miles	M – Glen Aulin = "Beautiful Valley"
	Tuolumne Meadows	Lembert Dome/Dog Lake (22, 23)	1.5 miles	E – Hike to Soda Springs and Parsons Lodge
	Lyell Canyon - ⚲	Lembert Dome/Dog Lake (22, 23)	8.0 miles	M – Creek crossings, follows John Muir Trail
	Dog Lake/Lembert Dome - ⚲	Lembert Dome/Dog Lake (22, 23)	2.8 miles	M – Begins with a steep grade, but flattens (4 miles to hike both)
	Elizabeth Lake - ⚲	Tuolumne Meadows Camp (24)	4.8 miles	M – Excellent hike to a glacially carved lake
	Vogelsang Area	John Muir Trailhead (24)	13.8 miles	S – John Muir Tr to Vogelsang Camp and Lake
	Cathedral Lakes - ⚲	Cathedral Lakes Trailhead (24)	7.0 miles	M – One of the most popular trails in the area
	Mono Pass - ⚲	Mono Pass Trailhead (25)	8.0 miles	M – Views of Mono Lake from the pass
	Gaylor Lakes - ⚲	Tioga Pass Entrance (26)	2.0 miles	M – Wonderful high country views
Hetch Hetchy	Lookout Point	Hetch Hetchy Entrance (27)	2.0 miles	M – Viewpoint overlooking Hetch Hetchy
	Smith Peak	Hetch Hetchy Entrance (27)	13.5 miles	M/S –Great Hetch Hetchy views
	Poopenaut Valley	Hetch Hetchy Entrance (27)	3.0 miles	S – Drops down to the Tuolumne River
	Wapama Falls - ⚲	O'Shaughnessy Dam (28)	5.0 miles	M – Waterfalls and wildflowers in spring
	Rancheria Falls	O'Shaughnessy Dam (28)	13.4 miles	M – Continues past Wapama Falls

Difficulty Ratings: E = Easy, M = Moderate, S = Strenuous

from mid-June through mid-September (7am to 7pm), connecting Tuolumne Meadows Lodge with Olmsted Point (and ten stops in between). It runs every half hour. Shuttles also make four trips between Tuolumne Meadows Lodge and Tioga Pass (the park's western entrance). Tioga Road shuttles cost a nominal fee.

Bus Tours

Yosemite Hospitality (888.413.8869, travelosemite.com) operates guided bus tours. They're a great, hassle-free way to explore the most popular areas of the park and a professional guide joins you every step of the way. Valley Floor Tour ($38/adult, $28/child) is a 2-hour drive through Yosemite Valley. It's offered all year, and on days leading up to the full moon a moonlight edition is available. Glacier Point Tour ($57/$36.50) is a 4-hour trip taking visitors from the valley floor to Glacier Point, seeing El Capitán, Bridalveil Falls, Half Dome, Yosemite Falls, and Tunnel View. It's offered from late May to late October. An 8-hour Grand Tour is offered in summer for $110/adult and $71/child. Reservations can be made online. And there's a hiker shuttle between Yosemite Valley and Tuolumne Meadows.

Hiking

More than 750 miles of hiking trails crisscross Yosemite National Park. Well-trod paths lead through lush meadows, meander along rivers to thunderous waterfalls, and climb to the crown of bald granite domes. Hiking in Yosemite is highly dependent on when you arrive. Winter and spring are fantastic for waterfalls. However, it's not all fun and waterfalls. Tioga Road is closed, and High Sierra trails are inaccessible without proper equipment. And each year is different, but you can expect mosquitoes to be worst the three weeks after the snow melts. Muddy trails and treacherous creek crossings are also likely.

Summer is the busiest season. Trails are crowded, but most are open by this time, spreading visitors out. Just because Tioga Road is open doesn't mean you should assume all its trails are accessible. Depending on the amount of winter snowfall, some in the highest elevations may not be passable until well into July. Check the park website or ask a ranger about conditions if you think you might encounter a snow-packed trail. Try hiking in late September or early October if you'd like pleasant temperatures, smaller crowds, and access to the entire trail network. Unfortunately, it's likely many of the waterfalls (including Yosemite Falls) will be bone dry or nothing more than a trickle. Hiking in winter without snowshoes or skis is limited to trails in Hetch Hetchy and Yosemite Valleys.

The grueling trek up Subdome

Yosemite Valley hikes are easily accessed via the free shuttle. **Mist** is one of the park's most popular trails. The scenery is magnificent as you hike to the top of Vernal Falls (continue to Nevada Falls, or ambitious hikers with a permit follow the trail all the way to the top of Half Dome or, without a permit, continue the long trek to Cloud's Rest). This trek begins at Happy Isles (Shuttle Stop) at the far eastern end of Yosemite Valley. Depending on water volume, **Yosemite and Bridalveil Falls** are well worth a look. You can even hike above Yosemite Falls from the valley. Wawona has a decent selection of trails beginning near the hotel and Mariposa Grove, including two loops around massive trees (busy in summer). Most trailheads in Tuolumne Meadows/Crane Flats/White Wolf areas are well-marked and accessed via Tioga Road. Hetch Hetchy is an excellent place to shake the crowds of Yosemite Valley, but hiking options are somewhat limited (unless you're headed to the backcountry). You really can't go wrong with any trail at Yosemite, but some of my favorites are marked with thumbs up in the hiking tables.

Half Dome

Half Dome is one of Yosemite's iconic landscapes, so renowned its image resides on the California state quarter alongside the likes of John Muir and the California condor. This famous granite dome is situated at the east end of Yosemite Valley, where it rises some 4,800 feet above the valley's floor. Up until the 1870s, Half Dome was declared "perfectly inaccessible." Seeking to access the inaccessible, George Anderson constructed his own route to its summit by drilling and placing iron eyebolts into the smooth granite surface, completing the first successful ascent in 1875.

Today, the dome is accessed by more than a dozen rock climbing routes and a hiking path along its rounded eastern face. Hikers are aided by metal cables strung between steel polls. Without these cables the final 700-foot ascent would be impossible. They are removed during winter and are usually installed before Memorial

Climbing that rock!

Day weekend (May) and taken down around Columbus Day (October). The hike to Half Dome should be taken seriously. Three separate routes reach its eastern face. They range from 14–16.4 miles (roundtrip). The trek gains nearly 4,800 feet in elevation. It's uphill the entire way from Happy Isles and things first start to get serious at Subdome. Wear shoes with good grip. Many people bring gloves for the cable section to prevent blisters. There's usually a pile of used gloves near the start of the cables but don't rely on it (and pack out your gloves—the park doesn't want trash back there, even if you think you're doing a kindness for non-glove-carrying hikers). All hikers expecting to scale Half Dome require a permit. Permits, good for up to four hikers, are only available by lottery through recreation.gov. There's a $10 non-refundable application fee plus $10 per person if you're successful. Enjoy the trip; this is one of the best hikes in the world. Up to 300 hikers are allowed per day, so it can get busy, especially on the cable section. When you're on the cable section, go at your pace. Be patient with slow hikers. Let fast hikers pass when possible. Don't go up if storm clouds are in the area. If the rock is wet, and it feels unsafe, there's no shame in turning around and living to try it again another day.

Guided Hikes

Rugged terrain, intimidating wildlife, and a plethora of trails often leave visitors bewildered when it comes to selecting their hiking adventure. To make things simple Yosemite Hospitality provides an array of guided or unguided, group or private, day or multi-day hiking tours. Day hikes cost between $40 and $100 and visit many of the most spectacular and popular locations. They are only offered between late May through early October. Trips can be reserved at (209) 372-8344 or travelyosemite.com.

Backpacking & Permits

Nearly 95% of Yosemite is designated wilderness, and more than 750 miles of trails traverse this undeveloped region. To plan a Yosemite backpacking trip, you should start with a good topographical map. If it's your first time, you will want to hike in one of the popular backcountry areas like Ten Lakes (White Wolf) or Cathedral Lakes (Tuolumne Meadows). Most of Yosemite Valley falls within a no-camping zone.

After selecting a route, the next step is getting a permit. Wilderness permits are required for all overnight trips. Day-hikers do not require one. Make your reservations online through the park's website as early as possible. Wilderness permit reservations are processed by lottery 24 weeks in advance. They cost $5 per confirmed reservation plus $5 per person. Permits for most of the popular trailheads fill the same day they become available. (Over 97% of all John Muir Trail through-hike permit applications are denied due to high demand. The park installed a rolling lottery for the JMT, which greatly increases the success rate for thru-hikers.) Of each trailhead's daily quota, 60% can be reserved ahead of time while the remaining 40% are available first-come, first-served no earlier than 11am the day before your hike begins. Permits can be obtained at Yosemite Valley Wilderness Center, Tuolumne Meadows Wilderness Center, Big Oak Flat Information Station, Wawona Visitor Center at Hill's Studio, Hetch Hetchy Entrance Station, and Badger Pass Ranger Station. Permit priority is given to the closest permit issuing station. (So you can't go to Wawona Visitor Center and get a permit for Cathedral Lakes.) From November through April, wilderness permits are available without reservation.

Rock Climbing

Thousands of visitors come to Yosemite National Park for one thing and one thing only: rock climbing. This is Mecca for climbers all around the world. Advanced climbers enjoy the challenges of multi-day ascents of Half Dome or 3,000-foot El Capitán (El Cap), but there's a little something here for people of all abilities. Experienced climbers new to Yosemite should head to Camp 4 to mingle among Yosemite's rock climbing communities or pick up a climbing-centric guidebook from one of the park's bookstores. Beginners can find plenty of good places for scrambling. Much of the high country is covered with granite boulders and Bridalveil Falls Trail has a nice collection of boulders to enjoy.

You can also join one of Yosemite Mountaineering School's (209.372.8344, travelyosemite.com) climbing lessons or guided climbs. Lessons are held as long as there are at least three participants. Their basic course costs $172/person. Crack Climbing and Anchoring classes are for novices at a cost of $175/person. They offer advanced courses as well. Guided climbs range from 6 hours ($175+/person) to a one-on-one 6-day El Cap climb ($6,032).

Water Activities

Rafts are available for rent at Curry Village Recreation Center (Yosemite Valley). Each raft holds four adults and costs $28.50/person. Trips begin at Curry Village and end 3 miles later at Sentinel Beach Picnic Area. Rafting season changes from year-to-year, but the Merced River is usually runnable from late May until the end of July. Visitors are welcome to bring their own floatables and purchase a ticket for the shuttle bus back to Curry Village for $5 per person. All river users should help protect the resource by entering and exiting the river on sandy beaches. Putting in at Stoneman Bridge (near Curry Village) and taking out at Sentinel Beach Picnic Area is the typical run. Personal flotation devices are required. Beyond Yosemite Valley, rafting is also permitted on the South Fork of the Merced River near Wawona. **Kayaking** is popular at Tenaya Lake. Fishing is permitted within the park. **Fishing** is permitted in the park, but you must follow all state and park regulations (including no fishing from bridges, and only artificial lures or flies with barbless hooks are allowed in Yosemite Valley).

Biking

Cyclists are free to enjoy the 12-mile Yosemite Valley Loop. This paved path is a fantastic alternative to driving congested park roads or riding packed shuttle buses. Cyclists are permitted on all park roads, but it's not recommended unless you plan on pedaling during the off-season or early morning. Bikes are prohibited from all hiking trails. Bike rental is available at Yosemite Valley Lodge and Curry Village Bike Kiosks. They are typically open from mid-June to fall. Rental rates are $24/half-day and $36/day. Strollers, trailers, and electric scooters are also available.

Horseback Riding

Yosemite Hospitality runs three stables within the park. They have two general offerings out of Wawona Stables (near Wawona Hotel). A 2-hour ride ($70/rider) is their all ages and abilities offering (as long as you're at least 7 years old, taller than 52 inches, and weigh between 52 and 225 pounds). It explores Wawona Meadow Loop. There's also an all-day ride ($144/rider) for fit, experienced riders. This ride is six hours long

and goes up to Mariposa Grove. Rides can be booked online through travelyosemite.com. If you'd like to go on a pack trip, Yosemite Hospitality will take you to the High Sierra Camps (549). Remember, you must also win the High Sierra Camp reservation lottery to head back there on a pack trip. Horse boarding is available at Yosemite Valley Stable in summer. Stock sites are available at Wawona, Bridalveil Creek, and Tuolumne Meadows Campgrounds.

Winter Activities

Snow rarely sticks in Yosemite Valley, but the higher elevations are often buried in the fluffy white stuff. Winter's cold and snow-capped mountains add a little more diversity to park activities. Cross-country skiing, snowshoeing, skiing, tubing, and ice-skating are popular. Marked trails are available at Badger Pass, along Glacier Point Road, in Mariposa Grove of Giant Sequoias, and around the Crane Flat area. Free ranger-guided snowshoe walks are also offered. You can usually find a current schedule of ranger programs at the park website or a visitor center.

Badger Pass (travelyosemite.com) is the oldest downhill skiing area in California. It has 5 lifts and most runs are easy to moderate, with an 800-ft elevation drop. Lift tickets cost $62/adult and $35/child for a full day. Badger Pass also offers snow-tubing ($25/person, per 2-hour session). Rentals, lessons, and multi-day cross-country tour packages are also available. Badger Pass is usually open from mid-December through mid-March (conditions permitting). Call (209) 372-8430 for information, lessons, or snow conditions. There's also a snowplay area near Crane Flat Campground.

Yosemite Hospitality (travelyosemite.com) also offers backcountry cross-country skiing tours, guided Glacier Point ski overnight trips ($423+/person), guided snowshoeing hikes ($75), and rental equipment.

And then there's an ice rink at Curry Village. You can skate around with Half Dome looming in the background. It's typically open from December until early March, but you may want to call (209) 372-8333 for up-to-date conditions. A 2-hour session costs $11/adult, $9.50/child, and $4.50 for skate rentals.

Photography & Art

Many Yosemite introductions are made through Ansel Adams' photos. Ansel became interested in this granite wonderland at the age of 14 after reading James Mason Hutchings' *In the Heart of the Sierras*. Yosemite helped drive Adams to become the preeminent

El Capitan

landscape photographer of the American West. Today, thousands of photographers try to recapture his famous images. Tunnel View (Wawona Road) and Glacier Point provide two of the most photographed vistas in the world. Then there's the February phenomenon known as the "Natural Firefall." There are no guarantees you'll see a "firefall," but with the right amount of water and light Horsetail Falls ignites against the granite wall. Interested photographers should park at Yosemite Falls parking area (just west of Yosemite Valley Lodge) and walk 1.5 miles (each way) to El Capitán Picnic Area on Northside Drive in mid-February. Yosemite Valley's Ansel Adams Gallery (anseladams.com) helps preserve the life, the work, and the vision of one of America's greatest photographers and conservationists. They give free camera walks and/or guided photography classes for $65–95/person. Daily art classes are offered at Happy Isles Art and Nature Center (yosemite.org) from spring through fall. They cost about $20–30 per adult. Kids' art classes are also offered for $10 per child or $30 per family.

Visitor Centers & Museums

Valley Visitor Center (All Year, 9am–5pm): Located just west of the main post office (shuttle stops #5 and #9), this visitor center is the main hub for information, maps, and books. Exhibits focusing on the park's geology and a 30-minute orientation film are available.

Yosemite Museum (All Year, 9am–5pm): Located next to Valley Visitor Center, the museum displays exhibits from Yosemite's past as well as a digital slide show of historic visitors and hotels.

Ansel Adams Gallery (All Year, 10am–3pm, anseladams.com): Located next to Valley Visitor Center, the gallery displays work of Ansel Adams as well as that of other photographers and artists.

Valley Wilderness Center (May–October, 8am–5pm): Adjacent to the post office, the Wilderness Center is here to help plan backcountry trips, obtain wilderness permits, and rent bear canisters.

Happy Isles Art and Nature Center (May–September, 9:30–5pm): Located near shuttle stop #16, it's the stop for nature-loving families and art enthusiasts.

Wawona Visitor Center at Hill's Studio (late May–early October, 8:30am–5pm): Wilderness permits, bear canister rentals, trail information, and books and maps are available.

Pioneer Yosemite History Center (Wawona): This time-period, open-air museum brings guests back to the days of log cabins and horse-drawn carriages. It's open 24/7.

Tuolumne Meadows Visitor Center (late May–late September, 9am–6pm): Trail information, books, and maps are available.

Tuolumne Meadows Wilderness Center (late May–mid-October, 8am–5pm): Maps, wilderness permits, bear canister rental, and guidebooks are available.

Yosemite Conservancy: The Yosemite Conservancy (800.469.7275, yosemite.org) is a non-profit organization helping to protect the park and educate its visitors via adventures ($700/day for 1–4 people) and art.

Ranger Programs & For Kids

Park rangers lead interpretive programs in every region of the park, from Mariposa Grove to Tuolumne Meadows (when accessible). There is, quite literally, something for everyone. Twilight strolls, junior ranger programs, campfire talks, and much more are at your disposal. And the best feature is that almost all these National Park Service programs are free. Visit the park's website prior to your arrival to check the event calendar for an up-to-date schedule of programs.

With so many kid-friendly activities, easy hiking trails, and awe-inspiring vistas, Yosemite is an exceptional family getaway. Children can also become Junior Rangers (ages 7–13) or Little Cubs (ages 3–6) while visiting. To do so, you must first purchase a Junior Ranger ($3.50) or Little Cub ($3) Booklet. They are available at Yosemite Valley Visitor Center, Happy Isles Nature Center (May–Sept), Wawona and Tuolumne Meadows Visitor Centers (June–Sept), and Big Oak Flat Information Station (May–Sept). Complete the booklet to become a Junior Ranger and receive an award.

Flora & Fauna
More than 400 mammals reside here. Most commonly seen are mule deer and black bear. Marmots are often seen in the rocky high country, even on top of Half Dome. Vegetation changes dramatically from Yosemite Valley to the high country. Dense forests and meadows cover the valleys and foothills, while the alpine zone is treeless and rocky.

Pets & Accessibility
Pets must be kept on a leash (less than six feet). They are only allowed in developed areas, on fully paved trails and roads (unless marked otherwise), and in campgrounds (except Camp 4 and group sites).

Yosemite Valley Visitor Center, Ansel Adams Gallery, Happy Isles Art and Nature Center, Tuolumne Meadows Visitor Center, and Mariposa Grove Museum are all accessible to wheelchair users. Several trails are accessible with assistance, including the eastern part of Yosemite Falls Loop, most of Valley Loop Trail, and Glacier Point Vista. Park shuttle buses are accessible. The Ahwahnee, Yosemite Valley Lodge, and Curry Village have accessible accommodations. Most campgrounds have a few accessible sites. All food-service facilities are accessible except The Loft, Tuolumne Meadows Lodge, and Wawona Hotel's dining room. For more details refer to the park's accessibility guide.

Weather
Yosemite Valley is warm in summer. The average high temperature for July and August is about 80°F. Overnight lows dip into the 50s°F. Summer averages less than 2 inches of precipitation each year, but

Vernal Falls

thunderstorms are a serious concern. You do not want to be caught on a massive, exposed slab of granite like Half Dome when an afternoon storm rolls in. During the winter, average highs are around 40°F in Yosemite Valley with lows in the 20s. Most precipitation falls between November and March. In the higher elevations snow can fall any month of the year. Regardless of when you hike, pack warm clothes and dress in layers.

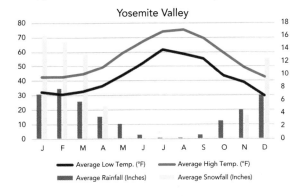

Yosemite Valley

Average Low Temp. (°F) — Average High Temp. (°F)
Average Rainfall (Inches) — Average Snowfall (Inches)

Glacier Point

Tips & Recommendations

About 75% of the park's visitors arrive between May and October, peaking in July/August. A best time to visit depends on what you're looking to do. In spring, flowers bloom and waterfalls roar. In summer, Tioga Road and the high-country open for exploration (but waterfalls dry up, and wildfires are common). In fall, crowds thin and colors change. In winter, activities transition, and snow begins to recharge the valley's waterfalls. Note that tire chains may be required, depending on conditions, fall through spring.

Because of the park's popularity, you may want to consider visiting in late fall or winter. If you're traveling with friends/family, or any group, do your best to carpool. And then, when you reach the park, use the shuttles as much as possible (you won't want to give up that parking space anyway).

Yosemite Valley can be ridiculously busy. I've been there when the line at the entrance is so long rangers conceded and let everyone drive in. No fees. No maps. Just a long stream of cars flowing down into Yosemite Valley until things clogged at the next bottleneck. If you're coming from outside the park to spend the day, plan on arriving early, especially if you're visiting between June and September. Arrive before nine to secure a parking spot, and then don't move your car. Remember to pack your patience. This is also a strong argument to secure camping or lodging accommodations inside the park. You'll have a place for your car.

Staying at Yosemite Valley's lodges comes at a premium (and you'll have to make reservations well in advance for peak season). However, this is one premium you shouldn't mind paying. Waking up and going to bed in the valley has immense value. The valley is the

place to be, and you won't have to make an hour-long (or more) drive to reach it. Not to mention, a late arrival means you'll likely be redirected to other areas of the park. More time spent in your car, means less time spent on the trails. Plus, wandering around a moon-lit valley is pure joy. Stay in the valley! Remember camping is an option, too! Although campsites are equally difficult to reserve during peak season.

Once you find a parking spot, leave your car there and use the free shuttle (or hike nearby trails). For many potential visitors, it's hard to imagine gridlock in an outdoor park, but it is true. Getting a parking spot after nine or ten is intense sport in Yosemite Valley (and many of the popular trailheads).

Keeping your car parked provides another perk: you won't need gas. However, you'll find gas stations at Wawona, El Portal, Crane Flat, and Tuolumne Meadows. There aren't any in Yosemite Valley. Yosemite is big, but not so big that gas becomes a problem.

While it's a good idea to bring food with you and prepare your meals, you don't have to. There are quite a few dining options (and a grocery store) in Yosemite Village. Wawona Hotel, White Wolf Lodge, and Tuolumne Meadows Lodge all serve food. There's also a grill at Tuolumne Meadows. And small markets are located at each of the gas stations. Also, if you're a backpacker, you do not need to stay at a High Sierra Camp to enjoy a hot meal or box lunch. Meal-only reservations are available.

Cell service is generally available in Yosemite Valley. Verizon has the broadest coverage, but you're still pretty limited once you get away from the valley. Free Wi-Fi is available at Degnan's Kitchen in Yosemite Valley and to overnight guests at The Ahwahnee, Yosemite Valley Lodge, Curry Village, and Wawona Hotel.

There's a funny story about a guest asking a park ranger what he should do with one hour in Yosemite Valley. The ranger points to a rock and says he'd sit right there and cry. The only tears you should shed at Yosemite are tears of joy from being in the presence of some of the most remarkable scenery on the planet. Allow a few days (at a minimum), not a few hours, for your trip to this unbelievably beautiful destination.

Yosemite Valley is certainly special, but the park's other areas aren't lousy. If Tioga Road is open, spend a night or two up at Tuolumne Meadows, explore Mariposa Grove, stop in at Hetch Hetchy (if you have time).

These areas aren't quite as accessible or accommodating as Yosemite Valley, but they are striking.

If you think you're up to climbing Half Dome, apply for a permit. Just know it's a pretty intense hike. You'll want to wear shoes with good grip, pack gloves for the cable section, and bring ample food and water. There's a good chance you'll be spent after climbing Subdome. Take a break and don't attempt the cable section up the spine of Half Dome until you feel ready for it. People have died here, and I've witnessed individuals cramping mid-cable section. These situations are not only dangerous for the individual in pain, but for others trying to ascend this massive rock. Don't be too disappointed if you don't get a permit. There are plenty of good alternatives, including Yosemite Falls, Four Mile, Cloud's Rest, and Panorama Trails.

Easy Hikes: Lower Yosemite (1 mile), Bridalveil Falls (0.5), Grizzly Giant (2)
Moderate Hikes: Sentinel Dome (2.2 miles), Cathedral Lakes (7), Elizabeth Lake (4.8), Glen Aulin (11), Gaylor Lakes (2), Mono Pass (8), Taft Point (1.8), Lembert Dome (2.8), Wapama Falls (5)
Strenuous Hikes: Vernal & Nevada Falls (8 miles), Yosemite Falls (7.2), Four Mile (9.6), Ostrander Lake (11.4), Panorama (8.3), Ten Lakes (12.6)
Extreme Hikes: Half Dome (14 miles)
Family Activities: Float the Merced River, visit in winter, check out the big trees at Mariposa, become Junior Rangers

Hetch Hetchy

Guided Tours: Go rock climbing, explore the backcountry, ride a horse
Rainy Day Activities: Stay close to your car or any of the museums/galleries/visitor centers if thunderstorms are in the forecast, you absolutely do not want to be on one of these massive rocks when lightning strikes
History Enthusiasts: Yosemite Museum, Pioneer Yosemite History Center
Sunset Spots: Stoneman Meadow (by Curry Village), Cook's Meadow, Sentinel Dome, Glacier Point, Washburn Point, Tunnel View, basically anywhere you can see Half Dome, but you can also have a cool sunset looking at it at spots like Taft Point
Sunrise Spots: Basically the same spots, since most of them are looking east toward Half Dome to see the last rays of light against it, just know you'd have to get very lucky and have an extremely colorful sunrise for it to light up the sky for onlookers in the valley (or even at Glacier Point). Many photographers like to leave the park to photograph Mono Lake for sunrise

Beyond the Park...

Dining
Around the Horn Brewing
17820 CA-120, Groveland
aroundthehornbeer.com

Savoury's • (209) 966-7677
5034 CA-140, Mariposa
savourys-restaurant.com

June Bug Café • (209) 966-6666
6979A CA-140, Midpines
junebugcafe.com

Oakhurst Grill • (559) 641-2477
40530 CA-41, Oakhurst
oakhurstgrillandwhiskey41.com

Grocery Stores
Pioneer Market • (209) 742-6100
5034 Coakley Cir, Mariposa

Vons • (559) 642-4250
40044 CA-49, Oakhurst

Raley's • (559) 683-8300
40041 CA-49, Oakhurst

Lodging & Camping
Blue Butterfly Inn • (209) 379-2100
11132 CA-140, El Portal
yosemitebluebutterflyinn.com

Sunset Inn • (209) 962-4360
33569 Hardin Flat Rd, Groveland

Rush Creek Lodge • (209) 379-2373
34001 CA-120, Groveland
rushcreeklodge.com
Yosemite Lakes RV • (209) 962-0103
31191 Hardin Flat Rd, Groveland

Yosemite RV Resort
34094 CA-41, Coarsegold
rvoutdoors.com • (866) 862-4059

Bass Lake RV Park • (559) 642-3145
39744 Rd 274, Bass Lake
basslakeatyosemite.com

Mono Vista RV Park • (760) 647-6401
57 Beaver Ln, Lee Vining
monovistarvpark.net

Festivals
Butterfly Fest • Mariposa
mariposabutterflyfestival.net

Attractions
National forests (fs.usda.gov) span the sierras, including Inyo (Mary Lake and endless amazing hiking), Humboldt-Toiyabe, Stanislaus, and Sierra. Within them are various wilderness areas, like Desolation (the popular Lake Aloha Trail), Ansel Adams, John Muir (popular Big Pine Lakes Trail), and Emigrant). This is a good place to look if you're tired of the national parks.

Devil's Postpile Nat Monument
Mammoth Lakes
nps.gov/depo • (760) 934-2289

Lake Tahoe
There are a number of state parks and scenic points around Lake Tahoe (in CA and NV)

Mono Lake Tufa State Reserve
million-year-old lake
US-395, Lee Vining
parks.ca.gov

Bodie State Historic Site
Gold-mining ghost town
CA-270, Bridgeport
parks.ca.gov

Calaveras Big Trees State Park
Two sequoia groves
1170 CA-4, Arnold
parks.ca.gov

Sugar Pine Railroad
56001 CA-41, Fish Camp
ymsprr.com • (559) 683-7273

Arta River Trips
Non-profit whitewater rafting co.
arta.org • (209) 962-7873

Yosemite Trail Pack Station
Horseback adventures
yosemitetrails.com

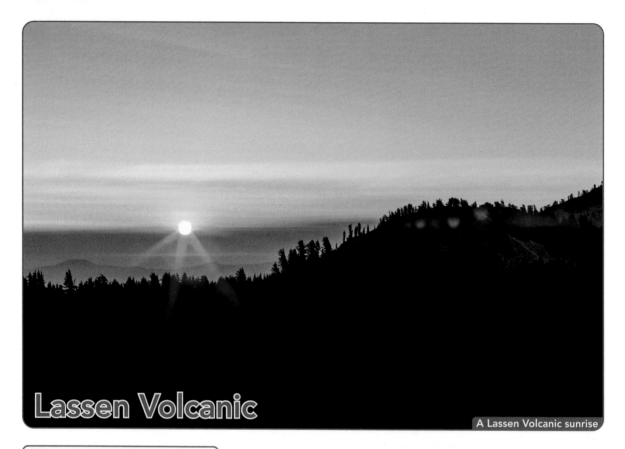

Lassen Volcanic

A Lassen Volcanic sunrise

Phone: (530) 595-4480
Website: nps.gov/lavo

Established: August 9, 1916
May 1907 (Nat'l Monument)
Size: 106,000 Acres
Annual Visitors: 500,000
Peak Season: June–September
Hiking Trails: 150 Miles

Activities: Hiking, Backpacking, Boating, Horseback Riding, Fishing, Stargazing, Cross-country Skiing, Snowshoeing

7 Campgrounds: $12–26/night
Backcountry Camping: Permitted
Drakesbad Ranch: $199–219/person/night

Park Hours: All day, every day
Entrance Fee: $30/25/15 (car/motorcycle/individual)

The Cascade Range stretches from Canada into northeastern California. Among these mountains is 10,457-foot Lassen Peak, the largest plug dome volcano in the world and the southernmost non-extinct volcano in the Cascade Range. Lassen Peak stands above its surroundings, serving as the centerpiece of Lassen Volcanic National Park. Beyond the prominent peak is a collection of deep blue alpine lakes, dense conifer forests, stinking fumaroles, belching mudpots, roiling hot springs, and boisterous streams. It's a place where features that are so obviously of this earth blend with those that are altogether otherworldly. Perhaps a greater mystery than how these landscapes were united is how today they go by relatively unnoticed.

Native Americans first took notice of the mountain and its surrounding landscapes, visiting seasonally to hunt and gather food. Lassen Peak served as a meeting site for four American Indian groups: Atsugewi, Yana, Yahi, and Maidu. Thanks were given for the food the region provided, but Natives eyed Lassen Peak with great suspicion. They knew it was filled with fire and water and believed there would come a day when it would blow apart, causing considerable damage to the region and potentially its people.

During the mid-19th century, California was flooded with gold-seeking 49ers. While trekking across the Cascades to fertile soils of the Sacramento Valley, they used the mighty peak as a landmark to assure their course was correct. One of the guides who led hopeful prospectors on this journey was Peter Lassen, a Danish blacksmith who settled in northern California in the 1830s. Together with William Nobles, they blazed the first two pioneer trails. Portions of Lassen and Nobles Emigrant Trail are still visible and used today. And Lassen's life is memorialized with a peak and a park.

As the gold rush subsided, Lassen Peak and the region it towered above returned to a life of relative anonymity. But the United States was growing, and forests were being cut at an astonishing rate. No tree was sacred to the lumberjacks. Neither the coastal redwoods nor the Sierra Nevada's giant sequoias were safe from the loggers' axe and saw. If these trees were in danger, so too were the pine and fir of the southern Cascades. With its forests in peril, a conservationist president took notice of this volcanic region. President Theodore Roosevelt preserved vast tracts of land for the enjoyment of the American people, including two regions in the southern Cascades: Cinder Cone National Monument and Lassen Peak National Monument. This designation spared the trees and opened the region to the nascent industry of commercial tourism.

But few Americans took notice. In May of 1915, as if to make people aware of its presence once more, the volcano woke up with a series of minor eruptions. These events created a new crater, released lava and ash, and razed several homes. Incandescent blocks of lava could be seen rolling down the flanks of Lassen Peak from 20 miles away. No one was killed by the eruptions, but people began to observe its fury. Scientists took interest in the park's volcanoes. Washington also was aware of these events, and in 1916, largely thanks to volcanic activity, the two monuments were combined and expanded to create Lassen Volcanic National Park. The eruptions stopped in 1921. Once again, the region was forgotten.

Perhaps some things are best left forgotten. Roads are rarely congested. Campgrounds aren't booked months in advance. If you're looking for a California getaway where volcanic past meets picturesque present, a place filled with wildlife not automobiles, a place where the mud boils and the earth steams, Lassen National Park is for you. Let this serve as your reminder that there's a national park in northern California brimming with natural beauty, rich history, and most importantly, peace and quiet from the busy everyday lifestyle that tends to make a person forget a few things.

Juniper Lake

When to Go
Lassen Volcanic National Park is open 24 hours a day, every day of the year, but the park's main road is usually closed or restricted due to snow coverage from fall through late spring. Many facilities are also seasonal. All campgrounds (except Southwest Walk-In) close for winter. Summer and early fall are the best times to visit.

Transportation & Airports
Public transportation does not provide service to the park. The closest major airports are Sacramento International (SMF), located 172 miles south of the park's Southwest Entrance, and Reno/Tahoe International (RNO), 151 miles to the southeast.

Directions
There are five entrances to Lassen Volcanic National Park. Southwest and Northwest, both on CA-89, are the primary points of entry/exit. Warner Valley, Juniper Lake, and Butte Lake entrances are accessible via unpaved roads from the south, southeast, and northeast, respectively.

Southwest Entrance from Sacramento (158 miles): Take I-5 north to Exit 649 for Antelope Blvd/CA-36. Follow signs for Lassen National Park, taking CA-36 E approximately 45 miles before turning north onto CA-89 into the park.

Northwest Entrance from Oregon (150 miles): Traveling south on I-5, take Exit 736 onto CA-89 S toward McCloud/Lassen National Park. CA-89 leads directly to the Northwest Entrance.

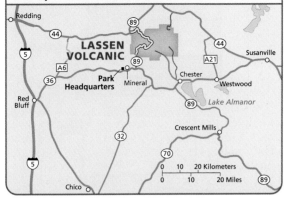

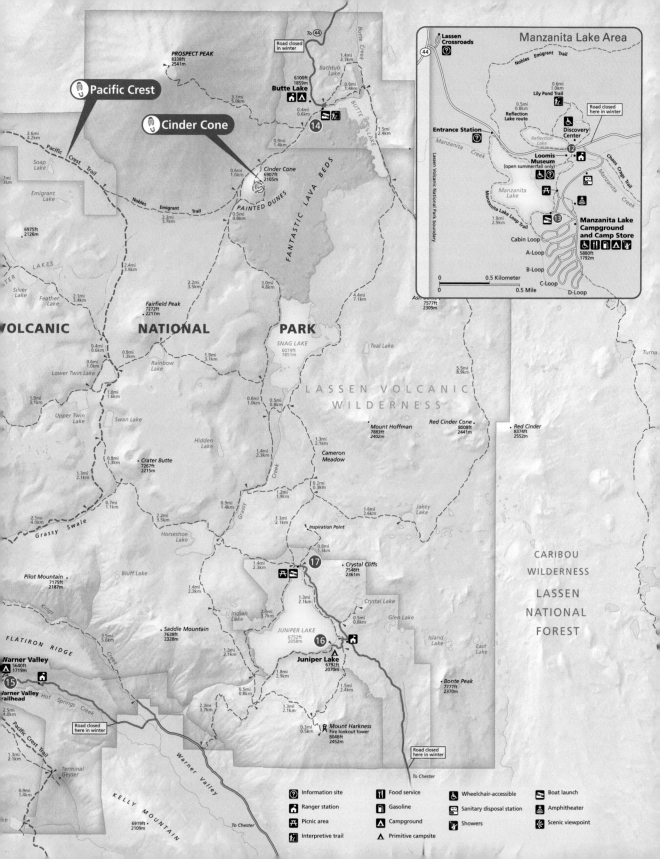

Pacific Crest

Cinder Cone

Manzanita Lake Area

To 44

Lassen Crossroads

44

Nobles Emigrant Trail

0.6mi
1.0km
Lily Pond Trail

0.5mi
0.8km
Reflection
Lake route

Road closed
here in winter

Entrance Station

Manzanita Creek

Reflection
Lake

Discovery Center

12

Chaos Crags Trail

Loomis Museum
(open summer/fall only)

Manzanita Lake

Manzanita Creek

13

Manzanita Lake Campground and Camp Store
5880ft
1792m

Cabin Loop

A-Loop

B-Loop

C-Loop

D-Loop

Manzanita Lake Loop Trail

1.8mi
2.9km

0   0.5 Kilometer
0   0.5 Mile

PROSPECT PEAK
8338ft
2541m

Road closed
in winter

1.4mi
2.3km

Butte Creek

Bathtub Lake

6100ft
1859m
Butte Lake

0.9mi
1.4km

0.4mi
0.6km

14

1.5mi
2.4km

BUTTE LAKE

3.1mi
5.0km

0.9mi
1.4km

0.6mi
1.0km
Cinder Cone
6907ft
2105m

2.6mi
4.2km

Pacific Crest Trail

Soap Lake

Nobles Emigrant Trail

7mi
3km

6975ft
2126m

0.5mi
0.8km

PAINTED DUNES

FANTASTIC LAVA BEDS

2.3mi
3.7km

2.2mi
3.5km

3.0mi
4.8km

4.4mi
7.1km

Ash Butte
7577ft
2309m

2.4mi
3.9km

Fairfield Peak
7272ft
2217m

LAKES

Silver Lake

Feather Lake

2.1mi
3.4km

Rainbow Lake

SNAG LAKE
6074ft
1851m

Teal Lake

Turna

0.4mi
0.6km

0.8mi
1.3km

1.9mi
3.1km

VOLCANIC

NATIONAL

PARK

LASSEN VOLCANIC

WILDERNESS

Mount Hoffman
7883ft
2402m

Red Cinder Cone
8008ft
2441m

Red Cinder
8374ft
2552m

CARIBOU

WILDERNESS

0.6mi
1.0km

Lower Twin Lake

0.6mi
1.0km

0.5mi
0.8km

Grassy Creek

1.3mi
2.1km

Cameron Meadow

1.9mi
3.1km

Upper Twin Lake

1.0mi
1.6km

Swan Lake

Hidden Lake

1.4mi
2.3km

1.2mi
1.9km

0.2mi
0.3km

LASSEN

NATIONAL

FOREST

0.8mi
1.3km

Crater Butte
7267ft
2215m

0.9mi
1.4km

1.3mi
2.1km

1.6mi
2.6km

Jakey Lake

1.3mi
2.1km

1.3mi
2.1km

2.5mi
4.0km

Grassy Swale

2.2mi
3.5km

Horseshoe Lake

Inspiration Point

0.8mi
1.3km

Pilot Mountain
7175ft
2187m

0.7mi
1.1km

Bluff Lake

1.4mi
2.3km

17

Crystal Cliffs
7548ft
2361m

FLATIRON RIDGE

3.5mi
5.6km

Saddle Mountain
7638ft
2328m

Indian Lake

1.4mi
2.3km

1.3mi
2.1km

2.3mi
3.7km

JUNIPER LAKE
6752ft
2058m

Crystal Lake

0.5mi
0.8km

Glen Lake

Island Lake

East Lake

Warner Valley
5640ft
1719m

15

Warner Valley Trailhead

Hot Springs Creek

1.8mi
2.9km

1.3mi
2.1km

0.5mi
0.8km

16

Juniper Lake
6792ft
2070m

1.5mi
2.4km

Bonte Peak
7777ft
2370m

2.5mi
4.0km

Road closed
here in winter

Kings Creek

2.3mi
3.7km

1.3mi
2.1km

0.3mi
0.5km

Mount Harkness
Fire lookout tower
8048ft
2452m

Road closed
here in winter

Pacific Crest Trail

1.3mi
2.1km

WARNER VALLEY

To Chester

0.9mi
1.4km

Terminal Geyser

KELLY MOUNTAIN

6919ft
2109m

To Chester

Legend

Information site	Food service	Wheelchair-accessible	Boat launch
Ranger station	Gasoline	Sanitary disposal station	Amphitheater
Picnic area	Campground	Showers	Scenic viewpoint
Interpretive trail	Primitive campsite		

outh-

Camping & Lodging

Along Main Park Road from Northwest to Southwest Entrance Stations are Manzanita Lake (179 sites, $26/night), Summit Lake North (46, $24), Summit Lake South (48, $22), and Southwest Walk-in (20, $16) Campgrounds. Warner Valley (18, $16), Juniper Lake (18, $12), and Butte Lake (101, $22) Campgrounds are accessed via rough and remote gravel roads. Coin-operated showers and laundry, and a dump station (fee) are only available near Manzanita Lake. Flush toilets are available at Butte Lake, Manzanita Lake, and Summit Lake North. Camping fees are reduced when water is not available. Juniper Lake Campground does not have potable water. You'll have to treat water from the lake. Southwest is the only year-round campground, but it's walk-in, tent-only camping. Sites at Manzanita Lake, Summit Lake, and Butte Lake can be reserved up to six months in advance at (877) 444-6777 or recreation. gov. **RV sites** are only available at Manzanita Lake, Lost Creek (group camp near Manzanita), Summit Lake North, Butte Lake, and Warner Valley. No sites have hookups. **Group sites** are available at Manzanita Lake (5, $72), Butte Lake (6, $62), Lost Creek (8, $62), and Juniper Lake (2, $32). Group sites must be reserved. All campgrounds (other than Southwest) open sometime between May and July and close between September and October (depending on the weather).

If you're looking for more comfortable lodging accommodations inside the park, you can book a stay at

Lassen Volcanic Hiking Trails (Distances are roundtrip)

	Name	Location (# on map)	Length	Difficulty Rating & Notes
Southwest Entrance	Brokeoff Mtn - ⚲	0.25 mile south of SW Entrance (1)	7.0 miles	S – Steep trail to summit, excellent views
	Mill Creek Falls - ⚲	Southwest Parking Area (2)	3.8 miles	M – Hike through forest to falls overlook
	Ridge Lakes	Sulphur Works Parking Area (3)	2.0 miles	S – Up ridge, through ravine to alpine lakes
	Bumpass Hell - ⚲	Bumpass Hell Parking Area (4)	3.0 miles	M – Boardwalk through a hydrothermal area
	Lassen Peak - ⚲	Lassen Peak Parking Area (5)	5.0 miles	S – Hike up mountain slope of loose rock
	Terrace, Shadow and Cliff Lakes	21 miles from NW Entrance (6)	4.0 miles	M – Great trail to view Lassen Peak
	Cold Boiling Lake	Kings Creek Picnic Area (7)	2.6 miles	E – Pass through forest to a bubbling lake
	Kings Creek Falls - ⚲	Kings Creek Falls Trailhead (8)	3.0 miles	M – Meadows, forest, flowers, and falls
Northwest Entrance	Echo Lake	Summit Lake Ranger Station (9)	4.4 miles	M – Can continue to Cluster Lakes
	Paradise Meadow	Hat Lake Parking Area (10)	2.8 miles	M – Footbridges to talus cliff-lined meadow
	Devastated Area	Devastated Parking Area (11)	0.25 mile	E – Interpretive trail discusses past eruptions
	Lily Pond	Across from Loomis Museum (12)	0.5 mile	E – Nature trail with interpretive brochures
	Manzanita Creek	Manzanita Lake (13)	7.0 miles	M – Switchbacks to meadow along creek
	Manzanita Lake - ⚲	Manzanita Lake (13)	1.8 miles	E – Flat trail around lake, birding area
	Chaos Crags and Crags Lake - ⚲	Manzanita Lake (13)	4.2 miles	M – Lake is often dry in summer
Butte Lake	Cinder Cone - ⚲	Butte Lake Parking Area (14)	4.0 miles	S – Pass lava beds and painted dunes
	Prospect Peak	Spur from Cinder Cone (15)	6.6 miles	S – Forested trail to rim of shield volcano
Warner Valley	Devil's Kitchen - ⚲	Warner Valley Rd (15)	4.4 miles	M – Mudpots, steam vents, and fumaroles
	Boiling Springs Lake	Warner Valley Rd (15)	3.0 miles	E – Mudpots, wildflowers, and 125°F lake
	Terminal Geyser	Warner Valley Rd (15)	5.8 miles	M – Not a geyser, a fumarole and steam
Juniper Lake	Mount Harkness	Juniper Lake Campground (16)	3.8 miles	S – Fire lookout provides wonderful views
	Crystal Lake	Juniper Lake Campground (16)	0.8 mile	E – Short trail to small tarn in rocky basin
	Inspiration Point	Juniper Lake Picnic Area (17)	1.4 miles	M – Views of the park's prominent peaks
	Horseshoe Lake	Juniper Lake Picnic Area (17)	2.8 miles	E – Gentle trail to a good fishing hole

Difficulty Ratings: E = Easy, M = Moderate, S = Strenuous

Drakesbad Guest Ranch (lassenlodging.com) in Warner Valley. Just know that comfortable is a relative term. Cabins do not have electricity, but meals are included at a cost of about $220 per person per night (two-night minimum). The ranch is typically open from mid-June through mid-October. Or there are **camping cabins** at Manzanita Lake starting at $76 per night (two-night minimum). Cabins are simple with thin/firm mattresses, a propane heater, and battery-powered lantern. You are responsible for bedding. Camper cabins can be reserved through recreation.gov.

Driving

The 29-mile Main Park Road weaves its way across the park, passing the majority of facilities and attractions. Only short sections of road at Northwest and Southwest Entrances are open all year. The remainder are closed beginning in late fall (with the first significant snowfall) until late spring or early summer.

Butte Lake, Warner Valley, and Juniper Lake Roads are unpaved roads leading to remote regions. All three are open seasonally (weather dependent). Butte Lake and Warner Valley Roads are at lower elevation and therefore open earlier and remain open later than Juniper Lake Road and the Main Park Road. If you're planning to visit in spring or fall, be sure to check with the park about current conditions prior to departing.

Hiking

You can see alpine lakes and peer up at Lassen Peak from your driver's seat, but it's impossible to appreciate them with your hands on a steering wheel. Visitors determined to explore the park to the fullest must hit the trails. Two of the most popular ones are Lassen Peak and Bumpass Hell, both located along Main Park Road. If you can arrange a shuttle, or cache a car/bike, it's possible to hike to Southwest Campground from Bumpass Hell by combining it with Cold Boiling Lake and Mill Creek Falls Trails (6.5 miles total). Together they offer a wide variety of scenery, including mudpots, hot springs, fumaroles, a boiling lake, and waterfall. Bumpass Hell looks, feels, and smells like a miniature Yellowstone.

Other popular trails along Main Park Road include Brokeoff Mountain, Devastation, and Manzanita Lake. You'll also find many trails beyond Main Park Road at Warner Valley, Juniper Lake, and Butte Lake. These locations provide plenty of solitude as you walk among a pristine wilderness filled with conifer forests and perfectly clear alpine lakes. (Note that these area's gravel access roads are long and rough.) **Cinder Cone Trail** in the Butte Lake area is a really nice strenuous hike to the top of the cinder cone that created Fantastic Lava Beds and Painted Dunes. Juniper Lake has a dense network of trails, allowing hikers to assemble looped routes of varying distances. Warner Valley features Devil's Kitchen and Drakesbad Ranch. Each area has its appeal.

Backpacking

More than 150 miles of trails, including 18 miles of the Pacific Crest Trail provides ample backpacking opportunities. All overnight trips in the backcountry require a free wilderness permit, available at self-registration stations found at Loomis Ranger Station, Kohm Yah-mah-nee Visitor Center, Butte Lake Ranger Station, Warner Valley Ranger Station, and Juniper Lake Ranger Station. Plan your route carefully. Do not expect to find a park ranger at any of the ranger stations (besides Loomis). Backpackers must use bear-resistant food canisters (required from mid-April through October) and camp at least 300 feet from other groups, 100 feet from streams and lakes, and at least 0.5 mile from any developed area. Bear canister rentals are available at park stores in Loomis Museum and Kohm Yah-mah-nee Visitor Center ($10 for 7 days).

Paddling

Paddlers must use the designated launch areas at Manzanita, Butte, and Juniper Lakes. Manzanita Lake Camper Store (lassenlodging.com) rents kayaks ($16/hr), canoes ($25), SUPs ($15), and catarafts ($30) on a first-come, first-served basis. Rentals are available from 10am until 4pm, late May through September. Boating is prohibited on Lake Helen, Reflection Lake, Emerald Lake, and Boiling Springs Lake. When we went to print, Manzanita Lake was temporarily closed to soft-sided floatation devices and swimming due to otter danger.

Horseback Riding

Visitors are welcome to bring their own stock, but overnight stays are only permitted in designated stock corrals at Butte Lake, Juniper Lake, and Summit Lake. A free wilderness permit must be obtained from any of the self-registration stations listed in the backpacking section above prior to trail use. An easier way to ride a horse is to stay at Drakesbad Guest Ranch (lassenlodging.com). They take guests on guided trail rides.

Fishing

Many of the park's waters possess rainbow and brown trout. Manzanita Lake is the most frequented fishing hole. You must practice catch and release and use single-hook, barbless, artificial lures. A California fishing license is required for all anglers 16 and older.

Stargazing

It's always a good idea to bring a reclining chair and blanket, and stay up late (or wake up early) to watch the stars (during a new moon or when it's below the horizon). Find a clear view of the sky (Lake Helen's shoreline is a great spot) and enjoy. The park even holds an annual Dark Sky Festival.

Winter Activities

In winter, Main Park Road may be closed but the fun doesn't stop where the road is not plowed. Southwest Parking Area is a great place to begin a snowshoe trek, cross-country ski adventure, or a family sledding excursion. Several sledding hills and miles of ski trails are available nearby Kohm Yah-mah-nee Visitor Center. Over at the Northwest Entrance, cross-country skiers and snowshoers can embark upon a 7-mile trail along Manzanita Creek (begins at Loomis Ranger Station) or the 5.6-mile Nobles Emigrant Trail (connects to Manzanita Lake Loop near entrance station). The park entrance fee is reduced to $10 in winter.

Visitor Centers & Museums

Kohm Yah-mah-nee Visitor Center, located at Southwest Entrance, provides park information, books, maps, exhibits, and a cafe. It houses an auditorium where visitors can view a short introductory film. The visitor center is open from 9am–5pm, daily from May through October, and Wednesday through Sunday for the rest of the year. **Loomis Museum**, near Manzanita Lake, is open daily, 9am–5pm, from late June through September. It features exhibits, a short park film, a bookstore, ranger programs, and access to several of the park's more popular trails. Ranger stations are found at Butte Lake, Warner Valley, and Juniper Lake.

Ranger Programs & For Kids

Lassen Volcanic offers free ranger-led activities during summer and winter. Summer programs run from mid-June to mid-August. They consist of a variety of walks, talks, and evening activities, including astronomy demonstrations. There are bird-watching hikes, junior ranger programs, and a slew of educational talks, discussing the park's unique ecology, geology, and history. During winter you can join park rangers on a 1–2 mile snowshoe adventure. These walks are held regularly from January through March, meeting at Kohm Yah-mah-nee Visitor Center (Southwest). Snowshoes are provided for the ranger-led hike. Wear water-resistant hiking boots and appropriate clothing. To view a complete and current schedule of events at the park, check bulletin boards at park facilities or view the park's online calendar before visiting.

The park offers ranger-led Junior Ranger Programs for kids. Junior Ranger Activity Booklets are available at Loomis Museum or Kohm Yah-mah-nee Visitor Center. Complete the activities and share your booklet with a park ranger at either location to be sworn in as a Junior Ranger and receive a patch. They also have a Junior Ranger Night Explorer Booklet, Volcano Club, and there's Volcano Adventure Camp, which offers outdoor programs for youth groups.

Flora & Fauna

Elevation ranging from 5,000 to nearly 10,500 feet creates an environment full of ecological diversity. More than 700 species of flowering plants reside in the park. Communities vary from dense conifer forests of the lower elevations to barren alpine mountaintops where trees are unable to survive. During the summer months meadows burst with color. Trails like Paradise Meadows and Kings Creek Falls guide hikers directly through beautiful foliage. Things are going to look quite different. The Dixie Fire burned nearly 70% of park land in 2021. More than 300 species of vertebrates, including 57 species of mammals, call the park home. Most famous are the black bears from whom you must lock your food away (use the bear lockers provided at the campgrounds). Bobcat, mountain lion, and Sierra Nevada and red fox live here, but are seldom seen. Animals you're most likely to see are the rodents (chipmunks, squirrels, and possibly skunks) and birds.

Pets & Accessibility

Pets are allowed on established roadways, at campgrounds, picnic areas, and other developed areas, but must be kept on a leash (less than six feet). Pets (except service animals) are not allowed in public buildings or on hiking trails.

Loomis Museum and Kohm Yah-mah-nee Visitor Center are accessible to wheelchair users. Devastated Trail is accessible, as are most restrooms. A wheelchair-accessible site is available at Manzanita Lake, Summit Lake (North), and Butte Lake Campgrounds.

Weather

There's more than 4,000 feet of elevation difference between Manzanita Lake and Lassen Peak. Such a dramatic change creates significant variations in temperature, wind, and weather. Expect temperatures to decrease about 4°F per 1,000 feet of increased elevation. Winters are cold and snowy in the high elevations; one year Lake Helen received some 40 feet of accumulated snow. At Manzanita Lake the average high temperature from December through February is nearly 50°F, with lows falling into the 20s. During summer average highs reach the 80s°F, with overnight lows dropping into the 40s°F. All campgrounds are above 5,600 feet so expect cool nights. Come prepared for wind, rain, and chilly evenings, and always dress in layers.

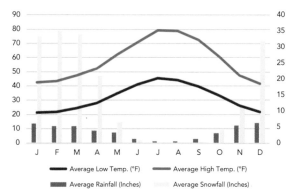

Average Low Temp. (°F) — Average High Temp. (°F)
■ Average Rainfall (Inches)   Average Snowfall (Inches)

Cinder Cone looming behind Butte Lake

Tips & Recommendations

Yosemite receives more visitors in June than Lassen gets in a year. But Lassen gets busy in summer. The park will be undergoing dramatic change as the Dixie Fire burned nearly 70% of park land in 2021.

Meals are provided at Drakesbad Ranch (summer). You can find food at Manzanita Lake Camper Store (summer). And there's a cafe inside Kohm Yah-mah-nee Visitor Center (year-round). Gas is available at the camper store in summer. EV charging and free Wi-Fi are available at Kohm Yah-mah-nee Visitor Center. Cell service is limited within the park.

Even if you only explore Main Park Road, it'll take a couple days to properly explore the main attractions:

Manzanita Lake, Summit Lakes, Kings Creek, Lassen Peak, and Bumpass Hell. And more remote areas like Butte Lake are worth a visit.

Easy Hike: Manzanita Lake (1.8 miles)
Moderate Hikes: Bumpass Hell (3 miles), Kings Creek Falls (3), Mill Creek Falls (3.8), Chaos Crags and Crags Lake (4.2)
Strenuous Hikes: Cinder Cone (4 miles), Lassen Peak (5), Brokeoff Mountain (7)
Family Activities: Paddle around Manzanita Lake, become Junior Rangers, hike Bumpass Hell, check out Loomis Museum
Sunset Spots: Manzanita Lake (here you're looking at the light on Lassen Peak), Hat Lake, Reflection Lake
Sunrise Spots: Lake Helen (you can be on the east side of the road to watch the sunrise or at the lake's shore to watch Lassen Peak light up)

Beyond the Park...

Dining
Tantardino's • (530) 596-3902
401 Ponderosa Dr, Westwood
tantardinosca.com

Burger Depot • (530) 258-1880
336 Main St, Chester

Grocery Stores
Holiday Market • (530) 317-1370
271 Main St, Chester

Peninsula Market • (530) 596-3500
309 Peninsula Dr, Lake Almanor

Lodging & Camping
Mill Creek Resort • (530) 595-4449
Campground & RV Park too
40271 CA-172, Mill Creek
millcreekresort.net

Lassen Mineral Lodge
38348 CA-36, Mineral
minerallodge.com • (530) 595-4422

Mt Lassen KOA
7749 KOA Rd, Shingletown
koa.com • (530) 474-3133

Attractions
Sierra Nevada Brewery
1075 E 20th St, Chico
sierranevada.com • (530) 899-4775

National Yo-Yo Museum
320 Broadway St, Chico
nationalyoyo.org • (530) 893-0545

Mossbrae Falls
Beautiful waterfall but it's on private property

Lava Beds National Monument
nps.gov/labe • *Lava tubes!*

National forests (fs.usda.gov)
include Shasta-Trinity (McCloud Falls, Mt Shasta), Plumas, Klamath, and Lassen (Subway Cave)

Whiskeytown-Shasta-Trinity NRA
Hiking, paddling, and biking
nps.gov/whis

McArthur-Burney Falls State Park
Popular, gorgeous waterfall
24898 CA-89 • parks.ca.gov

Castle Crags State Park
Very crag-y rock formation
20022 Castle Creek Rd, Castella
parks.ca.gov

Plumas-Eureka State Park
Gold rush history • parks.ca.gov
310 Johnsville Rd, Blairsden

Ahjumawi Lava Spring State Park
Only accessible by boat
parks.ca.gov

North Table Mountain ER
Waterfalls and wildflowers
2488 Cherokee Rd, Oroville
wildlife.ca.gov

Lake Shasta Caverns
2-hour cave tour ($32, includes a boat ride)
20359 Shasta Caverns Rd
lakeshastacaverns.com

Redwood

Trees aren't just tall at Tall Trees

Phone: (707) 464-6101
Website: nps.gov/redw

Established: January 1, 1968
Size: 131,983 Acres
Annual Visitors: 527,000
Peak Season: Summer

Activities: Hiking, Backpacking, Biking, Paddling, Horseback Riding

No National Park Campgrounds
4 State Park Campgrounds: $35/ night (RV sites are available but none have hookups)
Backcountry Camping: Permitted at designated sites with free permit ($5 fee at Gold Bluffs Beach, #23)
Lodging: None

Park Hours: All day, every day
National Park Fee: None
State Park Fee: $8 (day-use)

Redwood trees once grew all over the Northern Hemisphere. They have lived on the California coast for the last 20 million years, providing a link to the Age of Dinosaurs. As recently as 1850, more than two million acres of old-growth covered this coastline where fog supplies up to one-third their annual water intake. Today, Redwood National and State Parks protect less than 39,000 acres of old-growth forest, representing 45% of all remaining coastal redwoods. They are some of the oldest trees in the world, many of which have been growing here for more than 2,000 years. If they could speak, they'd tell stories of times long before Christopher Columbus discovered America. These are the tallest trees in the world. Some appear to pierce the sky, towering more than 370 feet into the air; at 379 feet, Hyperion is the tallest of them all. Credit bark more than 12 inches thick infused with tannin, which provides protection from disease, insects, and fire. Roots, no deeper than 10–13 feet but up to 80 feet long, support these monsters in becoming more than 22 feet in diameter at their base and weighing up to 500 tons. Until prospectors and loggers arrived on the scene, the only threat to the mighty redwood was itself. They simply grew too big and too tall for their shallow roots, planted in wet soil, to support themselves against the winds off the Pacific Ocean.

By the 1850s strong winds weren't the only threat these majestic giants faced. Jedediah Smith, trapper and explorer, was the first non-Native to reach California's northern coast by land in 1828. More than two decades later gold was found along the Trinity River. In 1850, settlers established the boom town of Eureka and miners steadily displaced Native Americans who had lived there for the past 3,000 years, just a bit longer than the oldest trees of the redwood forests. The Yurok, Tolowa, Karok, Chilula, and Wiyot Indian tribes all resided in the region. They used fallen redwoods for boats, houses, and small villages. Deer, elk, fish, nuts, berries, and seeds provided more than enough food to sustain tribes as large as 55 villages and 2,500 people. After two minor gold booms went bust, gold-seeking settlers who forced the Natives out, now had to seek something else on their own, a new way to survive and earn a living.

Gold fever became redwood fever, and more settlers were drawn to the area to exploit a seemingly endless supply of colossal trees. Harvested trees helped boost the rapid development of West Coast cities like San Francisco. In 1918, conservationists, appalled by the swaths of clear-cut coastal lands, formed the Save-the-Redwoods League. They drummed up support, which ultimately led to establishment of Prairie Creek, Del Norte Coast, and Jedediah Smith Redwoods State Parks. At the same time US-101, which would soon provide unprecedented access to untouched stands of coastal redwoods, was under construction. Conservationists spent the next four decades requesting creation of Redwood National Park. Demand for lumber during WWII delayed the park's inception, but finally, in the 1960s, the Save-the-Redwoods League, Sierra Club, and National Geographic Society made one last push for a national park. It was signed into law by President Lyndon B. Johnson in 1968. At the time more than 90% of old-growth forests had been logged.

Some of the trees have been saved. Native Americans still live among nature's sacred giants, even though treaties establishing reservations for the displaced Natives were never ratified. They perform traditional ceremonies, hunt and fish, and speak their native language. Guests are left awestruck by the soaring timber, sharing the same spiritual connection between nature and man. Hollywood has helped create a more tangible connection between man, nature, and the Age of Dinosaurs. Redwood Forest served as backdrop for Steven Spielberg's The Lost World: Jurassic Park. Another Spielberg flick, Star Wars: Return of the Jedi—a movie set "a long time ago, in a galaxy far, far away"—was also filmed here. Let's hope Redwood National Park goes back to the future, looking more like it did in 1850 than 1950.

Klamath River

When to Go
Redwood National Park is open all day, every day. Summer is less foggy but busy (about double the average monthly visitation). Winter is wet. Spring and fall are marked by visiting migratory birds. No matter when you visit, anticipate temperatures ranging between 40°F and 60°F along the coast. This fairly constant temperature is moderated by the Pacific Ocean. Smaller crowds, and a wide variety of visiting bird species make spring and fall ideal times to visit the Redwood Forest, but expect fog (especially in the morning). It's also a great time to cruise US-101/Redwood Highway and CA-1/Pacific Coast Highway.

Transportation & Airports
Public transportation does not provide service to or around the park. The closest large commercial airports are Portland International (PDX), 340 miles to the north, and San Francisco International (SFO), 330 miles to the south. Small regional airports are located nearby at Crescent City (CEC) and McKinleyville (ACV), CA; and Medford (MFR), OR.

Directions
Redwood National Park is oriented along US-101, one of the most scenic highways in the United States. The park does not have a formal entrance, but almost every area is accessed via US-101.

From the South: US-101 crosses San Francisco Bay via the Golden Gate Bridge, and then runs parallel to California's Coast all the way to the park.

From the North: Follow US-101 along the Oregon/California Coast (fantastic). You can also take I-5 South to Exit 58, where you'll merge onto CA-99 S toward US-100/Grants Pass. After 3 miles, turn right at US-199 S/Redwood Highway. Continue for 88 miles to the park.

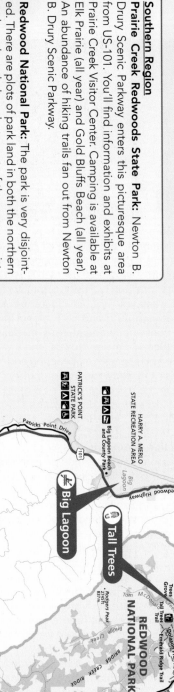

Southern Region

Prairie Creek Redwoods State Park: Newton B. Drury Scenic Parkway enters this picturesque area from US-101. You'll find information and exhibits at Prairie Creek Visitor Center. Camping is available at Elk Prairie (all year) and Gold Bluffs Beach (all year). An abundance of hiking trails fan out from Newton B. Drury Scenic Parkway.

Redwood National Park: The park is very disjointed. There are plots of park land in both the northern and southern halves, but most of the area consists of a large tract south of Prairie Creek where you'll find two of the most popular areas: Lady Bird Johnson Grove and Tall Trees Grove (permit required). These sites are accessed by Bald Hills Road.

Legend

Redwood National and State Parks boundary

State Park boundary

Unpaved road

Trail

Old-growth coast redwoods

Campground

Backcountry campsite (free permit required)

Fishing

Wheelchair-accessible

Boat access

Interpretive trail

Picnic area

North

0   5 Kilometers
0   5 Miles

1 Trailhead (see table on page 570)

Yurok Reservation
The lands within one mile of each side of the Klamath River from the Pacific Ocean to 43 miles upstream compose the Yurok Reservation.

PACIFIC OCEAN

Fern Canyon
Big Lagoon
Tall Trees

TRINIDAD STATE BEACH
PATRICK'S POINT STATE PARK
Patricks Point Drive
Trinidad
To Eureka 21mi 33km

HARRY A. MERLO STATE RECREATION AREA
Big Lagoon Beach and County Park
Big Lagoon

HUMBOLDT LAGOONS STATE PARK
Stone Lagoon Boat-in Camp
Dry Lagoon Beach
Stone Lagoon
Freshwater Lagoon

Kuchel Visitor Center
Redwood Creek
Trailer parking
Redwood National Park boundary

Gold Bluffs Beach
Fern Canyon
Coastal Trail

PRAIRIE CREEK REDWOODS STATE PARK
Prairie Creek Visitor Center
Elk Prairie
Big Tree Wayside

GOLD BLUFFS
Davison Road trailers prohibited
Elk Meadow
Trillium Falls Tr

REDWOOD NATIONAL PARK

McArthur
Orick
Orick Horse Trailhead
Berry Glen Trail
Lost Man Creek
Lady Bird Johnson

Elam Camp
Redwood Creek Trailhead
Permit required for overnight travel

Tall Trees Grove
Tall Trees Access Road by permit only
Emerald Ridge Trail
Spokoom Prairie Trail
Redwood Creek Overlook

Bald Hills Road

Dolason Prairie
HOLTER RIDGE

BRIDGE CREEK RIDGE

Rodgers Peak 2745ft 837m
Tom McDonald Creek

Lyons Ranch
Childs Hill Prairie
Schoolhouse Peak 3097ft 944m
To Weitchpec

Cal-Barrel Road trailers prohibited
Ah-Pah
Newton B. Drury Scenic Pkwy

Redwood Creek
Bridge Creek
Bald Hills Road motor homes and trailers not advised

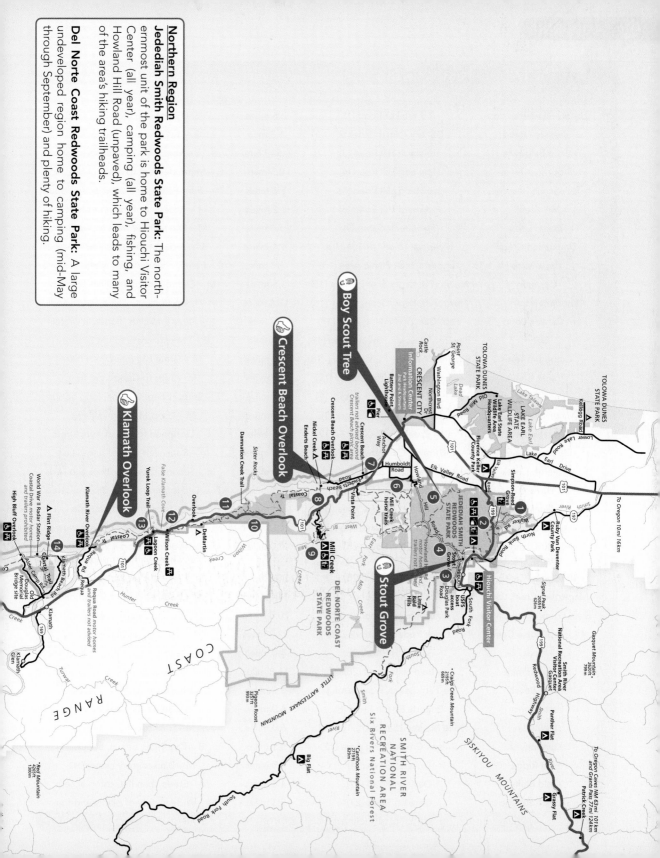

Northern Region

Jedediah Smith Redwoods State Park: The north-ernmost unit of the park is home to Hiouchi Visitor Center (all year), camping (all year), fishing, and Howland Hill Road (unpaved), which leads to many of the area's hiking trailheads.

Del Norte Coast Redwoods State Park: A large undeveloped region home to camping (mid-May through September) and plenty of hiking.

Boy Scout Tree

Crescent Beach Overlook

Klamath Overlook

Stout Grove

Hiouchi Visitor Center

Redwood Hiking Trails (Distances are roundtrip, except Coastal Trails)

	Name	Location (# on map)	Length	Difficulty Rating & Notes
Jedediah Smith	Leifer–Ellsworth Loop	Off Walker Road (1)	2.6 miles	E – Follows an old plank road
	Simpson–Reed	US-199 (North Side) (2)	1.0 mile	E – 1,000-year-old redwoods
	Little Bald Hills	Howland Hill Road (3)	6.6–9.6 mi	S – Backpack • Bikes/horses allowed
	Stout Grove - ♿	Howland Hill Road (4)	0.5 mile	E – Steep descent to great grove, loop
	Boy Scout Tree - ♿	Howland Hill Road (5)	5.6 miles	M – Fern Falls/giant redwood (via spur)
	Mill Creek	Howland Hill Road (6)	7.2 miles	M – Access for fishing or photos
Del Norte	Trestle Loop	Mill Creek Camp (9)	1.0 mile	M – Old railroad trestles, berries
	Damnation Creek	Milepost 16 on US-101 (10)	4.4 miles	S – Ancient redwoods and coast
	Yurok Loop	Lagoon Creek Picnic Area (13)	1.0 mile	E – Family-friendly/False Klamath Cove
Prairie Creek	Ossagon	Newton B. Drury Scenic Pkwy (15)	3.6 miles	M – Old rough road • Bikes allowed
	Rhododendron - ♿	Newton B. Drury Scenic Pkwy (16)	12.6 miles	M – Loop Brown Creek & South Fork
	Fern Canyon Loop - ♿	Fern Canyon Parking Area (17)	0.7 mile	E – Ferns and cliffs, floods in winter
	Circle	Big Tree Wayside Parking Area (18)	0.4 mile	E – Easiest access to the Big Tree
	Cathedral Trees	Big Tree Wayside Parking Area (18)	2.8 miles	M – Great big tree family hike
	Prairie Creek	Prairie Creek Visitor Center (19)	8.0 miles	M – Spur to Corkscrew Tree
	James Irvine - ♿	Prairie Creek Visitor Center (19)	8.4 miles	M – Ends at Fern Canyon, loop options
	Miner's Ridge - ♿	Prairie Creek Visitor Center (19)	8.2 miles	M – Loop with James Irvine
	Revelation	Prairie Creek Visitor Center (19)	0.6 mile	E – Designed for visually impaired
	Elk Prairie Loop	Elk Prairie Campground (20)	2.8 miles	M – Roosevelt elk sightings likely
	Streelow Creek	Davison Road (22)	3.6 miles	M – Second-growth • Bikes allowed
	Davison	Elk Meadow Day Use Area (23)	6.0 miles	M – Old logging road • Bikes allowed
Redwood NP	Trillium Falls	Elk Meadow Day Use Area (23)	2.5 miles	M – Loop to 10-ft cascade
	Lost Man Creek	Lost Man Creek Picnic Area (24)	20.0 miles	S – Big trees and ferns • Bikes allowed
	Lady Bird Johnson Grove - ♿	Bald Hills Road (25)	1.0 mile	E – Self-guided loop • Very popular, site where park was dedicated
	Redwood Creek	Bald Hills Road (26)	16.0–28.0 mi	M/S – All uphill to Dolason Prairie
	MacArthur Creek Loop	Orick Rodeo Grounds (27)	14.0 miles	M – Backpacker/horse-friendly
	Elam Loop/Horse Camp	Orick Rodeo Grounds (27)	20.0 miles	M – Backpacker/horse-friendly
	44 Loop/Horse Camp	Orick Rodeo Grounds (27)	32.0 miles	M – Backpacker/horse-friendly
	Tall Trees - ♿	Bald Hills Road (28)	4.0 miles	M – Tallest trees • Permit Req'd
	Dolason Prairie	Bald Hills Road (28)	11.8 miles	M – Open space, panoramic views
Coastal (One-way)	Crescent Beach - ♿	Crescent Beach Picnic Area (7)	3.5 miles	E – Beachcombing, Roosevelt elk
	Last Chance	Enderts Beach Road (8)	6.0 miles	S – Steep, Enderts Beach
	Demartin	Mile Marker 15.6 of US-101 (11)	6.0 miles	M – Backcountry campsites
	Klamath - ♿	Wilson Creek Picnic Area (12)	5.5 miles	S – Overlook, beach, tidepools
	Flint Ridge	Coastal Drive (14)	4.5 miles	M – Backcountry campsites
	Gold Bluffs	Davison Road (17)	4.8 miles	M – Steep then flat, camp access
	Skunk Cabbage	Davison Road (21)	5.3 miles	M – Wide variety of plants and trees

Difficulty Ratings: E = Easy, M = Moderate, S = Strenuous

Camping

There are no developed campgrounds in Redwood National Park, but three state parks (jointly administered with the national park) furnish four developed campgrounds. **Jedediah Smith Campground** is in an old-growth redwood grove on the banks of the Smith River. It is located on US-199, 10 miles east of Crescent City. You can hike, fish, and swim right at the campground. It's open all year, and offers 86 tent or RV sites (25-ft max length). **Mill Creek Campground** is in Del Norte Coast Redwoods State Park, 7 miles south of Crescent City on US-101. It offers 145 tent or RV sites (28-ft max length) from mid-May through September. **Elk Prairie Campground** is in Prairie Creek Redwoods State Park, 6 miles north of Orick, CA on Newton B. Drury Scenic Parkway. It's open all year, and offers 75 tent or RV sites (27-ft max length). **Gold Bluffs Beach Campground**, located in Prairie Creek Redwoods State Park on Davison Road, has 26 tent or RV sites (24-ft max length). It is open all year. All campgrounds do not offer hookups, but they have showers (solar showers at Gold Bluffs) and there are dump stations at Jedediah Smith and Mill Creek. Sites cost $35/night. Reservations (recommended between May and September) can be made up to six months in advance at reservecalifornia.com. Campgrounds fill, especially during summer, weekends, and holidays, but there are at least a dozen campgrounds located nearby.

Hiking

There are more than 200 miles of hiking trails. The best of the bunch explore the Pacific coastline or old-growth redwood forests.

Coastal Trail traces the coast almost continuously for some 35 miles. There's one major gap at the US-101 Bridge over Klamath River. The rest of the trail is broken into seven distinct sections that provide great opportunities for beachcombing, whale-watching, tide pool-exploring, and birding. Farthest north is the Crescent Beach Section. Before reaching the trail, Crescent Beach Overlook provides an excellent vantage point to survey the ocean for gray whales during their spring migration. Continuing south are the Last Chance and Demartin Sections. Longer and more strenuous, they provide greater solitude. Backcountry campsites are available along these portions. Further south you'll find the 5.5-mile Klamath Section and Klamath River Overlook (another excellent perch to peer across the Pacific). The 4.5-mile Flint Ridge Section provides a unique combination of old-growth redwood forests and ocean vistas. (Most redwoods grow at least a mile or two away from shore as salty water inhibits growth.) Gold Bluffs

Boy Scout Tree Trail

(4.8 miles)—where hikers can take the Fern Canyon loop (often flooded in winter) and spend the night at Ossagon Camp—is the next stretch. Last is Skunk Cabbage Section. If you can put up with the smell of the trail's namesake, you will be rewarded with views of grassy hills, massive redwoods, and wildflowers (seasonal) along this 5.25-mile trail.

At 379 feet, Hyperion is the world's tallest tree, but you won't find a trail leading to it. Its location is kept secret so visitors do not trample the surrounding soil. Still, there are plenty of great hiking trails with trees that tower more than twice as high as the Statue of Liberty. **Tall Trees Trail**, located off Bald Hills Road just north of Orick, is the best choice for giant redwoods. A free permit is required to visit the area. Only 50 permits are available each day. Reserve yours online from the park website up to two weeks in advance. If you're unable to secure a permit, check out Boy Scout or Stout (Memorial) Grove Trails in Jedediah Smith Redwoods State Park. **Boy Scout Trail** is 2.8 miles to Fern Falls. The waterfall isn't all that impressive, but the massive double redwood known as Boy Scout Tree is. Just make sure you see it. The spur trail to the big tree isn't marked. It's on the right-hand side of the trail, about a quarter-mile from the waterfall. It's only about 100 feet from the trail (up a small hill), so don't venture too far into the forest if you don't see a really huge double redwood with a "Boy Scout Tree" sign nailed to it. **Stout Memorial Grove Trail** is much shorter and easier (after the initial descent). Another alternative is **Lady Bird Johnson Grove Trail**, which begins just off Bald Hills Road. For a longer hike, the 12-mile James Irvine/Fern Canyon/Davison Road/Miners Ridge Loop in Prairie Creek Redwoods State Park is as good as it gets. Note that temporary footbridges are removed from some trails during the winter rainy season.

Tall Trees Access Road

Backpacking

Backcountry camping is only allowed at designated sites and along Redwood Creek gravel bars. There are four free sites: Nickel Creek, DeMartin, and Flint Ridge, located along the Coastal Trail; and Little Bald Hills, located on Little Bald Hills Trail. Little Bald Hills, Nickel Creek, and DeMartin are north of Klamath River. Five sites are located south of Klamath River. The hiker/biker site at Gold Bluffs Beach Camp requires a permit and $5 per person per night fee (payable at camp). Elam Creek and 44 Camp are located on Orick Horse Trail ($10 fee to park overnight at trailhead). Backcountry sites are also dispersed along Redwood Creek Trail. All sites feature picnic tables, fire pits, food storage lockers, and toilets. Proper food storage is required. Bear-resistant food canisters are available at Kuchel Visitor Center. A free permit is required for all overnight stays in the backcountry. They can be reserved online through the park's website.

Biking

Long distance road cyclists love the challenge and the scenery associated with pedaling along the Pacific Coast, including the section of US-101 passing through Redwood National Park. Summers are typically dry, but the roads are busiest. Little Bald Hills, Coastal (Last Chance and Gold Bluffs sections), Ossagon, Davison, Lost Man Creek, Streelow Creek, and many other trails permit bicycle use (mountain bikes). Howland Hill Road is another good choice. If you want to leave your bikes at home, Redwood Rides (707.951.6559, redwoodrides.com) offers guided bike (and paddling) tours, as well as mountain bike (and kayak) rentals. It costs $50/day for a Trek 3500, and tours start at $69/person for a 2-hour ride.

Paddling

Paddling is a great way to explore the coast, coves, and rivers. Big Lagoon, just south of the park, is popular among paddlers. Pacific Outfitters Adventures (pacificoutfittersadventures.com) offers guided Big Lagoon paddles ($79) as well as surf, SUP, and hiking tours. For something a little splashier, you can join Redwood Rides (707.951.6559, redwoodrides.com) on rafting trips down the Smith River ($129/full day). They also rent inflatable kayaks starting at $50 (3.5 hours) and offer biking, fishing, and hiking tours.

Horseback Riding

Many of the park's trails are open to horses. If you'd like to explore the majestic redwoods on a guided ride or overnight pack trip contact one of these outfitters: Crescent Trail Rides (707.951.5407, crescenttrailrides.com, $80/1.5 hours, beach or forest rides) Redwood Trail Rides (707.498.4837, redwoodhorserides.com, $65, forest), or Redwood Creek Buckarettes (707.499.2943, redwoodcreekbuckarettes.com, $70, forest). Rides are at a walk. Other durations are available. Reservations are recommended.

Visitor Centers

Jedediah Smith Visitor Center is open from June through September, 9am to 5pm. Hiouchi Visitor Center (9 miles northeast of Crescent City on US-199), Crescent City Information Center, Prairie Creek Visitor Center, and Thomas H. Kuchel Visitor Center are open daily, year-round, from 9am to 5pm. Winter hours are reduced to 9am to 4pm. They close New Year's Day, Thanksgiving, and Christmas. And Crescent City Information Center closes on Tuesdays and Thursdays in winter. Each one offers a variety of exhibits, books and maps, and restrooms. All the visitor centers offer ranger programs and hiking opportunities.

Ranger Programs & For Kids

Ranger programs at Redwood National Park are available from mid-May to mid-September. Time, location, and topics of current programs can be found at visitor centers, campground bulletin boards, or online. They offer everything from campfire programs (at the campgrounds), guided kayak tours (Smith River), tidepool walks, and more. Space for kayak tours is limited. You can sign up in person no sooner than one week before a scheduled tour at Hiouchi Visitor Center.

Children can become Redwood National Park Junior Rangers. Pick up an activity booklet from one of the park's visitor centers or download it from the park website to participate. Activities are designed for children (ages 7–12), but visitors of any age are welcome. Complete the requirements to earn a Junior Ranger badge.

Flora & Fauna

Coastal redwoods are the #1 attraction. They're the world's tallest trees soaring more than 300 feet into the air, but there's much more to the region's lush ecosystem. The park protects a variety of threatened species: brown pelican, tidewater goby, bald eagle, Chinook salmon, northern spotted owl, and Steller sea lion. Large mammals such as bear and Roosevelt elk are commonly seen. Not surprisingly, Elk Prairie and Elk Valley are two of the best places to spot their namesake grazing, so Davison Road is a good place to explore. Elk cross the roads, use the trails, and appear to be domesticated, but don't mistake their docile nature as an invitation to pose in a photograph with them. All the animals are wild and should be treated as such. Do not feed, provoke, or approach any native wildlife. Gray whale can be seen year-round, but the park states November, December, March, and April are the best times to spot them. And you can find tidepools at Endert's Beach (Coastal Trail from Crescent Beach Overlook) or Wilson Creek Beach (US-101, just north of Trees of Mystery). Be sure to consult a tide table to plan your visit around low tide.

Pets & Accessibility

Pets are allowed in the park but must be kept on a leash (less than six feet). They are prohibited from all hiking trails. Pets can essentially go anywhere your car can, like along roads, parking areas, viewpoints, picnic areas, and campgrounds, as well as Crescent, Freshwater, and Gold Bluffs beaches.

All the park's visitor centers are accessible to individuals with mobility impairments. Many of the park's campgrounds, picnic areas, beaches, and overlooks are also accessible. The map on page 568 designates all wheelchair-accessible sites.

Weather

Thunderstorms and fog are difficult to predict, but the temperature is not. Average high temperatures range from the mid-50s to 60s°F, all year. Average lows range from the low to high 40s°F. This consistency is due to the park's location along the Pacific Coast. The farther you travel from the coast, the greater the seasonal temperature difference becomes. On average the park receives 70 inches of rain each year, most of which falls between October and April. Come prepared for fog and rain any time of year, but you should expect it from fall through spring.

Smith River

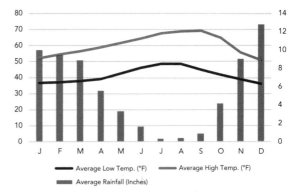

Average Low Temp. (°F) ——— Average High Temp. (°F)
Average Rainfall (Inches)

Tips & Recommendations

Most visitors come to Redwood National Park in summer, and it isn't just because it's time for summer vacations. The driest months are in summer, meaning more hiking trails are accessible. Many trails feature seasonal bridges, only available during this time. Of course, there are other reasons to visit throughout the year. Wildflowers bloom from February through September. Whales pass by in winter and spring. And witnessing the trees shrouded in patchy fog can be an interesting experience. However, thick fog isn't much fun.

Jedediah Smith, Del Norte Coast, and Prairie Creek State Parks charge an $8 day-use fee. As of 2018, they honor national park passes.

There's a pretty wide range of ways to experience Redwood National Park. Driving through with a quick detour along Newton B. Drury Scenic Parkway will take an hour or so, and you'll probably exit the park impressed with these towering trees (even if they're partially obscured by fog). Make a day of it and you could hike a few trails, do some tidepooling, and watch the sun sink into the Pacific. This is an even more satisfying adventure. Still, there's more than enough tree-based commercial opportunities surrounding the park to keep you busy for a couple days. You should spend more time, but the temptation to see it and leave it is understandable because there's so many sites along US-101. Do your homework. Figure out what you want to do. Map out an efficient way to make it happen, and then go to California and enjoy the heck out of it (just give yourself some time to relax).

With that said, Redwood is one of the more confusing national parks in the country. It's a mixture of federal and state land, including three state parks. Park names are a mere formality, the confusing part is finding the right roads to reach your desired destinations.

In addition to Newton B. Drury Scenic Parkway, there are three roads you should put at the top of your activity list. Bald Hills Road is where you'll find Tall Trees Trail. It's highly recommended. Just be sure to reserve a free permit online before going to the trailhead (they're distributed on a first-come, first-served basis, and are available up to two weeks before your intended visit). Davison Road is a good place to spot elk. It also leads to Gold Bluffs Beach and provides access to Fern Canyon Loop (summer). It's very easy to spend a couple hours (or more) in this area. And driving Howland Hills Road might make you feel like you're piloting a Star Wars speeder through the Redwood forest, but it also

provides access to some excellent hiking trails: Boy Scout Tree and Stout Grove, just to name two. There are many more sites and trails worth visiting, but this is a good starting point that will provide a wonderful introduction to Redwood National Park.

Cross your fingers for clear/mostly clear skies. Being among the redwoods as rays of light pierce through the dense canopy is pure bliss.

Hiking Trails: Tall Trees (Moderate, 4 miles), Boy Scout Tree (Moderate, 5.6), Fern Canyon (Easy, 0.7), Stout Grove (Easy, 0.5), Lady Bird Johnson Grove (Easy, 1), James Irvine (Moderate, 8.4), Miner's Ridge (Moderate, 8.2), Gold Bluffs (Moderate, 4.8), Klamath (Strenuous, 5.5), Rhododendron (Moderate, 12.6), Crescent Beach (Easy, 3.5)
Family Activities: Pretend you're ewoks hiking through Lady Bird Johnson Grove (nearby areas served as the "forest moon of Endor"), become Junior Rangers
Guided Tours: Paddle a kayak, ride a horse
Rainy Day Activities: Outside of summer, you should come prepared for rain and wet conditions
Sunset Spots: Endert's Beach, High Bluff Overlook, Dry Lagoon Beach, Crescent Beach, Crescent Beach Overlook, Klamath River Overlook, Klamath Beach, Big Lagoon Beach, Gold Bluffs Beach
Wildlife: Elk Prairie (Davison Road), Elk Valley (Howland Hill Road), coastal tidepools

Beyond the Park...

Dining
Headies Pizza and Pour
359 Main St, Trinidad • (707) 677-3077
headiespizzaandpour.com

Brick & Fire • (707) 268-8959
1630 F St, Eureka
brickandfirebistro.com

Café Waterfront • (707) 443-9190
102 F St, Eureka
cafewaterfronteureka.com

Grocery Stores
Grocery Outlet • (707) 630-5262
1581 Central Ave, McKinleyville

Eureka Natural Foods • (707) 839-3636
2165 Central Ave, McKinleyville

Safeway • (707) 840-9770
1503 City Center Rd, McKinleyville

Murphy's Market & Deli
1 Main St, Trinidad • (707) 677-3643

Shoreline Deli & Market
20025 US-101, Orick • (707) 488-5761

Lodging & Camping
Elk Meadow Cabins
7 Valley Green Camp Rd, Orick
elkmeadowcabins.com

The Historic Requa Inn
451 Requa Rd, Klamath
requainn.com • (707) 482-1425

View Crest RV • (707) 677-3393
3415 Patricks Point Dr, Trinidad
viewcrestlodge.com

Mystic Forest RV • (707) 482-4901
15875 US-101, Klamath
mysticforestrv.com

Ramblin' Redwoods • (707) 487-7404
6701 US-101, Crescent City
ramblinredwoodsrv.com

Redwoods KOA
4241 US-101, Crescent City
koa.com • (707) 464-5744

Festivals
Redwood Coast Music Festival
rcmfest.org • Eureka • Sept

Attractions
Trees of Mystery • (707) 482-2251
155500 US-101, Klamath
treesofmystery.net

Klamath River Jet Boat Tours
17635 US-101, Klamath
jetboattours.com • (707) 482-7775

Humboldt Redwoods State Park
Big park with tall trees
17119 Ave of the Giants, Weott
parks.ca.gov

Humboldt Lagoons State Park
15336 US-101, Trinidad
parks.ca.gov • (707) 677-3570

Battery Point Lighthouse &
South Beach • Crescent City

Tolowa Dunes State Park
Ancient dunes and wetlands
Kellogg Rd, Crescent City
parks.ca.gov

Trinidad State Beach
Peaceful cove • parks.ca.gov

Samuel P Taylor State Park
Redwoods and hiking
8889 Sir Francis Drake Blvd,
Lagunitas • parks.ca.gov

Point Reyes National Seashore
Wildcat Beach (Alamere Falls),
hiking, lighthouse, whales
nps.gov/pore

Sonoma Coast State Park
Coast with arches and coves
3095 CA-1 • parks.ca.gov

Mt Tamalpais State Park
Hiking/cabins north of Golden Gate Bridge • parks.ca.gov

Russian Gulch State Park
Good gulch with beaches and hiking (Fern Canyon)
CA-1, Mendocino • parks.ca.gov

Richardson Grove State Park
Redwoods 75 miles south of Eureka • parks.ca.gov
1600 US-101, Garberville

Tall Trees

Crater Lake

Wizard Island in winter

Phone: (541) 594-3000
Website: nps.gov/crla

Established: May 22, 1902
Size: 183,224 Acres
Annual Visitors: 700,000
Peak Season: July–September

Activities: Hiking, Backpacking, Guided Tours, Biking, Fishing, Swimming, Cross-country Skiing, Snowshoeing

2 Campgrounds: $5–43/night
Crater Lake Lodge: $197–255/night
Cabins at Mazama Village: $165
(Camping, cabin, and lodge reservations at travelcraterlake.com)
Backcountry Camping: Permitted with a free Backcountry Use Permit

Park Hours: All day, every day
Entrance Fee: $30/25/15
(car/motorcycle/individual)

Nearly 8,000 years ago a cataclysmic eruption of Mount Mazama caused the mountain to shatter and collapse into itself, forming a massive five-mile-wide caldera rimmed by cliffs almost 4,000 feet high. Sealed by molten rock, the caldera gradually filled with water from melted snow and rain. The lake's water level has finally settled, seepage and evaporation balancing the incoming flow. After 750 years, roughly five trillion gallons of almost perfectly pure water filled the caldera, creating one of the most impressive natural settings in the world. Crater Lake is so deep (up to 1,943 feet deep, 1,148 feet deep on average) and so pure the true blueness of water becomes obviously, almost indescribably, apparent. Viewed from soaring cliffs, the lake's brilliant deep blue hue leaves guests, past and present, spellbound.

Makalak Indians have a legend about the creation of Crater Lake. Llao, Chief of the Below World, sometimes came up from the earth to stand atop Mount Mazama. On one of his visits, Llao fell in love with the Makalak chief's beautiful daughter. Llao promised her eternal life if she would return with him to his home below the mountain. She refused. Enraged, Llao began pummeling the village with balls of fire. Skell, Chief of the Above World, witnessed Llao's rage from the top of Mount Shasta. He took pity on the helpless villagers and chose to wage war with Llao. The two chiefs hurled fiery hot boulders at one another from their respective mountains. The earth trembled in the wake of their violence. As villagers fled to the waters of Klamath Lake, two holy men remained behind. Their plan was to jump into the fiery pit hidden within Llao's mountain as a sacrifice to the Chief of the Below. Moved by their bravery, Skell ambushed Llao, driving him back into Mount Mazama, where the fight raged on through the night. The following morning Mount Mazama was gone. In its place was a gaping hole that filled with water from torrents of rain, which fell after the epic battle.

Makalak Indians may well have witnessed the formation of Crater Lake. Evidence of permanent ancient settlement has not been found, but the area was used for seasonal hunting and gathering, vision-quests, and prayer for at least 10,000 years. Mount Mazama erupted about 7,700 years ago. The event produced more than 100 times as much ash as Mount St. Helens' eruption in 1980, scattered as far south as central Nevada, as far east as Yellowstone National Park, and as far north as British Columbia. After its eruption, Natives were definitely aware of Mount Mazama's caldera gradually filling with water. They believed it took great strength to look at the saturated blue waters. Even today, Klamath (descendants of the Makalak) refuse to look at the lake for religious reasons.

John Wesley Hillman, the first white man to glimpse Crater Lake, had no such religious proclivities. After returning from a successful gold mining trip in California, Hillman funded a small gold mining expedition into Oregon's southern Cascades. On June 12, 1853, the group reached present day Discovery Point where a lake of incomprehensible majesty came into view. They named it Deep Blue Lake, returned to civilization to restock supplies, and continued their quest for gold. William Gladstone Steel visited the area in 1885. It was still used by local Indians for hunting, gathering, and religious purposes, but Steel spent the next 17 years campaigning for the creation of Crater Lake National Park (the name preferred by locals over the likes of Blue Lake, Lake Majesty, and the original, Deep Blue Lake). Steel named other features: Wizard Island, Llao Rock, and Skell Head. On May 22, 1902, Steel's efforts came to fruition when President Roosevelt signed legislation creating Crater Lake, the 6th oldest national park. Steel's focus shifted to making the area a spectacle, catering to wealthy tourists. It was a difficult task considering the rim receives more than 40 feet of snow annually. Erection of Crater Lake Lodge was constantly over-budget and behind schedule. In 1915 the lodge finally opened to popular fanfare, but it remained in a relatively constant state of construction. Three years later, Rim Drive was completed and the park was officially open for business.

A smoky sunset

When to Go
The park is always open, but most roads and facilities close from fall through spring. Only Rim Village Café and Gifts and Steel Visitor Center are open all year. Rim Drive and the North Entrance are closed from mid-October until mid-July (weather dependent). Most tourists arrive immediately after the snow melts and the roads open fully in July and August. During this time, Crater Lake Lodge is booked well in advance and campgrounds fill early. The same great views are available in September and October with smaller crowds. You can visit in winter. The road to Rim Village remains plowed. You're also free to snowshoe/ski and camp along the rim at this time (with a permit).

Transportation & Airports
Public transportation does not provide service to or around the park. Crater Lake Trolley (541.882.1896, craterlaketrolley.net) provides 2-hour, ranger-guided tours along Rim Drive during the summer months. Tickets cost $29/adult, $26/senior, and $18/child (5–13). They can be reserved online. Pick up or purchase tickets at the ticket booth near the Community House at Rim Village. The closest airports are Klamath Falls (LMT) and Rogue Valley–Medford (MFR). Portland International Airport (PDX) is about 244 miles to the north.

Directions
Crater Lake can be accessed by car from the south (all year) and the north (summer only). The North Entrance is reached via OR-138. From I-5 (west of the park), take Exit 124 at Roseburg to OR-138 E. From Bend, take US-97 S about 75 miles to OR-138. After 15 miles turn left at Crater Lake North Hwy. The South Entrance is reached via OR-62, which travels north from Medford and Klamath Falls on opposite sides of the park.

The Old Man

Old Man of the Lake is a 30-ft-tall tree stump, which has been floating about Crater Lake for more than a century. It is roughly 2 feet in diameter and stands 4 feet above the water. Old man is buoyant enough to support a person's weight. Tour boats may pass the stump.

Camping & Lodging

Mazama Campground (214 sites), located near the South Entrance, is typically open from mid-June through September. Sites are first-come, first-served in June. All sites can be reserved through Crater Lake Hospitality (888.292.6720, travelcraterlake.com) July through September. Walk-in, tent-only campsites cost $5/night. Standard tent sites cost $22/night. RV sites without hookups cost $32/night. RV sites with electric hookups costs $37/night. And an RV site with full hookups costs $43/night. Maximum RV length is 50 feet and 35 feet for trailers. Showers, laundry, and dump station are available. The nearby camper store sells groceries, firewood, and gasoline. **Lost Creek** offers 16 tent-only campsites located on the spur road to Pinnacles Overlook. These secluded sites are usually open from July through mid-October and are available on a first-come, first-served basis via self-registration for $5/night. Arriving at the park with Mazama Campground reservations is a good idea.

Crater Lake Lodge and the **Cabins at Mazama Village** (888.292.6720, travelcraterlake.com) are the in-park lodging options. The Lodge is part of Rim Village, and it overlooks Crater Lake. There are 71 rustic rooms (some only with a bathtub) available from mid-May through mid-October. Rates range from $197–255/night and they book up to a year in advance (particularly for July–September). Cabins at Mazama Village, located near the South Entrance, offers 40 basic rooms at $165/night from late May through late September. A restaurant is available at both locations.

Driving

Rim Drive is incredible. The narrow road winds its way around Crater Lake over the course of 33 miles. It's typically open from mid-July to late October. Open/close dates vary depending on snowfall. You can drive it in under an hour, but plan on spending at least two. There are more than two dozen overlooks and picnic areas.

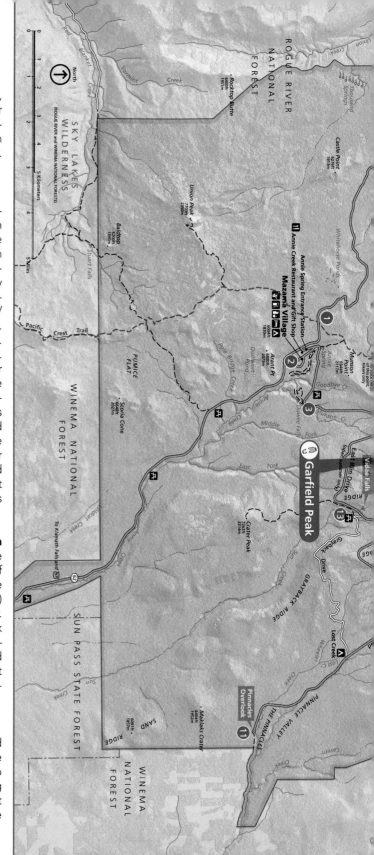

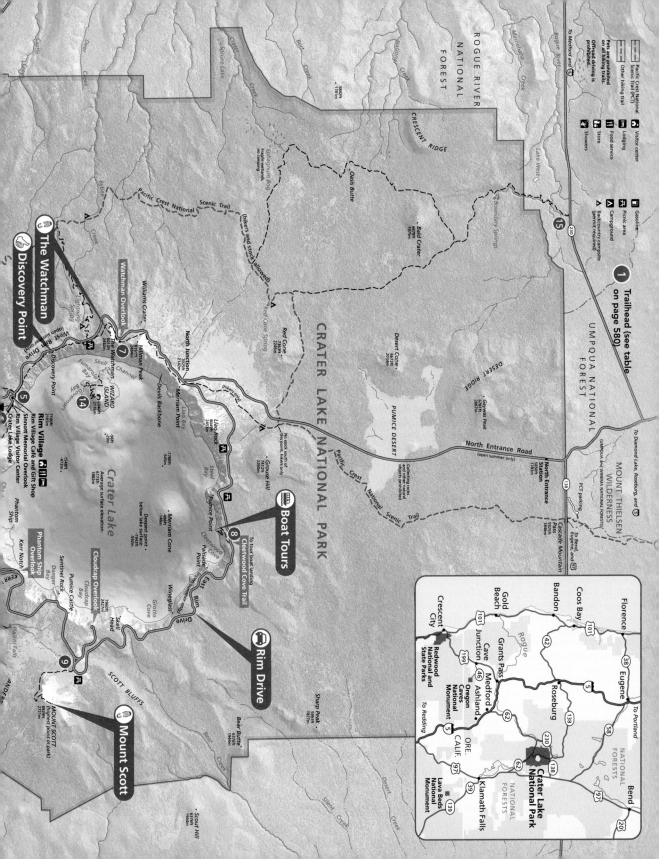

Hiking

Only 90 miles of maintained hiking trails penetrate the park's wilderness and explore the lake's rim. This place is buried in snow much of the year and Crater Lake is so magnificent and spellbinding it monopolizes most visitors' time, but you should take a few hours to explore the area on foot. A relatively small trail network makes choosing one very manageable. For unsurpassed views of Crater Lake, hike to Garfield Peak or Mount Scott. Both lead high into the Cascades where you can peer down into the lake's pure blue depths. For more easily accessible vantage points, try Discovery Point or Watchman Peak Trails. To reach the shore of Crater Lake, you'll have to hike 2.2-mile **Cleetwood Cove Trail**. The trail was improved recently, but it's no less steep than it was before. If you want to go swimming or join a boat tour, you'll have to make the moderately strenuous (700-ft descent) trip.

Backpacking

Comfortable cabins or developed campgrounds aren't for everyone. Some visitors seek solitude and solace. For them, Crater Lake offers more than 100,000 acres of wilderness. All overnight backcountry users must obtain a free backcountry permit and follow a few simple regulations. Permits are only available at the Park Headquarters Ranger Station. Pacific Crest Trail (PCT) thru-hikers do not require a permit, but should sign the trail registry upon entering the park. Backpackers must camp at least one mile from roads and facilities, out of sight of other campers and visitors, more than 100 feet away from any water source, and not within view of the lake. Winter backcountry camping adheres to the same rules, except you are free to camp at the lake's rim (at least one mile from the nearest plowed road).

Guided Tours

Crater Lake Hospitality (888.292.6720, travelcraterlake.com) offers **guided boat tours** of Crater Lake from July through early September (subject to weather). Standard Tours circle the lake as a ranger discusses its cultural and natural history (2 hours, $44/adult, $30/child, depart every hour from 9:30am–3:45pm). Wizard Island Tours drop guests off at Wizard Island, allowing time to explore the island (5 hours, $55/adult, $37/child, depart at 9:45am and 12:45pm). Both tours require hiking 1.1-mile (one-way) down Cleetwood Trail to the lake's shore. It's steep and strenuous, but short. Tours can be reserved online or purchased in person at the lodge, Mazama Village, or Cleetwood Cove kiosk. Joining a boat tour is a good idea.

Crater Lake Hiking Trails (Distances are roundtrip)

Name	Location (# on map)	Length	Difficulty Rating & Notes
Union Peak	Hwy 62, PCT TH (1)	9.8 miles	S – Interesting geology and ecology, no lake views
Annie Creek Canyon	Mazama Campground (2)	1.7 miles	M – Self-guided loop • Wildflowers July to mid-August
Godfrey Glen	Munson Valley Rd (3)	1.1 miles	E – Self-guided loop • Canyon views, old forest
Castle Crest	Park Headquarters (4)	0.5 mile	E – Self-guided loop • Wildflowers July to mid-August
Lady of the Woods	Steel Visitor Center (4)	0.7 mile	E – Self-guided pet-friendly loop • Architecture
Discovery Point - ⛲	Rim Village (5)	2.0 miles	E – Follows Crater Rim, stunning views
Garfield Peak - ⛲	Crater Lake Lodge (6)	3.6 miles	S – Highly rewarding wildflowers and lake views
Watchman Peak - ⛲	Watchman Overlook (7)	1.6 miles	M – Outstanding sunsets and views of Wizard Island
Cleetwood Cove	Rim Drive (8)	2.2 miles	S – Steep • Only access point to Crater Lake
Mount Scott - ⛲	Rim Drive (9)	4.4 miles	S – Highest point in the park • Wonderful lake views
Plaikni Falls	Pinnacles Road (10)	2.0 miles	E – Short trail to scenic waterfall
Pinnacles	Pinnacles Road (11)	0.8 mile	E – View volcanic spires
Sun Notch	Rim Drive (12)	0.8 mile	M – Uphill loop to views of Phantom Ship
Crater Peak	Rim Drive (13)	6.5 miles	M – Meadow, forest, volcano summit, no lake views
Fumarole Bay	Wizard Island (14)	1.8 miles	E – Rocky trail around Wizard Island's shoreline
Wizard Summit - ⛲	Wizard Island (14)	2.0 miles	M – Rocky trail to 90-ft deep crater atop Wizard Island
Boundary Springs	Hwy 230 Milepost 19 (15)	5.0 miles	M – Unmaintained trail to Rogue River headwaters

Difficulty Ratings: E = Easy, M = Moderate, S = Strenuous

Crater Lake Trolley (541.882.1896, craterlaketrolley.net) offers 2-hour **narrated trolley tours** of 33-mile Rim Drive during summer (typically beginning in July) and running through mid-September). Tickets cost $29/adult, $26/senior, and $18/child (6–13) and reservations are a good idea. Pick up or purchase tickets at the ticket booth near the Community House at Rim Village. Trolleys help alleviate traffic congestion and reduce pollution thanks to modern natural gas engines. They also run a shuttle between Klamath Falls Amtrak Station and the park ($40/adult).

Biking
Cyclists are allowed on all paved roads and on unpaved Grayback Drive. The 33-mile Rim Drive is the most popular biking destination. Bikers must be acutely aware of motorists, because the road twists, turns, climbs, and descends its way around the rim of Crater Lake. Strong winds are common, which make for not-so-enjoyable biking. To avoid traffic and winds, try pedaling early in the morning. Better yet, the park closes East Rim Drive to traffic two Saturdays each year (ridetherimoregon.com). During these days, cyclists have 24 miles of scenic road to themselves.

Fishing
Fish didn't inhabit the lake until 1888 when William Gladstone Steel stocked it with 6 species. Today, only rainbow trout and kokanee salmon thrive in the deep blue waters. Fishing licenses are not required and there are no catch limits. Anglers must use artificial lures and flies only. Cleetwood Cove Trail is the only route to the lake's shoreline. Fishermen are also welcome to cast their lines from Wizard Island (accessed via boat tour). There are no size restrictions or possession limits. Catch and keep as many as you like.

Swimming
Swimming in the lake is not for everyone, but it's allowed at Cleetwood Cove and Wizard Island. 55°F water is only fun for a little while (for most humans).

Winter Activities
Winter can be a remarkable time to visit Crater Lake, but Rim Village is the only car-accessible location (weather permitting) where the lake is visible. Park Rangers offer regular free snowshoe walks typically Saturdays, Sundays, and Holidays from late November through the end of April. Tours last two hours and snowshoes are provided. No experience is necessary. Reservations are required. Call (541) 594-3100 to make reservations. Cross-country skiing is gaining popularity as well. A few visitors set out to complete the 33-mile

Near Discovery Point

trek around the rim each year. Marked but ungroomed trails are available at Mazama and Rim Village for skiers of all ability levels. North Entrance Road is open and groomed for snowmobiles up to the rim of Crater Lake. Snowmobiles are not allowed on Rim Drive. Backcountry camping is allowed with a permit.

Visitor Centers
Steel Visitor Center is located at park headquarters, south of Crater Lake, near where East Rim Drive becomes West Rim Drive. It's open daily from 9am–5pm during summer and from 10am–4pm during winter (closed Christmas). Inside you'll find exhibits, a bookstore, a short film, and restrooms. **Rim Visitor Center**, located in Rim Village, is open daily from 9:30am–5pm (late May through September). It houses a bookstore, and you'll find exhibits at the nearby Sinnott Memorial Overlook. Backcountry permits are only available at Park Headquarters Ranger Station.

Ranger Programs & For Kids
In addition to trolley rides, boat tours and snowshoe treks, park rangers offer free talks, walks, and evening programs from late June to mid-September. Stop in at a visitor center or go online to view a current schedule of events. If you're staying at the lodge, they'll probably have evening talks on-site.

Children of all ages are invited to participate in Crater Lake's Junior Ranger Program. Pick up a free activity booklet from either visitor center (or download a copy online). Explore the park, completing activities as you go, return the book to a park ranger at one of the visitor centers, and your child will receive a Junior Ranger badge. The park also has a few fun scavenger hunts that may interest you and your child.

Pinnacles

Flora & Fauna

Crater Lake is home to 680 species of plants, 74 species of mammals, 26 species of reptiles and amphibians, and 158 species of birds. Threatened or endangered species include lynx, northern spotted owl, bull trout, and tailed frog. Elk, deer, and bear are often seen at dawn or dusk feeding in meadows. Hairy woodpeckers, bald eagles, and the American kestrel are frequently spotted during summer.

Pets & Accessibility

Pets are allowed in the park but must be kept on a leash (less than six feet). They are essentially allowed anywhere a car can go, including roadsides, parking areas, picnic areas, and developed campgrounds. Pets are not allowed in the backcountry, on most trails, or in public buildings (except service animals). Rim Village parking area (and promenade in summer) is a good place to walk your pet. In summer and fall you can walk your pet on Godfrey Glen or Lady of the Woods Trails.

Many of the park's facilities and trails are accessible to individuals with mobility impairments. The store, campground, and restaurant at Mazama Village are accessible, as is Godfrey Glen Trail, the upper section of Annie Creek Canyon Trail, and a portion of Plaikni Falls Trail. Facilities at Park Headquarters and Rim Village are accessible. Trolley tours also can accommodate wheelchair users.

Weather

It's important to consider the weather when planning a trip to Crater Lake. Most years the rim is buried beneath several feet of snow from October until July. Hwy 62 and the access road to Rim Village are plowed during winter, but Rim Drive is closed. Average daytime highs reach into the upper 60s°F during summer.

Temperatures cool off quickly in the evenings, often falling below freezing. Summer is typically dry and sunny, but visitors should come prepared for afternoon thunderstorms and high winds. The first major snowfall usually occurs by mid-October. Crater Lake is magnificent when the rim is covered in snow; the only real problem is there's just so much of it. In an average winter more than 500 inches of snow falls, making Crater Lake one of the snowiest regions of the Pacific Northwest. Winter temperatures are much less variable than the summer. Average highs are right around freezing and average lows are about 20°F.

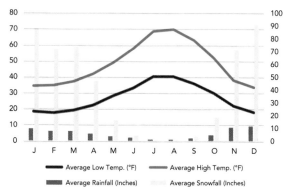

Tips & Recommendations

Crater Lake is one of those sites I could unfold a lawn chair and sit all day, just staring at that brilliant blue body of water. It's a powerful place. However, some visitors remain impervious to its powers. Road warriors, looking to see as much as possible, can race around the rim in an hour. The drive is only 33 miles (remember it typically opens in July and closes in October). Honestly, you only need a bit more time. One night is great. You can hike a few trails. See a sunrise. Two nights is better, allowing time to hike down to the shoreline and join a boat tour and step foot on Wizard Island.

Nearly half the park's annual visitors arrive in July and August. Things get a little busy at the rim. Lodge and camping reservations are hard to secure. Overlook parking is constantly at capacity.

Off-season trips deserve some consideration. This perfectly blue lake is even more entrancing when Wizard Island and the surrounding rim is blanketed in snow. The road to Rim Village is plowed year-round. As a bonus, snowshoers and cross-country skiers are permitted to camp along the rim in winter!

Drive the rim clockwise, simply because it's easier to make a right turn into the overlooks than a left.

All the overlooks are worth a stop, but the ones on the western end are more impressive as they overlook Wizard Island. On the eastern side, you get a decent look at the lake's other island, Phantom Ship, from Sun Notch and Phantom Ship Overlooks.

It's probably tempting to try and score a first-come, first-served campsite at Lost Creek. They're inexpensive and relatively close to the rim, but you better come with a backup plan if you strike out (especially in July or August). Remember, the only way to know whether or not a site is available is to drive there and see for yourself. You may get lucky. You may find yourself scrambling to find a place to spend the night and there are no designated dispersed camping areas close by.

Many visitors view the lake and never realize you can walk down to its shore or climb aboard a boat to Wizard Island. Not you. You know what's going on, and you should think about doing everything. Cleetwood Trail is short but steep. And you'll find some yahoos swimming in the lake. Join them!

This is another morning park, where sunrise is usually more interesting than sunset. If you don't get lucky with a few broken clouds off in the horizon, it's still fun to watch Wizard Island illuminate as the sun peeks over the crater's rim (it's a decent view from the lodge).

Speaking of the lodge, if you're only spending one night (which is enough time for most people to enjoy this lovely lake), book that night at Crater Lake Lodge. Just know it can be booked a year in advance.

Wizard Island

Hiking Trails: Watchman Peak (Moderate, 1.6 miles), Discovery Point (Easy, 2), Mount Scott (Strenuous, 4.4), Garfield Peak (Strenuous, 3.6), Wizard Summit (Moderate, 2), Cleetwood Cove (Strenuous, 2.2)
Viewpoints: Sinnott Memorial Overlook (Rim Village Visitor Center), Watchman Overlook, Discovery Point, Cloudcap Overlook, Phantom Ship Overlook
Family Activities: Catch a boat to Wizard Island, go swimming (seriously you can swim in the lake, but the water only warms up to about 55°F!), become Junior Rangers
Guided Tours: Take a boat tour, ride the trolley
Sunset/Sunrise Spots: Watchman Overlook, Sinnott Memorial Overlook, Crater Lake Lodge, Cloudcap Overlook (cloudless days: head to the eastern rim in the morning to watch the sun light up the western rim and Wizard Island; cloudy days: stay on the western rim and cross your fingers for a show; think in a similar fashion for sunset; sunrise is better as you'll have Wizard Island in the foreground)

Beyond the Park...

Dining
Prospect Pizza • (541) 560-4000
51 Mill Creek Dr, Prospect
prospectpizzacompany.com

South Shore Pizza • (541) 793-3333
3505 Diamond Lake Loop

Grocery Stores
Prospect Store • (541) 560-3655
500 Mill Creek Dr, Prospect

Walmart • (541) 885-6890
3600 Washburn Way, Klamath Falls

Lodging & Camping
Out 'n' About Treehouse Treesort
300 Page Creek Rd, Cave Junction
treehouses.com • (541) 592-2208

Diamond Lake Resort
350 Resort Dr, Diamond Lake
diamondlake.net • (541) 793-3333

Umpqua's Last Resort • (541) 498-2500
umpquaslastresort.com

Crater Lake North KOA
koa.com • (541) 643-0750

Crater Lake RV Park • (541) 560-3399
46611 OR-62, Prospect
prospectrvpark.com

Waterwheel RV • (541) 783-2738
200 Williamson River Dr, Chiloquin
waterwheelrvpark.com

Festivals
Winter Wings Festival • February
winterwingsfest.org • Klamath Falls

Oregon Shakespeare Festival
osfashland.org • Ashland • Feb

Britt Music & Arts Festival
brittfest.org • Jacksonville

Attractions
Mount Thielsen Wilderness
Mount Thielsen (lightning rod of the Cascades) & Diamond Lake, just north of the park

Rogue River • *Rafting trips!*

Waterfalls are everywhere, including nearby in Umpqua NF (*Toketee Falls—check this one out!, Watson Falls, Lemolo Falls*) and Prospext (*Mill and Barr Creek Falls*).

Oregon Caves NM • nps.gov/orca
Cave tours and hiking
19000 Caves Hwy, Cave Junction

Silver Falls State Park
Hiking, biking, horseback riding
20024 Silver Falls Hwy SE, Sublimity
stateparks.oregon.gov

The Oregon Coast is sensational, featuring many state parks (stateparks.oregon.gov) *like Harris Beach (hiking, camping), Samuel H. Boardman, Pistol River (viewpoint), Devil's Punchbowl, Ecola, Cape Lookout, and Oswald West. Then there's Oregon Dunes NRA (beaches and off-roading) in Reedsport and Thor's Well ("drainpipe of the Pacific) in Yachats. Driving the coast can be its own holiday.*

Smith Rock State Park
Beautiful site with camping
NE Crooked River Dr, Terrebonne
stateparks.oregon.gov

Hells Canyon NRA
Deep river gorge on Oregon/Idaho boundary, Buckhorn Overlook • fs.usda.gov

Mount Rainier

Mount Rainier from Burroughs Mountain Trail

Phone: (360) 569-2211
Website: nps.gov/mora

Established: March 2, 1899
Size: 235,625 Acres
Annual Visitors: 1.5 Million
Peak Season: June–September

Activities: Hiking, Backpacking, Mountaineering, Biking

5 Campgrounds: $20/night
Backcountry Camping: Permitted with a Backcountry Use Permit

Park Hours: All day, every day
Entrance Fee: $30/25/15 (car/motorcycle/individual)

Mount Rainier, the 14,410-foot volcano, towers above its surroundings, greeting visitors from more than 100 miles in all directions. Cowlitz, Nisqually, Puyallup, and Yakima tribes called the mountain Tahoma or "the Big Mountain where the waters begin." Much more than water begins here. Natives began vision-quests at this location. Today's guests depart on their own vision quest, and their search for respite begins and ends at majestic Mount Rainier. About 1.5 million visitors admire these mountain views each year, and some 10,000 climbers attempt to trek to its summit, where they can look down on 26 glaciers covering its upper reaches.

The snow-capped mountain's dramatic presence caught the attention of several groups, and soon commercial interests and conservationists were mired in a contentious debate over the best way to utilize the area. Intending to settle the dispute, federal government officials created the Pacific Forest Reserve in 1893, encompassing the mountain. Gifford Pinchot, head of the United States Forest Service, believed in "conservation through use," treating the nation's forests like a crop to be maintained and used. John Muir, a beloved naturalist who had successfully advocated for preservation of Yosemite Valley, formed a kinship with Mount Rainier in 1888 when he joined a group that completed the mountain's 5th recorded ascent. He wrote in a letter to his wife that he had absolutely no intention of climbing the mountain, but when five others showed interest in the idea, he couldn't help but tag along. Muir vehemently opposed the "conservation through use" idea. Not a single tree would fall at the hands of an ax or river be impeded by a dam if he had his way. Preservation, plain and simple, was his goal. These sublime works of nature were beyond the scope of anything man could ever make in terms of beauty and grandeur. They needed to be preserved and protected for the enjoyment of all, not looted and plundered for the benefit of private interests. Support from influential bodies with concerns of their own helped galvanize the conservationist movement. The National Geographic Society wished to study volcanism and glaciology in the area. The Northern Pacific Railroad was on board because a park could draw more passenger service on their trains—a proven method already yielding substantial benefits for Northern Pacific and Southern Pacific Railroads with the creation of Yellowstone and Yosemite National Parks, respectively. The Sierra Club and commercial leaders in Tacoma and Seattle joined the cause, supporting what would become a long and arduous battle. Over the course of five years of bitter debate and six attempts, a bill was finally passed with two provisions: the government needed assurances that no park land was suitable for farming or mining and that no government appropriations were required for its management and procurement. The provisions were met, and on March 2, 1899, Mount Rainier became the fifth national park and first to be created from a national forest.

Park establishment and construction of a road to Paradise in 1911 ushered in a new era of tourism. President William Howard Taft's touring car was the first vehicle to christen the road in incredibly unique fashion: muddy conditions resulted in his car being pulled through the upper portion by a team of mules. Six years later the National Park Service was established, and trails, facilities, roads, and campgrounds were developed in earnest, enhancing the overall visitor experience. Mountain climbers could experience summiting Rainier much like John Muir did, and now thousands of climbers make the trek each year. Today's visitors realize what Muir and Native Americans knew: Mount Rainier is more than a pleasure ground; it's a sacred place worthy of preservation and protection.

Lower tier of Comet Falls

When to Go
Mount Rainier National Park is open all year. Visitation peaks in July and August when the weather is best, most trails are free of snowpack, and wildflowers are in full bloom. Traffic can create considerable frustration during summer months and winter weekends. Traveling midweek or delaying your vacation until September or early October is a good way to avoid the crowds. The park's eastern half is not accessible during winter. Carbon River and Nisqually Entrances on the west side are open all year. However, unexpected road closures can occur at any time and the road to Paradise closes nightly in winter. Always check the park's website for current road status prior to your trip.

Transportation & Airports
In the past there has been a free shuttle between Longmire and Paradise on weekends, mid-June through early September. It was not running when we went to print. The closest large airports are Seattle–Tacoma International (SEA) and Portland International (PDX).

Directions
Directions to the Nisqually Entrance (Paradise), the most popular region, are provided below.

From Seattle (104 miles): Take I-5 S to WA-512 E (Exit 127) to WA-7 S. Take WA-7 to WA-706, which leads into the park.

From Portland (155 miles): Take I-5 N to US-12 E (Exit 68). Take US-12 to WA-7 N. Turn right at WA-706, which leads into the park.

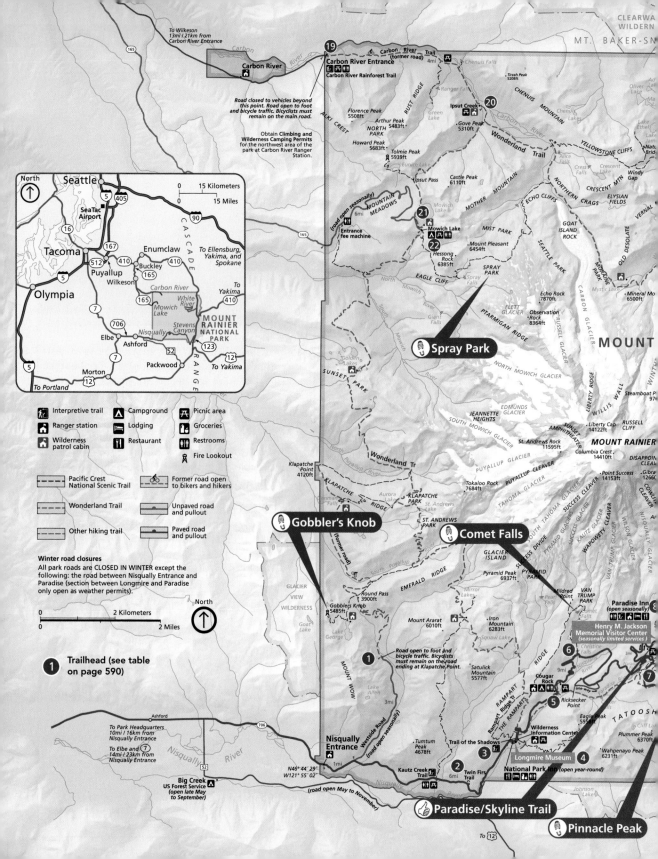

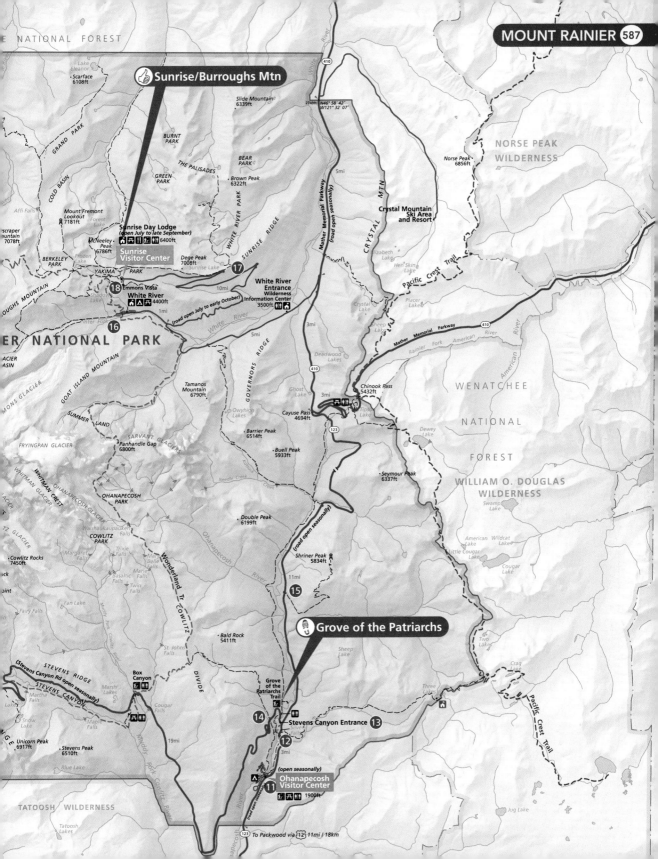

NATIONAL FOREST

NORSE PEAK
WILDERNESS

Lake
Eleanor

Scarface
6108ft

2749ft N46° 58' 42"
W121° 32' 07"

Slide Mountain
6339ft

BURNT
PARK

THE PALISADES

Norse Peak
6856ft

BEAR
PARK

Brown Peak
6322ft

Crystal Mountain
Ski Area
and Resort

Crystal MTN

Elizabeth
Lake

👍 **Sunrise/Burroughs Mtn**

GREEN
PARK

GRAND PARK

Affi Falls

Mount Fremont
Lookout 7181ft

Forest
Lake

Pacific Crest Trail

Hen Skin
Lake

Placer
Lakes

COLD BASIN

Scraper
mountain
7078ft

McNeeley
Peak
6786ft

Frozen
Lake

Sunrise Day Lodge
(open July to late September)
🏕🍴🚻 6400ft

Dege Peak
7008ft

Crystal
Lake

BERKELEY
PARK

YAKIMA
PARK

**Sunrise
Visitor Center**

Sunrise Lake

17

SUNRISE RIDGE

Mather Memorial Parkway
(road open seasonally)

Sheep
Lake

Placer
Lakes

WENATCHEE

18 Emmons Vista
White River 🏕🏕 4400ft

OUGHS MOUNTAIN

Shadow
Lake

10mi

**White River
Entrance**
Wilderness
Information Center
3500ft 🚻

NATIONAL

16

ER **NATIONAL PARK**

(road open July to early October)

1mi

White River

3mi

410

Deadwood
Lakes

Mather Memorial Parkway

Rainier Fork   American River

American River

410

FOREST

ACIER
ASIN

GOAT ISLAND MOUNTAIN

5mi

GOVERNORS RIDGE

Ghost
Lake

WILLIAM O. DOUGLAS

mons Glacier

SUMMER
LAND

Tamanos
Mountain
6790ft

Owyhigh
Lakes

3mi

Chinook Pass
5432ft

🏕

Hoso
Lake

Dewey
Lake

WILDERNESS

SARVANT GLACIERS

Cayuse Pass
4694ft

FRYINGPAN GLACIER

WHITMAN CREST

Panhandle Gap
6800ft

Barrier Peak
6514ft

123

Seymour Peak
6337ft

Swamp
Lake

OHANAPECOSH GLACIER

OHANAPECOSH
PARK

Buell Peak
5933ft

Needle Creek

American Wildcat
Lake

Little Cougar
Lake

Cowlitz Rocks
7450ft

COWLITZ
PARK

Wauhaukaupauken
Falls

Double Peak
6199ft

Cougar
Lake

Margaret
Falls

Marie
Belle
Falls

Trixie Falls

Basaltic
Falls

Mari
Bell
Falls

Wonderland Tr

Ohanapecosh

River

Shriner Peak
5834ft

🏕

(road open seasonally)

Fan Lake

Twin
Falls

COWLITZ

11mi

15

Fairy Falls

DIVIDE

Bald Rock
5411ft

Sheep
Lake

👣 **Grove of the Patriarchs**

Two
Lakes

STEVENS RIDGE

(Stevens Canyon Rd open seasonally)

STEVENS CANYON

Box Canyon
🏕

Marsh
Lakes

St. John
Falls

**Grove of the
Patriarchs Trail**
🚻

Three
Lakes

🏕

Crag
Lake

Martha
Falls

Snow
Lake

14

🏕

Stevens Canyon Entrance 13

Pacific Crest Trail

Unicorn Peak
6917ft

Stevens Peak
6510ft

Maple
Lake

12

Windy Fork Cowlitz River

19mi

3mi

🏕

**Ohanapecosh
Visitor Center**

Blue Lake

11

(open seasonally)

🚻🏕🍴 1900ft

TATOOSH WILDERNESS

Tatoosh
Lakes

Jug Lake

Ohanapecosh River

123 To Packwood via 12 11mi / 18km

Eagle Cliff (Mowich Lake)

Regions

Mount Rainier National Park is essentially broken into five road accessible regions.

Longmire (All Year) is located in the SW corner of the park, 7 miles east of Nisqually Entrance. Here you'll find Longmire Museum, National Park Inn, Trail of the Shadows (popular), and access to the 93-mile Wonderland Trail that circles the mountain. There's a Wilderness Information Center where you can plan a backcountry trip and pick up a permit. Cougar Rock Campground is about 2 miles beyond Longmire.

Paradise (All Year), the most popular destination, is located 12 miles east of Longmire. It receives almost 70% of all visitors. The region's wildflowers, glaciers, and dramatic mountain vistas provide some of the best scenery the Pacific Northwest has to offer. Henry M. Jackson Memorial Visitor Center provides a perfect venue to begin your trip to Mount Rainier with its exhibits and introductory film. Accommodations are available at Paradise Inn. Guide House is your spot for planning overnight hikes and climbs. Even though Paradise receives an average of 680 inches of snow per year, it is also the premier winter destination. Some sources have called it "the snowiest place on earth." Individuals familiar with the winter of '71–'72 wouldn't argue; 1,122 inches of snow were recorded that year.

Ohanapecosh (June–October) is located 42 miles east of Nisqually Entrance and 3 miles north of the park boundary on WA-123. Here you'll find dense old-growth forests of Douglas fir, western red cedar, and western hemlock. Camping and a visitor center are available.

Sunrise and White River (June/July–October) are located 60 miles NE of Nisqually Entrance. Sunrise is the highest point in the park that can be reached by vehicle and the second most popular destination. Excellent trails, spectacular wildflowers, White River Campground, Sunrise Visitor Center, and Sunrise Day Lodge are all at your disposal at the foot of mighty Rainier.

Carbon River and Mowich Lake (All Year) are in the park's northwest corner. Cars can travel as far as Carbon River Ranger Station. Unpaved and heavily wash-boarded Mowich Lake Road (mid-July–mid-October) leads to Mowich Lake Campground (walk-in sites) and a few exceptional trailheads.

Camping & Lodging

Choosing where to camp boils down to deciding which section(s) of the park you would like to visit. The most popular camp is Cougar Rock at Longmire/Paradise. Ohanapecosh, the largest campground, is located in the park's southeast corner. Sites at these two locations can be reserved up to six months in advance at (877) 444-6777 or recreation.gov. Reservations are a good idea. White River Campground, in the Sunrise/White River Region, is an excellent alternative. All 112 sites are available on a first-come, first-served basis. The campground fills almost every day of its season, and early on weekends. A more isolated experience is available at Mowich Lake Campground in the park's northwest corner. It offers primitive accommodations with walk-in, tent-only sites, located at the end of (rough and unpaved) Mowich Lake Road. No campsites have RV hookups, but many can accommodate large rigs. Cougar Rock can accommodate up to 35-ft RVs and 27-ft trailers. Ohanapecosh has sites for 32-ft RVs and 27-ft trailers. White River has sites for 27-ft RVs and 18-ft trailers.

Don't want to rough it? No problem. **National Park Inn** and **Paradise Inn** are located at Longmire and Paradise, respectively. The locations are unbeatable, and rates are fair (all things considered). A single room at either facility with basic accommodations and a shared bath will set you back about $225/night. A two-room unit with private bath costs right around $300/night.

Emmons Glacier

Rooms do not have TV, telephones, or internet. National Park Inn is the only year-round lodging facility in the park. A general store is located on-site with essential goods like food and camping supplies, and cross-country skis and snowshoes are available for rent in winter. Each inn has a dining room. Paradise Inn also has a cozy cafe. Both are operated by Mount Rainier Guest Services. Contact them at (855) 755-2275 or mtrainierguestservices.com for reservations. They also operate a snack bar at Sunrise Day Lodge (not a lodge) and cafe at Jackson Visitor Center. If you'd like to sacrifice location in favor of cost or are looking for more luxurious lodging facilities, there are many lodging options outside the park.

Mount Rainier Camping (Fees are per night)

Name	Location (# on map)	Open	Fee	Sites	Notes
Cougar Rock*	Between Longmire & Paradise (5)	late May–late September	$20	173	W, F, DS, 35-ft RV
Ohanapecosh*	Near Ohanapecosh VC (11)	late May–late September	$20	188	W, F, 32-ft RV
White River - ♨	White River (16)	late June–late September	$20	112	W, F, 25-ft RV
Mowich Lake	Mowich Lake (22)	July–early October	Free	13	Walk-in, tent-only • P

W = Potable Water, F = Flush Toilets, P = Pit Toilets, DS = Dump Station • RV hookups are not available at any camp
*Reservations can be made up to six months in advance at (877) 444-6777 or recreation.gov
Reservations are strongly recommended from late June through early September (especially for weekend travel)

Backcountry	Backcountry camping requires a free wilderness permit. Permits are available at Longmire Wilderness Information Center (WIC), Jackson Visitor Center, White River WIC, and Carbon River Ranger Station
Group	Group sites are available at Cougar Rock ($60/night) and Ohanapecosh ($60) Reservations (877.444.6777, recreation.gov) are required (available up to one year in advance)

Mount Rainier Lodging (Fees are per night)

Name	Open	Fee	Notes
National Park Inn	All Year	$224–308	Basic accommodations, rooms have shared or private baths
Paradise Inn	late May–early October	$226–268	Simple rooms with shared or private baths in historic building

Contact Mount Rainier Guest Services (855.755.2275, mtrainierguestservices.com) for information and reservations.

Mount Rainier Hiking Trails (Distances are roundtrip)

	Name	Location (# on map)	Length	Difficulty Rating & Notes
Longmire	Gobbler's Knob - 🐾	Westside Road (1)	11.2 miles	M – Can bike most of the way
	Trail of Shadows	Longmire Museum (2)	0.7 mile	E – Self-guided loop explores area's history
	Rampart Ridge	Trail of Shadows (3)	4.6 miles	M – Steep forested loop, stunning vistas
	Eagle Peak Saddle	Longmire (4)	7.2 miles	S – Steep trail through old-growth forest
	Carter/Madcap Fall	Cougar Rock Campground (5)	2.0 miles	M – Madcap Falls is just beyond Carter Falls
	Comet Falls - 🐾	4.4 mi east of Longmire (6)	3.8 miles	S – Steep, a short spur leads to Comet Falls
	Christine Falls	4.5 mi east of Longmire (6)	0.5 mile	E – 100-ft descent from road to view of falls
Paradise	The Lakes Loop - 🐾	Reflection Lakes (7)	5.0 miles	M – Intersects road and Skyline Trail
	Bench and Snow Lk	1.5 mi east of Reflection Lakes (7)	2.5 miles	M – Rolling hills, lakes, views, wildflowers
	Nisqually Vista	Lower Parking Lot (8)	1.2 miles	E – Stroller-friendly self-guided loop
	Deadhorse Creek	Lower Parking Lot (8)	2.5 miles	M – Can loop with Glacier Vista and Skyline
	Myrtle Falls	Upper Parking Lot (9)	1.0 mile	E – Stroller/Wheelchair (with assistance)
	Panorama Point	Upper Parking Lot (9)	4.0 miles	S – Via Skyline Trail and Golden Gate Trail
	Skyline Loop - 🐾	Upper Parking Lot (9)	5.5 miles	S – Best hike, Snowpack until summer
	Pinnacle Peak - 🐾	SE of Paradise (10)	2.5 miles	S – South of Paradise to peak and glacier
Ohanapecosh	Hot Springs	Visitor Center (11)	0.5 mile	E – Self-guided loop, access at campground
	Silver Falls	Multiple (11, 12, 13)	0.6–3.0 mi	M – Pretty falls, beautiful setting
	Laughingwater Crk	Route 123 (12)	12.0 miles	S – Long day hike, 2,700-ft elevation gain
	Grove of Patriarchs	Stevens Canyon Entrance (13)	1.3 miles	E – Self-guided, old, tall (300-ft) trees
	Cowlitz Divide - 🐾	Stevens Canyon Rd (14)	8.5 miles	S – Leads to Ollalie Creek and Wonderland
	Shriner Park	Route 123 (15)	8.4 miles	S – Traverses old burn area, minimal cover
Sunrise	Glacier Basin - 🐾	White River Campground (16)	7.0 miles	S – Spur to Emmons Moraine for glacier views
	Pallisades Lake	Sunrise Point (17)	7.0 miles	S – No views of Mount Rainier, alpine lakes
	Silver Forest	South of the Parking Lot (18)	2.0 miles	E – Leads to Emmons Vista Overlook
	Sunrise Nature	North of the Parking Lot (18)	1.5 miles	M – Views of Rainier over Sunrise Day Lodge
	Sourdough Ridge	North of the Parking Lot (18)	3.0 miles	M – Loop via Wonderland Trail
	Sunrise Rim	South of the Parking Lot (18)	5.2 miles	S – Leads to Shadow Lake/Glacier Overlook
	Burroughs Mtn - 🐾	North of the Parking Lot (18)	4.7 miles	S – 7 miles to Second Burroughs
	Freemont Lookout	North of the Parking Lot (18)	5.6 miles	S – Follow Sourdough Ridge Tr to Fremont Tr
	Berkeley Park	North of the Parking Lot (18)	7.0 miles	S – Follow Sourdough to Northern Loop
Carbon/Mowich	Rain Forest Loop	Carbon River Ranger Station (19)	0.3 mile	E – Self-guided loop through rain forest
	Green Lake	Carbon River Ranger Station (19)	10.8 miles	M – A short spur trail leads to Ranger Falls
	Chenuis Falls	Carbon River Ranger Station (19)	7.4 miles	M – Mostly along Carbon River Road
	Northern Loop - 🐾	Ipsut Creek (20)	30–40 miles	S – Start from Mowich, Ipsut Creek, or Sunrise
	Tolmie Peak	Mowich Lake Rd (21)	6.5 miles	M – Cross Ipsut Pass to Eunice Lake
	Spray Park - 🐾	Mowich Lake Campground (22)	6.0 miles	M – Short spur to Spray Falls (300-ft cascade)

Wonderland Trail - 🐾 • 93.0 miles • Circles Mount Rainier • Accessible from Longmire Wilderness Information Center, Mowich Lake, Ipsut Creek, Sunrise, Fryingpan Creek Trailhead and Box Canyon

Difficulty Ratings: E = Easy, M = Moderate, S = Strenuous

Driving

On a clear day, simply driving around Mount Rainier via WA-706, WA-123, and WA-410, including a side-trip up to Sunrise, can be a real treat. It also might be all you can do on a busy summer weekend. You should expect long waits at entrances, and, if you arrive late, it may be impossible to find parking at Paradise, Sunrise, and Grove of the Patriarchs (and trailheads in between). Make in-park camping/lodging reservations, travel midweek, or get an early start. If you're looking to hike and don't mind a long, unpaved road, head over to Mowich Lake. You could also go to Carbon River to hike/bike. (When we went to print, only the first 1.5 miles of Carbon River Road was accessible to bikers due to fallen trees.) The road to Paradise remains open through winter, but it closes nightly. It's always a good idea to check the park's website for current road status prior to visiting.

Hiking

There are more than 260 miles of maintained hiking trails. All five regions of the park have trails that explore pristine lakes, peaceful meadows, old-growth forests, and, of course, many offer exceptional views of Mount Rainier. But the best views are available at Paradise. When Martha Longmire first set eyes on the area's wildflower meadows and spectacular mountain vistas she exclaimed, "Oh, what a paradise!" Most visitors agree. And no trip to Paradise is complete without hitting the trails. At the very least hike a portion of **Skyline Trail**. Unfortunately, most visitors have the same agenda, making it busy, especially after 9am. It's a good idea to get an early start; if you begin by 7am you can complete the 5.5-mile circuit just as the crowd pours in. Beginning at Jackson Visitor Center, climb two miles to Panorama Point (restrooms available). Here you'll have outstanding views of Nisqually Glacier, which moves down the mountain's slope 6–12 inches each day in summer. You can complete a shorter loop via Golden Gate Trail, or return via Paradise Glacier Trail, which passes Sluiskin and Myrtle Falls. Skyline Loop is considered strenuous (1,700-ft elevation gain), but you'll be busy taking in a smorgasbord of scenic beauty along the way. If you're going to hike the whole thing, clockwise is best.

In Longmire you should hike to **Comet Falls**. The trailhead's small parking area, located near Christine Falls, fills early in summer, and there's no alternative parking nearby. This 300-ft falls earned its name because it resembles the tail of a comet. Note that you'll come to a "Comet Falls 200 feet" sign. It refers to your first view of the impressive waterfall. (Slightly

Mowich Lake sunset

confusing, if Comet Falls is obscured in fog and you missed the viewpoint, you may mistake Bloucher Falls, located near the spur trail and bridge to Comet Falls, as your final destination.) You can take a short obvious spur trail, crossing Van Trump Creek and hiking up and over a small ridge to the base of Comet Falls. The main trail continues (steeply) to Van Trump Park (commonly snow-packed into summer), offering tremendous views. This hike is quite steep and often inaccessible due to snow or avalanche conditions. The short hike to nearby Christine Falls is worth visiting, too.

Ohanapecosh offers a change of pace with **Grove of the Patriarchs Trail**. This relatively flat trail featuring massive trees more than 300 feet tall and 1,000 years old is a great family hike. To the north, you'll find one of the park's most popular trails, **Naches Peak Loop**. It's 3.5 miles, climbing briefly to Chinook Pass from Tipsoo Lake, then joining the Pacific Crest Trail (outside the park boundary). The PCT continues to Dewey Lake, while Naches Loop returns to Tipsoo Lake. This trail provides exceptional views of Mount Rainier.

If you're looking for a more rugged adventure, try **Glacier Basin Trail**, which begins at White River Campground (Loop D). The trail follows the White River to Glacier Basin Camp and Inter Glacier. **Burroughs Mountain Trail**, beginning at Sunrise and you can loop around Shadow Lake.

Be aware that many of these trails are inaccessible due to snow and mud until June or July. It is always a good idea to check trail conditions at a visitor center or the park website before arriving. Hikers should carry plenty of water, wear sunscreen, and stay on marked trails. Pets and bicycles are not permitted on any trails.

Grove of the Patriarchs

Backpacking

Mount Rainier has plenty to offer those looking to get deeper into the park's wilderness. The Pacific Crest Trail skirts the eastern boundary and Wonderland Trail spends 93 miles circling around Mount Rainier. These are the two most notable long-distance hiking trails in the park, but you'll find designated campsites throughout the backcountry. **North Loop** combined with **Wonderland Trail** is another good route with interesting spurs. You can access it from Mowich, Ipsut Creek or Sunrise. Begin planning your backcountry trip with a good topographical map.

Backpackers must obtain a wilderness camping permit (required for all overnight stays in the backcountry). About two-thirds of all permits can be reserved at recreation.gov during peak season (June through September) for $26 per confirmed reservation. The rest are available first-come, first-served in person ($6). A reservation is not your permit. Permits must be obtained in person at Longmire Wilderness Information Center, Paradise Wilderness Information Center, White River Wilderness Information Center, or Carbon River Ranger Station. From October through May, you must register in person at Longmire or Carbon River, or self-register at Paradise and White River. Demand outpaces availability for Wonderland Trail. In the spirit of fairness, the park holds an Early Access Lottery.

Mountaineering

Each year approximately 10,000 visitors attempt to climb 14,410-foot Mount Rainier. Less than half of them successfully reach the summit of the most heavily glaciated peak in the contiguous United States. Not only is Mount Rainier the ultimate in Lower 48 mountaineering, but it also serves as training ground for professional and amateur climbers. Physical preparation, specialized equipment, and finely tuned skills are required to ascend more than 9,000 feet over a distance of (at least) eight miles. All climbers who intend on traveling above 10,000 feet or on a glacier must register and pay a fee. Registration is available at Paradise Ranger Station, White River WIC, and Longmire WIC. The fee is $52/person (25 and older), and $36/person (24 and younger), payable at pay.gov. Passes are valid for the calendar year. You can also climb with an experienced guide. Rainier Mountaineering, Inc. (888.892.5462, rmiguides.com), Alpine Ascents International (206.378.1927, alpineascents.com), and Mount Rainier Alpine Guides (360.569.2889, mountainguides.com) offer a variety of routes and trips. Standard 3–4-day Muir Climbs cost about $1,800 (meals & permit included, gear rental costs extra).

Biking

Bikes are not allowed on hiking trails, but all park roads are open to cyclists. Roads are steep, narrow, and winding with unpaved shoulders. Bike rental is not available in the park. While you can bike to/from/around Paradise and Longmire between June and August, you may want to leave the roadways to motorists during this time. Midweek, after Labor Day is a better time to pedal. Somewhat hidden in the park's northwest corner, the unpaved five-mile **Carbon River Trail** (used to be a road) is closed to motorists but open to bikers and hikers (although downed trees prevent bikers from getting beyond the first 1.5 miles when we went to print). You can also bike unpaved **Westside Road**, located about one mile beyond Nisqually Entrance. The first three miles are open to vehicles (but parking at Dry Creek is extremely limited), after that bikers (and hikers) can continue all the way to Klapatche Park. If you're going to bike, bike the whole thing and park at one of the pullouts west of Westside Road. It's still a long haul. To get to **Gobbler's Knob**, you'll have to bike 6.8 miles each way down Westside Road to the trailhead beyond Round Pass (where you should find a bike rack). From the trailhead it's 0.8 mile to Lake George and another, much steeper, mile to the lookout tower at Gobbler's Knob. And then you have to hike/bike back to your car another 8.6 miles. (A little further down the road from Gobbler's Knob trailhead is Marine Memorial Airplane Crash Monument, dedicated to 32 marines who perished when their plane crashed into South Tahoma Glacier in December 1946.)

More intense pedalers should check out RAMROD (Ride Around Mount Rainier One Day, redmondcyclingclub.org). Every July cyclists test themselves against a 154-mile course with 10,000 feet of elevation gain.

Winter Activities

Abundant snow turns Paradise into a winter wonderland. Sledding is allowed in the snow play area located north of Paradise's upper parking lot (generally open from late December through mid-March). Westside Road is a rather good snowshoeing spot, or you can join a park ranger on a guided snowshoe walk. Skyline Trail is often trampled well enough snowshoes aren't necessary, but you definitely will want some sort of traction devices on your hiking boots (and/or hiking poles). Winter backcountry camping is allowed throughout the park (including Paradise) with a permit. Use a commercial toilet bag system to pack out your waste. Cross-country skis ($30/day) and snowshoes ($15/day) are available for rent at National Park Inn. Backcountry skiing and snowboarding are permitted. Snowmobiles are permitted 6.5 miles along Westside Road, on all the road loops of Cougar Rock Campground, and from the north boundary on WA-410 to the White River Campground (12 miles). Contact the park for snow conditions, avalanche danger, and the weather forecast before you arrive. You must carry tire chains with you from November through May.

Visitor Centers & Museum

Longmire Museum is open all year. It offers exhibits and a bookstore. **Jackson Visitor Center**, located in Paradise, is open daily in summer, and weekends only from October through May. It offers exhibits, a short film, ranger programs, bookstore, and a cafe. **Ohanapecosh Visitor Center** is open daily from June to early October, housing exhibits and a bookstore. **Sunrise Visitor Center** is open daily from early July to early September. **Sunrise Day Lodge**, offering food service and a gift shop, is located nearby. Call (360) 569-2211 for park road and facility status. Operating hours are extended in summer and shortened in winter.

Ranger Programs & For Kids

Ranger-led interpretive programs are an integral component of the national park experience. Free walks, talks, and campfire programs are offered daily during summer. In winter, you can join a ranger on a 1.8-mile snowshoe walk ($5 donation suggested). Event schedules are posted throughout the park as well as online.

Mount Rainier is one of the most family-friendly national parks. In summer, children enjoy walking along creeks and viewing wildflowers. Sledding, snowshoeing, and snowball fights are all fun-filled activities during winter. Any time of year, children are invited to participate in the park's Junior Ranger Program. Activity booklets can be picked up from any of the visitor

Spray Falls

centers. Complete an age-appropriate number of activities and return to a visitor center to receive an official Mount Rainier Junior Ranger badge.

Flora & Fauna

Mount Rainier is home to more than 800 species of vascular plants, including at least 100 species of wildflowers. Wildflower season typically peaks in August. Douglas, western red cedar, and western hemlock comprise most of the park's forests. Large mammals include elk, deer, black bear, and mountain lions.

Pets & Accessibility

Pets are allowed in the park but must be kept on a leash (less than six feet). Visitors with pets are limited to where they can travel as they are only allowed along paved roadways, in parking areas, and in developed campgrounds. They are not permitted in public buildings (except service animals), at ranger programs, in the backcountry, or on hiking trails (except the PCT).

Jackson Visitor Center (Paradise) is accessible to wheelchair users. Ohanapecosh and Sunrise Visitor Centers and Longmire Museum are accessible, but passages are narrow and may require assistance. Accessible rooms are available at Paradise Inn and National Park Inn. Accessible campsites are available at Cougar Rock and Ohanapecosh Campgrounds. Sourdough Ridge Trail, Trail of Shadows, and Paradise's Lower Meadow Trail are accessible with assistance.

Clouds breaching the mountains

Weather

Mountain weather is unpredictable. The best you can do is to have a contingency plan for all possible conditions. One of the most disappointing aspects of the park is that its 14,410-ft mountain is often hidden behind a blanket of clouds. July and August are typically the clearest, driest, and warmest months of the year. At Paradise (5,400-ft elevation), summer average highs are in the low 60s°F with lows in the mid-40s°F. The area's proximity to the Pacific Ocean helps moderate seasonal changes in temperature. Winter highs average in the mid-30s°F with lows in the low 20s°F. Expect Longmire (2,762 ft) to be 5–10 degrees warmer than Paradise and Ohanapecosh (1,950 ft) to be a few degrees warmer than Longmire.

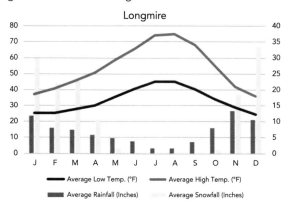

Longmire

- Average Low Temp. (°F)   — Average High Temp. (°F)
- Average Rainfall (Inches)   Average Snowfall (Inches)

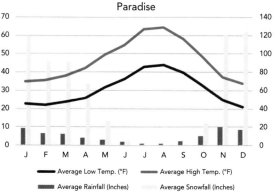

Paradise

- Average Low Temp. (°F)   — Average High Temp. (°F)
- Average Rainfall (Inches)   Average Snowfall (Inches)

Tips & Recommendations

About half of the park's visitors arrive in July or August, and with good reason: roads are open, weather is nice, and the mountain is usually "out" for you to see. Summer is not immune to rain or clouds, but those things are much more common from fall through spring. September is your best bet if you'd like to be able to access most of the park, enjoy decent weather, see the mountain, and have smaller crowds.

Outside of summer, the mountain serves as a beacon to all outdoorsy folk within a 100-mile radius. So, if you do visit during the offseason and are fortunate enough to experience a long stretch of clear skies, things still get busy, especially if it's a weekend. While visitation is substantially less, everyone congregates in Paradise since it's the only road-accessible region in winter.

For a winter trip, keep in mind that the road from Longmire to Paradise is generally open but it closes every night, and any time it is unsafe due to snow, ice, or avalanche potential. You must carry chains with you in winter (that includes 4WD vehicles).

Paradise and Sunrise are the popular summertime destinations. To escape the crowds, consider spending time at Ohanapecosh, Mowich Lake, and/or Carbon River. It's also a good idea to travel midweek.

Ohanapecosh can serve as a decent base camp to make daytrips up to Sunrise or over to Paradise. Carbon River or Westside Road are good places to bring your bikes (although fallen trees were making access difficult about 1.5 miles in on Carbon River Trail when we went to print). Mowich Lake offers primitive camping and similarly stunning hiking opportunities.

This is one of those places where it's best to plan a midweek trip (and avoid holidays). Arrive at Sunrise after the lots fill up and you'll find yourself waiting in line (potentially for more than an hour) as rangers let one car in for each car that leaves. Even for a midweek trip you'll want to arrive early in the day, find a parking space, and leave your car there.

If you're looking for a quick summer trip, spend two nights, allowing one day to explore Paradise, and another to explore Sunrise.

Wildflower blooms change year-to-year, but they usually begin in the low elevations around the middle of July and peak sometime in August. You'll want to check with the park website to be sure.

For hiking Skyline Trail, begin clockwise if you want to walk directly toward the mountain (and get the steepest section out of the way first), or counterclockwise to just do a short hike to Myrtle Falls and back. The scenery everywhere is tremendous, but this way, if you have an idea of what you'll see (and want to see), you can decide if you want to continue the entire five-mile loop once you're out there. Doing the entire loop is definitely worth the effort (and clockwise is probably the better way to go). The trail will be slippery in winter, so come prepared with traction devices for your boots and/or poles to keep from falling. Skyline Trail is usually busy, but, again, very much worth it.

Spending the night within the park's boundary is almost always your best option, but, since park lodging is located at Paradise and Longmire, spending the night outside Nisqually Entrance in Ashford is a pretty darn good alternative.

There are no gas stations within the park. Food is available at Paradise Inn, National Park Inn, Sunrise Day Lodge, and Jackson Visitor Center.

One of the best things about Mount Rainier is that it's great for every type of hiker/visitor. Since the mountain (volcano) is not surrounded by other mountains and valleys, you'll find (mostly) flat trails, steep trails, even glacier trails, and a whole lot of them feature impressive views of Mount Rainier.

If you're thinking about climbing Mount Rainier, know that less than half of all attempted summits are successful. It's not easy. If you want to try it with your own group, you'll need a permit. You can also join an outfit-

Sunset Nature Trail

ter on a multi-day climbing expedition where they take care of all the important details.

Hiking Trails: Skyline Loop (Strenuous, 5.5 miles), Burroughs Mountain (Strenuous, 4.7), Pinnacle Peak (Strenuous, 2.5), Gobbler's Knob (Strenuous, 11.2), Comet Falls (Strenuous, 3.8), The Lakes Loop (Moderate, 5), Spray Park (Moderate, 6), Glacier Basin (Strenuous, 7), Cowlitz Divide (Strenuous, 8.5)

Family Activities: Go sledding/tubing in winter, walk through the wildflower meadows at Paradise (just don't pick or step on them), become Junior Rangers

Guided Tours: Climb Mount Rainier

Rainy Day Activities: Narada Falls, Christine Falls, Reflection Lakes, Box Canyon, Grove of the Patriarchs/Silver Falls, these are all close to the road, but bring rain gear and plan on hiking to look for some ephemeral waterfalls regardless of conditions

History Enthusiasts: Longmire Museum

Sunset Spots: Sunrise, Tipsoo Lake/Chinook Pass, Reflection Lakes

Sunrise Spots: Reflection Lakes, Sunrise

Beyond the Park...

Dining
Cliff Droppers • (360) 494-2055
12968 US-12, Packwood

The Trailhead Bar & Grill
30319 WA-706 E, Ashford

Grocery Stores
Blanton's Market • (360) 494-6101
13040 US-12, Packwood

Suver's Store • (360) 569-2377
30402 WA-706, Ashford

Lodging & Camping
Crystal Mountain Resort
*Summit House Restaurant &
Snorting Elk Bar & Deli*
33914 Crystal Mtn Blvd, Enumclaw
crystalmountainresort.com

Stone Creek Lodge • (360) 569-2355
38624 WA-706, Ashford
stonecreeklodge.net

Stormking Cabins & Spa
37311 WA-706, Ashford
stormkingspa.com • (360) 569-2964

Packwood RV Park
12985 US-12, Packwood
packwoodrv.com • (360) 494-5145

Shady Firs RV • (360) 497-6108
10205 US-12, Randle

Attractions
NW Trek Wildlife Park
Wildlife drive ($90 non-member)
1161 Trek Dr, Eatonville
nwtrek.org

Gifford Pinchot National Forest
*Mt St Helens National Volcanic
Monument, High Rock Lookout
(short, steep hike to stunning
lookout), and Guler Ice Cave
(lava tubes near Trout Lake)*

Mount Hood
*Four hours south of Paradise,
Mount Hood offers year-round
attractions. Plenty to see here.*

Columbia River Gorge NSA
*Magnificent waterfalls, including
Multnomah, Oneonta, Latourell,
Wahkeena. Spectacular!*

Cape Disappointment State Park
Mouth of Columbia River
parks.state.wa.us

Twin Falls Natural Area
Waterfalls/hiking near North Bend

Alpine Lakes Wilderness in
Okanogan-Wenatchee NF
*Good hiking/backpacking
(Alpine Falls, Lake Ingalls)*

Lake Sammamish State Park
Day-use park on lake's south end
2000 NW Sammamish Rd, Issaquah
parks.state.wa.us

Palouse Falls State Park
*It's about five hours east of Paradise, but this is a place to have
on your radar if you're traveling
west along I-90. Very beautiful
setting, when much of eastern
Washington is a little blah.*

Olympic

Hurricane Ridge

Phone: (360) 565-3130
Website: nps.gov/olym

Established: June 29, 1938
March 2, 1909 (National Monument)
Size: 922,561 Acres
Annual Visitors: 3.2 Million
Peak Season: May–September

Activities: Hiking, Backpacking,
Boating, Biking, Swimming

14 Campgrounds: $15–40/night
Backcountry Camping: Permitted
4 Lodges: $157–395/night

Park Hours: All day, every day
Entrance Fee: $30/25/15
(car/motorcycle/individual)

Mount Olympus (7,980 feet), the park's centerpiece, was named by English explorer Captain John Meares in 1788 when he saw the mighty summit from a distance. He deemed it a worthy home of the Greek gods. Mount Olympus may have been named in the 18th century, but the Olympic Peninsula remained a blank spot on maps for another 100 years. Today, the mountainous region of western Washington State has been explored, but the landscape has not changed. Its temperate rain forests, steep cliffs, and high ridgelines remain relatively inaccessible. No roads enter the heart of the park where the Olympic Mountain Range is shaped by 13 rivers. Add 73 miles of wild Pacific coastline and Olympic National Park offers an unsurpassed diversity of relatively undisturbed ecosystems.

Juan de Fuca spotted the Olympic Peninsula in 1592. Captain Meares, Charles William Barkley, and George Vancouver explored the region nearly two centuries later, but Native Americans had lived here for more than 12,000 years. Ancestors of eight distinct tribes survived the decimation brought on by European diseases; the Hoh People still live along the Hoh River, and the Quileute People live at La Push on the

Pacific Coast. Americans did not explore the Olympic Range until the late 19th century. In 1885, Lieutenant Joseph P. O'Neil led an expedition into the mountains. Their journey began at Port Angeles, a small village at the time. It took one month to reach Hurricane Ridge. Today, 17-mile Hurricane Ridge Road follows roughly the same path O'Neil took, but allows visitors to reach the ridge with its scenic views of Mount Olympus in less than half an hour.

Lumber interests seeking untapped old-growth forests spent decades making the Olympic Peninsula more accessible. Aside from wet weather and rugged terrain, lumbermen couldn't have asked for a better location to cut trees than this lush environment. Forests of the Pacific Northwest produce three times the biomass of tropical rain forests. Lumber was being hauled out of the Olympic Peninsula as the general public gained interest in the outdoors, largely thanks to adoption of the automobile. These opposing sides helped fuel a controversial national park movement. President Theodore Roosevelt settled the dispute by establishing Olympic National Monument in 1909 to protect the calving grounds of the area's Roosevelt elk herds. But logging continued, and by the 1920s logging interests faced a swell of public dissent. In 1938, the monument was reestablished as a national park. A new title, but the same results. Largely due to increased demand caused by WWII, illegal logging continued long after the park was established.

Visitors no longer find fresh clear-cut swaths of land. About 366,000 acres of old growth are left unharmed, the largest of its kind in the Pacific Northwest. These impressive stands are nourished by ample rain. Mount Olympus receives as much as 220 inches of annual precipitation (half snow). Forks, located near Hoh Rainforest, receives more rain than any city in the contiguous U.S. Lush and lively, the Olympic Peninsula provides refuge and nourishment for hundreds of species of plants and animals, including several species found nowhere else in the world: Olympic marmot, Olympic torrent salamander, Olympic mudminnow, Olympic grasshopper, Flett's violet, and Piper's bellflower just to name a few. President Roosevelt's goal to preserve elk habitat worked. The park's population is the nation's largest unmanaged herd of Roosevelt elk. Not only does the park preserve an impressive collection of coastline, mountains, and rivers along with its incredible plant and animal diversity, but it also created a reservation for people. A refuge used to escape the doldrums of everyday life by immersing one's self in nature.

Third Beach

When to Go
Olympic National Park is open all day, every day. However, many of the park's roads, visitor centers, campgrounds, and lodging facilities close for winter. In winter, visitors head to the coast or Hurricane Ridge, where there are a multitude of snowplay activities on weekends and holidays. Still, most visitors arrive in summer and visitation peaks in August. At this time sunny skies are common, but so are mosquitoes and black flies.

Transportation & Airports
Ferry and bus service are available to the Olympic Peninsula, but not within the park. The closest large commercial airport is Seattle–Tacoma International (SEA). From Seattle, visitors can fly to William R. Fairchild International Airport (CLM) in Port Angeles.

Directions
Olympic is not the most convenient park for motorists. No road crosses the Olympic Mountain Range, but 12 separate roads penetrate the main park boundary encircling Mount Olympus. In addition, a sliver of Pacific coastline has three separate regions with their own access point. No matter where you're headed, you'll be traveling on US-101. Park Headquarters is located in Port Angeles, where most trips begin. Several different routes can be utilized between Port Angeles and Seattle. Motorists can use the Washington State Ferry System or drive south around Puget Sound via Tacoma or Olympia.

Port Angeles via Tacoma (~140 miles): Heading south on I-5, take Exit 132 to merge onto WA-16 W toward Bremerton. Cross the Tacoma Narrows Bridge (eastbound toll: $6). Just before Bremerton, WA-16 becomes WA-3. At Hood Canal Bridge WA-3 becomes WA-104. After about 15 miles, take the ramp to US-101 N. Continue north to Port Angeles.

Port Angeles via Olympia (~180 miles): Head south on I-5 from Seattle. After about 60 miles, take Exit 104 to merge onto US-101 N. Continue north for about 118 miles to Port Angeles.

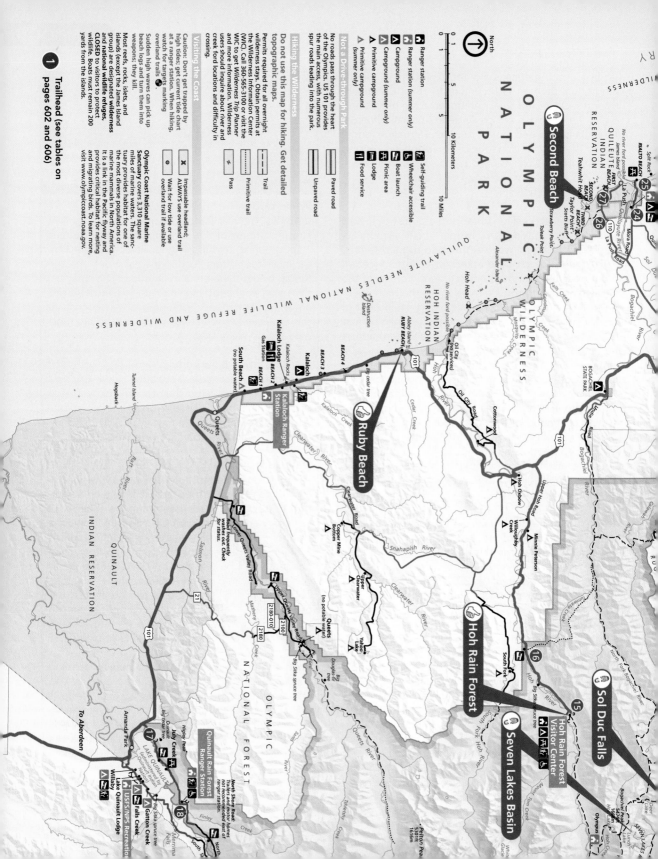

OLYMPIC NATIONAL PARK

North

	Ranger station
	Ranger station (summer only)
	Campground
	Campground (summer only)
	Primitive campground
	Primitive campground (summer only)

Not a Drive-through Park

No roads pass through the heart of the Olympics. US 101 provides the main access, with numerous spur roads leading into the park.

Hiking the Wilderness

Do not use this map for hiking. Get detailed topographic maps.

Permits required for all overnight wilderness stays. Obtain permits at the Wilderness Information Center (WIC). Call 360-565-3100 or visit the WIC to get Wilderness Trip Planner and more information. Wilderness users should inquire about river and creek ford locations and difficulty in crossing.

Visiting the Coast

Caution: Don't get trapped by high tides; get current tide chart at a ranger station. When hiking, watch for targets marking overland trails.

Sudden high waves can pick up beach logs and turn them into weapons; they kill.

Most reefs, rocks, islets, and islands (except the James Island group) are designated wilderness and national wildlife refuges. CLOSED to visitors to protect wildlife. Boats must remain 200 yards from the islands.

Olympic Coast National Marine Sanctuary covers 3,310 square miles of marine waters. The sanctuary provides habitat for one of the most diverse populations of marine mammals in North America. It is a link in the Pacific flyway and provides critical habitat for nesting and migrating birds. To learn more, visit www.olympiccoast.noaa.gov.

	Self-guiding trail
	Wheelchair accessible
	Boat launch
	Lodge
	Picnic area
	Food service

	Paved road
	Unpaved road
	Trail
	Primitive trail
	Pass

| ✗ | Impassable headland; ALWAYS use overland trail |
| ⊙ | Wait for low tide or use overland trail if available |

0 1 5 10 Kilometers
0 1 5 10 Miles

1 Trailhead (see tables on pages 602 and 606)

OLYMPIC WILDERNESS

QUILEUTE NEEDLES NATIONAL WILDLIFE REFUGE AND WILDERNESS

OLYMPIC NATIONAL FOREST

QUINAULT INDIAN RESERVATION

QUILEUTE INDIAN RESERVATION

HOH INDIAN RESERVATION

Second Beach

Ruby Beach

Hoh Rain Forest

Sol Duc Falls

Seven Lakes Basin

Hoh Rain Forest Visitor Center

Quinault Rain Forest Ranger Station

Kalaloch Ranger Station

Kalaloch Lodge

South Beach (no potable water)

LAKE QUINAULT

Lake Quinault Lodge

To Aberdeen

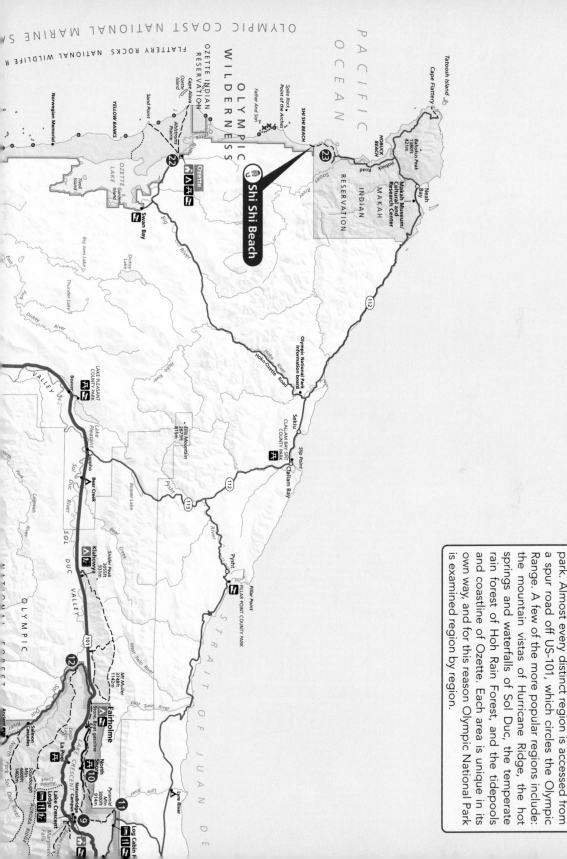

PACIFIC OCEAN

Tatoosh Island

Cape Flattery

Balahkus Peak
1380ft
421m

Neah
Bay

MAKAH INDIAN RESERVATION

HOBUCK BEACH

Hobuck Road

Makah Museum/
Cultural and
Research Center

Sooes River

SHI SHI BEACH

Shi Shi Beach

Ozette River

OLYMPIC WILDERNESS

OZETTE INDIAN RESERVATION

Cape Alava

Ozette
Island

Sand Point

Ahlstrom's Prairie

Spike Rock
Point of the Arches

Father And Son

YELLOW BANKS

Norwegian Memorial

Tivoli
Island

OZETTE LAKE

Ozette
Garden Island

22

Ozette

Swan Bay

Big River

Dickey Lake

Big Joes Lake

Thunder Lake

Dickey River

East Fork

North Fork

23

112

Hoko River

Hoko-Ozette Road

Olympic National Park
Information Board

Sekiu

Slip Point

Clallam Bay

CLALLAM BAY SPIT
COUNTY PARK

Pysht

Pysht River

Pillar Point

PILLAR POINT COUNTY PARK

STRAIT OF JUAN DE FUCA

VALLEY

Beaver

LAKE PLEASANT
COUNTY PARK

Lake Pleasant

Ellis Mountain
2671ft
81m

Sappho

Bear Creek

Beaver Lake

Bear Creek

112

113

Klahowya

Snider Peak
3055ft
931m

Mt Muller
3746ft
1142m

SOL DUC VALLEY

West Twin River

East Twin River

101

12

Fairholme
Store, Boat gasoline

La Poel

North Shore

Barnes Creek

Salmon Cascades

Scourdough Mtn
4600ft
1402m

Aurora Creek

Lake Crescent Lodge

9

10

NatureBridge
Olympic Campus

Pyramid
3005ft
914m

Lyre River

11

Log Cabin Resort

Lake Crescent

OLYMPIC NATIONAL FOREST

Sol Duc River

North Fork Sol Duc River

Ancient Groves

AURORA RIDGE

Barnes Creek

Buses & Ferries

Dungeness Line (360.417.0700, dungeness-line.com) provides two trips daily between Seattle-Tacoma International Airport and Port Angeles. Several stops are made in between. Roundtrip fare costs $78 from Seattle to Port Angeles. Clallam Transit (360.452.4511, clallamtransit.com) provides transportation around Port Angeles and northern Olympic Peninsula.

The Black Ball Ferry Line (360.457.4491, cohoferry.com) provides year-round transportation between Victoria, British Columbia and Port Angeles. One-way passenger fare is $19.50/ adult and $9.75/child (ages 5–11). Bicycles cost an additional $6.50. Vehicles cost an additional $67 plus an $11 online reservation fee. Car rental is available at the port. Taking the ferry is a great idea for cyclists. Victoria is a fantastic city for bicycle travel, and cyclists landing on the Olympic Peninsula may enjoy the challenge of pedaling up Hurricane Ridge. Washington State Ferry System (888.808.7977, wsdot.wa.gov) offers ferry service to multiple destinations on the Olympic Peninsula, but not to Port Angeles. Passenger fare is dependent on destination but one-way fare starts at $3.80 per passenger or $10.95 per passenger and vehicle (under 22 feet). Bicycles cost a nominal surcharge.

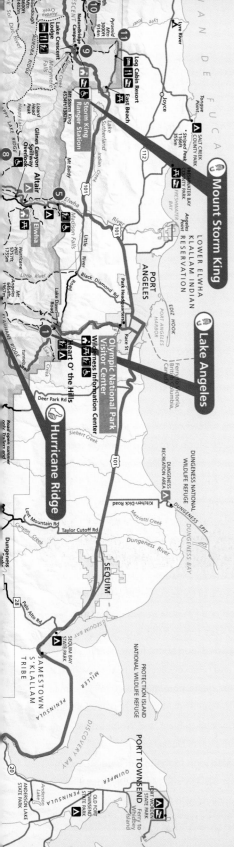

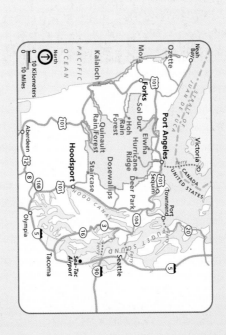

Olympic Mainland Hiking Trails (Distances are roundtrip)

	Name	Location (# on map)	Length	Difficulty Rating & Notes
Heart O' Hills/Hurricane Ridge	Heart O' the Forest	Campground Loop E (1)	4.0 miles	E – Trek through pristine old-growth forest
	Heather Park	Near Camp Entrance (1)	12.4 miles	S – Climbs 4,150 ft, 4 miles to meadow
	Lake Angeles - ♨	Near Camp Entrance (1)	12.6 miles	S – Loop w/ Heather Park, Lake Angeles at 3.4 mi
	Big Meadows	Near Visitor Center (2)	2.0 miles	E – Cirque Rim, Big Meadows, and High Ridge Tr
	Klahhane Ridge - ♨	Near Visitor Center (2)	5.6 miles	S – Switchbacks, connects to Heart O' the Hills
	Wolf Creek	Near Picnic Area A (3)	16.0 miles	M – Descends almost 4,000 ft to Whiskey Bend
	Hurricane Hill - ♨	End of Hurricane Hill Rd (4)	3.2 miles	M – First 0.25-mile is paved, panoramic views
	Little River	Hurricane Hill Trail (4)	16.0 miles	S – Descends 4,000+ feet to Little River Road
	Hurricane Hill/Elwha	Hurricane Hill Trail (4)	11.6 miles	S – Descends 5,250 feet to Whiskey Bend Road
Elwha	Madison Falls	Near Park Boundary (5)	0.2 mile	E – Wheelchair-accessible, 60-ft waterfall
	Humes Ranch - ♨	Whiskey Bend Rd (6)	6.5 miles	M – Loop, can shorten via intersecting trails
	Happy Lake Ridge	Near Observation Pt (7)	19.0 miles	M – Steep climb (4,100-ft gain) to ridge and lake
	Appleton Pass	Olympic Hot Springs Rd (8)	15.4 miles	S – Hot springs, Boulder Lake, can start at Sol Duc
Lake Crescent	Moments in Time	Whiskey Bend Rd (9)	0.6 mile	E – Self-guided loop through forest
	Marymere Falls - ♨	Storm King Ranger Station (9)	1.8 miles	E – Nice walk through old-growth to 90-ft falls
	Mt Storm King - ♨	Storm King Ranger Station (9)	4.2 miles	X – Must ascend steep sections aided by ropes
	Pyramid Peak - ♨	North Shore Picnic Area (10)	7.0 miles	S – Steep climbs, 2,350 feet elevation gain
	Spruce Railroad	Lyre River Trailhead (11)	4.0 miles	M – One-way, follows old rail line along north shore
Sol Duc	Ancient Groves	Near Park Boundary (12)	0.6 mile	E – Self-guided loop through old-growth forest
	Lover's Lane	Sol Duc Campground (13)	5.8 miles	M – Loop connects Sol Duc Resort and Falls
	Mink Lake	Sol Duc Campground (13)	5.2 miles	M – Climb through dense forest to small lake
	Sol Duc Falls - ♨	Sol Duc Falls Trailhead (14)	1.6 miles	E – Popular hike to a three-pronged falls
	Deer Lake	Sol Duc Falls Trailhead (14)	15.2 miles	M – Trail junction just before Sol Duc Falls
Hoh	Hall of Mosses - ♨	Visitor Center (15)	0.8 mile	E – Loop through old-growth rain forest
	Spruce Nature	Visitor Center (15)	1.2 miles	E – Skirts Hoh River (elk potential) for a bit
	Hoh River	Visitor Center (15)	37.0 miles	S – Ends at Glacier Meadows (Mt Olympus views)
	S Snider–Jackson	Near Entrance Station (16)	10.0 miles	M– Primitive trail to Bogachiel River (must ford)
Quinalt	Quinault Big Cedar	North Shore Road (17)	0.4 mile	E – Short and flat walk to huge cedar tree
	Maple Glade	Near Ranger Station (18)	0.5 mile	E – Short loop through big leaf maple grove
	Kestner Homestead	Ranger Station (18)	1.3 miles	E – Self-guided loop about homesteading life
	Irely Lake	Near North Fork Camp (19)	2.2 miles	E – Short and relatively flat hike to shallow lake
Staircase	Wagonwheel Lake	Ranger Station (20)	5.8 miles	S – Very steep, gains more than 1,000 feet per mile
	Shady Lane	Campground (20)	1.8 miles	E – Leads to Four Stream Rd and Lake Cushman
	Flapjack Lakes	Campground (20)	15.0 miles	S – Spur trail to Black and White Lakes
	N Fork Skokomish	Campground (20)	15.1 miles	S – Intersects Duckabush River Trail
Deer Park	Rain Shadow	Blue Mtn Parking Area (21)	0.5 mile	E – Self-guided loop to the top of Blue Mountain
	Obstruction Point	Ranger Station (21)	14.8 miles	M – Highest trail in park, Mount Olympus views
	Three Forks	Campground (21)	8.6 miles	S – Connects with Gray Wolf River Trail

Difficulty Ratings: E = Easy, M = Moderate, S = Strenuous, X = Extreme

Olympic National Park Visitor Center
Attractions: Visitor Center, Wilderness Information Center (WIC) • Backcountry Permits, Hiking

Olympic National Parks Visitor Center is located just south of Port Angeles on Mount Angeles Road. It has a variety of exhibits, including a hands-on "Discovery Room" for kids and a 25-minute introductory film. It's open daily, year-round, but closes for Thanksgiving and Christmas. If you want to get straight to exploring, **Living Forest and Peabody Creek Trails** are short, forested walks beginning outside the visitor center. Living Forest Loop is wheelchair accessible (with assistance).

Stop in at the **WIC** (360.565.3100), located inside the visitor center, for backcountry permits, bear cannisters, and current trail conditions. A permit is required for all overnight stays in the backcountry. This is an ideal place for an introduction to the Olympic Peninsula before continuing south along Hurricane Ridge Road to Heart O' the Hills and Hurricane Ridge.

Heart O' the Hills
Attractions: Ranger/Entrance Station, Camping, Hiking

Heart O' the Hills is located 5 miles south of Port Angeles and Olympic Visitor Center. The **campground** has 105 sites available on a first-come, first-served basis for $24/night. It's open all year, but may be walk-in only depending on the amount of snow. Interpretive programs are held at the campground from late June through September. Potable water and flush toilets are available. RV hookups and a dump station are not. All sites accommodate 21-ft RVs, some up to 35-ft. Sequim KOA (80 O'Brien Road, Port Angeles) is a nearby alternative camping option if you'd like more amenities and the comfort of a reservation. It's nice to spend at least one night at Heart O' the Hills Campground or Port Angeles to hike and explore Hurricane Ridge.

Heart O' the Forest Trail begins in Loop E of the campground. It's an easy 4.0-mile (roundtrip) hike through old-growth forest. For a much more strenuous trek, hikers can loop **Lake Angeles and Heather Park Trails** (seasonal, check trail conditions). Most people simply hike to picturesque Lake Angeles and back. The trailhead is located near the campground entrance on the west side of Hurricane Ridge Road. The loop covers nearly 13 miles, passes Lake Angeles, and the top of the loop intersects Klahhane Ridge/Heather Park/Switchback Junction where extremely ambitious hikers can continue hiking parallel to Hurricane Ridge Road another 3+ miles to Hurricane Ridge Visitor Center.

Deer near Hurricane Ridge

Hurricane Ridge
Attractions: Visitor Center, Driving, Biking, Hiking

If you have to choose one area of the park to visit, Hurricane Ridge is a good choice. Some of the most spectacular vistas are available here as you peer across river-carved valleys to the glacier-capped peak of Mount Olympus. The 17-mile **Hurricane Ridge Road** is an attraction in and of itself. Great for motorists, and a challenge for cyclists, it begins in Port Angeles. An avid biker can climb from sea level to 5,242 feet in about 20 miles. Rest your legs while soaking in the views from Hurricane Ridge before making the thrilling descent back to sea level (make sure your brakes work properly, because you'll need them). The main deterrent for exploring Hurricane Ridge is Mother Nature. The region earned its name thanks to winds that can gust up to 75 miles per hour, and as much as 30–35 feet of snow falls here annually. Trails are often snow-covered into May.

Hurricane Ridge Road is open 24 hours a day between June and October. The rest of the year it is primarily open on weekends and holiday Mondays from 9am until 5pm (weather permitting). Call (360) 565-3131 for up-to-date road and weather conditions. You must carry tire chains in winter (mid-December through March).

Hurricane Ridge Visitor Center offers exhibits, an introductory film, and restrooms. It's open daily in summer. Hours typically run from 9am–6pm in summer and 9am–4pm in winter (when the road is open). Interpretive programs are offered from late June to September. Snowshoe and ski rental are available at the gift shop in winter.

This is an excellent area for **hiking**. Cirque Rim, Big Meadow (accessible with assistance), and High Ridge Trails are one mile or less roundtrip. Klahhane Ridge Trail heads down toward Heart O' the Hills and intersects Lake Angeles/Heather Park Loop after 3.8 miles (one-way). At the end of Hurricane Ridge Road, you

Sol Duc Falls

can pick up **Hurricane Hill Trail**. It's a partially accessible (the first 0.25-mile is paved) 3.2-mile (roundtrip) initially-flat path (that gets steep) with stunning panoramic views. Most visitors do a quick out-and-back along Hurricane Hill Trail, but it continues to Elwha Valley if you're looking for a backcountry route or long (one-way) day hike (arrange a shuttle). Hurricane Ridge is also popular in winter among **cross-country skiers** and **snowshoers**. There are no marked trails, but unplowed roads are usually easy to follow. Or join a ranger-guided snowshoe walk ($7/adult, $3/youth). You'll also find a family-oriented **ski**, **snowboard**, and **tubing** area, complete with rope tows (usually open from 10am to 4pm). You will need a ticket or pass to use the ski/snowboard/tubing area. More information is available at hurricaneridge.com. There's also a small sled hill where children eight and under can sled for free.

Elwha
Attractions: Hiking

You used to be able to raft, hike, and camp in this area, but after a publicized dam removal, the road washed out and dangerous debris was found in the river. When we went to print, you could not drive beyond Madison Falls parking area, which is a 0.2-mile wheelchair-accessible trail to a 60-ft waterfall. We left a few of the hiking trails in the table, but if you want to visit Elwha, first check the status of Olympic Hot Springs Road.

Lake Crescent
Attractions: Lake Crescent Lodge and Log Cabin Resort, Boating, Camping, Hiking, Swimming

This area is difficult to miss. US-101 skirts the lake's southern shoreline for about 10 miles. From east to west you'll pass several short spur roads: East Beach Road to Log Cabin Resort (and campground) and East Beach, Lake Crescent Road to Storm King and Lake Crescent Lodge, and Camp David Jr. Road to Fairholme Campground and the North Shore.

Lake Crescent Lodge and their Roosevelt Cabins typically close after the winter holidays. Rates range from $157–327 per night. Boat ($27/adult) and kayak ($55) tours are available. **Log Cabin Resort** has everything from A-Frame Chalets ($191/night) to camper cabins ($84/night). Camper cabins do not have plumbing. Guests use communal restrooms and showers found at the campground. It is open from late May/mid-June through September. They also have a campground with RV sites with full hookups and tent sites. The setting is exceptional, and you'd have the perks of on-site boat rental, restaurant, general store, communal showers, and coin-operated laundry. Reservations for lodging can be made at olympicnationalparks.com. Camping reservations are only available at (888) 896-3818.

You can also camp at **Fairholme**. The campground has 88 sites available on a first-come, first-served basis for $24/night. It is open from May through fall. Sites can accommodate RVs up to 21 feet. Flush toilets, potable water, and a dump station ($10) are available. Canoe, kayak, and paddleboard rentals are available at **Fairholme General Store** (360.928.3020). Motorboats are allowed. **Boat launches** are located at Storm King, Fairholme, and Log Cabin Resort.

Swimming is popular at Fairholme, East Beach, and Devil's Punchbowl (via Spruce Railroad Trail, closer to the Lyre River Trailhead). A handful of hiking trails are available in the area. The 4.2-mile trek to **Mount Storm King** is fun but tricky due to a few steep ascents aided by ropes. Access the trail near Lake Crescent Lodge. From here you head south across US-101, turn right on Marymere Falls Trail (the easier, more popular alternative), then left onto Mount Storm King Trail, climbing 2,000 feet to the site where Native legend states the mountain spirit hurled a gigantic boulder down at two quarrelling tribes. The boulder struck the river, damming it up, creating Lake Crescent. Don't attempt Mount Storm King when the trail is muddy. On the lake's north shore, hikers can take **Pyramid Peak Trail** (7 miles, roundtrip) to an old WWII spotting tower with exceptional views of the lake. And **Spruce Railroad Trail** is a multi-use path for hikers (and pets), bikers, equestrians, and wheelchair-users. It runs along the north shore of Lake Crescent between Camp David Junior Road and Boundary Creek Road. It's flat and has a tunnel since it follows an old rail line.

Sol Duc

Attractions: Sol Duc Hot Springs Resort, Camping, Fishing, Hiking, Backpacking

Sol Duc Road, just west of Fairholme and Lake Crescent, closes for winter. It leads to the area's resorts, campground, and trailheads.

Sol Duc Hot Springs Resort (888.896.3818, olympic-nationalparks.com) offers basic cabins ($230), kitchen-cabins ($278), and a River Suite ($395). Pool admission is included. The resort is open from mid-April through October. The resort also operates three mineral hot spring soaking pools and one freshwater pool. A soak for anyone not staying at the resort costs $15/adult (ages 12 and older). Massages are also available.

Sol Duc Campground, operated by the resort, has 82 sites available from mid-April through October. 17 sites have water and electric hookups and can accommodate RVs up to 36 feet. A dump station is on site ($10). RV sites cost $40/night. Tent sites cost $21/night. Make reservations at recreation.gov. Access to the resorts pool is not included.

Every visitor should make the short walk to **Sol Duc Falls** (1.6 miles), but this is also a good location for backpacking. The Seven Lakes Basin Area, south of Sol Duc Road, offers an excellent loop trail with views of Mount Olympus.

Hoh Rain Forest

Attractions: Visitor Center, Camping, Rafting, Hiking

Hoh Rain Forest should not be skipped. It's located on the west side of the Olympics where winters are mild and wet. The area receives 140–170 inches of annual precipitation, which help make it one of the most spectacular examples of temperate rain forest in the world. **Hoh Rain Forest Visitor Center** offers exhibits, a bookstore, and guided walks and talks in summer. It's open daily in summer, (usually) on weekends in spring and fall, and closed from January through March. **Hoh Campground** has 78 sites available on a first-come, first-served basis for $24/night. Sites fit RVs up to 21 feet, with a few up to 35 feet. Flush toilets and potable water are available. No dump station.

Hoh River Rafters (360.683.9867, hohriverrafters.com) offers rafting trips on the Hoh River (Class I–II). These summer-only excursions cost $75 for a 3-hour float trip, where things may get a little "splashy" near the take-out. It's nothing wild.

Floating the Hoh River

Several hiking trails begin at Hoh Rain Forest Visitor Center and penetrate deep into the forest's depths. **Hall of Mosses Trail** (0.8 mile) and **Spruce Nature Trail** (1.2 miles) are wonderful self-guided options that explain the area's ecology. Hoh Rain Forest is also the gateway to Mount Olympus. The 18.5-mile (one-way) **Hoh River Trail** leads to Glacier Meadows, which provides excellent views of Mount Olympus and Blue Glacier (do not attempt to climb to its summit without proper equipment, experience, and a permit). Whether you're in the campground, rafting the river, or hiking the trails, you'll have an excellent chance of spotting Roosevelt elk. Olympic is home to the largest unmanaged herd, and about 400 reside in the Hoh area.

Queets

Queets is located in the park's southwest corner. This lightly visited region, accessed via an 11-mile unpaved road, is the perfect destination for some peace and solitude. The **campground** offers 20 primitive sites on a first-come, first-served basis for $15/night. It is open year-round. RVs are not recommended. There are pit toilets and no running water. Two **boat launches** are available to explore the water, and **Sam's River Loop** (2.8 miles) and **Queets River Trail** (15.8 miles, one-way) let you explore the land. You'll find some big trees in this area, but be aware that the road washes out on occasion. Check conditions before departing.

Quinault

Attractions: Lake Quinault Lodge, Camping, Hiking

Quinault is located along the park's southern boundary, just north of US-101 before it heads south along the Pacific Coast. **Lake Quinault Lodge** (888.896.3818, olympicnationalparks.com) is open year-round. Rooms range from basic hotel accommodations ($213/night) to luxury suites ($398/night). Reduced rates in winter.

Dining Room, pool, sauna, and a game room are on site. Boat ($35/adult, 1.5 hours) and hiking ($42/adult, 4 hours) tours are offered. And you can rent paddleboards ($25/hour), kayaks ($25), and canoes ($35). Motorboats are allowed. There are three **boat launches**.

Camping is available at Graves Creek (30 sites, $20/night, pit toilets, no water, no RVs or trailers) and North Fork (9, $20, pit toilets, no water, RVs and trailers not recommended). Olympic National Forest offers additional camping along the south shore of Lake Quinault.

Quinault is a good area to hear newborn elk in spring or bugling bulls in fall. The region is also known for record setting trees. Two of the largest are easily-accessible. A massive western red cedar is found at 0.4-mile **Quinault Big Cedar Trail**. The trailhead is located on North Shore Road on the northwest side of Lake Quinault, 2 miles north of US-101. The other is Big Sitka Spruce, which is located in Olympic National Forest. It stands at the northeastern edge of Lake Quinault and can be reached via a short spur road from South Shore Road. This is also a good **backpacking** destination. From the end of North Fork Road you can hike along Skyline Ridge and loop back to the trailhead following the North Fork of the Quinault River. Just be aware part of the trail is primitive and will require some route finding. At the end of Graves Creek Road you can hike East Fork Quinault River Trail to Enchanted Valley Chalet and keep going to several other trailheads if you can arrange a pickup or cache a vehicle.

Staircase
Staircase is located in the park's southeast corner. Staircase Road may not be accessible in winter. Call (360) 565-3131 for status or check online. The **campground** has 49 campsites available on a first-come, first-served basis for $24/night. A few sites can accommodate RVs up to 35 feet. During winter, sites may be walk-in only and water is not available. Most hiking trails follow the North Fork Skokomish River.

Deer Park
Deer Park Road runs south from US-101 between Port Angeles and Sequim. At the park boundary pavement gives way to gravel and the road twists, turns, and climbs nearly 6,000 feet to Deer Park on the east side of the Olympics. The road is narrow, steep, not suitable for RVs or trailers, and only open in summer. A ranger station is staffed intermittently during summer and fall. A total of 14 tent-only **campsites** are available on a first-come, first served basis from mid-June through mid-fall for $15/night. Water is not available.

Deer Park resides in the rain shadow of the Olympic Mountain Range, receiving only 18 inches of rain annually. Mount Olympus, just 20 miles to the west, receives more than 100 inches of annual precipitation. Another 10 miles to the west you'll find Hoh Rain Forest and Forks, which receive the most rain in the contiguous U.S., roughly 120 inches annually, an incredible contrast considering the two areas are only 100 miles apart (by car, even closer as the crow flies).

Olympic Coast Hiking Trails (Distances are roundtrip unless noted otherwise)

	Name	Location (# on map)	Length	Difficulty Rating & Notes
Ozette	Cape Alava	Ranger Station (22)	6.6 miles	E – Boardwalk through forest and prairie to beach
	Sandpoint	Ranger Station (22)	5.6 miles	E – Mostly boardwalk to sandy beach
	Ozette Loop - ♿	Ranger Station (22)	9.2 miles	E – Beach connects Cape Alava and Sandpoint Trails
	Shi Shi Beach - ♿	Hobuck Road (23)	4.0 miles	M – Steep descent to beach, Makah Rec. Pass required
Mora	James Pond	Ranger Station (24)	0.3 mile	E – Flat loop through forest to small pond
	Slough	Ranger Station (24)	1.8 miles	E – Hike through forest to the Quillayute River
	Rialto Beach - ♿	End of Mora Road (25)	3.0 miles	E – Hike to arch and tidepools at Hole-in-the-Wall
	N Coast Wilderness	End of Mora Road (25)	20.6 miles	E/M – Continue north beyond Rialto Beach (1-way)
La Push	Second Beach - ♿	La Push Road (26)	1.4 miles	E – Short trail, you'll have to crawl over some driftwood
	Third Beach - ♿	La Push Road (27)	2.8 miles	E – Short trail with somewhat steep descent to beach
	S Coast Wilderness	La Push Road	17.1 miles	E/M – Permit required for backcountry camping (1-way)

Kalaloch features 1-mile Kalaloch Nature Trail, which passes through coastal forest • Seven separate trails lead from US-101 to the ocean • Ruby Beach and Beach 4 have wheelchair-accessible viewpoints and restrooms

Difficulty Ratings: E = Easy, M = Moderate, S = Strenuous

There are some nice trails at Deer Park. Experienced hikers with good map-reading and route-finding skills can make a loop by hiking from Deer Park to **Obstruction Point** (7.4 miles, one-way) then heading south to Grand and Moose Lakes (~3 miles). From here, continue along a primitive trail across Grand Pass (~1 mile) and follow Cameron Creek Trail (~3 miles) to Three Forks Trail (2.1 miles) back to Deer Park. It's also one of the better areas to begin a **backpacking** trip.

Flora & Fauna

Over 1,450 types of vascular plants grow on the Olympic Peninsula. Most famous are the giant Sitka spruce, western hemlock, Douglas fir, and western red cedar of Queets, Quinault, and Hoh Rain Forest. You may see Roosevelt elk, black bear, mountain goats, beavers, or marmots. The park is also home to about 300 species of birds. Among them are bald eagles, osprey, and northern pygmy owl.

Ozette

Ozette is located on the northwestern coast of the Olympic Peninsula. It can be reached by taking WA-113/WA-112 north from US-101 to Hoko–Ozette Road, which eventually runs along the northern shoreline of Ozette Lake and to the coastline. Ozette is one of the more remote regions, at least an hour away from the next closest destination. The **campground** is open all year. All 15 sites (21-foot RV max) are first-come, first-served for $20/night. No water. Pit-toilets. Motorboats are allowed on Ozette Lake. **Boat launches** are located at Swan Bay and Ozette Ranger Station.

Cape Alava (6.6 miles) and **Sand Point** (5.6 miles) are popular thanks to the addition of boardwalks and stairs. You can connect both trails by a 3.1-mile stretch of sand and rock beach for a 9.2-mile loop. If you're looking for a more remote gem, look no further than **Shi Shi Beach**. It's located at the very northern corner of the Ozette area and is accessed via a short hiking trail beginning at the end of Hobuck Road in the Makah Indian Reservation. (Parking requires a Makah Recreation Pass, which can be purchased in Neah Bay at Makah Marina, The Museum at the Makah Culture and Research Center, Washburn's General Store, Makah Mini Mart, Makah Tribal Center, or Hobuck Beach Resort.) Reaching the beach requires a short but steep final descent (aided by a rope). You can also reach Shi Shi Beach from Ozette, following the coast for 15 miles. **Backpackers** can camp along the Ozette Coast (at Shi Shi Beach and beyond). Due to popularity, reservations are required from May through September. Contact the Wilderness Information Center in Port Angeles at

The World's Largest Spruce

(360) 565-3100 to make reservations. Animal-resistant food containers are required for storing food because of raccoons, not black bears. Make sure you have everything you need for your trip. The only close place to restock or purchase last minute supplies is a small store just outside the park boundary. It carries essentials and rents food storage buckets. All hikers exploring the coast should carry (and know how to use) a tide table. Several areas are only passable at low tides and getting trapped is a possibility.

Mora & La Push

WA-110 runs west from US-101, just north of Forks (of Twilight book fame). **Mora Campground**, located along the Quillayute River, is open all year. There are 94 sites, with flush toilets and running water for $24/night. Hookups are not available, but a dump station ($10) is. Some sites can accommodate RVs up to 35 feet. Sites can be reserved during peak season (late May through mid-September) at recreation.gov. Short hikes to **Second Beach** (1.4 miles), **Third Beach** (2.8 miles), and **Rialto Beach's Hole-in-the-Wall** (3.0 miles) explore the rocky shoreline that is pounded by waves and covered with giant drift logs. All three are great. If forced to choose one beach, Second would be first.

Shi Shi Beach

Kalaloch

Kalaloch, Olympic's southernmost stretch of Pacific Coast land, is easily accessed via US-101, which runs directly through the region. **Kalaloch Lodge** (866.662.9928, thekalalochlodge.com), located right on the beach, is open all year. During peak season, rooms cost anywhere from $251/night for a basic motel style room to $377/night for a suite. **Kalaloch Campground** features 170 campsites available year-round for $24/night. It has flush toilets and potable water. No hookups. Sites can be reserved from late May through mid-September at recreation.gov. A few sites have room for RVs up to 35 feet. A dump station ($10) is available. A few miles to the south you'll find **South Beach Campground**. It has 55 first-come, first-served sites available in summer for $20/night. A few can accommodate RVs up to 35 feet. It has flush toilets but no potable water.

Easy access and abundant overnight accommodations make Kalaloch one of the most popular regions of Olympic National Park. Beachcombers can rejoice as there are seven short trails leading to the waterfront. It's also a great location to watch for whales during their spring migration (April–May). Still, we prefer nearby Ruby Beach and La Push/Mora for beaches.

Flora & Fauna

Lucky guests may spot seals, sea lions, puffins, or sea otters while exploring the coast. Look for gray whales between March and May during their annual migration north to summer feeding grounds. In all, 29 species of marine mammals have been documented. Beach gives way to dense coniferous forests where you may see bald eagles perched atop towering western red cedar.

Visitor Centers

Visitor Centers are located at Port Angeles, Hurricane Ridge, and Hoh Rain Forest. They're briefly discussed in the regions. Ranger Stations are located at Storm King (Lake Crescent), Kalaloch (open daily in summer), Quinault, and Staircase.

Ranger Programs & For Kids

Ranger-led programs are available throughout the summer at popular locations and campgrounds. Activities include walks, talks, and campfire programs. Check online or at a visitor center or entrance station for an up-to-date schedule of events. It is highly recommended that you try to incorporate at least one ranger-led activity into your plans.

Children are invited to participate in the park's Junior Ranger and/or Ocean Stewards Programs. Pick up a free activity booklet at a visitor center, complete the activities, and return to receive a badge.

Pets & Accessibility

Pets are allowed in the park but must be kept on a leash (less than six feet). They are permitted only in park campgrounds, picnic areas, and parking lots. Pets are not allowed on trails or beaches, except the following: Rialto Beach (to Ellen Creek), all Kalaloch Beaches, Peabody Creek Trail, Madison Falls Trail, Spruce Railroad Trail, and July Creek Loop.

Visitor Centers, and most restrooms and picnic areas are fully accessible. Spruce Railroad and Madison Falls are two of the more easily-accessible trails in the park.

Weather

Extreme differences in elevation and rainfall make generalizing weather here exceptionally difficult. Elevation varies from sea level to 7,980 feet at Mount Olympus. Average annual rainfall varies from 18 to 120 inches depending on where you are. There are distinct dry and wet seasons. Dry season is the most popular time to visit and typically lasts from June through September.

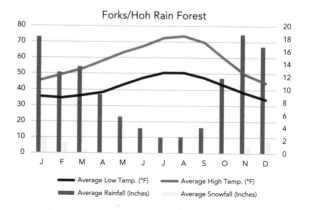

Forks/Hoh Rain Forest

— Average Low Temp. (°F)   — Average High Temp. (°F)
▬ Average Rainfall (Inches)   ▬ Average Snowfall (Inches)

Tips & Recommendations

Being close to Seattle, it's a good idea to plan a midweek trip. Even then, if you're visiting in summer, particularly August, make lodging and/or camping reservations early. Roughly two-thirds of Olympic's visitors arrive between May and September.

Olympic is one of the most difficult parks to plan for because it has incredible geographic diversity and more than a dozen vehicle-accessible regions (with no roads penetrating the heart of the park or connecting region to region). In a single day you can stroll through an alpine meadow while gazing at a distant glacier, stand in awe of a lush rainforest, and go tidepooling along the Pacific Coast. This place is incredible. In spring you could play in snow at Hurricane Ridge, play in the water at Crescent Lake or Lake Ozette, and go tidepooling along the ocean all in the same day!

Try to sample the three main environments: mountains, coast, and rain forest. Plan at least one day to explore Hurricane Ridge (hike to Lake Angeles, view Mount Olympus, maybe catch a ranger walk/talk) or Deer Park (hiking). Another day at Lake Crescent to hike and play in the water. And two days to explore the coast and Hoh Rain Forest (three if you'd like to spend the night at Shi Shi Beach—just know it can get crowded, as many as 250 campers have been out there on busy summer nights). Aside from Lake Quinault, the southern and eastern sides of the park are primarily departure points for backpacking trips or long hikes.

Speaking of backpacking, all overnight stays in the backcountry require a permit ($8 per person per night + $6 reservation fee). All permits were only available online (recreation.gov) for 2020/2021, but it seems likely they will go back to a mixture of reservation/walk-up permitting in the in the future at Wilderness Information Centers in Port Angeles and Quinault, where you can also borrow bear cannisters. There's also a free, walk-in, tent-only campground at Dosewallips on the park's eastern side. It has 30 sites, all first-come, first served, and there's pit toilets and no potable water.

If you'd like to set up a base camp, try Lake Crescent. 1). It's beautiful. 2). It's about as central as it gets, with decent access to the coast, rain forest, and Hurricane Ridge. It'd be a bit of a haul to get over to south and east sides, but, unless you have a lot of time, you're going to have to make some compromises.

It's a good idea to visit popular destinations like Hurricane Ridge or Second Beach early in the day (although you may want to be at the beach for sunset).

Easy Hikes: Second Beach (1.4 miles), Marymere Falls (1.3), Rialto Beach (3), Third Beach (2.8), Hall of Mosses (0.8), Sol Duc Falls (1.6), Ozette Loop (9.2)
Moderate Hikes: Shi Shi Beach (4), Hurricane Hill (3.2)
Strenuous Hikes: Lake Angeles (6.8 miles), Pyramid Peak (7), Klahhane Ridge (5.6, loop with Lake Angeles)
Extreme Hikes: Mount Storm King (4.2)
Family Activities: Go tidepooling, drive Hurricane Ridge, swim at Crescent Lake, chase a few waterfalls, wander through a rain forest, Become Junior Rangers
Guided Tours: Float the Hoh River
Rainy Day Activities: Hike to a waterfall
Sunset Spots: Second Beach, Shi Shi Beach, Rialto Beach, Ruby Beach, Hurricane Ridge, Lake Crescent
Sunrise Spots: Hurricane Ridge, Lake Crescent, Deer Park
Wildlife: Hoh Rain Forest (elk), Hurricane Ridge (deer)

Beyond the Park...

Dining
Granny's Café • (360) 928-3266
235471 US-101, Port Angeles
grannyscafe.net

Toga's Soup House • (360) 452-1952
122 W Lauridsen Blvd, Port Angeles
togassouphouse.com

Frugals • (360) 452-4320
1520 E Front St, Port Angeles
frugalburger.com

D&K BBQ • (210) 683-5357
275 N Forks Ave, Forks

Grocery Stores
Safeway • (360) 457-1461
2709 E US-101, Port Angeles

Thriftway • (360) 374-6161
950 S Forks Ave, Forks

Quinault Mercantile • (360) 288-2277
352 S Shore Rd, Quinault

Lodging & Camping
Angeles Motel • (360) 797-1779
812 E 1st St, Port Angeles
angelesmotel.com

Quillayute River Resort
473 Mora Rd, Forks
qriverresort.com • (360) 374-7447

Quinault River Inn • (360) 288-2237
8 River Dr, Amanda Park
quinaultriverinn.com

Port Angeles KOA • koa.com
80 O'Brien Rd, Port Angeles

Riverview RV Park • Forks
33 Mora Rd • forksriverviewrv.com

State Park (parks.state.wa.us)
camping: Dungeness, Fort
Townsend, Ebey's Landing,
Dosewalips, Penrose, Twanoh,
Jarrell Cove, Belfair, Scenic
Beach, and Lake Sylvia.

Festivals
Kite Festival • August
kitefestival.com • Long Beach

Crab Festival • October
crabfestival.org • Port Angeles

Attractions
Adventures through Kayaking
atkayaking.com • (360) 417-3015

Purple Haze Organic Lavender Farm
180 Bell Bottom Rd, Sequim
purplehazelavender.com

Wheel-In-Motor Drive-In
210 Theatre Rd, Port Townsend
ptwheelinmotormovie.com

Flattery Rocks NWR • fws.gov
Island just offshore Cape Alava
home to puffins and seals

Fort Flagler State Park
Old army fort
10541 Flagler Rd, Nordland

North Cascades

Phone: (360) 854-7200
Website: nps.gov/noca

Established: October 2, 1968
Size: 684,000 Acres
Annual Visitors: 30,000
Peak Season: July & August

Activities: Hiking, Backpacking, Boating, Mountaineering, Whitewater Rafting, Biking, Fishing, Cross-country Skiing, Snowshoeing

5 Campgrounds: Free–$24/night
Backcountry Camping: Permitted with a Backcountry Use Permit
2 Lodges: $154+/night

Park Hours: All day, every day
Entrance Fee: None
National Forest Day Pass: $5/day

The North Cascades are brimming with old-growth forests, more than one hundred glaciers, and pure alpine lakes. They are a hiker's paradise as unique in landscape as in name: North Cascades National Park Service Complex. The only one of its kind, this complex unites three park units: North Cascades National Park (North and South Units), Ross Lake National Recreation Area (NRA), and Lake Chelan NRA. The mountains, named for an abundance of waterfalls, form an imposing natural barrier, preventing all but the most determined visitors from entering their depths. Many people have tried their luck at making a living among these mountains, but few succeeded. Today, that task is easier thanks to considerable infrastructure and a burgeoning tourism industry. North Cascades Scenic Highway pierces the Cascades, crossing them from east to west as the roadway runs the entire length of Ross Lake NRA. Travel further from the beaten path—into river-carved valleys, on top of completely exposed rocky ridgelines, far away from the scenic byway—and you'll begin to see the landscape as its earliest inhabitants saw it, wild and free.

Native Americans lived in these mountains for thousands of years. Their lives were tied to the surroundings. Two major tribes lived in the region, one on each side of the Cascades. People of the Columbia

Diablo Lake

Blue Lake

When to Go
The park is open all year, but winter weather impacts when most visitors arrive. Roads and facilities are generally open between late April and late November. Visitation is rarely excessive, but almost all guests arrive between June and September, when weather is pleasant, and most trails are snow-free.

Transportation & Airports
Amtrak (1.800.872.7245, amtrak.com) and Greyhound (800.231.2222, greyhound.com) provide transportation along the I-5 corridor, but not directly to the park. Lady of the Lake ($43, one-way, 888.682.4584, ladyofthelake.com) and Stehekin Ferry ($39, one-way, 506.669.5045, stehekinferry.com) provide ferry service between Chelan and Stehekin, operating all year, daily in summer. Chelan Seaplanes (509.682.5555, chelanseaplanes.com) flies between Chelan, Seattle, and Stehekin. Roundtrip charter from Chelan with one hour in Stehekin costs $751 (up to six passengers). The closest major airport is Seattle–Tacoma International (SEA), 130 miles southwest of North Cascades Visitor Center.

Directions
North Cascades National Park Service Complex is not easy to access by vehicle. The South Unit is only accessed via unpaved Cascade River Road. No roads penetrate the North Unit or Lake Chelan National Recreation Area. Most visitors enter the complex via WA-20 (North Cascades Scenic Highway), which crosses the Cascades and Ross Lake National Recreation Area (NRA).

Ross Lake NRA via Seattle (~140 miles): Heading north on I-5, take Exit 230 for WA-20 toward Burlington/Anacortes/Skagit Airport. Turn right at WA-20 and follow it about 60 miles to the park.

Wenatchi lived to the east. People of the Puget Sound Salish lived to the west. They traded between each other, blazing trails across Stehekin (meaning "the way through"), and Cascade and Twisp Passes. They often followed high ridgelines to avoid navigating dense vegetation common in the lower elevations. Natives lived in harmony with the land; many Americans arrived seeking resources to sell.

Several American expeditions traversed the North Cascades, mapping and documenting what they witnessed. Fur trappers came and went. Hundreds of miners hoping to strike it rich arrived in the late 1870s. They panned for gold along the banks of the Skagit River, but found very little. The rush ended by 1880. Trees were felled and floated along the Skagit River and Lake Chelan, but inadequate transportation and infrastructure spared the forests. The most significant alterations to the landscape came in the form of three dams along the Skagit River, but for the most part this rugged land remains wild and free.

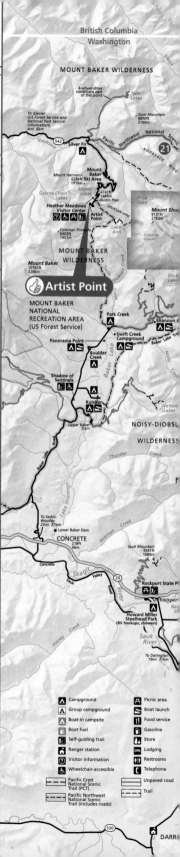

Regions

North Cascades is actually a National Park Service Complex, consisting of four distinct units: North Cascades National Park (North and South Units) and Ross Lake and Lake Chelan National Recreation Areas (NRA). The NRAs have more lenient preservation and protection regulations, allowing local interests like hydroelectric facilities, resorts, and hunting to continue with limited federal intervention. Stephen Mather Wilderness unites the units as it encompasses roughly 94% of the entire complex.

North Cascades National Park is the least accessible portion. It's broken into north and south units by Ross Lake NRA, which straddles North Cascades Highway and Ross Lake, bisecting the complex. The North Unit is only accessible by foot. **Cascade River Road** provides vehicle access to the South Unit and is the only vehicle access point into the park. The 23-mile dirt and gravel roadway is typically open from summer through fall. It's rough, but also one of the most gorgeous drives in the entire collection of parks. Along the way you'll pass two National Forest campgrounds before crossing the park boundary. Eventually the road terminates at Cascade Pass Trailhead. Cascade Pass and the spur trail to Sahale Glacier are two of the best hikes you'll find. Still, most visitors choose to hike into the north or south unit beginning at one of several trailheads located along WA-20 in Ross Lake NRA.

Ross Lake NRA serves as the centerpiece of the complex. Easy access via North Cascades Scenic Hwy/WA-20 and the majority of campgrounds, trailheads, and visitor facilities makes Ross Lake NRA the park's most popular region. The area protects stretches of the Skagit River, Diablo Lake, and 24-mile-long Ross Lake. Skagit River offers summer-long recreation. Diablo and Ross Lakes provide paddlers with the opportunity for some unique multi-day backcountry trips or casual day trips. Regularly scheduled boat tours are available on Ross Lake. But its only boat launch is accessed via a dirt and gravel road from Canada. **North Cascades Visitor Center**, located off WA-20 near Newhalem, is where you'll want to begin your trip. It's usually open daily, spring through fall, and on weekends in winter.

Lake Chelan NRA is located deep in the park's southern reaches, wrapping around the north end of 55-mile-long Lake Chelan, the nation's third-deepest lake (1,486 ft). Visitors must hike, fly, or boat into this picture-perfect setting. Even the ferry (ladyofthelake.com, stehekinferry.com) or plane (chelanseaplanes.com) trip is great for viewing waterfalls and shoreline of the glacially-carved lake. The sights don't stop once you've arrived. You can explore historic Buckner Orchard or marvel at 312-foot Rainbow Falls. Stehekin cannot be reached by car, but there is a lodge and road; a shuttle (one-way: $8/adult, $5/child, $8/bike or dog) transports visitors through the valley.

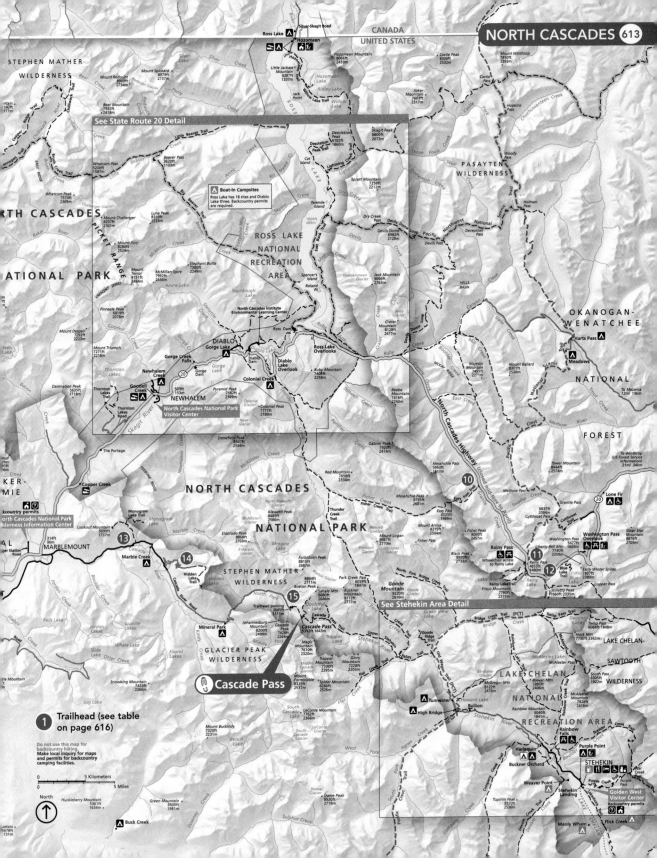

CANADA
UNITED STATES

STEPHEN MATHER
WILDERNESS

NORTH CASCADES

NATIONAL PARK

PICKET RANGE

ROSS LAKE
NATIONAL
RECREATION
AREA

PASAYTEN
WILDERNESS

OKANOGAN-
WENATCHEE

NATIONAL

FOREST

North Cascades Institute
Environmental Learning Center

North Cascades National Park
Visitor Center

DIABLO
Gorge Lake

Gorge Creek
Falls

Newhalem
Creek

Goodell
Creek

NEWHALEM

Thornton
Lakes Road

Colonial Creek

Ross Lake
Overlooks

Ross Lake
Overlook

Diablo
Lake Overlook

See State Route 20 Detail

Boat-In Campsites
Ross Lake has 18 sites and Diablo
Lake three. Backcountry permits
are required.

North Cascades National Park
Visitor Center

The Portage

Copper Creek

KER-
MIE

backcountry permits

North Cascades National Park
Wilderness Information Center

MARBLEMOUNT

13

Marble Creek

14

Hidden
Lake
Trail

STEPHEN MATHER
WILDERNESS

NORTH CASCADES

NATIONAL PARK

Mineral Park

15

Trailhead parking

GLACIER PEAK
WILDERNESS

See Stehekin Area Detail

Goode
Mountain

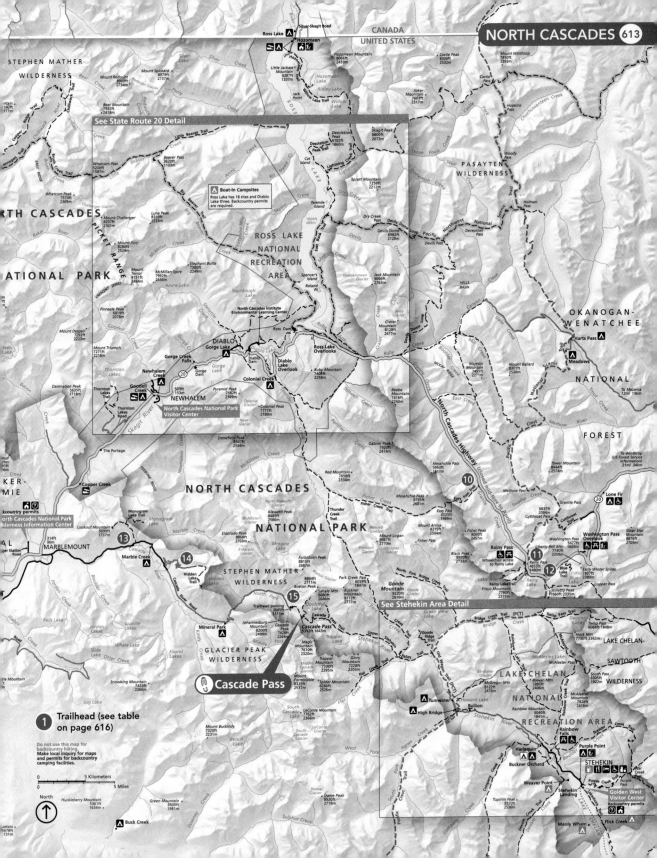
👣 **Cascade Pass**

LAKE CHELAN

SAWTOOTH

WILDERNESS

LAKE CHELAN

NATIONAL

RECREATION
AREA

Rainbow
Falls

① Trailhead (see table
on page 616)

Do not use this map for
backcountry hiking.
Make local inquiry for maps
and permits for backcountry
camping facilities.

0   5 Kilometers
0   5 Miles

North

Rainy Pass

Washington Pass
Overlook

10

11

12

Lone Fir

Rainy Lake

Blue
Lake

To Winthrop
(US Forest Service
Information) 21mi 34km

Harts Pass

Meadows

STEHEKIN

Golden West
Visitor Center
Backcountry permits

Purple Point

Stehekin
Landing

Weaver Point

Buckner Orchard

Harlequin

High Bridge

Bullion

Tumwater

Flick Creek

Manly Wham

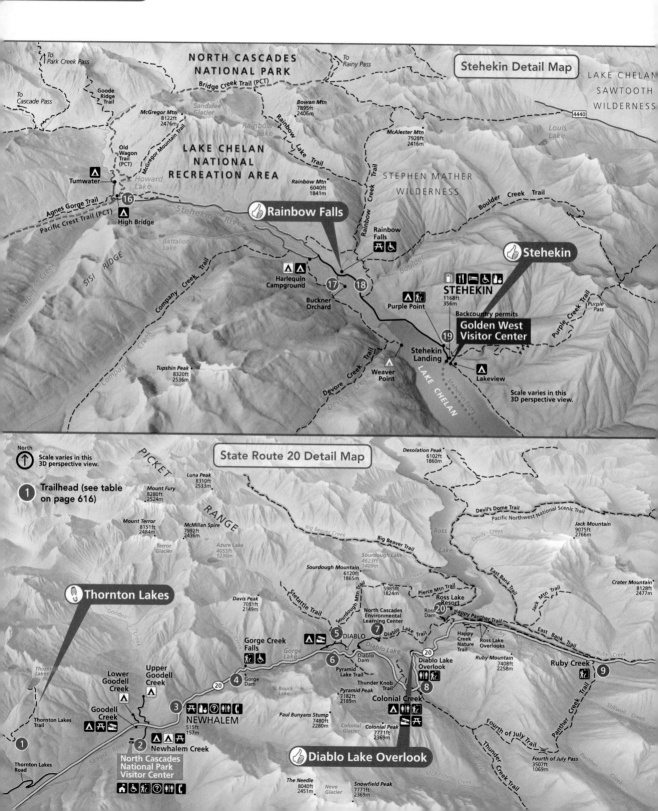

Rainbow Falls (Stehekin)

North Cascades Hiking Trails (Distances are roundtrip unless noted otherwise)

	Name	Location (# on map)	Length	Difficulty Rating & Notes
North Cascades Scenic Hwy (WA-20)	Thornton Lakes - 👍	Thornton Lake Road (1)	10.4 miles	M – Steep climb to classic cirque lakes
	Sterling Munro	North Cascades Visitor Center (2)	0.1 mile	E – Views of the Picket Range
	River Loop	North Cascades Visitor Center (2)	1.8 miles	E – Forested hike to river and camp
	Rock Shelter	New Halem Campground (3)	0.3 mile	E – Visits 1,400-year-old hunting camp
	Trail of the Cedars	River Loop/Linking Trails (3)	0.5 mile	E – Links Main Street and River Loop
	Ladder Creek Falls	Gorge Powerhouse (4)	0.4 mile	E – Pretty cool "downtown" waterfall
	Stetattle Creek	Near Diablo (5)	6.0 miles	M – Rock scrambling required
	Sourdough Mtn	Near Diablo (5)	11.1 miles	S – 5.2 miles to lookout (1-way)
	Pyramid Lake	WA-20 Milepost 126.8 (6)	4.2 miles	M – Small deep lake made by landslide
	Diablo Lake - 👍	North of Diablo Lake (7)	7.6 miles	M – Lower elevation trail, glacier views
	Thunder Creek - 👍	Colonial Creek Campground (8)	27.6 miles	E/S – Leads to Stehekin Valley
	Thunder Knob	Colonial Creek Campground (8)	3.6 miles	M – Kid-friendly, Diablo Lake views
	East Bank - 👍	WA-20 Milepost 138 (9)	31.0 miles	E – To Hozomeen (1-way) with spur trails
	Panther Creek	WA-20 Milepost 138 (9)	13.0 miles	M – 4th of July Pass, melts out early
	Easy Pass/ Fisher Creek	WA-20 Milepost 151 (US Forest Pass required to park) (10)	7.0 miles 14.5 miles	S – Good trail but definitely not easy S – Thunder Creek Trail junction (1-way)
	Rainy Lake - 👍	Rainy Pass on WA-20 (11)	1.0 mile	E – Excellent! Not in park, waterfalls
	Maple Pass - 👍	Rainy Pass on WA-20 (11)	7.5 miles	M – Loop to easier pass than Easy
	Blue Lake - 👍	Blue Lake Trailhead WA-20 (12)	4.4 miles	M – A beautiful mountain lake
Cascade RR	Monogram Lake	Travel 7 miles south on Cascade River Road from Marblemount (13)	10.0 miles	S – Climb 4,040 ft via switchbacks, and meander through subalpine meadows
	Hidden Lake - 👍	End of Sibley Creek Rd (14)	9.0 miles	M – 2,900-ft gain, popular day-hike
	Cascade Pass - 👍	End of Cascade River Rd (15)	7.4 miles 11.8 miles	M – Great views from the pass S – Or continue to Sahale Glacier
Stehekin (Lake Chelan)	Agnes Gorge	High Bridge (16)	5.0 miles	E – Wildflowers early and mid-summer
	Howard Lake	High Bridge/Bullion Camp (16)	2.6–3.8 mi	M – Mountain views (AKA Coon Lake)
	Old Wagon (PCT)	High Bridge (16)	Varies	E – Pacific Crest Trail • Connects valleys
	Goode Ridge	Old Wagon Trail (16)	10.0 miles	S – Views of Stehekin River drainage
	McGregor Mtn	Via Old Wagon Trail (16)	15.4 miles	S – Switchbacks to mountain summit
	Buckner Orchard	Near Rainbow Falls (17)	Varies	E – Self-guided, pick apples in fall
	Rainbow Creek	Stehekin Valley Road (18)	19.4 miles	M – To McAlester Pass/Trail
	Purple Creek - 👍	Golden West Visitor Center (19)	16.2 miles	S – To Juanita Lake, loop options
Backpack Loops	Beaver Loop	Ross Dam Trail, Milepost 134 (20)	34.2 miles	Big and Little Beaver • Water taxi req'd
	Rainbow and McAlester Pass	WA-20/Stehekin (12/18)	31.5 miles	M – Bridge Creek, McAlester Lake, Rainbow Creek and Lake Trail
	Copper Ridge/ Chilliwack River - 👍	Hannegan Road in Mount Baker Wilderness (21)	33.5 miles	S – Sites along Copper Ridge fill quickly • Ice axe required until July
	Devil's Dome	East Bank or Canyon Creek Trailhead on WA-20 (9)	40.4 miles	S – Through Okanogan National Forest, finishes on East Bank Trail (Lake Diablo)

Difficulty Ratings: E = Easy, M = Moderate, S = Strenuous

Camping & Lodging

Goodell Creek (Milepost 112, 19 sites, $24/night, water, all year), Newhalem Creek (MP 120, 111, $24, water, summer), Gorge Lake (MP 126, 8, $20, no water, all year), and Colonial Creek (MP 130, 137, $24, water, all year) Campgrounds are located along North Cascades Highway (WA-20). Reservations are accepted at Goodell Creek, Newhalem Creek, and Colonial Creek through (877) 444-6777 or recreation.gov during the peak summer season. The rest of the year they are first-come, first-served. Group sites are available at Upper and Lower Goodell Creek and Newhalem Creek. Reservations are required. Make them at recreation.gov up to one year in advance. Hozomeen Campground (75 sites, free, water, summer), located in the park's northeast corner, can be accessed via Skagit Road (39 miles, unpaved) from Canada, by foot (East Bank Trail, 31 miles), or boat (Ross Lake). There are also several small boat, road, and hiking camping areas (less than 10 sites each) in Stehekin. Lakeview, Purple Point, and Harlequin can be reserved from late May through early September at recreation.gov for $20/night. All other sites require a backcountry permit and a dock permit (if arriving by water). Additionally, there are more than 100 designated campsites for backpackers and boaters in the backcountry. Beyond park boundaries there are more than a dozen developed campgrounds in national forest, state park, and county park land.

There are two lodges within park boundaries. Neither are accessible by car, which adds a great deal to their charm. **Ross Lake Resort** (rosslakeresort.com, 206.486.3751) is just across from the Ross Dam, but you'll still need to catch a boat to access it. They're open from mid-June through October and reservations are available up to one year in advance (they're always fully booked). Pricing is extremely reasonable. $220–250/night for a little cabin. $240–304/night for a modern cabin (sleeps up to 6). $310–374/night for a private bunkhouse (sleeps up to 10). Or $400–520/night for a two-story cabin (sleeps up to 9). All cabins have wood stove heat, full kitchen, bathroom, and mountain vistas. You'll have to bring your own food. There's no restaurant or store. They also rent boats, portage kayaks (at Ross Dam). **North Cascades Stehekin Lodge** (lodgeatstehekin.com, 509.682.4494) is even more remote. It's located at the northern end of Lake Chelan, where the Lady of the Lake (ladyofthelake.com) or Stehekin ferry (stehekinferry.com) drop passengers off. Spending a night here is most highly recommended and rates are fair, starting at $154/night. A restaurant and general store are on site, and they're open from mid-May through mid-October.

Cascade Pass

Hiking

North Cascades Highway is nice, but to share a more intimate experience with the Cascades leave the car behind and set out on foot. Nearly 400 miles of hiking trails allow guests to explore the stunning beauty of the park's river-carved valleys and glacier-capped peaks. Most trailheads are located along North Cascades Highway and in Stehekin (Lake Chelan NRA), but the hiker's paradise is Cascade River Road (closed seasonally, typically opens in June). After mile 10, it becomes dirt and gravel, but should be passable by low-clearance 2WD vehicles. The trails to Hidden Lake and Cascade Pass are this area's gems and two of the best hikes in the Cascades. You'll also find several good day hikes along North Cascades Highway. They're listed in the hiking table, but backpacking unlocks a whole lot more majestic mountain scenery. If you'd like a local guide, try Skagit Guided Adventures (360.474.7479, skagitguidedadventures.com).

Backpacking & Boat-In Camping

Wilderness camping is only allowed at designated sites along trail corridors. All overnight stays in the backcountry require a backcountry permit. 60% of permits for backpacking trips from mid-May through September can be reserved through pay.gov. Applications are allowed between March 15 and April 15. Applying costs $20. Applications are processed in the order they were received. In summer it's open from 7am to 8pm on Friday and Saturday and 7am to 6pm from Sunday to Thursday. The rest of the permits are free and available in person no sooner than one day before your desired trip. Obtain permits at the ranger station closest to your destination. Permits are limited and popular areas like Cascade Pass, Ross Lake, Copper Ridge, and Thornton and Monogram Lakes often fill quickly. Backpacking trips should be planned in advance using a good topographic map. A few suggested loop trips are provided in the hiking table on the opposite page.

Lake Chelan

If you'd like to have someone take care of the details for you (and have a few gentle horses carry your stuff), reach out to Stehekin Outfitters (509.682.7742, stehekinoutfitters.com). They're based in Stehekin (accessed via ferry) and offer pack trips up the Stehekin River Valley (toward Cascade Pass).

Boat-in sites on Diablo Lake, Ross Lake, and Lake Chelan require a backcountry permit. In all there are 25 boat-in campsites. Most are on Ross Lake, with twenty sites spaced out along the 22 miles of open water between Ross Dam and Hozomeen. Permits follow the same procedure as backpacking sites. Boating can be a much more relaxing method of transportation, but it can also be a nightmare if you're unprepared or encounter unmanageable conditions. Be prepared.

Mountaineering

There are many technical mountaineering climbs within the park complex. Just like backpacking, permits are required for all overnight stays. There are composting toilets in popular climbing areas (Boston Basin, Sulphide Glacier on Mount Shuksan). If there isn't enough soil to bury your waste, you must carry and use a commercial toilet bag system. Permits for popular areas go quickly. If you're unfamiliar with the area and don't have access to someone who is, it's a good idea to hire a guide. If you choose to go it alone, always err on the side of caution. There are many dangerous ridgelines, glaciers, and summits. You have several options for climbing guides (including summits, rock climbing, ice climbing, and backcountry skiing/snowboarding): BC Adventure Guides (206.799.4092, bcadventureguides.com), Adventure Spirits (802.535.1498, adventurespiritguides.com), Kaf Adventures (206.413.5418, kafadventures.com),

Mountain Madness (206.937.8389, mountainmadness.com), Madison Mountaineering (206.494.5799, madisonmountaineering.com), Alpine Ascents (206.378.1927, alpineascents.com), Peak7 (509.467.5550, peak7.org), Northwest Mountain School (509.548.5823, mountainschool.com), Miyar Adventures (425.949.8634, miyaradventures.com), Pro Guide Service (425.888.6397, proguiding.com), Alpine Endeavors (877.486.5769, alpineendeavors.com), American Alpine Institute (360.671.1505, alpineinstitute.com), International Mountain Guides (360.569.2609, mountainguides.com), Northeast Mountaineering (978.799.3783, nemountaineering.com), North Cascades Mountain Guides (ncmountainguides.com), Pacific Alpine Guides (pacificalpineguides.com), and RMI Expeditions (888.892.5462, rmiguides.com). Rare Earth Adventures (503.308.9063, rareearthadventures.com) offers less-extreme offerings and moonlit snowshoeing trips. Most of them offer climbs of Mount Baker, Mount Shuksan, and a variety of peaks in Boston Basin (including Forbidden Peak).

Whitewater Rafting

There are several quality whitewater options in the Cascades, including the Skagit River (Class II–III) which runs alongside North Cascades Scenic Highway. Several outfitters offer rafting and tubing trips in the area. They include Alpine Adventures (800.7238386, alpineadventures.com), Blue Sky Outfitters (800.228.7238, blueskyoutfitters.com), Methow Rafting (509.866.6775, methowrafting.com), North Cascades River Expeditions (800.634.8433, riverexpeditions.com), and Triad River Tours (360.594.5117, triadrivertours.com). Wildwater River Guides (509.470.8558, wildwater-river.com) offers rafting, kayaking, and SUP trips.

Biking

Bikes are only allowed on park roads. Road cyclists have one option: North Cascades Highway. Traffic is usually bearable, but the elevation gain is sure to make your thighs burn. There are also two tunnels. Use lights on your bike, and activate the caution light on the longer tunnel east of Newhalem. Biking is also a great way to explore Stehekin Valley Road. Bicycles can be brought aboard Lady of the Lake Ferry ($15.50/one-way) or you can rent one from Discovery Bikes (stehekindiscoverybikes.com). Rentals cost $5 (hour), $25 (8am–5pm), and $30 (24 hours). Or join them for a breakfast ride ($37.50, bike included).

Fishing

You must follow state fishing regulations and purchase a fishing license to fish within the park complex.

Barbless hooks and knotless nets are recommended. Stehekin Fishing Adventures (stehekinfishingadventures.com) offers guided fishing trips on Lake Chelan and around Stehekin. Rates are $325 for a half-day (1–2 people) and $495 for a full day. Skagit River Guide Service (888.675.2448, skagitriverfishingguide.com) offers fishing and bald eagle viewing trips.

Winter Activities
Things are pretty limited in winter. Most roads close (even North Cascades Scenic Highway closes for winter, usually December through April). A few campgrounds stay open. You can camp in the backcountry yet, but you better be prepared for snow, ice, rain, wind, cold, avalanches. Just driving toward the park, you should be prepared for those things, traveling with a shovel, stove, sleeping bag, insulated pad, and anything else that will help you get through the night if you wind up getting stranded for a day or two.

Visitor Centers
North Cascades Visitor Center (206.386.4495 ext. 11), located on North Cascades Highway (NCH) near Milepost 120, is usually open daily, May through late September, and weekends in October. It's closed November through April. It's the place to stop and get oriented, featuring exhibits, a short film, bookstore, restrooms, and hiking trails. **Park and Forest Information Center** (360.854.7200), located on NCH in Sedro–Wooley, is open daily, late May through September and weekdays only for the rest of the year. **Wilderness Information Center** (360.854.7245), located on NCH near Marblemount (Milepost 105.3), is open daily from early May through mid-October. It's closed from mid-October through April. It's the place to get backcountry hiking and climbing information. **Golden West Visitor Center** (509.699.2080 ext. 14), located near the ferry landing in Stehekin, is open daily from mid-May through early October. It's closed from early October through mid-May. It has an information desk, bookstore, and you can get backcountry permits.

North Cascades Institute (360.854.2599, ncascades.org) offers a wealth of online courses and in-person experiences throughout northwest Washington. Many programs take place right in the heart of North Cascades National Park at **North Cascades Environmental Learning Center** on the north shore of Diablo Lake. Programs include birdwatching expeditions, photography classes, mountain hikes, and educational discussions. Cost varies depending on the duration and activity, but they're priced fairly. And meals and lodging are often included at the Learning Center campus.

Easy Pass

Ranger Programs & For Kids
Rangers offer red bus tours (fee) of Stehekin Valley Road, and a variety of free walks, talks, and evening programs in summer. Current schedules are available at the park website or at any visitor information center.

Children are welcome to participate in the Junior Ranger Program. Pick a booklet up at a visitor center, complete the activities appropriate for your age, and return to receive a Junior Ranger patch and certificate.

Flora & Fauna
North Cascades is home to more than 1,600 species of vascular plants and at least 500 species of animals. Wildflower meadows burst with color, some blooming as early as February and others as late as September. Trees, including western red cedar, Sitka spruce, Douglas fir, and western hemlock, dominate all but the highest elevations. You're most likely to spot black-tailed deer, Douglas squirrel, or playful pika, but you may encounter black bears, mountain goats, or wolves while exploring the park.

Pets & Accessibility
Bringing your pet severely limits what you can do here. First, wherever you are, your pet must be on a leash (less than six feet). In the national park, pets are only allowed on the Pacific Crest Trail and within 50 feet of roads. They are allowed in Ross Lake or Lake Chelan NRAs, as well as surrounding national forest lands.

North Cascades Visitor Center, Sedro–Woolley Information Station, and the Wilderness Information Office are fully accessible to wheelchair users. Golden West Visitor Center is accessible with assistance. Rock Shelter, River Loop, Happy Creek, and Linking Trail, all near North Cascades Visitor Center are accessible.

There's goats in these mountains

Weather

Mountain weather is downright baffling. Snow can fall any day of the year in the North Cascades. WA-20 can close and be buried in snow between November and February. Then there are outliers like the winter of 1976–'77 when North Cascades Highway/WA-20 remained open all year. The western slopes receive, on average, 76 more inches of rain and 407 more inches of snowfall than their eastern counterparts that reside in the mountain's rain shadow. You're never guaranteed beautiful weather in the Cascades, but the best bet for it is to travel between mid-June and late September.

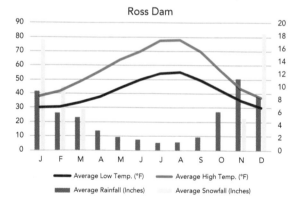

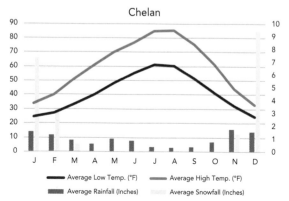

Tips & Recommendations

North Cascades is another National Park that may very well become an itch in need of regular scratching for you. Unless you're getting into the backcountry, staying in Stehekin, or paddling Ross Lake, most of it is left to the imagination. I know I want to return and start filling in some of those blank spaces.

North Cascades is undeveloped as far as national parks go. If you're just going to drive through Ross Lake NRA, you only need a few hours. To get a better taste of the place you'll need a few days (and it'll take multiple modes of transportation). Or stay at Ross Lake Resort (rosslakeresort.com) and you're almost guaranteed a good time.

Most visitors enter (and leave) the park via North Cascades Scenic Highway. That's fine. There's no denying the scenery, but things get even better in other corners of the park (and outside its boundary). The problem is these side trips are big commitments. Heading up unpaved Cascade River Road and hiking to Sahale Glacier is a full-day activity (and you'll need an early start). Taking a ferry or seaplane to Stehekin can be a day trip, but it's better to spend at least one night (camping or at the lodge). Outside the park, driving Mount Baker Highway to its conclusion for outstanding views of the national park's Mount Shuksan is another day. Or you can boat to Ross Lake Resort or camp in the backcountry (via boat or foot). And then there's Hozomeen in the park's northeast corner, which you access by boat, foot, or car (through Canada, bring your passport). There are other trails you can access through Canada as well that are worth looking into.

So, take your time, bring canoes or kayaks, and stay at Stehekin! There are multiple vacation's worth of activities waiting for you at North Cascades.

Easy Hikes: Rainy Lake (1 mile)
Moderate Hikes: Blue Lake (4.4 miles), Thornton Lakes (10.4), Hidden Lake (9), Diablo Lake (7.6), Maple Pass (7.5), Rainbow Creek (19.4, can loop with Stehekin Valley Road)
Strenuous Hikes: Cascade Pass (7.4 miles), Purple Creek (16.2)
Family Activities: Take a boat to Stehekin or around Diablo Lake, become Junior Rangers
Guided Tours: Climb a mountain, raft some whitewater
Sunset/Sunrise Spots: Diablo Lake Overlook, Picture Lake or Artist Point (Mount Baker-Wilderness with views of North Cascades National Park North Unit)

Ladder Creek

Beyond the Park...

Dining
Annie's Pizza Station • (360) 853-7227
44568 WA-20, Concrete
anniespizzastation.net

Birdsview Diner • (360) 840-1878
39974 WA-20, Concrete

Miga Asian Cuisine • (360) 853-8652
44618 WA-20, Concrete

Skagit Valley Burger Express
1172 WA-20, Sedro-Woolley
skagitvalleyburgers.com

River Time Brewing • (267) 483-7411
650 Emens Ave, Darrington
rivertimebrewing.com

Grocery Stores
Baker Lake Grocery • (360) 826-5467
38940 WA-20, Concrete

Lodging & Camping
Cascade Mountain Lodge
44618 WA-20, Concrete

Ovenell's Heritage Inn
46276 Saulk Valley Rd, Concrete
ovenells-inn.com • (360) 853-8494

North Cascades KOA
1114 WA-20, Winthrop
koa.com • (509) 996-2258

Festivals
Tulip Festival • April
tulipfestival.org • Skagit Valley

Attractions
Snoqualmie Falls
Easily-accessible waterfall
Snoqualmie Falls.com

Wallace Falls State Park
Waterfalls, hiking, camping
14503 Wallace Lake Rd, Gold Bar
parks.state.wa.us

Deception Pass State Park
Outstanding park with camping
41229 WA-20, Oak Harbor
parks.state.wa.us

Camano Island State Park
2269 Lowell Point Rd, Camano
parks.state.wa.us

San Juan Islands NHP
Known for orca sightings
nps.gov/sajh • (360) 378-2240

Mount Baker-Snoqualmie NF
Includes several wilderness areas (Boulder River, Glacier Peak, Stephen Mather, Noisy-Diobsud) and Mt Baker NRA. There are many exceptional hiking/ backpacking trails (Green Mountain Lookout, Boulder Lake, Nooksack Falls) • fs.usda.gov

Wenatche National Forest
Good hiking/backpacking (Silver Falls) and camping. Huge area.

Mount Baker Ski Resort
Heather Meadows Café
Mt Baker Hwy, Deming
mtbaker.us • (360) 734-6771

North Cascades Heli-skiing
heli-ski.com • (509) 996-3272

Lake Chelan State Park
South shore camping
7544 S Lakeshore Rd, Chelan
parks.state.wa.us

Lake Roosevelt NRA/Coulee Dam
Visitor Center, light show, water
activities, no dam tours
nps.gov/laro

Peshastin Pinnacles State Park
Pretty cool sandstone slabs
7201 N Dryden Rd, Cashmere
parks.state.wa.us

Steptoe Butte State Park
Grassy hills, ancient butte
parks.state.wa.us

Mount Spokane State Park
5,883-ft mountain
26107 N Mt Spokane Pk Dr, Mead
parks.state.wa.us

ALASKA

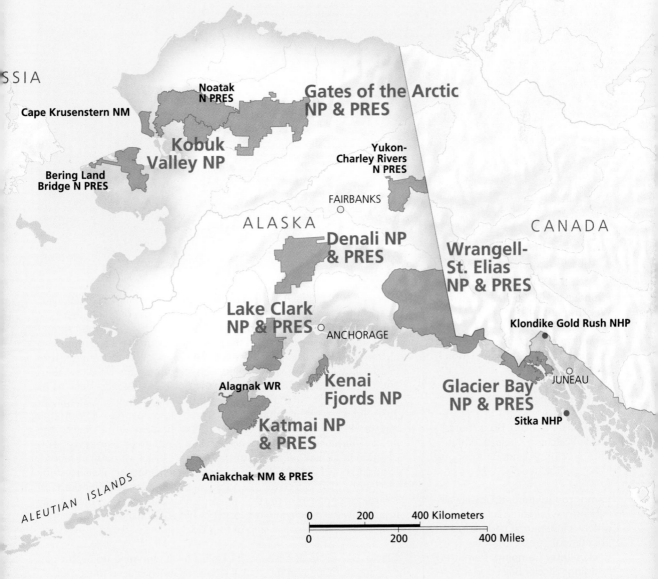

ALASKA (Washington, DC, minus 4 hours)

SSIA

Cape Krusenstern NM

Noatak
N PRES

Gates of the Arctic
NP & PRES

Kobuk
Valley NP

Bering Land
Bridge N PRES

Yukon-
Charley Rivers
N PRES

FAIRBANKS

ALASKA

CANADA

Denali NP
& PRES

Wrangell-
St. Elias
NP & PRES

Lake Clark
NP & PRES

ANCHORAGE

Klondike Gold Rush NHP

Alagnak WR

Kenai
Fjords NP

Glacier Bay
NP & PRES

JUNEAU

Katmai NP
& PRES

Sitka NHP

Aniakchak NM & PRES

ALEUTIAN ISLANDS

| 0 | 200 | 400 Kilometers |
| 0 | 200 | 400 Miles |

Glacier Bay

Watching for whales

Phone: (907) 697-2230
Website: nps.gov/glba

Established: December 2, 1980
February 25, 1925 (National Mon.)
Size: 3,283,000 Acres
Annual Visitors: 600,000
Peak Season: May–September

Activities: Paddling, Boat Tours, Whale Watching, Cruises, Whitewater Rafting, Hiking, Backpacking, Fishing, Flightseeing

Campground: Bartlett Cove (walk-in, tent-only, all campers must obtain a free permit and attend an orientation)
Backcountry Camping: Permitted*
Lodging: Glacier Bay Lodge
Rates: $250+/night

Park Hours: All day, every day
Entrance Fee: None

Glacier Bay National Park, located in southeastern Alaska just 60 miles west of the state capital of Juneau (reached by boat or plane, there are roads to the mainland), is an incredible world of ice, mountains, and sea. More than one quarter of the park is ice, permanent but retreating at a frightening rate. When Joseph Whidbey sailed to the mouth of Glacier Bay in 1794 it was choked with ice more than 4,000 feet thick and up to 20 miles wide. The immense glacier stretched back to its source, more than 100 miles away in the St. Elias Mountain Range. By 1879, John Muir found that ice had already retreated 48 miles into the bay. In 1916, Grand Pacific Glacier had withdrawn all the way to the head of Tarr Inlet, roughly 65 miles from the mouth of Glacier Bay. This phenomenon has been one of the fastest glacial retreats on record, exposing new land and providing opportunities for scientists to study glaciation, plant succession, and animal dynamics. And hundreds of thousands of guests come to witness giant icebergs as they break away from tidewater glaciers in explosive fashion—also known as calving—from the deck of a cruise ship or tour boat.

Glacier Bay protects 50 named glaciers (including nine tidewater glaciers that terminate in the sea). Climatic changes caused most glaciers in the eastern and southwestern regions, like McBride, Muir, Reid, and Riggs Glaciers to retreat. Muir Glacier, with a 2-mile calving face, was once the most impressive, but it completely receded in the 1990s. On the bay's western shoreline, Johns Hopkins, Lamplugh, and Margerie

Glaciers are stable or advancing and thickening. Today, most visitors stop and wait aboard a tour boat or cruise ship at the latter two, hoping ice will break from the glacier's face.

"To the lovers of pure wilderness Alaska is one of the most wonderful countries in the world...it seems as if surely we must at length reach the very paradise of the poets, the abode of the blessed."

– John Muir

John Muir, beloved naturalist and writer, became deeply interested in glaciers after years of hiking Yosemite Valley (which he proposed was carved by glaciers, not shaped by earthquakes). In 1879, Muir was first in a long line of scientists to visit Glacier Bay. He studied the recession of glaciers while enriching his spirit in the wilderness he loved so dearly. Muir visited again in 1899 as a member of the Harriman Alaska Expedition, organized by railroad tycoon Edward Harriman. His group of scientists, photographers, artists, and writers formed a who's who list of their respective fields. In September of that year, a massive earthquake shook Glacier Bay. Severed icebergs made the bay completely inaccessible to vessels for more than a decade, causing steamships to remove this destination from their itineraries. Visitation, exploration, and scientific research halted temporarily, but the area's beauty never diminished.

In 1925, President Calvin Coolidge established Glacier Bay National Monument. The area was preserved for its "tidewater glaciers in a magnificent setting, developing forests, scientific opportunities, historic interest, and accessibility." Commercial interests kept their eyes on the bay as well. In 1936, President Franklin D. Roosevelt reopened the area to mining. Ore was extracted from the mountains of Glacier Bay sporadically, and today there's still a claim on a significant nickel-copper bed that lies directly beneath Brady Glacier. In 1939, land was added to the national monument, doubling its size and making it the largest unit of the National Park System at the time. During WWII, the nearby city of Gustavus served as a strategic military location where a supply terminal was built. By 1943, 800 buildings, 3 large docks, and an airstrip were constructed on a 600-acre tract of land. After just a few months of use they were given to civilian control. Today, a short road linking Bartlett Cove and the airfield at Gustavus greatly increases park accessibility, allowing amateur scientists and lovers of nature to explore Glacier Bay on their own.

Exploring an ice cave

When to Go
Glacier Bay National Park is open all year, but you'd hardly know it come wintertime. Services in winter are extremely limited. Most visitors arrive via cruise ships from May through September. Humpback whales are seen during this entire period, but sightings increase in mid-June and peak around July and August. Regardless when you travel, be sure to dress in layers and pack rain gear.

Transportation & Airports
The park can only be reached by plane or boat. Within the park there is a 10-mile road connecting Gustavus and its airfield to the park headquarters at Bartlett Cove. It is possible to bring your vehicle via the Alaska Marine Highway Ferry System, but that's not recommended. Taxis run between Gustavus and Bartlett Cove upon request, and buses run a limited schedule. Cruise ships, tour vessels, and private boats all enter the bay. Private boaters entering Glacier Bay anytime from June through August must obtain a free (advance or short-notice) permit prior to arrival. Permits are limited. Application form is available at the park website.

Air travel is the easiest method of arrival. Alaska Airlines (800.252.7522, alaskaair.com) provides daily service from Juneau to Gustavus (~30 minutes, ~$100) during the busy summer season. Alaska Seaplanes (907.789.3331, flyalaskaseaplanes.com) also provides year-round service to Gustavus.

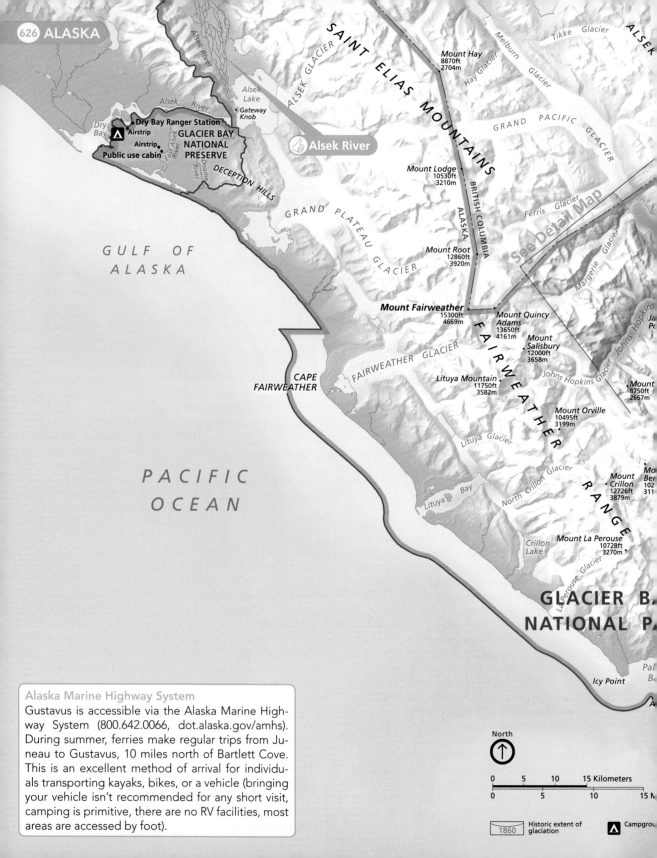

SAINT ELIAS MOUNTAINS

Tikke Glacier

ALSEK

Alsek River

ALSEK GLACIER

Mount Hay
8870ft
2704m

Melburn Glacier

Hay Glacier

GRAND PACIFIC GLACIER

Alsek River

Alsek Lake

• Gateway Knob

Dry Bay

Dry Bay Ranger Station
Airstrip
GLACIER BAY
NATIONAL
PRESERVE

Airstrip
Public use cabin

East Alsek River

Doame River

DECEPTION HILLS

Alsek River

👍 **Alsek River**

Mount Lodge
10530ft
3210m

BRITISH COLUMBIA

ALASKA

Ferris Glacier

See Detail Map

GRAND PLATEAU GLACIER

GULF OF
ALASKA

Mount Root
12860ft
3920m

Margerie Glacier

Mount Fairweather
15300ft
4669m

Mount Quincy
Adams
13650ft
4161m

Mount
Salisbury
12000ft
3658m

Johns Hopkins Glacier

Mount
8750ft
2667m

Ja...
Po...

CAPE
FAIRWEATHER

FAIRWEATHER GLACIER

Lituya Mountain
11750ft
3582m

F A I R W E A T H E R

Johns Hopkins Glacier

Mount Orville
10495ft
3199m

Glacier

Mount
Crillon
12726ft
3879m

Mo...
Ber...
102...
311...

PACIFIC
OCEAN

Lituya Bay

North Crillon Glacier

R A N G E

Crillon
Lake

Mount La Perouse
10728ft
3270m

Lituya Glacier

La Perouse Glacier

Glacier

GLACIER B...
NATIONAL P...

Pal...
Be...

Icy Point

A...

Alaska Marine Highway System

Gustavus is accessible via the Alaska Marine Highway System (800.642.0066, dot.alaska.gov/amhs). During summer, ferries make regular trips from Juneau to Gustavus, 10 miles north of Bartlett Cove. This is an excellent method of arrival for individuals transporting kayaks, bikes, or a vehicle (bringing your vehicle isn't recommended for any short visit, camping is primitive, there are no RV facilities, most areas are accessed by foot).

North
↑

0   5   10   15 Kilometers
0   5   10   15 M...

1860 Historic extent of glaciation

▲ Campgrou...

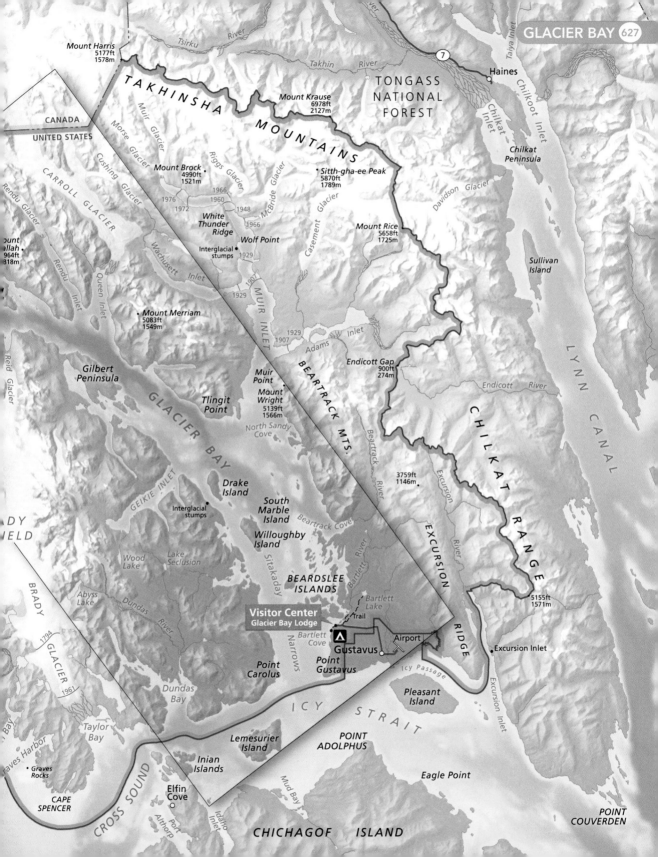

Mount Harris
5177ft
1578m

Tsirku River

Takhin River

7

Haines

Chilkoot Inlet

Taiya Inlet

CANADA

UNITED STATES

T A K H I N S H A

Mount Krause
6978ft
2127m

TONGASS
NATIONAL
FOREST

Chilkat
Inlet

Chilkat
Peninsula

CARROLL GLACIER

Muir Glacier

Morse Glacier

Cushing Glacier

M O U N T A I N S

Mount Brock
4990ft
1521m

Riggs Glacier

1966
1960

1976

1972

1948

McBride Glacier

1966

Sitth-gha-ee Peak
5870ft
1789m

Davidson Glacier

Sullivan
Island

Rendu Glacier

White
Thunder
Ridge

Wolf Point

Casement Glacier

Mount Rice
5658ft
1725m

ount
allah
964ft
318m

Rendu Inlet

Wachusett Inlet

Interglacial
stumps

1929

1907

1929

Adams Inlet

Mount Merriam
5083ft
1549m

Queen Inlet

M U I R I N L E T

1929
1907

Endicott Gap
900ft
274m

Endicott River

L Y N N C A N A L

Gilbert
Peninsula

Reid Glacier

Muir
Point

Mount
Wright
5139ft
1566m

B E A R T R A C K M T S.

Tlingit
Point

North Sandy
Cove

C H I L K A T R A N G E

G L A C I E R B A Y

Geikie Inlet

Drake
Island

Interglacial
stumps

South
Marble
Island

Beartrack Cove

Beartrack River

3759ft
1146m

Excursion River

Willoughby
Island

5155ft
1571m

DY
ELD

Wood
Lake

Lake
Seclusion

Sitakaday

B E A R D S L E E
I S L A N D S

Bartlett River

EXCURSION RIDGE

BRADY

Abyss
Lake

Dundas River

Narrows

Bartlett
Lake

Trail

1794

GLACIER

Visitor Center
Glacier Bay Lodge

Bartlett
Cove

Airport

Excursion Inlet

Excursion Inlet

1961

Point
Carolus

Dundas
Bay

Gustavus

Point
Gustavus

Icy Passage

Taylor
Bay

Pleasant
Island

Lemesurier
Island

I C Y   S T R A I T

POINT
ADOLPHUS

Eagle Point

Bay

Graves
Rocks

Inian
Islands

Mud Bay

CAPE
SPENCER

C R O S S   S O U N D

Elfin
Cove

Port Althorp

Idaho Inlet

C H I C H A G O F   I S L A N D

POINT
COUVERDEN

Park boundary

1925
1966

CANADA
UNITED STATES

Grand Pacific Glacier

Margerie Glacier

1907

Topeka Glacier

Johns Hopkins Glacier

1929 1966

Johns Hopkins Inlet

1912
1907

Jaw Point

Mount Cooper
6780ft
2066m

1941

Hoonah Glacier

Gilman Glacier

Lamplugh Glacier

Reid Glacier

1938

1892

1872

Russell Island

Mount Abdallah
5964ft
1818m

Rendu Glacier

Tarr Inlet

1892
1966

Gable Mountain
4780ft
1457m

CARROLL GLACIER

Cushing Glacier

Sentinel Peak
4355ft
1327m

👍 **Margerie Glacier**

Composite Island

1892

Rendu Inlet

Queen Inlet

1916
1966
1892

Mount Merriam
5083ft
1549m

Wachusett Inlet

1966

👍 **Johns Hopkins Glacier**

BRADY ICEFIELD

Scidmore Bay

Gilbert Peninsula

Mount Merriam

Gloomy Knob
1331ft
406m

-1416ft
-432m

1949

Blue Mouse Cove

Aurora Glacier

Hugh Miller Glacier

1892

1892

Hugh Miller Inlet

GLACIER BAY

Tribal Inlet

July Fourth Mountain
5007ft/1526m

Charpentier Inlet

Mount Bulky
3350ft
1021m

1966
1948

1892

1860

Tlingit Point

MUIR INLET

Sebree Island

Muir Point

🛶 **Muir Inlet**

GEIKIE INLET

Geikie Glacier

1892

Marble Mountain
3365ft
1026m

North Sandy Cove

1860

Blackthorn Peak
3789ft
1155m

Wood Lake

Tlingit Peak
3274ft
998m

Interglacial stumps

Drake Island

North Marble Island

1857

Spokane Cove

Abyss Lake

Serrated Peak
3327ft
1014m

Lake Seclusion

Whidbey Passage

Francis Island

South Marble Island

1845

Dundas River

Fingers Bay

Willoughby Island

Bong Bay

Beartrack Cove

White Cap Mountain
3299ft
1006m

Strawberry Island

🏕 **Bartlett Lake**

Dundas Bay

BEARDSLEE ISLANDS

Narrows

Sitakaday Narrows

1794

Visitor Center
Glacier Bay Lodge

Bartlett Cove

Trail

Bartlett Lake

Bartlett River

Park Headquarters

Point Carolus

-198ft
-60m

Point Gustavus

Park boundary

Glacier extent
1750–1780

North ↗

0   5 Kilometers
0   5 Miles

Lemesurier Island

ICY STRAIT

Gustavus

✈ Airport

9.3mi
15.0km

Falls Creek

1860 | Historic extent of glaciation

🏕 Campground

Camping & Lodging

Glacier Bay National Park has one primitive campground at **Bartlett Cove**. It's a free walk-in, tent-only camp, located 0.25-mile south of Bartlett Cove dock. It is open all year and features a bear-proof food cache, composting toilets, fire pit with firewood, and warming shelter near the shore. Group camping is available for groups of 12 or more. To use the campground, you must first obtain a free permit and participate in a 30-minute orientation program. The permit application is online. Showers are available at Glacier Bay Lodge during summer. Feel free to contact the Visitor Information Station (907.697.2627) about site availability prior to arrival.

Glacier Bay Lodge (888.229.8687, visitglacierbay.com) is the only hotel in the park. All rooms can accommodate up to four guests and have a private bath and/or shower. Fairweather Dining Room serves breakfast, lunch, and dinner. Rooms start at $250/night and they offer packages with boat tours and breakfast. The lodge is open from mid-May through early September.

Paddling

Looking to get up close and personal to whales, wildlife, and glaciers? If so, put a paddle in your hands, a boat in the water, and begin exploring the wonders of Glacier Bay.

Muir Inlet is a great place to paddle because it's off-limits to motorized boats in summer. Paddlers can bring their own boats via the Alaska Marine Highway System, but rental and guide services are available. Glacier Bay Sea Kayaks (907.697.2257, glacierbayseakayaks.com) provides rentals ($60/day, single, $75/day, double), and half-day ($95/person) and full-day ($150) guided tours. Day rentals include an hour-long safety orientation, and you must have a paddling partner. They also rent kayaks for extended paddling trips ($60/day, single; $75/day, double). Finally, they also offer guided backcountry trips (they provide kayaks and safety equipment; you bring clothes, camping equipment, food, and anything else you need). Glacier Bay Lodge's tour boat provides drop-offs at designated backcountry sites in summer. A free wilderness permit and camping orientation (at Bartlett Cove) are required for all overnight stays in the backcountry.

Spirit Walker Expeditions (800.529.2537, seakayakalaska.com), Mountain Travel Sobek (888.831.7526, mtsobek.com), and Alaska on the Home Shore (800.287.7063, homeshore.com) also offer multi-day kayaking expeditions.

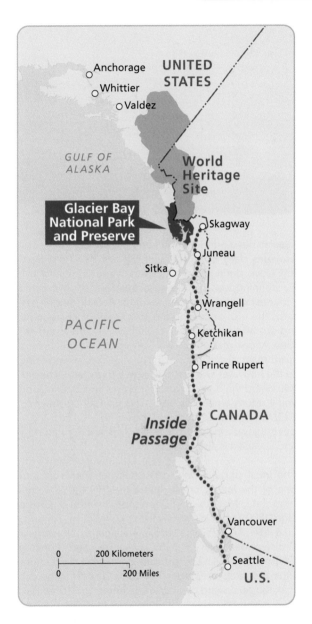

Boat Tours & Cruises

Commercial boat tours and cruises are the easiest, and in some respects, the best way to explore the inlets and coves of Glacier Bay. Kayaking is more peaceful. A boat tour is more efficient and flexible. Visitors spending the night in Bartlett Cove or Gustavus can embark on a full-day tour of the bay. Others come and go aboard massive luxury liners or specialized expedition cruise ships. Bring rain gear, binoculars, and warm layers of clothing no matter what time of year you plan on touring the bay.

A bear strolling the beach

Glacier Bay Lodge (888.229.8687, visitglacierbay.com) provides daily **boat tours** of Glacier Bay from Bartlett Cove during summer. The voyage is highlighted by stunning views of tidewater glaciers, snow-capped mountains, and abundant wildlife. A park ranger narrates the trip, discussing the area's history while pointing out whales, sea lions, coastal bears, seals, and eagles. At one glacier, you will wait up to 30 minutes for a giant mass of snow and ice to break free, plummeting to the icy water and crashing with a thunderous boom. You board the boat at 7am, departure is at 7:30am, and you'll return around 3:30pm. The full-day cruise costs $227/adult and $118/child (ages 3–12). Lunch and a beverage are included. One-way service for campers and kayakers is also available.

The most popular way to visit Glacier Bay is aboard one of the **luxury cruise liners** that ply these waters from late May to mid-September. Carnival Cruise Line (800.764.7419, carnival.com), Holland America Line (877.932.4259, hollandamerica.com), Norwegian Cruise Lines (866.234.7350, ncl.com), and Princess Cruises (800.774.6237, princess.com) offer 4–22-night trips that stop at Glacier Bay for a day (9–10 hours). Park rangers board the ship upon entering Glacier Bay. Cruise ships do not dock in the park, and they depart from various locations along the Pacific Coast including Vancouver, Seattle, and San Francisco. The base rate is around $100 per night per person.

Cruises are off-putting to some. Un-Cruise Adventures (888.862.8881, uncruise.com) or Linblad Special Expeditions (800.397.3348, expeditions.com) offer something slightly different. Groups are smaller, guides are knowledgeable experts and easily accessible, and all side trips are planned and included in the tour price. They are considerably more expensive. These tours cost about $600–1,200 per night per person.

Private Boating

Private boaters wanting to enter Glacier Bay from the beginning of June until the end of August must obtain a free permit and complete an annual boater orientation at the Visitor Information Station. 25 permits are available each day. 13 are available in advance (online application). 12 are available short notice (48 hours prior to entry date). Vessel operators may apply for permits by e-mail, phone, fax, VHF radio, mail, or in person at the Bartlett Cove Visitor Information Station (VIS). All motorized vessels are required to notify KWM20 Bartlett Cove before entering the park. Permits must be confirmed at least 48 hours before your scheduled entry date or your permit will be cancelled. Contact the VIS (907.697.2627) for more information.

Whitewater Rafting

Whitewater rafting is possible on the Alsek River and its major tributary, the Tatshenshini River. Both are large volume, swift glacial rivers that breach the coastal range passing through Tatshenshini–Alsek Provincial Park in Canada and Glacier Bay National Preserve in Alaska. A typical trip begins on the Tatshenshini at Shawshe (Dalton Post). This is the last road-accessible put-in off Haines Highway in Canada. The trip is 153 miles, including six miles of continuous Class III whitewater through a canyon below Shawshe. It usually takes about six days. A permit ($25 to be placed on waiting list, $100 fee for permit) is required for private trips.

Several outfitters provide 10+ day expeditions along the Alsek–Tatshenshini. Nahanni River Adventures (800.297.6927, nahanni.com), Chilkat Guides (907.313.4420, chilkatguides.com), and Tatshenshini Expediting (867.633.2742, tatshenshiniyukon.com) offer a multitude of Alaska/Yukon paddling trips. It costs around $3,500 per person for the Alsek.

Hiking

There are only four maintained trails. **Forest Loop** (1 mile) begins at Glacier Bay Lodge and passes through a temperate rain forest, returning along the shore. During summer, park rangers lead guided walks along this trail every afternoon. The 4-mile (roundtrip) **Bartlett River Trail** heads north from the road to Gustavus along an intertidal lagoon through spruce-hemlock forest before ending at Bartlett River estuary, an excellent place to spot wildlife such as ducks, geese, moose, bear, and river otter. In late summer you might come across hungry harbor seals feeding on salmon as they run up the river. The 10-mile (roundtrip) **Bartlett Lake Trail** diverges from Bartlett River Trail at a signpost located about 0.25-mile into the hike and then climbs to Bartlett Lake following a rugged primitive path. You can also reach the lake via **Towers Trail** (the first 1.7 miles is open to biking). **Tlingit Trail** (1 mile) strolls along the stretch of shoreline near the lodge. You can also hike the shore around Point Gustavus.

Backpacking & Mountaineering

With no maintained trails in the park's wilderness backpackers are left to their own devices when negotiating the unforgiving terrain of Glacier Bay's mountains and shorelines. Alpine meadows, rocky coasts, and deglaciated areas provide a wealth of hiking opportunity where you may not encounter another human for days at a time. One thing you're sure to stumble upon is alder. This successional plant grows in abundance along beaches, stream edges, avalanche chutes, and mountain slopes. Hiking is much more tedious than paddling largely due to alder's presence, which is notorious for slowing down and aggravating hikers. Wherever you plan on going, it is imperative that backpackers are well-prepared and have planned their trip thoroughly prior to heading into the backcountry. Areas of the park are often closed to campers due to animal activity. Always ask a park ranger for closure updates before you depart. A free permit and orientation program (Bartlett Cove) are required for overnight camping in the backcountry. This is also an opportunity to check out a bear-resistant food container (BRFC). Food and scented items must be stored in your BRFC. If you'd like to let someone else take care of logistics, Alaska Mountain Guides (800.766.3396, alaskamountainguides.com) offers guided hiking, climbing, and paddling tours.

Fishing

Anglers come to Glacier Bay in search of halibut and salmon. Fishermen 16 years and older require a valid Alaska State Fishing License, which can be purchased at Glacier Bay Lodge during summer. Elfin Cove Resort (888.922.3474, elfincoveresort.com), Alaska Anglers Inn (866.510.2800, alaskaanglersinn.com), Glacier Bay Sportfishing (907.697.3038, glacierbaysportfishing.com), Doc Warner's (801.298.8060, docwarners.com), Eagle Charters (907.239.2242, eaglecharters.com), Wild Alaska Inn (907.697.2704, glacier-bay.com), Taylor Charters (801.647.3401, taylorchartersfishing.com), Gull Cove Alaska (907.209.5149, gullcove.com), and Alaska Yacht Charters (206.780.0822, alaskansong.com) offer fishing and vacation packages near Glacier Bay.

Flightseeing

Leave the cruise ships behind and enjoy the spectacular scenery of Glacier Bay with a unique aerial

Bartlett Cove

view. Here's a list of Glacier Bay flightseeing companies along with contact info and their point of departure: Fly Drake (907.314.0675, flydrake.com, Haines & Skagway), Mountain Flying Service (907.766.3007, mountainflyingservice.com, Haines & Skagway), Ward Air (907.789.9150, wardair.com, Juneau), and Yakutat Coastal Airlines (907.784.3831, flyyca.com, Yakutat).

Visitor Center

The **Visitor Center** (907.697.2661), located on the second floor of Glacier Bay Lodge, is open daily from late May to early September. Exhibits are open 24-hours, and the information desk and bookstore are usually staffed from 11am to 9pm. The **Visitor Information Station** for boaters and campers, located at the head of the public-use dock in Bartlett Cove, is open Monday through Friday, May to September. Hours are typically from 8am to 5pm. **Yakutat Ranger Station** (907.784.3295) provides rafting info. Call before stopping in to make sure a ranger is present.

Ranger Programs & For Kids

From Memorial Day weekend to Labor Day weekend, park rangers host events from morning walks to evening talks. And rangers join cruise ships and tour boats to enhance the bay-viewing experience.

Your child can become the next Junior Ranger one of two ways (depending on your mode of transportation). If you come by plane or private boat, stop by the visitor center on the second floor of Glacier Bay Lodge. Here, you can obtain an activity booklet. Once completed, return the booklet to a park ranger to be inducted into this special club and earn a Junior Ranger badge. Most cruise ships have a children's center where they offer a Junior Ranger Program that can be completed over the course of the cruise. Park rangers offer a special program while they're onboard your ship.

A moose munching on flowers

Flora & Fauna

Life in and around Glacier Bay is constantly changing. As glaciers continue to recede a succession of plant life appears in its path. Lichens, moss, fireweed, cottonwood, and willows all grow where glaciers used to exist. Western hemlock and Sitka spruce make up the temperate rain forests. Moose immigrated to the park and were first spotted in 1966. Glacier Bay is part of humpback whales feeding grounds during their annual summer migration. Other large mammals include orca, black and brown bears, wolves, mountain goats, harbor seals, Steller sea lions, and porpoises. 281 species of birds have been recorded in the park. And you can look for a variety of shorebirds, waterfowl, and raptors right from Bartlett Cove.

Pets & Accessibility

Pets are only allowed at Bartlett Cove Public Use Dock, on the beach between the dock and the National Park Service Dock, within 100 feet of Bartlett Cove Developed Area's park roads and parking areas, and on a vessel in open water. Pets must be on a leash (less than six feet). They are prohibited from all trails, beaches (except already mentioned), and backcountry.

Glacier Bay Lodge has wheelchair-accessible rooms upon request. Forest Trail is partially accessible. Contact specific tour operators for accessibility.

Weather

Pack your rain gear! Bartlett Cove receives about 70 inches of precipitation each year. On average, 228 days of the year experience some form of precipitation. April, May, and June are usually the driest months. Most visitors arrive between late May and mid-September. September and October tend to be the wettest months. Temperature is greatly influenced by the Pacific Ocean. Summers are typically cool and moist, while winters are mild and cool. During the summer you can expect highs between 50 and 60°F near sea level. As elevation increases it becomes cooler and windier. Being Alaska, you probably expect long, harsh winters. That isn't exactly the case. Winters here are comparable to the Pacific Northwest. Snowy and cold but not unbearably so.

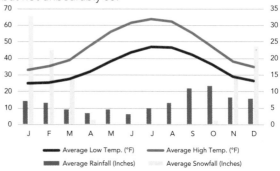

Tips & Recommendations

The park restricts Glacier Bay visitation during the summer months. Two cruise ships, three tour boats, six charter vessels, and 25 private vessels are allowed each day, so it's never excessively busy.

Something like 97% of all Glacier Bay visitors arrive aboard a cruise ship, so chances are that's how you'll visit too. But you can have a more personal experience by flying into Gustavus, spending the night at the lodge at Bartlett Cove, and arranging tours from there. (You're going to want to arrange kayak/boat tours well in advance.)

One of the first things you should do after boarding a cruise ship is scout it for good viewing locations.

Cruise ship passengers should consider going against the flow, watching for wildlife early in the morning or late in the evening.

Cruise ships typically spend a full day (9–10 hours) in Glacier Bay, with an hour at a major tidewater glacier, waiting for ice to calve (which is not guaranteed). Know what time your ship will be at the glacier! And spend as much of the time in the bay as you can enjoying the scenery and wildlife.

Humpback whales are more commonly seen closer to the mouth of Glacier Bay around Baranof Island, so choose a good perch and get your binoculars out long before reaching the tidewater glaciers.

Johns Hopkins Inlet

Be sure to take advantage of the park rangers who will be onboard your ship while cruising Glacier Bay. Join the ranger programs if you like that sort of thing, and encourage your children to participate in the special Junior Ranger Program.

Dress in layers and bring rain gear. It typically rains two out of every three days, and average highs are in the mid-50s/low 60s°F, made cooler by strong winds and icy glaciers.

There are additional lodging accommodations in Gustavus, as well as the primitive campground at Bartlett Cove, and more lodging accommodations and a public use cabin at Dry Bay. Glacier Bay Lodge is convenient, but it usually books early, leaving many visitors looking for lodging alternatives.

Beyond the Park...

If you don't arrive by cruise, it's likely you'll eat where you stay, but there are a few options at Gustavus. Juneau is not far away, but, like the park, it is not accessible by vehicle from the mainland. You must arrive via plane or ferry.

Dining
Fireweed Gallery, Coffee and Tea House • (907) 697-3013
4 Corners, Gustavus
fireweedcoffee.com

Grocery Stores
ToshCo • (907) 697-2220
Chinook Dr, Gustavus

Lodging
Glacier Bay Country Inn
35 Tong Rd, Gustavus
(907) 697-2288
glacierbayalaksa.com

Bear Track Inn • (907) 697-3017
5021 Rink Creek Rd, Gustavus
beartrackinn.com

Attractions
Sea Wolf Adventures
22 Glenn's Ditch Rd, Gustavus
(907) 957-1438
seawolfadventures.net

Glacier Bay Sea Kayaks
2 Parker Dr, Gustavus
(907) 697-2257
glacierbayseakayaks.com

Spirit Walker Expeditions
1 Grandpas Farm Rd, Gustavus
(800) 529-2537
seakayakalaska.com

Great Alaskan Lumberjack Show
420 Spruce Mill Way, Ketchikan
(907) 225-9050
alaskalumberjackshow.com

Alaska Raptor Center
1000 Raptor Way, Sitka
alaskaraptor.org • (907) 747-8662

Sockeye Cycle
24 Portage St, Haines
(907) 766-2869
381 5th Ave, Skagway
(907) 983-2851
sockeyecycle.com

Skagway Museum
700 Spring St, Skagway
Skagway.org

Klondike Gold Rush NHP
Skagway
nps.gov/klgo • (907) 983-9200

Misty Fjords National Mon

Alaskan Brewing Co
5364 Commercial Blvd, Juneau
alaskanbeer.com • (907) 780-5866

Mendenhall Glacier
Massive glacier in Tongass National Forest located about 12 miles from downtown Juneau.

Goldbelt Tram • (888) 461-8726
490 S Franklin St, Juneau
goldbelttram.com

Glacier Gardens Rainforest
7600 Glacier Hwy, Juneau
(907) 790-3377
glaciergardens.com

Alaska Icefield Expeditions
Dogsledding tours
1650 Maplesden Way, Juneau
akdogtour.com • (907) 983-2886

Alaska State Museum
395 Whittier St, Juneau
(907) 465-2901
museums.alaska.gov

Wrangell–St. Elias

Mount Drum

Phone: (907) 822-5234
Website: nps.gov/wrst

Established: December 2, 1980
November 16, 1978 (National Mon.)
Size: 13.2 Million Acres
Annual Visitors: 80,000
Peak Season: June–August

Activities: Hiking, Backpacking, Mountaineering, Flightseeing, Rafting, Floating, Hunting, Fishing

Campgrounds: None
Camping is allowed at pullouts along McCarthy and Nabesna Roads (no water; first-come, first-served)
Backcountry Camping: Permitted (backcountry permit not required)

Park Hours: All day, every day
Entrance Fee: None

"The region is superlative in its scenic beauty and measures up fully and beyond the requirements for its establishment as a National Monument and later as a National Park. It is my personal view that from the standpoint of scenic beauty, it is the finest region in Alaska. I have traveled through Switzerland extensively, have flown over the Andes, and am familiar with the Valley of Mexico and with other parts of Alaska. It is my unqualified view that this is the finest scenery that I have ever been privileged to see."

– Ernest Gruening
Director of U.S. Territories/Governor of Alaska/U.S. Senator

Wrangell–St. Elias National Park lies in the southeastern corner of Alaska, a few hundred miles south of the Arctic Circle. It's far from the northernmost point in Alaska, but these jagged mountains—including 9 of the 16 highest peaks on United States' soil—harbor more than 60% of Alaska's glacial ice. Scientists estimate 150 glaciers fill the valleys and ravines between mountain ridgelines. One of them, Malaspina, is larger than Rhode Island. Not only are the glaciers big, the park is monstrous, easily the largest in the United States. It's nearly four times the size of Death Valley, the largest national park in the contiguous United States. It isn't only big. It's beautiful. But few guests see the park's majesty beyond what's visible from two primitive roads and the coast.

Such a vast expanse of eye-catching mountains should not go unnoticed or unexplored for thousands of years, but this is the case of Wrangell–St. Elias. Mount St. Elias, the second highest mountain in the United States (at 18,008 feet), was unnamed until the feast day of St. Elias in 1741 when Vitus Bering spotted it while exploring the Alaskan coast. Mount Wrangell was named for Baron Ferdinand Petrovich von Wrangell, a Russian naval officer, arctic explorer, government administrator, and main opponent to selling Alaska to the United States. Despite his protest, in 1867 Alaska was sold for $0.03 per acre. And the rest, as they say, is history. Eyak and Tlingit people lived in villages along the coast for thousands of years and in the middle Copper Basin for at least the last 1,000, but Americans didn't penetrate the western Wrangell Mountains until 1885. Scientific expeditions occurred, but not until the gold rush in 1899 did the region receive any significant attention. More than one billion pounds of ore were hauled out of Kennecott mines during 27 years of operation. The mining boom went bust and tourism gradually took hold.

Camping & Lodging

There are no developed campgrounds, but visitors can **camp** at pullouts along McCarthy and Nabesna Roads. These pullouts are perfect for small to medium RVs, camper trailers, pick-up campers, or tents. All sites are primitive and available on a first-come, first-served basis. You'll find pullouts at Mileposts 6.1, 16.6, 21.8, 27.8, and 35.3 along Nabesna Road and Mileposts 1.6, 17.3, 29, and 55.2 along McCarthy Road.

There are also fourteen **backcountry cabins** (primitive, no water, pit toilet, bring toilet paper). Viking Lodge (Nabesna Road), Caribou Creek (Nabesna Road), Nugget Creek (Kotsina Road), and Esker Stream (Yakutat) accept reservations. The rest are first-come, first-served. Most cabins are extremely remote, requiring significant trip planning or access by air-taxi. All of them have a woodstove and bunks. Sleeping and dining gear are not provided. Leave the cabin stocked with firewood (if available) and at least as clean as it was when you arrived.

Lodging is available at **Devil's Mountain Lodge** (707.400.6848, devilsmountainlodge.com, $150–250/night, sheep and moose hunting trips), located at the end of Nabesna Road. **Ma Johnson's Historical Hotel** (907.554.4402, majohnsonhotel.com, $249–319/night) and **Kennicott Glacier Lodge** (800.582.5128, kenicottlodge.com, $210–330/night) are found at the end of McCarthy Road. The lodges are typically open from late May until early September. And then you

Climbing Mount Sanford

When to Go
Most visitors arrive at Wrangell–St. Elias National Park between early June and mid-September, peaking in July and August. The park never closes, but services are extremely limited beyond the tourism season and only the hardiest of visitors who possess extremely proficient winter survival skills visit from fall through spring.

Transportation
Interior Alaska Bus Line (800.770.6652, interioralaskabusline.com) and Soaring Eagle Transit (907.822.4545, gulkanacouncil.org) can get you around Alaska's interior. Traveling from Anchorage to Fairbanks costs about $160 per person. Wrangell Mountain Transport (wrangellmountaintransport.com), Kennicott Shuttle (907.822.5292, kennicottshuttle.com), and Blackburn Heritage Foundation (425.351.5021) provide shuttle service between Glennallen and McCarthy. Wrangell Mountain Air (907.554.4411, wrangellmountainair.com) will fly you to McCarthy from Chitina.

Directions
Wrangell–St. Elias is one of three road-accessible Alaskan national parks. Two rough gravel roads penetrate the park's interior. McCarthy Road begins at Chitina, where it enters the park and continues 60 miles into its heart at Kennecott. Nabesna Road enters the northern border at Slana and continues for 42 miles to Nabesna, an old mining town. Directions provided below begin at Glennallen, AK, which is about 170 miles east of Anchorage along AK-1.

McCarthy Road: From Glennallen head south for 31 miles on AK-4 toward Valdez. Continuing south you'll pass through Copper Center, where the main park visitor center, theater, and exhibit building are located, before turning left at Edgerton Highway/AK-10. Continue east for nearly 34 miles to Chitina, where McCarthy Road enters the park.

Nabesna Road: From Glennallen, head north on AK-1/AK-4. Continue almost 73 miles. Turn right at Nabesna Rd, pass through Slana and into the park.

have even more remote options like **Ultima Thule's fly-in lodge** (907.854.4500, ultimathulelodge.com, ~$9,000 per person for 4 nights, all meals and fly-out experiences included). With options for all budgets, you'll want to spend a night or three (unless your plan is to go flightseeing). You could look at 4-mile Root Glacier Trail and think you can do it in a day. It's two hours down McCarthy Road, but then you'll have to hike or shuttle another five miles to Kennecott, where the trailhead's located. And then you have to return. Long summer days will be on your side but it's a good idea to pace yourself. Plus, the lodges are quite charming.

Driving

McCarthy Road follows the path of an old railway constructed in 1909 to support the booming mining industry at Kennecott Mill. It's a dusty, winding, gravel road, but during summer most passenger vehicles can make the trip. The primitive journey from Chitina to Kennecott is 60 miles and takes about two hours (one-way). At the end of the road, you have a mile walk to McCarthy, and Kennecott Mines National Historic Landmark is five miles away. Shuttles should be available from the footbridge. Complimentary shuttle is provided if you're staying at a lodge. From Kennecott you can continue on to Root Glacier.

In 1934, **Nabesna Road** was built to simplify ore transportation to the coast. More than 75 years later very little has changed. It's a rough, twisting, 42-mile gravel road with unparalleled scenic value. It is typically accessible to all passenger vehicles, but at times creek crossings beyond Mile 29 can be problematic.

Both roads provide exceptional wildlife viewing opportunities. Do not travel without a full-size spare and an adequate jack. No fuel or services are available along these roads and cell phone service is extremely limited.

Hiking, Backpacking & Mountaineering

There are five short, maintained trails near Copper Center. **Boreal Forest Trail** (0.5-mile loop) begins at the Main Visitor Center. In Glennallen you'll find **Aspen Interpretive Trail** (1.0 mile, roundtrip). The trailhead is located on Co-op Road just off AK-1. **Tonsina River Trail** (2.0 miles) begins just beyond mile marker 12 of AK-10/Edgerton Highway. It leads to a perch overlooking Tonsina River. **Liberty Falls Trail** (2.5 miles) begins just before mile marker 25 of AK-10. **O'Brien to Haley Creek Trail** (10.0 miles) begins on O'Brien Creek Road near Chitina.

Several maintained trails begin from **Nabesna Road**, including **Caribou Creek** (6.0 miles, Mile 19.2, leads to backcountry cabin), **Skookum Volcano** (5.0 miles, Mile 36.2), and **Rambler Mine** (1.5 miles, Mile 42.5). They provide spectacular views of rugged terrain. Near **Kennecott/McCarthy Road** you can hike these trails: **Crystalline Hills** (2.5 miles, Mile 34.8), **Root Glacier** (4.0 miles, Kennecott Visitor Center), **Donoho Basin** (14 miles roundtrip to Donoho Summit, multi-day, follows Root Glacier Trail), or **Jumbo Mine** (10 miles, Root Glacier Trailhead). Most **backpackers** prefer to hike above the tree line where vegetation and mosquitoes are more manageable. Many day-hikes and multi-day trips require river crossings. Use proper judgment when selecting an area to cross. Hypothermia is a threat, even in summer. Adequate planning is required for a successful trip. Be sure you have the right gear, a good topographic map, and are comfortable camping in bear-country. Proper food storage is required. Bear-resistant food containers are available at any visitor center. And there are bear-proof lockers on the way to Root Glacier/Donoho Basin. Permits are not required for backcountry trips, but completing a backcountry itinerary (available at any park office) is encouraged. Leave your itinerary with friends or family. If you do not return on schedule, rangers will not administer a search party until a formal request is made by a friend or family member. Many hikers choose to hire a local guide to help ensure a safe and enjoyable trip. Guides also lead visitors on mountain climbing expeditions. With 9 of the 16 highest peaks on U.S. soil within park boundaries, Wrangell–St. Elias is a popular destination among mountain climbers.

A guide is a good idea. St. Elias Alpine Guides (907.231.6395, steliasguides.com) is the place to start. They do it all, day trips, rafting, backpacking, mountaineering, ski trips. They've been helping visitors make the most of their Wrangell–St. Elias trips for more than 40 years. Trek Alaska (907.795.5252, trekalaska. com, hiking & backpacking) and Kennicott Wilderness Guides (800.664.4537, kennicottguides.com, hiking, backpacking, ice climbing, rafting) are the next two to check out. There are many other companies leading trips here, including many of the outfitters listed in other park sections, but these are the ones based in the area who have been doing it for quite some time.

Flightseeing

To truly grasp the size of Wrangell–St. Elias National Park you should fly above it, peering across massive sheets of ice and jagged mountain ranges. Many local air taxi businesses provide flightseeing tours or backcountry drop-offs and pick-ups to otherwise unreachable regions. Wrangell Mountain Air (907.554.4411, wrangellmountainair.com), 40-Mile Air (907.883.5191, 40-mileair.com), Lee's Air Taxi (907.822.3574, leesairtaxi.com), Copper Valley Air Service (907.822.4200, coppervalleyairservice.com), Devil's Mountain Lodge (707.400.6848, devilsmountainlodge. com), Meekin's Air Service (907.745.1626, meekinsairservice.com), Ridgeline Aviation (907.429.6966, flyridgeline.com), and Tok Air Service (907.322.2903, flytokair.com) are here to help whenever you feel like lifting off to see some glaciers.

Rafting & Floating

Float trips, wild whitewater, and everything in between can be found at Wrangell–St. Elias. It's best to join an approved outfitter. McCarthy River Tours & Outfitters (907.302.0688, raftthewrangells.com) and Copper Oar (800.523.4453, copperoar.com) offer rafting trips. Guide companies also lead guests on sea kayaking trips at Icy Bay. Relatively "new" water, the bay was formed when four massive tidewater glaciers retreated beginning in 1900. Paddlers are usually dropped off at Kageet Point or Point Riou by air-taxi. Sea kayaking is a great way to spot marine and terrestrial wildlife.

Hunting & Fishing

Hunting is allowed in the preserve part of the park. Devil's Mountain Lodge (devilsmountainlodge. com) is the first place you should look into for a hunting trip. But Tim's Alaskan Guide Service (timsalaskanguideservice.com) and Wrangell Outfitters (wrangelloutfitters.com) offer horse-aided hunting trips and Tim also offers pack trips.

Sport fishing takes a backseat because of some of the more extreme activities in the area and legendary fishing sites further west in Alaska, but there are plenty of fish to catch here. Copper, Klutina, and Gulkana Rivers are accessible rivers where you might catch some salmon. Unfortunately, all the fishing guides frequent other Alaskan waters.

Visitor Centers

Copper Center Visitor Center (907.822.7250), located 10 miles south of the intersection of Glen and Richardson Highways, is a good place to start your trip to Wrangell–St. Elias. It houses exhibits, theater, bookstore, amphitheater, restrooms, and views of Mount Drum. Operating hours/dates change season-to-season, but it's usually open daily through summer, intermittently (as staffing allows) for spring and fall, and closed in winter. **Ahtna Cultural Center** (907.822.3535) is located next door. **Kennecott Visitor Center** (907205.7106) is located in Historic Kennecott Mill Town. It offers exhibits, film, ranger programs, bookstore, and backcountry trip planning. It's typically open in summer. **Slana Ranger Station** (907.822.7401) is located near the start of Nabesna Road and **Chitina Ranger Station** (907.823.2205) is located near the start of McCarthy Road. They can help with trip planning and area information, and are typically open in summer (staff permitting). At the end of McCarthy Road, you'll find a self-service information station that provides details on parking, shuttle service, Kennecott and McCarthy. For all these facilities, it's a good idea to call before visiting to verify they're open.

Ranger Programs & For Kids

In summer, Park Rangers provide talks, walks, and evening programs primarily at Copper Center Visitor Center and Kennecott. Go online or stop at a visitor center for a current schedule of activities. Note that the only way to tour Kennecott Mill is with St. Elias Alpine Guides (907.231.6395, steliasalpineguides.com). Tours cost $28/adult, $14/child and last two hours. Summer 2021 tours will be a little different than they were in the past as the National Park Service is busy working on construction and stabilization efforts in Kennecott.

Children are invited to learn about the park and its valuable resources by participating in the Junior Ranger Program. Visit the park's website, print an activity booklet, and complete it (either in the park or at home). Once it's finished, mail it to the park and a ranger will review your answers. For the effort, you'll be rewarded with a Wrangell–St. Elias Junior Ranger badge.

Flora & Fauna

Wrangell–St. Elias National Park features a variety of plants and animals. More than half of all Alaskan flora can be found in the Wrangells. Quaking aspen are the most prevalent tree, but paper birch and black and white spruce are also common. In all, more than 800 species of vascular plants color the landscape and provide nutrition for the park's residents. Animals include moose, bear (black and grizzly), lynx, caribou, mountain goats, wolves, bison, and the largest concentration of Dall sheep in North America.

Pets & Accessibility

Pets are allowed in the park but must be kept on a leash while in the Kennecott Historic Landmark area. Be aware that trapping is legal in Alaska from fall through spring.

Copper Center Visitor Center is accessible to wheelchair users, as are the recreation hall, visitor center, and Blackburn School at Kennecott. The mill is accessible by appointment only. An accessible backcountry cabin is available at Peavine (but you'll need to find an accessible bush plane).

Weather

Winters are long and cold (highs of 5–7°F). Summers are short but warm. Highs might sneak into the 80s°F on some days. Leaves typically begin to change by mid-August and the first significant snowfall arrives a month later.

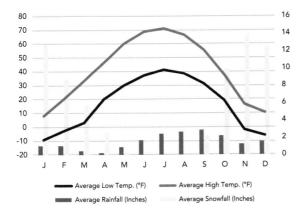

- Average Low Temp. (°F)
- Average High Temp. (°F)
- Average Rainfall (Inches)
- Average Snowfall (Inches)

Tips & Recommendations

If you'd like that truly once-in-a-lifetime Alaskan experience, think about staying at a lodge that intimately understands this vast region like Ultima Thule (ultimathulelodge.com). They'll be able to take you on bush plane-powered adventures deep into the Wrangells. I know that isn't in most traveler's budget, but still put strong consideration into flightseeing. Of all the Alaskan national parks, this would be my first choice to see the park and its many peaks and glaciers from above (a stop in the backcountry is even better). At the very least, go on a quick land-based day trip with St. Elias Alpine Guides (steliasalpineguides.com) in Kennecott.

Thanks to two dirt roads, there is a certain amount of accessibility, but you still have to come prepared, not full-on wilderness survival mode, but come prepared with snacks, toilet paper, a full tank of gas (fill up in Glenallen), and the spirit of adventure. A high-clearance vehicle is recommended, but most vehicles can navigate these roads under typical summer conditions. With that said, it's always a good idea to stop to speak with a ranger at Copper Center or near the start of the road before heading down it. Plan at least two hours each way for McCarthy Road and one and a half hours each way for Nabesna Road. Nabesna Road may be impassable beyond Mile 29 due to stream crossings, and the last four miles are unmaintained.

Most major rental car companies do not allow their vehicles to be driven on gravel roads. Many renters ignore these policies and drive wherever they like. Others will have to look for a smaller rental company like Alaska 4x4 Rentals (alaska4x4rentals.com) who allow their vehicles on maintained gravel roads. RVs and other oversized vehicles are not recommended.

Remember there are lodging options at the end of the roads, and it's a good idea to spend a night or two so you won't feel rushed reaching and exploring Kennecott. With that said, if you have to compromise between two nights in a remote lodge or a flightseeing tour of the Wrangells, sleep in a tent and get on board that plane.

From McCarthy, it's a five-mile hike to the historic Kennecott mine area. Shuttles are available in summer. Guided tours of Kennecott Mill are offered daily throughout summer by St. Elias Alpine Guides. They're two hours long and cost $28/adult. If you have a mixed-interest traveling party, St. Elias Alpine Guides has something for everyone.

Denali

Wonder Lake

Phone: (907) 683-9532
Website: nps.gov/dena

Established: February 26, 1917
Size: 6.1 Million Acres
Annual Visitors: 600,000
Peak Season: June–August

Activities: Bus/Shuttle Tours, Hiking, Backpacking, Mountaineering, Whitewater Rafting, Biking, Flightseeing, Fishing

6 Campgrounds*: $12–28/night
Backcountry Camping: Permitted
4 Private Backcountry Lodges

Park Hours: All day, every day
Entrance Fee: $15/individual (16 and older), Youth under 15 are free

*Reserve at reservedenali.com or (866) 761-6629

Denali, at 20,320 feet, is the tallest mountain in North America. It serves as the centerpiece and main attraction of Denali National Park. So tall and massive is this magnificent mountain that it creates its own weather, often in the form of clouds, which shroud its glory. When the clouds lift, Denali commands attention; from base to summit it is more prominent than Mount Everest, which rises 12,000 feet from its base on the Tibetan Plateau. Denali's base is at roughly 2,000-ft elevation, giving it a prominence of some 18,000 feet. Appropriately, the Koyukon Athabaskan people call the peak Denali or "The High One." It wasn't until 1869 that a failed businessman turned prospector named the mountain "McKinley" in honor of the presidential candidate who supported the gold standard. The name stuck just like its superlatives. In 1980, the park expanded and became Denali. However, North America's tallest peak was still officially McKinley until August 2015, when President Obama restored its native Alaskan name, Denali. To most, the name isn't what matters. This park and its majestic mountain, located in Alaska's interior, provide refuge for wildlife, respite for backpackers, and the ultimate challenge for mountain climbers.

People supposedly climb mountains because they're there, but the race to summit Denali was all about bragging rights. Frederick Cook, president of the Explorer's Club, claimed he reached the summit in 1903. And he returned with a picture to prove it. Another group retraced his route, duplicating the photo at a lower peak. In 1910 a group of prospectors boasted they were going to plant an American flag at the summit. It took them from January through April simply to reach the mountain's base and establish a camp. In May, two members wearing nothing but overalls and unlined parkas made a push for the summit with a thermos of hot chocolate and a bag of doughnuts. Amazingly, they backed up their words. The American flag was firmly planted at 19,470 feet, atop Denali's North Peak (850 feet lower than its South Peak). Three years later a group led by Alaska's Episcopal archdeacon, Hudson Stuck, climbed to the top of South Peak. The trek was so grueling and air so thin that Stuck blacked out repeatedly during ascent.

Just as the race to the summit was heating up, Charles Sheldon, a close friend of President Theodore Roosevelt, was wintering in a cabin on the Toklat River. While camped out in what was thought to be the last tract of unexploited American wilderness, he witnessed the slaughter of animals brought on by the rush of gold miners in 1903. He recorded his observations in a journal and later wrote *The Wilderness of Denali*. He described the idea of a park that would allow visitors to see Alaska as he saw it while living along the Toklat River, and spent years advocating a national park, delivering his proposal to Washington, D.C. by hand. On February 26, 1917, President Woodrow Wilson signed a bill creating Mount McKinley National Park, but it failed to include McKinley's summit in the preserved lands. Sheldon received additional disappointment when he learned the mountain and new park would not be returned to its original name, Denali. In 2015, the mighty mountain became Denali once more.

The area's distinctive wildlife and landscapes are protected from commercial interests, but the National Park Service can't shelter the environment from all threats. Changes in climate affect the environment in subtle ways. As you increase elevation there's a distinct tree line where average temperatures are too cold for trees to grow. As the climate warms, the tree line conspicuously rises. With continually increasing visitation, park staff must find new ways to manage and maintain the delicate habitat without ruining the experience. Limiting the 92-mile Denali Park Road to bus tours and enforcing backcountry permit quotas help maintain the pristine wilderness that Koyukon Athabascans, Charles Sheldon, and all past park visitors have enjoyed. With the work of the park rangers and conservation-minded patrons like yourself, Denali will remain the shining example of the Last Frontier.

Distant grizzlies

When to Go
The park is open all year, but Denali Park Road is first plowed beginning sometime in March (weather dependent) and is usually accessible to private vehicles sometime in April. Buses shuttling visitors along the road, begin in mid-May and run until mid-September. Most visitors arrive between June and August. The park usually turns green by the end of May and wildflowers begin to bloom in early June. Mosquitoes are most active in early summer. Chances of seeing the Northern Lights increase in fall as the days grow shorter.

Transportation & Airports
Denali Overland Transportation (907.733.2384, denalioverland.com) and Talkeetna Taxi (907.203.1381, talkeetnataxi.com) provide transportation service between Anchorage, Talkeetna, and the park.

Alaska Railroad (800.544.0552, alaskarailroad.com) connects Fairbanks and Anchorage, passing directly through the main park entrance. Car rental is available at each destination. One-way fare during peak season from Anchorage to Denali is $176/passenger and $79/passenger from Fairbanks to Denali.

Ted Stevens Anchorage International (ANC) and Fairbanks International (FAI) are the easiest destinations to fly into.

Directions
The 92-mile (one-way) Denali Park Road provides access to the park. Its first 15 miles are open to vehicles. The rest is only accessible on foot, bicycle, or shuttle bus during the summer tourism season.

From Anchorage (238 miles): Take AK-1/N/E 5th Ave north about 34 miles, where you continue onto Interstate A-4 W. Take AK-3 N/George Parks Way. After 201 miles, turn left onto Denali Park Road.

From Fairbanks (121 miles): Take AK-3 S/George Parks Highway 117 miles, and then turn right onto Denali Park Road.

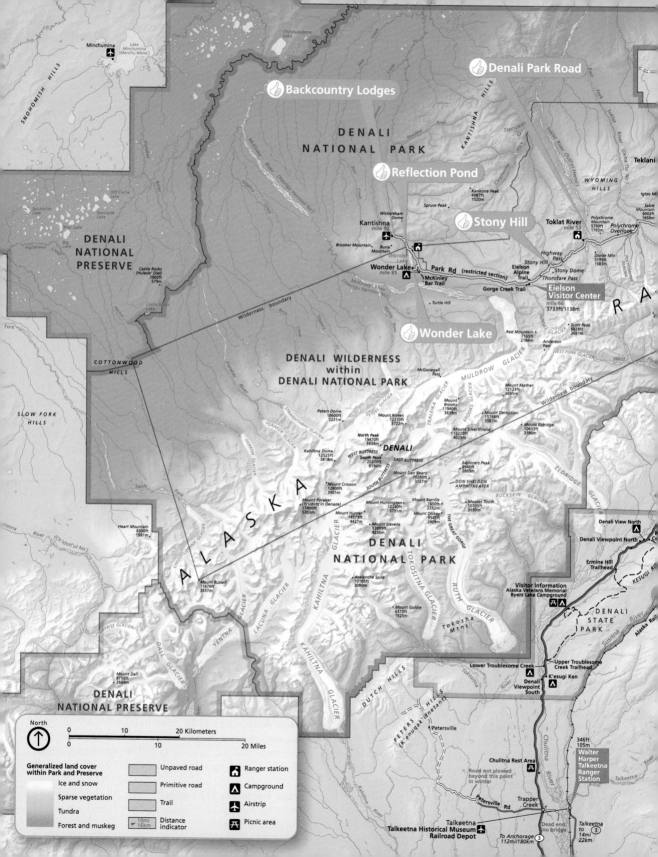

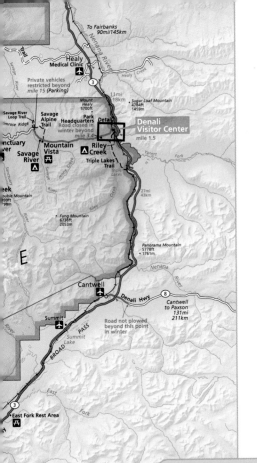

Camping & Lodging

There are six developed **campgrounds**, all located along Denali Park Road. Only two, Savage River and Wonder Lake, provide views of Denali. Since Riley Creek and Savage River Campgrounds are located within the first 15 miles of Denali Park Road, they are easily accessed via personal vehicles. You can also drive your vehicle/RV to Teklanika (Mile 29) if you spend a minimum of three nights there, but vehicles must stay at the campsite for the entire stay. You can also reach Teklanika via Camper Bus. A Tek Pass allows campers to use the park shuttle buses at will (space Permitting, but not beyond Teklanika) during your stay. Denali's most wondrous campground is the one located farthest from the park entrance: Wonder Lake (Mile 85). It is tent-only and accessible via Camper Bus. Just 26 miles from Denali, the behemoth of a mountain reflects upon the mirror-like water of Wonder Lake on clear days. This location is a wilderness lover's paradise, but there are a few drawbacks: cloudy skies often obscure Denali, and you're camping near water, a breeding ground for mosquitoes (often bad from mid-June until late August). A large food-storage building provides picnic tables where you can avoid the rain and bugs.

The park doesn't operate **lodging** facilities, but a few can be found on privately owned land within park boundaries around Kantishna. Denali Backcountry Lodge (800.808.8068, alaskacollection.com, Camp Denali & North Face Lodge (907.683.2290, campdenali.com, $675 per night per person, 3-night minimum), and Kantishna Roadhouse

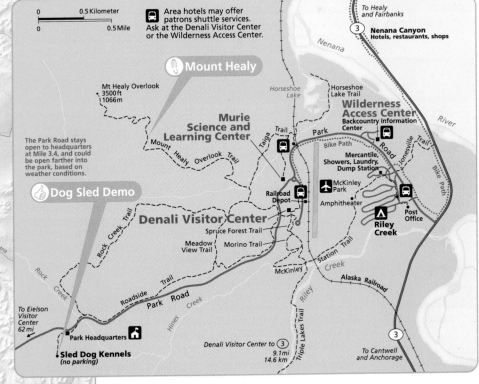

Beautiful views along Denali Park Road

Denali Shuttle Buses & Narrated Bus Tours

Name	Location	Duration	Fee	Notes
Toklat River*	Mile 53	6.5 hours	$50	Does not reach iconic Denali view at Stony Hill
Eielson Visitor Center*	Mile 66	8 hours	$60	45 minutes at the visitor center before turning around
Wonder Lake*	Mile 85	11 hours	$TBD	Heads to the south end of Wonder Lake
Kantishna* - ♨	Mile 92	13 hours	$TBD	Passes Reflection Pond, and north end of Wonder Lake
Camper Bus	Varies	Varies	$60	Must have camping reservation or backcountry permit
Natural History	Mile 17	4.5–5 hours	$101.75	Makes several stops, including a native presentation
Tundra Wilderness	Mile 53	7–8 hours	$162.50	Driving the road, looking for wildlife
Kantishna Experience	Mile 92	11–12 hours	$240.75	Complete Denali Park Road, all the way to Kantishna
*Reservations can be made beginning December 1 at (866) 761-6629 or reservedenali.com				
Three free courtesy buses connect popular points of interest in the park's main entrance area.				
Road Lottery	Every September for four days, lottery winners are permitted drive Denali Park Road as far as conditions allow. Single-day permit costs $25. The lottery is open during the month of June. Submit your name for the cost of a $15 non-refundable application fee at recreation.gov.			

Denali Camping (Fees are per night)

Name	Location	Open	Fee	Sites	Notes
Riley Creek*	Mile .25	All Year	$17/27/34	142	RVs up to 40 ft • W (summer), F, DS (free)
Savage River*	Mile 14	May–Sept	$27/34	32	Denali views, RVs up to 40 ft • W (summer), F
Sanctuary River**	Mile 22	May–Sept	$17	7	Tent-only, access via Camper Bus • P
Teklanika River*	Mile 29	May–Sept	$29	53	Vehicle/RV accessible with 3-night stay • W, P
Igloo Creek**	Mile 35	May–Sept	$17	7	Tent-only, access via Camper Bus • P
Wonder Lake* - ♨	Mile 85	June–Sept	$16***	28	Denali views, tent-only • W (summer), F

W = Water, F = Flush Toilets, P = Pit Toilets, DS = Dump Station; RV hookups are not available at any campground
Campground permits can be picked up at Riley Creek Mercantile located on Denali Park Road near the park entrance
Open and close dates subject to weather; Different fees apply to tent/RVs < 30 ft in length and RVs 30–40 ft in length
*Reservations can be made beginning December 1 at (866) 761-6629 or reservedenali.com
**Reservations are only available in person, no more than 2 days in advance at the WAC or Riley Creek Mercantile
***Prices do not include a one-time, non-refundable reservation fee of $6.50
Showers (fee), laundry (fee), Wi-Fi (free), and a camper convenience store are available at Riley Creek Mercantile

Backcountry	All overnight stays in the backcountry require a free wilderness permit. Permits are available at the Backcountry Information Center. You can apply for them online through the park's website. They must be obtained in person no more than 24 hours in advance of the first day of your trip.
Group	Sites available at Riley Creek ($49/night) and Savage Creek ($49) • Reserve at (866) 761-6629

(907.374.3041, kantishnaroadhouse.com, $560+ per person per night, 2-night minimum) are somewhat similar, offering all-inclusive stays and bus transportation to their property. Skyline Lodge (907.644.8222, katair.com, $501 per night for 2 guests, includes meals) can be reached by Camper Bus or fly-in (there's an airstrip in Kantishna).

And then Denali Bluffs Hotel (855.683.8600, denali-alaska.com) and Denali Princess Wilderness Lodge (800.426.0500, princesslodges.com) are near the park entrance. Additional overnight accommodations are available outside the park at Healy (11 miles north of the park entrance) and Cantwell (30 miles to the south).

Smoky/Cloudy Denali

Denali Park Road & Shuttle/Bus Tours

The 92-mile **Denali Park Road** provides the only easy access into the heart of the park. For all but four days, private vehicles are only allowed to travel to Savage River (Mile 15). Beyond this, traffic is restricted to shuttle buses and tour buses. **Shuttle buses** are less expensive and give passengers the freedom of being dropped off and picked up anywhere along the road (simply flag it down). They also make stops for wildlife viewing, restroom breaks, and beautiful scenery, including dramatic vistas of Denali (clouds permitting). If you want to hike, picnic, or just sit and admire mighty Denali, shuttles are the way to go. And even though they're "non-narrated," drivers usually add some context to what you're seeing. There are specially-designed camper shuttles for backpackers in which the rear seats are removed for packs and bikes. They stop at each campground and are reserved for individuals with camping reservations or backcountry permits. Shuttles typically run from late May through mid-September (weather permitting). Every September, once shuttles have stopped running, the park holds a **"Road Lottery"** through recreation.gov ($15 application fee). During these four days, lottery winners can purchase a single-day permit ($25) to drive the park road (as far as conditions will permit).

Bus tours are narrated by a trained naturalist (and driver), but they do not allow the freedom to exit and board wherever you please. Tours begin and end at various locations around the park entrance. They're listed in the table on the opposite page.

Shuttle bus and bus tour tickets can be reserved at (866) 761-6629 or reservedenali.com starting December 1. Reservations are recommended. If you plan on getting shuttle bus tickets upon arrival, you may have to wait a day or two before they become available.

Three free **courtesy buses** help visitors navigate the park entrance area while reducing parking requirements and traffic congestion. Bus stops are located at Wilderness Access Center and Denali Visitor Center. Shuttles serve Savage River Campground, Riley Creek Campground, and the Sled Dog Demonstration Area.

Hiking & Backpacking

Relative to its size there are very few hiking trails at Denali. Most exploration is done off-trail. Most maintained trails are located near the park entrance, and most of those are practical, connecting visitor facilities. McKinley Station Trail spans 1.6 miles between the Visitor Center and Riley Creek Campground. The Bike Path runs 1.7 miles from the Visitor Center to the Wilderness Access Center ending at the Park Entrance. Roadside (1.8 miles, one-way) and Rock Creek (2.4 miles, one-way) Trails connect the Visitor Center with Park Headquarters and the Sled Dog Kennels. Meadow View Trail is a 0.3-mile trail connecting Roadside and Rock Creek Trails. A few trails actually show off the area's impressive scenery. Spruce Forest Trail (0.2 miles, one-way) begins at Denali Visitor Center and explores a forested area where seasonal wildflowers and berries can be found. The 2-mile roundtrip hike to Horseshoe Lake circles the lake and extends to Nenana River. If you don't have enough time to explore the park's interior aboard one of the shuttle or tour buses, hike the 5.4-mile (roundtrip) **Mount Healy Overlook Trail**. It takes quite a bit of effort but shouldn't be a problem for the average day-hiker. You hike for a short distance along an exposed ridgeline where wind and weather are always unpredictable (pack a waterproof windbreaker). Mount Healy Overlook, Horseshoe Lake, and Rock Creek Trails are connected by the 0.9-mile Taiga Trail, beginning at the Visitor Center. Also from Denali Visitor Center, you can begin the 9.5-mile (one-way) Triple Lakes Trail. It loosely follows Riley Creek from

Mount Healy Overlook

McKinley Village to Hines Creek Bridge. To view Denali, stop at Mountain Vista Trailhead (Mile 13), where you'll find a short trail (0.7 miles). You can get there by private vehicle or the free Savage River Shuttle.

With proper preparation **backpacking** in Denali's wilderness can be one of the park's most rewarding adventures. You must craft your own itinerary, obtain a backcountry permit (online application up to two weeks before your trip), and practice proper backcountry hiking/camping techniques. Be conservative when estimating your daily mileage. Call the park to discuss itineraries. Or be prepared with several alternatives because many wilderness areas reach their quota during summer. There are no trails, terrain is challenging, and it's likely you'll have to make several river crossings. You'll pick up your permit at the Wilderness Access Center (Mile 0.75). They'll check to make sure you're ready for your trip. Each member must watch the summer backcountry safety videos (once per summer). Rangers will also update you on conditions. Make sure you have a camper bus ticket so you can reach your desired starting location along Denali Park Road. Backcountry campers must set-up camp at least a half-mile from and out of sight of the park road. Camp on durable surfaces where others have not camped before. Fires are not permitted, so bring a stove. Water should be filtered, treated, or boiled for one minute. Pack food and scented items in bear-resistant food containers. Backpackers can park their vehicle(s) at Riley Creek Camp's overflow parking area free of charge. Denali is huge. Bears are everywhere. Travel any significant distance and you're almost certain to encounter a creek in need of crossing. And there are no marked trails in the backcountry. These are just a few of the reasons visitors wishing to get in the backcountry should think about hiring a guide like Alaska Alpine Adventures (877.525.2577, alaskaalpineadventures.com).

Mountaineering

Denali is one of the premier mountaineering destinations in the world. Each year climbers from all over the globe test their climbing and wilderness survival skills against the 20,320-foot peak. If you plan on climbing Denali or Mt Foraker (17,400 feet), you must register with the park at least 60 days prior to your intended start date and pay a $375 per climber fee. (If you cancel prior to January 15 of the year in which the climb is scheduled, you will receive a $275 refund. Refunds will not be made for cancellations after January 15.) Pay the fee through pay.gov, and then apply for a special use permit online through the park's website. It's also a good idea to pay the park's entrance fee prior to arrival through pay.gov. All climbers must attend an in-person orientation at Talkeetna Ranger Station. Less than 1,000 climbers summit Denali each year, with a success rate around 50%. Climbing Denali requires much training, preparation, and experience. AK Mountaineering School (907.733.1016, climbalaska.org), Alpine Ascents International (206.378.1927, alpineascents.com), American Alpine Institute (360.671.1505, alpineinstitute.com), Mountain Trip International (970.369.1153, mountaintrip.com), N.O.L.S. (800.710.6657, nols.edu), and Rainier Mountaineering (888.892.5462, rmiguides.com) are authorized to lead intrepid individuals on summit attempts. Should you choose to use an unauthorized guide, your trip may be cancelled at any time. Contact Walter Harper Talkeetna Ranger Station (907.733.2231) with any mountaineering questions.

Whitewater Rafting

Private outfitters near the park entrance provide exhilarating whitewater adventures through the 10-mile Nenana River Canyon or float trips along its more placid stretches. Denali Raft Adventures (907.683.2234, denaliraft.com) and Raft Denali (800.789.7238, raftdenali.com) offer 2–6-hour trips ranging from $102 to $240 per person. Raft Denali also offers overnight trips.

Biking

Pedaling a mountain bike along the 92-mile Denali Park Road is a fantastic way to see the sights and get a bit (or an awful lot) of exercise along the way. The first 15 miles from the Park Entrance to Savage River are paved. The rest is narrow, graded gravel road without shoulders. Cyclists can shorten their trip by driving to Savage River or loading your bicycle onto one of the park buses. If you're overnighting it at the campgrounds or in the backcountry, camper buses have space for two bikes. It's a good idea to purchase your bus ticket over the phone and let them know you wish to bring a bike along. You must have a campground reservation or backcountry permit to reserve bike space. If you're planning to pedal all the way to Wonder Lake, know that it's a fairly steep descent from Eielson Visitor Center (Mile 66) to Wonder Lake (Mile 85), and that you have 50 miles between Igloo Creek and Wonder Lake Campgrounds. Cyclists are allowed on park roads, parking areas, campground loops, and the designated campground Bike Trail between Nenana River and Denali Visitor Center. Bikes are not permitted on any park trails or in the backcountry. Fat tire bikes do not fit in the buses bike racks. Rentals are available at Bike Denali (907.378.2107, bikedenali.com). Rates start at $75 for 24 hours (includes rain gear and bear spray). Or, if you stay at a place like Denali Backcountry Lodge (800.808.8068, alaskacollection.com), they have bikes you can check out and you'll start deep in the park's backcountry.

Flightseeing

Flightseeing gives visitors the opportunity to see Denali at eye level as you soar high above climbers attempting the much more laborious journey to its summit. From the air you gain a new appreciation for the park's immensity and its mountain. Flightseeing also provides the unique opportunity to land on a glacier where you can partake in a summertime snowball fight or make a snow angel. Fly Denali (907.683.2359, flydenali.com), Sheldon Air Service (907.733.2321, sheldonairservice.com), K2 Aviation (907.733.2291, flyk2.com), and Talkeetna Air Taxi (907.733.2218, talkeetnaair.com) are authorized park concessioners for flightseeing trips. They offer a variety of routes and itineraries, ranging in price from $220–549/person. Trips are weather dependent. Morning is usually better. Kantishna Air Taxi (907.644.8222, katair.com) provides taxi service to the Kantishna Airstrip (if you want to stay at one of the lodges and skip the bus ride in) as well as flightseeing tours.

Fishing

Denali is not renowned for its fishing like other Alaskan parks/areas, but fishermen enjoy dipping their line in Wonder Lake or one of the park's many streams. A state fishing license is required to fish at Wonder Lake or streams flowing into the Savage River. It's always a good idea to talk to the park about fishing locations, catch limits, and regulations before arriving.

Winter Activities

Just because the temperature drops below 32°F doesn't mean activities in the park come to a freezing halt. Winter visitors will find Murie Science & Learning Center open year-round, and from here you can head

Biking down Denali Park Road

into the park on cross-country skis, snowshoes, dog sleds, or snowmobiles (in designated areas). Chances are you won't bring your own sled dog team on vacation. EarthSong Lodge (907.683.2863, earthsonglodge.com) can help you out. They offer dog-sledding day trips starting at $140/person as well as overnight trips. Camping is available in the backcountry and at Riley Creek Campground. Spending a night in the park gives visitors an outstanding chance of seeing the Aurora Borealis (Northern Lights). This phenomenon occurs all year, but there's only enough darkness to see it between fall and spring. Remember that services are extremely limited. You'll have to head to Healy, 11 miles to the north, for the nearest service stations with essentials like food and gas.

Visitor Centers & Services

Denali Visitor Center (Mile 1.5, 907.683.9275) features exhibits, a film, ranger programs, and a bookstore. It's typically open from mid-May through mid-September. Near the visitor center you'll find a grill and bookstore. **Murie Science & Learning Center**

Snorkeling for lunch

(Mile 1.4, 907683.6432) features exhibits, classes, and field seminars w/ AK Geographic Institute. It's typically open all year, except major holidays. **Riley Creek Mercantile** (Mile 0.25) is where you check-in for all campgrounds. It's a small store with camping essentials, showers, and laundry. **Denali Bus Depot** (Mile 0.5) is the primary place to buy bus tickets and make same-day campground reservations. There's also a small coffee shop and store. **Wilderness Access Center** (WAC) (Mile 0.75, 907.683.9590) is where you go if you want to camp in the backcountry and didn't plan things out in advance. **Toklat Ranger Station** (Mile 53) is a pit-stop for all shuttle and tour buses. It features restrooms and a small bookstore. **Eielson Visitor Center** (Mile 66) is a pit-stop for some buses and features exhibits and ranger walks. **Walter Harper Talkeetna Ranger Station** (Downtown Talkeetna, 150 miles south of the park entrance, 907.733.2231) is where you go for mountaineering information.

Ranger Programs & For Kids

During summer, park rangers lead guests on walks, talks, demonstrations, and evening programs. These activities occur daily at both Denali and Eielson Visitor Centers. Discovery Hikes are a great way to explore the heart of the park with an experienced and engaging park ranger. "Disco" hikes are limited to 11 people, and you're only able to sign up in person, one-to-two days in advance at Denali Visitor Center. Park Rangers turn away unprepared hikers, so be sure to bring warm layers of clothing, wear proper shoes, have adequate food and water, and, most importantly, be prepared and excited to spend 11 hours (~5 hours hiking) in the park. You'll take a Disco Bus (fee) to the starting point.

You can also catch a **Sled Dog Demonstration** at the Sled Dog Kennels. These unique experiences are offered daily at 10am, 2pm, and 4pm during peak season (June–August). There is no parking. Arrive via shuttle bus or on foot. Program and shuttle are free.

Evening programs are held at Riley Creek, Savage River, Teklanika River, and Wonder Lake Campgrounds. And walks and talks are held regularly throughout the park in summer. Find a current schedule of activities online or in-person at a visitor center.

One of the best ways to introduce kids to the park's unique history and geography is the park's Junior Ranger Program. Get started by picking up a free Junior Ranger Activity Booklet at a visitor center. Complete the activities in any order, and then show your work to a park ranger. For a job well done you'll receive an official Denali National Park Junior Ranger certificate and badge. Children will also enjoy spotting wildlife during a bus ride, just make sure they're ready for a long journey.

Flora & Fauna

More than 650 species of flowering plants, 39 species of mammals, 167 species of birds, 10 species of fish, and one lonely species of amphibian live at Denali National Park. You are a visitor in their land, so protect it and respect it. The park is so far north very few species of trees can survive, but black and white spruce, quaking aspen, paper birch, and balsam poplar populate the lower elevations. Some descriptions of the park's wildlife may lead you to believe you're embarking upon an Alaskan safari. It's not quite like that, but you'll have a good chance of spotting a few of the big five: moose, grizzly bears, caribou, Dall's sheep, and wolves.

Pets & Accessibility

Pets are allowed in the park but must be kept on a leash (less than six feet). They may be walked on the Park Road, in parking lots, or on campground roads. They are not permitted on trails (except Roadside Trail and Bike Path), buses, or in the backcountry.

Denali Visitor Center, Wilderness Access Center, Murie Science & Learning Center, Eielson Visitor Center, Toklat Rest Area, and the Sled Dog Kennels are wheelchair accessible. The Bike Path, McKinley Station Trail, and Spruce Forest Trail are wheelchair accessible (with assistance). Savage River and Riley Creek Loop Shuttles are accessible. At least one of the Sled Dog Demonstration Shuttles is accessible. Many, but not all, Denali Park Road shuttle and tour buses are accessible. Many ranger programs, like theater talks at the visitor center, are accessible.

Weather

Warm weather from late May through early September attracts 90% of the park's visitors, but don't go expecting clear skies and temperatures in the 70s°F. Denali creates its own weather system. Clouds hide the prominent peak for about half the year. You have a better chance of viewing Denali early in the day, but for the best chance of seeing the massive mountain, spend a night or two camping in the park. Temperatures are just as unpredictable, ranging from 33°F to 75°F during summer. Winters can be nasty. On warm days the temperature might top out at 20°F, but it's not uncommon for the mercury to dip below -40°F. Extreme cold usually begins in late October and lasts through March. Don't forget a raincoat for your visit. June through August is the wettest period of the year, but precipitation is also difficult to predict. The table provided below gives you a general idea of what to expect.

Moose are excellent swimmers

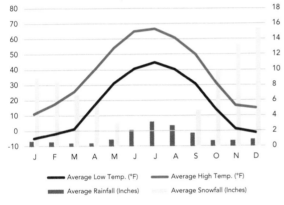

Legend:
— Average Low Temp. (°F)   — Average High Temp. (°F)
■ Average Rainfall (Inches)   Average Snowfall (Inches)

Tips & Recommendations

About three-quarters of all visitors arrive between June and August. It isn't the only time of year to visit, but it is the easiest thanks to park buses and warm afternoon temperatures.

Anything from a bus trip to a ranger-guided Discovery Hike is a full-day commitment. For many, one trip up and down Denali Park Road is more than enough, others repeat the ride as wildlife (and even Denali) is always different. There's no right or wrong way.

It is possible to get walk-up bus tickets and campsites. You have to decide what you're willing to risk: driving to Denali and not being able to get down the park road or making early reservations and rolling the dice with the weather Gods. It's not an easy decision.

This is a remote area. Come prepared with food and water. You can get water at either visitor center. There's

a grill near Denali Visitor Center and Riley Creek Mercantile is stocked with essentials. It's a good idea to call to see if they stock the specific type of fuel your camp stove requires before arriving. Gas is available near the park entrance in summer. (Food and gas are going to be more expensive than you're used to. But you're in Alaska!)

We're all accustomed to getting in a car and going where we want, but consider taking the train to Denali, especially if you're coming from Kenai Fjords/Seward. It's a beautiful stretch of rail.

And, once you reach the park, you'll have to leave your car behind. Denali Park Road (beyond Mile 15) can only be accessed by bus, bike, or foot during the busy summer tourism season.

If you plan on camping or staying at the park lodges, you'll need to plan ahead. Reservations often fill up minutes from when they become available.

Try to spend at least one night in the park camping or at one of the lodges near Kantishna. (Note: while the ride along Denali Park Road is great, it may not be everyone's idea of a good time as it is a long journey to go all the way to Kantishna. It's also possible to fly directly to Kantishna from Anchorage.)

When assessing the cost, consider the difficulty of running a lodge in a remote location like this. In addition to the operational/logistical challenges, you're treated to experienced guides, private buses, smaller groups, access to equipment, and, last but not least, superlative setting. I'm with most of us (I think), I do not want to blow my whole vacation budget on a couple nights in the Denali backcountry, but, if it's within your means, there's no better place to stay than at one of the lodges near Kantishna. And, if it isn't, camping is a great alternative.

Reflection Pond

Denali is often shrouded in clouds. But it's still a good idea to know where it is at all times, and watch for it as you drive/fly around the area. It can be seen from Anchorage on a clear day. While touring the park, it may be visible as early as Mile 9.

I prefer early tours with the sun at my back and wildlife looking for food. This is obviously hit and miss, as wildlife and conditions change (sometimes minute-by-minute), but more often than not, morning is better. Now, if your only chance to take a tour down Denali Park Road is in the afternoon, go for it.

Be engaged during your ride down Denali Park Road. More active eyes equal more wildlife sightings!

If you simply want to ride down the park road, looking around when you feel like it, take a shuttle bus (which is narrated by the driver, just not with a specific itinerary). If you prefer structure, spending the entire time with the same group, stopping at designated locations (and any points of interest for that day, including animal sightings), join a narrated tour. Both are great. If you have a personal preference, choose accordingly.

Bring binoculars. Close animal encounters do happen, but most are from a distance, sometimes great distances. Those golden grizzlies are surprisingly easy to spot by the naked eye, but help yourself out and bring a good pair of binoculars.

The left-hand side of the bus is better on the way out, and right-hand side is better on the way back. With that said, if you're traveling as a group, please take seats on both sides and rotate along the way.

Don't feel like you need to take more than one tour down the road. Camping or staying at Kantishna is a much better option. Now, if it's a beautiful day, and for some reason your schedule is open and you can get to the park and secure bus tickets, by all means get on that bus, but I wouldn't book several tours for one vacation unless you have an extremely specific wishlist of wildlife sightings or want to guarantee you see Denali but aren't able to spend a night or two deeper in the park.

Hike (remember, there are only a few marked trails): Mount Healy Overlook (Strenuous, 6+ miles)
Denali Viewing Locations: Stony Hill Overlook (Mile 62), Reflection Pond, Wonder Lake, Eielson Visitor Center, and Denali View (south of park on Parks Highway), or go flightseeing
Family Activities: Become Junior Rangers, Bus Tours (a few might be on the long side for some kids), Sled Dog Demonstrations
Guided Tours: Narrated Bus Tours, Whitewater Rafting, Flightseeing
Rainy Day Activities: Denali Visitor Center
Sunrise/Sunset Spots: Most visitors arrive in summer when there's a lot of daylight. Here, you might want to forget about getting a good sunrise/sunset photo and focus on early morning light on Denali or reflection at Reflection Pond. Those are your best bets, but it depends on condition and time of year.
Wildlife: Denali Park Road

Beyond the Park...

The following businesses are all located along George Parks Highway (AK-3) near the turn-off for Denali Park Road.

Dining (Denali)

Moose-Aka's
238.9 AK-3 • (907) 687-0003
moose-akas.com

229 Parks Restaurant
229.7 AK-3 • (907) 683-2567

Prospectors Pizzeria
238.9 AK-3 • (907) 683-7437
prospectorspizza.com

Alpenglow Restaurant
238 AK-3 • (907) 683-5150

Denali Park Salmon Bake
238.5 AK-3 • (907) 683-2733
denaliparksalmonbake.com

Denali Doghouse
238.6 AK-3 • (907) 683-3647
denalidoghouse.com

The Black Bear
238.5 AK-3 • (907) 683-1656
theblackbeardenali.com

Denali Thai Food
213 AK-3 • (907) 306-3545

Alaska Cabin Nite Dinner Theatre
231 AK-3 (Denali Park Village)
(907) 683-8900

The Perch
224 AK-3 • (888) 322-2523
denaliperchresort.com

Prey Bar and Eatery
229 AK-3 • (907) 683-2611
alaskacollection.com

Thai and Chinese Food To Go
238 AK-3 • (907) 306-3545

Rose's Café
249 AK-3 • (907) 683-7673

49th State Brewing
248 AK-3, Healy • (907) 683-2739
49statebrewing.com

Grocery Stores (Denali)

Three Bears
248.5 AK-3 • (907) 683-1300

Lodging (Denali)

McKinley Creekside Cabins & Café
224 AK-3 • (907) 683-2277
mckinleycabins.com

Denali Cabins
229 AK-3 • (800) 808-8068
alaskacollection.com

Denali Bluffs Hotel
238 AK-3 • (866) 683-8500
denalialaska.com

McKinley Chalet Resort
238.9 AK-3 • (800) 544-0970
westmarkhotels.com

Denali Park Hotel
247 AK-3 • (866) 683-1800
denaliparkhotel.com

Denali Hostel & Cabins
224.1 AK-3 • (907) 683-7503
denalihostel.com

Carlo Creek Cabins
224 AK-3 • (907) 683-2576
denaliparklodging.com

Princess Wilderness Lodge
238.5 AK-3 • (907) 683-2282
princesslodges.com

Grand Denali Lodge
238 AK-3 • (907) 683-5100
denalialaska.com

Denali Park Village
231 AK-3 • (800) 276-7234
denaliparkvillage.com

Tonglen Lake Lodge
230 AK-3 • (907) 683-2570
tonglenlake.com

Backwoods Lodge
133.7 AK-3 • (907) 987-0960
backwoodslodge.com

Black Diamond Resort
1 Otto Lake Rd, Healy
(907) 683-4653
blackdiamondtourco.com

Campgrounds (Denali)

Denali RV Park & Motel
245.1 AK-3 • (907) 683-1500
denalirvpark.com

Cantwell RV Park • (907) 888-6850

Nenana RV Park • (907) 750-4008
210 4th St, Nenana
nenanacamping.com

Caribou escaping a fire

The following businesses are near the western boundary of Wrangell-St Elias National Park.

Grocery Stores (Wrangell)

Kenny Lake Mercantile
7.1 Mile Edgerton Hwy, Copper Center

Lodging (Wrangell)

Wrangell Mountain Lodge
26 McCarthy Rd, Chitina
wrangellmountainlodge.com

Sawing Logzz B&B
Mile 105 AK-4, Copper Center
sawinglogzz.com • (907) 259-3242

Old Town Copper Center Inn & Rest
AK-4, Copper Center • (907) 822-3245
oldtowncoppercenter.com

Currant Ridge • (907) 554-2126
7, Mile 56 McCarthy Rd
currantridge.com

Caribou Hotel • (907) 822-3302
Mile 186.5 AK-1, Glenallen

Attractions

Denali, Wrangell-St Elias, and Kenai Fjords are get there and spend a few days destinations. There isn't much development in between the main attractions. However, there is quite a bit going on in Anchorage and Fairbanks.

Denali State Park • Trapper Creek
dnr.alaska.gov • (907) 745-3975

Fountainhead Auto Museum
212 Wedgewood Dr, Fairbanks
fountainheadmuseum.com

Running Reindeer Ranch
1470 Ivans Alley, Fairbanks
(907) 455-4998
runningreindeer.com

Morris Thompson Cultural & Visitors Center • (907) 459-3700
101 Dunkel St, Fairbanks
morristhompsoncenter.org

Large Animal Research Station
2220 Yankovich Rd, Fairbanks
uaf.edu

Anchorage Yoga • (907) 562-9642
701 W 36th Ave, Anchorage
anchorageyoga.com

Anchorage Trolley Tours
546 W 4th Ave, Anchorage
(907) 276-5603
anchoragetrolley.com

Anchorage Museum
625 C St, Anchorage
(907) 929-9200
anchoragemuseum.org

Alaska Native Heritage Center
8800 Heritage Center Dr, Anchorage
alaskanative.net • (907) 330-8000

Salmon Berry Tours • (907) 278-3572
515 W 4th Ave, Anchorage
salmonberrytours.com

Midnight Sun Brewing Co
8111 Dimond Hook Dr, Anchorage
(907) 344-1179
midnightsunbrewing.com

Chugach State Park
18620 Seward Hwy, Anchorage
dnr.alaska.gov • (907) 345-5014

Northern Lights
Summer isn't Aurora Borealis time due to nearly-constant daylight, but if you travel in the offseason (even March and September), you may be treated to brilliant light displays after dark. Fairbanks is a good place to set up base camp to hunt the northern lights.

Kenai Fjords

Exit Glacier

Phone: (907) 422-0500
Website: nps.gov/kefj

Established: December 2, 1980
Size: 699,983 Acres
Annual Visitors: 300,000
Peak Season: June–August

Activities: Hiking, Backpacking, Mountaineering, Boat Tours, Cruises, Kayaking (day and multi-day trips), Flightseeing, Fishing

Campground: Exit Glacier (12 free, walk-in, tent-only; first-come, first-served campsites)
Backcountry Camping: Permitted
Backcountry Cabins: 2 on Coast* ($75/night, summer only); 1 at Exit Glacier** ($50/night, winter only)

Park Hours: All day, every day
Entrance Fee: None

*Reserve at recreation.gov
**Reserve at (907) 422-0500

Kenai Fjords, located in south-central Alaska near the town of Seward, is the smallest of Alaska's national parks. Of course, small by Alaskan standards is large anywhere else. It's roughly the size of Grand Teton and Rocky Mountain National Parks combined. Along the coast, towering peaks rise abruptly from the sea. Glaciers slowly carved the fjords, and now they're receding. Tracing each glacier back to its origin inevitably leads to Harding Icefield. Named for President Warren G. Harding, the mile-high mass of ice covers more than 300 square miles (roughly the size of Crater Lake National Park). If you include some 40 glaciers fanning out from the icefield, it measures over 1,100 square miles. It accumulates as much as 400 inches of snow annually, and it is the largest of four icefields remaining in the United States.

From the first Russian navigators who explored the Kenai coast in search of harbors for whalers to today's visitors seeking nothing more than seclusion and grand natural beauty, everyone takes with them memories of the same dramatic landscape. Portraits of narrow, gradually deepening fjords bracketed by precipitous cliffs rising above the glaciers and icefield are burnt into their collective subconsciousness. Sea and land are home to Steller sea lions, puffins, Dall's porpoises, black and brown bears, mountain goats, and humpback and orca whales. Tens of thousands of seabirds migrate to the coastline in summer. Kenai Fjords National Park might be small by Alaskan standards, but it's big in scenery, untamed wilderness, and wildlife, and it possesses infinite opportunities to inspire awe in adventurers—traits that epitomize the Alaskan National Park.

Camping & Backcountry Cabins

There is a 12-site, walk-in, tent-only campground at **Exit Glacier**. Sites are available free of charge on a first-come, first-served basis. The camp features central food storage and a cooking and dining shelter. Water and pit-toilets are available.

Aialik (sleeps up to four) and **Holgate** (sleeps up to six) are rustic cabins located on the Kenai Fjords coast. They are available for public use from late May through mid-September. The cabins are accessible via float plane, water taxi, private vessel, or charter boat. Kayakers should be dropped off by boat due to extremely strong currents around Cape Aialik. All visitors must make their own transportation arrangements. Coastal cabins are equipped with heating stove (propane provided), table and chairs, and wooden bunks. You are responsible for bedding and sleeping pads, cook stove and utensils, drinking water (or means to treat it), and toilet paper, in addition to whatever food, clothing, gear, and emergency supplies you might need. You must pack out your waste. The cabins do not have electricity. Cost is $75/night. Reservations are required and can be made through recreation.gov. Stays are limited to three nights per group per season. Reservations must be cancelled at least 14 days in advance to receive a refund.

Willow Cabin (sleeps up to four) is available for public use after Exit Glacier Road closes due to snow, usually from mid-November through mid-April. The cabin can be reached by snowmobile, cross-country skis, snowshoes, or dogsled. It is located approximately 7 miles down Exit Glacier Road from Box Canyon Gate (1.5 miles off AK-9/Seward Highway). This rustic cabin has propane heat, propane stove, oven, refrigerator, lights, and basic cooking utensils. There is no running water. It sleeps four and costs $50/night. Stays are limited to three nights and must be reserved in person at the Park Headquarters or by calling (907) 422-0500.

Driving

The only road-accessible part of the park is Exit Glacier. From the Nature Center, visitors can hike a short trail to the glacier's base or make a more arduous journey to the top of Harding Icefield. During winter, visitors arrive at Exit Glacier by skis, dogsleds, snowshoes, and snowmobiles. PJS Taxi & Tours (907.224.5555, pjstaxi.com) can show you around.

Hiking, Backpacking & Mountaineering

Hiking is somewhat limited. All maintained trails are in or nearby Exit Glacier. The 8.2-mile (roundtrip)

Seward

When to Go

Kenai Fjords is open all year, but services and accessibility are limited during winter. Exit Glacier Road is typically closed from fall through spring due to snow. The park's coastal backcountry is inaccessible from late fall through early spring because of rough seas. Roughly 80% of all tourists arrive between June and August, most of those arriving by cruise ship. But it is possible to arrange flightseeing excursions and fishing charters year-round (weather permitting). April is typically the best time of year for experienced mountaineers to try and cross Harding Icefield. Guests also enjoy cross-country skiing, snowshoeing, or snowmobiling along Exit Glacier Road after it closes to cars in fall.

Transportation & Airports

Seward Bus Lines (sewardbuslines.net, 888.420.7788) provides year-round transportation between Anchorage and Seward. The trip takes 3 hours (one-way) and costs $39.95/adult (one-way). Alaska Cruise Transfer (sewardalaskabus.com, 907.350.6010) and The Park Connection (alaskacoach.com, 800.266.8625) provide seasonal motorcoach transportation between Seward and Denali/Anchorage.

Alaska Railroad (800.544.0552, alaskarailroad.com) serves Seward (port of call for many cruise lines) from May to September. The stretch of rail from Anchorage to Seward is widely regarded as the most stunning in America.

Ted Stevens Anchorage International (ANC) is the closest major airport.

Directions

Kenai Fjords National Park is located in south-central Alaska, just west of Seward and 132 miles south of Anchorage. Exit Glacier is the only portion of the park accessible by road.

Exit Glacier: From Anchorage, head south on AK-9/Seward Hwy. Continue for 122 miles. Turn right at Exit Glacier Rd (seasonal). Follow it into the park.

Harding Icefield

End of Trail

Emergency
Shelter

Harding Icefield Trail

Top of the Cliffs

Marmot
Meadows

Harding Icefield
Trail

Exit
Glacier

Glacier Overlook

Glacier
Overlook

Glacier
Overlook
Loop Trail

Exit Creek

Outwash Plain

Glacier View

Glacier View
Loop Trail

Exit Glacier
Nature Center

Pavilion

Restrooms

Picnic Area

Parking Area

Paddling by Pedersen Glacier

Harding Icefield Trail is as good as it gets. You'll pass through forests and meadows before climbing above tree line to outstanding views of the massive icefield (the largest icefield entirely in the United States). It is a strenuous trek. You gain about 1,000 feet of elevation each mile and may have to scramble over rocks. Before departing, inquire about trail conditions, pack plenty of water, and be prepared to hike in bear country.

A small network of shorter and easier trails originates at the Nature Center. From here you can hike to Exit Creek's shoreline (easy), to the toe of Exit Glacier (moderate), and/or to Exit Glacier Overlook (moderate). If you aren't going to make the strenuous trip up Harding Icefield Trail, I recommend at least going to **Exit Glacier Overlook**. The backcountry is trailless wilderness where hiking is not recommended due to dense vegetation and rugged terrain. **Backpackers** can camp along Harding Icefield Trail as long as you set up camp at least an eighth of a mile from the trail. If you're determined to explore the backcountry or Harding Icefield, it's recommended you hire a private outfitter.

Boat Tours & Cruises

In summer visitors can join boat tours exploring the coves and bays of Kenai Fjords. Major Marine Tours (907.224.8030, majormarine.com) and Kenai Fjords Tours (888.478.3346, kenaifjords.com) offer similar menus, offerings range from around $100 to $240 (3.5 to 9 hours). All tours focus on wildlife and tidewater glaciers—things this area has in abundance. You'll have a good chance of seeing Steller sea lions, sea otters, Dall's porpoises, orca whales, gray whales, humpback whales, and bald eagles. Each company offers specials and overnight packages. Lodging for Major Marine Tours is at Harbor 360 Hotel. Kenai Fjords Tours uses their privately owned lodging: Kenai Fjords Wilderness Lodge. It consists of eight beachfront cabins on Resurrection Bay's Fox Island, providing a peaceful setting

where meals (included in package price) are prepared by the island's private chef. Northern Latitude Adventures (907.422.0432, northernlatitudeadventures.com) and Alaska Fjords Charters (907.491.1075, alaskafjordcharters.com) also offer group and private boat tours. Miller's Landing (907.331.3113, millerslanding.com) offers water taxi service, fishing charters, kayaking trips, winter tours, lodging, camping, and rental equipment. Alaska Saltwater Lodge (907.224.5271, alaskasaltwaterlodge.com) also offers a little bit of everything.

Royal Caribbean (866.562.7625, royalcaribbean.com), Celebrity X Cruises (888.751.7804, celebritycruises.com), Holland America Line (855.932.1711, hollandamerica.com), Princess Cruises (800.774.6237, princesstours.com), and Norwegian Cruise Lines (866.234.7350, ncl.com) offer cruises that port at Whittier or Seward. From here, operators generally offer an optional cruise along the shores of Kenai Fjords. By this time, it's likely you've been through Glacier Bay and Wrangell–St. Elias's Icy Strait, so maybe you've seen enough tidewater glaciers and marine life. If not, the tours of Kenai Fjords are great too, and you never know what wildlife will be out.

Paddling

Kayakers are welcome to explore the seemingly endless supply of bays and coves. You don't need to be a paddling savant to kayak these waters, but it also shouldn't be your first time getting in a big sea kayak either. You should be a comfortable, confident sea kayaker, because this is a remote destination and any incident could prove deadly. Most kayakers are dropped off by boat at Bear Glacier Lagoon, Aialik Bay or Northwestern Lagoon, or by plane at Nuka Bay. From there you have many coves and beaches to explore. Day trips paddling Resurrection Bay from Seward are safe, but you should not attempt to round Aialik Cape because of treacherous waters. Weather Permitting (907.224.6595, watertaxiak.com) and Seward Ocean Excursions (907.599.0499, sewardoceanexcursions.com) offer water taxi service for kayakers as well as day boat tours. Seward Water Taxi (907.201.0542, sewardwatertaxi.com) also offers kayak/kayaker transportation. You could also stay at Kenai Backcountry Lodge (800.334.8730, alaskawildland.com), where they take care of everything for you, including paddling excursions, and their setting is sublime.

Flightseeing

Like all of Alaska's National Parks, flightseeing is a safe and enjoyable way to view some of the world's most exceptional scenery. But the thing is, the coast is often foggy. Most pilots focus on going to Lake Clark, Katmai, or Prince William Sound, where there are fishing/hiking destinations and impressive scenery. Talon Air Service (907.262.8899, talonair.com, Soldotna), High Adventure Air Charter (907.262.5237, highadventureair.com, Soldotna), or Northwind Aviation (907.235.7482, northwindak.com, Homer) can take you up and fly you around. They also offer bear-viewing and fishing trips. Most operators departing from Anchorage listed in the Lake Clark and Katmai sections of this book will take you above the Kenai Peninsula as well.

Fishing

If you'd like to try your hand at fishing (fresh or saltwater), you'll need an Alaska State fishing license for all fishermen over the age of 16. Before dipping your lines, visit adfg.alaska.gov for a list of up-to-date fishing regulations. Or put your fishing fortunes in the hands of a guide like Saltwater Safari Company (907.224.5232, saltwatersafari.com). Alaska River Adventures (907.595.2000, alaskariveradventures.com) offers river rafting and fishing adventures. Alaskan Wilderness (907.424.5552, alaskawilderness.com), Deep Creek Fishing Club (907.567.7373, alaskafishingclub.com), and All Alaska Outdoors Lodge (907.953.0186, allalaska.com) offer a variety of fishing, hunting, and bear-viewing trips.

Visitor Centers

Kenai Fjords Visitor Center, located at Seward's boat harbor, is typically open daily from early May to mid-September. It houses a bookstore, short film, and park rangers are available to answer your questions. **Exit Glacier Nature Center** is usually open daily from Memorial Day to Labor Day. It's at the Exit Glacier trailhead and home to a bookstore and exhibits.

Ranger Programs & For Kids

Programs are held regularly at Exit Glacier between Memorial Day and Labor Day. For a current schedule of all walks and interpretive talks visit the park website or stop in at Exit Glacier Nature Center.

Kenai Fjords has a few offerings designed specifically for kids. Art for Parks Backpack Program allows families to check out a backpack filled with art supplies. Packs are checked out free of charge and your artwork might be featured on the park website. Children are also invited to take part in the Junior Ranger Program. Pick up a booklet from the visitor center. Complete the activities appropriate for your child's age and show them to a ranger to receive an official Junior Ranger certificate and badge.

Touring the fjords

Flora & Fauna

Most land is bare or covered in ice and snow. The coastline supports vegetation and is covered with Sitka spruce and salmonberry. Sedges and grasses are the only plants capable of living in the park's Arctic–Alpine environments. In between the coast and the mountaintops you'll find alder, willow, and mature stands of spruce and hemlock trees.

Animals abound on land and in the sea. Black and brown bears, moose, mountain goats, and marmots live off the land. Whales, seals, sea lions, and sea otters patrol the seas.

Pets & Accessibility

Pets are only allowed on Exit Glacier Road and in the parking lot, and they must be kept on a leash (less than six feet). The only exceptions are dogs used for mushing or skijoring on Harding Icefield or in Exit Glacier when the road is closed.

Seward Information Center and Exit Glacier Nature Center are accessible to individuals in wheelchairs. The first one-third mile of Exit Glacier Trail is also accessible. Boat and flightseeing tours may be accessible; contact individual providers for details.

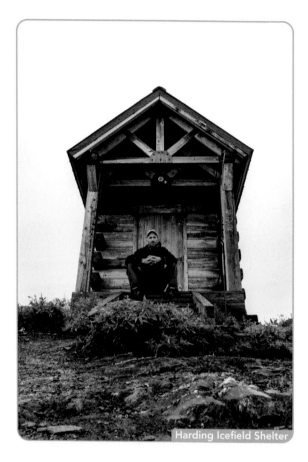

Harding Icefield Shelter

Weather

Visitors should come prepared for all sorts of weather. Mittens, hat, and a warm/waterproof windbreaker are essential gear for a boat tour. Even when the temperature is comfortable, the wind on the open water can make for a chilly afternoon. Summer highs range from the mid-40s to low 70s°F. Winter temperatures range from the low 30s to -20s°F. Rainy/snowy weather is common. The Exit Glacier area averages about 200 inches of snowfall each year.

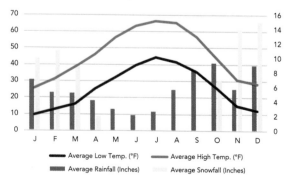

— Average Low Temp. (°F) — Average High Temp. (°F)
■ Average Rainfall (Inches) ■ Average Snowfall (Inches)

Tips & Recommendations

We won't blame you if your idea of visiting Kenai Fjords is driving up to Exit Glacier, taking a hike, and moving onto the next thing. But consider spending more time. The park is a paddler's paradise if you're willing to put in the effort planning the necessary logistics. And boat tours offer unlimited opportunities for sight seeing and wildlife viewing.

Parking is limited at Exit Glacier. If you're visiting in summer, mid-day, there's a good chance space will not be available. Prior to 2020, a shuttle ran between Seward and Exit Glacier. I'm not sure it will return.

Take the train! The stretch of rail from Anchorage to Seward is widely regarded as the most beautiful in the country. (Of course, the drive is pretty, too.) You can rent a car from the train station or coordinate with lodging/boat tours.

There are a variety of boat, paddling, flightseeing, and fishing tours. Weather greatly affects the enjoyment of these activities, but it's still a good idea to book in advance and cross your fingers, hoping for the best. Fortunately, June and July are the driest months of the year for this region and most storms pass quickly. Fog might be the biggest concern. Sometimes it adds to the experience, creating a mystical environment, other times it obscures everything worth seeing.

If you're looking for solitude, consider spending a night or two in one of the remote backcountry cabins. You'll need to reserve them in advance (or luck out on a cancellation). They're best for experienced sea kayakers paddling the fjords, but you could arrange drop-off by seaplane or water taxi. Remember that you'll have to pack in what you need and pack out all your waste. There's also a boat-in lodge, Kenai Fjords Glacier Lodge (alaskawildland.com).

Experienced open-water paddlers should do some paddling. You can explore Resurrection Bay from Seward (or possibly head over to Bear Glacier Lagoon) or arrange transport or a guide to paddle Aialik Bay or Bear Glacier Lagoon.

Hike: Exit Glacier Overlook (Moderate, 2+ miles), Harding Icefield (Strenuous, 8.2 miles)
Family Activities: Boat, Paddle, and Flight Tours
Guided Tours: Take a wildlife boat tour, see the fjords from the seat of a kayak, traverse Harding Icefield, go flightseeing above Harding Icefield
Wildlife: Kayaking, Boat Tours

Quite the view at Kenai Fjords Glacier Lodge

Beyond the Park...

Dining
Zudy's Café • (907) 224-4710
501 Railway Ave, Seward
zudyscafe.com

Lone Chicharron Taqueria
215B 4th Ave • (907) 422-0400
thelonechicharron.com

The Porthole • (907) 422-7335
1400 4th Ave, Seward • *Food truck*

Gold Rush Bistro • (907) 224-4782
203 4th St, Seward

Woody's Thai Kitchen
800 4th Ave • (907) 422-0338

The Highliner • (907) 224-3950
303 Adams St, Seward
highlinerseward.com

13 Ravens Coffee & Books
In an old railway car
411 Port Ave, Seward

Grocery Stores
Safeway • (907) 224-6900
1907 AK-9, Seward

Seward Marketplace
1711 AK-9 • (907) 224-2081

Lodging
Kenai Fjords Glacier Lodge
A lodge in the heart of the park
alaskawildland.com

Resurrection Lodge on the Bay
13970 Beach Dr • (907) 318-1450
resurrectionlodge.com

Angel's Rest • (907) 224-7378
13725 Beach Dr • angelsrest.com

Harbor 360 Hotel • (907) 224-2550
1412 4th Ave • harbor360hotel.com

Breeze Inn • (888) 224-5237
303 N Harbor St, Seward
breezeinn.com

Windsong Lodge • (907) 224-7116
31772 Herman Leirer Rd, Seward
alaskacollection.com

Exit Glacier Lodge
Herman Leirer Rd • (907) 224-6040
sewardalaskalodging.com

Campgrounds
Seward KOA
31702 Herman Leirer Rd, Seward
koa.com • (907) 224-4887

Stoney Creek RV Park
13760 Leslie Pl, Seward
(907) 224-6465
stoneycreekrvpark.com

There are a bunch of city camp-grounds all throughout Seward.

Attractions
Alaska SeaLife Center
301 Railway Ave, Seward
alaskasealife.org

Bardy's Trail Rides • (907) 362-7863
Horseback riding
Resurrection Bay Rd, Seward
sewardhorses.com

Ididaride Sled Dog Tours
Run by Iditarod champions
12820 Old Exit Glacier Rd
ididaride.com • (907) 224-8607

Trails End Horse Adventures
53435 East End Rd, Homer
(907) 235-6393

AK Islands & Ocean Visitor Center
95 AK-1, Homer • (907) 235-6961

Center for Alaskan Coastal Studies
708 Smoky Bay Way, Homer
(907) 235-6667
akcoastalstudies.org

Pratt Museum • (907) 235-8635
3779 Bartlett St, Homer
prattmuseum.org

Lake Clark

Bear-viewing at Chinitna Bay

Phone: (907) 781-2218
Website: nps.gov/lacl

Established: December 2, 1980
December 1, 1978 (National Mon.)
Size: 4 Million Acres
Annual Visitors: 18,000
Peak Season: June–September

Activities: Hiking, Backpacking, Flight-seeing, Boating, Hunting, Fishing

Campgrounds: None

Park Hours: All day, every day
Entrance Fee: None

When to Go

Lake Clark National Park is open all year, but almost all guests visit between June and September. You shouldn't get snowed on during this time, making it great for hiking, backpacking, fishing, and whatever else you'd like to do here.

Transportation & Airports

No roads reach the park. It's almost exclusively accessed by air taxi. Depending on your destination, you may arrive via float plane or wheeled plane. Commercial flights between Ted Stevens Anchorage International Airport (ANC) and Iliamna (30 miles outside the park boundary) are available.

Lake Clark provides a sample of all Alaska's parks. In this relatively small area of the Alaskan Peninsula (southwest of Anchorage) there are a variety of geographical features not found together in any of Alaska's other national parks. Three mountain ranges meet: the Alaska Range from the north, the Aleutian Range from the south, and the Chigmit Mountains in between. There are two active volcanoes: Iliamna and Redoubt, the latter erupting twice since 1966. Temperate hemlock-spruce rainforest covers the coast. Plateaus of arctic tundra are interrupted by turquoise lakes. Lake Clark is "the essence of Alaska." The very thing some people are searching for.

Richard Louis Proenneke was a man who understood the essence of Alaska, and he found it along the shores of Twin Lakes. Born in Iowa, he worked as a farmhand before enlisting in the Navy the day after Pearl Harbor was bombed. He was discharged for medical reasons in 1945. Four years later he made his first trip to Alaska, where he lived and worked intermittently for years, but not until 1962 did he visit the Twin Lakes area. By this time, demand for furs was waning and tourism was waxing. The indelible memories of his first journey drew him back in 1967 when he began working on a cabin. The modest abode was completed in 1968, built from the ground up using only hand tools, many of which he fashioned himself. He lived in this exquisite piece of craftsmanship from 1968 to 1998, when he was 82 years old. Throughout 30 years of life on the shores of Twin Lakes he created homemade furniture, filled journals with weather and wildlife observations, and set the standard for wilderness ethics: "Twin Lakes and the wildlife therein should not suffer for his presence." Today, like-minded individuals can admire Proenneke's foresight and vision by reading edited volumes of his journals: *One Man's Wilderness* and *More Readings from One Man's Wilderness*, or by watching the documentary film, *Alone in the Wilderness*. Better yet, come to Lake Clark National Park and see Proenneke's cabin for yourself. (Note: Dick Proenneke's cabin is locked from late September until late May.)

Camping & Lodging

There are no designated campgrounds. A backcountry permit is not required for hiking or camping, but it's a good idea to discuss your plans with a park ranger, especially if you aren't hiring a guide service. Bear-resistant food containers are recommended and available, free of charge, at the park visitor center in Port Alsworth. Tulchina Adventures (907.782.4720, tulchinaadventures.com) offers camping and cabin rental in Port Alsworth. Camping costs about $30 per night for 2 people, including fire pits, firewood, and outhouses included. They also have a cabin, offer a wide variety of excursions, and rent kayaks and camping gear. Several full-service lodges are listed in the activity sections.

Hiking & Backpacking

Two trails begin near Port Alsworth Visitor Center. **Beaver Pond Loop** (moderate) and **Falls and Lake Trail** are 1.7-mile legs that run parallel to one another and intersect **Tanalian Mountain Trail**. At the intersection, a left (north) leads to Tanalian Mountain (strenuous) after 2.6 miles. A right (south) leads to Tanalian Falls (moderate) and Kontrashibuna Lake after 1.1 miles. A short (unmarked) spur trail descends from the boardwalk to the base of the falls.

The trail ends at Kontrashibuna Lake, but you should be able to follow the shoreline, which requires crossing two (usually) shallow streams. Venturing any deeper into the park requires careful planning and route selection. **Upper to Lower Twin Lakes** is a relatively easy 10-mile backpacking trip (seaplane drop-off/pick-up) through Dick Proenneke's old haunt. The northwestern parts (Telaquana Lake, Turquoise Lake) offer the least challenging routes. **Telaquana Trail** (unmaintained) is an historic Dena'ina Athabascan route connecting Telaquana Lake to Kijik Village on Lake Clark. Originally blazed by the native Inland Dena'ina, and later by trappers, miners, and homesteaders. Today it's primarily used by backpackers. Alder, river crossings, and inclement weather will slow down travel. Expect your hiking rate to be about one mile per hour. A well-planned itinerary, good map, compass, warm layers of clothing, rain gear, knife, water, and snacks are imperative for hiking in Lake Clark's backcountry (even on day hikes). If you plan on hiking without a guide, be sure to contact the park before departing. Bear-resistant food containers (BRFC) are recommended, and the visitor center in Port Alsworth lends them out for free. Self-sufficiency is key. A properly prepared hiker/backpacker will find a trip into Lake Clark's wilderness to be nourishment for the soul and fulfilling

Proenneke Cabin

experience. If you aren't a confident outdoorsperson, hire a guide like Alaska Alpine Adventures (877.5252577, alaskaalpineadventures.com). They know the place as well as anybody, and can lead you on a backpacking, hiking, kayaking, or rafting trip of a lifetime.

Flightseeing

An air taxi is required to reach Port Alsworth, but they can also be used to access otherwise unreachable regions of the park; supply visitors with a bird's eye view of glacier-clad volcanoes, deep blue lakes, and endless expanses of open tundra; or go on bear-viewing missions. Lake Clark Air (907.278.2054, lakeclarkair.com, Anchorage), Rust's (907.243.1595, flyrusts.com, Anchorage), Alaska West Air (907.283.4292, alsakawestair.com, Nikiski), Beluga Air (907.235.8256, belugaair.com, Homer), Beryl Air (907.299.5494, berylair.com, Homer), Lake and Peninsula Airlines (lakeandpenair.com, multiple), Natron Air (907.262.8440, natronair.com, Soldotna), High Adventure Air (907.262.5237, highadventureair.com, Soldotna), Andrew Airways (907.487.2566, andrewairways.com, Kodiak), Smokey Bay Air (907.235.1511, smokeybayair.com, Homer), Alaska Air Service (907.694.8687, flyakair.com), and Sunlight Aviation (907.301.6993, sunlightaviation.com, Anchorage) all have permission to fly in Lake Clark (and other parks in the area).

Boating

If you're staying at a place like The Farm Lodge (907.781.2208, thefarmlodge.com) in Port Alsworth, you'll have the chance to take a guided boat tour of 42-mile-long Lake Clark. Alternatively, Catch-A-Lot Charters (907.567.7345, catchalotcharters.com) will motor two hours across Cook Inlet to Chinitna Bay to watch bears in summer, which is slightly less expensive than a bush plane and you'll have the chance to see some marine life along the way.

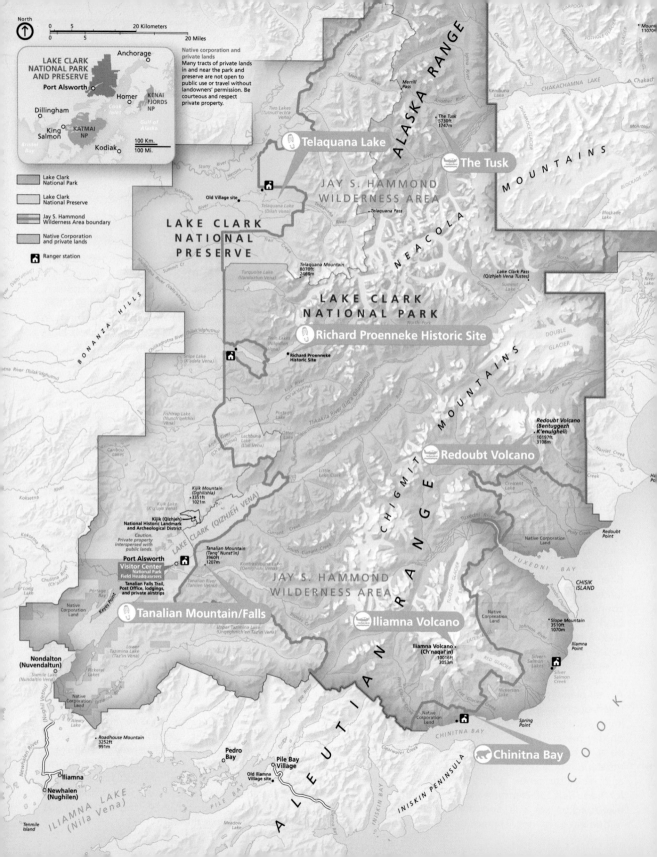

North

0   5   20 Kilometers
0   5   20 Miles

LAKE CLARK
NATIONAL PARK
AND PRESERVE

Port Alsworth

Anchorage

Homer

Dillingham

King
Salmon

KATMAI
NP

Kodiak

KENAI
FJORDS
NP

Cook Inlet

Gulf
of
Alaska

Bristol Bay

Native corporation and
private lands
Many tracts of private lands
in and near the park and
preserve are not open to
public use or travel without
landowners' permission. Be
courteous and respect
private property.

100 Km.
100 Mi.

Lake Clark
National Park

Lake Clark
National Preserve

Jay S. Hammond
Wilderness Area boundary

Native Corporation
and private lands

Ranger station

ALASKA RANGE

Merrill
Pass

Two Lakes
(Tutnuti'ech'a
Vena)

Mountain
11070ft

The Tusk
5730ft
1747m

NEACOLA

MOUNTAINS

CHAKACHAMNA LAKE

Telaquana Lake

The Tusk

JAY S. HAMMOND
WILDERNESS AREA

Old Village site

Telaquana Lake
(Dilah Vena)

Telaquana Pass

Telaquana River

Lake Clark Pass
(Qizhjeh Vena Tustes)

Summit
Lake

LAKE CLARK
NATIONAL
PRESERVE

Stony River

Necons River

Telaquana
River

Summit Cr.

Turquoise Lake
(Vandaztun Vena)

Telaquana Mountain
8070ft
2460m

LAKE CLARK
NATIONAL PARK

Richard Proenneke Historic Site

Richard Proenneke
Historic Site

BONANZA HILLS

Chilikadrotna River (Ndrul'atnuy)

Trail Creek

Twin Lakes
(Nilghilishla)

Snipe Lake
(K'adala Vena)

Kijik River
(Cha'qatnu)

Tlikakila River (Liq Qilunhtnu)

DOUBLE
GLACIER

Fishtrap Lake
(Nunch'qelchix
Vena)

Portage
Lake

Otter
Lake

Lachbuna Lake
(Łał Vena)

CHIGMIT MOUNTAINS

Redoubt Volcano
(Bentuggezh
K'enulgheli)
10197ft
3108m

Drift River

Harriet Creek

Kijik River (Cha'qatnu)

Little
Lake Clark

Redoubt Volcano

Crescent River

Crescent
Lake

Redoubt
Point

Caribou
Lakes

Koksetna River

Kijik Mountain
(Dghilishla)
3351ft
1021m

Kijik (Qizhjeh)
National Historic Landmark
and Archeological District

Caution.
Private property
interspersed with
public lands.

LAKE CLARK (QIZHJEH VENA)

Currant Creek

South Currant Creek

Tuxedni River

Tuxedni
Glacier

Polly Creek

Native Corporation
Land

TUXEDNI BAY

CHISIK
ISLAND

Port Alsworth
Visitor Center
National Park
Field Headquarters

Tanalian Mountain
(Tanq' Nunst'in)
3960ft
1207m

Tanalian Falls Trail,
Post Office, lodgings,
and private airstrips

Tanalian River
(Tanlien Vetnu)

Kontrashibuna Lake
(Qenlghishi Vena)

JAY S. HAMMOND
WILDERNESS AREA

ALEUTIAN RANGE

Iliamna Volcano

Tuxedni Glacier

Native
Corporation
Land

Slope Mountain
3510ft
1070m

Iliamna
Point

Silver
Salmon
Lakes

Silver Salmon Creek

Tanalian Mountain/Falls

Upper Tazimina Lake
(Ungeghnich'en Taz'in Vena)

Brusli Cr.

Iliamna Volcano
(Ch'naqal'in)
10016ft
3053m

RED GLACIER

Hickerson
Lake

Portage Bay

Keyes Point

Nondalton
(Nuvendaltun)

Sixmile Lake
(Nundaltin Vena)

Lower
Tazimina Lake
(Taz'in Vena)

Pickerel
Lakes

Tazimina River

Native
Corporation
Land

Pile River

Pile Glacier

Chinitna Bay

Native
Corporation
Land

Spring
Point

CHINITNA BAY

Clearwater Creek

COOK

Newhalen River (Nughil Vetnu)

Alexcy
Lake

Roadhouse Mountain
3252ft
991m

Pedro
Bay

Pile Bay
Village

Old Iliamna
Village site

INISKIN BAY

INISKIN PENINSULA

Iliamna

Newhalen
(Nughilen)

ILIAMNA LAKE
(Nila Vena)

Tenmile
Island

PILE BAY

Meadow
Lake

ALEUTIAN RANGE

Dena'ina Place Names

Present English	Dena'ina	Translation
Chilikadrotna River	Tsilak'idghutnu	Tongue stream
Chulitna River	Ch'alitnu	Flows out river
Iliamna Lake	Nila Vena	Islands lake
Iliamna Volcano	Ch'naqal'in	One that stands above
Kijik	Qizhjeh	Place where people gather
Kijik Lake	K'q'uya Vena	Red salmon lake
Kijik River	Ch'ak'daltnu	Animals-walk-out stream
Kontrashibuna Lake	Qenighishi Vena	Boiling lake
Lachbuna Lake	L'ali Vena	Dead fall collapses lake
Lake Clark	Qizhjeh Vena	People gather lake
Mulchatna River	Valts'atnaq'	River
Newhalen River	Nughil Vetnu	Flows down river
Nondalton	Nuvendaltun	Lake extends below
Redoubt Volcano	Bentuggezh K'enulgheli	One that has a notched forehead
Sixmile Lake	Nundaltin Vena	Lake extends below
Snipe Lake	K'adala Vena	Birds fly out lake
Tanalian River	Tanilen Vetnu	Flows into water stream
Tazimina Lake - Lower	Taz'in Vena	Fish trap lake
Telaquana Lake	Dilah Vena	Fish swim into lake
Tlikakila River	Łiq'a Qilanhtnu	Stream where salmon are
Turquoise Lake	Vandaztun Vena	Caribou hair lake
Twin Lakes	Nilqidlen Vena	Flows together lakes
Tyonek	Tubughnenq'	Beach land

Paddling

Rafting, canoeing, and kayaking opportunities abound. Muchatna, Chilikadrotna, and Tlikakila are three National Wild Rivers offering fast moving water with occasional whitewater. Popular trip lengths vary from 70 to 230 miles. June through September is the best time to paddle. You'll have to plan logistics with your bush plane. Sunlight Aviation (907.301.6993, sunlightaviation.com, Anchorage) supports rafting trips and rents inflatable rafts. You better be self-sufficient. Or stay at a lakeside lodge and you'll have kayaking and canoeing opportunities at your leisure.

Hunting & Fishing

Big game hunters with proper licenses and permits are allowed to hunt and trap in Lake Clark National Preserve. Hunting is not permitted within national park boundaries. It's best to join a knowledgeable guide. Bushwhack Alaska (907.571.2041, bushwhackalaska.com), Stony Mountain Lodge (907.250.4636, northwardboundak.com), and Alaska Trophy Outfitters (907.252.7413, alaskatrophyoutfitters.com) are the go-to guides for Lake Clark hunting trips. Just know that you'll have to plan some of these hunts more than one year in advance.

Saying that Lake Clark National Park is a good place to fish is like saying Lambeau Field is a good place to watch a football game. Lake Clark is home to some of the finest fishing grounds in the National Park System. The scenery isn't too shabby, either. Mountain lakes contain arctic grayling, Dolly Varden, several species of salmon, lake trout, and northern pike. July and August, during the salmon runs, are the most popular times to fish. Crescent Lake is the most popular destination. All fishermen 16 and older require an Alaska State fishing license and must comply with State of Alaska fishing regulations. Lodges already listed probably offer fishing excursions, but there are more. Redoubt Lodge (866.733.3034, redoubtlodge.com), Angry Eagle Lodge (angryeagle.com), Rainbow River Lodge (888.234.9552, rainbowriverlodge.com), All Alaska Outdoors Lodge (907.953.0186, allalaska.com), Within the Wild (907.274.2710, withinthewild.com), Rainbow King Lodge (800.458.6539, rainbowking.com), Stonewood Lodge (907.444.3892, stonewoodexpeditions.com), Chulitna Lodge (907.781.5772, chulitnalodge.com), Crystal Creek Lodge (907.357.3153, crystalcreeklodge.com), Island Lodge (islandlodge.com), Talarik Creek Lodge (907.388.8766, talarikcreeklodge.com), Redoubt Bay Lodge (907.776.7516, redoubtbaylodge.com), Lake Country Lodge (907.242.2331, lakecountrylodge.com), Alaska's Fishing Unlimited (907.781.2220, alaskalodge.com), Alaska Fly Anglers (907.252.2868, alaskaflyanglers.com). Newhalen Lodge (877.639.4256, newhalenlodge.com), And then there are fishing/hunting guides like Adventure Outfitters Alaska (907.690.2040, adventureoutfittersalaska.com) and

A fox surveys its surroundings

niche operators like Women's Flyfishing (907.274.7113, womensflyfishing.com). Finally, Ninilchik Charters (800.973.4742, ninilchik.com) offers fresh- and saltwater trips from Homer and Seward. And Mike Garcia (mgsfa.com) fishes for halibut in Cook Inlet from Homer.

Bear Viewing

Katmai gets most of the bear-viewing headlines but there are plenty of four-legged clam devourers within Lake Clark's boundaries too. Chinitna Bay and Silver Salmon Creek are prime bear-watching territory. The table below shows where and when to find bears. You can plan a bear-viewing adventure with the aforementioned flightseeing and boat tour operators or choose a specialist. AK Adventures (907.235.1805, goseebears.com), Bald Mountain Air (907.235.7969, baldmountain-air.com), Alaska Ultimate Safaris (888.696.2327, alaskaultimatesafaris.com), and J Bear Tours (907.435.1111, jbeartours.com) offer bear-viewing day trips from Homer. Bear Viewing Alaska (907.398.1744, bearviewinga-laska.com) offers boat and air bear-viewing trips from Homer. Or move in with the bears by sleeping at Silver Salmon Creek Lodge (907.252.5504, silversalmoncreek.com), Alaska Lodge Homestead (alaskawildlife.com), or Bear Mountain Lodge (907.252.1450, akbearmoun-tainlodge.com).

Visitor Center

Port Alsworth Field Headquarters (907.781.2218) and **Homer Field Office** (907.781.2117) are open in summer. Contact one of these facilities before arriving, especially if you intend on hiking, backpacking, rafting, mountaineering, or doing anything at Lake Clark without an authorized guide.

Ranger Programs & For Kids

Park rangers do not provide regularly scheduled walks and talks, but lectures and special programs are offered intermittently at Port Alsworth Visitor Center and Pratt Museum (907.235.8635, prattmuseum.org). For more information, contact Port Alsworth Visitor Center or Homer Field Office. The park does not offer any specific children's programs.

Flora & Fauna

Lake Clark's terrain varies from irregular coastlines to snow-clad volcanoes, forest to tundra to grassland, and glaciers of slow-moving ice to streams of fast-moving water. Diversity in terrain and ecosystem leads to top-rate wildlife viewing and bird watching. Caribou reside in the hills around Turquoise, Twin, and Snipe Lakes. Moose live below the tree line. Dall sheep scale the steep slopes of the Chigmit Mountains. Brown bears are found in all habitats, but are most common along the coast, particularly the Chinitna Bay Area. Throw in 125 species of birds and you won't want to forget your binoculars. And Neacola Mountain Air (907.350.3982, neacolamountainair.com, Wasilla) offers unique birding and walrus-viewing tours.

Pets & Accessibility

Leashed pets are allowed in the park, but for your safety, your pet's safety, and the health of the ecosystem, it is suggested you leave them at home.

Air charters may be able to transport wheelchair users, but no facilities or trails are accessible.

Bears: Where They Are and What They Are Eating

Location	Eating	June	July	August	September
Chinitna Bay	Vegetation & Clams	🐾🐾🐾	🐾🐾🐾	🐾🐾	🐾
Silver Salmon Creek	Vegetation, Clams & Salmon	🐾🐾	🐾🐾🐾	🐾🐾🐾	🐾🐾
Crescent Lake	Salmon	🐾	🐾🐾	🐾🐾	🐾🐾

🐾 = Few Bears, 🐾🐾 = Some Bears, 🐾🐾🐾 = Many Bears

River running below Iliamna Volcano

Weather

You never really know what sort of weather to expect while visiting Alaska, but there are two distinct climates at Lake Clark National Park. The coast is wet (40–80 inches of annual rainfall) with more moderate temperatures. The interior is drier (17–26 inches of annual rainfall) with more extreme temperature differences (-40°F in winter). Snow can fall most the year, but it's common from November through March. Lake Clark begins to freeze in November and thaw in April, but many lakes can be frozen into June.

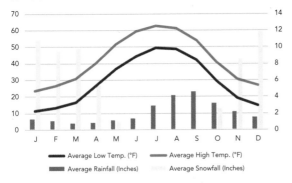

Average Low Temp. (°F) — Average High Temp. (°F)
Average Rainfall (Inches) — Average Snowfall (Inches)

Tips & Recommendations

It's a fly-in park and you basically have three options. 1). Fly with Lake Clark Air (lakeclarkair.com) or Lake and Peninsula Airlines (lakeandpenair.com) and fly into Port Alsworth and camp or stay at the Farm Lodge (the DIY approach). 2). Let someone else take care of the details by staying at one of the many lodges listed in these pages or hiring an adventure guide like Alaska Alpine Adventures (alaskaalpineadventures.com), Kenai Backcountry Adventures (kenaibackcountryadventures.com), or Great Alaska Adventures (greatalaska.com). Or 3). Charter a flight.

Dick Proenneke's cabin (locked late September through May) and Windsong Wilderness Retreat (windsongwildernessretreat.com), are located at Twin Lakes.

The sedge meadow between Sargent Creek confluence and Silver Salmon Creek is closed to human entry from mid-June through mid-September for habitat restoration. The meadow north of the slough at Chinitna Bay is closed to human entry from May through September, and you cannot picnic in Chinitna Bay from Glacier Spit to the Ranger Cabin, June through August.

Katmai

Phone: (907) 246-3305
Website: nps.gov/katm

Established: December 2, 1980
September 24, 1918 (National Monument)
Size: 4.7 Million Acres
Annual Visitors: 38,000
Peak Season: July & August

Activities: Bear Viewing, Flightseeing, Hunting, Fishing, Hiking, Backpacking, Paddling

Campgrounds: Brooks Camp*
Fee: $12 per person per night
Backcountry Camping: Permitted
Lodging: Brooks Lodge, Grosvenor Lodge, and Kulik Lodge
(800.544.0551, katmailand.com)

Park Hours: All day, every day
Entrance Fee: None

*Reservations are required and should be made as soon as they become available at recreation.gov or 877.444.6777

Originally created to protect features of the Novarupta Volcano eruption in 1912, Katmai has become a world-famous wildlife-viewing destination thanks to fishing bears who feast on salmon every summer at Brooks Falls. Bristol Bay is home to the world's largest run of Sockeye salmon. When they spawn in July, a small fraction make their way up the Naknek drainage to Brooks Camp. Sounds simple, but it's an incredibly treacherous journey. Along the way, they must pass a gauntlet of brown bears, sometimes numbering as many as one hundred. Each one is searching for dinner, and salmon is the main course. The best seats at the all-you-can-eat buffet are near Brooks Falls, where salmon back-up as they jump up the falls. It's dinner (for the bears) and a show (for you). And the show is spectacular.

To many visitors, bear terminology is a bit confusing. What's the difference between brown, grizzly, or Kodiak bears? They're actually the same species; they just come from different places. Kodiak bears reside on Kodiak Island, southeast of Katmai across Shelikof Strait. Browns refer to any bear living near the coast and grizzlies live in the interior. So, if a Kodiak bear moved to the Katmai coast it would become a brown, and if it traveled another 100 miles inland it would then be called a grizzly. Unfortunately bears do not carry birth certificates to prove their place of origin. However, habitat causes dramatic differences in appearance. Kodiaks are much larger, thanks to a steady diet of spawning salmon and very little competition for food. Kodiaks can weigh up to 1,500 pounds. Food for the inland grizzly is often less abundant; forced to scavenge, some full-grown grizzlies weigh as little as 350 pounds. At birth, the differences are superficial. Kodiaks, browns, and grizzlies are all born as one-pound baby cubs.

Tickets, please!

ALL passengers, please wait until your group is called

Brown bears of the Brooks River may be the headliner at Katmai, but the eruption of Novarupta and resulting Valley of Ten Thousand Smokes is an unforgettable encore. Novarupta Volcano erupted June 6–9, 1912. It was the single largest volcanic eruption of the 20th century. The explosion was heard for 140 miles. Nearby mountains were covered in ash up to 700 feet deep. Even Seattle, 1500 miles away, was dusted with ash from Novarupta. The sky over Kodiak Island was darkened for three days. Years later, Robert Griggs, a botanist on a National Geographic Expedition, recounted his visit to the devastated area: "The whole valley as far as the eye could see was full of hundreds, no thousands—literally tens of thousands—of smokes curling up from its fissured floor." The smoke stopped. The name stuck. Valley of Ten Thousand Smokes is a curiosity left behind to be explored by inquisitive backpackers. 15 active volcanoes remain in the park, and Alaska is by far the most volcanically active region of the Ring of Fire (an area in the basin of the Pacific Ocean where large numbers of earthquakes and volcanic eruptions occur). But volcanoes aren't the only hazard the park and its wildlife face. More than 1,055 tons of oiled debris was removed from shorelines following the Exxon Valdez oil spill in 1989. In some areas oil is still seen today. Enjoy the bears. Marvel the smokes. And remember the potential cost of procuring resources most of us rely on.

When to Go
Katmai National Park is open all year, but concessioner services are only offered from June through mid-September. Bear watching at Brooks Camp is best during July and September. Bears can be found in other areas like Hallo Bay, Geographic Harbor, Swikshak Lagoon, and Moraine/Funnel Creek during June and August.

Transportation & Airports
Katmai National Park is located on the Alaska Peninsula. Park Headquarters is in King Salmon, about 290 miles southwest of Anchorage as the crow flies. Brooks Camp, the main visitor destination, is 30 miles east of King Salmon. Neither area is accessible by car. Visitors can reach these remote destinations by plane or boat. Ted Stevens Anchorage International Airport (ANC) offers regularly scheduled commercial flights to King Salmon (AKN), which is the starting point for most Katmai adventures. Brooks Camp can also be accessed by boat from the villages of King Salmon or Naknek. Chances are you'll take a plane. Please refer to the flightseeing section for bush plane operators serving Katmai.

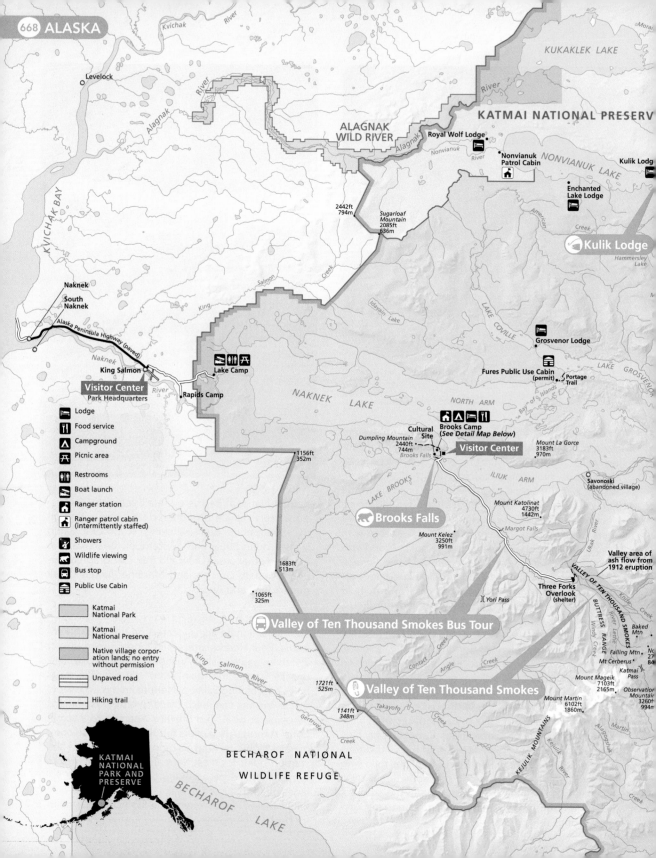

Kvichak River

Levelock

Alagnak River

ALAGNAK
WILD RIVER

KATMAI NATIONAL PRESERVE

KUKAKLEK LAKE

Royal Wolf Lodge

Nonvianuk River

Nonvianuk
Patrol Cabin

NONVIANUK LAKE

Kulik Lodg

2442ft
794m

Sugarloaf
Mountain
2085ft
636m

Enchanted
Lake Lodge

KVICHAK BAY

⊙ **Kulik Lodge**

Hammersley
Lake

Naknek

South
Naknek

Alaska Peninsula Highway (paved)

Naknek River

King Salmon

Visitor Center
Park Headquarters

Rapids Camp

Lake Camp

Salmon River

King River

Creek

Idavain Lake

LAKE COVILLE

Grosvenor Lodge

Fures Public Use Cabin
(permit)

Portage
Trail

LAKE GROSVENOR

NAKNEK LAKE

NORTH ARM

LAKE BROOKS

Bay of Islands

1156ft
352m

Cultural
Site

Dumpling Mountain
2440ft
744m
Brooks Falls

Brooks Camp
(See Detail Map Below)

Visitor Center

Mount La Gorce
3183ft
970m

ILIUK ARM

Savonoski
(abandoned village)

⊙ **Brooks Falls**

Mount Kelez
3250ft
991m

Mount Katolinat
4730ft
1442m

Margot Falls

Ukak River

Valley area of
ash flow from
1912 eruption

1683ft
513m

Three Forks
Overlook
(shelter)

VALLEY OF TEN THOUSAND SMOKES

Knife Creek

1065ft
325m

Yori Pass

Angle Creek

Contact Creek

⊟ **Valley of Ten Thousand Smokes Bus Tour**

BUTTRESS RANGE

Windy Creek

Baked
Mtn

Falling Mtn

Mt Cerberus

Katmai
Pass

No
27
84

King Salmon River

1721ft
525m

Takayofo Creek

⊙ **Valley of Ten Thousand Smokes**

Mount Mageik
7103ft
2165m

Observation
Mountain
3260f
994m

1141ft
348m

Gertrude Creek

Mount Martin
6102ft
1860m

KEJULIK MOUNTAINS

Kejulik River

Martin

Alagogshak

BECHAROF NATIONAL

WILDLIFE REFUGE

BECHAROF LAKE

Legend:

- 🛏 Lodge
- 🍴 Food service
- ⛺ Campground
- 🌲 Picnic area
- 🚻 Restrooms
- 🛶 Boat launch
- 🏠 Ranger station
- 🏚 Ranger patrol cabin
  (intermittently staffed)
- 🚿 Showers
- Wildlife viewing
- 🚌 Bus stop
- Public Use Cabin

Katmai
National Park

Katmai
National Preserve

Native village corpor-
ation lands; no entry
without permission

Unpaved road

Hiking trail

**KATMAI
NATIONAL
PARK AND
PRESERVE**

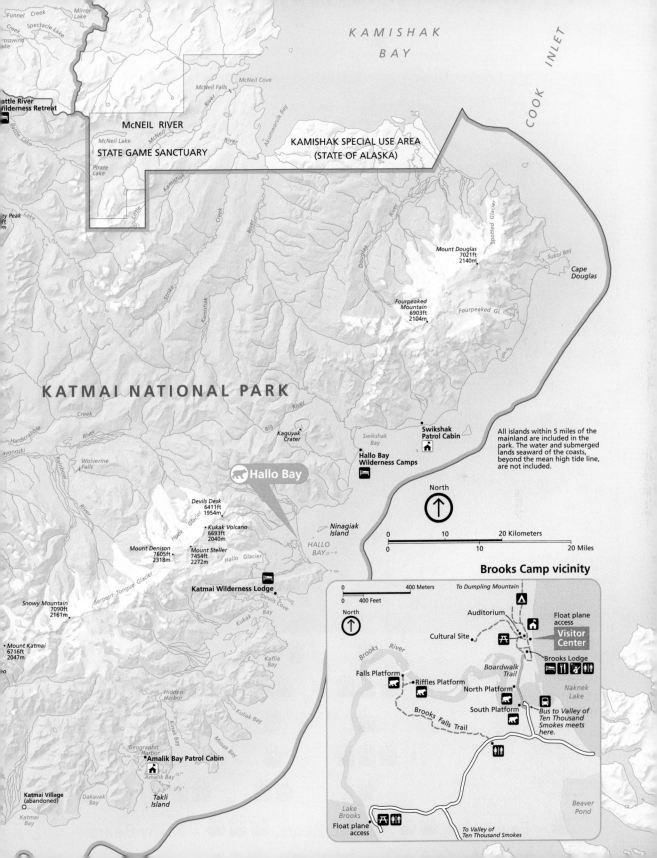

KAMISHAK BAY

COOK INLET

McNEIL RIVER
STATE GAME SANCTUARY

KAMISHAK SPECIAL USE AREA
(STATE OF ALASKA)

Battle River
Wilderness Retreat

McNeil Falls

McNeil Cove

McNeil Lake

Akumwarvik Bay

Pirate Lake

Mirror Lake

Spectacle Lake

Funnel Creek

Crossswind Lake

Mount Douglas
7021ft
2140m

Spotted Glacier

Sukoi Bay

Cape Douglas

Fourpeaked Mountain
6903ft
2104m

Fourpeaked Gl.

KATMAI NATIONAL PARK

Hardscrabble Creek

avonoski

Wolverine Falls

Rainbow River

Big Creek

Kaguyak Crater

Swikshak Bay

Swikshak Patrol Cabin

Hallo Bay Wilderness Camps

All islands within 5 miles of the mainland are included in the park. The water and submerged lands seaward of the coasts, beyond the mean high tide line, are not included.

⌕ **Hallo Bay**

North
↑

0   10   20 Kilometers
0   10   20 Miles

Devils Desk
6411ft
1954m

Kukak Volcano
6693ft
2040m

Mount Denison
7605ft
2318m

Mount Steller
7454ft
2272m

Snowy Mountain
7090ft
2161m

Mount Katmai
6716ft
2047m

Hook Glacier

Serpent Tongue Glacier

Hallo Glacier

Katmai Wilderness Lodge

Devils Cove Bay

Kukak Bay

Kaflia Bay

Ninagiak Island

HALLO BAY

Hidden Harbor

Kukak Bay

Kuliak Bay

Missak Bay

Geographic Harbor

Amalik Bay Patrol Cabin

Amalik Bay

Katmai Village (abandoned)

Dakavak Bay

Takli Island

Katmai Bay

Brooks Camp vicinity

0   400 Meters
0   400 Feet

North
↑

To Dumpling Mountain

Auditorium

Float plane access

Cultural Site

Visitor Center

Brooks River

Brooks Lodge

Falls Platform

Riffles Platform

Boardwalk Trail

North Platform

Naknek Lake

Brooks Falls Trail

South Platform

Bus to Valley of Ten Thousand Smokes meets here.

Lake Brooks

Float plane access

To Valley of Ten Thousand Smokes

Beaver Pond

Lunch time at Brooks Falls

Bears: Where They Are and What They Are Eating

Location	Eating	June	July	August	September
Brooks Camp	Salmon	🐾	🐾🐾🐾	🐾	🐾🐾🐾
Hallo Bay	Vegetation & Clams	🐾🐾🐾	🐾🐾	🐾🐾	🐾🐾
Geographic Harbor	Salmon	🐾	🐾	🐾🐾🐾	🐾🐾
Swikshak Lagoon	Vegetation	🐾🐾🐾	🐾	🐾	🐾
Moraine/Funnel Creek	Salmon	🐾	🐾🐾	🐾🐾🐾	🐾

🐾 = Few Bears, 🐾🐾 = Some Bears, 🐾🐾🐾 = Many Bears

Camping & Lodging

Brooks Camp (60-person capacity), located on the shores of Naknek Lake, is the only developed campground. Its scenic location and second-to-none wildlife viewing opportunities make this one of the best campgrounds in North America. Due to its unique setting in the midst of an extremely active bear habitat, campers must store all food and scented items in the food cache, cook in one of three shared cooking shelters, and wash dishes at the water spigot near the food storage cache. Campfires are allowed in three designated fire rings near each cooking shelter, but you may not cook over an open fire. Vault toilets are available. To help protect campers from the locals (bears), the campground is enclosed within an electric fence. The fence is not a physical bear barrier, but it deters most of them from entering. The campground is open from the beginning of June until mid-September. It costs $12 per person per night and sites must be reserved prior to arrival. Reservations can be made at (877) 444-6777 or recreation.gov. Be aware that reservations during peak bear viewing time fill within hours of becoming available (usually in January). During July, campsites can be reserved for a maximum of seven nights. The best time to visit Brooks Camp is July and September during prime bear viewing.

Brooks Lodge (katmailand.com), Kulik Lodge (kuliklodge.com), and Grosvenor Lodge (grosvenorlodge.com) are located in the park and operated by Bristol Adventures (800.544.0551). **Kulik Lodge** is the ideal destination for fly fishermen. Its cabins are situated along the shores of the Kulik River. Three nights starts at $4,495 per person (flights from Anchorage included, guided fly-out fishing not included). **Grosvenor Lodge** consists of three guest cabins with heat and electricity. Three nights costs $2,995 per person (flights from Anchorage and guided fly-out fishing not included). Lodging, meals, on-site boat and guide services, rods and waders, and complimentary evening cocktails are included. Fishing license and gratuities are not. **Brooks Lodge** consists of 16 modern rooms that can accommodate 2–4 persons. It's located in the heart of the park, just a short distance from Brooks Falls of salmon-fishing brown bears' fame. Pricing is variable depending on your choices (lodging, meals, rentals, fishing, Valley of 10,000 Smokes Tour, flightseeing), but expect it to cost somewhere around $3,000 per person for three nights at Brooks Lodge. Due to extremely high demand, rooms are distributed via online lottery through katmailand.com about 1.5 years in advance. Other lodging options are listed in the hunting and fishing section.

Valley of 10,000 Smokes

Bear Viewing

Katmai is home to as many as 2,200 brown bears. At times up to one hundred may be fishing for salmon along the Brooks River. This density and activity make Katmai one of the premier bear-viewing destinations in the world. There are several good areas to watch, but **Brooks Camp** is the most visited area of the park, where bear viewing is best during July and September. Three strategically located platforms provide safe viewing opportunities. Lower River Platform is located a short walk from the visitor center. An additional 0.9-mile (one-way) hike takes bear watchers to Falls and Riffles Platforms. A limited number of guests are allowed on each platform at a time. In July, bear can be seen at Brooks Falls as they fish for sockeye salmon swimming upriver to spawn. Bears return to the Brooks River to feed on dead/dying salmon in September but are usually found down river from the falls. Few bears are seen along the Brooks River during June and August, but they are active at this time in other areas. Katmai Air (800.544.0551, katmaiair.com, Anchorage), Emerald Air Service (907.235.4160, emeraldairservice.com, Homer), Bald Mountain Air Service (800.478.7969, baldmountainair.com, Homer), K Bay Air (877.522.9247, kbayair.com, Homer), Branch River Air Service (907.246.3437, branchriverair.com, King Salmon), Harvey Flying Service (907.487.2621, harveyflyingservice.com, Kodiak), and Sea Hawk Air (907.486.8282, seahawkair.com, Kodiak), as well as all the flight operators listed in the Lake Clark section, can get you here.

Flightseeing

The size of all these Alaskan parks is impossible to grasp. Going in a bush plane is a dramatic way to illuminate your perspective on the size and diversity of these stunning landscapes. Most of the bear-viewing planes and Lake Clark bush pilots will take you on a flightseeing tour. Valley of 10,000 Smokes, Mount Katmai, Mount Kaguyak, and American Creek are pretty good places to ask to fly over.

Hard to beat this fishing

Hunting & Fishing

Hunting is permitted within the preserve part of the park, pending you've procured the proper licenses. Your best bet is to join a specialized outfitter like Majestic Mountain Outfitters (406.347.5401, majesticmountainoutfitters.com) or Alaska Wild Wind Adventures (907.414.5434, alaskawildwind.com).

Fish here and the sport will never be the same. Several private lodges operate within or near the park's perimeter. No See Um Lodge 907.232.0729, noseeumlodge.com), Royal Wolf (866.428.1842, royalwolf.com), Deneki Outdoors (907.246.8345, deneki.com), Crystal Creek Lodge (907.357.3153, crystalcreeklodge.com), Tikchik Narrows (907.243.8450, tikchiklodge.com), Kvichak Lodge (907.230.6370, kvichaklodge.com), Naknek River Camp (907.439.2895, naknekrivercamp.com), and Blue Mountain Lodge (907.928.0023, bluemountainlodge.com) can take you to some of the best fishing you'll find anywhere on the planet. Or Frontier River Guides (877.818.2278, frontierriverguides.com) can take you on a multi-day float trip on Alagnak River, American Creek, or Moraine Creek.

Hiking & Backpacking

There are a handful of maintained hiking trails in the Brooks Camp area. The most popular is **Brooks Falls Trail**. It's an easy 1.2-mile hike leading from the visitor center to Brooks Falls, where Falls and Riffles Platforms are located (you'll use a new bridge built to prevent human traffic jams due to bear activity). **Cultural Site Trail** (0.1 mile) is an easy self-guided stroll through prehistoric camps and a reconstructed native dwelling. It begins at Brooks Camp Visitor Center. Park rangers lead guests on an hour-long interpretive walk of the area every day in summer. **Lake Brooks Road** begins at Lower Platform. This 1-mile path leads to the head of Brooks River and a large, glacially-carved lake. It's a good site to see salmon during spawning season (August), and bear occasionally fish here. **Dumpling Mountain Trail** begins at Brooks Camp Campground and climbs 800 feet over 1.5 miles to an overlook with outstanding views.

Katmai's other must-see attraction is **Valley of Ten Thousand Smokes**. The park is an expensive place to reach, but if you're determined to see the valley and save some money, frugal backpackers can make the 23-mile (one-way) hike along Valley of Ten Thousand Smokes Road, which begins at Lower Platform. The more sensible thing is to sign up for a bus tour provided by Katmailand (800.544.0551, katmailand.com). The bus driver is your guide and you'll be escorted on a fairly strenuous hike into the valley from Overlook Cabin (where the bus stops). The tour costs $96 (w/ lunch) or $88 (w/o), but those hoping to explore the region on their own can purchase a one-way ticket for $51. Valley of Ten Thousand Smokes is the site of the largest volcanic eruption of the 20th century, and it's a fantastic destination for **backpackers**. There used to be a pair of baked mountain huts 12 miles from the road toward Novarupta Volcano. The park says they were destroyed in a storm in 2018. It's still one of the better places to backpack within the park as bear activity is significantly less due to a lack of reliable food sources. River crossings in this area can be particularly dangerous. High volume of volcanic ash makes it nearly impossible to judge the depth. Always check river depth with a hiking pole or walking stick before each step. Bear-resistant food containers are required (available at King Salmon and Brooks Camp Visitor Centers). A backcountry permit is not required, but it is encouraged that you leave your hiking itinerary at Brooks Camp Visitor Center. Drinking water can be scarce in the valley. Make sure you know where you can find water before departing. The park is huge, with plenty of backpacking opportunities. Call the park to discuss or hire a guide like Alaska Alpine Adventures (877.525.2577, alaskaalpineadventures.com).

Paddling

The 80-mile Savonoski Loop follows the North Arm of Naknek Lake, where paddlers portage to Lake Grosvenor and continue on the Savonoski River to Iliuk Arm and back to Brooks Camp. Along the way you can spend the night at historic Fure's Cabin. It costs $45 per night. Reservations are required and can be made at recreation.gov.

Visitor Centers

There's a shared visitor center in King Salmon next to the airport. It's typically open in summer. Inside you'll find a small gift store and films. Upon arrival at Brooks Camp, you'll be greeted by a ranger to attend a mandatory bear etiquette and safety talk. It also has a small gift store. It's typically only open from June through September.

Ranger Programs & For Kids

Park rangers provide regularly scheduled cultural walks, hikes, and evening programs at Brooks Camp. Bus tours to the Valley of Ten Thousand Smokes ($96) are offered from early June through mid-September. Reservations are available at katmailand.com.

You'll have to decide if this is a good place for young children or not. There are a lot of bears, but the new elevated boardwalk and bridge are quite safe.

Fauna

Visitors come from around the world to see the bears, but they aren't the only animal roaming around this remote wilderness. Moose, caribou, red fox, wolf, lynx, wolverine, river otter, marten, porcupine, and other species live within the park's vast wilderness. Along the coast you may spot sea lions, sea otters, and beluga, killer, and gray whales.

Pets & Accessibility

This is not a good place for pets.

Most public buildings in Brooks Camp and all bear viewing platforms are accessible to individuals in wheelchairs, but the narrow dirt paths that connect facilities are often muddy, slippery, and difficult to navigate without assistance. Trails to Brooks Falls and Riffles are accessible. Close encounters with bears occur with some frequency, and there is a strong possibility visitors may need to leave the trail quickly and enter the woods to allow bears to pass. Air taxis may be accessible; contact the specific provider for details.

Weather

Visitors should come prepared for all types of weather. You might experience rain, sun, wind, or snow (unlikely in summer) during your stay, or even in a single day. Summer temperatures range from high 30s to low 80s°F. Winter is cold. Temps range from -40 to 40°F.

Behave in front of the humans

Tips & Recommendations

We know the bears are exciting, but don't forget about Valley of 10,000 Smokes. While a few people venture out here on their own, crossing silty streams and setting up camp in incredibly remote sites, most of its visitors only take the Bus Tour offered by Katmailand. It takes about 6–8 hours, but it's fascinating, and you'll go on a short hike to get an up-close view of the debris left behind by the largest volcanic explosion of the 20th century. Perhaps an even better way to view the region is to go on a flightseeing tour. That's something you can arrange with your lodge or flightseeing operator.

It's a good idea to get to know the bears before arriving. Thanks to technology and the wonderful Katmai park rangers, you can watch them from anyplace with a strong internet connection. The park operates several webcams, including a few at spots popular among the resident bears. Watch them fatten up over summer.

On one hand, it takes effort and money to get here, so it's a good idea to spend a few days and enjoy it. On the other hand, there's so much to see and do in Alaska, if you're spending multiple days, it's a good idea to add more activities (flightseeing, fishing, paddling, backpacking, etc.). The bears at Brooks Falls are amazing, but how much time do you want to spend watching them?

At first blush, the lodges look expensive, but when you consider that they'll fly you to-and-from Brooks Camp, take you fishing (fly-in options), and basically make sure you have an exciting itinerary every single day, the price becomes more palatable. In fact, I'd recommend it, especially if this is your dream vacation.

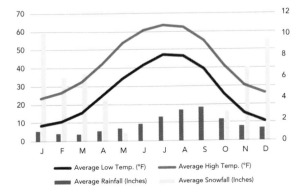

70												12
60												10
50												8
40												6
30												4
20												2
10												0
0	J	F	M	A	M	J	J	A	S	O	N	D

— Average Low Temp. (°F)   — Average High Temp. (°F)
■ Average Rainfall (Inches)   Average Snowfall (Inches)

Gates of the Arctic

River valley near Anaktuvuk

Phone: (907) 459-3730
Website: nps.gov/gaar

Established: December 2, 1980
December 1, 1978 (National Mon.)
Size: 8.5 Million Acres
Annual Visitors: 10,000
Peak Season: June–August

Activities: Backpacking, Packrafting, Flightseeing, Hunting, Fishing

Campgrounds: None
Backcountry Camping: Permitted
Lodging: Iniakuk Lake Wilderness Lodge and Wilderness Cabins
(877.479.6354, gofarnorth.com)

Park Hours: All day, every day
Entrance Fee: None

Gates of the Arctic, about the size of Switzerland, is the 2nd largest national park in the United States. The entire park resides north of the Arctic Circle, but it was still christened "Gates of the Arctic" by Bob Marshall while exploring the North Fork of the Koyukuk River. When he reached Frigid Crags and Boreal Mountain, one peak on each side of the river, he felt as though he had passed through the Arctic's stony gates. For explorers and outdoorsmen, the park is the gateway to a vast expanse of unspoiled wilderness and adventure. Rivers flow freely. Wildlife is undiminished. It represents nature at its purest, unscathed by roads, trails, and facilities. It's a land covered in snow and shrouded in darkness for much of the year. A land many people declare uninhabitable. A land that challenges outdoorsmen as they immerse themselves in nature. Wild, uninhibited, primitive nature.

Some 1,500 residents prove that this unforgiving landscape is in fact inhabitable. They reside in ten small communities within the park's "resident subsistence zone," where they still live lives similar to their ancestors who arrived more than 10,000 years ago from present-day eastern Siberia. Caribou, moose, and sheep provide sustenance. Caribou are of particular importance, used for food, shelter, clothing, and transportation. The animal's skin is fashioned into tents, parkas, pants, boots, socks, mittens, snowshoes, and sleds. Tendons are used to make nets to catch ptarmigan and fish. While exploring the park interior visitors may encounter relics of a caribou-dependent life. Remains of caribou skin tents are scattered throughout the wilderness. Inuksuit, or "stone people," are found along migratory routes; Nunamiut Eskimos used these stone effigies to drive caribou to locations where their hunters were waiting.

Throughout the years, gold miners, military officers, explorers, and government scientists came and went. Meanwhile, descendants of the original Inupiaq and Athabascan people continue to reside in the central region of the Brooks Mountain Range that crosses the park. A land filled with glacial cirques, six Wild and Scenic Rivers, and an undisturbed wilderness waiting to challenge the most seasoned backcountry explorers and winter survivalists. Indeed, Gates of the Arctic is the last American Frontier.

Hiking, Backpacking & Packrafting

Anyone traveling to Gates of the Arctic National Park must have a thorough agenda planned well in advance. There are no developed campgrounds or designated campsites. Rather than camping on fragile Arctic tundra, backpackers should search for durable surfaces like gravel bars, which have the added benefit of fewer mosquitoes. Just be sure to choose a location well above the water line since water levels can rise at any time. If you must camp on a vegetated site, choose a location with hardier plants like grasses and sedges rather than lichens and moss. You should make every effort to return your campsite to a natural appearance before leaving. Cooking should be done using a gas or propane stove. While open fires are allowed, wood and other burnable material is often scarce. Cook and eat all food at least 100 yards away from your camp. All food and scented items should be stored in a bear-resistant food container (BRFC). Visitor centers and ranger stations will loan BRFCs to visitors, free of charge, on a first-come, first-served basis. It is a good idea to call ahead to check availability.

Just as there are no designated backcountry campsites, there are no established hiking trails. Planning is essential to a safe and satisfying trip. Expect to move at a slower pace than usual. Vegetation can be dense, ground can be moist and boggy, and frequent river crossings will slow your travel. Going slowly isn't necessarily a bad thing. It affords time to savor this wild and rugged mountain wilderness. For easier travel,

Caribou

When to Go
Gates of the Arctic National Park is open all year. Summer is the best time to visit, but it's not perfect. Swarms of gnats and mosquitoes emerge once the snow melts (typically June–July). Like all Alaskan National Parks, weather can be extreme, and visitors must be prepared for all conditions. Snow can fall any day of the year, but precipitation is moderate. Hikers often rejoice when the sun comes out and the mercury rises, but heat causes rivers to swell, occasionally making them impassable. Visitors should have flexible plans and extra food in case your pick-up flight is delayed, or you need to wait out a storm or reroute your itinerary. Regardless of when you visit, all guests should be well versed in wilderness survival and self-rescue techniques.

Transportation & Airports
No roads enter the park, but Dalton Highway (AK-11) comes within 5 miles of its eastern boundary. Economically-minded hikers can begin on foot from Dalton Highway (river crossing required). Most visitors enter and exit the park via air taxi. Flights are available from Bettles (no road access), Coldfoot, and Anaktuvuk Pass (no road access), which can be reached by plane from Fairbanks International Airport (FAI).

NATIONAL PETROLEUM
RESERVE IN ALASKA

Continental Divide

Howard Pass

NOATAK   NATIONAL   PRESERVE

Iikhkluk Mountain
3650ft
1113m

Akiknaak Peaks
2880ft
878m

B   R   O   O   K   S

GATES OF THE ARCTIC
NATIONAL PARK AND PRESERVE

NATIONAL PARK
WILDERNESS

Continental Divide

👍 Arrigetch Peaks

Mount Igikpak
8510ft
2594m

Arrigetch Peaks
7190ft
2192m

🛶 Kobuk River

S C H W A T K A   M O U N T A I N S

Walker
Lake

HELPMEJACK HILLS

Shungnak

Kobuk

Kobuk   R.

ANGAYUCHAM
MOUNTAINS

NATIONAL
PRESERVE

NORUTAK HILLS

Norutak
Lake

Do not use this map
for hiking. Use USGS
topographical maps.

North
⬆

0	10	20 Kilometers
0	10	20 Miles

Approximate scale

National park area	National preserve area	🏠 Ranger station
National park wilderness area	Privately owned lands	✝ Airstrip
	Unpaved road	⛺ Primitive campground

Arctic   Circle

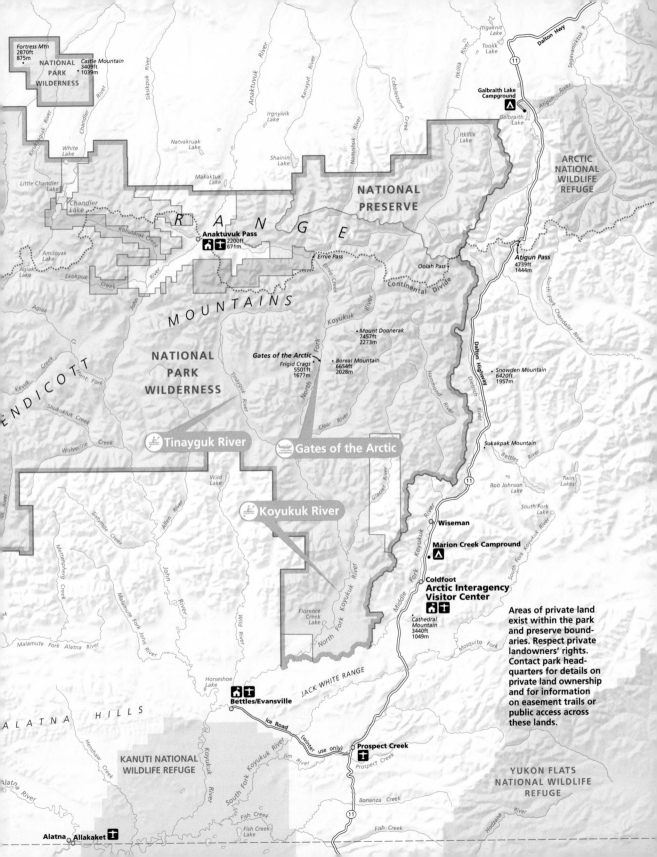

Fortress Mtn
2870ft
875m

NATIONAL
PARK
WILDERNESS

Castle Mountain
3409ft
1039m

Siksikpuk River

Anaktuvuk River

Kanayut River

Itigaknit Lake

Toolik Lake

Dalton Hwy

11

Galbraith Lake Campground

Galbraith Lake

Atigun River

ARCTIC
NATIONAL
WILDLIFE
REFUGE

Killukoguk River

Chandler River

Irgnyivik Lake

Natvakruak Lake

Shainin Lake

Cobbletone Creek

Nanushuk River

Itkillik Lake

White Lake

Little Chandler Lake

Chandler Lake

Makaktuk Lake

R A N G E

Anaktuvuk Pass
2200ft
671m

NATIONAL
PRESERVE

Amiloyak Lake

Kollutarak Creek

Agiak Lake

Ekokpuk Creek

Ernie Pass

Ernie Creek

Oolah Pass

Continental Divide

Atigun Pass
4739ft
1444m

North Fork Chandalar River

Aglak

M O U N T A I N S

Koyukuk River

Mount Doonerak
7457ft
2273m

Dalton Highway

Snowden Mountain
6420ft
1957m

Kevuk Creek

Hunt Fork

NATIONAL
PARK
WILDERNESS

Gates of the Arctic
Frigid Crags
5501ft
1677m

Boreal Mountain
6654ft
2028m

North Fork

Dietrich River

Hammond River

John River

Shukokluk Creek

Tinayguk River

Clear River

Sukakpak Mountain

E N D I C O T T

Wolverine Creek

🏊 Tinayguk River

🛶 Gates of the Arctic

Glacier River

11

Bettles River

Bob Johnson Lake

Twin Lakes

Sixtymile Creek

Allen River

Wild Lake

🏊 Koyukuk River

Koyukuk River

South Fork Lake

Mettenpherg Creek

John River

Wiseman

Marion Creek Campground

South Fork Koyukuk River

Malamute Fork John River

Florence Creek Lake

North Fork Koyukuk River

Wild River

Coldfoot
Arctic Interagency
Visitor Center

Middle Fork Koyukuk River

Malamute Fork Alatna River

Cathedral Mountain
3440ft
1049m

Mosquito Fork

Areas of private land
exist within the park
and preserve bound-
aries. Respect private
landowners' rights.
Contact park head-
quarters for details on
private land ownership
and for information
on easement trails or
public access across
these lands.

A L A T N A   H I L L S

Horseshoe Lake

Bettles/Evansville

JACK WHITE RANGE

Henshaw Creek

Koyukuk River

Ice Road
(winter use only)

Jim River

Prospect Creek

Prospect Creek

KANUTI NATIONAL
WILDLIFE REFUGE

South Fork Koyukuk River

11

Bonanza Creek

YUKON FLATS
NATIONAL WILDLIFE
REFUGE

Alatna River

Fish Creek

Fish Creek Lake

Fish Creek

Hodzana River

Alatna Allakaket

Prominent peaks

hike along the rocky riverbeds, where you won't face impassable ridgelines or boggy soil. Better yet, raft one of the six Wild and Scenic Rivers found in the park.

Rivers make for swifter travel. Many of the park's Wild and Scenic rivers can be navigated for hundreds of miles. Most are relatively easy floats, but the water is always cold and can be fast, especially when water levels peak in May and June or after particularly hot days or heavy rains. **Arrigetch Pass** (Kobuk River) and **Oolah Pass** (Koyukuk River) are two of the more popular areas of the park.

It's best to hire a guide. You have a few choices: Arctic Treks (907.455.6502, arctictreksadventure.com), Wilderness Alaska (907.345.3567, wildernessalaska.com), Arctic Wild (907.479.8203, arcticwild.com), Alaska Alpine Adventures (877.525.2577, alaskaalpineadventures. com), and Expeditions Alaska (770.952.4549, expeditionsalaska.com). All of them offer backpacking and packrafting trips in Gates of the Arctic. And Chulengo Expeditions (chulengo.org) does fly-in backpacking trips of the Brooks Range.

Flightseeing

And the easiest option is going on a flightseeing tour. Golden Eagle Outfitters (907.388.5968, alaskawildernessexpeditions.com), Brooks Range Aviation (800.692.5443, brooksrange.com), Wright Air Service (907.474.0502, wrightairservice.com), Coyote Air (907.678.5995, flycoyote.com), and Arctic Backcountry Flying Service (907.442.3200, arcticbackcountry.com), fly above the park or land on lakes and backcountry airstrips, transporting visitors deep into otherwise inaccessible wilderness. It is possible to see Gates of the Arctic and Kobuk Valley in the same day via plane, with short photo-stops at each. It's something worth discussing with the outfitter, but you're looking at a full day of flying at somewhere around $750/hour.

Hunting, Fishing & Wildlife Viewing

Just like the other activities at Gates of the Arctic, hunting and fishing are fly-in affairs. Arrowhead Outfitters (907.746.7744, arrowheadoutfitters.com) will take you hunting. Kobuk River Lodge (907.445.5235, kobukriverlodge.com) will take you fishing (although arctic waters have relatively low growth rates and productivity). And Bettles Lodge (907.692.5111, bettleslodge.com) and Iniakuk Lake Wilderness Lodge (877.479.6354, gofarnorth.com) offer all sorts of adventures, including fishing excursions and dog mushing. Speaking of dogs, Wild and Free Mushing (907.903.7707, wildandfreealaska.com) is another dog mushing option near the park.

Oolah Valley

Flora & Fauna

Gates of the Arctic is ideal for self-sufficient bird watchers and wildlife enthusiasts. Grizzlies, wolves, fox, caribou, and migratory birds gorge on food that becomes abundant during the short summer season. Talk with the park or plane operator about when and where to see wildlife.

Visitor Centers

If you're doing this on your own, leave your travel itinerary with a park ranger at one of the following facilities: Fairbanks Alaska Public Lands Information Center (101 Dunkel Street, 907.459.3730), Bettles Ranger Station (Bettles, 907.692.5495), Arctic Interagency Visitor Center (Coldfoot, 907.678.5209), or Anaktuvuk Pass Ranger Station (Anaktuvuk, 907.661.3520). Call to confirm hours of operation.

Ranger Programs & For Kids

The park does not offer regularly scheduled ranger or children's programs.

Pets & Accessibility

Pets are permitted but they should be leashed at all times in Bettles and Anaktuvuk Pass.

Gates of the Arctic is untamed wilderness. Terrain is unforgiving and difficult to navigate. Air taxis may be able to transport wheelchair users (call specific air taxi operators to verify), but there are no accessible park facilities or maintained trails.

Weather

Visitors should come prepared for all types of weather. The park's interior is relatively dry. The wettest months are June, August, and September. Summers are short, but the days are long (in summer the sun does not set for 30 straight days).

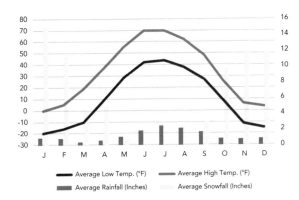

Kobuk Valley

Caribou crossing the Kobuk River

Phone: (907) 442-3890
Website: nps.gov/kova

Established: December 2, 1980
Size: 1.7 Million Acres
Annual Visitors: 15,000
Peak Season: June–August

Activities: Backpacking, Paddling, Flightseeing

Campgrounds/Lodging: None
Backcountry Camping: Permitted

Park Hours: All day, every day
Entrance Fee: None

Kobuk Valley National Park protects an arctic wilderness roughly the size of Delaware. It is a land so desolate and remote it can only be reached by foot, plane, boat, dogsled, or snowmobile. Unimaginable to modern people, natives have lived here for 10,000 years. Locals continue to follow in their ancestors' footsteps by hunting caribou at Onion Portage during the animal's southward migration in fall. The Western Arctic caribou herd is nearly half a million strong. Twice annually, they migrate across the park's southern reaches between summer calving grounds north of the Baird Mountains and winter breeding grounds south of the Waring Mountains. Along their journey, they leave tracks across Great Kobuk Sand Dunes, the largest active dune field in arctic North America. Today, it covers 23.5 square miles, but scientists believe the sand—ground down by glaciers of the last Ice Age—once covered an area more than ten times its present size. The landscape is constantly changing as wind and water reshape the dunes; some rise 200 feet above the tundra.

North of the Kobuk (Inupiaq for "Big") River are the Baird Mountains. Mount Angayukaqaraq (4,760 feet) is the park's highest peak. A modest mountain compared to Denali, but it presents an intimidating barrier for travelers. Lower in elevation, much of the tundra is soggy even though the park receives, on average, just 20 inches of snow and rain each year. Permafrost, many feet below the surface, prevents water from draining before everything freezes for the long, frigid winter. Life is forced to adapt or perish. The wood frog has found an interesting way to survive. In fall, it burrows beneath leaves and soil, where its body temperature drops below freezing. In spring, it thaws out only to hop about the valley and enjoy summer with a handful of humans seeking the ultimate adventure and solitude.

Activities

Visitors must possess a fairly unique set of skills. Self-sufficiency is paramount. Survival and self-rescue skills are, quite literally, a matter of life and death no matter when you travel. This is not a drive-thru vacation. No visitors park their cars and snap a picture of a grizzly bear lumbering across the tundra. There are no roads. No trails. No facilities. It's a vast expanse of relatively unexplored, completely wild wilderness. You are the guest of the grizzly, the caribou, and the gray wolf. It is not the sort of place for inexperienced paddlers or backpackers. If you get lost, you won't eventually "pop-out" at a fast-food joint, gas station, or even a road. The only thing that will be there to greet you is more wilderness. If you want to call for help, you better be carrying a satellite phone, because your cell phone won't work. Paddlers and hikers are completely alone out there. It's just you and Mother Nature, exactly what most of Kobuk Valley's visitors seek.

Unless you're flying over the park—viewing its rivers and mountains from above—trips into Kobuk Valley are usually extended expeditions. If you're going to plan your own backpacking or packrafting trip, do it with the help of a park ranger. Most trips begin with an air taxi ride to your starting point. Air taxis are available from nearby towns of Kotzebue and Bettles (also serving Gates of the Arctic). Golden Eagle Outfitters (alaskawildernessexpeditions.com) and Arctic Backcountry (arcticbackcountry.com) fly out of Kotzebue. You can reach Kotzebue from Anchorage using Alaska Airlines. In Kotzebue you'll find one hotel (nullagvikhotel.com) and a B&B. Before your trip, it's a very good idea to stop at Northwest Arctic Heritage Center in Kotzebue to drop off a copy of your trip itinerary and borrow a bear-resistant food container if you don't have one. The easiest hiking is along

Looking down on the Kobuk River

When to Go
The park is open all year, but only the hardiest adventurers (if any) enter the park during winter when the days are incredibly short, if the sun rises at all. All visitors should have extensive backcountry experience and advanced survival skills. Summer is the time to visit. The season is short (June–September), but the days are long (the sun doesn't set for more than a month around the Summer Solstice). Mosquitoes and gnats hatch in late May/early June. Daytime highs peak in July. August is often wet. The caribou migration, between winter breeding grounds south of the Waring Mountains and summer calving grounds north of the Baird Mountains, begins in September. Summer high temperatures average a comfortable 54°F, but visitors must come prepared for all types of weather. Snow and freezing temperatures may occur at any time, and temperatures exceeding 90°F have been recorded in certain regions of the park in July.

Transportation & Airports
No roads enter Kobuk Valley. Air taxis provide access to remote villages, lakes, and landing strips inside the park. Kotzebue and Bettles are the primary launch points for air taxi trips, but they aren't accessible by road either. Commercial airlines from Ted Stevens Anchorage International Airport (ANC) provide service to Kotzebue. Fairbanks International Airport (FAI) provides service to Bettles.

In summer, it's possible to access the park via motorized/non-motorized watercraft, or by foot. In winter, the park can be accessed via snowmobile or dogsled. Entering the park by foot is not recommended for anyone but the most skilled outdoorsmen.

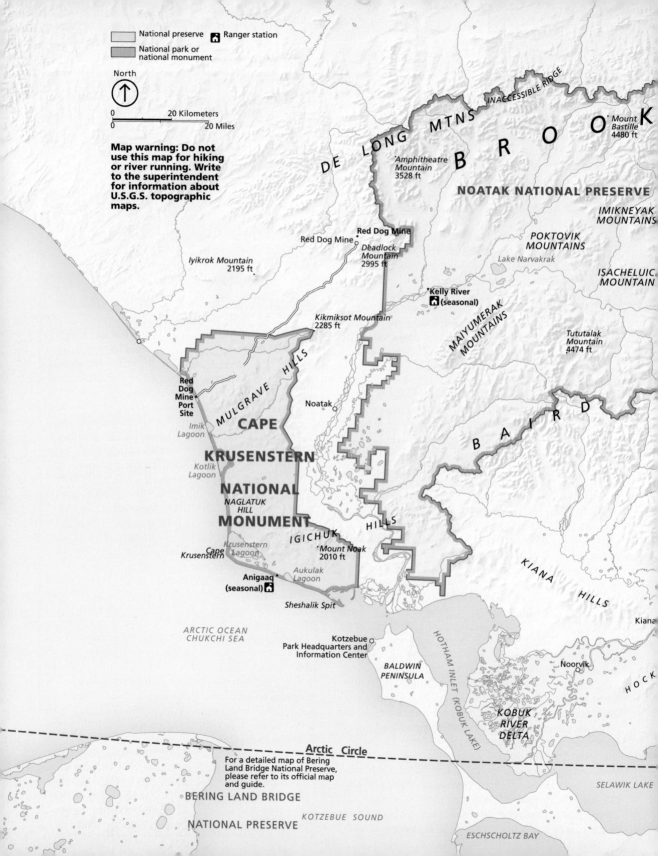

National preserve
National park or national monument
Ranger station

North

0   20 Kilometers
0   20 Miles

Map warning: Do not use this map for hiking or river running. Write to the superintendent for information about U.S.G.S. topographic maps.

DE LONG MTNS

INACCESSIBLE RIDGE

B R O O K

Mount Bastille 4480 ft

'Amphitheatre Mountain 3528 ft

NOATAK NATIONAL PRESERVE

IMIKNEYAK MOUNTAINS

POKTOVIK MOUNTAINS

ISACHELUIC MOUNTAIN

Red Dog Mine

Red Dog Mine

Iyikrok Mountain 2195 ft

Deadlock Mountain 2995 ft

Lake Narvakrak

Kelly River (seasonal)

Kikmiksot Mountain 2285 ft

MAIYUMERAK MOUNTAINS

Tututalak Mountain 4474 ft

Red Dog Mine Port Site

MULGRAVE

HILLS

CAPE

Noatak

B A I R D

Imik Lagoon

Kotlik Lagoon

KRUSENSTERN

NATIONAL

NAGLATUK HILL

MONUMENT

IGICHUK   HILLS

KIANA HILLS

Krusenstern Lagoon

Cape Krusenstern

'Mount Noak 2010 ft

Aukulak Lagoon

Anigaaq (seasonal)

Sheshalik Spit

ARCTIC OCEAN CHUKCHI SEA

Kotzebue Park Headquarters and Information Center

BALDWIN PENINSULA

HOTHAM INLET (KOBUK LAKE)

Kiana

Noorvik

HOCK

KOBUK RIVER DELTA

Arctic   Circle

For a detailed map of Bering Land Bridge National Preserve, please refer to its official map and guide.

SELAWIK LAKE

BERING LAND BRIDGE

KOTZEBUE SOUND

NATIONAL PRESERVE

ESCHSCHOLTZ BAY

NATIONAL PETROLEUM RESERVE IN ALASKA

R A N G E

Mount Bupto
4131 ft

Kivliktort
Mountain
4449 ft

Howard Pass

IGGIRUK
MOUNTAINS

Desperation
Lake

Aniralik
Lake

Feniak
Lake

Iikhkluk
Mountain
3730 ft

Okoklik
Lake

Anigaaq (seasonal)

Lake
Kangilipak

Kanaktok Mountain
3320 ft

Akiknaak Peaks
2890 ft

Lake
Matcharak

Mount
Angayukaqsraq
4760 ft

GATES OF THE ARCTIC
NATIONAL PARK

M T N S

AKIAK MOUNTAINS

SCHWATKA MTNS

KOBUK VALLEY
NATIONAL PARK

JADE MOUNTAINS

UK HILLS

Onion Portage
(seasonal)

GATES OF THE ARCTIC
NATIONAL PRESERVE

Kallarichuk
(seasonal)

GREAT KOBUK
SAND DUNES

Ambler

LITTLE KOBUK
SAND DUNES

Kobuk

M O U N T A I N S

Shungnak

River

Kobuk

Caribou Crossing (September)

Great Kobuk Sand Dunes

RING

SELAWIK NATIONAL WILDLIFE REFUGE

SHEKLUKSHUK RANGE

Field Station
(seasonal)

Selawik

Arctic   Circle

INLAND
LAKE

KOYUKUK NATIONAL
WILDLIFE REFUGE

Caribou

the ridgelines of the Baird Mountains. Ridgelines are exposed to chilling winds, but travel is free of swampy soil and impenetrable vegetation. Paddlers can float the 350-mile Kobuk River. This may be the best way to experience the park. The river is wide (up to 1,500 feet) but shallow as it crosses the park's southern half from east to west. The 80-mile trip from Ambler to Kiana can be made in about a week. This journey provides plenty of opportunities to explore on foot, too. In late August/September you may be able to stop and watch caribou as they swim across the Kobuk River at Onion Portage, near the park's eastern boundary. Further down river you can hike along Kavet Creek to Great Kobuk Sand Dunes. And paddling makes for much easier gear transportation. Alaska Alpine Adventures (877.525.2577, alaskaalpineadventures.com) is the only company offering regularly scheduled trips in Kobuk Valley. There aren't any lodges within the park's perimeter, but Kobuk River Lodge (907.445.5235, kobukriverlodge.com) is just upstream on the Kobuk River between Kobuk Valley and Gates of the Arctic.

Visitor Centers

The park's headquarters and office, located at **Northwest Arctic Heritage Center** (907.442.3890) in Kotzebue, is open year-round. Call to verify hours of operation before arriving. Ranger stations at Onion Portage and Kallarichuk are staffed intermittently.

Ranger Programs & For Kids

The park does not offer regularly scheduled ranger-led activities, but rangers are available to provide assistance over the phone or in person at Northwest Arctic Heritage Center in Kotzebue. This site also holds community activities throughout the year. Topics include natural and cultural history, local research, local crafts, and children's activities. Call (907) 442-3890 before your arrival for a current schedule of events.

Kobuk Valley isn't a very kid-friendly park, but children are invited to complete the Western Arctic Parklands Junior Ranger Book (available online) to earn a badge.

Flora & Fauna

Kobuk River is the lifeblood of an otherwise inhospitable region. North of this ribbon of scenic waterway rise the Baird Mountains. Each year several hundred thousand caribou, the largest herd in Alaska, cross the Kobuk River as they migrate from summer calving grounds north of the Baird Mountains to winter breeding grounds south of the Waring Mountains. Caribou are vitally important to the region's people. Nearly 1,500 locals reside in ten small communities within the park's "resident subsistence zone." These residents still hunt caribou at Onion Portage, just like their ancestors did for hundreds of years. Seeing the migrating herd of caribou can be just as rewarding as watching grizzlies

Landing at the Great Kobuk Dunes (Thanks, Justin!)

fish at Brooks Falls of Katmai National Park or whales swimming in Glacier Bay.

Caribou aren't the only show in the valley. It is estimated that there are 32 mammals, 23 fish, 119 birds, and 1 amphibian that live in or visit the park. Other popular mammals include grizzly bear, wolf, black bear, mink, lynx, fox, wolverine, moose, and Dall's sheep.

Great Kobuk Sand Dunes and the northernmost reaches of boreal forest lie south of the Kobuk River. Caribou walk across the 23.5-square-mile dunefield during their biannual migration (north in the spring, south in the fall). Little Kobuk and Hunt River dunes also reside south of the Kobuk River. Much of the southern reaches are covered in sand created by the grinding action of ancient glaciers, and then sculpted by wind and water, eventually stabilizing thanks to vegetation. More than 400 species of plants grow here, remarkable diversity for an area with such a harsh climate.

Pets & Accessibility
It's not a particularly good idea to bring your pet.

There are no visitor facilities or designated trails inside park boundaries. This is an extremely wild and undeveloped region that should not be accessed by anyone other than people with significant backcountry experience and skill. Individuals in wheelchairs may be able to tour the park by plane. Please contact specific transportation providers for details.

Weather
Visitors must come prepared for all types of weather. Snow, wind, rain, and clouds can occur any time of year. Average summer temperatures in the mid-60s°F sounds pleasant, but they may reach into the mid-80s°F one day in July only to fall below freezing the next. Average January lows are below zero, and they can fall below -40°F. Due to extreme day-to-day temperature variance, average temps are not always a good guideline. One thing you can be sure of is that there will be long summer days. The sun never sets between June 3 and July 9. In winter, twilight lasts for hours each day, but the sun is only above the horizon for 1.5 hours on December 21. The northern lights (Aurora Borealis) are active year-round, but it is best seen on dark winter nights.

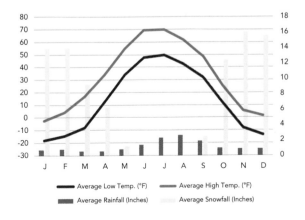

— Average Low Temp. (°F)   — Average High Temp. (°F)
■ Average Rainfall (Inches)   Average Snowfall (Inches)

REMOTE ISLANDS

HAWAII

🕐 **HAWAII (Washington, DC, minus 5 hours; minus 6 hours during daylight saving time)**

KAUA'I

NI'IHAU

O'AHU

World War II Valor in the Pacific NM

Honouliuli NM

HONOLULU

Kalaupapa NHP

MOLOKA'I

Haleakalā NP

H A W A I I

MAUI

Pu'ukoholā Heiau NHS

HAWAI'I

Kaloko-Honokōhau NHP

Pu'uhonua o Hōnaunau NHP

Hawai'i Volcanoes NP

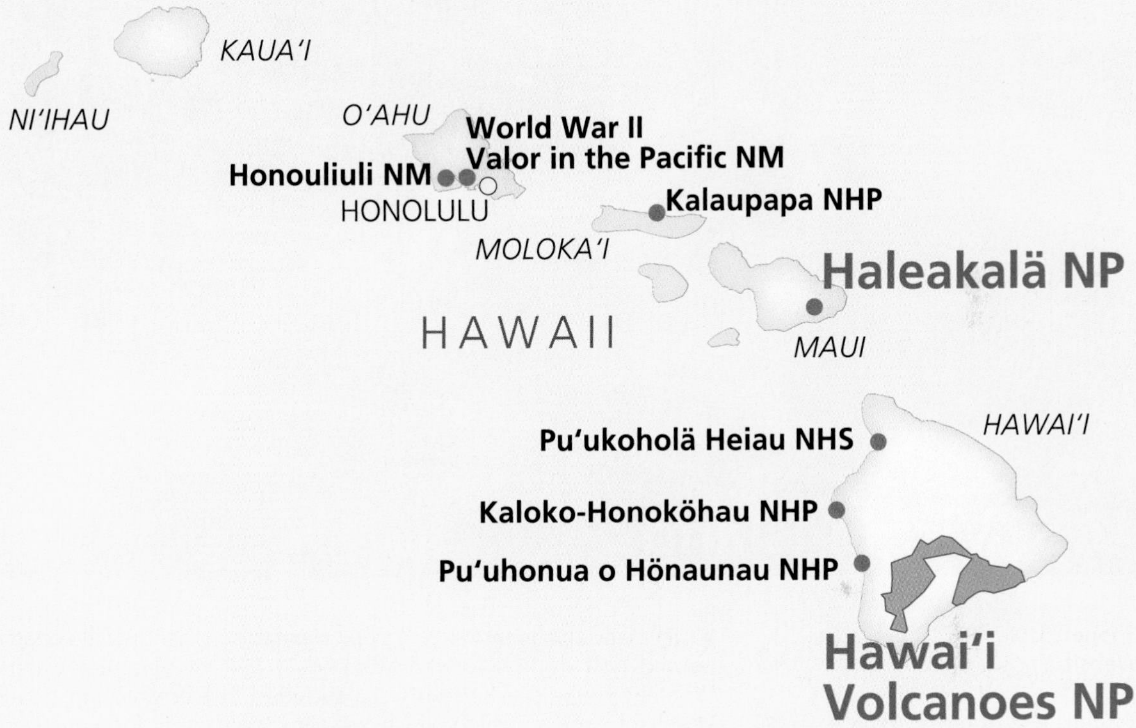

AMERICAN SAMOA

🕐 **AMERICAN SAMOA (Washington, DC, minus 5 hours; minus 6 hours during daylight saving time)**

National Park of American Samoa

TUTUILA   *OFU*   *TA'Ü*

PAGO PAGO

AMERICAN SAMOA

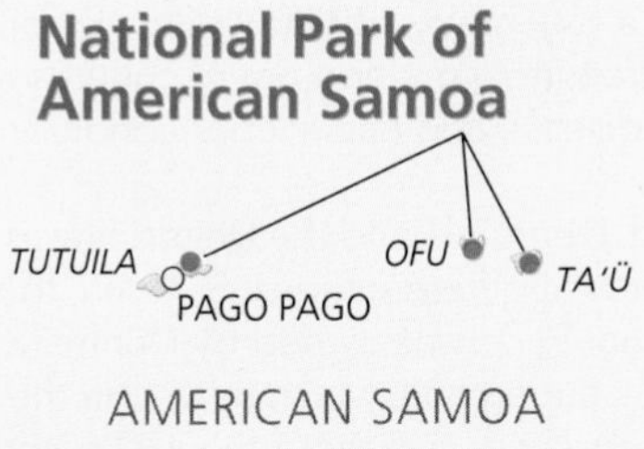

U.S. VIRGIN ISLANDS

🕐 **PUERTO RICO and VIRGIN ISLANDS (Washington, DC, plus 1 hour; same time during daylight saving time)**

PUERTO RICO   VIRGIN ISLANDS

SAN JUAN
San Juan NHS

Virgin Islands NP

CHARLOTTE AMALIE

Virgin Islands Coral Reef NM

Buck Island Reef NM

Salt River Bay NHP and Ecological Preserve

Christiansted NHS

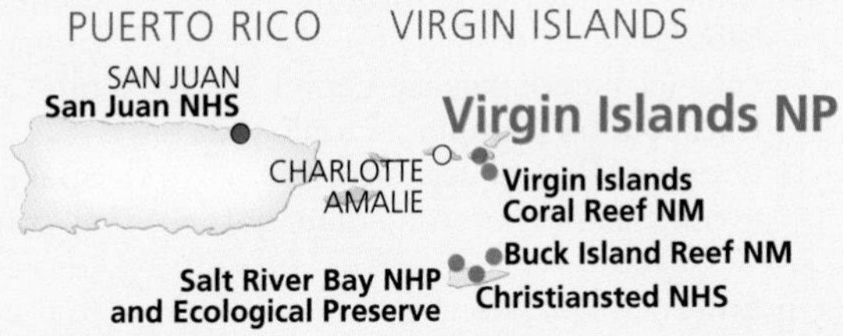

U.S. Virgin Islands

Trunk Bay

Phone: (340) 776-6201 ext. 238
Website: nps.gov/viis

Established: August 2, 1956
Size: 14,689 Acres
Annual Visitors: 400,000
Peak Season: December–April

Activities: Hiking, Paddling, Sailing, Snorkeling, SCUBA, Fishing

Best Beaches: Trunk Bay, Salomon/Honeymoon Beach, Maho Bay

Cinnamon Bay Campground
Closed for restoration after hurricane (cinnamonbayresort.com)
Backcountry Camping: Prohibited
Lodging: Caneel Bay Resort
(closed due to hurricane damage)

Entrance Fee: None
Trunk Bay Day Pass: $5/person
Overnight Anchoring: $26/night

Virgin Islands National Park is a tropical paradise of sandy white beaches and lush tropical forests wrapped in brilliant turquoise waters. Whether you're perched above a secluded bay or watching gentle waves roll onto a pristine beach, the views here are fit for a postcard. Stray away from the leisurely comforts of the bays and beaches, and you can learn of the area's not-so-perfect past. A past at odds with such an idyllic environment.

It's believed humans have inhabited the Virgin Islands since 1,000 BC. Like many primitive people, they progressed from a nomadic village lifestyle to a complex religious culture with ceremonial sites for worshipping the spirits of the cassava (their main crop) and the sea. Europeans arrived in 1493, when Christopher Columbus, on his second voyage to the West Indies, spotted more than 100 emerald isles. He named them after Saint Ursula's legendary 11,000 virgins. Europeans began to colonize the islands, creating a melting pot of cultures where pre-Columbians perished from disease and harsh labor conditions.

Spain, France, Holland, England, Denmark, and the United States have all controlled various Virgin Islands at different times. St. John, the centerpiece of Virgin Islands National Park, was owned by Denmark prior to the United States. At this time, sugarcane, which thrived in the tropical climate, was the primary cash crop, and more than 90 percent of the island's native vegetation was stripped away in favor of farming. For nearly two centuries, Danes produced huge quantities of sugar, rum, and molasses, which were shipped back to Europe. Such impressive production was a boon to the plantation owners, but the burden was placed squarely on the shoulders of enslaved Africans and their descendants. More than 80 plantations were constructed on St. John alone. Decades of growth left an island where slaves outnumbered the plantation owners by a rate of five to one. In 1848, a slave revolt led by General Buddhoe resulted in the release of Danish slaves in Frederikstad, St. Croix. Emancipation, low sugar prices, and nutrient-depleted soil marked the end of the "sugar is king" era of the Virgin Islands.

In 1917, construction of the Panama Canal and rise of German naval strength spurred the United States to purchase St. Croix, St. Thomas, St. John, and about 50 smaller islands from Denmark for $25 million. The islands served a role in military strategy, but they gained notoriety as a vacation destination. St. John's heavenly beaches have served as sun-bathing ground for millions of tourists. The sight of Little Maho Bay was enough to make Ethel McCully jump out of her boat and swim to shore. Once the eccentric American arrived, she never left; throwing caution to the wind, she lived her life in a setting most people only dream about. With six donkeys and two laborers she built a home, and then sat down to pen a book about the experience.

Ethel wasn't the only person smitten by the island's allure. Developers began purchasing land and building extravagant resorts and hotels. Laurance Rockefeller, philanthropist, conservationist and son of John D. Rockefeller, Jr., also took notice of the island's unique beauty and its rapid development. In 1956, he purchased 5,000 acres, half of St. John Island, for $1.75 million. He ended up donating this tract of land to the United States for use as a national park. Today, Rockefeller's personal estate in Caneel Bay serves as the park's only resort (closed due to hurricane damage).

Tourism is currently king, but ruins of plantations, factories, and mills serve as reminders of the islands' past. You can learn all about the history and process of sugar production at Catherineberg and Annaberg Sugar Mill Ruins. Still, the park's main attractions are its warm and crystal-clear water, ideal tropical climate, and powdery beaches. It's a setting that many of the park's roughly 400,000 annual visitors can only dream about, but maybe you'll be the next person so enthralled with its beauty that you refuse to leave paradise, much like Ethel McCully.

Salt Pond Bay

When to Go

The park is open all year, but most travelers visit between December and mid-April. Trunk Bay's bathhouse, snack bar, and souvenir shop are open until 4pm. Lifeguards are on duty daily at Trunk Bay Beach. Cinnamon Bay Campground closes to unregistered guests at 10pm.

Transportation

Due to its remote location in the Caribbean, Virgin Islands National Park must be reached by plane or boat. The park consists of half of the Island of St. John plus a few other isolated smaller islands. Its visitor center is situated near the dock at Cruz Bay on St. John.

Cyril E. King Airport (STT) in Charlotte Amalie, St. Thomas serves as gateway to the U.S. Virgin Islands. From here you can reach Cruz Bay by ferry from two different docks. To reach the downtown Charlotte Amalie ferry dock you will need to take a short taxi ride (~$6/person). The ferry takes about 40 minutes and costs $13 each way. Ferry service from Charlotte Amalie to Cruz Bay departs three times per day. You can also take a taxi or bus from Charlotte Amalie to Red Hook (~$9/person). A taxi ride provides a decent tour of St. Thomas Island. Ferries depart Red Hook for Cruz Bay every hour between 6am and midnight. The ferry takes about 20 minutes and costs $6 each way. Contact Varlack Ventures (340.693.9933, varlack-ventures.com) for additional information on ferry services. Visitors can also find private water-taxis and car ferries. Car rental is available near the dock at Cruz Bay ($75–120/day, $450–720/week). Remember to drive on the left-hand side of the road. Star Fish Tours (340.998.6139, stjohnislandtours.com) and Aqua Blu (340.776.2782, aquablucarrental.com) offer driving tours.

Public transportation is available on St. John. VITRAN buses travel between Cruz Bay and Saltpond Bay, leaving the dock at 20 minutes after the hour from 6am until 7:25pm.

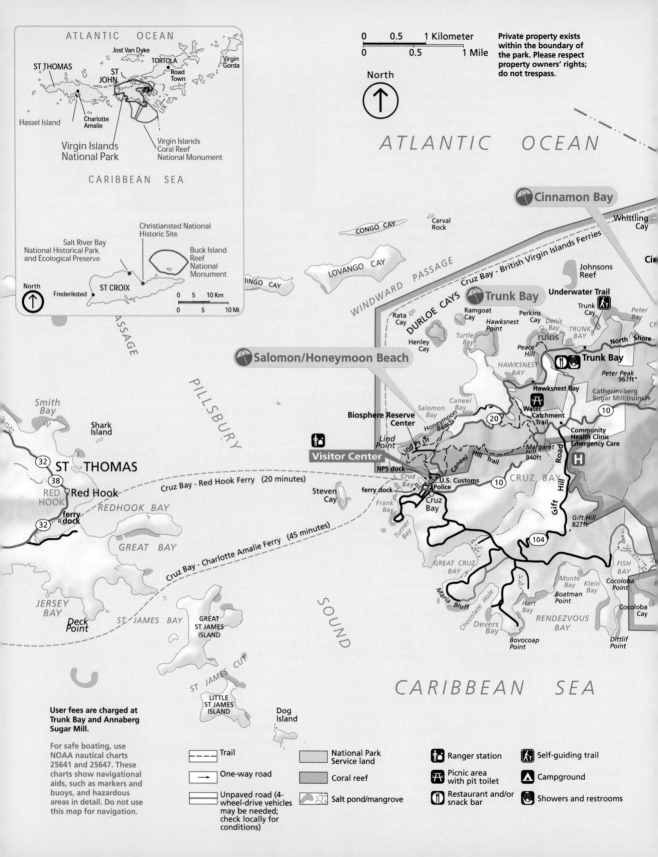

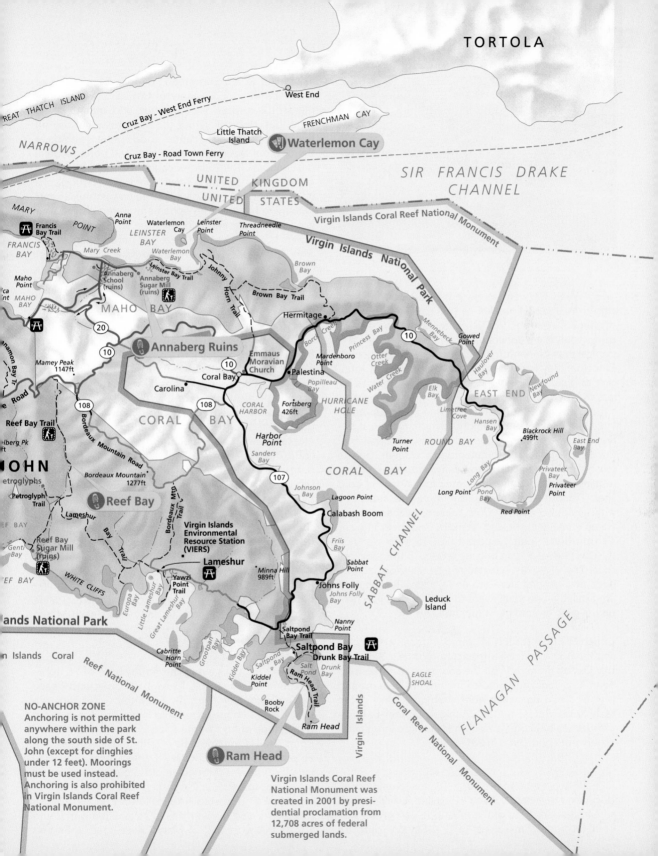

TORTOLA

GREAT THATCH ISLAND

West End

Cruz Bay – West End Ferry

FRENCHMAN CAY

NARROWS

Cruz Bay – Road Town Ferry

Little Thatch Island

Waterlemon Cay

SIR FRANCIS DRAKE CHANNEL

UNITED KINGDOM
UNITED STATES

Virgin Islands Coral Reef National Monument

MARY

POINT

Anna Point

Waterlemon Cay

Leinster Point

Threadneedle Point

Virgin Islands National Park

Francis Bay Trail

FRANCIS BAY

LEINSTER BAY

Mary Creek

Waterlemon Bay

Leinster Bay Trail

Brown Bay

Maho Point

Annaberg School (ruins)

Annaberg Sugar Mill (ruins)

Johnny Horn Trail

Brown Bay Trail

MAHO BAY

Hermitage

Mennebeck Bay

Gowed Point

MAHO BAY

20

Mamey Peak 1147ft

10

Annaberg Ruins

Emmaus Moravian Church

Coral Bay

Borck Creek

Princess Bay

Mardenboro Point

Otter Creek

10

Haulover Bay

Newfound Bay

EAST END

Carolina

Palestina

Popilleau Bay

HURRICANE HOLE

Water Creek

Elk Bay

Limetree Cove

Hansen Bay

Blackrock Hill 499ft

East End Bay

Reef Bay Trail

108

Bordeaux Mountain Road

CORAL   BAY

108

107

Fortsberg 426ft

CORAL HARBOR

Harbor Point

Sanders Bay

Turner Point

ROUND BAY

CORAL   BAY

Long Bay

Long Point

Pond Bay

Red Point

Privateer Bay

Privateer Point

JOHN

Petroglyphs

Petroglyph Trail

Reef Bay

Bordeaux Mountain 1277ft

Bordeaux Mtn Trail

Virgin Islands Environmental Resource Station (VIERS)

Johnson Bay

Lagoon Point

Calabash Boom

SABBAT   CHANNEL

Reef Bay Sugar Mill (ruins)

Lameshur

Reef Bay Trail

Lameshur

Friis Bay

Sabbat Point

Yawzi Point Trail

Minna Hill 989ft

Johns Folly

Johns Folly Bay

Leduck Island

Europa Bay

Little Lameshur

Great Lameshur Bay

WHITE CLIFFS

Cabritte Horn Point

Grootpan Bay

Kiddel Bay

Saltpond Bay Trail

Nanny Point

FLANAGAN   PASSAGE

lands National Park

Saltpond Bay

Drunk Bay Trail

Islands   Coral

Reef National Monument

Kiddel Point

Saltpond Bay

Salt Pond

Drunk Bay

EAGLE SHOAL

Booby Rock

Ram Head Trail

Coral Reef National Monument

NO-ANCHOR ZONE
Anchoring is not permitted anywhere within the park along the south side of St. John (except for dinghies under 12 feet). Moorings must be used instead. Anchoring is also prohibited in Virgin Islands Coral Reef National Monument.

Ram Head

Ram Head

Virgin Islands

Virgin Islands Coral Reef National Monument was created in 2001 by presidential proclamation from 12,708 acres of federal submerged lands.

Cinnamon Bay

Camping & Lodging

When we went to print the campground was closed for restoration due to hurricane damage (re-opening December 2021). As far as national park campgrounds are concerned, they don't get any more tropical than **Cinnamon Bay** (cinnamonbayresort.com). Cinnamon Bay, located on the north side of Saint John, isn't as beautiful as neighboring Trunk Bay, but it's far less crowded. It's the park's only campground as well as a great place for snorkeling, swimming, and sun-bathing. Bare campsites ($45/night), similar to typical national park camping accommodations, are available, but they also offer platform tents and cottages. Guests must bring (or rent from the camp store) everything required (tent, sleeping mat, etc.) to stay at the bare sites. Platform tents are 10'-by-14' canvas structures with mosquito netting. Cots, lantern, propane stove, water container, cooking utensils, and bedding are also provided. Cottages are 15'-by-15' with electricity, 4 twin beds, and an outside terrace. Bathrooms are shared by all guests. A restaurant, beach shop, laundry (fee), and general store are on location. Reservations are available and you'll want to book early if you plan on traveling around the winter holidays.

Concordia Eco-Resort (340.690.0561, concordiaecoresort.com), offers Eco-Tents and studios near Saltpond Bay just off Route 107 on the southeastern side of St. John. Eco-Tents and Studios feature full kitchens and private bathrooms that were designed using green techniques. Rates start at $99/night. **Caneel Bay Resort** (caneelbay.com) is also undergoing a lengthy recovery from hurricanes in 2017.

Hiking

Visitors come to the Virgin Islands to enjoy powdery white beaches, but you'll also find 20 hiking trails within the park. One of the most popular is **Reef Bay Trail**, located 4.9 miles east of Cruz Bay on Route 10/ Centerline Road. This steep, 2.2-mile (one-way) trail descends through a variety of tropical plant life to a pleasant bay (pack your swimsuit and snorkel if you want, but it's certainly not the most beautiful bay on the island—snorkeling can be good on the west side of the bay, but again there are easier and better snorkel destinations). You'll also encounter ruins of four sugar mill estates. There's a 0.3-mile spur trail to petroglyphs (rock carvings of pre-Columbian Taino people), a small swimming hole, and an ephemeral waterfall. The spur is one of the best parts of the hike, so don't skip it. It's about 1.5 miles into the hike, just before the junction with Lameshur Bay Trail. You should notice a sign for "Petroglyph Trail." (Note: Taking Lameshur Bay Trail to Europa Bay is a pretty good alternative hike-and-snorkel adventure.) Wear hiking boots (or at least don't wear flip-flops) because the trail can be very slippery. The park periodically offers ranger-led hikes of Reef Bay and L'Esperance Trails, where you hike down to Reef Bay and boat back to Cruz Bay. (L'Esperance Trail also begins on Route 10/Centerline Road and ends at Reef Bay.) For reservations and inquiries, stop by the Friends of the Park Store (340.779.4940, friendsvinp. org), located in Cruz Bay Visitor Center. The hike requires a fee to cover transportation expenses (boat and taxi rides). Located on the south shore of St. John is **Bordeaux Mountain Trail**. It's a 1.2-mile (one-way) path leading to the highest point in the park, Bordeaux Mountain (1,300 ft). The trail connects Bordeaux Mountain Road with Lameshur Bay. Southeast of Lameshur Bay off Route 107 near Saltpond Bay you'll find three short trails. **Ram Head Trail** is the best of the bunch. It's a 1.0-mile (one-way) walk to a rock outcropping 200 feet above the Caribbean. The views are awe-inspiring. The other two trails are Saltpond Bay and Drunk Bay. **Drunk Bay Trail** offers opportunities to see wading birds (and plenty of visitor-created coral artwork) while **Saltpond Bay Trail** leads to Salt Pond Beach, where you'll find a picnic area and good swimming and snorkeling, although the seafloor is a bit rough.

There are 12 trails along the north shore of St. John. Lind Point, Caneel Hill, Caneel Hill Spur, and Peace Hill Trails are near Cruz Bay. From the visitor center in Cruz Bay, it's about 1.5 miles to **Salomon/Honeymoon Beach** (one of my favorite spots on the island) via **Lind Point Trail**. **Cinnamon Bay Trail** is located near the entrance to Cinnamon Bay Campground. This 0.5-mile loop passes through an old sugar mill estate and a tropical forest. You'll also find Cinnamon Bay Trail nearby. It's a forested hike, following an old Danish plantation road for 1.1 miles to its junction with Route 10. At the west end of Mary Creek Road is **Francis**

Bay Trail. This 0.5-mile (one-way) trail is a favorite of snorkelers, swimmers, and birdwatchers. Just south of Mary Point are **Annaberg School Ruins** and a bit further east are **Annaberg Sugar Mill Ruins**, where you'll find a self-guided tour that helps explain the Danes' sugar industry during the 18th and 19th centuries.

Paddling, Sailing & Boating

You don't need to bring your own kayak or sailboat to the Virgin Islands. Rentals are available at Cinnamon Bay Campground (when it's open) and Salomon/Honeymoon Beach. Virgin Islands Eco Tours (340.779.2155, viecotours.com) and Arawak Expeditions (340.693.8312, arawakexp.com) offer rentals and paddle/snorkel tours all over the island. Kekoa (340.244.7245, blacksailsvi.com), Cruz Bay Watersports (340.776.6234, cruzbaywatersports.com), and Virgin Caribe (888.545.9198, virgincaribe.com) offer private charters and snorkeling adventures. Lion In Da Sun (340.626.4783, lionindasun.com) will take you snorkeling or drop you off and pick you up from any of the park's smaller islands. Bad Kitty (340.777.7245, calypsovi.com) has a variety of boats you can charter to explore the park's waters or beyond (like Coral Bay's floating taco bar or the British Virgin Islands).

Snorkeling

More than one-third of the park is underwater, and several reefs can be reached directly from its beaches. There's even a snorkel trail at Trunk Bay where underwater plaques describe the marine life as you swim by it (although much of the coral has been ruined by overuse). Nearly the entire St. John's shoreline is a snorkeler's playground. If you enjoy seeing colorful fish and feisty sea life, you'll want to have snorkel gear with you every day you're on the island. You should be able to rent gear at Cruz Bay, Salomon/Honeymoon Beach, Trunk Bay, and Cinnamon Bay. Rental costs about $8/day or $40/week. Trunk Bay, Cinnamon Bay, Hawksnest Beach, Saltpond Bay, Francis Bay, and Maho Bay are some of the best locations to hop in the water for a little underwater exploration. **Waterlemon Cay** offers a unique snorkeling experience where visitors must complete a 10-minute walk from Annaberg Sugar Mill Ruins Parking Area to the edge of Waterlemon Bay. From here, Waterlemon Cay is just to the northeast across the bay. Swim out to the small emerald island, but be sure to circle it in a counter-clockwise fashion; swimming in this direction will be easier thanks to the water's current. Snorkeling this fairly-long stretch provides excellent opportunities to see turtles, starfish, stingrays, sharks, and barracudas. Strong swimmers might also consider snorkeling from Francis Bay across

Salomon Beach

Fungi Passage, and around Whistling Cay. If you'd like to snorkel with an experienced guide, Virgin Islands Eco Tours (340.779.2155, viecotours.com) and Arawak Expeditions (340.693.8312, arawakexp.com) have you covered. Otherwise the park offers ranger-led trips for a nominal fee. Stop by or call Cruz Bay Visitor Center (340.776.6201, ext. 238) for a current schedule of ranger-led snorkel tours.

SCUBA Diving

The U.S. Virgin Islands' wealth of water and reefs make it a great place to SCUBA dive. When it was open you could take SCUBA lessons at Cinnamon Bay Campground. Courses are offered for beginners and certified divers. Diving arrangements can be made at the activities desk. **Buck Island Reef National Monument** (nps.gov/buis), just north of Saint Croix Island, is a popular SCUBA diving destination close to the park. Numerous outfitters provide SCUBA lessons and charters for divers of all experience levels. They offer beginner courses, certification courses, night dives, wreck dives, and multi-dive discounts. Low Key Watersports (340.693.8999, divelowkey.com), and Patagon Dive Center (340. 690.7223, patagondivecenter.com) offer dives, diving certification, and private charters. And you can SNUBA at Trunk Bay (340.693.8063, visnuba.com, $80 for 2 hours).

Fishing

Just Fish St. John (340.201.9329, justfishstjohn.com), Offshore Adventures (340.513.0389, sportfishingstjohn.com), Salty Daze (340.690.7258, saltydaze-usvi.com), and Rockhoppin' Adventures (340.514.5527, rockhoppin.com) offer fishing charters (or private snorkel/adventure charters). Most charters provide four- and eight-hour excursions. Fishing is allowed in park waters with the exception of Trunk Bay and other swim

Cruz Bay

areas. A fishing license is not required if you fish from the shore. The Virgin Islands may be best known for world record blue marlins pulled from its waters, but you'll also find bonito, tuna, wahoo, sailfish, and skipjack. Fishing is good year-round, but you're likely to have the most success between May and October.

Birdwatching

Approximately 144 species of birds have been documented within the park. This includes both resident and migratory species. Not only is winter the best time for tourists, it's the birds' favorite season as well. Brown pelicans, brown boobies, magnificent frigatebirds, and royal terns are commonly seen near the shorelines. Mangrove cuckoos, zenaida cloves, Antillean-crested hummingbirds, gray kingbirds, pearly-eyed thrashers, and bananaquits are commonly seen in the park's dry forests. A bird checklist is available at the park website or visitor center. It includes information regarding breeding status, habitat, abundance, and best season to spot each species.

Visitor Center

Cruz Bay Visitor Center is open daily from 8:30am to 4:30pm. You'll find exhibits, a bookstore, park rangers, and restrooms. Trunk Bay's restrooms and showers are open from 8am until 4pm.

Ranger Programs & For Kids

The park offers a handful of ranger-led activities, including free tours of Cinnamon Bay Estate ruins, one of the first plantations on the island. You can explore the sea with a park ranger on a snorkel trip (nominal fee). The ranger-led Reef Bay Hike (or L'Esperance Hike) offered by Friends of Virgin Islands National Park (friendsvinp.org) is a 3.1-mile trek through the history

of St. John Island. Bring along a lunch and your swimsuit for this tour. It costs about $40/person, but transportation to and from the trailhead is provided. A taxi takes you to the trailhead. A boat brings you back to Cruz Bay Visitor Center (no uphill hiking required!). Several other hikes and early morning birdwatch tours are also offered. For a current schedule, meeting locations, and to make reservations stop in at the visitor center or check out the park's online calendar.

Virgin Islands National Park offers a Junior Ranger Program for children. Workbooks can be picked up at the park's visitor center. When completed, return to receive a certificate and badge. An abundance of snorkeling, swimming, beaches, and short hiking trails make the Virgin Islands one of the most kid-friendly national parks in the United States, but you'll be tempted to leave the children at home for this one, because it's also one of the most romantic.

Flora & Fauna

More than 90% of St. John's native vegetation was destroyed in favor of cash crops like cotton and sugarcane and to graze livestock. It wasn't until the 1950s—when Laurance Rockefeller donated more than half of St. John Island to the National Park Service—that natural reforestation began. From underwater seagrass to mangrove shorelines, moist forests to dry cactus scrubland, the landscapes of the U.S. Virgin Islands are once again changing and adapting in a more natural manner.

Very little is natural about the islands' mammals. Bats are the only natives. Goats, donkeys, and mongoose were all introduced by humans. Dolphins are frequently seen in the winter months, and sea turtles are commonly spotted by snorkelers and SCUBA divers. In fact, Trunk Bay got its name from Danes who believed the leatherback turtle resembled a great leather traveling trunk. You'll also find a multitude of coral and mosquitoes can be bothersome.

Pets & Accessibility

Pets are not allowed on beaches, in campgrounds, or in picnic areas. They are permitted on trails but must be on a leash (less than six feet).

Wheelchair-accessible campsites are available at Cinnamon Bay Camp. The visitor center and picnic areas at Trunk Bay and Hawksnest are accessible. Most trails are steep, slippery, and relatively inaccessible. Cinnamon Bay Self-Guided Trail, Francis Bay Boardwalk, and Annaberg Plantation are accessible.

Weather

Virgin Islands National Park is a tropical paradise. All year-long high temperatures are in the mid-80s°F with lows in the 70s°F. While the weather is always out-of-this-world, most visitors arrive between December and April. The summer months from June through August are hottest. Hurricane season spans from June until November. September through November tend to be the wettest months. Water temperature is about 83°F in summer and 79°F in winter.

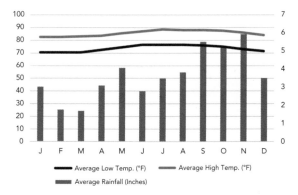

Legend:
— Average Low Temp. (°F)   — Average High Temp. (°F)
▬ Average Rainfall (Inches)

Tips & Recommendations

If you're renting a car, the rental company will probably pick you up at the dock. Double check to make sure.

You definitely can get by without a car rental, but you'll be somewhat limited. The best beaches are all on the west side of St. John, a short distance from Cruz Bay. Taxis can get you to Trunk Bay or take you on a 2-hour tour of St. John, stopping at popular spots (for about $30/person). Think about it. Not having a car often creates a more relaxed vacation, and you won't have to drive on the left side of the road.

Hummingbird near Salt Pond Bay

If you don't want to camp in the heat or Caneel Bay Resort is still closed or beyond your budget, there are plenty of choices in between, including AirBnBs.

Hiking Trails: Lind Point (Easy, 3 miles), Ram Head (Moderate, 2), Reef Bay (Moderate, 4.4)
Beaches: Trunk Bay, Salomon/Honeymoon, Denis, Caneel Bay, Maho Bay, Cinnamon Bay
Family Activities: You're on a tropical island...go to the beach, become a Junior Ranger
Guided Tours: SCUBA diving, sailing
Rainy Day Activities: It's usually sunny and warm, but if things turn gloomy, you can always duck into a bar or the visitor center for a bit
History Enthusiasts: Annaberg Ruins, Petroglyph Trail, Catherineberg Ruins
Sunset Spots: Just about any of the beaches facing west (like Maho Bay, Caneel Bay, or Francis Bay), Bordeaux Mountain, Ram Head, restaurants in Cruz Bay
Sunrise Spots: Ram Head, Coral Bay

Beyond the Park...

Dining
Sun Dog Café • (340) 693-8340
Mongoose Jct
sundogcafe.com

The Banana Deck • (340) 693-5055
Bay St, Cruz Bay
thebananadeck.com

The Longboard
Cruz Bay • (340) 715-2210
thelongboardstjohn.com

Extra Virgin Bistro
6D Cruz Bay • (340) 715-1864
extravirginbistro.com

The Lime Inn • limeinn.com
Cruz Bay • (340) 776-6425

Lime Out • limeoutvi.com
Floating taco bar (Coral Harbor)

Grocery Stores
Starfish Market
Cruz Bay • (340) 779-4949

Dolphin Gourmet Market
Chocolate Hole St • (340) 779-6001

Love City Market • (340) 693-5790
King Hill Rd, Coral Bay

Lodging
Treetops • Pelican Rd
treetops.vi • (340) 779-4490

St John Inn • stjohninn.com
Cruz Bay • (340) 693-8688

Gallows Point Resort
Cruz Bay • (800) 323-7229
gallowspointresort.com

Grande Bay Resort • (340) 693-4600
Quarter St, Cruz Bay
grandebayresort.com

The Hills • (800) 727-6610
11 Bay View Terrace
thehillsstjohn.com

Festivals
8 Tuff Miles Race • February
8tuffmiles.com

Attractions
Arawak Expeditions
arawakexp.com

Island Roots Charters
islandrootscharters.com

Big Blue Excursions
bigblue-usvi.com

SUP St John
sup-stjohn.com

Buck Island Reef National Mon
Uninhabited island near St Croix that's good for SCUBA diving
nps.gov/buis • (340) 773-1460

Ultimate Bluewater Adventures
St Croix • stcroixscuba.com

Paul & Jill's Equestrian Stables
St Croix • paulandjills.com

Haleakala

Haleakala Visitor Center

Phone: (808) 572-4400
Website: nps.gov/hale

Established: August 1, 1916
Size: 30,183 Acres
Annual Visitors: 1 Million
Peak Season: All Year

Activities: Hiking, Backpacking, Stargazing, Swimming, Birdwatching

2 Campgrounds: Free
3 Backcountry Cabins: $75/night*
Backcountry Camping: Permitted at designated sites and cabins*
Cabin Reservations: recreation.gov or (877) 444-6777

Park Hours: All day, every day (may close for severe weather)
Entrance Fee: $30/25/15 (car/motorcycle/individual)

*Permit required for backcountry camping and cabins

A sea of clouds floats below you. Burnt-red rocky slopes lie in front of you. Haleakala Summit is the sort of scene that can make a person feel like you've woken up in another world. A world where myths seem like reality, rather than a story as colorful as the crater itself. Haleakala National Park consists of two distinct regions. Haleakala summit, nearly two miles above sea level, is a seemingly lifeless landscape that should require a space shuttle and rover to reach. Lower Kipahulu's lush rainforest brimming with life, forests of bamboo, and waterfalls stirring sacred pools, provide yin to the summit's yang.

Clouds often surround Haleakala like a barrier between worlds. On one side is civilization and everything else you find familiar. On the other side is the sun and brilliant blue sky as you're transported to the heavens above. The experience of walking through the clouds may have inspired ancient Hawaiians to name the volcano Haleakala or "house of the sun." Legend has it that Maui, the Hawaiian demigod who had raised the Hawaiian Islands with a homemade fishhook and line, knew where the sun resided. Maui overheard his mother complain that the days were too short, and that there wasn't enough time for her kapa (bark cloth) to dry. He climbed Haleakala to lasso the sun with his sister's hair. Caught, the sun pled for its life and agreed the days would be longer in summer and shorter in winter. In a paradise like this, who wouldn't want longer days?

Haleakala Summit, at 10,023 feet above sea level, is the island's highest peak. From here, sure-footed visitors can descend 2,600 feet into the crater. Geologically speaking, it is a dormant volcano that hasn't erupted for more than 400 years. It's not a crater either, but two valleys joined when the ridgeline between them eroded away. Pipiwai Spring, at the very southeast corner of the park, is continuously wearing away the land as water tumbles some 400 feet over Waimoku Falls and on into 'Ohe'o Gulch. This area is Kipahulu. A location where you can spend the long summer days bathing in its idyllic, nay, sacred swimming pools, hiking Pipiwai Trail, or just enjoying the sights along Hana Highway (one of the most scenic—and stressful—drives in the world). The only visitors who want the sun to set are those who wish to gaze at the night sky or arrive at the summit with blankets and coffee early enough to see the sun's glorious return above Haleakala, its home. Those who do will learn the night is often as spectacular as the day.

As the sun rises over Haleakala there are few places in the world that appear so lifeless yet so beautiful. Volcanic islands, like Hawai'i, begin as barren masses of molten rock. It takes hundreds of thousands of years for species to arrive by wind, water, or wings. Prior to civilization, a species arrived every 10,000 to 100,000 years, in part because the destination was the most isolated significant island chain in the world. This remote setting—nearly complete isolation from life—is exactly what makes the species that survived and evolved here even more unique.

Haleakala silversword, a relative of the sunflower, is found nowhere else in the world. Reaching maturity after seven years, it blooms, sending forth a stalk three to eight feet tall containing several hundred tiny sunflowers, then it dies. Silversword was once so abundant the crater floor looked as if it was covered with glistening snow. Vandalism and grazing by cattle and goats nearly led to its extinction.

More endangered species live in Haleakala than any other national park in the United States, and the park's unique ecosystems make for one of the world's most interesting and studied living laboratories. Scientists hope to preserve the biology found here, so areas like upper Kipahulu Valley and Waikamoi are closed to tourism or accessible only when guided by a ranger or naturalist. Invasive species and destructive tourism are constant threats. Today, aided by over a million annual visitors, about 20 alien species arrive on the islands each year. We must find a way to strike a balance between nature and tourism so that this one park—two worlds, part Marscape, part jungle—can be preserved for future generations.

Haleakala Sunrise

When to Go
The park is open all year, but it closes occasionally for severe weather. Visitation is steady, although winter holidays are particularly busy. I feel the best time to visit is between December and May, when humpback whales migrate to surrounding waters.

Transportation & Airports
The park is located on the Island of Maui. Most visitors arrive via commercial airline from the U.S. mainland or another Hawaiian Island. Maui's primary airport is Kahului Airport (OGG). There are smaller airports near Kapalua (JHM) and Hana (HNM). Public transportation does not serve the park. Car rental is available at each airport.

Directions
The park's two regions, Haleakala Summit and Kipahulu Valley, are not directly connected by roads. In fact, from the airport they are opposite directions from one another.

To Haleakala Summit (37 miles): Exit the airport on HI-37. Turn left onto HI-377. After about 6 miles, turn left at Crater Road (HI-378/Haleakala Highway). After 1.5 miles, turn right to stay on Crater Road. Continue on Crater Road for approximately 20 miles to Haleakala Summit. The road to the summit is steep. You leave near sea level in Kahului and arrive at the 10,023-ft summit after less than 40 miles.

To Kipahulu (60 miles from airport/80 miles from Haleakala Summit): Exit the airport on HI-36 (Hana Highway). Continue to follow Hana Highway, one of the most scenic roadways in the United States, to Kipahulu Visitor Center. This region of the park can also be reached going the other way around the island via HI-37 and HI-31 from the summit (about 60 miles), but you must traverse a section of unpaved road that is a little more than 3 miles long. This is many visitor's preferred route to Kipahulu/Hana, but your rental agreement may void if you explore unpaved roadways (although the road is quite good).

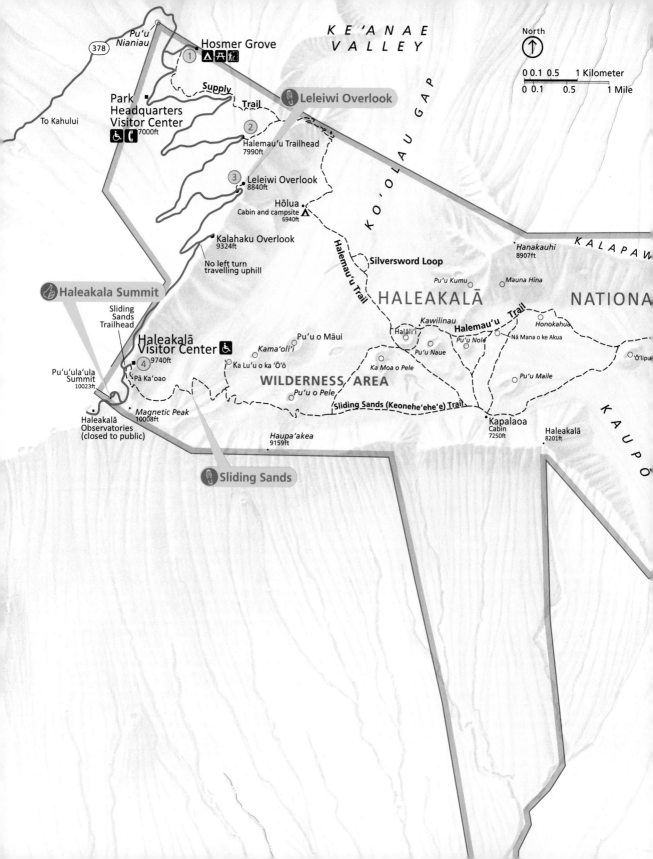

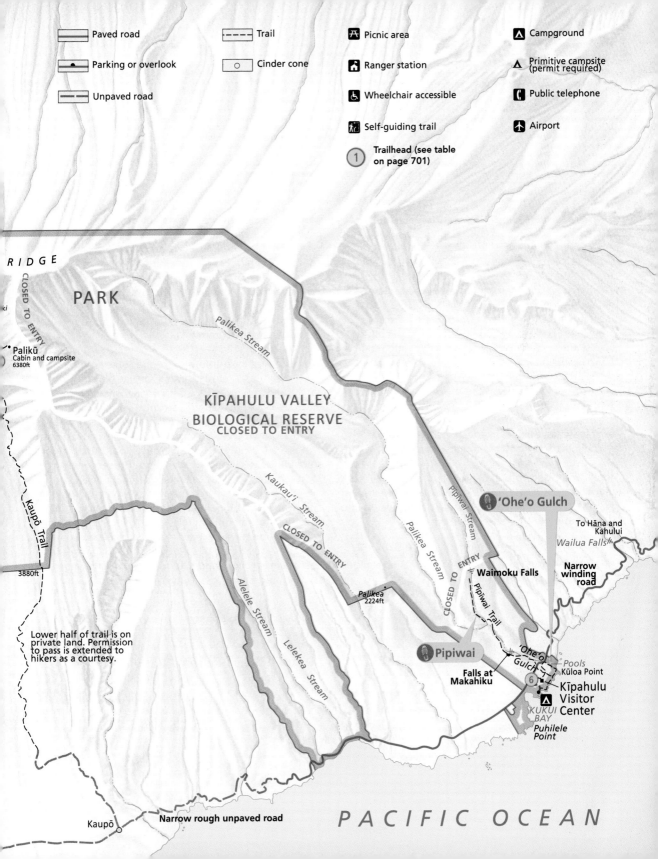

▭ Paved road	▭ Trail	⛺ Picnic area
▭ Parking or overlook	○ Cinder cone	⌂ Ranger station
▭ Unpaved road		♿ Wheelchair accessible
		🚶 Self-guiding trail
		① Trailhead (see table on page 701)

▲ Campground

△ Primitive campsite (permit required)

☎ Public telephone

✈ Airport

R I D G E

CLOSED TO ENTRY

PARK

Palikū
Cabin and campsite
6380ft

Palikea Stream

KĪPAHULU VALLEY
BIOLOGICAL RESERVE
CLOSED TO ENTRY

Kaupō Trail

3880ft

Kaukau'i Stream

CLOSED TO ENTRY

Pipiwai Stream

🚶 'Ohe'o Gulch

To Hāna and
Kahului
Wailua Falls

Narrow
winding
road

Waimoku Falls

Palikea Stream

CLOSED TO ENTRY

Palikea
2224ft

Alelele Stream

Lelekea Stream

Lower half of trail is on
private land. Permission
to pass is extended to
hikers as a courtesy.

🚶 Pipiwai

Pipiwai Trail

'Ohe'o
Gulch

Pools
Kūloa Point

Falls at
Makahiku

⑥ 🏕 Kīpahulu
Visitor
Center

*KUKUI
BAY*

Puhilele
Point

Kaupō   Narrow rough unpaved road

PACIFIC OCEAN

Camping & Backcountry Cabins

The park offers two frontcountry campgrounds. **Hosmer Grove** is located near Haleakala Summit, where it's windy and cold, often near freezing at night. **Kipahulu Campground** is located south of the visitor center, a short walk from 'Ohe'o Gulch. Both campgrounds are free of charge and available on a first-come, first-served basis. You can camp three nights per month in each campground.

Backpackers can camp at Holua or Paliku camps, which are located in the park's wilderness area and are only accessible by trails. Space is available on a first-come, first-served basis. A free permit, available at Headquarters Visitor Center up to one day in advance, is required. Additionally, there are three trail-accessible wilderness cabins. Holua is the closest cabin to a trailhead at 3.7 miles via Halemau'u Trail. Paliku is the farthest at 9.3 miles via Sliding Sands Trail. Cabins feature 12 bunks, non-potable water (filter or treat before drinking, check water status with the park before relying on it), a wood-burning stove, cookware, and dishes. These are simple cabins without electricity. Cabins can be reserved up to 180 days in advance at recreation.gov or (877) 444-6777 for $75 per cabin per night. Cancel at least three weeks in advance and you will receive a full refund, less a $10 per night service fee.

Hotels and resorts are expensive and packing all your gear can be a hassle, but please don't buy camping gear at Walmart and leave it on the island. Hostels and AirBnB are more cost-effective alternatives.

Hiking

Most visitors drive up to the summit, have a look around, maybe watch the sunrise, and then leave. Don't follow the path of the average tourist. The park boasts more than 30 miles of hiking trails in the summit area and another 10 miles or so around Kipahulu. Do you enjoy hiking? Want to explore the crater? Are you trying to escape the crowds? If you answered "yes" to any of these questions, hike **Sliding Sands Trail** into the valley below Haleakala Summit. You can even make a semi-loop with **Halemau'u Trail** and hitching a ride back to where you parked. Both trails are strenuous. But they're also great, offering short spurs to cinder cones and silverswords, as well as access to the park's backcountry campsites and cabins. For the semi-loop, start with Sliding Sands to hike more down than up (it begins at a higher elevation). Before departing on either of these journeys, be sure to honestly assess your energy-level and amount of free time. The trails are challenging (plenty of loose rocks and steep climbs to navigate), and it may take twice as long on the return trip uphill to the summit.

You can also hike a few short and relatively flat trails in the summit area. **Hosmer's Grove Nature Trail** is a self-guided hike through a forest of different tree species planted by Ralph Hosmer while experimenting with what plant species would grow best. The hike from **Leleiwi Overlook** is a short walk packed with amazing panoramic vistas. In addition, park rangers provide guided tours of **Waikamoi Preserve** (reservation required) that focus on birdwatching.

Pipiwai Trail at Kipahulu is one of the best, if not the best hiking trail on Maui. It's an uphill climb, but your effort will be rewarded with 400 feet of Waimoku Falls. It's a very good idea to spend a night in Hana (or at the park campground) and hike to the falls in the morning before getting back on Hana Highway.

Haleakala Camping (Fees are per night)

Name	Location	Fee	Notes
Kipahulu	Kipahulu Area	Free	50 camper limit, pit toilets, no water
Hosmer Grove	Summit Area	Free	25 camper limit, pit toilets, water
Holua (backcountry)	Sliding Sands (7.4 mi) or Halemau'u (3.7 mi) Trails	Free	Pit toilets, non-potable water
Paliku (backcountry)	Sliding Sands (9.3 mi) and Halemau'u (10.4 mi) Trails	Free	Pit toilets, non-potable water
Backcountry Cabins (Holua, Kapalaoa, and Paliku)	Holua: Halemau'u Trail (3.7 mi) Kapalaoa and Paliku: Sliding Sands Trail (5.5 mi and 9.3 mi)	$75	Bunks, cook & dinnerware, and stove

All Campsites are open all year and available on a first-come, first-served basis • Cabins can be reserved up to 180 days in advance at (877) 444-6777 or recreation.gov • Camping is limited to a maximum of 3 nights per 30 day period • Permits are required for all backcountry campsites and cabins (available at Headquarters Visitor Center)

Stargazing

Haleakala is such a great spot for viewing what exists beyond earth's atmosphere, the government built an observatory at its summit. This lair is reserved for scientists and professionals, but everyone has access to the stars shining brightly on clear Hawaiian nights. There is little artificial light to dim the sky, allowing you to see more stars than you ever knew existed. Note that it's cold (40°F) by Hawaiian standards at the summit and often windy. Stargazers may be leery of the return drive down the mountain's slope, but traffic will be scarce and the usually distracting scenery will be hidden under cover of darkness. Still, the best option is to camp at Hosmer's Grove (or in the park's backcountry), where you can see the stars at night and the sun as it rises in the morning. (You'll need a permit to see the sunrise from the summit. Reserve yours for $1 at recreation.gov up to seven days in advance.)

Swimming

Swimming is a popular pastime at Kipahulu Valley. Most visitors bathe or swim in the waterfall pools of **'Ohe'o Gulch** known as the seven sacred pools. Arrive early because the gulch can get busy. (It's also best to drive Hana Highway very early in the morning; there are only a few parking spots at each viewpoint or attraction.) More secluded swimming holes are found further upstream. Note that these pools are a part of the park and you will have to pay the entrance fee. If your heart is set on soaking in the sacred pools, you're going to want to call the park to inquire about their status (they close intermittently for a variety of reasons—usually safety). Even if they aren't open, Pipiwai Trail and a few other sites along Hana Highway make Kipahulu a worthwhile destination.

Hosmer Grove

Birdwatching

A large collection of rare birds, including many found nowhere else in the world, makes Haleakala National Park a popular destination among birdwatchers. Hawaiian petrel (or 'ua'u) and Hawaiian goose (or nene, also the state bird of Hawai'i) nest at the summit. One of the most popular avian attractions is the park's unique family of honeycreepers. Several species have evolved from one common ancestor, and over thousands of years they have become strikingly different due to variations in their individual habitats. Hosmer's Grove is one of the best places to see birds.

Visitor Centers

Park Headquarters Visitor Center (808.572.4459), Haleakala VC, and Kipahulu VC (808.248.7375) are open daily, except for Christmas and New Year's Day. They're all great places for a quick stop to get yourself oriented, and they have 24/7 restrooms.

Haleakala Hiking Trails (Distances are roundtrip unless noted otherwise)

	Name	Location (# on map)	Length	Difficulty Rating & Notes
Summit	Hosmer Grove	Hosmer Grove Camp (1)	0.5 mile	E – Self-guided nature trail
	Halemau'u	8,000 Foot Parking Area (3.5 miles above Park HQ) (2)	11.7 miles	S – Hike into the valley to view cinder cones and Haleakala silverswords
	Leleiwi Overlook	Leleiwi Parking Area (3)	0.3 mile	E – Uncrowded spot with excellent photo-ops
	Sliding Sands (Keonehe'ehe'e) - ♿	Haleakala Visitor Center Parking Area (4)	11.2 miles	S – Steep descent into valley • Leads to cinder cones, backcountry camps and cabins
	Kaupo	Junction with Sliding Sands near Paliku Camp (5)	8.6 miles	S – Unmaintained trail across private property to Kaupo on the coast (1-way)
Kipahulu	Kuloa Point	Kipahulu Ranger Station (6)	0.5 mile	M – A bluff overlooking 'Ohe'o Gulch
	Pipiwai - ♿	North end of the visitor center (6)	4.0 miles	M – Hike through bamboo forest to 400-foot Waimoku Falls

Difficulty Ratings: E = Easy, M = Moderate, S = Strenuous

Silverswords

Ranger Programs & For Kids

Ranger-led activities are held regularly at Hosmer Grove and the summit area. Waikamoi Cloud Forest Hike is most common, but stargazing programs, hikes, and talks are also held periodically. Stop at a visitor center or go online for a current schedule.

Children find Haleakala's otherworldly Marscapes and pristine swimming holes more than agreeable. Kids of all ages may participate in the Junior Ranger Program. Stop at a visitor center to pick-up a free activity booklet. Complete the booklet and return to a visitor center for a badge.

Flora & Fauna

There are approximately 370 species of native plants living at Haleakala National Park. Of these, about 90% are found only on the Hawaiian Islands. Haleakala silversword, found at and around the summit and nowhere else in the world, is the most famous.

The Hawaiian Islands are home to just two native mammal species: monk seal and hoary bat. No land amphibians or reptiles are native to the park. Some of the most sought-after animals are found in the ocean. Whales, turtles, dolphins, and seabirds are occasionally seen offshore from Kuloa Point near Kipahulu.

Pets & Accessibility

Pets are permitted but must be kept on a leash (less than six feet). They are only allowed in parking lots, drive-up campgrounds, and along paved roads and paths. Visitors are not allowed to take pets on hiking trails or leave them unattended.

The park's visitor centers are wheelchair accessible. Haleakala's summit building is accessible with assistance via a steep ramp. Wheelchair-accessible campsites are available. Trails are unpaved and difficult for wheelchairs or individuals requiring assistance.

Weather

Haleakala National Park's two distinct locations have completely contrasting climates. Haleakala summit is cool and dry (in summer) while Kipahulu is wet and hot. Visitors can expect a 20–30°F temperature difference from sea level to Haleakala summit at 10,023 feet, where high winds and intense solar radiation are common. Snowstorms can even occur in the higher elevations. Kipahulu enjoys the tropical climate Hawai'i vacationers have come to expect, with year-round warm temperatures and frequent showers. Pack clothes for all conditions, especially if you plan on going to the summit. Check the weather forecast prior to leaving, because conditions change rapidly with little warning.

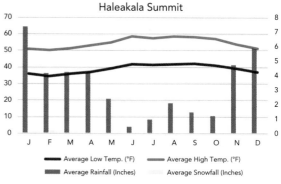

Haleakala Summit
— Average Low Temp. (°F) — Average High Temp. (°F)
■ Average Rainfall (Inches) Average Snowfall (Inches)

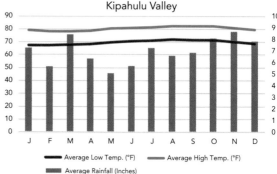

Kipahulu Valley
— Average Low Temp. (°F) — Average High Temp. (°F)
■ Average Rainfall (Inches)

Tips & Recommendations

Visit both areas, Haleakala Summit and Kipahulu. The contrast from one to the other is so dramatic you won't believe they're two sides of the same volcano.

The summit can be explored in a day, especially if you wake up for sunrise (don't forget to secure a sunrise permit through recreation.gov up to one week in advance for $1). The main reason you'd need more time is if you want to go backpacking (which is a good idea). Don't underestimate the amount of time required to reach the summit. Without traffic, it'll take 2.5 hours from Kapalua on the west end of the island.

Speaking of good ideas, plan on spending a night in Hana or camping at Kipahulu. The drive to Hana can be a stressful experience. An abundance of bends, one-lane bridges, and waterfall-seeking tourists make for an often-congested roadway. Not to mention, the desirable pull-offs become occupied quickly. You'll need another source to find where to stop, but there's a lot to see, and by the time you reach Hana, there's a good chance you'll want to relax a bit. Spend the night and you can get an early start at the park to explore 'O'heo Gulch and hike Pipiwai Trail, and then you can leave the area in more relaxed fashion, continuing the circle around Haleakala (which is a breeze). Many people make a big deal about how part of the road beyond Kipahulu is unpaved and taking your rental car across it voids the agreement. The road is usually in good condition, and, if you're worried about breaking the rental agreement, you can find local companies who allow their cars on dirt roads.

Driving up to Haleakala Summit is third on my list of Maui's most nerve-racking drives (after Highway 340 and Hana Highway), but some people have a great deal of fun driving up and down the big red hill's relatively gentle slope. If you possess a strong aversion to switchbacks and exposed roadways, you can let someone else do the driving by hiring a guide like Valley Isle Excursions (tourmaui.com). You can also hire them to take you down Hana Highway.

A few intense individuals are drawn to the challenge of pedaling from sea level to the 10,023-foot summit of Haleakala. If you're one of them, be prepared for a narrow, winding road, with no shoulder and steady traffic. You also should be prepared for cooler weather and wind. Don't let it deter you. Many cyclists make the trip. It's just not one to be taken lightly.

Pipiwai Trail

Haleakala sunrise gets all the buzz, but sunset is good too (and with much smaller crowds). Not to mention, after sunset you can stick around for the stars to come out. An observatory wasn't built up here for show. With that said, sunrise is better. Clouds typically bank against the volcanos eastern flank, and you're looking straight across the dormant volcano. Imagine if your first sight of Haleakala was in-person, standing at the rim as the sun slowly rises? The view from Haleakala Visitor Center is best (and busiest), but you can also go to Leleiwi Overlook, Kalahaku Overlook, or the summit for a similar experience. Plan on arriving at least a half-hour before first light. Dress warm. Bring blankets and coffee or hot chocolate.

Hiking Trails: Sliding Sands (Strenuous, 11.2 miles), Pipiwai (Moderate, 4), Leleiwi Overlook (Easy, 0.3)
Rainy Day Activities: Fortunately, storms typically pass through quickly. If one hits on your way to Kipahulu, you'll be treated to swollen streams and ephemeral waterfalls (be extra cautious hiking). If things look ominous atop Haleakala, you might want to hold off on driving up there. The drive is a little bit stressful, and it's usually cold and windy at the summit. Add rain and you're likely to have an unenjoyable experience.
History Enthusiasts: Hosmer Grove
Sunset Spot: Haleakala Summit
Sunrise Spots: Haleakala Summit, Leleiwi Overlook

Beyond the Park...

Choosing where to stay and eat on Maui is no easy decision. Most visitors opt for beachside resorts at Kapalua, Kaanapali, Kihei, or Wailea. Nearby you'll find way more (of everything) than you could ever possibly require. Upcountry stays at Makawao or Kula have the benefit of cooler temperatures and less commotion. Spending a night in Hana is a great idea. It'll break up a stressful drive, and give you an opportunity to explore the sleepy town or go back up Hana Highway before the afternoon rush passes through. It will make the entire experience much more enjoyable. One private campground and several public campgrounds are sprinkled around the island's many beaches. But, if you're thinking about spending your nights here in a tent, Haleakala is the place to do it. You can find groceries near Haleakala Summit at Kula Marketplace, but there are grocery stores in Kihei, Lahaina, even a Costco in Kahului.

Choosing what to do once you've arrived is equally difficult. We all know Haleakala looks pretty darn amazing, but there's so much more. Each island warrants its own guidebook, but these attractions are a good starting point for a Maui vacation.

Attractions
Whale Watching
Winter/Spring you'll have all kinds of whale watching options from two-story cruise boats to zodiacs, or you might want to join a kayak tour (or rent them and go out on your own—just be sure to get detailed information on currents and swell. If you aren't a strong paddler/swimmer, things could get dangerous in a hurry if you paddle into some tricky water.

Maui Ocean Riders
These guys zip around the island of Lanai, snorkeling along the way. It's fantastic.

Molokai Helicopter Tour
Kauai is most visitor's #1 choice for a helicopter tour, but Maui and Molokai have some sights too.

Also think about these things: Waihee Ridge (hike), Makena State Park (Big Beach), Molokini (snorkel back wall), Waianapanapa State Park (black sand), Kaihalulu (red sand) Beach, Kapalua Beach, Wailea Beach

Hawaii Volcanoes

Halemaumau Crater

Phone: (808) 985-6011
Website: nps.gov/havo

Established: August 1, 1916
Size: 323,431 Acres
Annual Visitors: 1.3 Million
Peak Season: All Year
International Biosphere
World Heritage Site

Activities: Lava Viewing, Hiking,
Backpacking, Biking

Campgrounds: Namakanipaio ($15/
night) and Kulanaokuaiki (free)
Cabins: 10 at Namakanipaio
Cabin Rates: $80/night
Lodging: Volcano House Hotel
Rates: $239–339/night
Backcountry Camping: Permitted
with a permit ($10) (Backcountry
Cabins on Mauna Loa)

Park Hours: All day, every day,
except Kahuku Unit (9am–3pm)
Entrance Fee: $30/25/15
(car/motorcycle/individual)

Hawai'i Volcanoes National Park is fire and water, rock and sand, rain forest and desert, desolation and beauty, creation and destruction. Such contradictions have the power to leave visitors speechless. Short of words. Lost in thought. The mind flooded with questions. Where does the lava come from? When will it erupt again? How did plant and animal life reach the island? Was there ever a massive eruption? Musings range from genesis to apocalypse. Hawai'i Volcanoes is a world where creation never looked so destructive.

To native Hawaiians, Kilauea Volcano is a holy place. They consider it the "body" of Pele, the volcano goddess of ancient Hawaiian legends. Today, Kilauea is the center of the park and #1 attraction. The Pu'u 'O'o Cone erupted nearly continuously from 1983 until 2018. Pele roils at Halema'uma'u Crater, where a lava lake returned in 2020 and again September 2021, lighting up the night's sky. A sky admired by visitors from around the world. And Loihi, an underwater volcano 22 miles offshore, continues to spew molten rock.

Mauna Loa is equally impressive. Rising 13,679 feet above sea level, it towers above 4,000-foot Kilauea. When measured from its base, some 18,000 feet below the water's surface, Mauna Loa is earth's largest mountain, taller and more massive than Mount Everest. It's hard to believe such a gargantuan land mass could go unnoticed, undisturbed, and unsettled for thousands of years.

About 1,500 years ago, Polynesian pioneers, probably from Samoa, steered double-hulled canoes more than 2,500 miles to the Hawaiian

Islands. Scientists believe they followed the path of the koleo (or golden plover), a small bird that flies more than 2,500 miles non-stop to Alaska every summer, where they mate before returning to Hawai'i. Some choose to continue another 2,500 miles to Samoa. It's plausible that early Samoans, curious as to where these birds were going, hopped in their canoes, following their feathered friends only to learn the closest significant land was more than one-tenth of the way around the globe (Insert punch line: "and man were their arms tired.") Luckily, they were prepared for settlement. Pigs, dogs, chickens, taro, sweet potato, and seeds of coconut, sugar cane, banana, and other edible and medicinal plants accompanied them on their voyage. Very little is known beyond the arrival of Hawai'i's original culture. It is widely believed they were assimilated, killed, or forced into exile by a second wave of colonists, this time from Tahiti.

Tahitian colonists brought with them practices of human sacrifice and a distinct class structure. Professionals, commoners, and slaves were ruled by chiefs. Settlements with new leadership began to be established across all the Hawaiian Islands. War was common between rival tribes. Canoes were used for fishing rather than exploring. Samoa and Tahiti were long forgotten. Hawai'i was now their home.

It was a home without room for Western explorers like Captain James Cook, who stumbled upon the Hawaiian Islands in January 1778 while on his way to Alaska. He returned three more times, and on his third visit he sailed into Kealakekua Bay of the Big Island, where he and his crew were greeted by villagers, many of whom believed Cook was Lono, the god of fertility (land). Cook and his crew left the island but returned shortly after departing to make repairs to a broken mast. This time they were greeted with hostility. Natives stole a small rowboat and Captain Cook attempted to hold the tribe's king hostage (a common practice) in exchange for their boat. The attempt failed; Natives struck Captain Cook on his head, stabbing him to death before he could flee.

By the 1840s, visitors were once again a welcome sight on the Big Island. Tourism had become the island's leading industry, and just as it is today, Hawai'i Volcanoes was the most popular attraction. In 1916, a national park was created to protect this spectacular area from grazing cattle, over-development, and ultimately, its destruction. And now visitors like you are free to conjure questions about this land filled with contradictions.

Thurston Lava Tube

When to Go

The park is open all year. Visitation is steady with peaks during winter and summer. Weather is also fairly consistent throughout the year, but it varies greatly depending on your location in the park. It's warm and breezy by the west coast, comfortable and wet at Kilauea (4,000 ft), and temperatures occasionally dip below freezing at the summit of Mauna Loa (13,677 ft). To make the weather even more interesting, temperatures can exceed 100°F near sites of volcanic activity. Pack for all conditions if you intend on exploring all the park's ecosystems.

Transportation & Airports

Hawai'i Volcanoes National Park is on the island of Hawai'i (also known as the Big Island). Hilo International (ITO) and Kona International at Keahole (KOA) are the major airports. Direct flights from the continental U.S. to Kona and Hilo are available. Car rental is available at both airports. Car rental and lodging have gotten considerably more expensive in Hawaii. They're taking the Iceland approach—inexpensive flights, expensive everything else.

Directions

Kona is farther from the park, but the drive is more interesting as you'll pass beautiful beaches and the road to the southernmost point of the United States, cleverly named South Point. From Hilo it is a relatively short drive through villages and forest. Kahuku Unit is west of the main park and rarely visited.

From Kona (~111 miles): From Keahole Airport Road take HI-19 south for about 7 miles, where it turns into HI-11. Continue for a little more than 93 miles, and then turn right at HI-11/Crater Rim Road. Follow Crater Rim Road to the visitor center.

From Hilo (~30 miles): Take Airport Road to HI-11 and head south for about 27 miles. Turn left at Crater Rim Road to the park.

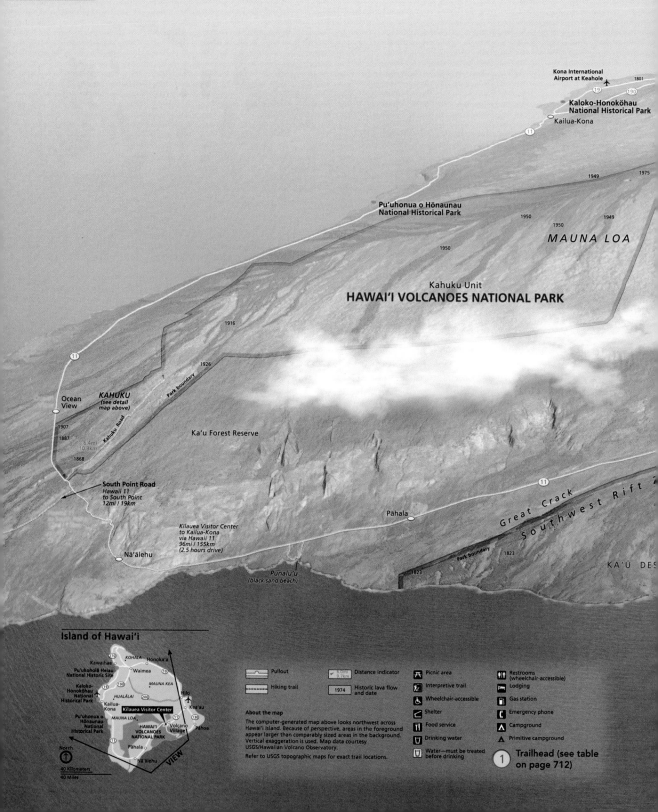

1801

Kona International
Airport at Keahole

Kaloko-Honokōhau
National Historical Park

Kailua-Kona

1949   1975

1950

1949

Pu'uhonua o Hōnaunau
National Historical Park

1950

1950

MAUNA LOA

1890

Kahuku Unit
HAWAI'I VOLCANOES NATIONAL PARK

1916

Park boundary

1926

Ocean
View

KAHUKU
(see detail
map above)

Ka'u Forest Reserve

1907

1887

6.4mi
10.3km

1868

South Point Road
Hawaii 11
to South Point
12mi / 19km

Pāhala

Great Crack

Southwest Rift Z

Kīlauea Visitor Center
to Kailua-Kona
via Hawaii 11
96mi / 155km
(2.5 hours drive)

Nā'ālehu

1823

Park boundary

1823

KA'Ū DES

Punalu'u
(black sand beach)

Island of Hawai'i

KOHALA   Honoka'a

Kawaihae

Pu'ukoholā Heiau
National Historic Site

Waimea

Kaloko-
Honokōhau
National
Historical Park

MAUNA KEA

HUALĀLAI

Kailua-
Kona

Hilo

Kīlauea Visitor Center

Kea'au

Pu'uhonua o
Hōnaunau
National
Historical Park

MAUNA LOA

HAWAI'I
VOLCANOES
NATIONAL
PARK

Volcano
Village

Pāhoa

North

Pāhala

VIEW

Nā'ālehu

40 Kilometers

40 Miles

Pullout	Distance indicator	Picnic area
Hiking trail	1974 Historic lava flow and date	Interpretive trail

6.0mi
9.7km

Wheelchair-accessible

Shelter

Food service

Drinking water

Water—must be treated
before draining

Restrooms
(wheelchair-accessible)

Lodging

Gas station

Emergency phone

Campground

Primitive campground

Trailhead (see table
on page 712)

About the map

The computer-generated map above looks northwest across
Hawai'i Island. Because of perspective, areas in the foreground
appear larger than comparably sized areas in the background.
Vertical exaggeration is used. Map data courtesy
USGS/Hawaiian Volcano Observatory.
Refer to USGS topographic maps for exact trail locations.

KOHALA

Pu'ukoholā Heiau
National Historic Site

Kawaihae

Waimea

Honoka'a

13796ft
4205m

MAUNA KEA

19

1801

190

200

ku'āweoweo
dera

2.6mi
4.2km

11150ft
3399m
Mauna Loa
Weather Observatory

1859

1843

6632ft
2022m

Mauna Kea
Visitor Center
9300ft
2835m

6.0mi
9.7km

3.8mi
6.1km

Cabin
)

na
3.4km

1942

1975

12.2mi
19.6km

3250ft
4039m

1899

9.5mi
15.3km

10035ft
3059m
Pu'u'ula'ula
Red Hill Cabin

Mauna Loa Observatory Road

1855

1855

1984

2.1mi
3.4km

1984

1942

Mauna Loa

1881

Cabin
ged)

1880

Park boundary

Mauna Loa
Trail

7.5mi
12.1km

6662ft
2031m
Mauna Loa
Lookout

1

11.5mi
18.5km

Mauna Loa
Road
(paved, one lane)

KĪLAUEA
(see detail map
above)

1984

gate

'Ainapo Road
(4-wheel drive)

Kipukapuaulu

3980ft
1213m

'Ōla'a Forest
HAWAI'I VOLCANOES
NATIONAL PARK
'ŌLA'A WILDERNESS

5.7mi
9.2km

3040ft
926m
Ka'ū Desert Trailhead

Nāmakanipaio

2

Volcano
House

Kīlauea Visitor Center

Access road gate
800ft
244m

Maunaiki

0.7mi
1.1km

1974

1974

CLOSURES IN EFFECT
Crater Rim Drive

Volcano
Village

Wright Road

11

1.8mi
2.9km

Ka'ū Desert Trail

1971

6.3mi
10.1km

Maunaiki Trail

Thurston
Lava Tube (Nāhuku)

Escape Road

1974

Kulanaokuaiki

3.5mi
5.6km

Hilina Pali Road (closed to vehicles)

Pauahi Crater

4.0mi
6.4km

3

Pu'u
Huluhulu

Pu'u O'o

2280ft
695m
Hilina Pali
Overlook

6

Hiking trail (seasonally closed and unmaintained)

4

1969

Mauna Ulu
3200ft
975m

EAST RIFT
WILDERNESS

1969

2600ft
792m
Nāpau

11.8km

1974

Ka'ū Desert Trail

Hilina

Pali

HAWAI'I
VOLCANOES
NATIONAL PARK

Makaopuhi
Crater

1969-1974

Nāpau
Crater

680ft
512m

ERNESS

1.4mi
2.3km

Hilina Pali Trail

3.0mi
4.8km

Keauhou Trail

3.6mi
5.8km

Niulu Trail

Kalapana Trail (unmaintained)

Pu'u O'o

eiao
in

4.8mi

Mau Loa o
Mauna Ulu
2680ft
817m

1969

Chain
of
Craters
Road

Ka'aha Trail

Ka'aha

1.3mi

1.6mi
2.6km

Halapē

1.6mi
2.6km

Keauhou

1.0mi
1.6km

2.0mi
3.2km

Kealakomo
2000ft
610m

Hōlei

1972

Pali

Ka'aha

Halape

1973

'Āpua Point

Puna Coast Trail

1971

1972

Pu'u Loa
Petroglyphs

5

0.7mi
1.1km

1983-2018

Road closed by
lava flow

Hōlei
Sea Arch

Pu'u Loa Petroglyphs

PACIFIC OCEAN

The glow from Kilauea's lava lake

1.2mi
2.0km

Kīpukapuaulu

Park boundary

Pi'i Mauna Dr

Tree Molds

Kīlauea
Military Camp

St

Crater Rim Drive

Highway 11 to
Mauna Loa Lookout
11.5mi/18.5km

Mauna Loa Road

1.5mi
2.4km

Crater Rim Drive

1.0mi
0.6km

0.
1.

Steaming Bluff
(Wahinekapu)

Nämakanipaio
Campground
and Cabins

Crater Rim Trail

11

Lava flows before 19

Kīlauea Overlook

KĪLAUEA CAL

To Kailua-Kona
96mi/155km

CLOSURES IN EFFECT
Check with rangers for current conditions

1982 lava

Halema'uma'u
Crater

1971 lava

1971 lava

Ko

Lava flows
before 1924

0.3mi
0.5km

Southwest
Rift Zone
KA'Ü
DESERT

Holoholoakōlea

1971 lava

1982 lava

Halema'uma'u Crater

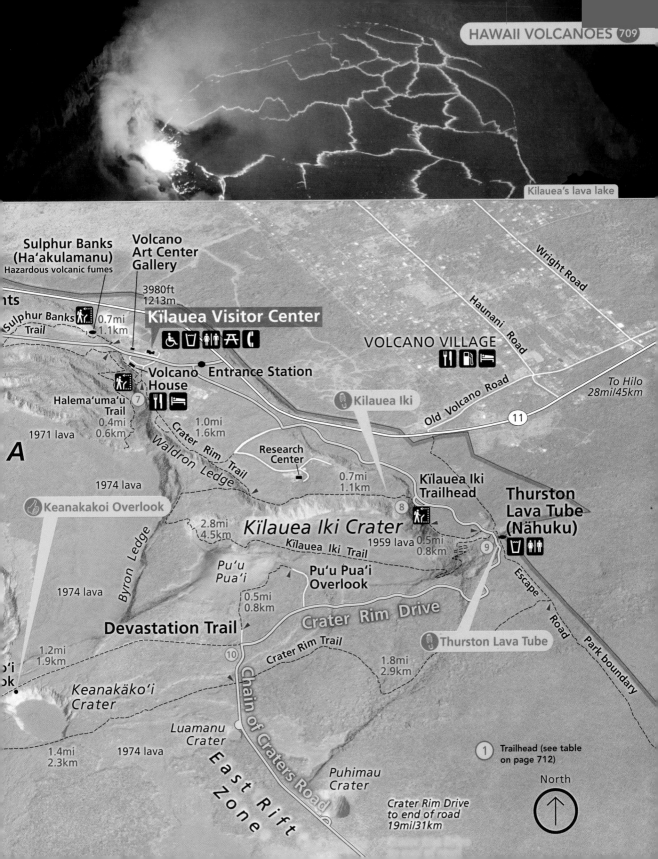

Kilauea's lava lake

Sulphur Banks (Haʻakulamanu)
Hazardous volcanic fumes

Volcano Art Center Gallery

3980ft
1213m

Sulphur Banks Trail
0.7mi
1.1km

Kīlauea Visitor Center

VOLCANO VILLAGE

Wright Road

Haunani Road

Volcano House
Entrance Station

Kīlauea Iki

Old Volcano Road

To Hilo
28mi/45km

11

nts

Halemaʻumaʻu Trail
0.4mi
0.6km

7

1971 lava

A

Crater Rim Trail

Waldron Ledge

Research Center

1.0mi
1.6km

0.7mi
1.1km

Kīlauea Iki Trailhead

8

Thurston Lava Tube (Nāhuku)

1974 lava

Keanakakoi Overlook

Byron Ledge

2.8mi
4.5km

Kīlauea Iki Crater

Kīlauea Iki Trail

1959 lava

0.5mi
0.8km

9

1974 lava

Puʻu Puaʻi

Puʻu Puaʻi Overlook

0.5mi
0.8km

Escape Road

Park boundary

Devastation Trail

Crater Rim Drive

Thurston Lava Tube

1.2mi
1.9km

oʻi ok

Keanakākoʻi Crater

10

Crater Rim Trail

1.8mi
2.9km

1.4mi
2.3km

1974 lava

Luamanu Crater

Chain of Craters Road

East Rift Zone

Puhimau Crater

1 Trailhead (see table on page 712)

Crater Rim Drive to end of road
19mi/31km

North

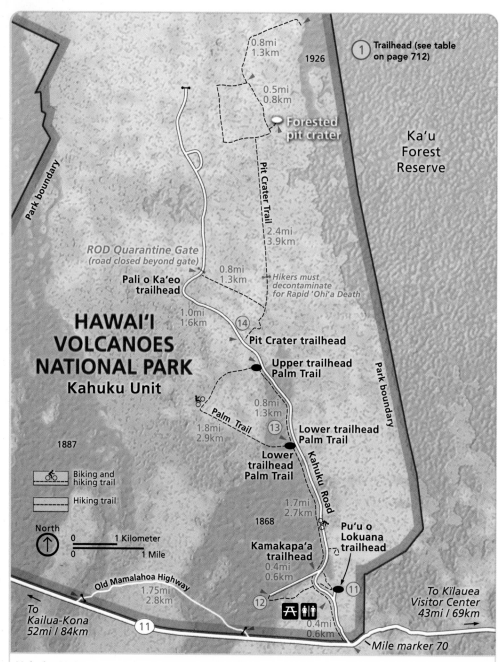

0.8mi
1.3km

1926

0.5mi
0.8km

Forested
pit crater

① Trailhead (see table
on page 712)

Ka'u
Forest
Reserve

Pit Crater Trail

2.4mi
3.9km

ROD Quarantine Gate
(road closed beyond gate)

0.8mi
1.3km

Hikers must
decontaminate
for Rapid 'Ohi'a Death

Pali o Ka'eo
trailhead

1.0mi
1.6km

⑭

Pit Crater trailhead

HAWAI'I
VOLCANOES
NATIONAL PARK
Kahuku Unit

Upper trailhead
Palm Trail

0.8mi
1.3km

Palm Trail

1.8mi
2.9km

⑬ Lower trailhead
Palm Trail

1887

Lower
trailhead
Palm Trail

Kahuku Road

Biking and
hiking trail

Hiking trail

1.7mi
2.7km

1868

Pu'u o
Lokuana
trailhead

North

0	1 Kilometer
0	1 Mile

Kamakapa'a
trailhead
0.4mi
0.6km

Old Mamalahoa Highway

1.75mi
2.8km

⑪

⑫

To
Kailua-Kona
52mi / 84km

11

To Kīlauea
Visitor Center
43mi / 69km

0.4mi
0.6km

Mile marker 70

Kahuku Unit

Located 40 miles west of the main park entrance (near Mile Marker 70.5), this unknown region offers everything from volcanic craters to grassy ranchlands. The unit is 116,000 acres of mostly undeveloped land. The 6-mile gravel road is accessible to all vehicles up to Upper Palm Trailhead, beyond that a high-clearance 4WD vehicle is recommended. The draw here is hiking. A handful of trails explore the area's ecology and volcanic features. Ranger-guided hikes are offered regularly (check the park website for a current schedule of events). Note that the unit is only open from 9am until 4pm, Thursdays through Sundays.

Camping & Lodging

Two drive-in campgrounds are available. **Namakanipaio Campground**, located on State Highway 11 just a few miles west of Kilauea Entrance, costs $15/night. It features restrooms, water, picnic tables, and grills. Pack for cool evenings. Temperatures here can drop into the 30s°F at night and rain is common. **Kulanaokuaiki Campground**, about 5 miles west on Hilina Pali Road, features nine campsites with vault toilets and picnic tables, but no water. Camping here is $10/night. Temperatures can drop into the 40s°F at night and rain is less common. Sites at both campgrounds are available on a first-come, first-served basis. Campgrounds occasionally fill, but there's an overflow walk-in camping area at Namakanipaio.

If you'd rather leave your camping gear at home, Namakanipaio also features 10 rustic, one-room **cabins**, each with one full bed and a bunk bed for $80/night. Cabins have electricity and a communal shower/restroom is nearby. Another option is to pay for camping gear rental and set-up. For $40, plus $15/night campsite fee, a tent for two (with a foam mattress, hotel linens, cooler, lantern, and two chairs) will be yours. They even take it down. Guests can check-in at 3pm and must check-out by noon. Contact Volcano House (808.756.9625, hawaiivolcanohouse.com) for cabin and tent rental details and reservations. For a more luxurious stay spend the night at recently-renovated **Volcano House Hotel**. Nightly rates range from $239–339, and a few rooms have views of Halema'uma'u Crater, allowing you to watch the volcano's glow (if glowing) from your bedroom. Even if you don't spend the night, I recommend checking out the hotel. Maybe have a meal at The Rim (reservations at 808.756.9625) or a drink at Uncle George's Lounge, or skip them and have a look at the views across the caldera. It's a pretty incredible setting. You'll also find a couple shops and a communal fireplace (in case you didn't dress for Hawaii at 4,000+ feet). Reservations can be made at (808) 756-9625 or hawaiivolcanohouse.com.

Driving

Hawai'i Volcanoes is essentially a drive-in volcano. The 11-mile **Crater Rim Drive** circling Kilauea Crater has been closed between Kilauea Overlook and Chain of Craters Road since this book's first edition. A few years ago, a portion of the road collapsed into the crater. It's unlikely the loop will be reopening anytime soon. Still, Crater Rim Drive provides access to many of the park's main attractions: Kilauea Visitor Center, Volcano House, Kilauea Overlook, Jaggar Museum (permanently closed), Halema'uma'u Overlook

Lava Boat tours run during coastal flows

(closed), Thurston (Nahuku) Lava Tube (recently reopened), Kilauea Iki Trail, and Chain of Craters Road. **Chain of Craters Road** ends at an emergency-use-only gravel road after 19 miles. It also provides access to Hilina Pali Road and several popular hiking trails like the self-guided Mauna Ulu and Pu'u Loa Petroglyphs Trails. **Mauna Loa Road** is a one-lane stretch of pavement ending at Mauna Loa Lookout (and the trailhead for the long way to the summit of Mauna Loa).

Lava Viewing

Hawaii Volcanoes is an incredibly dynamic place. The best way to learn if and where you can see lava is to stop at Kilauea Visitor Center, give them a call (808.985.6011), or visit the USGS website (usgs.gov/volcanoes/kilauea/volcano-updates). Things change. After erupting nearly continuously since 1983, the lava stopped in December 2018. And then a lava lake formed once more at the bottom of Halema'uma'u Crater in December 2020.

It stopped and started once more, but when we went to print, **Halema'uma'u Crater** was active. The lava lake illuminates the night's sky (best seen from Keanakakoi Overlook)! If the lava lake is active during your visit, spending a night in the park is a wonderful idea. If there are surface flows, businesses will pop up, leading visitors to them. If lava is flowing into the ocean, lava boat tours will cruise the coast from Isaac Hale Beach Park.

Regarding **Pu'u 'O'o** (the previously active vent), visitors are permitted as far as the backcountry campsite at Napau. However, it is possible to hike to view Pu'u 'O'o from outside the park via Kahauale'a Trail. It's accessed from South Glenwood Road between mile markers 19 and 20 on HI-11, about 20 miles from Hilo.

Follow South Glenwood Road, which becomes Captain's Drive/Ala Kapena and continue to its end, 3.5 miles from the highway. Do not leave valuables in your car. This hike is about 5 miles (one-way) through thick rain forest to the 500-ft cone built up during the last eruption. (An eruption that wiped out Kapoho Tidepools!) Restrictions change for visitor safety. Please obey park closures and advisories. Visit the park website for current updates.

Hiking

Hawai'i Volcanoes is one of the best destinations for hiking in Hawai'i. More than 150 miles of trails crisscross black sand shores, arid deserts, lush rain forests, and delicate volcanic surfaces. Expect a few trail closures even when the volcano isn't active. Stop at the visitor center for up-to-date information.

The most popular hike is **Kilauea Iki Trail.** Kilauea means "spewing," and the hike leads you on an up-close-and-personal look at the volcanic geology of Kilauea's last "spew." Its trailhead is located at Kilauea Iki Overlook. Walking counter-clockwise you will pass through rain forest before Pu'u Pua'i cinder cone, the main vent of an eruption on November 14, 1959, comes into view. Lava gushed out of the vent, shooting arcs as high as 1,900 feet. That's a personal record for Pele, the goddess of fire. Next you'll pass through a forest destroyed by the eruption, which is followed by another view of Pu'u Pua'i. Hike past a few large boulders and through another forest before descending into the caldera. Here you'll notice cones, fractures, and the "bathtub ring" that marks the high lava mark of a 2,000°F lake of molten rock that once filled the caldera. The lake didn't cool completely until the mid-

Hawaii Volcanoes Hiking Trails (Distances are roundtrip)

Name	Location (# on map)	Length	Difficulty Rating & Notes
Mauna Loa - ⛰	Mauna Loa Lookout (1)	38.2 miles	S – 9.4 more miles to true summit (13,679 ft)
Kipukapuaulu	Mauna Loa Road (2)	1.2 miles	E – Loop trail through island forest (kipuka)
Mauna Ulu	Chain of Craters Road (3)	2.5 miles	E – Lava fields, fissures, and flows
Pu'u Huluhulu	Mauna Ulu Trailhead (3)	18.6 miles	S – Old lava flows, lava trees, and kipuka
Napau	Mauna Ulu Trailhead (3)	14.0 miles	S – Recent lava flows and rain forest
Keauhou	Chain of Craters Road (4)	Varies	S – Cross open lava field to coastal camps
Pu'u Loa Petroglyphs	Chain of Craters Road (5)	1.5 miles	E – Boardwalk trail across old lava flows where ancient petroglyphs were drawn
Hilina Pali	Hilina Pali Road (6)	Varies	S – Cross open lava fields to coast
Ka'u Desert	Hilina Pali Road (6)	Varies	S – Open lava fields, 13.9 miles to Highway Belt Rd
Waldron Ledge	South of Volcano House (7)	1.0 mile	E – A section of Old Crater Rim Drive (Earthquake)
Halema'uma'u	Behind Volcano House (7)	1.8 miles	M – Significant portion closed due to gas
Sulphur Banks	West of Volcano House (7)	1.2 miles	E – Colorful thermal area, loop with Sandalwood
Kilauea Iki - ⛰	Kilauea Iki Overlook (8)	3.3 miles	M – Loop trail (proceed counter-clockwise)
Nahuku (Thurston) - ⛰	Crater Rim Drive (9)	1.5 miles	E – Lava tube equipped with lights formed by a massive flow
Devastation	Crater Rim Drive (10)	1.0 mile	E – View effects of 1959 eruption
Crater Rim	Accessible from several locations along Crater Rim Drive	11.6 miles	M – Closed from Kilauea Overlook south to the junction with Chain of Craters Rd
Pu'u o Lokuana Cinder Cone	Kahuku Road (11)	0.4 mile	M – Short but steep climb to the top of a cinder cone, stay back from the edge
Pu'u o Lokuana	Kahuku Road (12)	2.0 miles	E – Historic ranch, tree molds and lava flows
Palm	Kahuku Road (13)	2.6 miles	M – Connect the loop via Kahuku Road, big views
Glover	Kahuku Road (14)	3.0 miles	M – Loop through rain forest, pit crater
Kona	Kahuku Road (14)	4.7 miles	M – Loop through ranching era relics

Difficulty Ratings: E = Easy, M = Moderate, S = Strenuous

1990s. Today you can walk across its solid surface. Before exiting the crater and returning to the overlook, look back and imagine a lake of spouting and spitting lava, waves of thick molten rock oozing at your feet. (The lava lake that was active when we went to print is nothing like that. It's much more sedate.) You'll exit near **Thurston (Nahuku) Lava Tube**. Take a short walk through the tube. It was created when the outer layer of lava cooled, acting as insulation to the inner lava as it continued to flow downhill to the ocean. Devastation Trail and Byron Ledge are pretty decent, too.

Pu'u Loa Petroglyphs Trail is located near the end of Chain of Craters Road at Milepost 16.5. There are more than 23,000 cryptic symbols scrawled onto lava rocks in this region of the park. The 2-mile boardwalk traverses old lava flows to one of Hawai'i's most extensive petroglyph fields. Please stay on the boardwalk to protect the fragile environment and its artifacts. At first sight these images could pass as the handiwork of a 14-year-old vandal, but with a bit of explanation their meaning becomes clearer. For example, you may see petroglyphs consisting of a dot with concentric circles around it. The dot signifies a man, and each circle represents a voyage around the island. Anthropologist Martha Beckwith visited Pu'u Loa in 1914 and argued that holes in the lava's surface were created to deposit umbilical cords at birth. She believes that natives placed the cord in the hole, setting a rock on top. If the cord was gone in the morning, it ensured a long life. So, no one really knows. Feel free to come to your own conclusion.

Fossilized footprints are found along **Ka'u Desert Trail**. They were created in 1790 after a massive eruption of Kilauea. Years of erosion have taken their toll, but the outlines of ancient feet can still be seen today. The trail is accessed via Ka'u Desert Trailhead, adjacent to Highway 11 near Mile Marker 38. It can also be reached via Ka'u Desert Trail from Crater Rim Drive. The prints are fragile, so please remain on the path. Legend holds that a retreating army was passing by Kilauea Volcano in 1782. The volcano was angry that day. To appease the goddess Pele, they chose to stay near the volcano's rim offering sacrifices for several days. Upon leaving the summit, the army split into three companies. The first company had not gone far when Kilauea exploded, emitting ash and gas. Unable to escape, everyone in the second company died, except a lone pig. Members of the third company survived, but they encountered the remains of the second party lying dead, face first in the ashes. Ash provided an excellent medium for fossilization of the warriors' footprints. It's impossible

Kilauea Iki

to know exactly whose footsteps have been preserved along Ka'u Desert Trail, but there most certainly was an eruption in 1790. Reports state that anywhere from 80 to over 5,000 individuals were killed by it. What's the truth? We'll never know, but it's fun to hike and imagine that day's events for yourself.

Backpacking

Backcountry camping is allowed with a permit ($10), available in person up to one week in advance from the Backcountry Office (808.985.6178). You are allowed a maximum stay of three consecutive nights per site, and just 16 people/night are allowed at each backcountry location. All sites have pit toilets. Do not dispose of trash in toilets. You must pick up your permit at the Backcountry Office no earlier than one day before your departure. To get there, take an immediate left after the Entrance Station, and then an immediate right. Park in the parking area on your left and walk to the nearby building. That's it. Backpackers must check out upon completion at Kilauea Visitor Center.

More than half the park is designated wilderness, providing ample opportunity for solitude and volcanic exploration. Take proper precautions before heading out. Pack the essentials: water, first-aid kit, stove, map, flashlight and batteries, rain gear, toilet paper, and food (pack out what you pack in). You must camp at designated sites, so plan your route in advance. There are three main backpacking areas. Mauna Loa and Halape are my favorite spots, but it takes some work to reach them.

Mauna Loa: The 19.1-mile (one-way) Mauna Loa Trail to Mauna Loa Cabin begins at the end of Mauna Loa Road. (It's an additional 9.4 miles out-and-back to the

The hike to Mauna Loa

true summit from the cabin.) Rock piles, commonly called cairns, mark the trail. From the trailhead it is 7.5 miles to **Pu'u'ula'ula Red Hill Cabin**. It has 8 bunks with mattresses. Rest here because it's another 11.6 miles to **Mauna Loa Cabin**. It has 12 bunks. Both cabins have water catchments (the only reliable source of water along the trail). Check on water levels while registering, and then treat the water before drinking. Plan on spending a night at each cabin to acclimatize. Mauna Loa's summit is 13,679 feet, so altitude sickness can be a problem. Extreme weather conditions can also occur at any time of year. Eruptions are possible, but unlikely. Campfires are not permitted due to the prevalence of flammable grasses and brush. You can also hike to Mauna Loa Summit from Mauna Loa Observatory Road on the mountain's north flank. Aggressive hikers can make it a day-hike, but you'll probably want to spend a night acclimatizing by sleeping in your car at the trailhead or at Mauna Kea State Recreation Area. A permit is required if you plan on spending the night at Mauna Loa Cabin. Fortunately, you do not have to drive all the way to the Backcountry Office to get one. You can call (808) 985-6178 to request a permit and receive trail/water updates the day of your hike.

East Rift Zone: The trail to Pu'u 'O'o vent is closed, but backpackers can still hike Napau or Naulu Trails and camp near Napau Crater Overlook. This campsite does not have shelter or water. Due to extreme instability, these trails can close at any time.

Coastal Areas: From Pu'u Loa Petroglyphs Parking Area backpackers can take Puna Coast Trail to one of three backcountry camps. **Ka'aha, Halape, and Keauhou campsites** have three-walled shelters, but tents are advised due to bugs and mice. These sites and Pepeiao (farther west along Ka'aha Trail) have water catchments (check water level during the permitting process). Water must be treated before drinking. **'Apua Point** has no shelter and no water. You can make a semi-loop by hiking in via Keauhou Trail (follow the cairns carefully) and out via Puna Coast Trail, but you'll need to arrange a shuttle or hitch back up the hill to Keauhou trailhead on Chain of Craters Road. Hiking across open lava field is pretty brutal, especially after noon when dark lava rock has had a chance to absorb the sun's heat. There's very little shade, and while the terrain is more-or-less level from point A to point B, you're constantly going up and down on these gnarly lava folds. With that said, a little oasis, like Halape, in the barren lava field is all the more refreshing. Also note that rodents may try to get at your food.

Biking
Cyclists on the Big Island typically stick to the Ironman route or test their iron legs taking a mountain bike from sea level to the summit of Mauna Kea. However, there are biking opportunities. It can also be frustrating if the roads are packed with tour buses and rental cars, so it's best to pedal early in the morning before the afternoon rush. Crater Rim Drive is closed from Kilaeua Overlook to Chain of Craters Road. The open portion passes several short trails. Climbers can go from Kilauea to the Coastal Plains and back up the 19-mile (one-way) Chain of Craters Road. You could also pedal the recently graded emergency route of Chain of Craters/Kalapana Road along the coast. Mauna Loa Road (3,700-ft climb) offers another excellent challenge. It ascends nearly 3,000 feet in 13.5 miles before terminating at Mauna Loa Trailhead. Climb it and then turn around and enjoy the rapid descent back to where you started (Kipukapuaulu is a good choice). Hilina Pali Road (off Chain of Craters Road) is 9 miles long and open to cyclists. Escape Road (a dirt escape route in case of eruption) runs mostly parallel to Chain of Craters Road and can be accessed from Thurston Lava Tube (Nahuku) or Highway 11. You can bike at Kahuku Unit as well.

Visitor Center & Museum
Kilauea Visitor Center is open daily. It's the central hub of information, filled with exhibits, a bookstore, and a short film is played regularly. Unfortunately, **Jaggar Museum** is permanently closed. **Kahuku** (no visitor center), between Mile Markers 70 and 71, is open Thursdays through Sundays from 9am to 4pm, but closed weekdays and federal holidays.

Ranger Programs & For Kids
A current schedule of ranger programs can be found at the park website or on the ranger activity bulletin board at Kilauea Visitor Center. Visitors can expect rangers to give a 20-minute talk on "How It All Began" outside the visitor center every day. Attending a ranger program is a great use of your time in the park.

If a miniature papier-mâché volcano with a vinegar-baking soda eruption draws "ooohs" and "ahhhs" from your children (like they're viewing 4th of July fireworks), imagine what they'll think about seeing a real volcano? Here you can (maybe) see lava, hike through a lava tube, and view a collection of ancient Hawaiian

Nenes

artifacts. If that's not enough entertainment, children (ages 7–12) can take part in the park's Junior Ranger Program. A free activity booklet (available at the visitor center) helps families learn more about the park, and kids earn a badge for completing its activities.

Flora & Fauna
Hawai'i, the world's most isolated island group, is a fascinating biological laboratory. After hundreds of thousands of years of volcanic activity, the Hawaiian Islands finally broke the surface of the Pacific Ocean, creating a new and unique habitat for life. Life faced one major obstacle. The islands were more than 2,000 miles from the nearest significant land mass. Plant life would have to be carried there by wind, water, or birds. Eventually several species of plants and animals made the seemingly impossible journey. After millions of years of evolution and adaptation, a unique world was created where more than 90% of the species of flora and fauna are only found on these islands.

The park is home to many fascinating creatures: happyface spiders, carnivorous caterpillars, picture wing flies, and honeycreepers. It's also refuge to a variety of endangered species: hawksbill turtles, nene, dark-rumped petrel, and hoary bat. Hawksbill turtles use some of the park's beaches as nesting areas, and backpackers should not camp in areas posted as turtle nesting habitat. This is also a great area for birdwatching. Sea birds can be seen from the end of Chain of Craters Road. Kipukapuaulu Loop is another exceptional birding location; this 100-acre island of vegetation contains the richest concentrations of native plants and bird life in Hawai'i. Nenes (Hawaiian geese, descendent of Canadian geese) nest in the park. Motorists should always drive cautiously, as nenes tend to get in the way.

Steam Vents

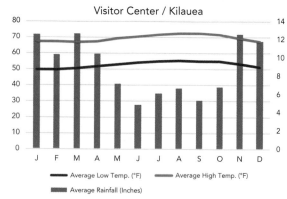

Visitor Center / Kilauea

Average Low Temp. (°F) Average High Temp. (°F)
Average Rainfall (Inches)

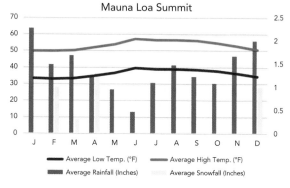

Mauna Loa Summit

Average Low Temp. (°F) Average High Temp. (°F)
Average Rainfall (Inches) Average Snowfall (Inches)

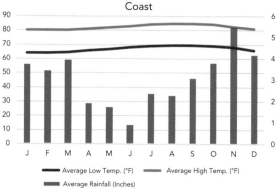

Coast

Average Low Temp. (°F) Average High Temp. (°F)
Average Rainfall (Inches)

Pets & Accessibility

In general it's not a good idea to bring your pets to Hawai'i. They are permitted in the park, but must be kept on a leash (less than six feet). Pets are permitted in developed areas including paved roadways, parking areas, and Namakanipaio Campground, but are prohibited in all undeveloped areas, Hilina Pali Road, and Kulanaokuaiki Campground. Do not leave your pets unattended in a vehicle.

Many facilities are wheelchair accessible. These include Kilauea Visitor Center, Volcano House Hotel, and Volcano Art Center. The visitor center has a wheelchair available for use. Namkanipaio and Kulanaokuaiki Campgrounds have accessible campsites and restrooms. Sulphur Banks Trail is accessible if you begin from the Steam Vents parking lot to the west. Devastation Trail is accessible from the Devastation Trail Parking Area.

Weather

Weather on the Big Island is unpredictable. Visitors should come prepared for rain, wind, sun, and maybe even a little snow if you plan on trekking around the summit of Mauna Loa. A good example of the weather's unpredictability is to compare rainfall measurements at Kilauea Visitor Center. In March of 2006, rainfall measured 34 inches. In March of 2008 it was 4.5 inches. In December of 2007 more than 40 inches of rain fell. December 2005, 1.6 inches. With stats like this it's difficult to generalize, but if you had to pick the driest months (on average) choose somewhere between May and October.

Tips & Recommendations

If the volcano is active, start at the visitor center. They'll provide current lava/safety information, which will help you choose what to do.

Hawaii Volcanoes is an incredibly dynamic national park. A volcanic eruption that began in 1983 ended in 2018, culminating with the largest lower East Rift Zone eruption in at least 200 years (and part of Crater Rim Drive sliding into Halema'uma'u Crater!). Lava buried Kapoho tidepools (a shame because it was a wonderful place). Halema'uma'u Crater began to fill with water, and then, to close out 2020, the lake turned to steam, and lava appeared. It turned off, only to turn on again September 2021. The point is, you have to stay tuned to the volcano's activity. If it's putting on a show when you visit, you need to determine where to see it (Keanakakoi Overlook as of November 2021) and that's why you should first stop at the visitor center.

You can safely view the destruction from the crater's collapse during the 2018 eruption by parking at Devastation Trailhead and walking down Chain of Craters Road toward the volcano.

Hawaii Volcanoes is always worth visiting, but there's a lot to do on the Big Island. If the volcano is active, the lava lake is lighting up the night's sky, and you feel like it still will be when you arrive, book a night at Volcano House (or somewhere nearby). Without lava, the park is an interesting day trip, where you cruise Chain of Craters Road and hike Kilauea Iki and Thurston Lava Tube (Nahuku). There are more than enough trails to warrant spending a few nights, especially if you're thinking about backpacking to the coast or Mauna Loa, but I'd plan some time outside the park too (see below).

If you don't want to rent a car but still want to visit the park, Roberts Hawaii (robertshawaii.com, $144) offers coach tours. It's a full day and you'll spend most of the time in a bus. You'll also miss out on other fun things along the way (Kealakekua Bay, Honaunau, South Point, Green Sand Beach, etc.).

If you're flying all the way to Hawaii, don't come only for the national park. You can swim with manta rays, backpack to majestic valleys, stargaze at Mauna Kea,

Surface flow

and there's plenty of premium sand and snorkeling you expect on a tropical island paradise like this.

Hiking Trails: Mauna Loa (Strenuous, multi-day), Kilauea Iki (Moderate, 3.3 miles), Thurston (Nahuku) Lava Tube (Easy, 1.5)
Guided Tours: There isn't much you'd need a guide for if lava isn't flowing into the ocean. Spend your money on a manta ray snorkel instead.
Rainy Day Activities: Rainstorms are typically brief and nothing to alter your plans for (although it is relatively cool at Kilauea Visitor Center, and gets cooler further up Mauna Loa, so make sure you have a few extra layers packed with you or else you'll be buying them at the gift shop like many other guests)
Sunset Spots: Keanakakoi Overlook (if lava is present at Halemaumau Crater, it was when we went to print, but the lava had only been on since September 2021)

Beyond the Park...

Choosing where to stay and eat on the Big Island is no easy decision. Most visitors opt for beachside resorts on the west coast between Kawaihae and Captain Cook. Commercial comforts are sparser than other islands, but there are grocery stores in Waimea, Waikoloa, Kona, and Hilo, as well as a Costco near the Kona airport. There are several public campgrounds along the island's coast and a few in the interior. Try to spend at least one night in or near the park (perhaps more if the volcano is making interesting things happen and you want to see them).

Choosing what to do once you've arrived is equally difficult. If you can get over to the national park and ogle a little lava, great!, but there's a whole lot more to see here, and you should stick around for a while to have a look. As its name implies, the island is big. You could have a grand old time spending

your entire Hawaiian vacation at a beachside resort. That's definitely an option. It'll take quite a bit of driving to see what this magnificent island has to offer, and, if you want to see most of the highlights, you'll want to book accommodations at a few different locations. Again, each island warrants its own guidebook, but these attractions are a good starting point for a Big Island vacation. Take a closer look into them, see what interests you, and then plan where to stay from there.

Attractions
Swim with manta rays!
You have the option to snorkel or SCUBA in two different locations. I prefer the traditional offering, where you paddle out into Keauhou Bay and slide into the water with a few of these graceful giants. The other option takes you near the airport.

South Point & Green Sand Beach (Papakolea) These two destinations are along the way to Hawaii Volcanoes from Kona. People cliff jump at South Point when conditions allow it, the Green Sand Beach is a decent hike, but locals camp out to give tourists a ride (fee).

And there's so much more: Waimanu Valley (backpacking), Honaunau (AKA Two Step) (snorkeling), Captain Cook Monument/Kealakekua Bay (snorkeling, kayaking), Kekaha Kai State Park/Makalawena (Beach, 4x4 or hike required), Kekaha Kai State Park/Kua Bay (beach, sometimes the sand washes away), Mauna Kea (sunset, sunrise, stargazing, hiking), Hapuna Beach State Park (beach, fee), Mauna Kea, Pe'e Pe'e Falls (sacred waterfall), Rainbow Falls, Akaka Falls State Park, Waipio Valley (hiking, waterfalls, black sand beach, trailhead to Waimanu Valley), Kaloko-Honokohau National Historical Park (snorkel)

American Samoa

A traditional woven mat

Phone: (684) 633-7082
Website: nps.gov/npsa

Established: October 31, 1988
Size: 10,550 Acres
Annual Visitors: 30,000
Peak Season: All Year

Activities: Snorkeling, SCUBA Diving, Hiking

Campgrounds: None

Homestay Program
Rates: Determined by the host (typically between $50–150/night)
Lodging: Available on all islands except Olosega*
Rates: $40–200/night

Park Hours: Open all year
Entrance Fee: None
Visitation Requirements: Passport

*Homestay lodging is the only type available on the island of Ta'u

American Samoa is one of the least visited and least developed national parks the United States has to offer. Culturally and geographically, it's one of the most unique. Park land spans four separate islands located deep in the South Pacific on the only United States territory south of the equator. It's a park that isn't built for motorists. Like the Hawaiian Islands, American Samoa was created by volcanoes. What's different is that most of the region is free of man-made improvements. The climate is tropical. The mountains are rugged. The land is covered with dense rain forest, and there are beaches sprinkled along the coast. The waters are home to some of the oldest coral colonies in existence. In short, it's a small park overflowing with cultural and tropical treasures.

American Samoa is extremely isolated. Even in today's global world, traveling to Tutuila, the largest and most populous island, can be a challenge. However, the journey is much easier today than it was for the first Samoans. Historians believe that some 3,000 years ago a few adventurous souls left Southeast Asia in boats with absolutely no idea where the ocean currents would take them. After covering 5,000 miles of open water, they arrived at an island oasis. A land they embraced and made their home. They continued to worship the same gods and upheld their Polynesian traditions. For centuries, the early Samoans were left undisturbed by the outside world. Whalers, pirates, missionaries, and European explorers simply came and went. But in the 1870s their world was torn apart from the inside. An argument between kings started a contentious civil dispute dividing eastern and western halves of Samoa.

Years later, Great Britain, Germany, and the United States were offered exclusive rights to build a naval base in Tutuila's Pago Pago Bay in return for military protection. Each nation ignored the offer, but they remained to pursue private interests. German interests involved invading a Samoan village, an act resulting in destruction of American property. American response was swift; two warships were sent to Pago Pago Harbor. Before either side fired, a typhoon swept through the area, wrecking three German warships and both American vessels. Time settled their differences—or, perhaps more accurately, things cooled off to a semblance of civility—and the United States began to formally occupy Samoa in 1900.

Samoans were forced to make many difficult decisions about American occupation. Most importantly was the choice to be Samoan or American? Many Samoans still weave mats, paint bark of the mulberry tree, and decorate their bodies with traditional tattoos. Samoan women still dance the siva and the sasa. Men do the fa'ataupati, a slap dance performed without music. The 'ava ceremony is a highly ritualistic ceremonial drink with specific gestures and phrases. It is considered a great honor if a visitor is asked to share 'ava (do not decline, embrace the gesture). Samoans also continue the ritual of Fa'aaloaloga. It's the process of exchanging gifts at formal events. Most people are bilingual, speaking both Samoan and English.

That said, the American influence on Samoa is clear. Schools, a hospital, roads, sewage treatment facilities, and canneries were built in the 1960s. Many of these structures proved far too costly to maintain and have since fallen into a state of disrepair. (But you'll still find popular fast-food restaurants in Pago Pago, so not all ventures were unprofitable.) However, not all local politicians were interested in mimicking the rest of the United States. Laws were passed to curb exploitation and development. For example, non-Samoans cannot own land and foreign companies must partner with a Samoan before starting any venture on the islands. These laws, and the islands' remote location, have helped prevent coastlines from being littered with ostentatious resorts. Roads don't weave past every scenic vista. Visitors aren't piling into the park by the busload. There isn't any bumper-to-bumper traffic to deal with like a summer weekend in Yosemite Valley. In American Samoa you'll find nothing but seclusion and peace in a laid-back environment. The park may be small in stature, but it's rich in culture, and with only a few thousand outsiders visiting each year, it may feel like your own tropical paradise.

Ofu Lagoon

When to Go

In an entire year National Park of American Samoa receives roughly the same number of visitors Grand Canyon sees on an average day. So overcrowding isn't a problem. Don't plan on being shoulder-to-shoulder with fellow hikers trekking to Mount 'Alava or having to wake up at the crack of dawn to secure a sliver of prime beach realty. Weather is what you have to worry about. Tropical storms are most common during the rainy season (October–April), but visitors are treated to year-round warmth and rain (June–September is slightly drier than the rest of the year). Humpback whales might be seen late summer/early fall.

Transportation & Airports

American Samoa is an unincorporated territory of the United States located in the South Pacific Ocean. The island chain is some 2,500 miles southwest of Hawai'i. Most trips begin and end at Tafuna International Airport (PPG) in Pago Pago on the island of Tutuila. Currently two flights per week arrive in Pago Pago from Honolulu, HI. The International Airport at Upolo, (Western) Samoa receives weekly flights from Australia, Fiji, and New Zealand (a less expensive alternative if you have time and want to explore this side of the world a bit).

Car rental is available at or near the airport (about $120/day), but there is only one main road on the island of Tutuila. 'Aiga or "family" buses provide transportation. Buses originate and terminate at Fagatogo market and fares are reasonable. Buses do not run on Sundays. Taxis are also available at the airport or market. Inter Island Vacations (interislandvacations.com), Samoa Airways (samoaairways.com), and Manua Airways (manuaair.com) provide infrequent flights between islands. There are no set schedules to these remote islands, so contact the provider for more information.

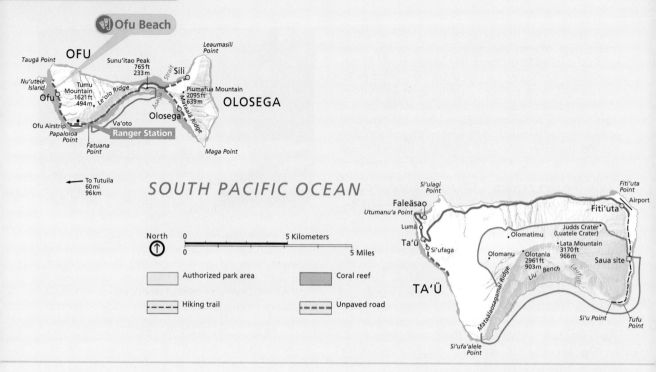

Ofu Beach

OFU

Taugā Point

Nu'utele Island

Ofu

Ofu Airstrip

Papaloloa Point

Fatuana Point

Tumu Mountain 1621 ft 494 m

Va'oto

Ranger Station

Sunu'itao Peak 765 ft 233 m

Le'olo Ridge

Asaga Strait

Sili

Olosega

Mata'ala Ridge

Leaumasili Point

Piumafua Mountain 2095 ft 639 m

OLOSEGA

Maga Point

To Tutuila 60 mi 96 km

SOUTH PACIFIC OCEAN

North

0 ___ 5 Kilometers
0 ___ 5 Miles

Authorized park area

Coral reef

Hiking trail

Unpaved road

Si'ulagi Point

Faleāsao

Utumanu'a Point

Lumā

Ta'ū

Si'ufaga

Olomatimu

Olomanu

Olotania 2961 ft 903 m

Mata'alaosagama'i Ridge

Liu Bench

Fiti'uta Point

Airport

Fiti'uta

Judds Crater (Luatele Crater)

Lata Mountain 3170 ft 966 m

Saua site

Laufuti

Si'u Point

Tufu Point

TA'Ū

Si'ufa'alele Point

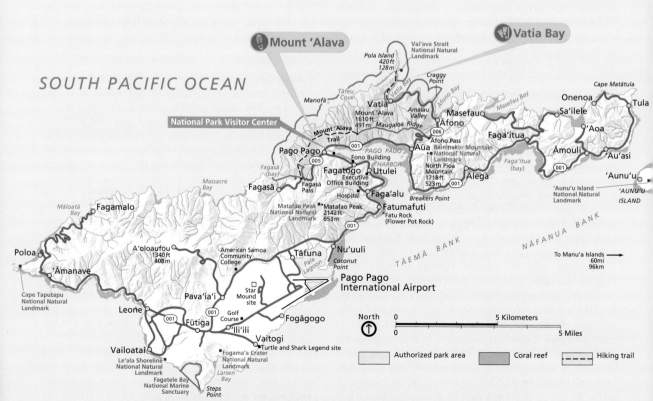

Mount 'Alava

Vatia Bay

SOUTH PACIFIC OCEAN

National Park Visitor Center

Tāfeu Cove

Manofā

Pola Island 420 ft 128 m

Vai'ava Strait National Natural Landmark

Vatia

Mount 'Alava 1610 ft 491 m

Mount 'Alava Trail

Maugaloa Ridge

Amalau Valley

Craggy Point

Vatia Bay

Afono Bay

Afono

Afono Pass

006

Masefau Bay

Masefau

Faga'itua

Cape Matātula

Onenoa

Sa'ilele

'Aoa

Tula

'Au'asi

Pago Pago

005

001

Fono Building

Fagatogo

Utulei

Executive Office Building

Fagasā (bay)

Fagasā

Fagasā Pass

Hospital

Massacre Bay

Rainmaker Mountain National Natural Landmark

Aūa

North Pioa Mountain 1718 ft 523 m

Breakers Point

001

Āleaga

Faga'itua (bay)

Āmouli

'Aunu'u

'Aunu'u Island National Natural Landmark

'AUNU'U ISLAND

Faga'alu

Fatumafuti

Fatu Rock (Flower Pot Rock)

Matafao Peak National Natural Landmark

Matafao Peak 2142 ft 653 m

001

TĀEMĀ BANK

NĀFANUA BANK

Māloatā Bay

Fagamalo

A'oloaufou 1340 ft 408 m

American Samoa Community College

Tāfuna

Nu'uuli

Coconut Point

Pala Lagoon

Pago Pago International Airport

To Manu'a Islands 60 mi 96 km

Poloa

'Āmanave

Cape Taputapu National Natural Landmark

Leone

001

Fūtiga

'Ili'ili

Vaitogi

Pava'ia'i

Star Mound site

Golf Course

Fogāgogo

Turtle and Shark Legend site

Vailoatai

Fogama'a Crater National Natural Landmark

Le'ala Shoreline National Natural Landmark

Fagatele Bay National Marine Sanctuary

Larsen Bay

Steps Point

North

0 ___ 5 Kilometers
0 ___ 5 Miles

Authorized park area

Coral reef

Hiking trail

Regions

Tutuila: Roughly 2,500 acres of land and 1,200 acres of water on the north end of Tutuila are leased by the National Park Service. This is the only section of park accessible by car. 'Alava Trail is located here.

Ofu and Olesega: Home of the best reefs and snorkeling in the park, and the most beautiful beach in American Samoa (Ofu Beach).

Ta'u: The park protects 5,400 acres of land, including Lata Mountain, American Samoa's highest peak, and another 1,000 acres of water.

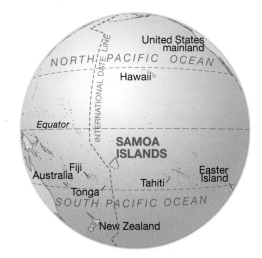

Samoa is an American territory, but many Samoans remain loyal to their traditions and culture. As a visitor, respect and follow local customs.

- Always ask villagers or the village mayor for permission to walk in the village, take photographs, or use the beach.
- Take your shoes off before entering a traditional home or fale. Cross your legs while sitting on the floor.
- Sunday is a day of rest. Even activities like swimming are sometimes not permitted.
- Every evening around dusk villagers observe a special time of prayer called Sa. If you are in a village during this time, stop and wait quietly until Sa ends.
- It is considered an honor to share a drink called 'ava. 'Ava is a local drink made from the root of the pepper plant.
- Do not eat or drink while walking through a village.
- Do not begin eating until prayer has finished and the head of the house begins eating.
- It is impolite to reject food.
- Only stay with one host family in a village to prevent embarrassing your hosts.
- Samoans of all ages swim in shorts and shirts. Avoid short shorts, bathing suits, and bikinis unless you wear a T-shirt over it. In villages, wear long shorts, pants, skirts, or sarongs. Dress modestly.
- Like at home, excuse yourself when crossing someone's path. Lower your head and say excuse me ("tulou").
- Women and men holding hands is acceptable, but other public displays of affection are frowned upon.
- Time on the island goes a bit slower and plans change frequently. To avoid frustration, simply go with the flow.

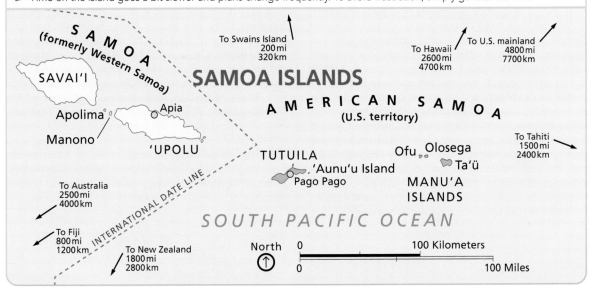

Ofu Lagoon

The best snorkeling of all the islands is here too but be sure to bring your own gear because you won't find any outfitters nearby. People in general are hard to come by. (More than 95% of American Samoa's population lives on the island of Tutuila.) In fact, it's difficult for tourists to reach Ofu; an interisland flight from Samoa Airways (samoaairways.com), Manua Airways (manuaair.com), or Inter Island Vacations (interislandvacations.com) is required to reach this secluded tropical paradise. Or you may be able to catch a ride aboard a supply ship or private boat. Vatia Bay on Tutuila is the alternative for those that cannot make the trip to Ofu. The tiny village of Vatia is situated at the bay's edge where guests can enjoy the water and impressive views of the uninhabited island of Pola. You can also find good snorkeling and swimming locations beyond park boundaries on Tutuila. Pago Pago Marine Charters (684.699.9234, pagopagomarinecharters.com) offers fishing and SCUBA charters, as well as coastline tours. Dive Adventures (diveadventures.com), based out of Australia, offers an American Samoa SCUBA trip.

Hiking

There is a 7-mile (roundtrip) trail leading to the summit of 1,610-ft **Mount 'Alava**, which follows a ridgeline across the national park's portion of Tutuila. The trailhead is located at Fagasa Pass, a short drive west of Pago Pago. From the summit, hikers can view Pago Pago Harbor and the surrounding islands. The trail continues to Vatia Village where you can swim or snorkel in Vatia Bay. A short hiking trail along **Lower Sauma Ridge** begins at Alamau Valley Scenic Overlook and leads to archeological sites. The upper trail connects to Mount 'Alava's ridgeline. You can also find easy hikes to historic WWII gun emplacements at Breaker's Point and Blunt's Point. **Tuafanua Trail** (2.2 miles) rises up switchbacks from Vatia Village to views of Pola Island. On Ta'u you can hike 5.7 miles along an old road to Si'u Point. On Olosega you can hike 2.7 miles to Oge Beach. And on Ofu, you can hike the 5.5-mile **Tumu Mountain Trail** which affords views of the Manu'a Islands. A bridge connects Ofu and Olosega.

Homestay Program

American Samoa's Homestay Program allows visitors to become more closely acquainted with Samoan people and culture. Participants live in the home of local residents associated with the park. This living situation has its advantages. You may be invited to make crafts, weave a mat, fish the Samoan way (with poles and nets), or collect giant clams and spear octopus. It is an incredibly unique opportunity where visitors are not only welcomed into a local home, but into their lives. If you're looking for a truly authentic Samoan experience that you'll never forget, the Homestay Program is for you. All fees, including accommodations and cultural activities, are set by the local host. The park encourages you to contact hosts directly, but you'll have to contact the park for a list of potential hosts.

Water Activities

All the best water activities are found on the island of Ofu, where you'll find the park's true gem: Ofu Beach.

Visitor Center

The visitor center, located in Pago Pago across from Pago Way Service Station, is open on weekdays, 8am until 4:30pm. It's closed on weekends and federal holidays. It houses a few exhibits and a small store.

Ranger Programs & For Kids

Due to limited visitation the park does not offer any regularly scheduled ranger programs. If you'd like to talk to a ranger, call (684) 633-7082.